FROMMER'S

COMPREHENSIVE TRAVEL GUIDE

GERMANY '94

C0-AKI-678

by Darwin Porter
Assisted by Danforth Prince

PRENTICE HALL TRAVEL

NEW YORK • LONDON • TORONTO • SYDNEY • TOKYO • SINGAPORE

FROMMER BOOKS

Published by Prentice Hall General Reference
A division of Simon & Schuster Inc.
15 Columbus Circle
New York, NY 10023

ISBN: 0-671-84904-2
ISSN: 1044-2405

Design by Robert Bull Design
Maps by Geografix Inc.

Frommer's Editorial Staff

Editorial Director: Marilyn Wood
Editorial Manager/Senior Editor: Alice Fellows
Senior Editor: Lisa Renaud
Editors: Charlotte Allstrom, Thomas F. Hirsch, Peter Katucki, Sara Hinsey Raveret, Theodore Stavrou
Assistant Editors: Margaret Bowen, Christopher Hollander, Ian Wilker
Editorial Assistants: Gretchen Henderson, Bethany Jewett
Managing Editor: Leanne Coupe

Special Sales

Bulk purchases (10+ copies) of Frommer's Travel Guides are available to corporations at special discounts. The Special Sales Department can produce custom editions to be used as premiums and/or for sales promotion to suit individual needs. Existing editions can be produced with custom cover imprints such as a corporate logo. For more information write to: Special Sales, Prentice Hall Travel, 15 Columbus Circle, New York, New York 10023.

Manufactured in the United States of America

CONTENTS

LIST OF MAPS

INVITATION TO THE READERS

In researching this book, we have come across many fine establishments, the best of which we have included here. We are sure that many of you will also come across appealing hotels, inns, restaurants, guest houses, shops, and attractions. Please don't keep them to yourself. Share your experiences, especially if you want to comment on places that have been included in this edition that have changed for the worse. You can address your letters to:

Darwin Porter
Frommer's Germany '94
Prentice Hall Travel
15 Columbus Circle
New York, NY 10023

A DISCLAIMER

Readers are advised that prices fluctuate in the course of time and travel information changes under the impact of the varied and volatile factors that affect the travel industry. Neither the author nor the publisher can be held responsible for the experiences of the readers while traveling. Readers are invited to write to the publisher with ideas, comments, and suggestions for future editions.

SAFETY ADVISORY

Whenever you're traveling in an unfamiliar city or country, stay alert. Be aware of your immediate surroundings. Wear a moneybelt and keep a close eye on your possessions. Be particularly careful with cameras, purses, and wallets, all favorite targets of thieves and pickpockets.

GERMAN POSTAL CODE

A new German postal code system was scheduled to be implemented beginning in mid-1993. The new system calls for five numbers set before the name of the city or town (for instance, 10351 Berlin) rather than four numbers before the name and in some cases one or two numbers after the name (for instance, 1000 Berlin 33). The new system was not available at presstime, but the codes in this book will continue to be handled by the German postal service.

CHAPTER 1

GETTING TO KNOW GERMANY

A unified, wealthy, industrial—yet beautiful—Germany awaits you.

Many of its treasures were lost in World War II, but much remains and much has been restored in the original style. Natural scenery, particularly in the Black Forest, the Mosel Valley, the Harz Mountains, and the Bavarian Alps, was and is a potent lure.

For those who want to see history in the making, I'd also recommend visiting Potsdam, Leipzig, Dresden, Meissen, and Weimar—centers of East Germany before German unification in October 1990. Keep in mind, however, that although political developments have been fast-paced, the infrastructure of the five new states (old East Germany) cannot change overnight, and living standards there are different from those in western Germany.

The people of Germany—in both the western and the eastern sections—are of varied ethnic backgrounds. What you'll most likely meet are people of learning and sophistication, boasting a long cultural heritage, people who are forging a powerful nation in central Europe with advanced technology and industry that are the wonder of much of the rest of the world.

Germany is both modern and traditional—a land that knows how to harmonize contrasts. To learn something of German culture should be the goal of every traveler. The businesslike lifestyle of the Germans hasn't stifled their creative spirit. Their admiration and devotion to the arts has existed from early times, when the nobility, wealthy merchants, and others encouraged and gave financial aid to talented painters, musicians, and artisans. Ordinary citizens staged morality plays, took part in folk dancing and singing, and honored compatriots who showed creative abilities.

This guide is meant to help you decide where to go in Germany, but ultimately the most gratifying experiences will be your own serendipitous discoveries—drinking beer in a yard shaded by chestnut trees, picnicking in a Bavarian meadow, spending an hour chatting with a winemaker in the Mosel Valley—whatever it is that will stay in your memory for years to come.

We'll spend time in popular destinations like Munich, Frankfurt, Heidelberg, and Berlin, focusing on both obvious and hidden treasures. But to seek out the wonders of this diverse and complicated country, we must also go to the Bavarian Alps, Lake

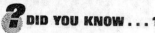

DID YOU KNOW . . . ?

- The Rhine, the "most German" of all rivers, isn't necessarily German since it begins in the Swiss Alps and washes the borders of six countries.
- Berlin has been the capital of all Germany for only about 75 years, from 1871 to 1945 and again beginning in 1991.
- In 1945, 24% of Germany was ceded to Poland.
- Between 1820 and 1920, Germany sent more immigrants to the United States than did England.
- The Nazis considered "degenerate" all painting that did not faithfully reproduce natural objects, and they destroyed vast collections.
- In sections of Germany, it is not only the stork that is said to deliver children, but also the swan, the owl, and even the crow.
- Some scholars believe that Martin Luther started the Christmas tree tradition.
- In olden days, mistletoe wasn't meant to invite a kiss but to ward off evil spirits and disease.
- In Berlin it's a tradition to eat carp on New Year's Day and to keep a fish scale in one's coin purse to prevent it from becoming empty.
- Germany has the highest proportion of wage-earning women in the world.
- In spite of a worldwide cliché, Germans aren't the leading beer drinkers. Belgians, per capita, drink more of the brew.

Constance, the Rhine and Mosel valleys, and the coast of the North Sea.

1. GEOGRAPHY, HISTORY & POLITICS

GEOGRAPHY

Germany lies in the heart of Europe, bordered by Switzerland and Austria on the south, France, Luxembourg, Belgium, and The Netherlands on the west, Denmark on the north, and Poland and the Czech Republic on the east. It encompasses an area of 137,535 square miles and has a population of about 80 million. At the apex of its political expansion, when the country was known as the Third Reich under Hitler, its lands included Austria, the Sudeten districts of former Czechoslovakia, and much of what is now western Poland, as well as the old city of Danzig (Gdańsk).

The country embraces many different physical terrains. It is generally divided into several major zones: the Rhine Valley; southern Germany, which includes the Bavarian Alps; the Danube Basin; the Neckar and Main river basins; the Franconian and Swabian Jura; the north German plain; and the central German hills, which stretch from the Ardennes in the west to the northern side of the Bohemian landmass in the east. These zones include the following regions.

THE REGIONS IN BRIEF

Frankfurt District On the Main River, this thriving metropolis, the gateway to Germany for many visitors, is a leading commercial and financial center of the country It was rebuilt in a modern high-rise style from the debris of World War II.

Munich and Bavarian Alps Bouncing back from the rubble of World War II, Munich is one of the most visited cities of Europe. It is the best base for exploring the Bavarian Alps, which lie between the city and Austria, and include such resorts as Berchtesgaden and Garmisch-Partenkirchen.

Rhineland Beginning in Switzerland as a mountain stream, this mighty river of legend and lore flows for some 850 miles. For 2,000 years it has been a major European trade route. Bonn, Cologne, Düsseldorf, and Koblenz are on its banks.

Heidelberg and the Neckar Valley Heidelberg, with a famous university and castle, is one of Germany's most popular sightseeing attractions. From here, you can explore the Neckar River.

Stuttgart and Swabia The capital of the state of Baden-Württemberg, Stuttgart is an industrial center, home of Mercedes and Porsche automobiles. It is also a city of historic interest and the base of the highly acclaimed Stuttgart Ballet and Stuttgart State Opera.

Westphalia Perhaps because it contains the industrial Ruhr Valley, this part of west-central Germany tends to be shunned by North American tourists. However, it has many country inns, half-timbered houses, forests, castles, and spas.

Black Forest Called *Schwarzwald* in German because of its dense fir forests, it actually receives more sunshine than most other forests in Germany. It is filled with beauty and charm; its major center is Freiburg and its most visited city is Baden-Baden.

Romantic Road Called the *Romantische Strasse* in German, this road winds its way south from the imperial city of Würzburg to the little town of Füssen at the foot of the Bavarian Alps. Rothenburg, Nördlingen, and Dinkelsbühl are among the best-preserved medieval towns in Germany.

Mosel Valley Known as the Moselle in France, this river weaves a snakelike path through the mountains west of the Rhineland, and many of its vineyards—on both sides of the river—produce wines superior to those of the Rhine.

Lake Constance The 162-mile coastline of this inland sea, called *Bodensee* in German, is shared with two other countries, Switzerland and Austria. Its chief German town is medieval Constance (Konstanz), now a summer resort.

Franconia and the German Danube Some of Germany's greatest medieval and Renaissance treasures came from this land, which gave the world such artists as Albrecht Dürer and Lucas Cranach. An annual Wagner festival attracts music lovers to the city of Bayreuth. Ulm is famed for its cathedral, and Bamberg is a medieval ecclesiastical center. Nürnberg, its largest city, was carefully restored after massive Allied bombing in World War II.

Lower Saxony and North Hesse Many visitors come here to travel the "Fairy Tale Road" of the Brothers Grimm, whose work has been translated into every major world language. This district is one of the country's most neglected tourist regions.

Hamburg This city of canals was severely bombed in 1943 but has been rebuilt in an impressive style on the banks of the Alster river. It is known for nightlife and good food and has a very busy port.

Schleswig-Holstein Its capital is Kiel, an old Hanseatic port that became a Free Imperial City in 1242. You are never far from the roaring waves here; the North Sea borders its western side, and the more peaceful Baltic Sea its eastern coast. A long, narrow island, Sylt is one of the major summer resorts of Germany, where nudity is the rule of the day. Lübeck is a popular tourist destination.

Berlin Berlin is more interesting than ever, now that it has reached out to embrace its old eastern sector again. The city is slowly reasserting its former identity as capital of a united Germany. The attractive city of Potsdam is nearby.

Harz Mountains and Thuringian Forest Long a tourist mecca for workers from the former Eastern bloc countries, the Harz mountains are filled with old churches, castles (many in ruins), and medieval fortresses. In Weimar you follow in the footsteps of Goethe and Schiller.

Leipzig and Dresden Leipzig is the most important industrial city in the east, known for its annual trade fair. With some 80% of its center destroyed in an infamous 1945 air raid, Dresden has bounced back and is now a high point of a visit to the eastern sector of the country.

IMPRESSIONS

The most civilized nations of modern Europe issued from the woods of Germany, and in the rude institutions of those barbarians we may still distinguish the original principles of our present laws and manners.
—EDWARD GIBBON, *THE DECLINE AND FALL OF THE ROMAN EMPIRE* (1776–88)

5546
DENMARK
North Sea
Baltic Sea
Sylt
Westerland
Flensburg
North
Frisian
Is.
Schleswig
Kiel Bay
Kiel
Mecklenburg
Bay
Hiddensee
Stralsund
Rügen
Pomeranian
Bay
Greifswald
Rostock
Wismar
Lübeck
East
Frisian Is.
West
Frisian Is.
Cuxhaven
Elbe
Wilhelmshaven
Bremerhaven
Emden
Hamburg
Schwerin
Neubrandenburg
Stettin
Bay
Lake Müritz
(Müritz)
Lüneburg
Oldenburg
Weser
Bremen
Elbe
Oder
Havel
Aller
Celle
Brandenburg
BERLIN
POLAND
THE NETHERLANDS
Osnabrück
Hannover
Minden
Braunschweig
Havel
Potsdam
Spree
Frankfurt
Münster
Hildesheim
Magdeburg
Bielefeld
Hameln
Oder
Detmold
Weser
Bad Pyrmont
Harz
Lippe
Dessau
Wittenburg
Lübbenau
Essen
Dortmund
Rhine
Ruhr
Göttingen
Elbe
Spree
Neisse
Cottbus
Düsseldorf
Kassel
Leipzig
N
0
50 mi
80 km

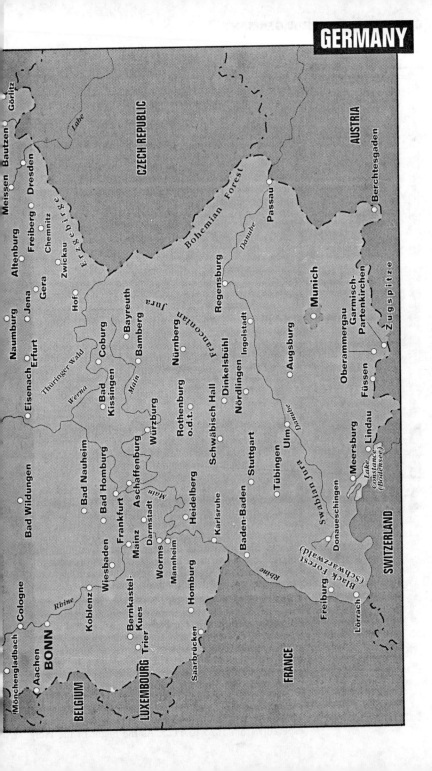

GERMANY

HISTORY

- **1800 B.C.E.**
  Celts establish permanent living sites and cultivate crops and raise animals.
- **9 B.C.E.–C.E.9**
  Romans attempt to conquer Teutonic tribes.
- **C.E. 300** Huns invade central Europe from the east.
- **486** Clovis founds Frankish kingdom, ruling from Paris.
- **496** Franks are converted to Christianity.
- **800** Charlemagne is crowned in Rome by the Pope.
- **962** Pope crowns Otto I as Holy Roman Emperor.
- **1138** Frederick Barbarossa's reign leads to a recentralization of power, but the emperor fails to bring the pope under German control.
- **1158** Munich founded by Henry the Lion, duke of Saxony.
- **1241** Hanseatic League founded to protect the trade of such cities as Bremen, Hamburg, and Lübeck.
- **Mid-1200s**
  Gothic style blooms throughout Germany.
- **1432** Maximilian I, "last of the German knights," becomes emperor, marking the begin-
  (continues)

PREHISTORY The land that today is Germany has been inhabited since prehistoric times. Ethnic groups ranged through the forested country, where they found plentiful streams, rivers, fish, and game. At Mauer near Heidelberg, at Steinheim an der Murr, and in the Neander valley near Düsseldorf, remains of ancient humans have been found.

These rootless people moved as crops were exhausted or animals migrated. It wasn't until between 8000 B.C.E. and the arrival of the Bronze Age, about 1800 B.C.E., that the Celts began to settle in more or less permanent spots, where they cultivated crops, domesticated animals, and eventually established commerce with their neighbors.

Indo-Europeans known as Teutons, or Germanic tribes, began to move in and establish themselves in the Rhine and Oder valleys and areas that today comprise southern Germany and northern Italy. The Celts and their hilltop forts were overrun, and they were forced to flee west across the Rhine. They were replaced by the Germanic tribes— Alemanni, Burgundians, Franks, Lombards, Ostrogoths, and Visigoths. Then, from 9 B.C.E. to C.E. 9, Romans came with a view to extending their empire north. They succeeded briefly, building forts at strategic spots, including Cologne, Trier, Mainz, Wiesbaden, and Passau. The inhabitants of the area resisted ferociously, forming large, combined West Germanic groups whose descendants are still in the land. They stopped the Romans; later, some of these people invaded Italy and helped destroy the Roman Empire.

Beginning about 300, the Huns came from the east into central Europe. Their migration signaled permanent fixing of home ground by the Bavarians in the south, Alemanni in Swabia, Thuringians in central Germany, Franks in the west, and Saxons and Frisians in the north.

Gradually, Christianity spread, and the people took on the gloss of civilization and culture. By 486, Clovis had founded the Frankish kingdom, the court being in Paris, and by 496 the Franks had converted to Christianity. In 800, a Frankish king, Charlemagne, was crowned as emperor, and his rule marks the high point of cultural and political development of that period. Emperors who followed him, however, did not match him in ability and power, and control decentralized.

HOLY ROMAN EMPIRE The Holy Roman Empire was a political entity that formally came into being when the pope crowned Otto I as Holy Roman Emperor in 962. Supposedly this empire was an extension of the Western Christian Unity established by Charlemagne. It represented the temporal power of united Christendom in western Europe against its enemies from outside, much as the pope represented Christendom's spiritual powers.

The idea of unity, however, did not prevail. Little nations, dukedoms, bishoprics, and principalities arose, and subsequent struggles pitted church against state as well, especially from 1025 to 1125. As the might of the Holy

Roman Empire declined, emperors were forced to seek alliance with rich German cities; with such powerful political alliances as the Swabian League; and with the Hanseatic League, a commercial city league founded to protect the trade of such north German cities as Bremen, Hamburg, and Lübeck.

In 1432, Maximilian I, "the last of the German knights," became Holy Roman Emperor. This marked the beginning of the hegemony of the Hapsburgs, which was to last for four centuries. Maximilian's marriage to Mary of Burgundy brought him her dowry and the Netherlands; and, in time, through marriages and other means, Bohemia, Hungary, and Spain came under Hapsburg influence.

The 15th century witnessed a major historical event, in 1456 when Johannes Gutenberg (ca. 1397–1468) produced the first book in Europe printed with movable type.

THE REFORMATION AND BEYOND Practices such as the sale of "indulgences," which purchased absolution of sin for the wealthy, greatly enriched the Roman Catholic Church, and discontent grew. It was in Germany that the first major attack upon these abuses was launched. An Augustinian monk, fired by burning religious conviction, became convinced that the church was corrupt. When Martin Luther ushered in the Reformation by nailing his theses on a church door in Wittenberg in 1517, he created a political as well as religious schism. The Reformation divided the Catholic emperors from the Protestant princes and set the stage for the devastating Thirty Years' War (1618–48), which fragmented Germany more than ever. The only powerful German state to emerge from these conflicts was the little kingdom of Prussia in the northeast on the Baltic Sea. The rise of Prussian power continued throughout the 18th century; under Frederick II (the Great) it became a major kingdom, with Berlin as its capital. Frederick reigned from 1740 to 1786 and, along with his many important military victories, introduced the Age of Enlightenment to Germany.

NAPOLEONIC PERIOD Under the War of the First Coalition of 1792 to 1797, the left bank of the Rhine came under the influence of France. Prussia stayed out of the War of the Second Coalition, in which Austria was defeated in 1802. In 1806, during the War of the Third Coalition, the Holy Roman Empire officially came to an end. Napoleon's armies invaded Prussia, making it part of the French empire. The following year, the serfs were freed—finally—and the Prussian army began to rebuild. In 1813, Napoleon's armies were defeated at Leipzig, and two years later, Britain and Prussia crushed Napoleon at the Battle of Waterloo.

RISE OF PRUSSIA The Congress of Vienna (1814–15), following the Napoleonic wars, redrew the map of Germany, giving more territory to Prussia but making Austria the leader in a German Confederation. During these events, there was a rising spirit of nationalism, exploited to good effect by Prince Otto von Bismarck when he became Prussia's chief minister in 1862. In the Austro-

DATELINE

ning of the hegemony of the Hapsburgs.

• **1456** Johannes Gutenberg prints the first book in Europe using movable type.

• **1517** Protestant Reformation begins in Germany, as Martin Luther nails his Ninety-five Theses to a church door in Wittenberg.

• **1618–48** Thirty Years' War fragments Germany more than ever as Protestant forces defeat Catholic Hapsburgs.

• **1740–86** Prussian might grows under Frederick the Great in the Age of Enlightenment.

• **1806** Armies of Napoleon invade Prussia, and it briefly is incorporated into the French Empire.

• **1813** Prussians fdefeat Napoleon at Leipzig.

• **1815** At the Congress of Vienna, the German Confederation of 39 independent states is created.

• **1862** Otto von Bismarck (1815–98) becomes prime minister of Prussia.

• **1866** Prussia defeats the Austrians as Bismarck sets up a Northern German Confederation the following year.

• **1870** Franco-
(continues)

Prussian War of 1866, Prussia triumphed over its rival to create a North German Confederation with Prussia as its leader. After the Franco-Prussian War, in which Prussia laid siege to Paris, Bismarck succeeded in his goal: Wilhelm I was crowned emperor of Germany, and the German Empire was established in 1871. Unity was achieved and a strong Germany took shape; an advanced social welfare system was adopted, and industrial production as well as technical and scientific pursuits advanced to new heights. The nation also grew in military might, but Bismarck kept the country out of wars.

At the accession of Wilhelm II in 1888, Bismarck came into conflict with the ambitions of the new emperor, whose efforts to make Germany a world power upset the fragile balance in Europe. The Kaiser dismissed Bismarck in 1890 and launched an aggressive foreign policy, while expanding the Germany navy. The disastrous result was World War I.

WORLD WAR I By 1907, Europe was divided into two armed camps, with Russia, France, and Great Britain forming the Triple Entente on one side, which was set against the Triple Alliance of Germany, Austria-Hungary, and Italy. All that was needed was a match to ignite the powder keg.

That came at Sarajevo in 1914, with the assassination of the Austrian Archduke Franz Ferdinand, heir to the throne of the Austro-Hungarian Empire. The German invasion of France launched the costly war. With Russia to its east, Germany faced a war on two fronts. The Germans were forced to dig trenches along the northern part of France and Belgium, which led to a new kind of war, "trench warfare." Casualties were staggering. The decision of the Germans to launch unrestricted U-boat submarine warfare in the Atlantic led eventually to U.S. involvement in the war.

A temporary reprieve came in 1917 when the Russian Revolution forced Russia out of the war, but this was only a lull. In the west, the situation was hopeless, as the German high command realized on August 8, 1918, when the Allies penetrated its lines.

In an attempt to get more favorable treatment from the Allies, the Germans declared a parliamentary democracy, ending the reign of the kaiser. However, in 1918, Germany was forced to sign the humiliating Treaty of Versailles, surrendering its colonies abroad and also lands in Europe, including beloved Alsace-Lorraine, which went to France. Germans still speak of that region as "the lost province." The Allies also demanded huge reparations.

WEIMAR REPUBLIC Once a center of German Enlightenment, Weimar became the headquarters of the new but shaky democracy and saw the adoption of a democratic constitution, hailed as "the most progressive in the world."

In the turbulent years following the aftermath of World War I, extremists from both the left and the right launched savage attacks against the idealistic government. The reparations demanded by the allies crippled the German economy; when payments stopped, France occupied the Ruhr in

1923. Inflation—perhaps the worst in history—destroyed what was left of the German economy; it virtually took wheelbarrows of money to purchase a loaf of bread.

When Gustav Stresemann became chancellor, he temporarily brought relief to the country. He took a number of measures to save the economy, including securing vast U.S. loans. By 1924, the situation had reversed: German marks meant something again, and high levels of employment were reached. Stresemann wanted to reestablish Germany upon the world stage, and with the Locarno Pact of 1925, he reached a rapprochement with France. In 1926, Germany was admitted to the League of Nations. More U.S. aid poured in, and reparation payments were lowered. The country's future looked better, but trouble loomed. The presidential election of 1925 was won by the 78-year-old Paul von Hindenburg.

Stresemann, who had done so much for the republic, died in October 1929, only weeks before world stock markets came tumbling down in the wake of America's Wall Street crash.

RISE OF NAZISM Throughout the Weimar Republic, Adolf Hitler was a player on the stage of German politics, with his "Beer Hall Putsch" in 1923, a failed rightist revolt, and the publishing of his notoriously anti-Semitic *Mein Kampf (My Struggle)* in 1925. Racism was the basis of his policies, and he firmly believed in an almost divine right of "Aryans" to rule the world, convinced as he was of their superior powers. Blaming the Jews for most of the ills of Germany, he at first failed to gain popular support. Nazi membership in the Reichstag had gone from 25 in 1925 to only a dozen following the elections of 1928.

In 1932, Hitler ran against the increasingly senile Hindenburg for president, but lost. Hindenburg made a disastrous decision: Seeking to secure a majority in the Reichstag, he accepted Hitler as chancellor, with himself as deputy. Hitler assumed power on January 30, 1933, and he proceeded to make his position secure, launching a National Socialist revolution. At the death of Hindenburg in 1934, Hitler declared himself *Führer* ("Leader" in German) of the German empire or Third Reich. In his virulently racist and anti-Communist government, Hitler made his position absolute.

The Reichstag fire in 1933, although blamed on the Communists, was probably the work of the Nazis themselves, to give Hitler an excuse to pursue his enemies. Hitler's policy of *Gleichschaltung* (coordination) Nazified Germany. Joseph Goebbels became minister of popular enlightenment; Communists and Social Democrats were sent to concentration camps; Jews were ostracized and persecuted; and the Gestapo, or secret police, launched a reign of terror.

On June 30, 1934, the "Night of Long Knives," hundreds of perceived enemies within Hitler's own party were massacred, including SA chief Ernst Röhm. Heinrich Himmler's black-shirted *Schutzstaffel*, or SS, became a powerful political force. Hitler now viewed his empire as a worthy successor to those of Charlemagne and Bismarck.

DATELINE

rer (leader) of the Third Reich.

• **1936** Germany militarizes the Rhineland, and Hitler signs agreements with Italy and Japan to form the Axis.

1938 Germany occupies Austria and the Sudetenland in Czechoslovakia.

• **1939** Hitler signs a pact with the Soviet Union in August and invades Poland on September 1, launching World War II.

• **1940–45** After early successes, German armies begin their retreat, as the Soviet Union moves in from the east and the Allied armies from the west. Germany is in ruins by 1945.

• **1945** The Yalta Conference divides Germany into zones of occupation. Each Allied country—France, the Soviet Union, the United States, and Great Britain—also occupies part of Berlin.

• **1948–49** The Soviet Union attempts by blockade to exclude Allies from Berlin. City is saved by a massive airlift.

• **1949** Soviets establish the country of East Germany, the German Democratic Republic (DDR). Konrad *(continues)*

In 1936, Hitler remilitarized the Rhineland, and signed agreements with Japan and Italy, forming the Axis powers. In 1938, he forced the *Anschluss* of Austria and marched triumphantly into the country of his birth. That same year, he occupied the Sudetenland in Czechoslovakia, an act the other Western powers unfortunately did not oppose forcefully.

WORLD WAR II   In August 1939, Hitler signed with the Soviet Union a pact that gave him the security to launch an invasion against Poland on September 1, 1939. France and Britain honored their treaty agreements with Poland, and World War II began. Since Germany was the only country prepared for war, it scored early victories, forcing France, within weeks, to sign an armistice. Hitler, in 1941 at the epitome of his power, chose not to launch an invasion of England but to attack instead his nominal ally, the Soviet Union. At the same time, he began to implement his racial theories in concentration camps, where his "final solution" was meant to wipe out Jews, Slavs, and all others he considered inferior.

On December 7, 1941, Japan, pursuing its own agenda, attacked Pearl Harbor and brought the United States into the war. Hitler had not intended for this to happen—he had hoped Japan would instead attack the Soviet Union from the east.

After defeats in North Africa in 1942 and at Stalingrad in 1943, the story of the war was one of Nazi retreat. The D-day landings on June 6, 1944, on the coast of Normandy began the steady advance of the Allied armies toward the east, while Soviet armies relentlessly advanced toward the west. Along with his mistress, Eva Braun, Hitler committed suicide in Berlin in April 1945. Hitler's dream of a "thousand-year Reich" ended on an inglorious note, as much of Europe, including Germany, lay in rubble.

DIVISION OF GERMANY   At war's end, Germany and its capital city were divided. The nation shrank in size, losing long-held territories (among them East Prussia). The United States, Great Britain, France, and the Soviet Union divided the country into four zones of occupation, with Berlin lying in the Soviet area. However, it was decided that the capital would also be divided among the four powers. The Soviet Union tried to cut off access by the other three nations into Berlin in the late 1940s, but the attempt failed. The Soviet-directed government of East Germany erected the Berlin Wall in 1961 and sealed off the borders to stop emigration from East to West, at the same time making visits to the East very difficult for the people of the West. That wall stood until 1989.

Starting in 1949, Great Britain, the United States, and France allowed their zones of occupation to be self-governing. The Soviet Union, on the other hand, made its zone into a virtual police state, severely limiting the freedom of its citizens until the liberating events that began in late 1989.

In all the zones of occupation, the destruction caused by World War II was tremendous. The task of rebuilding has

IMPRESSIONS

To be an Englishman is in Germany to be an angel—they almost worship you.
—S.T. COLERIDGE, LETTER TO THOMAS POOLE (1798)

been one of the miracles of the 20th century. Much was reconstructed in the old style, although much of the Germany of old was lost forever.

ECONOMIC MIRACLE In the west, the German Federal Republic was founded along liberal democratic principles. In the 1950s, aided in part by the Marshall Plan, but mainly by the hard work of its people, Germany rebuilt not only its devastated cities but also its wrecked economy. The word applied was *Wirtschaftswunder* or "economic miracle." Ending decades of hostilities, West Germany and France concluded the European Coal and Steel Pact in 1951, which led, six years later, to the formation of the European Economic Community (EEC).

The elderly chancellor, Konrad Adenauer, led the Federal Republic from 1949 until his retirement in 1963. In 1961, during Adenauer's long time in office, the East Germans erected the Berlin Wall to stem the tide of fleeing refugees. Willy Brandt became chancellor of West Germany in 1969, and for a while his *Ostpolitik*—opening to the east—led to a thawing in the Cold War.

UNIFICATION The year 1989 was a time of great change and turmoil. Uprisings in East Germany led to a stream of refugees to the west. Communist power began to collapse across Eastern Europe, symbolized by the fall of the Berlin Wall.

The following year was perhaps one of the most significant in modern German history. In March elections in East Germany, Communists suffered heavy defeats. German unification was the main issue. The two German nations announced economic unification in July of that year, followed by total unification—with its inherent problems—on October 3, 1990.

A nationwide debate ended in 1991 when Parliament voted to eventually quit Bonn, seat of the West German government since 1949, and go to the old capital of Berlin once more.

Since unification, the heady promises of Chancellor Helmut Kohl and other politicians of western Germany did not materialize. Disillusionment set in in much of former East Germany. The rate of unemployment was high, and resentment against immigrant workers led to violent Neo-Nazi marches, bombings, and physical assaults. In 1992, the German government faced annual bills of some $80 billion in their task of rebuilding the eastern part of their nation. The influential newspaper *Frankfurter Rundschau* editorialized, "The terms of east and west are not so much geographical expressions as they are descriptions of states of mind." In the two years following unification, it was estimated that nearly every second job in eastern Germany had simply vanished.

POLITICS

Government affairs in Germany were centered in Berlin from 1871 until the end of World War II. In the late 1940s, the capital of the German Federal Republic (West Germany) was moved west to Bonn in the Rhineland. East Berlin, became the capital of the German Democratic Republic (East Germany).

IMPRESSIONS

The Germany praised by the pro-Germans is much nastier than the Germany abused by the anti-Germans.
—G.K. CHESTERTON, AS I WAS SAYING (1936)

At present, the government of Germany is run from both Berlin and Bonn. The political capital of newly united Germany was officially designated as Berlin in 1990, and in June 1991 the Bundestag (German Parliament) voted to move the seat of government to Berlin from Bonn. The actual transfer of government institutions to Berlin was expected to be very slow, however.

In western Germany, the country comprises ten Länder (states): Baden-Württemberg, Rhineland-Palatinate (Rheinland-Pfalz), the Saar, Bavaria (Bayern), North Rhine–Westphalia (Nordrhein-Westfalen), Lower Saxony (Niedersachsen), Schleswig-Holstein, Hesse, Hamburg, and Bremen (the last two have been city-states since the days of the Hanseatic League in medieval times).

From the east following unification (or "reassociation," as some prefer to call it) came five states, Brandenburg, Mecklenburg-Vorpommern, Saxony, Saxony-Anhalt, and Thuringia. The two halves of a once divided but now united Berlin form their own federal state.

Since its establishment, the Federal Republic's government has been stable. It is parliamentary in structure, with a democratic constitution. The chief of state is a president, with mainly ceremonial duties. The chancellor (prime minister) heads the executive branch of government. The two houses of parliament are the Bundestag (lower chamber, with the most power) and the Bundesrat (upper chamber).

2. FAMOUS GERMANS

Konrad Adenauer (1876–1967) The first chancellor of postwar West Germany (1949–63), who had twice been imprisoned by the Nazis, he supervised the reconstruction of the country from a morass of bombed-out rubble to the leading economic power of Europe.

Robert Wilhelm Everhard von Bunsen (1811–99) He is considered the epitome of the kind of scientific methodology that made German technology admired around the world. His discoveries helped to boost the productivity of the industrial revolution in Germany.

Marlene Dietrich (1901–92) Her face recognizable to millions around the world, this Berlin-born actress was a legend for half a century. From the femme fatale of *The Blue Angel* to a series of memorable Hollywood films, Dietrich stood for ambiguously erotic glamour.

Albrecht Dürer (1471–1528) The son of a Hungarian-born goldsmith, Dürer introduced the Renaissance to German painting and is regarded as the foremost painter and engraver of his period. He was equally successful in woodcutting. For seven years he was court painter to Holy Roman Emperor Maximilian I.

Frederick William, The Great Elector (1620–88) This German Elector of Brandenburg forcibly created the centralized state of Brandenburg/Prussia from a loosely governed collection of local estates, and under his guidance and force of will, the Prussian army became one of the most feared in Europe. Before he died, he set in motion a series of marriages and alliances whereby his son, Frederick I (1657–1713), was crowned as the first full-fledged king of Prussia in 1701.

Johann Wolfgang von Goethe (1749–1832) One of the world's greatest writers, Goethe was a novelist, philosopher, dramatist, and poet. A devotee of science, he believed in the common origin of all human life. His masterpiece is *Faust*, a poetic drama in two parts.

Jacob Grimm (1785–1863) and **Wilhelm Grimm** (1786–1859) Two brothers, philologists and folklorists, they are famous for their collection of folktales, which they culled from hundreds of farms and villages in the countryside. Their best-known work is *Kinder- und Hausmärchen* (known in English as *Grimm's Fairy Tales*) published in 1841; they also wrote books on German and Danish sagas.

Johannes Gutenberg (ca. 1397–1468) Inventor of a form of movable type, using oil-based inks, he introduced a revolution in the dissemination of information, spurring education and laying the foundation for the publishing industry as we know it today. The most famous book he printed was the Gutenberg Bible (ca. 1455), followed soon after with school grammars.

Immanuel Kant (1724–1804) Kant's ideas on the nature of reason and logic later influenced everyone from classical philosophers to the proponents of existentialism. Professor of logic and metaphysics at the University of Königsberg (1770–97), he infuriated the Prussian governmental leaders with his liberal religious views. Influenced by David Hume and the English empiricists, he slowly developed a philosophy obsessed with the limitations of human knowledge, categories of human consciousness, and the aesthetic and moral consequences of a world where human acts and decisions are based on paradigms whose nature is unclear.

Baron Richard von Krafft-Ebing (1840–1902) A Mannheim-born neuropsychiatrist and professor at the universities of Strasbourg and Vienna, he studied sexual obsessions and sexual psychopathology. His most influential work, closely studied by Freud and Jung, was *Psychopathia Sexualis* (1886).

Friedrich Krupp (1787–1826); **Alfred Krupp** (1812–87); **Gustav Krupp von Bohlen und Halbach** (1870–1950); and **Alfred Krupp** (1907–67) This Ruhr Valley steel-manufacturing family was intimately associated with the political fortunes of Europe throughout the 19th and 20th centuries. In World War I, the firm's largest and deadliest cannon, Big Bertha, bombarded Paris from an astonishing range of 76 miles. The company's vast foundries before and during World War II worked aggressively to arm the Third Reich. After 1945, many of the company's remaining factories were disassembled and shipped to the Soviet Union as war reparations, and Alfred Krupp was forced to sell in a depressed market an estimated 75% of the value of his family holdings into public ownership.

Martin Luther (1483–1546). Instigator of the Reformation and one of the most influential religious and political forces in western history, he became the focal point of controversies that had been simmering for centuries between Rome and the powerful mercantile states of northern Europe. His most famous act was nailing his Ninety-five Theses to the door of his local church, an act that led to his excommunication. Luther translated the Old and New Testaments from Hebrew and Greek into German, significantly influencing the development of the modern language and laid the groundwork for Protestantism. He married Katarina von Bora, a former nun.

Friedrich Nietzsche (1844–1900) A philosopher and poet, he was known for his denunciation of religion and espousal of the doctrine of man's perfectability through self-assertion. His most famous work, *Thus Spake Zarathustra*, develops the notion of *Übermensch* (usually translated as Superman), the self-perfected human being able to influence and change the world. Later his ideas were frequently used and often distorted, especially by the Nazis.

3. ART & ARCHITECTURE

HISTORY

BEGINNINGS The earliest known Germanic art, as with many prehistoric people, was bone ornament, later replaced by metal objects. This applied art changed in northern Germany during the Bronze Age, from simple circles and other geometric forms to objects decorated with spirals and scrolls. When the Germanic people spread out over the plain in what is today North Germany, different cultures added to the art forms. Grotesque animal figures made their appearance among these pagan people of the north on ornaments and sculpture a few centuries after the birth of Christ.

The Romans left traces of their stay in southern Germany between the Danube and

Rhine rivers. The ruins of buildings, little statues, earthenware, and glass have been found in the area.

In the Christian era, which took a firm hold under Charlemagne and the Holy Roman Empire, new architectural forms came into play. German art, as we know it today, had its beginning during the 10th and early 11th centuries—known as the Ottonian period, for Emperor Otto I. The Romanesque period was roughly from 1000 to 1300. German architects, virtually all of whom are anonymous, built churches that were adaptations of the Roman basilica style. St. Michaelis-Kirche in Hildesheim is an outstanding example from this period. The present structure was reconstructed after World War II damage.

Decorative ivories, crucifixes, and book illumination were also characteristic of the period. Monasteries set up painting schools, and wall paintings of the time—around 1000—still exist on the island of Reichenau in Lake Constance.

The typically Romanesque Cathedral of Speyer was the 12th-century prototype for the imperial cathedrals in Mainz and Worms. Door carvings, bronze figures of Christ, and stained glass from this period show striking force despite their crudity.

CHANGING STYLES   Gothic architecture flowered in Europe, notably in France, from the 13th to the 16th century. The Romanesque influence was still strong, however, and Gothic did not establish as strong a foothold in Germany. The greatest of the German Gothic cathedrals, the Dom at Cologne, was started in 1284 but was not completed, as astonishing as it may sound, until 1880. The cathedral needed restoration after World War II. High Gothic is best represented by the Münster at Freiburg im Breisgau (see Chapter 9 on the Black Forest), which is famous for its pierced octagonal belfry crowned by a delicate openwork spire.

Perhaps more representative of the period is the hall-type church, which had its origins in Westphalia. Called Hallenkirche, this type of church was characterized by aisles constructed at the same height as the nave. They were separated from the nave by tall columns. Many of these churches were built during the late Gothic period, the 14th and 15th centuries, which was a period of great artistic growth in Germany.

The Renaissance, which began around 1520 and lasted a century, did not take hold in Germany as it did in Italy. The finest German Renaissance town is perhaps Rothenburg (see Chapter 11, "The Romantic Road").

Baroque style, an Italian import, brought a different kind of renaissance to Germany. The baroque swept southern Germany, especially Bavaria, though builders in the north tended to resist it. The baroque period began about 1660 and continued into the 18th century. Architectural forms no longer followed regular patterns. There was more freedom and more variety in design. The German and Danubian baroque artists, such as those of the Vorarlberg School, sought to give an impression of movement to their florid building designs. The splendor of the period is exemplified in the designs of such architects as Lukas von Hildebrandt and J. B. Fischer von Erlach. Berlin, as the center of an emerging Prussian state, moved into prominence as a seat of art and architecture. The baroque movement eventually dipped its brushes into the flippant paint of the rococo, and that movement brought even greater freedom and gaiety.

By the 19th century, many members of the rising and prosperous middle class in Germany preferred to decorate their homes in the Biedermeier style, with its lighter designs and flowing lines. By now the baroque and rococo styles were dead (the French Revolution had seen to that). Neoclassicism was strong. Once again, the south of Germany brought a lighter touch to this style than did the north. The Romantic Movement followed the neoclassical period. For inspiration in this Neo-Gothic era, architects looked back to medieval days.

Historicism is a word often used to describe an era that characterized German architecture in the latter 1800s. No one represented this flamboyant movement better than Ludwig II of Bavaria at his palace Neuschwanstein, which even today is one of the major tourist attractions of the country (see Chapter 11).

FROM JUGENDSTIL TO MODERN   By the end of the 19th century, the art nouveau movement—called Jugendstil in German after the magazine *Jugend* ("youth")—swept the country and marked the beginning of contemporary architecture. It was characterized by mass production and solid construction, as architects used such materials as glass, steel, and concrete.

In the aftermath of World War I, Walter Gropius gained prominence as leader of the Bauhaus movement. Art and technique were wed at this architectural school whose primary aim was to unify arts and crafts in architecture. Founded at Weimar and directed there by Gropius from 1919, it moved to Dessau in 1925. (Gropius eventually settled in the United States.) This movement was dissolved in 1933. By then the so-called National Socialist, or "Third Reich," architecture was the law of the land, and under Hitler and his lieutenants, architecture as well as art became a form of propaganda. The Führer's dream of rebuilding Germany collapsed, of course.

One of the sad legacies of World War II was that many of Germany's greatest architectural treasures were virtually leveled by Allied bombing raids. Notable among these tragedies was the destruction of Dresden, one of the most beautiful cities of Europe until 1945.

In the years after the war, both Germanies, East and West, set for themselves the formidable task of rebuilding. In some cases, the past was swept away never to be rebuilt. However, many cathedrals and other buildings were restored in the old style, even though they were extensively damaged. In some instances, entire buildings were carefully reconstructed in their original style.

As Germany advances through the 1990s, rebuilding continues on some structures. Cologne, for example, has already reconstructed a dozen Romanesque churches that had been destroyed. Buildings, both domestic and commercial, erected immediately after the war were hastily put up for convenience more than for architectural grandeur. However, in the prosperous Germany of today, there has also been a renewed interest and concern for style in modern architecture. The country weds a respect for its past with the expanding needs of a growing population.

ARTISTS & ARCHITECTS

Before the 1400s, the names of individual German artists did not stand out. But by the 15th century, individual artists and sculptors, as well as architects, began to enter the art history books. Notable among these was Tilman Riemenschneider (1460–1531), "the master of Würzburg." A sculptor, he carved splendid altars at Würzburg, Bamberg, and Rothenburg.

Veit Stoss (1445–1533), another sculptor, was often called a "tormented genius." His celebrated *Annunciation* is displayed in the Gothic church of St. Lawrence in Nürnberg. Stephan Lochner, who died in 1451, was a leading member of the Cologne school. Lochner's altarpiece is today one of the outstanding artistic treasures of the cathedral at Cologne.

The premier name of the 16th century—indeed the best-known and most praised artist of the German school—was Albrecht Dürer (1471–1528), who was noted for his very imaginative, often symbolic, works and his incredible attention to detailed workmanship. Not only was this Nürnberg artist a master of painting, but also he excelled at drawing and the woodcut and wrote a treatise on his theories of art.

No roster of 16th-century German artists would be complete without the name of Lucas Cranach the Elder (1472–1553), who is known for having painted the portraits of the leaders of the Reformation, most notably Martin Luther. Cranach the Younger (1515–86) followed in his father's footsteps. The other major member of this Danubian school was Albrecht Altdorfer (1480–1538). Matthias Grünewald, or Mathis Gothart Nithart, continued to show a healthy respect for the Middle Ages, even though he lived from 1460 to 1528. A master colorist, he excelled in realistic studies of the crucifixion of Christ. His greatest work, the *Isenheim Altar*, is in Colmar, France. Another portrait painter, Hans Holbein the Younger (1497–1543), also turned to religious themes for his strikingly realistic works. With his graceful and inventive mature style, he became court painter to Henry VIII of England. He was the son of the famous German painter of religious art Hans Holbein the Elder (1460–1524).

The 17th century produced fewer great artists and architects than the 16th. An exception was Elias Holl (1573–1646), a Renaissance architect whose notable works included the large Rathaus at Augsburg with its golden chamber. The building (see Chapter 11), was hit by bombs in 1944 but has been restored. Among sculptors in North Germany, Andreas Schlüter (1660–1714), praised for his virile style, is represented today by such works as the bronze equestrian statue of the Great Elector, his masterpiece, in the Court of Honor at Charlottenburg in Berlin.

Many artists and architects of the 18th century left a rich legacy. Dominikus Zimmermann (1685–1766) was the master of the Bavarian rococo style. On the slopes of the Ammergau Alps, he created his masterpiece, the Wieskirche, completed in 1754. Another architect (and in this case an engineer as well) was Balthazar Neumann (1687–1753), who was a master at creating both religious and secular buildings. He is today remembered for his pilgrimage church, Vierzehnheiligen (northeast of Bamberg), and his Residenz at Würzburg, one of the biggest baroque palaces in the country.

Often in the baroque era, an architect would work with a painter or sculptor. One of the most successful collaborations was that of the Asam brothers. Egid Quirin Asam (1692–1750), a sculptor, and his brother, Cosmas Damian Asam (1686–1739), a painter, worked on churches at Weltenburg, Rohr, and Munich.

In the 19th century, Wilhelm Leibl (1844–1900), a master of the realist school, known for his scenes of common life in Bavaria, and Caspar David Friedrich (1774–1840), acclaimed painter of the romantic movement, distinguished themselves.

20TH CENTURY   The often dreary, imitative art of the 19th century in Germany gave way in the 20th to schools and movements noted for their vigor and vitality. Often deliberately "revolutionary" and shocking (at least for their time), the works of many of these artists were labeled decadent or destroyed during the Third Reich, when painting was supposed to express the "ideals" of National Socialism. The new century began with the expressionist school, whose haunted, tormented view of the world was inspired by van Gogh as well as Scandinavia's greatest painter, Edvard Munch. Expressionism grew out of Die Brücke (The Bridge), a group founded in 1905. Until the outbreak of World War I, this controversial but influential group brought together such artists as Karl Schmidt-Rottluff, Erich Heckel, and Ernst Ludwig Kirchner. Kirchner, who committed suicide in 1938, did pictures that were sharply patterned and colored, with distorted figures.

For a time, Emil Hansen (1867–1956) was a member of the group. Better known by the name Emil Nolde, the painter lived in a house in the marsh in Seebull in Schleswig-Holstein. He was known for his aggressive use of color and for his juxtaposition of the sacred and the profane. One of the most prominent expressionists was Ernst Barlach, a sculptor who was born in 1870 and died a year before the outbreak of World War II. His large, tormented works in bronze and wood include Man in Doubt and The Avenger.

Another major artistic movement, Der Blaue Reiter (The Blue Rider), was developed in Munich in 1911 by Franz Marc and Wassily Kandinsky, a Russian. Later, August Macke and Paul Klee reinforced the movement. Absorbed by the romantic and the lyrical, their dreamy works influenced abstract painting in the decades to come.

If the Blue Riders wanted to free art from rigid constraints, the Dadaists carried such a desire to the ultimate extreme. However, at the same time, such eminent artists as George Grosz (1893–1959) practiced a brutal realism. This painter and graphic artist, who came to the United States in 1932, was noted for his satirical pictures of German society and of war and capitalism.

Walter Gropius (1883–1969) is considered one of the most celebrated and influential architects of the 20th century. He was the founder, in Weimar in 1919, of the Bauhaus school of art and design. Stressing functional designs that reflected the robust tastes of the postindustrial revolution, his buildings were controversial. He designed many of Germany's buildings during the 1930s as well as many of urban America's after he adopted the United States.

Gropius's Bauhaus also attracted a number of painters and sculptors, such as Wassily Kandinsky and Lyonel Feininger.

Art bounced back in the postwar era with a number of movements. For example, Max Ernst (1891–1976), a German painter who lived for many years in the United States, was a leader in the Dada and surrealist movements and is credited with adapting the cubist technique of collage in a highly original manner.

In the 1980s and 1990s, the painting scene in Germany was very lively, with notable centers in Berlin, Hamburg, Cologne, and Düsseldorf.

4. LITERATURE

Even before Gutenberg invented the first printing press in the Western world in the 15th century, German literature, both oral and written, was being produced. The first written literary work known is *The Lay of Hildebrand,* a narrative poem handed down by ancient storytellers and copied by monks at the Benedictine abbey at Fulda. Such tales of valor, love, sorrow, and death were strong in oral tradition, with the Rhine Valley giving rise to many legends and songs through the centuries— Lohengrin, Roland, the Lorelei, and the Nibelungen among the subjects.

The age of chivalry gave birth to lyric poetry in Germany. Like the troubadors in France, *Minnesingers* of the Middle Ages roamed the land singing songs of love and derring-do inspired by the Crusades. One of these, Walther von der Vogelweide, a knight of the late 12th and early 13th centuries, is seen as the father of lyric poetry in Germany. Another early 13th-century poet of note was Wolfram von Eschenbach, whose epic *Parzival* glorifies chivalry and religious devotion. By the 16th century, another "hero" had joined German folklore and literature—Til Eulenspiegel, a clownish fellow whose life around 1300 became the subject of story and song.

From the time of the Reformation (16th century), Martin Luther's influence can be traced in many fields of the German life of the mind and spirit. His translation of the Bible into modern German was hailed as the first great literary work in the language. A Luther contemporary, Hans Sachs, a *Meistersinger,* was a prolific author of stories, poems, plays, and songs.

Publication of the picaresque novel *Simplicissimus* by Hans Jakob Christoffel von Grimmelshausen (17th century) marked the start of production of long prose narratives in the country. The Age of Enlightenment in German literature dawned in the late 17th century, inaugurated by Friedrich Gottlieb Klopstock in his epic *Der Messias* and his *Odes,* and it continued into the 18th century. Rationalization was the watchword in this period. Also in this era, the principles of German drama were laid out by Gotthold Lessing.

STURM UND DRANG As a reaction to rationalization, a literary movement known as *Sturm und Drang* ("storm and stress") was born in the 18th century, marked especially by poetry and drama extolling both sentiment and grand passions and rejecting previous social, political, moral, and literary authority. It was at this time, that Johann Wolfgang von Goethe (1749–1832) arrived on the scene, a giant of letters. Dramatist, novelist, philosopher, and Germany's greatest poet, Goethe followed the pattern of the times in youth and early manhood (the *Urfaust* [or *Early Faust*], *Egmont,* and *The Sorrows of Young Werther*). However, he soon became disenchanted with Sturm und Drang, turning in midlife after a stay in Italy to a classical mode (*Nausikaa*). During this period, he reworked *Faust,* so that the final product begins with storm and stress and then levels off into tranquil classicism. It was after his sojourn in Italy that he also produced *Wilhelm Meisters Lehrjahre,* a novel that served for decades as the prototype of the best German fiction.

Another literary immortal, Friedrich von Schiller (1759–1805), playwright and poet, a contemporary and friend of Goethe, also turned away from Sturm und Drang with the presentation of *Don Carlos,* a powerful historical drama honoring liberty.

Similar dramas were *Wallenstein* and *Wilhelm Tell*. Schiller's outlook placed his interests in the fields of history and philosophy.

As the literary world moved from classicism to romanticism to historical romanticism, such names of world note appear as the brothers Jacob (1785–1863) and Wilhelm (1786–1859) Grimm, famous for their collection of fairy tales, folktales, and myths, and Heinrich Heine (1797–1856), second only to Goethe as Germany's greatest poet. Forced out of Germany for politics considered "too liberal" at the time, Heine lived in France from 1848. He wrote many celebrated lyrics, including the *Lorelei*. *Sketchbooks* was his attack on conservatism.

20TH CENTURY Rainer Maria Rilke (1875–1926) wrote verse considered mystical and symbolic. Concerned with death and the nature of human existence, he is known for his *Poems from the Book of Hours,* which in 1905 brought him fame, and *Duino Elegies,* published in 1923.

Another German, the novelist Erich Maria Remarque (1898–1970), moved to France to escape the political conditions of his homeland. He is best known for several novels that became popular films as well: *All Quiet on the Western Front, A Time to Love and a Time to Die,* and *Arch of Triumph.*

Franz Kafka (1883–1924) was actually an Austrian novelist born in Prague, although he become a major figure in German literature. Most of his work was published posthumously. He explored a person's efforts to find identity in a baffling, often hostile universe, as exemplified by such novels as *Amerika* and *The Trial.*

Bertolt Brecht (1898–1956), a poet and playwright, chose to live in East Germany after World War II. He created his own "epic theater" company, and his plays often expressed Marxist or antimilitary establishment themes. His best-known work is *The Threepenny Opera;* another powerful play is *Mother Courage.*

Germany's winners of the Nobel Prize for Literature have been Theodor Mommsen (1902), classical scholar and historian; Rudolf C. Eucken (1908), philosopher; Paul J. L. Heyse (1910), novelist, dramatist, and poet; Gerhart J. R. Hauptmann (1912), dramatist; and novelists Thomas Mann (1929), Hermann Hesse (1946), and Heinrich Böll (1972).

Of them all, Thomas Mann (1875–1955) and Hermann Hesse (1877–1962) achieved the largest world audience. It seemed that every young person in America in the late 1960s was reading Hesse's *Siddhartha.* Almost violently anti-Nazi in his time, he is also known for such works as *Steppenwolf.* He was passionately interested in the religions of the East. Mann went on to greater fame, and such masterpieces as *The Magic Mountain* (1925) and *Death in Venice* (1912), a novella, have placed him in the foreground of the most significant writers of the 20th century. He, too, opposed the Nazi regime, and from 1938 to 1953 he lived in the United States.

Günter Grass wrote *The Tin Drum* and *Dog Years.* One of Germany's best-known postwar novelists, he has attempted in his writing to come to terms with Germany's horrendous recent past. Heinrich Böll, known for such works as *The Lost Honor of Katharina Blum* and *The Clown,* won the Nobel Prize for Literature in 1972.

Writers who subsequently won a wide following include Siegfried Lenz, Martin Walser, Michael Ende, Patrick Süskind, and Austrian-born Peter Handke.

5. MUSIC & FILM

MUSIC

Music is an important facet of life in Germany. No other country has produced so many composers of indisputable greatness.

In the Middle Ages, music and dancing was important in towns and villages. Dances included an elaborate *Moresche* similar to the English morris dance. Bagpipes, shawms, hurdy-gurdies, and dulcimers sounded the tunes. *Stadtpfeifer* (professional musicians) guilds played trumpets and drums to accompany dances and religious processions. In monasteries, the plain chant of Roman origin came into use, and art music slowly took shape. Latin was the language used by the monks, but from their chants the early vernacular hymns (religious folk songs) developed.

From about the 11th century, the *Minnesang* (love song) became widely known; courtly love lyrics were accompanied by bowed and wind instruments. In later centuries the *Meistergesang* (master song), a conservative form used by singing schools (guilds) developed in such towns as Augsburg and Nürnberg, bringing music into focus in middle-class culture.

Development of the organ, an instrument known from the 8th century, was rapid. By the end of the 15th century, its use in Germany was widespread and was the most highly developed in Europe.

Musical establishments began to spring up based on church, court, and town. Court musicians, usually made up of a number of different groups, performed both sacred and secular music. One group was the ecclesiastical court *Kapelle,* with choirboys and clerics, replaced after the Reformation in Lutheran courts by *Kantorei* (professional voices). Vocalists were much higher up the social ladder than instrumentalists, except for trumpeters, who were the highest-ranking players, paid by the military. In cities and towns without courts, professional musicians' guilds were formed, sometimes paid by the town council. These performed for civic entertainment and also were used to sound the hours of the day from a tower in the town. The idea for the fable "The Town Musicians of Bremen," by the Brothers Grimm, was based on such performers.

In the 16th century, music came to play a major role in university curricula in the Protestant north of Germany, both as a discipline and as a practical subject, with emphasis on church music. Martin Luther, who wrote both words and music of hymns, was an important influence on church music. Protestant hymns, borrowing from the style of secular tunes, gained popularity through much of Germany with the spread of music printing, although not in the Catholic south. The organ dominated the instrumental music of the 16th century, becoming larger, more sophisticated, and more widely used. A 17th-century leader in the field of church music was Heinrich Schütz.

BAROQUE MUSIC German baroque music that developed from an adoption and fusing of foreign ideal and native tradition prepared the way for the great works that date from the 18th century on, especially in the art of the harpsichord and other keyboard instruments. In the course of about a century, German opera grew from vernacular works on religious and moral subjects to the operatic masterpieces of Wagner.

Early in the 18th century, in the baroque period, the names of musical geniuses whose works are known throughout the world began to resound in Germany. Ensembles became a part of life among university and town groups, one of which was started at Leipzig by Georg Philipp Telemann, whose descriptive music became popular. This ensemble later was headed by Johann Sebastian Bach (1685-1750), who was a master of all musical forms of his time. The baroque church cantata was one of the main German musical genres of the century, and Bach produced many fine ones for the Lutheran churches in which he served as cantor. After his death, he grew still more influential in German music in the last half of the 18th century because of his keyboard works; the tradition was maintained especially by two of his talented sons.

During the baroque period also, George Frideric Handel (1685-1759), known for the *Messiah* and other oratorios and operas, rose to prominence in his role as musician to the courts of Hannover and St. James in England. Christoph Willibald von Gluck (1714-87) was an operatic composer, who fused music and text into a dramatic whole. Many of his operas were based on classical themes, including *Orpheus and Eurydice.*

Wolfgang Amadeus Mozart (1756-91), although an Austrian, cannot be omitted from any discussion of German music. His operas, *The Marriage of Figaro, The Magic Flute,* and *Don Giovanni* are without equal for their dramatic effectiveness and for their musical characterization, and his orchestral and instrumental music left a lasting influence. Franz Joseph Haydn (1732–1809), like Mozart, was an Austrian who exerted great influence on German music. The classical sonata form reached perfection in his symphonies.

Musical theater was developing in Germany in the 18th century, a specialty of the stage being the Lied, an art song used with chamber instrumental music in its early stages and then with symphony orchestras. The German musical stage produced the Singspiel, which combined dialogue with music, following introduction of the form in Vienna. The hearty acceptance of the Singspiel became the base for the popularity of 19th-century German opera. Mozart's *Die Zauberflöte* (*The Magic Flute*) was the point of departure for German opera.

19TH & 20TH CENTURIES   Ludwig van Beethoven (1770–1827) helped usher in romanticism. His works—showing that music could be a personal statement—included 9 symphonies, 5 piano concertos, and 32 piano sonatas. He lost his hearing completely in 1819.

Riches of music poured across Germany in the 19th century. Franz Schubert (1797–1828) developed the song (*Lied*) to a high art. Felix Mendelssohn (1809–47) combined a romantic mood with a classical form; Robert Schumann (1810–56) wrote passionately romantic works, such as *Piano Concerto in A Minor;* and Johannes Brahms (1833–97) was a master of classical forms. Carl Maria von Weber (1786–1826) is considered the founder of German romantic opera.

A giant in the music world, Richard Wagner (1813–83) and his theories of music drama exerted a tremendous influence on all opera that followed him. Perhaps his greatest work is his cycle *The Ring of the Nibelungs.* Following in his footsteps was Richard Strauss (1864–1949). His works include *Salome* (based on a work by Oscar Wilde), *Elektra,* and *Don Quixote.* Max Reger (1873–1916), especially gifted as a contrapuntist, is known for his chamber music and piano concertos, among other works.

During the Nazi era, several eminent composers had to leave their homeland and work abroad. Among these was Kurt Weill (1900–50), whose best-known music is the score of *The Threepenny Opera.* Paul Hindemith (1895–1963) also went to the United States. He experimented with atonality in his early works, and his best-known pieces include the opera *Mathis der Maler.* Arnold Schoenberg (1874–1951), born in Austria, fled Germany in 1933. He is notable for the "12-tone technique" for structuring his atonal music.

In the present day as in the past, music is important in Germany. Notable modern and experimental composers are Karlheinz Stockhausen, Carl Orff, and Hans Werner Henze.

The Länder and cities keep alive the music of the masters and encourage modern composers by holding operatic weeks and various music festivals. Among major events is the Bayreuth Festival instituted by Wagner, who made the town a music landmark. Throughout the country, music lovers can pretty well take their pick of what to hear at most times, with opera, symphonic music, chamber music, vocal recitals, and choral singing—and just about everything else—available.

FILM

German cinema came into its own in the aftermath of World War I—although it had actually begun in 1895 when the Brothers Skladanowsky presented their Bioscop in the Wintergarten at Berlin. The famous UFA was formed, a German film company that was to continue making films until the very twilight of the Nazi era.

No film did more to earn Germany a place in cinema history than *Das Cabinet des Dr. Caligari* (*The Cabinet of Dr. Caligari*), directed by Dr. Robert Wiene, released in Berlin in 1920. Some press reviews hailed it "as the first work of art on the screen."

After viewing the film the French coined the term *Caligarisme,* to describe the "all upside down" postwar world.

The 1920s saw the production of many notable German films, such as Fritz Lang's *Dr. Mabuse, The Gambler* (1922), a screen version of a novel by Norbert Jacques. In 1924, Lang achieved far greater success with his two *Die Nibelungen* films, which became classics, recounting the legend of Siegfried and Kriemhild. Another notable Lang film, *Metropolis,* was released in 1927. Lang's *The Spy* (1928) became the forerunner of the Hitchcock thrillers. Carl Mayer achieved renown for his scripts, which were called "screen poems." These include the expressionist film *Genuine* (1920) and *Backstairs* (1921). *The Last Laugh* was a powerful film, released at the end of 1924. Mayer is said to have "unchained" the camera.

In 1925, Paramount and Loew's Inc. bailed UFA out of its financial woes. But it was only a temporary bailout, and in 1927 it again faced financial ruin. Hollywood outbid UFA for some of the brightest stars, who went to California, including directors Ernst Lubitsch and F. W. Murnau (*Faust,* 1926) and stars such as Conrad Veidt and Emil Jannings.

The Wall Street crash of 1929 greatly hurt film production in Germany. The most notable film to come out of the subsequent troubled period was *Der Blaue Engel* (*The Blue Angel*), released in 1930. It starred Emil Jannings and brought world acclaim to its female lead, Marlene Dietrich. It was directed by Josef von Sternberg, who brought Dietrich to Hollywood and even greater glory.

When the Nazis came to power, German films became a propaganda instrument. Nazi propaganda films reached the zenith of their power in Leni Riefenstahl's 1934 *Triumph of the Will,* acclaimed for its cinematic techniques in spite of the glorification of Nazism enveloping the film.

In the first decades after World War II, the German film industry was not very creative. By the 1970s, however, a group of talented directors was emerging. Notable directors included Rainer Werner Fassbinder, Werner Herzog, Wim Wenders, and Volker Schlöndorff.

6. RELIGION, MYTH & FOLKLORE

Germany possesses a rich trove of legend and myth, plus some of the most compelling folklore of any nation in Europe, and its allure and allegorical symbols have strongly influenced many of the historic yearnings and values of the German people. Richly idealistic and passionate in its defense of those ideals, Germany has also produced some of the leading theologians of the Christian era and spawned on its soil the ideas that led to the Protestant Reformation.

RELIGION

Except for a handful of previously converted small areas, Germany was Christianized in the 700s by such saints as Willibrord (658–739) and Boniface (673–754). In the late 700s, Charlemagne, from his capital at Aachen, forcibly converted many other non-Christian people, partly as an assurance of control over them. However, intense conflicts between the Vatican and the German states developed as early as the 11th century, much of it based on power, influence, and income. The dissatisfaction that led to the Protestant Reformation, whose roots were sown in Germany during the early 1500s by such theologians as Martin Luther, had already been present for almost 400 years.

After the Reformation, central, northeastern, and northern Germany was largely Protestant (Lutheran and Calvinist), while the west, south, and southwest remained mostly Roman Catholic. In both areas, however, enclaves of other religions remained, including communities of Jews. This traditional geographic division of Germany into Protestant and Catholic zones remained unchanged, except for some occasional differences brought about by movement of rural folk into urban industrial zones, until the large-scale migrations of German refugees after 1945.

After the unification of Germany under the Prussia-based Hohenzollerns (staunch Protestants) in 1871, the official life of the country was more Protestant than Catholic, although during the ill-fated Weimar Republic, the Catholic hierarchy asserted itself by reorganizing its followers into a more efficient and broad-based series of ecclesiastical provinces, with increased numbers of dioceses and archbishops.

The Nazis made concentrated efforts to assimilate the Protestant and Catholic churches of Germany into the government machinery, and in many cases completely dominated both their clergy and their memberships.

After World War II, the Communist regime of East Germany oppressed all aspects of organized religion as actively as possible, with especially intense persecution of its members in 1952 and 1953. In 1953, the East German representatives of the Protestant church formally agreed to refrain from unconstitutional interference in economic and political life, and the pressure abated somewhat.

Since 1945 there has emerged a German synthesis, studied and adapted throughout the world, of existentialism and Christian dogma. This synthesis (Christianized existentialism) has influenced every aspect of modern Christian thought.

MYTH

The great Swiss historian Carl Burckhardt observed that Germany's primeval myths and pagan legends have always been intoxicating to the Germans.

The most visible and universal of these myths is, of course, the *Niebelungenlied*. First written down in 1200, possibly as a compilation of 20 shorter and much older poems, its heroes, heroines, and villains—Siegfried, Günther, Brunhilde, Kriemhild, and Hagen—have become a part of German legend. Echoes of this saga are found everywhere, from Wagner's great operas to Fritz Lang's 1920s movie. Hitler's use of the myth as nationalist and racist propaganda has somewhat tainted it for the present day, and modern German writers tend to shy away from using it.

The plot involves the hoarded treasure (the Rheingold) of the Niebelungs, who—depending on the interpretation—might have been either the Burgundians or a mythical group of migratory forest dwellers under the direction of Siegfried. Siegfried's power derived from his bravery; his organizational ability; and also the mystical virtue of his sword, which had been forged by elves working in fiery smithies in the caverns of mountains and tempered with the blood of slain dragons.

When Hagen, killer of the heroic Siegfried, cast his opponents into the Rhine, the river swallowed the treasure of the Niebelungs, ingesting it into the bowels of Germany, where it has remained, cursed and hidden, ever since.

This saga, stripped of many of its complicated subplots and infused with a different kind of sexual love from that expressed within the original epic, was the basis for Richard Wagner's masterpiece, *Ring of the Niebelungs*. The epic was also updated by Hitler with his designation of the fortifications along the German-French border as "the Siegfried Line."

Other myths have tended to transform flesh-and-blood historical figures into semideified allegorical symbols. As in Britain's King Arthur legend, these characters, resurrected from death, will supposedly return to save Germany in a moment of crisis. Two examples are Hermann the Cherusker and Barbarossa.

Hermann the Cherusker (also known as General Auminius) defended the Teutoburgerwald (a region near the Ruhr Valley) against a far greater Roman force in 9 C.E., and he has ever since been viewed as the quintessential Teutonic savior of his people. From the shelter of a German forest, he annihilated the Roman force, capturing the sacred eagle-shaped standards of three Roman legions. Six years later, a larger Roman force, fighting in an open field, slaughtered the German tribes, murdered Hermann with the daggers of his chieftains, and dragged his visibly pregnant young wife in chains through the streets of Rome. Some German historians have seen this single set of events as the historical catalyst that led Teutonic people to invade Italy and cause the downfall of the Roman empire, but regardless of his historical fact, Hermann is forever assured a place in German myth.

The legend of Barbarossa plays an even more prominent part than that of Hermann in German myth and yearning. Emperor Friedrich I (1123–90), called Barbarossa, was leader of the loose confederation of states known as the Holy Roman Empire. He filled a vacuum in central Europe in his time, and his semibarbaric grandeur dazzled Christendom. Considered by the Germans to be one of their great kings, he enlarged the empire, encouraged city and town development, and maintained peace and prosperity. He was drowned while embarking on the Third Crusade. His legend and his power have long intrigued Germany, and myth has him alive and asleep, like Britain's Arthur, within the protective womb of a German mountain. The exact spot differs—most sources designate Kyffhauser in Thuringia, with a splinter group arguing for the Untersberg near Salzburg, Austria. Asleep, he is believed to be waiting for his country to need him, at which moment he will be awakened by ravens encircling his mountain lair, to propel his fatherland to the glory of a new Golden Age.

No one can deny the psychological potency of this legend, a myth that Hitler and the Nazi propaganda machine played upon insidiously to reinforce their self-appointed role as the saviors of Germany. Hitler appropriated this myth as code name for Nazi Germany's invasion of the Soviet Union—it was designated as Operation Barbarossa.

FOLKLORE

German folklore survived in rural areas at least until the mid-19th century, and much of its charm is still visible and nostalgically remembered today. The earliest scholars of German folklore were Jacob and Wilhelm Grimm, who traveled to far-flung corners of German-speaking areas in the early 19th century to record the tales they heard. Their compendium *Tales of the Brothers Grimm* is the second most frequently translated book, after the Bible. The book's contents belong to the intimate dreams of children and adults throughout the Western world, and its characters are familiar symbols in all European-based cultures. Children and adults even today rarely miss the fundamental messages about good and evil, wisdom and beauty, the supernatural and the mundane, concepts that have significance for all humanity.

Many of these tales occur within the sheltering darkness of a forest, a setting which has always been of prime importance to the German consciousness. During the heyday of the Teutonic people, trees and the forest were considered sacred objects of worship. (Even today, the German word *Wald* can be translated as either "forest" or "religious sanctuary" depending on its context.) They punished anyone who stripped the bark off a tree by skinning him alive and wrapping his hide around the wounded tree. Even today, the forests of Germany (and also the waters of the Rhine) exert a potent aura. Especially powerful were the linden, the oak, and the parasite of the oak, the mistletoe, which was considered the spirit of the oak because of its verdancy even in winter.

Supposedly, the death of winter and the rebirth of summer was the time of the Walpurgisnacht celebrations, when witches rubbed their naked bodies with ointments of fat, hemlock, and nightshade and danced themselves into an orgiastic trance in company with the devil. As they passed over German villages, they supposedly gnawed off pieces of every church bell they passed. German villages built bonfires to protect themselves from the witches' powers. There are many other folk customs, similar to those practiced all over Europe, of which we see vestiges today.

One final point to be mentioned is the pithy wisdom and emotive charm of old German folk wisdom. You may notice historic buildings that have pieces of advice prominently painted on the walls, both inside and out. Understanding their tone adds enormously to the fun of an evening in an old German inn. Translated examples include these: "The House's jewelry is cleanliness." "We all build well but we are foreign guests here, and in the place where we are to be forever, we build very little." "One's own stove is worth gold; if it is poor, it is yet warm." And finally (the favorite of any homeowner), "Building is a delightful pleasure, but I didn't know it would cost so much. May God shelter us always against masons and carpenters."

7. CULTURAL & SOCIAL LIFE

THE PEOPLE

The nature and appearance of the German people vary from region to region, ranging from the highland denizens of the south to the gregarious Rhinelanders to the more reserved inhabitants of the industrialized north. Descended from the several Germanic peoples mentioned above, the Germans today reflect the religious and cultural traditions of their forebears.

Prussian characteristics are not admired or emulated among Germans, especially not among young people. Germans tend in the main to be conformists, although some of the more progressive political and environmental movements in Europe have arisen in Germany, notably the Green Party. Among the people of the south, you'll find an informality and a joie de vivre that are sometimes lacking in the north. As a rule, the people of Germany are methodical; hardworking; and also hard-playing at such scheduled times as Oktoberfest, carnivals, weddings, and other festive occasions. Germany long ago pretty well did away with the class system, and the people as a whole are genial, outgoing, and friendly and helpful to visitors.

Many old traditions are still followed. You can see age-old costumes at folk festivals, particularly in Bavaria, the Black Forest, and Hesse. The land of castles and fairy tales, cuckoo clocks, oompah bands, and beer-hall frivolity still exists, although sometimes you may be startled at the regimentation of German festivities.

The Germans are nature lovers, treasuring their woods and parklands. Physical fitness is almost a religion to many, from childhood until they can no longer hike along mountain trails or follow the fitness courses laid out in most parks and playgrounds. They are also neat, tidy, and aesthetically oriented, as you'll appreciate when you observe their almost litter-free and flower-decked public places, and even more, their homes and their immediate surroundings.

LANGUAGE

High German is the official language, but some dialects persist. In the North German coastal regions and the Frisian islands, Lower Saxony, and Westphalia, the Low German dialect (Plattdeutsch) is both spoken and written, while the distinctive Frisian tongue is almost gone, used in only a tiny area. The Alemanni dialect is heard in the Black Forest, mingling with Franconian in the north and Swabian in the east. In eastern Germany, the Wendish language is occasionally used. The Wends (Sorbs), descended from western Slav tribes, live in the southeastern part of the country.

In general, Germanic languages are said to be composed of both early and modern forms of English, Dutch, Flemish, German (both High and Low), Frisian, and all of the Scandinavian languages except Finnish. The vocabulary also consists of some extinct languages, such as Gothic.

Early records come from fragments or inscriptions from the third to the first centuries B.C.E. Around the 1st century B.C.E., fragmented words and proper names were recorded by such writers as Pliny and even Caesar. The first extant major text in a Germanic language was part of a Gothic Bible, translated by a Visigothic bishop in 350 C.E. It was written in a 27-letter alphabet language largely "invented" by the scholar. Scholars stress that no written records of the parent language remain.

Of course, many German words came from Latin, as did English ones. *Vinum* in Latin became *wine* in English and *Wein* in German. Some German and English words were borrowed from French. *Danse* in French became *dance* in English and *Tanz* in German.

8. SPORTS & RECREATION

CAMPING AND CARAVANING   Some 2,100 German camping sites, located in the most beautiful and popular resort districts, and with all the necessary facilities, welcome visitors from abroad. Blue signs bearing the international camping symbol—a black tent on a white background—make it easy to find camping sites. Some 400 camping sites are kept open during the winter. Information on camping matters and camping sites is available on request from the **Allgemeiner Deutscher Automobil-Club (ADAC)**, Am Westpark 8, D-8000 München 70; and the **Deutscher Camping-Club**, Mandlstrasse 28, D-8000 München 40.

FISHING   If you'd like to do some fishing on your holiday, you can obtain complete information from the **German Anglers Association**, Bahnhofstrasse 37, D-6050 Offenbach. In Germany some local catches include char, grayling, river and sea trout, carp, pike, perch, pike perch, rockfish, eel, and bream. An official license—called a Fischereischein—is required, and it's available from local district or municipal authorities. Tourist offices in the various regions will supply details.

GLIDING   This is a fast-growing sport in Germany, offered by some 1,000 branches of the **Deutscher Aero Club**. For more information, contact its main branch at Rudolf-Braas-Strasse 20, D-6056 Heusenstamm (tel. 06104/6996-0).

GOLF   Most German golf clubs welcome foreign players. Weekday greens fees usually are 30 DM ($19.80), rising to as much as 60 DM ($39.60) on Saturday and Sunday. For information about the various golf courses in Germany, write the **German Golf Association**, Leberberg 26, D-6200 Wiesbaden.

HIKING AND MOUNTAIN CLIMBING   These sports have been a popular activity in the German uplands. It is estimated that there are more than 80,000 marked hiking and mountain-walking tracks in the country. The trails are serviced by the **German Hiking and Climbing Association**, which provides information from its address at Hospitalstrasse 21B, D-7000, Stuttgart 1. This outfit offers details not only about trails but also about shelters and huts and addresses of hiking associations in the various regions. The **German Alpine Association**, Praterinsel 5, D-78, 8000 München 22, owns and operates in and around the Alps 252 huts that are open to all mountaineers. The association also maintains a 9,500-mile network of alpine trails.

HORSEBACK RIDING   Throughout Germany are numerous riding schools or clubs, although this is a rather expensive sport. Charges vary from region to region. The school will expect you to have some experience of riding before venturing out, however. Pony trekking tours are also available in many parts of the country. Ask at local tourist offices.

SAILING   More than 30 sailing schools are found in the north, along the North Sea or Baltic Sea coastlines. In the south, the most popular place for sailing is Lake Constance. German national tourist offices abroad provide a list of sailing schools, or you can write to **Verband Deutscher Segelschulen**, Graelstrasse 45, D-4400, Münster 44.

SWIMMING   Almost every town in Germany has at least one indoor pool and one outdoor pool open to the public, and more and more hotels are offering swimming pools, either indoors or outdoors, or both. Beaches are found along the North Sea and Baltic Sea coastlines, although temperatures may be so low for many visitors they'd prefer the indoor seawater pools instead.

German spas contain mineral water or thermal indoor pools as well. Many

Germans, however, prefer to swim in lakes, especially the alpine lakes of Bavaria. River swimming is not recommended, mainly because of pollution, although shipping traffic could be a problem too. Look for signs *Baden Verboten,* which means no swimming allowed.

To swim in either indoor or outdoor pools, you must wear a bathing cap, which usually can be rented for a nominal fee. Germans are fond of nude bathing. Signs found on beaches that read *FKK* mean that nudity is permitted.

TENNIS Courts are available all over in Germany, and the sport is practiced in both winter and summer. Ask the local tourist office for a list of available courts in whatever region you're traveling in. If you're staying at a resort or spa hotel, you'll often find courts right on the hotel grounds. Many courts are indoors. Most indoor courts cost from 25 DM to 35 DM ($16.50 to $23.10) per game played, with outdoor charges generally ranging from 20 DM to 30 DM ($13.20 to $19.80) per game.

WINTER SPORTS More than 300 winter-sports resorts are in the German Alps and such wooded hill country as the Harz Mountains, the Black Forest, and the Bavarian Forest at altitudes of up to 4,905 feet. In addition to outstanding ski slopes, trails, lifts, and jumps, toboggan slides, and skating rinks, many larger resorts also offer ice hockey, ice boating, and bobsledding. Curling is very popular, especially in Upper Bavaria. The Olympic sports facilities at Garmisch-Partenkirchen enjoy international renown, as do the ski jumps of Oberstdorf and the artificial-ice speed-skating rink at Inzell. More than 250 ski lifts are in the German Alps, the Black Forest, and the Harz Mountains. Information on winter-sports facilities is available from local tourist bureaus and the offices of the German National Tourist Board.

9. FOOD & DRINK

REGIONAL SPECIALTIES

The Germans like to eat, and they take food preparation and consumption seriously. Calorie- and cholesterol-conscious Americans may recoil at the sight of meals of dumplings, potatoes, some of the hundreds of *Würste* (sausages), breads, and pastries. The beer that may accompany such a meal is not in the "light" category, and helpings of food served in this country are not small. Heavy meals, however, do not keep many of the German people from their cake and coffee break, considered a compulsory afternoon event.

The German love affair with sausage is of ancient lineage, Wurst having been a major part of the national diet almost since there were people in the area. However, Germans get German cooking at home, and so more and more restaurants are offering foreign foods and *neue Küche* (cuisine moderne), although the people of the country still like large helpings. Young people have become health-conscious and are eschewing the overrich, overabundant fare of their ancestors. Health-food shops are seen more and more frequently, and it is considered chic to patronize them. Young chefs, trained in Switzerland, France, or Italy, are returning to Germany in droves and opening continental restaurants. Italians, many who came originally to Germany as "guest workers," have stayed to open up trattorias.

Every region has its own specialties, ranging from A (*Aalsuppe,* or eel soup) to Z (*Zwiebelbrot,* or onion bread). You might begin with a Hamburg herring dish, then follow with red-wine soup from the Palatinate and (for a main course) Berlin liver with Bavarian potato dumplings, then some Allgau cheese, with some *Zwetschenkuchen* (plumcake) for dessert, rounded off by a glass of cherry brandy from the Black Forest. Fish comes from two seas in the north and also from the south and from the many lakes.

The most common German food is the already mentioned sausage (Wurst), not sauerkraut, as the world often mistakenly assumes. Germans take their Wurst with a bun and a dab of mustard (often smoky). Every region of Germany has its own sausage, but everybody's favorite seems to be Bratwurst from Nürnberg, made of seasoned and spiced pork. White sausage is called Weisswurst, and it's often a medley of veal, calves' brains, and spleen. As tradition has it, this sausage should be eaten only between midnight and noon. *Bauernwurst* (farmer's sausage) and Knockwurst are variations of the Frankfurter. The Frankfurter originated in Frankfurt, although another country made it even more famous as the hot dog. Small Frankfurters, which are called wieners or Vienna sausages in the United States and Wienerwurst in Germany, are, surprise of surprises, known as Frankfurters in Austria. Leberwurst is a specialty of Hesse. *Rinderwurst* and *Blutwurst* (beef sausage and blood sausage) are specialties of Westphalia and are often consumed with *Steinhager* (corn brandy).

Bavarians are hearty eaters, devouring such dishes as *Züngerl* (pig's tongue) and *Wammerl* (pig's stomach), most often with cabbage. Potato dumplings, or *Klösse*, also are served with many dishes, and *Leber* (liver) dumplings enjoy a great popularity. *Semmel* (bread) dumplings most often accompany the most famous meat dish of Bavaria, *Schweinebraten* (roast pork). Also with their devotees are *Kalbshaxen* (veal shank) and *Schweinshaxen* (roast knuckle of pork). At Altmühl, carp is praised by gastronomes, as is a superb trout (Forelle). Lake Constance has almost three dozen types of fish, of which the salmonlike Felchen is the most prized.

Berlin has its own hearty cuisine, no dish being more famous than *Eisbein* (knuckle of pork). The "backup" dishes to this main course are sauerkraut and *Erbsenbrei* (pease pudding), the latter a thick pea purée. Soul food to a Berliner is *Erbsensuppe* (yellow split-pea soup) served with Bockwurst. If you're not a true carnivore, you might skip the *Berliner Schlachtplatte*, most often containing pig's kidneys, boiled pork, along with liver and fresh blood sausage. Goose, prepared in several different ways, is popular in Germany, especially Berlin. A favorite of the famed Berlin conductor, Herbert von Karajan, was *Königsberger Klopse* (meatballs with capers and herring). A leg of pork with red cabbage is also a classic.

Along with Wurst, herring has long enjoyed a place on the German table. It is prepared in countless ways, including herring tartare or Bismarck. Perhaps the most common is Matjeshering, served with boiled potatoes.

From the Lüneburg Heath in the north comes the most delectable lamb in Germany. Called *Heidschnuckenbraten,* it is most often served roasted. Most visitors will prefer this lamb to such local dishes as *Braunkohl mit Bragenwurst* (kale with brain sausage).

The chefs of Bremen and Hamburg are known for an *Aalsuppe* (eel soup), which is often cooked with fruit. Neptune rules on the tables of the East Frisian islands, where local tables feature everything from fresh crab to eggs laid by seagulls. Fish is also a staple of the diet of Schleswig-Holstein, along with that sailors' favorite, Labskaus, a medley of such ingredients as potatoes, pickled meat, beer, and herring. The Holstein Schnitzel from this region is similar to the Wiener Schnitzel. From Lübeck comes the famed Marzipan.

Westphalia is best known for its delectable hams, which often weigh as much as 30 pounds, but it also produces a number of other plates. Ham is invariably accompanied by a dark pumpernickel bread. A highly spiced boiled beef, *Pfefferpotthast,* is the peppery local goulash. From the many freshwater rivers of the area come a wide variety of fish.

One dish from the Rhineland that has crossed the oceans of the world is Sauerbraten, which is braised pickled beef. This dish is often marinated for three days in a spicy vinegar before it is slowly cooked in robust red wine. *Rotkohl* (red cabbage), another famous German dish, is its usual accompaniment. *Himmel und Erde* (heaven and earth) is a medley of potatoes and apples with blood sausage, and Hase im Topf is a tasty rabbit pâté flavored with various "brews."

Pork is king in Hesse. Everything from that animal goes into the pot, including pig's trotters and ears. Bacon pie, or *Speckkuchen,* is a tasty concoction, as is *Kasseler Rippchen* (smoked pickled loin of pork).

Swabia and Franconia enjoy their own cuisines and if you indulge in them you may need to start a *Diät,* or diet, when you return home. The most popular soup of the region is *Flädlesuppe* (crêpelike pancakes are cut into strips and added to this soup). Instead of dumplings, *Spätzle* (pasta made of eggs, salt, and flour) often accompanies the Sunday roast. This noodle dish is a golden yellow in color. The Swabians have their own version of ravioli, Maultaschen, which are filled with minced meat and often flavored with onions and spinach. This is served in a rich broth or browned in fat. One of the best-known German confections comes from the Black Forest; a cherry cake called *Schwarzwälderkirschtorte*, it is usually eaten with afternoon coffee. The people of this region also consume a lot of *Speck* (smoked bacon).

The people of Franconia are known for their honest cookery—that means it's rather plain and homelike fare without a lot of fancy adornments. This cuisine is represented by such dishes as the *Bamberger Krautbraten* (meat-stuffed cabbage served with potato dumplings).

DRINKS

BEER Nowhere else are there so many good and different kinds of beer. Nowadays, many inns brew their own. The world's oldest brewery is in Bavaria, but the Bavarians are not the only ones who know about beer, which in Germany, incidentally, comes straight from the barrel. Export beers and the rather more bitter Pils, the most popular kinds, are also produced in Berlin, Hamburg, the Ruhr, Hesse, and Stuttgart. Altbier, a very early product of the brewer's art, is today to be found all over Germany. Berliner Weisse is another kind of beer (made from wheat, like a Bavarian white beer), but with a dash of raspberry or woodruff syrup. Malt beer is dark and sweet and contains hardly any alcohol, whereas "March beer" is also dark but considerably stronger.

In Germany, if you go into a beer hall and ask the bartender for *ein Bier,* you'll probably get the standard stock beer, Vollbier, which is 4% proof. More potent is Export at 5% or Bockbier at 6%. Helles Bier is light and brewed from malt that the local brewery, or Brauerei, has dried and baked. When the malt has been darkly roasted and fermented for much longer, it becomes dunkles Bier, or dark beer. Pils, or Pilsener, beers are light and contain more hops. Dortmund has earned a reputation in this field. In summer, Bavarians flock to beer gardens to enjoy their local brews, which are sometimes accompanied by white or red radishes and crisp pretzels.

WINE For centuries, Germany has made delightful, thirst-quenching wines, renowned for their natural lightness and their balance of sweetness and acidity. Climate, soil, and grape varieties all contribute to the success of the wine industry. Most vineyards flourish on steep hillsides, with protection from harsh winds provided by wooded neighboring hills. These vineyards rise mainly from the Rhine River and its tributaries, profiting by the reflected warmth from the sunlit water. Slow maturing of the grapes gives the German wines their typical fresh, fruity acidity.

There are 13 German wine-growing districts: Ahr, Mosel-Saar-Ruwer, Mittelrhein, Rheingau, Nahe, Rheinhessen, Rheinpfalz, Hessische Bergstrasse, Franken, Württemberg, Baden, Saale/Unstrut, and Sachsen. Wines range from vigorous reds to fragrant, aromatic whites, with Rheingau being the home of one of the most popular and best known, Riesling. There are German wines for every taste and occasion. *Trocken* (dry) and *Halbtrocken* (semidry) are often indicated on the labels, which also give other vital statistics about the bottles' contents, such as the growing region, the year the grapes were harvested, the town and vineyard from which the grapes came, the grape variety, the quality level, and other data.

There are two basic categories of wine allowed in European Community countries: table wine and quality wine from specified regions. In addition, Germany produces its famed *Qualitätswein mit Prädikat* (quality wines with special attributes). This latter category includes Kabinett, Spätlese, Auslese, Beerenauslese, Eiswein, and Trockenbeerenauslese, the crowning achievement of German viticulture. Qualitätswein b.A. is a light, fruity wine, which, along with Kabinett, is good with lightly seasoned dishes. Spicy dishes call for Qualitätswein (quality wines) or Prädikat Spätlese, while such dishes as roasts and game go best with white and red wines: Riesling, Rulander, Spätburgunder, or Lemberger. Delicate, medium-dry wines are best with mild cheeses, spicy or fragrant ones with strong cheeses. For a leisurely drink after your meal, perhaps with savory snacks, try a noble, full-bodied wine such as a fine Spätlese or Auslese.

A visit to Germany is not complete without a tour of one of the wine-growing districts, which stretch from the middle Rhine at Bonn south to Lake Constance, filled with classic scenery of imposing castle ruins, cathedrals, black-and-white gabled houses, elegant spas, and little Brothers Grimm villages. For information on a trip through one or more of these regions, ask at the **German Wine Information Bureau,** 79 Madison Ave., New York, NY 10016 (tel. 212/213-7028), or at the **German National Tourist Office,** 122 E. 42nd St., New York, NY 10168-0072 (tel. 212/661-7200).

OTHER LIBATIONS A clear corn brandy and juniper Schnaps are made in North Germany and Westphalia and are often served in earthenware bottles. From the Black Forest come clear fruit brandies and delicate herb liqueurs, often produced in places where, centuries ago, they were invented by monastic friars.

10. RECOMMENDED BOOKS, FILMS & RECORDINGS

BOOKS

HISTORY

A. James McAdams, *Germany Divided: From the Wall to Reunification,* Princeton University Press (1992). German unification came unexpectedly, and this study shows how ill prepared both sides were to meet the challenges.

Golo Mann, *The History of Germany Since 1787,* Praeger (1968). The son of Thomas Mann, the author writes evocatively of the politics and culture of a land he obviously knows well.

Detlev J. K. Puekert, *The Weimar Republic: The Crisis of Classical Modernity* (translated by Richard Deveson), Hill & Wang (1992). The late German historian Peukert documents both the cultural breakthroughs under Weimar and the economic crisis.

Peter Schneider, *The German Comedy: Scenes of Life After the Wall* (translated by Leigh Hafrey and Philip Boehm), Farrar, Straus & Giroux (1992). Comic absurdities surrounding the collapse of the Wall fill this book, but Schneider (author of *The Wall Jumper*) also explores resurgent anti-Semitism and how Germans are coping with the flood of refugees from the east.

William L. Shirer, *The Rise and Fall of the Third Reich: A History of Nazi Germany,* Simon & Schuster (1959–60). This story has never been told better—the complete saga of Hitler's empire from its unpromising beginnings until its tragic end.

Rebecca West, *A Train of Powder,* Viking (1955). This English novelist and historian covered the Nürnberg Trials for the *Daily Telegraph.* She provides a keen insight into the moral and legal judgments rendered there.

John Willett, *Weimar Years: A Culture Cut Short,* Abbeville Press (1983). Willett is known for translating Brecht's works into English, but in this book he provides his own insight into the culture and politics of this ill-fated republic.

BIOGRAPHY

Steven Bach, *Marlene Dietrich: Life and Legend,* William Morrow (1992). Better than Donald Spoto's "quickie" biography of Dietrich (*Blue Angel*), this book explores much of her often-scandalous life but pays special attention to her unique show-business career. Also notable is *Marlene Dietrich* (Knopf 1993) by the star's daughter, Maria Riva.

Roland Bainton, *Here I Stand: A Life of Martin Luther*, NAL (1989). This is a highly readable biography of the reformer who changed the religious face of Germany.

Einhard and Notker the Stammerer, *Two Lives of Charlemagne*, Penguin (1969). These are medieval biographers. One, Einhard, a courtier to Charlemagne, provides a well-written but short work. Notker's book was penned a century later.

Sam H. Shirakawa, *The Devil's Music Master: The Controversial Life and Career of Wilhelm Fürtwangler*, Oxford University Press (1992). Some have called Fürtwangler "the greatest conductor of this century." This is the finest book ever published on him.

A. J. P. Taylor, *Bismarck: The Man and the Statesman*, Random House (1967). This is the story of the "Iron Chancellor," who was instrumental in the unifying of the German states into the German empire.

John Toland, *Adolf Hitler*, Doubleday (1976). The Pulitzer Prize–winning author of *The Rising Sun* has written a monumental and revealing biography of the man who changed the face of Europe.

Hugh Trevor-Roper, *The Last Days of Hitler*, Macmillan (1986). This is an insightful reconstruction of the twilight of the Third Reich.

Renate Wind, *A Spoke in the Wheel: The Life of Dietrich Bonhoeffer* (translated by John Bowden), William B. Eerdmans (1992). This book sheds new light on the German theologian killed by the Nazis. The portrait is kind, but Wind also details Bonhoeffer's torment and narcissism.

FICTION

Johann Wolfgang von Goethe, *The Sorrows of Young Werther*, Random House (1990). This is virtually required reading by every German schoolchild. One of the world's great writers, Goethe explored the theme of suicide in this early epistolary novella.

Günter Grass, *Dog Years*, Harcourt Brace Jovanovich (1989); *The Tin Drum*, Random House (1990); and *The Flounder*, Harcourt Brace Jovanovich (1989). His works deal with the German psyche coming to terms with the dreadful legacy of Nazism and World War II. The latest work by Glass, *The Call of the Toad*, Harcourt Brace Jovanovich (1993), is a good read—part love story and part political lampoon.

Christoph Hein, *The Tango Player*, Farrar, Straus & Giroux (1992). Following in the tradition of the German expressionists, Hein uses satire and symbolism to warn against the state curbing freedom. Critics have found it evocative of *The Trial* by Kafka.

Hermann Hesse, *Narcissus and Goldmund*, Bantam (1981). Set in Germany of the Middle Ages, this book tells the story of two monks.

Christopher Isherwood, *The Berlin Stories*, New Directions (1954). Isherwood lived in Berlin from 1929 to 1933. His most famous story was "Goodbye to Berlin," which became the source for the stage and film versions of *Cabaret*.

Siegfried Lenz, *The Training Ground*, Henry Holt (1992). Author of *The German Lesson*, Lenz writes about the "heavy hand" of the state (ca. 1985). The plot centers on German chauvinism and warns against the rise of militarism.

Thomas Mann, *The Magic Mountain*, Random House (1969). This is the most celebrated masterpiece of this writer. It is set in a Swiss sanatorium (Davos); the sickness of the characters is a metaphor for the sickness of Europe as a whole.

Erich Maria Remarque, *All Quiet on the Western Front*, Fawcett (1987). This is a classic novel of World War I.

TRAVEL

Mark Twain, *A Tramp Abroad*, Hippocrine Books (1989). The American humorist was one of the original "Grand Tour" Americans viewing Europe. His travels through Germany are humorously detailed, including his description of life in Heidelberg. Read also his comments on "The Awful German Language."

POLITICS & SOCIETY

John Borneman, *After the Wall: East Meets West in the New Berlin,* Basic Books (1991). An anthropologist writes of East Germans before the revolution and discusses the "headlong rush into the embrace of capitalism."

Ralf Dahrendorf, *Society and Democracy in Germany,* W. W. Norton (1979). The question "What made Auschwitz happen" leads to a thoughtful analysis of the psyche of the German people.

Robert Darnton, *Berlin Journal 1989–90,* W. W. Norton (1991). This American scholar writes of the near bloodless revolution that led to the unification of Germany.

FOLKLORE & LEGENDS

Jacob and Wilhelm Grimm, *Complete Grimm Tales,* Pantheon (1974). This is the world's most famous collection of folktales—everybody from Little Red Riding Hood to Tom Thumb.

The Nibelungenlied, Penguin (1965). This is the great German epic.

FILMS

Cabaret (1972), directed by Bob Fosse. Although given a glossy Hollywood treatment with Liza Minnelli, Michael York, and Joel Grey, this film made some serious points about life in Berlin in 1931 as the Nazis were rising to power.

Berlin Alexanderplatz (1980), directed by Rainer Werner Fassbinder, won world attention, tracing the life of a man in Berlin from 1927 to 1978.

Abraham's Gold (1990), directed by Jörg Grave, provides a compelling look into how people deal with the "brown-shirted past" of Germany. Winner of a prize at the Cannes Film Festival, the film was called "fascinating, unsparing."

The Nasty Girl (1990), directed by Michael Verhoeven, deals with ostracism of a schoolgirl by members of her community after she sets out to learn the town's history during the Nazi era.

Europa Europa (1991), a French-German coproduction—and a controversial one at that—has been one of the most acclaimed foreign films of recent years. Written and directed by Agnieszka Holland, the film tells of the travails of a good-looking teenage boy (a German Jew), first with the Russians and later with Nazi soldiers.

The Other Eye (1991), written and directed by Johanna Heer and Werner Schmiedel, examines the career of G. W. Pabst, the Austrian director known for his work with Louise Brooks, including *Diary of a Lost Girl* and *Pandora's Box.* This documentary traces Pabst's work, including films made under the auspices of the Third Reich.

Schtonk (1992), written and directed by Helmut Dietl, deals in part with neo-Nazis and a forgery of Hitler's supposed diaries.

RECORDINGS
CLASSICAL

There's no denying the timeless allure of the music of Johann Sebastian Bach. Trevor Pinnock's performances of the *Brandenburg Concertos nos. 1–6,* present an authentic interpretation of the German master's music that is both clear and refreshing (DG Digital/410500/BWV 1046/51). Bach can be enjoyed with the Munich Orchestra's *Concertos for Flute, Violin, and Harpsichord nos. 1, 4, and 6* (DG Digital 413421-4GW).

Daniel Barenboim and the New Philharmonia Orchestra's Klemperer present works by one of Germany's immortal composers, Ludwig van Beethoven. His *Piano Concertos nos. 1–5* and *Choral Fantasia, opus 80* (EMI/CMS/63360-2 [3]) is considered a truly great recording.

Sir Thomas Beecham with Ilse Hollweg and the Royal Philharmonic Orchestra (EMI/CDM7 63374-2) present the gavotte and scherzo movements of G. F. Handel's *Amaryllis Suite;* also Handel's *The Gods Go a-Begging (Ballet) Suite,* and *The Great*

Elopement Serenade Part One (Love in Bath). Each of these is considered an infrequently performed work by a German-born composer whose recording represents one of the pinnacles of Sir Thomas Beecham's career.

Pianist Andreas Schiff, accompanied by the Bavarian Radio Symphony Orchestra, performs Felix Mendelssohn's *Piano Concertos no. 1 in G Minor* and *no. 2 in D Minor* (Decca 414 672-2). This has been reviewed as one of the most authoritative interpretations of the brilliant German composer.

No survey of German classical music should omit Wagner's *Siegfried Idyll,* performed by Europe's most colorful conductor, the late Herbert von Karajan. This was Wagner's birthday present to his wife, Cosima. Karajan's account has been critically received as unsurpassed. The reverse side of this recording (also by Karajan) is by a composer (Bruckner) rapidly gaining popularity as a competitor and contemporary of Brahms: Bruckner's *Symphony no. 8* (DG 419 196-2 [2] [id]).

One of the most influential forces in modern music was Kurt Weill. His *Violin Concerto* and his *Kleine Dreigroschen Musik* (Suite for Wind Orchestra from *The Threepenny Opera*) are performed by L. Lidell and the Sinfonia Atherton (DG 423 255-2).

JAZZ

Playing as smooth a horn as you'll find on any continent is German-born trombonist Albert Mangeldorf, whose album *Purity* has been a best-seller for jazz enthusiasts (Mood/DA Music 201/530 6887).

ROCK

One group that is rocking audiences from Lübeck to Los Angeles is a quartet of German men known collectively as Van der Graff Generator. One of their most successful albums is *The Quiet Zone* (Blue Plate/Caroline 61640).

CHAPTER 2

PLANNING A TRIP TO GERMANY

This chapter is devoted to the where, when, and how of your trip—the advance-planning issues that are usually required to get it together and take it on the road.

After people decide where to go, most have two fundamental questions: What will it cost? and How do I get there? This chapter will respond to those questions and then follow with additional practical information that any visitor to Germany will need.

1. INFORMATION, ENTRY REQUIREMENTS & MONEY

SOURCES OF INFORMATION

Nearly all larger towns and all cities in the Federal Republic have tourist offices. The headquarters of the **German National Tourist Board** is at Beethovenstrasse 69, D-6000 Frankfurt am Main 1 (tel. 069/75-72-0).

Before you go, you'll find a German National Tourist Office in **New York** at 122 E. 42nd St., 52nd Floor, New York, NY 10168-0072 (tel. 212/661-7200); in **Los Angeles** at 11766 Wilshire Blvd., Suite 750, Los Angeles, CA 90025 (tel. 310/575-9799); in **Toronto** at 175 Bloor St. E., North Tower, Suite 604, Toronto, ON M4W 3R8 (tel. 416/968-1570); and in **London** at Nightingale House, 65 Curzon St., London W1Y 7PE (tel. 071/495-3990). There are also tourist offices in about 20 other international cities, including Hong Kong, Johannesburg, Milan, Paris, and Sydney.

Other useful sources are, of course, newspapers and magazines. To find the latest articles that have been published on the destination, go to your library and consult the *Readers' Guide to Periodical Literature* and look under the city/country for listings.

You may also want to obtain **U.S. State Department** background bulletins. Contact the Superintendent of Documents, U.S. Government Printing Office, Washington, DC 20402 (tel. 202/783-3238).

A good travel agent can also be a source of information. Make sure that the agent is a member of the **American Society of Travel Agents** (ASTA). If you get poor service, write to ASTA Affairs Department, 1101 King St., Alexandria, VA 22314.

And, finally, we come to the best source of all—friends and other travelers who have just returned from Germany.

ENTRY REQUIREMENTS

PASSPORTS AND VISAS Every U.S. traveler entering Germany must hold a valid passport. It is not necessary to obtain a visa unless you are staying longer than three continuous months. For information on permanent residence in Germany and work permits, contact the nearest German consulate. Once you gain entry into Germany, you don't have to show your passport again at the borders with Belgium, France, Italy, Luxembourg, the Netherlands, Portugal, and Spain, according to an agreement signed among these European Community countries that went into effect on January 1, 1993.

In the **United States,** you can apply for passports in person at one of 13 regional offices or by mail. To apply, you will need a passport application form, available at U.S. post offices and federal court offices, and proof of citizenship, such as a birth certificate or naturalization papers; an expired passport is also accepted. Two identical passport-size photographs are required. First-time applicants for passports pay $65 ($40 if under 18 years of age). Persons 16 or older who have an expired passport that's not more than 12 years old can reapply by mail. The old passport must be submitted along with new photographs and a pink renewal form (DSP-82). The fee is $55. Call 202/647-0518 at any time for information.

In **Canada,** citizens can go to one of 25 regional offices or mail an application to the Passport Office, External Affairs and International Trade Canada, Ottawa ON K1A 0G3. Applicants residing in a city with a passport office are requested to apply in person. Passport applications are available at passport offices, post offices, and most travel agents. Passport requirements are stated on the application form. The fee is Can $35. Passports are valid for five years and are not renewable.

In **Great Britain,** citizens may apply at one of the regional offices in Liverpool, Newport, Glasgow, Peterborough, and Belfast, or in London if they reside there. You can also apply in person at a main post office. The fee is £15, and the passport is good for 10 years. Two photos must accompany the application.

In **Australia,** citizens can apply at the nearest post office. Provincial capitals and other major cities have passport offices. Application fees are subject to review every three months. Telephone 02/13-12-32 for the latest information. An adult's passport is valid for 10 years; for people under 18, a passport is valid for 5 years. Australians must also buy a departure tax stamp at a post office or airport.

New Zealand citizens should contact the nearest consulate or passport office to obtain an application. One can file in person or by mail. Proof of citizenship is required. A passport is valid for 10 years. The fee is $NZ56.25.

In **Ireland,** contact the Passport Office, Setanta Centre, Molesworth Street, Dublin 2, Ireland (tel. 01/780-822). The charge is IR £45. Applications are sent by mail. Irish citizens living in North America can contact the Irish Embassy, 2234 Massachusetts Ave. NW, Washington, DC 20008 (tel. 202/462-3939). The embassy can issue a new passport or direct you to one of the three North American consulates that have jurisdiction over a particular region; the charge is U.S.$65.

GERMAN CUSTOMS In general, items required for personal and professional use or consumption may be brought in duty-free. No duty is levied for a private car, provided that it is reported. Gifts are duty-free up to a total value of 620 DM ($409.20) and can include a maximum of 155 DM ($102.30) in items destined for non-European Community countries.

The following items are permitted into Germany duty-free (imports from European Community countries in parentheses): 200 (300) cigarettes or 100 (150) cigarillos, or 50 (75) cigars, or 250 (400) grams of tobacco. Americans or Canadians not residing in Europe may import double the tobacco allowance. You are also allowed 1 (1.5) liter(s) of liquor above 44 proof, or 2 (3) liters of liquor less than 44 proof, or 2 (3) liters of sparkling wines and 2 (4) liters of other wines; 50 (75) grams of perfume and 0.25 (0.375) liters of eau de cologne; 250 (750) grams of coffee; 100 (150) grams of tea. The duty-free tobacco and alcoholic beverage allowances are authorized for persons age 17 and above only, the coffee quota for persons age 15 and above only. All duty-free allowances are authorized only when the items are carried in the traveler's personal baggage.

MONEY

While this book documents the best hotels, restaurants, and attractions in Germany, my ultimate aim is to stretch your buying power—to show that you don't need to pay scalper's prices for charm, top-grade comfort, and gourmet food. You'll generally find prices very similar to those in the United States—but sometimes you'll pay far more. Germany is not the travel bargain of Europe.

CASH/CURRENCY The unit of German currency is the Deutsche mark (DM), which is subdivided into pfennigs. Bills are issued in denominations of 10, 20, 50, 500, and 1,000 marks; coins come in 1, 2, and 5 marks and 1, 2, 5, 10, and 50 pfennigs. What the Deutsche mark is worth in terms of U.S. money is a tricky question, the answer to which you determine by consulting the market quotations from day to day.

If you need a check in German marks before your trip, for example, to pay a deposit on a hotel room, or if you wish to buy traveler's checks in German marks, you can contact **Ruesch International,** 1350 Eye St. NW, Washington, D.C. 20005 (tel. 202/408-1200, or toll free 800/424-2923). Ruesch performs a wide variety of conversion-related services, usually for U.S. $2 per transaction. You can also inquire at a local bank.

TRAVELER'S CHECKS Traveler's checks are the safest way to carry cash while traveling. Most banks will give you a better rate on traveler's checks than for cash. Checks denominated in U.S. dollars are accepted virtually anywhere, but in some cases (perhaps for ease of conversion into local currencies), travelers might want checks denominated in other currencies.

THE MARK & THE U.S. DOLLAR

The following DM-to-dollar table should be used only as a gauge; check the rate of exchange immediately before you leave. The table is based on an exchange rate of approximately 1.50 DM to U.S. $1.

DM	U.S.$	DM	U.S.$
1.00	0.65	20.00	13.20
2.00	1.30	25.00	16.50
3.00	2.00	30.00	19.80
4.00	2.60	35.00	23.10
5.00	3.30	40.00	26.40
6.00	4.00	50.00	33.00
7.00	4.60	60.00	39.60
8.00	5.30	70.00	46.20
10.00	6.60	80.00	52.80
15.00	9.90	100.00	66.00

THE MARK & THE BRITISH POUND

The following DM-to-pound table should be used only as a gauge; check the rate of exchange immediately before you leave. The table is based on an exchange rate of approximately 2.50 DM to U.K.£1.

DM	British £	DM	British £
1.00	0.40	20.00	8.00
2.00	0.80	25.00	10.00
3.00	1.20	30.00	12.00
4.00	1.60	35.00	14.00
5.00	2.00	40.00	16.00
6.00	2.40	50.00	20.00
7.00	2.80	60.00	24.00
8.00	3.20	70.00	28.00
10.00	4.00	80.00	32.00
15.00	6.00	100.00	40.00

Each agency listed below will refund your checks if lost or stolen, provided that you produce sufficient documentation. When purchasing checks, ask about refund hotlines. American Express has probably the greatest number of offices around the world.

American Express (tel. toll free 800/221-7282 in the U.S. and Canada) charges a 1% commission. Checks are commission free to members of the American Automobile Association. Checks are denominated in U.S. dollars, Canadian dollars, British pounds, Swiss francs, French francs, German marks, Saudi riyals, and Japanese yen.

Citicorp (tel. toll free 800/645-6556 in the U.S., or 813/623-1709, collect, in Canada) issues checks in U.S. dollars, British pounds, German marks, and Japanese yen.

MasterCard International/Thomas Cook International (tel. toll free 800/223-9920 in the U.S., or 212/974-5695, collect, from the rest of the world) issues checks in U.S. dollars, French francs, German marks, Dutch guilders, Spanish pesetas, Australian dollars, Japanese yen, Swiss francs, and Hong Kong dollars.

Barclays Bank/Bank of America (tel. toll free 800/221-2426 in the U.S. and Canada) offers VISA traveler's checks denominated in U.S. dollars, British pounds, Swiss francs, French francs, German marks, and Japanese yen.

CREDIT CARDS American Express, Diners Club, VISA, and MasterCard are widely accepted in Germany. If you see Eurocard or Access displayed at an establishment, MasterCard is accepted. Credit cards can spare your valuable cash and give financial flexibility for large purchases or last-minute changes. The exchange rate used to compute credit-card charges can be quite favorable.

WHAT WILL IT COST?

Germany is one of the more expensive destinations in the world.

Although there are many variations in hotel price structure, based on size and type of rooms, hotels ranked **very expensive** generally charge 300 DM ($198) and up for a double room. **Expensive** means that doubles cost about 200 DM to 300 DM ($132 to $198); **moderate** rooms run about 120 DM to 200 DM ($79 to $132). A double priced under about 120 DM ($79) is considered **inexpensive.** Prices are for two persons occupying one room and include tax and service. All rooms are with bath unless stated otherwise. If **parking** is not specifically mentioned in a listing, the hotel has no garage or other parking facility. You'll need to find a place on the street or at a nearby garage. Parking rates are per day.

Germany offers a wide range of dining, in both cuisine and price. In the listings in this guide, a restaurant is considered **very expensive** if a meal costs more than about 70 DM ($50) without wine. **Expensive** dining runs about 50 DM to 70 DM ($33 to $50); **moderate,** about 30 DM to 50 DM ($20 to $33); and **inexpensive,** less than about 30 DM ($20).

If you want to see the country while not breaking your travel budget, you will need to cut short your time in Frankfurt, Munich, or Berlin and concentrate on regional capitals such as Freiburg in the Black Forest, where you can cut your travel costs by anywhere from 20% to 40%. A moderately priced rail pass will allow you to see a lot of Germany in a short time.

Though prices are high, you generally get good value for your money. The inflation rate, unlike that of most of the world, has remained low. Hotels usually are clean and comfortable, and restaurants generally offer a good cuisine and ample portions made with quality ingredients. The trains run on time, and they're fast, and most service personnel treat you with respect.

Many people come to Germany just for its winter sports. The most expensive resorts are such places as Garmisch-Partenkirchen. You can still enjoy winter fun, all at a moderate cost, if it is not important to you to be seen in chic places. At about two-thirds the price—or even less—you can patronize some of the less fabled winter spots in the Bavarian Alps. Sometimes if you stay in the village next to a chic resort, prices are 30% cheaper.

In Germany, many prices for children (generally defined as aged 6 to 17) are considerably lower than for adults. Children under 6 often are charged no admission or other fee.

WHAT THINGS COST IN BERLIN

	U.S. $
Taxi from Tegel Airport to Europa-Center	19.10
Underground from Kurfürstendamm to Brandenburger Tor	2.00
Local telephone call	.20
Double at Hotel Bristol Kempinski (very expensive)	345.80
Double at Bogotá (moderate)	128.70
Double at Cortina (inexpensive)	62.70
Lunch for one at Goldene Gans (moderate)	20.00
Lunch for one at Hard Rock Café (inexpensive)	15.00
Dinner for one, without wine, at Bamberger Reiter (very expensive)	60.00
Dinner for one, without wine, at Bacco (moderate)	30.00
Dinner for one, without wine, at San Marino (inexpensive)	15.00
Half a liter of beer	3.00
Coca-Cola in a restaurant	1.80
Cup of coffee	2.10
Glass of wine	3.10
Roll of 200 ASA color film, 36 exposures	6.50
Admission to Dahlem Museums	2.60
Movie ticket	6.00
Ticket at Schiller-Theater	6.60–34.30

WHAT THINGS COST IN MUNICH	U.S. $
Taxi from airport to Hauptbahnhof	52.80
Underground from Hauptbahnhof to Schwabing	1.60
Local telephone call	.20
Double at Vier Jahreszeiten Kempinski (very expensive)	379.50
Double at Hotel Reinbold (expensive)	155.80
Double at Adria (moderate)	112.20
Double at Pension Westfalia (inexpensive)	62.70
Lunch for one at Zum Bürgerhaus (moderate)	22.40
Lunch for one at Ratskeller (moderate)	16.00
Dinner for one, without wine, at Aubergine (very expensive)	70.00
Dinner for one, without wine, at Halali (expensive)	38.00
Dinner for one, without wine, at Weinstadl (inexpensive)	15.00
Glass of wine	2.20
Liter of beer	5.35
Cup of coffee	2.10
Coca-Cola in a restaurant	1.75
Roll of 200 ASA color film, 36 exposures	6.75
Admission to Schloss Nymphenburg	4.00
Movie ticket	6.00
Ticket to Nationaltheater	4.60–125.40

2. WHEN TO GO — CLIMATE, HOLIDAYS & EVENTS

CLIMATE

Germany's climate varies from the relatively temperate but damp north to the snowy Alps in the south. Northern winters tend to be mild, and summers are most agreeable. In the south and in the Alps, it can sometimes be very cold in winter, especially in January, and very warm in summer, but with cool, rainy days even in July and August. Spring and fall are often "stretched out"—in fact, I've enjoyed many a Bavarian-style "Indian summer" until late in October. The most popular tourist months are from May through October, although winter travel to Germany is becoming increasingly popular, especially to the ski areas in the Bavarian Alps.

Berlin's Average Daytime Temperature & Rainfall

	Jan	Feb	Mar	Apr	May	June	July	Aug	Sept	Oct	Nov	Dec
Temp. (°F)	30	32	40	48	53	60	64	62	56	49	40	34
Rainfall (in.)	2.2	1.6	1.2	1.6	2.3	2.9	3.2	2.7	2.2	1.6	2.4	1.9

Frankfurt's Average Daytime Temperature & Rainfall

	Jan	Feb	Mar	Apr	May	June	July	Aug	Sept	Oct	Nov	Dec
Temp. (°F)	33.6	36.1	41.5	48.9	57.0	63.1	65.8	65.8	58.3	49.5	41.0	34.9
Rainfall (in.)	6.5	5.1	5.6	5.7	5.9	5.5	5.0	5.1	4.2	4.8	6.5	6.0

Munich's Average Daytime Temperature & Days of Rain

	Jan	Feb	Mar	Apr	May	June	July	Aug	Sept	Oct	Nov	Dec
Temp. (°F)	33	35	40	50	60	65	70	73	65	50	39	33
Days rain	19	16	19	19	21	24	18	17	18	15	17	18

HOLIDAYS

Public holidays are January 1; Easter (Good Friday and Easter Monday); May 1 (Labor Day); Ascension Day (10 days before Pentecost); Whit Monday (day after Pentecost); October 3 (Day of German Unity); November 17 (Day of Prayer and Repentance); and December 25 to 26 (Christmas). In addition, the following holidays are observed in some German states only: January 6 (Epiphany); Corpus Christi (10 days after Pentecost); August 15 (Assumption); and November 1 (All Saints' Day).

GERMANY
CALENDAR OF EVENTS

Actual dates of events vary from year to year. Contact one of the branches of the German National Tourist Office (see "Sources of Information," above) for exact dates or more information.

The German National Tourist Board (GNTB) publishes a free calendar of forthcoming events three times a year: in April, October, and January, of which the first two are half-yearly calendars and the latter is a yearly preview. They give the dates of trade fairs and exhibitions, theatrical and musical performances, local and folk festivals, sporting events, conferences, and congresses throughout Germany.

JANUARY

☐ **New Year's Day International Ski Jumping,** Garmisch-Partenkirchen. One of Europe's major sporting events. For more information, contact the tourist bureau there at Dr.-Richard-Strauss-Platz (tel. 088/21-18-06).

☐ **Fasching.** Carnival festivals take place throughout Germany, reaching their peak preceding Ash Wednesday. Famous ones are presented in such Rhineland cities as Bonn, Cologne, and Düsseldorf, as well as in Munich.

FEBRUARY

☐ **Frankfurt International Fair.** This is one of the principal consumer-goods trade fairs of Europe, its origins actually going back centuries. For information, contact the Frankfurt Tourist Bureau, at the Hauptbahnhof (tel. 069/21-23-88-49). Late February.

MARCH

☐ **Spring fairs.** These events highlight the calendar throughout Germany, especially in Augsburg, Münster, Nürnberg, Hamburg, and Stuttgart.

☐ **Leipzig Trade Fair.** One of Europe's oldest and most venerated trade fairs. For information and dates, contact Leipzig Information, Sachsenplatz (tel. 0341/7-95-90).

APRIL

☐ **Walpurgis Festivals.** Celebrated, as in Scandinavia, throughout towns in the Harz Mountains. Festivities occur on the night preceding May 1.

MAY

☐ **"Hamburg Summer."** A whole series of cultural events, including concerts, plays, festivals, and special exhibitions. For various dates and venues, contact the Hamburg Tourist Bureau, Burchardstrasse 14 (tel. 040/7-30-05-10).

☐ **The International May Festival,** Wiesbaden. This city near Frankfurt hosts a premier cultural event, a series of "artistic celebrations" lasting a month. For information, contact the Wiesbaden Tourist Bureau, Rheinstrasse 15 (tel. 0611/172-97-80).

☐ **Red Wine Festival,** Rüdesheim/Assmannshausen. This is held in Assmannshausen, the most famous Rhine village for red wines. For information, contact Rüdesheim Tourist Bureau, Rheinstrasse 16 (tel. 06722/2962). May 12–15.

JUNE

☐ **Frankfurt Summertime Festival.** A series of cultural and artistic celebrations, plus outdoor events, staged throughout the city. For more information, contact the Frankfurt Tourist Bureau, at the Hauptbahnhof (tel. 069/21-23-88-49).

☐ **Floodlighting of the Castle,** Heidelberg. Fireworks enliven the display in this storied university city. For more information, contact the Heidelberg Tourist Bureau, Pavillon am Hauptbahnhof (tel. 06221/2-13-41). June 1.

☐ **Mozart Festival,** Würzburg. Aficionados of the composer flock to this major cultural event in the baroque city. For more information, contact the Mozart Festival Bureau, Haus Zum Falken, Marktplatz (tel. 0931/3-73-36). June 4–25.

JULY

☉ *RICHARD WAGNER FESTIVAL   This major cultural event takes place in Bayreuth, drawing Wagner lovers from around the world. The great opera composer built a Festspielhaus here and lived in this city, which is the capital of Upper Franconia.*
  Where: *Bayreuth Festspielhaus.* ***When:*** *End of July to end of August.* ***How:*** *Reserve hotel rooms well in advance. For more information, contact Tourist-Information, Luitpoldplatz 9 (tel. 0921/8-85-88).*

AUGUST

☐ **Freiburg Wine Tasting.** Local residents and visitors enjoy the first vintages from grapes grown in the Black Forest district. For more information, contact the Freiburg Tourist Bureau, Rotteckring 14 (tel. 0761/3-68-90-90). August 10–18.

SEPTEMBER

☐ **Leipzig Autumn Fair.** This is another trade fair in Leipzig with a long tradition. For more information, contact Leipzig Information, Sachsenplatz (tel. 0341/7-95-90). September 1–7.

OCTOBER

☐ **Frankfurt Book Fair.** A major international event for publishers, book dealers, agents, and authors. For more information, contact the Frankfurt Tourist Bureau, at the Hauptbahnhof (tel. 069/21-23-88-49). Usually mid-October.

NOVEMBER

☐ **Winter Dom,** Hamburg. An annual amusement fair (sometimes called Hamburg Dom) at the Heiligengeistfeld. For more information, contact the Hamburg Tourist Bureau, Burchardstrasse 14 (tel. 040/30-05-10). November 4–December 4.

DECEMBER

☐ **Christmas fair,** Mainz. Mainz stages its Christmas fair on the Rhine for three weeks preceding Christmas. For more information, contact the Mainz Tourist Bureau, Bahnhofstrasse 15 (tel. 06131/28-62-10). Other towns hold Christmas fairs in November.

MUNICH
CALENDAR OF EVENTS

For details on the following observances, consult the Munich Tourist Bureau, at the Hauptbahnhof (tel. 089/239-12-56).

JANUARY

☐ **Fasching (Carnival).** Pre-Lenten revelry characterizes this bash with a whirl of colorful parades and masked balls. The celebration lasts from January 7 to Shrove Tuesday, peaking on Fasching Sunday and Shrove Tuesday. Special events are staged at the Viktualienmarkt.

APRIL

☐ **Munich Fashion Week.** The latest and often the most elegant parades of fashion are staged at various venues throughout the city.

JUNE

☐ **Munich Film Festival.** This festival isn't as well attended as the February International Film Festival in Berlin, but it draws a serious audience. June 22–30.

SEPTEMBER

✪ *OKTOBERFEST Germany's most famous festival takes place principally in September, not October, as the name would suggest. Hotels are packed as the beer and revelry flow from tent to tent. Millions show up to recall Ludwig I's wedding to Princess Theresa back in 1810.*

__Where:__ Most activities are on Theresienwiese, where gigantic tents are sponsored by local breweries. Tents can hold up to 6,000 beer drinkers. __When:__ Middle of September to the first Sunday in October. __How:__ Contact the Munich Tourist Bureau for particulars or just show up. Always reserve hotel rooms well in advance.

BERLIN
CALENDAR OF EVENTS

Details on the precise dates and venues of the following festivals are available from the Berlin Tourist Information Office, at Europa-Center (tel. 030/262-6031).

FEBRUARY

✪ *__INTERNATIONAL FILM FESTIVAL__ Stars, would-be stars, directors, and almost anyone with a film to peddle show up here at this well-attended festival. It lasts for two weeks and is often a showcase for not only the latest German films but also the work of international film directors.*
   __Where:__ It takes place at various theaters announced in local newspapers. __When:__ Late February. __How:__ Tickets range from 10 DM to 15 DM ($6.60 to $9.90) and can be purchased at the box office or at a special booth at the Europa-Center.

SEPTEMBER

☐ **Berliner Festwochen.** One of the highpoints on the cultural calendar of Germany, the Berlin Festival Weeks bring an international array of performing artists to Berlin. There are fine opera, symphony, and concert performances and major theatrical presentations.

OCTOBER/NOVEMBER

☐ **Jazz-Fest Berlin.** This annual festival staged at the Philharmonie attracts some of the world's finest jazz artists, ranging from classical to experimental. Tickets at the box office cost from 10 DM to 30 DM ($6.60 to $19.80).

---

3. HEALTH, INSURANCE & OTHER CONCERNS

HEALTH

German medical facilities are among the best in the world. No endemic contagious diseases exist. Immunization for contagious diseases is required only if a traveler has been in an infected area within 14 days preceding arrival in Germany.

Take whatever medication or drugs you'll need with you to avoid the time and trouble of getting a prescription filled. German, not American, pharmaceutical brands prevail.

If a medical emergency arises, your hotel staff can usually put you in touch with a reliable doctor. If not, contact the American embassy or a consulate, as each one maintains a list of English-speaking doctors.

Before you leave home, you can obtain a list of English-speaking doctors from the **International Association for Medical Assistance to Travelers (IAMAT),** in the United States at 417 Center St., Lewiston, NY 14092 (tel. 716/754-4883); in Canada, at 40 Regal Rd., Guelph, ON N1K 1B5 (tel. 519/836-0102). For some chronic conditions, a Medic Alert Identification Tag will tell a doctor about your condition and provide the telephone number of Medic Alert's 24-hour hotline so your medical records can be obtained. For a lifetime membership, the cost is a well-spent $35. Contact the **Medic Alert Foundation,** P.O. Box 1009, Turlock, CA 95381-1009 (tel. toll free 800/432-5378).

Tap water in Germany is generally safe to drink. However, do not drink from mountain streams and rivers regardless of how clear and clean they appear to be.

At some point in a journey, a mild upset stomach, primarily a result of a change in diet and eating habits, may occur. This usually doesn't mean you've had bad or contaminated food and water, and such upsets typically pass quickly without medication.

INSURANCE

Credit-card companies often insure users in case of a travel accident, providing the travel was paid with their card. Sometimes fraternal organizations have policies that protect members in case of sickness or accidents abroad.

Many homeowners' insurance policies cover luggage theft and loss of documents. Coverage is usually limited to about U.S.$500. To submit a claim, remember that you'll need police reports or a statement from a local medical authority.

Some insurance policies provide advances in cash or arrange funds transfers so you won't have to dip into your travel money to settle medical bills. Seniors should be aware that Medicare does not cover the cost of illness in Europe.

You may want insurance against a cancellation. Some travel agencies provide coverage. Often such insurance is written into tickets paid for by credit card. Insurance agents can also provide coverage.

If you feel you need additional insurance, try **Travel Guard International,** 1145 Clark St., Stevens Point, WI 54481 (tel. toll free 800/826-1300), which offers a comprehensive seven-day policy for about $52. **Travel Insurance PAK,** Travelers Insurance Co., One Tower Sq., 10 NB, Hartford, CT 06183-5040 (tel. toll free 800/243-3174), offers illness and accident coverage, costing from $10 for 6 to 10 days. Other types of insurance are at an additional cost. **Mutual of Omaha** (Tele-Trip), 3201 Farnam St., Omaha, NB 68131 (tel. 402/345-2400, or toll free 800/228-9792), provides foreign medical coverage up to $50,000. It maintains a 24-hour hotline and offers other policies. Plans differ from state to state.

TRAVEL ASSISTANCE A number of companies offer policies and help in case you're stranded abroad in an emergency. These include **Wallack & Company,** 107 W. Federal St., P.O. Box 480, Middleburg, VA 22117-0480 (tel. 703/687-3166, or toll free 800/237-6615), and **Access America,** 6600 W. Broad St., Richmond, VA 23230 (tel. 804/285-3300, or toll free 800/284-8300).

4. WHAT TO PACK

Older Germans dress both stylishly and conservatively; younger Germans, like young Americans, wear what they want. In the big cities, men feel comfortable in suits or sports jackets. Suits, skirts and sweaters, simple dresses, or pants are suitable for women. Posh restaurants may require ties for men. Both men and women should dress up for nightclubs and for the casinos in the posh spas.

As for the country, a great deal depends on where you go, the time of year, and the activities you engage in. Although many Germans travel in shorts, you could be denied entry to churches and cathedrals, which are prime attractions, if you are wearing shorts. If you sun along a lake, remember to wear a cover-up (both men and women) when you leave the beach to promenade along lakeside quays. Bring along a bathing cap for use in a swimming pool.

Whatever the season, bring a raincoat and umbrella. Summer days can be warm and mild, but chilly nights, especially in the Alps, call for a sweater or jacket. For sightseeing, bring along comfortable walking shoes—preferably two pairs.

Above all, pack as lightly as possible. Sometimes it's hard to get a porter or a baggage cart in rail and air terminals. Airlines are increasingly strict about how much luggage you can bring aboard, particularly when flights are fully booked (or overbooked). Checked baggage should not be more than 62 inches (width plus length plus height). Bags shouldn't weigh more than 70 pounds.

5. TIPS FOR THE DISABLED, SENIORS, SINGLES, FAMILIES & STUDENTS

FOR THE DISABLED

For more information to help plan your trip, a good source is the **Travel Information Service,** MossRehab Hospital, 1200 W. Tabor Rd., Philadelphia, PA 19141-3099 (tel. 215/456-9600). It charges a postage and handling fee for material mailed. Each package contains names and addresses of accessible hotels, restaurants, and attractions.

You can also obtain a copy of **"Air Transportation of Handicapped Persons,"** published by the U.S. Department of Transportation. The copy is sent free by writing for Free Advisory Circular No. AC12032, Distribution Unit, U.S. Department of Transportation, Publications Division, M-4332, Washington, DC 20590.

You may also want to consider joining a tour specifically for disabled visitors. Names and addresses of such tour operators can be obtained by contacting the **Society for the Advancement of Travel for the Handicapped,** 347 Fifth Ave., New York, NY 10016 (tel. 212/447-7284). Yearly membership dues are $45, $25 for senior citizens and students. Send a stamped self-addressed envelope.

The **Federation of the Handicapped,** 211 W. 14th St., New York, NY 10011 (tel. 212/206-4200), offers summer tours for members, who pay a $4 yearly fee.

For the blind and visually impaired, the best information source is the **American Foundation for the Blind,** 15 W. 16th St., New York, NY 10011 (tel. toll free 800/232-5463; in New York, 212/620-2147), which offers publications and products for visually challenged travelers. It also issues $10 identification cards for those who are legally blind.

FOR SENIORS

Many discounts are available for men and women who have reached what the French call "the third age." Be advised, however, that you often have to be a member of an association to obtain certain discounts.

"Travel Tips for Older Americans" (publication #8970) is distributed for $1 by the Superintendent of Documents, U.S. Government Printing Office, Washington,

DC 20402-9375 (tel. 202/512-2164). Another booklet, this one free, is called **"101 Tips for the Mature Traveler."** It's available from Grand Circle Travel, 347 Congress St., Suite 3A, Boston, MA 02210 (tel. 617/350-7500, or toll free 800/221-2610). Grand Circle Travel offers extended vacations, escorted programs, and cruises featuring unique learning experiences at competitive prices.

Mature Outlook, 6001 North Clark Street, Chicago, IL 60660 (tel. toll free 800/336-6330), a travel club for people over 50, is operated by Sears Roebuck & Co. Annual membership is $9.95 and includes a bimonthly newsletter featuring hotel discounts.

SAGA International Holidays is known for its "low-price but not cheap" all-inclusive tours for persons 60 and older. Insurance is included in the price. Contact SAGA International Holidays, 222 Berkeley St., Boston, MA 02116 (tel. toll free 800/343-0273).

The **American Association of Retired Persons (AARP),** 601 E St. NW, Washington, DC 20049 (tel. 202/434-AARP), offers members discounts on car rentals, hotels, and airfares. Group travel is provided by AARP Travel Experience from American Express. Tours may be purchased through any American Express office or travel agent or by calling toll free 800/927-0111. Cruises may be purchased only by telephoning toll free 800/745-4567. Flights to the various destinations are handled by either of the toll-free numbers as part of land arrangements or cruise bookings.

Information is also available from the nonprofit **National Council of Senior Citizens,** 1331 F St. NW, Washington, DC 20005 (tel. 202/347-8800). The council charges $12 per person/couple, and you receive a monthly newsletter partly devoted to travel tips. Discounts on hotel rates and auto rentals are also provided.

FOR SINGLES

Even though millions of adult Americans are single, the travel industry is far better geared for double occupancy of hotel rooms. One company, **Travel Companion Exchange,** has made heroic efforts to match single travelers with like-minded companions. Jens Jurgen, the German-born founder, charges $36 to $66 for a six-month listing. New applicants fill out a form stating their preferences and needs; then they receive a minilisting of potential partners who might be suitable travel companions. The same or the opposite sex can be requested. A bimonthly newsletter averaging 34 large pages also gives numerous money-saving tips of special interest to solo travelers. A sample copy is available for $4. For an application and more information, contact Jens Jurgen, Travel Companion Exchange, P.O. Box P-833, Amityville, NY 11701 (tel. 516/454-0880).

Singleworld, 401 Theodore Fremd Ave., Rye, NY 10580 (tel. 914/967-3334, or toll free 800/223-6490), is a travel agency that operates tours geared to solo travel. Two basic types of tours are available, either a youth-oriented tour for people under 35 or jaunts for any age. Annual dues are $25.

Another agency to check is **Grand Circle Travel,** which offers escorted tours and cruises for retired people, including singles. Once you book one of their trips, membership is included, and, in addition, you get vouchers providing discounts for future trips. Contact Grand Circle Travel at 347 Congress St., Boston, MA 02210 (tel. 617/350-7500, or toll free 800/221-2610).

FOR FAMILIES

If you're planning to take your family abroad, you'll need to do some advance planning. You may want to discuss your vacation plans with your family doctor.

Special children's menus on airlines must be requested at least 24 hours in advance. If baby food is required, however, bring your own and ask a flight attendant to warm it to the right temperature.

Take along a "security blanket" for your child. This might be a pacifier, a favorite toy or book, depending on age, to make the child feel at home in different surroundings. Arrange ahead of time for such necessities as a crib and a bottle warmer, plus a car seat, if you're driving. Remember that in Germany small children aren't allowed to ride in the front seat. Find out if the place you're staying stocks baby food. If not, it can easily be bought in German supermarkets.

Draw up rules for your family to follow during your holiday. These should be flexible, of course—after all, this is a trip for fun. But guidelines on bedtime, eating, keeping tidy, protection against the sun if you're at one of the alpine or lakeside resorts, even shopping and spending, can help make everyone's vacation more enjoyable.

Sitters can be found for you at most hotels and always insist on a sitter with at least a rudimentary knowledge of English. This should be no problem in Germany.

Family Travel Times newsletter, published ten times a year by **TWYCH,** (Travel with Your Children), includes a weekly call-in service for subscribers ($55 a year). Order from TWYCH, 45 W. 18th St., 7th floor, New York, NY 10011 (tel. 212/206-0688). TWYCH also publishes two nitty-gritty information guides, *Skiing with Children* and *Cruising with Children,* that sell for $29 and $22, respectively, and are discounted to newsletter subscribers. A TWYCH information packet, including a sample issue, is available by sending $3.50 to the above address.

FOR STUDENTS

A leading organization in educational exchange and student travel is the **Council on International Educational Exchange (CIEE),** 205 E. 42nd St., New York, NY 10017 (tel. 212/661-1414). CIEE provides details about budget travel, study abroad, working permits, and insurance. It also sells a number of helpful publications, including *Work, Study, Travel Abroad: The Whole World Handbook* ($12.95), and distributes its *Student Travel Magazine* free. To bonafide students, it issues an International Student Identity Card, which provides an array of travel benefits.

Membership in **International Youth Hostel Federation (IYHF)** is recommended to help keep costs down. Many countries support branch offices, including American Youth Hostels (AYH), P.O. Box 37613, Washington, DC 20013-7613 (tel. 202/783-6161). Membership is $25 per year, unless you're under 18 ($10) or over 55 ($15).

6. ALTERNATIVE/SPECIALTY TRAVEL

Some of America's respected travel visionaries have perceived a change in the needs of many experienced (and sometimes jaded) travelers. There has emerged a demand for specialized travel experiences with clearly defined goals.

Note: The inclusion of an organization in this section is in no way to be interpreted as a guarantee. Information about the organizations is presented only as a preview, to be followed by your own investigation.

SPA VACATIONS

The natural curative springs of Germany are said not only to help cure the sick but also to ward off disease. Proponents of spa therapy point to the quiet and relaxation found in the health resorts as remedies for psychological stress and the pressures of everyday life.

Some 260 registered spas and health resorts are in Germany. They feature the most modern therapeutic facilities and provide numerous medical treatments, sports, and amusements for recuperation, weight reduction, and rest. Most German spas today contain "Beauty Farms." Information on spas and health resorts may be obtained by

writing **Deutscher Bäderverband e.V.,** Schumannstrasse 111, D-5300 Bonn.
Also refer to Chapter 5 in this guide, "Leading Spa Resorts."

In the United States, **Health and Pleasure Tours, Inc.,** 165 W. 46th St., New
York, NY 10036 (tel. 212/586-1775), will provide information about spa vacations.

CULTURAL EXCHANGE

Servas, 11 John St., Suite 407, New York, NY 10038 (tel. 212/267-0252)—the
name means "to serve" in Esperanto—is a nonprofit, nongovernmental, international,
interfaith network of travelers and hosts. The goal of the program is to bridge cultural
gaps through personal interaction among people of diverse backgrounds. Servas
travelers are invited to stay in a private home for up to two days. Visitors pay a $55
annual membership fee, fill out an application, and are checked for suitability by one
of more than 200 Servas interviewers throughout the country. They then receive a
Servas directory listing the names and addresses of Servas hosts who accept visitors in
their homes.

Friendship Force, 575 South Tower, 1 CNN Center, Atlanta, GA 30303 (tel.
404/522-9490), is a nonprofit organization that fosters and encourages friendship
among people worldwide. Dozens of branch offices throughout North America
arrange en masse visits, usually once a year. Because of group bookings, the airfare to
the host country is usually less than the cost of individual APEX tickets. Each
participant is required to spend two weeks in the host country. One full week is spent
as a guest in the home of a family; most volunteers spend the second week traveling in
the host country.

EDUCATIONAL

INTERHOSTEL An international series of programs for persons over 50 interested
in combining travel and learning is offered by Interhostel, developed by the University
of New Hampshire. Each two-week trip is led by a university faculty or staff member
and is arranged in conjunction with a host university or cultural institution. Programs
consist of cultural and intellectual activities, such as field trips to museums, and
participants can extend a stay beyond two weeks if they wish. For information,
contact the University of New Hampshire, Division of Continuing Education, 6
Garrison Ave., Durham, NH 03824 (tel. 603/862-1147, or toll free 800/733-9753).
It's best to phone between 1:30 and 4pm ET.

CIEE The best information for students is provided by the **Council on International Educational Exchange (CIEE),** 205 E. 42nd St., New York, NY 10017
(tel. 212/661-1414). CIEE not only arranges low-cost travel opportunities through its
Council Travel offices but also offers information about working, volunteering, and
studying abroad. It's best to request a copy of the 500-page *Work, Study, Travel
Abroad: The Whole World Handbook,* costing $12.95. If you'd like it mailed, add
another $1.50 for shipping. Outlined are some 1,000 study opportunities abroad.

FOREIGN SCHOOLS ABROAD The **National Registration Center for
Studies Abroad (NRCSA),** 823 N. 2nd St., Milwaukee, WI 53203 (tel. 414/278-
0631), publishes a catalog ($2) of schools in Germany and Austria. They will register
you at the school of your choice, arrange for room and board, and make airline
reservations—all for no extra fee. Ask for a free copy of their newsletter. Costs range
from $350 to $600 per week, depending on the location and the number of meals
included. Rates include tuition, registration, and lodging at all schools—and books,
learning materials, and meals at others.

SENIOR-CITIZEN VACATIONS

ELDERHOSTEL One of the most dynamic educational organizations for senior
citizens is **Elderhostel,** 75 Federal St., Boston, MA 02110-1941 (tel. 617/426-7788),

which was established in 1975. Elderhostel maintains an array of liberal arts programs throughout Europe, including Germany. Most courses last for three weeks and are good values considering that airfare, accommodations in student dormitories or modest inns, all meals, and tuition are included. Although participants do not receive homework or grades, this experience should be considered an academic experience, not a luxury vacation. Participants must be more than 60. However, if two members go as a couple, only one member need be over 60. Contact Elderhostel for a free newsletter and a list of upcoming courses and destinations.

GOLDEN COMPANIONS If you're between 45 and 89 and need a travel companion, **Golden Companions,** P.O. Box 754, Pullman, WA 99163 (tel. 208/858-2183), might provide the answer. A research economist, Joanne R. Buteau, founded this helpful service and is quick to point out that it's not a dating service. Travelers meet potential companions through a confidential mail network. Members, once they have "connected," make their own travel arrangements. Created in 1987, this organization draws members from many walks of life. Members also receive a bimonthly travel newsletter, *The Golden Traveler.* Membership for a full year costs $85 per person.

HOME EXCHANGES

One of the most exciting breakthroughs in modern tourism is the home exchange, whereby, for instance, the Hauzenberger family of Munich and the Phillips family of North Carolina can exchange homes. Sometimes the family automobile is included. Of course, you must be comfortable with the idea of having relative strangers in your home, and you must be content to spend your vacation in one place.

Home exchanges cut costs. You don't pay hotel bills, and you can also save money by shopping in markets and eating in. One potential problem, though, is that you may not be offered a home in the area you request.

Intervac U.S./International Home Exchange, P.O. Box 590504, San Francisco, CA 94159 (tel. 415/435-3497, or toll free 800/756-HOME), is the largest worldwide home exchange network. Each year it publishes three catalogues that contain more than 8,800 homes in some 36 countries.

Vacation Exchange Club, P.O. Box 650, Key West, FL 33041 (tel. 305/294-3720, or toll free 800/638-3841), will send you four directories a year—in one of which you're listed—for $60.

OPERA TOURS

On a cultural note, **Dailey-Thorp Travel,** 330 W. 58th St. Suite 610, New York, NY 10019-1817 (tel. 212/307-1555), in business since 1971, is probably the best-regarded organizer of music and opera tours operating in America. Because of its "favored" relations with European box offices, it is often able to purchase books of otherwise unavailable tickets to such events as the Bayreuth Festival in Germany and the Salzburg Festival in Austria, as well as to performances in other German and European opera houses. Tours range from 7 to 21 days and include first-class or deluxe accommodations and meals in top-rated restaurants. Dailey-Thorp is also known for its breakthrough visits to opera houses in eastern Europe and in the less traveled cities of Italy.

7. GETTING THERE

Much of Germany's history has been influenced by its position at the crossroads of Europe, and today, many travelers opt to begin their exploration of the Continent by landing in the area's heartland. Not only is Germany jam-packed with atmosphere, nightlife, and sightseeing interests, but its central position also makes it a perfect gateway to the rest of Europe.

BY PLANE

There are several available methods of cutting air transportation costs. The best strategy for securing the most economical airfare is to shop around. Keep calling the airlines. Sometimes you can purchase a cheaper ticket at the very last minute, because if the flight is not fully booked, an airline may discount tickets to achieve full capacity.

For those who don't want to or can't leave everything to the last minute, there are certain things that you should know about airfare structures. Most airlines charge different fares according to season. Peak season, usually during the summer months if you're flying to Europe, is most expensive; basic season, during winter months, except the Christmas holidays, offers the least expensive fares. Shoulder season is in between. Most airlines also offer an assortment of fares from first class, the most expensive, through business class to economy class, the lowest-priced regular airfare carrying no special restrictions or requirements. Most airlines also offer promotional fares, which carry stringent requirements such as advance purchase, minimum stay, and cancellation penalties. The most common such fare is the APEX (advance purchase excursion).

Because they're faced with stiff competition, many airlines offer promotional fares that offer substantial savings if your timing is right. Lufthansa, Germany's national airline, sometimes offers promotional fares lower than the best APEX (advance purchase excursion) fare. Lufthansa also offers seniors over 62 a 10% discount; the reduction applies to a traveling companion as well.

Flying time to Frankfurt from New York is about 7½ hours; from Chicago, 10 hours; and from Los Angeles, 12 hours.

THE AIRLINES Responding to the political changes within central Europe, an increasing number of regularly scheduled airlines fly directly to Germany. They include Lufthansa, American, Delta, TWA, Continental, and United.

Of the six, **Lufthansa** (tel. toll free 800/645-3880; fax 800/522-2329) operates the most frequent service and flies to the greatest number of the country's airports. Within Germany, Lufthansa flies to dozens of regional population centers, including such eastern cities as Berlin, Dresden, and Leipzig.

From North America, Lufthansa serves 14 gateway cities, 11 in the United States. In any season, there are more than 100 weekly flights from these cities to Germany. The largest of the gateways are in the New York City area, where flights depart from both JFK and Newark airports. From JFK, daily flights depart nonstop for Frankfurt and Düsseldorf. After a brief touchdown in Düsseldorf, the Lufthansa flight continues to Munich. From Newark International, Lufthansa offers daily flights to Frankfurt. Lufthansa's other gateways include Atlanta; Boston; Chicago; Dallas/Fort Worth; Houston; Los Angeles; Miami; San Juan (Puerto Rico); San Francisco; and Washington, D.C. From Canada and Mexico, Lufthansa flies to Germany from Montreal, Toronto, Vancouver, Calgary, and Mexico City.

American Airlines (tel. toll free 800/443-7300), flies to Frankfurt, Munich, and Düsseldorf (sometimes with stops along the way) from New York, Dallas/Fort Worth, and Chicago. The airline also flies every day from Chicago to Berlin, with connections through Chicago from many other parts of North America. In the early 1990s, **Continental Airlines** (tel. toll free 800/231-0856) became an important player with daily nonstop service between Newark and Frankfurt and Munich. The airline maintains excellent connections between Newark and hubs in cities like Denver, Cleveland, Los Angeles, and Houston. Continental offers some of the most attractively priced and most comfortable (with expandable sleeper seats) business-class passage to Germany in the airline industry. (Year-round business-class fares from Newark to Munich are $1,426 each way.) The airline also offers discounts and other benefits to seniors 62 and over and their traveling companions.

Delta Airlines (tel. toll free 800/241-4141), long known as a strong regional airline, has become one of the strongest forces in Germany since its acquisition of the now-defunct Pan Am's routes from around the world to Frankfurt. As part of the same transaction, it also acquired the architecturally acclaimed Pan Am terminal at JFK Airport in New York, thereby initiating daily nonstop service from JFK to both Frankfurt and Hamburg. Delta is especially strong in service from its headquarters in Atlanta to Frankfurt (offering at least one, and sometimes two, nonstops per day), as well as daily nonstops from Atlanta to Munich and Hamburg. Delta's service to Stuttgart departs daily from Atlanta with a touchdown (and sometimes a change of aircraft) in Amsterdam. Delta also offers frequent nonstops to Frankfurt from Cincinnati (a major midwestern hub) and Orlando. Through either of those two cities, good connections are available with Dallas/Fort Worth and many other cities in North America.

Despite the financial problems of **TWA** (tel. toll free 800/892-4141), the airline, at presstime, offered daily nonstop service between New York and Frankfurt. Through Paris, it also makes daily connections to Munich, and through Brussels, it makes daily connections to Berlin.

United Airlines (tel. toll free 800/241-6522) joined the German-bound battalions in 1991 by acquiring several of Pan Am's North Atlantic routes. These include daily nonstops from Washington, D.C., to Frankfurt, daily nonstops from Chicago to Frankfurt, and service from London's Heathrow airport to Munich, Berlin, and Hamburg.

British Airways (tel. 081/897-4000 in London) and **Lufthansa** (tel. 071/408-0442 in London) are the most convenient carriers from London to major German cities like Düsseldorf, Cologne, Frankfurt, Munich, and Berlin. Both carriers have two flights a day to Cologne (flying time, 75 minutes). BA has seven flights and Lufthansa six flights from London to Frankfurt (85 minutes). Both airlines offer three daily flights to Munich (100 minutes). BA also offers three nonstop and three one-stop flights to Berlin (100, 40 minutes), as does Lufthansa. Lufthansa also flies daily from London to Nürnberg, plus both carriers service Bremen, Hannover, and Stuttgart.

Small carriers plying some of the routes include **Connectair** (tel. 0293/862971 in England), with twice-daily service between Gatwick (outside London) and Düsseldorf. **Air UK** (tel. 0345/666777 in England) also flies from Stansted (outside London) to Frankfurt (115 minutes). Another carrier, **Dan Air** (tel. 071/229-2474 in London), offers regular charters from Gatwick—at least four per week to both Munich and Berlin and two per week to Düsseldorf, Hamburg, Hannover, and Stuttgart.

AIRLINE FARES The airlines compete in offering the most economical fares encumbered with the least number of restrictions. Any promotional fare announced without advance notice by one will probably be quickly matched by competitors. Insofar as airline fares go, the early bird almost always merits lower fares, since price structures are specifically geared to reward travelers who reserve and arrange payment for their tickets in advance. Watch the newspapers, consult your travel agent, and remain as flexible as possible about travel dates so that you can profit from last-minute price changes.

For example, at presstime, Lufthansa offered a complicated but very appealing series of promotional early-saver fares from each of its U.S. gateways to Germany. Allowing a maximum stay abroad of 30 to 60 days, they undercut the cheapest regularly available APEX or Super-APEX fares by between $200 and $400, depending on circumstances and projected dates of departure. Although valid for travel during the height of the midsummer season, these fares required full booking and payment before early March. For passengers interested in traveling during midwinter (when Germany is presumably at its most untrammeled best), similar, but even less expensive, arrangements existed that required booking before the end of October.

At presstime, Delta offered roughly similar arrangements for fares to Germany from several cities. This promotional fare (sometimes referred to as a Winter Sale Fare) carried restrictions equally stringent as those attached to more expensive charter tickets: A trip to Germany must begin between mid-January and mid-March and be booked before mid-February. To qualify, participants are required to remain in Europe over a Saturday night and not more than 30 days. Round-trip tickets were priced at around $450 for travel Monday through Thursday to Frankfurt from Atlanta, New York, or Cincinnati. Tickets were nonrefundable, though credit could be applied toward more expensive fares later in the season. Slightly higher promotional fares applied to travel scheduled for specific dates in April, May, September, and October.

APEX Fares The tickets mentioned above are suitable only for passengers who can plan trips many months in advance. For passengers who can't, Lufthansa offers a Super-APEX fare that requires payment 30 days in advance and a relatively nonrestrictive delay of 7 days to 3 weeks before you must use the return half of your round-trip ticket. If you cancel a ticket, you'll lose between $250 and the full value of the ticket. Despite the drawback, this type of APEX ticket (or one roughly similar) has been among the most popular fare options in airline history.

On all airlines, midweek travel is less expensive than weekend travel. (Lufthansa defines "midweek" as Monday to Thursday and "weekend" as Friday, Saturday, and Sunday.) The difference in price between the two categories for most APEX tickets averages about $30 for each leg of a round-trip ticket.

The lowest APEX fares are available for passage during low season, roughly November 1 to late March, with a slight price increase over Christmas. Somewhat more expensive is passage during most of April, May, and October, periods defined as shoulder season, when many visitors find Germany at its least heavily visited and most appealing. Midsummer (June to September) is the period when APEX tickets are most expensive.

Business Class and First Class Each airline recognizes that part of its profit comes from business travelers who need to be as rested as possible on arrival for what might be a tightly scheduled set of meetings and business problems. Each offers a category of service midway between tourist and the most luxurious class, first class. Known as business class, it features larger seats, upgraded food and service, and more room to spread out papers, calculators or battery-operated computers, and briefcases. Since business travel is not seasonal, prices remain the same year-round. Lufthansa charges $1,426 each way from New York to Munich, but imposes absolutely no restrictions concerning length stay, advance reservation, or prepayment. First class offers extra comfort and service. The first-class Lufthansa fare from New York to Munich costs $2,539 each way, and the amenities can be very pleasant and refreshing.

The competition for first- and business-class passengers is fierce throughout the industry. Delta's first-class fare between Atlanta and Munich costs $2,654 each way; its business fare for the same route costs about $1,618 each way.

Important Note All fares, rules, and regulations are subject to change. The best way to benefit from promotional fares is to ask for them specifically when shopping around and to remain as flexible as possible about travel plans.

OTHER GOOD-VALUE CHOICES Bucket Shops (Consolidators)
The name *bucket shop* originated in the 1960s in Great Britain, where mainstream airlines gave the then pejorative name to resellers of blocks of unsold tickets consigned to them by major transatlantic carriers. Bucket shop has stuck as a label, but it might be more polite to refer to them as "consolidators." They exist in many shapes and forms. In its purest sense, a bucket shop acts as a clearinghouse for blocks of tickets that airlines discount and consign during normally slow periods of air travel.

Charter operators (see below) and bucket shops once performed separate functions, but their offerings in many cases have been blurred in recent times. Many outfits perform both functions.

Tickets are sometimes—but not always—priced at up to 35% less than full fare. Terms of payment can vary—say, from anywhere from 45 days prior to departure to last-minute sales offered in a final attempt by an airline to fill a craft. Tickets can be purchased through regular travel agents, who usually mark up the ticket 8% to 10%, maybe more, thereby greatly reducing your discount. A survey conducted of fliers who use consolidator tickets voiced only one major complaint. Use of such a ticket doesn't qualify you for an advance seat assignment, and you are therefore likely to be assigned a "poor seat" on the plane at the last minute.

The survey revealed that most fliers estimated their savings at around $200 per ticket off the regular price. Nearly a third of the passengers reported savings of up to $300 off the regular price. But—and here is the hitch—many persons who booked consolidator tickets reported no savings at all, as the airline will sometimes match the consolidator ticket by announcing a promotional fare. The situation is a bit tricky and calls for some careful investigation on your part to determine just how much you are saving.

Bucket shops abound from coast to coast, and here are some recommendations. Also look for ads in your local newspaper's travel section. They're usually very small.

In New York, try **TFI Tours International**, 34 W. 32nd St., 12th floor, New York, NY 10001 (tel. 212/736-1140 in New York State, or toll free 800/825-3834 elsewhere in the U.S.).

In Miami, check **25 West Tours**, 2490 Coral Way, Miami FL 33145 (tel. 305/856-0810 in Miami, or toll free 800/423-6954 in Florida, 800/225-2582 elsewhere in the U.S.).

On the West Coast, contact **Sunline Express Holidays, Inc.**, 607 Market St., San Francisco, CA 94105 (tel. 415/541-7800, or toll free 800/786-5463).

In New England, a possibility is **Travel Management International**, 18 Prescott St., Suite 4, Cambridge, MA 02138 (tel. toll free 800/245-3672), which offers a wide variety of discounts, including youth fares. Its contract fares often are lower then rebate prices (see below).

Charter Flights   For reasons of economy, not convenience, some travelers opt for a charter flight to Germany. Strictly speaking, a charter uses an aircraft reserved months in advance for a one-time-only transit to some predetermined point. Before paying for a charter, check the restrictions on your ticket or contract. You may be asked to purchase a tour package and pay far in advance. You'll pay a stiff penalty (or forfeit the ticket entirely) if you cancel. Charters are sometimes canceled when the plane doesn't fill. In some cases, the charter-ticket seller will offer an insurance policy for a cancellation for good cause (hospital confinement or death in the family, for example).

Some charter companies have proved unreliable in the past. Among reliable charter operators is **Council Charter**, 205 E. 42nd St., New York, NY 10017 (tel. 212/661-0311, or toll free 800/800-8222). This firm can arrange "charter seats on regularly scheduled aircraft" to most major European cities.

Schwaben International, Inc., a German charter operator, maintains a U.S. office at 1 World Trade Center, Suite 1145, New York, NY 10048 (tel. toll free 800/457-0009 from within the Northeast; from other points call 212/432-0116). Schwaben is one of the sales agents for the charter flights of three different airlines, American Transair, Balair, and LTU. Flights depart from New York's JFK for Stuttgart once a week in summer only. Currently, passage between New York and Stuttgart on one of Schwaben's charters ranges from $589 to $689 round trip, depending on season. Penalties of $100 are imposed for cancellation or alteration of flight days more than 14 days prior to takeoff, and after that, tickets are completely nonrefundable. (Flight insurance can be purchased for an additional $24. This provides a refund of the ticket price if a passenger can't fly on the predetermined dates because of a health-related emergency.) Payment and bookings for any flight is accepted, if space is available, until the date of departure. The company also arranges domestic airfares within the United States and operates cost-conscious motorcoach tours of Germany. The tours last one week or more and cost $900 and up without airfare but with double-occupancy hotel accommodations and some meals.

There is no way to predict whether a proposed flight to Germany will cost less on a charter or in a bucket shop. You'll need to investigate at the time of your trip.

Rebators   Rebators are firms that pass along to the passenger part of their commission, though many assess a fee for the services. They are not the same as travel agents but can sometimes offer similar service. Most rebators offer discounts averaging 10% to 25%, plus a $20 handling charge.

Rebators include **Travel Avenue,** 641 W. Lake St., Suite 201, Chicago, IL 60606-1012 (tel. 312/876-1116, or toll free 800/333-3335), and **The Smart Traveller,** 3111 SW 27th Ave., Miami, FL 33133 (tel. 305/448-3338, or toll free 800/448-3338). The latter offers rebates on air, tours, rail passes, cruises, rental cars, hotels, and so on.

Traveling as a Courier Couriers are hired by overnight air-freight firms hoping to skirt customs hassles and delays on the other end. With a courier, the checked freight sails through customs as quickly as regular luggage.

Don't worry—the courier service is absolutely legal, and for the service, the courier gets greatly discounted airfare or sometimes even flies free. You're allowed one piece of carry-on luggage only (your baggage allowance is used by the courier firm to transport its cargo). As a courier, you don't actually handle the merchandise you're "transporting" to Europe, you just carry a manifest to present to customs.

Upon your arrival, an employee of the courier service will reclaim the cargo. Incidentally, you fly alone, so don't plan to travel with anybody. Most operate from Los Angeles or New York, but some operate out of Chicago or Miami. Courier services are often listed in the yellow pages or in advertisements in travel sections of newspapers.

You might contact **Halbart Express,** 147-05 176th St., Jamaica, NY 11434 (tel. 718/656-8189), 10am to 3pm daily, or **Now Voyager,** 74 Varick St., Suite 307, New York, NY 10013 (tel. 212/431-1616), 11:30am to 6pm daily.

The **International Association of Air Travel Couriers,** P.O. Box 1349, Lake Worth, FL 33460 (tel. 407/582-8320), publishes *Shoestring Traveler,* a newsletter, and *Air Courier Bulletin,* a directory of courier bargains around the world. The annual membership fee is $35.

BY TRAIN

Many passengers, especially holders of the Eurailpass, travel to Germany by train, since it lies in the heart of Europe and has connections with major capitals. BritishRail, for example, runs 10 trains a day to Germany from London under its division, Rail Europe. Tickets are purchased through **British Rail** travel centers in London (tel. 071/834-2345 for a location near you). Eight daily trains leave from Victoria Station in London, going by way of the Dover-Ostende ferry or jetfoil. Two

---

 FROMMER'S SMART TRAVELER: AIRFARES

1. Take off-peak-season flights—autumn-to-spring and Monday-through-Thursday departures.
2. Avoid last-minute changes of plans to avoid airline penalties.
3. Keep checking the airlines and their fares. One airline discounted a New York–to-Munich fare by $195 in seven days.
4. Shop all the airlines that fly to your destination.
5. Always ask for the lowest fare, not just a discount fare.
6. Ask about frequent-flier programs.
7. Check bucket shops for last-minute, even cheaper discount fares.
8. Ask about air/land packages.
9. Fly free or at a heavy discount as a courier.
10. Call Lufthansa about any special off-season discounted or promotional fares.

trains depart from Liverpool Street Station in London, going by way of Harwich-Hook of Holland. If you go by jetfoil, Cologne is just 9 hours away; it's 12 hours via the Dover-Ostende ferry. Most trains change at Cologne for destinations elsewhere in Germany. Travel from London to Munich—depending on the connection—can mean a trip of 12, 19, or even 22 hours. Most visitors find it cheaper to fly from London to Munich than take the train. Berlin can be reached in about 20 hours, with connections via Hannover.

From Paris, the Orient Express leaves from Gare de l'Est at 7:43pm daily and arrives in Munich at 4:26am. If you're in Rome, you can take the Michelangelo Express daily at 7:45am. It arrives in Munich at 6:58pm.

The Bavaria Express leaves Zurich at 7:07am daily, arriving in Munich at 11:24am. The Zurich-Hamburg Express leaves Zurich daily at 9pm, arriving in Hannover at 5:57am and in Hamburg at 8:01am.

See also Section 8, "Getting Around," below, for information on purchasing the Eurailpass.

BY BUS

From London, the best and most efficient service is by Europabus, with three daily departures from Victoria Station. Buses cross the English Channel on the Dover-Zeebrugge ferry operated by Sealink. The bus then traverses the Netherlands and Belgium, arriving in Cologne in 14½ hours. From Cologne, connections are available to Frankfurt (17½ hours) and Munich (about 23 hours). In London make reservations by calling **Transline** (tel. 0708/86-4911).

BY CAR & FERRY

If you're driving to Germany from England and plan to start your German trip in the north, then go via a port in the Netherlands. If you plan to explore central or south Germany, then leave England on a sea connection headed to a port in Belgium. In England, ferries leave from Harwich for Hook of Holland. **Sealink** (tel. 071/834-8122 in London) has two departures daily year round; the crossing takes 8 hours. For Belgium, **P&O European Ferries** (tel. 071/734-4431 in London) operates Channel-crossing services from Dover (England) to both Zeebrugge and Ostende in Belgium. Trip time to Ostende is 4 hours; to Zeebrugge it's 4½ hours.

Once you reach these continental ports (either in the Netherlands or Belgium), you can drive to the German border in from 1 to 2 hours.

Germany also has Autobahn (express highway) links to its neighbors. Motorists from Brussels take the E5 into Cologne. From Innsbruck (Austria) the E17, E86, and E11 lead directly to Munich. From Italy, most motorists go from Bolzano in the north along the E6 to Innsbruck, where the road continues north to Munich.

It is a bit slow going from France. From Paris you must take the Autoroute du Soleil to Switzerland and then take Swiss expressways until you reach the German frontier. If you're going to Frankfurt, use Basel (Switzerland) as your departure point north from Switzerland. If you're going to Munich, you can continue east from Zürich heading for Innsbruck in the east, where you can then make Autobahn connections to Munich.

BY FREIGHTER

Many people think travel by freighter might be fun, something out of a Humphrey Bogart movie. Actually, it's more prosaic than that. If you're interested, try **Anytime, Anywhere Travel,** 91 N. Bedford Rd., Chappaqua, NY 10514 (tel. 914/238-8800). A maximum of 12 passengers are allowed on board, and a freighter voyage to Europe takes 9 to 10 days. Reservations should be made at least 6 months in advance. Ships leave several times a month from Newark, NJ; Baltimore; or Wilmington, NC, to

Bremerhaven. Not only will you enjoy a double-occupancy cabin with private bath, but also you'll dine with the ship's officers. The cost is $1,000 and up one way.

Lykes Brothers Steamship Co., Lykes Center, 300 Poydras St., New Orleans, LA 70130 (tel. toll free 800/235-9537), is owned and operated by a Florida-based family. This American-registered shipping company runs four freighters, one of which carries goods every 30 days between New Orleans, Antwerp in Belgium, and Bremerhaven. On the way back from Bremerhaven, it stops at Felixstowe in England; Le Havre in France; Norfolk, VA; and Galveston, TX, before returning to New Orleans. No more than six passengers are accommodated at one time, in three double cabins. There is no entertainment.

For more information, contact **Ford's Freighter Travel Guide,** 19448 Londelius St., Northridge, CA 91324 (tel. 818/701-7414).

PACKAGE TOURS

Many questions arise for people planning their first European trip, whether to Germany or elsewhere: How do I plan my trip so as not to miss the most outstanding sights of the country? Will I have a problem moving from place to place, complete with luggage? Am I too old to embark on such a journey? How will I cope with a foreign language?

My answer to these questions—indeed, my advice to many people traveling to Europe for the first time—is simple: Take a tour during which your needs are looked after from arrival at a European airport to departure back to the United States. Taking a tour is often cheaper than exploring a country on your own.

Leading tour operators include the following: **Lufthansa German Airlines,** 680 Fifth Ave., New York, NY 10019 (tel. 718/895-1277), features air-and-hotel packages throughout the country.

American Express Vacations, P.O. Box 5014, Atlanta, GA 30302 (tel. toll free 800/241-1700), offers an array of tours featuring Germany, including air-and-land packages. You can contact the Atlanta address or go to the nearest North American office for information.

DER Tours, 11933 Wilshire Blvd., Los Angeles, CA 90025 (tel. 310/479-4411, or toll free 800/937-1234), shapes tours for independent travelers and offers air-and-land packages. Some tours feature B&B (bed-and-breakfast) accommodations.

Delta Airlines (tel. toll free 800/872-7786) offers both fly/drive and fly/rail packages for touring Germany. For tourists with limited time, it features three-day "city sprees" in cities like Hamburg and Munich.

U.K. residents can go to any travel agent for an array of package tours to Germany. They can also telephone the German national carrier, Lufthansa (tel. 071/408-0442 in London), to learn of the latest package deals. Another option is **Transline** (tel. 0708/86-4911 in England), the booking agent for Europabus, a European-wide network of buses, with one section devoted to German railroads. This section offers tours (usually seven days long) through scenic parts of Germany, including the Romantic Road.

8. GETTING AROUND

BY PLANE

The commercial airports of Germany are linked with one another by scheduled service. From Frankfurt am Main, most Lufthansa destinations in Germany can be reached in an average of 50 minutes, with at least four flights daily. Contact your

Lufthansa travel agency or Lufthansa town office for the most economical current offers.

All German cities with commercial airports have an airport shuttle service, offering reduced fares and fast connections between the city proper and the airport. Departure points are usually the airlines' town offices and the city's Hauptbahnhof terminal. Luggage can be turned in at the DB (GermanRail) baggage counter at the airport for delivery to railroad stations in Germany.

Once in Germany, many visitors take advantage of the efficient Lufthansa Airport Express, a high-speed train that travels between the Frankfurt and Düsseldorf airports, with stops at Bonn, Stuttgart, Dortmund, and Cologne, giving the traveler an opportunity to view the Rhine Valley.

BY TRAIN

Whether you travel first or second class, you'll find that the trains of **GermanRail** (tel. 708/692-4141 in Rosemont, Ill.) deserve their good reputation for comfort, cleanliness, and punctuality. They are modern and fast, running smoothly over welded tracks. Both first- and second-class trains carry smoker and nonsmoker compartments. A snack bar or a dining car serving German and international cuisine, as well as good wine and beer, will usually be on your train (unless you're taking a local), and you can enjoy the landscape through picture windows.

Actually, GermanRail's customer service begins long before you board. Special features of major rail stations include information desks and ticket offices, pictorial directional signs (eliminating language problems), and posted timetables listing departures and arrivals chronologically. In addition, each car carries signs, inside and out, describing its routing, point of origin, destination, and important stops en route. Restaurants, snack bars, post and money-exchange offices, newsstands and bookstores, flower shops, beauty parlors, pharmacies, and a cinema are some of the facilities major railroad stations offer. And they're usually located right in the center of the city.

For city sightseeing, you can leave your baggage in a locker or check it at the station's baggage counter. In many cities GermanRail provides door-to-door baggage service, allowing passengers to have luggage picked up or delivered to their hotels. Accompanying baggage can be checked for a nominal fee. Suitcases, baby carriages, skis, bicycles, and steamer trunks are permitted as baggage. Insurance policies of various kinds, including a travel medical plan, are obtainable.

About 20,000 passenger trains per day comprise the network of InterCity (IC) trains offering express service every hour among most of the large and medium-size cities of Germany. IC trains carry first as well as coach class. These trains require a surcharge (but not from holders of the Eurailpass and the first- and second-class GermanRail Pass). The luxurious interiors of IC trains have adjustable cushioned seats and individual reading lights. Business travelers appreciate the telephone and secretarial services offered on most of these trains. Bars, lounges, and dining rooms are available too. A network of EuroCity trains in 13 countries of Europe, designated EC, offers the same high standards of service as those of IC.

Germany's high-speed rail networks, known as the InterCity Express (ICE), are among the fastest in Europe. One of these trains runs from Hamburg through Würzburg and Nürnberg to Munich, and another from Frankfurt through Stuttgart to Munich. Each of these makes stops along the way, and reaches speeds of 165 mph. An ICE significantly reduces travel time from point to point within Germany, making transits north to south across the country easily possible in the course of a single day. Some 200 east-west connections have been added to the GermanRail timetable to link the Deutsche Bundesbahn (west) and the Deutsche Reichsbahn (east). Additional connections make Berlin, Leipzig, and Dresden more accessible.

Advance reservations for sleeping accommodations on GermanRail trains are necessary. Travelers wanting to avoid the fatigue of long-distance driving can reach their destination on special car-sleeper trains (Auto Trains). Some daytime automobile trains are also operated.

Children below the age of 4, provided they do not require a separate seat, travel free; those between 4 and 12 pay half fare.

Before leaving for Germany, you can get complete details about the German Federal Railroad and the many plans it offers, as well as information about Eurailpasses, at the following offices: 9501 W. Devon Ave., Rosemont, IL 60018-4832 (tel. 708/692-4141, or toll free 800/782-2424); 222 W. Las Colinas, Suite 1050, Irving, TX 75039 (tel. 214/402-8377); 3400 Peachtree Rd. NE, Lenox Towers, Suite 1229, Atlanta, GA 30326 (tel. 404/266-9555); 11933 Wilshire Blvd., Los Angeles, CA 90025 (tel. 213/479-2772); and 20 Park Plaza, Boston, MA 02116 (tel. 617/542-0577). In Canada, contact the office at 904 The EastMall, Etobicoke, ON M9B 6K2 (tel. 416/695-1211).

GERMANRAIL TOURIST PASSES & OPTIONS The German Federal Railroad offers discount fares to Americans and Canadians who buy tickets before leaving home, as well as cheaper round-trip fares for long-distance trips inside Germany if you buy tickets in advance. GermanRail passes are available from travel agents and GermanRail offices in the United States.

Since the fall of the Berlin Wall, the opening of Eastern Europe, and the completion of German unification, GermanRail has increased service and offered new rail passes, packages, and additional trains. Its **Flexipass** includes unlimited travel on the entire German rail system. Under the Flexipass, you can travel for 5 days in coach for $170 or $250 in first class; for 10 days, $268 in coach and $390 in first class; and for 15 days, $348 in coach and $498 in first class. A junior Flexipass costs $130 for 5 days, $178 for 10 days, and $218 for 15 days.

The Flexipass is good for unlimited rail travel for any 5, 10, or 15 days (nonconsecutive) within a 1-month period. The pass also entitles the bearer to the following exclusive bonuses: free travel on selected routes operated by Deutsche Touring/Europabus, such as the Romantic Road and the Castle Road; free travel on KD German Rhine Line day steamers on the Rhine, Main, and Mosel rivers; and free admission to the Museum of Transportation in Nürnberg.

Other travel plans include "Rail and Drive" packages, programs for senior and junior citizens, city-to-city weekend tours, and district tickets. In addition, GermanRail offers reduced fares for minigroups of more than ten, holiday tickets (Vorzugskarten), and conference compartments and cars in IC and ICE trains.

EURAILPASS This ticket entitles North American residents to unlimited first-class rail travel over the 100,000-mile national railroad networks of 17 western European countries (except Great Britain) plus Hungary in eastern Europe. It is also valid on some lake steamers, ferries, and private railroads. Passes may be purchased for 15 days to 3 months.

Here's how it works: The pass cannot be purchased in Europe. It must be bought before you go. The pass costs $460 for 15 days, $598 for 21 days, $728 for 1 month, $998 for 2 months, or $1,260 for 3 months. If you're under 26, you can obtain unlimited second-class travel wherever Eurailpass is honored on a Eurail Youthpass, which costs $508 for 1 month or $698 for 2 months. In addition, a Eurail Youth Flexipass offers 15 days of unlimited second-class rail travel in a 2-month period for $474.

Eurailpasses eliminate the hassles of buying tickets—just show your pass to the ticket collector. Note, however, that some trains require seat reservations. Also, many trains have couchettes (sleeping cars) for which an additional fee is charged. Obviously, the two- or three-month traveler gets the greatest economic advantages; the Eurailpass is ideal for extensive trips. To obtain full advantage of the ticket in 15 days or a month, however, you'd have to spend a great deal of time on the train.

Travel agents or national rail offices of European countries can provide further details. General brochures are available by contacting **GermanRail**, 9501 W. Devon Ave., Rosemont, IL 60018-4832 (tel. 708/692-4141, or toll free 800/782-2424).

Eurail Saverpass Groups of three can purchase a ticket that allows 15 days of discounted travel, valid from April 1 and September 30. To get the discount the individuals must always travel as a group. The price of a Saverpass, valid all over Europe and good for first-class travel only, is $390 for the 15 days. Off-season, only two people need travel together.

Eurail Flexipass This pass offers 5 days of unlimited first-class rail travel during a 2-month period for $298; 10 days during a 2-month period, $496; and 15 days during a 2-month period, $676.

BY CAR

CAR RENTALS Competition in the European car-rental industry is almost as fierce as in the transatlantic airline industry. All the big U.S. car-rental companies, including Avis, Budget, and Hertz, are represented in Germany. You can make reservations and do comparison shopping by calling their toll-free numbers in the United States: **Avis** at 800/331-2112, **Budget** at 800/472-3325, and **Hertz** at 800/654-3001.

Cars at all three companies can usually be rented at one German city and returned at another for no additional charge. An understanding of insurance and its many legal and financial implications is all-important during your initial paperwork. A collision damage waiver (CDW) is an optional insurance policy that can be purchased when you sign a rental agreement. For an extra fee, the rental agency agrees to eliminate all but a small percentage of your financial responsibility for liability and collision damage in case of an accident. If you don't have a CDW and do have an accident, you'll usually pay for all damages, up to the cost of actually replacing the vehicle if the accident is serious enough.

Certain credit-card companies, usually including American Express and Diners Club, agree to reimburse card-users for the deductible in the event of an accident. Because of that, many renters have chosen to waive the cost of the extra CDW. However, although the credit-card issuers will usually (several weeks after the accident) reimburse the renter for the cost of damages, payments have sometimes been delayed with such coverage until after the completion of certain documents. Unless there's enough of a credit line associated with your particular credit card, some car renters involved in an accident will be required to pay cash on the spot (sometimes a large sum).

To avoid misunderstandings, the large car-rental companies offer clients the option of either automatically including the CDW as part of the rental price, or to forgo it completely in favor of the insurance that sometimes applies automatically through your credit-card company. Although this confusion has sometimes resulted in "double coverage," it has nonetheless prevented hundreds of renters from having to shell out cash while waiting for reimbursement.

Regardless of the insurance-related options you select, all three of the companies maintain competitive rates that are attractive only if you reserve your car from North America *before departure*. Rental of the smallest car (a Ford Fiesta or Opel Corsa with manual transmission) at all three companies differed by only a few dollars per week for pickup on equivalent dates. At Budget, the cost for this car was around $151 per week, plus payment of a 15% government tax. The cost of the (optional) CDW ranged, depending on the company, from $17 to $31 per day. The truly unpleasant surprise, however, awaited travelers who simply walked into a local branch without prereserving. In that event, the cost of a rental of an equivalent car was sometimes increased threefold.

Some passengers prefer the convenience of prepaying their rental in dollars before leaving the United States. In such circumstances, an easy-to-understand net price (including the CDW and additional personal accident insurance and, in some cases, the local government tax) is quoted and prepaid at least 14 days before departure by credit card. The main benefit to those who opt for this is a somewhat more streamlined rental process, a price structure easier to understand, and an ability to avoid unpleasant surprises caused by sudden unfavorable changes in exchange rates. Rental companies usually assess a penalty for changes or cancellations, for instance, $25 per change at Budget and $50 per change at Hertz.

Don't overlook the availability of cars with automatic transmission (viewed as somewhat of a luxury in Europe) or one of the sleekly styled German sports cars or luxury sedans. All three companies inventory these cars in abundance, usually at correspondingly elaborate prices.

MOTOR HOMES Some families, particularly those traveling with children, have found the rising prices of Europe to be prohibitive. To stretch vacation dollars, they've turned to renting motor homes (recreational vehicles — RVs) as a relatively inexpensive substitute for hotels and restaurants. **Executive Motorhome,** Opelstrasse 28, D-6082 Morefelden (tel. 06105/3037), established in 1964, is the oldest motor-home rental company in Europe, with a location about 9 miles south of the Frankfurt airport. Free pickup can be arranged by calling in advance. RVs come in two sizes, 16 feet and 19 feet long, suitable for five or six persons, respectively. They're furnished with bedding, crockery, cutlery, and minikitchens and can be driven out of Germany as far as Moscow without restriction. Rentals include all insurance. Costs range from $80 to $160 per day, depending on vehicle and season. Additional charges apply for such things as cooking gas and cleaning.

GASOLINE Gasoline is readily available throughout Germany, and service stations appear frequently along the Autobahns. The cheapest gasoline is at stations marked SB-Tanken, or self-service. Gasoline pumps labeled *Bleifrei* offer unleaded gas.

DRIVING RULES In Germany, you drive on the right. Easy-to-understand international road signs are posted throughout Germany. Road signs are in kilometers, not miles. In congested areas the speed limit is about 50 kmph (or around 30 mph). On all other roads except the Autobahns the speed limit is 100 kmph or about 60 mph. In theory, there is no speed limit on the Autobahns (in the left, fast lane), but many drivers reportedly going too fast have written that they have been stopped by the police and fined on the spot. So reasonable precaution is recommended here, for safety if not other reasons. A German driver on the Autobahn can be a ferocious creature, and you may prefer the slow lane. The government nevertheless recommends an Autobahn speed limit of 130 kmph or 80 mph. Both front-seat and back-seat passengers are required to wear safety belts.

Note: Drinking and driving is a very serious offense in Germany. Therefore, be sure to keep any alcoholic beverages in the trunk or some other storage area. Avoid even the appearance of drinking alcohol while driving.

BREAKDOWNS/ASSISTANCE There are two major automobile clubs in Germany: **DTC** (Deutscher Touring Automobile Club), Amalienburgstrasse 23, D-8000 Munich 60 (tel. 089/811-1212), and **AvD** (Automobilclub von Deutschland), Lyoner Strasse 16, D-6000 Frankfurt 71 (tel. 069/660-60). If you don't belong to an auto club and have a breakdown, call from an emergency phone on the Autobahn. These are spaced about 1 mile apart. On secondary roads, go to the nearest phone and call 01308/19211. In English, ask for "road service assistance." Emergency assistance is free, but you pay for parts or materials.

MAPS The best maps, available at all major bookstores throughout Germany, are published by Michelin, which offers various regional maps. Other good maps for those who plan to do extensive touring are published by Hallwag.

DRIVER'S LICENSES If you or your car is from an EC country, all you need is a domestic license and proof of insurance. Otherwise, an international driver's license is required.

For an international driver's license, apply at a branch of the **American Automobile Association (AAA).** You must be at least 18 years old and have two 2-inch by 2-inch photographs, a $10 fee, and a photocopy of your U.S. driver's license with an AAA application form. AAA's nearest office will probably be listed in your local telephone directory or you can contact AAA's national headquarters at 1000 AAA Drive, Heathrow, FL 32746-5080 (tel. 407/444-4240). Remember that an international driver's license is valid only if physically accompanied by your original driver's license. In Canada, you can get the address of the Canadian Automobile Club closest to you by calling toll-free, 800/336-HELP.

Both in Germany and throughout the rest of Europe, you must have an international insurance certificate, known as a green card (carte verte) to legally drive a car. Any car-rental agency will automatically provide one of these as a standard part of the rental contract, but it's a good idea to double check the documents the counter attendant gives you at the time of rental just to be sure you can identify it if asked by a border patrol or the police.

BY BUS

An excellent network of efficient buses service Germany. Many are operated by **Bahnbus,** the railway line. They are integrated to complement the rail service. Where rail service is light, the bus takes you the rest of the way. Bus service in Germany is particularly convenient during slow periods for rail travel, normally around midday and on Saturday and Sunday. Local bus services are usually operated by German post offices (contact local post offices for schedules and prices).

The most popular bus ride is along the Romantic Road (see Chapter 11), beginning in Würzburg and ending at Füssen. Any travel agent in Germany will reserve you a seat on this bus, which operates daily in each direction in the summer.

BY BOAT

You can travel Germany by boat or ship on its lakes and rivers. The longest river in the country, the mighty Rhine, is the country's most traveled waterway, and it's covered by boats, motorships, and hydrofoils. You can go, for example, from Düsseldorf in the north up the river to Mainz by hydrofoil.

German cruise ships also operate on the Rhine as far as Basel in the north of Switzerland. They also run on the Main River between Mainz and Frankfurt, and sail the Danube to Linz (Austria), going on to Vienna. Cruises also operate on the Mosel between Koblenz and Trier.

The most services are operated by **KD River Cruises of Europe,** Frankenwerft 15, D-5000 Köln 1 (tel. 0221/20880). Eurailpasses are valid for most KD excursions. The ship company also offers several luxury cruises, the most popular being a four-day cruise along the Rhine from Amsterdam to Basel.

BY BICYCLE

Many athletic visitors tour the country by bicycle. At rail depots throughout the country, bicycles can be rented for 10 DM ($6.60) per day. If you have a valid rail ticket, the cost can be reduced by 50%. If arrangements are made, bicycles can be rented at one rail depot and returned at another. More than 300 railroad stations participate in this "Bicycle at the Station" plan.

Information about cycling possibilities is available by contacting **Bund Deutscher Radfahrer,** Otto Fleck Schneise 4, D-6000 Frankfurt 71. This is the association of German cyclists.

BY HITCHHIKING

Germany offers some of the best and safest hitchhiking possibilities in Europe. Seemingly every German owns an auto, and there is a splendid network of Autobahns. *Der Weg-Wanderer,* as a hitchhiker is known, isn't frowned upon here, as in some countries. However, you should never hitch a ride while actually on an Autobahn. It is also illegal to hitch a ride near an exit or entrance to an Autobahn. Therefore, you'll have to stand far enough away so you won't get picked up by the police. You'd better have a sign. Always use the German name for a city, not the English one—for example, Köln not Cologne.

Note: The golden days of hitchhiking in Europe are gone, and it is no longer viewed as a completely safe practice anywhere in the world. You could always be picked up by a dangerous person, so be alert for possible trouble.

SUGGESTED ITINERARIES

IF YOU HAVE 1 WEEK

Day 1 Most visitors begin their one-week "Grand Tour of Germany" in Frankfurt am Main, because of its superior air links to the rest of the world. From here, you can "work" your way south to Munich.

Day 2 After a night in Frankfurt, head south on the Autobahn to Heidelberg, a distance of some 60 miles. Explore the castle of *The Student Prince* fame and visit one of the student taverns in the evening.

Day 3 From Heidelberg, head east for a night in Würzburg, one of the loveliest baroque cities in Germany.

Day 4 Begin your exploration of the Romantic Road, stretching for 180 miles between Würzburg in the north and Füssen in the foothills of the Bavarian Alps. Stop for lunch in Rothenburg, 40 miles south of Würzburg, one of the finest medieval cities in Europe. Continue south, passing through the picture-book towns in Dinkelsbühl and Nördlingen, then continue along the Romantic Road to Füssen, near the Austrian frontier. (If accommodations can't be found there, go east to Garmisch-Partenkirchen.)

Day 5 While based in or around Füssen explore the royal castles of Bavaria, including Neuschwanstein, the fairy-tale castle of the "mad king," Ludwig II, and Hohenschwangau.

Days 6 and 7 Head north to Munich, capital of Bavaria, where two nights will give you only enough time to cover the highlights (see Chapter 4).

IF YOU HAVE 2 WEEKS

Spend the first week as outlined above.

Day 8 Begin your tour with a stopover in Wiesbaden on the Rhine, 8 miles north of Mainz, one of the world's leading belle époque spas.

Day 9 From Wiesbaden, it is a 64-mile drive northwest to Koblenz, which stands at the confluence of the Rhine and Mosel rivers. On the way there pass through the famous Rheingau, with stopovers at one of the little wine towns, such as Rüdesheim.

Day 10 In the morning, you can explore the Mosel Valley, which many visitors find more appealing than the Rhine. Your final destination, a distance of 77 miles, will be Trier, considered the oldest city in Germany, some 6 miles from the Luxembourg border. The most intriguing stopovers along the Mosel include Zell, Traben-Trarbach, Bernkastel-Kues, Beilstein, Cochem, and Eltz Castle (take your pick).

Day 11 Return to Koblenz, exploring whichever riverbank of the Mosel you missed the preceding day. From Koblenz, it is a 55-mile ride north to Cologne. Along the way, you can see the longtime postwar capital of West Germany, Bonn, which lies 17 miles south of Cologne.

Day 12 Since you will reach Cologne late in the afternoon, you should spend two nights here, to give yourself a full day to see Cologne, the largest city in the Rhineland and one of the premier attractions of Germany, known for its famous cathedral.

Days 13 and 14 Continue north from Cologne to Hamburg, the port city that's filled with attractions and nightlife. It has superior air and rail links with the rest of Europe.

IF YOU HAVE 3 WEEKS

Spend weeks one and two as outlined above.

Days 15 and 16 Head for Berlin, at the geographical heart of Europe, about halfway between Lisbon and Moscow. You could spend weeks here, but two nights will give you a chance to explore some of the highlights in both the eastern and western sections, including the Pergamon Museum and the Brandenburg Gate.

Day 17 Visit Potsdam to see, among other attractions, Sans Souci, the summer residence of Frederick II. You can overnight in Potsdam or take the train back for a sample of Berlin's nightlife.

Day 18 Head south from Berlin for an overnight visit to Dresden. You should be there in time for lunch, leaving your afternoon free to explore its many sights, including the Zwinger quadrangle of pavilions and galleries. At night you can attend a performance at the restored Semper Opera House (reserve tickets ahead).

Day 19 Drive northwest from Dresden to Meissen and tour the famous porcelain factory. Continue to Leipzig (about a two-hour drive or train ride). Visit, among other attractions, Thomaskirche, the burial place of its one-time choirmaster, Johann Sebastian Bach.

Day 20 Continue to Weimar, the 1,000-year-old town on the edge of the Thuringian Forest, which for so long was a seat of German culture. Visit the Goethe National Museum and other principal attractions. The train or car ride from Leipzig to Weimar takes about an hour.

Day 21 After an overnight in Weimar return to Berlin for a final visit. From there, you can make air or rail links to your next destination.

9. WHERE TO STAY

In general, Germany has one of the highest standards of innkeeping in the world. With notable exceptions, the hotels in the eastern section of Germany—once geared to tourism from the old East bloc countries—are not of the same standard as those in the west.

Hotels throughout Germany range from some of the most luxurious five-stars to plain country inns. There is a huge variation in rates, ranging from citadels of luxury and comfort down to the simple *Gasthäuser* (guesthouses). Many pensions or boardinghouses are called *Fremdenheime,* and throughout the country you'll see *Zimmer frei* signs. The latter offers the cheapest method of living in the country, as these are rooms for rent in private homes.

Hotels listed as garni provide no meals other than breakfast. Often tourist offices will book you into a room for a small charge. Obviously, the earlier you arrive in these offices, the more likely you are to get a desirable room at a price you want.

When you don't have time to make reservations on your own, **ADZ,** Corneliusstrasse 34, D-6000 Frankfurt am Main (tel. 069/74-07-67), can do so throughout the country, for only a small service charge.

Of course, if you're traveling on the big-chain route, such as Steigenberger, Hilton, Sheraton, Ramada, Holiday Inn, or others, you can use toll-free numbers in the United States or Canada to make reservations.

BUNGALOW, VILLA & APARTMENT RENTALS

All over the country, many Germans who own vacation homes or units make them available for visitors when the homes are vacant. These villas, apartments, and bungalows—called *Ferienwohnungen* or *Ferienapartments*—shelter from two to eight people in most cases. The longer you stay, the better the rate. Sometimes extra charges are imposed for utilities, but these matters have to be worked out, as does the arrangement for bed linens. Regional, city, or town tourist offices have details of rentals available in their areas, or you can write to **ADAC Reisen,** Am Westpark 8, D-8000 München 70.

CASTLE HOTELS

Perhaps the most romantic way to stay in Germany, castle hotels—called *Schlosshotels* in German—are available in most regions of the country. Some of them are relatively plain, without adequate plumbing, whereas others offer some of the most luxurious amenities in the country, often with four-poster beds in rooms decorated with German baronial splendor. Many are resorts, with pools and a number of sporting activities available on their grounds, including horseback riding. Contact one of the offices of the German National Tourist Office and ask for a brochure called "Castle Hotels in Germany." Bookings can be made through any travel agent. Several of the better castle hotels in Germany will be recommended in this guide. Castle hotels throughout Germany are also represented by **Romantic Hotels Reservations,** P.O. Box 1278, Woodinville, WA 98072 (tel. 206/485-6985, or toll free 800/826-0015 in the U.S.}.

FARM VACATIONS

Growing in its appeal to tourists, a vacation down on the farm—*Urlaub auf dem Bauernhof* in German—cuts costs and is an adventure as well. Nearly every local tourist office has a list of farmhouses in its area that take in paying guests. Sometimes only a bed and breakfast are offered; at other places a farm-style home-cooked dinner can be included if you wish. For data before you go, you can contact **DLG** (German Agricultural Association), Zimmerweg 16, D-6000 Frankfurt am Main 1, for a list of some 1,500 farms. You must send the equivalent of 7.50 DM ($4.95), plus an International Reply Coupon.

ROMANTIK HOTELS

Throughout Germany you'll encounter hotels with a "Romantik" in their names. This is not a chain but a voluntary association of small inns and guesthouses that have only one element in common: They are usually old and charming as well as romantic in architecture. If you like traditional ambience, as opposed to modern, then a Romantik Hotel might be for you. The requirement is that the hotel be in a historic building (or at least one of vintage date) and managed by the owner. Usually you get a regional cuisine and good, personal service, along with an old-fashioned setting and cozy charm. Whenever possible, I always book myself into one, savoring a life known to travelers years ago. Sometimes the plumbing could be better, and standards of comfort vary widely, but all of them have been inspected.

For complete information about these hotels and restaurants, send $7.50 to **Romantik Hotels Reservations,** P.O. Box 1278, Woodinville, WA 98072 (tel. 206/485-6985). If you decide to make reservations in one of these hotels, call toll free 800/826-0015 in the United States.

YOUTH HOSTELS

Germany has some of the finest youth hostels in the world. There are more than 700 of them, many in old castles or bucolic settings. Visitors up to 26 years of age pay 12.50 DM to 18 DM ($8.30 to $11.90) per night. Persons over 26, provided there is room, are charged 15 DM to 22 DM ($9.90 to $14.50). Space allowing, adults are given a bed only after 6pm. In Bavaria, adults over 27 may not stay in youth hostels. For young people up to 26, a junior membership card is issued for 18 DM ($11.90); adult membership costs 30 DM ($19.80). Membership cards that are stamped for families also cost 30 DM ($19.80). These are annual dues. An additional 2 DM ($1.30) is charged when the card is first issued.

Membership cards of associations affiliated with Hostelling International/American Youth Hostels are regarded as the equivalent of German membership cards. Foreigners who are not members of an association affiliated with the IYHF and are staying only temporarily in Germany, must obtain an international guest card for 36 DM ($23.80). The average price for a meal in one of these hostels is 9 DM ($5.90). Breakfast, however, is included in the rate.

Application should be made in writing to **Deutsches Jugendherbergswerk** (German Youth Hostel Association), Postfach 1455, D-4930 Detmold, or to **Hostelling International/American Youth Hostels,** P.O. Box 37613, Washington, DC 20013.

10. FOR BRITISH TRAVELERS

A NOTE ON CUSTOMS

On January 1, 1993, the borders between European countries were relaxed as the European markets united. When you're traveling within the EC, this will have a big impact on what you can buy and take home with you for personal use.

If you buy your goods in a duty-free shop, then the old rules still apply—you're allowed to bring home 200 cigarettes and 2 liters of table wine, plus 1 liter of spirits or 2 liters of fortified wine. But now you can buy your wine, spirits, or cigarettes in an ordinary shop in France or Belgium, for example, and bring home *almost* as much as you like. (U.K. Customs and Excise does set theoretical limits.) If you are returning home from a non-EC country, the allowances are the standard ones from duty-free shops. You must declare any goods in excess of these allowances.

GETTING TO EUROPE

BY PLANE   There are no hard and fast rules about where to get the best deals for European flights, but do bear the following points in mind. (1) Daily papers often carry advertisements for companies offering cheap flights. Highly recommended companies include Trailfinders (tel. 071/938-3366) and Platinum Travel (tel. 071/937-5122). (2) In London, there are many bucket shops around Victoria and Earls Court that offer cheap fares. Make sure that the company you deal with is a member of the IATA, ABTA, or ATOL. (3) CEEFAX, a British television information service included on many home and hotel TVs, runs details of package holidays and flights to Europe and beyond.

BY TRAIN   Many different rail passes are available in the U.K. for travel in Britain and Europe. Stop in at the **International Rail Centre,** Victoria Station, London SW1V 1JY (tel. 071/834-2345) or **Wasteels,** 121 Wilton Rd., London SW1V 1JZ (tel. 071/834-7066). The most popular rail ticket for U.K. residents is the **InterRail card,** available for travelers under 26 years of age. It costs £240, is valid for one month, and entitles you to unlimited second-class travel in 26 European countries. Recently, an InterRail card for those over 26 was introduced, costing £260 for a month, or £180 for 15 days. According to BritRail, there is some doubt about its availability for 1994. **Eurotrain** tickets are another good option for travelers under 26. Valid for two months, they allow you to choose your own route to a final destination and stop off as many times as you like along the way.

BY COACH & FERRY   If you want to take your time, coach travel is a relaxing way to see Europe. **Cosmos Tourama** (081/464-3477) provides a wide range of trips all over Europe. **Eurolines,** 52 Grosvenor Gardens, London SW1W 0AU (tel. 071/730-0202) has a range of budget coach trips around Europe. The U.K. ferry company **Sally Line** (tel. 081/858-1127) runs a cheap coach/ferry service from Liverpool Street to Copenhagen between April and November. If you're looking for a cheap camping/coach tour, try **Contiki Concept** (tel. 081/290-6422).

BY CAR & FERRY   Taking your car abroad gives you maximum flexibility to travel at your own pace and to set up your own itinerary. **Brittany Ferries** is the U.K.'s largest ferry/drive company. Sailings depart from Portsmouth to St. Malo and Caen (tel. 0705/827-701); from Poole to Cherbourg (tel. 0202/666-466); and from Plymouth to Roscoff and Santander, Spain (tel. 0752/221-321). Brittany also runs ferries from Cork in Northern Ireland to Roscoff and St. Malo (tel. 0752/269-926 for a brochure). **Stena Sealink Lines** (tel. 0233/647-047) runs ferries from Dover to Calais; Southampton to Cherbourg; Newhaven to Dieppe; Harwich to the Hook of

Holland; and from the west coast of England to Ireland. **P&O Ferries** (tel. 081/575-8555) sails from Portsmouth to Cherbourg and Le Havre in France and to Bilbao, Spain; from Dover to Calais, France and Ostend, Belgium; and from Felixstowe to Zeebrugge, Belgium.

BY HOVERCRAFT Traveling by Hovercraft or SeaCat cuts your journey time from the U.K. to the continent. A hovercraft trip is definitely a fun adventure, as the vessel is technically "flying" off the water. The SeaCat (or catamaran) is a recent addition to the U.K.'s sailing fleet, and its channel crossing requires only a fraction of the time a ferry would take. SeaCats also travel to the Isle of Wight, Belfast, and the Isle of Man. For more details call 0304/240-101 for Dover sailings, or 0303/221-281 for Folkestone crossings.

VIA THE CHANNEL TUNNEL The tunnel is scheduled to open in 1994. Running between Folkestone and Calais, in France, the Channel Tunnel will reduce the travel time to France to 30 minutes. You can travel via the tunnel on a train from London's Waterloo station. If you take a car, it will be stowed away on the shuttle trains, for you to drive off at the destination. For up-to-the-minute information, call 0302/270-111.

ALTERNATIVE/ADVENTURE SPECIALISTS

Cycling tours are a good way to see a country. **Anglo Dutch Sports** (tel. 081/650-2347) offers a series of economical packages in Holland. **Alternative Travel Group Limited,** 69–71 Banbury Rd., Oxford OX2 6PE (tel. 0865/310-555) runs cycling tours in Italy and France, through scenic countryside and medieval towns. Other good alternatives are **Bike Tours** (tel. 0225/480-130) and the **Cyclists' Touring Club** (tel. 0483/417-217). There is a wide range of **hiking holidays,** all generally quite pricey. Try **Waymark Holidays** (tel. 0753/516-477) and **Sherpa Expeditions,** 131a Heston Rd., Hounslow, Middlesex TW5 0RD (tel. 081/577-7187). Choose a walk or trek that's suited to your fitness level. **Walking holidays** can be cheaper and less rigorous. **HF Holidays,** Imperial House, Edgware Road, Colindale, London NW9 5AL (tel. 081/905-9388 for a brochure) offers a range of one- to two-week packages. You may have read a lot about **archaeology tours**— but most only let you look, not dig. **Earthwatch Europe** (tel. 0865/311-600) is different, though, allowing you to take part in one of its 150 projects. Botanical tours and wine- and food-tasting packages are also popular, but can be expensive. **Cox & Kings** (tel. 071/834-7446) specialize in unusual, if pricey, holidays.

TIPS FOR SPECIAL TRAVELERS

FAMILIES The best deals for families are often package holidays. **Skytours** (tel. 081/200-8733) offers thousands of free holidays for children under 18, on a first-come, first-served basis. **Airtours** (tel. 0706/26000) operates a similar program for children under 19. Both companies have clubs for children between the ages of 3 and 11.

SINGLES For single people, there is a wealth of holidays. **Explore** (tel. 0252/344-161) has a well-justified reputation for fascinating offbeat tours. **HF Holidays** (tel. 081/905-9388) also runs a range of packages throughout Europe for travelers aged 18 to 35.

STUDENTS Check **Campus Travel,** 52 Grosvenor Gardens, London SW1W 0AG (tel. 071/730-3402), which provides a wealth of information and offers for the student traveler. The **International Student Identity Card** (ISIC) is an internationally recognized proof of student status that will entitle you to savings on flights, sightseeing, food, and accommodation. It costs only £5 and well worth the cost. **Youth hostels** are the place to stay if you're a student. You'll need an International

Youth Hostels Association card, which you can purchase from the youth hostel store at 14 Southampton Street, London (tel. 071/836-8541) or Campus Travel.

SENIORS Wasteels, 121 Wilton Rd., London (tel. 071/834-7066) currently provides an over-60s Rail Europe Senior Card, and **Scandinavian Sea Ways** offers 50% discounts to senior citizens for most sailings. Coach tours also cater to those over 60, with excellent offerings available from **Wallace Arnold** (tel. 081/464-9696) and **Cosmos Tourama** (tel. 081/464-3477).

THE DISABLED   British Rail offers 34% or 50% discounts on some fares to those using wheelchairs and one companion. RADAR (Royal Association for Disability and Rehabilitation) publishes two annual holiday guides for the disabled: "Holidays and Travel Abroad" and "Holidays in the British Isles." RADAR also provides a number of holiday fact sheets. There is a nominal charge for all publications, available by calling 071/637-5400 or by writing RADAR, 25 Mortimer St., London W1N 8AB. Another good resource is the **Holiday Care Service,** 2, Old Bank Chambers, Station Road, Horley, Surrey RH6 9HW (tel. 0293/774-535; fax 0293/784-647).

TRAVEL INSURANCE

You might contact **Columbus Travel Insurance Ltd.** (tel. 071/375-0011) or, for students, **Campus Travel** (tel. 071/730-3402). If you're unsure about who provides the best deal, contact **Association of British Insurers,** 51 Gresham St., London EC2V 7HQ (tel. 071/600-333).

 GERMANY

American Express   There are offices in such major cities as Frankfurt, Hamburg, Berlin, and Munich. See the "Fast Facts" in individual city chapters.

Business Hours   Most banks are open Monday to Friday from 8:30am to 1pm and 2:30 to 4pm (on Thursday until 5:30pm). Money exchanges at airports and border crossing points are generally open daily from 6am to 10pm. Exchanges at border railroad stations are kept open for arrivals of all international trains. Many businesses are open Monday to Friday from 9am to 5pm and Saturday from 9am to 1pm. Store hours can vary from town to town. Most shops are open Monday to Friday from 9am (or 10am) to either 6 or 6:30pm (8:30pm on Thursday). Saturday hours are generally from 9am to 1 or 2pm, except on the first Saturday of a month, when stores may remain open to 4pm.

Camera/Film   Every major town and city in Germany has outlets for selling and processing popular brands and sizes of films. In some of the smaller villages, color shots have to be mailed to city labs for processing.

Cigarettes   Most popular U.S. brands can be found in Germany. However, there are many British or German products you may want to try, especially if you like a mild cigarette. Cigars and pipe tobacco are widely available.

Climate   See "When to Go" in this chapter.

Crime   See "Safety," below.

Currency   See "Information, Entry Requirements & Money" in this chapter.

Currency Exchange   See "Information, Entry Requirements & Money" in this chapter.

Customs   U.S. residents returning from abroad are allowed to bring back $400 in duty-free items for personal use. To qualify, you must have been outside the United States at least 48 hours and not have claimed an exemption in the past 30 days. Articles valued in excess of $400 will be assessed at a flat-duty rate of 10%. Antiques and original works of art produced 100 years prior to the date that you return to the United States may be brought home duty-free, but you must be able to prove their authenticity. Gifts for your personal use, but not for business purposes, may be excluded from the $400 exemption. You can send home unsolicited gifts amounting to a total of $50 per day without declaring them on your Customs declaration. Liquor is limited to one 32-ounce bottle; tobacco, to 200 cigarettes and 100 cigars. Keep all your receipts for purchases made in Germany or elsewhere on your trip abroad as you may be asked for proof of the prices you paid.

Documents Required See "Information, Entry Requirements & Money" in this chapter.

Driving Rules See "Getting Around" in this chapter.

Drug Laws Penalties for illegal drug possession in Germany are severe. You could go to jail or be deported immediately. *Caveat:* Drug pushers often turn in their customers to the police.

Drugstores There are two types: the Apotheke, which sells pharmaceuticals, and the Drogerie, which sells cosmetics and over-the-counter drugs. German pharmacies are open during regular business hours. All post lists of pharmacies that are open nights, on Sunday, and on holidays. It's always possible to get a prescription filled outside of business hours.

Electricity In most places the electrical current is 220 volts AC, 50 cycles. Therefore, adapters will be needed for your U.S. appliances. Many leading hotels will supply an adapter.

Embassies/Consulates Offices of various governments are being moved and changed, so check with local tourist offices if you can't locate an embassy or consulate at one of the addresses below. The **United States** embassy is at Deichmannsaue 29 in Bonn (tel. 0228/339-1); there is a U.S. embassy office at Neustaedtische Kirchstrasse 4-5 in Berlin (tel. 030/238-51-74). Passports and visa problems are handled at the U.S. consulate at Clayallee 170 in Berlin (tel. 030/819-74-85). In Munich, a U.S. consulate is at Amalienstrasse 62 (tel. 089/381-62-80), and in Frankfurt at Seismayerstrasse 21 (tel. 069/7535-0). The **United Kingdom** embassy is at Unter den Linden 32-34 in Berlin (tel. 030/220-24-31). The British consulate-general, handling passport and visa applications, is at Yorkstrasse 19 in Düsseldorf (tel. 0211/9448-0). The U.K. also has a consulate office at Bochenheimer Landstrasse 51-53 (tel. 069/170-00-20) in Frankfurt, and a consulate-general office at Bürkleinstrasse 10 in Munich (tel. 089/21-10-90). The **Canadian** Embassy is at Godesburger Allee 119 in Bonn (tel. 0228/81-00-60). Canada maintains consulate offices at Friedrichstrasse 95 in Berlin (tel. 030/261-11-61), and at Tal 29 in Munich (tel. 089/29-06-50). The **Australian** embassy is at Godesburger Allee 107 in Bonn (tel. 0228/810-30). There are consulate offices at Gutleustrasse 85 in Frankfurt (tel. 069/273-90-90), and at Mohrenstrasse 30 in Berlin (tel. 030/2382-2041). The **New Zealand** embassy is at Bundeskanzlerplatz in Bonn (tel. 0228/228-07-25).

Emergencies Throughout Germany the emergency number for police is **110;** for fire or to call an ambulance, **112.**

Etiquette When a man or woman is introduced to a group of people, it is considered polite for both men and women to shake hands. Although Germans are often loud and boisterous in beer halls, at more formal gatherings they tend to be polite but reserved.

Gambling Roulette and baccarat are just some of the international games that can be played in the spa resorts of Germany, the most famous of which is Baden-Baden in the Black Forest. It was from Bad Homburg, close to Frankfurt, that roulette was "exported" to Monte Carlo. Other famous casinos are at Wiesbaden and Garmisch-Partenkirchen, south of Munich. Admission tickets are available to persons over 21 upon presentation of a valid passport.

Hitchhiking See "Getting Around" in this chapter.

Holidays See "When to Go" in this chapter.

Information See "Information, Entry Requirements & Money" in this chapter, plus individual chapters for local information offices.

Language The official language, of course, is German, but English is often spoken, at least at major hotels and restaurants and in the principal tourist areas. A good phrase book to carry with you is the *Berlitz German for Travellers,* available in most big bookstores in the United States.

Laundry Upper-bracket hotels have facilities for laundering, but the service is very expensive. To cut costs, you can use a launderette, available in all major cities and towns. They are called *Wäscherei* in the telephone directories. Coin laundries are called *Munzwäscherei*. See individual city listings for specific recommendations.

Legal Aid This may be hard to come by in Germany. The government advises foreigners to consult their embassy or consulate (see "Embassies/Consulates," above), in case of a dire emergency, such as an arrest. Even if a consulate or embassy declines to offer financial or legal help, officials will generally offer advice as to how to obtain help locally. For example, they will provide a list of attorneys who might represent you for a fee.

Liquor Laws As in many European countries, the application of laws that apply to drinking are flexible and enforced only if a problem develops or if decorum is broken. Officially, someone must be 18 to consume any kind of alcoholic beverages in Germany, although at family gatherings, wine or schnapps might be offered to underage imbibers. For a bar or café to request proof of age of a prospective client is very rare. Drinking and driving, however, is treated as a very serious offense.

Mail General delivery—mark it "Poste Restante"—can be used in any major town or city in Germany. Your mail may be picked up upon presentation of a valid identity card or passport. To post a letter on the street, look for a mailbox painted yellow. To send an airmail letter to the United States or Canada, the cost is 1.65 DM ($1.10) for the first 5 grams (about 0.2 oz.), whereas postcards are 1.05 DM (70¢). To mail a package, go to one of the larger post offices in Germany, preferably the main branch if you have a choice (see individual city listings). All letters to the United Kingdom cost 1 DM (66¢), 0.60 DM (40¢) for postcards.

Maps See "Getting Around" in this chapter.

Medical Assistance Most major hotels in Germany have a physician on staff or on call. If you can't get hold of a doctor, the best thing to do is to dial the emergency service, which is open day and night. The number is listed in every telephone directory under the heading of *Ärztlicher Notdienst* (emergency medical service). The Red Cross can also help in cases of illness or accident. Medical and hospital services in the Federal Republic aren't free. It is therefore advisable, before departure, to be sure you have appropriate insurance coverage.

Newspapers/Magazines Most German papers are published in German, of course. However, news kiosks in major cities stock British dailies plus the *International Herald Tribune* or *USA Today*. International editions of *Time* and *Newsweek* and other U.S. and British magazines are also widely available.

Passports See "Information, Entry Requirements & Money" in this chapter.

Pets Dogs and cats brought into Germany from abroad will require a veterinary certificate stating that the animal has been vaccinated against rabies not less than 30 days and not more than 1 year prior to entry into the country. This regulation also applies to dogs and cats returning after a temporary absence from Germany, but is not applicable to animals transported through the country by rail or air traffic.

Police Throughout the country, dial **110** for emergencies.

Radio/TV English-speaking visitors can tune to the American Forces Network (AFN) at 1107 AM and the Voice of America on 1197 AM. The BBC from London can often be picked up. TV channels broadcast in German, but films are sometimes telecast in the original language, which is often English, with German appearing in the subtitles. Many big hotels subscribe to CNN, with up-to-the-minute news broadcasts, available in the individual bedrooms.

Religious Services Roman Catholic and Protestant services are found throughout Germany. Your hotel should be a helpful source in locating a church near you, whatever your faith. Tourist bureaus also have lists with times of services.

Restrooms Women's toilets are usually marked with an "F" for *Frauen,* and men's toilets with an "H" for *Herren*. Germany, frankly, doesn't have enough public toilets, except in transportation centers. The locals have to rely on bars, cafés, or restaurants, which isn't always appreciated unless you're a paying customer. In a public toilet, a small tip is customary. If you need soap and towel, give something extra.

Safety   Whenever you're traveling in an unfamiliar city or country, stay alert. Be aware of your immediate surroundings. Wear a moneybelt or keep your wallet in an inside pocket. Hold onto your camera or purse; leave your valuables in your hotel safe. This will minimize the possibility of your becoming a victim of crime. Every society has its criminals. It's your responsibility to be aware and alert even in the most heavily touristed areas.

Taxes   As a member of the European Community, the Federal Republic of Germany imposes a tax on most goods and services known as a **value-added tax** (VAT), or, in German, *Mehrwertsteuer*. Tax on books and materials of educational or cultural content is only 7%, but nearly everything else is taxed at 14%. That includes a vital necessity such as gas and luxury items such as jewelry. Note that the purchase of goods, such as a German camera, has the 14% already factored into the price, whereas services, such as paying a garage mechanic to fix your car, will have the 14% added to the bill. Foreigners who purchase more than 60 DM ($39.60) worth of merchandise in any one store are entitled to a refund of the VAT. Refunds are granted for only 6% to 11% of the 14% tax. Stores issue Tax Free Cheques when you make a purchase. Foreign shoppers must fill in the reverse side of this cheque, then present the cheque, along with the merchandise, to German customs upon leaving the country. The customs agent stamps the check. The stamped cheque can then be mailed to the store where you purchased the merchandise, and the refund will be mailed to your home address.

Telephone/Telex/Fax   Local and long-distance calls may be placed from all post offices and coin-operated public telephone booths. The unit charge is 0.30 DM (20¢) or three 10-pfennig coins. Coin-operated phones are dwindling. By 1995, it is estimated that more than half the phones in Germany will require an advance-payment telephone card from Telekom, the German telephone company. Phone cards are sold at such places as post offices and newsstands, costing 6 DM ($4), 12 DM ($7.90), and 50 DM ($33). The 6- and 12-DM cards have 20 or 40 units at 0.30 DM (20¢) each, and the 50-DM card has 200 units at 0.25 DM (20¢) each. Rates are measured in units rather than minutes. The farther the distance, the more units are consumed. For example, a three-minute call to the United States costs 41 units. All towns and cities in the Federal Republic may be dialed directly by using the prefix listed in the telephone directory above each local heading. Telephone calls made through hotel switchboards can double, triple, or whatever, the charge. Therefore try to make your calls outside your hotel at a post office where you can also send telexes and faxes. For telephone information within Germany, dial 1188. For international telephone information, phone 0118.

Time   Germany is 6 hours ahead of eastern time (ET) in the United States. Germany operates on central European time (CET), which places it 1 hour ahead of Greenwich mean time. Summer time begins in Germany in April and ends in September—there is a slight difference in the dates from year to year—so there may be a period in early spring and in the fall when there is a 7-hour difference between U.S. ET and CET. Always check carefully if you're traveling at these periods, especially if you need to catch a plane.

Tipping   If a restaurant bill says *Bedienung,* that means a service charge has already been added, so just round up to the nearest mark. If not, add 10% to 15%. Round up to the nearest mark for taxis. Bellhops get 2 DM ($1.30) per bag, as does the doorman at your hotel, restaurant, or nightclub. Maids aren't tipped in Germany, but tip concierges who perform some special favor such as obtaining hard-to-get theater or opera tickets. Tip hairdressers or barbers 5% to 10%.

Tourist Offices   See "Information, Entry Requirements & Money" in this chapter.

Water   Tap water is safe to drink in all German towns and cities. However, do not drink from rivers or mountain streams, regardless of how clean the water may appear.

CHAPTER 3

FRANKFURT AM MAIN & ENVIRONS

Your first glimpse of Germany may well be this thriving industrial metropolis—the country's fifth-largest city and its most important transportation center. Its huge airport, Flughafen Frankfurt/Main, serves just about every major international airline. More than 1,600 trains run in and out of its massive 19th-century station, the busiest in Germany.

As the home of the Bundesbank (Germany's central bank), Frankfurt is also the financial center of the Federal Republic. Since the Rothschilds opened their first bank here in 1798, it has been a major banking city, currently containing more than 220 banks and a leading stock exchange. It is also a heavily industrial city, with more than 2,450 factories operating around the ford (*Furt*) on the Main where the Frankish tribes once settled.

Frankfurt has also been the site of important trade fairs since about 1200. The international Frankfurt fairs in spring and autumn bring some 1.2 million visitors to the city and to its Messengelände (fairgrounds), causing a logjam at its hotels. Fairs include the Motor Show, the Textile Fair, the Chemical Industries Fair, the Cookery Fair, and the International Book Fair. The International Book Fair, perhaps the best known, is the most important single meeting place for the acquisition and sale of book rights and translations, drawing some 5,500 publishers from nearly 100 countries.

In spite of its commerce and industry, Frankfurt is also a tourist city, offering numerous attractions to its many visitors. One out of 11 persons in Frankfurt on any given day is actually a stranger. The city's population is about 635,000.

1. ORIENTATION

ARRIVING

BY PLANE   Flughafen Frankfurt/Main, D-6000 Frankfurt, lies 7 miles from the city center at the Frankfurter Kreuz, the intersection of two major expressways (A3

WHAT'S SPECIAL ABOUT FRANKFURT

Literary Shrines

☐ Goethe-Haus, where the greatest German writer was born in 1749. Restored after World War II bombing.

Museums

☐ Frankfurter Goethe-Museum, adjoining Goethe-Haus, with the world's largest collection of the writer's memorabilia and manuscripts, including *Faust*.

☐ Städel Museum, the city's most important art gallery. Nearly all schools and periods of European painting.

Parks/Gardens

☐ Palmengarten, one of Germany's greatest botanical gardens— everything from a monsoon forest to tropical waterplants.

For the Kids

☐ Zoologischer Garten, one of Europe's great zoos—animals in enclosures that resemble native habitats.

Streets/Neighborhoods

☐ Altstadt, the old town, though largely a restoration, still evokes memories of yesterday.

☐ Alt-Sachsenhausen, on the left bank, site of the Apfelweinstuben, or apple wine taverns, where there's a party every night.

Events/Festivals

☐ Frankfurt's the site of more than 100 annual festivals and special outdoor markets, more than half of which are organized by the city itself.

☐ International Book Fair, drawing some 5,500 publishers from some 100 countries.

and A5). As continental Europe's busiest airport, Frankfurt serves more than 220 destinations in about 100 countries worldwide and is Germany's major international gateway. There are daily direct flights to and from American cities, and all major German airports can be reached via Frankfurt. Flying time from Frankfurt to Berlin and Hamburg is 70 minutes, and to Munich it's 60 minutes. For airport information, call 069/690-3051. In addition, regular rail services are available at the Airport Train Station beneath Terminal 1, including the German Federal Railroad InterCity trains, Lufthansa's Airport Express, and S-Bahn commuter trains to nearby cities (Frankfurt, Mainz, Wiesbaden). The new terminal 2, scheduled to open in autumn 1994, will be linked to Terminal 1 by a people-mover system, providing quick transfers and maintaining the airport's standard of a 45-minute maximum connecting time. Train information is available at the **GermanRail** ticket counter at Arrivals Hall B (tel. 069/69-1844). **S-Bahn** lines between the airport and Frankfurt center run every 10 minutes and deposit passengers at the main rail station. Take trains S-14 or S-15. Travel time is 11 to 15 minutes, and a one-way ticket costs 3.80 DM ($2.50), raised to 4.80 DM ($3.20) during rush hours.

BY TRAIN & BUS Frankfurt's main rail station, **Hauptbahnhof,** Am Hauptbahnhof, D-6000 Frankfurt/Main, is the busiest rail station in Europe, arrival point for some 1,640 trains per day carrying about 260,000 passengers. From most major cities of Germany, a train arrives every hour. Most big European cities also have direct rail links with Frankfurt. For travel information about long-distance trains, call 069/19-419; for ticket reservations 069/265-38-46; and for train schedule information 069/75-432.

Frankfurt also offers long-distance bus service to about 200 German and European cities. Buses depart from the south side of the Hauptbahnhof. For information contact **Deutsche Touring Gesellschaft,** Mannheimer Strasse 17 (tel. 069/17-90-30).

BY CAR Frankfurt is reached by expressway (Autobahn) from all directions. The

A3 and A5 intersect at Frankfurt, with the A3 coming in from the Netherlands, Cologne, and Bonn, and continuing east and south to Würzburg, Nürnberg, and Munich. The A5 from the northeast (Hannover, Bad Hersfeld) continues south to Heidelberg, Mannheim, and Basel (Switzerland). From the west A60 connects with A66, which leads to Frankfurt and the inner city, hooking up with A3. Road signs and directions are frequently posted.

TOURIST INFORMATION

The official tourist office, dispensing information for the whole country, is the **German National Tourist Board,** Beethovenstrasse 69, D-6000 Frankfurt (tel. 069/75-72-0). For information bureaus, which will also help you find accommodations, see Section 3, "Accommodations," below.

CITY LAYOUT

At the western edge of the center of town, the Hauptbahnhof opens onto a large street called Am Hauptbahnhof. As you walk out of the station, Düsseldorferstrasse will be on your left, Baselerstrasse on your right, heading south toward the Main River. You have a choice of three streets heading east to the center of the Altstadt (old town): Taunusstrasse, Kaiserstrasse, and Münchner Strasse. Münchner Strasse leads directly into Theaterplatz, with its opera house. Taunusstrasse leads to three of the major Altstadt squares in the southern part of the city: Goetheplatz, Rathenauplatz, and (most important) the Hauptwache, with its good U-Bahn connections. In this section of Frankfurt, along Kaiserstrasse, some of the best shops are found; major attractions, including Goethe-Haus, are nearby.

The Main River flows slightly south of the Altstadt. Many bridges, including the Alte Brücke and the Obermainbrücke, cross this vital river. On the south bank of the Main is a popular district, Alt-Sachsenhausen, center of the apple-wine taverns (more about them later). For other major attractions, you'll have to branch out, heading east to the Frankfurt Zoo or northwest to the Palmengarten (both easily reached by public transportation).

NEIGHBORHOODS IN BRIEF

Altstadt The only way to discover Frankfurt's old town is to walk. Rebuilt after Allied bombing raids leveled it in 1944, it never regained its old style but is interesting nonetheless. The gently sloping Römerberg, the geographical heart of Frankfurt, was once the principal headquarters of this "city of merchants."

Alt-Sachsenhausen Called a "city-within-a-city," Frankfurt's south bank apple-wine district is filled with taverns where patrons consume vast quantities of *Ebbelwei*. Incorporated into Frankfurt in 1390, it has the safest and most lively nightlife. Take your pick of the dozens of apple-wine houses around Affentorplatz, the center of this town.

Museumsufer Running between Eiserner Steg and Friedensbrücke, this district is the site of major museums, seven in all. It's called variously "museum row" and a "cultural feast." The district is split by a major road, Schaumainkai. Note that all museums are closed on Monday.

Westend The financial district, this area grew rapidly in the prosperous 19th century and—before the Nazis—had the second largest Jewish settlement in Germany, plus it was the abode of the Rothschilds. Today, its bustling streets are filled with skyscrapers and offices, which earn for Frankfurt the label "*Main*hattan."

Bockenheim This is primarily a working class district. Because of its low prices, as reflected by its bars, cafés, and restaurants, it also has a heavy concentration of students and a big *Gastarbeiter* (foreign guest worker) population. Its main street—good for shopping—is Leipziger Strasse. Take U-Bahn line 6.

STREET MAPS Arm yourself with a detailed street map, not the general overview handed out by the tourist office. Even if you're in Frankfurt for just a day or two and plan to see only the major monuments, you'll need a detailed map. The best ones are published by **Falk,** and they are carefully indexed. These maps are sold at most bookstores and at general news kiosks. See "Bookstores" under "Fast Facts: Frankfurt" below.

FINDING AN ADDRESS Most of Frankfurt's streets are numbered with the evens on one side and the odds on the other.

2. GETTING AROUND

BY PUBLIC TRANSPORTATION The city and its environs, up to a radius of 24 miles, are connected by a number of fast, modern means of transport, under the Frankfurt Transport Federation (FVV), Mannheimer Strasse 15 (tel. 069/26-94-62). City and overland buses, trams, subways, and district trains can be used within fare zones at one price, including transfers. Tickets are obtained at *blue* coin-operated automatic machines labeled *Fahrscheine.* These machines will change up to 5 DM ($3.30). A 24-hour ticket with unlimited travel costs 8 DM ($5.30), half price for children. Zone charts and additional information in six languages are displayed on all the automatic machines. Be sure to buy your ticket before you board. If you are caught traveling without the proper card, you are subject to a fine of 60 DM ($39.60).

Tickets for the GermanRail within a 30-mile radius of Frankfurt, plus necessary additional tickets, may be obtained from the *red* coin-operated machines in the main section foyer of the railway station in front of the platforms. The machines give change.

BY TAXI If for some reason public transport is not feasible, you'll have to rely on taxi service. Radio taxis are on call day and night, either at marked taxi stands or by calling 23-00-33, 54-50-11, or 25-00-01. There is no extra charge for pickup. The fare is by trip not passenger or piece of luggage. The rate is 3.60 DM ($2.40), plus 2.05 DM ($1.40) per kilometer traveled.

BY CAR The big rental companies have offices at the airport and at central locations. Rentals are available at such agencies as **Avis,** Schmidtstrasse 39 (tel. 069/23-01-01), and **Hertz,** Schwalbacher Strasse 47–49 (tel. 069/730-404).

If you're planning to tour the country, you might want to check with an automobile club, **AvD,** Lyoner Strasse 16, D-6000 Frankfurt 71 (tel. 069/660-60), for membership possibilities. This club can be useful if you experience difficulties on the road.

ON FOOT The center of Frankfurt is a relatively compact area, and because of heavy traffic it is best explored on foot. A few streets are reserved for pedestrians only. These include the Römer complex, south of the Hauptwache. From this point, you can cross the Main, taking the Eisener Steg, or "iron bridge," to Alt-Sachsenhausen, site of the famous apple-wine taverns.

FAST
FACTS **FRANKFURT**

American Express Centrally located at Kaiserstrasse 8 (tel. 069/21-05-48), the offices are open Monday to Friday from 9:30am to 5:30pm (Saturday 9am to noon). Unless you have an American Express card or traveler's checks, you'll be assessed 2 DM ($1.30) for using the mail service.

Area Code   The telephone area code is **069.**

Babysitters   Most hotels can arrange for a sitter who speaks English.

Bookstores   The best English-language bookstore is **British Bookshop,** Börsenstrasse 17 (tel. 069/28-04-92). Many English-language editions are also for sale at **Internationale Buchhandlung,** Zeil 127 (tel. 069/29-89-04-10).

Car Rentals   See "Getting Around" in this chapter.

Climate   See "When to Go," in Chapter 2.

Cultural Institute   Amerika-Haus is at Staufenstrasse (tel. 069/72-27-94).

Currency   See "Information, Entry Requirements & Money," in Chapter 2.

Currency Exchange   To exchange dollars into marks, go to the Hauptbahnhof's **Deutsche Verkehrs-Kredit Bank** (tel. 069/264-82-01), open daily from 6:30am to 10pm, or the airport branch (tel. 069/690-35-06), open daily from 7:30am to 9pm.

Dentist   For an English-speaking dentist, call 069/660-727-11 to arrange an appointment.

Doctor   For an English-speaking doctor, call 069/79-50-22-00 to arrange an appointment.

Drugstores   For information about pharmacies open near you, call 069/115-00.

Consulates   If you lose a passport or have some such emergency, contact the U.S. consulate, Siesmayerstrasse 21 (tel. 069/7535-0). The U.K. consulate is at Bockenheimer Landstrasse 51–53 (tel. 069/170-00-20). The Australian consulate is at Gutleustrasse 85 (tel. 069/273-90-90).

Emergencies   Frankfurt has several emergency numbers that might come in handy. Among them are: **110**—accident; **112**—fire and first aid; **069/792-02-00**—emergency medical service; and **069/660-72-71**—emergency dental service.

Eyeglasses   Go to **Hertie,** An der Zeil 390 (tel. 069/2961), the city's major department store. The optician's hours are Monday through Friday from 9am to 6:30pm and Saturday from 9am to 2pm.

Hairdressers/Barbers   For both men and women, **Friseur Salon Kraiss** (tel. 069/23-22-28), located on Level B of the Hauptbahnhof, is open Monday through Saturday from 6:30am to 8:30pm.

Holidays   See "When to Go" in Chapter 2.

Hotlines   The rape/battered women's hotline is 069/70-94-94.

Information   See "Information, Entry Requirements & Money" in Chapter 2.

Laundry/Dry Cleaning   Try **Kingsgad Reinigung,** Franken Allee (tel. 069/73-80-035). Hours are Monday through Friday from 8:30am to 1pm and 3 to 6:30pm and Saturday from 8:30am to 1pm.

Libraries   Deutsche Bibliothek, Zeppelin Alle 4–8 (tel. 069/75-661), is open daily from 9am to 7pm. Take Bus no. 2.

Lost Property   Go to **Bundesbahn-Fundstelle,** Hauptbahnhof-Nordseite (track 24; tel. 069/265-56-45) Monday to Friday from 7:30am to 4pm.

Luggage Storage/Lockers   Lockers can be rented and luggage stored at the Hauptbahnhof.

Newspapers/Magazines   If you read German, the leading newspaper of Frankfurt, the *Frankfurter Allgemeine Zeitung,* contains data on films, theater, exhibitions, and local concerts. You'll also find copies of the *International Herald Tribune* and *USA Today* at most newsstands and in several of the larger hotels, along with European editions of magazines like *Time* and *Newsweek.*

Photographic Needs   Check out **Foto Netthold,** Schillerstrasse 13 (tel. 069/28-25-61).

Police   Telephone **110.**

Post Office   In Frankfurt, the **central post office** is at Zeil 108–110, near the Hauptwache (tel. 069/211-44-40). It is open Monday to Saturday from 8am to

6pm. Go here to pick up general delivery mail (called "poste restante" in Europe). There is also a post office in the Hauptbahnhof, open day and night.

Radio   If you know German, you can listen to one of nine radio stations operated by ARD. For radio programs in English, tune to 90.2 FM (87.6 on cable) for the BBC, or 87.9 AM (94 on cable) for the American Forces Network.

Religious Services   For information about Protestant services in Frankfurt, call 11101; for Catholic services, call 11102. For Jewish services, contact the Jewish Community, Westendstrasse 43 (tel. 069/74-07-21).

Restrooms   Don't ask for the "bathroom" in Germany, because it will be assumed you truly want to take a bath. Use the word *Toilette*. Often it is labeled WC in public places, meaning "water closet." Sometimes there's only an H (*Herren,* for men) on the door or F (*Frauen,* for women). In central Frankfurt are several public facilities, especially in the Altstadt. You can also use facilities at terminals, restaurants, bars, cafés, department stores, hotels, and pubs.

Safety   Frankfurt is a relatively safe city, but crime is on the increase, so you should stay alert at all times. Pickpockets and thieves are especially fond of lifting wallets, cameras, and purses. Keep valuables in a safety deposit box at your hotel, wear a money belt, and keep a close eye on possessions such as cameras. Stay out of the area around the Hauptbahnhof at night, as muggings are frequent.

Shoe Repairs   Go to the Hertie department store, An der Zeil 390 (tel. 069/2961) and seek out **Mister Minit** on the ground level. Hours are Monday through Friday from 9am to 6:30pm and Saturday from 9am to 2pm.

Television   There are two national TV broadcasters, ARD and ZDF, but you'll need to understand German. Many of the better hotels offer cable TV with CNN broadcasts from the United States, plus a sports channel in English, and Super Channel with programs from Great Britain.

Taxes   Value-added tax (VAT) is included in all bills for goods, services, hotels, and restaurants in Germany. There are, however, no special city taxes in Frankfurt, nor is there an airport departure tax.

Taxis   See "Getting Around" in this chapter.

Telegrams/Telex/Fax   You can send all of these at the post office at the Hauptbahnhof (tel. 069/261-51-13), is open 24 hours.

Useful Telephone Numbers   Police **110;** fire **112;** medical emergency **069/792-0200.**

Weather   See the temperature chart for Frankfurt in section 2 of Chapter 2.

3. ACCOMMODATIONS

If you arrive during a busy trade fair, you may find all the better hotels fully booked. You can generally reserve a room on the spot by going to the tourist office in the Hauptbahnhof, across track 23. It's called **Verkehrsamt Frankfurt am Main** (tel. 069/212-38849). In season (May to October), the office is open Monday through Saturday from 8am to 10pm; Sunday and holidays, 9:30am to 8pm. In off-season (November to April), the office is open Monday to Saturday from 8am to 9pm; Sunday and holidays, 9:30am to 8pm. Another tourist information center is at Römerberg 27 (tel. 069/212-38-708). It's open March to October Monday to Friday from 9am to 7pm and Saturday, Sunday, and holidays from 9:30am to 6pm; during November to February, hours are Monday to Friday from 9am to 6pm. The offices charge 5 DM ($3.30) for the room-finding service and 8 DM ($5.30) as partial prepayment for the accommodation.

IN THE CENTER
VERY EXPENSIVE

ARABELLA GRAND HOTEL, Konrad-Adenauer-Strasse 7, D-6000 Frankfurt. Tel. 069/2-98-10. Fax 069/29-818-10. 378 rms, 11 suites. A/C MINIBAR TV TEL **U-Bahn:** Konstablerwache.

$ Rates: 355 DM–505 DM ($234.30–$333.30) single; 405 DM–555 DM ($267.30–$366.30) double; from 1,110 DM ($732.60) suite. Breakfast 30 DM ($19.80) extra. AE, DC, MC, V. **Parking:** 25 DM ($16.50).

This is one of the most modern and glamorous hotels in Frankfurt, laden with international big-city style. Rising six stories in the heart of the financial district, the hotel has an atrium-style lobby warmly decorated in brown and white marble. There are upholstered furniture, lots of plants, and a carefully trained staff. Bedrooms are large and outfitted in dusty rose and brown, with furniture inspired by art deco.

Dining/Entertainment: The hotel boasts Dynasty, one of the best Chinese restaurants in Frankfurt, and also operates a successful Brasserie serving international dishes. Its principal restaurant is appropriately called Premiere (see "Dining," below).

Services: 24-hour room service, laundry, babysitting.

Facilities: Fitness center, beauty parlor, sauna, solarium, pool.

FRANKFURT MARRIOTT HOTEL, Hamburger Allee 2, D-6000 Frankfurt. Tel. 069/7-95-50. Fax 069/795-52-432. 585 rms. 25 suites. A/C MINIBAR TV TEL **Tram:** 16 or 19.

$ Rates: 365 DM–560 DM ($240.90–$369.60) single; 415 DM–620 DM ($273.90–$409.20) double; from 675 DM ($445.50) suite. Buffet breakfast 28 DM ($18.50) extra. AE, DC, MC, V. **Parking:** 20 DM ($13.20).

Across the street from the Messegelände, the Marriott is packed to the rafters during Frankfurt's book and trade fairs, with top publishers reserving rooms a year in advance. This chain-run hotel, one of the most inviting in Frankfurt, is within walking distance of the heart of town, the Palmengarten, and the Senckenberg Museum (just around the corner). Its guest rooms have private baths and are equipped with radios, color TVs, in-house videos, trouser presses, and hairdryers. Traffic noise is left far below, and you can look out over the city and the surrounding countryside, framed against a backdrop of the Taunus Mountains.

Dining/Entertainment: The hotel offers two restaurants, the luxuriously appointed Geheimratsstube, and the Bäckerei, where you can watch the hotel's bakers turn out fresh bread and rolls each morning.

Services: Laundry, babysitting, 24-hour room service.

Facilities: Car-rental facilities, shopping boutiques, business center.

MÖVENPICK PARKHOTEL FRANKFURT, Wiesenhuttenplatz 28–38, D-6000 Frankfurt. Tel. 069/2697-884. Fax 069/269-78-849. 299 rms, 14 suites. A/C MINIBAR TV TEL **S-Bahn:** 15.

$ Rates: 298 DM–488 DM ($196.70–$322.10) single; 398 DM–538 DM ($262.70–$355.10) double; from 748 DM ($493.70) suite. Buffet breakfast 22 DM ($14.50) extra. AE, DC, MC, V. **Parking:** 25 DM ($16.50).

This fine hotel provides not only warmth but also personal attention for its guests. Near the Hauptbahnhof, it opens onto a quiet square. The hotel has been built in two sections—an ornately decorated, recently renovated 19th-century building alongside a sleek 1970s wing. In the older part, rooms have a luxurious atmosphere and are individually designed (the largest suite is done in Louis XVI style), while the newer section boasts a modern decor. All rooms and suites are in the five-star category.

Dining/Entertainment: The hotel's gourmet restaurant, La Truffe, dishes out some of the best hors d'oeuvres in Frankfurt and has one of Germany's best wine lists, recognized by the Deutsche Sommelier Union. The Mövenpick restaurant offers German regional cooking.

Services: Laundry, dry cleaning, babysitting, room service, overnight shoe cleaning.

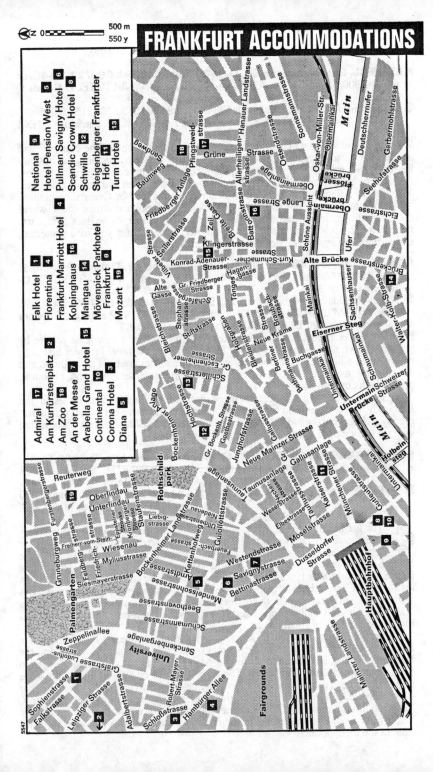

FRANKFURT ACCOMMODATIONS

0   500 m
    550 y

National **9**	Falk Hotel **1**
Hotel Pension West **5**	Florentina **4**
Pullman Savigny Hotel **6**	Frankfurt Marriott Hotel **4**
Scandic Crown Hotel **8**	Kolpinghaus **16**
Schwille **12**	Maingau **14**
Steigenberger Frankfurter Hof **11**	Mövenpick Parkhotel Frankfurt **8**
Turm Hotel **13**	Mozart **19**

Admiral **17**	
Am Kurfürstenplatz **2**	
Am Zoo **18**	
An der Messe **7**	
Arabella Grand Hotel **15**	
Continental **10**	
Corona Hotel **3**	
Diana **5**	

Facilities: Sauna, solarium, shopping boutiques, business center.

NATIONAL, Baselerstrasse 50, D-6000 Frankfurt. Tel. 069/27-39-40, or toll free 800/528-1234. Fax 069/23-44-60. 95 rms. MINIBAR TV TEL **U-Bahn:** 1, 2, or 3.

$ Rates (including buffet breakfast): 198 DM–228 DM ($130.70–$150.50) single; 299 DM–384 DM ($197.30–$253.40) double. AE, DC, MC, V. **Parking:** 20 DM ($13.20).

With an ambience unmatched by larger, more impersonal hotels, the National will appeal to the traditionalist. A first-class hotel of Best Western affiliation, the hostelry lies only two minutes from the Hauptbahnhof. The fairgrounds are also nearby. Antiques or handsome reproductions are in both public rooms and private chambers. Many of the rooms are spacious, with decoration enhanced by Oriental carpeting.

You might want to dine in the hotel's beautifully appointed dining room, where the international menu features a 45-DM ($29.70) dinner as well as à la carte selections. The lobby bar, decorated in classical style, invites you to a protected, comfortable rendezvous before dinner or after the theater.

SCANDIC CROWN HOTEL, Wiesenhuttenstrasse 42, D-6000 Frankfurt. Tel. 069/27-39-60. Fax 069/27-39-67-95. 144 rms. MINIBAR TV TEL **U-Bahn:** 1, 2, or 3.

$ Rates (including buffet breakfast): 250 DM–390 DM ($165–$257.40) single; 295 DM–420 DM ($194.70–$277.20) double. AE, DC, MC, V. **Parking:** Multistory car park nearby, 20 DM ($13.20). **Closed:** Dec 23–Jan 3.

Formerly the Frankfurt Savoy, this hostelry has been given a new lease on life by Scandic Crown management. Near the Hauptbahnhof, the hotel provides first-class comfort and a lighthearted ambience. Swedish furnishings are used throughout, and the guest rooms contain color TVs, radios, trouser presses, hairdryers, and, of course, private baths or showers.

Guests can enjoy a continental menu with many international dishes in the Rhapsody, or they can head for the hotel's premier (and more expensive) restaurant, the Savoy, honoring the old name of the establishment. Facilities include a fitness club with an indoor pool, along with a sauna and solarium.

STEIGENBERGER FRANKFURTER HOF, Am Kaiserplatz, D-6000 Frankfurt. Tel. 069/2-15-02, or toll free 800/223-5652 in the U.S. and Canada. Fax 069/21-59-00. 350 rms, 30 suites. MINIBAR TV TEL **U-Bahn:** 1, 2, or 3.

$ Rates (including breakfast): 322 DM–515 DM ($212.50–$339.90) single; 380 DM–570 DM ($250.80–$376.20) double; from 1,300 DM ($858) suite. AE, DC, MC, V. **Parking:** 25 DM ($16.50).

The grand hotel of Frankfurt, run by the Steigenberger chain, is the number-one choice of traditionalists. Its position in the center of the city is ideal for tourists and businesspeople alike, for it's just a few short blocks from the Hauptbahnhof and near the sights of the Altstadt. Behind an 1876 neobaroque facade, the Frankfurter Hof has successfully combined the classic and the modern. Its art collection, particularly its Gobelin tapestries, is outstanding. In spite of its size, this well-maintained hotel offers both comfort and a personalized atmosphere. The rooms and suites, all with well-equipped baths, are furnished in a restrained and dignified modern style; 75% of them are airconditioned.

Dining/Entertainment: In keeping with the management's belief that a fine hotel is more than just a place to sleep, Frankfurter Hof boasts several attractions: the Restaurant Français, decorated in Empire style, and the thatch-roofed Hofgarten Restaurant, which has grilled meats. The Kaiserbrunnen offers light meals and wines and champagne in a cozy setting with a Biedermeier decor. The hotel's Lipizzaner Bar is regarded by discerning visitors as the most elegant in the city (see Section 8, "Evening Entertainment"). The favorite spot in the hotel is the provincial-style Frankfurter Stubb, recommended in the dining section below. A pianist plays at tea time in the lobby lounge.

Services: Same-day laundry and valet service; dry cleaning; shoeshine service; babysitting; 24-hour room service; and full business services, including a Lufthansa counter.

Facilities: Shopping arcade with hairdresser and beauty parlor, wine and gourmet boutique.

EXPENSIVE

AN DER MESSE, Westendstrasse 104, D-6000 Frankfurt. Tel. 069/74-79-79, or toll free 800/221-6509. Fax 069/74-83-49. 46 rms. MINIBAR TV TEL **Bus:** 32.

$ Rates (including breakfast): 210 DM–290 DM ($138.60–$191.40) single; 260 DM–440 DM ($171.60–$290.40) double. AE, DC, MC, V. **Parking:** Underground garage, 20 DM ($13.20).

Its white facade is pierced by smoked-glass windows and a canopied entrance, and its quiet location is just a five-minute walk from the university, the Hauptbahnhof, the banking district, and the fairgrounds. The staff does much to make guests feel comfortable in the elegantly furnished rooms, each with private bath or shower, color TV, and radio. Only half a dozen singles are rented, and they're hard to come by unless you reserve well in advance. Breakfast is served in a light, airy room.

AM ZOO, Alfred-Brehm-Platz 6, D-6000 Frankfurt. Tel. 069/49-07-71. Fax 069/43-98-68. 85 rms (all with shower or bath). TEL **Tram:** 11, 14, or 16.

$ Rates (including continental breakfast): 120 DM–150 DM ($79.20–$99) single; 190 DM–240 DM ($125.40–$158.40) double. AE, DC, MC, V. **Parking:** Behind the hotel, 8 DM ($5.30). **Closed:** Dec 20–Jan 5.

Just across from the zoo entrance is this modern hotel with a nice restaurant. The rooms are clean, with simple but comfortable modern pieces; 80 contain minibars and TVs. The street-level breakfast room is the hotel's most charming feature, with linen-covered tables and stained-glass windows. Trams stop across the street, and the U-Bahn connects with the Hauptbahnhof and the airport.

CONTINENTAL, Baselerstrasse 56, D-6000 Frankfurt. Tel. 069/23-03-41. Fax 069/23-29-14. 80 rms, 4 suites. TV TEL **U-Bahn:** 1, 2, or 3.

$ Rates (including continental breakfast): 155 DM–190 DM ($102.30–$125.40) single; 220 DM–260 DM ($145.20–$171.60) double; from 325 DM ($214.50) suite. AE, DC, MC, V. **Parking:** 20 DM ($13.20).

A leader among middle-bracket hotels near the Hauptbahnhof is the Continental. Founded in 1889, it enjoyed its heyday in the belle époque era. From the ashes of World War II, it was reconstructed in 1952 and refurbished in 1985. Around the corner are lively bars, but serenity prevails inside, where the rooms—especially those with modern plumbing—are comfortable. Windows have been soundproofed to keep out traffic din. The hotel—the choice of many businesspeople, including Japanese clients—has a pleasant restaurant, Conti, with an international cuisine.

FALK HOTEL, Falkstrasse 38A, D-6000 Frankfurt. Tel. 069/70-80-94. Fax 069/70-80-17. 32 rms. TV TEL

$ Rates (including breakfast): 140 DM–165 DM ($92.40–$108.90) single; 205 DM–245 DM ($135.30–$161.70) double. No credit cards. **Parking:** 15 DM ($9.90).

The Falk may be stark outside, but inside there is much to recommend it. Bright and modern, it has enough traditional touches to lend warmth and coziness. It rents small and uncluttered guest rooms that are spotlessly maintained. A rustic bar with Spanish tiles and hanging lights is called the Toledo-Stil.

MOZART, Parkstrasse 17, D-6000 Frankfurt. Tel. 069/55-08-31. Fax 069/596-45-59. 35 rms. MINIBAR TV TEL **U-Bahn:** 1, 2, or 3.

$ Rates (including buffet breakfast): 145 DM–160 DM ($95.70–$105.60) single; 210 DM ($138.60) double. AE, DC, MC, V.

Perhaps the best small hotel in Frankfurt, the Mozart stands on the periphery of the Palmengarten, right off the busy Fürstenbergerstrasse, near the Alte Oper. The hotel is recognized by its marble facade, softened by curtains at the windows. Everything inside—walls, furniture, bed coverings—is white or pink. The breakfast room, incidentally, could easily pass for an 18th-century salon with crystal chandeliers and Louis XV–style chairs. The staff is polite and helpful.

PULLMAN SAVIGNY HOTEL, Savignystrasse 14–16, D-6000 Frankfurt. Tel. 069/7-53-30, or toll free in U.S. 800/223-98-62. Fax 069/753-31-75. 124 rms, 2 suites. MINIBAR TV TEL **U-Bahn:** 1, 2, or 3.

$ Rates: 208 DM–308 DM ($137.30–$203.30) single; 266 DM–366 DM ($175.60–$241.60) double; from 466 DM ($307.60) suite. Buffet breakfast 22 DM ($14.50) per person. AE, DC, MC, V. **Parking:** Nearby garage, 20 DM ($13.20).

In the center of the banking and business districts, the first-class Pullman Savigny has undergone extensive upgrading. The foyer, restaurant, and bar have been renovated and redesigned, and the newly furnished guest rooms are equipped with luxury modern baths.

The restaurant offers creative cuisine and outstanding service, with meals priced from 50 DM to 80 DM ($33 to $52.80). The elegant hotel bar has a welcoming atmosphere. Services include laundry and dry cleaning, car rentals, and booking of sightseeing tours. The hotel is an eight-minute walk from the main railway station and the Messegelände, but the location is quiet.

TURM HOTEL, Eschersheimer Landstrasse 20, D-6000 Frankfurt. Tel. 069/15-40-50. Fax 069/55-35-78. 75 rms. TV TEL **U-Bahn:** 1, 2, or 3.

$ Rates (including breakfast): 130 DM ($85.80) single; 195 DM–245 DM ($128.70–$161.70) double. AE, DC, MC, V. **Parking:** Free.

A centrally located six-story structure, the Turm offers compact, boxy rooms that are

---

Ⓕ **FROMMER'S SMART TRAVELER: HOTELS**

1. In inexpensive or moderately priced hotels, a room with a shower is cheaper than a room with a private bath. Even cheaper is a room with hot and cold running water and a corridor bathroom.
2. Consider a package tour (or book land arrangements with your air ticket). You'll often pay 30% or more less than individual "rack" rates (off-the-street, independent bookings).
3. If Frankfurt hotels are not full, a little bargaining can bring down the cost of a room. Be polite: Ask if there's a "businessperson's rate?" or if teachers get a discount. The technique works best when the hotel has a 40% vacancy at night and wants to fill those empty rooms.
4. At less expensive hotels that take credit cards, ask if payment by cash will get you a reduction.
5. If you're going to spend at least a week in Frankfurt, ask about long-term discounts.
6. Ask about weekend discounts, which can add up to 50% at certain city hotels patronized mainly by businesspeople.
7. Try to take advantage of special rates, if offered. Hotel chains often grant them, especially in July and August, when German business travel falls off.

uncluttered, in Spartan taste. The innkeeper has a helpful staff. Most winning is the hotel restaurant, an Argentine-style steakhouse called La Pampa.

MODERATE

ADMIRAL, Hölderlinstrasse 25, D-6000 Frankfurt. Tel. 069/44-80-21. Fax 069/43-94-02. 67 rms (all with bath or shower). MINIBAR TV TEL **U-Bahn:** 6 or 7.

$ Rates (including breakfast): 100 DM–120 DM ($66–$79.20) single; 150 DM–190 DM ($99–$125.40) double. AE, DC, MC, V. **Parking:** 5 DM ($3.30).

The Admiral is often favored by families. Perhaps they like its location near the zoo, a short haul from the center of Frankfurt. It rents 67 plainly but comfortably furnished guest rooms and has a natural wood decor in Scandinavian style. The hotel serves breakfast only.

DIANA, Westendstrasse 83-85, D-6000 Frankfurt. Tel. 069/74-70-07. Fax 069/74-70-79. 26 rms. TEL **Bus:** 19.

$ Rates (including buffet breakfast): 85 DM–100 DM ($56.10–$66) single; 148 DM ($97.70) double. AE, DC, MC, V. **Parking:** 6 DM ($4).

Spotless and homey, the Diana stands as a leader in its price class. A copy of a private villa, with a drawing room and an intimate breakfast salon, it is situated in the Westend on a pleasant residential street, where it maintains a tone of quiet dignity. Double rooms have TVs.

FLORENTINA, Westendstrasse 23, D-6000 Frankfurt. Tel. 069/74-60-44. Fax 069/74-79-24. 35 rms (28 with bath or shower). A/C TV TEL **U-Bahn:** 1, 2, or 3.

$ Rates (including buffet breakfast): 70 DM ($46.20) single without bath or shower, 110 DM–135 DM ($72.60–$89.10) single with bath or shower; 160 DM–200 DM ($105.60–$132) double with bath or shower. AE, DC, MC, V. **Parking:** 10 DM ($6.60).

Solid and modern, the Florentina lies on a one-way street about 500 yards from the Hauptbahnhof. Guests are made welcome in this well-run hotel, with pleasantly comfortable rooms reached by elevator. Although the hotel serves only breakfast, drinks can be ordered at any time, as can snacks in the evening.

INEXPENSIVE

AM KURFÜRSTENPLATZ, Kurfürstenplatz 38, D-6000 Frankfurt. Tel. 069/77-78-16. Fax 069/70-77-027. 34 rms (10 with shower). TV TEL **U-Bahn:** 1, 2, or 3.

$ Rates (including continental breakfast): 77 DM ($50.80) single without bath, 92 DM ($60.70) single with shower; 117 DM ($77.20) double without bath, 127 DM ($83.80) double with shower. No credit cards. **Parking:** Free.

The English-speaking owner has decorated this hotel in a mixture of styles, perking up each room with bright, cheerful colors and boxes of plants at the windows. The combination breakfast room/lounge sparkles. The front rooms face a park complete with fountain, church spire, and lots of baby carriages. The hotel provides one bath and toilet for every three rooms; some have private showers but no toilets.

KOLPINGHAUS, Langestrasse 26, D-6000 Frankfurt. Tel. 069/28-85-41. Fax 069/29-05-59. 48 rms (33 with bath or shower). TEL **Tram:** 11 from the Hauptbahnhof.

$ Rates (including breakfast): 80 DM ($52.80) single without bath, 110 DM ($72.60) single with shower; 125 DM ($82.50) double without bath, 165 DM ($108.90) double with bath. MC, V.

The Kolpinghaus is a modern hotel whose most winning feature is the little garden out back, where café tables are placed in fair weather. The rooms are small, like

American university dorm rooms, but well maintained, with crisp white sheets. The location is within walking distance of the zoo and the shopping street, the Zeil.

ALT-SACHSENHAUSEN

MODERATE

MAINGAU, Schifferstrasse 38-40, D-6000 Frankfurt. Tel. 069/61-70-01. Fax 069/62-07-90. 100 rms, 10 suites. MINIBAR TV TEL **Bus:** 62. **Tram:** 16.
$ Rates (including buffet breakfast): 110 DM–130 DM ($72.60–$85.80) single; 130 DM–180 DM ($85.80–$118.80) double; from 200 DM ($132) suite. AE, MC, V.

Opening onto a small park in the apple-wine district, just across the Main from the Altstadt, Hotel Maingau, is appropriate for those who want to live among Frankfurters rather than with fellow visitors on the right bank. Blondwood Nordic furnishings characterize both the old building and its newer annex. The hotel is a good point from which to launch a nighttime pub crawl of the apple-wine district, perhaps starting at the hotel's restaurant. Meals cost 25 DM ($16.50) to 81 DM ($53.50) there.

GRAVENBRUCH

VERY EXPENSIVE

GRAVENBRUCH-KEMPINSKI-FRANKFURT, Neu-Isenburg 2, D-6078 Frankfurt. Tel. 06102/5050. Fax 06102/50-54-45. 288 rms, 29 suites. A/C MINIBAR TV TEL **Transportation:** Free transfers to and from airport and city center.
$ Rates: 345 DM–485 DM ($227.70–$320.10) single; 485 DM–575 DM ($320.10–$379.50) double; from 800 DM ($528) suite. Buffet breakfast 30 DM ($19.80) extra. AE, DC, MC, V. **Parking:** Free.

In the suburbs, a 20-minute taxi ride from the center of the city via A3 and B459 across Gravenbruch, is a recommendation for guests wanting to escape the bustle of a commercial setting. Here you'll find luxury combined with rural charm. Only 10 minutes from the Frankfurt airport, the hotel is set back from route B459 on 37 acres of parkland, complete with a lake. The structure was built on the foundation and old walls of a former manor house dating from 1568. More modern residential wings are positioned along the lakeshore, but some touches of the old country-mansion character remain, such as the large atrium-style courtyards. The hotel provides attractive, sleep-inducing bedrooms.

Dining/Entertainment: Many in-the-know Frankfurters journey here just to sample the cuisine. The elegant Restaurant Forsthaus, with a view of the park, was converted from a 16th-century hunting lodge. It serves meals costing 50 DM to 80

Ⓕ FROMMER'S COOL FOR KIDS: HOTELS

Mövenpick Parkhotel Frankfurt *(see page 76)* Children under 16 stay free in their parents' room at this chain-run hotel across from a city park.

Am Zoo *(see page 79)* This clean, well-furnished, and comfortable hotel lies just across from the zoo entrance in a quiet, safe neighborhood.

Admiral *(see page 81)* This family favorite near the zoo has rooms that are simply furnished but comfortable—and the price is right.

DM ($33 to $52.80). Torschänke has a stone-slab floor, as well as draft beer from a barrel, and is housed in what were horse stables in the 16th century. The hotel bar offers dancing to music from international trios and entertainers.

Services: Room service, laundry facilities, babysitting.

Facilities: Heated indoor and outdoor pools, fitness center, sauna, solarium, tennis courts, boutiques, hairdressing salon; beauty and fitness farm, with massage service; golf and horseback riding available nearby.

4. DINING

IN THE CENTER

VERY EXPENSIVE

PREMIERE, in the Arabella Grand Hotel, Konrad-Adenauer-Strasse 7. Tel. 069/2-98-10.

Cuisine: CONTINENTAL. **Reservations:** Recommended. **U-Bahn:** Konstablerwache.

$ **Prices:** Appetizers 15 DM–35 DM ($9.90–$23.10); main courses 43 DM–52 DM ($28.40–$34.30); fixed-price menus 85 DM ($56.10) and 132 DM ($87.10). AE, DC, MC, V.

Open: Dinner only, daily 6–11pm (last order).

One of Frankfurt's most stylish and elegant restaurants lies just above lobby level of the city's newest five-star hotel. Entirely sheathed in mirrors interspersed with slabs of polished cherrywood, it's a preferred venue of the city's discreetly wealthy industrial and financial moguls. Its repertoire is defined by the chefs as *cuisine vitale,* stressing healthful and succulent preparations of fresh ingredients, presented artfully. Examples include duckling Schnitzel in vinaigrette-and-truffle sauce, liaison of salmon and John Dory with rice in chervil sauce, truffled breast of guinea fowl, and a "composition of seafood" featuring several fish and shellfish served with leaf spinach and two sauces (lobster and champagne-butter). The dessert menu is appropriately elegant, with a particular favorite being an Irish coffee tart.

RESTAURANT FRANÇAIS, in the Steigenberger Frankfurter Hof, Am Kaiserplatz. Tel. 069/2-15-02.

Cuisine: FRENCH. **Reservations:** Required. **U-Bahn:** 1, 2, or 3.

$ **Prices:** Appetizers 28 DM–48 DM ($18.50–$31.70); main courses 42 DM–66 DM ($27.70–$43.60); fixed-price lunch 98 DM ($64.70); fixed-price dinner 150 DM ($99). AE, DC, MC, V.

Open: Lunch Tues–Sat noon–2pm; dinner Tues–Sat 7–11pm. **Closed:** June–July 4, holidays.

⭐ On the main floor of this previously recommended hotel sits one of the most outstanding restaurants of Frankfurt. Cookery, in the main, is from Lyon and Provence. Lyon, is, of course, the gastronomic capital of France; Provence may come as a bit of a surprise.

The chef is a perfectionist, insisting on not only professionalism but also enthusiasm. One of the local favorites is stuffed quail in a truffle butter sauce. You might begin with a velvety smooth cream of wild mushroom soup or a gâteau of mostelle, a delicately flavored fish found mainly in the Mediterranean, covered with orange butter. A magret of duckling is prepared with black currants and a confit of onions. Try also the Angus beef grillé Villette or roast pork "like your grandmother used to make." In season, game is a specialty.

For lunch, the place fills up with businesspeople, while at dinner the ambience is more romantic. A seven-course menu dégustation is available in the evening; you can also order à la carte.

WEINHAUS BRÜCKENKELLER, Schützenstrasse 6. Tel. 069/28-42-38.

Cuisine: GERMAN/FRENCH. **Reservations:** Required. **U-Bahn:** 1, 2, or 3.

$ **Prices:** Appetizers 25 DM–68 DM ($16.50–$44.90); main courses 48 DM–65 DM ($31.70–$42.90); fixed-price menus 138 DM–168 DM ($91.10–$110.90). AE, DC, MC, V.

Open: Dinner Mon–Tues and Thurs–Sat 6pm–1am. **Closed:** Dec 20–Jan 7.

A leading restaurant, Weinhaus Brückenkeller is perhaps the favorite watering spot of well-heeled North American visitors. In the heart of the Altstadt, you dine under medieval-looking arches at candlelit tables. Strolling musicians encourage singing. Franconian carvings adorn the alcoves, and huge wooden barrels are decorated with scenes from Goethe's *Faust* and from the life of Martin Luther.

A typical meal might begin with cream of sorrel soup or a more substantial goose liver terrine, followed by saddle of venison or saddle of young lamb. For a perfect finish, you might order a soufflé of strawberries with vanilla sauce. Their Tafelspitz is the best in town, as good as any you might have in Vienna. The evening repast includes homemade sourdough bread. The wine cellar holds an excellent collection of German wines, 180 in all, including the best from the Rhineland. Personal attention and efficient service are hallmarks.

ZAUBERFLÖTE, Opernplatz 1. Tel. 069/134-03-86.

Cuisine: FRENCH. **Reservations:** Recommended. **U-Bahn:** 1, 2, or 3.

$ **Prices:** Appetizers 18 DM–42 DM ($11.90–$27.70); main courses 56 DM–75 DM ($37–$49.50); fixed-price menu 135 DM–155 DM ($89.10–$102.30). AE, DC, MC, V.

Open: Dinner only, Tues–Sat 6pm–midnight. **Closed:** July 6–Aug 16.

This is the perfect place for an after-theater supper in a setting that Offenbach himself might have found stimulating. Surely the composer of *The Tales of Hoffmann* would gravitate to the elegant pink-and-blue decor with discreet lighting, brass-framed mirrors, superb china, not to mention the 240-bottle selection of wine, along with a good assortment of liqueurs. The entrance is hidden in the Alte Opera (opera house), opposite the opera café. You might begin with herring filet in a potato crust, apple-and-cucumber soup, or perhaps smoked salmon with an apple/mustard crust. You can order excellent fish such as John Dory for a main dish or one of the meat selections. For dessert, try the hazelnut soufflé or another of the many specialties. Adjoining is the Opernbistro, operated by the same management, open daily from 11am to midnight, with meals from 36 DM to 52 DM ($23 to $34.30).

EXPENSIVE

BÖRSENKELLER, Schillerstrasse 11. Tel. 069/28-11-15.

Cuisine: CONTINENTAL. **Reservations:** Recommended. **U-Bahn:** 1, 2, or 3.

$ **Prices:** Appetizers 20 DM–30 DM ($13.20–$19.80); main courses 32 DM–48 DM ($21.10–$31.70). AE, DC, MC, V.

Open: Mon–Fri 11am–11pm.

Börsenkeller, a favorite with stockbrokers and bankers, conceals its old-world atmosphere behind a modern exterior. Dining takes place on the lower level, with arched cellar rooms and lots of nooks and recessed areas. During the evening, accordion music is played. Typical dishes include rumpsteak Rothschild with croquettes and pork chops Swiss style.

MÖVENPICK AM OPERNPLATZ, Opernplatz 2. Tel. 069/2-06-80.

Cuisine: INTERNATIONAL. **Reservations:** Not necessary. **U-Bahn:** 1, 2, or 3.

$ **Prices:** Appetizers 22 DM–36 DM ($14.50–$23.80); main courses 32 DM–55 DM ($21.10–$36.30). AE, DC, MC, V.

Open: Lunch daily 11:30am–3pm; dinner daily 5pm–midnight.

The Swiss have invaded Frankfurt and have given Hesse cuisine a real challenge in the process. Having long enjoyed an outstanding reputation for cooking in their own

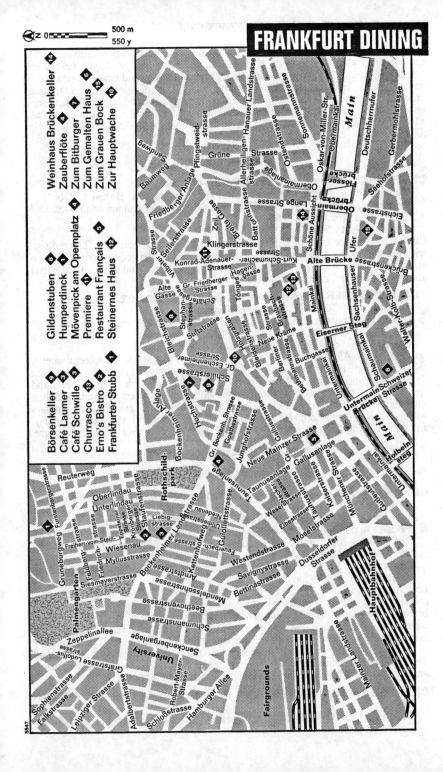

FRANKFURT DINING

Börsenkeller 9
Café Laumer 3
Café Schwille 3
Churrasco 13
Erno's Bistro 2
Frankfurter Stubb

Gildenstuben 8
Humperdinck
Mövenpick am Opernplatz 4
Premiere 11
Restaurant Français 5
Steinernes Haus 12

Weinhaus Brückenkeller 14
Zauberflöte
Zum Bitburger 7
Zum Gemalten Haus 6
Zum Grauen Bock 10
Zur Hauptwache 15

500 m
550 y

country, the Mövenpick interests have created dramatic dining in this German city. In the main restaurant, Baron de la Mouette, the roast rib of Angus beef with horseradish cream, Warwick mustard sauce, beef pan gravy, and baked potato is the daily specialty. Seductive French and international dishes include scampi in tarragon sauce and entrecôte Bordelaise. The restaurant serves apéritifs, liquor, steak, warm snacks, seafood, and salad; specialties include a crayfish cocktail and Angus entrecôte. Meals range from 38 DM ($25.10) for a business lunch to 88 DM ($58.10) for a big dinner.

INEXPENSIVE

CHURRASCO, Domplatz 6. Tel. 069/28-48-04.
   Cuisine: ARGENTINE. **Reservations:** Recommended. **U-Bahn:** 1, 2, or 3.
$ **Prices:** Appetizers 7 DM–10 DM ($4.60–$6.60); main courses 14 DM–30 DM ($9.20–$19.80). AE, DC, MC, V.
   Open: Daily 11:30am–11:30pm.
Churrasco is where Frankfurters go for succulent Argentine beefsteak. The red sign with the steer marks this dimly lit tavern. Lower-priced orders of rumpsteak are also available. All cuts are charcoal grilled to your specifications. Rounding out the menu are fresh salads and a limited list of desserts.

ZUM BITBURGER, Hachstrasse 54. Tel. 069/28-03-02.
   Cuisine: CONTINENTAL. **Reservations:** Required.
$ **Prices:** Appetizers 5.50 DM–35 DM ($3.60–$23.10); main courses 14.50 DM–35 DM ($9.60–$23.10). AE, DC, MC, V.
   Open: Mon–Fri 11:30am–1am. **Closed:** July 15–Aug 15.
Near the Alte Oper in the center of Frankfurt, run by the Bitburger Brauerei, this is one of the finest brewery-operated restaurants in Frankfurt, with a long and proud tradition. Waiters hurry back and forth with mugs of beer, and somehow they also manage to slip through with hearty platters of food, including such standard but well-prepared dishes as grilled rumpsteak, goulash, and sausages with red cabbage and home-fried potatoes. You can begin with the soup of the day, and there is always a fresh seasonal salad. The kitchen serves hot food until midnight.

ALT-SACHSENHAUSEN
EXPENSIVE

BISTROT 77, Ziegelhüttenweg 1, Frankfurt-Sachsenhausen. Tel. 069/ 61-40-40.
   Cuisine: FRENCH. **Reservations:** Required. **Bus:** 62. **Tram:** 16.
$ **Prices:** Appetizers 22 DM–32 DM ($14.50–$21.10); main courses 42 DM–55 DM ($27.70–$36.30); fixed-price lunch 60 DM ($39.60); fixed-price dinner 145 DM ($95.70). AE, DC, MC, V.
   Open: Lunch Mon–Fri noon–2pm; dinner Mon–Sat 7–10pm. **Closed:** June 15–July 15, Dec 24–Jan 6.
Less than a mile from the heart of the city, Bistrot 77 is one of the most chic restaurants in town. The overall impression is one of light and glass, with a black-and-white tile floor and an airy latticework ceiling. In summer the preferred tables are on the terrace. Dominique and Guy Mosbach, two French citizens, have made a name for themselves with their cuisine moderne, a frequently changing array of imaginatively prepared fish and meat dishes, along with intriguing appetizers and desserts. The bill of fare depends on the shopping of the day. A seven-course dinner is available, as are a less expensive set luncheon menu and à la carte meals.

DIE GANS IN SACHSENHAUSEN, Schweizerstrasse 76. Tel. 069/61-50-75.
   Cuisine: CONTINENTAL/GAME. **Reservations:** Recommended. **U-Bahn:** Schweizerplatz.

**FROMMER'S SMART TRAVELER:
RESTAURANTS**

1. Some of the great restaurants of Frankfurt offer fixed-price luncheons at such reasonable prices that the kitchen actually loses money.
2. Select set luncheons or dinners—many represent at least a 30% savings over à la carte menus.
3. Look for the daily specials on any à la carte menu. They're invariably fresh and often carry a lower price tag than regular à la carte listings.
4. Drink the house wine served in a carafe—it's a fraction of the price of bottled wine.

$ Prices: Appetizers 12 DM–45 DM ($7.90–$29.70); main courses 40 DM–45 DM ($26.40–$29.70); fixed-price menus 68 DM ($44.90) and 108 DM ($71.30). AE, DC, MC, V.
Open: Dinner only, daily 6–11pm. **Closed:** Dec 23–Jan 2.

Stylish, sophisticated, and relatively casual, this is a refreshing tribute to the combined cuisines of Europe, with a special emphasis on the game dishes that have always been dear to Germans. You might enjoy an apéritif at the well-accessorized bar before heading into the intimate, bistrolike dining room. You'll be offered a choice of such dishes as zesty fish soup with strips of smoked salmon, mousse of smoked ham, several different preparations of seasonal dishes like venison and rabbit, North Atlantic lobster, ravioli of seafish with spinach sauce, breast of goose in raspberry-vinegar sauce, and roast rack of lamb with provençal herbs.

WESTEND

VERY EXPENSIVE

ERNO'S BISTRO, Liebigstrasse 15. Tel. 069/72-19-97.
Cuisine: FRENCH. **Reservations:** Required. **U-Bahn:** 6 or 7 to Westend.
$ Prices: Appetizers 30 DM–40 DM ($19.80–$26.40); main courses 55 DM–95 DM ($36.30–$62.70); fixed-price menus 50 DM ($33) and 120 DM ($79.20). AE, DC, MC, V.
Open: Lunch Mon–Fri noon–2pm; dinner Mon–Fri 7–10pm. **Closed:** Mid-June to mid-July.

Erno's, a chic midtown rendezvous between the Alte Oper and the Palmengarten, draws everybody from visiting film stars to bank executives. At this small place with an English-speaking staff, the fine service and appointments, plus a commendable cuisine that seems to improve year by year, are hallmarks. The menu changes daily, and the kitchen serves only fish brought fresh from Paris by air or from European waters. The chef offers both cuisine moderne and what is known as *cuisine formidable.* The most exciting—and most expensive—appetizer is the foie gras natural à l'ombre. For a main course, I'd suggest the grilled brill, whose flesh is very delicate and light, served with a rare type of mushroom.

HUMPERDINCK, Grüneburgweg 95. Tel. 069/72-21-22.
Cuisine: FRENCH. **Reservations:** Required. **U-Bahn:** 1, 2, or 3.
$ Prices: Appetizers 35 DM–45 DM ($23.10–$29.70); main courses 42 DM–52 DM ($27.70–$34.30); fixed-price lunch 75 DM ($49.50); fixed-price dinner 140 DM ($92.40). AE, DC, MC, V.
Open: Lunch Mon–Fri noon–2pm; dinner Mon–Sat 7–10:30pm. **Closed:** June–July 3.

Humperdinck is named after composer Engelbert Humperdinck (*Hänsel und Gretel*), who once lived at this fashionable address near the Palmengarten in the western sector of Frankfurt. The setting is classical, refined, and elegant, with tones of subtle ivory and dove gray complementing the cracklewood paneling. Specialties are likely to include ravioli stuffed with crayfish in the chef's special sauce, rich herb soup with butter croûtons, or salmon Schnitzel with vegetable risotto.

GÖTZENHAIN

MODERATE

GUTSSCHÄNKE NEUHOF, 6072 Dreieich-Götzenhain. Tel. 06102/32-00-14.
Cuisine: GERMAN. **Reservations:** Required. **Bus:** 963 from Frankfurt.
$ Prices: Appetizers 12 DM–32 DM ($7.90–$21.10); main courses 22 DM–52 DM ($14.50–$34.30). AE, DC, MC, V.
Open: Lunch daily noon–2:30pm; dinner daily 6–9:30pm.

Some 8 miles south of the center of Frankfurt, Gutsschänke Neuhof, between Neu Isenberg and Götzenhain, is a dining adventure. Surrounded by woods, meadows, and fields of flowers, the inn is part of a huge farm estate (Hofgut Neuhof) dating from 1499. In summer, tables are set out on the wide terrace overlooking the pond. Inside, the former manor farmhouse is a maze of connecting rooms for dining. It's a rustic atmosphere, with pewter candlesticks and fresh-cut field flowers on the tables; on the walls hang antlers, maps, old prints, swords, and rifles.

English-speaking waiters proffer excellent service, and the food is exceptional, beginning with the Vorspeise Neuhof, an array of hors d'oeuvres served at your table from a cart and priced by size. Two house specialties are gespickte Rehkeule Hubertus (leg of venison, in season) and roast duck. The owner supplements the excellent wine cellar with wines from his own Herzheim/Weinstrasse (Rhenish Palatinate) vineyards.

While you're visiting, browse in the gift shop which sells pottery and linens as well as homemade sausages, candy, applecakes, and aromatic breads.

SPECIALTY DINING

APFELWEINSTUBEN

For your best dining bargains, head across the Main to a district known for its many apple-wine taverns, or *Apfelweinstuben*. These taverns are in the Alt-Sachsenhausen section of the south or left bank. It was here that composer Paul Hindemith once lived in a watchtower dating from the 1400s. Sachsenhausen has been called the most

---

FROMMER'S COOL FOR KIDS: RESTAURANTS

Churrasco *(see page 86)* Kids delight in the atmosphere of the pampas at this Argentine restaurant, serving charcoal-grilled savory beef and children's portions.

Gutsschänke Neuhof *(see above)* Perfect for a luncheon excursion into the countryside, this historic inn from 1499 grew out of an old farmstead. Rustic atmosphere abounds.

Zum Gemalten Haus *(see page 89)* You can dine early at this apple wine tavern where children will discover some of the biggest—and tastiest-franks they've ever eaten.

Frankfurtish neighborhood in the city. But now the main street, Schweizerstrasse, is filled with bistros, cafés, and boutiques catering to tourists. The area, especially in summer, is often overrun with tour buses, so much of the old character is gone. Here you drink local apple wine, which some Frankfurters enjoy and some foreigners consider a cousin to vinegar. My verdict: An acquired taste. Tradition says that you won't like the apple wine until you've had three big steins. After that, what does taste matter?

Inexpensive

ZUM GEMALTEN HAUS, Schweizerstrasse 67. Tel. 069/61-80-26.
   Cuisine: GERMAN. **Reservations:** Not accepted. **Tram:** 16.
$ Prices: Appetizers 5 DM–6 DM ($3.30–$4); main courses 14 DM–20 DM ($9.20–$13.20). No credit cards.
   Open: Wed–Sun 10am–midnight.

⑤ Don't bother to call—no one takes reservations here. You simply arrive, and chances are you'll share a table with other patrons, perhaps in the garden if the weather is fair. All of you will enjoy the ample portions of good Hessian cooking. If your taste dictates "Frankfurter Platte" (specialties of the house) with sauerkraut or perhaps Knockwurst with sauerkraut or potato salad, you won't be disappointed. The Eisbein, or pork knuckle with mashed potatoes, washed down with apple wine, is the cook's specialty. The apple wine is homemade. The raw or cooked sauerkraut is very healthful, making this place a spot even for the diet-minded. Don't forget to taste the various types of sausages.

ZUM GRAUEN BOCK, Grosse Rittergasse 30–54. Tel. 069/61-80-26.
   Cuisine: GERMAN. **Reservations:** Recommended. **U-Bahn:** Lokalbahnhof.
$ Prices: Appetizers 4 DM–8.80 DM ($2.60–$5.80); main courses 12 DM–38 DM ($7.90–$25.10); three-course fixed-price menu 33.50 DM ($22.10). AE, MC, V.
   Open: Dinner only, Mon–Sat 5pm–1am.
A gemütlich atmosphere prevails in this smoke-filled tavern run by the Elsässer family. Sometimes the communal singing is so robust it's necessary to slide back the roof on a summer night. An accordionist goes from table to table, involving everyone in song. Contact is made and instant friendships are formed, at least for the evening. Featured on the menu is Handkas mit Musik (cheese with vinegar, oil, and onions). You may want to let the locals enjoy the subtle pleasures of this repast, selecting instead a German specialty known as Schweinhaxen, a huge pork shank with sauerkraut and boiled potatoes. A good beginning is the Frankfurter Bohnensuppe (bean soup). A fixed-price menu is offered, along with daily specials and à la carte selections.

LATE-NIGHT DINING
Inexpensive

GILDENSTUBEN, Bleichstrasse 38. Tel. 069/28-32-28.
   Cuisine: BOHEMIAN. **Reservations:** Not necessary. **U-Bahn:** 1, 2, or 3.
$ Prices: Appetizers 3 DM–5 DM ($2–$3.30); main courses 7.50 DM–18.80 DM ($5–$12.40). AE, DC, MC, V.
   Open: Daily 10am–2am.
This is one of the most popular beer taverns in Frankfurt, with a sprawling garden opening onto a park. The specialties are Bohemian, and the Czech dishes are reasonably priced. *Svickova* is a kind of meatloaf of smoked beef with dumplings and a berry sauce. Goose is a specialty. Meat eaters might be drawn to the unattractively named *Schlachtfest* ("slaughter feast") with various meats. Diners wash down all this fare with Budvar and Pilsener Urquell beers.

LOCAL FAVORITE
Inexpensive

STEINERNES HAUS, Braubachstrasse 35. Tel. 069/28-34-91.

Cuisine: GERMAN. **Reservations:** Not necessary. **Tram:** 11.

$ Prices: Appetizers 5.50 DM–7.50 DM ($3.60–$5); main courses 16 DM–32 DM ($10.60–$21.10). No credit cards.

Open: Daily 11am–11pm.

One of the most historic inns of the city, Steinernes Haus was restored after World War II; management at the time decided to keep it simple and unpretentious, the way it had always been. Around the corner from the Rathaus (town hall), it lies in the historic heart of Frankfurt. Locals come here for the good-tasting German beer, beginning at 3.80 DM ($2.50), along with hearty rib-sticking fare. The 15-DM ($9.90) daily main dish specialty also includes salad and potatoes, so you can enjoy an inexpensive meal. A selection of sausages is presented, along with beef filet and such popular German dishes as Zigeunerhackbraten (spicy meatloaf) and Frankfurter Rippchen (smoked pork).

HOTEL DINING

Inexpensive

FRANKFURTER STUBB, in the Steigenberger Frankfurter Hof, Am Kaiserplatz. Tel. 069/2-15-02.

Cuisine: GERMAN. **Reservations:** Recommended. **U-Bahn:** 1, 2, or 3.

$ Prices: Appetizers 8 DM–22 DM ($5.30–$14.50); main courses 10.50 DM–42 DM ($6.90–$27.70). AE, DC, MC, V.

Open: Mon–Sat noon–midnight.

A dependable dining spot, Frankfurter Stubb specializes in regional German cooking of the past century. The food here is straightforward and honest, the ambience that of an elegant wine cellar, with cozy dining nooks. The attentive English-speaking servers in regional garb are most helpful in translating the German menu. For openers, try the excellent lentil soup. One of the house specialties is Tafelspitz with Frankfurt green sauce, served with potatoes cooked in bouillon. The featured dessert is Rote Grüte, a jelly of fresh fruit served with either vanilla sauce or cream.

PICNIC FARE & WHERE TO EAT IT

There are many delis in Frankfurt, and usually the reception desk at your hotel will pinpoint a good one for you on the map. Otherwise, you can go to the deli department at **Hertie,** An der Zeil 390 (tel. 069/2961), the leading department store.

Sufficiently supplied, you can head for **Palmengarten** (see "Attractions," below), with its wide, open lawns and flower borders. Later you can rent a rowboat and take the kids on a little excursion. Sometimes concerts take place here, and there'll be a musical background to your picnic.

CAFÉS

As in most German cities the café is an important institution where people enjoy morning or afternoon coffee and cake, read newspapers, or eat light meals.

CAFÉ LAUMER, Bockenheimer Landstrasse 67. Tel. 069/72-79-12.

Café Laumer enjoys an enviable location between the Palmengarten and the Alte Oper. The service is helpful and welcoming, and the habitués often have their favorite marble-topped tables. There they enjoy a light lunch for 19 DM ($12.50) or snacks and a selection of cake and torte throughout the afternoon. In summer, try for a table on the open terrace.

Open: Mon–Sat 8am–7pm, Sun 11am–7pm.

CAFÉ SCHWILLE, Grosse Bockenheimerstrasse 50. Tel. 069/92-01-00.

If you have a sweet tooth, head for the Café Schwille, the most famous place in

Frankfurt for pastry and sweets. Light snacks begin at 9.50 DM ($6.30), pastries at 5 DM ($3.30).

Open: Mon–Sat 7am–7:30pm, Sun 12:30–7pm. In summer, if the weather's good, it stays open as late as 11pm.

ZUR HAUPTWACHE, An der Hauptwache. Tel. 069/28-10-26.

The café nearly everybody finds without any guidance is Zur Hauptwache, which is 250 years old and is at the strategic heart of Frankfurt, now a pedestrian zone. The present building was reconstructed after World War II. The menu appears in English, among other languages. On a warm evening the street-level café, attracting coffee drinkers and pastry eaters, is a delight. Don't fail to ask for the special beer, Römer Pilsner. Coffee costs 3.50 DM ($2.30), and main dishes cost 8.50 DM ($5.60) and up.

Open: Mon–Sat 7:30am–7pm.

5. ATTRACTIONS

When bombs rained on Frankfurt in 1944, nearly all the old half-timbered buildings were leveled to mere piles of rubble. In what must have been a record reconstruction, however, the Frankfurters not only rebuilt their city into a fine mélange of modern and traditional architecture but also faithfully restored some of their most prized old buildings as well.

ALTSTADT

The Altstadt centers around three Gothic buildings with stepped gables, known collectively as the **Römer.** These houses were originally built between 1288 and 1305 and bought by the city a century later for use as the Rathaus. The second floor of the center house is the **Imperial Hall (Kaisersaal),** lined with the romanticized portraits of 52 emperors; 13 of them celebrated their coronation banquets here. You can visit this hall Monday to Saturday from 9am to 1pm and 1:30 to 5pm, Sunday from 10am to 4pm. Tickets can be purchased at the entrance to the Römer. The charge is 1 DM (70¢) for adults and 0.50 DM (30¢) for children.

The elaborate facade of the Römer, with its ornate balcony and statues of four emperors, overlooks **Römerberg Square.** On festive occasions in days gone by, the square was the scene of oxen roasts that featured flowing wine. Today, unfortunately, the Fountain of Justitia pours forth only water, but oxen are still roasted on special occasions.

The dominant feature of the Altstadt is the 15th-century red-sandstone tower of the **Dom St. Bartholomaus,** Domplatz 14 (tel. 069/29-07-87), in whose chapel emperors were elected and crowned for nearly 300 years. In the cloister of the church is the **Dom Museum** (tel. 069/28-92-29), which exhibits robes of the imperial electors. It is open Tuesday through Friday from 10am to 5pm and Saturday and Sunday from 11am to 5pm. Admission is 2 DM ($1.30).

The **Alte Nikolaikirche,** Römerberg 9 (tel. 069/28-42-35), is a historic church drawing thousands of visitors annually to its location across from the Rathaus. After a three-year renovation, archeologists "redated" its origins as a 12th-century church. The old church is open daily from 10am to 8pm. The early Gothic church has a court chapel from the mid-1100s and interesting Gothic sandstone sculptures. Inside are ancient gravestones and a variety of sculpture, including a Schmerzensmann dating from 1370.

At the northern edge of the Altstadt is the **Hauptwache,** an old guard house, which is the heart of modern Frankfurt. Under it is the main U-Bahn station with a modern shopping promenade.

MORE ATTRACTIONS

GOETHE-HAUS, Grosser Hirschgraben 23–25. Tel. 069/28-28-24.

⭐ Goethe was born in the house in 1749. It's been a shrine for Goethe enthusiasts since it was opened to the public in 1863. One critic wrote that the restoration was carried out "with loving care and damn-the-expense craftsmanship."

Reflecting the fashion trends of the 18th century, the house was decorated in different styles: neoclassical, baroque, and rococo. You can view the library where Goethe's father worked and often watched the street for the return of his son. A portrait of the severe-looking gentleman hangs behind the door of his wife's room.

On the second floor is an unusual astronomical clock built about 1749 and repaired in 1949 to run for another 200 years. One room contains a picture gallery with paintings collected by Goethe's father. Most by contemporary Frankfurt artists, these works influenced Goethe's artistic views for a great part of his life. The poet's rooms contain a puppet theater that was one of his most important childhood possessions and played a significant role in his *Wilhelm Meister*.

Annexed to the house is the **Frankfurter Goethe-Museum,** built after the war on the site of its predecessor. The museum contains a library of 120,000 volumes and a collection of about 30,000 manuscripts, as well as 16,000 graphic artworks and 400 paintings associated in some way with Goethe and his works.

Admission: 3 DM ($2) adults, 2 DM ($1.30) children.

Open: Mon–Sat 9am–6pm Apr–Sept (to 4pm Oct–Mar), Sun 10am–1pm. **U-Bahn or S-Bahn:** Hauptwache.

STÄDEL MUSEUM, Schaumainkal 63. Tel. 069/61-70-92.

⭐ On the south bank of the Main stands Frankfurt's most important art gallery, containing a fine representative collection of most European schools and periods of painting. The French impressionists are represented on the first floor by Renoir and Monet, mixed in with notable German painters of the 19th and 20th centuries. One of the best of these is Ernst Ludwig Kirchner (1880–1938); see in particular his *Nude Woman with Hat.* Also on the first floor is Johann Heinrich Wilhelm Tischbein's portrait of Goethe in the Campagna in Italy. If you're short on time, however, go directly to the second floor to view the outstanding collection of Flemish primitives, 17th-century Dutch painting, German 16th-century masterpieces, and other European painting. Works by Dürer, Grünewald, Memling, Hans Holbein, Mantegna, Elsheimer, Rembrandt, Vermeer, Claude Lorrain, Tiepolo, and many others have been brought together here. One of the most impressive paintings is Jan Van Eyck's *Madonna* (1433). Lucas Cranach is represented by several works, including a large winged altarpiece and his rather impish nude *Venus.* The museum also includes a display from the Italian school, including a *Madonna* by Bellini. One department contains 30,000 drawings and 70,000 prints of European schools. Recent acquisitions include Jean Antoine Watteau's *L'Ile de Cythère* (1709). In the Department of Modern Art are works by Bacon, Dubuffet, Tapiès, and Yves Klein.

Admission: 6 DM ($4). Free Sun.

Open: Tues and Thurs–Sun 10am–5pm, Wed 10am–8pm. **U-Bahn:** 1, 2, or 3.

LIEBIEGHAUS, Schaumainkal 71. Tel. 069/212-38-617.

The city's largest collection of sculpture spans thousands of years, from ancient Egyptian to neoclassicist. One of the most impressive is a bas relief by Andrea della Robbia. Along with the Bargello in Florence, this sculpture museum is considered one of the most important in Europe. At a tiny café you can order tasty little fruit pies baked by the caretaker.

Admission: Free.

Open: Tues and Thurs–Sun 10am–5pm, Wed 10am–8pm. **Bus:** 61.

PARKS & GARDENS

PALMENGARTEN, Siesmayerstrasse 61. Tel. 069/212-36-316.

More than a botanical garden, this is a park area for recreation throughout the year. During the last decade, the gardens have been totally renewed and conservatories completely reconstructed, as were the historical greenhouses. Thousands of flowers bloom. A garden for perennials, an expanded rock garden, a beautiful rose garden, and rich and varied beds of annuals at all seasons can be admired. The 1869 palmhouse is now surrounded by a huge gallery that serves as an exhibition hall for flower shows as well as for botanical exhibitions from early spring to Christmas. During recent years, a complex of conservatories, the **Tropicarium,** has been built. It has seven parts: semidesert, thorn forest, savannah, monsoon forest, lowland rain forest, highland rain forest, and mangrove with tropical waterplants. Huge collections of orchids, palms, bromeliads, succulents, waterlilies, insectivorous plants, and many others are on display. In summer, concerts are given in the bandshell, and evening events include open-air dancing, jazz, and fountain illumination. Some facilities for food are provided in the garden.

Admission: 5 DM ($3.30) adults, 2 DM ($1.30) children.
Open: Daily 9am–dusk. **Bus:** 36. **U-Bahn:** 6 or 7 line to Palmengarten.

COOL FOR KIDS

Children take delight in visiting the Palmengarten (see above), and the zoo is also a favorite. Try to schedule a visit, if possible, to the **Senckenberg Museum of Natural History,** Senckenberganlage 25 (tel. 069/75-41-7), which has an interesting collection of fossils of extinct animals (including dinosaurs). Hours are Monday through Friday from 9am to 5pm, Saturday and Sunday until 6pm.

ZOOLOGISCHER GARTEN, Alfred-Brehm-Platz 16. Tel. 069/222-33-715.

Because it's a multifaceted institution intent on education as well as entertainment, the zoo is interesting for both young and old. Most animals are in enclosures that resemble their native habitats: One of the best examples is the **African Veldt Enclosure,** landscaped with hills and bushes so that the animals living there can avoid encounters with other breeds. In this single exhibit, antelopes and ostriches roam freely. In the **Exotarium,** fish and various reptiles live under special climatic conditions; and in an artificially cooled polar landscape, king and gentoo penguins swim and dive. In keeping with its educational policy, the zoo has, in addition to many typical animal exhibits, a nursery where young apes are cared for by zookeepers when the mother cannot care for the baby properly, as well as a breeding aviary where you can watch birds preparing unusual nests. A building for small mammals, with a nocturnal section, is one of the largest and most diversified of its kind in the world and also contains many educational facilities.

Admission: 9.50 DM ($6.30) adults, 4.50 DM ($3) children 6–17.
Open: Daily 8am–5pm Nov–Mar (to 7pm Apr–Oct). **U-Bahn:** 6 or 7.

SPECIAL-INTEREST SIGHTSEEING

FOR THE LITERARY ENTHUSIAST

The major sight in Frankfurt for devotees of German literature is **Goethe-Haus** (see above).

FOR THE ARCHITECTURE ENTHUSIAST

DEUTSCHES ARCHITEKTURMUSEUM, Schaumainkal 43. Tel. 069/212-388-44.

This is Germany's only museum devoted solely to architecture. Drawings, models, and photos, among other exhibits, alternate with special exhibitions staged throughout the year. The museum is housed in an avant-garde conversion of a Frankfurt villa.

Admission: 4 DM ($2.60) adults, 2 DM ($1.30) children.
Open: Tues–Sat 10am–8pm. **U-Bahn:** 1, 2, or 3.

WALKING TOUR — FRANKFURT

Start: Alte Oper (Opera House).
Finish: Goethe-Haus.
Estimated Time: 90 minutes.
Best Times: Any daylight hours during good weather.
Worst Times: Mon–Sat 8–9:30am and 4:30–6:30pm.

Despite its skyscraping modernity and daunting traffic, Frankfurt contains charming sights best appreciated by pedestrians. Begin your tour at the:

1. **Alte Oper,** the old opera house. Built in 1880, destroyed by incendiary bombs in 1944, and rebuilt in 1981, it affords sweeping views of Frankfurt from its portico. From the Opernplatz's southeast corner, follow the Fressgasse, a street lined with specialty food shops, taverns, and cafés. Within five blocks, turn left on the Börsenstrasse, where, on the right side of the street, you'll see the:
2. **Börse** (Stock Market), where the economic pulse of Germany throbs to the beat of world finance. Just beyond the Börse, turn right onto the Taubenstrasse, which will lead to one of the oldest fortified gates of medieval Frankfurt, the:
3. **Eschenheimer Tor.** From here, head southeast along the Stiftstrasse, which in about a block will intersect with one of the city's legendary shopping streets, the:
4. **Zeil.** Explore its shops (which at this point run in either direction) at your leisure, but for the moment, turn right and walk for two blocks until you reach the:
5. **Hauptwache,** a single-story 18th-century building originally built as a jail. The adjacent square serves as the public transportation hub of the city. On the square's southern edge rises one of the most noteworthy Protestant churches of Frankfurt, the:
6. **Katharinenkirche,** reconstructed after damage from Allied bombs in World War II. In 1522, Frankfurt's first Protestant sermon was given here. After admiring its somber grandeur, head south along the Kornmarkt, then east along Berlinerstrasse, to the rounded walls of the:
7. **Pauluskirche,** whose 18th-century walls (redesigned and rebuilt after World War II) were the site of a revolutionary congress in 1848, which, though soon after disbanded, offered the crown of Germany to the king of Prussia. Just beyond the Pauluskirche, turn left on Bethmannstrasse. Very soon, you'll enter the large expanse of:
8. **Römerberg Square.** The Römer (City Hall) at its center has a symmetrical facade and an ornate balcony. Frankfurt's official symbol, it is composed of three separate buildings (Alt Limpurg, Zum Römer, Löwenstein) and has been used for centuries for ceremonial, commercial, and political functions. The elegant 16th-century statue in the plaza represents Justice. At the 1612 coronation of Emperor Matthias, wine instead of water flowed from this fountain, a grace note that almost caused a riot as citizens rushed to drink.

REFUELING STOP Although you'll find cafés and taverns at virtually every street corner of this walking tour, **Römer Restaurant,** inside the building, offers typical Frankfurt dishes and wine from city-owned vineyards.

After your snack, stop to admire the massive:

9. **Alte Nikolaikirche (Church of St. Nicholas),** rising from the southern edge of the square. Built during the 12th century as a royal chapel for the Holy Roman Emperors, it's fronted with a carillon of glockenspiels that ring out every

WALKING TOUR—FRANKFURT

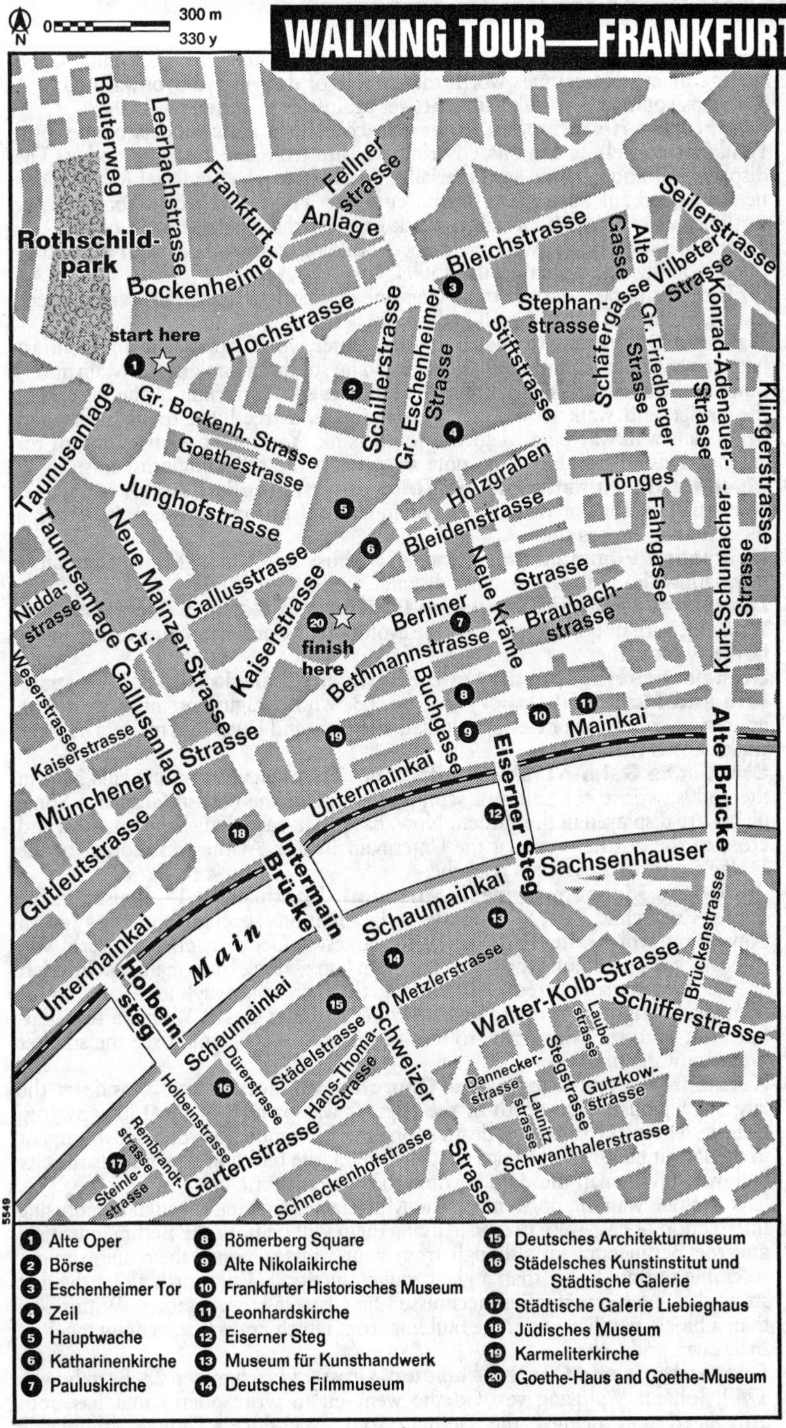

0   300 m   330 y

N

Rothschild-park

start here
1 ☆

finish here
20 ☆

Main

Streets and labels:
Reuterweg, Leerbachstrasse, Frankfurter Anlage, Fellner strasse, Seilerstrasse, Bockenheimer, Hochstrasse, Bleichstrasse, Stephanstrasse, Schäfergasse, Alte Gasse, Gr. Friedberger Strasse, Vilbeter Strasse, Konrad-Adenauer-Strasse, Klingerstrasse, Taunusanlage, Gr. Bockenh. Strasse, Schillerstrasse, Gr. Eschenheimer Strasse, Stiftstrasse, Goethestrasse, Holzgraben, Tönges, Junghofstrasse, Bleidenstrasse, Neue Mainzer Strasse, Gallusstrasse, Kaiserstrasse, Berliner Strasse, Neue Kräme, Braubach-strasse, Fahrgasse, Schumacher-strasse, Nidda strasse, Gr. Gallusanlage, Kaiserstrasse, Weserstrasse, Münchener Strasse, Gutleutstrasse, Bethmannstrasse, Buchgasse, Untermainkai, Mainkai, Alte Brücke, Eiserner Steg, Untermain Brücke, Sachsenhauser, Schaumainkai, Walter-Kolb-Strasse, Schifferstrasse, Brückenstrasse, Metzlerstrasse, Schweizer Strasse, Laube strasse, Stegstrasse, Gutzkow-strasse, Dannecker-strasse, Launitz strasse, Schwanthalerstrasse, Schaumainkai, Städelstrasse, Hans-Thoma-Strasse, Dürerstrasse, Holbeinsteg, Holbeinstrasse, Rembrandt-strasse, Steinle-strasse, Gartenstrasse, Schneckenhofstrasse

Legend

1. Alte Oper
2. Börse
3. Eschenheimer Tor
4. Zeil
5. Hauptwache
6. Katharinenkirche
7. Pauluskirche
8. Römerberg Square
9. Alte Nikolaikirche
10. Frankfurter Historisches Museum
11. Leonhardskirche
12. Eiserner Steg
13. Museum für Kunsthandwerk
14. Deutsches Filmmuseum
15. Deutsches Architekturmuseum
16. Städelsches Kunstinstitut und Städtische Galerie
17. Städtische Galerie Liebieghaus
18. Jüdisches Museum
19. Karmeliterkirche
20. Goethe-Haus and Goethe-Museum

5549

day at 9am, noon, and 5pm. Local citizens set their watches by these chimes, and hearing them is sometimes worth the trouble of delaying your onward path. A few steps south of the Nikolaikirche, set against the river quays, is the:

10. **Frankfurter Historisches Museum,** containing scale models of medieval Frankfurt as well as exhibits covering city life from the 1500s to today. The displays of antique silver are especially noteworthy. The medieval fortifications near the riverbank adjacent to the museum once controlled access from the river to the town center. About half a block east rise the dignified walls of the:

11. **Leonhardskirche,** a well-maintained building constructed from the 1200s (most notably, the porch) to the 1500s.

Take this opportunity to cross over one of Germany's most influential rivers, the Main, by traversing the all-pedestrian:

12. **Eiserner Steg** (iron bridge). From its center, you'll appreciate the contrast between medieval and modern Frankfurt. The southern bank of the Main at this point is the ancient district of **Sachsenhausen.** Turn right at the far end of the bridge and walk west along Schaumainkai, a tree-lined traffic artery and pedestrian walkway parallel to the south bank. You might want to return for extended visits later. However, note as you pass the following museums:

13. **Museum für Kunsthandwerk (Museum of Applied Arts),** at no. 17, containing exhibits of virtually every handcraft of Europe and Asia. Less than a block to the west is the:

14. **Deutsches Filmmuseum,** at no. 41, whose exhibits celebrate Germany's fascinating film industry. A short distance to the west is the:

15. **Deutsches Architekturmuseum (Museum of German Architecture),** at no. 43, with notable displays on the evolution of German architecture. Slightly farther west is the:

16. **Städelsches Kunstinstitut und Städtische Galerie (Städel Art Institute and Municipal Gallery),** at no. 63, whose august premises shelter an impressive collection of German, Italian, Flemish, and Dutch old masters. A short walk west is the:

17. **Städtische Galerie Liebieghaus,** at no. 71, originally a private villa built in the 1600s, whose collection of sculpture is one of the best in Germany. Some pieces are displayed in the garden. Now, backtrack east along Schaumainkai and cross to the northern end of the Untermain Bridge. At the west corner of the bridge's northern terminus rises the:

18. **Jüdisches Museum (Jewish Museum),** Untermainkai 15, housed in the former Rothschild Palace. Its library and exhibitions spotlight the city's Jewish population, which, after Berlin's, was the largest in Germany prior to World War II. Now, walk east along the river's northern bank, along Untermainkai. Turn left at the first narrow street (little more than an alleyway) and cut almost immediately right onto the somewhat wider Mainzer Gasse. Within a few steps (turn left onto the Münzgasse to find its main entrance), you'll see the somber masonry walls of the:

19. **Karmeliterkirche (Carmelite Church and Monastery).** Inside is the largest religious fresco north of the Alps. It was painted in the 1500s by Jörg Ratgeb, who was tortured to death soon after its completion for his involvement in the Peasant's Revolt. Deconsecrated in 1803, the building now houses the city archives and a small museum devoted to the prehistoric era.

Continue walking north along the Münzgasse, crossing through a confusing intersection of east-west streets. (Among them will be both the Bethmannstrasse and the Berlinerstrasse, although from your vantage point, their union might resemble nothing more than a giant traffic junction.) Walk north along the first street that intersects the Berlinerstrasse (the Grosser Hirschgraben). Within less than a block, you'll arrive at the building from which Frankfurters draw much of their civic pride, the:

20. **Goethe-Haus and Goethe-Museum,** Grosser Hirschgraben 23. Born here in 1749, Johann Wolfgang von Goethe went on to write poetry that has both articulated and defined the German soul ever since. Though completely

destroyed during World War II, the building has been rebuilt to look almost exactly as it did when young Goethe played here.

ORGANIZED TOURS

CITY TOURS   The tourist office sponsors a daily bus tour that newcomers will find interesting. It departs every day throughout the year from the tourist information office in the Hauptbahnhof. Participants assemble in the office, opposite track 23, and are led by an English-speaking guide to a waiting bus. The 2½-hour tours depart every day at 1:15pm and cost 30 DM ($19.80) or 20 DM ($13.20) for children under 15. You'll get glimpses of the Altstadt and some of the more interesting modern buildings, with stops at Goethe-Haus every Monday through Saturday. (On Sunday, when Goethe-Haus is closed, the tour substitutes a visit to Frankfurt's telecommunications tower.)

Tram Tours, organized by the Stadtwerke Frankfurt am Main, Borneplatz 3 (tel. 069/13-68-24-25), are a nice way to experience the pleasures of old-time Frankfurt. They depart at hourly intervals between 2:06 and 6:06pm every Saturday and Sunday from the tram station in front of the Sudbahnhof. Tours last around 50 minutes. Participation costs 3 DM ($2) per adult and 2 DM ($1.30) for children under 15. You'll recognize the touring tram by its red, blue, and painted flowers.

GAMING EXCURSION   The 19th-century resort of Bad Homburg (see Chapter 5) has always exerted a powerful allure for Frankfurters eager for a visit to the suburbs. The resort's well-established casino operates a free bus, departing daily on the hour from 3pm to 10pm. The bus leaves from the south side of the Hauptbahnhof, takes 40 minutes to reach its destination, and requires that passengers pay a visit to Bad Homburg's casino as part of the experience. For up-to-date information, call 069/212-388-49.

6. SPORTS & RECREATION

BICYCLING   Bicycles can be rented (April to October) at **Goetheturm,** on the northern edge of the city's sprawling Stadtwald. The rental kiosk is in the car park at the intersection of Sachsenhäuser Landwehrweg and Wendelsweg. Per-hour charges range between 2.40 DM ($1.60) and 4 DM ($2.60), depending on the bike. For more information, contact Karl Breidert & Co., Kurt-Schumacher-Ring 21 at Egelsbach (tel. 06103/49111).

FITNESS   Many hotels in Frankfurt maintain health clubs, but if your hotel does not, consider a day ticket at such semiprivate health clubs as **Sport and Fitness Center Judokan,** Taubenstrasse 9 (tel. 069/28-05-65), with a branch on Frankfurt's busiest shopping street, Zeil 109 (same phone); or the **Sportschule Petrescu,** Bleichstrasse 55–57 (tel. 069/29-59-06).

GOLF   A suitable choice near Frankfurt might be **Golf-und-Landclub,** Schloss Friedrichshof, 6242 Kronberg/Taunus (tel. 06173/14-26). Clubs can be rented.

ICE SKATING   Throughout the year, with extended hours during winter, ice skating is available at the **Eissporthalle,** Bornheimer Hang 4, Ratsweg (tel. 069/41-91-41).

JOGGING   A good jogging route is along quays of the River Main, using both sides of the river and the bridges to create a series of loops. Another choice is the centrally located Gruneberg Park, whose walkways are suitable for jogging.

RIDING   Call the **Frankfurter Reit-und Fahrclub e.V,** Hahnstrasse 85 (tel. 069/666-7585).

SQUASH AND TENNIS   Both indoor and outdoor tennis courts, squash, and a reasonably constant selection of partners are available at the **Europa Tennis & Squash Park,** Ginnheimer Landstrasse 49 (tel. 069/53-20-40). Outdoor tennis, in summer only, is available on the 20 courts of the **Waldstadion,** Moerfelder Landstrasse 362 (tel. 069/67-80-40).

7. SAVVY SHOPPING

For shoppers, Frankfurt has everything—the specialty shops are so much like those back in the States that most visitors from America will feel right at home. Shops in the downtown area are open Monday to Friday from 9am to 6:30pm and Saturday from 9am to 2pm (to 4 or 6pm on the first Saturday of the month).

THE SHOPPING SCENE

In Frankfurt, the street or area rather than the specific shop is important. For example, the **Zeil** is one of the most famous shopping streets on the Continent. A pedestrian zone between the Hauptwache and the Konstablerwache, it has the highest sales of any shopping area in Germany. It was a cattle round-up market as early as the 14th century; by the 19th century it had become a major shopping center. Destroyed in the war, it was redesigned in the 1980s but has not regained its former prestige. Here you will find department stores, clothing shops, shoe stores, and furniture outlets. Nearby is the **Kleinmarkthalle,** a covered market with international grocery products.

In the center of Frankfurt, the **Hauptwache** consists of two shopping areas, one above and one below ground. Groceries, flowers, clothing, tobacco, photo supplies, recordings, and sporting equipment abound. In the Hauptwache-Passage are restaurants, travel agencies, and banks.

Schillerstrasse, another pedestrian zone, lies between the Hauptwache and Eschenheimer Turm, near the stock exchange. Walking from Schillerstrasse northeast toward Eschenheimer Tor, you'll pass many elegant boutiques and specialty shops.

Southwest of the Hauptwache is the Alte Oper. You can reach it either by taking **Goethestrasse,** with its exclusive stores, evocative of Paris or Milan, or making your way via the parallel **Grosse Bockenheimerstrasse,** traditionally nicknamed "Fressgasse." Most wine dealers, delis, and butcher shops here look back on a long and venerable past. At Opernplatz you find a variety of restaurants and cafés. West from the Hauptwache is the **Rossmarkt,** leading to Kaiserstrasse. It passes the BFG skyscraper, which has three floors of exclusive retail stores, boutiques, and restaurants and directly connects the downtown area to the Hauptbahnhof. **Kaiserstrasse** is known for its large selection of stores selling clothing, audio and photography equipment, and stainless-steel ware. The heart of the fur trade in Frankfurt is **Düsseldorfer Strasse,** opposite the Hauptbahnhof. Most book dealers are located around the **Hauptwache** and **Goetheplatz.** You will find antiques, old books, etchings, and paintings in Braubachstrasse near the Römer, at the Dom, and in Fahrgasse.

Art and antiques are the domain of **Alt-Sachsenhausen.** In this appealing and original part of Frankfurt, the famous **Frankfurt Flea Market** takes place every Sunday morning at the Schlachthof, where anything and everything is for sale. The Flea Market is an El Dorado for fervent collectors of every creed and color.

GERHARD WEMPE, An der Hauptwache 7. Tel. 069/29-17-77.
One of the best centers of elegant jewelry in Frankfurt is Gerhard Wempe. They also have one of the biggest collections of watches for sale in Germany, with the famous Swiss brands featured.

KINDERHAUS PFÜLLER, Goethestrasse 12. Tel. 069/28-45-47.
Kinderhaus Pfüller concentrates on children's wear, from baby clothes all the way up to teenage fashions. It also sells bath towels and linens.

LOREY, Schillerstrasse 16. Tel. 069/29-99-50.
Lorey carries one of the best selections of Hummel and Meissen figurines.

MODEHAUS PFÜLLER, Goethestrasse 15-17. Tel. 069/28-45-47.
Since 1878 Modehaus Pfüller has specialized in traditional fashions for women, men, and children, offering a line of exclusive lingerie, woolens, and beachwear, among other merchandise.

8. EVENING ENTERTAINMENT

THE PERFORMING ARTS

You can purchase tickets at the tourist office at the Hauptbahnhof for many major cultural presentations, or you can go to the theater box offices.

ALTE OPER, Opernplatz. Tel. 069/13-40-400.
The pride of Frankfurt, even though opera is presented elsewhere today, this building was reopened in 1981 following its reconstruction after World War II bombings. The original building had been officially opened in 1880 by Kaiser Wilhelm I. At that time, it was hailed as one of the most beautiful theaters in Europe. Today, the "old opera" is part of the intrinsic cultural life of the city, the site of frequent symphonic and choral concerts.
Prices: Tickets 30 DM–125 DM ($19.80–$82.50).

THEATER DER STADT FRANKFURT, Theaterplatz 1–3. Tel. 069/23-60-61.
One auditorium at this cultural center is devoted to opera, two stages to drama. Productions of the Frankfurt Municipal Opera have received worldwide recognition in recent years.
If your German is adequate, at the same address you can attend a performance of the Städtische Bühnen/Schauspiel (tel. 069/212-37-444), which is a forum for classic German plays as well as modern drama.
Prices: Tickets 15 DM–110 DM ($9.90–$72.60).

FRITZ RÉMOND THEATER IM ZOO, at Zoologischer Garten, Alfred-Brehm-Platz. Tel. 069/44-40-04.
This theater often stages American and British productions in German.
Prices: Tickets 22 DM–38 DM ($14.50–$25.10). **Closed:** July–Aug.

DIE KOMÖDIE, Theaterplatz at Neue Mainzerstrasse 18. Tel. 069/28-45-80.
Light comedy—often called boulevard theater—is presented here. Tickets are sold daily from 10am to 1:30pm and 2 to 8pm.
Prices: Tickets 18 DM–32 DM ($11.90–$21.10).

HESSISCHER-RUNDFUNK, Bertramstrasse 8. Tel. 069/15-51.
This is a concert hall with a changing repertoire of musical events, including chamber music concerts.
Prices: Tickets 15 DM–30 DM ($9.90–$19.80).

THE CLUB & BAR SCENE

In a 16-square-block area in front of the Hauptbahnhof, you'll find a rowdy kind of entertainment: what the Germans call *erotische Spiele*. Doormen will practically pull you inside to view porno movies, sex shows, sex shops, even discos teeming with prostitutes. *Warning:* This area is dangerous; don't go there alone.

COOKY'S, Am Salzhaus 4. Tel. 069/28-76-62.
Cooky's presents live music every Monday, including rock, acid, funk, and the blues. Acts change frequently. You can dance, eat, drink, or just listen to the music.

Open: Sun–Thurs 10:30pm–4am, Fri–Sat 10:30pm–6am.
Admission: 6 DM–18 DM ($4–$11.90), depending on act and night of week.

DORIAN GRAY, O Level of Section C, in the Frankfurt airport. Tel. 069/69-15-21.

In the catacombs of the Frankfurt airport is Dorian Gray, reached from the heart of the city in about 15 minutes aboard an S-train, departing from the Hauptbahnhof every 20 minutes or so. (This place should not be confused with Dorian Gay, a self-styled "gaymen sexshop" in another part of the city.) Dorian Gray is a disco that enjoys a wide popularity, as well as a continental bistro, with well-appointed lounges and a clubroom, often drawing an elegant well-dressed crowd. You can order from a wide range of drinks. Beer is the cheapest, of course, costing from 6.50 DM ($4.30) a mug.
Open: Wed–Thurs 9pm–4am, Fri 9pm–6am, Sat 9am–6am.
Admission: Wed–Thurs free; Fri–Sat 20 DM ($13.20).

JAZZ HAUS, Kleine Bockenheimerstrasse 12. Tel. 069/28-71-94.

Although it once attracted some big names of international jazz, Jazz Haus now offers only recorded music. No one dances here, yet it's known as a "discotheque for jazz." Enthusiasts prefer the smoky, permissive, and relaxed ambience of the club, which has a distinctive personality. A medium-size beer goes for 4.50 DM ($3), and there's a selection of small snacks.
Open: Daily 6pm–1am.
Admission: Free.

JAZZ-KNEIPE, Berlinstrasse 70. Tel. 069/28-71-73.

Jazz-Kneipe has some lively jam sessions—it's considered the number-one place in Frankfurt for traditional swing, with live music from 10pm to 3am. A beer costs from 4 DM ($2.60), with drinks beginning at 8 DM ($5.30).
Open: Daily 8pm–4am.
Admission: 5 DM–20 DM ($3.30–$13.20).

JIMMY'S, in the Hotel Hessischer Hof, Friedrich-Ebert-Anlage 40. Tel. 069/75-40-0.

In this luxurious atmosphere you'll find snacks and other specialties served in candlelit calm with soft background music. You can enjoy drinks, with prices beginning at 21 DM ($13.90), in the midst of a social gathering or while you relax after a busy day. Beer costs from 11 DM ($7.30).
Open: Daily 8pm–4am.

LIPIZZANER BAR, Steigenberger Frankfurter Hof, Am Kaiserplatz. Tel. 069/2-15-02.

This is regarded as the most elegant bar in town, with crystal mirrors, wood paneling, and international drinks that begin at 16 DM ($10.60). Beer starts at 11 DM ($7.30). A pianist provides nightly entertainment.
Open: Mon–Sat 6pm–2am.

MAIER GUSTL'S BAYRISCH ZELL, Münchnerstrasse 57. Tel. 069/23-20-92.

One of the best-known beerhalls in Frankfurt, this heavily timbered re-creation of a mountain chalet is perfect for a checkered-tablecloth kind of Teutonic nostalgia. Two bands play nightly, one a typical Bavarian brass group and one a modern show band, changing every half hour so that the music is nonstop. About 1,000 persons can be fitted onto the two dance floors. Some tables have private phones for electronic contact with a person you fancy. Meals are available, with the famous Eisbein mit sauerkraut (leg of pork) the most expensive dish at 18 DM ($11.90). Beer, depending on size, costs 8 DM to 14 DM ($5.30 to $9.20).
Open: Daily 7pm–4am.

ST. JOHN'S INN, Grosser Hirschgraben 20. Tel. 069/29-25-18.

St. John's Inn is across from Goethe-Haus, a short walk from the Hauptwache. Its cozy old-world ambience is created in part by its large brick-and-timber fireplace with raised hearth, Windsor chairs, and candlelit tables. It's possible to drop in just for drinks, but you may order food as well; the house specialty is a pot of Irish stew. Meals cost 25 DM to 55 DM ($16.50 to $36.30). If you don't order food, there's a two-drink minimum of 12 DM ($7.90). Beer is 6 DM ($4). A disc jockey plays international favorites. Often it's so crowded that you can't get in.

Open: Daily 9pm–4am.

MUNICH

The people of Munich don't need much of a reason for celebrating. If you arrive here in late September, you'll find them in the middle of a festival honoring Ludwig I's wedding to Princess Theresa—and that took place in 1810! The Oktoberfest, for which more than 7 million may show up, starts on a Saturday, lasts 16 days, and ends the first Sunday in October. Although this is the most famous of Munich's festivals, when beer flows as freely as water, the city is actually less inhibited and more individualistic during the pre-Lenten Fasching (Carnival). Even the most reserved Germans are caught up in this whirl of colorful parades, masked balls, and revelry.

Munich remains lively all year—fairs and holidays seem to follow one on top of the other. But this is no "oompah" town. Here you'll find the most sophisticated clubs, the best theaters, and the finest concert halls. Don't go to Munich to rest—it's a city mainly for having fun, and it has a wealth of cultural events and sights.

MUNICH — PAST AND PRESENT

One of Europe's most-visited cities, filled with monuments and fabulous museums, Munich is a city with memories of yesterday, both good and bad, but it is very much a city living in its present. Don't worry about feeling lost and bewildered here. You'll be like most everybody else: Two-thirds of the population are newcomers.

WHAT IT WAS Munich owes its name to a tiny settlement of monks living near the banks of the Isar River more than 1,200 years ago. Their cloister and the little villages that grew up around it were referred to as *Münichen,* the little monks. In modern German, that nickname has become *München.* A little monk is incorporated into the city's coat-of-arms—he raises his hands as if he wants to speak. If so, he'll probably say, "Gruss Gott!" the welcome still used around here.

Munich lay on the Salzstrasse (salt route) linking Augsburg with Salzburg, and in 1158, when Duke Henry the Lion of the house of Wittelsbach diverted the salt trade over the bridge "by the monks," Munich began to thrive as the trading center for Upper Bavaria. In time the little town grew into a walled city with entrance through five gates. One was near what is now the Alte Rathaus on Marienplatz; this was once the grain market and very early in the city's history formed its heartbeat. By the end of

WHAT'S SPECIAL ABOUT MUNICH

Museums/Galleries

☐ Alte Pinakothek, a once royal art collection that grew into one of the most important in Germany.

☐ Deutsches Museum, the largest technological museum in the world, with priceless holdings, including the first automobile.

☐ Bavarian National Museum, the richest display of the historical treasures of Bavaria.

Castles/Palaces

☐ Schloss Nymphenburg, summer residence of the Wittelsbach dynasty.

☐ The Residenz, the official home of the rulers of Bavaria from 1385 to 1918.

Ace Attractions

☐ Olympiapark, site of the 1972 Olympic Games, now a residential and recreational area.

☐ Beer gardens and halls, dozens of them, including the most famous in the world: the state-owned Hofbräuhaus am Platzl.

Architectural Highlight

☐ Cuvilliés Theater, from the mid-1700s, the grandest rococo theater in the country.

Special Events

☐ Fasching or Carnival, a joyous season extending from just after Epiphany right up to Shrove Tuesday.

☐ Oktoberfest, the world's greatest beer-drinking blast (actually mostly in September).

---

the 13th century, the city had increased its size fivefold. The Wittelsbachs were to retain power until the end of World War I (1918). Autocratic and proud, they ruled with an iron hand, though many historians have called them "benevolent despots."

During the centuries that followed, Munich went through many vicissitudes. From 1314 to 1347, it was an imperial city when its duke, Ludwig IV, called "Ludwig the Bavarian," became Holy Roman emperor. In 1327, a great fire destroyed much of the city. During the Reformation, Munich remained Roman Catholic and became the chief city of the Counter-Reformation in Germany.

In 1799, Bavaria became a sovereign state when Napoleon Bonaparte crowned Maximilian IV Joseph as King Maximilian I, a position it held for the better part of the 19th century. It was in the 19th century that real growth took place, and the art-loving kings, Ludwig I, Maximilian II, and Ludwig II, built it up into "a modern Athens." Ludwig I attracted artists, writers, sculptors, and painters to the city, but his notorious love affair with the dancer Lola Montez (subject of countless movies) threatened his reign. Finally, in 1848, Ludwig abdicated; Ms. Montez fled to Mexico; and Ludwig's son, Maximilian, assumed power.

Interested in the arts and sciences, Maximilian II ushered in a liberal era, which included the founding in 1855 of the Bavarian National Museum. The railway arrived in 1839. When Maximilian II died in 1864, Ludwig II became the ruler. He is the Bavarian king best known around the world today, mainly because of his "fairy-tale castles."

In 1871, under the unification plan for Germany, Bavaria lost its status as an independent state. Ludwig died by mysterious drowning in 1886. Under his successor, Prince Regent Luitpold, Munich became known as a cultural city, and played an important part in the development of art in the 19th and early 20th centuries, attracting such artists as Wassily Kandinsky and Paul Klee. By this time the city had gained a reputation for drinking, merrymaking, and festivals.

World War I brought hunger and deprivation to the city. Demonstrations and social unrest followed the war. A Munich republic was established, but it did not last long. Reaction set in. Julius Streicher, later to become a henchman of Hitler's, founded the anti-Semitic German Freedom Party. Unemployment and inflation plagued the city, problems to be exploited by Hitler. In 1923, Hitler's "beerhall putsch" attempted—and failed—to overthrow the government. He was sentenced to five years in prison, during which time he wrote *Mein Kampf*. After he was released in 1924, he established his headquarters in the city.

By 1933, as Hitler came to power, Munich was in the grip of a National Socialist dictatorship. The Bavarian government, led by Heinrich Held, was dissolved, the first concentration camp, Dachau, was established outside Munich, and a torture chamber was set up in the former Wittelsbach Palace. The city at the time had 10,000 Jews, but only 200 were to survive.

Hitler and Chamberlain came to the city in 1938 to sign the infamous Munich Pact. Then came World War II, and the face of Munich was to be changed forever. Air raid followed air raid, especially in 1942, and nearly half the city had been destroyed by the time American troops arrived on April 30, 1945. Over 200,000 people had lost their lives.

WHAT IT IS NOW With something approaching a miracle, Munich bounced back from the disaster of World War II. Rubble was removed, the city rebuilt, and restorations made with taste and discretion. In 1949, upon establishment of the Federal Republic of Germany, it became the capital of the Federal Land of Bavaria. It was to be—and still is—a major economic city, a center of north-south trade in Europe. The largest industrial city of the Federal Republic, it soon attracted such famous names as Siemens and BMW, becoming a center for high-tech microelectronics. It has a big publishing industry, as well as burgeoning film studios, and is the largest university town in Germany.

By 1957, the population had jumped from 470,000 to 1 million. In 1972, the city played host to the Olympic Games.

Today, with some 1.2 million inhabitants, of which 16% are foreigners, Munich is the third-largest city in Germany. It is also the Germans' first choice as a place to live, according to various polls. Still a city of art and culture, it remains one of the most beautiful of German cities—although much of the older beauty is gone forever.

1. ORIENTATION

Munich is just slightly smaller than Berlin and Hamburg. Trying to see all of it would be a major undertaking; however, you can explore the heart of Munich on foot. Many attractions are in the environs, so you'll have to rely on a car or public transportation.

ARRIVING

Munich is easily reached from major cities of Europe. From Frankfurt, it's a 50-minute flight aboard Lufthansa; from Hamburg or Berlin, 65 minutes. It takes 3 hours and 45 minutes to reach Munich from Frankfurt by car or train. From Berlin, it's 8 hours by car or rail, and from Hamburg, it's 8 or 9 hours by car and 7 hours by train.

IMPRESSIONS

Bavarians say that the difference between a rich farmer and a poor farmer is that the poor farmer cleans his Mercedes himself.
—J.W. MURRAY, OBSERVER (1979)

BY PLANE The **Münchner Flughafen,** inaugurated in 1992, is among the most modern, best-equipped, and most efficient airports in the world. The $5.3-billion facility handles more than 100 flights a day, serving 60 cities worldwide. Passengers can fly nonstop to such cities as New York, Miami, Chicago, and Toronto. It lies 19 miles northeast of central Munich at Erdinger Moos. Facilities include parking garages; car-rental centers; restaurants, bars, and cafés; money-exchange kiosks; lockers; and luggage storage facilities. For flight information, call the airline of your choice.

S-Bahn trains connect the airport with the Hauptbahnhof (main railroad station) in downtown Munich. Departures are every 30 minutes for the 40-minute trip. The fare is 10 DM ($6.60); Eurailpass holders ride free. A taxi into the center costs 80 DM ($52.80). For more information, call Munich Verkehrs and Tarifverband (tel. 089/23-80-30). Airport buses, such as those operated by Lufthansa, also run between the airport and the center.

BY TRAIN Munich's main rail station, **Hauptbahnhof,** Bahnhofplatz, D-8000 München 2, is one of the largest in Europe. It is located near the city center and the trade-fair grounds, containing a hotel, restaurants, shopping, car parking, and banking facilities. All major German cities are connected to this station, most with a train arriving and departing almost every hour. Many major European cities have rail links to Munich. For example, Munich is connected to Frankfurt by some 67 daily trains. There are about 20 daily rail connections to Berlin.

The rail station is connected with the S-Bahn rapid transit system, a network of 260 miles of tracks, providing service to various city districts and outlying suburbs. The major subway serving Munich (the U-Bahn) is also centered at the rail station. In addition, buses fan out in all directions. Long-distance buses arrive and depart in the section of the station known as Westwing-Starnberger Bahnhof. For information about long-distance trains, call 089/194-19; for S-Bahn trains, 089/55-75-75.

BY BUS Munich has long-distance bus service to many German and European cities. Buses depart from the section of the Hauptbahnhof called Westwing-Starnberger Bahnhof. For information about connections, tariffs, and schedules, call **Deutsche Touring GmbH,** Arnulf Strasse 3 (tel. 089/59-18-24). It covers many major cities and also runs buses to The Romantic Road (see Chapter 11). **Bayern Express Reisen,** Arnulf Strasse 16–18 (tel. 089/55-30-74), offers daily service to Berlin via Nürnberg. Excursions to such popular Bavarian destinations as Berchtesgaden, Schwangau-Neuschwanstein, Garmisch-Partenkirchen, and Chiemsee are offered by several local bus companies, including **Panorama Tours** at a number of locations (call 089/59-15-04 for more information).

TOURIST INFORMATION

Tourist information can be obtained at the Hauptbahnhof or at the Münchner Flughafen in the central area (tel. 089/975-92-815); the latter is open Monday to Saturday from 8:30am to 10pm and Sunday from 1 to 9pm. The main tourist office (Fremden Verkehrsamt) at the Hauptbahnhof is found at the south exit opening onto Bayerstrasse. Open Monday through Saturday from 8am to 10pm and Sunday from 11am to 7pm, it offers a free map of Munich and will also reserve rooms (see "Accommodations," below). For information, call 089/239-11. To find out about museum opening hours (in English), call 089/2391-256.

CITY LAYOUT

Munich's **Hauptbahnhof** lies just west of the town center and opens onto Bahnhofplatz. From the square you can take Schützenstrasse to one of the major centers of Munich, **Karlsplatz** (nicknamed Stachus). Many streetcar lines converge on this square. From Karlsplatz, you can continue east along the pedestrian-only streets of Neuhauserstrasse and Kaufingerstrasse until you reach Marienplatz, where you'll be deep in the **Altstadt** (old town) of Munich (for a more complete description of this sector, refer to "Attractions" later in this chapter).

From **Marienplatz,** with its daily Glockenspiel performance, you can head north on the Dienerstrasse, which will lead you to Residenzstrasse and finally, to **Max-Joseph-Platz,** a landmark square, with the Nationaltheater and the former royal palace, the Residenz. East of this square runs **Maximilianstrasse,** perhaps the most fashionable shopping and restaurant street of Munich, containing the prestigious Hotel Vier Jahreszeiten Kempinski München. Between Marienplatz and the Nationaltheater is the Platzl quarter, where you'll want to head for nighttime diversions, as it's the seat of some of the finest (and some of the worst) restaurants in Munich, along with the landmark Hofbraühaus, the most famous beer hall in Europe.

North of the old town is **Schwabing,** a former bohemian section whose main street is Leopoldstrasse. The large, sprawling municipal park grounds, the Englischer Garten, are found due east of Schwabing. Northwest of Schwabing is the Olympic complex (more about that later).

NEIGHBORHOODS IN BRIEF

Altstadt   This is the historic part of Munich, the site of the original medieval city. Three gates remain to indicate the borders of the town. It's bounded by the Sendlinger Tor and the Odeonsplatz to the north and the south, whereas the Isar Tor and Karlstor limit its eastern and western periphery. You can virtually walk across the district in 15 minutes. The hub is the Marienplatz, with its Rathaus or town hall.

Schwabing   This is a large northern section, reached by U-Bahn from the Marienplatz. After 1945 it became known as the Bohemian district of Munich, similar to Greenwich Village. Leopoldstrasse makes almost a straight axis through the center of it. The Englischer Garten forms one border, and Schwabing extends as far north as the Studentenstadt, with Olympiapark and Josephplatz marking its western border.

Olympiapark   Host to rock and pop concerts on weekends, this residential and recreational area was the site of the 1972 Olympics, which is remembered for the terrorist attack by the Arab "Black September" group against Israeli athletes. Today, the park is the site of a Greek theater and a lake used for boating.

Museum Quarter   Between Altstadt and Schwabing is the museum district, containing such great museums as the Alte Pinakothek (see "Attractions," below). Bordered by Briennerstrasse and Theresienstrasse, it actually covers only two blocks but could take days to explore in depth if you visit the state-owned museums.

Nymphenburg   Take the U-Bahn to Rotkreuzplatz, then tram 12 to reach the Nymphenburg district, site of the summer palace of the Wittelsbach dynasty, who once ruled Bavaria (see "Attractions," below).

FINDING AN ADDRESS/MAPS   Locating an address is relatively easy in Munich, as even numbers run up one side of a street and odd numbers down the other. In Altstadt, "hidden" squares may make it a little difficult; therefore you'll need a detailed street map, not the more general maps handed out free by the tourist office and many hotels. The best ones are published by Falk, and they're available at nearly all bookstores and at many news kiosks. These pocket-size maps are easy to carry and contain a detailed street index at the end.

2. GETTING AROUND

BY PUBLIC TRANSPORTATION   The city's rapid transit system is preferable to streetcars (trams) and certainly to the high-priced taxis. The underground network contains many convenient electronic devices, and the rides are relatively noise-free. The same ticket entitles you to ride the U-Bahn and the S-Bahn, as well as streetcars and buses. The U-Bahn, or Untergrundbahn, is the line you will use most frequently; the S-Bahn, or Stadtbahn, services suburban locations.

At the transport hub, Marienplatz, U-Bahn and S-Bahn rails crisscross each other.

It's possible to use your Eurailpass on S-Bahn journeys, as it's a state-owned railway. Otherwise, you must purchase a single-trip ticket or a strip ticket for several journeys at one of the blue vending machines positioned at the entryways to the underground stations. These tickets entitle you to ride both the S and U lines, and they're also good for rides on streetcars and buses. If you're making only one trip, a single ticket will average 2.50 DM ($1.70), although it can reach as high as 12 DM ($7.90) to an outlying area.

Costing less per ride is the strip ticket, called *Streifenkarte* in German. It's good for several rides and sells for 10 DM ($6.60). It consists of strips worth about 1 DM (66¢) each. A short ride requires only one strip. A day ticket, called a *Tageskarte,* is also a good investment if you plan to stay within the city limits. It costs 8 DM ($5.30). If you'd like to branch out to Greater Munich (that is, within a 50-mile radius), you can purchase a day card for 16 DM ($10.60). A trip within the metropolitan area costs you two strips, which are valid for two hours. In that time, you may interrupt your trip and transfer as you like, traveling in one continuous direction. When you reverse your direction, you must cancel two strips again. Children aged 4 to 14 use the red *Kinderstreifenkarte* costing 5 DM ($3.30) for six strips. For a trip within the metropolitan area, they cancel only one strip. Above the age of 15, children must pay adult fares. For public transport information, dial 089/23-80-30.

Where the U-Bahn comes to an end, buses and streetcars take over; you can transfer as many times as you need to reach your destination, using the same ticket. Fares are expected to rise in the lifetime of this edition.

BY TAXI   Cabs are relatively expensive—the average ride costs 8 DM to 12 DM ($5.30 to $7.90). In an emergency, call 2-1610 for a radio-dispatched taxi.

BY CAR   It is usually best to rent a car before leaving for Germany (see "Planning a Trip to Germany," in Chapter 2). You can also rent cars on the spot but often at substantially higher tariffs. Major car-rental companies are represented in Munich, with easy-to-spot offices at the airport.

You can rent cars within the city center as well. Companies include **Avis,** Nymphenburger Strasse 61 (tel. 089/12-60-00-20), and **Sixt/Budget Autovermietung,** Seitzstrasse 9–11 (tel. 089/22-56-25). It's wise to call a number of agencies as prices can vary widely. Rental companies are found under *Autovermietung* in the yellow pages of the Munich phone book. One-day rentals often range from 155 DM to 175 DM ($102.30 to $115.60), unlimited mileage and tax included.

Because of the heavy traffic, don't attempt to see Munich by car. If you're driving into Munich, call your hotel and ask if parking is available on site. Hotel recommendations (see "Accommodations," below), indicate if parking is available at the hotel. Otherwise, drive to your hotel, unload your luggage, and ask one of the staff to direct you to the nearest parking garage. Charges tend to be high in most of these garages, often 19 DM to 30 DM ($12.50 to $19.80) per night.

ON FOOT AND BY BICYCLE   Of course, the best way to explore Munich is on foot, since it has a vast pedestrian zone in the center. Many of its attractions can, in fact, be reached only on foot. Pick up a good map and set out.

The tourist office also sells a pamphlet called "Radl-Touren für unsere Gäste," costing only 0.50 DM (30¢). It outlines itineraries for touring Munich by bicycle.

One of the most convenient places to rent a bike is **Lothar Borucki,** Hans-Sachs-Strasse 7 (tel. 089/26-65-06), near the U-Bahn station at Frauenhoferstrasse. It is open Monday to Friday from 9am to 1pm and 3 to 6pm and Saturday from 9am to noon. Charges are 18 DM ($11.90) for a full day.

FAST FACTS: *MUNICH*

Besides the general information given under "Fast Facts: Germany" in Chapter 2, some specific data may help you have a more pleasant stay in Munich.

American Express Your lifeline back to the States might be American Express, Promenadeplatz 6 (tel. 089/290-90-0), which is open for mail pickup and check cashing Monday to Friday from 9am to 5:30pm, Saturday from 9am to noon. Unless you have an American Express card or traveler's checks, you'll be charged 2 DM ($1.30) for picking up your mail.

Area Code The area code for Munich is **089.**

Babysitters Call 089/22-92-91 for this service. If you need a sitter in the evening, try to call before noon.

Bookstores Try **Anglia English Bookshop,** Schellingstrasse 3 (tel. 089/28-36-42), in the Schwabing district, which sells English-language titles and travel books. Hours are Monday to Friday from 9am to 6:30pm and Saturday from 10am to 2pm.

Business Hours Most **banks** are open Monday to Friday from 8:30am to 12:30pm and 1:30 to 3:30pm (many banks stay open until 5:30pm on Thursday). Most **businesses** and **stores** are open Monday to Friday from 9am to 6pm and Saturday from 9am to 2pm. During *langer Samstag* (the first Saturday of the month) stores remain open until 6pm. Many stores in Munich observe a late closing on Thursday, usually 8 or 9pm.

Car Rentals See "Getting Around" in this chapter.

Climate See "When to Go" in Chapter 2.

Currency See "Information, Entry Requirements & Money" in Chapter 2.

Currency Exchange You can get a better rate at a bank rather than at your hotel. American Express traveler's checks are best cashed at the local American Express office (see above). On Saturday and Sunday or at night, you can exchange money at the Hauptbahnhof exchange, Bahnhofplatz, which is open daily from 6am to 11:30pm.

Dentist For an English-speaking dentist, go to **Universtäts-Zahrnarzt Klinik,** Lindwurmstrasse 2A (tel. 089/5160-2911), the dental clinic for the university. It deals with emergency cases and is always open.

Doctor The British, American, and Canadian consulates (see below) keep a list of recommended English-speaking physicians.

Drugstores For an international drugstore where English is spoken, go to **International Ludwig's Apotheke,** Neuhauser Strasse 8 (tel. 089/260-30-21), in the pedestrian shopping zone. It is open Monday to Friday from 9am to 6:30pm and Saturday from 9am to 2pm.

Embassies/Consulates In case you should lose your passport or have an emergency, the **U.S. consulate** is at Königstrasse 5, D-8000 München 22 (tel. 089/28-881). It's open Monday to Friday from 8am to noon. The **British consulate** is at Bürkleinstrasse 10 (tel. 089/21-10-90). It's open Monday to Friday from 8:45 to 11:30am and from 1 to 3:15pm. The **Canadian consulate** is at Tal 29 (tel. 089/29-0650). It's open Monday to Thursday from 9am to noon and from 2 to 5pm and Friday from 9am to 1:30pm.

Emergencies For emergency medical aid, phone **089/55-86-61.** Call the police at **110.**

Eyeglasses German optics are among the most precise in the world, and dozens of opticians in central Munich could quickly and rapidly prepare new eyeglasses or contact lenses. **Hertie Department Store,** Bahnhofplatz 7 (tel. 089/55-120) has a department selling both eyeglasses and cameras, but a somewhat different selection of frames is available from **Apollo Optik,** Neuhauserstrasse 15 (tel. 089/260-9457).

Hairdresser/Barber One of the best unisex hair salons is **Dieter Beil,** Neuhauser Strasse 24 (tel. 089/26-57-35), which is open Monday to Friday from 8:30am to 6pm (by appointment only).

Holidays See "When to Go" in Chapter 2.

Hospitals Munich has many hospitals. Americans, British, and Canadians can contact their consulates (see above) for a recommendation of a particular hospital. For emergency medical service, call **089/55-86-61.**

Information   See "Tourist Information" in this chapter.

Laundry/Dry Cleaning   Two good dry-cleaning establishments are **Paradies-Sofortreiningung,** 11 Lerchenfeldstrasse 11 (tel. 089/22-34-65) and **Tommaselli,** Landsbergerstrasse 102 (tel. 089/50-55-64). Look in the yellow pages under either *Wäscherei* or *Waschsalon* for a coin-operated laundry near your hotel. A 24-hour one is found at Landshuter Allee 77, near Rotkreuzplatz.

Lost Property   Go to the local lost and found office at Ruppertstrasse 19 (tel. 089/23-31), open Monday to Friday from 8:30am to noon. On Tuesday, it is also open from 2 to 5:30pm. If you should lose an item on the S-Bahn or one of the German trains, then go to the lost and found office at the Hauptbahnhof (track 25; tel. 089/128-66-64). Hours there are from 6:30am to 11:30pm daily.

Luggage Storage/Lockers   Facilities are available at the Hauptbahnhof, Bahnhofplatz, which is open daily from 5am to 12:30am.

Newspapers/Magazines   The *International Herald Tribune* is the most widely distributed English-language newspaper in the city. You can also find copies of *USA Today* and the European editions of *Time* and *Newsweek.*

Photographic Needs   Munich abounds with photographic shops in every neighborhood. You can also go to Hertie Department Store, Bahnhofplatz 7 (tel. 089/55-120).

Post Office   The **Postamt München** (main post office) is across from the Hauptbahnhof at Bahnhofplatz 1 (tel. 089/5388-27-32). It's open day and night, and you can also make long-distance calls here (far cheaper than at your hotel, where you'll be charged for service). If you want to have your mail sent to you, mark it *"poste restante"* for general delivery (take along your passport to reclaim any mail and go to counter 14, 16, or 17). Have it addressed D-8000 München 32. For long-distance calls and telegrams, it is open 24 hours.

Radio   The BBC World Service broadcasts to Munich as does the American Forces Network (AFN), which you can hear on 1107AM. For the Voice of America, tune in to 1197AM. English news broadcasts are presented frequently on the Bavarian Radio Service (Bayerischer Rundfunk).

Religious Services   From the tourist office (see "Orientation" in this chapter) you can obtain a copy of "Monatsprogramm" for 2 DM ($1.30), listing churches of various denominations in Munich, along with hours of weekly services.

Restrooms   Use the word *Toilette,* which is pronounced "TWA-leh-teh." Often they are labeled WC in public places, sometimes H (*Herren* for men) or F (*Frauen* for women). In the center of Munich are several public facilities. You can also patronize the facilities at terminals, restaurants, bars, cafés, department stores, hotels, and pubs.

Safety   Munich, like all big cities of the world, has its share of crime. Innocent tourists are often victims. The major crimes are pickpocketing and purse- and camera-snatching. It is your responsibility to keep your guard up and to be alert. Wear a moneybelt. If necessary, store valuables in a hotel safe. Most robberies occur in the much-frequented tourist areas, such as the one around Marienplatz and the area around the Hauptbahnhof, which is particularly dangerous at night. Many tourists lose their valuables when they carelessly leave clothing unprotected as they join the nude sunbathers in Englischer Garten.

Shoe Repairs   Offering the quickest service is **Mister Minit,** at the Hertie Department Store, Bahnhofplatz 7 (tel. 089/55-120).

Taxis   See "Getting Around" in this chapter.

Telegrams/Telex/Fax   These can be sent from the Postamt München, Bahnhofplatz 1 (tel. 089/5388-27-32), open 24 hours a day.

Television   There are two national TV channels, ARD (channel 1) and ZDF (channel 2). Sometimes these stations show films in their original language (most often English). The more expensive hotels often have cable TV, with such programs as 24-hour news on CNN.

Transit Info   For S-Bahn information, dial **089/55-75-75.**

Water   Tap water is safe to drink in Munich.

3. ACCOMMODATIONS

Finding a room in Munich is comparatively easy, but tabs tend to be high. Bargains are few and hard to find, but exist.

If you arrive without a reservation, go to the **Munich Tourist Information Office** on platform 12 at the Hauptbahnhof (tel. 089/239-12-57, where general information is also available), open daily from 8am to 10pm. There, Bavarian personnel (most speak English), with some 34,000 listings in their files, will come to your rescue. Tell them what you can afford, pay a fee, and get a receipt—as well as a map with instructions on how to reach the accommodation into which they have booked you. You pay a fee of 5 DM ($3.30) per room. Keep your receipt. If you don't like the room to which you have been sent, go back to the tourist office and they will try to find you another lodging at no extra charge. Correspondence, however, should be addressed to the administration offices at Sendingerstrasse/Ruffinihaus, D-8000 München 2. These offices are open Monday to Friday from 9am to 3pm.

CENTRAL MUNICH

VERY EXPENSIVE

AUSTROTEL MÜNCHEN, Arnulfstrasse 2, D-8000 München 2. Tel. 089/5-38-60. Fax 089/538-62-255. 174 rms. MINIBAR TV TEL **Tram:** 19 or 25. **Bus:** 55. **U-Bahn or S-Bahn:** Hauptbahnhof stop.

$ Rates (including buffet breakfast): 205 DM–215 DM ($135.30–$141.90) single; 370 DM ($244.20) double. AE, DC, MC, V. **Parking:** 19 DM ($12.50).

The high-rise Austrotel München has been refurbished and upgraded to four-star status. All the modern guest rooms have radios, TVs, and city views. The handsome 15th-floor Belvedere restaurant serves international menus, including Austrian and Bavarian specialties. As you dine, you can look out on Munich—with the Alps visible in the distance on clear days. A coffee bar, Amadeus, and a gift shop are also on the premises. The Austrotel is at the Hauptbahnhof and the air terminal, as well as the U- and S-Bahn stations. Laundry and room service are offered.

BAYERISCHER HOF & PALAIS MONTGELAS, Promenadeplatz 2–6, D-8000 München 2. Tel. 089/2-12-00, or toll free 800/223-6800. Fax 089/21-20-906. 440 rms, 45 suites. MINIBAR TV TEL **Tram:** 19.

$ Rates (including buffet breakfast): 287 DM–350 DM ($189.40–$231) single; 425 DM–545 DM ($280.50–$359.70) double; from 750 DM ($495) suite. AE, DC, MC, V. **Parking:** 27 DM ($17.80).

Considered by many travelers a Bavarian version of New York's Waldorf-Astoria, the Bayerischer Hof & Palais Montgelas is in a swank location, across from American Express, opening onto a little tree-filled square. The tastefully decorated central lounge, with English and French reproductions and Oriental rugs, is practically the living room of Munich: "Meet you in the lounge of the Bayerischer Hof" is heard often. The integration of the sumptuously decorated Palais Montgelas into the hotel brought deluxe suites and double rooms, as well as a number of conference and banqueting rooms. All the guest rooms have radios and TVs, and 80 are air-conditioned.

Dining/Entertainment: The major dining room, the Garden-Restaurant, evokes the grandeur of a small palace, with an ornate ceiling, crystal chandeliers, and French provincial chairs. Generous drinks and charcoal specialties from the rôtisserie are served in the clublike bar, where the tables are lit by candles and the reflected glow from the octagonally paned stained-glass windows. There's also the Kleine Komödie Theater, a Trader Vic's, and the best nightclub in Munich, recommended separately.

Services: Room service, laundry, babysitting.

Facilities: Rooftop pool and garden with bricked sun terrace, sauna, massage rooms.

EDEN-HOTEL-WOLFF, Arnulfstrasse 4-8, D-8000 München 2. Tel. 089/ 55-11-50. Fax 089/551-15-555. 214 rms. MINIBAR TV TEL **U-Bahn or S-Bahn:** Hauptbahnhof.

$ Rates (including buffet breakfast): 175 DM–330 DM ($115.50–$217.80) single; 280 DM–450 DM ($184.80–$297) double. AE, DC, MC, V. **Parking:** 19 DM ($12.50).

Opposite the Hauptbahnhof, the Eden-Hotel-Wolff misleads with its sedate exterior. The interior is decorated in a richly traditional style. In the main dining room the theme is Bavarian—a natural pine ceiling, gleaming brass lantern sconces, and thick stone arches. Another paneled dining room has oil paintings and brass chandeliers. The guest rooms are also in Bavarian style.

GRAND HOTEL CONTINENTAL, Max-Joseph-Strasse 5, D-8000 München 2. Tel. 089/55-15-70. Fax 089/55-15-75-00. 148 rms, 21 suites. MINIBAR TV TEL **Tram:** 19.

$ Rates: 295 DM–375 DM ($194.70–$247.50) single; 350 DM–490 DM ($231– $323.40) double; from 850 DM ($561) suite. Buffet breakfast 30 DM ($19.80) extra. AE, DC, MC, V. **Parking:** 25 DM ($16.50).

This is perhaps the nicest place to stay in Munich if you appreciate a stylish, antique-filled hotel run in a personal manner. It belongs to a small deluxe chain, Royal Classic Hotels, and is affectionately known as the "Conti." The elegant lounge sets the tone. The formal dining room has a wood-beamed ceiling, an open château fireplace, and high antique cupboards. That the Continental deserves its "Grand" appellation is reflected everywhere: in the French provincial coffee and card room; in the formal sitting salon, with ornate Louis XVI–style furniture, brocaded walls, and baroque doors; and in the garden room, with its arbor, vines, and planters of red geraniums. The suites are elegant and filled with antiques.

Dining/Entertainment: The hotel's dining room serves an excellent international and Bavarian cuisine, with meals ranging from 65 DM to 95 DM ($42.90 to $62.70).

Services: Room service, laundry, babysitting, currency exchange, express checkout, translation service.

Facilities: Business center.

KÖNIGSHOF, Karlsplatz 25, D-8000 München 2. Tel. 089/55-13-60, or toll free 800/44-UTELL. Fax 089/55-13-61-13. 106 rms, 9 suites. A/C MINIBAR TV TEL **Tram:** 11. **S-Bahn:** S3, S7, or S8 to Karlsplatz.

$ Rates: 298 DM–310 DM ($196.70–$204.60) single; 345 DM–460 DM ($227.70–$303.60) double; from 600 DM ($396) suite. Breakfast 30 DM ($19.80) extra. AE, DC, MC, V. **Parking:** 19 DM ($12.50) in 180-car underground garage.

In the heart of Munich, the Königshof overlooks the famous Stachus (Karlsplatz) and the old part of the city, where interesting walking and shopping areas are found. Opened in 1862, the hotel has enjoyed great renown, and the proprietors, the Geisel family, have seen that it maintains its legend. The hotel offers traditional comfort plus up-to-date facilities. All of its sleekly styled rooms have soundproofing and picture windows.

Dining/Entertainment: On the second floor is the well-known Restaurant Königshof, serving French and international cuisine. Entertainment is provided by a piano bar. The lobby houses an intimate club bar, the Königshof-Bar.

Services: Room service, laundry, babysitting.

Facilities: Car-rental facilities, shopping boutiques.

MÜNCHEN PARK HILTON, Am Tucherpark 7, D-8000 München 22. Tel. 089/3-84-50, or toll free 800/USA-0130. Fax 089/384-51-845. 477 rms, 21 suites. A/C MINIBAR TV TEL **Bus:** E54 from Schwabing.

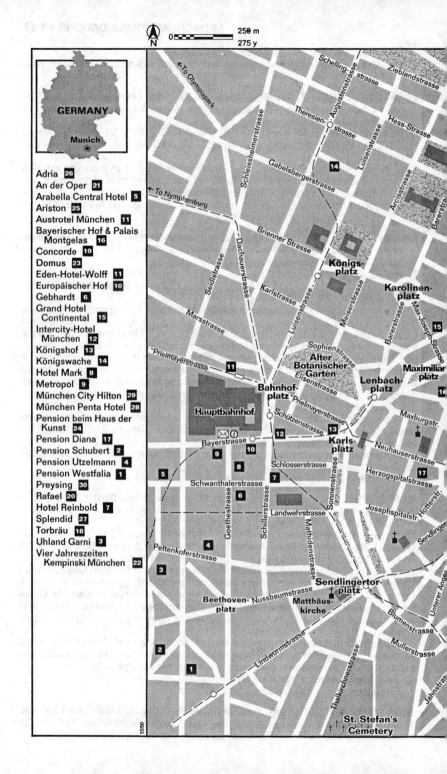

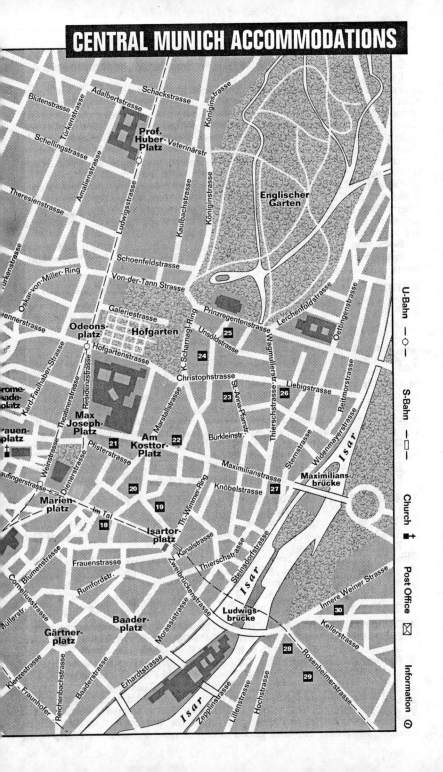

CENTRAL MUNICH ACCOMMODATIONS

Blütenstrasse
Schackstrasse
Adalbertstrasse
Türkenstrasse
Schellingstrasse
Amalienstrasse
Theresienstrasse
Königinstrasse
Prof. Huber-Platz
Veterinärstr
Ludwigstrasse
Kaulbachstrasse
Königinstrasse

Englischer Garten

Türkenstrasse
Oskar-von-Miller- Ring
Schoenfeldstrasse
Von-der-Tann Strasse
Galeriestrasse
iennerstrasse
Odeons-platz
Hofgarten
Prinzregentenstrasse
Lerchenfeldstrasse
Oettingenstrasse
K.-Scharnagl-Ring
Wagmullerstrasse
Kard.-Faulhaber-Strasse
Hofgartenstrasse
Residenzstrasse
Unsöldstrasse
25
24
Christophstrasse
St.-Anna-Pfarrstr.
Liebigstrasse
Reitmorstrasse
rome-ade-platz
Theatinerstrasse
Marstallstrasse
23
Thierschstrasse
Sternstrasse
26
Max Joseph-Platz
Am Kosttor-Platz
22
Bürkleinstr.
Widenmayerstrasse
Isar
rauen-platz
Weinstrasse
Pfisterstrasse
21
Maximilianstrasse
aufingerstrasse
Dienerstrasse
20
Knöbelstrasse
27
Maximilians-brücke
Marien-platz
Im Tal
19
Th.-Wimmer-Ring
18
Isartor-platz
Kanalstrasse
Steinsdorfstrasse
Frauenstrasse
Thierschstrasse
Corneliusstrasse
Blumenstrasse
Rumfordstr.
Zweibrückenstrasse
Morassistrasse
Isar
Müllerstr.
Baader-platz
Ludwigs-brücke
Innere Weiner Strasse
30
Kellerstrasse
Gärtner-platz
Reichenbachstrasse
Baaderstrasse
Erhardtstrasse
28
Rosenheimerstrasse
Klenzestrasse
Fraunhofer
Zepplinstrasse
Lilienstrasse
Hochstrasse
29
Isar

U-Bahn —○—

S-Bahn —□—

Church ✚

Post Office ⊠

Information ⊙

$ Rates: 295 DM–450 DM ($194.70–$297) single; 360 DM–515 DM ($237.60–$339.90) double; from 800 DM ($528) suite. Breakfast 31 DM ($20.50) extra. AE, DC, MC. V. **Parking:** 19 DM ($12.50).

A newly refurnished 15-story modern hotel between the Isar River and the Englischer Garten, the Park Hilton was built in 1972 in the center of the former Tivoli Park, about a 10-minute ride from the central shopping areas. The guest rooms contain floor-to-ceiling picture windows, plus balconies affording a distant view of the Alps. Units are contemporary yet elegant, with dark Macassar-wood furniture perfectly complementing the autumnal colors used throughout. Opened in 1988 was the deluxe Executive Floor, providing handsomely decorated guest rooms and a private lounge where continental breakfasts, drinks, and small snacks are served.

Dining/Entertainment: Overlooking the pool is Isar Terrassen, which offers a buffet and an à la carte menu. In summer the restaurant opens onto the garden. International and creative dishes are offered in the Hilton Grill on the ground floor, and there is also a Chinese restaurant, Tse Yang. The Piano Bar features a pianist and the best martinis in town.

Services: 24-hour room service, babysitting, laundry, dry cleaning, hairdresser.

Facilities: Health club facing the Englischer Garten, with heated indoor pool, sauna, Turkish bath, solarium.

RAFAEL, Neuturmstrasse 1, D-8000 München 2. Tel. 089/29-09-80. Fax 089/22-25-39. 74 rms, 18 suites. A/C MINIBAR TV TEL **Tram:** 19.

$ Rates (including breakfast): 420 DM–560 DM ($277.20–$369.60) single; 520 DM–720 DM ($343.20–$475.20) double; from 820 DM ($541.20) suite. AE, DC, MC. V. **Parking:** 30 DM ($19.80).

One of Munich's smallest hotels is also one of its most sophisticated and luxurious. A wedge-shaped neo-Renaissance building within sight of the symbol of Munich, the Marienplatz Church, this hotel was inaugurated in 1990 in a marble-fringed format of style and elegance. Originally built in 1880 on city fortifications dating from the 13th century, the hotel's interior has neoclassical and Biedermeier touches. A marble staircase beginning near the reception desk sweeps upward to the very comfortable guest rooms, each of which has a TV with VCR, a richly appointed bathroom, and especially crafted furniture or original antiques.

Dining/Entertainment: The culinary showplace is Mark's Restaurant, deliberately small, with only 75 seats and an adjacent cocktail bar.

Services: Valet parking, concierge, 24-hour room service, laundry, babysitting.

Facilities: Rooftop pool with view over historic district, boutiques.

TORBRÄU, Tal 37, D-8000 München 2. Tel. 089/22-50-16. Fax 089/22-50-19. 86 rms. TV TEL **U-Bahn:** Isator.

$ Rates (including buffet breakfast): 210 DM ($138.60) single; 300 DM–350 DM ($198–$231) double. AE, MC, V. **Parking:** 20 DM ($13.20). **Closed:** Dec 22–Jan 11.

This inviting choice in the center of old Munich is within easy reach of the Rathaus, the pedestrian shopping mall, the Deutsches Museum, the Residenz, and the opera house. It's much more charming than some of its bandbox competitors, with traditionally furnished guest rooms. The restaurant, Firenze, is bright and festive, serving Italian specialties, and there's also a Café-Conditorei on the premises.

VIER JAHRESZEITEN KEMPINSKI MÜNCHEN, Maximilianstrasse 17, D-8000 München 22. Tel. 089/23-03-90, or toll free 800/426-3155. Fax 089/230-39-693. 344 rms, 25 suites. A/C MINIBAR TV TEL **Tram:** 19.

$ Rates: 395 DM–695 DM ($260.70–$458.70) single; 575 DM–753 DM ($379.50–$497) double; from 1,580 DM ($1,042.80) suite. Breakfast 30 DM ($19.80) extra. AE, DC, MC, V. **Parking:** 30 DM ($19.80).

The most elegant place to stay in Munich is this grand hotel with a tradition stretching back to 1858. King Maximilian II took a personal interest in the establishment of this hotel and helped the founder, restaurateur August Schimon, financially. The hotel gained worldwide fame under the ownership of the

Walterspiel family, who brought it to the peak of its prominence and still owned it when it was mostly destroyed in a 1944 air raid. They rebuilt it and brought it back to its number-one position, selling it in 1970 to its present proprietors, Kempinski AG and Lufthansa German Airlines.

The guest rooms and suites, which have hosted royalty, heads of state, and famed personalities from all over the world, combine the charm of days gone by with modern amenities. Each bedroom contains a TV and radio. The windows opening onto Maximilianstrasse are double-glazed, and quiet is assured in the units facing the three inner courts. The hotel is not connected to other Vier Jahreszeiten hotels found throughout Germany.

Dining/Entertainment: Vier Jahreszeiten Restaurant, its finest dining spot (open nightly), is recommended separately. The Four Seasons lies under a magnificent glass roof (with emblems representing the four seasons) above the lobby. Guests like to linger in the Jahreszeiten Bar, where piano music is played nightly during the cocktail hour, with an international trio performing until 2am. The completely refurnished Bisto Eck surprises guests with its modern yet classical atmosphere. The Theaterkeller welcomes you at night to a comfortable setting; every Saturday from 6pm to midnight, a romantic candlelit buffet awaits you there. On Sunday from 10:30am to 2:30pm, the Theaterkeller invites you to a buffet brunch.

Services: Room service, laundry facilities, babysitting.

Facilities: Indoor pool and sauna, solarium.

EXPENSIVE

AN DER OPER, Falkenturmstrasse 11, D-8000 München 2. Tel. 089/ 290-02-70. Fax 089/290-02-729. 55 rms. TEL **Tram:** 19.
$ Rates (including continental breakfast): 140 DM–190 DM ($92.40–$125.40) single; 215 DM–235 DM ($141.90–$155.10) double. AE, DC, MC, V.

Located just off Maximilianstrasse, near Marienplatz, this hotel is superb for sightseeing or shopping in the traffic-free malls, just steps from the Bavarian National Theater. In spite of its basic, clean-cut modernity, there are touches of elegance: the crystal chandeliers in the little reception area, for example. Adjoining the luxurious

---

 FROMMER'S SMART TRAVELER: HOTELS

1. In inexpensive or moderately priced hotels, a room with a shower is cheaper than a room with a private bath. Even cheaper is a room with hot and cold running water and a corridor bathroom.
2. Remember that with a package tour (land arrangements booked with your air ticket) you'll often pay 30% less.
3. If Munich hotels are not full, a little bargaining can bring down the cost of a hotel room. Be polite: Ask if there's a "businessperson's rate" or if schoolteachers get a discount. The technique works best when the hotel has a 40% vacancy at night and wants to fill those empty rooms.
4. At less expensive hotels that take credit cards, ask if payment by cash will get you a reduction.
5. If you're going to spend at least a week in Munich, ask about long-term discounts.
6. Ask about weekend discounts, which can add up to 50% at certain city hotels patronized mainly by businesspeople.
7. Try to take advantage, if offered, of special summer rates. Hotel chains often grant them, especially in July and August, when German business travel falls off.

cellar bar, the Opern Taverne, is one of Munich's most prestigious restaurants, the Bouillabaisse. The guest rooms offer first-class amenities, each containing a small sitting area with armchairs and tables for breakfast. Traditional and modern elements have been combined throughout.

ARABELLA-CENTRAL HOTEL, Schwanthalerstrasse 111, D-8000 München 2. Tel. 089/510-83-0. Fax 089/51-08-32-49. 102 rms, 24 suites. MINIBAR TV TEL **Tram:** 16.

$ Rates (including buffet breakfast): 205 DM–310 DM ($135.30–$204.60) single; 260 DM–365 DM ($171.60–$240.90) double; from 350 DM ($231) suite. AE, DC, MC, V. **Parking:** 18 DM ($11.90). **Closed:** Dec 22–Jan 8.

Managed by the Arabella conglomerate, this is called in German *das kleine Grosstadthotel*, or "the little metropolitan hotel." A hotel garni, it lies only five minutes from the Messegelände and the Oktoberfest grounds, half a mile from the Hauptbahnhof. Everything is modern, often attractively so. The hotel was designed for convenience, and each unit is equipped with a balcony, a color TV, a radio, and an alarm clock. The hotel has a sauna and solarium and provides laundry and babysitting.

CONCORDE, Hernstrasse 38, D-8000 München 22. Tel. 089/22-45-15. Fax 089/22-83-282. 71 rms, 4 suites. MINIBAR TV TEL **U-Bahn:** U3 or U6 to Isartor Platz, a three-minute walk from the hotel.

$ Rates (including buffet breakfast): 180 DM–240 DM ($118.80–$158.40) single; 240 DM–310 DM ($158.40–$204.60) double; from 350 DM ($231) suite. AE, DC, MC, V. **Parking:** 18 DM ($11.90). **Closed:** Dec 23–Jan 6.

This is a suitable choice for those seeking an intimate hotel in the center of Munich. Though not very well known and located on a side street, it's only a few minutes' walk from some of the major sightseeing attractions of the Bavarian capital. The guest rooms, all with comfortable large beds, have been newly furnished and decorated.

DOMUS, St.-Anna-Strasse 31, D-8000 München 22. Tel. 089/22-17-04. Fax 089/228-53-59. 45 rms, 2 suites. MINIBAR TV TEL **U-Bahn:** U4 or U5 to Lehel.

$ Rates (including buffet breakfast): 200 DM–250 DM ($132–$165) single; 230 DM–260 DM ($151.80–$171.60) double; from 290 DM ($191.40) suite. AE, DC, MC, V. **Parking:** 18 DM ($11.90).

The Domus may sound like a university dormitory, but it isn't. Sleekly modern, this hotel near the Englischer Garten and the Haus der Kunst is about a 10-minute ride from the Hauptbahnhof. After a hectic day of sightseeing, you return here to comfort as you would to a private home, even though the Domus is a good-size hotel. The guest rooms are tastefully furnished. To give you an undisturbed night's rest, the hotel pays special attention to the quality of its carpeting and doors. You can breakfast in your room or downstairs.

INTERCITY-HOTEL MÜNCHEN, Bayerstrasse 10, D-8000 München 2. Tel. 089/54-55-60. Fax 089/54-55-6-610. 203 rms (all with bath or shower), 8 suites. A/C MINIBAR TV TEL **S-Bahn or U-Bahn:** Hauptbahnhof.

$ Rates (including buffet breakfast): 189 DM–282 DM ($124.70–$186.10) single; 235 DM–365 DM ($155.10–$240.90) double; from 450 DM ($297) suite. DC, MC, V. **Parking:** 18 DM ($11.90).

Making up part of the railway station complex—in fact, right inside it—is the Intercity-Hotel München. However, you shut out that dreary world as soon as you enter its doors. A dignified, traditional lounge greets you. You can unwind in the snug leather-coated bar or enjoy good German cooking in the Bavarian restaurant. The accommodations, all behind soundproof windows and each with its own personality, combine French and art nouveau designs.

KÖNIGSWACHE, Steinheilstrasse 7, D-8000 München 2. Tel. 089/52-20-01. Fax 089/52-32-114. 39 rms. MINIBAR TV TEL **U-Bahn:** U2 to Königsplatz.

$ Rates (including buffet breakfast with champagne): 155 DM–210 DM ($102.30–

$138.60) single; 205 DM–265 DM ($135.30–$174.90) double. MC, V. **Parking:** 18 DM ($11.90).

Though not as regal as its name, the Königswache has much to recommend it. The location, about a 10-minute ride from the Hauptbahnhof and only 2 minutes from the technical university, is between the Stachus and Schwabing—a section of Munich preferred by many clients who find the railway station area dangerous, especially at night. The hospital staff speaks English. Rooms are modern and comfortable, with writing desks. The attractive restaurant serves Korean food, offered by a Korean staff, and the hotel bar is decorated in a cozy, rustic style.

METROPOL, Bayerstrasse 43, D-8000 München 2. Tel. 089/53-07-64. Fax 089/53-28-134. 260 rms (223 with bath). TV TEL **S-Bahn or U-Bahn:** Hauptbahnhof.

$ Rates (including continental breakfast): 130 DM ($85.80) single with shower but no toilet, 145 DM–165 DM ($95.70–$108.90) single with complete bath; 170 DM–200 DM ($112.20–$132) double with shower but no toilet, 230 DM ($151.80) double with complete bath. AE, DC, MC, V. **Parking:** 18 DM ($11.90).

This modern businessperson's hotel stands in the center of Munich, directly across from the Hauptbahnhof. English-speaking receptionists literally roll out the red carpet in the cavernous lobby and reception area. Sleek, contemporary lines and styling attract those who are tired of the rustic and traditional. The guest rooms are furnished in a functional style, with soundproofed windows. The hotel also has a restaurant if you (wisely) don't want to venture out into the railway station area at night.

HOTEL REINBOLD, Adolf-Kolping-Strasse 11, D-8000 München. Tel. 089/59-79-45. Fax 089/59-62-72. 63 rms, 2 suites. A/C MINIBAR TV TEL **S-Bahn or U-Bahn:** Hauptbahnhof stop.

$ Rates (including continental breakfast): 126 DM–196 DM ($83.20–$129.40) single; 236 DM–396 DM ($155.80–$261.40) double; from 425 DM ($280.50) suite. AE, DC, MC, V. **Parking:** 20 DM ($13.20).

A no-nonsense, no-frills hotel, the Reinbold delivers what it promises: a clean, decent room and efficient and polite service. It's right in the heart of Munich, about a three-minute walk from the Hauptbahnhof and only a five-minute stroll from the fair and exhibition site. The rooms are compact and comfortably (but not lavishly) furnished. Room service and babysitting and laundry services are provided.

SPLENDID, Maximilianstrasse 54, D-8000 München 22. Tel. 089/29-66-06. Fax 089/29-131-76. 40 rms (32 with bath), 1 suite. TV TEL **Tram:** 19 or 20.

$ Rates (including buffet breakfast): 140 DM ($92.40) single without bath, 150 DM–215 DM ($99–$141.90) single with bath; 135 DM–240 DM ($89.10–$158.40) double without bath, 195 DM–335 DM ($128.70–$221.10) double with bath; from 390 DM ($257.40) suite. AE, DC, MC, V. **Parking:** Free.

The Splendid is one of the most attractive old-world hotels in Munich. Each room reflects the owner's ability to achieve a harmonious style that evokes the aura of a country home. Room prices are scaled according to size, furnishings, and plumbing, with the higher prices charged only at fair and festival times. On sunny mornings many guests prefer to have breakfast on the paved and trellised patio. Babysitting can be arranged, and room service is provided.

MODERATE

ADRIA, Liebigstrasse 8a, D-8000 München 22. Tel. 089/29-30-81. Fax 089/22-70-15. 47 rms. MINIBAR TV TEL **Tram:** 20.

$ Rates (including buffet breakfast): 120 DM–180 DM ($79.20–$118.80) single; 170 DM–210 DM ($112.20–$138.60) double. No credit cards. **Closed:** Dec 23–Jan 6.

The Adria is a revamped hotel, offering many special appointments that remove it from the ordinary. With red-shaded lamps, global maps behind the reception desk, wood panels, planters of greenery, and Oriental rugs, the lobby sets the stylish contemporary look. The guest rooms are furnished with armchairs or sofas and small desks. Breakfast is served in the garden room, and arrangements can be made for snacks and small meals.

ARISTON, Unsöldstrasse 10, D-8000 München 80. Tel. 089/22-26-91. Fax 089/291-35-95. 61 rms (all with bath or shower). TV TEL **U-Bahn:** U4 or U5 to Lehel.

$ Rates (including buffet breakfast): 130 DM–180 DM ($85.80–$118.80) single; 150 DM–220 DM ($99–$145.20) double. AE, DC, MC, V. **Parking:** 12 DM ($7.90). **Closed:** Jan.

A modern hotel in the center of Munich, not too far from the Haus der Kunst and the Bavarian National Museum, the Ariston is a straightforward, no-frills place. Its rooms are furnished very simply, but a small entryway to each unit allows for greater quiet and privacy.

HOTEL MARK, Senfelderstrasse 12, D-8000 München 2. Tel. 089/55-98-20. Fax 089/559-82-333. 91 rms. A/C MINIBAR TV TEL **S-Bahn or U-Bahn:** Hauptbahnhof stop.

$ Rates (including buffet breakfast): 135 DM–155 DM ($89.10–$102.30) single; 180 DM–210 DM ($118.80–$138.60) double. AE, DC, MC, V. **Parking:** 12 DM ($7.90).

This hotel near the south exit of the Hauptbahnhof should be considered for its comfort and moderate prices. Rebuilt in 1956, it offers serviceable amenities and modern plumbing. The guest rooms are modern and functionally furnished. Breakfast is the only meal served.

INEXPENSIVE

EUROPÄISCHER HOF, Bayerstrasse 31, D-8000 München 2. Tel. 089/55-15-10. Fax 089/55-15-12-22. 153 rms (131 with bath or shower). TEL **S-Bahn or U-Bahn:** Hauptbahnhof.

$ Rates (including buffet breakfast): 85 DM ($56.10) single without bath, 130 DM ($85.80) single with bath or shower; 108 DM ($71.30) double without bath, 160 DM ($105.60) double with bath or shower; AE, DC, MC, V. **Parking:** 12 DM ($7.90).

Ⓢ This nine-floor hotel opposite the Hauptbahnhof was originally built by a group of Catholic sisters (there's even a chapel on the premises). Now run by the Sturzer family, it's one of the best buys in Munich. Many of the accommodations overlook an inner courtyard. A total of 131 rooms contain TVs, and there are minibars in 37 rooms. Most of the rooms are of fair size, with built-in headboards, double-glazed windows, radios, desk tables, sofas, armchairs, coffee tables, luggage racks, and entry-hall wardrobes. Despite its dreary station location, the

---

Ⓕ FROMMER'S COOL FOR KIDS: HOTELS

Holiday Inn Crowne Plaza Munich *(see page 119)* Children under 19 stay free in their parents' room at this well-run chain hotel near the Olympiapark area.

Gästehaus Englischer Garten *(see page 120)* An oasis of calm and tranquility near the Englischer Garten, this ivy-covered villa provides an old-fashioned family atmosphere.

Arabella Olympiapark Hotel München *(see page 121)* Right at Europe's biggest sports and recreation center, this hotel rents many triple rooms—ideal for families.

hotel couldn't be more immaculate; constant dusting, polishing, buffing, and waxing make spring cleaning a year-round activity here.

PENSION AM MARKT, Heiliggeiststrasse 6, D-8000 München 2. Tel. 089/22-50-14. 32 rms (13 with bath). TEL **S-Bahn:** From the Hauptbahnhof, take any S-Bahn train headed for the Marienplatz, a two-stop ride from the station.

$ Rates (including continental breakfast): 58 DM ($38.30) single without bath, 90 DM ($59.40) single with bath; 104 DM ($68.60) double without bath, 150 DM ($99) double with bath. No credit cards. **Parking:** 10 DM ($6.60).

This popular Bavarian hotel with many decorative trappings that reflect the glory of another era stands in the heart of the older section. The hotel is not luxurious, and owner Harald Herrler has wisely maintained a nostalgic decor in the lobby and dining room. Behind his reception desk is a wall of photographs of friends or former guests, including the late Viennese chanteuse Greta Keller. As Mr. Herrler points out, when you have breakfast here, you are likely to find yourself surrounded by opera and concert artists who like to stay here because they're close to the houses in which they perform. The guest rooms are basic modern—small but trim and neat. All units have hot and cold running water, with free use of the corridor baths and toilets.

PENSION BEIM HAUS DER KUNST, Bruderstrasse 4, D-8000 München 22. Tel. 089/22-21-27. 9 rms (none with bath), 1 apt with bath. **U-Bahn:** Lehel.

$ Rates (including breakfast): 90 DM ($59.40) double; 180 DM ($118.80) apt for four. AE. **Parking:** Free on street when available.

Noted for its ideal location near the Englischer Garten, its copious breakfasts, and its warm hospitality, this is one of the most inexpensive and well-run small pensions of Munich. Early reservations are important here. The establishment's apartment contains the only private bath; guests in the other rooms (no singles) must share the facilities in the hallways. Built in 1956, the hotel is low-key and decent.

PENSION DIANA, Altheimer Eck 15, D-8000 München 2. Tel. 089/260-31-07. 17 rms (none with bath). **U-Bahn:** Karlsplatz.

$ Rates (including breakfast): 70 DM–80 DM ($46.20–$52.80) single; 100 DM ($66) double; 120 DM ($79.20) triple; 160 DM ($105.60) quad. AE, MC, V. **Parking:** 17 DM ($11.20).

Set behind a grand stone facade, the Diana occupies a section of what used to be a grand palace in an interesting central district of Munich. There's no elevator, so you'll have to climb a wide baroque staircase to the third floor. There you'll find bright, sunny guest rooms, each with simple but comfortable pinewood furnishings, plus hot and cold running water.

PENSION WESTFALIA, Mozartstrasse 23, D-8000 München 2. Tel. 089/53-03-77. Fax 089/54-39-120. 19 rms (11 with bath). TEL **Bus:** 58 from the Hauptbahnhof.

$ Rates (including buffet breakfast): 60 DM ($39.60) single without bath, 80 DM ($52.80) single with bath; 85 DM ($56.10) double without bath, 95 DM–115 DM ($62.70–$75.90) double with bath. No credit cards. **Parking:** Free on street when available.

Facing the meadow where the annual Oktoberfest takes place, this four-story town house near Goetheplatz is one of the best pensions in Munich, offering immaculately maintained guest rooms, many with TVs. Owner Peter Deitritz speaks English.

SCHWABING

VERY EXPENSIVE

HOLIDAY INN CROWNE PLAZA MUNICH, Leopoldstrasse 194, D-8000 München 40-Schwabing. Tel. 089/38-179-0. Fax 089/38-179-888. 364 rms, 3 suites. A/C MINIBAR TV TEL **Bus:** 54, 85, 143, or 185.

$ Rates: 250 DM–420 DM ($165–$277.20) single; 330 DM–450 DM ($217.80–$297) double; from 550 DM ($363) suite. Buffet breakfast 28 DM ($18.50) extra. Children under 19 stay free in parents' room. AE, DC, MC, V. **Parking:** 19 DM ($12.50).

The Holiday Inn acquainted Munich with this American motel chain. And this one's quite a glamorous introduction. Long a leading Munich hotel, it was created originally to lure business in the year of the Olympics but today touts its position 25 minutes from the new airport. Every room is well furnished, with a queen-size bed (two in doubles). The decor is streamlined, with natural woods and picture windows. Some rooms are reserved for nonsmokers. The inn is near the Olympic area, right at the Autobahn Nürnberg-Berlin-Frankfurt.

Dining/Entertainment: Beside the Old Munich cocktail bar, there's the restaurant Omas Küche or Muhackl, serving both international and Bavarian food.

Services: Room service, babysitting, laundry.

Facilities: Award-winning indoor pool, sauna, solarium, steambath, massage service.

RESIDENCE MÜNCHEN, Artur-Kutscher-Platz 4, D-8000 München 40-Schwabing. Tel. 089/38-17-80. Fax 089/381-78-951. 165 rms, 3 suites. MINIBAR TV TEL **U-Bahn:** U3 to Münchner Freiheit.

$ Rates (including buffet breakfast): 198 DM–290 DM ($130.70–$191.40) single; 274 DM–370 DM ($180.90–$244.20) double; from 480 DM ($316.80) suite. AE, DC, MC, V. **Parking:** 10 DM ($6.60).

A breath of fresh modernity in Schwabing is provided at the eight-floor Residence, a corner honeycomb structure. The lounge is attractive, its vibrant colors intermixed with chalk-white and wood paneling. Color and style are also notable features of the spacious guest rooms, most of which have balconies. Prices are set according to the floor you're assigned—those nearer the ground are cheaper. All rooms have radios.

Dining/Entertainment: You can dine here at the elegant Le Pavillon restaurant, with its glass-globe lighting, bentwood chairs, and filmy white curtains; patronize the cozy bar-restaurant, Die Kutsche (air-conditioned); or meet for drinks in the wood-paneled bar.

Services: Room service, laundry, babysitting.

Facilities: Sauna-style pool, with wall and ceiling of natural pine, subtropical plants, lounge chairs.

MODERATE

GÄSTEHAUS ENGLISCHER GARTEN, Liebergesellstrasse 8, D-8000 München 40-Schwabing. Tel. 089/39-12-33. 27 rms (24 with bath). A/C MINIBAR TV TEL **U-Bahn:** U3 or U6 to Münchner Freiheit.

$ Rates: 98 DM–130 DM ($64.70–$85.80) single without bath, 136 DM–158 DM ($89.80–$104.30) single with bath; 130 DM–140 DM ($85.80–$92.40) double without bath, 148 DM–175 DM ($97.70–$115.50) double with bath. Continental breakfast 6 DM ($4) extra. No credit cards. **Parking:** 8 DM ($5.30).

Among my most preferred stopovers in the Bavarian capital, this oasis of charm and tranquility was named for its proximity to the Englischer Garten. The ivy-covered villa was once the site of a mill. It later became a private villa, but for some two decades now it has been operated as a hotel by Frau Irene Schlüter-Hubscher. All the rooms are attractively furnished, and half of them lie in an annex across the street. Try for room 20, a particular favorite. In fair weather, breakfast is served in a rear garden.

INTERNATIONAL HOTEL, Hohenzollernstrasse 5, D-8000 München 40-Schwabing. Tel. 089/33-30-43. Fax 089/39-80-06. 70 rms (all with bath or shower), 2 suites. TEL **U-Bahn:** U3 or U6 to Münchner Freiheit or Gieslastrasse.

$ Rates (including buffet breakfast): 150 DM ($99) single; 190 DM ($125.40) double; from 220 DM ($145.20) suite. Children 12 and under stay free in parents' room. AE, DC, MC. **Parking:** 10 DM ($6.60).

The International, built in 1968, ranks as one of the best-run little hotels in Schwabing. The owners have created a hospitable environment, with up-to-date comfort. Each of the modern rooms has a radio, a TV, and carpeting, along with a little balcony. The location is only a few steps from Leopoldstrasse, near the Englischer Garten. The U-Bahn station is a five-minute walk from the hotel. A cozy café provides breakfast, and in summer tables are placed out on the sidewalk.

LEOPOLD, Leopoldstrasse 119, D-8000 München 40-Schwabing. Tel. 089/36-70-61. Fax 089/36-70-61. 78 rms. TV TEL **U-Bahn:** U3 or U6 to Münchner Freiheit.

$ Rates (including breakfast): 145 DM–160 DM ($95.70–$105.60) single; 175 DM–215 DM ($115.50–$141.90) double. AE, DC, MC, V. **Parking:** 6 DM ($4).

A unique hotel in a 1924 villa, the Leopold offers a modern annex behind its garden, connected to the main building by a glassed-in passageway. Passing the hotel is the exit road of the Autobahn Nürnberg-Würzburg-Berlin. Think of the Leopold as a kind of motel, with plentiful parking. Two U-Bahn stations are 250 yards away, allowing you access to the city center in about 10 minutes. Finally, the Englischer Garten is only a few minutes away by foot. Most of the public rooms are furnished in Bavarian style. The guest rooms are nicely designed, many with built-in beds and all with armchairs. Whether in the old or new wing (which has an elevator), you'll have doors that have been double soundproofed.

OLYMPIAPARK

EXPENSIVE

ARABELLA OLYMPIAPARK HOTEL MÜNCHEN, Helene-Mayer-Rin 12, D-8000 München. Tel. 089/351-60-71. Fax 089/35-43-730. 105 rms. MINIBAR TV TEL **U-Bahn:** U2 or U3 to Olympia Centrum.

$ Rates (including buffet breakfast): 200 DM ($132) single; 288 DM ($190.10) double; 318 DM ($209.90) triple. AE, DC, MC, V. **Parking:** Free.

Right at Europe's biggest sports and recreation center stands Arabella Olympiapark Hotel München. The hotel is near the stadium, site of so many major sports events. For fitness-minded people who want to be near all the action, it's appealing. Its guest rooms are among the most modern and well kept in the city, and sports heroes, both European and American, casually stroll through the lobby. There's no need to drive into the city center: The U-Bahn will whisk you there in minutes. If you want to unwind after a tough night in the beer halls, you'll find a refreshing pool, a sauna, and a massage room.

HAIDHAUSEN

VERY EXPENSIVE

MÜNCHEN CITY HILTON, Rosenheimerstrasse 15, D-8000 München. Tel. 089/48-04-0, or toll free 800/445-8667 in the U.S. or Canada. Fax 089/48-04-48-04. 480 rms, 22 suites. A/C MINIBAR TV TEL **S-Bahn:** 1, 2, 3, 4, 5, 6, or 7 to Rosenheimer Platz.

$ Rates: 280 DM–440 DM ($184.80–$290.40) single; 495 DM ($326.70) double; from 550 DM ($363) suite. Breakfast 29 DM ($19.10) extra. AE, DC, MC, V. **Parking:** 19 DM ($12.50).

When it opened in 1989, München City Hilton became the second Hilton to grace the Munich skyline. Owned by a Dutch pension fund, it lies beside the Deutsches Museum and the performing arts center, Gasteig. It was designed in a low-rise format of red brick, shimmering glass, and geometric windows divided by white bands of metal reminiscent of a Mondrian painting. The historic center of Munich is an invigorating 25-minute walk across the river. On the premises are a pair of well-designed restaurants, a lobby-level café, a bar, and a staff sensitive to the needs of visitors. The traditional guest rooms contain modern adaptations of Biedermeier furniture, plush carpeting, radios, and cable color TVs.

Dining/Entertainment: The Hilton offers good drinking and dining facilities, including Zum Gasteig, a Bavarian restaurant decorated in a typical style; Löwen-Schanke, a Bavarian pub; and Café Lenbach, where you can order a leisurely breakfast or afternoon tea.

Services: 24-hour room service, laundry, dry cleaning, babysitting.

Facilities: Flower shop, newsstand.

MÜNCHEN PENTA HOTEL, Hochstrasse 3, D-8000 München 80. Tel. 089/4803-0, or toll free 800/448-55-55. Fax 089/448-82-77. 582 rms, 12 suites. A/C MINIBAR TV TEL **S-Bahn:** Rosenheimer Platz.

$ Rates: 270 DM–320 DM ($178.20–$211.20) single; 320 DM–380 DM ($211.20–$250.80) double; from 500 DM ($330) suite. Breakfast 30 DM ($19.80) extra. Weekend rates sometimes available. AE, DC, MC, V. **Parking:** 18 DM ($11.90).

One of the largest hotels in the city is rated four stars by the government. It enjoys a prime location in the city center, a 10-minute walk from Marienplatz. The S-Bahn, which stops at the hotel complex, will whisk you to wherever you're going. The hotel offers attractively furnished guest rooms with first-class comfort, including cable TVs.

Dining/Entertainment: The hotel serves a classic German and a regional Bavarian cuisine, offering three choices for dining: the Gasteig Taverne, Münchner Kindl Stuben, and the Münchner Kindl Bar. The latter has an excellent selection of German beers.

Services: Room service, babysitting, laundry, dry cleaning.

Facilities: Lufthansa check-in counter, Sixt Budget Rent-a-Car agent, indoor pool.

EXPENSIVE

PREYSING, Preysingstrasse 1, D-8000 München 80. Tel. 089/48-10-11. Fax 089/44-70-998. 76 rms, 5 suites. A/C MINIBAR TV TEL **Tram:** 18.

$ Rates (including breakfast): 175 DM–265 DM ($115.50–$174.90) single; 300 DM ($198) double; from 375 DM ($247.50) suite. No credit cards. **Parking:** 19 DM ($12.50). **Closed:** Dec 23–Jan 6.

If you don't mind the inconvenience of a hotel on the outskirts and want a quiet location, one of the best places to stay is the Preysing, across the Isar near the Deutsches Museum. (A short tram ride will whisk you into the center of the city.) When you first view the building, a seven-story modern structure, you may feel I've misled you. However, if you've gone this far, venture inside for a pleasant surprise.

The family who runs it has one of the most thoughtful staffs in Munich. The style of the hotel is most agreeable, with dozens of little extras to provide homelike comfort. Fresh flowers are everywhere, and the furnishings, traditional combined with modern, have been thoughtfully selected. Each room has many amenities.

Dining/Entertainment: Preysing's restaurant is one of the finest in Munich (see "Dining" below).

Services: Room service, laundry, babysitting.

Facilities: Outdoor pool, sauna, solarium, hot whirlpool.

MODERATE

HABIS, Maria-Theresia-Strasse 2A, München 80-Haidhausen. Tel. 089/470-50-71. Fax 089/47-05-101. 25 rms. TV TEL **U-Bahn:** U4 or U5 to Max-Weber-Platz.

$ Rates (including buffet breakfast): 135 DM–150 DM ($89.10–$99) single; 170 DM–190 DM ($112.20–$125.40) double. AE, DC, MC, V.

This small hotel of special character is across from Isarpark overlooking the river; across the bridge are some of Munich's leading museums. The renovated hotel, built on a corner, has five floors of individualized guest rooms and a wine restaurant. Also on the premises is the unusual Komödientheater, where shows are presented nightly except Monday. The hotel's general decor, especially that of the entrance with its curving staircase, is in modified art nouveau. The bedrooms have strong earth colors, with painted built-in pieces, trim beds, casual wicker armchairs, and balloon lights.

BOGENHAUSEN

VERY EXPENSIVE

ARABELLA HOTEL BOGENHAUSEN, Arabellastrasse 5, D-8000 München 81. Tel. 089/9-23-20. Fax 089/923-24-447. 467 rms, 32 suites. A/C MINIBAR TV TEL **Tram:** 18 or 20. **Bus:** 44.
$ Rates (including buffet breakfast): 305 DM–366 DM ($201.30–$241.60) single; 350 DM–476 DM ($231–$314.20) double; from 860 DM ($567.60) suite. AE, DC, MC, V. **Parking:** 25 DM ($16.50).

Situated in the Bogenhausen section, 10 minutes from the city center, the Arabella has a freewheeling contemporary design, with many dramatic public rooms. All of the chic accommodations have radios, color TVs with English-language programs, trouser presses, hairdryers, and balconies. The hotel has good transportation connections and easy access to all major motorways.

Dining/Entertainment: Two hotel restaurants serve Bavarian and international cuisine daily. Meals cost from 45 DM to 75 DM ($29.70 to $49.50).

Services: Room service, laundry, babysitting.

Facilities: Pool on 23rd floor, with waterfall, five whirlpools, three Roman steam baths, two saunas, solariums, health club, palm trees, pool bar.

MÜNCHEN SHERATON, Arabellastrasse 6, D-8000 München. Tel. 089/ 192-26-40, or toll free 800/325-3535. Fax 089/191-68-77. 637 rms, 16 suites. A/C MINIBAR TV TEL **Tram:** 18 or 20. **Bus:** 44.
$ Rates: 282 DM–420 DM ($186.10–$277.20) single; 320 DM–492 DM ($211.20–$324.70) double; from 1,060 DM ($699.60) suite. Breakfast 30 DM ($19.80) extra. AE, DC, MC, V. **Parking:** 18 DM ($11.90).

If you're in Munich on a convention, chances are good that you'll be housed here. In the Bogenhausen section, east of the heart of Munich, this 22-story structure, with attractively furnished guest rooms, opens onto the Englischer Garten. All rooms, many quite large, contain TVs and radios. With so many facilities, it's hardly necessary to leave, but if you do, you'll find bus and tram connections nearby; the center of town is less than 15 minutes away.

Dining/Entertainment: The Sheraton is almost a world unto itself, offering two bars, three restaurants, a beer garden, a coffee shop, and a nightclub where international bands and dance music entertain guests until 4am.

Services: 24-hour room service, laundry, concierge service.

Facilities: Health club, 65-foot pool, solarium, fitness room, sauna, massage parlor, shopping arcade, car-rental agency.

4. DINING

It is said that Münchners consume more beer and food than the people in any other German city. Bernd Boehle once wrote: "If a man really belongs to Munich he drinks beer at all times of the day, at breakfast, at midday, at teatime; and in the evening, of course, he just never stops."

Some of the local fare may frighten the timid. The classic dish of Munich is, of course, Weisswürste, herb-flavored white veal sausages that have been blanched in water. Traditionally, they are consumed before noon. Munich is definitely the place to practice *Edelfresswelle* ("high-class gluttony"). Don't assume, however, that the cuisine is all about ample quantities—outside of Paris and Brussels, Munich is one of the very few European cities that has more than one "three-star" restaurant, and some of its other sophisticated restaurants are considered among the finest anywhere.

CENTRAL MUNICH
VERY EXPENSIVE

A. BOETTNER, Theatinerstrasse 8, off Marienplatz. Tel. 089/22-12-10.
Cuisine: INTERNATIONAL. **Reservations:** Required. **Tram:** 19.
$ **Prices:** Appetizers 12 DM–198 DM ($7.90–$130.70); main courses 56 DM–265 DM ($37–$174.90). AE, DC, MC, V.
Open: Lunch Mon–Sat 11am–4pm; dinner Mon–Fri 6–11pm.

⭐ One of the choicest special restaurants of Munich is tiny and totally intimate—at times everybody seems to know everybody else. It's been run by the same family since 1901. Here you're assured such savory fare as saddle of venison and fried goose liver on a bed of green beans. Lobster is a specialty, and it sometimes appears within a soufflé of pike. For dessert, the chocolate mousse makes a particularly velvety choice. Your tab could skyrocket if you go crazy with the caviar and lobster. The wine cellar is excellent, the relatively unadorned surroundings are pleasant, and the service is polite and skilled. It's for the discriminating gourmet only. The location is within a pedestrian zone, a five-minute walk from the opera.

AUBERGINE, Maximilianplatz 5. Tel. 089/59-81-71.
Cuisine: FRENCH. **Reservations:** Required. **Tram:** 19.
$ **Prices:** Appetizers 39 DM–45 DM ($25.70–$29.70); main courses 50 DM–78 DM ($33–$51.50); fixed-price lunch 175 DM ($115.50); fixed-price dinner 235 DM ($155.10). AE, DC, MC, V.
Open: Lunch Tues–Sat noon–2pm; dinner Tues–Sat 7–11pm. **Closed:** Public holidays, Dec 23–Jan 7.

⭐ Discreet and distinguished, Aubergine is a citadel of fine taste, good food, impeccable service, and lethal tariffs. It's chic, elegant, and fashionable. The noted chef, Austria-born Eckart Witzigmann, studied with the famous Paul Bocuse of Lyons, France. His cuisine is a mixture of classic French dishes along with cuisine moderne offerings. One food expert has divided Germany's gastronomic history into two parts—"before Witzigmann and after." Many experts consider the Aubergine the finest restaurant in Germany today. The great chef told Craig Claiborne of *The New York Times* that "the important things are slow cooking and patience and freshness of ingredients." Sometimes his guests are very special indeed, as when the master prepared a private banquet for King Carl XVI Gustaf of Sweden and his queen.

At lunch you can order a set menu, and at dinner there's an eight-course table d'hôte menu. The set menu is almost invariably good and contains an array of widely varying specialties, including a sorbet served between courses to clear your palate. Menus change daily and can't be written until the owner returns from the market with the freshest of ingredients. You can order à la carte, selecting such tempting treats as sole filet in champagne sauce or crab salad with broccoli in vinaigrette. Many specialties are for two, including venison with wild berries.

KÄFER-SCHÄNKE, Prinzregentenstrasse 73. Tel. 089/416-82-47.
Cuisine: GERMAN/INTERNATIONAL. **Reservations:** Essential. **Bus:** 55.
$ **Prices:** Appetizers 30 DM–40 DM ($19.80–$26.40); main courses 30 DM–60 DM ($19.80–$39.60). AE, DC, MC, V.
Open: Mon–Sat 11:30am–midnight. **Closed:** Holidays.
On the main floor of this famous spot is a deluxe gourmet shop. The decor suggests the home of a wealthy country gentleman, with a few antiques placed here and there.

You select your own hors d'oeuvres from the most dazzling display in Munich and are billed according to how many pâtés or croûtes you make off with. The main dishes are served by waiters. Often Käfer-Schänke features a week devoted to a particular country's cuisine. On one visit I enjoyed the classic loup (sea bass) with fennel as presented on the French Riviera. The salads have what one reviewer called "rococo splendor." From a cold table, you can select such temptations as smoked salmon or smoked eel. Venison, quail, and guinea hen are regularly featured.

LE GOURMET SCHWARZWÄLDER, Hartmannstrasse 8. Tel. 089/212-09-58.
   Cuisine: FRENCH. **Reservations:** Required. **U-Bahn:** U2 or U3 to Marienplatz. **Tram:** 19.
$ **Prices:** Appetizers 28 DM–38 DM ($18.50–$25.10); main courses 42 DM–72 DM ($27.70–$47.50); three-course fixed-price lunch 75 DM ($49.50); seven-course fixed-price dinner 172 DM ($113.50). AE, DC, MC, V.
   Open: Lunch Tues–Sat noon–2pm; dinner Tues–Sat 7–11pm. **Closed:** Dec 23–Jan 7.

⭐ Specializing in cuisine moderne served amid a classical and elegant decor, chef/owner Otto Koch is the motivating force behind the success of this place. He graciously circulates, attending to the well-being of his guests. Your meal might have such outstanding specialties as mushroom cake Le Gourmet with truffle sauce; sautéed goose liver with red cabbage; or rack of lamb roasted in mustard seed. The soufflé café chocolat makes a luscious dessert. A seven-course set dinner is available, but you can spend less by ordering from the à la carte offerings.

SABITZER, Reitmorstrasse 21. Tel. 089/29-85-84.
   Cuisine: FRENCH. **Reservations:** Required. **Tram:** 20. **Bus:** 53.
$ **Prices:** Appetizers 32 DM–43 DM ($21.10–$28.40); main courses 52 DM–58 DM ($34.30–$38.30); seven-course fixed-price dinner 168 DM ($110.90). AE, DC, MC, V. **Closed:** Jan 7–24 and Aug 10–22.

⭐ This gourmet citadel of cuisine moderne also serves classical French specialties. The Austrian head chef, Herwig Sabitzer, made his debut on the Munich restaurant scene in 1981, and within months he was the "talk of the town." Mr. Sabitzer is assisted by his wife, Dorothea, and together they offer seasonal specialties and only the freshest of products, based on the shopping of the day. The menu changes so frequently one hesitates to recommend a specific dish. However, turbot is often cooked en paupiette and salmon in saffron sauce. You can order a fixed-price meal or from an à la carte menu.

EXPENSIVE

GASTHAUS GLOCKENBACH, Kapuzinerstrasse 29. Tel. 089/53-40-43.
   Cuisine: BAVARIAN/FRENCH. **Reservations:** Required. **U-Bahn:** Goetheplatz.
$ **Prices:** Appetizers 15 DM–25 DM ($9.90–$16.50); main courses 35 DM–45 DM ($23.10–$29.70); fixed-price menu 70 DM–110 DM ($46.20–$72.60). MC.
   Open: Lunch Tues–Sat noon–3pm; dinner Tues–Sat 7pm–1am. **Closed:** Dec 24–Jan 2.

Consistently competent traditional cookery is offered here in a half-paneled and vaulted dining room with arched windows. Menu items include skillful preparations of whatever fresh fish was available that day in the marketplace. You might enjoy a potato-and-lettuce salad garnished with strips of grilled salmon, perhaps a flavorful ragoût of freshwater fish, or a confit of goose, followed by an array of tempting desserts.

HALALI, Schonfeldstrasse 22. Tel. 089/28-59-09.
   Cuisine: BAVARIAN. **Reservations:** Recommended. **Tram:** 20. **Bus:** 53.
$ **Prices:** Appetizers 14 DM–30 DM ($9.20–$19.80); main courses 34 DM–48 DM ($22.40–$31.70). AE, MC.
   Open: Mon–Sat 11am–11pm. **Closed:** Holidays.

N

0 ⊏⊏⊏⊏⊏ 250 m
275 y

GERMANY

Munich ⦿

A. Boettner ㉒
Alois Dallmayr ㉑
Aubergine ❺
Austernkeller ㉖
Biergärten Chinesischer
  Turm ㉚
Donisl ⑰
El Toulà ❻
Gaststätte zum
  Flaucher ❶
Goldene Stadt ⑪
Halali ㉔
Haxnbauer ⑳
Hirschgarten ⑫
Hundskugel ⑩
Käfer-Schänke ㉙
Kay's Bistro ⑬
Königshof ❸
Le Gourmet
  Schwarzwälder ❽
Mövenpick Restaurant ❹
Nürnberger Bratwurst
  Glockl am Dom ❾
Palais Keller ❼
Preysing-Keller ㉗
Prinz Myshkin ⑰
Ratskeller München ⑯
Restaurant Vier
  Jahreszeiten ㉕
Sabitzer ㉘
Spatenhaus ㉓
Straubinger Hof ⑭
Weinhaus Neuner ❷
Weinhaus
  Schwarzwälder ❽
Weinstadl ⑲
Weisses Bräuhaus ⑯
Zum Alten Markt ⑮
Zum Bürgerhaus ㉛

5551

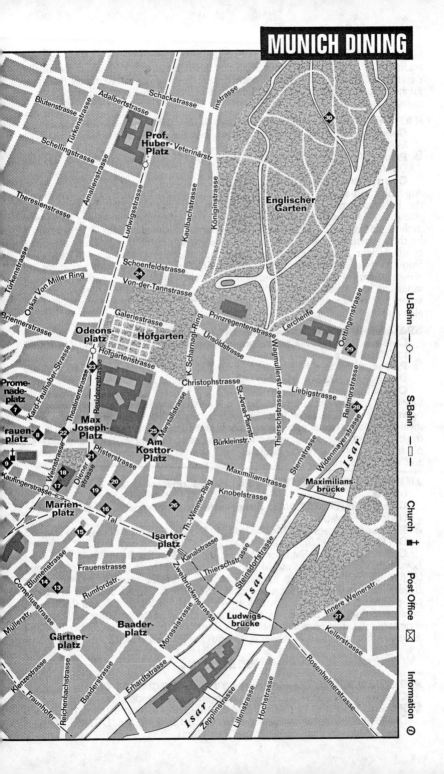

MUNICH DINING

U-Bahn ──◇──

S-Bahn ──□──

Church ∎✝

Post Office ⊠

Information ⊙

Halali can be roughly translated as "tallyho." The huntsman-style decor and the traditions of this old-fashioned charming restaurant are about as authentically Bavarian as anything in Munich. Typical dishes, derived from the Germanic tradition, might include terrine of smoked fish, salad of braised quail, and filets of veal in mustard sauce, plus the kind of desserts that are caloric but tempting.

KAY'S BISTRO, Utzschneiderstrasse 1. Tel. 089/260-35-84.
   Cuisine: FRENCH. **Reservations:** Required. **U-Bahn:** U2 or U3 to Marienplatz.
$ **Prices:** Appetizers 12 DM–30 DM ($7.90–$19.80); main courses 45 DM–50 DM ($29.70–$33). MC.
   Open: Dinner only, daily 7pm–1am.

Arguably the most sophisticated dining rendezvous in the Bavarian capital, Kay's is off the historic market of Munich, the Viktualienmarkt. It's filled nightly with a glamorous (sometimes media-related) clientele that appreciates the value of being seen in the right places. The decoration is changed four or five times a year—perhaps you'll be there when the walls are laden with Hollywood souvenirs. The French-inspired cuisine is light, nouvelle, and avant-garde; many ingredients are shipped in fresh daily from the wholesale food market, Rungis, in Paris. You might on any night be presented with veal cutlets with mango, carpaccio with parmesan, turbot with fresh asparagus in a Riesling sauce, followed with white chocolate mousse with mocha sauce. Kay Wörsching greets his guests personally. A gracious, welcoming host, he is also a magazine columnist.

SPATENHAUS, Residenzstrasse 12. Tel. 089/290-70-60.
   Cuisine: BAVARIAN. **Reservations:** Recommended. **U-Bahn:** U3, U4, or U6 to Odeonsplatz or Marienplatz.
$ **Prices:** Appetizers 16 DM–24 DM ($10.60–$15.80); main courses 30 DM–36 DM ($19.80–$23.80). AE, DC, MC, V.
   Open: Daily 11am–midnight.

One of the best-known beer restaurants in Munich has wide windows overlooking the opera house on Max-Joseph-Platz. Of course, to be loyal, you should accompany your meal with the restaurant's own beer, called Spaten-Franziskaner-Bier. You can choose to sit in the intimate, semiprivate dining nooks or at a big table. The Spatenhaus has old traditions, offering typical Bavarian food, and it is known for its generous portions and reasonable prices.

WEINHAUS SCHWARZWÄLDER, Hartmannstrasse 8. Tel. 089/212-09-79.
   Cuisine: INTERNATIONAL. **Reservations:** Recommended. **U-Bahn:** U2 or U3 to Marienplatz.
$ **Prices:** Appetizers 22 DM–33 DM ($14.50–$21.80); main courses 34 DM–45 DM ($22.40–$29.70). AE, DC, MC.
   Open: Lunch Mon–Sat noon–2:30pm; dinner Mon–Sat 6–11:30pm.

Loyal habitués come to this old Munich wine restaurant to order meals accompanied by fine German wines from an extensive list. From the moment you enter, the atmosphere sets the mood for a fine meal. The menu is international, but in season, game is the specialty prepared with flair by the chef. Freshwater fish and shellfish are other specialties. For dessert, try the walnut parfait with nougat sauce or Viennese-style apple pie. The restaurant lies only a short walk from the Bayerischer Hof and American Express, both of which open onto the Promenadeplatz.

MODERATE

ALOIS DALLMAYR, Dienerstrasse 14. Tel. 089/213-51-00.
   Cuisine: CONTINENTAL. **Reservations:** Recommended. **Tram:** 19.
$ **Prices:** Appetizers 12 DM–28 DM ($7.90–$18.50); main courses 28 DM–46 DM ($18.50–$30.40); fixed-price menu 90 DM ($59.40). AE, DC, MC, V.
   Open: Mon–Fri 9am–midnight, Sat 9am–3pm.

The Fauchon's of Munich is Alois Dallmayr, tracing its history back to 1700. Near the Rathaus, it is perhaps the most famous delicatessen in Germany and one of the most renowned in the world. After walking through it, looking at its tempting array of delicacies from around the globe, you'll think you're lost in a millionaire's supermarket. Dallmayr has been a purveyor to many royal courts.

Here you'll find the most elegant consumers in all of Munich, looking for that "tinned treasure," perhaps Scottish salmon, foie gras, English biscuits, wines and spirits, as well as out-of-season fresh produce.

In the upstairs dining room, the food is a subtle German version of continental cuisine, owing a heavy debt to France. The food array is dazzling, ranging from the best herring and sausages I've ever tasted to such rare treats as perfectly vine-ripened tomatoes flown in from Morocco and papayas from Brazil. The famous French poulet de Bresse, believed by many gourmets to be the finest in the world, is also shipped in. The smoked fish is outstanding. The soups are superb (especially one made with shrimp). If you're dining alone, you might prefer to anchor at the counter instead of a table. The bustling restaurant is crowded at lunchtime.

AUSTERNKELLER, Stollbergstrasse 11. Tel. 089/29-87-87.
   Cuisine: SEAFOOD. **Reservations:** Required. **U-Bahn:** Isartorplatz.
$ Prices: Appetizers 8.50 DM–25 DM ($5.60–$16.50); main courses 32 DM–46 DM ($21.10–$30.40). AE, DC, MC, V.
   Open: Tues–Sun 6pm–1am. **Closed:** Dec 23–26.
The "oyster cellar" of Munich is a delight to both visitors and the local trade. You get the finest oysters and the largest selection in town; many gourmets make an entire meal of raw oysters. Others prefer them elaborately prepared—for example, oysters Rockefeller. A delectable beginning to a meal would be the shellfish platter with fresh oysters as well as mussels, clams, scampi, and sea snails. Or you might begin with one of the excellent soups or cold hors d'oeuvres. French meat specialties are offered, but most guests prefer one of the fish dishes—everything from lobster thermidor to shrimp grilled in the shell. The decor, under a vaulted ceiling, is a kitsch collection of everything from plastic lobsters to old porcelain.

PALAIS KELLER, Palais Montgelas, Promenadeplatz 2. Tel. 089/21-20-990.
   Cuisine: GERMAN. **Reservations:** Recommended. **Tram:** 19.
$ Prices: Appetizers 10 DM–20 DM ($6.60–$13.20); main courses 20 DM–45 DM ($13.20–$29.70). AE, DC, MC, V.
   Open: Daily 11:30am–1am.
Palais Keller lies deep in the cellar of one of Munich's finest hotels, but its prices are easily competitive with those of beer halls and Weinstubes in far less desirable places. You descend a flight of stone steps to reach the massively beamed and wood-sheathed interior of this charming restaurant. Waitresses speak English and wear frilly aprons and genuine smiles. There is a tempting array of such German dishes as veal in sour cream sauce with glazed turnips, cabbage, and carrots; pike balls on buttery leaf spinach with shrimp sauce; and Tafelspitz with vinaigrette sauce. A wide selection of German wines is sold by the bottle or the glass.

RATSKELLER MÜNCHEN, Im Rathaus, Marienplatz 8. Tel. 089/22-03-13.
   Cuisine: BAVARIAN. **Reservations:** Required. **U-Bahn:** U2 or U3 to Marienplatz.
$ Prices: Appetizers 12.50 DM–18.50 DM ($8.30–$12.20); main courses 15 DM–31 DM ($9.90–$20.50); fixed-price menus 32 DM–42 DM ($21.10–$27.70). AE, MC, V.
   Open: Daily 9am–midnight.
Throughout Germany you'll find "Ratskellers," traditional cellar restaurants in Rathaus basements, serving inexpensive good food and wine. The decor is much what

you'd expect: lots of dark wood and carved chairs. The most interesting tables, the ones staked out by the in-the-know locals, are the semiprivate dining nooks in the rear, under the vaulted painted ceilings. Bavarian music adds to the ambience. The menu is a showcase of regional fare, but it also includes some international dishes. A freshly made soup of the day is always featured, and you can help yourself from the salad bar.

WEINHAUS NEUNER, Herzogspitalstrasse 8. Tel. 089/260-39-54.
   Cuisine: BAVARIAN. **Reservations:** Recommended. **U-Bahn:** U4 to Stachus.
$ **Prices:** Appetizers 14 DM–28 DM ($9.20–$18.50); main courses 28 DM–39 DM ($18.50–$25.70). AE, DC, MC.
   Open: Lunch Tues–Sat noon–2pm; dinner Mon–Sat 6pm–1am.

This is an *Altestes Weinhaus Münchens* divided into two parts. Its history dates back to the end of the 15th century, and it is the only building in Munich that has its original Tyrolean vaults. Once young priests were educated here, but after secularization by Napoleon the place became a wine tavern and a meeting place for artists, writers, and composers, including Richard Wagner. Its rooms have been renovated and its paintings restored.

The less expensive place to dine in is the casual Weinstube, with lots of local atmosphere, where you can order typical Bavarian dishes. The restaurant, on the other hand, is elegant with candles and flowers. The chef makes a happy marriage between cuisine moderne and regional specialties.

ZUM ALTEN MARKT, Am Viktualienmarkt, Dreifaltigkeitsplatz 3. Tel. 089/29-99-95.
   Cuisine: BAVARIAN/INTERNATIONAL. **Reservations:** Recommended. **U-Bahn:** U2 or U3 to Marienplatz. **Bus:** 52.
$ **Prices:** Appetizers 15 DM–21 DM ($9.90–$13.90); main courses 30 DM–40 DM ($19.80–$26.40). No credit cards.
   Open: Lunch Mon–Sat noon–2pm; dinner Mon–Sat 6–10pm.

Snug and cozy, Zum Alten Markt serves beautifully presented fresh cuisine at a good price. Located on a tiny square just off the large outdoor food market of Munich, the restaurant has a mellow charm, and the welcome is from its owner, Josef Lehner. The interior decor, with its intricately coffered wooden ceiling, came from a 400-year-old Tyrolean castle that was torn down. In summer, there are outside tables. Fish and fresh vegetables come from the nearby market. You might begin with a tasty homemade soup, such as cream of carrot, or perhaps black-truffle tortellini in cream sauce with young onions and tomatoes. The chef makes some of Munich's best Tafelspitz (the elegant boiled beef dish so beloved by Emperor Franz Josef of Austria). You can also order such classic dishes as Bavarian goose and roast suckling pig.

INEXPENSIVE

DONISL, Weinstrasse 1. Tel. 089/22-01-84.
   Cuisine: BAVARIAN/INTERNATIONAL. **Reservations:** Recommended. **U-Bahn:** U2 or U3 to Marienplatz.
$ **Prices:** Appetizers 5 DM–10 DM ($3.30–$6.60); main courses 9.80 DM–26.50 DM ($6.50–$17.50). AE, DC, MC, V.
   Open: Daily 8am–12:30am.

Donisl is reputedly the oldest beer hall in Munich, dating from 1715. Some readers praise this Munich-style restaurant as gemütlich, with its relaxed and comfortable atmosphere. Seating capacity is about 350, and in summer one can enjoy the hum and bustle of Marienplatz while dining in the garden area out front. The restaurant has two levels, the second of which is a gallery. English is spoken. The standard menu offers traditional Bavarian food as well as a daily-changing specials menu. Specialties include Weisswürste, the little white sausages that have been a tradition of this place for decades. Or perhaps try the Bavarian meatloaf (Leberkäs), grilled sausages, or a traditional Sauerbraten. Select beers from Munich's own Hacker-Pschorr Brewery top the evening. A zither player at noon and an accordion player in the evening entertain the guests.

HAXNBAUER, Münzstrasse 8. Tel. 089/22-19-22.

Cuisine: GERMAN. **Reservations:** Not necessary. **U-Bahn:** U2 or U3 to Marienplatz.

$ Prices: Appetizers 5.50 DM–16 DM ($3.60–$10.60); main courses 12.50 DM–26 DM ($8.30–$17.20); fixed-price menus 32 DM–48 DM ($21.10–$31.70). AE, DC, MC, V.

Open: Daily 11am–midnight.

More than 100 years in the same family, this restaurant could get by on atmosphere alone. One of the most typical Bavarian restaurants in Munich, with a devoted following, it offers a choice of dining rooms. A specialty is Radi mit Hausgeräuchertem Schinken—razor-thin slices of ham with white radishes and chive bread, a traditional appetizer. Other specialties of the house are Schweinhaxen and Kalbshaxen (pork or veal shank), priced according to weight; you can also order Truthahnhaxen (turkey shank). They are spit roasted, the skin cooked to a crusty brown. The meat or poultry is guaranteed fresh, as the restaurant has its own butcher. For dessert, the chef's pride is Apfelkucherl flambé.

NÜRNBERGER BRATWURST GLÖCKL AM DOM, Frauenplatz 9. Tel. 089/22-03-85.

Cuisine: BAVARIAN. **Reservations:** Not necessary. **U-Bahn:** U2 or U3 to Marienplatz.

$ Prices: Appetizers 5 DM–10 DM ($3.30–$6.60); main courses 16 DM–30 DM ($10.60–$19.80). No credit cards.

Open: Daily 9am–midnight.

In the coziest and warmest of Munich's local restaurants, you sit in chairs that look as if they came from some carver's shop in the Black Forest, among memorabilia that includes pictures, prints, pewter, and beer steins. The restaurant first opened in 1893 but had to be rebuilt after an allied bombing raid at the close of World War II. It stands near one of the most famous Munich churches, Frauenkirche. Upstairs, reached through a hidden stairway, is a dining room decorated with reproductions of Dürer prints. The restaurant has a strict policy of shared tables, and service is on tin plates. The homesick Nürnberger comes here just for one dish: Nürnberger Schweinwurstl mit Kraut—those delectable little sausages. A short walk from Marienplatz, the restaurant faces the cathedral.

STRAUBINGER HOF, Blumenstrasse 5. Tel. 089/260-8444.

Cuisine: GERMAN. **Reservations:** Recommended.

$ Prices: Appetizers 3.50 DM–6.50 DM ($2.30–$4.30); main courses 13.80 DM–25 DM ($9.10–$16.50). AE, MC.

Open: Mon–Fri 9am–9:30pm (last food order), Sat 9am–3pm. **Closed:** Sun, holidays, and Aug 25–Sept 10.

One of the most traditional restaurants in the Viktualienmarkt district serves heaping portions of such perennial favorites as Weisswurst, Blutwurst and Leberwurst, roast pork, veal knuckles with potatoes and sauerkraut, and Tafelspitz (boiled beef). Beer, either light or dark, arrives in foaming steins.

WEINSTADL, Burgstrasse 5. Tel. 089/523-27-01.

Cuisine: GERMAN. **Reservations:** Required. **U-Bahn:** U2 or U3 to Marienplatz.

$ Prices: Appetizers 6.50 DM–22 DM ($4.30–$14.50); main courses 10 DM–30 DM ($6.60–$19.80). No credit cards.

Open: Mon–Sat 11am–11:15pm, Sun 5–11:15pm.

A Weinhaus since 1850 and reputedly the oldest in Munich, Weinstadl was built in 1551 for use as a municipal wine cellar. Real old-world charm is to be found here: vaulted ceilings, a trompe l'oeil facade, and wrought-iron sconces. Dining is on three levels. Hearty Bavarian food and Palatinate wines are served; especially hearty is the bean soup with ham. A typical main dish is roast pork with potato dumplings and mixed salad. Watch for the daily specials. The beer garden is popular in summer.

WEISSES BRÄUHAUS, Tal 10. Tel. 089/29-98-75.
   Cuisine: BAVARIAN. **Reservations:** Recommended, especially for back room.
   U-Bahn: U2 or U3 to Marienplatz.
$ **Prices:** Appetizers 6.20 DM–8.90 DM ($4.10–$5.90); main courses 10 DM–25 DM ($6.60–$16.50). AE, DC, MC, V.
   Open: Daily 9am–midnight.
In the heart of the city, Weisses Bräuhaus is big, bustling, and Bavarian with a vengeance. Not for the pretentious, this informal place does what it has for centuries: serves home-brewed beer. At one time the famous salt trade route between Salzburg and Augsburg passed by its door, and salt traders were very thirsty back then.

In a world of smoke-blackened dark-wood paneling and stained glass, the front room is for drinking and informal eating; the back room has white tablecloths and black-outfitted waiters, and you can sample typical Bavarian dishes. Begin with smoked filet of trout or rich-tasting potato soup, then try roast pork with noodles and sauerkraut or Viennese veal Gulasch with mushrooms and cream sauce. You'll invariably share your table, but that's part of the fun here.

SCHWABING

This district of Munich, which used to be called "Bohemian," overflows with restaurants, some of them cheap, attracting a youthful clientele. Evening is the best time for a visit.

VERY EXPENSIVE

TANTRIS, Johann-Fichte-Strasse 7, Schwabing. Tel. 089/36-20-61.
   Cuisine: FRENCH/INTERNATIONAL. **Reservations:** Required. **U-Bahn:** U6 to Dietlindenstrasse.
$ **Prices:** Appetizers 28 DM–62 DM ($18.50–$40.90); main courses 52 DM–82 DM ($34.30–$54.10); five-course fixed-price lunch 152 DM ($100.30); eight-course fixed-price dinner 200 DM ($132). AE, DC, MC, V.
   Open: Lunch Tues–Fri noon–3pm; dinner Mon–Sat 6:30pm–1am. **Closed:** Public holidays; annual holidays in Jan and May.

 **FROMMER'S SMART TRAVELER:
RESTAURANTS**

1. Some of the great restaurants of Munich offer fixed-price luncheons at such reasonable prices that the kitchen actually loses money.
2. Select set luncheons or dinners when offered—many represent at least a 30% savings over à la carte menus.
3. Look for the daily specials on any à la carte menu. They're invariably fresh, and often carry a lower price tag than regular à la carte listings.
4. Drink the house wine served in a carafe—it's only a fraction of the price of bottled wine.

★ Tantris serves some of the finest cuisine in Munich. The setting is unlikely—near the Holiday Inn and gas station—but once you're inside, you're transported into an ultramodern atmosphere with fine service. Many leading members of Munich's business colony like to entertain here.

The food is a treat to the eye as well as the palate, with especially interesting soups. The choice of dishes is wisely limited, and the cooking is both subtle and original, the beautiful interior adding to one's enjoyment. There's an eight-course menu that changes daily, plus a five-course table d'hôte, served at noon. You might begin with a terrine of smoked fish served with green cucumber sauce, then follow with classic roast duck on mustard-seed sauce or perhaps a delightful concoction of lobster medallions on black noodles.

EXPENSIVE

BISTRO TERRINE, Amalienstrasse 89. Tel. 089/28-17-80.
   Cuisine: FRENCH. **Reservations:** Required. **Tram:** 18. **Bus:** 53.
$ **Prices:** Appetizers 8.50 DM–34 DM ($5.60–$22.40); main courses 38 DM–50 DM ($25.10–$33); fixed-price lunch 45 DM ($29.70); fixed-price dinner 106 DM ($70). AE, MC.
   Open: Lunch Mon–Sat noon–1:45pm; dinner Mon–Sat 6:30–10:30pm.
   Closed: Jan 1–7.
Bistro Terrine has an inviting outdoor terrace where you might like to sit in warm weather. Locals, however, request a table in the art nouveau interior, even in summer. This is a popular bistro where small tables are set between high-ceilinged walls festooned with old mirrors, tassel-bottomed lamps, and turn-of-the-century bric-a-brac. The chef uses the freshest possible ingredients in his French-inspired cuisine moderne. Menu items vary, depending on the season and the day's shopping. Few guests are able to resist the tempting light desserts.

MODERATE

PARAISO ESPAÑOL, Schraudolphstrasse 24. Tel. 089/272-24-39.
   Cuisine: SPANISH. **Reservations:** Recommended. **Tram:** 18. **U-Bahn:** U6 to Josephsplatz.
$ **Prices:** Appetizers 9.50 DM–15 DM ($6.30–$9.90); main courses 25 DM–31 DM ($16.50–$20.50). No credit cards.
   Open: Dinner only, Mon–Sat 6–11pm (last order).

 FROMMER'S COOL FOR KIDS: RESTAURANTS

Tower Restaurant, Olympiapark (see page 138) For a spectacular view of the Alps as well as the Olympic grounds, take your kid here to dine and later out onto one of the observation platforms.

Nürnberger Bratwurst Glöckl am Dom (see page 131) Hot dogs will never taste the same again after your child has tried one of those delectable little sausages from Nürnberg.

Café Glockenspiel (see page 138) Your kid can down delectable Bavarian pastries while enjoying the miniature "tournament" staged each day by the clock on the Rathaus facade.

Its cuisine and wines celebrate a land that has always intrigued Müncheners—Spain. Within a carefully decorated interior ringed with mirrors and murals of the pueblo villages of central Spain, you can enjoy an array of Iberian specialties. These include paella; gambas à la plancha; cordera asado; clams in green sauce; and a wide array of seafood.

INEXPENSIVE

WEINBAUER, Fendstrasse 5. Tel. 089/39-81-55.
   Cuisine: BAVARIAN. **Reservations:** Recommended. **U-Bahn:** U6 to Münchener Freiheit.
$ Prices: Appetizers 6 DM–8 DM ($4–$5.30); main courses 17 DM–30 DM ($11.20–$19.80). No credit cards.
   Open: Thurs–Tues 11:30am–11:30pm.

Just off Leopoldstrasse is one of the preferred budget favorites in the area. It's a rather small Gaststätte full of students and smoke. No glossy accessories are found here, just wood tables and passable food. Generous platters range from a Wurst and Leberwurst (liver sausage) platter to a filet steak. Try the pepper steak or Wiener Schnitzel, washed down with half a liter of beer costing 3.40 DM ($2.20).

HAIDHAUSEN
EXPENSIVE

PREYSING-KELLER, Innere-Wiener-Strasse 6. Tel. 089/48-10-15.
   Cuisine: GERMAN/INTERNATIONAL. **Reservations:** Recommended. **Tram:** 18.
$ Prices: Appetizers 18 DM–32 DM ($11.90–$21.10); main courses 32 DM–46 DM ($21.10–$30.40); fixed-price menu 120 DM ($79.20). No credit cards.
   Open: Dinner only, daily 6pm–1am.

Preysing-Keller is a "find," but you have to cross the Isar to discover its superb cookery and wines. It's connected to the Hotel Preysing, already previewed.
   You'll dine in a 300-year-old cellar, with massive beams and high masonry arches; the decor is simple, with wooden tables and chairs. Daily market excursions are made by the staff, who are told to select only the freshest ingredients. The fish and seafood are stored in aquariums on the premises prior to cooking. The goose-liver pâté is a specialty, as is lobster in butter sauce and steak tartare of venison. In addition to original recipes, the chef prepares old-fashioned Bavarian dishes.

SPECIALTY DINING
HOTEL DINING
Very Expensive

RESTAURANT KÖNIGSHOF, in the Hotel Königshof, Karlsplatz 25 (Am Stachus). Tel. 089/55-13-60.
   Cuisine: INTERNATIONAL. **Reservations:** Required. **Tram:** 11. **S-Bahn:** S3, S7, or S8 to Karlsplatz.
$ Prices: Appetizers 24 DM–38 DM ($15.80–$25.10); main courses 45 DM–75 DM ($29.70–$49.50); fixed-price menus 120 DM ($79.20) and 142 DM ($93.70). AE, DC, MC, V.
   Open: Lunch daily noon–3pm; dinner daily 6:30–11pm.

The owners of this deluxe hotel (already reviewed) want the Königshof to surface near the top in sophisticated culinary delights. The Geisel family has made major renovations to the dining room, with its oyster-white panels of oak, polished bronze chandeliers, silver candelabra, and porcelain. The black-jacketed waiters in long white aprons are polite and skilled. Chef Wolfgang Abrell is both inventive and creative. His "culinary masterpieces" depend on his whim of the moment and, almost as important, upon what is available in season. He likes extremely fresh ingredients, and the food here reflects his passion. Perhaps you'll get to try his foie gras with sauternes, lobster soufflé, loin of lamb with fine herbes, lobster with vanilla butter, or sea bass suprême.

RESTAURANT VIER JAHRESZEITEN, in the Hotel Vier Jahreszeiten, Maximilianstrasse 17. Tel. 089/23-03-90.
  Cuisine: FRENCH. **Reservations:** Required. **Tram:** 19.
  $ Prices: Appetizers 30 DM–40 DM ($19.80–$26.40); main courses 42 DM–49 DM ($27.70–$32.30); seven-course fixed-price menu 120 DM ($79.20). AE, DC, MC, V.
  Open: Lunch Tues–Fri and Sun noon–3pm; dinner daily 6pm–midnight. **Closed:** Aug to mid-Sept.

The Restaurant Vier Jahreszeiten is in a quiet and elegant location within walking distance of the opera house. The atmosphere is dignified and refined, the service extremely competent, and the food prepared along classic French lines, with many imaginative variations. Appetizers are likely to include mushroom soufflé served with artichoke cream sauce, freshly made vegetable soup flavored with pesto, or turbot encased in basil-flavored crust. For a main course, you might try breast of Bresse chicken with scampi, flavored with a ginger sauce, or roast medallions of venison with cherry-pepper sauce. Another main dish specialty is blanquette of veal and lobster. Desserts include such specialties as strawberries Walterspiel, or, for two, tangerine soufflé served with foamy vanilla sauce.

LOCAL FAVORITES
Moderate

ZUM BÜRGERHAUS, Pettenkoferstrasse 1. Tel. 089/59-79-09.
  Cuisine: BAVARIAN/FRENCH. **Reservations:** Required. **S-Bahn:** Sendlinger Tor.
  $ Prices: Appetizers 12 DM–26 DM ($7.90–$17.20); main courses 27 DM–50 DM ($17.80–$33); fixed-price lunch 34 DM ($22.40); fixed-price dinner 68 DM–78 DM ($44.90–$51.50). DC, MC, V.
  Open: Mon–Fri noon–midnight, Sat 6pm–midnight.

Zum Bürgerhaus dates from 1827 and has furnishings typical of that era. Little known to visitors, it has a loyal German patronage attracted to its good home-style cookery. There are about two dozen tables seating about 65 diners, and this place can really fill up.

Inexpensive

HUNDSKUGEL, Hotterstrasse 18. Tel. 089/26-42-72.
  Cuisine: BAVARIAN. **Reservations:** Required. **U-Bahn:** U2 or U3 to Marienplatz.
  $ Prices: Appetizers 5.50 DM–7.50 DM ($3.60–$5); main courses 15.80 DM–38 DM ($10.40–$25.10). No credit cards.
  Open: Daily 11am–11pm.

Reportedly the oldest tavern in the city, Hundskugel dates back to 1440. Built in an alpine style, it is within easy walking distance of Marienplatz. Perhaps half the residents of Munich at one time or another have made their way here to be wined and dined in style. The cookery is honest Bavarian with no pretensions. Though the chef makes a specialty of Spanferkel, or roast suckling pig with potato noodles, you might prefer Tafelspitz in dill sauce or roast veal stuffed with goose liver. To begin, try one of the hearty soups, made fresh daily.

CONTINENTAL FAVORITES
Expensive

EL TOULÀ, Sparkassenstrasse 5. Tel. 089/29-28-69.
  Cuisine: ITALIAN. **Reservations:** Required. **U-Bahn:** U2 or U3 to Marienplatz.
  Bus: 52.

$ Prices: Appetizers 15.50 DM–32.50 DM ($10.20–$21.50); main courses 38 DM–45 DM ($25.10–$29.70); fixed-price lunch 55 DM ($36.30); fixed-price dinner 125 DM ($82.50). AE, DC, MC, V.
Open: Lunch Tues–Sat noon–2pm; dinner Tues–Sat 7pm–1am.
Closed: First 3 weeks in Aug.

This elegant restaurant, serving Italian haute cuisine, is one of the finest links in a chain that stretches from Rome to Tokyo. The turn-of-the-century decor, with wickered bentwood chairs, features a work of the well-known artist Dudovic, called *Woman with Hound.* All pasta is homemade on the premises, and the fish and meat specialties use only the freshest ingredients. The cookery style ranges from the cuisine of Piedmont to Lombardy, with a stopover in Venice. Care is taken with the vegetables, and desserts are luscious. Prices are a bit luscious as well. A business lunch is offered, and there's a six-course fixed-price dinner.

PICNIC FARE & WHERE TO EAT IT

There is no better place in all of Germany to get the makings for an elegant picnic than at **Alois Dallmayr** (see previous recommendation). Its selection of foodstuff—much of it prepared and ready to go—includes delectable sausages, wines, grilled chicken, and pastries. You can find less expensive picnic fare at one of the major department stores, such as **Hertie** across from the Hauptbahnhof, or **Kaufhof,** at the Marienplatz.

Another good place to obtain picnic supplies is **Viktualienmarkt,** the famous open-air market of Munich, a tradition since the early 19th century. Here you can stock up on cakes, pastries, wine, fresh fruit and vegetables, sausages, freshly baked breads, and the like.

Head for the **Englischer Garten,** preferably away from the nude sunbathers, and enjoy your afternoon delight.

DINING WITH A VIEW

Try the **Tower Restaurant** at Olympiapark (see recommendation below). It has perhaps the finest view of any restaurant in Bavaria.

VEGETARIAN

Moderate

PRINZ MYSHKIN, Hackenstrasse 2. Tel. 089/26-55-96.
Cuisine: VEGETARIAN. **Reservations:** Not necessary. **U-Bahn:** U2 or U3 to Marienplatz.
$ Prices: Appetizers 10 DM–15 DM ($6.60–$9.90); main courses 17 DM–27 DM ($11.20–$17.80); fixed-price lunch 15 DM ($9.90). No credit cards.
Open: Mon–Thurs 11am–midnight, Fri–Sat 11am–1am.

This is one of the better-known vegetarian restaurants in Munich, certainly one of the most centrally located, near the Marienplatz. You can enjoy freshly made crisp salads here, then follow perhaps with a vegetarian main dish. Pizza is the most popular item on the menu. Wine is also sold, but not beer.

BEER GARDENS

If you're in Munich anytime between the first sunny spring day and the last fading light of a Bavarian-style autumn, you might head for one of the city's celebrated beer gardens (Biergarten). Traditionally, beer gardens were tables placed under chestnut trees planted above the storage cellars to keep beer cool in summer. People, naturally, started to drink close to the source of their pleasure, and the tradition has remained.

Lids on beer steins, incidentally, were meant to keep out flies. It is estimated that today Munich has at least 400 beer gardens and cellars. Food, drink, and atmosphere are much the same in all of them.

BAMBERGER HAUS, Brunnerstrasse 2. Tel. 089/308-89-66.

In a century-old house northwest of Schwabing at the edge of Luitpold Park, Bamberger Haus is named after the city most noted for the quantity of its beer drinking. Most visitors head for the street-level restaurant. Bavarian and international specialties include well-seasoned soups, grilled steak, veal, pork, and sausages. If you want only to drink, you might visit the rowdier and less expensive beer hall in the cellar. Meals begin at 35 DM ($23.10) each, and beer starts at 5.50 DM ($3.60).

Open: Restaurant, daily noon–midnight; beer hall, daily 6pm–1am. AE, MC.

BIERGÄRTEN CHINESISCHER TURM, Englischer Garten 3. Tel. 089/39-50-28.

⭐ My favorite is in the Englischer Garten, the park lying between the Isar River and Schwabing. The biggest city-owned park in Europe, it has several beer gardens, of which the Biergärten Chinesischer Turm is preferred. It is the largest and most popular of its kind in Europe, taking its name from its location at the foot of a pagodalike tower, a landmark that is easy to find. Beer and Bavarian food, and plenty of it, are what you get here. A large glass or mug of beer (ask for *ein Mass Bier*), enough to bathe in, costs 9 DM ($5.90). It will likely be slammed down, still foaming, by a server carrying 12 other tall steins as well. Food is very cheap, with a simple meal costing from 15 DM ($9.90). Homemade dumplings are often a specialty, as are all kinds of tasty sausage. You can get a first-rate Schweinbraten (a braised loin of pork served with a potato dumpling and rich brown gravy), which is Bavaria's answer to the better-known Sauerbraten of the north. Leberknödl is classic, served in a broth with fresh chives. Huge baskets of pretzels are passed around, and they are eaten with radi, the large, tasty white radishes famous in these parts. Oompah bands often play, and it's most festive.

Open: May–Oct, daily 10am–midnight. MC, V.

GASTSTÄTTE ZUM FLAUCHER, Isarauen 1. Tel. 089/72-32-677.

If you're going to the zoo, which I'll recommend later, you might want to stop over for fun and food at the Gaststätte zum Flaucher, which is close by. "Gaststätte" tells you that it's a typical Bavarian inn. This one is mellow and traditional, with tables set in a tree-shaded garden overlooking the river. Here you can order the local specialty, Leberkäse, which many foreigners mistakenly think is "liver cheese." It's neither— rather, a large loaf of sausage eaten with black bread and plenty of mustard, a deli delight. Beer costs 9 DM ($5.90) for a large mug, and the most expensive platter of food goes for 16 DM ($10.60). Full meals range from 15 DM to 28 DM ($9.90 to $18.50).

Open: May–Oct, daily 10am–10pm; Nov–Apr, Fri–Tues 10am–10pm. No credit cards.

HIRSCHGARTEN, Hirschgartenstrasse 1. Tel. 089/17-25-91.

In the Nymphenburg Park sector (near one of Munich's leading sightseeing attractions, Schloss Nymphenburg), west of the heart of the town, this beer garden is part of a 500-acre park with hunting lodges and lakes. This is the largest open-air restaurant in Munich, seating some 8,000 beer drinkers and Bavarian merrymakers. Full meals cost from 18 DM to 42 DM ($11.90 to $27.70). A 1-liter stein of Augustiner tap beer goes for 9 DM ($5.90).

Open: Daily 10:30am–11pm. MC, V. **Tram:** Romanplatz. **S-Bahn:** Laim.

ZUM AUMEISTER, Sondermeierstrasse 1. Tel. 089/32-52-24.

If you're motoring, you might visit a hunting lodge that was once owned by the kings of Bavaria. It's Zum Aumeister, which lies off the Frankfurter Ring at

München-Freimann. It offers a daily list of seasonal Bavarian specialties, and you might end up with cream of cauliflower soup or perhaps a rich oxtail. Meals range from 16 DM to 40 DM ($10.60 to $26.40). Beer costs 9 DM ($5.90).

Open: Tues–Sun 10am–10pm. AE, DC, MC, V.

CAFÉS & PASTRIES

CAFÉ EXTRABLATT, Leopoldstrasse 7, Schwabing. Tel. 089/33-33-33.
Very much like a Parisian café, it's complete with Piaf recordings, bentwood chairs, and a wide terrace. Operated by Michael Grater, a well-known newspaper columnist, the café offers drinks or open-air dining. Light meals cost from 12 DM ($7.90), drinks from 5 DM ($3.30), and beer from 5 DM ($3.30). Inside, you can admire the photo gallery of celebrities.

Open: Mon–Fri 7am–midnight, Sat 9am–1am, Sun 9am–midnight.

CAFÉ GLOCKENSPIEL, Marienplatz 28. Tel. 089/26-42-56.
About 10:30am or before (to make sure you have a good seat), head for the Café Glockenspiel, right in the heart of Munich. From there you can watch the miniature tournament staged each day by the clock on the Rathaus facade. In addition to its view, the café has good coffee, which costs from 3.50 DM ($2.30). Pastries begin at 4.40 DM ($2.90).

Open: Daily 8:30am–8pm.

CAFÉ LUITPOLD, Briennerstrasse 11. Tel. 089/29-28-65.
Opened in 1888, in its day it attracted such notables as Ibsen, Kandinsky, Johann Strauss the Younger, and other great musicians, authors, and artists as well as members of the royal court of Bavaria. Rebuilt after World War II, it's a favorite rendezvous with Münchners, who enjoy its whipped-cream pastries, costing from 5.50 DM ($3.60). Coffee goes for about 4 DM ($2.60). A fixed-price menu is offered for 15 DM ($9.90).

Open: Mon–Fri 9am–8pm, Sat 8am–7pm.

DINING COMPLEXES

MÖVENPICK RESTAURANT   A lot of Swiss gastronomic know-how has been poured into the **Mövenpick Restaurant,** Im Künstlerhaus, Lenbachplatz 8 (tel. 089/55-78-65), a cluster of five different dining spots in a historic building that used to be called "the house of the artists," where the literary elite once gathered for coffee. Posted at the door is a menu bulletin for each of the restaurants. In summer the terrace, seating 250, is one of the most popular rendezvous places in Munich. Depending on which restaurant you select, meals can range from 18 DM to 42 DM ($11.90 to $27.70). Open daily from 10am to midnight. Take the U-Bahn 4 or 5 to Stachus. Credit cards: AE, DC, MC, V.

AT THE OLYMPIC GROUNDS   A choice of dining experiences is offered at the **Olympia Tower,** Olympiapark (tel. 089/3067-2818). The television tower, open daily from 9am to midnight, is 950 feet tall, making it one of the most visible buildings on the Munich skyline. A combined ticket for a tour of the park and a ride up the tower, the speediest elevator on the Continent, costs 7 DM ($4.60) for adults and 4 DM ($2.60) for children below 15.

The most expensive dining spot is the **Tower Restaurant,** featuring a selection of French and German dishes. Food is served daily from 11am to 5:30pm and 6:30pm to midnight. A complete dinner costs between 62 DM and 75 DM ($40.90 to $49.50). Before or after dinner, you'll want to take in the view, which reaches to the Alps. Four observation platforms look out over the Olympiapark. The Tower Restaurant revolves

- Munich is called "the secret capital" of Germany.
- The city officially dates from 1158, but a document from C.E. 777 mentions the settlement.
- Ludwig III, the last Bavarian king, abdicated in November 1918, at the close of World War I.
- It took just 70 Allied air raids in World War II to reduce Munich to rubble.
- The average Münchner drinks 35 gallons of beer—"liquid bread"—per year.
- One of Germany's oldest inhabitants rests in the Deutsches Museum—the fossil of a 140-million-year-old ichthyosaur.
- The neoclassical buildings constructed during the reign of Ludwig I earned for Munich the title of "Isar Athens."
- The famed Hofbräuhaus beer hall of Munich was once a battleground between Hitler's German Workers Party and other Bavarians.
- Germany's greatest artist wrote an inscription under his *Self-Portrait* in the Alte Pinakothek: "Thus I, Albrecht Dürer from Nürnberg, painted myself in imperishable colors at the age of 28."

around its axis in 36, 53, or 70 minutes, giving the guests who linger a changing vista of the entire Olympic grounds. Credit cards: AE, DC, MC, V.

At the base of the tower is the **Am Olympiasee,** Spiridon-Louis-Ring 7 (tel. 089/306-13-309), serving genuine Bavarian specialties, with meals costing from 18 DM ($11.90). Favored items include half a roast chicken and various hearty soups, and food is served daily from 9:30am to 7pm (until 9pm in summer). The restaurant is popular in summer because of its terrace. No credit cards are accepted. Take the U-Bahn to Olympiazentrum.

5. ATTRACTIONS

Munich is stocked with so many treasures and sights that the visitor who plans to "do" the city in one or two days makes a mistake. Not only will many of the highlights be missed, but also the visitor will fail to grasp the spirit of Munich and to absorb fully its special flavor, unique among the cities of the world. But faced with an enormous list of important attractions, sightseeing may have to be limited to a few of the more vital ones. After a quick trip through the old city center with its numerous sights, I'll survey the most important museums and churches, then suggest interesting excursions from the city.

SUGGESTED ITINERARIES

IF YOU HAVE 1 DAY For decades, local tourist tradition always calls for a morning breakfast of Weisswürste (little white sausages). Head for Donisl (see "Dining," above), which opens at 8am. A true Münchner downs them with a mug of beer. Then walk to the **Marienplatz** (see "City Center," below), with its Glockenspiel and Altes Rathaus (town hall). Later stroll along **Maximilianstrasse,** one of the great shopping streets of Europe.

In the afternoon visit **Alte Pinakothek** and see at least *some* of the exhibits at the Deutsches Museum. Cap the evening with a night of Bavarian food, beer, and music at the Hofbräuhaus am Platzl (see "Evening Entertainment," below).

IF YOU HAVE 2 DAYS Spend Day 1 as detailed above. In the morning of Day 2, visit **Neue Pinakothek** and, if the weather's right, plan a lunch in one of the beer gardens of the **Englischer Garten.** In the afternoon visit **Nymphenburg Palace,** summer residence of the Wittelsbach dynasty, rulers of Bavaria.

IF YOU HAVE 3 DAYS Spend Days 1 and 2 as outlined above. Occupy Day 3 exploring the sights you've missed so far: **Residenz,** the **Städtische Galerie im**

Lenbachhaus, and the **Bavarian National Museum.** If you have any more time, pay a return visit to the **Deutsches Museum.** Have dinner or at least a drink at Olympiapark, enjoying spectacular views of the Alps.

IF YOU HAVE 5 DAYS Spend Days 1–3 as outlined above. As fascinating as Munich is, tear yourself away for a day's excursion to the **Royal Castles** once occupied by the "mad king" Ludwig II. (See Chapter 11, "The Romantic Road.") On Day 5, take an excursion to **Dachau,** the notorious concentration camp of World War II (see "Easy Excursions," below), and in the afternoon visit **Berchtesgaden** for a taste of the Bavarian Alps (see Chapter 12).

THE TOP ATTRACTIONS

CITY CENTER

The **Marienplatz,** dedicated to the patron of the city whose statue stands on a huge column in the center of the square, is the heart of the Altstadt (Old Town). On its north side is the **Neues Rathaus** (New City Hall) built in 19th-century Gothic style. Each day at 11am and also at noon and 5pm in summer, the Glockenspiel on the facade performs a miniature tournament, with enameled copper figures moving in and out of the archways. Since you're already at the Rathaus, you may wish to climb 55 steps to the top of its tower (an elevator is available if you're conserving energy) for a good overall view of the city center. The **Altes** (Old) **Rathaus,** with its plain Gothic tower, is to the right. It was reconstructed in the 15th century, after being destroyed by a fire.

South of the square you can see the oldest church in Munich, St. Peter's. The **Viktualienmarkt,** just off the Marienplatz and around the corner from St. Peter's Church, has been a gathering place since 1807. Here people not only buy fresh country produce, wines, meats, and cheese, but also they gossip, browse, and snack.

To the north lies **Odeonsplatz,** Munich's most beautiful square, surrounded by the **Residenz** (Royal Palace) and the **Theatinerkirche.** Adjoining the Residenz is the restored **Nationaltheater,** home of the acclaimed Bavarian State Opera and Bavarian National Ballet.

Running west from Odeonsplatz is the wide shopping avenue, Briennerstrasse, leading to **Königsplatz.** Flanking this large Grecian square are three classical buildings constructed by Ludwig I—the **Propyläen,** the **Glyptothek,** and the **Antikensammlungen.** Returning to Odeonsplatz, take the busy Ludwigstrasse north to the section of Munich known as **Schwabing.** This is the Greenwich Village, Latin Quarter, or Chelsea of Munich, proud of its artist and writer element, numbering among its own such literati as Ibsen and Rilke. The Blue Rider group, which so influenced abstract art in the early 20th century, originated here. Today Schwabing still retains a frankly offbeat flavor, with racks of handmade jewelry for sale along the streets and sidewalk tables filled with young people from all over the world.

Isartor (Isar Gate) is one of the most-photographed landmarks of Munich. Take the S-Bahn to Isartor. This is the only tower left from the town gates that once encircled Munich, forming part of the city's fortifications against invaders. It was erected by Ludwig the Bavarian in the first part of the 14th century.

The other major gate of Munich is the **Karlstor,** once known as Neuhauser Tor, lying northeast of Karlsplatz (also called Stachus). Take the S-Bahn to Karlsplatz. Karlstor lies at the end of Neuhauser Strasse, which formed part of the town's second circuit of walls, dating from the 1500s. It takes its present name from Elector Charles Theodore in 1791. Unlike Isartor, Karlstor lost its main tower (built 1302) in an 1857 explosion.

MUSEUMS & PALACES

ALTE PINAKOTHEK, Barerstrasse 27. Tel. 089/23-805-215.

✪ If you have time to visit only one museum during your Munich stay, it definitely should be this one. The nearly 900 paintings on display (many thousands more are in storage) in this huge neoclassical building represent the greatest European artists of the 14th through the 18th century. Begun as a small court collection by the royal Wittelsbach family in the early 1500s, the collection is now one of the most important in Germany. There are only two floors with exhibits, but the museum is immense, and I do not recommend that you try to cover all the galleries in one day, but try to see the works below.

The landscape painter par excellence of the Danube school, Albrecht Altdorfer, is represented by no fewer than six monumental works. The works of Albrecht Dürer include his greatest—and final—*Self-Portrait* (1500). Here the artist has portrayed himself with almost Christ-like solemnity. Also displayed is the last great painting by the artist, his two-paneled work called *The Four Apostles* (1526).

Several galleries are given over to works by Dutch and Flemish masters. The *St. Columba Altarpiece* (1460–62), by Roger van der Weyden, is one of the greatest of these, in size as well as importance. Measuring nearly 10 feet across, this triptych is a triumph of van der Weyden's subtle linear style, and one of his last works (he died in 1464).

A number of works by Rembrandt, Rubens, and Van Dyck are displayed. Included are a series of religious panels painted by Rembrandt for Prince Frederick Hendrick of the Netherlands. A variety of French, Spanish, and Italian artists are found in both the larger galleries and the small rooms lining the outer wall. The Italian masters are well represented by Fra Filippo Lippi, Giotto, Botticelli, Raphael (*Holy Family*), and Titian.

You'll also find a *Madonna* by da Vinci, a famous self-portrait by the young Rembrandt (1629), and a number of works by Lucas Cranach, including his *Venus*. In the *Land of Cockaigne,* Pieter Brueghel has satirized a popular subject of European folk literature: the place where no work has to be done and where food simply falls into one's mouth. Note the little egg on legs running up to be eaten, and the plucked and cooked chicken laying its neck on a plate. In the background you'll see a knight lying under a roof with his mouth open, waiting for the pies to slip off the eaves over his head.

Important works are always on display, but exhibits are changed in two rooms on the first floor. You'd be wise to buy a map of the gallery to guide you through the dozens of rooms.

Admission: 6 DM ($4) adults, 1 DM (66¢) children; free Sun.
Open: Daily 9:15am–4:30pm, with additional hours Tues and Thurs 7–9pm. U-Bahn: (U2) to Königsplatz. **Tram:** 18. **Bus:** 53.

DEUTSCHES MUSEUM [German Museum of Masterpieces of Science and Technology], Museumsinsel 1. Tel. 089/2-17-91.

✪ On an island in the Isar River, in the heart of Munich, this is the largest technological museum of its kind in the world. Its huge collection of priceless artifacts and historic originals includes the first electric dynamo (Siemens, 1866), the first automobile (Benz, 1886), the first diesel engine (1897), and the laboratory bench at which the atom was first split (Hahn, Strassmann, 1938), to mention just a few. There are hundreds of buttons to push, levers to crank, and gears to turn, as well as a knowledgeable staff in every department to answer questions and demonstrate the workings of steam engines, pumps, or historical musical instruments.

Among the most popular displays are those on mining, with a series of model coal, salt, and iron mines, as well as the electrical power hall, with high-voltage displays that actually produce lightning. There are also exhibits on transportation, printing, photography, textiles, and many other activities, including demonstrations of glass-blowing and paper-making. The air-and-space hall is the largest in the museum. The new hall for high-tech exhibits, computer science, automation, microelectronics, and telecommunications enjoys great popularity. Recently the museum opened an astronomy exhibition, which shows the development of this science from its beginnings in early civilizations to its current status. This is the largest permanent

GERMANY

Munich

0 — 250 m
275 y

To Olympiapark →

To Nymphenburg →

Schelling-strasse
Zieblandstrasse
Augustenstrasse
Theresien-strasse
Hess-Strasse
Luisenstrasse
Arcisstrasse
Barerstr.
Gabelsbergerstrasse
Schleissheimerstrasse
Brienner Strasse
Dachauerstrasse
Königs-platz
Karolinen-platz
Seidlstrasse
Karlstrasse
Meiserstrasse
Barerstrasse
Max-Joseph-Strasse
Marsstrasse
Sophienstrasse
Alter Botanischer Garten
Maximilia-platz
Prielmayerstrasse
Elisenstrasse
Bahnhof-platz
Lenbach-platz
Luisenstrasse
Hauptbahnhof
Prielmayerstrasse
Maxburgstr.
Bayerstrasse
Schützenstrasse
Karls-platz
Neuhauserstrasse
Schlosserstrasse
Herzogspitalstrasse
Schwanthalerstrasse
Sonnenstrasse
Josephspitalstr.
Hotterstr.
Goethestrasse
Schillerstrasse
Landwehrstrasse
Sendlinge-
Pettenkoferstrasse

Kleiner See
Nymphenburger Kanal
Magdalenen-Klause ㉛
Bishofgarten ㉜
Schloss ㉝
Marstall Museum ㉞
Pagodenburg ㉚
Schlosspark ㊲
Amalienburg ㉟
Grosser See
Badenburg ㊱
Hirschgartenallee
Nymphenburg
Zuccalistrasse
Richildenstrasse
St. Stefan's Cemetery

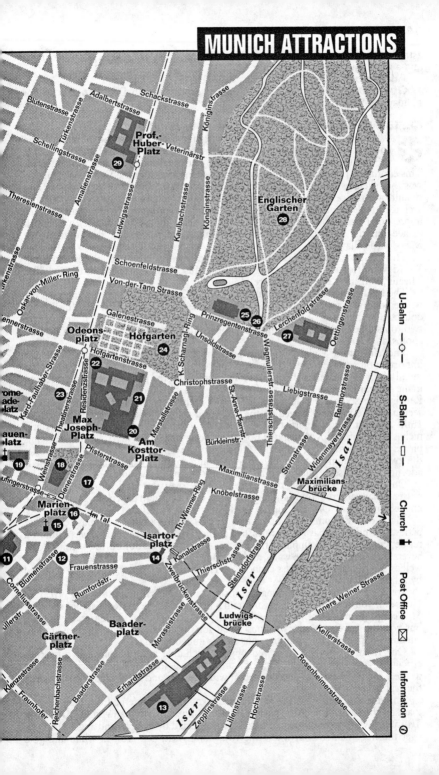

MUNICH ATTRACTIONS

Blütenstrasse
Adalbertstrasse
Schackstrasse
Königinstrasse
Türkenstrasse
Amalienstrasse
Schellingstrasse
Theresienstrasse

Prof.-Huber-Platz
Veterinärstr
㉙

Ludwigsstrasse
Kaulbachstrasse
Königinstrasse

Englischer Garten
㉘

Schoenfeldstrasse
Von-der-Tann Strasse

Oskar-von-Miller-Ring

Galeriestrasse
Odeonsplatz
Hofgarten
㉔
Hofgartenstrasse
Prinzregentenstrasse
㉕ ㉖
Lerchenfeldstrasse
Oettingenstrasse
㉗
Unsöldstrasse
K.-Scharnagl-Ring

Wagmüllerstr.
Thierschstrasse
Reitmorstrasse
Liebigstrasse

㉒
㉓
Residenzstrasse
㉑
Christophstrasse
St.-Anna-Platz
St.-Anna-Strasse

Max Joseph-Platz
Theatinerstrasse
㉒⓪
Am Kosttor-Platz
Marstallstrasse
Bürkleinstr.
Sternstrasse
Widenmayerstrasse

auen-latz
㉙
㉘
Weinstrasse
Dienerstrasse
㉗
Pfisterstrasse
Maximilianstrasse

Maximiliansbrücke

ufingerstrasse
Marien-platz ㉖
㉕
Im Tal
Knöbelstrasse
Th.-Wimmer-Ring
㆒

⓫
㉒
Frauenstrasse
Rumfordstr.
Isartor-platz
㉔
Kanalstrasse
Zweibrückenstrasse
Thierschstrasse
Steinsdorfstrasse
Innere Weiner Strasse

Cornelliusstrasse
Blumenstrasse
Gärtner-platz
Baader-platz
Morassistrasse
Ludwigs-brücke
Kellerstrasse

üllerstr.
Klenzestrasse
Fraunhofer
Reichenbachstrasse
Baaderstrasse
Erhardtstrasse
⓭
Zepplinstrasse
Lillenstrasse
Hochstrasse
Rosenheimerstrasse

Isar

U-Bahn —◇—

S-Bahn —□—

Church ∎✝

Post Office ⊠

Information ⊙

astronomy exhibition in Europe—and perhaps the world. There are a good restaurant and a museum shop on the premises.

Admission: 8 DM ($5.30) adults, 2.50 DM ($1.70) children.

Open: Daily 9am–5pm. Closes at 2pm second Wed in Dec. **Closed:** Major holidays. **S-Bahn:** Isartor. **Tram:** 18.

RESIDENZ, Max-Joseph-Platz 3. Tel. 089/29-06-07.

✪ When a member of the royal Bavarian family said he was going to the castle, he could have meant any number of places, especially if he was Ludwig II. But if he said he was going home, it could only be the Residenz to which he referred. This enormous palace, with a history almost as long as that of the Wittelsbach family, was the official residence of the rulers of Bavaria from 1385 to 1918. Added to and rebuilt over the centuries, the complex is a conglomerate of various styles of art and architecture. Depending on the direction from which you approach the Residenz, your impression can be one of a German Renaissance hall (the western facade), a Palladian palace (on the north), or a Florentine Renaissance palace (on the south facing Max-Joseph-Platz).

The Residenz has been completely restored since its almost total destruction in World War II and now houses the Residenz Museum, a concert hall, the Cuvilliés Theater, and the Residenz Treasure House.

The **Residenz Museum,** Max-Joseph-Platz 3 (tel. 089/29-06-71), takes up the whole southwestern section of the palace, some 100 rooms of art and furnishings collected by centuries of Wittelsbachs. To see the entire collection, you'll have to take two tours, one in the morning and the other in the afternoon. You may also visit the rooms on your own.

The Ancestors' Gallery is designed almost like a hall of mirrors, with one important difference: Where the mirrors would normally be, there are portraits of the members of the Wittelsbach family, set into gilded, carved paneling. The largest room in the museum section is the Hall of Antiquities, possibly the finest example of interior Renaissance styling in Germany (outside of churches, that is). Frescoes adorn seemingly every inch of space on the walls and ceilings alike, painted by dozens of 16th- and 17th-century artists. The room is broken into sections by pilasters and niches, each with its own bust of a Roman emperor or a Greek hero. The hall contains pieces of furniture dating from the 16th century as well, but the center of attraction is the two-story chimney-piece of red stucco and marble. Completed in 1600, it is adorned with Tuscan pillars and a large coat-of-arms of the dukes of Bavaria.

On the second floor of the palace, directly over the Hall of Antiquities, the museum has gathered its enormous collection of Far Eastern porcelain. Note also the fine assemblage of Oriental rugs in the long narrow Porcelain Gallery.

Many of the rooms have been organized as exhibit salons with glass cases and pedestals, and some have been furnished as they were when the palace was actually a residence. The best example is the Elector's bedroom (1730) on the second floor. Several tapestries adorn the walls, and the room is lit by carved and gilded sconces as well as by the massive cut-glass chandelier. The focal point is the ornate bed enclosed by a balustrade.

You'll have to pay an additional admission to visit the **Schatzkammer** (Treasure House). If you've time to see only one item here, it should be the Renaissance statue of *St. George Slaying the Dragon* (16th century). The equestrian statue is made of gold, but you can barely see the precious metal for the thousands of diamonds, rubies, emeralds, sapphires, and semiprecious stones imbedded in it.

One room is devoted to sacred objects, including several icons and numerous crucifixes, carved in ivory or ebony or hammered in gold. The Wittelsbach equivalent to the Crown Jewels is in another room, with scepters and royal orbs. The crown of the realm is also on display.

Both the Residenz Museum and the Schatzkammer are entered from Max-Joseph-Platz on the south side of the palace. From the museum, you can visit the **Cuvilliés Theater,** whose rococo tiers of boxes are supported by nymphs and angels. Directly over the huge center box, where the royal family sat, is a crest in white and gold topped by a jewel-bedecked crown of Bavaria held in place by a group of cherubs in flight. In summer this theater is the scene of frequent concert and opera performances. Mozart's *Idomeneo* had its first performance here in 1781.

The Italianate **Hofgarten,** or Court Garden, is one of the special "green lungs" of Munich. To the north of the Residenz, it is enclosed on two sides by arcades; the garden dates from the time of Duke Maximilian I and was laid out in 1613 to 1617. In the center is the Hofgarten temple, a dozen-sided pavilion dating from 1615.

Admission: Museum 4 DM ($2.60); Treasure House 4 DM ($2.60); Theater 2.50 DM ($1.70); children below 15 free.

Open: Museum and Treasure House, Tues–Sun 10am–4:30pm. **U-Bahn:** U3 or U6 to Odeonsplatz.

BAYERISCHES NATIONAL MUSEUM (Bavarian National Museum), Prinzregentenstrasse 3. Tel. 089/21-68-0.

King Maximilian II in 1855 began an ever-growing institution that today presents the largest and richest display of the artistic and historical riches of Bavaria, all found in the Bayerisches Nationalmuseum. So rapidly has its collection grown in the past 100 years that the museum has been moved to larger quarters several times. Its current building, near the Haus der Kunst, contains three vast floors of sculpture, painting, folk art, ceramics, furniture, and textiles, as well as clocks and scientific instruments.

Entering the museum, turn to the right and go into the first large gallery (called the Wessobrunn Room). Devoted to early church art, from the 5th through the 13th century, this room holds some of the oldest and most valuable works. The desk case contains ancient and medieval ivories, including the so-called Munich ivory, from about C.E. 400. The carving shows the women weeping at the tomb of Christ while the resurrected Lord is gingerly stepping up the clouds and into heaven. At the crossing to the adjoining room the stone figure of the *Virgin with the Rose Bush* is from Straubing (ca. 1300). This is one of the few old Bavarian pieces of church art to be influenced by the spirit of mysticism.

The Riemenschneider Room is devoted to the works of the great sculptor Tilman Riemenschneider (ca. 1460–1531) and his contemporaries. Characteristic of the sculptor's works is the natural, unpainted wood of his carvings and statuary. Note especially the 12 apostles from the Marienkapelle in Würzburg (1510), St. Mary Magdalene, the central group of the high altar in the parish church of Münnerstadt (1490–92), and the figure of St. Sebastian (1490). Also on display are famous collections of arms and armor from the 16th to the 18th century.

Other main-floor salons are devoted to various periods of German and northern Italian art (which is closely tied to the cultural evolution of Bavaria). One room is occupied by scale models of important Bavarian towns as they looked in the 16th century.

The second floor contains a fine collection of stained and painted glass—an art in which medieval Germany excelled. Other rooms on this floor include baroque ivory carvings, Meissen porcelain, and ceramics. One of the novelty additions to the museum is the collection of antique clocks, dating from as early as the 16th century.

In the east wing of the basement level are many Christmas Cribs, not only from Germany but also from Austria, Italy, and Moravia. The variety of materials competes with the styles themselves—wood, amber, gold, terra-cotta, and even wax were used in making these nativity scenes. Also on this level is a display of Bavarian folk art, including many examples of woodcarving.

Admission: 5 DM ($3.30) adults, 3 DM ($2) children; free Sun.

Open: Tues–Sun 9:30am–5pm. **Tram:** 20. **Bus:** 53. **U-Bahn:** U4 or U5 to Lehel.

SCHLOSS NYMPHENBURG, Schloss Nymphenburg 1. Tel. 089/17-908-654.

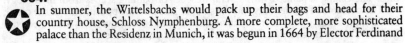

In summer, the Wittelsbachs would pack up their bags and head for their country house, Schloss Nymphenburg. A more complete, more sophisticated palace than the Residenz in Munich, it was begun in 1664 by Elector Ferdinand

Maria in Italian villa style and took more than 150 years and several architectural changes to complete. The final plan of the palace was due mainly to Elector Max Emanuel, who in 1702 decided to enlarge the villa by adding four large pavilions connected by arcaded passageways. Gradually, the French style took over, and today the facade is a subdued baroque.

The interior of the palace is less subtle, however. Upon entering the main building, you're in the great hall, decorated in rococo colors and stuccos. The frescoes by Zimmermann (1756) depict incidents from mythology, especially those dealing with Flora, goddess of the nymphs for whom the palace was named. This hall was used for both banquets and concerts during the reign of Max Joseph III, elector during the mid-18th century. Concerts are still presented here in summer. The smaller rooms are devoted to tapestries, paintings, and period furniture.

From the main building, turn left and head for the arcaded gallery connecting the northern pavilions. The first room in the arcade is the Great Gallery of Beauties, painted for Elector Max Emanuel in 1710, containing portraits of five of the loveliest ladies in the court of Louis XIV. More provocative, however, is Ludwig I's Gallery of Beauties in the south pavilion (the apartments of Queen Caroline). Ludwig commissioned no fewer than 36 portraits of the most beautiful women of his day. The paintings by J. Stieler (painted from 1827 to 1850) include the *Schöne Münchnerin* (lovely Munich girl) and one of the dancer Lola Montez, whose "friendship" with Ludwig I caused such a scandal that it was a factor in the Revolution of 1848.

To the south of the palace buildings, in the rectangular block of low structures that once housed the court stables, is the Marstallmuseum, containing carriages, coaches, sleighs, and riding accessories from the 18th and 19th centuries. As soon as you enter the first hall, look for the coronation coach of Elector Karl Albrecht. Built in Paris in 1740, this glass coach is ornamented with everything from acanthus leaves to dolphins. On the flat panels on the side of the coach are oil paintings of Justitia, Bellona, and Ecclesia. From the same period comes the hunting sleigh of Electress Amalia, with the statue of Diana, goddess of the hunt; even the sleigh's runners are decorated with shellwork and hunting trophies.

The coaches and sleighs of Ludwig II are displayed in the third hall. In keeping with his constant longing for the grandeur of the past, his state coach was ornately designed for his marriage to Duchess Sophie of Bavaria, a royal wedding that never came off. The fairy-tale coach wasn't wasted, however, since Ludwig often rode off through the countryside to one of his many castles in it, creating quite a picture. The coach is completely gilded, inside and out. Rococo carvings cover every inch of space except for the panels, faced with paintings on copper. In winter the king would use his state sleigh, nearly as elaborate as the Cinderella coach.

Nymphenburg's greatest attraction is the park. Stretching for 500 acres in front of the palace, it is divided into two sections by the canal that runs from the pool at the foot of the staircase to the cascade at the far end of the gardens. From the palace steps, you can see the formal design of the gardens, laid out in English style, with lakes, greenery, and beds of flowers.

Within the park are several pavilions. On the guided tour, you begin with the Amalienburg, whose plain exterior belies the rococo decoration inside. Built as a hunting lodge for Electress Amalia (1734), the pavilion carries the hunting theme through the first few rooms and then bursts into salons of flamboyant colors, rich carvings, and wall paintings. The most impressive room is the Hall of Mirrors, a symphony of silver ornaments on a faintly blue ground.

The Badenburg Pavilion sits at the edge of the large lake of the same name. As its name implies, it was built as a bathing pavilion, although it's difficult to visualize Ludwig dashing in from the water with swimming suit dripping on those elegant floors. A trip to the basement, however, will help you appreciate the pavilion's practical side. Here you'll see the unique bath, surrounded by blue-and-white Dutch tiles. The ceiling is painted with several frescoes of bathing scenes from mythology.

The octagonal Pagodenburg, on the smaller lake on the opposite side of the canal, looks like a Chinese pagoda from the outside. The interior, however, is decorated with pseudo-Chinese motifs, often using Dutch tiles in place of the Chinese ones.

The Magdalenenklause may look like a ruin, but it was intended that way when it was built in 1725. Also called the Hermitage, it was planned as a retreat for prayer and solitude. The four main rooms of the one-story structure are all paneled with uncarved stained oak. All the furnishings are simple and the few paintings, religious. It's really a drastic change from the other buildings.

Admission: If you have the better part of a day, buy the 6-DM ($4) ticket to the palace, carriage museum, and the pavilions in the park. Kids (6–14) pay 4 DM ($2.60). For Nymphenburg Palace, Amalienburg, and the Marstallmuseum only, 4.50 DM ($3) for adults, 3 DM ($2) for children.

Open: Apr 1–Sept 30, Tues–Sun, the main palace 9am–12:30pm and 1:30–5pm; the Amalienburg 9am–12:30pm and 1:30–5pm; the Marstallmuseum 9am–noon and 1–5pm; the Badenburg, Pagodenburg, and Magdalenenklause 10am–12:30pm and 1:30–5pm. In winter, Tues–Sun, the main palace 10am–12:30pm; the Amalienburg 10am–12:30pm; the Marstallmuseum 10am–noon and 1–4pm. **Closed:** Mon. **Tram:** 12 to Auffahrtsallee. **Bus:** 41 **Parking:** Beside the Marstallmuseum.

MORE ATTRACTIONS

NEUE PINAKOTHEK, Barerstrasse 29. Tel. 089/23-80-51-95.

The Neue Pinakothek offers a survey of 18th- and 19th-century art. Across the Theresienstrasse from the Alte Pinakothek, the museum was reconstructed after its destruction in World War II, reopening again in 1981.

The museum has paintings by Gainsborough, Goya, David, Manet, van Gogh, and Monet. Among the more popular German artists represented are Wilhelm Leibl and Gustav Klimt; you should encounter a host of others whose art is less well known. Note particularly the genre paintings by Carl Spitzweg.

Placed throughout the gallery are sculptures, mainly in bronze, by German artists, with a Degas and Rodin here and there. I've especially enjoyed the French paintings, including several Cézannes, Corots, and Gauguins.

Admission: 6 DM ($4) adults, 3.50 DM ($2.30) children; free Sun. Combination ticket for both Alte Pinakothek (see above) and Neue, 10 DM ($6.60) adults, 5 DM ($3.30) children.

Open: Tues–Sun 9:15am–4:30pm, with additional hours Tues 7–9pm. **U-Bahn:** U2 to Königsplatz. **Tram:** 18. **Bus:** 53.

 ### FROMMER'S FAVORITE MUNICH EXPERIENCES

A Morning at the Deutsches Museum   It would take a month to see all of the largest technological museum in the world, but a morning will whet the appetite. Everything is here: the first Benz of 1886, original Wright brothers' airplanes, Ludwig II's state coach.

An Afternoon at Nymphenburg Palace   The Wittelsbach family (rulers of Munich) considered it the best place to be on a hot afternoon—and so might you. The palace grounds of Germany's largest baroque palace are filled with lakes, waterfalls, and park pavilions.

A Night at the Opera [Cuvilliés Theater]   Some consider it the most beautiful theater in the world: a small rococo tier-boxed theater from the mid-18th century that was designed by a dwarf who began life as a court jester.

A Weekend in the Beer Gardens   Münchners gather on weekends in summer to down huge *Masse* of beer and watch the world go by, especially at Chinesischer Turm in the Englischer Garten.

ANTIKENSAMMLUNGEN [Museum of Antiquities], Königsplatz 1. Tel. 089/59-83-59.

After 100 years of floating from one museum to another, the Museum of Antiquities finally found a home in the 19th-century neoclassical hall on the south side of the Königsplatz. The collection grew around the vase collection of Ludwig I and the Royal Antiquarium, both of which were incorporated after World War I into a loosely defined group called the Museum Antiker Kleinkunst (Museum of Small Works of Ancient Art). Many of the pieces may be small in size but never in value or artistic significance.

Entering the museum, you find yourself in the large central hall. The five main-floor halls house more than 650 Greek vases, collected from all parts of the Mediterranean. The pottery has been restored to a near-perfect condition, although most of it dates as far back as 500 B.C.E. The oldest piece is "the goddess from Aegina," dating from 3000 B.C.E. Technically not pottery, this pre-Mycenaean figure, carved from a mussel shell, is on display along with the Mycenaean pottery exhibits in Room I. The upper level of the Central Hall is devoted to large Greek vases discovered in Sicily and to the art of the Etruscans.

Returning to the Central Hall, take the stairs down to the lower level to see the collection of Greek, Roman, and Etruscan jewelry. Note the similarities with today's fashions in design. Included on this level as well are rooms devoted to ancient colored glass, Etruscan bronzes, and Greek terracottas.

Admission: 3.50 DM ($2.30) adults. Joint ticket to Museum of Antiquities and Glyptothek, 6 DM ($4) adults; children below 14 free. Free Sun.

Open: Tues and Thurs–Sun 10am–4:30pm, Wed noon–8:30pm. **U-Bahn:** U2 to Königsplatz.

GLYPTOTHEK, Königsplatz 3. Tel. 089/28-61-00.

The ideal neighbor for the Museum of Antiquities, it supplements the pottery and smaller pieces of the main museum with an excellent collection of ancient Greek and Roman sculpture. Included are the famous pediments from the temple of Aegina, two marvelous statues of Kuroi from the 6th century B.C.E., the colossal figure of a *Sleeping Satyr* from the Hellenistic period, classical masterpieces of sculpture from ancient Athens, and a splendid collection of Roman portraits. In all, the collection is the largest assemblage of classical art in the country. It was ordered built by King Ludwig I, who had fantasies of transforming Munich into another Athens.

Admission: 3.50 DM ($2.30) adults. Joint ticket to Museum of Antiquities and Glyptothek, 6 DM ($4) adults; children below 14 free. Free Sun.

Open: Tues–Wed and Fri–Sun 10am–4:30pm, Thurs noon–8:30pm. **U-Bahn:** U2 to Königsplatz.

STAATSGALERIE MODERNER KUNST [State Gallery of Modern Art], Haus der Kunst, Prinzregentenstrasse 1. Tel. 089/29-27-10.

Munich's State Gallery of Modern Art is housed in the west wing of the massive Haus der Kunst, which was constructed in 1937. Some art critics claim that it has one of the 10 finest collections of modern art in the world. It shows about 400 paintings, sculptures, and art objects from the beginning of the 20th century to the present. The largest exhibit is devoted to modern German art. You'll see paintings by Klee, Marc, Kirchner, and Beckmann as well as Italian art, with stars such as Marino Marini and Renato Guttuso; American abstract expressionism; minimalist art; and a host of celebrated artists from Bacon to Braque, de Chirico to Dali, Dubuffet to Giacometti, Matisse to Mondrian that round out the collection. Picasso is especially honored, with 14 works, the earliest dating from 1903.

The east wing of the Haus der Kunst, Prinzregentenstrasse 1 (tel. 089/22-26-51-3), is entered separately and requires a separate ticket. It is devoted to changing exhibitions, which often consist of the works of exciting new artists whose canvases are for sale as well as display. Many traveling exhibitions of worldwide importance come here.

Admission: To the Staatsgalerie, 5 DM ($3.30) adults, 3 DM ($2) children; free Sun. To the east wing, from 5 DM ($3.30), depending on exhibit.

Open: Tues–Sun 9:15am–4:30pm; Thurs also 7–9pm. **Closed:** Mon, some holidays. **U-Bahn:** Odeonsplatz. **Bus:** 53.

MÜNCHNER STADTMUSEUM [Municipal Museum], St. Jakobsplatz 1. Tel. 089/233-22-370.

Munich's Municipal Museum is to the city what the Bavarian National Museum is to the whole state. In what was once the armory building, its collections give you an insight into the history and daily lives of the people of this unique community. A wooden model shows how Munich looked in 1572. Special exhibitions about popular arts and traditions are frequently presented. The extensive collection of furnishings is changed annually so that visitors will have a chance to see various periods from the vast storehouse.

The museum's most important exhibit is its Moorish Dancers (*Moriskentanzer*) on the ground floor. These 10 figures, each 2 feet high, carved in wood and painted in bright colors by Erasmus Grasser in 1480, are among the best examples of secular Gothic art in medieval Germany. In the large Gothic hall on the ground floor you can admire an important collection of armor and weapons from the 14th to the 18th century.

The second-floor photo museum traces the early history of the camera back to 1839. Cabinet after cabinet of early cameras line the walls. Every day, at 6 and 9pm, the film museum shows two different films from its extensive archives. The historical collection of musical instruments on the fourth floor is one of the greatest of its kind in the world. In addition, there is an ethnological collection of instruments from Africa, Oceania, the Americas, the Far East, the Middle East, Byzantium, and early Europe.

Enter the Municipal Museum through the main courtyard with its cafeteria.

Admission: 5 DM ($3.30) adults, 2.50 DM ($1.70) children; free Sun and holidays.

Open: Tues–Sun 10am–5pm, with additional hours Wed until 8:30pm. **S-Bahn or U-Bahn:** Marienplatz.

STADTISCHE GALERIE IM LENBACHHAUS, Luisenstrasse 33. Tel. 089/52-10-41.

The ancient villa of Franz von Lenbach, this gallery exhibits works by that 19th-century artist (1836–1904) and others. Entering the gold-colored mansion through the gardens, you'll first be greeted with a large collection of early works by Paul Klee (1879–1940)—mainly those predating World War I. There's an outstanding group of works by Kandinsky, leader of the Blue Rider movement in the early 20th century. There are many 19th-century paintings throughout the villa, along with a few earlier works. The enclosed patio is pleasant for a coffee break.

Admission: 6 DM ($4) adults; children 14 and below free.

Open: Tues–Sun 10am–6pm. **Closed:** Mon. **U-Bahn:** U2 to Königsplatz.

SCHACK-GALERIE, Prinzregentenstrasse 9. Tel. 089/238-05-224.

Near the Haus der Kunst, the Schack Gallery houses a collection of art bequeathed to the German emperor by Prussian civil servant Count Schack. The comprehensive collection is devoted to 19th-century German art and has paintings by such artists as Bocklin, Lenbach, Spitzweg, Schwind, and others. The building, erected in 1907, also housed the headquarters of the Prussian Embassy in Bavaria.

Admission: 3 DM ($2) adults, 2 DM ($1.30) children; free Sun.

Open: Wed–Mon 9:15am–4:30pm (Fasching, Sun and Dec 31 9:15am–noon). **Closed:** Tues and holidays. **Tram:** 20. **Bus:** 53.

CHURCHES

Other than the major churches documented below, those visitors with more time might also consider visits to the **Asamkirche,** Sendlinger Strasse (S-Bahn: Marienplatz), which is a beautiful rococo church built between 1733 and 1746 and dedicated to St. John of Nepomuk; the **Michaelskirche,** or St. Michael's Church, Neuhauser Strasse 52 (U-Bahn: Marienplatz), the largest Renaissance church north of the Alps, built by Duke William the Pious in 1583 to 1597; and the **Matthäuskirche,** or St. Matthew's Church, Nussbaumstrasse 1 (U-Bahn: Sendlinger-Tor-Platz), an Evangelical cathedral built from 1953 to 1955.

FRAUENKIRCHE [Cathedral of Our Lady], Frauenplatz.

★ When the smoke cleared from the bombings of 1945, only a fragile shell remained of Munich's largest church. Workmen and architects who restored the 15th-century Gothic cathedral used whatever remains they could find in the rubble, along with modern innovations. The overall effect of the rebuilt Frauenkirche is strikingly simple, yet dignified.

The twin towers (which remained intact), with their strangely un-Gothic onion domes, have been the city's landmark since 1525. The red-brick exterior of the cathedral has retained its Gothic appearance. Instead of the typical flying buttresses, the edifice is supported by huge props on the inside that separate the side chapels. The Gothic vaulting over the nave and chancel is borne by 22 simple octagonal pillars.

Entering the main doors at the west end of the cathedral, you first notice no windows (they are actually hidden, except for the tall chancel window, by the enormous pillars). According to legend, the devil laughed at the notion of hidden windows, and you can still see the strange footlike mark called "the devil's step" in the entrance hall where he stamped in glee at the stupidity of the architect. As you enter the left aisle of the three-aisled nave, you'll see photographs showing the cathedral as it looked after it was destroyed in the air raids of World War II. Many of the works of art formerly housed in the church were safely put away before that time and are displayed in the chapels along the nave and behind the chancel.

In the chapel directly behind the high altar is the most interesting painting in the cathedral: *The Protecting Cloak,* a 1510 work by Jan Polack, showing the Virgin holding out her majestic robes to shelter all humankind. The collection of tiny figures beneath the cloak includes everyone from the pope to peasants. At the entrance to the vestry, just to the left of the choir, is a huge painting of *The Ascension of the Virgin Mary* by Peter Candid. In the south chapel adjoining the Chapel of the Holy Sacrament is one of the modern works, *The Immaculate Virgin,* a graceful bronze statue (1959) hung over a simple altar.

The baptistry, to the right of the choir, contains the cathedral's oldest work, a stone sculpture of the suffering Christ, dating from 1380.

Returning to the entrance via the south nave, you'll pass the mausoleum of Emperor Ludwig IV, built in 1622. The elaborately carved tomb is guarded at each corner by armored soldiers with banners of the realm. In the front stands a sculpted likeness of the emperor, sword in hand. The cathedral is open daily from 6am to 6:30pm. U-Bahn and S-Bahn: Marienplatz.

PETERSKIRCHE [St. Peter's Church], Rindermarkt 1. Tel. 089/260-48-28.

Munich's oldest church (1180) has turned over a new leaf, and it's a gold one at that. The white-and-gray interior has been decorated with painted medallions of puce and lots of gilded baroque. It contains a series of murals by Johann Baptist Zimmermann, but nothing tops the attraction of the bizarre relic in the second chapel on the left: the gilt-covered and gem-studded skeleton of St. Mundita staring at you with two false eyes in its head, which rests on a cushion. Jewels cover the mouth of rotten teeth, quite a contrast to the fresh roses usually kept in front of the black-and-silver coffin.

Near the Rathaus, St. Peter's, known locally as Old Peter, also has a high steeple, although you may be discouraged from going up it by the lack of an elevator. Colored circles on the lower platform tell you whether the climb is worthwhile: If the circle is white, you can be assured of a spectacular view as far as the Alps. Admission to the tower is 2 DM ($1.30) for adults and 0.50 DM (30¢) for children; it's open Monday to Friday from 9am to 5pm, Saturday from 8:30am to 7pm, and Sunday from 10am to 7pm. U-Bahn: Marienplatz.

THEATINERKIRCHE, Theatinerstrasse 22.

Named for a small group of Roman Catholic clergy (the Theatines), this church is the finest example of Italian baroque in Munich. Dedicated to the scholar-saint Kajetan, it was begun in the mid-17th century by two Italian architects, Barelli and Zucalli. It was completed in 1768 by the son of the dwarf court jester–cum–architect, François de Cuvilliés. On the facade and interior are cherubs, some quite mischievous, especially the "Angel of Silence," who points the way with one hand while he holds the other to his lips to form an obvious "shh."

The arched ceiling of the nave is supported by fluted columns that line the center aisle. Above the transept, dividing the nave from the choir, the ceiling breaks into an open dome with an ornate gallery decorated with large but graceful statues. Nothing seems to detract from the whiteness of the interior, except the dark wooden pews and the canopied pulpit. U-Bahn: Odeonsplatz.

PARKS & ZOOS

About 4 miles south of the city center, the **Hellabrunn Zoo** stands in the Tierpark Hellabrunn, Tierparkstrasse 30 (tel. 089/62-50-80). It is one of the largest zoos in the world, and may be visited daily from 8am to 6pm (in winter, from 9am to 5pm), for an admission of 7 DM ($4.60) for adults and 3 DM ($2) for children. To reach the park, you can take a bus leaving from Marienplatz, no. 52, or the U-Bahn to Thalkirchen. Hundreds of animals roam in a natural habitat. A walk through the park is so attractive that it's recommended even if you're not a zoo buff. There is also a big children's zoo, as well as a large aviary.

Bordering Schwabing on the east and extending almost to the Isar River is Munich's city park, the 18th-century **Englischer Garten,** laid out by Sir Benjamin Thompson. Here you can wander for hours along the walks and among trees, flowers, and summer nudes, even stopping for tea on the plaza near the Chinese pagoda.

THE OLYMPIC GROUNDS

The Olympiapark, site of the 1972 Olympic Games, is 740 acres at the northern edge of the city. More than 15,000 workers from 18 countries transformed the site into a park of nearly 5,000 trees, 27 miles of roads, 32 bridges, and a lake.

Olympiapark has its own railway station, U-Bahn line, mayor, post office, churches, even an elementary school. It broke the skyline of Munich by the addition of a 960-foot television tower in the center of the park.

The showpiece of this city is a huge stadium, capable of seating 80,000 spectators, and topped by the largest roof in the world—nearly 90,000 square yards of tinted acrylic glass. The supports for the stadium are anchored by two huge blocks, each capable of resisting 4,000 tons under stress. The roof serves the additional purpose of collecting rainwater and draining it into the nearby Olympic lake.

Nearly 5,000 apartments and cottages were built on the grounds to house members of the Olympic staffs and teams. After the games were over, these were turned into modern housing for some 10,000 residents.

Smaller halls throughout the park are used for exhibitions and such competitive events as wrestling, judo, fencing, and weight lifting. The covered swimming stadium, with four large pools, is now open to the public.

The park is open daily from 8:30am to 6pm, charging 1 DM (66¢) admission for adults and 0.50 DM (30¢) for children. You can also snack or eat at the park in either the Tower Restaurant or Am Olympiasee; many visitors come just for a view of the Alps from the Olympia Tower (see "Specialty Dining" above). Take U-Bahn 3 or 8 to Olympiazentrum.

Near Olympiapark, you can visit the **BMW Museum,** Petuelring 130 (tel. 089/38-95-33-07), where the history of the automobile is stunningly displayed in an atmosphere created by Oscar winner Rolf Zehetbauer, a "film architect." The museum, housed in a demisphere of modern architecture, takes you into both the future and the past. You can also view 24 video films and 10 slide shows (an especially interesting one shows how people of yesterday imagined the future). The museum is open daily from 9am to 5pm, charging 4.50 DM ($3) for adults and 3 DM ($2) for children. While there, you might also ask about tours of the BMW factory. Take U-Bahn 3 or 8 to Olympiazentrum.

6. COOL FOR KIDS

From the Circus Krone to the Marionetten Theater, to the Bavarian Film Studio, kids love Munich.

Take your children to the **Münchner Stadtmuseum,** St. Jakobsplatz 1 (tel. 089/233-22-370). On the third floor is an array of puppets from around the world, with star billing going to the puppeteer's art. The comical and grotesque figures include both marionettes and hand puppets. Like a Lilliputian version of the world of the stage, the collection also includes detailed puppet theaters and miniature scenery. A special department is devoted to fairground art, including carousel animals, shooting galleries, models of roller coasters, and wax and museum figures. The main exhibit contains the oldest known carousel horses, dating from 1820. For opening hours, see the previous write-up in "Attractions."

If children have a favorite museum in Munich, it's the **Deutsches Museum,** Museumsinsel 1 (tel. 089/2-17-91), which has many "hands-on" exhibits. For details, refer to the previous write-up.

The **Spielzeugmuseum,** in the Altes Rathaus, Marienplatz 15 (tel. 089/29-40-01), is a historic collection of toys. Open Monday to Saturday from 10am to 5:30pm; Sunday 10am to 6pm. Admission is 4 DM ($2.60) for adults and 1 DM (66¢) for children.

At the **Münchner Marionetten Theater,** Blumenstrasse 29A (tel. 089/26-57-12), you can attend puppet shows and the theatre de marionnettes. Adults as well as children are delighted with these productions, many of which are of operas. Performances are Wednesday, Thursday, Saturday, and Sunday at 3pm. Admission is 5 DM ($3.30) for adults and 8 DM ($5.30) for children. To reach the theater, take the U-Bahn to Sendlinger Tor.

The **Bavaria Film Studio,** Bavariafilmplatz 7, Geiselgasteig (tel. 089/64-90-67), is the largest filmmaking center in Europe. It is Munich's version of Hollywood. Guided 1½-hour tours are possible from March 1 to October 31, daily from 9am to 4pm. Take tram 25 to Bavariafilmplatz. Admission is 12 DM ($7.90) for adults and 8 DM ($5.30) for children.

Hellabrunn Zoo, already described, has a large children's zoo where children are allowed to pet the animals.

Not to be ignored is the **Circus Krone,** Marstrasse 43 (tel. 089/55-81-66). It might be compared to London's Albert Hall, its productions are so varied—one night, a jazz festival; the next night, a hard-rock concert; yet another night, gospel singers; and from December 25 to March 31, a circus show every night. In season, performances are daily at 3pm and 8pm, with admission at 15 DM ($9.90) for children and 18 DM ($11.90) for adults. To reach the circus, take the S-Bahn to Hackerbrücke.

WALKING TOUR — MUNICH

Start: Frauenkirche.
Finish: Königsplatz.
Time: 2½ hours, not counting visits to interiors or shopping.
Best Time: Daylight hours during clement weather.

With a history spanning centuries of building and rebuilding, Munich is one of the

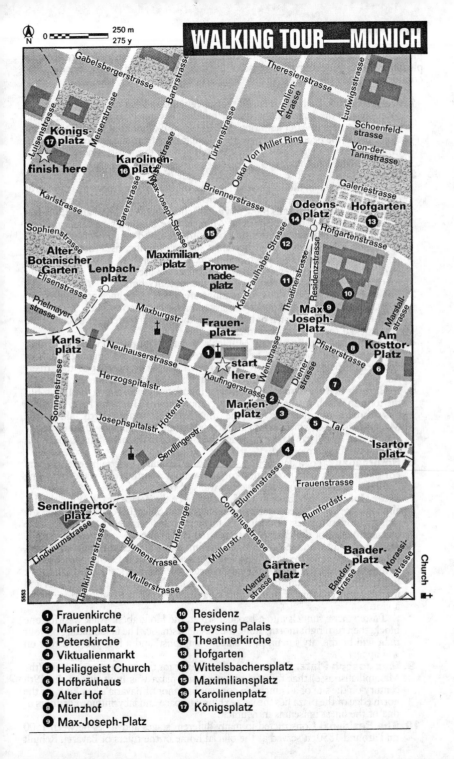

WALKING TOUR—MUNICH

0 — 250 m
0 — 275 y

N

Königsplatz ⑰
finish here

Karolinenplatz ⑯

Odeonsplatz ⑭
Hofgarten ⑬

Alter Botanischer Garten

Lenbachplatz

Maximilianplatz

Promenadeplatz

Max Joseph-Platz ⑨

Am Kosttor-Platz ⑥

Karlsplatz

Frauenplatz ①
start here ☆

Marienplatz ②

Isartorplatz

Sendlingertorplatz

Baaderplatz

Gärtnerplatz

Church ✝

① Frauenkirche
② Marienplatz
③ Peterskirche
④ Viktualienmarkt
⑤ Heiliggeist Church
⑥ Hofbräuhaus
⑦ Alter Hof
⑧ Münzhof
⑨ Max-Joseph-Platz
⑩ Residenz
⑪ Preysing Palais
⑫ Theatinerkirche
⑬ Hofgarten
⑭ Wittelsbachersplatz
⑮ Maximiliansplatz
⑯ Karolinenplatz
⑰ Königsplatz

most interesting cities of Europe, especially for pedestrians with time to savor its pleasures. Begin your tour at the base of the dignified cathedral whose brickwork is considered among the most impressive in Europe, the:

1. **Frauenkirche.** Built in a mere 20 years, beginning in 1468 on the site of a much older church, the majestically somber building is capped with twin towers, the symbol of Munich. After admiring their design, walk for about a block southeast along any of the pedestrian alleyways radiating away from the rear of the church. In about two minutes, you'll find yourself within the most famous medieval square of Munich, the:

2. **Marienplatz,** in whose center a golden statue (the *Mariensäule*) rises above a pavement first laid in the 1300s when the rest of the city's streets were a morass of mud and sewage. On the square's northern boundary rises the richly ornamented bulk of the Neues Rathaus (new town hall), built between 1867 and 1908 as a neo-Gothic symbol of the power of Munich. The building's mechanical clock and Glockenspiel are two of the most carefully preserved monuments of Munich. At the square's eastern border, beyond a stream of traffic, rises the simpler and smaller Altes Rathaus (old town hall), which was rebuilt in its present form in 1470 after an even earlier version was destroyed by fire. From the square, walk south along the Rindermarkt, encircling the masonry bulk of:

3. **Peterskirche.** Although its foundations are much more ancient, dating from 1000, the interior is a sunflooded fantasy of baroque stucco and gilt. Walk to the rear of this church, at which point you'll see the sprawling premises of one of the best-stocked food emporiums in Europe, the:

4. **Viktualienmarkt.** Known as "Munich's stomach," it's packed with opportunities for snacking, picnicking, beer drinking, or watching the ongoing rituals of European grocery shopping. At the northern end, at the corner of the streets Rosen Tal and Im Tal, rise the richly ornate baroque walls of the:

5. **Heiliggeist (Holy Ghost) Church.** Its foundations were laid in the 1100s, but the form in which you see it today was completed in 1730. From here, cross the busy boulevard identified as the Im Tal and walk north along the Maderbraustrasse (which within a block will change its name to Orlandostrasse and then to Am Platz). There, look for the entrance to the most famous beer hall in Europe, the state-owned:

6. **Hofbräuhaus.** For a description, refer to the "Evening Entertainment" section. For the moment, note its location for an eventual return. Now, walk east along the Pfisterstrasse. To your left rise the walls of the:

7. **Alter Hof,** originally built in 1255. It was once the palace of the Wittelsbachs, although greatly eclipsed later by grander palaces. Since 1816, it has housed the rather colorless offices of Munich's financial bureaucracies. On the opposite (northern) edge of the Pfisterstrasse rise the walls of the:

8. **Münzhof** (built 1563–67). During its lifetime it has housed the imperial stables, the first museum north of the Alps, and (between 1809 and 1986) a branch of the government mint. Today, it is the headquarters for Munich's office for Landmark Preservation (Landesamt für Denkmal-schutz). If it's open, the double tiers and massive stone columns of the building's Bavarian renaissance courtyard are worth a visit.

Pfisterstrasse funnels into a broader street, the Hofgraben. Walk west for one block, then turn right (north) along the Residenzstrasse. The first building on your right will be the city's main post office (Hauptpost) and a few paces further on will appear the:

9. **Max-Joseph-Platz.** Designed as a focal point for the monumental avenue (the Maximilianstrasse) that radiates eastward, the plaza was built during the 19th century on the site of a Franciscan convent in honor of Bavaria's first king. At the north edge of the plaza lies the vast exhibition space and labyrinthine corridors of one of the finest museums in Munich:

10. **The Residenz.** Constructed in many different stages and styles between 1500 and around 1850, it served as the official home of the rulers of Bavaria. Rebuilt

after the bombings of World War II, in a design re-creating its labyrinthine floor plan, it contains seven semiconcealed courtyards, lavish apartments for the housing of such foreign visitors as Queen Elizabeth II and Charles de Gaulle, as well as museums that include the Residenz Museum, the Treasure House of the Residenz, the Cuvilliés Theater (a richly gilded rococo theater built in 1753), the State Coin Collection of Egyptian Art, the National Theater, and a baroque concert hall noted for its decorations, the Herkulessaal.

If you haven't already done so, walk from the Max-Joseph-Platz north along the Residenzstrasse. Take the first left turn and walk west along the Salvatorstrasse; then, within another block, turn right (north) along the Theatinerstrasse. On your right, you'll immediately notice the imposing walls of Munich's first baroque palace, the:

11. **Preysing Palais.** Built between 1723 and 1728, it is still associated with the oldest surviving family of aristocratic lineage in Bavaria today. Adjacent to the Palais' northern wall, and faced with an Italian-inspired loggia, is the Felherrnhalle (1841–44), originally built to honor the military greats of Bavaria. On the western (opposite) side of the same street (Theatinerstrasse) is the:

12. **Theatinerkirche** (Church of St. Kajetan). Completed in 1690, with a triple-domed Italian baroque facade added about a century later, it has a crypt containing the tombs of many of the Wittelsbachs. Now, continue walking north passing through the Odeonsplatz, below which several subway lines converge. On the northeastern side of this square lie the flowers, fountains, and cafés of one of the most pleasant gardens in Munich, the:

13. **Hofgarten.** Originally built for members of the royal court in 1613, it was opened to the public in 1780. Along the edges of the Hofgarten, as well as along the avenues radiating away from it, lie many opportunities for your much-awaited:

REFUELING STOP Do as the Münchners do and enjoy the panorama of the Odeonsplatz and the nearby Hofgarten. One particularly attractive choice is **Café Luitpold,** Briennerstrasse 11. Rebuilt in a streamlined design after the bombings of World War II, it has in the past welcomed such café-loving habitués as Ibsen, Johann Strauss the Younger, and Kandinsky.

Now, walk westward along the Briennerstrasse, through a neighborhood lined with impressive buildings. On your right, notice the heroic statue of Maximilian I, the Great Elector (1597–1651) rising from the center of the:

14. **Wittelsbachersplatz.** In short time, the gentle fork to your left leads into the verdant and stylish perimeter of the:

15. **Maximiliansplatz.** Shop at your leisure or plan to return later for a more in-depth sampling of this prestigious neighborhood. For the moment, return to the Briennerstrasse, turn left (west), and head toward the 85-foot obelisk (erected 1833) that soars above the:

16. **Karolinenplatz.** Its design commemorates Bavarians killed in the Napoleonic invasion of Russia. Continuing west, you'll come upon the:

17. **Königsplatz.** Its formal neoclassical design was selected by Crown Prince Ludwig after an architectural competition during the early 19th century. Its perimeter is ringed with some of the most impressive museum buildings in Germany, the Doric-inspired Propylaen monument (west side), the Antikensammlungen (south side), and the Ionic-fronted Glyptothek (north side).

ORGANIZED TOURS

Blue buses, with conducted sightseeing tours in both German and English, leave from the square in front of the Hauptbahnhof, at Hertie's, all year round. Tickets are sold on the bus, and no advanced booking is necessary.

A one-hour tour—costing 15 DM ($9.90) for adults and 8 DM ($5.30) for children

6 to 12—leaves daily at 10 and 11:30am and 2:30pm from May 1 to October 31. Winter departures, November 1 to April 30, are daily from 10am and 2:30pm. A 2½-hour tour, including the Olympic Tower, costs 27 DM ($17.80) for adults and 14 DM ($9.20) for children from May 1 to October 31; departures are at 10am and 2:30pm. In winter, November 1 to April 30, departures are at 10am and 2:30pm.

A second 2½-hour tour, costing 27 DM ($17.80) for adults and 14 DM ($9.20) for children, visits the famous Alte Pinakothek (painting gallery), Liebfrauendom (landmark of Munich) and the chiming clocks at Marienplatz every day except Monday, at 10am.

A third 2½-hour tour, costing from 27 DM ($17.80) for adults and 14 DM ($9.20) for children, visits Nymphenburg Palace and the Schatzkammer every day, except Monday, at 2:30pm.

If you'd like to go farther afield and visit some of the major attractions in the environs of Munich, you can get information from **Panorama Tours,** an affiliate of Gray Line. The office is at Arnulfstrasse 8 (tel. 089/59-15-04) to the north of the Hauptbahnhof. Hours are 7:30am to 6pm Monday to Friday and 7:30am to noon on Saturday and Sunday.

7. SPORTS & RECREATION

BEACHES, SWIMMING POOLS, AND WATER SPORTS On hot weekends, much of Munich embarks for nearby lakes, the Ammersee and the Starnbergersee, where bathing facilities are clearly marked. You can also swim at Maria-Einsiedel, in the frigid, snow-fed waters of the Isar River. The city has several public swimming pools. The largest of these includes the giant competition-sized pool within the Olympiapark, the **Olympia-Schwimmhalle** (tel. 089/52-01-51). Information on both sailing and windsurfing is available from the **Bayerischer Segler-Verband,** Georg-Brauchle-Ring 93, D-8000 München 50 (tel. 089/157-02-366).

FITNESS CENTERS AND HEALTH CLUBS Several of Munich's larger hotels have installed state-of-the-art exercise equipment. These include the Bayerischer Hof, the München Sheraton, the Park Hilton München, and the Vier Jahreszeiten Kempinski München, (see "Accommodations," above). In addition, there are gyms and health clubs scattered throughout the city, many of which sell temporary passes to newcomers. For information, ask your hotel receptionist or contact the **Bayerischer Landessportverband,** Georg-Brauchle-Ring 93, D-8000 Munchen 50 (tel. 089/157-02-0).

HIKING AND HILLCLIMBING Bavaria is packed with well-marked hiking trails. For information about nearby terrains and itineraries, contact the **Deutscher Alpeinverein,** Praterinsel 5, D-8000 München 22 (tel. 089/235-0900).

ICE SKATING During the coldest months of winter, one of the lakes in the Englischer Garten freezes over and is opened to ice skaters. Also blocked off for skaters is a section of the Nymphenburger Canal. Be alert to the *Gefahr* (Danger) signs which are posted whenever temperatures rise and the ice becomes too thin. The indoor rink is the **Olympic Icestadium** in the Olympiapark, Spiridon-Louis-Ring 3 (tel. 089/3067-2150). Information on hockey matches and other aspects of ice skating is available from **Bayerischer Eissportverband,** Georg-Brauchle-Ring (tel. 089/157-02-0).

JOGGING Regardless of the season, the most lushly landscaped place in Munich is the **Englischer Garten** (U-Bahn: Münchner Freiheit), which has a circumference of 7 miles and an array of dirt and asphalt tracks. Also appropriate are the grounds of the **Olympiapark** (U-Bahn: Olympiazentrum), or the park surrounding **Schloss**

Nymphenburg. More convenient to the center of the city's commercial district is a jog along the embankments of the Isar River.

RAFTING Raft trips on the Isar River are conducted between the town of Wolfratshausen and Munich between early May and late September. You might find yourself in a raft containing up to 60 other passengers, but if the idea appeals to you, one company that can usually accommodate you is **Franz and Sebastian Seitner,** Heideweg 9, D-8190 Wolfratshausen (tel. 08171/18320).

ROWING Rowboats add to the charm of the lakes in the Englischer Garten. (There's a kiosk located at the edge of the Kleinhesseloher See renting them during clement weather.) You can also find rowboat rentals on the southern bank of the Olympiasee, in the Olympiapark.

SKIING Because of the proximity of the Bavarian and Austrian alps, many residents of Munich are avid skiers. For information on resorts and getaway snow-related activities, contact the **Bayerischer Skiverband,** Georg-Brauchle-Ring 93, D-8000 München 50 (tel. 089/157-02-0).

SPECTATOR SPORTS If you want to participate in Munich's soccer craze by attending a match between opposing teams from different ends of Europe, chances are good that there'll be one in Munich's enormous Olympiapark (tel. 089/30613-204). Originally built for the 1972 Olympics, it's the largest recreational and sports facility in Europe, and has facilities for competitions of virtually every kind. Two organizations that keep close tabs on all spectator events within Munich and its environs (including the Olympiapark), and sometimes act as an outlet for ticket sales, are the **Haus des Sports,** Georg-Brauchle-Ring 93 (tel. 089/157-02-0), and the **Stadtischen Sportamt,** Neuhauserstrasse 26 (tel. 089/23-36-224).

TENNIS At least 200 indoor and outdoor tennis courts are scattered around greater Munich. Many can be booked in advance through **Sport Scheck** (tel. 089/21-660). For information on Munich's many tennis tournaments and competitions, contact the **Bayerischer Tennis Verband,** Georg-Brauchle-Ring 93, D-8000 München 50 (tel. 089/157-02-640).

8. SAVVY SHOPPING

The most interesting shops are concentrated on Munich's pedestrians-only street, lying between Karlsplatz and Marienplatz at the Rathaus.

The following recommended stores keep the same hours: 8:30am to 12:30pm and 3 to 6pm Monday to Friday; on Saturday, they operate "half days"—that is, 8:30am to noon. They are closed Sunday.

ART & ANTIQUES

ILEANA ELLENBOGEN, Frauenstrasse 12. Tel. 089/29-27-98.

This gallery, across from one of Munich's best-known outdoor vegetable markets, sells original art nouveau stained-glass windows. This Romanian-born art historian sells glass carefully extracted from old houses and public buildings in Belgium, Germany, France, England, and Austria, with a scattering from 19th-century America as well.

KUNSTHANDLUNG TIMBERG, Maximilianstrasse 15. Tel. 089/29-52-35.

In the central shopping mall, this outlet—almost a miniature museum—has the best collection of new and antique Meissen porcelain. Look for both an old or new Meissener coffee set with the blue-and-white onion design. *Important:* Any purchase here can be packed and shipped safely. They've had a lot of experience in doing just that.

BOOKSTORE

HUGENDUBEL, Marienplatz 22. Tel. 089/23-89-1.
Not only is this the biggest bookstore in Munich, but also it enjoys the most central location. It sells a number of English-language titles, both fiction and nonfiction. It also offers a number of travel books and helpful maps.

CAMERAS

PHOTO-KOHLROSER, Maffeistrasse 14. Tel. 089/22-10-19.
Germany's cameras are magnificent, and Leica is perhaps the most famous name. This shop carries a good assortment of cameras and equipment. The location is within an easy walk of the Bayerischer Hof and American Express. Look also for the Minox cameras (sometimes referred to humorously as "spy cameras"). The shop also carries Japanese cameras, field glasses, and video cameras. It also does photo express developing.

CHOCOLATE

ELLY SEIDL, Am Kosttor 2. Tel. 089/22-15-22.
This is the premier shop for delectable homemade chocolates. Whatever your taste, this store can generally meet your demand.

CRAFTS

BAYERISCHER KUNSTGEWERBEVEREIN [Bavarian Association of Artisans], Pacellistrasse 7. Tel. 089/29-35-21.
At this showcase for Bavarian artisans, you'll find excellent handcrafts: ceramics, glasses, jewelry, wood carvings, pewter, and Christmas decorations.

KARL STORR, Kaufingerstrasse 25. Tel. 089/22-95-14.
Here you'll find the finest selection of Bavarian wood carvings, both machinemade and handmade items.

LUDWIG BECK AM RATHAUSECK, Am Marienplatz 11. Tel. 089/236-91-0.
This outlet is a four-floor shopping bazaar selling handmade crafts from all over Germany, both old and new. Items include decorative pottery and dishes, beer steins and vases of etched glass, painted wall plaques depicting rural scenes, and decorative flower arrangements. There is much unusual kitchenware, colored flatware, calico hot pads and towels, and a collection of leather-trimmed canvas purses that are casually chic. The shop also offers fashions and textiles.

WALLACH, Residenzstrasse 1. Tel. 089/22-08-71.
Wallach is the preferred place to shop for folk art and handcrafts. In fact, I consider it the finest place in Germany to obtain handcrafts, both new and antique. It can save much time in your search for a memorable object that will remind you of your trip to Germany. You'll find such items as antique churns, old kitchenware, brass hunting horns, rag-rug lengths sold by the yard, paintings on glass, charmingly hand-painted wooden boxes and trays, milking stools, painted porcelain clocks, wooden wall clocks, doilies, napkins, and towels.

FASHION

FOR THE SKIER

BOGNER HAUS, Residenzstrasse 15. Tel. 089/29-07-04-0.
Bogner Haus is the place to shop for the latest in ski clothing and styles before you head for the slopes. All this flamboyant attire is sold by Willy Bogner, the filmmaker

and Olympic downhill racer. The store also sells more formal clothing for men and women.

TRADITIONAL CLOTHING

DIRNDL-ECKE, Am Platzl 1-Sparkassenstrasse 10. Tel. 089/22-01-63.

★ One block up from the famed Hofbräuhaus, this shop gets my unreserved recommendation as a stylish place specializing in high-grade dirndls, feathered alpine hats, and all clothing associated with the alpine regions. Everything sold is of fine quality—there is no tourist junk. Other merchandise includes needlework hats, beaded belts, and pleated shirts for men. You may also be attracted to the stylish capes; the silver jewelry in old Bavarian style; the leather shoes; or the linen-and-cotton combinations, such as skirts with blouses and jackets. Bavarian clothing for children is also sold.

FRANKONIA, Maximilianplatz 10. Tel. 089/291-31-31.

This store has the most prestigious collection of traditional Bavarian dress (called *Tracht* in German) in Munich. If you see yourself dressed hunter style, this place can outfit you well. It has a fine collection of wool cardigan jackets with silvery buttons.

LODEN-FREY, Maffeistrasse 7–9. Tel. 089/23-69-30.

The twin domes of the Frauenkirche are visible above the soaring glass-enclosed atrium of this shop's showroom. Go here for the world's largest selection of Loden clothing and traditional costumes, as well as for international fashions from top such European designers as Armani, Valentino, and Ungaro.

JEWELRY & WATCHES

ANDREAS HUBER, Weinstrasse 8. Tel. 089/29-82-95.

This store sells all the big names in Swiss and other European wristwatches as well as clocks. They offer some jewelry, but their main focus is on timepieces.

GEBRUDER HEMMERLE, Maximilianstrasse 14. Tel. 22-01-89.

This is the place for jewelry. The original founders of this stylish place made their fortune designing bejeweled fantasies for the Royal Bavarian Court of Ludwig II. Today, within a shop paneled in southern baroque pastel-painted wood, you can buy some of the most desirable jewelry in the capital. All pieces are designed and made in-house by Bavarian craftspeople whose editions are limited. The company also designs a wristwatch of its own, the Hemmerle, and distributes what is said to be one of the world's finest watches, the Breguet.

PORCELAIN

KUSTERMANN [ROSENTHAL], Theatinerstrasse 8. Tel. 089/22-04-22.

Set near the Rathaus, this is a prestigious shop for porcelain and glass manufactured by the noted Rosenthal firm. Several Bavarian factories combine to produce the high-quality china, known throughout the world. You'll also find matching crystal and gift items. The store will wrap and mail your purchases virtually anywhere. Another, somewhat larger, branch of this store lies at the Viktualienmarkt 2 (tel. 089/23-72-50).

NYMPHENBURGER PORZELLANMANUFAKTUR, Nordliches Schloss-rondell 8. Tel. 089/17-91-970.

At Nymphenburg, about 5 miles northwest of the heart of Munich, this is one of the most famous porcelain factories in Germany, on the grounds of Schloss Nymphenburg. You can visit its exhibition and sales rooms, where shipments can be arranged if you make purchases, Monday to Friday only from 8am to noon and 12:30 to 5pm.

9. EVENING ENTERTAINMENT

To find out what's happening in the Bavarian capital, go to the tourist office (see "Accommodations," above) and request a copy of *Monatsprogramm*, costing 2 DM ($1.30). It contains a complete cultural guide for visitors to Munich, telling you not only what is being presented—from concerts to opera, from special exhibitions to museum hours—but also how to purchase tickets.

PERFORMING ARTS

Perhaps nowhere else in Europe, other than London and Paris, will you find so many musical and theatrical performances. And the good news is the low cost of the seats—so count on indulging yourself and going to several concerts. You'll get good tickets if you're willing to pay anywhere from 15 DM to 70 DM ($9.90 to $46.20).

If you speak German, you'll find at least 20 theaters offering plays of every description: classic, comic, experimental, contemporary—take your pick. The best way to find out what current productions might interest you is to go to a theater-ticket agency: The most convenient one is at Marienplatz at the entrance to the S-Bahn.

GASTEIG KULTURZENTRUM, Rosenheimer Strasse 5. Tel. 089/48-09-80.

Gasteig Cultural Center is the home of the Münchner Philharmoniker (Munich Philharmonic Orchestra), which was founded in 1893. Its present home, which opened in 1985, also shelters the Richard Strauss Conservatory and The Munich Municipal Library. The orchestra performs in Philharmonic Hall, which has the largest seating capacity of the center's five performance halls. In the district of Haidhausen, Gasteig stands on the bluffs of the Isar River. It is reached by taking the S-Bahn or bus 51. You can purchase tickets to events at the ground-level Glashalle, Monday to Friday from 10:30am to 2pm and 3 to 6pm and Saturday from 10:30am to 2pm. The Philharmonic season begins in mid-September and runs to July.

Tickets: 20 DM–120 DM ($13.20–$79.20).
Tram: 18 to Gasteig. **S-Bahn:** Rosenheimer Platz.

NATIONALTHEATER, Max-Joseph-Platz 2. Tel. 089/22-13-16.

Practically any night of the year, except August to mid-September, you'll find a performance at the opera house, the home of the Bavarian State Opera, one of the world's great companies. The Bavarians give their hearts, perhaps their souls, to opera. Productions are beautifully mounted and presented and sung by some of the world's greatest singers. Hard-to-get tickets may be purchased Monday to Friday from 10am to 1pm and 3:30 to 5:30pm, plus one hour before each performance (during the weekend, only on Saturday from 10am to 12:30pm). The National theater is also the home of the highly praised Bavarian National Ballet. For ticket information, call 089/29-36-49.

Tickets: 7 DM–190 DM ($4.60–$125.40), including standing room.
U-Bahn or S-Bahn: Marienplatz.

DEUTSCHES THEATER, Schwanthalerstrasse 13. Tel. 089/55-234-0.

The regular season of the Deutsches Theater lasts from March to June and July to December. Musicals are popular, but operettas, ballets, and international shows are performed as well. It's the only theater in Germany that is both a theater and a ballroom. During the carnival season in January and February, the seats are removed and stored, replaced by tables and chairs for more than 2,000 guests. Handmade decorations by artists combined with lighting effects create an enchanting ambience. Waiters serve wine, champagne, and food. There are costume balls and official black-tie festivities, famous throughout Europe.

Tickets: 17 DM–29 DM ($11.20–$19.10).
U-Bahn: Karlsplatz/Stachus.

STAATSTHEATER AM GÄRTNERPLATZ, Gärtnerplatz 3. Tel. 089/20-167-67.

This is yet another theater where the presentations are varied and entertaining. The programs include ballet, opera, operettas, and musicals. The ticket office is open during the same hours as that of the Nationaltheater.

Tickets: 10 DM–85 DM ($6.60–$56.10).

U-Bahn: Fraunhoferstrasse.

ALTES RESIDENZTHEATER (Cuvilliés Theater), Residenzstrasse 1. Tel. 089/22-13-16.

⭐ A part of the Residenz (see "The Top Attractions," above), this theater is a sightseeing attraction in its own right. The Bavarian State Opera and the Bayerisches Staatsschauspiel (Bavarian National Theater) perform smaller works here in keeping with the more intimate character of the tiny theater. Box-office hours are the same as those for the Nationaltheater. The theater is celebrated as the most outstanding example of a rococo tier-boxed theater in the country. Seating an audience of 550, it was designed by court architect Francois de Cuvilliés in the mid-18th century. During World War II, the interior of the theater was dismantled and stored; after the war it was reassembled in the reconstructed building. For an admission of 2 DM ($1.30), visitors can look at the theater Monday to Saturday from 2 to 5pm and Sunday from 10am to 5pm.

Tickets: Opera tickets 10 DM–175 DM ($6.60–$115.50); play tickets 7 DM–48 DM ($4.60–$31.70).

U-Bahn: U3, U5, or U6 to Odeonsplatz.

MÜNCHNER KAMMERSPIELE, Maximilianstrasse 26-28. Tel. 089/237-21-328.

Contemporary plays, as well as classics from German or international playwrights, ranging from Goethe to Brecht, from Shakespeare to Goldoni, are performed here in season. The season lasts from early October to the end of July. Tickets can be reserved by phone Monday through Friday from 10am to 6pm but must be picked up at least two days before a performance. The box office is open Monday through Friday from 10am to 6pm and Saturday from 10am to 1pm.

Tickets: 8 DM–43 DM ($5.30–$28.40).

Tram: 19 to Maximilianstrasse.

BEER HALLS

The Bierhalle is a traditional Munich institution, offering food, entertainment, and, of course, beer.

AUGUSTINERBRAU, Neuhauserstrasse 16. Tel. 089/55-199-257.

On the principal pedestrians-only street of Munich, this beer hall offers generous helpings of food, good beer, and mellow atmosphere. Dark-wood panels and ceilings in carved plaster make the place look even older than it is. It's been around for less than a century, but beer was first brewed on this spot in 1328, or so the literature about the establishment claims. The long menu changes daily, and the cuisine is not for dieters: It's hearty, heavy, and starchy, but that's what the customers want.

Prices: Half a liter of beer from 4.95 DM ($3.30); meals 25 DM–55 DM ($16.50–$36.30).

Open: Mon–Sat 10am–midnight. **U-Bahn or S-Bahn:** Marienplatz. Tram: 19.

HOFBRÄUHAUS AM PLATZL, Am Platzl 9. Tel. 089/22-16-76.

⭐ This is the most famous beer hall in the world, a legend among beer halls. Visitors with only one night in Munich usually target the Hofbräuhaus as their number-one nighttime destination. Owned by the state, the present Hofbräuhaus was built at the end of the 19th century, but the tradition of a beer house on this spot dates from 1589. In the 19th century it attracted artists, students, and civil servants. It was called the Blue Hall because of its dim lights and smoky atmosphere. When it grew too small to contain everybody, architects designed another in 1897. This one was the 1920 setting for the notorious meeting of Hitler's newly launched German Workers Party. Fistfights erupted as the Nazis attacked their Bavarian enemies, right in the beer palace.

Today 4,500 beer drinkers can crowd in here on a given night. There are several rooms spread over three floors, including one on the top floor for dancing every night in summer. But with its brass band (which starts playing in the afternoon), the ground-floor Schwemme is most typical of what you always expected of a beer hall—here it's eternal Oktoberfest. In the second-floor restaurant, strolling musicians, including an accordion player and a violinist, entertain. Dirndl-clad servers place mugs of beer at your table between sing-alongs. In season, from mid-March to October Hofbräuhaus am Platzl presents a typical Bavarian show in its Fest-Hall every evening, starting at 7pm and lasting until midnight. The entrance fee is 8 DM ($5.30), and the food is the same as that served in the other parts of the beer palace.

Prices: Liter of beer, 8.20 DM ($5.40); meals 15 DM–35 DM ($9.90–$23.10).
Open: Daily 9am–midnight. **U-Bahn or S-Bahn:** Marienplatz.

LOWENBRÄUKELLER, Nymphenburgerstrasse 2. Tel. 089/52-60-21.

This beer hall is gargantuan, busy inside and out. Admittedly, it's somewhat removed from the center of town, yet it offers one of the best gemütlich evenings in Munich. On the à la carte menu, a typical main dish would be Sauerbraten with dumplings and red cabbage. Such Bavarian specialties are served in the open-air beer garden. A simple meal might cost 15 DM ($10), but you could spend a lot more, of course—from 30 DM ($19.80) and beyond. The Lowenbräukeller is especially known for its musical programs, including "Bavarian Evenings" and "Royal Bavarian Nights," when live entertainment is featured.

Prices: Stein of beer from 6.50 DM ($4.30).
Open: Daily 9am–1am. **Tram:** 12.

MATHÄSER BIERSTADT, Bayerstrasse 5. Tel. 089/59-28-96.

Mathäser Bierstadt is a rough and rowdy beer city, filled both afternoons and evenings with happy imbibers. To reach the Bierhalle, walk through to the back, then go upstairs. Featured is a brass band oompahing away. The largest of all Bavarian taverns, the Mathäser contains tables of drinkers joining in the songs. Even at midafternoon the place is often packed, making you wonder if anybody is working in the entire city. In addition to the main hall, there are a rooftop garden and a downstairs tavern. Lowenbräu kegs spill out onto the sidewalk for stand-up sausage and Kraut nibblers. Specialties of the house include knuckles of veal and pork. At certain times of the year you can order soups made with fresh white asparagus.

During the spring "strong beer season," two weeks after the end of Fasching, and during Oktoberfest, the Mathäser holds a special program featuring a big brass band and yodeling. The place is also famous for its Bavarian breakfasts with Weisswürste and beer.

Prices: Liter of beer from 8.40 DM ($5.50); meals 15 DM–35 DM ($9.90–$23.10).
Open: Daily 8am–midnight. **U-Bahn or S-Bahn:** Stachus.

PLATZL, Am Platzl 1. Tel. 089/23-70-30.

Platzl faces its more famous competitor, the Hofbräuhaus. It presents a Bavarian folk program nightly in the large beer-hall area. The women dancers wear dirndls, the men dress in lederhosen, loden jackets, and felt hats. Together they perform the Schulplattler, the thigh-slapping folk dance of the Bavarian Alps. The entrance charge for the two-hour show is 15 DM ($9.90). The inn offers fine Bavarian food and sausages; Platzl draft beer from a keg is placed at the table.

Prices: Half a liter of beer from 4.90 DM ($3.20); meals 20 DM–50 DM ($13.20–$33).
Open: Tues–Sat 11am–2pm and 6:30pm–midnight. **Tram:** 19. **U-Bahn:** Marienplatz.

WALDWIRTSCHAFT GROSSHESSLOHE, Georg-Kalb-Strasse 3. Tel. 089/79-50-88.

This popular summertime rendezvous has seats for some 2,000 drinkers. The gardens are open daily from 10:30am to 10pm (they have to close early because of complaints from neighborhood residents). Music ranging from Dixieland to English jazz to Polish bands is played throughout the week. Entrance is free and you bring your own food. The location is above the Isar River in the vicinity of the zoo.
Prices: Liter of beer 10 DM ($6.60).
Open: Daily 10:30am–10pm. **Tram:** 7.

CLUB & MUSIC SCENE
NIGHTCLUBS

BAYERISCHER HOF NIGHT CLUB, Hotel Bayerischer Hof, Promenade-platz 2-6. Tel. 089/212-09-94.
Contained within the extensive cellars of the previously recommended Bayerischer Hof, is some of the most sophisticated entertainment in Munich. Within one very large room is a piano bar where a musician plays melodies every night between 6 and 10pm. Behind a partition that disappears after 10pm is a bandstand for live orchestras, which play to a crowd of dancing patrons every night between 10pm and between 3 and 4am, depending on business. Entrance to the piano bar is free, but there's a cover charge to the nightclub on Friday and Saturday nights.
Admission: 18 DM ($11.90) on Fri–Sat to nightclub. **Prices:** Drinks from 18 DM ($11.90); meals from 60 DM ($39.60).
Open: Daily 6pm–3 or 4am. **Tram:** 19.

WELSER KUCHE, Residenzstrasse 27. Tel. 089/29-69-73.
Welser Kuche offers hearty medieval feasts. Guests can begin a meal any night of the week from 8pm, and they must be prepared to stick around for three hours, as they are served by "Magde" and "Knechte" (or wenches and knaves) in 16th-century costumes, as was the custom 450 years ago. In many ways this is like a takeoff on one of the many medieval Tudor banquets that enjoy such popularity with tourists in London. Food is served in hand-thrown pottery, and guests eat these medieval delicacies with their fingers, aided only by a stilettolike dagger.
You can order a 6- or 10-course menu, called a Welser Feast; for smaller appetites, 4-course meals are also served. Many of the recipes were found in a cookbook that belonged to a 16th-century baroness. Discovered in 1970, the cookbook serves as a culinary guide. The place can be good fun if you're in the mood, but because it is likely to be overflowing, reservations are recommended.
Prices: Menus 44.50 DM ($29.40), 64.50 DM ($42.60), and 74.50 DM ($49.20).
Open: Daily 8pm–1am. **U-Bahn:** U3 to Odeonsplatz.

CABARET

RATIONALTHEATER, Hesseloherstrasse 18. Tel. 089/33-50-40.
In Munich when you "come to the cabaret"—political, that is—you may end up at the Rationaltheater. It has existed since 1963, and some critics claim its political satire is so pointed that it has the power to topple governments. The show is performed every day except Sunday and Monday, starting at 8:30pm. Tickets must be reserved by phone, beginning at 10am.
Tickets: 25 DM–30 DM ($16.50–$19.80).
Open: Shows Tues–Sat 8:30pm.

JAZZ

JAZZCLUB UNTERFAHRT, Kirchenstrasse 96. Tel. 089/448-27-94.
This is the leading jazz club of Munich, lying near the Ostbahnhof in the district of Haidhausen. Within a gemütlich ambience of pinewood paneling and flickering candles, its management presents live music every night of the week but Monday. Off to one corner of the 120-seat establishment is an art gallery where a changing collection of paintings and sculpture are sold. Live music begins at 9pm. Wine, small

snacks, beer, and hard drinks are sold as well. Sunday night there's a special jam session for improvisation.

Admission: 13 DM–18 DM ($8.60–$11.90); Sun jam session 5 DM ($3.30). **Prices:** Beer from 7.90 DM ($5.20); snacks 4.50 DM–7.50 DM ($3–$5). **Open:** Daily 6pm–1am. **S-Bahn or U-Bahn:** Ostbahnhof.

SCHWABINGER PODIUM, Wagnerstrasse 1. Tel. 089/39-94-82.

This club offers varying nightly entertainment. Some evenings are devoted to jazz, and on other occasions I've been entertained by Dixieland as well as rock.

Admission: 5 DM–8 DM ($3.30–$5.30). **Prices:** Beer from 5.80 DM ($3.80). **Open:** Daily 8pm–1am. **U-Bahn:** U3 or U6 to Munchner Freiheit.

DISCOS

NACHCAFÉ, Maximilianplatz 5. Tel. 089/59-59-00.

It hums, it thrives, and it captures the nocturnal imagination of everyone: No other nightspot in Munich attracts such an array of soccer stars, film celebrities, literary figures, and, as one employee put it, "ordinary people, but only the most sympathetically crazy ones." Waves of patrons appear at different times of the evening: at midnight, when live concerts begin; at about 2am, when restaurants close; and at about 4am, when diehard revelers seek a final drink as they face the predawn hours. There are no fewer than four indoor bars (and an additional three on an outdoor terrace in summertime), and lots of tiny tables. There's no cover charge. The decor is updated 1950s (lots of neon), the music a sort of "retro-fun" beat, with electric rhythms.

Prices: Beer 5.50 DM–6 DM ($3.60–$4); drinks 11 DM ($7.30); meals 15 DM–30 DM ($9.90–$19.80). **Open:** Daily 7pm–5am. **Tram:** 19.

PARK-CAFÉ, Sophienstrasse 7. Tel. 089/59-83-13.

This is a Tanzpalast (dance palace) with a disc jockey, located near the Hauptbahnhof in an imposing building whose massive neoclassical porch belies the theatrical kitsch decor within. The only cover imposed is on Friday and Saturday. Sandwiches are the only food served.

Admission: 15 DM ($9.90) Fri–Sat; otherwise free. **Prices:** Beer from 8.90 DM ($5.90); sandwiches 12 DM–15 DM ($7.90–$9.90). **Open:** Tues–Sun 10:30am–4am. **S-Bahn or U-Bahn:** Hauptbahnhof.

BAR & CAFE SCENE

SCHUMANN'S, Maximilianstrasse 36. Tel. 089/22-90-60.

Located on Munich's most desirable shopping street, Schumann's doesn't waste any money on decor. It doesn't have to, as it depends on the local beau monde to keep it fashionable. In cold weather, guests retreat inside, but once the sun heats up, they prefer the terrace that spills out onto the street. Schumann's is known as "a thinking man's bar." Charles Schumann, author of three bar books, conceived of a bar that would serve as an artistic, literary, and communicative social focus of the metropolis. Popular with the film, advertising, and publishing worlds, his place is said to have contributed to a remarkable renaissance of bar culture in the city.

Prices: Drinks 8.90 DM–30 DM ($5.90–$19.80). **Open:** Sun–Fri 5pm–3am. **Closed:** Sat. **Tram:** 19.

HARRY'S NEW YORK BAR, Falkenturmstrasse 9. Tel. 089/22-27-00.

Near the Hofbräuhaus, the establishment takes its name from the first American bar in Paris in the 1920s and features such drinks as the Sidecar cocktail, created in 1931, and the Monkey's Gland, created in 1930. Attentive waiters will bring you food as well, including salads, chili tacos, and a shrimp plate. Every evening from 9pm there is a singing piano player featured in the "Downstairs Room."

Prices: Beer from 9 DM ($5.90); drinks from 15 DM ($9.90); snacks 15 DM–20 DM ($9.90–$13.20).

Open: Mon–Sat 4pm–3am. **Tram:** 10.

ALTER SIMPL, Türkenstrasse 57. Tel. 089/272-30-83.

Once a literary café, Alter Simpl takes its name from a satirical review of 1903. There is no one around any more who remembers the revue of that name, but Alter Simpl remained on the scene and was made famous by its legendary owner, Kathi Kobus. Lale Andersen, who made the song "Lili Marlene" famous, frequented the café when she was in Munich always maintaining that the correct spelling of the song was "Lili Marleen," as pointed out repeatedly in her autobiography (she died while promoting the book). Today it attracts a wide segment of locals, including a lot of young people, even counterculturists and Gastarbeiters. Food is served, including sausages, potato salad, rumpsteak, and omelets. The real fun of the place occurs after 11pm, when the iconoclastic artistic ferment is more reminiscent of Berlin than Bavaria.

Prices: Drinks from 10 DM ($6.60); light meals from 28 DM ($18.50).
Open: Mon–Sat 6pm–3 or 4am. **Tram:** 18. **Bus:** 53.

SCHULTZ, Barerstrasse 47. Tel. 089/271-47-11.

Schultz is a New York–style bar in Schwabing popular with a clientele of theater people who crowd in as they do at Schumann's for lots of smoke-filled chatter. The food is uncomplicated. The decor, as they say here, is "unobvious and understated."

Prices: Beer from 4.50 DM ($3); drinks from 12.50 DM ($8.30).
Open: Daily 5pm–1am. **U-Bahn:** U3 or U6 to Münchner Freiheit.

WEINSCHENKE AM MARKT, Dreifaltigkeitsplatz 1. Tel. 089/22-61-33.

Since about 1400, Münchners have patronized this ancient winehouse. At the edge of the city's huge outside vegetable and fruit market, the Viktualienmarkt, the winehouse has arched ceilings and hand-painted country furnishings. You can have cheese, Black Forest ham, and herb bread to accompany one of the Austrian, French, or German wines.

Prices: Wine from 9 DM ($5.90) per glass.
Open: Mon–Sat 11am–1am. **U-Bahn:** Marienplatz.

GAY CLUBS

NEW YORK, Sonnenstrasse 25. Tel. 089/59-10-56.

The strident rhythms and electronic sounds might just have been imported from New York, Los Angeles, or Paris. The sound system is sophisticated and accompanied by shows of laser-driven light. This is the premier gay (male) disco of Munich. Most clients, whose ages range from 20 to 35, wear jeans.

Admission: 10 DM ($6.60) Fri–Sun; otherwise free. **Prices:** Beer from 7 DM ($4.60); drinks 14.50 DM ($9.60).
Open: Daily 11pm–4am. **U-Bahn:** U1, U2, U3, or U6 to Sendlinger-Tor-Platz.

TEDDY BAR, Hans-Sachsstrasse 1. Tel. 089/260-33-59.

Teddy Bar is a small, cozy 100% gay bar decorated with teddy bears. It draws a congenial crowd, both foreign and domestic. There's no cover. From October to April, a Sunday brunch is given from 11am to 3pm.

Prices: Beer 4.50 DM–5 DM ($3–$3.30); drinks 13 DM ($8.60).
Open: Daily 24 hrs. **Tram:** 18 or 25. **U-Bahn:** Sendlingertor.

10. EASY EXCURSIONS

The whole of the Bavarian Alps awaits within commuting distance of Munich (see Chapter 12), or you can head for Neuschwanstein (see Chapter 11) to see Ludwig II's fairy-tale castle.

DACHAU In 1933 what had once been a quiet little artists' community just 10 miles from Munich, **KZ-Gedenkstätte Dachau,** Robert-Bosch-Strasse (tel. 089/ 08131/17-41), became what was to be a tragic symbol of the Nazi era. Himmler and the SS set up the first German concentration camp in March of that year, on the grounds of a former ammunition factory. Dachau saw countless prisoners arrive between 1933 and 1945. Although the files show a registry of more than 206,000, the exact number of people imprisoned here is unknown.

Entering the camp today, you are faced by three memorial chapels—Catholic, Protestant, and Jewish—built in the early 1960s. Immediately behind the Catholic chapel is the "Lagerstrasse," the main camp road lined with poplar trees, once flanked by the 32 barracks, each housing 208 prisoners. Two of these barracks have been rebuilt to give visitors an insight into the horrible conditions endured by the prisoners.

The museum is housed in the large building that once contained the kitchen, laundry, and shower baths where prisoners were often brought for torture by the SS. Photographs and documents show the rise of the Nazi regime, the superpower of the SS, as well as exhibits depicting the persecution of Jews and other prisoners. Every effort has been made to present the facts. The tour of Dachau is a truly moving experience.

You can get to the camp by taking the frequent S-Bahn trains (train S2) from the Hauptbahnhof to the Dachau station (direction: Petershausen), and then bus no. 722 from the station to the camp. Admission is free, and the camp is open Tuesday to Sunday from 9am to 5pm. The English version of a documentary film, *KZ-Dachau*, is shown at 11:30am and 3:30pm. All documents are translated in the catalog, available at the entrance of the museum.

LEADING SPA RESORTS

Even if you wander into the most out-of-the-way places in Germany, you'll never get away from one of the greatest of all Teutonic institutions, the spa. Dozens are spread throughout the country; some have been known since Roman times, while others are of much more recent vintage, but they all have one thing in common—"healing" waters.

From seawater to thermal or radioactive springs, the Germans have learned to make the best use of all types of water for all types of ailments. Ever since the Kneipp treatment, commonly called hydrotherapy, was formulated by a Bavarian pastor, natural mineral springs are no longer a prerequisite for the establishment of a spa. Spas exist in every imaginable location, from seaside resorts to mountaintops in the Bavarian Alps. Besides mud baths and hydrotherapy, they offer a wide range of activities and facilities. From the casinos in Baden-Baden, Bad Homburg, and Westerland to golf courses and horse racing, there's never a dull moment during the busy summer spa season. Some of the larger spas are active all year.

In this chapter I'll sample some of the variety to be found among the spas. In addition to the seven spas detailed, you'll find other important German resorts, such as Baden-Baden in Chapter 9, Bad Godesberg in Chapter 6, and Westerland in Chapter 16.

THE GERMAN SPA

More than any other country in Europe, Germany developed the spa process to a high art. Although immersing overtired, arthritic, or overindulged bodies in mineral springs has been actively promoted for thousands of years (and brought to a highly debauched art by the ancient Romans), in Europe (especially in Germany) the practice developed into an intensely ritualized social process. The noble families of Central Europe understood for many years the value of immersing gouty feet, overtaxed kidneys, and enlarged livers into heated mineral waters, but the heyday of German spa construction occurred during the 19th century. Then, almost as a symbol of the newly emerging power of the German bourgeoisie, a lavish series of resorts was built above the dozens of mineral springs that bubbled out of the German soil. Many of these springs had been known since the Middle Ages, and each was attributed specifically with cures for arthritis, gout, infertility, hypertension, and/or gynecological problems.

Inspired by the universal yearning for health and longevity of their clientele, the new spas richly incorporated the most lavish architecture, landscaping, service, and

WHAT'S SPECIAL ABOUT THE SPA RESORTS

Great Towns/Villages

☐ Wiesbaden, the most international of spas, one of Germany's oldest cities. Its hot springs attracted Roman legions 2,000 years ago.

☐ Bad Homburg, a popular watering spot since Roman times, a favorite of royalty at the turn of the century.

☐ Bad Reichenhall, an old salt town that's the most curative spa in the Bavarian Alps.

Ace Attractions

☐ Wiesbaden's Bath Quarter (Kurviertel), from the beginning of the century an international meeting place.

☐ Bad Homburg's Spielbank (Casino), called the "Mother of Monte Carlo"—the gaming capital of Europe in the 19th century.

☐ Bad Reichenhaller Quellenbau, the old salt works of Bavaria, ordered constructed by Ludwig I of Bavaria.

Parks/Gardens

☐ Bad Pyrmont's Spa Park (Kurpark), among the most beautiful in Germany, planted with hundreds of different species of palms.

☐ Wiesbaden's Spa Park (Kurpark), with its century-old trees and attractive lake stretching for half a mile of landscaped lushness.

Religious Shrine

☐ Bad Wildungen's Stadtkirche, from the 14th century, owner of the *Niederwildungen Altarpiece*, one of the best examples of early German painting (1403).

cuisine then available in Europe. As 19th-century Europe industrialized and grew wealthy, the recently prosperous bourgeoisie flooded into the spa towns (especially when their gardens were at their most lavish), scheduling for itself rounds of parties, musical concerts, and receptions that were judiciously interspersed with rest, relaxation, and—sometimes as an afterthought or as an excuse for the entire process—carefully controlled immersions in the mineral springs.

Recently, modern and up-to-date spas, many imitating (and modifying) the format, have developed in the United States and France. Stressing weight control, cholesterol counts, and the kinds of stress reduction that are appropriate for overworked American urbanites, they draw a devoted clientele who spend thousands in their search for health and well being. The new (North American) spas tend to serve updated cuisine and to stress exercise regimes and (occasionally) well-presented introductions to yoga and Eastern mysticism. In response, the German spas have modified their cuisine to incorporate diet and weight-reduction programs, and updated many of their health programs to reflect modern tastes in health and beauty. These changes within the German spas have been subtle, however, and have in no way detracted from the time-honored rituals that make attendance at a German spa town so interesting.

Don't expect frenzied nightlife or nonstop activities. The reason for being at a spa is to escape pressure, and the spas wisely seem to pad the emotional corners of life for their clientele, providing a soothing and unruffled environment that almost anyone could appreciate for a day or two. Even if you choose not to visit the innards and bowels of the clinics (most of which are disturbingly reminiscent of hospitals and are usually connected with hotels), the insight into the ritualization of German social life is worth the effort. Enjoy a leisurely meal in one of the resort's airy and elegantly formal restaurants, preferably one that overlooks a sprawling garden accented with thousands of flowers. Sit in a café, perhaps with a glass of wine, and watch a rather conservative clientele engaged in the rituals of the prosperous bourgeoisie. And, if you choose, elect for a spa treatment, subjecting your travel-weary body to everything from mud baths to immersions in sulphur-rich water, and endure the massages and skin treatments that will at least have you emerging from them in decidedly more relaxed form than when you initially began them.

There are more than 250 health resorts in Germany today. The word *Bad* before the name of any town (i.e., Bad Godesberg, Bad Orb) is a sure sign that somewhere within that town lies some kind of ritualized process for taking the waters. Most spa directors insist on a brief medical checkup—performed on site by resident doctors—before any treatments can begin.

A complete list of spas is available by writing to the **Deutsch Baderverband** (The German Health Resort and Spa Association), Schumannstrasse 111, 5300 Bonn 1 (tel. 0228/26-20-10), or by going to any branch of the German National Tourist Office.

SUGGESTED ITINERARY

Days 1–2   Relax in Wiesbaden, enjoying its elegant hotels, gardens, and mineral baths. On the second day, make a sightseeing excursion to Frankfurt (see Chapter 3).

Day 3   Join well-heeled Frankfurters on their favorite outing: a weekend at Bad Homburg in the Taunus woods, famed for its Spa Park and Spielbank (Casino), founded in 1840.

Days 4–5   Head for Bavaria's best-known spa, Bad Reichenhall, a holiday combined not only with sampling the resort's curative springs, but sightseeing in the Alps.

GETTING THERE

Unlike the other regional chapters in this guide, the "Spa country" is not a geographical section of Germany but a group of spas selected from dozens of possibilities—a selection, we hope, that will appeal to a wide array of taste. Therefore, each spa has its own transportation network, outlined in the introduction to each town.

---

1. BAD PYRMONT

45 miles SW of Hannover, 30 miles SE of Bielefeld

GETTING THERE   By Train   The nearest airport is at Hannover, but good rail connections from that city hook up with Bad Pyrmont. There are frequent trains throughout the day on the Hannover Paderborn main rail line. For rail information, call 05281/19419.

By Bus   Regional buses run between Hameln (see Chapter 14) and Bad Pyrmont. The service is provided by RVH Busline Hameln (tel. 05151/12015).

By Car   From Hannover, Route 215 leads southwest to Bad Pyrmont.

ESSENTIALS   For information, go to **Kur-und Verkehrsverein,** Arkaden 14 (tel. 05281/46-27).

This attractive spa has enjoyed a reputation for more than 2,000 years. Its springs vary from the brine variety in the fields to the medicinal iron waters on the southern side of the valley of the Weser Hills. In the center of town you can drink a medicinal cocktail from the fountain at the Hyllige Born spring. Another popular pastime is taking mud baths. But Bad Pyrmont is a good place to vacation even if you don't come to take the waters. Horseback riding in the hills, hiking, tennis, and swimming, as well as concerts and shows, make the resort a lively place.

⭐ The **Spa Park (Kurpark)** is among the most beautiful in Germany, with little temples, flowering trees, and even a palm garden, an unusual touch in the temperate climate. The concert house in the Kurpark has shows during the busy summer. At night the central promenade is glamorously lit, giving the spa a festive air, while guests sit at sidewalk tables drinking beer.

WHERE TO STAY
VERY EXPENSIVE

BERGKURPARK, Ockelstrasse 11, D-3280 Bad Pyrmont. Tel. 05281/ 40-01. Fax 05281/40-04. 57 rms (54 with bath), 3 suites. TEL **Bus:** 3.

$ Rates (including continental breakfast): 59 DM ($38.90) single without bath, 158 DM ($104.30) single with bath; 158 DM ($104.30) double without bath, 360 DM ($237.60) double with bath; from 450 DM ($297) suite. AE, MC, V. **Parking:** 5 DM ($3.30).

The most distinguished hotel at the spa, the Bergkurpark is certainly the most glamorous architecturally. Its entryway has a thatched roof covering a combination hewn-stone and stucco facade with half-rounded picture windows—most dramatic. After checking in, you're shown your room, which might be in a modern block with private terraces overlooking a park. The hotel rents singles, twin-bedded rooms, and a few suites.

Room service, laundry, and dry cleaning are arranged. The hotel has its own park, a forest, a heated pool, and a terrace with sun parasols overlooking the garden. There are also exercise rooms and a sauna. Its restaurant serves the best food at the spa (see below). The hotel also has an elegant café, Sans Souci, and the rustic-style Wilhelm Busch-Stube, where beer, wine, and good food are served.

MODERATE

HOTEL BAD PYRMONTER HOF, Brunnenstrasse 32, D-2380 Bad Pyrmont. Tel. 05281/60-93-03. Fax 05281/60-93-06. 45 rms (38 with bath). TV TEL **Bus:** 3.

$ Rates (including continental breakfast): 70 DM ($46.20) single without bath, 110 DM ($72.60) single with bath; 140 DM–170 DM ($92.40–$112.20) double with bath. AE, MC, V. **Parking:** 5 DM ($3.30).

Providing a personal atmosphere, good service, and comfort, this place has been considerably modernized. The guest rooms are immaculate, restful, and comfortably furnished. The hotel restaurant is only for guests.

HOTEL KAISERHOF, Kirchstrasse 1-2, D-3280 Bad Pyrmont. Tel. 05281/40-11. Fax 05281/30-06. 49 rms (all with bath or shower). TV TEL **Bus:** 3.

$ Rates (including continental breakfast): 110 DM–120 DM ($72.60–$79.20) single; 150 DM–180 DM ($99–$118.80) double. Half-board rates 18 DM ($11.90) per person extra. AE, MC. **Parking:** Free.

When it was originally built in 1910, the Kaiserhof was the finest hotel at the resort, with a glittering clientele from throughout Germany. Today, although supplanted by many younger rivals, it retains its green-and-white facade, its elegant multipaned windows, and its quiet location on a tree-lined street near the Kurpark and the casino. The elegant ground-floor dance café is the best-known one at the spa. The rooms are well furnished, many with balconies opening onto the promenade.

PARK-HOTEL RASMUSSEN, Hauptalle 8, D-3280 Bad Pyrmont. Tel. 05281/44-85. Fax 05281/60-68-72. 12 rms (all with bath or shower). TV TEL **Bus:** 3.

$ Rates (including continental breakfast): 85 DM–120 DM ($56.10–$79.20) single; 160 DM–190 DM ($105.60–$125.40) double. AE. **Closed:** Nov–Feb. **Parking:** 7.50 DM ($5).

This completely renovated villa in the heart of Bad Pyrmont stands on the traffic-free promenade. The spacious rooms are well furnished, with comfortable beds; many have balconies overlooking the promenade. The staff is pleasant.

The hotel's quiet dining room offers lunches costing from 38 DM ($25.10); in the evening, diners are presented such dishes as trout au bleu and wild game (in season) for two, with meals costing from 65 DM ($42.90) per person. The bar adjoining the dining room has a clublike atmosphere.

WHERE TO DINE

MODERATE

RESTAURANT SEPARÉE, in the Hotel Bergkurpark, Ockelstrasse 11. Tel. 05281/40-01.
   Cuisine: INTERNATIONAL. **Reservations:** Not necessary. **Bus:** 3.
$ Prices: Appetizers 8 DM–15 DM ($5.30–$9.90); main courses 21.50 DM–45 DM ($14.20–$29.70); fixed-price menus 28 DM–75 DM ($18.50–$49.50). AE, MC, V.
   Open: Lunch daily noon–2:30pm; dinner daily 6–10pm.

The Separée is part of the finest hotel in town, already previewed. In summer many diners, both foreign and domestic, like to eat on the beautifully decorated terrace. Otherwise, food is served in an elegantly decorated restaurant, with large, comfortable chairs. I was impressed by the size and cleanliness of the kitchen, which turns out an array of international specialties, such as medallions of veal with cream morels. Trout and lobster are kept in a tank.

2. BAD WILDUNGEN

27 miles SW of Kassel; 100 miles NE of Frankfurt am Main

GETTING THERE   By Train   The nearest airport is at Frankfurt, 100 miles away, so rail is preferred. There is very frequent service on the Kassel-Fritzlar line from Kassel.

By Bus   Bus service in the region is provided by Regionalverkehr Kurhessen GmbH (tel. 905661/50401 for schedules and information).

By Car   Access by car is via autobahn A33 from the north and also from federal highway 3. From Kassel take Route 49 southwest, then west on Route 251.

ESSENTIALS   For tourist information, contact the **Kurverwaltung,** Lange-marckstrasse 2 (tel. 05621/7-04-01).

The healing mineral springs of Bad Wildungen have long attracted northern Europeans to the rolling hills and deep forests of the Waldeck region southwest of Kassel. Thousands of annual visitors seek treatment for kidney and gallbladder disorders, or simply come for rest and relaxation and the numerous cultural activities.

The spa gardens augment the natural wooded surroundings with carefully planted flowers from all parts of the world, as well as with several attractive buildings, including two bandshells where outdoor concerts are frequently given. Lawn chairs are placed throughout the grounds for the convenience and comfort of strollers. The modern horseshoe-shaped arcade houses the Georg-Viktor spring, plus several exclusive shops and a small auditorium.

Bad Wildungen is more than 700 years old. Rising above the Altstadt is the massive tower of the 14th-century ✪ **Stadtkirche,** the most impressive (and oldest) structure in the town. The highlight of the church, with its interesting Hallenkirch architecture, is its remarkable *Niederwildungen Altarpiece,* one of the best examples of early German painting. Painted in 1403 by Master Konrad von Soest, the wing-paneled altarpiece contains a large dramatic scene of the Crucifixion, flanked by six smaller scenes depicting the birth, passion, and resurrection of Christ. The work shows an obvious French influence in the use of delicate colors and figures, made even more vivid by the use of actual gold. It is open daily from 8am to 5pm.

WHERE TO STAY

EXPENSIVE

MARITIM BADEHOTEL, Dr.-Marc-Strasse 4, D-3590 Bad Wildungen. Tel. 05621/79-99. Fax 05621/79-97-99. 127 rms, 15 suites. MINIBAR TV TEL
$ Rates (including continental breakfast): 189 DM–283 DM ($124.70–$186.80) single; 264 DM–344 DM ($174.20–$227) double; from 430 DM ($283.80) suite. AE, DC, MC, V. **Parking:** 10 DM ($6.60).

At the entrance to the gardens, in the Kurpark, the Maritim Badehotel, dating from 1855, is located in the center of the clinical and cultural activities. Evoking the grandeur of another era, it's large and rambling, branching out in two great wings from the circular, domed entrance. Aside from a large heated indoor pool, it has its own therapeutic facilities, including carbon dioxide baths, massages, and complete medical attention by a fine professional staff. The renovated hotel rooms are large, sunlit, and airy, all with views of the Waldeck woodlands and spa gardens. Furnishings are sleek, comfortable, and modern. Prices of rooms vary according to size and location.

The hotel's restaurant offers a rich cuisine if you're not worried about calories, although special diets are available, including vegetarian meals. Veal dishes are the specialty, and the *Kalbsschnitzel* (veal scallops) cooked with herbs is a tasty choice. Other dishes include trout au bleu, filet of sole, and *nasi-goreng* (Indonesian fried rice cooked with various spices and ingredients). A carafe of Mosel wine comes with most meals, which cost 42 DM to 76 DM ($27.70 to $50.20).

MODERATE

HOTEL-PENSION DIE HARDTMÜHLE, Im Urfftal 5–7, D-3590 Bad Wildungen. Tel. 05621/7-41. Fax 05621/7-43. 36 rms, 1 apt. TEL
$ Rates (including continental breakfast): 70 DM–85 DM ($46.20–$56.10) single; 120 DM–166 DM ($79.20–$109.60) double; 215 DM ($141.90) family room for three; 315 DM ($207.90) apt for four. MC. **Parking:** 4 DM ($2.60). **Closed:** Jan 10–Feb 5.

⑤ Set in the countryside, with lazy cows grazing the pastureland, this family-run hotel where English is spoken places a strong accent on sports, including swimming in an indoor pool, tennis, and other activities. The rooms are cozy and warmly inviting, and there are units suitable for three to four. Five rooms have TVs. Sometimes a buffet is set out, or the cook may have a barbeque. Meals cost from 30 DM ($19.80). This place is so popular in summer that reservations should be made well in advance.

INEXPENSIVE

HOTEL-CAFÉ SCHWARZE, Brunnenallee 42, D-3590 Bad Wildungen. Tel. 05621/40-64. Fax 05621/74-279. 26 rms. TV TEL

$ Rates (including continental breakfast): 44 DM–75 DM ($29–$49.50) single; 72 DM–110 DM ($47.50–$72.60) double. No credit cards.

Ⓢ Founded in 1876, this has been one of the most popular rendezvous points at the spa for decades. You can drink and dine al fresco at one of the tables in front of the large main building. Antiques and typical furnishings of the region have been used, giving the place a rustic character. Comfortably furnished rooms are rented at very reasonable rates.

3. WIESBADEN

25 miles W of Frankfurt; 94 miles SE of Bonn

GETTING THERE   By Train   The Frankfurt airport (see Chapter 3) is the nearest plane connection. Trains between the airport and Wiesbaden depart about every hour (trains leave from the lower level of the airport). You can purchase tickets (in German marks only) at automatic machines posted within the station area, or else you can go to the airport's railway ticket counter. There is also frequent train service making the 30- to 40-minute trip from the center of Frankfurt on the S-Bahn line. For rail information, call 0611/11531.

By Bus   Deutsche Touring GmbH in Frankfurt (069/790-30) operates frequent service throughout the day to Wiesbaden (Line T81 or T82). Bus service for the surrounding region is provided by Omnibusverkehr Rhein Nahe GmbH in Wiesbaden (tel. 0611/70-70-88 for schedules and more information).

By Car   Wiesbaden lies at a major crossroads, with access via autobahn (A3) from the north and south, connecting with autobahn (A66) from the west and east. Travel time by car from Frankfurt (Route 66) is about 20 to 30 minutes, depending on traffic. From the Frankfurt airport to Wiesbaden by car is about 20 minutes.

ESSENTIALS   For information, go to the **Verkehrsbüro**, Rheinstrasse 15 (tel. 0611/17-29-780), or the **Tourist Information Office** at Im Hauptbahnhof (tel. 0611/17-29-781).

A health resort has been firmly established in this sheltered valley between the Rhine and the Taunus Mountains since Roman times. Although part of its success as a spa is because of its 26 hot springs, with temperatures ranging from 117° to 150°F, its proximity to Germany's larger cities and transportation centers has made Wiesbaden the most international of spas. Retaining much of its turn-of-the-century splendor, Wiesbaden competes with Baden-Baden as Germany's most fashionable resort.

It is also one of the most important cultural centers in the country. Every spring it plays host to the International May Festival of music, dance, and drama. Most of these cultural activities take place in Wiesbaden's **Bath Quarter** (Kurviertel), around the Kurhaus and Kurhauskolonnade opposite the Theaterkolonnade). The major concert halls are in the ✪ **Kurhaus,** a big, lively structure centering around a cupola-crowned hall that opens into rooms in all directions. In addition to concerts, the complex hosts plays and ballets, plus a variety of social gatherings. Since its complete renovation in 1988, it has established itself as a center for international conferences, congresses, exhibitions, and trade fairs. There is also a casino, plus a lively restaurant and an outdoor café.

If you prefer the outdoors, Wiesbaden offers horseback riding, a golf course, indoor and outdoor swimming, tennis, and hiking. The streets of the city are enjoyable for rambling, and the **Spa Park** has a lake surrounded by old shade trees. It is especially beautiful at night, when the lights of the spa and the huge fountains in the lake are reflected in the water. The park (called *Kurpark* in German) stretches for half a mile northward along the Kuranlagen ending in a fancy residential quarter, the Sonnenberg.

Johannes Brahms was a resident of Wiesbaden in and around 1880 to 1890, and he composed three symphonies here. The famous painter Alexej von Jawlensky also lived in Wiesbaden from 1921 to 1941. He is buried at the Russian graveyard at Neroberg.

WHERE TO STAY

VERY EXPENSIVE

AUKAMM HOTEL, Aukamm-Allee 31, D-6200 Wiesbaden. Tel. 0611/57-60. Fax 0611/576-264. 160 rms, 14 suites. MINIBAR TV TEL **Bus:** 5, 18, or 25.
$ Rates (including hot and cold buffet breakfast): 291 DM–331 DM ($192.10–$218.50) single; 362 DM–402 DM ($238.90–$265.30) double; from 652 DM ($430.30) suite. AE, DC, MC. **Parking:** 18 DM ($11.90).
Built in 1970, one of the leading first-class hotels in Wiesbaden sits in a fashionable residential area across from the spa gardens and next to the Clinic for Diagnostics. All the rooms have balconies, color TVs, in-house videos (some in English), and radios. There are also luxury suites with two to five rooms.

The hotel has a Japanese restaurant, Imari; a European restaurant, Rosenpark; a day bar for snacks and drinks; a cocktail bar serving international drinks, draft beer, and light meals; and the Bierkathedralsche, a rustic pub with regional dishes as well as live organ music. A cosmetic studio, an underground garage, and ample parking on the hotel premises are plus factors at the Aukamm. Room service, dry cleaning, and laundry are available. The hotel offers a nonsmoking area on the 11th floor. It lies only about 15 miles from the Frankfurt airport.

NASSAUER HOF, Kaiser-Freidrich-Platz 3–4, D-6200 Wiesbaden. Tel. 0611/13-36-06, or toll free 800/223-6800. Fax 0611/133-614. 210 rms, 14 suites. A/C MINIBAR TV TEL **Bus:** 1, 8, 16.
$ Rates: 395 DM ($260.70) single; 480 DM–550 DM ($316.80–$363) double; suites from 680 DM ($448.80). Breakfast buffet 26 DM ($17.20) extra. AE, DC, MC, V. **Parking:** 25 DM ($16.50).
Nassauer Hof is an old favorite with up-to-date conveniences. In 1987, renovations preserved the baroque facade, but the interior was completely modernized. With the addition of two restaurants, this hotel now ranks with the most appealing in Germany. The Orangerie features local German specialties at moderate prices, while Die Ente vom Lehel boasts the finest deluxe fare in Wiesbaden. The cozy Nassauer Hof Bar has an open fireplace and piano entertainment. The staff provides cordial service in understandable English. The spacious rooms feature soundproof windows, some with air conditioning. Room service is available 24 hours a day. On the premises is the Lancaster beauty spa. The hotel stands in the city center, within walking distance of the Kurhaus, Spielbank, theaters, and the shopping area.

EXPENSIVE

HOTEL BÄREN, Bärenstrasse 3, D-6200 Wiesbaden. Tel. 0611/30-10-21. Fax 0611/30-10-24. 60 rms (56 with bath), 2 suites. TV TEL **Bus:** 1 or 8.
$ Rates (including buffet breakfast): 140 DM ($92.40) single without bath, 160 DM ($105.60) single with bath; 200 DM–230 DM ($132–$151.80) double with bath; from 270 DM ($178.20) suite. AE, DC, MC, V.
A three-minute walk from the Schloss and the Marktkirche, the Bären is standard modern, with guest rooms that are clean and efficiently appointed. Thirty-six rooms have minibars. Guests are welcome to use the thermal pool, and there's a cocktail bar and restaurant, König im Bären, that serves international food and drink. Room service and laundry are available.

HANSA HOTEL, Bahnhofstrasse 23, D-6200 Wiesbaden. Tel. 0611/3-

99-55. Fax 0611/30-03-19. 86 rms (all with bath or shower). TV TEL **Bus:** 5, 18, 25.

$ Rates (including continental breakfast): 130 DM ($85.80) single; 220 DM ($145.20) double. AE, DC, MC, V. **Closed:** Dec 15–Jan 3. **Parking:** 10 DM ($6.60).

Near the Rhein-Main-Halle, the Hansa is like a big town house, offering streamlined modern rooms. A real German pub, dark and mellow, serves good beer and continental food.

HOTEL KLEE AM PARK, Parkstrasse 4, D-6200 Wiesbaden. Tel. 0611/ 30-50-61. Fax 0611/30-40-48. 60 rms, 2 suites. MINIBAR TV TEL **Bus:** 2 or 8.

$ Rates (including buffet breakfast): 195 DM–215 DM ($128.70–$141.90) single; 245 DM–285 DM ($161.70–$188.10) double; from 375 DM ($247.50) suite. AE, DC, MC, V. **Parking:** Free.

A square, modern hotel in a tranquil setting at the edge of a park, the Klee am Park is surrounded by its own informal gardens. The theater is nearby, as are the casino and shopping area. All the guest rooms have French doors opening onto balconies; some have sitting areas large enough for entertaining. The baths are tiled, many containing double sinks.

Guests will find a café and restaurant where French cuisine is served, plus a comfortable English-style bar. The hotel is highly recommended for those who find the older, superluxurious hotels a bit too monumental. Meals range in price from 55 DM to 85 DM ($36.30 to $56.10).

RAMADA HOTEL WIESBADEN, Abraham-Lincoln-Strasse 17, D-6200 Wiesbaden. Tel. 0611/79-70, or toll free 800/272-6232 in U.S. Fax 0611/76- 13-72. 157 rms, 8 suites. A/C MINIBAR TV TEL **Bus:** 5, 18, or 25.

$ Rates: 217 DM–345 DM ($143.20–$227.70) single; 250 DM–385 DM ($165– $254.10) double; from 500 DM ($330) suite. Breakfast 22 DM ($14.50) extra. AE, DC, MC, V. **Parking:** Free.

Since it lies in a region where top-name companies make their homes, lots of businesspeople stay at the Ramada instead of in Frankfurt, as it is only 20 minutes from the Frankfurt airport. Its modern guest rooms have been redecorated, and each has a color TV and VCR.

For recreation, a pool, sauna, and solarium are available. The restaurant, Friesenstube, offers a variety of regional and international dishes. Try a glass of Rhine wine or draft beer in the Bierpumpe Bar or a snack on the terrace bordering the indoor pool. Laundry and babysitting are avaiable.

WIESBADEN PENTA HOTEL, Augusta-Viktoria-Strasse 15, D-6200 Wiesbaden. Tel. 0611/37-70-41. Fax 0611/30-39-60. 200 rms, 5 suites. MINIBAR TV TEL **Bus:** 5, 18, or 25.

$ Rates: 205 DM–265 DM ($135.30–$174.90) single; 245 DM–305 DM ($161.70–$201.30) double; from 330 DM ($217.80) suite. Buffet breakfast 26 DM ($17.20) extra. AE, DC, MC, V. **Parking:** 12 DM ($7.90).

This member of the Penta chain can't be beat for up-to-date amenities. It stands in the heart of Wiesbaden, opposite Rhein-Main-Halle, a five-minute walk from the main station. Glamorously modern, it offers well-furnished soundproofed rooms, all with balconies, many of which overlook the gardens that surround the hotel.

A lunch buffet is served in the split-level restaurant, Globetrotter, and coffee shop or, in summer, on the terrace. German beer and snacks are the feature of the hotel's Bierstube. Recreation is important here, with a health club, sauna, plunge pool, and tanning studio. Room service, laundry, and dry cleaning are available.

MODERATE

HOTEL AM LANDESHAUS, Moritzstrasse 51, D-6200 Wiesbaden. Tel.

0611/37-30-41. Fax 0611/37-30-44. 21 rms (all with bath or shower). TV TEL
Bus: 10, 14, or 16.

$ Rates (including buffet breakfast): 125 DM–135 DM ($82.50–$89.10) single;
175 DM–180 DM ($115.50–$118.80) double. AE, V. **Parking:** 5 DM ($3.30).
Closed: Dec 20–Jan 6.

Located in central Wiesbaden within walking distance of the railroad station,
this hotel opened in the spring of 1984. It's since been recognized as one of the
spa's best reasonably priced hotels. Completely modern, with an elevator, the
place is warm, cozy, and inviting, a choice for the traditionalist. The rooms are well
kept, and guests can enjoy drinks in a rustic ale tavern.

**HOTEL ORANIEN, Platterstrasse 2, D-6200 Wiesbaden. Tel. 0611/52-
50-25.** Fax 0611/52-50-20. 87 rms (all with bath or shower). TV TEL **Bus:** 3, 10,
or 13.

$ Rates (including buffet breakfast): 135 DM–158 DM ($89.10–$104.30) single;
210 DM–230 DM ($138.60–$151.80) double. AE, DC, MC, V. **Parking:** 12 DM
($7.90)

Dating from 1879, and frequently renovated since its original construction, the
Oranien is in the spa center, surrounded by a small park. It offers traditionally
furnished rooms. Regular meals cost from 36 DM ($23.80) to 75 DM ($49.50).
There's a popular summer terrace.

INEXPENSIVE

**HOTEL IM PARK, Danziger Strasse 104, D-6200 Wiesbaden. Tel. 0611/
54-11-96.** 14 rms (none with bath). MINIBAR TV **Bus:** 16.

$ Rates (including buffet breakfast): 80 DM ($52.80) single; 110 DM ($72.60)
double. AE, DC, MC, V. **Parking:** 5 DM ($3.30).

This bed-and-breakfast accommodation next to the Café Hahn and the lovely
Kurpark, run by English-speaking hotelier Christian Kollman, is quiet, inviting, and
maintained in good taste. Each room has a wash basin, and guests use communal
baths on the floors. The city bus stop, Tennelbach, is in front of the hotel.

WHERE TO DINE

VERY EXPENSIVE

**DIE ENTE VOM LEHEL, in the Hotel Nassauer Hof, Kaiser-Friedrich-Platz
3–4. Tel. 0611/13-36-06.**
Cuisine: CONTINENTAL. **Reservations:** Required. **Bus:** 5, 18, 25.

$ Prices: Appetizers 28 DM–35 DM ($18.50–$23.10); main courses 50 DM–60
DM ($33–$39.60); fixed-price dinners 130 DM–170 DM ($85.80–$112.20). AE,
DC, MC, V.

Open: Restaurant and wine cellar, Tues–Sat 6pm–1am; bistro, Tues–Sat 10am–
midnight.

In an intimate restaurant seating 85 on two levels, an innovative chef prepares a
cuisine as pleasing to the eye as to the palate. Specialties change from week to
week, based on seasonal availability of ingredients. The cuisine is light modern
German. Typical offerings might include parfait of duck livers, roast medallions of
venison with chanterelles, and clams in puff pastry.

A boutique, delicatessen, wine cellar, and bistro are attached. The bistro offers a
three-course menu at 68 DM ($44.90).

EXPENSIVE

LE GOURMET, Bahnhofstrasse 42. Tel. 0611/30-16-54.

Cuisine: FRENCH/TURKISH. **Reservations:** Required.
$ **Prices:** Appetizers 13.50 DM–22.50 DM ($8.90–$14.90); main courses 28.50 DM–45 DM ($18.80–$29.70); fixed-price lunch 22.50 DM ($14.90); fixed-price dinner 70 DM ($46.20). AE, MC.
Open: Lunch Mon–Sat noon–2:30pm; dinner Mon–Sat 6–10pm.

Elegantly modern, Le Gourmet is unusual in specializing in both French and Turkish cookery. Although the combination may sound bizarre, this citadel of good food achieves harmony between the cuisines. The Turkish coffee is divine, naturally, as is the eggplant kebab over grilled lambsteak. Full of Near Eastern charm, this restaurant is run by Akin Soykandar, who is proud of his large wine and champagne list.

RISTORANTE LANTERNA, Westendstrasse 3. Tel. 0611/40-25-22.
Cuisine: ITALIAN/FRENCH. **Reservations:** Required. **Bus:** 5, 18, 25.
$ **Prices:** Appetizers 18 DM–25 DM ($11.90–$16.50); main courses 42 DM–46 DM ($27.70–$30.40); fixed-price dinner 118 DM ($77.90). AE, DC, MC, V.
Open: Lunch Sat–Thurs noon–2pm; dinner Sat–Thurs 6–11pm.

Ristorante Lanterna is both rustic and elegant, featuring Italian and French cuisine moderne. A big wine list accompanies the menu, which offers at least 15 main dishes, including such light dishes as seafood salad with lemon sauce and, the specialty, wild game (particularly woodcock and pheasant) in season. A six-course set meal is available, or you can order à la carte. There are only a dozen indoor tables, but in summer, you might request a table on the fully planted terrace, which seats another 20 diners.

MODERATE

ZUR ROSE, Bremthaler Strasse 1. Tel. 06127/40-06-07.
Cuisine: FRENCH/GERMAN. **Reservations:** Recommended. **Bus:** 21, 22, or 23.
$ **Prices:** Appetizers 15 DM–21 DM ($9.90–$13.90); main courses 24 DM–35 DM ($15.80–$23.10); fixed-price menus 35 DM ($23.10) and 50 DM ($33). AE, DC, MC, V.
Open: Lunch Mon–Fri noon–2pm; dinner Mon–Sat 6–10pm.

This is a half-timbered building, nearly two centuries old, offering a nostalgic decor, with a ceramic tile oven, rose-colored lace tablecloths, and candlelight. In this cozy setting, you can enjoy the freshly baked and buttered rolls as you peruse the menu. Various fresh fish dishes (often served with shrimp) are offered, with smoked salmon and trout regularly featured. You might begin with cucumber cream soup flavored with dill and containing shrimp, then select Barbarie duck breast with goose-liver sauce. For dessert, try puff pastry filled with fresh fruits or poppyseed mousse with rum-marinated fruits.

EVENING ENTERTAINMENT

Rien ne va plus is the call when the ball starts to roll on the gaming tables at **Spielbank Wiesbaden,** Im Kurhaus, Kurhausplatz 1 (tel. 06121/536-100), which is open daily from 3pm to 2am and charges an admission of 5 DM ($3.30). Roulette and baccarat are the featured games. Here the great Russian writer Fyodor Dostoyevski attempted to win a fortune, but nearly lost everything. The casino, reached by bus 1, 8, or 16, is located at the end of the Wilhelmstrasse, one of the most famous streets of Wiesbaden. To enter the place, it is necessary to present a passport or an identification card. Beer costs from 7 DM ($4.60), with a whisky and soda going for 15 DM ($9.90). Käfer's Bistro, a restaurant within the Kurhaus, is open from noon to midnight daily, serving meals for 48 DM ($31.70) and up.

On a more cultural note, the greatest event, already mentioned, is the **International May Festival** throughout the month of May. The festival features artists of stature from all over Europe, and comprises instrumental music, opera, dance, drama, folk music, and other offerings.

Music and theater flourish at Wiesbaden throughout the year. For information on performances during your visit (plus the availability of tickets), check at the Wiesbaden Tourist Office (see above). It's open Monday through Friday from 8am to 6:30pm. There's another office at Im Hauptbahnhof (tel. 0611/17-29-781), open daily from 8am to 9pm.

The **Hessisches Staatstheater,** Christian-Zais-Strasse (tel. 0611/132-1), is one of the most beautiful theaters in Germany. Built in 1894 by Emperor Wilhelm II, it presents a program of operas, musicals, ballets, and plays by its resident companies. Its season lasts from September 15 to June 30, and tickets range from 10 DM to 50 DM ($6.60 to $33).

For information about any of the facilities within the Kurhaus compound, including the casino and the theater, call 06121/31-28-33.

If you're in Wiesbaden on a summer night, you can wander in the **Kurpark,** enjoying the concerts and the garden festivals—the latter with illumination and fireworks displays that beat most after-dark activity likely to be going on behind any nearby walls.

Wiesbaden even has its own version of the Via Veneto. Here it's called **Wilhelmstrasse.** On this street you can find a café where you can stake out a post to people watch, a favorite pastime of both locals and visitors.

---

4. BAD NAUHEIM

22 miles N of Frankfurt; 40 miles NE of Wiesbaden

GETTING THERE **By Train** Bad Nauheim can be easily reached from Frankfurt, site of the nearest airport. Trains arrive during the day at least once per hour (every 30 minutes during rush hours). Trip time is 30 minutes. Service is on the Westerbahn Line–Frankfurt–Giessen.

By Bus Buses run frequently between Frankfurt and Bad Nauheim, service provided by Regionalverkehr Kurhessen GmbH (tel. 0641/79-72-33 for information and schedules).

By Car Access is via autobahn (A5) from the north (Cologne) and from the south (Frankfurt). Driving time from Frankfurt is about half an hour.

ESSENTIALS For tourist information, go to **Verkehrsverein,** Pavillon in der Parkstrasse (tel. 06032/21-20).

Like many similar spas throughout Germany, Bad Nauheim grew popular in the early part of this century when the railroad became a convenient and inexpensive means of transportation. Still going strong today, the resort at the northern edge of the Taunus Mountains is a center for golf, tennis, and ice skating, as well as the beginning point for energetic hikers to scale the 773-foot Johannisberg, towering over the town.

The warm carbonic acid springs of the spa are beneficial in the treatment of heart and circulatory disorders, and rheumatic diseases. The Kurpark is attractive, well-maintained, and filled with promenaders all summer long.

Bad Nauheim offers a number of hotels that sprouted up to cater to the turn-of-the-century crowds who flocked to "take the waters," as well as hostelries of recent vintage. Many famous guests have visited this spa, including Bismarck (1859); Richard Strauss (1927); and William Randolph Hearst with his mistress, Marion Davies (1931).

All the important sights, including the bathhouse complex, can be visited in half a day. The resort has a busy activity calendar, with concerts twice daily, along with operas, plays, dances, park illuminations, and fashion shows. The tourist office (see above) will have details.

WHERE TO STAY

EXPENSIVE

HOTEL AM HOCHWALD, Carl-Oelemann-Weg 9, D-6350 Bad Nauheim. Tel. 06032/34-80. Fax 06032/34-81-95. 124 rms. A/C MINIBAR TV TEL
$ Rates (including continental breakfast): 140 DM–180 DM ($92.40–$118.80) single; 196 DM–240 DM ($129.40–$158.40) double; from 480 DM ($316.80) suite. AE, DC, MC, V. **Parking:** 12 DM ($7.90).

In a quiet location near woodlands on the eastern outskirts, this stylish modern hotel boasts facilities ranging from a pool with a bar to a sauna, solarium, massage room, and facilities for table tennis. The comfortably furnished guest rooms contain balconies, radios, and many other thoughtful touches; some are reserved for nonsmokers. The hotel offers interesting dining possibilities at its Hessenstube and Terrassen Restaurant (see below).

PARKHOTEL AM KURHAUS, Nördlicher Park 16, D-6350 Bad Nauheim. Tel. 06032/30-30. Fax 06032/30-34-19. 99 rms, 8 suites. MINIBAR TV TEL
$ Rates (including continental breakfast): 164 DM–192 DM ($108.20–$126.70) single; 250 DM–330 DM ($165–$217.80) double; from 390 DM ($257.40) suite. AE, DC, MC, V. **Parking:** 12 DM ($7.90).

Built of concrete pierced by big sliding glass windows, with expanses of balconies, this modern hotel is the finest in town. It's located in the middle of the park that rings the resort's thermal springs. You get all the calm, quiet, and conservative comfort you expect in a spa hotel here.

Its public rooms are filled with green plants, arching windows, and two restaurants and a café, in addition to a Bierstube, wine tavern, and bar. Special diets and vegetarian menus are offered. Room service, laundry, and babysitting are provided, and nonsmoking rooms are available.

HOTEL ROSENAU, Steinfurther Strasse 1, D-6350 Bad Nauheim. Tel. 06032/8-60-61. Fax 06032/8-60-63. 54 rms. A/C MINIBAR TV TEL
$ Rates (including continental breakfast): 157 DM–207 DM ($103.60–$136.60) single; 224 DM–298 DM ($147.80–$196.70) double. AE, DC, MC, V. **Parking:** Free. **Closed:** Dec 27–Jan 4.

⑤ One of the better choices at the resort is this updated version of a German manor house, with white walls and a red-tile hip roof. Two fan-shaped arches announce its entrance. Inside, the decor is one of light-toned wood and pastel colors. The guest rooms are modern and attractively furnished, with such amenities as radios and electric trouser presses. The hotel has both a bistro and a restaurant on the premises, plus a small pool. The hotel is west of Grosser Telch, the town lake.

MODERATE

HOTEL INTER-EUROPA, Bahnhofsallée 13, D-6350 Bad Nauheim. Tel. 06032/20-36. Fax 06032/71-254. 35 rms (all with shower). TV TEL
$ Rates (including continental breakfast): 110 DM–125 DM ($72.60–$82.50) single; 160 DM–180 DM ($105.60–$118.80) double. AE, DC, MC, V.

A lively and modern hotel north of the Kurpark, the Inter-Europa is across the street from the Bahnhof. Oriental carpets and antique paintings add warmth to the public areas. The guest rooms are compact, clean, and comfortable. There is a restaurant and a grill room that serve many international specialties, a Wienstube, and a popular café. Meals cost from 32 DM ($21.10).

INEXPENSIVE

GAUDESBERGER, Hauptstrasse 6, D-6350 Bad Nauheim. Tel. 06032/25-08. 8 rms (none with bath). TEL

$ Rates (including continental breakfast): 43 DM ($28.40) single; 80 DM ($52.80) double. AE, DC, MC, V.

Known mainly for its restaurant, this centrally located hotel offers guest rooms that are simply but comfortably furnished. Even if you don't stay here, you might want to patronize the dining room (see "Where to Dine," below).

WHERE TO DINE

MODERATE

RESTAURANT GAUDESBERGER, in the Hotel Gaudesberger, Hauptstrasse 6. Tel. 06032/25-08.
   Cuisine: INTERNATIONAL. **Reservations:** Recommended.
$ Prices: Appetizers 15.50 DM–34.50 DM ($10.20–$22.80); main courses 29 DM–45 DM ($19.10–$29.70); fixed-price lunch 18.80 DM ($12.40); fixed-price dinner 28 DM ($18.50). AE, DC, MC, V.
   Open: Lunch Thurs–Tues 11:30am–2pm; dinner Thurs–Tues 6:30–9pm.
   Closed: Feb.

A large menu of dishes, well prepared by the chef, is offered here. You can stick to the tried-and-true specialties, such as chateaubriand with béarnaise sauce or mixed grill. Or you can dip into the international specialties: pork in curry-cream sauce or ox tongue in madeira sauce. The English-speaking staff is most cooperative and courteous.

ROSENAU—LA ROSE, in the Hotel Rosenau, Steinfurther Strasse 1. Tel. 06032/8-60-61.
   Cuisine: INTERNATIONAL. **Reservations:** Not required.
$ Prices: Appetizers 10.50 DM–16 DM ($6.90–$10.60); main courses 26 DM–42 DM ($17.20–$27.70); fixed-price lunch 46 DM–68 DM ($30.40–$44.90). AE, DC, MC, V.
   Open: Lunch daily noon–2pm; dinner daily 6–10pm. **Closed:** Dec 27–Jan 4.
Contained within a previously recommended hotel, this restaurant is known as one of the best moderately priced eateries in town. It serves two fixed-price lunch menus and à la carte evening meals. The flavorful dishes might include cream of tomato and young vegetable soup, roasted breast of young hen, and filet of salmon with fresh herbs, plus several different pork and game dishes, depending on the season.

TERRASSEN RESTAURANT, in the Hotel Am Hochwald, Carl-Oelemann-Weg 9. Tel. 06032/34-80.
   Cuisine: GERMAN/INTERNATIONAL. **Reservations:** Recommended.
$ Prices: Appetizers 9.50 DM–18 DM ($6.30–$11.90); main courses 28 DM–45 DM ($18.50–$29.70). AE, DC, MC, V.
   Open: Lunch daily 11:30am–2:30pm; dinner daily 6:30–11:30pm.
Terrassen offers good service in a modern decor with provincial motifs. The menu includes all the typical German dishes as well as a selection of international specialties. You can also be served a beer and a cold snack or salad throughout the day. Warm food is served during the hours listed above. The restaurant is in one of the town's larger hotels, recommended previously, on the eastern outskirts of town, reached along the Hochwaldstrasse.

5. BAD HOMBURG

10 miles N of Frankfurt; 28 miles NE of Wiesbaden

GETTING THERE By Train There's rail service by S-Bahn (S5) from the center of Frankfurt. Phone 069/26-94-62 for more information.

By Bus The "Alpine-Airport-Express" is Bad Homburg's special, hourly nonstop shuttle service (deluxe motor coach) to and from Frankfurt airport, the nearest airport (see Chapter 3). Trip time is 20 minutes. Regional bus service to the surrounding area is provided by Verkehrsgesellschaft GmbH Untermain (tel. 06172/21-286 for more information).

By Car Access by car is from the north or south via autobahn A5, exiting at Bad Homburg.

ESSENTIALS For tourist information, go to **Verkehrsamt im Kurhaus,** Louisenstrasse 58 (tel. 06172/12-13-10).

Bad Homburg is one of Germany's most attractive spas, still basking in the grandeur of turn-of-the-century Europe. The 1,200-year-old town was the official residence of the counts of Hessen. Actually, Bad Homburg has been a popular watering spot since Roman times. Royalty from all over the world have visited the spa and left their mark. King Chulalongkorn of Siam was so impressed by it that he built a Siamese temple in the Kurpark. Czar Nicholas I erected an onion-domed Russian chapel nearby. The name of the town was popularized by Edward VII of England when, as Prince of Wales, he visited the spa and introduced a new hat style, which he called the homburg. The town became the gaming capital of Europe when the Blanc brothers opened the casino in 1841.

The spa park is an oasis in the middle of a large, rather commercial town. The spa's saline springs are used to treat various disorders, especially heart and circulatory diseases. The Kurpark extends into the foothills of the Taunus Mountains, stretching in front of the Kurhaus. The gardens are filled with brooks, ponds, and arbors. The generous pedestrian zones within the town center offer an abundance of shops, stores, restaurants, and cafés.

WHAT TO SEE & DO

BAD HOMBURG PALACE, Schlossverwaltung. Tel. 06172/2-60-91.

A few short blocks from the spa gardens sits what was the residence of the Landgraves of Hesse-Homburg from its construction in 1680 until the mid-19th century. Its builder, Prince Friedrich II von Homburg, preserved the White Tower from the medieval castle that stood on the site and incorporated it into the structure of his baroque palace. In the late 19th century, the palace became a summer residence for Prussian kings and, later, German emperors. After World War I the state assumed ownership.

The interior contains 18th-century furniture and painting, including a bust of Prince Friedrich II by Andreas Schluter, Germany's greatest baroque sculptor. The former "telephone room of the empress" includes a Cleopatra by Pellegrini.

Admission: 3 DM ($2) adults, 1.50 DM ($1) children.

Open: Palace and formal gardens, Mar–Oct, Tues–Sun 10am–5pm; Nov–Feb, Tues–Sun 10am–4pm.

SPIELBANK, Im Kurpark. Tel. 06172/170-10.

Called the "Mother of Monte Carlo," Spielbank was the site of endless series of diplomatic, industrial, and romantic intrigues during the 19th and early 20th centuries. It's especially popular in summer. Roulette, blackjack, and baccarat are the games people play. Passports are required for entrance.

Admission: 5 DM ($3.30).

Open: Daily from 3pm; closing time varies.

THE TAUNUS THERME, Seedammweg. Tel. 06172/48-78.

A large, fascinating recreation area, the Taunus Therme boasts several pools, a sauna, solarium, and health center, plus TVs, cinemas, and two restaurants.

Open: Thurs and Sun–Tues 9am–11pm, Wed and Fri–Sat 9am–midnight.

WHERE TO STAY

VERY EXPENSIVE

MARITIM KURHAUS-HOTEL, Kurpark, Ludwigstrasse, D-6380 Bad Homburg. Tel. 06172/2-80-51. Fax 06172/24-341. 148 rms, 10 suites. TV TEL

$ Rates (including buffet breakfast): 239 DM–399 DM ($157.70–$263.30) single; 288 DM–480 DM ($190.10–$316.80) double; from 600 DM ($396) suite. Summer reductions July 1–Aug 22. AE, DC, MC, V. **Parking:** 10 DM ($6.60).

With modern spa facilities nearby, this hotel offers visitors plush accommodations, many illuminated with tall bay windows. Some units have balconies or terraces, permitting wide-angle views over the greenery of the surrounding park. The hotel's big-windowed indoor pool tempts guests with the opportunity to exercise away any weight they might gain in either of the well-managed restaurants or at the café terrace. There's a sauna for additional relaxation. Copious buffet breakfasts are a part of the many offerings at this attractive place.

PARKHOTEL, Kaiser-Friedrich-Promenade 53-55, Am Kurpark, D-6380 Bad Homburg. Tel. 06172/80-10. Fax 06172/80-18-01. 100 rms, 10 suites. MINIBAR TV TEL **Tram:** 5.

$ Rates (including buffet breakfast): 194 DM–260 DM ($128–$171.60) single; 264 DM–350 DM ($174.20–$231) double; from 400 DM ($264) suite. AE, DC, MC, V. **Parking:** 10 DM ($6.60).

At least some of the appeal of this hotel derives from its position in the middle of the Kurpark's well-maintained gardens, near the thermal springs at the spa. Although its design is modern and angular, its edges are softened with windowboxes. Each guest room contains a cable-connected TV and radio, along with comfortably conservative furnishings. On the premises are a bar and a sunny room for writing letters and postcards. Restaurant Jade serves a Chinese cuisine. Facilities include a sauna, health club, and solarium, and room service and laundry are available.

STEIGENBERGER BAD HOMBURG, Kaiser-Friedrich-Promenade 69–75, D-6380 Bad Homburg. Tel. 06172/181-0, or toll free 800/223-5652 in U.S. or Canada. Fax 06172/18-16-30. 169 rms, 17 suites. A/C MINIBAR TV TEL **Tram:** 5.

$ Rates: 245 DM–375 DM ($161.70–$247.50) single; 290 DM–420 DM ($191.40–$277.20) double; 480 DM–680 DM ($316.80–$448.80) suite. Buffet breakfast 25 DM ($16.50) extra. AE, DC, MC, V. **Parking:** 20 DM ($13.20).

The resort's prestige hotel lies in the center, directly opposite the spa gardens and the casino. It offers beautifully furnished guest rooms, each with individually adjustable air conditioning, color TV, radio, minibar, and extra long beds, along with a large and spacious bath. Fifty-three are reserved for nonsmokers.

Restaurants include Ritter's in the Park, an elegant enclave offering creative cuisine moderne of light dishes, along with the French-style Charly's Bistro. There is a lobby bar, plus a patio restaurant and a summer restaurant offering al fresco dining. Facilities include a sauna and solarium, and services include babysitting, room service, laundry facilities, and dry cleaning.

MODERATE

HARDTWALD HOTEL, Philosophenweg 31, D-6380 Bad Homburg. Tel. 06172/8-10-26. Fax 06172/82-512. 39 rms. MINIBAR TV TEL **Bus:** 3 from the Bahnhof.

$ Rates (including continental breakfast): 125 DM–185 DM ($82.50–$122.10) single; 165 DM–295 DM ($108.90–$194.70) double. AE, DC, MC, V. **Parking:** Free.

Resembling a chalet set in a forest, the Hardtwald is a 20-minute walk from the center. Run by the Kurze family since 1868, the hotel is an ideal retreat near the spa gardens. Its rooms, overlooking the forest, have TVs and radios. The hotel's dining room, planted with flowers, is noted for its food, with meals costing from 40 DM ($26.40). In summer, tables are set on the large patio. Next to the hotel is a stable where you can rent horses.

HAUS DAHEIM, Elisabethenstrasse 42, D-6380, Bad Homburg. Tel. 06172/2-00-98. Fax 06172/25-580. 19 rms. TEL **Tram:** 5.

$ Rates (including continental breakfast): 105 DM–145 DM ($69.30–$95.70) single; 175 DM–215 DM ($115.50–$141.90) double. AE, DC, MC, V. **Parking:** 8 DM ($5.30).

In a light-blue corner building, only a short stroll from the Kurhaus, innkeeper Horst Stiegmann sees to your needs, and his is one of the finest of the small hotels of the spa. All the comfortable rooms have good beds and radios.

INEXPENSIVE

VILLA KISSELEFF, Kisseleffstrasse 19, D-6380 Bad Homburg. Tel. 06172/2-15-40. Fax 06172/2-08-68. 14 rms (8 with bath or shower). **Tram:** 5.

$ Rates (including continental breakfast): 60 DM ($39.60) single without bath, 100 DM ($66) single with shower; 120 DM ($79.20) double without bath, 150 DM ($99) double with bath. MC, V.

In the Kurpark, close to the curative springs, sits this symmetrical four-story baroque villa, originally built in the early 19th century. A restful atmosphere pervades the place, which is run by Frau Elfriede Yuen. Breakfast is served in your room at the hour you request it.

WHERE TO DINE

EXPENSIVE

ASSMANN'S RESTAURANT IM ROMERBRUNNEN, Kisseleffstrasse. Tel. 06172/2-47-10.
 Cuisine: FRENCH. **Reservations:** Required. **Tram:** 5.
$ Prices: Appetizers 18 DM–26 DM ($11.90–$17.20); main courses 38 DM–50 DM ($25.10–$33); fixed-price lunch 56 DM ($37); fixed-price dinner 86 DM ($56.80) and 112 DM ($73.90). AE, MC.
 Open: Thurs–Tues noon–midnight; hot food served noon–2:30pm and 6–10:30pm. **Closed:** Jan 1–18.
The beautiful roofed terrace here (only used in summer) is surrounded by big old trees amid the green of the Kurpark. The restaurant and the bistro were both completely renovated in 1988, and a wine boutique with delicatessen is attached. Lothar Assmann himself stays in the kitchen, creating a cookery that is as pleasing to the eye as to the palate. Fixed-price or à la carte meals are available.

OBERLE'S RESTAURANT, Obergasse 1. Tel. 06172/246-62.
 Cuisine: CONTINENTAL. **Reservations:** Required. **Tram:** 5.
$ Prices: Appetizers 20 DM–32 DM ($13.20–$21.10); main courses 36 DM–52 DM ($23.80–$34.30); fixed-price menus 60 DM–93 DM ($39.60–$61.40). MC.
 Open: Lunch Tues–Sun noon–2:30pm; dinner Tues–Sun 6:30–midnight.
The Weitzel-Oeth family owns and operates what is considered one of the best restaurants of Bad Homburg. Surrounded by an art nouveau and art deco decor, you

are served fixed-price or à la carte meals. The kitchen staff prides itself on a sophisticated cuisine, which includes goose-liver mousse, marinated and warmed filets of salmon served in saffron-and-Pernod sauce, sweetbreads of veal in a sauce of white wine and mustard, and a comfortably caloric version of cream and wild mushroom soup.

SÄNGERS RESTAURANT, Kaiser-Friedrich-Promenade 85. Tel. 06172/ 24425.
  Cuisine: FRENCH. **Reservations:** Required. **Tram:** 5.
$ **Prices:** Two-course fixed-price lunch 55 DM ($36.30); lunch or dinner appetizers 18 DM–40 DM ($11.90–$26.40); lunch or dinner main courses 35 DM–55 DM ($23.10–$36.30). AE.
  Open: Lunch Tues–Fri noon–2pm; dinner Mon–Sat 6:30–11pm. **Closed:** Two weeks in midsummer.

⬤ Stylish and elegant, this restaurant offers a pair of pale-blue dining rooms outfitted in the style of Louis XIV, plus a desirable location adjacent to the Steigenberger Bad Homburg. The cuisine, a sophisticated blend of fresh ingredients and culinary skill, might include carpaccio of turbot with Iranian caviar, gooseliver terrine served with brioche and gelatin of wild berries, an unusual foam-capped version of celery soup with quail eggs, roasted breast of duck on bed of rhubarb, stuffed oxtail in the style of the house, and a succulent array of desserts.

MODERATE

CASINO-RESTAURANT, Im Kurpark. Tel. 06172/170-10.
  Cuisine: FRENCH/GERMAN. **Reservations:** Required. **Tram:** 5.
$ **Prices:** Appetizers 12 DM–22 DM ($7.90–$14.50); main courses 24 DM–35 DM ($15.80–$23.10). AE, DC, MC, V.
  Open: Dinner only, daily 6–11pm.
Proud of its role as one of the finest restaurants in town, this is said to be the only restaurant in Germany that directly adjoins the gaming tables of a casino. Decorated in a formal, vaguely English style, it maintains impeccable service and offers a winning selection of modern and classic French and German dishes. The frequently changing menu features seasonal specialties that contain only the freshest of ingredients. Head chef Gunther Schwanitz begins each workday at the local markets. Lobster, prepared in about five ways according to client wishes, is a universal favorite here, supposedly attracting diners from as far away as Frankfurt. Other specialties include sautéed chicken with sweetbreads in mushroom-cream sauce, accompanied by a salad of fresh dandelion greens. Men should wear jackets and ties.

EVENING ENTERTAINMENT

Close to the Spielbank, the **Tennis Bar,** Im Kurpark (tel. 06172/2-60-41), is the most famous spot in town, with dancing and live music. Many Frankfurters visit it just for the evening. It is open nightly from 9pm to 4am, charging 15 DM ($9.90) admission. Mixed drinks cost from 17.50 DM ($11.60).

---

6. BAD WIESSEE

33 miles S of Munich; 11 miles SE of Bad Tölz

GETTING THERE   By Train   The nearest airport is Munich (see Chapter 4), so most passengers arrive by train. The nearest Bahnhof (rail station) is at Gmund, 2 miles away; however, buses to Bad Wiessee meet arriving trains from Munich. Trip time between Munich and Gmund is 1 hour and 10 minutes.

By Bus   As mentioned, buses from Gmund meet arriving trains and transport passengers on the 15-minute ride to Bad Wiessee. For more bus information, call 08022/86-03-23.

By Car   Access from either Munich or Salzburg (Austria) is via autobahn (A8). Take the Holzkirchen exit in the direction of Bad Wiessee and follow the signposts.

ESSENTIALS   For tourist information, go to **Kuramt**, Adrian-Stoop-Strasse 20 (tel. 08022/8-60-30).

If you've always believed that the best medicine is the worst tasting, you should feel right at home in Bad Wiessee—the mineral springs of this popular spa on the Tegernsee are saturated with iodine and sulfur. However, the other attractions of this small town more than make up for this discomfort. This spa, with a huge lake at its feet and towering Alps rising behind it, is a year-round resort. In summer, swimming and boating are popular; in winter, you can ski on the slopes or skate on the lake.

The springs are used for the treatment of many diseases, including rheumatism and heart and respiratory conditions. In spite of its tiny size, Bad Wiessee is advanced in its medicinal facilities as well as in its accommodations and restaurants. There's even a small gambling casino.

The main season begins in May and ends in October. Bad Wiessee in recent years has become increasingly popular with holidaymakers from Munich to the north. During these busy times, you should definitely make a reservation. Many hotels close in winter, so be warned if you're an off-season visitor.

From Bad Wiessee, any number of tours are possible, including visits to Munich; Chiemsee; and the royal castles of Neuschwanstein, Herrenchiemsee, and Linderhof. You can also visit Salzburg and Innsbruck in Austria. Tours are offered by **Reiseburo Sareiter**, Lindenplatz 6 (tel. 08022/81338).

WHERE TO STAY & DINE

EXPENSIVE

LANDHAUS HOTEL SAPPLFELD, Im Sapplfeld 8, D-8182 Bad Wiessee. Tel. 08022/8-20-67. Fax 08022/83-560. 17 rms TV TEL
$ Rates (including continental breakfast): 125 DM–205 DM ($82.50–$135.30) single; 198 DM–258 DM ($130.70–$170.30) double. DC, MC, V. **Parking:** Free. **Closed:** Nov 10–Dec 20.
A typical Bavarian inn, with geranium-filled balconies and a roof overhang, this is a real alpine resort, where people come to have a good time when they're not involved in a fitness program or swimming in the indoor pool. Men go nude with women into the sauna. The hotel is bi-seasonal, attracting scenery lovers in summer, skiers in winter. The guest rooms are completely modern, each with a balcony.

HOTEL LEDERER AM SEE, Bodenschneidstrasse 9–11, D-8182 Bad Wiessee. Tel. 08022/82-90. Fax 08022/82-92-61. 115 rms, 3 suites. TV TEL
$ Rates (including continental breakfast): 125 DM–180 DM ($82.50–$118.80) single; 220 DM–320 DM ($145.20–$211.20) double; from 330 DM ($217.80) suite. AE, DC, MC. **Parking:** Free. **Closed:** Nov to mid-Dec.
Clearly the most distinguished choice in the town is this spa and holiday hotel. From the balcony of your room, you'll most likely look out onto the Tegernsee and the Lower Bavarian Alps. The atmosphere is pleasant, with good service and rooms that are attractively furnished and well maintained.

The hotel stands in a large park, and there are a dock for bathing and a meadow for sunbathing. However, if the weather is bad, the place also has an indoor pool. Sometimes there is a barbecue on the terrace facing the lake, followed by entertainment or dancing in the Martinsklause. The hotel has its own medical staff and "beauty farm." The kitchen turns out an international cuisine of good standard, meals costing 41 DM to 59 DM ($27.10 to $38.90).

MODERATE

HOTEL MARINA, Furtwänglerstrasse 9, D-8182 Bad Wiessee. Tel. 08022/8-60-10. Fax 08022/86-01-40. 52 rms. TV TEL
$ Rates (including continental breakfast): 70 DM–95 DM ($46.20–$62.70) single; 160 DM–170 DM ($105.60–$112.20) double. AE, MC. **Parking:** Free. **Closed:** Mid-Nov to mid-Dec.

In summer, potted plants grace the balconies of this typical Bavarian house with a roof overhang. Every guest here (well, almost) seems on a fitness campaign, swimming in the indoor pool or patronizing the solarium and sauna (no one objects to a little nudity). The place has a lovely gardenlike setting in summer, and on a cold winter's night, it's ablaze with lights. The guest rooms are furnished in a warm, traditional Bavarian style. The service is personal.

PARK HOTEL RESI VON DER POST, Zilcherstrasse 14, D-8182 Bad Wiessee. Tel. 08022/8-27-88. Fax 08022/83-216. 35 rms, 4 suites. TV TEL
$ Rates (including continental breakfast): 85 DM–120 DM ($56.10–$79.20) single; 150 DM–210 DM ($99–$138.60) double; from 240 DM ($158.40) suite. AE, DC, MC, V. **Parking:** 10 DM ($6.60).

This enduring favorite has been around much longer than many of its fast-rising competitors. The hotel has been considerably modernized, with well-furnished traditional guest rooms. The atmosphere in the hotel's restaurant is often bustling, as diners who live nearby fill up the place; many show up in Bavarian costumes. They know they can get fresh fish from the lake, as well as hearty Bavarian fare. Ask for a special cheese of the Tegernsee district, Miesbacher.

KURHOTEL REX, Münchnerstrasse 25, D-8182 Bad Wiessee. Tel. 08022/8-20-91. Fax 08022/83-841. 57 rms, 1 suite. TV TEL
$ Rates: 100 DM–132 DM ($66–$87.10) single; 180 DM–220 DM ($118.80–$145.20) double; from 250 DM ($165) suite. Half-board rates 120 DM–170 DM ($79.20–$112.20) per person daily. No credit cards. **Parking:** Free. **Closed:** Nov–Mar.

A modern hotel with much charm and character, the Kurhotel Rex is set against a backdrop of the Lower Bavarian Alps. Run by the Beil family, it's one of the nicer choices at the spa—in fact, an ideal choice for a holiday by the lake. The decorator tried to make the place as warm and inviting as possible. Its guest rooms are furnished in Bavarian style.

The hotel has good food and also caters to special dieters. Its main restaurant is only for hotel guests. Its Bierstüberl is often a lively gathering place for holidaymakers.

INEXPENSIVE

KURHOTEL EDELWEISS, Münchnerstrasse 21, D-8182 Bad Wiessee. Tel. 08022/8-60-90. Fax 08022/83-883. 40 rms. TV TEL
$ Rates (including continental breakfast): 65 DM–85 DM ($42.90–$56.10) single; 105 DM–135 DM ($69.30–$89.10) double. No credit cards. **Parking:** Free. **Closed:** Mid-Nov to Christmas.

The main body of this chalet guesthouse is ornamented with wooden balconies and painted detailing around its doors and windows. Additional units are available in the motel-like outbuildings that stretch beside the main structure, affording comfortable and well-maintained lodging in summer and winter. The colorfully modern public rooms have a certain German kitsch. The main guest rooms are comfortably but functionally furnished. The restaurant is only for hotel guests.

WIESSEER HOF, Sanktjohanserstrasse 456, D-8182 Bad Wiessee. Tel. 08022/86-70. Fax 08022/86-71-65. 58 rms. TV TEL
$ Rates (including buffet breakfast): 48 DM–120 DM ($31.70–$79.20) single; 88 DM–190 DM ($58.10–$125.40) double. AE, DC, MC, V. **Parking:** Free.

Most of the rooms in this modern hotel have balconies that in summertime are festooned with boxes of geraniums. The style of the place is like an overgrown chalet, with four floors of rooms, many with views over a lawn dotted with greenery, leading up to the blue expanse of the Tegernsee. The guest rooms are up-to-date, and the stuccoed wooden walls of the public rooms create a gemütlich warmth.

The Eberle family, which runs the Wiesseer Hof, has a healthy respect for traditional styles. The kitchen features many Bavarian specialties, and an elevator comes in handy when you've overindulged in them.

7. BAD REICHENHALL

84 miles SE of Munich; 12 miles SW of Salzburg

GETTING THERE   By Train   An airport is at Munich (see Chapter 4), to which Bad Reichenhall is connected by frequent train service, the rail connection going through Rosenheim.

By Bus   Regional bus service to and from Bad Reichenhall is provided by Regionalverkehr Oberbayern Betrieb (tel. 08652/5473 for information). From the spa, you can take a bus to various tourist spots in the Bavarian Alps, including Berchtesgaden.

By Car   Access is by autobahn (A8), Munich from the north and Salzburg from the south. Exit on federal highway 21 into Bad Reichenhall.

ESSENTIALS   For tourist information, go to **Kur-und Verkehrsverein im Kurgstzentrum,** Wittelsbacherstrasse 15 (tel. 08651/30-03).

The most excellent German spas can call themselves *Staatsbad,* and Bad Reichenhall bears that title with pride. This old salt town is the most important curative spa in the Bavarian Alps. Mountain chains surround it, protecting it from the winds. Its brine springs, with a salt content as high as 24%, are the most powerful saline springs in Europe, and the town has been a source of salt for more than 2,400 years. The combination of the waters and the pure air has made Bad Reichenhall a recognized spa for centuries.

In 1848, King Maximilian of Bavaria stayed here, popularizing Bad Reichenhall as a fashionable resort. Today visitors come from all over the world to take the waters, which supposedly treat asthma and other respiratory ailments. Treatment sessions are almost exclusively in the morning at the seven resort institutes, therapy ranging from simply drinking the water to pneumato-therapy—even electronic lungs for the most serious cases. Although Bad Reichenhall takes the medical side of the cure seriously, spa authorities encourage visitors to enjoy its many attractions as well.

There's a wide choice of activities, from symphony concerts to folklore presentations. The State Gaming Rooms are popular, and the ideal climate permits a complete spectrum of outdoor events, from excursions into the mountains for hikes or skiing to tennis tournaments. Incidentally, the spa gardens are unusual in that the sheltered location of the town amid the lofty Alps permits the growth of several varieties of tropical plants, giving the gardens a lush, exotic appearance.

The ✪ **Bad Reichenhaller Saltmuseum,** Saline Bad Reichenhall, Reichenbachstrasse 4 (tel. 08651/70-02-51), just a short walk from the Kurgarten, is the home of the ancient industry responsible for the growth and prosperity of Bad

Reichenhall from Celtic times to the present. Parts of the old plant still stand today, but most of it was reconstructed in the mid-19th century in the troubadour style by Ludwig I of Bavaria. The large pumps and huge marble caverns are impressive. Tours are provided daily from April 1 to October 31; hours are 10 to 11:30am and 2 to 4pm. Admission is 6.50 DM ($4.30) for adults and 3 DM ($2) for children.

The great fire of 1834 destroyed much of the town, but many of the impressive churches survived. One outstanding memorial is **St. Zeno,** a 12th-century Gothic church showing a later baroque influence. Its most remarkable feature is the painted interior, centering on the carved altarpiece of the *Coronation of the Virgin.*

WHERE TO STAY

VERY EXPENSIVE

STEIGENBERGER AXELMANNSTEIN, Salzburger Strasse 2–6, D-8230 Bad Reichenhall. Tel. 08651/777-0, or toll free 800/223-5652 in the U.S. or Canada. Fax 08651/59-32. 151 rms, 8 suites. MINIBAR TV TEL **Bus:** 941.

$ **Rates** (including continental breakfast): 205 DM–280 DM ($135.30–$184.80) single; 290 DM–500 DM ($191.40–$330) double; from 550 DM ($363) suite. AE, DC, MC, V. **Parking:** 15 DM ($9.90).

Set in its own 7½-acre garden, Steigenberger Axelmannstein is a first-class hotel attracting a mature clientele. It offers a cure department, a sauna, a solarium, a fitness center, a cosmetic studio, a hairdresser, an indoor pool, and a tennis court. Many of the well-furnished rooms have views of the encircling Bavarian Alps, and each contains a color TV and radio.

The public rooms are traditionally furnished with antiques and reproductions, including some Gobelin tapestries. The Parkrestaurant, opening onto a garden, attracts many nonresidents, as does the cozy wood-paneled Axel-Stuberl, offering regional dishes. The cozy wood-paneled Axel-Bar features live entertainment daily. Room service, laundry, and dry cleaning are provided.

EXPENSIVE

HOTEL PANORAMA, Badenstrasse 6, D-8230 Bad Reichenhall. Tel. 08651/779-0. Fax 08651/78985. 83 rms. TV TEL **Bus:** 9541.

$ **Rates** (including buffet breakfast): 96 DM–152 DM ($63.40–$100.30) single; 162 DM–284 DM ($106.90–$187.40) double. AE, DC, MC, V. **Parking:** 7 DM ($4.60).

The pristine, modern Panorama overlooks the spa, with a scenic mountain backdrop. The hotel is for those who demand the latest in spa facilities, and the many it offers range from a large pool to a sauna to cure treatments. Accommodations, compact and sleekly contemporary, are divided into category "A" and category "B." Naturally, the most expensive are those with the better views. The hotel offers rooms with balconies and radios. Good meals are served in an attractive setting, and you can enjoy the café and bar when you've finished your fitness program.

KURHOTEL LUISENBAD, Ludwigstrasse 33, D-8230 Bad Reichenhall. Tel. 08651/60-40. Fax 08651/629-28. 83 rms, 3 suites. MINIBAR TV TEL **Bus:** 9541.

$ **Rates** (including continental breakfast): 134 DM–165 DM ($88.40–$108.90) single; 240 DM–314 DM ($158.40–$207.20) double; from 394 DM ($260) suite. DC, MC, V. **Closed:** Nov 20–Dec.

A world unto itself, the Kurhotel Luisenbad is an older hotel with a newer guest room wing in a garden setting. Its most outstanding feature is its indoor pool with a glass wall bringing the outdoors inside. The lounges and atmosphere are inviting—nothing austere here, as the emphasis is on informality and comfort. The more modern rooms are quite handsome, with bold colors and tasteful furnishings. There are facilities for thermal baths, inhalations, massages, and mud baths, plus a Finnish sauna. Room service, laundry, and dry cleaning are available.

MODERATE

HOTEL BAYERISCHER HOF, Bahnhofplatz 14, D-8230 Bad Reichenhall. Tel. 08651/60-90. Fax 08651/60-91-11. 64 rms. MINIBAR TV TEL **Bus:** 9541.
$ Rates (including buffet breakfast): 112 DM–174 DM ($73.90–$114.80) single; 178 DM–230 DM ($117.50–$151.80) double. AE, DC, MC, V. **Parking:** 10 DM ($6.60).

Modern and inviting, the Bayerischer Hof is in the center of the spa on the main street. The staff is well trained, and those at the reception desk are helpful in arranging excursions to Obersalzberg, Berchtesgadener Land, and Salzburg. If you're there in winter, they'll help arrange such sports as cross-country and downhill skiing. Many of the guest rooms are furnished in a well-maintained functional modern style; each contains a TV and radio.

The hotel is equipped with such facilities as a roof-garden indoor pool with Finnish sauna and a salon for massage and cosmetic treatments. In addition to the main restaurant, there is a café with live music, as well as the Tiffany Bar and a nightclub with international acts.

HANSI AM KURPARK, Rinckstrasse 3, D-8230 Bad Reichenhall. Tel. 08651/31-08. 19 rms. TV TEL **Bus:** 9541.
$ Rates (including buffet breakfast): 64 DM–95 DM ($42.20–$62.70) single; 130 DM–140 DM ($85.80–$92.40) double. MC. **Parking:** 6 DM ($4). **Closed:** Dec–Jan.

A late 19th-century building of pleasing symmetry with a tile mansard roof and flower-bedecked verandas, the Hansi am Kurpark lies a two-minute walk from the Hauptbahnhof. The owners of this well-maintained establishment offer their guests a good cuisine, with vegetarians and dieters catered to. The rooms are furnished in a homelike modern style.

SALZBURGER HOF, Mozartstrasse 7, D-8230 Bad Reichenhall. Tel. 08651/20-62. Fax 08651/60-91-11. 25 rms. MINIBAR TV TEL **Bus:** 9541.
$ Rates (including continental breakfast): 85 DM–104 DM ($56.10–$68.60) single; 140 DM–184 DM ($92.40–$121.40) double. AE, DC, MC, V. **Parking:** 6 DM ($4).

⑤ One of the best buys if you're shopping for a moderately priced choice is the Salzburger Hof. Although the hotel was recently built and is architecturally contemporary, most of its public rooms have been given an overlay of old Bavarian charm. Lounges have been sacrificed to make room for unique dining rooms and nooks. Best of all are the compact guest rooms, most of which contain streamlined sofas, window desks, beds with built-in headboards, and armchairs around a breakfast table; all open onto tiny balconies.

INEXPENSIVE

HOTEL-PENSION ERIKA, Adolf-Schmid-Strasse 3, D-8230 Bad Reichenhall. Tel. 08651/30-93. 36 rms. TV TEL **Bus:** 9541.
$ Rates (including buffet breakfast): 60 DM–80 DM ($39.60–$52.80) single; 112 DM–160 DM ($73.90–$105.60) double. AE, MC, V. **Parking:** 6 DM ($4). **Closed:** Nov–Feb.

⑤ This grand 19th-century salmon-colored villa welcomes guests into the high-ceilinged splendor of a renovated palace, now updated into a modern hotel. The Erika is known for its garden, and the rooms are warm and comfortably furnished. Home-cooked meals cost from 18 DM to 34 DM ($11.90 to $22.40).

HOTEL KÜRFURST, Kürfurstenstrasse 11, D-8230 Bad Reichenhall. Tel. 08651/27-10. 12 rms, 1 suite. MINIBAR TV TEL **Bus:** 9541.

$ Rates (including buffet breakfast): 50 DM–75 DM ($33–$49.50) single; 104 DM–130 DM ($68.60–$85.80) double; from 134 DM ($88.40) suite. AE, DC, MC, V. **Parking:** Free. **Closed:** Dec 15–Jan 15.

The Kürfurst is under the personal management of its conscientious owner, Renate Voitz. Hers is a family-run hotel near the outskirts of Bad Reichenhall, close to the river and about a 10-minute walk to anywhere else in town. A trim and well-maintained modern facade in white stucco opens into a lobby with Oriental rugs and a staircase that curves to the upper floors. The rooms are spacious and sunny, some having terraces with tables and chairs. Lunch and dinner can be served here, but only to hotel guests.

WHERE TO DINE
EXPENSIVE

SCHWEIZER STUBEN, Kirchberg Schlössl, Thumseestrasse 11. Tel. 08651/27-60.
Cuisine: INTERNATIONAL. **Reservations:** Required. **Directions:** SW of town in the center of the suburb of Kirchberg.

$ Prices: Appetizers 18 DM–32 DM ($11.90–$21.10); main courses 25 DM–42 DM ($16.50–$27.70); fixed-price lunch 38 DM–75 DM ($25.10–$49.50); fixed-price dinner 95 DM–105 DM ($62.70–$69.30). AE, DC, MC, V.
Open: Lunch Fri–Wed 11am–3pm; dinner Fri–Wed 6pm–1am.

⭐ If you want to throw a party, this is the place to do it. The chef will feed "any number of guests," or so he promises. However, even if your "party" is confined just to yourself or one or two others, Messrs. Schwab and Anfang will open to you the delights of what is known as Bad Reichenhall's "rendezvous point for gourmets." They feature a light cuisine, along with specialties from Bavaria and the Berchtesgaden region. The decor is appropriately rustic, the ambience gemütlich, and the choice of food attractively poised between international and regional.

STEIGENBERGER AXELMANNSTEIN PARKRESTAURANT & AXEL-STÜBERL, Salzburger Strasse 2–6. Tel. 08651/777-0.
Cuisine: CONTINENTAL/INTERNATIONAL. **Reservations:** Recommended. **Bus:** 9541.

$ Prices: Appetizers 12 DM–32 DM ($7.90–$21.10); main courses 36 DM–41 DM ($23.80–$27.10); fixed-price menus 75 DM–105 DM ($49.50–$69.30). AE, DC, MC, V.
Open: Parkrestaurant, lunch daily noon–2pm; dinner daily 6:30pm–9pm; Axel-Stüberl, lunch daily noon–2pm, dinner daily 6–11pm.

The Parkrestaurant and the Axel-Stüberl are in the Steigenberger Axelmannstein, previewed above. The Parkrestaurant is known for international specialties, while the Axel-Stüberl features original Bavarian and Austrian cooking. The head chef uses his skills to prepare cuisine moderne specialties—tasty and of low calorie count. The fish served in both restaurants is particularly good, as is the standing rack of lamb provençal, with fresh herbs and homemade bread.

MODERATE

RESTAURANT DIE HOLZSTUBE, in the Hotel Luisenbad, Ludwigstrasse 33. Tel. 08651/60-40.
Cuisine: GERMAN. **Reservations:** Recommended. **Bus:** 9541.
$ Prices: Appetizers 15 DM–28 DM ($9.90–$18.50); main courses 28 DM–42 DM ($18.50–$27.70). DC, MC, V.
Open: Lunch daily noon–2pm; dinner daily 6:30–10pm.

The old-fashioned tradition and service here have always had a seductive pull on its many regular patrons. It's a place where you can watch the flowers bloom and enjoy a world-class cuisine (with many diet-conscious selections). You might try one of the original recipes developed here: for example, marinated and roasted medallions of venison Königin Luise, served with bacon, chanterelles, and whortleberries.

THE RHINELAND

Few rivers of the world can claim such an important role in the growth of a nation as the Rhine. The Rhine begins in Switzerland and ultimately reaches the Netherlands in its progress to the sea, but most of its 850 miles snake through the mountains and plains of Germany. For more than 2,000 years it has been a chief trade route, its deep waters enabling modern sea vessels to travel upstream from the North Sea as far as Cologne.

Trade was not the only commodity carried along the waters of the Rhine. From earliest times, it was also the magnet for the intellectual, artistic, and religious minds of Europe. It has been called "a triumphal avenue of the muses," and a trip along its banks today reveals historic and artistic treasures. Legend and history seem to wait around every bend of the river.

From Mainz north to Koblenz, the winding river cuts through steep vine-covered hillsides dotted with towns whose names are synonymous with fine German wine. In this section is the legendary Lorelei, from which rock a Siren lured men to doom. The saga of the Nibelungen, the best known of the Rhine legends, is associated with the topography from the Siebengebirge (the Seven Mountains) near Bonn, where Siegfried slew the dragon, to the city of Worms, where Brünnhilde plotted against the dragon-slayer.

The Rhine is also the home of many of Germany's largest and most modern cities. Cologne and Düsseldorf vie for trade and tourism. Bonn was the postwar provisional capital of West Germany and continues as the de facto capital of Germany, even though Berlin has been designated as the capital of the united country.

SUGGESTED ITINERARY

Day 1 Head for Düsseldorf, city of fashion and industry. Explore its Altstadt (Old Town).

Days 2–3 Go south to Cologne to see its cathedral and major museums. While still based in Cologne, spend Day 3 making a side trip west to Aachen.

Day 4 Spend a night in Bonn and see the Beethoven House. It's also possible to find accommodations in adjoining Bad Godesburg.

Day 5 Spend the morning sightseeing at Koblenz, and in the evening anchor into one of the wine towns of the Rheingau, enjoying vineyards and wine.

Day 6 Head for a morning of sightseeing at Mainz, before moving south to overnight in Worms.

Day 7 In the morning sightsee in Worms, then continue south to the ancient city of Speyer for a final night.

WHAT'S SPECIAL ABOUT THE RHINELAND

Great Towns/Villages
☐ Cologne, largest city on the Rhine, known for its cathedral, artist community, and scented toilet water.
☐ Aachen, on the border with France, the city of Charlemagne.
☐ Düsseldorf, a sophisticated and glittering showcase of the "economic miracle."

Ace Attractions
☐ Rhine cruises, a 500-mile tour along a river of legend and scenic beauty.
☐ The Rheingau, Rhine wine towns, filled with vineyards and drinking taverns—a tribute to Bacchus.

Religious Shrines
☐ Cologne Cathedral, the largest Gothic cathedral in Germany.

☐ St. Peter's Cathedral, in Worms, the purest Romanesque basilica in the Rhine valley.
☐ Domkapitel, in Speyer, evocative of the medieval German empire, perhaps the greatest building of its time.

Museums
☐ Beethoven House, in Bonn, where the great composer was born in 1770.
☐ Roman-Germanic Museum, in Cologne, with its precious collection of Roman glass and other priceless artifacts.

SEEING THE REGION

BY TRAIN EuroCity and InterCity trains connect all the major cities along the Rhine, including Cologne, Düsseldorf, Bonn, and Mainz. Rail service also extends as far north as Hamburg and as far south as Munich. The most scenic part is between Mainz and Bonn, alongside the mighty river. Many passengers travel this particular stretch just for the scenic views.

RHINE CRUISES The best way to get a really intimate look at the river valley that helped shape the history of Europe is to travel on its waters by ship. A wide range of cruises, from a single afternoon to a week or more, are available from several shipping lines. These range from a 500-mile tour in a luxury yacht to one-day cruises between a variety of preselected sites of historical and/or artistic importance.

The premier carrier for both categories is **KD River Cruises of Europe** (Köln-Düsseldorfer Deutsche Rheinschiffahrt), Frankenwerft 15, D-5000 Köln 1 (tel. 0221/20880-318-319). Established early in the 19th century and today the owner of a fleet of more than 20 vessels, the company offers elegant, nonglitzy river tours on compact but comfortable ships equipped with open-air pools, dining rooms, bars, and highly competent multilingual staffs. Although a singer might provide entertainment over dinner each night, the main entertainment comes from dialogue with fellow passengers and the sweeping views of the landscape and water views nearby.

A five-day Amsterdam-to-Strasbourg cruise costs between $760 and $1,715 per person, double occupancy, all-inclusive. A three-day cruise between Strasbourg and Cologne costs from $370 to $835 per person, double occupancy. Ships always dock overnight at cities of historical interest and offer, for an extra fee, an array of motorcoach touring options at each of the ports of call.

You can also opt instead for a trip on the company's day steamers—for example, traveling down the river from Cologne, stopping overnight in Koblenz, then continuing the next day to Mainz. One-way fares from Cologne to Koblenz or from Koblenz to Mainz are 76 DM ($50.20). A 10-hour return from Mainz to Cologne costs 150 DM ($99).

Though the day cruises don't stop for very long, passengers can embark or disembark at such historic towns as Bonn, Linz, Braubach, St. Goarshausen, and Rüdesheim. For the purposes of day excursions, children up to 4 years and holders of Eurailpasses travel free and children under 14 pay half price. Although tickets for day excursions cannot be reserved and should be bought directly on the pier before departure, arrangements for multiday tours can be booked through the company's U.S.-based sales representative. For more information, contact **Rhine Cruises,** 170 Hamilton Ave., White Plains, NY 10601 (tel. toll free 800/346-6525), or **Rhine Cruises,** 323 Geary St., San Francisco, CA 94102 (tel. toll free 800/858-8587).

BY CAR   The advantage of driving, of course, is being able to stop whenever and wherever you want without the restrictions of train or boat schedules. If your schedule can accommodate the time, allow at least a week—although this will enable you only to scratch the surface.

Highways and autobahns along the Rhine tend to be heavily trafficked, so allow adequate time. Highways, not autobahns, hug both the left and right banks of the Rhine, and at many points you'll come across car ferries crossing the river. The most scenic stretch for driving is the mid-Rhine, between Koblenz and Mainz.

1. DÜSSELDORF

25 miles N of Cologne; 19 miles SW of Essen; 143 miles NW of Frankfurt

GETTING THERE   By Plane   Lufthansa connects New York and Düsseldorf with a daily nonstop flight. There is also service from Miami and Toronto. You land at Lohausen Airport, 4 miles north of the city, the second-largest airport in Germany. From here, you can take regularly scheduled connections to 14 German, 47 European, and 19 international airports. Lufthansa will fly you from Frankfurt to Düsseldorf in just 45 minutes or from Munich in an hour.

The airport is linked to the GermanRail network. Transfer to the Düsseldorf main rail station is via S-Bahn no. 7, offering service daily from 5:30am to 11:09pm, with trains every 20 minutes. Trip time is 13 minutes. The one-way fare is 2.60 DM ($1.70). Regular airport buses also connect Düsseldorf airport with Bonn and Cologne. Four daily Lufthansa express trains connect the airport to Frankfurt, Cologne, and Bonn (tel. 0211/13-21-68 for information). A taxi ride from the airport to central Düsseldorf takes about 20 to 30 minutes and costs 30 DM ($19.80) and up.

By Train   The main station, Düsseldorf Hauptbahnhof (tel. 0211/36-801), offers frequent connections to all major cities. For example, trip time to Frankfurt is about 2½ hours and to Munich, about 7 hours. For rail information, call 0211/19-419. Düsseldorf also has extensive regional rail links (for information on regional trains or trams, call 0211/58-228).

By Bus   Bus service to nearby cities is provided by Westfalen Bus GmbH, W-5758 Froedenberg (tel. 02373/73-56 for information). Long-distance buses run from Düsseldorf to Berlin on coaches owned by Linienverkehrder Deutschen Land- und Seereisen GmbH. Information is via a toll-free number, 0130/66-62.

By Car   Access to Düsseldorf is by autobahn A3 north and south or A46 east and west.

ESSENTIALS   Luggage storage facilities are available at the Hauptbahnhof and at the airport. For questions about transportation, boat trips, or other matters, ask at the tourist office, the **Verkehrsverein,** Konrad-Adenauer-Platz (tel. 0211/17-20-20).

Although Düsseldorf got its start as a settlement on the right bank of the Rhine, today it is built on both sides—the older sections on the right and the modern, commercial, and industrial parts on the left. The two parts are connected by five

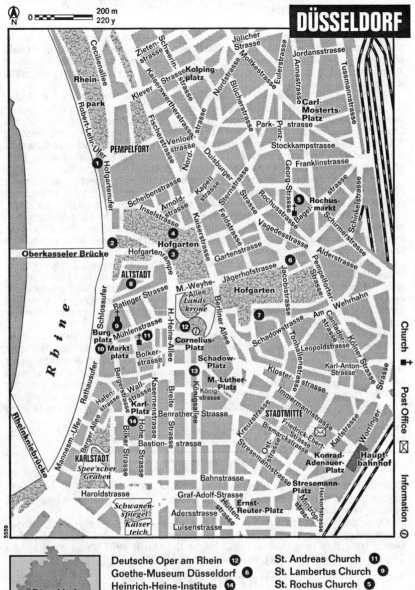

DÜSSELDORF

0 ⊨⊨⊨⊨ 200 m
220 y

N

Rhein-park

Cecilienallee

Robert-Lehr-Ufer

Hofgartenufer

Zieten-strasse

Schwerin-strasse

Kaiserswertherstrasse

Kolping-platz

Klever

Fischerstrasse

Kaiserstrasse

Nord-strasse

Venloer-strasse

PEMPELFORT

1

Scheibenstrasse

Arnold-Inselstrasse

Kapell-strasse

Duisburger Strasse

Jülicher Strasse

Moltkestrasse

Nordstrasse

Blücherstrasse

Eulerstrasse

Jordansstrasse

Annastrasse

Tussmannstrasse

Carl-Mosterts-Platz

Park- Prinz- strasse

Stockkampstrasse

Franklinstrasse

Georg-Strasse

strasse

Sternstrasse

Rochusstrasse

Schinkelstrasse

5 **Rochus-markt**
Bagel-

Hofgarten

4

3

Hofgartenrampe

Kaiserstrasse

Feldstrasse

Gartenstrasse

Vagedesstrasse

Schirmerstrasse

Alderstrasse

ALTSTADT

8

Ratinger Strasse

Schlossufer

M.-Weyhe-Allee

Landskrone

12

H.-Heine-Allee

Berliner Allee

Jägerhofstrasse

Hofgarten

6

Jacobistrasse

Pempelforter-strasse

Am Cantador-strasse

Adlerstrasse

Wehrhahn

Kölner Strasse

R h i n e

Mühlenstrasse

11

Burg-platz

9

10 **Markt-platz**

Bolker-strasse

Cornelius-Platz

Schadow-Platz

7

Schadowstrasse

Tonhallenstrasse

Leopoldstrasse

Karl-Anton-Strasse

Kölner Strasse

Rathausufer

Bergerstrasse

Wall-strasse

Kasernenstrasse

Karl-Platz

14

Breite Strasse

13

M.-Luther-Platz

König-strasse

Königsallee

Benrather Strasse

Kloster-strasse

Immermannstrasse

STADTMITTE

Hafenstrasse

Mannesm.-Ufer

Berger Allee

Hohe Strasse

Bilker Strasse

Bastion- strasse

Kreuzstrasse

Stresemannstrasse

Ost-

Bismarckstrasse

Friedrich-Ebert-Strasse

Karlstrasse

Worringer Strasse

Konrad-Adenauer-Platz

Haupt-bahnhof

KARLSTADT

Spee'scher Gräben

Haroldstrasse

Schwanen-spiegel

Kaiser-teich

Graf-Adolf-Strasse

Adersstrasse

Luisenstrasse

Bahnstrasse

Hütten-strasse

Ernst-Reuter-Platz

Stresemann-Platz

Mintropstrasse

Harkortstrasse

Oberkasseler Brücke

2

Rheinkniebrücke

5559

Church ✝

Post Office ✉

Information ①

● Düsseldorf
GERMANY

Deutsche Oper am Rhein **12**	St. Andreas Church **11**
Goethe-Museum Düsseldorf **6**	St. Lambertus Church **9**
Heinrich-Heine-Institute **14**	St. Rochus Church **5**
Hofgarten **4**	Schauspielhaus **7**
Königsallee **13**	Thyssen-House **3**
Kunstmuseum Düsseldorf **1**	Tonhalle (Düsseldorf Symphony Orchestra) **2**
Kunstsammlung Nordrhein-Westfalen **8**	Town Hall (Rathaus) **10**

bridges, the most impressive being the Oberkassel. Parks and esplanades line the riverbanks. After 85% of the right bank city was destroyed in World War II, it could have easily grown into just another ugly manufacturing town, but Düsseldorf followed a modern trend in reconstruction, and today it is the most elegant metropolis in the Rhine Valley.

As in most German cities, there is an **Altstadt,** with a marketplace, a Gothic Rathaus (town hall), and a few old buildings and churches. Near the Rathaus in Burgplatz are two of the city's most famous landmarks, the twisted spire of **St. Lambertus Church** and the round **Schlossturm** (Castle Tower), both of 13th-century origin. A short walk to the east takes you to **St. Andreas Church,** one of the most important in Düsseldorf, originally a Jesuit foundation dating from 1629. Düsseldorf was the former seat of the Electors of the Palatinate.

The Altstadt has been called "the longest bar in the world" because of the some 200-plus bars and restaurants found there. The favorite drink here is a top-fermented Altbier (old beer), a dark, mellow brew that must be consumed soon after it's made.

A walk up **Königsallee,** affectionately called the "Kö" by Düsseldorfers, will give the outsider a quick look at what the city and its residents are like. This street flanks an ornamental canal, shaded by trees and crossed by bridges. While one bank is lined with office buildings and financial centers, the other is filled with elegant shops, cafés, and restaurants. Here you'll see women dressed in the very latest styles, as Düsseldorf is also the fashion center of Germany. It is known for its Fashion Weeks, which attract designers and buyers from all over Europe. Retail shops are generally open Monday to Friday from 9am to 6:30pm, Saturday from 9am to 2pm. On the first Saturday of the month, shops stay open until 6pm. Big stores stay open on Thursday until 8pm.

As the capital of North Rhine–Westphalia, Düsseldorf is a wealthy city—the richest in Germany. It's a big, commercial city full of banks and industrial offices, yet it's refreshingly clean. It has managed to incorporate parks and gardens throughout the city, some of them wedged comfortably between skyscrapers. The most impressive of these buildings is the **Thyssen-House,** in the bustling center of town, towering over the Hofgarten (see below). Residents call the office tower the *Dreischeibenhaus* (three-slice house), because it actually looks like three huge monoliths sandwiched together.

Famous Düsseldorf citizens have included the poet, Heinrich Heine, who was born here on December 13, 1797. He wrote a famous poem about the Lorelei.

GETTING AROUND

Düsseldorf is a big, sprawling city, and it's not easy to get around on foot. It's best to rely on public transportation. The Hauptbahnhof lies in the southeastern sector, opening onto Konrad-Adenauer-Platz.

Düsseldorf and environs are served by a network of S-Bahn railways that fan out to the suburbs, along with buses and streetcars (Strassenbahn). A U-Bahn Düsseldorf system went into operation in 1988. Ask at the tourist office about purchasing a 24-hour visitor's ticket, a *Tagesnetzkarte,* for 8.50 DM ($5.60).

WHAT TO SEE & DO

If you walk up the Kö toward the triton fountain at the northern end of the canal, you'll reach the **Hofgarten,** a huge, rambling park. You could wander along the walks or sit and relax amid shade trees, gardens, fountains, and statues, almost forgetting you're in the very center of the city. Among the monuments is one to the poet Heinrich Heine. The Hofgarten is a good central point for seeing the city's major attractions—nearly all museums and cultural attractions are on its perimeter.

KUNSTSAMMLUNG NORDRHEIN-WESTFALEN, Grabbeplatz 5. Tel. 0211/838-10.
Opposite the Kunsthalle, this museum has an outstanding collection of modern art, including works by Picasso, Braque, Juan Gris, Fernand Léger, Max Ernst,

Salvador Dalí, René Magritte, Joan Miró, Kirchner, Kandinsky, Chagall, Jackson Pollock, Robert Rauschenberg, Roy Lichtenstein, Andy Warhol, Frank Stella, and others, plus a big collection of works by Julius Bissier. The museum also has 94 works by Paul Klee—so many, in fact, that the Klee exhibition is rotated at regular intervals since all the works cannot be shown at the same time. Furthermore, there are about six temporary exhibitions of contemporary art in the large exhibition hall every year.

Admission: 10 DM ($6.60) adults, 5 DM ($3.30) children.
Open: Tues–Sun 10am–6pm. **Bus:** 705, 717.

GOETHE-MUSEUM DÜSSELDORF, Schloss-Jägerhof, Jacobistrasse 2. Tel. 0211/899-62-62.

In the 18th-century Jägerhof Castle at the Hofgarten, near the city, the Anton and Katharina Kippenberg Foundation has sponsored a literary museum dedicated to the memory of Goethe's life and work. It emerged from the Kippenbergs' private collection of Goetheana containing some 35,000 items, consisting of autographs, books, busts, paintings, coins, medals, plaques, and china, among other objects. Anton Kippenberg, the owner and managing director of the Insel publishing house in Leipzig from 1904 to 1945, began collecting Goethe memorabilia when he was a young bookseller. About a thousand pieces of his collection are shown in the permanent exhibition, including the first draft of Goethe's poem "Noble Be Man"; a special copy of the fifth *Roman Elegy,* which Goethe sent to his friend Jacobi from Düsseldorf; the love poem "Ginkgo Biloba" from *The Divan;* and the world-famous "Chorus Mysticus" from *Faust II.* The displays present a chronology of Goethe's life and work. There are also exhibits on certain topics of the Goethe era. Just to the north of the castle is St. Rochus, one of the city's finest modern churches.

Admission: 3 DM ($2) adults, 1.50 DM ($1) children.
Open: Tues–Fri noon–5pm, Sat 1–5pm, Sun 11am–5pm. **Tram:** 704, 707.

KUNSTMUSEUM DÜSSELDORF, Ehrenhof 5. Tel. 0211/899-24-60.

One of the largest and most comprehensive museums in the Rhineland is famous for its collection of painting (Rubens, Caspar David Friedrich, Die Brücke and Der Blaue Reiter schools) and sculpture from the late Middle Ages to the 20th century, as well as for its print room with a collection of Italian drawings. There are also early Persian bronzes and ceramics; textiles from late antiquity to the present; and a glass collection with a strong showing of art nouveau, Jugendstil, and art deco items.

Admission: 5 DM ($3.30) adults, 2.50 DM ($1.70) children.
Open: Tues–Sun 11am–6pm. **Tram:** 725.

HEINRICH-HEINE-INSTITUT, Bilker Strasse 12–14. Tel. 0211/899-55-71.

More than 10,000 volumes, as well as the manuscript bequest of this Düsseldorf-born poet (1797–1856), are found here. One of Germany's greatest lyric poets, Heine is the author of the famous "Die Lorelei," the legend that later inspired such musicians as Schubert, Wagner, and Hugo Wolf. He also wrote satires criticizing society, as well as *Reisebilder,* or travel sketches. Born into a Jewish family, he nominally converted to Christianity so that he could attend law school. His work was prohibited during the Nazi era, and "Die Lorelei" officially attributed to an unknown author. (In the Altstadt, you can pay your respects at the house where the poet was born. It's at Bolkerstrasse 53 and is marked by a plaque.)

Admission: 3 DM ($2).
Open: Tues–Sun 11am–5pm. **Tram:** 704, 707.

WHERE TO STAY

VERY EXPENSIVE

BREIDENBACHER HOF, Heinrich-Heine-Allee 36, D-4000 Düsseldorf 1. Tel. 0211/130-30. Fax 0211/13-03-830. 132 rms, 31 suites. A/C MINIBAR TV TEL **U-Bahn:** Heinrich-Heine-Allee. **Tram:** 76, 78, or 705.
$ Rates (including continental breakfast): 290 DM–440 DM ($191.40–$290.40)

single; 440 DM–613 DM ($290.40–$404.60) double; from 1,050 DM ($693) suite. AE, DC, MC, V. **Parking:** 25 DM ($16.50).

★ Dating back to 1806 (although it was rebuilt after World War II), Düsseldorf's leading traditional hotel sits just around the corner from Königsallee. Everything for plush living is found here. The main drawing rooms and lounges have traditional furnishings, glamorized by antiques, gilt mirrors, paintings, and bronze chandeliers. Each guest room is uniquely decorated. The service is excellent.

Dining/Entertainment: The Bar Royal is a select meeting place, with leather chairs and soft piano music—small and intimate. Next door, the Grill Royal serves a traditional European cuisine and is considered one of the finest restaurants in Germany. In the Breidenbacher Eck, an informal bistro atmosphere prevails. A full menu is offered at lunch and dinner; here you can also order snacks throughout the day until late at night. Trader Vic's is a Polynesian restaurant and bar, with Caribbean cocktails and exotic South Seas dishes.

Services: 24-hour room service, laundry, dry cleaning.

Facilities: Car-rental facilities, nearby health club.

DÜSSELDORF HILTON, Georg-Glock-Strasse 20, D-4000 Düsseldorf 30. Tel. 0211/43-77-0, or toll free 800/445-8667 in the U.S. Fax 0211/437-76-50. 372 rms, 9 suites. A/C MINIBAR TV TEL **Bus:** 834.

$ **Rates:** 325 DM–490 DM ($214.50–$323.40) single; 385 DM–490 DM ($254.10–$323.40) double; from 950 DM ($627) suite. Continental breakfast 28 DM ($18.50) extra. AE, DC, MC, V. **Parking:** 18 DM ($11.90).

This is one of the most outstanding Hiltons in the chain and one of the best run. Both the Düsseldorf Hilton and its adjoining congress centers are near the Rhine, close to the city, airport, and fairgrounds. It is exactly what you would expect from a Hilton, plus a lot more. Each well-designed and streamlined guest room has a handsomely equipped tile bath. The Executive Floor has a separate check-in/check-out desk and a lounge for drinks and a breakfast buffet. But no matter what you pay, the view is good and the rooms attractively styled. Added conveniences are there too: VCRs, radios, direct-dial phones, and more. The public lounges reflect a sleek modern decor, utilizing free-form sculpture and contemporary paintings.

Dining/Entertainment: Most agreeable is the Hofgarten-Restaurant, a glassed-in garden room for informal dining. The hotel also offers the Golden Orchid Garden, one of the famous Baan Thai restaurants.

Services: 24-hour room service, laundry, dry cleaning.

Facilities: The popular Neptune's Club, with pool, sauna, massage facilities, fitness center, solarium.

SAVOY HOTEL, Oststrasse 128, D-4000 Düsseldorf 1. Tel. 0211/36-03-36. Fax 0211/35-66-42. 123 rms. MINIBAR TV TEL **Tram:** 709, 719. **Bus:** 834.

$ **Rates** (including continental breakfast): 225 DM–290 DM ($148.50–$191.40) single; 305 DM–390 DM ($201.30–$257.40) double. AE, DC, MC, V. **Parking:** 16 DM ($10.60).

Owned by one of Germany's largest chains, the Savoy gives personalized service in a gracious setting. Its facade is of heavily sculptured white limestone, and its guest rooms are comfortable and inviting, with all the modern conveniences. Guests can use the Savoy's pool.

Bierhoff, the court confectioners in the Savoy, is more than 125 years old. When the old Savoy had to make way for the new U-Bahn, this famous city café was relocated on Oststrasse. Today, in its reincarnation, the Bierhoff Konditorei, has reemerged with most of its old splendor. Massages are available, as are room service, laundry, and dry cleaning.

STEIGENBERGER PARK-HOTEL, Corneliusplatz 1, D-4000 Düsseldorf 1. Tel. 0211/13-81-0, or toll free 800/223-5652 in the U.S. and Canada. Fax 0211/13-16-79. 160 rms, 12 suites. MINIBAR TV TEL **Bus:** 778. **Tram:** 78, 79, 705, 710.

$ Rates (including continental breakfast): 315 DM–415 DM ($207.90–$273.90) single; 440 DM–570 DM ($290.40–$376.20) double; from 950 DM ($627) suite. AE, DC, MC, V. **Parking:** Free.

One of the traditional deluxe German hotels that survived World War II has been completely modernized and re-equipped to meet modern demands. It's right at the beginning of Königsallee, overlooking Hofgarten Park, next to the German Opera on the Rhine. A prestigious place, the Steigenberger maintains a high level of service in old-world style. All the guest rooms, refitted to the latest standards, are cozy and comfortable with TVs and radios.

Dining/Entertainment: The Rôtisserie attracts gourmets from all over the world, drawn to its modern French cuisine. Before-dinner drinks are served in the Etoile Bar. In summer, a terrace overlooking the parks and gardens of Düsseldorf invites you for a leisurely meal. Special seasonal meals are offered in a little bistro.

Services: 24-hour room service, laundry, dry cleaning, shoe-shine service.

Facilities: Sauna, car-rental facilities.

EXPENSIVE

AM RHEIN SCHNELLENBURG, Rotterdarnerstrasse 120, D-4000 Düsseldorf 30. Tel. 0211/43-41-33. Fax 0211/437-09-76. 49 rms, 3 suites. MINIBAR TV TEL **Bus:** 722 from Düsseldorf Bahnhof to Messe Center.

$ Rates (including buffet breakfast): 160 DM–260 DM ($105.60–$171.60) single; 220 DM–320 DM ($145.20–$211.20) double; from 380 DM ($250.80) suite. AE, DC, MC, V. **Parking:** Free. **Closed:** Dec 20–Jan 6.

Located on the outskirts, this hotel was built on the ruins of a medieval castle opening directly onto the Rhine. In a traditional style, with windowboxes of flowers in summer, it is an engaging choice, lying about 2½ miles from Düsseldorf's international airport and within walking distance of both the convention center and the Japanese Garden. All rooms are completely modern.

The hotel has a good restaurant with a terrace overlooking the river. Sightseeing boats leave from the hotel's own pier. The place manages to be cosmopolitan yet still comfortably informal. English is spoken.

EDEN, Adersstrasse 29–31, D-4000 Düsseldorf 1. Tel. 0211/3-89-70. Fax 0211/389-77-77. 130 rms. MINIBAR TV TEL **Tram:** 709 or 719. **Bus:** 834.

$ Rates (including buffet breakfast): 188 DM–359 DM ($124.10–$236.90) single; 241 DM–424 DM ($159.10–$279.80) double. AE, DC, MC, V. **Parking:** 18 DM ($11.90).

The centrally located Eden, in spite of its name, is more solid than lush. A lot of care has gone into making the completely renovated guest rooms comfortable. The third floor is reserved for nonsmokers. Beer, snacks, or full meals are served in the hotel's Bierstube. The hotel has a lobby bar; a hairdresser; a flower shop; and a good location, only two minutes from the Kö shopping area and five minutes from the Hauptbahnhof.

FÜRSTENHOF, Fürstenplatz 3, D-4000 Düsseldorf 1. Tel. 0211/37-05-45. Fax 0211/37-90-62. 43 rms. MINIBAR TV TEL **Tram:** 709 or 719. **Bus:** 834.

$ Rates (including buffet breakfast): 210 DM ($138.60) single; 305 DM ($201.30) double. AE, DC, MC, V. **Closed:** Dec 24–Jan 2.

This hotel has been totally revamped. Modern, but not glaringly so, it opens onto an attractive tree-filled square. All its handsomely furnished guest rooms are equipped with color TVs and radios. Nonsmoker rooms are available, and half of the breakfast room is reserved for nonsmoking guests. The hotel is a good, safe choice in the center of town. A sauna and fitness room are available, and the buffet breakfast is one of the best in town.

REMA HOTEL CENTRAL, Luisenstrasse 42, D-4000 Düsseldorf. Tel. 0211/37-90-91. Fax 0211/37-90-94. 72 rms. TV TEL **Tram:** 709 or 719. **Bus:** 834.

$ Rates (including buffet breakfast): 185 DM–260 DM ($122.10–$171.60) single; 260 DM–460 DM ($171.60–$303.60) double. AE, DC, MC, V. **Closed:** Dec 20–Jan 1.

In the heart of the business and fair world, this hotel is well located, lying near Königsallee. Its rooms are modern and clean. The shopping center of the Altstadt, theaters, cabarets, and museums lie only a short walk from the hotel, as does the Hauptbahnhof. Breakfast is the only meal served, but many restaurants with varied cuisines lie only a few minutes' walk from its doorstep.

MODERATE

HOTEL GROSSER KURFÜRST, Kufürsterstrasse 18, D-4000 Düsseldorf. Tel. 0211/35-76-47. Fax 0211/16-25-97. 22 rms (all with bath or shower). TV TEL **Tram:** 709 or 719.
$ Rates (including continental breakfast): 115 DM–165 DM ($75.90–$108.90) single; 145 DM–220 DM ($95.70–$145.20) double. AE, MC, V. **Closed:** Dec 22–Jan 4.

The Grosser Kurfürst is housed in a modern building. The rooms are well organized, but there's no furniture to spare, and accommodations are equipped with radios (in some cases, TVs). Breakfast is the only meal served.

LANCASTER, Oststrasse 166, D-4000 Düsseldorf 1. Tel. 0211/35-10-66. Fax 0211/16-28-84. 40 rms. MINIBAR TV TEL **Tram:** 709 or 719. **Bus:** 834.
$ Rates (including buffet breakfast): 155 DM–175 DM ($102.30–$115.50) single; 185 DM–205 DM ($122.10–$135.30) double. AE, MC, V.

Attractively situated in the center of town, the Lancaster is a five-minute walk from the Hauptbahnhof. The mirrored reception area efficiently registers guests before packing them off to comfortable and often sunny rooms. Breakfast includes an assortment of sausages that might make a Wurst fan of you.

RHEINPARK, Bankstrasse 13, D-4000 Düsseldorf 30-Golzheim. Tel. 0211/49-91-86. Fax 0211/49-02-24. 29 rms (3 with bath). **Bus:** 718, 772.
$ Rates (including continental breakfast): 68 DM ($44.90) single without bath; 125 DM ($82.50) double without bath, 140 DM ($92.40) double with bath. No credit cards. **Parking:** Free.

The Rheinpark is an antiseptically modern little hotel, about three blocks from the Rhine, in the Golzheim section. You are quite far away from the center, but a bus stopping nearby will quickly bring you to the Königsallee. The hotel's in a colorless concrete building, with no proper reception area, but the rooms are nicely decorated with old pictures. All rooms have running water, and there's a shower on each floor.

WURMS HOTEL, Scheurenstrasse 23, D-4000 Düsseldorf 1. Tel. 0211/37-50-01. Fax 0211/37-50-03. 27 rms (24 with bath or shower). TV TEL **Bus:** 835. **Tram:** 734, 741, or 752.
$ Rates (including continental breakfast): 95 DM ($62.70) single without bath, 130 DM ($85.80) single with bath or shower; 140 DM–180 DM ($92.40–$118.80) double with bath or shower. AE, DC, MC, V.

In a five-story stucco building, close to the Graf-Adolf-Strasse and about four blocks from the Hauptbahnhof, the Wurms Hotel is most recommendable. The accommodations are done in dark wood offset by bright bedspreads and curtains. The continental breakfast is the only meal served. The hotel lies only a short walk from the central landmark square Graf-Adolf-Platz.

WHERE TO DINE
VERY EXPENSIVE

IM SCHIFFCHEN, Kaiserwerther Markt 9. Tel. 0211/40-10-50.
Cuisine: FRENCH/SEAFOOD. **Reservations:** Required. **Tram:** 79 to Kelmensplatz.

$ Prices: Appetizers 25 DM–49 DM ($16.50–$32.30); main courses 52 DM–98 DM ($34.30–$64.70); fixed-price menus 169 DM–186 DM ($111.50–$122.80). AE, DC, MC, V.

Open: Dinner only, Tues–Sat 7–9:30pm.

On the outskirts, at Kaiserwerth, Im Schiffchen offers what many gourmets consider the finest food in Düsseldorf, if you don't mind the journey here to enjoy it. The featured piece of decor in this 18th-century house is the steering wheel from an old Rhine cruiser, and looking past it through the large windows, one has the feeling of being in a boat. The menu, in German and French, features such French-inspired cuisine moderne dishes as homemade goose-liver pâté with green peppercorns, Norwegian salmon in Vouvray sauce, lobster cooked in chamomile tea, and pike or perch in puff pastry. For dessert, you might try a granulated fruit mélange with almond cream.

RESTAURANT SAVINI, Stromstrasse 47. Tel. 0211/39-39-31.

Cuisine: ITALIAN. **Reservations:** Recommended. **Bus:** 834.

$ Prices: Appetizers 29 DM–45 DM ($19–$29.70); main courses 39 DM–54 DM ($25.70–$35.60); fixed-price lunch 65 DM ($42.90); fixed-price dinner 110 DM ($72.60). DC, MC, V.

Open: Lunch Tues–Sat noon–2:30pm; dinner Tues–Sat 6–10:30pm. **Closed:** July–Aug 2.

This restaurant, run by Mr. and Mrs. Carlo Caputo, is often cited as being one of the five best Italian restaurants in Germany. In a white-walled room with tastefully colored banquettes, diners are served a menu featuring a creative Italian cuisine. Produce comes fresh from the market and is deftly handled in the kitchen, as reflected by the carpaccio of beef with warm king prawns, black spaghetti with scallops, or seabass with risotto of mushrooms. The fixed-price menus change daily. The restaurant also has one of the best Italian wine cellars in Germany, with some 500 offerings.

VICTORIAN RESTAURANT, Königstrasse 3a. Tel. 0211/32-02-22.

Cuisine: CONTINENTAL. **Reservations:** Required for restaurant, recommended for lounge. **Tram:** 709 or 719. **Bus:** 834.

$ Prices: Appetizers 23 DM–50 DM ($15.20–$33); main courses 38 DM–60 DM ($25.10–$39.60); fixed-price menus 125 DM ($82.50) and 155 DM ($102.30). AE, DC, MC, V.

Open: Lunch Mon–Sat noon–3pm; dinner Mon–Sat 7–11pm. **Closed:** Mid-July through Aug.

Set behind a sign richly lettered with gilded characters, this establishment has a meticulously crafted environment of sparkling crystal, black-leather banquettes, and masses of flowers. The food represents the best of both traditional and modern schools of cuisine. Examples include deep-fried zucchini flowers stuffed with lobster mousse and flavored with a sauce of champagne vinegar and coriander; apple salad with slices of goose liver; and a trio of vegetable purées. The delectable desserts change with the inspiration of the pastry chef but might include terrine of oranges served with raspberry liqueur and fresh mint.

Between May and August, less expensive and simpler variations of the cuisine are served in the Victorian Lounge, which highlights regional dishes. Here, meals costing from 50 DM ($33.35) might include such typical dishes as Tafelspitz, goose-liver terrine flavored with aged cognac, and apple strudel.

EXPENSIVE

DE' MEDICI, Amboss-Strasse 3. Tel. 0211/59-41-51.

Cuisine: FRENCH/ITALIAN. **Reservations:** Required. **U-Bahn:** 76 to Amboss-Strasse.

$ Prices: Appetizers 18 DM–22 DM ($11.90–$14.50); main courses 30 DM–40 DM ($19.80–$26.40). AE, DC, MC, V.

Open: Lunch Mon–Sat noon–3pm; dinner Mon–Sat 6pm–midnight.

On the outskirts, at Oberkassel, De' Medici is elegantly modern, serving two culinary traditions, French and Italian. The oversize menu reflects the constant array of tried-and-true dishes, with concessions to whatever was available in the market that day. An unusual choice might be marinated sweetbreads over sautéed eggplant or medallions of veal in puff pastry.

MODERATE

RHEINTURM-TOP 180 RESTAURANT, Stromstrasse 20. Tel. 0211/84-85-80.

Cuisine: INTERNATIONAL. **Reservations:** Recommended. **Bus:** 725 or 834. **Tram:** 709.

$ Prices: Appetizers 10 DM–28 DM ($6.60–$18.50); main courses 28 DM–48 DM ($18.50–$31.70); fixed-price lunch 48 DM ($31.70); fixed-price dinner 85 DM ($56.10). AE, DC, MC, V.

Open: Lunch daily noon–2:30pm; dinner daily 6:30–10:30pm.

The international cuisine here is competently served and decently prepared, but most of the restaurant's clientele consider the view as important as the cuisine. Set atop a spool-shaped summit of the city's tallest tower, it boasts a futuristic design that incorporates a 360-degree panorama of Düsseldorf, its buildings, and its parks. Many of the people who share the elevator with you might only intend to use the tower's observation lookout. (It costs 5 DM [$3.30] to go up in the elevator.) Menu items include grills, game dishes, fish, and soups. Try the slices of smoked duck breast with creamy Savoy cabbage or rolls of salmon stuffed with turbot filling and served in Riesling-and-saffron sauce.

ZUM CSIKOS, Andreastrasse 9. Tel. 0211/32-97-71.

Cuisine: HUNGARIAN. **Reservations:** Recommended. **U-Bahn:** Opernhaus.

$ Prices: Appetizers 12 DM–24 DM ($7.90–$15.80); main courses 26 DM–38 DM ($17.20–$25.10). AE, DC, MC.

Open: Dinner only, Mon–Sat 6pm–3am. **Closed:** Mid-July to mid-Aug.

When you tire of Germanic cookery, Zum Csikos makes a refreshing change of pace with its Hungarian cuisine and music and a name that translates as "Hungarian cowboy." The structure dates from 1697. This charming place is arranged on three levels; candlelight gives the place (and the diners) a mellow glow. The home-style Hungarian food is well prepared, and the portions are hefty. The beef goulash is excellent, as is the chopped liver. The restaurant follows the Hungarian tradition of late-late closings.

ZUM SCHIFFCHEN, Hafenstrasse 5. Tel. 0211/13-24-21.

Cuisine: RHINELAND. **Reservations:** Required. **Tram:** 705.

$ Prices: Appetizers 5.50 DM–26 DM ($3.60–$17.20); main courses 18 DM–42 DM ($11.90–$27.70). AE, DC, MC, V.

Open: Lunch Mon–Sat noon–3pm; dinner Mon–Sat 5pm–midnight.

S There's plenty of atmosphere at Zum Schiffchen. A golden model ship on top of the step-gabled building reminds you of its location, only a block from the Rhine. The interior of the 1628 structure is in the tavern tradition of scrubbed wooden tables and rustic artifacts. Good, hefty portions of regional cuisine are the rule of the kitchen. The Schiffchen roast plate is served for two. The menu is large, and the service rather hectic. Zum Schiffchen is the perfect place to sample Düsseldorf's own beer. Over the years, it has attracted a host of famous diners, ranging from Napoleon to Heinrich Heine, from Curt Jurgens to Arthur Miller.

INEXPENSIVE

Instead of dining at a restaurant, an inexpensive alternative is to put together a meal right on the street (especially Flingerstrasse and Bölkerstrasse). Reibekuchen is a tasty potato pancake popular with Düsseldorfers. It's very fattening, filling, and good—and always inexpensive. Most Americans shun Blutwurst, a black (blood) pudding accompanied by raw onions. However, Bratwurst with one of those savory German mustards is delectable, as is Spanferkel Brötchen, a hefty slice of tender roast suckling pig served on rye bread. In winter, mussels are offered at several little *intime* restaurants (where you stand up to eat); sometimes they've been cooked in a Rhine-wine sauce.

IM ALTEN BIERHAUS, Alt-Niederkassel 75. Tel. 0211/55-12-72.
   Cuisine: RHINELAND. **Reservations:** Required. **Bus:** 834.
$ Prices: Appetizers 5.50 DM–10.50 DM ($3.60–$6.90); main courses 10.50 DM–17.50 DM ($6.90–$11.60). No credit cards.
   Open: Tues–Sat 3–11pm, Sun 11am–11pm. **Closed:** 3 weeks in summer (dates vary).

The centuries-old look of this guesthouse on the outskirts of Düsseldorf dates from 1641, when much of the place was built. Connoisseurs of German handcrafts will recognize the style of the Rhine's left bank (as opposed to the right). Typical German specialties, many sautéed, are served here. This is actually more a Weinstube than a restaurant. On Sundays the beer drinkers pile in at 11am. The specialty of the house is a dark and foamy brew known as *Altbier,* a specialty of the region of Düsseldorf. Beer begins at 2 DM ($1.30).

ZUM SCHLÜSSEL, Gatzweilers beer hall, Bölkerstrasse 43–47. Tel. 0211/32-61-55.
   Cuisine: GERMAN. **Reservations:** Recommended. **U-Bahn:** Opernhaus.
$ Prices: Appetizers 6 DM–7.50 DM ($4–$5); main courses 12 DM–28 DM ($7.90–$18.50). No credit cards.
   Open: Daily 10am–11pm; hot food served 11am–10pm.

On the original site of the famous Gatzweilers Alt brewery is Zum Schlüssel. The decor is that of a classic German Gasthaus, with the aura of a country inn. The service, proffered by courteous, shirtsleeved waiters, is swift. The food has both aroma and taste, and there's plenty to eat (try the Eisbein or a huge bowl of soup). This establishment is as Germanic as the Rhine. There are more than 30 meals from which to choose, but if you want only to drink, there's a snack bar. Try a quarter of a liter of the house beer, Gatzweilers Alt.

EVENING ENTERTAINMENT

The place to go is the Altstadt. Between Königsallee and the Rhine River, this half square mile of narrow streets and alleyways is jam-packed with restaurants, discos, art galleries, boutiques, nightclubs, restaurants, and some 200 song-filled beer taverns. If Düsseldorfers spend the night cruising the Old Town, they refer to the experience as an *Altstadtbummel.*

PERFORMING ARTS

Theater offerings are diverse. The **Schauspielhaus,** Gustaf-Grundgens-Platz 1 (tel. 0211/36-87-0), is well known for classical and modern drama. There are also many cinemas in Düsseldorf. Foreign films are almost always dubbed into German. Evening performances start at 8 or 8:30pm.

DEUTSCHE OPER AM RHEIN, Heinrich-Heine-Allee 16A. Tel. 0211/899-36-06.

Rated as one of the outstanding opera companies in Europe, Deutsche Oper am Rhein offers innovative productions. The season usually closes for about seven weeks between June and September, depending on a variable schedule.
   Prices: Tickets 12 DM–52 DM ($7.90–$34.30), but vary widely depending on presentation.

DÜSSELDORF SYMPHONY ORCHESTRA, performing in the Tonhalle, Ehrenhof 1. Tel. 0211/899-61-23.

This first-class orchestra, among the top dozen or so in Germany, usually sells out long before each performance, often to regular subscribers. The hall closes for six weeks in summer (dates vary).

Prices: Tickets 13 DM–50 DM ($8.60–$33).

BAR SCENE

In the town's dozens of taverns, you can sample the leading beers of the city. I especially recommend that you try the Schlösser and Frankenheim brews.

BRAUEREI ZUM UERIGE, Bergerstrasse 1. Tel. 0211/84-455.

A lot of beer is drunk every night in the Altstadt, and many locals prefer Brauerei, a unique beer that can be purchased only at this brewer-operated tavern. In half a dozen hearty drinking rooms, often filled with young people, nearly 10,000 mugs of beer are tossed across the counter every day. The cost is 2.50 DM ($1.70) for a quarter of a liter. They also serve apple cider and food, with simple plates ranging from 5 DM to 8 DM ($3.30 to $5.30). Open from 10am to midnight except for four days a year, usually religious holidays.

THE IRISH PUB, Hunsrückenstrasse 13. Tel. 0211/13-31-81.

⭐ On the nightlife circuit, The Irish Pub (also called Bei Fatty), is a sentimental favorite, housed in a building dating from 1648. Nowadays the alley out front is bombarded by disco music from every door, but this place tenaciously holds on to its Irish-pub atmosphere, the owner and most of the staff being Irish born-and-bred. It's a haven for anyone looking for the Bohemian auld lang syne of Düsseldorf artists, who made this their traditional dining and drinking spot. Artist-guests have contributed the paintings on the walls, and the decor is cluttered and charming, with gingham cloths, copper kettles and pots, and frosted lights shining softly on pewter plates. At a horseshoe-shaped bar, you can drink up, ordering anything from good beer to Irish coffee. A pint of Guinness costs 5.50 DM ($3.60). Open Monday to Friday from 2:30pm to 3am, Saturday from 1pm to 3am, and Sunday from noon to 3am. There's no cover charge, and often the establishment presents live entertainment every Friday and Saturday beginning at 10pm.

---

2. AACHEN (AIX-LA-CHAPELLE)

40 miles W of Cologne; 50 miles SW of Düsseldorf

GETTING THERE   By Train   The Hauptbahnhof at Aachen receives some 200 trains a day from all parts of Germany, with easy connections from such cities as Cologne, Berlin, Munich, Frankfurt, and Düsseldorf. Trains also arrive from Paris. Frankfurt is 5½ hours away, and Munich 8½ hours. Travel time between Cologne and Aachen is 45 minutes. For rail schedules and information, call 0241/19-419.

By Bus   It's best to take the train, but once you arrive in Aachen regional bus service is provided by BRV Busverkehr Rheinland GmbH at Simmerath (tel. 02473/6646 for schedules and information).

By Car   Access is by autobahn A4 east and west or A44 north or south. Frankfurt is 3½ hours away by car, Munich 6½ hours.

ESSENTIALS   You'll find the **Tourist Office Aachen** at Bahnhofplatz 4 (tel. 0241/180-29-65).

At the frontiers of Germany, Belgium, and the Netherlands is the ancient Imperial City of Aachen (Aix-la-Chapelle), inseparably associated with Charlemagne, who selected this spa as the center of his vast Frankish empire.

As a spa, Aachen has an even longer history than as an imperial city. Roman legionnaires established a military bath here in the 1st century C.E. At the end of the 17th century, it became known as the Spa of Kings, attracting royalty from all over Europe. In 1742, Frederick the Great took the cure here, and in 1818, the "Congress of Monarchs" brought Czar Alexander from Russia. After World War II, which badly damaged the town, the spa was rebuilt and today enjoys a mild reputation as a remedial center. Its springs are among the hottest in Europe. The treatment includes baths and the Trinkkur (the drinking of water). The spa gardens are the center of the resort activity, with attractive ponds, fountains, and shade trees.

Most travelers visit Aachen on a day trip from Cologne, via the Cologne-Aachen Autobahn, usually dining at the Ratskeller before returning to the larger city on the Rhine. However, those interested in the spa facilities can stay at one of the hotels described below.

The **Altstadt** of Aachen is small enough to be covered on foot. Marktplatz is in the heart of town, overshadowed by the Gothic Rathaus. From here, you can head down one of the most popular and busiest pedestrian precincts in the city, Krämerstrasse, which will lead to Münsterplatz and the famous cathedral, one of the masterpieces of architecture in the Western world.

From Cathedral Square you can go through the great iron gate to the Fischmarkt, with old merchants' houses and the Fischpuddelchen fountain with spouting fish. On the other side you can see Aachen's Rathaus, which contains the city archives. Past the Dom you reach the Elisengarten, bordered to the south by the symbol of Bad Aachen, the Elisenbrunnen, a rotunda with a thermal drinking fountain.

The Wingertsberg Kurgarten and the Stadtgarten with its thermal bath and casino lie to the northeast of town, and the Hauptbahnhof is on the southern ring, opening onto Romerstrasse.

WHAT TO SEE & DO

IMPERIAL CATHEDRAL, Münsterplatz. Tel. 0241/477-09-27.

About C.E. 800 the emperor built the octagon, the core of the Imperial Cathedral. Within the cathedral stands the marble "Königsstuhl," Charlemagne's throne, considered one of the most venerable monuments in Germany. For 600 years the Holy Roman emperors were crowned here, until Frankfurt became the coronation city in the mid-16th century.

The cathedral is an unusual mixture of Carolingian (the well-preserved dome), Gothic (the choir, completed in 1414), and baroque (the roof), all united into a magnificent upward sweep of architecture. The treasury, in the adjoining treasure house, is the most valuable and celebrated ecclesiastical treasure store north of the Alps. But the cathedral holds its own share of wealth. The elaborate gold shrine in the chancel contains the relics of the Emperor Charlemagne. The pulpit of Henry II is copper studded with precious gems. Visitors to the cathedral can view the throne of Charlemagne only with a guide (request one at the treasury).

Admission: Treasury, 3 DM ($2) adults, 2 DM ($1.30) children.

Open: Treasury, Apr–Sept, Mon 10am–2pm, Tues–Sat 10am–6pm, Sun 10:30am–5pm; Oct–Mar, Mon 10am–2pm, Tues–Sat 10am–5pm, Sun 10:30am–5pm. **Bus:** 1, 11, or 21.

RATHAUS, Am Markt. Tel. 0241/432-73-10.

The 14th-century Rathaus was built on the original site of Charlemagne's palace. Part of the old structure can still be seen in the so-called Granus Tower at the east side of the hall. The richly decorated facade of the Rathaus facing the marketplace is adorned with the statues of 50 German rulers, 31 of them crowned in Aachen. In the center, standing in relief, are the "Majestas Domini" and the two most important men in the Holy Roman Empire, Charlemagne and Pope Leo III.

On the second floor of the Rathaus is the double-naved and crossbeamed **Imperial Hall,** dating from 1330, the scene of German coronation meals from 1349 to 1531, built as the successor to the Carolingian Royal Hall. This hall today contains exact replicas of the Imperial Crown Jewels, true in size and material to the originals, presently in the Vienna Secular Treasury. On the walls are the Charlemagne frescoes, painted in the 19th century by Alfred Rethel, illustrating the victory of the Christian Franks over the Germanic heathens.

Admission: 2 DM ($1.30) adults, 1 DM (66¢) children.
Open: Mon–Fri 8am–1pm and 2–5pm, Sat–Sun 10am–1pm and 2–5pm.
Closed: Sometimes for official events. **Bus:** 1, 11, or 21.

COUVEN MUSEUM, Huhnermarkt 17. Tel. 0241/432-44-21.

A lovely rococo residence, the Couven Museum is filled with elegant household furnishings from the 1600s and 1700s. On the ground floor is a dispensary set up as it existed in the 1700s, and on the second landing is a spacious chamber with a chimney of decorated sculptured wood. In fact, there's a little bit of everything here: lots of hidden treasures.

Admission: 2 DM ($1.30) adults, 0.50 DM (30¢) children.
Open: Tues–Fri and Sun 10am–5pm, Sat 10am–1pm. **Bus:** 1, 11, or 21.

SUERMONDT-LUDWIG MUSEUM, Wilhelmstrasse 18. Tel. 0241/432-44-00.

The impressive collection of medieval German sculpture here is one of the finest in the land. It has some exceptional art, including a *Madonna in Robes* from 1420 from the Swabian school and a *Virgin and Child* from the 14th-century Tournai school. The second landing has a good collection of primitive Flemish and German works, along with 17th-century Dutch and Flemish paintings. Look for works by major masters such as Van Dyck and Rubens. The museum also has modern works, everything from Picasso to Roy Lichtenstein, Andy Warhol, and Jasper Johns.

Admission: 2 DM ($1.30) adults, 0.50 DM (30¢) children.
Open: Tues–Sat 10am–5pm, Sun 10am–1pm. **Bus:** 1, 11, or 21.

WHERE TO STAY

VERY EXPENSIVE

STEIGENBERGER HOTEL QUELLENHOF, Monheimsallee 52, D-5100 Aachen. Tel. 0241/15-20-81, or toll free 800/223-5652 in the U.S. and Canada. Fax 0241/15-45-04. 160 rms, 5 suites. TEL Bus: 1, 11, or 21.

$ Rates: 175 DM–280 DM ($115.50–$184.80) single; 280 DM–420 DM ($184.80–$277.20) double; from 650 DM ($429) suite. Half-board $55 per person extra. AE, DC, MC, V. **Parking:** Free.

A palacelike structure in a tranquil setting, the Steigenberger is as inviting as it is impressive. Architecturally neoclassical, it's furnished with a combination of antique reproductions and modern pieces. True to spa tradition, it is stately and elegant. All of the comfortable, tastefully furnished guest rooms have radios; most have TVs and are quite spacious.

Dining/Entertainment: The large Parkrestaurant Quellenhof, the best of the hotel's several eating places, is known for its cuisine moderne. Seating more than 80, it combines elegance and refined service with stylistic harmony; in summer, windows open onto the terrace, and cakes and coffee can be enjoyed under bright sun umbrellas. Both international and regional dishes are served, and a complete wine list is featured. A meal costs 70 DM to 105 DM ($46.20 to $69.30). The Parkrestaurant is open daily from noon until shortly before midnight. Nonresidents are welcome to dine here but should make reservations first. You can also eat in the Parkstube bar, where meals begin at 45 DM ($29.70). The Nationenbar is a good place to enjoy a drink from an almost unlimited variety of libations.

Services: Room service, laundry, dry cleaning.
Facilities: Large indoor thermal pool with picture windows and garden view.

EXPENSIVE

AQUIS GRANA CITY HOTEL, Büchel 32, D-5100 Aachen. Tel. 0241/4-43-0. Fax 0241/44-31-37. 94 rms, 2 suites. MINIBAR TV TEL **Bus:** 1, 11, or 21.
$ Rates (including buffet breakfast): 165 DM–185 DM ($108.90–$122.10) single; 205 DM–235 DM ($135.30–$155.10) double; from 410 DM ($270.60) suite. Children up to 10 years stay free in their parents' room. AE, DC, MC, V. **Parking:** 10 DM ($6.60) per night.

On a downtown street corner, the Aquis Grana City Hotel offers all the modern amenities. The rooms are warm, comfortable, and inviting, with quilts in autumnal colors on the single or twin beds. There is a direct entrance from the hotel into the spa facilities, Thermalhallenbad Römerbad. Room service, laundry, and dry cleaning can be arranged.

The hotel has a good restaurant where a meal costs from 36 DM to 75 DM ($23.80 to $49.50), featuring international and regional specialties. Favorite dishes include creamed soup with "herbs from Charlemagne's garden," fresh sole meunière, and roast beef with home-fried potatoes. Low-calorie diets are also catered to.

HOTEL ROYAL, Jülicherstrasse 1, D-5100 Aachen. Tel. 0241/1-50-61. Fax 0241/15-68-13. 31 rms. TV TEL **Bus:** 1, 11, or 21.
$ Rates (including continental breakfast): 145 DM–170 DM ($95.70–$112.20) single; 205 DM–260 DM ($135.30–$171.60) double. AE, DC, MC, V.

The Royal is modern, its brick facade curving slightly to follow the contour of one of Aachen's peripheral ringed streets. The hotel offers cozy comfort within 200 yards of the casino. The rooms are carpeted, with colorfully tiled baths. Triple glazing on the windows keeps out the noise. In the attractive bar of the Royal, you can order a drink or a light meal.

MODERATE

AM MARSCHIERTOR, Wallstrasse 1–7, D-5100 Aachen. Tel. 0241/3-19-41. Fax 0241/3-19-44. 50 rms. TV TEL **Bus:** 1, 11, or 21.
$ Rates (including buffet breakfast): 110 DM–130 DM ($72.60–$85.80) single; 155 DM–175 DM ($102.30–$115.50) double. DC, MC, V. **Parking:** 8 DM ($5.30), opposite the hotel.

Am Marschiertor stands in the center of Aachen, not far from the Hauptbahnhof and next to the medieval town gate, Marschiertor—a beautiful and historical part of town. It's in a quiet position, with a courtyard and a view over the Altstadt and the cathedral. Run by the Bott family, the hotel has an attractive lobby and connecting hall with antique furniture. The recently furnished rooms have a cozy atmosphere.

HOTEL BACCARA, Turmstrasse 174, D-5100 Aachen. Tel. 0241/8-30-05. Fax 0241/87-48-76. 33 rms (all with bath or shower). MINIBAR TV TEL **Bus:** 3 or 23.
$ Rates (including buffet breakfast): 100 DM–130 DM ($66–$85.80) single; 125 DM–170 DM ($82.50–$112.20) double. AE, MC, V. **Parking:** 15 DM ($9.90).

Relaxed and inviting, the Baccara lies a few minutes from central Aachen. The rooms are contemporary and clean, with blond-wood furniture and predominant use of black and white. Some of the units contain private balconies.

HOTEL BENELUX, Franzstrasse 21, D-5100 Aachen. Tel. 0241/2-23-43. Fax 0241/22-3-45. 33 rms (all with bath or shower). TV TEL **Bus:** 1, 2, 3, 5, 11, 12, or 21.
$ Rates (including continental breakfast): 120 DM–150 DM ($79.20–$99) single; 145 DM–205 DM ($95.70–$135.30) double. AE, DC, MC, V. **Parking:** 10 DM ($6.60).

S The warm and inviting Benelux is centrally located within walking distance of most everything. Tastefully decorated and personalized, it's a small family-run hotel, a favorite for those watching their marks. Americans from the Southwest will feel at home in the lobby/reception area—it has probably the only cactus collection in Aachen. Antiques are scattered throughout the corridors, and the rooms are streamlined. On the premises is a Chinese/Mongolian restaurant.

HOTEL BUSCHHAUSEN, Adenauerallee 215, D-5100 Aachen. Tel. 0241/6-30-71. Fax 0241/60-28-30. 80 rms. MINIBAR TV TEL **Directions:** Autobahn exit at Lichtenbusch, toward Aachen. **Bus:** 33 or 56.
$ Rates (including continental breakfast): 115 DM ($75.90) single; 175 DM ($115.50) double. AE, DC, MC, V. **Parking:** Free.

Set beside the bypass highway encircling the outskirts of Aachen, this hotel lies just over a mile south of the city center. Built in 1950, it offers three floors of simple but quiet and comfortable guest rooms, easy access to a garden and a surrounding forest, two saunas, and a pool. There are also an in-house bistro, a mini-golf course, and an outdoor terrace where barbecues are held in midsummer.

INEXPENSIVE

HOTEL DANICA, Franzstrasse 38, D-5100 Aachen. Tel. 0241/3-49-91. Fax 0241/40-84-54. 26 rms. TEL **Bus:** 1, 2, 3, 5, 11, 12, or 21.
$ Rates (including continental breakfast): 90 DM–130 DM ($59.40–$85.80) single; 130 DM–140 DM ($85.80–$92.40) double; 160 DM ($105.60) triple. AE, DC, MC, V. **Parking:** 15 DM ($9.90).

This "breakfast-only" hotel is modern, efficient, and centrally located. It has a family atmosphere and a small staff. Rooms are clean and functionally furnished.

WHERE TO DINE

EXPENSIVE

LA BÉCASSE, Hanbrucherstrasse 1. Tel. 0241/7-44-44.
  Cuisine: GERMAN/CONTINENTAL. **Reservations:** Recommended. **Bus:** 5, 25, or 35.
$ Prices: Appetizers 25 DM–32 DM ($16.50–$21.10); main courses 40 DM–55 DM ($26.40–$36.30); six-course menu 105 DM ($69.30). AE, DC, MC, V.
  Open: Lunch Mon–Sat noon–2:30pm; dinner Mon–Sat 7–10:30pm.

Full of greenery, this modern restaurant serves a pleasing combination of traditional German recipes and light, modern continental specialties. Daily and seasonal dishes are served. Christof Lang, realizing early his "calling" of reproducing the fine foods of France, has been the owner since 1981. The food is imported every day from the wholesale markets at Rungis, outside Paris. Try, for example, his ragoût of fish or his cassoulet.

RESTAURANT GALA, Monheimsallee 44. Tel. 0241/15-30-13.
  Cuisine: GERMAN. **Reservations:** Required. **Bus:** 13.
$ Prices: Appetizers 22 DM–28 DM ($14.50–$18.50); main courses 38 DM–48 DM ($25.10–$31.70); fixed-price menus 150 DM ($99) and 180 DM ($118.80). AE, MC.
  Open: Dinner only, Tues–Sun 7pm–midnight.

★ One of the best dining places in Aachen is the Restaurant Gala. Light plays merrily through the crystal-draped decor onto the oak-paneled walls of this elegant restaurant, which is loosely linked to one of the country's busier casinos. Some of the paintings are by the late Salvador Dalí. The restaurant is named for his former wife. The Gala, owned by Gerhard Gartner, is reputed to be able to soothe the frayed nerves of even the heaviest gamblers. The kitchen turns out frequently updated menus in a "reformed regional style," such as gamecock in calvados-and-mustard sauce or filet of venison in blood sauce. Ingredients are trucked in daily from Rungis markets in Paris. The wine list is impressive; the confections are French and delectable.

MODERATE

ELISENBRUNNEN, Friedrich-Wilhelm-Platz 13A. Tel. 0241/2-97-72.

Cuisine: CONTINENTAL. **Reservations:** Recommended. **Bus:** 1, 11, or 21.
$ Prices: Appetizers 15 DM–28 DM ($9.90–$18.50); main courses 25 DM–46 DM ($16.50–$30.40); fixed-price lunch 34 DM ($22.40). AE, DC, MC, V.
Open: Daily 9am–10:30pm.

Elisenbrunnen belongs to one of Germany's biggest concerns, offering a large and well-maintained terrace for summertime dining. The menu boasts more than 50 items, many of which will appeal to vegetarians or the calorie conscious. On a warm day, seated on the terrace in the shade of the Kaiserdom and the historic Rathaus, a diner can contemplate the splendors of the Altstadt. In the kitchen you'll find the chef whipping up the latest in a light, modern continental cuisine.

RATSKELLER, Am Markt. Tel. 0241/3-50-01.

Cuisine: FRENCH/GERMAN. **Reservations:** Recommended. **Bus:** 1, 11, or 21.
$ Prices: Appetizers 12 DM–22 DM ($7.90–$14.50); main courses 28 DM–50 DM ($18.50–$33); seven-course fixed-price dinner 160 DM ($105.60). AE, DC, MC, V.
Open: Postwagen daily 10am–1pm; Ratskeller noon–3pm and 6pm–midnight.

⑤ The Ratskeller is a charming place to dine, with its rustic atmosphere of brick and stone, oak benches, and tables. Most intimate and attractive is an extension containing a pub where patrons gather to drink and play cards. In the pub, Postwagen, you can grab a quick lunch; otherwise à la carte and a fixed-price dinner are available in the more formal Ratskeller. Obviously, if you order the most expensive items on the menu, the cellar is no longer a budget choice. Regional cuisine, both French and German, is served in both places, including several grills and even vegetarian food. Locals come here to order Nürnberger sausages with sauerkraut.

EVENING ENTERTAINMENT

Behind the portals of what were formerly pump rooms is **Spielcasino Aachen,** Kurpark, Monheimsallee 44 (tel. 0241/18-080), where many gaming possibilities are offered in spacious, elegant surroundings. Roulette, blackjack, and baccarat are played by international rules, from 3pm to 2am daily and to 3am on Friday and Saturday. Visitors, who must be over 18, are required to show their passports to enter. Jackets and ties are required for men. Minimum stakes are 5 DM to 20 DM ($3.30 to $13.20) for roulette, 10 DM ($6.60) for blackjack, and 100 DM ($66) for baccarat. There are also slot machines. Admission is 5 DM ($3.30).

---

3. KÖLN (COLOGNE)

17 miles N of Bonn; 25 miles S of Düsseldorf; 117 miles NW of Frankfurt

GETTING THERE By Plane Cologne and Bonn share the same airport, Köln-Bonn Flughafen, lying 9 miles southeast of Cologne. Air connections are possible to most major German cities, such as Berlin, Frankfurt, and Munich. Cologne also has several air links to major European cities. For complete information, call 02203/40-24-04. Buses from the airport to the center of Cologne run every 30 minutes from 6am to 10:30pm. Travel time is 20 minutes, and the fare is 3.60 DM ($2.40). A taxi costs 35 DM ($23.10) and up. Four daily Lufthansa Express train connections link the Köln-Bonn airport with Frankfurt and Düsseldorf.

By Train   The Cologne Hauptbahnhof lies in the heart of the city next to the Cathedral. For schedules, call 0221/11-531. This depot has frequent rail connections to all major German cities and many continental destinations. For example, 30 trains per day depart for Berlin (trip time: 6 to 7 hours); 30 trains to Frankfurt (trip time: 2½ hours); and 20 trains to Hamburg (trip time: 4½ hours).

By Bus   Cologne is linked to several major cities, such as Frankfurt by Europabus. For complete information and schedules, call Deutsche Touring GmbH, Omnibusbahnhof, Breslauer Platz, in Cologne (tel. 0221/12-48-03). Regional bus service to nearby cities such as Trier (see Chapter 8) is provided by Regionalverkehr Köln GmbH at Euskirchen (tel. 02251/56-031).

By Car   Cologne is easily reached from major German cities. It is connected north and south by autobahn A3, and east and west by autobahn A4. From Frankfurt, for example, head northwest along A3.

ESSENTIALS   For tourist information, go to the **Verkehrsamt,** Am Dom (tel. 0221/221-33-45).

The largest city in the Rhineland is so rich in antiquity that every time a new foundation is dug, the excavators come up with archeological finds. Tragic though the World War II devastation of Cologne was—nearly all buildings of the Altstadt were damaged—reconstruction brought to light a period of Cologne's history that had been steeped in mystery for centuries. Evidence showed that Cologne was as important and powerful during the early Christian era as it was during Roman times and the Middle Ages.

Cologne traces its beginnings to 38 B.C.E., when Roman legions set up camp here. As early as C.E. 50, it was given municipal rights as a capital of a Roman province by the emperor Claudius. In the early Christian era a bishopric was founded here and a number of saints were martyred, including the patron of the city, St. Ursula. During the Middle Ages, as Cologne became a center for international trade, Romanesque and Gothic churches were built with prosperous merchants' gold. There is much to see from every period of the city's 2,000-year history—from the old Roman towers to the modern opera house.

The city is the birthplace of Jacques Offenbach, and the Offenbachplatz, a large square in front of the Cologne Opera, commemorates that fact. Offenbach was born on June 20, 1819, at Grosser Griechenmarkt 1; a plaque on the building there honors the event.

The very word *Cologne* has become a part of the common language since the introduction to the world many years ago of the scented water called *eau de cologne,* first made by the Italian chemist Giovanni Maria Farina, who settled in Cologne in 1709. Cologne water is still produced in the city.

ORIENTATION

The major sightseeing attractions of this ancient city lie within the **Altstadt,** the section along the Rhine in the shape of a semicircle. The streets enclosing the Altstadt follow the route of the original medieval city wall; remnants of three gates remain. Cutting through the center of the town is **Hohestrasse,** a straight street connecting the north and south Roman gates. This main shopping artery of Cologne is so narrow

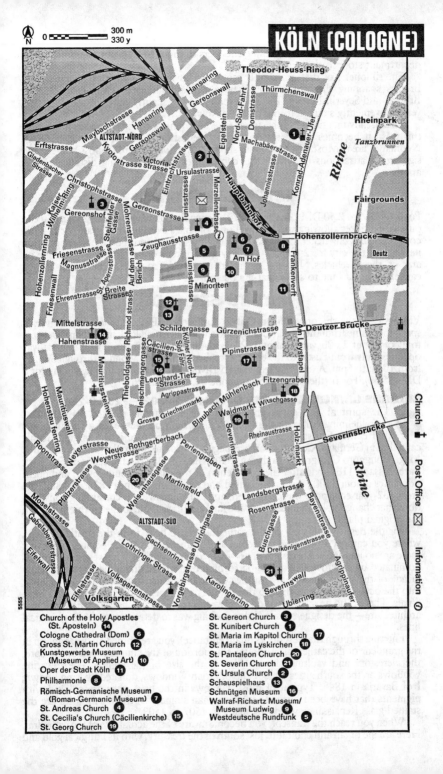

KÖLN (COLOGNE)

0 — 300 m
0 — 330 y

N

Theodor-Heuss-Ring

Rheinpark

Tanzbrunnen

Rhine

Fairgrounds

Deutz

Rhine

Church ✝

Post Office ⊠

Information ⓘ

Church of the Holy Apostles (St. Aposteln) **14**
Cologne Cathedral (Dom) **6**
Gross St. Martin Church **12**
Kunstgewerbe Museum (Museum of Applied Art) **10**
Oper der Stadt Köln **11**
Philharmonie **8**
Römisch-Germanische Museum (Roman-Germanic Museum) **7**
St. Andreas Church **4**
St. Cecilia's Church (Cäcilienkirche) **15**
St. Georg Church **19**

St. Gereon Church **3**
St. Kunibert Church **1**
St. Maria im Kapitol Church **17**
St. Maria im Lyskirchen **18**
St. Pantaleon Church **20**
St. Severin Church **21**
St. Ursula Church **2**
Schauspielhaus **13**
Schnütgen Museum **16**
Wallraf-Richartz Museum/ Museum Ludwig **9**
Westdeutsche Rundfunk **5**

that vehicles are prohibited, enabling shoppers to move freely from one boutique or department store to the next.

The silhouette of the cathedral is prominent as you cross any of Cologne's eight bridges spanning the Rhine. The major ones are Hohenzollernbrücke, Deutzer Brücke, and Severinsbrücke. The Hauptbahnhof lies slightly north of the cathedral, very conveniently situated to the center of town.

The already mentioned Hohestrasse runs south into Gürzenichstrasse. If you take this west, it becomes Schildergasse, another pedestrian zone leading into the huge Neumarkt area. Most of the hotels, shops, attractions, nightlife possibilities, and sightseeing attractions lie within this central area, within walking distance of one another.

GETTING AROUND

For 1.60 DM to 2.50 DM ($1.10 to $1.70), depending on where you're going, you can purchase a ticket allowing you to travel on Cologne's excellent bus, tram, or U-Bahn connections. A day ticket for 8 DM ($5.30) allows you to travel on the transportation network of the city for 24 hours. You buy your ticket from a dispensing machine on any of these vehicles. Tickets are interchangeable. You stick the ticket into a cancellation machine to show that it's been used.

WHAT TO SEE & DO

Visitors can take the only **Rhine Cable Railway** in Europe that spans a river. It spans the Rhine from the zoo in Cologne-Riehl to the Rhine Park in Cologne-Deutz, a total of about 1,000 yards; about 525 yards are over the river. The cable railway operates daily from Easter to the end of October. Hours are Monday through Sunday from 10am to 6pm. A one-way trip costs 5 DM ($3.30), with a round trip going for 8 DM ($5.30). For further information, phone 0221/76-42-69.

COLOGNE CATHEDRAL [DOM], Domplatz. Tel. 0221/23-10-25.

✪ The spiritual and geographical heart of the city is marked by the most overwhelming edifice in the Rhine Valley. Built on the site of a pagan temple and earlier Christian churches, the majestic structure is the largest Gothic cathedral in Germany. Construction was begun in 1248 to house the relics of the three Magi brought to Cologne by Archbishop Reinald von Dassel, chancellor of Frederick Barbarossa in 1164, but after the completion of the chancel, south tower, and north side aisles (about 1500), work was halted and not resumed until 1823. In 1880, the great 632-year enterprise was completed, and unlike many time-consuming constructions that change styles in midstream, the final result was true to the Gothic style as in the original plans.

For the best overall view of the cathedral, stand back from the south transept, where you can get an idea of the actual size and splendor of the edifice. Note that there are no important horizontal lines—everything is vertical. The west side (front) is dominated by two towering spires, perfectly proportioned and joined by the narrow facade of the nave. The first two stories of the towers are square, gradually merging into the octagonal form of the top three stories and tapering off at the top with huge finials. There is no great rose window between the spires, so characteristic of Gothic architecture—the designers insisted that nothing was to detract from the lofty vertical lines.

Entering through the west doors (main entrance), you are immediately caught up in the grandeur of the cathedral. Although this portion of the church is somewhat bare, the clerestory and vaulting give an idea of the size of the edifice. The towering windows on the south aisles include the Bavarian Windows, donated by King Ludwig I of Bavaria in 1848. Typical of most windows in the nave, they are colored with pigments that have been burned on rather than stained. In the north aisles are the stained-glass Renaissance windows, made in 1507 to 1509.

When you reach the transept, you become aware of the actual size of the cathedral. Here are the organ and choir loft, just south of the treasury, with its liturgical gold and silver pieces. In the center of the transept is an elegant bronze-and-marble altar, which can be seen from all parts of the cathedral. This was to have been the site of the Shrine of the Three Kings, but the reliquary actually stands behind the high altar in the chancel.

The Shrine of the Three Magi is the most important and valuable object in the cathedral. Designed in gold and silver in the form of a triple-naved basilica, it is decorated with relief figures depicting the life of Christ, the Apostles, and various Old Testament prophets. Across the front of the chancel are two rows of choir stalls divided into richly carved partitions. The unpainted oak choir dates from 1310 and is the largest extant in Germany.

Surrounding the chancel are nine chapels, each containing important works of religious art. The Chapel of the Cross, beneath the organ loft, shelters the painted, carved oak cross of Archbishop Gero (969–976), the oldest full-size cross in the Occident. Behind the altar in Our Lady's Chapel, directly across the chancel from the Chapel of the Cross, is the famous triptych masterpiece painted by Stephan Lochner (1400–51). When closed, the Dombild, as it is called, shows the Annunciation, and when opened, it reveals the Adoration of the Magi in the center, flanked by the patron saint of Cologne, St. Ursula, and St. Gereon.

Tours: Daily 10 and 11am and 2:30, 3:30, and 4:30pm.

Admission: Treasury and cathedral tower each 3 DM ($2) adults, 1.50 DM ($1) children.

Open: Cathedral, daily 7am–7pm, except during religious services. Treasury and cathedral tower, summer Mon–Sat 9am–5pm, Sun and holidays noon–5pm; winter Mon–Sat 9am–4pm, Sun and holidays noon–4pm. **U-Bahn:** Hauptbahnhof.

KUNSTGEWERBE MUSEUM [Museum of Applied Art], An der Rechtsschule. Tel. 0221/221-29-95.

This is a showcase for the arts and crafts of Germany, dating back to the Middle Ages. Of course, the 20th century is prominently featured. The museum is considered one of the best of its kind in Germany.

Admission: 5 DM ($3.30) adults, 2.50 DM ($1.70) children.

Open: Tues–Sun 10am–5pm. Every first Thurs in month 10am–8pm. **U-Bahn:** Hauptbahnhof.

RÖMISCH-GERMANISCHE MUSEUM [Roman-Germanic Museum], Roncalliplatz 4. Tel. 0221/221-23-01.

The most compelling treasure housed in the museum is the Dionysos-Mosaik, from the 3rd century B.C.E., discovered in 1941 when workmen were digging an air-raid shelter. This mosaic once was the floor of an *oecus* (main room) of a large Roman villa. The elaborately decorated and colored work, made up of octagons and squares, depicts Dionysus, the Greek god of wine and dispeller of care.

On the second floor of the museum is an unusual collection of Roman antiquities found in the Rhine Valley, including Roman glass from the 1st to the 4th centuries, as well as pottery, marble busts, and jewelry.

Admission: 5 DM ($3.30) adults, 2.50 DM ($1.70) children.

Open: Tues–Sun 10am–5pm. **U-Bahn:** Hauptbahnhof.

SCHNÜTGEN MUSEUM, Cäcilienstrasse 29. Tel. 0221/221-23-10.

A curator's dream, this is Cologne's best collection of religious art and sculpture displayed in an original setting, St. Cecilia's Church (Cäcilien-kirche). The church is a fine example of Rhenish-Romanic architecture. The works displayed include several medieval ivories and woodwork, and medieval tapestries, especially one showing rosy-cheeked Magi bringing gifts to the Christ child (1470). There are many madonnas, of all sizes and descriptions, carved in stone, wood, and metal.

Admission: 5 DM ($3.30) adults, 2.50 DM ($1.70) children.

Open: Tues–Sun 10am–5pm; until 8pm on Thurs. **U-Bahn:** Neumarkt.

WALLRAF-RICHARTZ MUSEUM/MUSEUM LUDWIG, Bischofsgarten-strasse 1. Tel. 0221/221-26-29.

Just a short walk from Domplatz is Cologne's oldest museum, begun in the 19th century with a collection of Gothic works by Cologne artists. That group of works is still one of the main attractions, although today the Wallraf-Richartz shows art from 1300 to 1900, and the Ludwig art from 1900 until today. Representative of the Gothic style in Germany is Stephan Lochner, best shown in his *Madonna in the Rose Garden,* painted in 1450. Several works from the cathedral are exhibited here, including the triptych of the *Madonna with the Vetch Flower* (1410). The museum is proud of its collection of German artists, spanning more than 500 years. It houses Germany's largest collection of works by Wilhelm Leibl as well as paintings by Max Ernst, Paul Klee, and Ernst Ludwig Kirchner. There is also a representative collection of nearly every period and school of painting, from the Dutch and Flemish masters to the French impressionists to American art of the 1960s and 1970s (the famous Ludwig Donation).

Admission: 8 DM ($5.30) adults, 4 DM ($2.60) children.
Open: Tues–Sun 10am–6pm. **U-Bahn:** Hauptbahnhof.

CHURCHES

Cologne has 12 important Romanesque churches, all within the medieval city wall. Devastated during World War II, they have been almost completely restored and again recapture Cologne's rich early medieval heritage. **St. Pantaleon,** Am Pantaleonsberg 2, built in 980, has the oldest cloister arcades remaining in Germany. Claiming an even earlier foundation, in the late 4th century, is **St. Gereon,** Gereonsdriesch 2–4. **St. Severin,** on Severinstrasse, originated in a late 4th-century memorial chapel; the present church dates from the 13th to the 15th century.

The church of **St. Ursula** (1135), on Ursulaplatz, is on the site of a Roman graveyard. St. Ursula, patron saint of Cologne, was supposedly martyred with 11,000 virgin followers. **St. Maria im Kapitol,** Kasinostrasse 6, is in the place where Plectrudis, wife of Pippin, built a church in the early 8th century. The cloverleaf choir of the present structure was modeled on that of the Church of the Nativity in Bethlehem. **St. Aposteln,** Neumarkt 30, and Gross St. Martin, on the Rhine in the Altstadt, also have the cloverleaf choir design.

St. Georg, Am Waidmarkt, the only remaining Romanesque pillared basilica in the Rhineland, contains an impressive forked crucifix from the early 14th century. **St. Cecilia's (Cäcilienkirche),** Cäcilienstrasse 29, near Neumarkt, is the site of the Schnütgen Museum for sacred art. **St. Andreas,** near the cathedral, contains a wealth of late Romanesque architectural sculpture. The remaining two Romanesque churches are on the Rhine—**St. Kunibert,** Kunibertskloster 2, and **St. Maria Lyskirchen,** An Lyskirchen 12, both of 13th-century origin.

ORGANIZED TOURS

The easiest way to get a comprehensive look at Cologne's many attractions is to take one of the tours departing from the Verkehrsamt (tourist information office), opposite the cathedral. From May 1 to October 31, two-hour tours in English are offered daily at 10 and 11am and at 1, 2, and 3pm. From November 1 to April 30, tours are at 11am and 2pm. Costing 22 DM ($14.50) for adults and 8 DM ($5.30) for children, they cover the major sights, including a large number of Gothic and Romanesque churches, a Roman tower, the medieval city gates, the Gothic (15th-century) Rathaus, the Roman Praetorium, and the modern opera house. The tour also includes a stop at a major museum.

From July through August 31, evening tours of the city are offered every Friday and Saturday, departing from the tourist information office at 8pm. The price of 45 DM ($29.70) includes a cold platter. Advance bookings can be made through the **ETRAV-Travel Agency** (tel. 0221/258-07-91-94).

Of course, the most popular excursions are offered on the Rhine. The best ones are by **Köln-Düsseldorfer Deutsche Rheinschiffahrt,** Frankenwerft 15 (tel. 0221/20-880). This company offers regular passenger service—either day trips or longer cruises—on its fleet, nearly two dozen craft, including hydrofoils, motorships, steamers, and paddleboats. Many day trips costs 50 DM ($33).

WHERE TO STAY

VERY EXPENSIVE

DOM HOTEL, Domkloster 2A, D-5000 Köln 1. Tel. 0221/2-02-40, or toll free 800/225-5843 in the U.S. Fax 0221/20-24-444. 126 rms. MINIBAR TV TEL **U-Bahn:** Hauptbahnhof.
$ Rates: 330 DM–370 DM ($217.80–$244.20) single; 490 DM–570 DM ($323.40–$376.20) double. Breakfast 26 DM ($17.20) extra. AE, DC, MC, V. **Parking:** 30 DM ($19.80).

⭐ Standing within the shadow of Germany's most famous cathedral, the Dom is assured a steady clientele because of its location alone. Few hotels in Germany, however, have been so consistently awarded five stars or have so consistently maintained such a standard of excellence.

Founded in 1857 by Theodore Metz, whose afternoon concerts welcomed such performing artists as Paganini and Mendelssohn, the hotel has been rebuilt since 1945. It received a boost and an elegant redecorating in 1987, shortly after its reservations facilities were acquired by Forte hotel chain. Today the side portico overlooking the square to the side of the cathedral is filled in summer with café tables. To reach it, drive your car into the square to the side of the Dom's flying buttresses. Each guest room contains all the modern conveniences and an interesting collection of period furniture.

Dining/Entertainment: On the premises is an elegant French restaurant, ringed with lustrous dark paneling and upholstered in golden beige, plus a winter-garden bistro.
Services: Room service, laundry, dry cleaning.
Facilities: Terrace garden, conference facilities.

EXCELSIOR HOTEL ERNST, Trankgasse, D-5000 Köln 1. Tel. 0221/27-01. Fax 0221/13-51-50. 160 rms, 20 suites. MINIBAR TV TEL **U-Bahn:** Hauptbahnhof.
$ Rates (including continental breakfast): 325 DM–440 DM ($214.50–$290.40) single; 440 DM–610 DM ($290.40–$402.60) double; from 700 DM ($462) suite. AE, DC, MC, V. **Parking:** 30 DM ($19.80).

Cologne's long-time prestige hotel, with plenty of traditional style and ambience, faces the cathedral square, in the center of the city's finest shopping and business area, only a couple of hundred yards from the Hauptbahnhof. The guest rooms are spacious, with many facilities for comfort, including built-in wardrobes, bedside reading lamps, and traditional furnishings, as well as color TVs and radios. Most rooms are air-conditioned.

Dining/Entertainment: The hotel has an outstanding restaurant, Hanse-Stube (see my dining recommendations), and guests can enjoy the intimate and cozy Piano Bar as well as the Excelsior Keller, where regional and seasonal delicacies are served amid elegant rustic surroundings.
Services: Room service, laundry, dry cleaning.
Facilities: Shopping arcades, hairdresser, barber shop.

HYATT REGENCY, Kennedy-Ufer 2A, D-5000 Köln 21-Deutz. Tel. 0221/ 828-12-34, or toll free 800/228-9000 in the U.S. Fax 0221/828-13-70. 307 rms, 18 suites. A/C MINIBAR TV TEL **Tram:** 1 or 2.
$ Rates: 320 DM–570 DM ($211.20–$376.20) single; 295 DM–695 DM ($194.70–$458.70) double; from 980 DM ($647.80) suite. Breakfast 26 DM ($17.20) extra. AE, DC, MC, V. **Parking:** 20 DM ($13.20).

⭐ On the Cologne banks of the Rhine is the most spectacular and up-to-date hotel in Cologne. Owned by a Dutch company but managed by one of North America's finest hotel groups, it is considered an architectural triumph: a mixture of reddish granite, huge expanses of glass, and a facade incorporating elements of neo-Aztec and art deco. The location is next to the Messe/Exposition halls, a short walk from the Hauptbahnhof. You can take the Hohenzollernbrücke across the Rhine to the Dom and the Altstadt.

The lobby is dramatic, with a 12-foot waterfall cascading into a reflecting pool. Each guest room is comfortably and stylishly furnished with plush carpets and richly grained hardwood furniture. Many have views of the Rhine and of the cathedral across the river. A total of 35 Regency Club rooms are in five suites occupying the top floor. These are the most expensive, of course.

Dining/Entertainment: Graugans offers a Germanic version of cuisine moderne, with meals beginning at 48 DM ($31.70). It also serves Asian food. You can also dine in the lobby café with its views of the river, the cathedral, and old town. The intimate bar, Schael Sick, serves the locally brewed Koelsch beer, which can also be enjoyed, along with a selection of international wines, on the garden terrace.

Services: 24-hour room service, laundry, dry cleaning.

Facilities: Fitness center with pool, sauna, steam room, massage facilities, solarium, whirlpool, fully equipped exercise room; business center.

SENATS HOTEL, Unter-Goldschmied 9, D-5000 Köln 1. Tel. 0221/2-06-20. Fax 0221/24-78-63. 60 rms. MINIBAR TV TEL **U-Bahn:** Hauptbahnhof.
$ **Rates** (including continental breakfast): 208 DM–255 DM ($137.30–$168.30) single; 295 DM–345 DM ($194.70–$227.70) double. AE, DC, MC, V. **Closed:** Dec 21–31.

In a secluded corner within the heart of the city shopping center, five minutes' walk from the cathedral, the Rhinegardens, and the Altstadt, the Senats offers attractive rooms, all with radios. The restaurant is known for its cuisine and wide range of European wines and beverages.

EXPENSIVE

ANTIK-HOTEL BRISTOL, Kaiser-Wilhelm-Ring 48, D-5000 Köln 1. Tel. 0221/12-01-95. Fax 0221/13-14-95. 44 rms, 3 suites. TV TEL **Tram:** Christophstrasse.
$ **Rates** (including continental breakfast): 165 DM–275 DM ($108.90–$181.50) single; 195 DM–360 DM ($128.70–$237.60) double; from 380 DM ($250.80) suite. AE, DC, MC, V. **Parking:** 18 DM ($11.90).

The Bristol is exceptional in that each of its rooms is furnished with genuine antiques, either regal or rustic. There is a different antique bed in almost every room, ranging from French baroque and rococo to something reminiscent of High Rhenish ecclesiastical art; the oldest four-poster dates from 1742. The hotel is conveniently located near an underground stop and is within walking distance of the cathedral. Bathroom amenities include hairdryers and magnifying makeup mirrors, and rooms have phones and TVs. The hotel has the Bristol Bar for guests, but breakfast is the only meal served. The Bristol stands in a little park, removed from traffic, with lots of greenery, flowers, and fountains.

HAUS LYSKIRCHEN, Filzengraben 26-32, D-5000 Köln 1. Tel. 0221/20-97-0. Fax 0221/209-77-18. 94 rms. MINIBAR TV TEL **U-Bahn:** Heumarkt. **Tram:** 1, 2, or 7.
$ **Rates** (including continental breakfast): 170 DM–250 DM ($112.20–$165) single; 200 DM–340 DM ($132–$224.40) double. AE, DC, MC, V. **Parking:** 14 DM ($9.20). **Closed:** Dec 23–Jan 2.

Four blocks from the cathedral, Haus Lyskirchen offers a rustic country decor in an inner-city hotel. The facade has one of those baroque yellow-stuccoed step-gabled rooflines. The units, with unfinished wood planking on parts of the ceilings and walls, look more like something from a chalet in the Alps than rooms in central Cologne. The hotel has a 19-foot by 37-foot heated pool, a sauna, and a solarium, along with two warmly decorated restaurants and an attractive wood-paneled pub. The well-furnished rooms have color TVs, radios, hairdryers, and trouser presses.

KOMMERZ HOTEL, Breslauer Platz, D-5000 Köln 1. Tel. 0221/1-61-00. Fax 0221/161-01-22. 77 rms. TV TEL **U-Bahn:** Hauptbahnhof.

$ Rates (including continental breakfast): 165 DM–205 DM ($108.90–$135.30)
single; 215 DM–285 DM ($141.90–$188.10) double. AE, DC, MC, V.
Near the cathedral and Hauptbahnhof, this tangerine-colored modern hotel looks
glaringly conspicuous when viewed with the Dom in the background. But despite this
juxtaposition of the old with the new, the rooms are convenient, with full-length
windows and utilitarian furnishings. The sunny wood-paneled bar has an attractive
U-shaped serving area where you're likely to meet anyone in Cologne.

HOTEL SAVOY, Turiner Strasse 9, D-5000 Köln 1. Tel. 0221/1-62-30.
Fax 0221/162-32-00. 112 rms. TV TEL **U-Bahn:** Hauptbahnhof.
$ Rates (including continental breakfast): 175 DM–325 DM ($115.50–$214.50)
single; 230 DM–500 DM ($151.80–$330) double. AE, DC, MC, V.
Residents of this recently renovated hotel need walk only a short distance to either the
railway station or the Dom. The hotel, designed in an angular format of strong
horizontal lines and sweeping bands of glass, includes comfortably furnished guest
rooms. The streamlined decor includes warmly monochromatic color schemes,
French-style armchairs, and green plants. The Intermezzo Bar offers a hideaway for a
drink, and lunch and dinner are served in a restaurant decorated with artworks. A
sauna, steam bath, and solarium are available for guests.

MODERATE

ALTSTADT-HOTEL, Salzgasse, D-5000 Köln 1. Tel. 0221/257-78-51. Fax
0221/257-79-63. 28 rms, 1 suite. MINIBAR TV TEL **U-Bahn:** Hauptbahnhof.
$ Rates (including buffet breakfast): 105 DM–110 DM ($69.30–$72.60) single;
120 DM–190 DM ($79.20–$125.40) double; from 250 DM ($165) suite. AE, DC,
MC, V. **Closed:** Dec 20–Jan 10.
In the old section, the Altstadt-Hotel is just two minutes from the Rhine
boat-landing dock. Guests have passed the word along to their friends, making
this place a big success. Herr Olbrich learned about catering to international
guests while a steward on the German-America Line, and he has furnished his little
hotel beguilingly. Each room is individually decorated, a restful haven with a radio
and TV. A sauna is on the premises. Advance reservations are recommended.

HOTEL CRISTALL, Ursulaplatz 9, D-5000 Köln 1. Tel. 0221/12-00-55.
Fax 0221/163-0330. 100 rms. MINIBAR TV TEL **U-Bahn:** Hauptbahnhof or
Breslauer Platz.
$ Rates (including continental breakfast): 135 DM–210 DM ($89.10–$138.60)
single; 175 DM–290 DM ($115.50–$191.40) double. AE, DC, MC, V.
Originally built around 50 years ago, this hotel was radically upgraded in 1992 and
was enlarged with the addition of an additional story, giving it a total of five. Its very
modern guest rooms are pleasantly furnished, and the hotel has a polite English-
speaking staff. Despite the modernity of the lobby and the rooms, the hotel contains
one of the most deliberately old-fashioned restaurants in Cologne, the Weinhaus Lenz,
with woodcarvings that create a fantasy version of a building in the Black Forest. The
hotel is convenient to the railway station, the cathedral, and the city's major points of
touristic interest.

DAS KLEINE STAPELHÄUSCHEN, Fischmarkt 1–3, D-5000 Köln 1. Tel.
0221/25-77-862. Fax 0221/257-42-32. 33 rms (14 with bath). TV TEL
U-Bahn: Heumarkt. **Bus:** 136.
$ Rates (including continental breakfast): 70 DM ($46.20) single without bath, 100
DM ($66) single with bath; 105 DM ($69.30) double without bath, 195 DM
($128.70) double with bath. MC, V. **Parking:** 30 DM ($19.80) nearby.
Stapelhäuschen was originally built in the 1100s near the city site where fish was sold
by Benedictine monks from Scotland. Since then, it figured in occasional references in
the city's chronicles as the home of one or another of Cologne's leading merchants
until it was converted into a hotel in 1950. The two tall, narrow town houses are on a
corner of a historic square, and their ironwork announces the year of their

construction—1235. Inside you'll find a richly evocative decor and an occasional portrait of Irish-born St. Brigit. They offer an old-fashioned decor of patterned wallpaper and clean, if slightly faded, furniture. On the premises is a good restaurant, recommended separately.

INEXPENSIVE

BRANDENBURGER HOF, Brandenburgerstrasse 2-4, D-5000 Köln 1. Tel. 0221/12-28-89. Fax 0221/13-53-04. 45 rms (28 with bath). **U-Bahn:** Hauptbahnhof.

$ Rates (including continental breakfast): 60 DM ($39.60) single without bath, 75 DM ($49.50) single with bath; 80 DM ($52.80) double without bath, 100 DM ($66) double with bath; 100 DM ($66) triple without bath; 120 DM ($79.20) quad without bath. No credit cards. **Parking:** Free.

In this family-style hotel, you can get the best rates for accommodations sheltering three or four persons without baths. All rooms are small, warm, and equipped with running water, and there's a bath on each floor. Breakfast with orange juice and eggs is served in a cozy room or, in summer, in the garden. The hotel is behind the Hauptbahnhof, about three blocks from the river and within walking distance of the cathedral.

WHERE TO DINE
VERY EXPENSIVE

CHEZ ALEX, Mühlengasse 1. Tel. 0221/23-05-60.
 Cuisine: FRENCH. **Reservations:** Required. **U-Bahn:** Heumarkt.
$ Prices: Appetizers 22 DM–46 DM ($14.50–$30.40); main courses 36 DM–55 DM ($23.80–$36.30); fixed-price lunch 40 DM–60 DM ($26.40–$39.60); fixed-price dinner 120 DM–155 DM ($79.20–$102.30). AE, DC, MC, V.
 Open: Lunch Mon–Fri noon–2pm; dinner Mon–Sat 7–11pm. **Closed:** Holidays.

⭐ The finest restaurant in the city itself greets guests with a festive vista of hot-pink linen. The decor of this elegant "Maison de Champagne" is belle époque, with paneled walls and dark-velvet banquettes. Established in 1978, Chez Alex quickly moved to the foreground of Cologne restaurants serving a French cuisine moderne. The menu is in French with German subtitles. Among the offerings, you're likely to find coquilles St.-Jacques en feuilletage or mousse of smoked salmon with caviar. In season, you can order suckling lamb marinated in Pauillac. A nine-course menu gastronomique is available, as are à la carte dinners.

DIE BASTEI, Konrad-Adenauer-Ufer 80. Tel. 0221/12-28-25.
 Cuisine: CONTINENTAL. **Reservations:** Required. **U-Bahn:** Ebertplatz.
$ Prices: Appetizers 28 DM–42 DM ($18.50–$27.70); main courses 45 DM–50 DM ($29.70–$33); fixed-price lunch 55 DM ($36.30); fixed-price dinner 85 DM ($56.10). AE, DC, MC, V.
 Open: Lunch daily noon–3pm; dinner daily 7–10:30pm.

Die Bastei is the favored spot for your "watch on the Rhine," the trick being to aim for a window table. The split-level dining room is on the second floor of a circular, towerlike building jutting out into the river, and the view is dramatic. The restaurant is as high-class as its prices. In addition to German specialties, many dishes are presented from neighboring Switzerland, Austria, and France. Dinner and dance music is played on Saturday evening.

GOLDENER PFLUG, Olpener Strasse 421. Tel. 0221/89-55-09.
 Cuisine: FRENCH. **Reservations:** Required. **Tram:** 1 to Merheim.
$ Prices: Appetizers 39 DM–68 DM ($25.70–$44.90); main courses 49 DM–79 DM ($32.30–$52.10); fixed-price lunch 55 DM ($36.30); fixed-price dinner 99 DM–198 DM ($65.30–$130.70). AE.
 Open: Lunch Mon–Sat noon–3pm; dinner Mon–Sat 6pm–midnight. **Closed:** 3 weeks in summer (dates vary).

★ On the outskirts in the suburb of Merheim, the Goldener Pflug should be visited for "that special occasion." Owned by Ludwig Robertz, it's one of the top restaurants in Germany. The chef appreciates impossibly demanding clients with jaded palates and takes pleasure in sending them away satisfied. Top-quality ingredients are used in his imaginative blend of classical repertoires. Try, for example, any of his truffled specialties, ranging from soups to a wide choice of delicately seasoned main courses. For dessert, the most exciting choices are apple cake flambé and soufflé à la Rothschild with strawberries. The decor of what was a former tavern is simple, with a golden motif repeated in the walls, draperies, and upholstery. A fixed-price gourmet "surprise" menu consists of eight courses, or you can order à la carte.

EXPENSIVE

BÖRSEN RESTAURANT, Unter Sachsenhausen 10. Tel. 0221/13-30-21.
   Cuisine: CONTINENTAL. **Reservations:** Recommended. **U-Bahn:** Hauptbahnhof.
$ Prices: Appetizers 15 DM–45 DM ($9.90–$29.70); main courses 42 DM–52 DM ($27.70–$34.30); fixed-price menus 62.50 DM–82.50 DM ($41.30–$54.50). AE, DC, MC, V.
   Open: Lunch daily noon–3pm; dinner Mon–Sat 6–10pm. **Closed:** Aug.
Börsen, near the stock exchange, is not too far from the cathedral. This busy place welcomes the clerks, clients, and administration of Cologne's financial community. It offers not only good value but also a glimpse of everyday Cologne life, particularly at noon. Seasonally adjusted fixed-price meals offer classic, conservative cookery.

HANSE-STUBE, on the ground floor of the Excelsior Hotel Ernst. Domplatz. Tel. 0221/27-01.
   Cuisine: FRENCH. **Reservations:** Recommended. **U-Bahn:** Hauptbahnhof.
$ Prices: Appetizers 12 DM–48 DM ($7.90–$31.70); main courses 38 DM–60 DM ($25.10–$39.60); five-course fixed-price menu 115 DM ($75.90). AE, DC, MC, V.
   Open: Lunch daily noon–2:30pm; dinner daily 6–10:30pm.
Rightly considered one of the best restaurants in Cologne, Hanse-Stube offers top-drawer cuisine and service. The setting is that of a tavern, which you can enter through the hotel. Main-dish specialties include poached salmon in sorrel sauce and filet of veal Excelsior style. For dessert, try the parfait of hazelnut with Rémy Martin sauce.

RESTAURANT BADO—LA POELE D'OR, Komödienstrasse 50–52A. Tel. 0221/13-41-00.
   Cuisine: FRENCH. **Reservations:** Recommended. **U-Bahn:** Apostelstrasse.
$ Prices: Appetizers 12 DM–38 DM ($7.90–$25.10); main courses 36 DM–52 DM ($23.80–$34.30); fixed-price lunch 50 DM ($33); fixed-price dinner 72 DM–165 DM ($47.50–$108.90). AE, DC, MC, V.
   Open: Lunch Tues–Sat noon–2pm; dinner Mon–Sat 6:30–10pm. **Closed:** Dec 23–Jan 4.
The idea of a new philosophy in French cookery is nothing new to the chef of this sophisticated restaurant. Jean-Claude Bado has used fresh ingredients and a lighter approach to classical French recipes for years: Try the salmon in lemon sauce, goose salad with wild mushrooms, or filet of John Dory in caviar sauce. The decor is elegantly simple, the service impeccable.

RINO CASATI, Ebertplatz 3–5. Tel. 0221/72-11-08.
   Cuisine: ITALIAN. **Reservations:** Required. **U-Bahn:** Ebertplatz.
$ Prices: Appetizers 22 DM–32 DM ($14.50–$21.10); main courses 35 DM–48 DM ($23.10–$31.70); fixed-price menus 115 DM–165 DM ($75.90–$108.90). AE, DC, MC, V.
   Open: Lunch Tues–Sat noon–2:30pm; dinner Tues–Sat 6–10pm.

✪ The trappings of this elegant restaurant are rich and old world. The cuisine is light and modern, the entire show orchestrated with flair and panache by Guerino Casati, who diligently supervises the service and advises clients on the freshest delicacies available on his seasonal menu. Dining does indeed resemble an evening's entertainment, and "the production" isn't cheap.

SOUFFLÉ, Hohenstaufenring 53. Tel. 0221/21-20-22.

Cuisine: CONTINENTAL. **Reservations:** Required. **U-Bahn:** Rudolfplatz.

$ **Prices:** Appetizers 10.50 DM–28 DM ($6.90–$18.50); main courses 35 DM–45 DM ($23.10–$29.70); fixed-price lunch 42 DM ($27.70); fixed-price dinner 92 DM ($60.70). AE, DC, MC, V.

Open: Lunch Mon–Fri noon–2:30pm; dinner Sun–Fri 6:30–11pm. **Closed:** Sat and Jan 1–7.

As its continental name suggests, this restaurant incorporates about a dozen versions of soufflés into its menu. You might begin with spinach soufflé as an appetizer, finishing with one of the dessert soufflés. However, the creative chefs here also produce such typical dishes as rack of lamb, a rosy-pink preparation of calves' liver, ragoût of sweetbreads and kidneys in a champagne-flavored mustard sauce, and succulent desserts—the last likely to include whatever fresh fruit happens to be in season served with amaretto sabayon.

DINING IN THE ALTSTADT
Expensive

WEINHAUS IM WALFISCH, Salzgasse 13. Tel. 0221/257-78-79.

Cuisine: GERMAN. **Reservations:** Required. **U-Bahn:** Hauptbahnhof.

$ **Prices:** Appetizers 12 DM–30 DM ($7.90–$19.80); main courses 38 DM–52 DM ($25.10–$34.30). AE, DC, MC, V.

Open: Lunch Mon–Fri noon–3pm; dinner Mon–Fri 6–10pm. **Closed:** Sat–Sun and Dec 22–Jan 6.

Ⓢ Dating back to 1626, Weinhaus im Walfisch is a step-gabled inn with a black-and-white-timbered facade behind which you'll find the leading atmospheric choice for dining. More important, it serves some of the best food in the city. Not too easy to find, it's on a narrow street set back from the Rhine. There are many German specialties, or you might try the sole meunière or venison for two.

Moderate

DAS KLEINE STAPELHÄUSCHEN, Fischmarkt 1–3. Tel. 0221/25-77-862.

Cuisine: GERMAN. **Reservations:** Recommended. **U-Bahn:** Heumarkt.

$ **Prices:** Appetizers 9 DM–30 DM ($5.90–$19.80); main courses 22 DM–42 DM ($14.50–$27.70); seven-course fixed-price menu 85 DM ($56.10). MC, V.

Open: Daily noon–11:30pm. **Closed:** Dec–Jan.

Ⓢ One of the most popular wine taverns in Cologne is just a few minutes from the cathedral, housed in an office building and opening onto the old fish market square and the Rhine. The two-story dining room and service bar are antique in style, and provincial cabinets hold a superb wine collection. A carved Madonna on the wall, brass objects hanging against paneled wainscoting, a copper coffee urn—everything here is rustic. A wide wooden cantilevered staircase leads to mezzanine tables. While wine is the main reason for coming here (it's that special), the cuisine is excellent. Soups are hearty and flavorful, and main dishes such as medallions of veal in a creamy sauce are well prepared. A specialty is Rheinischer Sauerbraten with almonds, raisins, and potato dumplings. Desserts are appropriately luscious.

BEER TAVERNS

ALT-KÖLN AM DOM, Trankgasse 7–9. Tel. 0221/13-74-71.

This place seemingly can feed half the visitors to Cologne on any busy day. Its location across from the cathedral and the Hauptbahnhof, right in the heart of the city, is hard to miss. It has a mechanical clock on its face; when it chimes the hour, a parade of figures emerges and disappears. Alt-Köln is a re-creation of a group of old taverns, including one done in the Gothic style. You can come here for a beer or a good hot meal of Westphalian dishes. Some of the upper-floor tables provide box-seat views of the cathedral. The favorite main dishes include Wiener Schnitzel, Schweinehaxen (pork knuckle), and a platter of sausage specialties with spicy mustard. Try also the braised beef Rhineland style. Meals begin at 25 DM ($16.50), and a small beer costs only 3 DM ($2). Hours are 11am to 1am daily. Credit cards: AE, DC, MC, V. U-Bahn: Hauptbahnhof.

BRAUHAUS SION, Unter Taschenmacher 5. Tel. 0221/20-81-70.
If you want a traditional local Brauhaus where the wood paneling is a little smoky with time and frequent polishings, where the portions are inexpensive and generous, where you can sit alone or with friends and enjoy a few glasses of draft beer, this is the place. It's an institution that has been around for a long time and will change only under great pressure. Traditional and filling Westphalian meals range from 22 DM to 50 DM ($14.50 to $33). You'll get such hearty fare as pig knuckles with sauerkraut or the inevitable Bratwurst with savoy cabbage and fried potatoes. But the traditional dish to order here is Kölsch Kaviar (blood sausage decorated with onion rings). You can also ask for halve Hahn, which translates as "half a rooster." On tap is the famed local beer, Kölsch, which is light with an alcohol content of about 3%. It is served in Stangen (rods) about 7 inches tall. The Brauhaus is open every day of the year (except Christmas Eve) from 11:30am to 11:30pm. No credit cards. Bus: 131, 132.

FRÜH AM DOM, Am Hof 12–14. Tel. 0221/23-66-18.
Within the cathedral precincts is Früh Am Dom—the best all-around choice for economy and hearty portions. Well-cooked meals are served on scrubbed wooden tables, with a different German specialty offered every day of the week. Meals cost up to 40 DM ($26.40). To make things easier, the menu is in English. A favorite dish is a Cologne specialty of cured smoked knuckle of pork cooked in root-vegetable broth and served with sauerkraut and potato purée; apple purée and dumplings go well with this dish. Hot meals are served daily from noon to midnight. Früh-Kolsch, a very special beer, is available. It's a top-fermented brew with a dry, inimitable taste and a tradition stretching back 1,000 years. In summer, the beer garden overflows. No credit cards are accepted. U-Bahn: Hauptbahnhof.

EVENING ENTERTAINMENT
PERFORMING ARTS

Cologne is one of the major cultural cities of Germany. The **Oper der Stadt Köln** Offenbachplatz (tel. 0221/221-82-10), seating 1,330, is one of Europe's finest modern opera houses, built between 1954 and 1957. The city's **Philharmonie,** Bischofsgartenstrasse 1 (tel. 0221/204-080), is a circular concert hall with a beamless roof 130 feet in diameter. It has a changing repertoire of some of the finest classical music. Two local symphony orchestras, the **Gürzenich** and the **Westdeutsche Rundfunk,** perform here. Pop and jazz programs are also presented. Tickets cost from 15.50 DM to 55 DM ($10.20 to $36.30). For ticket information, call 0221/8201.

For classical and modern drama (if you speak German), it's the **Schauspielhaus** (tel. 0221/22-18-40), next door to the opera. The **Kefka,** Albertasstrasse (0221/24-01-688), is the only theater in Europe devoted solely to pantomime.

NIGHTCLUBS & BEER HALLS

Papa Joe's Jazzlokal "Em Streckstrumf," Buttermarkt 37 (tel. 0221/21-79-50), is the best jazz center in Cologne. It's open Monday to Saturday from 7pm to 3am and on Sunday from 11am to 4pm. Every night a different band plays. The walls are hung with "Berliner Illustrete" from 1903. Beer costs 6.50 DM ($4.30), and admission is free.

Papa Joe's Biersalon "Klimperkasten," Alter Markt 50–52 (tel. 0221/21-

67-59), is Cologne's most unusual beer hall in turn-of-the-century style. Its center of attraction is a collection of mechanical instruments that play every night, in the original sound. And from 8pm on, well-known pianists provide background music. The Biersalon is open daily from 11am to 3am. Beer costs 6.50 DM ($4.30), and admission is free.

4. BONN

45 miles S of Düsseldorf; 17 miles S of Cologne; 108 miles NW of Frankfurt

GETTING THERE   By Plane   The nearest airport is Köln-Bonn Flughafen (see Köln [Cologne], above). Buses from the airport to Bonn's main rail station run every 30 minutes daily from 6am to 10:30pm.

By Train   The Bonn Hauptbahnhof is on a major rail line, with connections to most German cities. There are 12 trains daily to Berlin (trip time: 7 hours); more than 30 trains to Frankfurt (trip time: 2 hours); and service to Cologne every 15 minutes (trip time: 20 minutes). For rail information call 0221/19-419; for schedules, call 0221/11-531.

By Bus   Long-distance bus service is provided by Europabus to such cities as Munich, Stuttgart, Aachen, Brussels, and London. For information and schedules, call Deutsches Touring GmbH in Frankfurt (tel. 069/79-030). Regional bus service to Bad Godesberg and nearby towns is provided by Regionalverkehr Köln GmbH at Meckenheim (tel. 0225/6087).

By Car   Access is by autobahn A565 connecting with the A3 from the north or south.

ESSENTIALS   For tourist information, go to **Informationsstelle,** Cassius-Bastel, Münsterstrasse 20 (tel. 0228/77-34-66).

SPECIAL EVENTS   Visitors come from all over the world for the Beethoven Festival, held every three years in Beethovenhalle, a modern concert hall renowned for its acoustics. The next festival is 1995.

U ntil 1949 Bonn was a sleepy little university town, basking in its glorious 2,000 years of history. Suddenly it was shaken out of this quiet life and made provisional capital of the Federal Republic of Germany. Bonn's role as capital was only meant to be "provisional," as the German government thought at the time that the country would soon be united. But 1949 gradually stretched out until 1991, when Berlin was designated as newly united Germany's capital. By 1993, few government offices had been transferred to Berlin, and Bonn remained de facto capital of Germany.

Within sight of the Siebengebirge of Nibelungen legend, Bonn has been a strategic city since Roman times. From the 13th through the 18th centuries it was the capital of the electors of Cologne, princes of the Holy Roman Empire, who had the right to participate in the election of the emperor. However, the city is proudest of its intellectual and musical history—Beethoven was born here, Schumann lived here, and Karl Marx and Heinrich Heine studied in Bonn's university.

In the 1990s, Bonn is developing as a center of science, culture, education, research, and service companies. Bonn's latest achievement, called "Museum Mile," consists of the Bundeskunsthalle (Federal Art and Exhibition Hall), presenting a changing array of exhibitions, and the Kunstmuseum (Art Museum), displaying the works of Rheinish Expressionists.

ORIENTATION

Bonn lies on the west bank of the Rhine; its major link to the right bank is across the Kennedybrücke. One of three bridges crossing this river, this bridge will lead you to the heart of the Altstadt, with its important attractions. This area still has many baroque buildings, is the seat of the university, and is also the main shopping center, with a large area set aside for pedestrians only. Just southwest of the Altstadt, but within easy access, is the Bahnhof.

From the Altstadt, bypassing the university grounds, the major boulevard of Bonn, Adenauerallee, heads south (on the west bank). This big artery, which passes many public buildings, will take you to the Bonn Center, the postwar seat of the federal government. Some government ministries are also here. Bad Godesberg, the diplomatic residential suburb, is to the south (see next section).

WHAT TO SEE & DO

The best way to become oriented to what Bonn has to offer is to take a guided tour. From April to October, tours are offered daily from 10am to 12:30pm; from July to September, from 2 to 4:30pm, except Sunday. The meeting point is the **Bonn Tourist Information Office,** Cassius-Bastel, Münsterstrasse 20 (tel. 0228/77-34-66). The cost is 16 DM ($10.60) per person.

The government quarter, along the west bank of the Rhine, is a complex of modern white buildings, rather nondescript when compared to the architecture of the Altstadt. The two most impressive structures, both along Koblenzerstrasse, are the former residence of the president and chancellor (prime minister). These Empire villas are more reminiscent of old Bonn, long before it became an international center of diplomatic activity. They are not open to the public. Running north along the Rhine from the government buildings is a promenade, lined with trees and flowers as far as the **Alter Zoll,** an ancient fortress whose ruins make a good viewing point from which visitors can see across the Rhine to the Siebengebirge and the old village of Beuel.

BEETHOVEN HOUSE, Bonngasse 20. Tel. 0228/63-51-88.

Beethoven House, Bonn's pride and joy, is in the old section of town, just north of the marketplace. Beethoven was born in 1770 in the small house in back, which opens onto a little garden. On its second floor is the room where he was born, decorated only with a simple marble bust of the composer. Within the house are many personal possessions of Beethoven, including manuscripts and musical instruments. In the Vienna Room, in the front of the house overlooking the street, is Beethoven's last piano. The instrument was custom-made, with a special sounding board meant to amplify the sound enough so that the composer might hear it in spite of his deafness.

Admission: 5 DM ($3.30) adults, 1.50 DM ($1) children.
Open: Mon–Sat 10am–5pm, Sun 10am–1pm. **Tram:** 61 or 62.

RHINELAND MUSEUM, Colmantstrasse 14–16. Tel. 0228/7-29-41.

Housing a fine collection of art and artifacts from the Rhine Valley, the Rhineland Museum has treasures that include the first skull of Neanderthal man ever discovered, found in 1856 a few miles east of Düsseldorf. The most interesting collection, however, is in the Roman department, with altars, stones, glass, and artifacts found in the Roman settlements in the Rhineland. A fascinating exhibit is the altar to the Aufanic Matrons, a group of deities worshipped by the landowners of the Rhine. The galleries continue with the Frankish period and with the art and applied arts of the Middle Ages to modern times, including paintings by noted German, Dutch, and Flemish artists; furniture; earthenware; glass; goldsmiths' art; and sculpture. Ten galleries exhibit contemporary Rhineland art.

Admission: 4 DM ($2.60) adults, 2 DM ($1.30) children.
Open: Tues and Thurs 9am–5pm, Wed 9am–8pm, Fri 9am–4pm, Sat–Sun 10am–5pm. **Tram:** 61 or 62.

KUNSTMUSEUM BONN, Friedrich-Ebert-Allee 2. Tel. 0228/77-62-62.

One of the major buildings along the new "Museum Mile," this triangular-shaped structure, flooded with light, contains one of the most important art collections along the Rhine. It is known for its premier collection of 20th-century art, including

Rhenish Expressionism. The celebrated works of the painter August Macke form the nucleus of the collection. In addition, there are works by Kirchner, Schmidt-Rottluff, Campendonk, Ernest, Seehaus, and Thuar.

Admission: 5 DM ($3.30) adults, 3 DM ($2) children.

Open: Tues–Sun 10am–7pm. **U-Bahn:** 16, 63, or 66 to Heussallee.

KUNST UND AUSSTELLUNGSHALLE DER BUNDESREPUBLIK DEUTSCHLAND, Friedrich-Ebert-Allee 4. Tel. 0228/91-71-200.

Located next door to the Kunstmuseum Bonn, this new building is devoted to contemporary exhibitions and may develop into one of the country's most important museums. It is a showcase not only of art, architecture, and science, but also of the cultural history and technology of Germany. Two major and three minor exhibitions are presented annually. Its roof garden is a modern sculpture gallery.

Admission: 8 DM ($5.30) adults, 4 DM ($2.60) children.

Open: Tues–Sun 10am–7pm. **U-Bahn:** 16, 63, or 66 to Heussallee.

WHERE TO STAY

VERY EXPENSIVE

GÜNNEWIG BRISTOL HOTEL, Prinz-Albert-Strasse 2, D-5300 1. Tel. 0228/2-69-80. Fax 0228/269-82-22. 120 rms, 4 suites. A/C MINIBAR TV TEL **Tram:** 61 or 62.

$ **Rates** (including continental breakfast): 295 DM ($194.70) single; 410 DM ($270.60) double; from 570 DM ($376.20) suite. AE, DC, MC, V. **Parking:** 15 DM ($9.90).

One of the most luxurious hotels in Bonn is perched in the heart of the capital near the Bahnhof. All of its attractive, up-to-date units offer soundproofed windows.

Dining/Entertainment: Dining facilities include the Restaurant Majestic, the Hofkonditorei Bierhoff, and the Brasserie Kupferklause. There is also a gemütlich lounge-bar.

Services: Room service, laundry, dry cleaning.

Facilities: Sun terrace, indoor pool.

KAISER KARL, Vorgebirgstrasse 56, D-5300 Bonn. Tel. 0228/65-09-33. Fax 0228/63-78-99. 41 rms. MINIBAR TV TEL **Tram:** 61 or 62.

$ **Rates:** 200 DM–330 DM ($132–$217.80) single; 280 DM–400 DM ($184.80–$264) double. Breakfast buffet 24 DM ($15.80) extra. AE, DC, MC, V. **Parking:** 25 DM ($16.50).

⭐ The Kaiser Karl is one of Bonn's gems. Its stately, symmetrical facade is illuminated at night. Constructed in 1905 as a private town house, it was converted in 1983 into a stylish hotel. The attractive decor includes lacquered Japanese screens, English antiques, Oriental carpets, Venetian mirrors, and Edwardian potted palms. Each beautifully furnished guest room has a TV with video, a safe for valuables, and phones in both bedroom and private bath.

Dining/Entertainment: Though breakfast is the only meal served, there is an elegant piano bar and a garden where you can order drinks.

Services: Room service, laundry, dry cleaning.

Facilities: Indoor pool.

STEIGENBERGER HOTEL VENUSBERG, An der Casselsruhe 1, D-5300 Bonn. Tel. 0228/28-80, or toll free 800/223-5652 in the U.S. and Canada. Fax 0228/28-82-88. 84 rms, 6 suites. MINIBAR TV TEL **Directions:** 3 miles southwest on Trierer Strasse.

$ **Rates** (including continental breakfast): 265 DM–295 DM ($174.90–$194.70) single; 340 DM–380 DM ($224.40–$250.80) double; from 550 DM ($363) suite. AE, DC, MC, V. **Parking:** 15 DM ($9.90).

The elegant and intimate Steigenberger opened in 1988 under the management of one of Europe's most respected hotel chains. The hotel is 2½ miles south of Bonn, surrounded by the beauty of the fabled Venusberg nature reserve, which is a part of the larger Kottenforst. Built in a style evocative of a French country home, the hotel extends symmetrical wings around either side of a forecourt, where some of the most luxurious automobiles in Europe are likely to deposit their occupants.

Each accommodation contains a TV, a radio, and a well-accessorized bathroom in cream-colored or black-and-white marble. There are six air-conditioned suites, and about half the units offer private balconies overlooking the hills.

Dining/Entertainment: A gourmet dining room called Restaurant Venusberg has an outdoor terrace overlooking the seven nearby hills of local legends. A piano bar provides live music (except Monday) from 5 to 11pm.

Services: Room service, laundry, dry cleaning.

Facilities: Sauna, health club, massage facilities.

EXPENSIVE

HOTEL DOMICIL, Thomas-Mann-Strasse 24-26, D-5300 Bonn. Tel. 0228/72-90-90, or toll free 800/528-1234 in the U.S. Fax 0228/69-12-07. 42 rms, 3 suites. MINIBAR TV TEL

$ Rates: 175 DM–340 DM ($115.50–$224.40) single; 235 DM–380 DM ($155.10–$250.80) double; from 440 DM ($290.40) suite. Buffet breakfast 19.50 DM ($12.90) extra. AE, DC, MC, V. **Parking:** 5 DM ($3.30). **Closed:** Dec 22–Jan 3.

Built in 1985, this modern and convenient hotel lies about four blocks north of the cathedral in the center of town near the Bahnhof. In the front a glass-and-steel portico stretches over the sidewalk. The interior is one of the most elegantly decorated in the capital, with a stylishly angular lobby and an art deco bistro. The handsomely designed guest rooms have radios and TVs.

Dining/Entertainment: You can enjoy a drink in the piano bar before heading for the Krull restaurant, where French and Italian meals run from about 50 DM to 75 DM ($33 to $49.50). Specialties include fresh fish, well-seasoned lamb, noodles laden with crabmeat, and Tafelspitz. Meals are offered from noon to 2:30pm and 7 to 11:30pm; closed Sundays and for several weeks in midsummer. The hotel also has a nightclub, Joyce Evening Club.

Services: Room service, laundry, dry cleaning.

Facilities: Sauna, car-rental facilities.

MODERATE

HOTEL BEETHOVEN, Rheingasse 24-26, D-5300 Bonn. Tel. 0228/63-14-11. Fax 0228/69-16-29. 59 rms. TV TEL **Tram:** 61 or 62.

$ Rates (including buffet breakfast): 100 DM–160 DM ($66–$105.60) single; 160 DM–180 DM ($105.60–$118.80) double. DC, MC, V. **Parking:** Free.

A 10-minute walk from the Bahnhof, the Beethoven stands across the street from the Stadttheater, with one of its wings facing the Rhine. Its main attraction is a panoramic view of the river traffic from the high-ceilinged dining room, where first-class meals are served, supervised by the owner. Double-glazed windows prevent urban noises from disturbing the calm in the comfortable rooms.

STERNHOTEL, Mark 8, D-5300 Bonn. Tel. 0228/726-70, or toll free 800/223-6764. Fax 0228/726-71-25. 75 rms (all with bath or shower). TV TEL **Bus:** 624, 625, or 626.

$ Rates (including buffet breakfast): 135 DM ($89.10) single with shower, 160 DM ($105.60) single with bath; 195 DM ($128.70) double with shower, 225 DM ($148.50) double with bath. AE, DC, MC, V.

One of the best of Bonn's moderately priced hotels is the Sternhotel, in the heart of town, next door to Bonn's most colorful building, the baroque Rathaus. The Stern has been in the hands of the Haupt family since 1902, and they offer an informal, homelike place for guests. A reception lounge has been combined with a cafeteria; furnishings harmoniously blend the traditional and the contemporary. Equally homelike are the guest rooms, the larger of which have sitting areas. International meals are served in the dining room.

INEXPENSIVE

HAUS HOFGARTEN, Fritz-Tillmann-Strasse 7, D-5300 Bonn. Tel. 0228/ 22-34-82. Fax 0228/21-39-02. 15 rms (8 with bath). **Tram:** 61 or 62.

$ Rates (including continental breakfast): 69 DM ($45.50) single without bath, 115 DM ($75.90) single with bath; 110 DM ($72.60) double without bath, 160 DM ($105.60) double with bath. AE, DC, MC, V.

Haus Hofgarten is a five-minute walk from the Bahnhof. A hardworking couple presides over this unique establishment with the charm of another era. The good-size breakfast room makes it a bit like living in a private home. A wide mahogany staircase leads to the simply but comfortably furnished rooms, nine of which have phone and TVs.

WHERE TO DINE

EXPENSIVE

LE MARRON, Provinzialstrasse 35. Tel. 0228/25-32-61.
Cuisine: CONTINENTAL. **Reservations:** Recommended. **Bus:** 622.
$ Prices: Appetizers 28 DM–45 DM ($18.50–$29.70); main courses 42 DM–52 DM ($27.70–$34.30); fixed-price lunch 48 DM ($31.70); fixed-price dinner 95 DM–120 DM ($62.70–$79.20). AE, DC, MC, V.
Open: Lunch Mon–Fri noon–2pm; dinner Fri–Wed 7–10pm.

Le Marron is a popular place at Lengsdorf, 3 miles southwest of Bonn. It's a warmly rustic restaurant where, in winter, an open fireplace burns in the intimate dining room. A favorite dish is fresh mussels in a truffle-butter sauce or with chervil and wild mushrooms, or Norwegian salmon in a Riesling sauce. À la carte or fixed-price meals are available.

LE PETIT POISSON, Wilhelmstrasse 23A. Tel. 0228/63-38-83.
Cuisine: FRENCH/SEAFOOD. **Reservations:** Required. **Tram:** 61 or 62.
$ Prices: Appetizers 18 DM–36 DM ($11.90–$23.80); main courses 30 DM–60 DM ($19.80–$39.60); fixed-price dinner 78 DM–115 DM ($51.50–$75.90). AE, DC, MC, V.
Open: Dinner Mon–Sat 6–10pm.

Le Petit Poisson reflects the personality of the couple who owns it. Ludwig Reinarz and his wife, Johanna, have decorated this place elegantly in an art nouveau bistro style. Cuisine moderne has made itself felt here: All ingredients are fresh, and many concoctions are temptingly light. Try the cream of fish and mushroom soup. Savory meat and game dishes are available, including venison in vermouth sauce. Fixed-price dinners are offered, or you can order à la carte.

RISTORANTE GRAND'ITALIA, Bischofsplatz 1. Tel. 0228/63-83-33.
Cuisine: ITALIAN. **Reservations:** Required. **Tram:** 62 or 66.
$ Prices: Appetizers 16 DM–23 DM ($10.60–$15.20); main courses 36 DM–60 DM ($23.80–$39.60). AE, DC, MC, V.
Open: Lunch daily noon–2:30pm; dinner daily 6–11:30pm.

Right off the old market square is what's rightly considered one of the best Italian restaurants along the Rhine. It makes an excellent change of pace, and the service is good. Pasta is prepared with a number of sauces. The pizza oven turns out many different sizzling pies. In season, the chef buys the white truffle of Piedmont to use in a variety of ways and also prepares pheasant. For dessert, you may want to sample the classic Italian zabaglione.

MODERATE

EM HÖTTCHE, Markt 4. Tel. 0228/65-85-96.
Cuisine: GERMAN. **Reservations:** Not accepted. **Tram:** 47. **Bus:** 625.
$ Prices: Appetizers 9.50 DM–18.50 DM ($6.30–$12.20); main courses 20 DM–42 DM ($13.20–$27.70). AE, DC, MC, V.
Open: Lunch Mon–Sat noon–2:30pm; dinner Mon–Sat 6pm–midnight. **Closed:** Last 2 weeks in Dec.

Tracing its origin back to 1389, Em Höttche has a long and colorful history. Next to the baroque Rathaus, it has been restored by the Mieboch-Grünwald family, with carved wood paneling, natural brick, old beamed ceilings, decoratively painted plaster, and curlicued chandeliers. Favorite dining spots are the tables set inside the walk-in fireplace. The front room is mostly for drinks. On the à la carte list, you'll find filet Gulasch Stroganoff and specialties for two, including entrecôte. Fresh salmon is often available. You can complement your meal with a carafe of local wine—the best buy in the house.

ZUR LESE, Adenauerallée 37. Tel. 0228/22-33-22.
Cuisine: GERMAN. **Reservations:** Required.
$ Prices: Appetizers 9.50 DM–20 DM ($6.30–$13.20); main dishes 25 DM–40 DM ($16.50–$26.40); fixed-price lunch 25 DM–40 DM ($16.50–$26.40). AE, DC, MC, V.
Open: Tues–Sun 10am–10pm.

Zur Lese is a wine restaurant with a terrace café, one of the finest in Bonn. Hartmut Wicht, your English-speaking host, believes that care and precision should go into a cuisine. Zur Lese opens for morning coffee and serves throughout the day. It's especially popular in the afternoon, when visitors drop in for coffee and cakes. It lies a 5-minute walk through the Hofgarten, and on a summer night the view of the Rhine from the terrace is dramatic.

A menu of German specialties is presented (with English translations). You might begin your meal with French onion soup or smoked salmon from Norway (a favorite is crayfish soup laced with cognac). Among the specialties, pork is served with curry sauce, and the chef prepares a superb filet Gulasch Lese. You can also choose rainbow trout or lobster from the terrace aquarium.

INEXPENSIVE

IM BÄREN, Acherstrasse 1–3. Tel. 0228/63-32-00.
Cuisine: GERMAN. **Reservations:** Recommended. **Tram:** 61 or 62.
$ Prices: Appetizers 8 DM–22 DM ($5.30–$14.50); main courses 18 DM–26 DM ($11.90–$17.20). No credit cards.
Open: Tues–Sun 10am–midnight.

In this Gasthaus dating from 1385, the quality of the hearty Rhineland food is high, and the antique atmosphere is in keeping with the style of the building. It's one of the best bargains of Bonn. Service is polite and attentive.

IM STIEFEL, Bonngasse 30. Tel. 0228/63-48-06.
Cuisine: RHINELAND. **Reservations:** Recommended. **Tram:** 61 or 62.
$ Prices: Appetizers 6 DM–17.20 DM ($4–$11.40); main courses 16 DM–30 DM ($10.60–$19.80); fixed-price lunch 15 DM ($9.90). AE, MC, V.

Open: Lunch Mon–Sat 11am–2:15pm; dinner Mon–Sat 6–10pm.

Ⓢ A few doors down from the Beethoven House, this atmospheric restaurant is a local favorite. Dining is at bare bleached tables in several rooms with wood paneling and stained glass. There's a stand-up bar for mugs of beer. The menu is short, featuring Rhineland dishes, including a local dish, Hämmchen, served with sauerkraut and mashed potatoes. A specialty is braised beef marinated in almond-raisin sauce and served with sauerkraut and mashed potatoes.

WEINHAUS JACOBS, Friedrichstrasse 18. Tel. 0228/63-73-53.
  Cuisine: GERMAN. **Reservations:** Recommended. **Tram:** 61 or 62.
$ **Prices:** Appetizers 8 DM–19 DM ($5.30–$12.50); main courses 15 DM–29.50 DM ($9.90–$19.50). No credit cards.
  Open: Mon–Sat 4:30pm–1am. **Closed:** 3 weeks in Aug (dates vary).
You'll find lots of hand-carved wood decorating this traditional winehouse, which serves an unusual array of regional Rhineland specialties—many recipes date from the days of the Holy Roman Empire. The food and drink are reasonable.

---

5. BAD GODESBERG

4 miles S of central Bonn

GETTING THERE   See Bonn, Section 4, above.

ESSENTIALS   For information about the town, consult the tourist office in Bonn at **Cassius-Bastei,** Münsterstrasse 20 (tel. 0228/77-34-66).

Part of greater Bonn, Bad Godesburg is built around one of the Rhine's oldest resorts. Just opposite the Siebengebirge, it has a view of the crag Drachenfels (Dragon's Rock) where Siegfried slew the dragon. The dragons are gone from the Rhine, but you can still see some ancient castle ruins on the hills. The most interesting is Godesberg Castle, built in the 13th century by the electors of Cologne (its ruins have been incorporated into a hotel described below). From the promenade along the Rhine, you can watch a flow of boats and barges wending their way up and down the river.

Most of the spa's activity centers around the Redoute Palace, a small but elegant 18th-century castle. Beethoven Hall, the main ballroom, was the scene of the meeting between the young Beethoven and Haydn. Although the town is mainly a residential center, there is seemingly no end to the entertainment and cultural facilities here. Theaters, concerts, and social functions offer a constant whirl of events. There are many diplomatic missions.

WHERE TO STAY

EXPENSIVE

GODESBERG CASTLEHOTEL, Auf dem Godesberg 5, D-5300 Bonn 2–Bad Godesberg. Tel. 0228/31-60-71. Fax 0228/31-12-18. 14 rms. TV TEL **Tram:** 16 or 63 from Bonn.
$ **Rates** (including continental breakfast): 145 DM ($95.70) single; 190 DM–300 DM ($125.40–$198) double. AE, DC, MC, V. **Parking:** Free.
A winding road leads up to this hilltop castle ruin, now converted into a distinctive and highly recommended place to stay. Its tall tower and many of its rugged stone walls were erected in 1210 by the archbishop of Cologne and are still intact. A lounge, built against one of the stone walls, provides a sunny perch and a view of the spa and

the river. There's also a roof terrace, with tables for drinks. The guest rooms have been picture windows. The food is especially good here (see my restaurant recommendations).

RHEINHOTEL DREESEN, Rheinstrasse 45–49, D-5300 Bonn 2–Bad Godesberg. Tel. 0228/8-20-20. Fax 0228/82-02-153. 72 rms, 2 suites. MINIBAR TV TEL **Tram:** 16 or 63 from Bonn.
$ Rates (including continental breakfast): 155 DM–305 DM ($102.30–$201.30) single; 218 DM–468 DM ($143.90–$308.90) double; from 750 DM ($495) suite. AE, DC, MC, V. **Parking:** 20 DM ($13.20).

A traditional five-story elevator building with gardens and terraces, directly on the Rhine, the Rheinhotel Dreesen has been receiving guests since 1893. It's a sentimental favorite of old-timers, as well as a holiday resort center for businesspeople and families. The guest rooms, all recently renovated, contain TVs and radios. Units are elegant and of generous size, with prices based on the view.

The Gobelin restaurant features a view of the river, with meals costing from 55 DM to 80 DM ($36.30 to $52.80). Among the amenities are room service and valet and laundry service.

MODERATE

INSEL HOTEL, Theaterplatz 5–7, D-5300 Bonn 2–Bad Godesberg. Tel. 0228/36-40-82. Fax 0228/35-28-78. 66 rms, 1 suite. MINIBAR TV TEL **Tram:** 16 or 63 from Bonn.
$ Rates (including continental breakfast): 138 DM ($91.10) single; 195 DM ($128.70) double; from 350 DM ($231) suite. AE, MC, V. **Parking:** Free.

If you stay in this comfortable establishment in the heart of this spa city, you'll be but a short car ride from the Rhine. The hotel has pleasantly furnished rooms. In the restaurant or at the sidewalk café terrace, both German dishes and international specialties are served, with a fine selection of Rhine wines. Meals cost from 35 DM ($23.10).

ZUM ADLER, Koblenzerstrasse 60, D-5300 Bonn 2–Bad Godesberg. Tel. 0228/36-40-71. Fax 0228/36-19-33. 39 rms, 2 suites. TV TEL **Tram:** 16 or 62 from Bonn.
$ Rates (including continental breakfast): 115 DM–125 DM ($75.90–$82.50) single; 160 DM–190 DM ($105.60–$125.40) double; from 250 DM ($165) suite. AE, DC, MC, V. **Parking:** 8 DM ($5.30).

⑤ With a 19th-century atmosphere, the prestigious Zum Adler, dating back to 1860, was once a private villa, built right on the street, with a small rear garden. It is furnished with good antiques, and the plumbing has been completely improved. A substantial breakfast is the only meal served.

WHERE TO DINE

EXPENSIVE

CÄCILIENHÖHE, Goldbergweg 17. Tel. 0228/32-10-01.
Cuisine: GERMAN/ITALIAN/SEAFOOD. **Reservations:** Recommended. **Bus:** 610 or 611.
$ Prices: Appetizers 16 DM–25 DM ($10.60–$16.50); main courses 36 DM–43 DM ($23.80–$28.40); fixed-price lunch 69 DM–78 DM ($45.50–$51.50); fixed-price dinner 89 DM–105 DM ($58.70–$69.30). AE, DC, MC, V.
Open: Lunch Mon–Fri noon–2:30pm; dinner Mon–Sat 6:30–11pm.

Besides a panoramic view, this restaurant, with only a dozen tables, offers an array of classic German dishes along with Tuscan specialties and fish from both the Atlantic and the Mediterranean. Top-quality natural and fresh ingredients are used in the kitchen.

The hotel also has 10 pleasantly furnished rooms attached, renting for 120 DM to 160 DM ($79.20 to $105.60) daily for a double.

HALBEDEL'S GASTHAUS, Rheinallee 47. Tel. 0228/35-42-53.
   Cuisine: CONTINENTAL. **Reservations:** Recommended. **Tram:** 16 or 63 from Bonn.
$ **Prices:** Appetizers 18 DM–36 DM ($11.90–$23.80); main courses 45 DM–50 DM ($29.70–$33); seven-course fixed-price dinner 105 DM ($69.30). MC.
   Open: Dinner Tues–Sun 6pm–midnight. Last order, 10:30pm. **Closed:** July–Aug 3.

✪ Amid many nostalgic souvenirs and antique tables and chairs, you are greeted by the courtly owners of this turn-of-the-century villa. The kitchen prides itself on using mostly German-grown ingredients. Menu choices might include a flavorful and stylish array of light-textured modern dishes (including a soup made of wild mushrooms), rack of lamb prepared French style, and a salad of dandelion greens and wild lettuce, followed by flavorful desserts. Fixed-priced or à la carte menus are available.

MODERATE

GODESBERG CASTLEHOTEL RESTAURANT, Auf dem Godesberg 5. Tel. 0228/31-60-71.
   Cuisine: INTERNATIONAL. **Reservations:** Not necessary. **Tram:** 16 or 63 from Bonn.
$ **Prices:** Appetizers 8.50 DM–18 DM ($5.60–$11.90); main courses 25 DM–33 DM ($16.50–$21.80); three-course lunch 32 DM ($21.10); six-course dinner 95 DM ($62.70). AE, DC, MC, V.
   Open: Lunch daily noon–2pm; dinner daily 6–9pm.

Part of the previously recommended 13th-century castle that was turned into a hotel, this spot offers excellent meals in a romantic setting. The former knights' hall has been converted into a spacious dining room with picture-window views—true eagle's-nest style. The adjoining Weinstube is warmer in tone, with its inner wall paneled in grainy wood. The international menu appeals to the widest possible tastes.

WIRTSHAUS ST. MICHAEL, Brunnenallee 26. Tel. 0228/36-47-65.
   Cuisine: CONTINENTAL. **Reservations:** Required. **Tram:** 16 or 63 from Bonn.
$ **Prices:** Appetizers 12 DM–15 DM ($7.90–$9.90); main courses 24 DM–48 DM ($15.80–$31.70); fixed-price menu 48 DM ($31.70). AE, DC, MC, V.
   Open: Dinner Mon–Sat 6–10pm.

Some of the best cuisine in Bad Godesberg is served at Wirtshaus St. Michael. The beautifully coffered ceiling of this elegant and revered restaurant is painted white, and century-old antiques and intimate lighting are also part of its charm. In summer, you can dine on the terrace with a view of the Godesberg castle. Diners feast on lobster, shrimp, homemade goose-liver pâté, or Norwegian salmon on a bed of freshly picked spinach leaves.

ZUR KORKEICHE, Lyngsbergstrasse 104. Tel. 0228/34-78-97.
   Cuisine: CONTINENTAL. **Reservations:** Recommended. **Bus:** 14.
$ **Prices:** Appetizers 8.50 DM–18 DM ($5.60–$11.90); main courses 25 DM–40 DM ($16.50–$26.40); six-course dinner 72 DM ($47.50). MC.
   Open: Dinner Tues–Sun 6pm–midnight. **Closed:** 2 weeks in Jan, 2 weeks in Sept (dates vary).

Ⓢ Zur Korkeiche lies outside Bad Godesberg in the village of Lannesdorf, but it's such a tranquil and satisfying choice that it's worth arming yourself with a road map to find. Advertised as a wine and sherry house, it's a well-maintained half-timbered building with two stories of gemütlich comfort and tradition; the decor is rustic in a country-elegant way. The head chef prepares a light cuisine, including delicately seasoned smoked salmon in champagne sauce.

6. KOBLENZ

55 miles SE of Cologne; 39 miles SE of Bonn; 62 miles NW of Frankfurt

GETTING THERE **By Plane** The nearest airports to Koblenz are Frankfurt (see Chapter 3) and Köln (see Section 3, above).

By Train The Koblenz Hauptbahnhof lies on a major rail line with frequent connections to major German cities. For train information, tariffs, and schedules, call 0261/19-419. Thirty trains per day connect Koblenz with Frankfurt (trip time: 2 hours); 16 trains per day to Berlin (trip time: 8½ hours); and 50 trains to Cologne (trip time: 45 minutes to one hour).

By Bus Long-distance bus service to major cities such as Frankfurt is provided by Europabus. Information is available from the Deutsches Touring GmbH in Frankfurt (tel. 069/79-030). Regional bus service to nearby towns along the Rhine and Mosel rivers (see chapters 7 and 8) is provided by RMV Rhine-Mosel Verkehrsgesellschaft at Koblenz (tel. 0261/17-383).

By Car Access by car to Koblenz is via autobahn A48 east and west, connecting with A6 or A3 north to south.

ESSENTIALS For information about tours, boat trips on the Rhine, and bus and train connections, contact the **Koblenz Tourist Office,** Pavillon gegenüber dem Hauptbahnhof (tel. 0261/3-13-04), opposite the Hauptbahnhof.

Koblenz has stood at the confluence of the Rhine and Mosel for more than 2,000 years. Its strategic point in the mid-Rhine region has made the city a vital link in the international river trade routes of Europe. Visitors often find themselves here at either the start or finish of a steamer excursion through the Rhine Valley. Right in the heart of wine country, Koblenz is surrounded by vine-covered hills dotted with castles and fortresses.

The town was heavily bombed during World War II, but many of the historic buildings have been restored. For the best overall view of the town, go to the point where the two rivers meet. This is called **Deutsches Eck** (corner of Germany). From the top of the base where a huge statue of Wilhelm I once stood, you can see the Altstadt and across the Rhine to the Ehrenbreitstein Fortress.

The focal point of the Altstadt is the **Liebfrauenkirche** (Church of Our Lady), a 13th-century Gothic basilica built on a Romanesque foundation. Of interest are the onion-shaped spires on the top of the church's twin towers. The early 18th-century **Rathaus** was formerly a Jesuit college. In the courtyard behind the hall is a fountain dedicated to the youth of Koblenz called *The Spitting Boy,* and that's just what he does. At the edge of the old town, near the Deutsches Eck, is Koblenz's oldest and most attractive church, **St. Castor's,** dating from 836. This twin-towered Romanesque basilica was the site of the Treaty of Verdun in the 9th century, dividing Charlemagne's empire.

The ✪ **Ehrenbreitstein Fortress,** across the Rhine from Koblenz, can be reached by chair lift, but if you have a fear of heights, you can drive via the Pfaffendorfer Bridge just south of the Altstadt. The fortress was built on a rock, towering 400 feet above the Rhine. The present walls were built in the 19th century by the Prussians, on the site of the 10th-century fortress of the archbishops of Trier. It was the headquarters of the American Occupation Army following World War I. From the stone terrace you can see for miles up and down the Rhine, a view that includes not only Koblenz but also several castles along the Rhine and the terraced vineyards of the region. This is considered one of the most panoramic vistas along the Rhine. To reach the fortress, make the 1.20-DM (80¢) one-way passage across the river from the main Rhine dock. Ferries run Monday through Friday from 7am to 7pm, Saturday from 8am to 7pm, and Sunday from 8:30am to 7pm. The chairlift (*Sesselbahn*) operates daily in May through October from 9am to 5pm, costing 7 DM ($4.60) for a round-trip ticket.

WHERE TO STAY

EXPENSIVE

HOTEL BRENNER, Rizzastrasse 20–22, D-5400 Koblenz. Tel. 0261/3-20-60. Fax 0261/36-278. 25 rms. TV TEL **Bus:** 1 or 5.

$ Rates (including continental breakfast): 110 DM–165 DM ($72.60–$108.90) single; 180 DM–250 DM ($118.80–$165) double. AE, DC, MC, V. **Parking:** 8 DM ($5.30). **Closed:** Nov to mid-Dec and Jan.

Close to the Kurfürstl Schloss (castle) and about five city blocks from either the Rhine or the Mosel, this is a leading contender for top honors in Koblenz. The hotel might vaguely remind you of the famed institution of Baden-Baden with the same name. The owners offer four floors of gilt detailing on white walls, with lots of little tables and chairs. Everything looks Louis XIV. The garden retreat is a nice place in which to get back to nature. Each room has remote-control cable TV.

DIEHLS, Am Pfaffendorfer Tor 10, Ehrenbreitstein, D-5400 Koblenz. Tel. 0261/7-20-10. Fax 0261/72-021. 65 rms, 4 suites. TV TEL **Bus:** 7, 8, 9, or 10.

$ Rates (including continental breakfast): 118 DM–168 DM ($77.90–$110.90) single; 160 DM–250 DM ($105.60–$165) double; from 300 DM ($198) suite. DC, MC, V. **Parking:** 8 DM ($5.30).

Since it's on the banks of the Rhine across the river from the town, all of the Diehl's public rooms, lounges, dining rooms, and guest rooms face the river directly. You can watch the sun set on the water from your room. The hotel has a pool, sauna, and solarium. It's an old-style hotel and often accommodates groups. Rooms are well-furnished; most have minibars. Another advantage, besides the magnificent views, is the sliding scale of room prices.

SCANDIC CROWN HOTEL, Julius-Wegeler-Strasse 6, D-5400 Koblenz. Tel. 0261/13-60. Fax 0261/136-11-99. 167 rms, 1 suite. A/C MINIBAR TV TEL **Bus:** 1 or 5.

$ Rates (including buffet breakfast): 225 DM–265 DM ($148.50–$174.90) single; 285 DM–325 DM ($188.10–$214.50) double; from 480 DM ($316.80) suite. AE, DC, MC, V. **Parking:** 10 DM ($6.60).

Modern, glittering, and stylish, the Scandic Crown, a Swedish-owned hotel, sits on a hillock at the edge of the Rhine. Opened in 1986, it easily qualifies as the newest, best, and most dramatic hotel in town. Its streamlined architecture contrasts with the century-old trees and the ancient stones of the medieval town surrounding it. On the premises are two elegant restaurants: Rhapsody and Le Gourmet. The hotel offers comfortably furnished and well-insulated guest rooms, each with radio and color TV with VCR. On the premises is a Swedish sauna as well as a solarium and hot whirlpool. Room service, laundry, and dry cleaning are available. One of the city's loveliest riverside promenades lies just a short walk away.

MODERATE

HOTEL HAMM, St-Josef-Strasse 32, D-5400 Koblenz. Tel. 0261/3-45-46. Fax 0261/16-09-72. 30 rms. TV TEL **Bus:** 1 or 5.

$ Rates (including buffet breakfast): 70 DM–85 DM ($46.20–$56.10) single; 120 DM–145 DM ($79.20–$95.70) double. AE, DC, MC, V. **Closed:** Mid-Dec to mid-Jan.

This cozy, informal hotel is run by the English-speaking Volker-Dick family. The public rooms are modern and the guest rooms well maintained (half offer minibars). The Hamm lies near the railway station, a five-minute walk from the Rhine.

HOTEL HÖHMANN, Bahnhofplatz 5, D-5400 Koblenz. Tel. 0261/3-50-11. Fax 0261/1-87-23. 41 rms. TV TEL
$ Rates (including buffet breakfast): 98 DM–105 DM ($64.70–$69.30) single; 166 DM–190 DM ($109.60–$125.40) double. AE, DC, MC, V. **Parking:** 5 DM ($3.30).

The Höhmann stands across from the Hauptbahnhof, a symmetrical structure recently renovated inside and out. The rooms have comfortable beds and color TVs. The hotel has an elevator. English is spoken here.

KLEINER RIESEN, Kaiserin-Augusta-Anlagen 18, D-5400 Koblenz. Tel. 0261/3-20-77. Fax 0261/16-07-25. 27 rms. TEL
$ Rates (including continental breakfast): 100 DM–150 DM ($66–$99) single; 180 DM–220 DM ($118.80–$145.20) double. AE, DC, MC, V. **Parking:** 10 DM ($6.60).

One of the few city hotels on the banks of the Rhine is the Kleiner Riesen. In fact, its dining room terrace and most of its guest rooms are close enough for viewing the boats as they go by. The hotel is a large, overgrown chalet, informal, with several living rooms and comfortable, clean bedrooms. Nicely situated away from the town traffic, it has a peaceful small-town quiet.

HOTEL SCHOLZ, Moselweisserstrasse 121, D-5400 Koblenz. Tel. 0261/40-80-21. Fax 0261/40-80-26. 62 rms (all with shower). MINIBAR TV TEL **Bus:** 6.
$ Rates (including continental breakfast): 85 DM ($56.10) single; 140 DM ($92.40) double. AE, DC, MC, V. **Closed:** Dec 20–Jan 7. **Parking:** Free.

The Scholz is a personally run family hotel that has been under the same management for half a century. Only a five-minute bus ride from the town center, it offers sparsely furnished units that make for a comfortable, reasonably priced overnight stopover. A traditional German cuisine is served.

TRIERER HOF, Clemensstrasse 1, D-5400 Koblenz. Tel. 0261/3-10-60. Fax 0261/16-04-39. 36 rms. TV TEL **Bus:** 10.
$ Rates (including continental breakfast): 95 DM–99 DM ($62.70–$65.30) single; 160 DM–190 DM ($105.60–$125.40) double. AE, DC, MC, V. **Parking:** 5 DM ($3.30).

A private hotel built in 1786, the Trierer Hof was converted into a Gasthof as early as 1789—something considered "revolutionary" at the time. It is behind the Schloss in the midst of gardens and only a quarter of a mile from the Deutsches Eck, where the Rhine meets the Mosel. Most of the guest rooms and lounges are overscale, and the furnishings are simple and most adequate. On the premises is an independently run Argentine steakhouse, Buffalo.

WHERE TO DINE
EXPENSIVE

LE GOURMET, in the Scandic Crown Hotel, Julius-Wegeler-Strasse 6. Tel. 0261/13-60.
Cuisine: CONTINENTAL. **Reservations:** Recommended. **Bus:** 1 or 5.
$ Prices: Appetizers 18 DM–22 DM ($11.90–$14.50); main courses 28 DM–42 DM ($18.50–$27.70). AE, DC, MC, V.
Open: Lunch daily noon–3pm; dinner daily 6–11pm.

In the previously recommended Scandic Crown, Le Gourmet is elegantly modern in both design and flavor, very much a statement of Scandinavia. It is also considered one of the leading restaurants of Koblenz. You dine on a wide flower-trimmed terrace in summer or inside in a Nordic ambience of pastel and polished wood. Typical continental dishes are beef filet, grilled veal steak, fresh herring from Holland, marinated salmon or fresh shrimp from a cold deli case, or sole strips in Riesling with truffles and carrot purée. Desserts are served from a well-stocked trolley.

WINE TAVERN

WEINHAUS HUBERTUS, Florinsmarkt 6. Tel. 0261/3-11-77.
   Cuisine: GERMAN. **Reservations:** Recommended. **Bus:** 1.
$ Prices: Appetizers 5.50 DM–17.50 DM ($3.60–$11.60). No main courses. No credit cards. **Open:** Wed–Mon 4pm–1am.

Across from the Old Rathaus Museum in the Altstadt, Weinhaus Hubertus offers various German wines accompanied by a choice of homemade dishes. Dating from 1696, it looks like a timbered country inn, with boxes of red geraniums at the windows. The furnishings and the decor of the rooms are family style, providing a homelike atmosphere. It is the oldest wine tavern in town and offers a choice of 100 wines (a broad selection from all over Germany), of which 30 can be served by the glass. Glasses of wine begin at 3.50 DM ($2.30). In the summer, the terrace lets you enjoy the view.

WINE TASTING

At the foot of the Pfaffendorfer Bridge, **Weindorf,** Julius-Wegeler-Strasse 2 (tel. 0261/3-16-80), right on the Rhine, is the center for tasting the wines of the vineyards of the Mosel and Rhine regions. It's a timbered wine village where everyone gathers on festive evenings. In fair weather you'll prefer to do your sampling in the open beer garden or on the river-view terrace. Let someone else do the driving afterward. Meals, costing from 25 DM ($16.50), feature a hearty German cuisine, including such dishes as pork filet in a mushroom-cream sauce and Sauerbraten. Perhaps you'd prefer something more continental—a rumpsteak Café de Paris. Weindorf is open daily from 10am to midnight. Live music is presented after 7pm. A glass of wine costs from 4.50 DM ($3). Credit cards: AE, MC.

7. THE RHEINGAU

When God was looking for a place to set up Paradise, so goes the story, the sunny slopes between the Taunus Mountains and the Rhine nearly won the prize. Today the Rheingau is the kingdom of another god, Bacchus, who reigns supreme here. Nearly every town and village from Wiesbaden to Assmannshausen, no matter how small, is a major wine producer. The names suddenly seem familiar—Bingen, Johannisberg, Rüdesheim, Oestrich—because we have seen them on the labels of many favorite wines.

The Rheingau is also rich in old churches and castles, as well as landmarks. The **Niederwald Monument,** on a hill halfway between Rüdesheim and Assmannshausen—it can be reached by cable car from either town—is a huge statue of Germania, erected by Bismarck in 1883 to commemorate the unification of Germany. Below it, on a small island at the bend of the Rhine, is the infamous **Mäuseturm** (Mouse Tower), where, according to legend, the harsh bishop of Mainz was devoured by a swarm of hungry mice. But the real attraction of the Rheingau is the cheerful character of the wine villages and their people.

GETTING THERE

Rüdesheim and Assmannshausen are the most visited towns. Assmannshausen is part of Rüdesheim, its center lying 3 miles to the northwest on the Rhine River. Rüdesheim is 17 miles west of Wiesbaden and 37 miles south of Koblenz. The nearest airport is at

Frankfurt (see Chapter 3), 30 miles away. Access by car is via autobahn A61 from the west and state highway 42 connecting with A671 from the west.

From Frankfurt, motorists can take A66 until they reach the junction of B42, which will be signposted and lead them right into Rüdesheim. Motorists heading from Koblenz on the west bank of the Rhine can use A61 to Bingen, then follow the signs for the ferry boats that cross the river to Rüdesheim. For ferry service information about crossing the Rhine to Bingen, call 06721/14-140. From Koblenz you can also take B42 along the east bank of the river, which will lead directly into Rüdesheim.

The main rail station at Rüdesheim is on the Wiesbaden/Koblenz line, with frequent service to regional towns and connections to all major cities. For rail information and schedules, call 06722/194-19.

Rüdesheim and Assmannshausen can be reached from Munich by train or car in about five hours, but by car or train from Frankfurt takes only one hour. By train from Frankfurt is via Wiesbaden.

Bus service for the region is provided by ORN, Omnibusverkehr Rhein-Nahe GmbH at Mainz (tel. 0611/70-00-88).

RÜDESHEIM

With its old courtyards and winding alleyways lined with timbered houses, Rüdesheim is the epitome of a Rhine wine town. The vineyards around the village date back to the Roman emperor Probus. Besides the full-bodied Riesling, brandy and champagne (Sekt) are also produced here. Rüdesheim is the scene of the annual August wine festival, when the old taverns on the narrow Drosselgasse are filled with jovial tasters from all over the world. Drosselgasse has been called "the smallest but the happiest street in the world." From April through November, you can listen to the music and dance in these taverns daily from noon to 1am.

To prove how seriously Rüdesheimers take their wines, they have opened a wine museum in Bromserburg Castle. The **Rheingau-und Weinmuseum,** charging 3 DM ($2) for admission, is open daily, May to November, from 9am to 6pm. It traces the history of the grape and has an exhibition of wine presses, glasses, goblets, and drinking utensils dating from Roman times to the present.

Brahms (1833–97), the composer, lived at Rüdesheim for some time. Bismarck, the "Iron Chancellor," stayed at Rüdesheim many times in the past century, as did Emperor Wilhelm I. Other famous visitors have included Thomas Jefferson in 1788, Goethe in 1793, and James Fenimore Cooper, the American novelist, in 1832.

For tourist information about both Rüdesheim and Assmannshausen (see below), go to **Stadt Verkehrsamt,** Rheinstrasse 16 (tel. 06722/29-62).

WHERE TO STAY & DINE

Moderate

HOTEL UND WEINHAUS FELSENKELLER, Oberstrasse 39–41, D-6220 Rüdesheim. Tel. 06722/20-94. Fax 06722/47-202. 60 rms. MINIBAR TV TEL

$ Rates (including buffet breakfast): 95 DM–130 DM ($62.70–$85.80) single; 148 DM–212 DM ($97.70–$139.90) double. AE, MC, V. **Closed:** Nov–Easter. **Parking:** 10 DM ($6.60).

The beautifully carved timbers on the facade of this popular guesthouse and Weinhaus in the center of the old part of town suggest the kind of traditional aura you can expect inside. Since 1898, it's been run by the Rolz family. The establishment dates from 1613, and a 1982 addition was constructed in the half-timbered style of the original. A sampling of Rhine wine can be enjoyed in a room of vaulted ceilings stuccoed and muraled with vine leaves and pithy pieces of folk wisdom. In fair weather, guests are served on the terrace. The guest rooms are attractively modern and freshly painted, opening onto views of the vineyards surrounding the house.

RÜDESHEIMER HOF, Geisenheimerstrasse 1, D-6220 Rüdesheim. Tel. 06722/20-11. Fax 06722/4-81-94. 42 rms (all with bath or shower).

$ **Rates** (including buffet breakfast): 85 DM–100 DM ($56.10–$66) single; 130 DM–150 DM ($85.80–$99) double. AE, MC, V. **Parking:** Free. **Closed:** Dec to mid-Feb.

This village inn set back from the Rhine, a 10-minute walk from the Bahnhof, boasts a side garden and terrace where wine tasters gather at rustic tables. Most of the accommodations are roomy and comfortably furnished; four have TVs and 30 have phones. The atmosphere is informal; staying here is like sampling the pulse of a Rhine village—seeing the townspeople mingling with visitors, eating the regional food, and drinking the Rheingau wines.

If you're stopping by just to eat, you'll find set meals from 34 DM to 80 DM ($22.40 to $52.80). Guests dine at café tables placed under a willow tree. Food is served daily from 11:30am to 9:30pm.

ZUM BÄREN, Schmidtstrasse 24–31, D-6220 Rüdesheim. Tel. 06722/10-91. Fax 06722/10-94. 26 rms. TV TEL

$ **Rates** (including buffet breakfast): 85 DM–115 DM ($56.10–$75.90) single; 110 DM–170 DM ($72.60–$112.20) double. Half-board supplement 35 DM ($23.10) per person. AE, DC, MC, V.

Zum Bären is a well-run hotel presided over by Karl-Heinz Willig and his family. The Willigs offer comfortably furnished guest rooms with TVs (on request) and a sauna. The half board supplement, considering the quality of the food, is a good value. The restaurant offers good Rhineland cooking. Guests enjoy sitting on the cozy terrace and seem to like the central location. Meals costing 36 DM ($23.80) are served on Wednesday to Monday from noon to 2pm and 6 to 10pm.

Inexpensive

HOTEL GARNI DRIES, Kaiserstrasse 1, D-6220 Rüdesheim. Tel. 06722/24-20. Fax 06722/26-63. 50 rms (all with bath or shower).

$ **Rates** (including continental breakfast): 90 DM ($59.40) single; 125 DM ($82.50) double. AE, MC, V. **Closed:** Dec–Mar.

In this wine-producing region, it seems appropriate for a tastefully decorated Weinstube to carve *In Vino Veritas* into one of the rustic beams. The slogan, plus a sculpted ceiling and sea-green exterior balconies, identifies this cozy modern establishment, run by the Dries family. The hotel has its own pool, along with a sun terrace decorated with flowerpots. Naturally there's a wide choice of local wines. The hotel rents well-furnished and comfortable rooms. Breakfast is the only meal served.

GASTHOF KRANCHER, Eibinger-Oberstrasse 4, D-6220 Rüdesheim. Tel. 06722/27-62. Fax 06722/47-870. 62 rms (all with bath or shower). TV TEL

$ **Rates** (including continental breakfast): 65 DM–70 DM ($42.90–$46.20) single; 100 DM–120 DM ($66–$79.20) double. Half board 25 DM ($16.50) extra. AE, MC, V. **Closed:** July.

Gasthof Krancher has been in the Krancher family for four generations. The location is about a 10-minute walk from the town center, next to the inn's own vineyards. Naturally, the Kranchers make their own wines, and they'll gladly show you the cellar where they store bottles that have won gold and silver medals. The cuisine is first-class, and certainly the wines are. Everything is decorated in a regional motif. From your window, you can look out at the vineyards. Perhaps you'll be there when the grapes are harvested in the autumn.

HOTEL RHEINSTEIN, Rheinstrasse 20, D-6220 Rüdesheim. Tel. 06722/20-04. Fax 06722/47-688. 40 rms (all with bath or shower). TEL

$ **Rates** (including continental breakfast): 70 DM ($46.20) single with shower, 100 DM ($66) single with bath; 100 DM ($66) double with shower, 160 DM ($105.60) double with bath. Half board 65 DM–110 DM ($42.90–$72.60) per person daily. AE, DC, MC, V. **Closed:** Dec–Mar.

The Rheinstein's elongated terrace facing the street is one of the most popular gathering places in Rüdesheim. Many locals drop in during the afternoon to enjoy the excellent cakes, all baked on the premises. Irene Gehrig offers well-kept and comfortable rooms furnished with modern styling. The location is across from the landing stage along the Rhine of the Cologne-Düsseldorf Anlegestelle.

EVENING ENTERTAINMENT

Rüdesheimer Schloss, Drosselgasse (tel. 06722/20-31), is one of the most colorful restaurants along the Rhine. The intricately carved timbers of this castle date from 1729. There is no cover charge for entrance here, where a band often plays the Rüdesheimer Polonaise (conga!). The restaurant offers well-prepared traditional foods in a wide price range. Every vintage since 1929 is available, plus some older rare ones that include an 1893 Rheingau wine. Food service is from 11am until 10pm anytime daily except January. Dishes are likely to include Sauerbraten, roast wild boar, or stuffed suckling pig. A three-course "musical meal" with a small bottle of the local wine costs 48 DM ($31.70); with a large bottle it costs 59 DM ($38.90). Inexpensive lunches cost from 19 DM ($12.50) and dinner from 28 DM ($18.50). The revelry overflows into the garden in summer.

The establishment's wine cellars at Grabenstrasse 8 (tel. 06722/10-27), called **Georg Breuer,** have been recently renovated and include a modern vinotheque (wine shop) where all the estate-bottled wines can be tasted and purchased. The shop is open daily from March to November (9am to 6pm), and in winter if you call first. There are modern toilet facilities, a waiting room, and a cobblestoned courtyard. A cellar visit with a "tasting" costs from 12 DM ($7.90). The location is half a mile from the rail station.

ASSMANNSHAUSEN

At the northern edge of the Rheingau, this old village is built on the slopes of the east bank of the Rhine. The half-timbered houses and vineyards seem precariously perched on the steep hillsides, and the view of the Rhine Valley from here is awe-inspiring. Assmanshausen is known for its fine burgundy-style wine. It lies 3 miles northwest of Rüdesheim and 37 miles west of Frankfurt.

WHERE TO STAY & DINE

Very Expensive

KRONE ASSMANNSHAUSEN, Rheinuferstrasse 10, D-6220 Rüdes-heim-Assmannshausen. Tel. 06722/40-30. Fax 06722/30-49. 65 rms, 9 suites. MINIBAR TV TEL
$ **Rates:** 210 DM ($138.60) single; 490 DM ($323.40) double; 850 DM ($561) suite. Breakfast 22 DM ($14.50) extra. DC, MC, V. **Closed:** Jan–Feb. **Parking:** Free.

This hotel has a distinguished pedigree. Built on the banks of the Rhine, surrounded by lawns, gardens, and a pool, it traces its origins back 400 years. The inn is overscale, a great big gingerbread fantasy. A small second-floor lounge is virtually a museum, with framed letters and manuscripts of some of the more celebrated personages who have stayed here—Goethe, for one. There's a stack of 37 autograph books signed by writers, painters, diplomats, and composers.

You may stay in a medieval building, a Renaissance structure, or a postwar house. The guest rooms have an old inn character and are spacious, with traditional furnishings.

Dining/Entertainment: Even if you're not overnighting, you may want to stop to sample one of the finest meals you're likely to be served on the Rhine, costing 65 DM to 110 DM ($42.90 to $72.60). Specialties are homemade pâtés, fresh salmon or eel from Lake Constance in a dill sauce, and saddle of venison in season. For dessert, try the Eisbecher Krone. The owners, the Hufnagel family, whose domain is the famous Assmannshauser Höllenberg Pinot Noir, maintains one of the finest assortments of Rhine wines in the world in the rock-hewn cellars of the inn.

Services: Breakfast room service, babysitting, laundry.

Facilities: Pool, sauna.

Moderate

ALTE BAUERNSCHANKE-NASSAUER HOF, Niederwaldstrasse 23, D-6220 Rüdesheim-Assmannshausen. Tel. 06722/23-13. Fax 06722/47912. 52 rms. TV TEL

$ Rates (including continental breakfast): 90 DM–100 DM ($59.40–$66) single; 140 DM–180 DM ($92.40–$118.80) double. AE, MC, V. **Closed:** Nov–Mar.

The wine-grower owners have renovated two of the oldest mansions of the town, turning them into a hotel and restaurant. The interior decor is luxurious, the comfort fine, and the welcome hearty. Near the church, the hotel lies about a quarter mile from the Rhine. Units are beautifully furnished with traditional styling.

The restaurant provides a folkloric experience, with musicians playing every night. Try Gulasch soup, peppersteak with fresh green beans and french fries, plus a half bottle of the growers' red wine, which cost a maximum of 56 DM ($37) per person. If you select less lavish dishes, you can get away for 36 DM ($23.80).

ANKER, Rheinuferstrasse 5–7, D-6220, Rüdesheim-Assmannshausen. Tel. 06722/29-12. Fax 06722/48-130. 48 rms. TEL

$ Rates (including continental breakfast): 85 DM–115 DM ($56.10–$75.90) single; 120 DM–200 DM ($79.20–$132) double. AE, DC, MC, V. **Parking:** Free. **Closed:** Mid-Dec to mid-Mar.

The Anker was already old when Bismarck stayed here in 1842. Constructed in baroque yellow stucco in 1660, the building served as a guesthouse for the passengers and crews of the horse teams that pulled the barges, Erie Canal style, along this section of the Rhine. Today it's a renovated hotel, with an arbor-covered Rhine terrace fronting the river. Many of the rooms have views of the Rhine, along with high ceilings and Oriental rugs. The restaurant—charmingly decorated with old porcelain, brass tankards, and copper pots—serves full-course meals that begin as low as 35 DM ($23.10) and climb to 66 DM ($43.60).

SCHÖN, Rheinuferstrasse 3, D-6220 Rüdesheim-Assmannshausen. Tel. 06722/22-25. Fax 06722/21-90. 27 rms. TV

$ Rates (including continental breakfast): 80 DM–100 DM ($52.80–$66) single; 120 DM–185 DM ($79.20–$122.10) double. Half board 95 DM–130 DM ($62.70–$85.80) per person. MC, V. **Parking:** Free. **Closed:** Nov–Mar.

A family-run riverside hotel, Schön offers comfortable rooms and a café terrace fronting the river. Its original home was an olive-green baroque house; the building next door has been added on, painted harmoniously in the same color. Most rooms have balconies facing the river and are furnished with simple modern tastes. Half have private phones, and 20% have minibars. The hotel has an excellent restaurant, serving food daily from noon to 2pm and 6 to 9pm. It has had its own winery since 1752, and guests can visit the wine cellar.

UNTER DEN LINDEN, Rheinallee 1, D-6220 Rüdesheim-Assmannshausen. Tel. 06722/22-88. Fax 06722/47-201. 28 rms. TV

$ Rates (including continental breakfast): 75 DM–110 DM ($49.50–$72.60) single; 130 DM–170 DM ($85.80–$112.20) double. MC. **Parking:** Free. **Closed:** Mid-Nov to Mar.

This converted Rhine-fronting villa places emphasis on its cuisine and terrace wine drinking. All the guest rooms are pleasantly decorated, each with a TV. A building was added at the rear, offering units for overnight, but avoid the location because of heavy railroad traffic (the line runs 30 yards from your window, and a train passes by every three minutes).

Up front, the dining room overflows onto part of an open terrace. In front is a wide terrace shaded by a grape arbor and linden trees. In summer, revelers fill up every table. English is spoken, the food is good, and the wine is superb. A dish of the day is featured in the dining room. Meals range from 32 DM to 75 DM ($21.10 to $49.50).

Inexpensive

EWIGE LAMPE UND HAUS RESI, Niederwaldstrasse 14, D-6220 Rüdesheim-Assmannshausen. Tel. 06722/24-17. Fax 06722/48-459. 24 rms.
$ Rates (including continental breakfast): 60 DM–80 DM ($39.60–$52.80) single; 100 DM–160 DM ($66–$105.60) double. No credit cards. **Parking:** Free. **Closed:** Jan 3–Feb 14.

You'll find a lot to do in this wine-producing center. You're within a few miles of some historic vineyards, not to mention woodland trails through Rhenish forests. Hosts Engelbert and Renate Uri will welcome you to their cozy, tastefully furnished guesthouse. Many of their rooms have wooden ceilings, some have colorfully tiled baths, and all are impeccably clean. The fortifying breakfast is often served on a sun terrace under parasols. Meals cost 20 DM to 35 DM ($13.20 to $23.10) per person.

8. MAINZ

8 miles S of Wiesbaden; 51 miles NW of Mannheim; 25 miles SW of Frankfurt

GETTING THERE   By Plane   The nearest airport is at Frankfurt (see Chapter 3). There is direct rail service from the airport (S14 train) via Wiesbaden to Mainz. For information, phone FVV, Mannheimer Strasse 15–19, in Frankfurt (tel. 069/26-94-62).

By Train   From Frankfurt, an express train takes 25 minutes to reach Mainz, while a slower S-Bahn train takes 40 minutes. There are also trains leaving Mainz for outlying points of interest, including Heidelberg and Koblenz, which can be reached in an hour, or Cologne in two hours. There are daily trains to and from Munich that take about 4½ hours. For more rail information, phone 06131/19-419.

By Bus   Long-distance bus service by Europabus Line (1013) runs to Frankfurt, Trier, and Luxemburg. Information is available from Deutsche Touring GmbH in Frankfurt (tel. 069/79-030). Regional bus service is provided by ORN Omnibusverkehr Rhein-Nahe GmbH at Mainz (tel. 06131/67-10-26).

By Car   Access by car to Mainz is via autobahn, A60 east and west, or A63 south and A643 north.

ESSENTIALS   For tourist information, go to **Verkehrsverein,** Bahnhofstrasse 15 (tel. 06131/23-37-41).

SPECIAL EVENTS   In festive Mainz, the most celebrated merrymaking is at the All Fools capers at Carnival each spring, broadcast throughout Germany like an annual Macy's parade. In June each year, the Gutenberg Festival sponsors a cultural season, a living memorial to the city's favorite son, the inventor of the movable-type printing press. There's also the annual Wine Fair in August and September of each year.

A 2,000-year-old city, once a powerful episcopal see, Mainz had its origin in prehistoric times on the left bank of the Rhine across from the point where the Main River adds its waters to those of the Rhine. It is thought today that there may have been wine-producing vines in the area before the coming of the Romans in 38 B.C.E., although it was from that time that the regions of the Rheingau and Rheinhessen became widely known for fine viticulture.

At the beginning of the Christian era, the settlement on the Rhine's left bank and the Roman fortifications opposite were connected by a bridge. Christianity came early to Mainz, which in the 8th century became a primary archbishopric. By the 15th century, church politics grew into a war between two rival archbishops. The city later became a military center, and target in several conflicts, being sometimes ruled by France (and called Mayence), sometimes by German states. Because of all these drastic changes Mainz never became the great commerce center its location would seem to assure. However, the Rhenish wine traffic and other trade activities have given it prosperity.

The city of Mainz sprawls over a large district, but the only part that interests most visitors is the **Altstadt,** which is relatively compact and can be covered on foot. The heart of town is Marktplatz, which is dominated by the majestic Dom, or cathedral, and the sister square, Liebfrauen-Platz. From here you can branch out to explore satellite streets, which are about all that is left of the Altstadt following heavy aerial bombardment in World War II. The most interesting streets and squares include Gutenbergplatz, Augustinerstrasse, Schillerplatz, and Ludwigstrasse. Head east from the Altstadt to reach the convention and concert center, the Rheingoldhalle. This area is also the home of the Hilton Hotel and the contemporary Rathaus and is the departure point for vessels cruising the Rhine.

WHAT TO SEE & DO

ST. MARTIN'S CATHEDRAL AND THE DIOCESAN MUSEUM, Domstrasse 3. Tel. 06131/25-33-44.

✪ Above the roofs of the half-timbered houses in the Altstadt rise the six towers of St. Martin's Cathedral, the most important Catholic cathedral in the country after Cologne. The Romanesque basilica, dating from A.D. 975, has been continually rebuilt and restored, until it reached its present form, dating mainly from the 13th and 14th centuries. Below the largest dome, a combination of Romanesque and baroque, is the transept, separating the west chancel from the nave and smaller east chancel. Many of the supporting pillars along the aisles of the nave are decorated with carved and painted statues of French and German saints.

A collection of religious art is housed in the cathedral's Diocesan Museum. Within it are exhibitions of reliquaries and medieval sculpture, including works by the Master of Naumburg. In the 1,000-year-old cathedral crypt is a contemporary gold reliquary of the saints of Mainz. Among the most impressive furnishings in the sanctuary are the rococo choir stalls and a pewter baptismal font from the early 14th century.

Admission: Free.

Open: Cathedral Mon–Fri 9am–6:30pm, Sat 9am–4pm, Sun 1–5pm; museum Mon–Wed and Fri 10am–4pm, Thurs 10am–5pm, Sat 10am–2pm. **Bus:** 1, 7, 13, 17, or 23.

GUTENBERG MUSEUM, Liebfrauenplatz 5. Tel. 06131/12-26-40.

Opposite the east towers of the cathedral is a unique memorial to the city's most famous son. In the modern display rooms, visitors can trace the history of printing from Gutenberg's hand press, on which he printed the 42-line Bible from 1452 to 1455, to the most advanced typesetting processes. The collections cover the entire spectrum of the graphic arts as well as book production and printing, illustration, and binding in all countries, past and present. Two Gutenberg Bibles are the most popular exhibits.

Admission: Free.
Open: Tues–Sat 10am–6pm, Sun 10am–1pm. **Closed:** Jan. **Bus:** 1, 7, 13, 17, or 19.

LANDESMUSEUM MAINZ [Provincial Museum of the Central Rhineland], Grosse Bleiche 49–51. Tel. 06131/23-29-55.

It's worth a visit here to get a pictorial history of Mainz and the middle Rhine, from prehistoric times to the present. The most impressive exhibits are the Roman marble head of the Emperor Augustus (or his nephew, Gaius Caesar), about C.E. 14, and the towering Column of Jupiter, erected in Mainz by the Romans in C.E. 67. Although the original is in the museum, you may, if you are pressed for time, see the true-to-life replica in front of the Parliament building. The Lapidarium shows one of the most important collections of Roman monuments in Europe.
Admission: Free.
Open: Tues–Thurs and Sat–Sun 10am–5pm, Fri 10am–4pm. **Bus:** 6, 15, or 23.

WHERE TO STAY

VERY EXPENSIVE

EUROPAHOTEL, Kaiserstrasse 7, D-6500 Mainz. Tel. 06131/97-50. Fax 06131/97-55-55. 104 rms. TV TEL **Bus:** 16 or 23.

$ Rates (including continental breakfast): 158 DM–293 DM ($104.30–$193.40) single; 296 DM–486 DM ($195.40–$320.80) double. AE, DC, MC, V.

The Europahotel is in the center near the Hauptbahnhof, its bright lights making it easy to find. Its bar and restaurants, as well as the Corona Classic Club, serve as attractive meeting places. The hotel offers guest rooms with all the up-to-date amenities you're likely to need, including VCRs. Regional and international specialties are served in the hotel restaurant, where meals begin at 51 DM ($33.70).

MAINZ HILTON, Rheinstrasse 68, D-6500 Mainz. Tel. 06131/24-50, or toll free 800/445-8667 in the U.S. Fax 06131/24-55-89. 421 rms, 21 suites. A/C MINIBAR TV TEL **Bus:** 6, 15, or 23.

$ Rates: 380 DM–460 DM ($250.80–$303.60) single; 460 DM–510 DM ($303.60–$336.60) double; from 1,150 DM ($759) suite. Children under 17 stay free in parents' room. Continental breakfast 19 DM ($12.50) extra. AE, DC, MC, V. **Parking:** 2 DM ($1.30) per hour.

⭐ The Hilton is one of the most imaginatively designed and strikingly modern hotels in Germany and certainly one of the most alluring along the Rhine Valley. It occupies two desirable plots of land near the center of town, a five-minute walk from the cathedral. Sheathed in reflective mirrors and soaring spans of steel, the hotel's twin sections are connected with a glass-sided covered walkway spanning the traffic below. There are enough bars, restaurants, nightlife possibilities, and health club facilities to amuse one for a week. Within each of its soaring yet still intimate meeting points, the hotel provides a lavish and elegant charm that is not lost on its up-market clientele. Within the labyrinthine interior are sun-flooded atriums with live plants, piano bars encrusted with polished mahogany and brass, and acres of marble flooring, along with some of the most plushly decorated guest rooms in the region, all with color TVs and radio.

Dining/Entertainment: The Rheingrill restaurant, overlooking the flowing waters of its namesake, is a fine dining place. However, many visitors prefer either the French-inspired Bistro or the rustic Romische Weinstube. At night, one of the bars becomes a disco, open until very late.

Services: Room service, laundry, dry cleaning, hairdresser.
Facilities: Sauna, supervised health and exercise club.

EXPENSIVE

ATRIUM HOTEL KURMAINZ, Flugplatzstrasse 44, D-6500 Mainz-Finthen. Tel. 06131/491-0. Fax 06131/49-11-28. 85 rms, 6 suites. MINIBAR

TV TEL **Directions:** Take the A60, exiting at the signposted turnoff for Mainz-Finthen. Drive through Finthen; the hotel is the last building on the right. **Bus:** 16.

$ **Rates** (including continental breakfast): 150 DM–220 DM ($99–$145.20) single; 190 DM–290 DM ($125.40–$191.40) double; from 320 DM ($211.20) suite. AE, DC, MC, V. **Parking:** Free in parking lot on grounds; 12 DM ($7.90) per night in 12-car indoor garage.

A modern hotel lying in the midst of orchards in the Rhine Valley, the Kurmainz is convenient to the nearby cities of Frankfurt and Wiesbaden and only 15 minutes from the Frankfurt airport. The atmosphere is inviting; the bar has an open fireplace, and the atrium garden has a brook, pond, and exotic plants. The accommodations are comfortable, with such extra amenities as personal safes and hairdryers. A wide range of sports facilities is available, including an indoor pool, sauna, steam bath, fitness center, and tennis court. The hotel has a French restaurant, Heinrich's Bar & Restaurant.

HOTEL MAINZER HOF, Kaiserstrasse 98, D-6500 Mainz. Tel. 06131/ 23-37-71. Fax 06131/22-82-55. 99 rms, 2 suites. MINIBAR TV TEL. **Bus:** 9 toward Schierstein, getting off at Kaisertor.

$ **Rates** (including continental breakfast): 159 DM–195 DM ($104.90–$128.70) single; 200 DM–290 DM ($132–$191.40) double; from 390 DM ($257.40) suite. AE, DC, MC, V. **Parking:** 8 DM ($5.30).

The Mainzer Hof is six floors of modernity directly on the Rhine, almost at the point where some of the boats dock. It's a clean-cut, convenient stopover on your journey down the Rhine. The rooms were completely renovated in 1987 and equipped with TVs and radios. Each is well furnished and comfortably maintained. In the basement is an Italian specialty restaurant, Rimini, and on the sixth floor is the restaurant Panorama Salon, which is reserved for groups. There is an inviting atmosphere in the lobby bar. Room service, laundry, and dry cleaning are provided. The Hauptbahnhof is a 10-minute walk from the hotel.

MODERATE

HAMMER, Bahnhofplatz 6, D-6500 Mainz. Tel. 06131/61-10-61. Fax 06131/61-10-65. 40 rms. MINIBAR TV TEL **Bus:** 16 or 23.

$ **Rates** (including buffet breakfast): 120 DM–150 DM ($79.20–$99) single; 150 DM–190 DM ($99–$125.40) double. AE, DC, MC, V. **Parking:** 10 DM ($6.60).

The Hammer has been completely renewed, with an inviting lobby and a breakfast room. The furnishings are modern, and the reception is bright. The rooms are comfortable and of good size, all accommodations coming with hairdryers, radios, and color TVs. The Hammer has a sauna, solarium, and fitness center.

INEXPENSIVE

HOTEL MIRA, Bonifaziusstrasse 4, D-6500 Mainz. Tel. 06131/96-01-30. Fax 06131/63-27-00. 42 rms (20 with bath or shower). TEL **Bus:** 16 or 23.

$ **Rates** (including continental breakfast): 65 DM ($42.90) single without bath, 105 DM ($69.30) single with bath; 98 DM ($64.70) double without bath, 165 DM ($108.90) double with bath. AE, DC, MC, V. **Parking:** 8 DM ($5.30).

The delicate pink of the facade hides a quiet but central elevator hotel. The Mira beckons warmly to tourists from its location near the Hauptbahnhof. Your host, Alfred Kohl provides maps (if available) and lots of useful information. Twenty units have TVs.

WHERE TO DINE

EXPENSIVE

DREI LILIEN, Ballplatz 2. Tel. 06131/22-50-68.
   Cuisine: FRENCH. **Reservations:** Required. **Bus:** 16 or 23.
$ **Prices:** Appetizers 15 DM–26 DM ($9.90–$17.20); main courses 39 DM–45

DM ($25.70–$29.70); fixed-price lunch 80 DM ($52.80); fixed-price dinner 85 DM–115 DM ($56.10–$75.90). AE, DC, MC, V.
Open: Lunch Tues–Sat noon–2pm; dinner Tues–Sat 6:30–10:30pm. **Closed:** 2 weeks in July–Aug (dates vary).

⭐ A good place to have an inspired French meal is Drei Lilien, where the chef practices a form of cuisine moderne that he has dubbed *cuisine du marché*. Everything is cooked with imagination and concern based on fresh seasonal ingredients. The decor of this wood-beamed, chandeliered eatery could be called "graciously rustic," the linens are impeccable, and the service is deferential. Try grilled steak with wild trumpet mushrooms in cognac sauce with grape leaves or delicately poached baby turbot in mushroom sauce. Table d'hôte dinners are offered along with à la carte meals.

MODERATE

GEBERT'S WEINSTUBEN, Frauenlobstrasse 94. Tel. 06131/61-16-19.
   Cuisine: FRENCH. **Reservations:** Required. **Bus:** 7 or 21.
$ **Prices:** Appetizers 12 DM–25 DM ($7.90–$16.50); main courses 24 DM–42 DM ($15.80–$27.70). AE, DC, MC, V.
   Open: Lunch Mon–Fri 11:30am–2pm; dinner Mon–Sat 6–10pm. **Closed:** Mid-July to mid-Aug.
A traditional Weinstube is housed in one of the oldest buildings of Mainz, with a decor that is almost Spartan when compared to the opulence of some of the city's other restaurants. But decor is not the reason people come here, and they patronize it in great numbers. Once seated, you are treated to a traditional meal of game, fish, or regional specialties, such as goose à l'orange.

HAUS DES DEUTSCHEN WEINES, Gutenbergplatz 3. Tel. 06131/22-86-76.
   Cuisine: INTERNATIONAL/GERMAN. **Reservations:** Recommended. **Bus:** 6, 15, or 23.
$ **Prices:** Appetizers 12 DM–22 DM ($7.90–$14.50); main courses 26 DM–48 DM ($17.20–$31.70); fixed-price lunch 28 DM–45 DM ($18.50–$29.70); fixed-price dinner 60 DM–95 DM ($39.60–$62.70). AE, DC, MC, V.
   Open: Lunch Mon–Sat 11:30am–3pm; dinner Mon–Sat 5pm–midnight. **Closed:** Holidays.

💲 The shields outside represent the German wine districts, and the cellar inside stocks the finest bottles from the Rheingau. An easy walk from the Dom and the Gutenberg Museum, the House of German Wines makes a fine dining choice. The cuisine is essentially modern international and "new German." Game is featured in season. Because the restaurant is affiliated with both the city of Mainz and the German Wine Institute, you can find a cross section of wines from the 11 leading wine regions of Germany.

ZUM AUGUSTINER, Augustinerstrasse 8. Tel. 06131/23-17-37.
   Cuisine: CONTINENTAL. **Reservations:** Recommended for dinner. **Bus:** 6, 15, or 23.
$ **Prices:** Appetizers 10 DM–16 DM ($6.60–$10.60); main courses 20 DM–25 DM ($13.20–$16.50). AE, DC, MC, V.
   Open: Daily noon–1am.
This was a popular beer hall before entrepreneur Thomas Heinecke took charge. Today, much of its space is devoted to a convivial pub counter, with a handful of simple tables set up in another part of its large premises. Set one floor above street level, it serves copious amounts of beer, the most prominent of which is a relatively weak light-colored brew from Cologne known as Kolsch. Don't overlook the excellent turkey salads that comprise one of the most popular lunchtime main courses. Equally popular are any of the fish dishes, the breast of Bresse hen, the filet of pork, and the beefsteaks, whose sauces and preparation change every day. The tempting desserts are made fresh daily.

INEXPENSIVE

WEINSTUBE LÖSCH, Jakobsbergstrasse 9. Tel. 06131/22-03-83.
  Cuisine: RHINELAND. **Reservations:** Recommended. **Bus:** 6, 15, or 23.
$ Prices: Appetizers 6.80 DM–10 DM ($4.50–$6.60); main courses 9.80 DM–
  28.50 DM ($6.50–$18.80). No credit cards.
  Open: Daily 4pm–1am.

⑤ This old-fashioned Weinstube in the heart of the Altstadt is popular with generations of Mainzers and rich in tradition. Meals offer both hot and cold dishes, plus lots of Rhine wine. The daily changing bill of fare offers regional dishes and interesting salads. There are only 12 tables, but they seat 85 guests. Now that the Jakobsbergstrasse has been changed into a pedestrian mall, the Weinstube places six additional tables out front in summer.

9. WORMS

28 miles S of Mainz; 27 miles SW of Darmstadt

GETTING THERE   **By Train**   The nearest airport is at Frankfurt (see Chapter 3), 43 miles away. But Worms enjoys good rail connections to major German cities. It lies on the main Mainz-Mannheim line, with frequent service. For rail information and schedules, call 06241/19-419.

By Bus   Regional bus service for the area is provided by BRN Busverkehr Rhein-Neckar GmbH (tel. 06241/43-178) in Worms.

By Car   From Mainz (see above), continue south along Route 9.

ESSENTIALS   For more tourist information, go to **Verkehrsverein,** Neumarkt 14, Rathausplatz (tel. 06241/85-35-60).

This ancient city traces its beginnings back to the earliest civilizations. Before the Romans settled here, Germanic peoples had made Worms their capital. Here Siegfried began his legendary adventures, recorded in *The Nibelungenlied*. The town's most famous visitor, Martin Luther, arrived under less desirable circumstances. He was "invited" to appear before the Imperial Diet at Worms, and after refusing to retract his grievances against the Church of Rome, he was declared an outlaw by the Holy Roman Emperor Charles V. Now that the majority of Worms is Protestant, it has erected a huge monument to Luther and other giants of the Reformation.

Worms also has one of the oldest Jewish communities in Germany, with a synagogue dating to the 11th century. The Hebrew cemetery is interesting, with hundreds of tombstones, some going back more than 900 years.

Towering physically and historically above all the other ancient buildings of the city is the majestic **✪ St. Peter's Cathedral,** Lutherring 9 (tel. 06241/61-15), considered the purest Romanesque basilica in the Rhine Valley. The east choir, with a flat facade and semicircular interior, is the oldest section, dating from 1132. This was designed as the sanctuary, where the clergy performed the rites of the divine service. Lavishly decorated in baroque style during the 18th century by the famous architect Balthasar Neumann, the chancel glows with the gold and marble of the pillared enclosure for the high altar. This opulent work was so large that there was no place for a proper transept. In Gothic times the choir stalls had stood in the apse, but later they were built into the transept. The interior has a quiet elegance, with little decoration other than the rosette window and several memorial slabs and monuments to the dead buried beneath the cathedral. Between these two extremes, which symbolize the coordination of ecclesiastical and secular power, is the nave. A new organ built like a bird's nest has been placed where an organ was situated until its destruction in 1689. Well worth seeing is the highly decorated 14th-century side Chapel of St. Nicholas, with its Gothic baptismal font and new stained-glass windows. The cathedral is open for visitors in spring through autumn, daily from 8am to 6pm; in winter, daily from 9am to 5pm. Bus: 2.

WHERE TO STAY

MODERATE

CENTRAL HOTEL WORMS, Kämmererstrasse 5, D-6520 Worms. Tel. 06241/64-58. Fax 06241/27-439. 19 rms. TV TEL **Bus:** 2.

$ Rates (including continental breakfast): 88 DM–98 DM ($58.10–$64.70) single; 140 DM–150 DM ($92.40–$99) double. AE, DC, MC, V. **Parking:** 8 DM ($5.30). **Closed:** Dec 20–Jan 6.

Completely renovated in 1988, this is now one of the best of the small hotels of the city. Innkeeper Agnes Labidi rents comfortably furnished rooms in her family-run hotel. The reception staff speaks English, and the hotel has an ideal central location, within walking distance of all the major historical monuments.

DOM-HOTEL, Am Obermarkt 10, D-6520 Worms. Tel. 06241/69-13. Fax 06241/23-515. 60 rms, 2 suites. A/C MINIBAR TV TEL

$ Rates (including buffet breakfast): 110 DM–125 DM ($72.60–$82.50) single; 145 DM–165 DM ($95.70–$108.90) double; from 220 DM ($145.20) suite. AE, DC, MC, V. **Parking:** Free.

This all-purpose hotel, about a block from the cathedral in the pedestrian zone, is a postwar structure that was recently renovated, built in a complex of shops and boutiques. The glass-walled guest rooms have an assortment of contemporary furnishings and offer adequate comfort. All contain TVs and radios.

The guest lounge is a good place for relaxation. In the wood-paneled dining room, a breakfast buffet is spread out, and later on, a French cuisine is served in the dining room, where meals begin at 46 DM ($30.40). Altogether, it's an ideal little hotel for an in-and-out traveler.

HOTEL NIBELUNGEN, Martinsgasse 16, D-6520 Worms. Tel. 06241/69-77. Fax 06241/872-10. 46 rms. MINIBAR TV TEL **Bus:** 2.

$ Rates (including buffet breakfast): 120 DM–140 DM ($79.20–$92.40) single; 180 DM–210 DM ($118.80–$138.60) double. AE, DC, MC, V. **Parking:** 12 DM ($7.90). **Closed:** Dec 24–Jan 3.

The newest and most luxuriously appointed place to stay in Worms is the Nibelungen, in the center of town. It offers modern comfort behind a yellow-and-mustard facade. Each room has a radio and TV. The well-furnished guest rooms are the best in town. Breakfast is the only meal served.

WHERE TO DINE

EXPENSIVE

RÔTISSERIE DUBS, Kirchstrasse 6, at Rheindurkheim. Tel. 06242/20-23.

Cuisine: CONTINENTAL. **Reservations:** Required. **Directions:** Route 9 north for 5 miles.

$ Prices: Appetizers 19 DM–32 DM ($12.50–$21.10); main courses 48 DM–52 DM ($31.70–$34.30); fixed-price menus 85 DM ($56.10) and 110 DM ($72.60). MC.

Open: Lunch Sun–Mon and Wed–Fri noon–2pm; dinner Wed–Mon 6pm–midnight.

Despite the rustic beams of the ceiling and the massive stonework of the fireplace, Rôtisserie Dubs has a feeling of elegant lightness. The light continental cuisine adds to that impression. After traveling through France, the owner, Wolfgang Dubs, decided to feature such dishes as salmon in champagne marinade and delicately seasoned pike-and-cabbage soup.

MODERATE

LE BISTRO LÉGER, Siegfriedstrasse 2. Tel. 06241/46-27-7.
Cuisine: RHINELAND. **Reservations:** Recommended. **Bus:** 2.
$ **Prices:** Appetizers 6 DM–14 DM ($4–$9.20); main courses 10.50 DM–34 DM ($6.90–$22.40). MC.
Open: Lunch Mon–Sat noon–2pm; dinner Mon–Sat 5pm–midnight.

Le Bistro Léger is stylish and nostalgically decorated, with a regional cuisine and a middle-bracket price structure. An outdoor terrace is much favored in warm weather. Fresh ingredients go into the food; try, for example, veal cutlets prepared in the style of the Rhineland, fish filet, oysters in season, or roast beef. The well-chosen wine list is mainly French.

10. SPEYER

58 miles S of Mainz; 13 miles SW of Heidelberg

GETTING THERE By Train You can reach Speyer by train from either Heidelberg or Mannheim, the biggest cities near Speyer. Trains run several times during the day. Trains from Munich take five to six hours. Call 06232/19-419 for schedules.

By Bus Buses from Heidelberg arrive at the rate of about one per hour. A "City Shuttle" (bus) runs from the Speyer Hauptbahnhof through the town to the Festplatz near the Dom (Cathedral) at the east of the old town. It connects most of the major hotels and restaurants.

By Car You can drive from Frankfurt in about an hour (or allow a trip time of two hours by train). It takes about four hours to drive from Munich. Access is by autobahn A61 east and west connecting with Route 9, a state highway south. Regional service is provided by BRN Busverkehr Rhein-Neckar GmbH at Ludwigshafen (tel. 0621/51-21-22).

ESSENTIALS For tourist information, go to **Verkehrsamt,** Maximillianstrasse 11 (tel. 06232/143-95).

As one of the oldest Rhine cities of the Holy Roman Empire, Speyer celebrated its 2,000th jubilee in 1990. It early became an important religious center, culminating in the Diet of Speyer, which in 1529 united the followers of Luther in a protest against the the Church of Rome. Nothing recalls this medieval German empire as much as the ○ **Domkapitel** (Imperial Cathedral), Domplatz 3 (tel. 06232/10-22-59), in Speyer, perhaps the greatest building of its time. The Cathedral of Speyer, consecrated in the early 11th century, is the largest Romanesque edifice in Germany. Having weathered the damage of fires and wars and other restorations, the cathedral was restored from 1957 to 1961 to its original shape. Entering the church through the single west door set in a stepped arch, you are immediately caught up in the vastness of the proportions, as the whole length of the nave and east chancel opens up before you. Lit by the muted daylight from above, it contains the royal tombs of four Holy Roman emperors and four German kings, as well as a row of bishops' tombs. The cathedral is open April 1 to September 30, Monday to Friday from 9am to 7pm; Saturday from 9am to 4pm; Sunday from 1:30 to 4:30pm. In winter, hours are 9am to 5pm on weekdays; Saturday 9am to 4pm; and Sunday 1:30 to 4:30pm. Entrance to the crypt is free.

WHERE TO STAY

MODERATE

AM WARTTURM, Landwehrstrasse 30, D-6720 Speyer. Tel. 06232/360-66. 13 rms (all with shower). TEL **Transportation:** City shuttle.
$ Rates (including continental breakfast): 90 DM–110 DM ($59.40–$72.60) single; 140 DM–160 DM ($92.40–$105.60) double. No credit cards. **Parking:** Free.
In this modern little guesthouse, owner Herr Koithahn rents simply furnished units. He will arrange for an evening meal if you request it. Service is polite and attentive.

GRAF'S HOTEL LÖWENGARTEN, Schwerdstrasse 14, D-6720 Speyer. Tel. 06232/7-10-51. Fax 06323/26-452. 42 rms. MINIBAR TV TEL **Transportation:** City shuttle.
$ Rates (including continental breakfast): 129 DM–155 DM ($85.10–$102.30) single; 165 DM–205 DM ($108.90–$135.30) double. AE, DC, MC, V. **Parking:** 8 DM ($5.30).
Karl-Heinz Graf is your host at this well-known hotel and restaurant several blocks from the cathedral. The rooms, all with color TVs, are simply but comfortably furnished with modern styling. Regional meals in the restaurant begin at 40 DM ($26.40).

RHEIN-HOTEL LUXHOF, D-6832 Hockenheim. Tel. 06205/30-30. Fax 06205/303-25. 45 rms. TV TEL **Transportation:** City shuttle.
$ Rates (including buffet breakfast): 75 DM–92 DM ($49.50–$60.70) single; 115 DM–160 DM ($75.90–$105.60) double. AE, DC, MC, V. **Parking:** Free.
⑤ At the Rhine Bridge just outside the town is a hotel of unusual character. It's modern in style, but somehow the spirit of a rambling country inn has been retained. The dining rooms are charming and colorful. The guest rooms are well designed and compact, often featuring small sitting areas that open onto tiny balconies. The hotel has a sauna, a solarium, and other fitness facilities.

INEXPENSIVE

TRUTZPFAFF, Webergasse 5, D-6720 Speyer. Tel. 06232/7-83-99. 8 rms. **Transportation:** City shuttle.
$ Rates (including continental breakfast): 69 DM ($45.50) single; 95 DM ($62.70) double. No credit cards. **Parking:** 5 DM ($3.30).
Conveniently located near the cathedral, this family-run guesthouse offers personalized service from the English-speaking owner, Edgar Ulses. Rooms are pleasantly furnished. The location is in the city center.

WHERE TO DINE

EXPENSIVE

BACKMULDE, Karmeliterstrasse 11–13. Tel. 06232/7-15-77.
Cuisine: FRENCH/SEAFOOD. **Reservations:** Required. **Transportation:** City shuttle.
$ Prices: Appetizers 18 DM–26 DM ($11.90–$17.20); main courses 36 DM–48 DM ($23.80–$31.70); fixed-price lunch 48 DM ($31.70); fixed-price dinner 110 DM–130 DM ($72.60–$85.80). AE, DC, MC, V.

Open: Lunch Tues–Sat 11:30am–1:30pm; dinner Mon–Sat 7–9pm. **Closed:** 3 weeks end of Aug to mid-Sept.

In what used to be a bakery, the Backmulde is owned by Gunter Schmidt, who has researched the centuries-old recipes of the Palatinate, added a modern touch, and come up with a combination that has made this the most important restaurant in Speyer. You can savor such unusual delicacies as gratinée of oysters in champagne sabayon, quail stuffed with well-seasoned sweetbreads, and roast baby lamb with freshly picked spinach.

CHAPTER 7

HEIDELBERG, STUTTGART & THE NECKAR VALLEY

- **WHAT'S SPECIAL ABOUT HEIDELBERG, STUTTGART & THE NECKAR VALLEY**
1. **HEIDELBERG**
2. **THE NECKAR VALLEY**
3. **STUTTGART**
4. **TÜBINGEN**
5. **SCHWÄBISCH HALL**

Ancient castle ruins in the midst of thick woodlands, quiet university towns, busy manufacturing centers—all this truly belongs to the countryside of southwestern Germany, extending along the Neckar River from Heidelberg past medieval towns and modern cities as far as Tübingen. The Neckar flows between the Black Forest and the Schwäbische Alb; although the river is open to commercial shipping vessels as far as Stuttgart, much of the valley has remained unspoiled. This area has been the cradle of German royal families for centuries. The castles that rise around every bend in the river were once home to the Hohenstaufen and Hohenzollern. Some ruins were once summer palaces of kings and emperors. Today, some castles and country palaces offer bed and board to travelers.

SUGGESTED ITINERARY

Day 1 Explore Heidelberg, visiting its historic castle, and see nearby Schloss Schwetzingen, before spending the evening in the student drinking clubs.

Day 2 Travel east in the Neckar Valley, stopping for the night in a historic town like Hirschhorn or Eberbach.

Day 3 Devote a day to Stuttgart, seeing its State Gallery of Stuttgart and the Porsche and Mercedes-Benz museums. Try to attend a performance of the Stuttgart Ballet in the evening.

Day 4 Cap your tour of the region by heading south to Tübingen for a day strolling the old streets of this university town, which some visitors like even more than Heidelberg.

GETTING THERE

Heidelberg and Stuttgart are your principal gateways to the region. The nearest major airports are at Frankfurt (see Chapter 3) and Stuttgart (see below). There's easy access by rail or auto to all major towns along the Neckar. Express trains connect Heidelberg

WHAT'S SPECIAL ABOUT HEIDELBERG, STUTTGART & THE NECKAR VALLEY

Great Towns

- ☐ Heidelberg, of *The Student Prince* fame, a university town since 1386. Known for its castle, largely in ruins.
- ☐ Tübingen, often compared to Heidelberg, a university town on the upper Neckar, with gabled medieval houses.
- ☐ Stuttgart, home of Mercedes and Porsche automobiles, the leading cultural center of southwest Germany.

Ace Attractions

- ☐ The Neckar Valley, a lovely river valley with medieval towns like Hirschhorn.
- ☐ Student Drinking Clubs of Heidelberg, a historic tradition at such places as Zum Roter Ochsen (Red Ox Inn). Notables like Mark Twain and Bismarck have raised a stein in them.

Historic Castles

- ☐ Heidelberg Castle, a dignified red-sandstone ruin today after plundering and burning.
- ☐ Schloss Schwetzingen, outside Heidelberg, summer residence of the Palatine electors.

Museum

- ☐ State Gallery of Stuttgart, noted for 19th- and 20th-century art, especially works of German Expressionists.

Architectural Highlight

- ☐ Marktplatz at Schwäbisch Hall, possibly the most attractive market square in Germany, with fine half-timbered patrician houses.

Cultural Highlight

- ☐ The Stuttgart Ballet, one of the world's premier ballet troupes.

and Stuttgart. Heidelberg and Heilbronn (see below) are linked by both autobahn and train.

1. HEIDELBERG

75 miles NW of Stuttgart; 12 miles SE of Mannheim; 55 miles S of Frankfurt

GETTING THERE By Plane The nearest major airport is at Frankfurt (see Chapter 3), with a direct bus link to Heidelberg. Call 06221/10-099 for more travel information.

By Train Heidelberg's Hauptbahnhof is an important railroad station, lying on the Mannheim line with frequent service both to regional towns and major cities, including Cologne, Munich, and Basel (Switzerland). Forty trains per day connect Heidelberg with Frankfurt (trip time: 1 hour); and 20 trains per day run to Stuttgart (trip time: 45 minutes to 1 hour and 15 minutes, depending on train). Travel by rail to and from Munich takes about 3½ hours. For rail information, call 06221/20-845.

By Bus Regional bus service in the Neckar Valley (see below) is provided by BRN Busverkehr Rhein-Neckar at Heidelberg (tel. 06221/16-24-46).

By Car Access by car to Heidelberg is via autobahn A5 on German routes north or south and by state highway 45 east and north. From autobahn A5, head east at the junction with Route 45.

ESSENTIALS Information Contact the **Tourist-Information,** Pavillon am Hauptbahnhof (tel. 06221/2-13-41).

Orientation The Neckar River forms the northern periphery of the heart of Heidelberg, but wherever you go, Heidelberg Castle looms over you (locals refer to it as *das Schloss*). If you arrive by train, you'll be deposited at the Hauptbahnhof in the "west end," a modern sector that hardly lives up to the image of romantic Heidelberg. It opens onto a street, Kurfüstenanlage, that leads east to the Altstadt via Adenauerplatz.

If Heidelberg has a main street, it is the Hauptstrasse, where you'll find the city's major taverns, shops, and many restaurants. This street begins just north of Adenauerplatz on another square, Bismarckplatz, and stretches to Karlsplatz, a long but interesting walk. The major bridge of town is the Theodor Heuss Brücke. In the heart of the Altstadt is the Alte Brücke, dating from the late 18th century. The more contemporary part of Heidelberg is west of Bismarckplatz.

Summertime in Heidelberg, according to the song from the popular operetta *The Student Prince,* is a time for music and romance. Today it's also a time when droves of visitors invade this city on the Neckar—and with cause. Heidelberg is one of the few large German cities not leveled by air raids in World War II, and important buildings date from the latter part of the Middle Ages and early Renaissance.

Heidelberg is, above all, a university town and has been since 1386. Students make up much of the population. The colorful atmosphere that university life imparts to the town is felt especially in the old student quarter, with its narrow streets and lively inns. This oldest university in Germany is officially named **Ruprecht-Karl-University,** honoring its founder, Elector Ruprecht I of the Palatinate, and the man who in 1803 made it the leading university in the state of Baden, Margrave Karl Friedrich. The school was founded after the Great Schism of 1378, when conflicting claims to the papacy created unrest, and German teachers and students fled the Sorbonne in Paris. A papal bull from Urban VI in Rome authorized the founding of the University of Heidelberg.

The university grew rapidly. Monastic in character at first, it changed in the 16th century with the appointment of a married rector. The so-called Old University was built in the early 18th century, the New University constructed nearby from 1930 to 1932. Funds for this structure came from many American sources, including Henry Ford. Today lecture halls, institutes, seminar buildings, and clinics are scattered all over town, but a new university quarter is being developed on the plain in the Neuenheim district, with multistory buildings and a modern cancer research center. Seven university scientists have been recipients of Nobel prizes in chemistry, physics, and medicine.

Modern Heidelberg is centered around Bismarck Square at the foot of the Theodor Heuss Brücke. The tall buildings and shopping plazas contrast with the Altstadt nearby. In the new city you will find many of the best hotels and restaurants. Across the Neckar are sports grounds, a zoo, and a large botanical garden.

WHAT TO SEE & DO

All the important sights of Heidelberg lie on or near the south bank of the Neckar, and you must cross the river (via the 18th-century Karl Theodore Bridge) for the best overall view. **Philosophen Weg** (Philosopher's Way), halfway up the mountain on the north bank, is best for viewing. And above the brown roofs of the town on the opposite bank is the rose-pink major attraction of Heidelberg, the castle.

THE TOP ATTRACTION

HEIDELBERG CASTLE. Tel. 06221/2-00-70.

✪ In its magnificent setting of woodland and terraced gardens, the huge red-sandstone castle is reached from the town below by several routes. If you're not taking the cable car (see below), you may drive to the winding Neue Schlosstrasse, past the old houses perched on the hillside. This is also a walking route, rewarding because of the constantly changing view of the town and surrounding countryside. For a shorter walk, you can climb the steep Burgweg from the Kornmarkt or take the more gradual walk from the Klingentor.

The castle is only a dignified ruin today. Even in its deteriorated state, it's considered one of the finest Gothic-Renaissance castles in Germany. Entering the castle walls at the main gate, you first come upon the huge **Gun Park** to your left, from which you can gaze down upon Heidelberg and the Neckar Valley. Straight ahead is the Thick Tower, or what remains of it after its 25-foot walls were blown up by the French in the late 17th century. Leaving the Gun Park via Elizabeth's Gate, erected by Friedrich V in 1615 for his Scottish wife, Elizabeth Stuart, daughter of James I, you come to the Bridge House and the bridge crossing the site of the former moat.

Through the entrance tower lies the **castle courtyard,** the heart of the complex of structures. Surrounding it are buildings dating from the 13th to the 17th century. You'll notice that nature has done its best to repair the ravages by covering the gaping holes and roofless sections with ivy and shrubbery. Walking around the courtyard in a clockwise fashion, you come first to the Gothic **Ruprecht Building,** built about 1400. Adjacent is the **library,** with a Gothic oriel window dating from the early 16th century. It once housed the library of Ludwig V.

The **Frauenzimmer** (Women's Room) was originally a three-story Gothic-Renaissance building housing the ladies of the court, but today only the ground level, the King's Hall, remains.

Along the north side of the courtyard stretches the stern palace of Friedrich IV, erected from 1601 to 1607. Less damaged than other parts of the castle, it has been almost completely restored, including the gallery of princes and kings of the German Empire from the time of Charlemagne. The palace has its own terrace, the Altan, which offers a splendid view of the plain of the Neckar. The ancient bell tower, at the northeast end of the Altan, dates from the early 1500s.

At the west end of the terrace, in the cellars of the castle, is the Wine Vat Building, built in the late 16th century and worth a visit for a look at the **Great Cask,** symbol of the abundant and exuberant life of the Rhineland-Palatinate. This huge barrel-like monstrosity, built in 1751, is capable of holding more than 55,000 gallons of wine.

On the east, connecting the palace of Friedrich IV to the **Ottheinrich Building,** itself an outstanding example of German Renaissance architecture, is the **Hall of Mirrors Building,** constructed in 1549—a Renaissance masterpiece. Only the shell of the original building remains, enough to give you an idea of its former glory, with its arcades and steep gables decorated with cherubs and sirens.

Next to Ottheinrich's palace is the Chemist's Tower, housing the **Pharmaceutical Museum.** The museum, on the tower's ground floor, shows a chemist's shop with utensils and laboratory equipment from the 18th and 19th centuries. It is open during the usual castle visiting hours, and admission is 3 DM ($2).

Returning to the Castle Gate, you will pass the old barracks for the soldiers of the garrison. Next to the barracks is the former well house, its roof supported by ancient Roman columns. Some of the household buildings, such as the bakery, kitchen, smithshop, and butchery nearby, have been restored.

In summer you can enjoy serenades and concerts in the large castle courtyard. But the biggest spectacle is the **castle illumination,** commemorating the battles of the 17th century. Several times throughout the summer, at dates rescheduled yearly, the castle is floodlit and fireworks are set off above it.

Tours: Interior can be visited only on 1-hour guided tour for 5 DM ($3.30) adults, 2.50 DM ($1.70) children. Tours are frequent, especially in summer.

Admission: Grounds free; visit to Great Cask without tour, 2 DM ($1.30) adults, 1 DM (66¢) children.

Open: Daily 9am–4pm. **Cable car:** Two-minute ride from platform near Kornmarkt (Grain Market)—4.50 DM ($3) round trip.

MORE ATTRACTIONS

Back in the town itself, a tour of the main attractions begins with the **Marktplatz** in front of the Rathaus. On market days the square is filled with stalls of fresh flowers, fish, and vegetables. At the opposite end of the square is the late Gothic **Church of the Holy Ghost,** built about 1400. For nearly 300 years the church was the burial place of the electors, but most of the graves were destroyed in the French invasion late in the 17th century. In 1706, a wall was erected to divide the church, giving both Catholics and Protestants a portion in which to worship. The wall has since been removed and the church restored to its original plan. Around the corner from the church is the famous old mansion **Zum Ritter,** recommended in the hotel listings below.

KURPFÄLZISCHES MUSEUM [Museum of the Palatinate], Hauptstrasse 97. Tel. 06221/58-34-00.

If you follow the Hauptstrasse, you'll arrive at the Museum of the Palatinate, housed in a baroque palace. The museum presents a large collection of painting and sculpture from six centuries, among them the Riemenschneider Altar from Windsheim (1509) with Christ and the Twelve Apostles. There is also a cast of the jawbone of the Heidelberg Man, some 500,000 years old; an archeological collection; examples of history and culture of the Palatinate; and paintings from the Romantic period.

Admission: 1 DM (66¢) adults; children free.
Open: Tues and Thurs–Sun 10am–5pm, Wed 10am–9pm. **Bus:** 10, 12, or 35.

STUDENTKRANZER [Student Jail], Augustinergasse 2. Tel. 06221/54-23-34.

The walls and even the ceilings of the prison are covered with graffiti and drawings, including portraits and silhouettes. The last prisoners were held here in 1914. Ring the caretaker's bell (same address) for admission.

Admission: 1 DM (66¢) adults; 0.70 DM (50¢) students.
Open: Mon–Sat 9am–5pm. **Closed:** Holidays. **Bus:** 10, 12, or 35.

A NEARBY ATTRACTION

SCHLOSS SCHWETZINGEN, D-6830 Schwetzingen. Tel. 06202/81-481.

The 18th-century Palatine electors journeyed 7 miles west of Heidelberg to their summer residence, Schloss Schwetzingen. Along this route came Voltaire, a host of other famous visitors, and some of the artistic and intellectual elite of their era. In 1991, after years of restoration, the famous castle reopened to visitors. Guided tours depart on the hour, sweeping through the largest of the castle's 40 rooms. The gardens, laid out in rococo style, are adorned with artfully arranged ruins, temples, and sculptures. A mosque suggests the Middle East; watercourses, fountains, live animals, and flower beds complete the picture, which the electors found "a paradise on earth." The best time to visit the gardens is during late spring and early summer, when lilacs and linden trees are in bloom.

Tours: Daily 9am–4pm, departing within castle on the hour.
Admission: Castle tour and gardens, 8 DM ($5.30) adults, 4 DM ($2.60) children. Gardens (without castle tour), 2.50 DM ($1.70) adults, 1.50 DM ($1) children.
Open: Gardens Apr–Sept, daily 8am–8pm; Oct–Mar, daily 9am–6pm. **Transportation:** From Heidelberg, take a tram labeled "Eppelheim" from the Bismarckplatz. At the end of the line, change to a bus labeled "Schwetzingen." The

combined one-way passage to the town of Schwetzingen costs 7.10 DM ($4.70). Buses stop in front of the palace.

WHERE TO STAY

VERY EXPENSIVE

DER EUROPÄISCHE HOF-HOTEL EUROPA, Friedrich-Ebert-Anlage 1, D-6900 Heidelberg. Tel. 06221/515-0, or toll free 800/223-5652 or 800/223-6800 in the U.S. or Canada. Fax 06221/51-55-55. 121 rms, 14 suites. A/C MINIBAR TV TEL **Tram:** Bismarckplatz.

$ Rates: 279 DM–299 DM ($184.10–$197.30) single; 370 DM–400 DM ($244.20–$264) double; from 680 DM ($448.80) suite. Buffet breakfast 25 DM ($16.50) per person extra. AE, DC, MC, V. **Parking:** 25 DM ($16.50).

✪ Fronting the city park in the heart of town, within walking distance of the castle and the university, is Heidelberg's glamour hotel. Its interior is like that of a gracious home, with antiques, crystal chandeliers, and Oriental rugs. Some rooms and several suites with separate bedrooms and sitting rooms face a quiet inside garden. Each room is individually decorated with rich, traditional taste and has a radio, room safe, and trouser press. Most are air-conditioned, and the more expensive doubles contain alcoves. Nineteen units have whirlpool tubs.

Dining/Entertainment: Meals are served in the Louis XVI restaurant, in the Garden Room (where windows can be lowered to floor level), or in the finely paneled Kurfürstenstube. Before dinner, guests congregate around the curved bar in the wood-paneled lounge. In summer, meals are served on the open terrace with a view of the water fountains.

Services: Room service, laundry, dry cleaning.

Facilities: Shopping arcade, cafeteria Europ-Treff, fitness center, pool, massage room, sun terrace.

HEIDELBERG PENTA HOTEL, Vangerowstrasse 16, D-6900 Heidelberg. Tel. 06221/90-80. Fax 06221/22977. 251 rms, 12 junior suites, 4 senior suites. A/C MINIBAR TV TEL **Tram:** Bergheimer Strasse.

$ Rates: 340 DM ($224.40) single; 600 DM ($396) double; 500 DM and 1,000 DM ($330 and $660) suite. Buffet breakfast 25 DM ($16.50) extra. AE, DC, MC, V. **Parking:** Free.

This modern building sits on the river opposite the University Medical Research complex and just minutes from the city center, with easy access by bus or car. Most of the comfortable rooms have views over the river or the hills.

Dining/Entertainment: The elegant Globetrotter Restaurant (open daily from 6:30am to 10pm), with a terrace, has views over the gardens and river. It offers local and international specialties as well as health foods. The pub Pinte serves draft beer, wines, and light meals (daily from noon to 10pm). The lobby bar is the ideal meeting place for relaxing over drinks.

Services: Room service, laundry, dry cleaning.

Facilities: Health club with indoor pool, sauna, solarium, massage parlor, exercise area; hair and beauty salon; boutique; boat landing area.

HOLIDAY INN CROWNE PLAZA, Kurfürstenanlage 1, D-6900 Heidelberg. Tel. 06221/91-70. Fax 06221/21-007. 232 rms, 4 suites. A/C MINIBAR TV TEL **Bus:** 10, 12, or 35.

$ Rates: 284 DM–324 DM ($187.40–$213.80) single; 338 DM–378 DM ($223.10–$249.50) double; from 550 DM ($363) suite. Continental breakfast 24 DM ($15.80) extra. AE, DC, MC, V. **Parking:** 2 DM ($1.30) per hour.

Opened in 1988, the Holiday Inn quickly became one of the best-rated hotels in the city. In the center of Heidelberg, at Adenauerplatz, it is convenient for touring the major attractions. This first-class hotel with a number of facilities offers well-furnished guest rooms.

Dining/Entertainment: The stylish restaurants include the Palatina, open only for dinner, and the less expensive Atrium. There is also a cozy cocktail bar.

Services: Room service, laundry.
Facilities: Fitness center with an indoor pool.

HOTEL HIRSCHGASSE, Hirschgasse 3, D-6900 Heidelberg. Tel. 06221/403-21-60. Fax 06221/40-32-161. 20 suites. MINIBAR TV TEL

$ **Rates:** 295 DM ($194.70) junior suite for two; 350 DM–450 DM ($231–$297) senior suite for two; 550 DM–650 DM ($363–$429) executive suite for two. Buffet breakfast 25 DM ($16.50) per person extra. AE, DC, MC, V. **Parking:** 20 DM ($13.20). **Closed:** Dec 23–Jan.

⭐ This historic guesthouse dating from 1472 figured in the well-known love story of the poet Friedrich von Soest and the daughter of the Hirschgasse's innkeeper. Among its stellar lodgers have been the noted 18th-century German poet Hölderlin; Mark Twain; and Bismarck, honored with a suite named after him, including a Jacuzzi no less. The Hirschgasse, nestled on the hillside of a historic lane adjoining Philosopher's Way, is today a country home–style hotel, owned by the English-speaking Kraft family, who run the superb Prinzhotel Heidelberg.

In 1988 its guest rooms were reconstructed as suites, decorated in Laura Ashley designs. Each has a salon, a separate toilet, double wash basins, and a Jacuzzi. For American guests there is cable TV news from home.

Dining/Entertainment: Regional, traditional, and modern cuisine is offered in the hotel restaurant, which since 1472 has been attracting diners from Europe and abroad. It is open Monday to Saturday from 6pm to midnight, charging from 82 DM ($54.10) per person for dinner. The Studentenstube keeps alive the atmosphere of the old student fraternities.

Services: Laundry, babysitting, room service.
Facilities: Horseback riding and golf arranged, terrace garden.

EXPENSIVE

ACOR, Friedrich-Ebert-Anlage 55, D-6900 Heidelberg. Tel. 06221/2-20-44. Fax 06221/28-609. 18 rms. MINIBAR TV TEL **Bus:** 33 or 34.

$ **Rates** (including buffet breakfast): 165 DM ($108.90) single; 235 DM ($155.10) double. AE, DC, MC, V. **Parking:** 20 DM ($13.20).

Acor is a recommendable hotel that was converted from an old patrician house. An elevator has been installed, and the furnishings have been updated. Most rooms are compact (although a few are large) and quite comfortable. The buffet breakfast is served in a little room overlooking a small rear garden. The street is busy with traffic, but soundproof windows have been installed.

PRINZHOTEL HEIDELBERG, Neuenheimer Landstrasse 5, D-6900 Heidelberg. Tel. 06221/4-03-20. Fax 06221/40-32-196. 50 rms, 5 penthouse suites. MINIBAR TV TEL **Bus:** 10, 12, or 35.

$ **Rates:** 185 DM–295 DM ($122.10–$194.70) single or double; 295 DM–350 DM ($194.70–$231) suite. Buffet breakfast 25 DM ($16.50) extra. AE, DC, MC, V. **Parking:** 20 DM ($13.20).

⭐ In the center of town and near the Congress Hall is this first-class hotel owned and managed by the Kraft family. Each accommodation is furnished with sleek modern styling and is well maintained, complete with bathrobes, a laid-out toilet set, and a hairdryer. The hotel offers personal service.

Dining/Entertainment: Breakfast, the only meal provided, is served in the restaurant, Stars, with a view of the Neckar.

Services: Room service, laundry, babysitting.
Facilities: Pool club, with hot whirlpool and Roman steambath.

ZUM RITTER ST. GEORG, Hauptstrasse 178, D-6900 Heidelberg. Tel. 06221/2-42-72, or toll free 800/826-0015 in the U.S. Fax 06221/126-83. 40 rms. MINIBAR TV TEL **Bus:** 10, 11, or 12.

$ **Rates** (including buffet breakfast): 140 DM–240 DM ($92.40–$158.40) single; 230 DM–320 DM ($151.80–$211.20) double. AE, DC, MC, V.

A glorious old inn right out of the German Renaissance, Zum Ritter is a well-preserved rarity. Built in 1592 by the Frenchman Charles Bélier, it is now listed among the major sightseeing attractions of this university town, having survived the destruction wrought by Louis XIV's troops in 1693. Deep in the heart of the student area of drinking houses and nightclubs, Zum Ritter holds its own. There are no public lounges; the guest rooms play second fiddle to the fine restaurant downstairs. Furnishings are in a functional modern style.

MODERATE

HOTEL ANLAGE, Friedrich-Ebert-Anlage 32, D-6900 Heidelberg. Tel. 06221/2-64-25. Fax 06221/16-44-26. 20 rms (all with bath or shower). TV TEL **Bus:** 12 or 33.
$ Rates (including continental breakfast): 99 DM–119 DM ($65.30–$78.50) single; 140 DM–179 DM ($92.40–$118.10) double. AE, DC, MC, V.

In the heart of the city, Hotel Anlage stands on the street leading up to *das Schloss,* the castle. With its richly ornate facade, it occupies one wing of a lavishly built late 19th-century palace of orange brick and carved stone. The structure, built in 1892, has been well adapted to its present use as one of the best budget hotels in the city. It rents cozy guest rooms, each with cable TV (with English programs). The pleasant restaurant is reserved for guests.

HOLLÄNDER HOF, Neckarstaden 66, D-6900 Heidelberg. Tel. 06221/1-20-91. Fax 06221/22-085. 40 rms. TV TEL **Bus:** 10, 12, or 35.
$ Rates (including continental breakfast): 120 DM–235 DM ($79.20–$155.10) single; 180 DM–285 DM ($118.80–$188.10) double. AE, DC, MC, V.
Holländer Hof, in the heart of old Heidelberg, has an enviable position opening onto Alte Brücke. A pink-and-white building, it was one of the town's 12 guesthouses in medieval days. Rebuilt after a fire in 1693, it has hosted many celebrated visitors over the years. Today it offers renovated and attractively furnished rooms, all with hair-dryers, safes, radios; some also offer minibars. Six rooms are wheelchair-accessible.

HOTEL MONPTI, Friedrich-Ebert-Anlage 57, D-6900 Heidelberg. Tel. 06221/2-34-83. Fax 06221/24-395. 14 rms. MINIBAR TV TEL **Bus:** 10, 11, 12, and 33.
$ Rates (including continental breakfast): 145 DM ($95.70) single; 170 DM ($112.20) double. MC. **Parking:** Free.

A small hotel with sophisticated charm, the Monpti is run on a personal basis. The owner, Peter Mack, was born in this stately little town house in 1939. After traveling extensively, especially in Spain, he returned to his native town and converted his home into a super guesthouse, utilizing both his inherent and his acquired tastes. Built in the neoclassical style, the Monpti is painted an olive green with a distinctive architectural trim in white. Each guest room has color and freshness. All the practical items are behind doors, and your chamber is furnished like a little salon.

There's a petite breakfast room where guests gather over morning coffee. The owner has transformed the lower level (built on a hillside) into the bodega Vinothek, where he, his wife, and his friends gather in the evening to enjoy paella. Perhaps a Spanish guitarist will provide background music when you are there. The restaurant is open daily from 7am to 1am.

NECKAR-HOTEL HEIDELBERG, Bismarckstrasse 19, D-6900 Heidelberg. Tel. 06221/1-08-14. Fax 06221/23-260. 35 rms. TV TEL **Bus:** 10, 12, or 35.
$ Rates (including continental breakfast): 140 DM–180 DM ($92.40–$118.80) single; 180 DM–230 DM ($118.80–$151.80) double. AE, MC, V. **Parking:** Free. **Closed:** Dec 20–Jan 7.
The Neckar-Hotel Heidelberg enjoys an enviable position on the Neckar River near

the center of the university town. There is no garden, but a superb view. The facilities are substantial and comfortable, the guest rooms fitted with Germanic-modern pieces. Breakfast is the only meal served.

PARKHOTEL ATLANTIC, Schloss-Wolfsbrunnen-Weg 23, D-6900 Heidelberg. Tel. 06221/2-45-45. Fax 06221/16-40-54. 23 rms. MINIBAR TV TEL **Directions:** From the Hauptbahnhof, head east along Kürfursten-Anlage going through the tunnel. After the tunnel, take the second right, bringing you to Heidelberg Castle. Continue straight beyond the castle until you see the hotel.

$ Rates (including buffet breakfast): 135 DM–200 DM ($89.10–$132) single; 180 DM–220 DM ($118.80–$145.20) double. DC, MC, V. **Parking:** 10 DM ($6.60).

On the wooded outskirts of Heidelberg, near Heidelberg Castle, this rather grand hotel offers modern comfort in annexes built around the core of an older villa. The surrounding park is full of trees, and visitors are assured of calm and comfort. Often they take advantage of the many woodland trails extending through the Neckar Valley. The rooms are decorated in circa-1965 modern.

HOTEL VIER JAHRESZEITEN, Haspelgasse 2, D-6900 Heidelberg. Tel. 06221/2-41-64. Fax 06221/16-31-10. 22 rms (16 with bath). TV TEL **Bus:** 35.

$ Rates (including continental breakfast): 75 DM ($49.50) single without bath, 155 DM ($102.30) single with bath; 120 DM ($79.20) double without bath, 210 DM ($138.60) double with bath. AE, DC, MC, V. **Parking:** 15 DM ($9.90).

The Vier Jahreszeiten lives up to its name and is a worthy choice in any of the "four seasons." The location is by the Alte Brücke in the heart of Heidelberg, the starting point for many interesting walks. You can walk not only to the castle but also to many old student inns. The hotel has been improved over the years, and rooms are comfortable if perhaps dated.

HOTEL ZUM PFALZGRAFEN, Kettengasse 21, D-6900 Heidelberg. Tel. 06221/2-04-89. 28 rms (16 with shower). **Bus:** 33 from Hauptbahnhof to Peterskirche.

$ Rates (including continental breakfast): 65 DM–70 DM ($42.90–$46.20) single without shower, 95 DM–105 DM ($62.70–$69.30) single with shower; 90 DM–100 DM ($59.40–$66) double or twin without shower, 140 DM–145 DM ($92.40–$95.70) double with shower. AE, DC, MC, V. **Parking:** Available on street.

A simple town inn, this hotel stands in the heart of old Heidelberg, only a 15-minute walk from most major sights. The best rooms contain private showers and are priced accordingly. The bargains, however, are the rooms with hot and cold running water only. Showers are on the same floor.

WHERE TO DINE

VERY EXPENSIVE

KURFÜRSTENSTUBE, in Der Europäische Hof-Hotel Europa, Friedrich-Ebert-Anlage 1. Tel. 06221/515-0.
Cuisine: FRENCH. **Reservations:** Required. **Tram:** Bismarckplatz.
$ Prices: Appetizers 12 DM–36 DM ($7.90–$23.80); main courses 42 DM–58 DM ($27.70–$38.30); fixed-price lunch 48 DM ($31.70); fixed-price dinner 120 DM ($79.20). AE, DC, MC, V.
Open: Lunch daily noon–2:30pm; dinner daily 6:30–11pm.

⭐ The best dining spot in Heidelberg is the Kurfürstenstube, occupying a ground-floor wing of this outstanding hotel. The wood-paneled grill room is attractively decorated with provincial furnishings, pewter plates, and a stein collection. The menu is in English, but the cuisine is mainly French, with both fixed-price and à la carte meals. Specialties include homemade goose-liver pâté with apples, soup of Odenwald brook trout, consommé with green rye quenelles, slices of pike-perch fried in butter, and vegetables of the season. Rounding out the meal might be flamed pancakes with bananas and maple sauce. The wine list is impressive.

SIMPLICISSIMUS, Ingrimstrasse 16. Tel. 06221/18-33-36.
   Cuisine: FRENCH. **Reservations:** Required. **Bus:** 10, 12, or 35.
$ **Prices:** Appetizers 14 DM–30 DM ($9.20–$19.80); main courses 38 DM–52 DM ($25.10–$34.30); fixed-price menus 78 DM ($51.50), 88 DM ($58.10), and 110 DM ($72.60). AE, MC, V.
   Open: Dinner only, Wed–Mon 6–11pm. **Closed:** Aug 1–15.

★ Simplicissimus is elegant, ideal for a gourmet rendezvous for those tired of student drinking clubs. A cuisine moderne is prepared with consummate skill by the owner and perhaps the finest chef in Heidelberg, Johann Lummer. His restaurant in the Altstadt is decorated simply but with taste and style, featuring white paneling, globe lights, and touches of crimson. *Gourmet* magazine said Herr Lummer "paints with food," and in so many ways he does. Not only are his platters delectable to the tastebuds, but also their presentation seems equally important. The menu varies but is likely to include fresh mushrooms in cream sauce with homemade noodles, crayfish with fresh melon and herb-flavored cream sauce, or monkfish with crayfish. Two four-course set menus are offered, and there's an elaborate seven-course repast; also, you can order à la carte.

ZUR HERRENMÜHLE, Hauptstrasse 239. Tel. 06221/1-29-09.
   Cuisine: FRENCH. **Reservations:** Recommended. **Bus:** 35.
$ **Prices:** Appetizers 15 DM–38 DM ($9.90–$25.10); main courses 38.50 DM–55 DM ($25.40–$36.30); fixed-price menus 98 DM–125 DM ($64.70–$82.50). AE, DC, MC, V.
   Open: Dinner only, Mon–Sat 5:30pm–midnight.
The house that contains this restaurant was originally built in the 17th century, as you'll quickly realize thanks to the thick walls, antique paneling, and frequently polished patinas. Maintained as a restaurant by the Ueberle family, the dining room prepares succulent versions of a classical cuisine based on fresh ingredients and a rigorous culinary training. It has a sophisticated maître d' to add both glamour and an appropriate kind of theatricality. Meals might include rack of lamb with herbs and homemade green noodles; roast roebuck with vinegar-and-honey sauce; and an array of desserts, perhaps a sorbet flavored with blood oranges and served with a parfait of mandarin oranges.

EXPENSIVE

KURPFÄLZICHES MUSEUM RESTAURANT, Hauptstrasse 97. Tel. 06221/2-40-50.
   Cuisine: GERMAN. **Reservations:** Required. **Bus:** 10, 12, or 35.
$ **Prices:** Appetizers 16 DM–28 DM ($10.60–$18.50); main courses 25 DM–42 DM ($16.50–$27.70); six-course fixed-price menus 85 DM–105 DM ($56.10–$69.30). AE, DC, MC, V.
   Open: Daily 11am–midnight.
This is a quiet culinary oasis in the precincts of the Kurpfälziches Museum. Housed in a baroque palace, the museum makes an interesting stopover before lunch. You can order such dishes as rump steak Madagascar (with green pepper), and from your table you can enjoy the little garden and splashing fountain.

MODERATE

MERIAN-STUBEN, Neckarstadten 24. Tel. 06221/2-73-81.
   Cuisine: FRENCH. **Reservations:** Recommended. **Bus:** 10 or 12.
$ **Prices:** Appetizers 8.50 DM–16.50 DM ($5.60–$10.90); main courses 22 DM–35 DM ($14.50–$23.10). AE, DC, MC, V.
   Open: Lunch Tues–Sun noon–2pm; dinner Tues–Sun 6–10pm. **Closed:** Jan.
One of the best restaurants in Heidelberg is housed in the Kongresshaus Stadthalle,

offering attentive service and good food. The menu is printed in English. You might begin with Alsatian snails cooked in a pan with onions, mushrooms, and fresh herbs, or frogs' legs sautéed in light garlic butter with glazed onions and tomatoes. For a fish selection, poached pike comes in creamy mustard sauce, and you can also order pork filet à la Dijon (spit broiled, basted with a mustard sauce). For dessert, try the cherry-flavored ice cream served with slivered chocolate and whipped cream.

SCHÖNBERGER HOF, Untere Neckarstrasse 54. Tel. 06221/2-26-15.
   Cuisine: GERMAN. **Reservations:** Recommended. **Bus:** 10 or 35.
$ Prices: Appetizers 8 DM–25 DM ($5.30–$16.50); main courses 30 DM–38 DM ($19.80–$25.10); four-course fixed-price dinner 60 DM ($39.60). MC, V.
   Open: Dinner only, Mon–Fri 6pm–midnight. **Closed:** 2 weeks in summer.

 Soothing and *satisfying* best describe this gaily painted old German Weinstube, where Rheingau and French wines and hearty Germanic cookery prevail. The chef regularly features fish and game specialties. Only fresh food from the day's market are featured. It stands between Montpellier Park on the Neckar and the Stadthalle.

ZUM RITTER ST. GEORG, Hauptstrasse 178. Tel. 06221/2-42-72.
   Cuisine: GERMAN/INTERNATIONAL. **Reservations:** Recommended. **Bus:** 10, 11, or 12.
$ Prices: Appetizers 15 DM–25 DM ($9.90–$16.50); main courses 28 DM–48 DM ($18.50–$31.70); fixed-price menus 35 DM–78 DM ($23.10–$51.50). AE, DC, MC, V.
   Open: Lunch daily noon–2pm; dinner daily 6–10pm.

 Zum Ritter is popular with both students and professors, for they know they can get not only good German cooking here but also delectable Dortmunder Actien-Brauerei beer. You dine either in the first-class Great Hall (the Rittersaal) or in the smaller Councillors' Chamber. I like the elegant larger room, with its sepia ceilings, wainscoting, and Oriental rugs. The house specialty is saddle of venison for two (in season). A good beginning might be game soup St. Hubertus with brandy foam, and a fine end would be crêpes Suzette for dessert.

INEXPENSIVE

KONDITOREI-CAFÉ SCHAFHEUTLE, Hauptstrasse 94. Tel. 06221/2-13-16.
   Cuisine: PASTRIES/GERMAN. **Reservations:** Not necessary. **Bus:** 10 or 12.
$ Prices: Appetizers 7 DM–11 DM ($4.60–$7.30); main courses 15 DM–16 DM ($9.90–$10.60). No credit cards.
   Open: Mon–Fri 9am–7:30pm, Sat 9am–6pm. **Closed:** Holidays.
Rain need never ruin your summer outing in this partially roofed café-garden. Light meals are presented with attentive service. There is a large choice of pastries, which are best accompanied with a cup of coffee.

STUDENT DRINKING CLUBS

ZUM ROTER OCHSEN [Red Ox Inn], Hauptstrasse 217. Tel. 06221/2-09-77.

 Heidelberg's most famous and revered student tavern, Zum Roter Ochsen opened in 1703. For six generations it's been in the Spengel family, who have welcomed everybody from Bismarck to Mark Twain. It seems that every student who has attended the university has left his or her mark on the walls—or at least his or her initials. Revelers sit at long oak tables under smoke-blackened ceilings. Distinguished patrons of yore have left mementos, often framed photographs of themselves. The series of rooms is arranged in horseshoe fashion; the U part has a pianist who sets the musical pace. As the evening progresses, the songs become more festive and vigorous. By midnight the sounds are heard blocks away. Motherly-looking waitresses bring in huge steins of beer and plates of food. A mug of beer costs from 5 DM ($3.30). Dishes include Gulaschsuppe, Sauerbraten Rhineland style, and veal steak Cordon Bleu. Meals cost 20 DM to 35 DM ($13.20 to $23.10).

Open: Mon–Sat 5pm–midnight. **Closed:** Dec 20–Jan 20. **Bus:** 33.

ZUM SEPP'L, Hauptstrasse 213. Tel. 06221/2-30-85.

Next door to Roter Ochsen, right off Karlsplatz, is the second famous drinking club of Heidelberg. It is filled with photographs of former students at the university (hundreds have carved their initials), along with memorabilia that range from old Berlin street signs to Alabama license plates. The building itself dates from 1407. You can order platters of food, such as farmer's sausages, and meals cost 24 DM to 29.50 DM ($15.80 to $19.50). A mug of beer goes for 4.50 DM ($3). When the university is closed, the activity here dies down considerably, except for tourist merrymaking, but it remains a long-enduring favorite. No credit cards.

Open: Apr–Oct, daily 11am–midnight; Nov–Mar, Mon–Thurs 5pm–midnight, Fri–Sun 11am–midnight. **Bus:** 33.

2. THE NECKAR VALLEY

Heidelberg is a good point from which to explore the romantic Neckar Valley. From June to early September, you can take a boat tour along the river as far as Neckarsteinach and back. You can order drinks or snacks on the boat. There are usually four or five round trips daily, and you need not return immediately on the same boat. That gives time to explore the various sights (including four castles). Boats are operated by the **Rhein-Neckar-Fahrgastschiffahrt GmbH**, Stadthalle, Heidelberg (tel. 06221/2-01-81). Trips between Heidelberg and Neckarsteinach cost 14 DM ($9.20) round trip, and those between Heidelberg and Hirschhorn cost 19 DM ($12.50) round trip. Some of the people who take you on this pleasant trip may be descended from the Neckar fishermen who helped Mark Twain when he rafted down from Hirschhorn. The same families have been working the Neckar since the early 1600s.

Another way to get a close look at the many attractions along the banks of the Neckar is by car, driving eastward along the right bank of the river.

HIRSCHHORN

Called the gem of the Neckar Valley, this medieval town, 16 miles east of Heidelberg, still carries an aura of the past. It obtained municipal rights in 1391. Overlooking the town and the Neckar from a fortified promontory is the 18th-century **Hirschhorn Castle.** The castle was erected on the site of an earlier Renaissance palace built by Ludwig von Hirschhorn in the late 16th century. The castle defenses are from the 14th century, and wall paintings from that period can be seen in the chapel. The castle is now a hotel and restaurant. For a view of the sharp bend of the Neckar below the town, climb to the top of the tower.

Access by car is via Route 45 east from Heidelberg. Hirschhorn lies on the Neckarelz/Heidelberg rail line with frequent local service between the two towns. For more information call 06272/19-419. Regional bus service from Heidelberg is provided by VGO Lines (#41 and #45). For information, call 06068/16-78.

IMPRESSIONS

The Neckar is in many places so narrow that a person can throw a dog across it, if he has one.
—MARK TWAIN, *A TRAMP ABROAD* (1880)

WHERE TO STAY & DINE

MODERATE

SCHLOSS-HOTEL, Auf Burg Hirschhorn, D-6932 Hirschhorn. Tel. 06272/13-73. Fax 06272/32-67. 34 rms. TV TEL **Directions:** Looms over the center of town.

$ Rates (including continental breakfast): 120 DM–170 DM ($79.20–$112.20) single; 175 DM–215 DM ($115.50–$141.90) double. AE, MC, V. **Parking:** Free. **Closed:** Dec–Jan.

On Route B37 (Heidelberg-Eberbach), you'll come across an opportunity to stay in a hilltop castle. Accommodations are divided between a palace and a guesthouse annex. The double rooms are furnished in modern style, each with a river view and a collection of good antiques. Central heating and an elevator have been installed.

The restaurant serves meals to nonresidents, but only if they phone in advance. Specialties are prepared in traditional ways and include various kinds of game, smoked trout, and home-baked bread. Food service is daily from noon to 2pm and 6 to 8pm. A fixed-price meal costs 38 DM ($25.10), while à la carte meals can run as high as 65 DM ($42.90).

EBERBACH

Four miles farther along the Neckar is the medieval Imperial City of Eberbach, which traces its municipal rights back to 1227. Its castle is even older, dating from 1012. The fortress was destroyed in the 15th century, but its ivy-covered ruins attract many visitors today, as does the old Pfarr Hof, the medieval center of the town within the city walls. *Historical note:* Queen Victoria was conceived at Eberbach, a momentous event commemorated by a plaque outside her parents' home, Haus Thalheim.

Motorists find that routes 37 and 45 connect to autobahn A5 heading north and south or A6 going east and west. From Heidelberg, head west along Route 45. Eberbach lies on the Neckarelz/Heidelberg line with frequent service. Phone 06271/4899 for more information. Regional buses run along the Neckar, the service provided by VGO lines (#41 or #45). For schedules, phone 06068/16-78.

For tourist information, contact the **Kurverwaltung,** Im Kurzentrum, Kellereistrasse 32 (tel. 06271/48-99).

WHERE TO STAY

MODERATE

HOTEL KETTENBOOT, Friedrichstrasse 1, D-6930 Eberbach. Tel. 06271/24-70. 15 rms (8 with bath). TV TEL **Directions:** Near rail station.

$ Rates (including continental breakfast): 50 DM ($33) single without bath, 60 DM ($39.60) single with bath; 120 DM ($79.20) double without bath, 150 DM ($99) double with bath. No credit cards. **Parking:** Free.

This is one of the better-known hotels in town, with a thriving street-level restaurant where everyone in town has arrived for at least one meal. This restaurant is a trustworthy place to get a well-cooked meal and sample German, French, and international specialties. Full meals cost from 30 DM to 65 DM ($19.80 to $42.90). The restaurant is open from noon to 2pm and from 6 to 9pm; closed Friday and during November.

HOTEL KRONE-POST, Hauptstrasse 1, D-6930 Eberbach. Tel. 06271/ 20-13. Fax 06271/16-33. 42 rms (all with bath or shower). TEL **Directions:** In the town center.

$ Rates (including continental breakfast): 75 DM–120 DM ($49.50–$79.20) single; 118 DM–195 DM ($77.90–$128.70) double. AE, DC, MC, V. **Parking:** Free.

In the center of town, this inn was originally built in the 1600s as the coach-and-buggy station. Today, it's a spacious and well-maintained hotel. The guest rooms are comfortably and conservatively furnished, most with TVs and minibars. The restaurant is of a good standard, specializing in regional cuisine.

HOTEL ZUM KARPFEN, Alter Markt 1–4, D-6930 Eberbach. Tel. 06271/7-10-15 or 06271/71010. 90 rms (70 with bath), 2 suites. **Directions:** In town center near river.

$ Rates (including buffet breakfast): 50 DM ($33) single without bath; 115 DM ($75.90) single with bath; 75 DM–125 DM ($49.50–$82.50) double without bath; 115 DM–190 DM ($75.90–$125.40) double with bath; from 185 DM ($122.10) suites. AE, MC, V. **Parking:** Free.

Ⓢ This is one of the most colorful hotels in town. To be found on its facade are authentic *sgraffito* (scratched on) paintings depicting the history of Eberbach.

Built more than two centuries ago near the river, the hotel still welcomes guests into its darkly paneled interior. The guest rooms are comfortably furnished, most with phones, and about half with TVs.

At the restaurant you can have well-prepared meals in an old-world setting; at the informal Weinstube, less formal platters are served in generous portions. Meals in both sections are served from noon till 2pm and 6 to 9pm. The restaurant, but not the Weinstube, is closed every Tuesday at lunchtime.

WHERE TO DINE

VERY EXPENSIVE

HOTEL ALTES BADHAUS, Am Lindenplatz 1. Tel. 06271/710-57.
  Cuisine: CONTINENTAL. **Reservations:** Required. **Directions:** Town center.
$ Prices: Appetizers 18 DM–26 DM ($11.90–$17.20); main courses 48 DM–68 DM ($31.70–$44.90); fixed-price menus 98 DM ($64.70), and 148 DM ($97.70). AE, DC, MC, V.
  Open: Dinner daily 6–10pm; lighter meals served on the terrace daily noon–2pm and 6–11pm.

★ The Hotel Altes Badhaus is one of the most interesting buildings in Eberbach. Its name, Old Bath House, stems from its original 16th-century function. The finest surviving example of its kind in southern Germany, it was painstakingly restored about 10 years ago, and its beautiful vaulted ground floor is now a gourmet restaurant. Upstairs, diners can enjoy the creations of one of Germany's most distinguished chefs, Heinrich Gotzenberger. Typically regional dishes, along with French and Italian specialties, are served. Fixed-price menus are available, as are à la carte meals.

Fourteen guest rooms are rented, each with a private bath, minibar, TV, and phone. Singles cost 115 DM to 175 DM ($75.90 to $115.50) daily, with doubles at 205 DM ($135.30). One suite for two costs 275 DM ($181.50). A buffet breakfast is included in the rates, and parking costs 8 DM ($5.30).

HEILBRONN

The city on the Neckar is a very old town—documents show that a Villa Heilbrunna existed here in 741. In 1371 the city was made an Imperial City by Emperor Karl IV. The town owes its name to a holy spring (Heiligbronn) that bubbled up from beneath the high altar at **St. Kilian's Church,** the city's most important monument. The old city was largely destroyed in World War II, but the church has been rebuilt in its original Gothic and High Renaissance style. The original church was begun in 1020 and completed in 1529. Its 210-foot-high tower is considered the earliest example of

Renaissance architecture in Germany. Inside are excellent original wood carvings, preserved during the war, including an elaborate choir and altar.

Opposite the church is the **Rathaus,** also reconstructed, a combination of Gothic and Renaissance architecture. On its balcony is an astronomical clock going back to 1580. It was designed by the best-known horologist of the time, Isaak Habrecht, who created the famous clock inside the cathedral at Strasbourg, France.

Heilbronn is the largest producer of wine in the Neckar Valley, growing mainly Trollinger and Riesling grapes. The best Neckar wine grows in Heilbronn, or so goes an old German saying. The 550 acres of vineyards around the town yield about 5 million liters of wine annually. Every September, a large arena around the Rathaus is converted into a **"wine village."** At various booths you can sample the vintage, often at bargain prices. Merriment and music fill the gap when you aren't drinking. Local food is sold as well, including Zwiebelkuchen (onion cake) and Dicker Hund, which has been compared to a "pork hamburger" (don't order it rare).

Centuries-old traditional festivals and fêtes take place here, including a **Volksfest** at the end of July and the beginning of August.

The play *Das Käthchen von Heilbronn* was written by Heinrich von Kleist in 1808 and performed for the first time in Vienna in 1810. It became so popular over the years that Käthchen is now the symbol of Heilbronn. Every two years a jury selects a "Käthchen," who represents the city at various functions. In addition, there are Käthchen dolls, a Käthchen Fountain, the Käthchen House, and even a Käthchen beer.

Today Heilbronn is a major commercial and cultural center of Franconia. In addition, the city definitely believes in "keeping fit" (perhaps to compensate for the wine and beer drinking). Some 10,000 acres of wooded parkland surround the city, accessible by footpaths and nature trails.

Access by car is via autobahn A6 east and west and A81 north and south. From Heidelberg, drive south along Route 45, then take A6 east. Heilbronn lies on the major Stuttgart/Würzburg rail line with frequent service. Call 07131/19419 for more information. Bus service to Stuttgart is provided by Regional Bus Stuttgart GmbH at Heilbronn (tel. 07131/62-450 for more information).

For tourist information, contact the **Stadtisches Verkehrsamt,** Rathaus (tel. 07131/56-22-70).

WHERE TO STAY

EXPENSIVE

INSEL HOTEL, Friedrich-Ebert-Brücke, D-7100 Heilbronn. Tel. 07131/ 63-00. Fax 07131/62-60-60. 120 rms, 4 suites. TV **Bus:** Am Rathaus city bus.
   $ Rates (including buffet breakfast): 150 DM–200 DM ($99–$132) single; 228 DM–320 DM ($150.50–$211.20) double; from 440 DM ($290.40) suite. AE, DC, MC, V. **Parking:** Free.
A modern hotel, renovated in 1978, is built on an island (*Insel* in German) in the middle of the river, right in the heart of Heilbronn. The rooms are well designed, most with balconies opening onto weeping willows and the hotel's park.

The buffet breakfast offers rolls, cheese, sausages, juices, cereals, and fruits. The front terrace is the beer and gossip center of town, a beehive of a place. Within, there's the cozy Swabian Restaurant, where you can have homemade Spätzle and other well-known specialties. The Insel also has a nightclub, an indoor pool, a sauna, and a solarium.

MODERATE

HOTEL GÖTZ, Moltkestrasse 52, D-7100 Heilbronn. Tel. 07131/15-50. Fax 07131/15-58-81. 90 rms. TV TEL **Bus:** Am Rathaus city bus.
   $ Rates (including continental breakfast): 144 DM–164 DM ($95–$108.20) single;

182 DM–225 DM ($120.10–$148.50) double. AE, DC, MC, V. **Parking:** 8 DM ($5.30).

The Götz is in a modern complex of business-related inner-city buildings. Many of the establishment's clients are connected with conventions and come here for annual meetings and policy discussions. The well-designed accommodations have modern furnishings, TVs, and radios. There's a plushly furnished dining room, as well as a Bierstube restaurant. Room service is provided 24 hours a day.

WHERE TO DINE

MODERATE

RATSKELLER, Im Rathaus, Marktplatz 7. Tel. 07131/8-46-28.
    Cuisine: SWABIAN. **Reservations:** Recommended. **Bus:** Am Rathaus city bus.
$ Prices: Appetizers 8.50 DM–24 DM ($5.60–$15.80); main courses 22 DM–40 DM ($14.50–$26.40). No credit cards.
    Open: Mon–Sat 8am–midnight. **Closed:** Aug 30–Sept. 20.

    This is one of your best bets for dining in Heilbronn. Although a true Ratskeller, unlike so many others, it's been given the modern treatment, with upholstered banquettes and wrought-iron grillwork. Tables are set on two levels. The prices are modest for such typical main dishes as Gulasch, peppersteak with french fries and salad, and grilled sole. There's an impressive wine list, although many diners consider "the wine of the cellar" (house wine) perfectly adequate.

WIRTSHAUS AM GÖTZENTURM, Allerheiligenstrasse 1. Tel. 07131/8-05-34.
    Cuisine: SWABIAN. **Reservations:** Recommended. **Bus:** Am Rathaus city bus.
$ Prices: Appetizers 9.50 DM–18 DM ($6.30–$11.90); main courses 20 DM–28 DM ($13.20–$18.50). No credit cards.
    Open: Dinner only, Mon–Sat 6pm–midnight.

The food here is well prepared and reasonable in price, but many diners come as much for the charming antique-inspired decor as for the cuisine. By the light of oil-burning lamps, you'll appreciate the brightly polished copper pots, the small-paned windows, the time-blackened paneling, and the elaborate table settings. The food is an updated version of Swabian cuisine, with a sophisticated cheese board and delectable desserts.

---

3. STUTTGART

126 miles SE of Frankfurt; 138 miles NW of Munich;
78 miles SE of Heidelberg

GETTING THERE   By Plane   You arrive at the Stuttgart Echterdingen Airport, 9 miles south of the city near Echterdingen. The airport has connections with most major German and many European cities. For airport information, phone 0711/790-14-67. Trip time by air from Frankfurt is 55 minutes; from Hamburg or Berlin, 1 hour and 10 minutes. Buses run from the airport to the City Air Terminal, Lautenbergerstrasse 14, in Stuttgart. Bus A leaves every 25 minutes, taking 20 to 30 minutes to reach the heart of the city. A one-way fare is 6 DM ($4). A taxi to downtown Stuttgart costs 32 DM ($21.10) and up. The Stuttgart airport has four daily Lufthansa Express trains to the Frankfurt airport (trip time: 90 minutes).

    By Train   Stuttgart has rail links to all major German cities, with frequent connections. Your arrival is at the Hauptbahnhof, directly north of the historical area. Forty-five daily trains run to Munich (trip time: 2 to 3 hours, depending on train), and 30 trains run to Frankfurt (trip time: 1½ hours to 2 hours). For Stuttgart rail information, phone 0711/19-419.

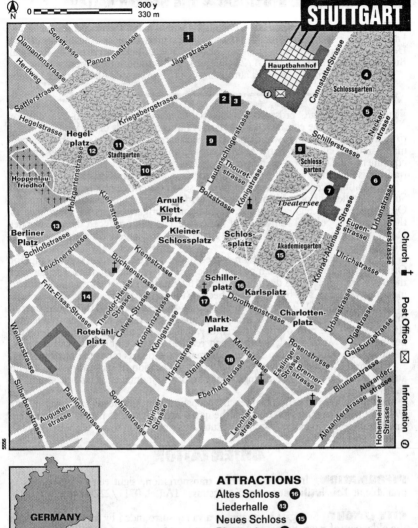

N 0 ⊨⊨⊨⊨⊨ 300 y / 330 m

STUTTGART

GERMANY

● Stuttgart

ACCOMMODATIONS

Hotel Am Schlossgarten **8**
Kronen Hotel **1**
Rieker **2**
Hotel Ruff **10**
Steigenberger Hotel Graf Zeppelin **3**
Hotel Unger **9**
Wartburg **14**

ATTRACTIONS

Altes Schloss **16**
Liederhalle **13**
Neues Schloss **15**
Planetarium **5**
Rathaus **18**
Schlossgarten **4**
Staatsgalerie
  (State Gallery of Stuttgart) **6**
Staatstheater **7**
Stadtgarten **11**
Stiftskirche **17**
Universität **12**
Württembergisches Landesmuseum
  (Altes Schloss) **15**

By Bus Long-distance bus service from several major German cities, including Frankfurt, is provided by Europabus Line 1012. Information is available by calling Deutsche Touring GmbH in Frankfurt at 069/79-030. Local service is by Regional Bus Stuttgart GmbH (tel. 07031/25-003 for schedules and information).

By Car Access by car is via autobahn A8 east and west or A81 north and south.

Unlike many large, prosperous industrial centers, Stuttgart is not a city of concrete—on the contrary, within the city limits two-thirds of the land is devoted to parks, gardens, and woodland. Yet Stuttgart is one of Germany's largest manufacturing cities, the home of Mercedes and Porsche automobiles, Zeiss optical equipment, and many other industrial concerns. As a city interested in export and trade, it is also the site of international trade fairs and congresses.

As a cultural center, it is without peer in southwestern Germany. The acclaimed Stuttgart Ballet performs throughout the world. Its State Opera and Philharmonic Orchestra are also highly regarded. In addition, Stuttgart boasts an abundance of theater groups, cultural festivals, and museums. The city produced the philosopher Hegel, who in turn inspired Marx and Engels. It is the largest wine-growing city in Germany.

Its name comes from a stud farm owned by the Duke of Swabia, son of Emperor Otto the Great, and a horse can be seen today in the city's coat-of-arms. The name of the town first appears in a document from 1160. Stuttgart experienced major growth in the 13th century, and by 1428 it had become the capital and residence of the counts of Württemberg. In 1803 Württemberg became an electorate, and three years later, a kingdom. The city grew and prospered under the reign of Kaiser Wilhelm I (1816–64). At the turn of the 20th century, it had a population of 175,000. By the beginning of World War I, Stuttgart had reached out to embrace several districts, notably ancient Cannstatt, so that its land mass extended as far as the Neckar River.

In World War II it experienced the worst devastation in its history—53 bomb attacks leveled 60% of its buildings. Not one of its landmarks or historic structures came through intact.

Following a short period of French occupation, the Americans took over in July 1945. Stuttgart became the capital of the newly formed state of Baden-Württemberg (many still prefer to call it "Swabia"). Stuttgart's population today is about 580,000.

ORIENTATION

INFORMATION Information about transportation, sightseeing, and hotels is available at **Touristik-Zentrum,** Königstrasse 1A (tel. 0711/2228-240).

CITY LAYOUT Stuttgart is situated in a valley surrounded by forested hills. From the older part of town, houses and streets climb up the slopes of the hills. The historic Königstrasse, the main street of the city, is lined with stores and restaurants. Along it are found such important sights as St. Eberhard's Cathedral and shop-lined Königsbau. It follows the former town moat, which King Friedrich had built in 1806, into Schlossplatz where Neues Schloss, the last castle of the Württemberg royals, stands. Directly south is another landmark square—the center of Stuttgart—Schillerplatz, and south of Schillerplatz is the Marktplatz and Rathaus. In back of Schillerplatz stands the **Stiftskirche,** the most historic church of Stuttgart. Originally built between 1433 and 1531, it replaced a Roman basilica from the 12th century. This late Gothic church was reconstructed from 1950 to 1959.

In the northwest, near the Ministry of Economy, is the massive Design Center, with changing and temporary exhibitions. It lies near the **Stadtgarten,** which contains the Technological University. The home of Mercedes-Benz, oldest automobile factory in the world, is in the suburb of Untertürkheim, on the right bank of the Neckar.

It's easy to discover the city by using the walking tour mapped out for you by city officials. Starting at the Hauptbahnhof, follow the yellow-and-black signs through the most important historical districts as well as the **Schlossgarten,** one of Stuttgart's vast parks, which extends from the Neues Schloss to Spa Hall at Bad Cannstatt on the Neckar River. This is Stuttgart's answer to New York's Central Park. A free organized walking tour through historical Stuttgart leaves from the inner courtyard of the Altes Schloss on Schillerplatz on Saturday at 10am, lasting until about 12:30pm.

GETTING AROUND

Stuttgart and environs are serviced by a streamlined bus and streetcar system. It also has a modern U-Bahn, with more lines planned for the future. The 24-hour ticket for 13 DM ($8.60) is most economical, allowing visitors to travel on all city transportation facilities. For information, call 0711/66-06-200.

WHAT TO SEE & DO

Many of the most remarkable structures in today's Stuttgart are of advanced design, created by such architects as Ludwig Miĕs van der Rohe, Walter Gropius, Hans Scharoun, and Le Corbusier. The **Liederhalle,** Schloss-Strasse, constructed in 1956 of concrete, glass, and glazed brick, is fascinating inside and out. The hall contains three auditoriums so acoustically perfect that all can stage concerts at the same time and not disturb the others. Clustered around the Schillerplatz and the statue of that great German poet and dramatist is the older section. The modern **Rathaus** faces the old Marktplatz, where flowers, fruit, and vegetables are sold in open stalls.

For the best view of Stuttgart, climb to the top of the 1,680-foot **Birkenkopf,** west of the city. The hill is composed of debris of Stuttgart gathered after air raids in World War II. The 20-minute walk to the top will be rewarded by a view of Stuttgart and the surrounding Swabian Hills, covered with vineyards and woods.

Neues Schloss at Schlossplatz, can be visited only by group tour. Constructed between 1746 and 1807, the castle was rebuilt beginning in 1958. Today it houses state government rooms.

FERNSEHTURM [Television Tower], Jahnstrasse 124, Stuttgart-Degerloch, south of the city, just off the B3. Tel. 0711/288-30-37.

Designed and built in 1956 using radically innovative applications of aluminum and prestressed reinforced concrete, this 712-foot tower was later used as a prototype for larger towers in such cities as Toronto and Moscow. Capped with a red and white transmitter, the tower soars above a forested hillock south of Stuttgart. You'll find one restaurant at the tower's base, and another restaurant, a café, a bar, an observation platform, and information about the tower's construction at the top of a 492-foot elevator. Look for several mobile platforms around the exterior for use by window washers. Views from the top are breathtaking.

Admission: 5 DM ($3.30) adults, 2.50 DM ($1.70) children.
Open: Daily 8am–10:30pm.

ALTES SCHLOSS AND WÜRTTEMBERGISCHES LANDESMUSEUM, Schillerplatz. Tel. 0711/279-34-00.

One of Stuttgart's oldest standing structures, the huge ducal palace was originally a moated castle built in the 13th century, but it was renovated in the 16th century into a Renaissance style. It now houses the Württembergisches Landesmuseum, which traces the art and culture of Swabia from the Stone Age to the present day. The most valuable items are displayed in the Dürnitzbau, including a survey of European handcrafts through the ages, the ducal art chamber, and the crown jewels. The museum houses a large collection of Swabian sculptures, and don't miss the exhibition of clocks, coins, and musical instruments. The world-famous treasures of the tomb of the Celtic prince of Hochdorf (circa C.E. 530) are here, as well as one of the biggest collections from the Merovingian period in the early Middle Ages.

Admission: Free.

Open: Tues and Thurs–Sun 10am–5pm, Wed 10am–7pm. **U-Bahn:** Schloss-platz.

STAATSGALERIE [State Gallery of Stuttgart], Konrad-Adenauer-Strasse 30–32. Tel. 0711/212-50-50.

⭐ The city's finest art museum exhibits works spanning some 550 years. However, the best collection is from the 19th and 20th centuries, especially the works of the German expressionists—Kirchner, Barlach, and Beckmann—as well as representatives of the Bauhaus movement, Klee and Feininger. The largest collection of non-German painters is the group of works by French artists of the 19th and 20th centuries, including Manet, Cézanne, Gauguin, Renoir, Picasso, Braque, and Léger, and by the European and American avant-garde after World War II.

Admission: Free.

Open: Wed and Fri–Sun 10am–5pm, Tues and Thurs 10am–8pm. **U-Bahn:** Staatsgalerie.

PLANETARIUM, Neckarstrasse 47. Tel. 0711/29-09-40.

In terms of technology, this Planetarium is one of the most advanced in the world, drawing some 200,000 visitors a year. Every two months or so, the program is changed. Public showings in the planetarium last about 45 minutes, and children under 6 aren't admitted so as not to disturb the viewers.

Admission: 8 DM ($5.30) adults, 5 DM ($3.30) children.

Open: Public shows, Tues 10am and 3pm; Wed 10am and 3 and 8pm; Thurs 10am and 3pm; Fri 10am and 3 and 8pm; Sat–Sun 2, 4, and 6pm. **U-Bahn:** Schlossgarten.

WILHELMA ZOO, Neckartalstrasse, Stuttgart-Bad Cannstatt. Tel. 0711/54-02-0.

Just outside of town is one of the largest and most beautiful zoological and botanical gardens in Europe. Created in 1842 for King Wilhelm I of Württemberg as a Moorish garden, it contains more than 8,000 animals, along with important orchid cultures, an aquarium with a crocodile hall, and a famous coral fish collection.

Other attractions include a magnolia grove, an ape house, a camellia and azalea house, plus a restaurant and café-terrace.

Admission: 9 DM ($5.90) adults, 4.50 DM ($3) children.

Open: May 1–Aug 31, daily 8am–6pm. Rest of year, daily 8am–4 or 5:30pm, depending on season. **Tram:** 13 or 14.

PORSCHE MUSEUM, Porschestrasse 42, Stuttgart-Zuffenhausen. Tel. 0711/827-53-84 for tour reservations.

Ferdinand Porsche, of Bohemia, was the creator of the Volkswagen Beetle; he founded the Porsche company after World War II. This museum is devoted to the world-famous manufacturer of racing and sports cars, with tours of the production lines.

Tours: Free tours by reservation Mon–Fri 9am–noon and 1:30–4pm.

S-Bahn: No. 6 to Neuwirtshaus station.

MERCEDES-BENZ MUSEUM, Mercedesstrasse 136, Stuttgart-Unter-türkheim. Tel. 0711/172-32-56.

A museum devoted to the oldest automobile factory in the world was established to honor the separate invention of the motorcar by Carl Benz and Gottlieb Daimler. (The Daimler-Benz company was formed through merger in 1926.) Nearly 75 historical vehicles are shown, including a Daimler Reitwagen from 1885, the first motor bicycle. You can also see the Daimler company's first Mercedes. The year was 1902. Both utility and luxury cars are displayed (one made for the royal family of Japan). There are also racing cars, built between 1899 and 1989. Among them you can see the Blitzen-Mercedes, the Silver Arrows, and the Sauber Mercedes. There are also some cars specially built to achieve speed records.

Admission: Free.
Open: Tues–Sun 9am–5pm. **Transportation:** Take S-Bahn no. 1 to Neckarstadion. Head on foot to the entrance to the plant, where you'll be taken on a special bus to the museum.

WHERE TO STAY

No matter when you come to Stuttgart, you will probably find an international trade fair in progress, from the January glass and ceramics exposition to the December book exhibition. (Stuttgart is also southern Germany's most important publishing center.) Because of this, suitable accommodations may be difficult to find unless you reserve in advance.

VERY EXPENSIVE

HOTEL AM SCHLOSSGARTEN, Schillerstrasse 23, D-7000 Stuttgart. Tel. 0711/2-02-60. Fax 0711/202-68-88. 121 rms. MINIBAR TV TEL **U-Bahn:** Hauptbahnhof.
$ Rates (including buffet breakfast): 255 DM–340 DM ($168.30–$224.40) single; 390 DM–490 DM ($257.40–$323.40) double. AE, DC, MC, V. **Parking:** 18 DM ($11.90).
A tasteful top contender, the 10-floor Hotel am Schlossgarten was totally renovated in 1989—it's not splashy but offers convenience and comfort on the Hauptbahnhof square. The guest rooms are well furnished, and the public rooms consistently sedate.
Dining/Entertainment: The bar is warm and cozy, but most intimate is the Zirbelstube, with knotty-pine walls and ceiling and birch armchairs. You dine by candlelight in this tavern atmosphere.
Services: Room service, laundry, dry cleaning.
Facilities: Terrace garden, conference facilities.

HOTEL ROYAL, Sophienstrasse 35, D-7000 Stuttgart. Tel. 0711/62-50-50. Fax 0711/62-88-09. 94 rms, 3 suites. A/C MINIBAR TV TEL **S-Bahn:** Stadtmitte.
$ Rates: 218 DM–410 DM ($143.90–$270.60) single; 285 DM–510 DM ($188.10–$336.60) double; from 650 DM ($429) suite. Breakfast 18 DM ($11.90) extra. AE, DC, MC, V. **Parking:** 10 DM ($6.60).
Just a few paces from a major pedestrian walkway, a plain facade opens into a well-designed interior, with attractive geometric carpets whose design is repeated in the glass of some of the wall dividers. An octagonal-shaped bar could serve as a rendezvous point.
The rooms are warmly lit and comfortable. The hotel dining room serves both a regional and continental cuisine, with meals beginning at 45 DM ($29.70). Room service, laundry, and dry cleaning are available.

STEIGENBERGER HOTEL GRAF ZEPPELIN, Arnulf-Klett-Platz 7, D-7000 Stuttgart. Tel. 0711/2048-0, or toll free 800/223-5652 in the U.S. and Canada. Fax 0711/29-21-41. 280 rms, 16 suites. A/C MINIBAR TV TEL **U-Bahn:** Hauptbahnhof.
$ Rates (including buffet breakfast): 295 DM–425 DM ($194.70–$280.50) single; 455 DM–535 DM ($300.30–$353.10) double; from 650 DM ($429) suite. AE, DC, MC, V. **Parking:** 25 DM ($16.50).
The best hotel for those who want to wheel and deal with Stuttgart businesspeople is the Steigenberger. Although right at the Hauptbahnhof, it's not only attractive but possesses dignity and style. The soundproof guest rooms are colorfully decorated.
Dining/Entertainment: Guests congregate in the Apéritif-Bar before making their way to the Restaurant Graf Zeppelin with its French cuisine; the Zeppelin-Stube,

serving Swabian dishes; the Maukenescht (Swabian wine corner); or the ZEPP 7 (bistro-café). Later in the evening there is dancing in the Scotch-Club.

Services: Room service, laundry, dry cleaning.

Facilities: Sauna, indoor pool with wood-paneled waterside lounge.

EXPENSIVE

KRONEN HOTEL, Kronenstrasse 48, D-7000 Stuttgart. Tel. 0711/29-96-61. Fax 0711/29-69-40. 90 rms. MINIBAR TV TEL **U-Bahn:** Hauptbahnhof.

$ **Rates** (including buffet breakfast): 180 DM–220 DM ($118.80–$145.20) single; 220 DM–320 DM ($145.20–$211.20) double. AE, DC, MC, V. **Parking:** 15 DM ($9.90).

A seven-minute walk from the train station, with a view over the vineyards near Stuttgart, this completely renovated hotel offers spacious and elegant rooms. Units are furnished with upholstered armchairs in a variety of styles, along with Oriental rugs. The hotel has an interior patio, a sauna and a whirlpool, plus an elevator designed to accommodate wheelchairs. Breakfast is the only meal served.

RIEKER, Friedrichstrasse 3, D-7000 Stuttgart. Tel. 0711/22-13-11. Fax 0711/29-38-94. 63 rms. TV TEL **U-Bahn:** Hauptbahnhof.

$ **Rates:** 165 DM–190 DM ($108.90–$125.40) single; 208 DM–230 DM ($137.30–$151.80) double. Breakfast 20 DM ($13.20) extra. AE, DC, MC, V.

Across the street from the Hauptbahnhof is this well-furnished hotel where English is spoken. Its public rooms have lots of comfortably upholstered armchairs and Oriental rugs scattered over the parquet or terrazzo floors. Some of the virtually soundproof guest rooms are designed with sleeping alcoves and draw curtains. All accommodations have radios and TVs. You'll be only a one-minute walk from Stuttgart's Municipal Air Terminal, where buses leave frequently for Echterdingen Airport.

PARK HOTEL STUTTGART, Villastrasse 21, D-7000 Stuttgart. Tel. 0711/28-01-0. Fax 0711/28-64-353. 75 rms, 3 suites. MINIBAR TV TEL **Tram:** 1, 2, or 14.

$ **Rates** (including buffet breakfast): 200 DM–240 DM ($132–$158.40) single; 280 DM–330 DM ($184.80–$217.80) double; 580 DM ($382.80) suite. AE, DC, MC, V. **Parking:** 12 DM ($7.90).

This is the choice for those who seek a first-class accommodation in a secluded and quiet area. It's out of the center, in the midst of the gardens of the Villa Berg, within walking distance of a mineral-water pool surrounded by a park. The rooms are well designed with a decidedly personal aura. Room service, laundry, and dry-cleaning services are provided.

In the Villa Berg French Restaurant, a handsome decor features wood paneling and fabric screens to provide semiprivacy; roses adorn the white tables, and glass-bowl droplights make a colorful setting. Meals cost from 57 DM ($37.60). In addition, Radio Stüble serves a Swabian cuisine.

HOTEL UNGER, Kronenstrasse 17, D-7000 Stuttgart. Tel. 0711/20-99-0. Fax 0711/209-91-00. 80 rms. MINIBAR TV TEL **U-Bahn:** Hauptbahnhof.

$ **Rates** (including continental breakfast): 169 DM–199 DM ($111.50–$131.30) single; 239 DM–259 DM ($157.70–$170.90) double. AE, DC, MC, V. **Parking:** 10 DM ($6.60).

The renovated, fairly distinguished facade of this modern hotel welcomes visitors, and there is a helpful reception staff. All rooms are soundproof and furnished with cable color TVs and radios. The hotel stands beside the City Air Terminal, a two-minute walk from the Hauptbahnhof, bus depot, and major U-Bahn terminus.

WARTBURG, Langestrasse 49, D-7000 Stuttgart. Tel. 0711/20-45-0. Fax 0711/20-45-450. 81 rms. MINIBAR TV TEL **Bus:** 43.

$ Rates (including buffet breakfast): 145 DM–185 DM ($95.70–$122.10) single; 240 DM–250 DM ($158.40–$165) double. AE, DC, MC, V. **Parking:** 7 DM ($4.60).

One block off a main thoroughfare, the Theodor-Heuss-Strasse, this boxy hotel has balconies with flowerboxes and comfortable guest rooms decorated in earth tones. In the spacious lobby, guests register. Continental and Swabian food is offered in both its main dining room and its open-air restaurant.

MODERATE

MACK UND PFLIGER, Kriegerstrasse 7–11, D-7000 Stuttgart. Tel. 0711/29-29-42. Fax 0711/29-34-89. 85 rms (69 with bath or shower). TEL **U-Bahn:** Hauptbahnhof.

$ Rates (including buffet breakfast): 85 DM ($56.10) single without bath or shower, 145 DM ($95.70) single with bath or shower; 150 DM ($99) double without bath or shower, 215 DM ($141.90) double with bath or shower. AE, DC, MC, V. **Parking:** Free.

This fairly modern little hotel on a hillside ledge is an eight-minute walk from the Hauptbahnhof. Homelike and cozy, it offers up-to-date guest rooms that are small and basic but quite adequate.

HOTEL RUFF, Friedhofstrasse 21, D-7000 Stuttgart. Tel. 0711/25-87-0. Fax 0711/25-87-404. 85 rms. TV TEL **U-Bahn:** U15 from the Hauptbahnhof.

$ Rates (including buffet breakfast): 135 DM–175 DM ($89.10–$115.50) single; 176 DM–198 DM ($116.20–$130.70) double. AE, DC, MC, V. **Parking:** Free. **Closed:** Dec 22–Jan 2, Apr 8–12, and July 17–Aug 1.

Some of the side benefits of this modern hotel, located in the city center about 1 mile from the station, include subtly lit tile bathrooms, an attractively tiled indoor pool with a sauna, and a manicured garden where a waiter will take your drink order. The dining room is an attractive place in which to eat, with both Swabian and international food. Rooms are comfortably furnished with modern styling.

WÖRTZ-ZUR WEINSTEIGE, Hohenheimerstrasse 30, D-7000 Stuttgart. Tel. 0711/236-70-01. Fax 0711/236-70-07. 25 rms (20 with bath or shower). TV TEL **S-Bahn:** Dobelstrasse.

$ Rates (including buffet breakfast): 85 DM ($56.10) single without bath or shower, 230 DM ($151.80) single with bath or shower; 115 DM ($75.90) double without bath or shower, 270 DM ($178.20) double with bath or shower. AE, DC, MC, V.

The amber lights of a Weinstube welcome visitors to this local favorite in Stuttgart. The guest rooms are paneled and sometimes have massive hand-carved armoires; all are soundproof. The Weinstube is perfect for relaxing with a beer or glass of wine after a long trip. It evokes the feeling that you're in some remote corner of Swabia. The hotel is known for its garden terrace. Breakfast is the only meal served.

WHERE TO DINE

EXPENSIVE

ALTE POST, Friedrichstrasse 43. Tel. 0711/29-30-79.
Cuisine: FRENCH. **Reservations:** Required. **U-Bahn:** Hauptbahnhof.
$ Prices: Appetizers 20 DM–32 DM ($13.20–$21.10); main courses 38 DM–52 DM ($25.10–$34.30); fixed-price lunch 46 DM–60 DM ($30.40–$39.60). DC, MC, V.
Open: Lunch Mon–Fri noon–2:30pm; dinner Mon–Sat 6–11pm. **Closed:** Late July to mid-Aug.

⭐ I recommend the Alte Post for both its cuisine and its high standard of service. Featuring an old tavern ambience, it provides the finest food in Stuttgart. The hors d'oeuvres are superb, including goose-liver parfait. Among fish dishes, I'd suggest the marvelous sole soufflé Alte Post. A special dish is saddle of venison Waidmannsheil with Spätzle. You can choose your dessert from the buffet. Stuttgart is modern, but this mellow inn, with its antique interior, provides a comfortable link with the Germany of old.

ALTER SIMPL, Hohenheimerstrasse 64. Tel. 0711/24-08-21.
   Cuisine: SWABIAN. **Reservations:** Required. **S-Bahn:** Dobelstrasse.
$ **Prices:** Appetizers 19 DM–26 DM ($12.50–$17.20); main courses 38 DM–48 DM ($25.10–$31.70); fixed-price menus 80 DM–140 DM ($52.80–$92.40). AE, DC, MC, V.
   Open: Dinner only, Mon–Fri 6pm–1am.

Rustic and cozy warmth are the trademarks here, from the filtered light streaming in through the bull's-eye glass in the leaded windows to the sympathetic chatter of the other guests. The chef prepares predominantly Swabian specialties, with some light, modern dishes. Because all the ingredients used are likely to be very fresh, the food is expensive, served on à la carte or fixed-price menus, including a menu gastronomique of gourmet specialties.

RESTAURANT GRAF ZEPPELIN, in the Steigenberger Hotel Graf Zeppelin, Arnulf-Klett-Platz 7. Tel. 0711/2048-0.
   Cuisine: FRENCH/CONTINENTAL. **Reservations:** Recommended. **U-Bahn:** Hauptbahnhof.
$ **Prices:** Appetizers 18 DM–26 DM ($11.90–$17.20); main courses 38 DM–62 DM ($25.10–$40.90); fixed-price menus 70 DM ($46.20), 125 DM ($82.50), and 175 DM ($115.50). AE, DC, MC, V.
   Open: Lunch Mon–Fri noon–2:30pm; dinner Mon–Sat 6:30–10:30pm. **Closed:** Public holidays.

In this elegantly appointed restaurant, each dish is individually prepared from fresh ingredients, according to the season. Gourmets ask for lobsters and coquilles St-Jacques in puff pastry, veal liver in cassis sauce with leeks, or Viennese Tafelspitz. Twice a week, duck, lamb, and fresh herbs are delivered directly from Paris markets. The cheese selection is stunning—40 types (the oldest from 1891). The restaurant offers about 75 types of German wines.

MODERATE

ALTE KANZLEI, Schillerplatz 5A. Tel. 0711/29-44-57.
   Cuisine: SWABIAN. **Reservations:** Recommended. **U-Bahn:** Schlossplatz.
$ **Prices:** Appetizers 8 DM–16 DM ($5.30–$10.60); main courses 20 DM–40 DM ($13.20–$26.40). AE, DC, MC, V.
   Open: Daily 11am–midnight.

This popular folkloric restaurant is contained within the section of the old castle (Den Alten Schloss) that was originally built in 1533 as the depot for government records and the payment of taxes. Its warmly rustic street-level interior has been serving Swabian specialties since around 1910 within one enormous dining room and a handful of more private satellite rooms. One of the most popular specialties is Maultaschen, a Stuttgart version of ravioli stuffed with ham or spinach. Equally popular are Swabian Rostbraten (roast beef) and Stuttgarter Ratsherrenteller, laden with filets of pork and beef and served with Spätzle, fresh vegetables, and mushroom gravy. You can also ask for the local pils beer or some of the region's fine wines. Perhaps try the pale rosé known as Tuniberg or one of the full-bodied red wines made from the Trollinger grape.

ZUR WEINSTEIGE, in the Hotel Wörtz, Hohenheimerstrasse 30. Tel. 0711/236-70-01.
   Cuisine: INTERNATIONAL. **Reservations:** Recommended. **S-Bahn:** Dobelstrasse.

$ Prices: Appetizers 10 DM–22 DM ($6.60–$14.50); main courses 28 DM–48 DM ($18.50–$31.70). AE, DC, MC, V.
Open: Tues–Sat 7am–midnight; warm food served noon–2pm and 6–10pm.
Closed: Holidays.

The interior of this place might be called a celebration of German handcrafts. Everything looks handmade, from the hand-blown leaded glass in the small-paned windows to the carved columns and tables and chairs. International cuisine, with numerous Swabian specialties, is offered. In summer, you'll be tempted to sit among the grape vines stretching over the sun terrace. Also worth seeing is the wine cellar, well stocked with the best regional wines and a good selection of German and international wines, about 12,000 bottles. Next to the cellar is a room for sitting and tasting the wines.

NEARBY DINING
EXPENSIVE

HIRSCH-WEINSTUBEN, Maierstrasse 3, Möhringen. Tel. 0711/71-13-75.
Cuisine: SWABIAN. **Reservations:** Recommended. **Tram:** 5 or 6.
$ Prices: Appetizers 12 DM–38 DM ($7.90–$25.10); main courses 39 DM–49.50 DM ($25.70–$32.70); fixed-price menus 65 DM–155 DM ($42.90–$102.30). AE, DC, MC, V.
Open: Lunch Tues–Fri noon–1:30pm; dinner Mon–Sat 6–9:30pm. **Closed:** Holidays.

In Möhringen, a few miles outside Stuttgart, is this attractively rustic spot, with a wooden ceiling and lots of hand-painted plates hanging on the walls. This popular restaurant serves the kinds of specialties that the locals prefer. These are likely to include ragoût of oxtail, Rostbraten with cabbage, and game dishes in season. Lighter dishes might include basil soup with quails' eggs and brains.

EVENING ENTERTAINMENT

The state theater, ✪ **Staatstheater,** Oberer Schlossgarten (tel. 0711/2-03-20), is the leading cultural venue in Stuttgart. The theater consists of a Grosses Haus for opera and ballet, a Kleines House for theater, and the Kammertheater, which puts on experimental works. The theater is the home of the world-class **Stuttgart Ballet,** established by the American choreographer John Cranko in the 1960s. Tickets for events here can be purchased at the tourist office (see "Orientation," above), near the Hauptbahnhof. Tickets range from 10 DM to 90 DM ($6.60 to $59.40).

Classical and other concerts may be heard in the three halls of the **Liederhalle,** Schloss-Strasse (tel. 0711/29-94-71). If your German is good, there are a variety of theatrical offerings in the city. Consult the tourist office for information.

---

4. TÜBINGEN

29 miles S of Stuttgart; 95 miles NE of Freiburg

GETTING THERE By Train The nearest major airport, at Stuttgart, has good connections to Tübingen, including a direct bus link. Tübingen lies on the Stuttgart/Tübingen rail line with frequent service between the cities. For rail information, call 07071/19-419. Tübingen also has good rail ties to major cities in Germany, including Frankfurt (trip time: 3½ hours), Berlin (trip time: 11 hours), and Hamburg (trip time: 8½ hours).

By Bus Long-distance buses link Tübingen with major German cities like Stuttgart. Call Deutsche Touring GmbH in Frankfurt for information (tel. 069/79-030). Regional Bus Stuttgart GmbH (tel. 07031/250-03) operates buses between Tübingen and regional towns like Freudenstadt and Baden-Baden.

By Car Access is via Route 27 west from autobahn A8 running east and west and autobahn A81 running north and south.

ESSENTIALS For tourist information, contact the **Verkehrsverein,** An der Eberhardsbrücke (tel. 07071/3-50-11).

Often compared to Heidelberg, this quiet old university town on the upper Neckar has a look and personality all its own. Gabled medieval houses are crowded against the medieval town wall at the bank of the river. In summer, the only movement to break this peaceful picture is of students poling gondolalike boats up and down the river. This far upstream, the Neckar is too shallow for commercial vessels, so Tübingen has been spared the industrial look of a trading community.

Progress has not passed the city by, however. In spite of its medieval aspect, it has a new residential and science suburb in the shadow of the Schoenbuch Forest north of the city, with medical facilities, research institutes, and lecture halls affiliated with the university. North of the botanical garden stand buildings of the old university, founded in 1477. The humanist Melanchthon taught here in the 16th century, and later on, Schiller, Hegel, and Hölderlin were students. Most of the buildings are in a functional neoclassical design, but they fit right in with the old city around them.

A unique feature of Tübingen is an artificial island in the Neckar, with a promenade lined with plane trees. This street, known as **Platanenallee,** is always alive with summer strollers who cross from the main town via the wide Eberhardt Brücke. The island also offers the best view of the town, with its willows and houses reflected in the river. Towering above the roofs is the Renaissance castle, used by the university. Visitors to Tübingen should see the castle, at least for the dramatic view from the terraces.

The narrow streets of the Altstadt wind up and down the hillside, but they all seem to lead to the **Marktplatz,** where festive markets are held on Monday, Wednesday, and Friday. You'll feel like you're stepping into the past when you come upon the scene of country women selling fruit and vegetables in the open square. In the center of all this activity stands the softly murmuring Renaissance fountain of the god Neptune. Facing the square is the Rathaus, dating from the 15th century but with more recent additions, including the 19th-century painted designs on the facade overlooking the Marktplatz.

On a hillside above the Marktplatz is **St. George's Church,** the former monastery church of the Stift, an Augustinian monastery. The monastery became a Protestant seminary in 1548, and its church, the Collegiate Church. Worth seeing inside are the tombs of the dukes of Württemberg in the chancel and the French Gothic pulpit and rood screen, dating from the 15th century.

WHERE TO STAY

EXPENSIVE

KRONE HOTEL, Uhlandstrasse 1, D-7400 Tübingen. Tel. 07071/3-10-36. Fax 07071/38-718. 50 rms (all with bath or shower), 2 suites. TV TEL **Bus:** 1.
$ Rates (including buffet breakfast): 145 DM–170 DM ($95.70–$112.20) single; 200 DM–295 DM ($132–$194.70) double; from 320 DM ($211.20) suite. AE, DC, MC, V. **Parking:** 12 DM ($7.90). **Closed:** Dec 22–30.

The university town's most prestigious hostelry is right off the river, in the heart of Tübingen. Dating from 1885, the hotel is traditional and conservative. The interior has a homelike atmosphere with a liberal use of antiques or good reproductions. The rooms are all personalized, with cable TV. Many of the baths are decoratively tiled, with stall showers.

The owners, Karl and Erika Schlagenhauff, provide some of the best meals in town (recommendable even if you're not an overnighter). There are three dining rooms: the formal dining salon; the Uhlandstube, with an old-tavern atmosphere; and a country-style room, all served by one kitchen. The menu is international, typical dishes including filet of sole in butter, Wiener Schnitzel, and tournedos Rossini. Meals cost 26 DM to 42 DM ($17.20 to $27.70); fixed-price menus are available for 49 DM and 93 DM ($32.30 to $61.40). Service is daily from noon to 2:15pm and 6 to 10:30pm.

MODERATE

HOTEL AM BAD, Am Freibad 2, D-7400 Tübingen. Tel. 07071/7-30-71.
Fax 07071/75-336. 36 rms (all with bath or shower). MINIBAR TV TEL **Bus:** 1.
$ Rates (including buffet breakfast): 74 DM–102 DM ($48.80–$67.30) single; 136 DM–164 DM ($89.80–$108.20) double. **Parking:** 7 DM ($4.60). AE, MC, V. **Closed:** Dec 20–Jan 10.

In the center of one of Tübingen's well-maintained public parks, this hotel has the added advantage of an Olympic-size public pool practically at its back door. Its rambling yellow exterior contrasts vividly with the masses of red flowers planted on the sun terrace. Inside, the comfortable rooms offer woodland calm not far from the city center. The hotel has one restaurant and one bar, specializing in the food of Bavaria.

WHERE TO DINE
MODERATE

LANDGASTHOF ROSENAU, Beim Neuen Botanischen Garten. Tel. 07071/6-64-66.
Cuisine: SWABIAN. **Reservations:** Recommended. **Bus:** 1.
$ Prices: Appetizers 14 DM–24 DM ($9.20–$15.80); main courses 26 DM–36 DM ($17.20–$23.80); fixed-price menu 51 DM–120 DM ($33.70–$79.20). AE, DC, MC, V.
Open: Lunch Wed–Mon noon–2:30pm; dinner Wed–Mon 6–9:30pm.
Near the botanical gardens, the Landgasthof Rosenau is like a roadhouse with a café-annex. The owner serves superb Swabian specialties along with modern cuisine. The typical regional fare is listed under the gutbürgerliche selections. Among these, for example, is a tasty and filling Swabian hot pot with Spätzle and fresh mushrooms. From the section of the menu "reserved for gourmets," you might choose veal steak with morels. Desserts are often elaborate concoctions. In fair weather, guests can order drinks out in the sun.

RESTAURANT MUSEUM, Wilhelmstrasse 3. Tel. 07071/2-28-28.
Cuisine: INTERNATIONAL. **Reservations:** Recommended. **Bus:** 1.
$ Prices: Appetizers 12 DM–24 DM ($7.90–$15.80); main courses 28 DM–35 DM ($18.50–$23.10). AE, DC, MC, V.
Open: Tues–Sun 10am–midnight.

Outside of the hotel dining rooms, the Restaurant Museum is one of Tübingen's foremost eateries. Its lunches are considered by many locals (including students) to be not only the best meals in town but also the best value as well. The restaurant is a pleasant place to dine on international specialties, such as Marseille snail soup, or a regional dish, such as Swabian medallions of veal.

INEXPENSIVE

ALTE WEINSTUBE GÖHNER, Schmiedtorstrasse 5. Tel. 07071/228-70.
Cuisine: SWABIAN/LEBANESE. **Reservations:** Recommended. **Bus:** 1.
$ Prices: Appetizers 7 DM–10 DM ($4.60–$6.60); main courses 13 DM–26 DM ($8.60–$17.20). No credit cards.
Open: Dinner only, daily 6–11pm.

In one of Tübingen's most reasonably priced restaurants and wine bars, in the heart of town, you will find students as well as locals. Containing only about five tables and a prominent bar, it was established in the 1860s within a much older building whose facade has since been blandly modernized. The owner offers local specialties, as well as a small assortment of Lebanese dishes (the cook was born in Beirut), along with many kinds of wine. Beer costs from 4 DM ($2.60); a glass of wine begins at 6.50 DM ($4.30).

NEARBY DINING

EXPENSIVE

GASTHOF WALDHORN, Schönbuchstrasse 49. Tel. 07071/6-12-70.
Cuisine: GERMAN/FRENCH. **Reservations:** Required.
$ Prices: Appetizers 16 DM–26 DM ($10.60–$17.20); main courses 38 DM–58 DM ($25.10–$38.30); fixed-price menu 100 DM–160 DM ($66–$105.60). No credit cards.
Open: Lunch Sat–Wed noon–2pm; dinner Fri–Wed 6:30–9pm. **Closed:** 3 weeks sometime in summer.

⭐ The finest restaurant in the area is not in Tübingen but on its outskirts. At the Gasthof Waldhorn, at Tübingen-Bebenhausen, about 4 miles from the heart of the university town, Herr and Frau Schilling operate a restaurant decorated like a large farmhouse. They offer a light German and French cuisine based on regional ingredients, backed up by an impressive wine list (many half-bottles). The menu changes daily but is likely to include trout terrine and wild venison with mushrooms, along with whatever vegetable is in season, perhaps asparagus or forest mushrooms. The dessert specialty is a soft cream concoction flavored with rose hips.

5. SCHWÄBISCH HALL

16 miles NE of Stuttgart; 86 miles W of Nürnberg

GETTING THERE   By Train   Daily service is from Stuttgart (see above) to the Bahnhof Schwäbisch Hall.

By Bus   Regional bus service is provided by Bus Stuttgart GmbH (tel. 07131/62-450 for schedules and information).

By Car   Access is via autobahn A6 running east and west and Route 14 south.

ESSENTIALS   Tourist-information, Am Markt 9 (tel. 0791/75-12-46), supplies information about the town.

Technically, this medieval town is not in the Neckar Valley; however, if you skip it in your travels through this region, you will have missed one of the treasures of southwestern Germany. In the heart of the forests of the Schwäbische Alb, the town clings to the steep banks of the Kocher River, a tributary of the Neckar. The houses of the Altstadt are set on terraces built into the hillside, and from the opposite bank they appear to be arranged in steps, overlooking the old wooden bridges on the river.

The ✪ **Marktplatz** is possibly the most attractive market square in all Germany. Flanking the square are fine half-timbered patrician houses, and at the lower end of the sloping square, stands the baroque Rathaus. In the center of the square is a 16th-century Gothic fountain, decorated with statues of St. Michael with St. George and Samson. Behind the fountain is a decorative wall holding the pillory where offenders in days gone by were left to be jeered at by the townspeople. Today the square is the scene of festive occasions, such as the annual **Kuchenfest** (Salt Maker's Festival), celebrating the ancient salt industry that grew around springs in Schwäbisch Hall.

On the northern side of the Marktplatz, facing the Rathaus, are the imposing 54 large stone steps, delicately curved, leading to **St. Michael's Cathedral.** The cathedral is a 15th-century Gothic Hallenkirche with a 12th-century tower. Many pews date from the 15th century, as does St. Michael's altarpiece in the side chapel. Admission to the tower is 1 DM (66¢). The church is open Monday from 2 to 5pm,

Tuesday through Saturday from 9am to noon and 2 to 5pm, and Sunday from 11am to noon and 2 to 5pm.

WHERE TO STAY & DINE
EXPENSIVE

DER ADELSHOF, Am Markt 12, D-7170 Schwäbisch Hall. Tel. 0791/7-58-90. Fax 0791/60-36. 46 rms, 3 suites. TV TEL

$ Rates (including continental breakfast): 145 DM–210 DM ($95.70–$138.60) single; 200 DM–240 DM ($132–$158.40) double; from 430 DM ($283.80) suite. AE, DC, MC, V. **Parking:** Free.

Right on the Marktplatz, the Adelshof is an attractive stone building, much of it dating from 1400. The hotel has been completely renewed, and its rooms are now of a good standard. A heated pool is a further lure, and sauna baths are available for an extra charge. Downstairs, the restaurant (closed Monday) serves some of the best food in town, with meals ranging from 38 DM to 75 DM ($25.10 to $49.50).

HOTEL HOHENLOHE, Am Weilertor 14, D-7170 Schwäbisch Hall. Tel. 0791/75-87-0. Fax 0791/75-87-84. 102 rms, 7 suites. MINIBAR TV TEL

Directions: Left bank of river, opposite town center.

$ Rates: 149 DM–219 DM ($98.30–$144.50) single; 186 DM–268 DM ($122.80–$176.90) double; from 350 DM ($231) suite. Breakfast buffet 22 DM ($14.50) extra. AE, DC, MC, V. **Parking:** 7.50 DM ($5).

The Hohenlohe is built beside the Kocher River in the historic Freie Reichsstadt district. A good view unfolds from its several floors of rooms. The accommodations are comfortable and compact, with bright color accents.

Breakfast is served on an open-view roof deck. The hotel's restaurant offers meals for 45 DM ($29.70) and up, and there are also a cafeteria and a bar on the premises. Other facilities include an indoor and an outdoor pool, sauna, solarium, and massage parlor.

MODERATE

HOTEL GARNI SCHOLL, Klosterstrasse 3, D-7170 Schwäbisch Hall. Tel. 0791/7-10-46. 32 rms (all with bath or shower). TV TEL

$ Rates (including continental breakfast): 88 DM ($58.10) single; 130 DM–140 DM ($85.80–$92.40) double. No credit cards.

Beautifully located on the medieval square to the side of St. Michael's, this hotel is the union of three very old half-timbered houses, one pumpkin-colored, another olive green. You'll find plenty of visitors enjoying the café's front terrace, overlooking the Marktplatz. The guest rooms are comfortably and nicely furnished.

NEARBY ACCOMMODATIONS & DINING
VERY EXPENSIVE

WALD UND SCHLOSSHOTEL FRIEDRICHSRUHE, D-7111 Friedrichs-ruhe-Zweiflingen. Tel. 07941/60-870. Fax 07941/614-68. 49 rms, 11 suites. TEL **Bus:** 5.

$ Rates (including continental breakfast): 165 DM–302 DM ($108.90–$199.30) single; 291 DM–390 DM ($192.10–$257.40) double; from 407 DM ($268.60) suite. AE, DC, MC, V. **Parking:** 10 DM ($6.60).

About 17 miles from Schwäbisch Hall on the Hohenlohe plateau—named for one of the great German princely families of centuries past—stands the Wald und Schlosshotel Friedrichsruhe. It's about 4 miles north of the little village of Ohringen. One of the three buildings comprising the hotel was built between 1712 and 1719 by Prince Johann Friedrich of the Ohringen branch of the Hohenlohe family. Constructed as a hunting lodge, the three-story edifice, with a tile roof and baroque central gable, was called Friedrichsruhe, or Friedrich's Refuge. A second building, added in 1953, about a three-minute walk from the original lodge, is modern inside—rooms with up-to-date conveniences, two restaurants, saunas, and a heated indoor pool—but it was constructed to look old outside. Some rooms have TVs and minibars. There are also an outdoor pool and tennis courts. The present Hohenlohe-Ohringen prince is the owner.

You can dine in the main dining room amid red walls, snow-white damask napery, and brass chandeliers, or in the less formal Stube, with a regional ambience produced by mounted antlers, carved-back chairs, and an old porcelain stove. Expect to pay 63 DM to 195 DM ($41.60 to $128.70) for a meal, depending on your selection.

CHAPTER 8

THE MOSEL VALLEY

- **WHAT'S SPECIAL ABOUT THE MOSEL VALLEY**
- **1. TRIER (TRÈVES)**
- **2. ZELL**
- **3. BERNKASTEL-KUES**
- **4. TRABEN-TRARBACH**
- **5. BEILSTEIN**
- **6. COCHEM**

Those returning from Germany singing the praises of the Rhine as the most scenic of German rivers have definitely not toured the lovely Mosel River Valley. Weaving a snakelike path through the mountains west of the Rhineland, the Mosel (Moselle in French) encounters town after town whose sole purpose seems to be to beautify the banks of the river. Nearly every village and hill has its own castle or fortress, surrounded by vineyards where green grapes are grown for the popular wines.

Many Mosel wines are superior to those of the Rhine Valley, and in spite of lightness, they are rich and full-bodied. Mosel wines have the lowest alcoholic content (about 9%) of any white wine in the world. Because of this, they are best enjoyed in their youth. The freshness of some vintages deteriorates with age.

The Mosel begins in the hills of France, and its most scenic portion is the last 120 miles before it enters the Rhine at Koblenz. Along these banks, the visitor enjoys the lively landscapes, the legend-rich countryside, and, of course, the best wines. In recent years, locks have been built at strategic points along the river to enable vessels to sail waters that once transported Roman ships. The locks have been incorporated into the landscape and thus far have not hurt the appearance of the river.

If you enter Germany via France or Luxembourg, the Mosel route is a good way to begin your tour of the German countryside. You'll arrive first at the major city of Trier before weaving through the Hunsrück and Eifel mountains.

SUGGESTED ITINERARY

Day 1 From Koblenz drive along the north bank of the Mosel to the village of Moselkern, where you can explore Eltz Castle in the morning. Spend the night at one of the Mosel wine towns farther west, perhaps Cochem, Zell, or Traben-Trarbach.

Day 2 Leisurely explore either the north or south bank of the Mosel as you continue west to Trier. Arrive in Trier in the late afternoon and walk through the town.

Day 3 Spend the day in Trier exploring its many monuments. Overnight there again before heading to your next destination.

GETTING THERE

The Mosel Valley is reachable by train, boat, or car. The nearest major airports are at Luxembourg, Cologne, and Frankfurt. Access is via autobahn A1 north or south, A48

WHAT'S SPECIAL ABOUT THE MOSEL VALLEY

Great Towns/Villages
- [ ] Trier, as Augusta Treverorum "the second Rome," one of German's oldest cities.
- [ ] Traben-Trarbach, halfway between Koblenz and Trier, twin towns that are the wine capitals of the Mosel.
- [ ] Cochem, a medieval town lying in one of the best wine regions of the Mosel.

Historic Castles
- [ ] Burg Eltz, in Moselkern, one of the few intact medieval castles in the region.
- [ ] Reichsburg Cochem, above Cochem, built in 1027, largely destroyed in 1689 and restored in the 19th century.

Ace Attraction
- [ ] Wine-tasting in Mosel River towns, such as Traben-Trarbach, and at little country inns and taverns, each with a wine cellar.

Ancient Monuments
- [ ] Porta Nigra (Black Gate), in Trier, the best preserved Roman relic in Germany, only survivor of "the great wall."
- [ ] Imperial Baths, in Trier, a relic of what once were among the largest baths in the Roman Empire.

Religious Shrine
- [ ] Liebfrauenkirche, in Trier, a parish church that is the first example of French Gothic in Germany, from 1235.

Museum
- [ ] Rheinisches Landesmuseum, in Trier, one of the outstanding museums of Roman antiquities north of the Alps.

Literary Shrine
- [ ] Karl-Marx-Haus, in Trier, the house in which the author of *Das Kapital* was born, with a large collection of Marx memorabilia.

---

north and east, or Route 51 from the north. An ideal tour is a boat ride between Trier and Cochem (see "Trier," below).

---

1. TRIER [TRÈVES]

77 miles SW of Koblenz; 89 miles SW of Bonn; 120 miles SW of Frankfurt

GETTING THERE   By Train   Trier Hauptbahnhof is on the Wasserbillig-Trier-Koblenz "Moselbahn" line and also the Trier/Saarbrücken rail line. Trier has frequent regional connections. Twenty trains per day run to Koblenz (trip time: 1 hour, 20 minutes); 20 trains to Cologne (2 hours, 25 minutes), and 20 trains to Saarbrücken (1 hour, 20 minutes). For rail information, call 0651/19-419. Regional rail service along the Mosel is via the Moselbahn between Trier and Bullay. For information, call Moselbahn GmbH at Trier (tel. 0651/28-315).

By Bus   Long-distance buses run between Frankfurt, Trier, and Luxembourg, operating on Europabus Line 1013. For information, call Deutsche Touring GmbH at Frankfurt (tel. 069/79-030).

By Boat   Boat rides on the Mosel River operate between Trier and Cochem (see Section 6, below). Service is by Mosel Personen Schiffahrt Gebr., Kolb, Brieden/Mosel (tel. 02673/15-15).

By Car   Access by car to Trier is via autobahn A1 north and south, A48 north and east, or Route 51 from the north.

ESSENTIALS Information Contact **Tourist-Information,** An der Porta Nigra (tel. 0651/97-80-80).

Orientation If you arrive by rail, you'll be deposited at the Hauptbahnhof, opening onto Bahnhofplatz in the eastern part of town very near the old quarter. From here you can walk west (following the Mosel) along Theodor-Heuss-Allee to the major landmark of Trier, the Porta Nigra. From the Porta Nigra, you can take a pedestrians-only street, Simeonstrasse, which leads to the Hauptmarkt, the major square of Trier. At this "living room of Trier," you'll be at several of the town's major attractions, including its Dom and Liebfrauenkirche. The city's two major bridges spanning the Mosel are the Romerbrücke (which still possesses its old Roman pilings) and the Kaiser-Wilhelm-Brücke (which crosses over an islet known as Moselinsel).

As the Romans spread over Europe, they established satellite capitals and imperial residences for ruling their distant colonies. Augusta Treverorum (Trier) eventually became known as Roma Secunda—the second Rome. For nearly five centuries, well into the Christian Era, Trier remained one of Europe's political, cultural, and ecclesiastical power centers.

Officially founded by the Romans under Augustus in 16 B.C.E., Germany's oldest city actually dates back much further. In 2000 B.C.E., according to legend, the Assyrians established a colony here, and archeological findings indicate a pre-Roman (Celtic) civilization. The buildings and monuments still standing today, however, date from Roman and later periods.

Trier is an important gateway, lying on the western frontier of Germany, where the Ruwer and Saar rivers meet the Mosel. Just 6 miles from the Luxembourg border, it is the first major German city on the Mosel—and one rich in art and tradition. It was an important market by 958, a fact commemorated by the market cross placed on the old Hauptmarkt by the archbishop. Because of its location, it is one of Germany's largest exporters of wine. Karl Marx was born and grew up in Trier; his birthplace is now a museum (see "What to See & Do," below). As a young man, he traveled down the Mosel Valley and was shocked by the exploitation of vineyard workers, wrote articles about such practices, and so began his career.

WHAT TO SEE & DO

When the last Roman prefect departed Trier in about 400, he left behind a vast collection of monuments to the centuries of Roman domination. The ✪ **Porta Nigra** (Black Gate) is the best-preserved Roman relic in Germany, the only survivor of the great wall that once surrounded Trier. The huge sandstone blocks, assembled without mortar, were held together with iron clamps, the marks of which can still be seen. From outside the gate, the structure appeared to be simply two arched entrances between rounded towers leading directly into the town, but intruders soon discovered that the arches opened into an inner courtyard where they were at the mercy of the town's protectors.

During the Middle Ages the Greek hermit Simeon, later canonized, chose the east tower as his retreat. After his death the archbishop turned the gate into a huge double church. When Napoleon came this way, however, he ordered all the architectural changes to be removed and the original Roman core restored. The Porta Nigra is open from 9am to 1pm and 2 to 6pm (to 5pm in winter); closed Monday. Admission is 2 DM ($1.30) for adults and 1 DM (66¢) for children.

The **Imperial Palace** district, stretching along the site of the former medieval wall of the city, begins with the huge Roman room known today as the Basilica. Although much of the original structure has been demolished, the huge hall that remains gives some idea of the grandeur of the original palace. Believed to be the throne room, the hall is 220 feet long, 90 feet wide, and 98 feet high. The two tiers of windows are arranged within high-rising arches in which fragments of some of the original wall paintings can be seen. The unique method of Roman central heating through a hollow floor was used to warm this hall from five large heating chambers outside the walls. Today the hall serves as the main Protestant church in the city.

Adjacent to the Basilica is the **Kurfürstliches Palais** (Electoral Palace), built in the 17th century as the residence for the archbishop-electors. Originally designed in German Renaissance style, the wing facing the **Palace Gardens** (Palastgarten) received a more rococo appearance in an 18th-century remodeling. These formal gardens, full of ponds and flowers, are decorated with rococo statues.

The **Imperial Baths** (Kaiserthermen), at the south end of the Palace Gardens, were erected in the early 4th century by Constantine I. Of the huge complex, more than 284 yards long, only the ruins of the hot baths remain. These baths were among the largest in the Roman Empire, and although never completed, they were used in connection with the Imperial Palace and built about the same time. Some older Roman baths, the Baths of St. Barbara, are on Sudallee near the Roman bridge.

The **Amphitheater,** incorporated into the old Roman walls, is the oldest Roman construction in Trier, dating from C.E. 100. The stone seats, arranged in three circles separated by broad promenades, held at least 20,000 people.

✪ **St. Peter's Cathedral** (Dom), north of the Palace Gardens and Basilica, stands above the former palace (4th century) of Empress Helena, mother of Constantine. This structure influenced the style adopted by the archbishop when he added the Romanesque facade in the 11th century. The Gothic and baroque additions in later centuries only helped to pull the ecclesiastical architecture into a timeless unity. The interior is also unique, combining baroque furnishings with the Gothic vaulting and archways. The treasury contains many important works of art, including the 10th-century St. Andrew's Altar, an unusual portable altar (if you could lift it) made of wood and covered with gold and ivory. But the most valuable treasure, the Holy Robe alleged to be the seamless robe of Christ, is so fragile that it was last displayed in 1959. The cathedral is open daily from 6am to 6pm April through October. From November through March, hours are 6am to noon and 2 to 5:30pm. Admission to the cathedral is free, but it costs 1 DM (66¢) to visit the treasury.

✪ **Liebfrauenkirche,** Liebfrauenstrasse 2 (tel. 0651/42-554), separated from the cathedral by a narrow passageway, is a parish church that is more pleasing aesthetically than its older neighbor. The first example of French Gothic in Germany, it was begun in 1235. The ground plan is in the shape of a Greek cross, creating a circular effect with all points equidistant from the central high altar. The structure is supported by 12 circular columns, rather than the typical open buttresses. The interior is bathed in sunlight, which streams through the high transoms. Although the restoration after the war changed some of the effect of the central construction, the edifice is still unique among German churches. Some of the important works of art have been placed in the Bischofliches Museum; the sepulcher of Bishop Karl von Metternich is among the most interesting of those remaining. On the black-marble sarcophagus is a sculptured likeness of the canon, who represented the archbishopric during the Thirty Years' War. The church is open daily from 8am to 6pm.

✪ **Rheinisches Landesmuseum,** Weimarer Allee 1 (tel. 0651/4-35-88), between the Imperial Baths and the Basilica, at the edge of the Palace Gardens behind the medieval city wall, is one of the outstanding museums of Roman antiquities north of the Alps. Numerous reliefs from funerary monuments show daily life in Roman times. The museum's most popular exhibit is the *Mosel Ship,* a sculpture of a wine-bearing vessel crowning a big funerary monument of the 3rd century C.E. Many ornamental and figurative mosaics and frescoes, ceramics, glassware (especially the great diatret-vessel), an outstanding numismatic collection, and prehistoric and medieval art and sculpture are also exhibited. The museum is open Monday from 10am to 4pm, Tuesday through Friday from 9:30am to 4pm, Saturday from 9:30am to 1pm, and Sunday from 9am to 1pm. Admission is free. To reach the museum, take bus 2, 6, 16, 26, or 30.

Bischöfliches Museum, Windstrasse 8 (tel. 0651/710-52-55), also near the cathedral, contains valuable pieces of religious art from the Trier diocese. Among the most important is the ceiling painting from Constantine's palace, recently discovered under the cathedral. Also included are medieval sculptures and other works of art from the treasures of the churches of Trier. The museum is open Monday to Saturday from 9am to 1pm and 2 to 5pm, Sunday from 1 to 5pm. Admission is 1 DM (66¢) for adults and 0.50 DM (30¢) for children.

Karl-Marx-Haus, Brückenstrasse 10 (tel. 0651/4-30-11), is the old burgher's house in which Marx was born in 1818. It has been made into a museum exhibiting his handwritten volumes of poetry, original letters, photographs with personal dedications, and first editions of such works as *Das Kapital.* The personal history of Marx is documented here as well as the development of socialism in the 19th century. The house contains one of the largest collections in the world of international editions of the *Communist Manifesto,* including rare first editions and printings that appeared before 1900. From April to October, the museum is open on Monday from 1 to 6pm and Tuesday to Sunday from 10am to 6pm. From November to March, it is open on Monday from 3 to 6pm and Tuesday to Sunday from 10am to 1pm and 3 to 6pm. Admission is 3 DM ($2) for adults and 2 DM ($1.30) for children under 15. At Simeonstrasse 8 is a plaque stating that it was the residence of the Marx family from 1819. Marx lived here until he finished school in 1835. In the vicinity of the museum is a study center, Studienzentrum Karl-Marx-Haus, for research on Marx and Engels. The study center, among its other riches, contains much of the literature that influenced both Marx and Engels. To reach the museum, take bus 1, 2, 3, or 4.

Because of the importance of Trier as a wine export center, a visit to the huge wine vaults beneath the city is recommended. Tours of the vaults and special wine tastings (daily from 10am to 6pm) can be arranged through the city tourist office (see "Information," above). There you can also purchase a "Go-As-You-Please" ticket for one day, which is valid for use on all public transport in the central zone of Trier. The cost is 6 DM ($4). From May to October, the tourist office offers a two-hour English-language tour on Monday to Friday, costing 10 DM ($6.60) per person.

In summer, there are regular cruises and occasional excursions by boat starting from the city dock, Zurlauben. Some boats go from Trier to Koblenz, a two-day tour, stopping at little Mosel villages along the way. The tourist office has the details about these excursions, which fluctuate seasonally and vary widely in price.

WHERE TO STAY

EXPENSIVE

DORINT PORTA NIGRA, am Porta-Nigra-Platz 1, D-5500 Trier. Tel. 0651/2-70-10. Fax 0651/270-11-70. 106 rms, 2 suites. MINIBAR TV TEL **Bus:** 1, 2, or 12.

$ Rates (including continental breakfast): 170 DM–215 DM ($112.20–$141.90) single; 235 DM–270 DM ($155.10–$178.20) double; from 340 DM ($224.40) suite. AE, MC, V. **Parking:** 13 DM ($8.60).

Across from the Roman ruins, the Dorint Porta Nigra combines style, comfort, and position. It is a six-story building whose interior is decorated with primary colors and contemporary furnishings. The guest rooms usually have sitting areas; baths with each room are ornately tiled.

Guests enjoy drinks in the intimate bar before dining in the traditional restaurant where meals begin at 42 DM ($27.70). A café with an entire wall of glass provides a view of the Roman ruins. The hotel also houses a casino offering roulette and blackjack. Room service, laundry, and dry cleaning are provided, and some facilities for the disabled are available.

RAMADA HOTEL TRIER, Kaiserstrasse 29, D-5500 Trier. Tel. 0651/9495-0, or toll free in U.S. 800/272-6232. Fax 0651/9495-666. 122 rms, 8 suites. A/C MINIBAR TV TEL **Bus:** 1, 2, or 12.

$ Rates (including continental breakfast): 178 DM–196 DM ($117.50–$129.40) single; 246 DM–266 DM ($162.40–$175.60) double; from 356 DM ($235) suite. AE, DC, MC, V. **Parking:** 13 DM ($8.60).

In the heart of the monumental sightseeing zone, near the old Roman monuments, this is one of the most important hotels to be built in Trier in many a year. It operates in conjunction with Europa-Halle, a major venue for conferences. The rooms are among the finest in the city, with streamlined modern furnishings. They also include many amenities, like radios, self-dial phones, and color TVs. Some 42 rooms are air-conditioned. Babysitting, laundry, room service, and a first-aid room are provided.

The Park Restaurant specializes in an international cuisine. In summer, diners overflow onto a terrace. Meals begin at 46 DM ($30.40).

SCANDIC CROWN HOTEL, Zurmaiener Strasse 164, D-5500 Trier. Tel. 0651/14-30. Fax 0651/143-20-00. 216 rms. MINIBAR TV TEL **Bus:** 5.

$ Rates: 195 DM–235 DM ($128.70–$155.10) single; 245 DM–285 DM ($161.70–$188.10) double. Children under 16 stay free in parents' room. Buffet breakfast 25 DM ($16.50) per person extra. AE, DC, MC, V. **Parking:** Free.

One of the leading hotels in Trier lies on the banks of the Mosel, near the autobahn exit labeled Trier-Nord-Verteilerkreis, some five minutes by car from the city center. A former Holiday Inn, this is a newly refurbished first-class hotel offering well-furnished rooms, most of which open onto views of the river.

The hotel offers two good restaurants, serving not only international and regional food but also a Swedish cuisine, as befits the owners of the hotel. Other facilities include a pool and sauna. In the evening, guests relax in the bar with live piano music. Room service, laundry, and dry cleaning are available.

MODERATE

ALTSTADTHOTEL, am Porta-Nigra-Platz, D-5500 Trier. Tel. 0651/4-80-41. Fax 0651/41-293. 32 rms, 1 suite. MINIBAR TV TEL **Bus:** 1, 2, or 12.

$ Rates (including buffet breakfast): 95 DM–110 DM ($62.70–$72.60) single; 150 DM–210 DM ($99–$138.60) double; 220 DM ($145.20) suite. AE, DC, MC, V. **Parking:** Free.

In a refurbished charming turn-of-the-century house with all modern conveniences (including elevator and parking lot), the Altstadthotel sits one block from the Porta Nigra, extending into a quiet side street. Rooms are simply but comfortably furnished. The highly praised buffet breakfast is the only meal served.

DEUTSCHHERRENHOF, Deutschherrenstrasse 32, D-5500 Trier. Tel. 0651/4-83-08. Fax 0651/42-395. 15 rms (all with shower). MINIBAR TV TEL **Bus:** 1, 2, or 12.

$ Rates (including buffet breakfast): 80 DM–100 DM ($52.80–$66) single; 120 DM–160 DM ($79.20–$105.60) double. AE, DC, MC, V. **Parking:** 5 DM ($3.30).

The Deutschherrenhof is identified by its elegantly discreet entrance. Rooms are clean and comfortable, furnished in a functional modern style. Breakfast is the only meal served. The hotel, which stands in the middle of the town, has an attractive bar.

KESSLER, Brückenstrasse 28, D-5500 Trier. Tel. 0651/7-67-71. Fax 0651/76-773. 21 rms (all with shower), 1 suite. MINIBAR TV TEL **Bus:** 1, 2, 3, or 4 from the Hauptbahnhof.

$ Rates (including buffet breakfast): 90 DM–120 DM ($59.40–$79.20) single; 135 DM–160 DM ($89.10–$105.60) double; 180 DM ($118.80) suite. AE, DC, MC, V. **Parking:** 10 DM ($6.60).

The Kessler stands next to the Karl-Marx-Haus. Because of its position on an acute angle of a downtown street corner, there's direct sunlight from three sides. Units are attractively maintained and furnished in a clean modern style. Guests gather in the evening in the hotel's cozy bar. The hotel is under the administration of Jörg Mueller, who speaks English and does everything he can do to make your stay pleasant. He also serves a very good breakfast.

PETRISBERG, Sickingenstrasse 11, D-5500 Trier. Tel. 0651/4-11-81. Fax 0651/732-73. 35 rms, 3 suites. TV TEL **Bus:** 6.

$ Rates (including continental breakfast): 90 DM–95 DM ($59.40–$62.70) single; 135 DM–160 DM ($89.10–$105.60) double; 200 DM ($132) suite for three. No credit cards. **Parking:** 6 DM ($4).

With a view over the city of Trier, the Petrisberg is beautifully situated at a point where a forest, a vineyard, and a private park meet. This intelligently designed four-story hotel offers accommodations that each contain a virtual wall of glass, opening onto a view of the greenery outside. Furnishings may include 7-foot armoires or reproductions of slant-topped antique desks. The ground-floor Weinstube is the gathering place for many residents who live nearby, particularly on weekends.

VILLA HÜGEL, Berhnhardstrasse 14, D-5500 Trier. Tel. 0651/3-30-66.
Fax 0651/37-958. 30 rms. TV TEL **Bus:** 2 or 8.
$ Rates (including continental breakfast): 95 DM–120 DM ($62.70–$79.20) single; 145 DM–200 DM ($95.70–$132) double. AE, DC, MC, V. **Parking:** 10 DM ($6.60).

All the views from the windows of this lovely white house overlook either a private garden with old trees or the city of Trier. You can order food and beverages while sitting on a panoramic terrace. The sitting room/lobby area is decorated with masonry detailing and Oriental rugs, while the guest rooms are spacious and high ceilinged. Four double rooms are so spacious that they're almost like suites, making them favorites with families.

INEXPENSIVE

HOTEL KURFÜRST BALDUIN, Theodor-Heuss-Allee 22, D-5500 Trier. Tel. 0651/2-56-10. Fax 0651/13-770. 17 rms (5 with bath or shower). **Bus:** 1, 2, 5, 6, 12, or 13.
$ Rates (including continental breakfast): 55 DM ($36.30) single without bath or shower, 80 DM ($52.80) single with bath or shower; 80 DM ($52.80) double without bath or shower, 120 DM ($79.20) double with bath or shower. AE, DC, MC, V. **Parking:** 5 DM ($3.30).

Only one block from the Hauptbahnhof, this hotel is most convenient, yet far enough away to escape the noise coming from the station. The rooms have been remodeled, and each is neat, clean, and comfortable; TVs are available upon request.

The innkeeper, Hella Schwarz, will give recommendations and directions for shops, restaurants, and sightseeing and is in general a warm, friendly person. Readers have liked the old-fashioned charm of the hotel. Guests don't seem to mind the lack of an elevator and often gather in the lounge/coffee room to watch TV.

HOTEL MONOPOL, Bahnhofsplatz 7, D-5500 Trier. Tel. 0651/71-40-90.
Fax 0651/71-409-10. 35 rms (22 with bath or shower). TEL **Bus:** 1, 2, 5, 6, 12, or 13.
$ Rates (including buffet breakfast): 60 DM ($39.60) single without bath or shower, 75 DM ($49.50) single with bath or shower; 105 DM ($69.30) double without bath or shower, 120 DM–150 DM ($79.20–$99) double with bath or shower. AE, DC, MC, V.

If you're seeking a reasonably priced accommodation, the Monopol, across from the Hauptbahnhof, may fill the bill. Reached by elevator, its rooms are both good-sized and well maintained. The management has employed a helpful staff.

WHERE TO DINE

EXPENSIVE

PFEFFERMÜHLE, Zurlaubener Ufer 76, Zurlauben. Tel. 0651/2-61-33.
Cuisine: FRENCH. **Reservations:** Required. **Bus:** 5.

$ Prices: Appetizers 19 DM–26 DM ($12.50–$17.20); main courses 35 DM–48 DM ($23.10–$31.70); fixed-price menus 78 DM–105 DM ($51.50–$69.30). MC.
Open: Lunch Mon–Sat noon–2pm; dinner Mon–Sat 6–10pm. **Closed:** Holidays; 3 weeks from mid-July.

How do you make a restaurant successful in Trier? Siegberg and Angelika Waldes use fresh ingredients, work long hours, and welcome diners to the bright, well-decorated dining room (with river view) where they are served a delectable cuisine. Many critics consider this the best restaurant in Trier. Try the assorted fish—cooked *à point*—with homemade noodles, followed by petits fours. Fixed-price and à la carte meals are available.

MODERATE

BRASSERIE, Fleischstrasse 12. Tel. 0651/7-52-31.
Cuisine: GERMAN. **Reservations:** Recommended. **Bus:** 1.
$ Prices: Appetizers 7.50 DM–9 DM ($5–$5.90); main courses 20 DM–33 DM ($13.20–$21.80); fixed-price menu 68 DM ($44.90). DC, MC, V.
Open: Mon–Sat 10:30am–10:30pm.

The Brasserie is on the bottom floor of a beautifully maintained neoclassical house near the Hauptmarkt. A pub-style restaurant, it serves the finest fish and wild-game dishes in its price range. Everything is fresh here. Recipes feature international dishes at night, but at lunch there's a special emphasis on seasonal regional cookery. Try, for example, filet of sole in wild mushroom cream sauce or marinated pork cooked by a special recipe.

ZUM DOMSTEIN, Hauptmarkt and Dom 5. Tel. 0651/7-44-90.
Cuisine: RHINELAND. **Reservations:** Recommended. **Bus:** 1, 2, or 12.
$ Prices: Appetizers 9.50 DM–13.80 DM ($6.30–$9.10); main courses 18 DM–27 DM ($11.90–$17.80). MC, V.
Open: Lunch daily 11:30am–1:45pm; dinner daily 6–9:30pm.

A preferred choice for dining is Zum Domstein, overlooking the flower stands and the fountain on the Hauptmarkt. Opening onto an inner courtyard, it features an authentic local cuisine and sets a high culinary standard. The three dining rooms have a true gemütlich atmosphere, in the best German-tavern tradition. English is spoken. For 12 DM ($7.90), you're given six different wines of the Mosel, Saar, and Ruwer regions, lined up so that you can drink them in proper order. In addition, 18 open wines and about 250 bottled ones are in the cellar awaiting your selection. The food is tempting; a typical offering is a platter of pike balls in Riesling sauce with noodles. In winter, you'll want to find a spot near the huge tile stove.

You can also have a look at the **Romischer Weinkeller**. This room is near the double cathedral (C.E. 326), excavated in 1970. Original Roman artifacts, many connected with food and cooking, decorated the cellar room. In the Romischer Weinkeller you are served dishes prepared according to recipes attributed to Marcus Gavius Apicius, said to have been the foremost chef at the court of the Roman emperor Tiberius. One food critic labeled this banquet "a curious mixture of flavors, unforeseen combinations, and sudden surprises." Meals cost from 43 DM to 51 DM ($28.40 to $33.70).

2. ZELL

43 miles NE of Trier; 65 miles W of Mainz; 22 miles S of Cochem

GETTING THERE   By Train   The Zell Bahnhof lies on the private Moselbahn rail line, with frequent service to Trier and Bullay, the latter 2½ miles from Zell. For train schedules and information, call 0651/21-075.

By Bus Regional bus service is provided by RMV Rhein Mosel Verkehrsgesellschaft GmbH at Wittlich (tel. 0651/71-41) with connections to Trier.

By Car Access by car is via autobahn A1 north and south or Route 53 east and west.

ESSENTIALS Check with **Tourist-Information,** Rathaus, Balduinstrasse 44 (tel. 06541/7-01-22).

This old town, stretching along the east bank of the Mosel, is best known for its excellent wine, Schwarze Katz (Black Cat). The grape is king here, as you'll realize if you come to Zell during the annual autumn wine festival.

On the left bank of the Mosel, 5 miles from Zell and 20 from Cochem, stands the little wine village of **Alf.** The surroundings are idyllic, especially if you climb up to the Marienburg. From there, you get a fine view overlooking the Mosel and the vineyards of Zell.

WHERE TO STAY & DINE

MODERATE

WEINHAUS MAYER, Balduinstrasse 15, D-5583 Zell. Tel. 06542/45-30. 30 rms (all with shower).

$ Rates (including continental breakfast): 55 DM–65 DM ($36.30–$42.90) single; 110 DM–150 DM ($72.60–$99) double. MC. **Parking:** Free. **Closed:** Dec–Mar.

This five-story balconied rustic hotel in the town center is named after its founder. It offers personalized comfort in simply furnished rooms, usually with a view over the Mosel. Many guests come here just to sample Mosel wine.

INEXPENSIVE

ZUR POST, Schlosstrasse 21, D-5583 Zell. Tel. 06542/42-17. 16 rms (all with bath or shower).

$ Rates (including continental breakfast): 58 DM–60 DM ($38.30–$39.60) single; 110 DM–120 DM ($72.60–$79.20) double. AE, DC, MC, V. **Parking:** Free. **Closed:** Feb to mid-Mar.

S This beflowered hotel sits directly on the river. Its rooms are carpeted, with French doors opening onto balconies. The sun terrace is the kind of inviting space where you sit, drink Mosel wine, and watch the river traffic. The warmly decorated Weinstube is a venue for sampling Mosel wine. Meals, served Tuesday to Sunday, cost from 28 DM to 50 DM ($18.50 to $33).

---

3. BERNKASTEL-KUES

30 miles NE of Trier; 70 miles W of Mainz

GETTING THERE By Train Bernkastel-Kues lies on the Moselbahn line between Trier and Bullay, with frequent regional service. For information and schedules, call 0651/21-075.

By Bus Long-distance buses (Europabus Line 1013), running between Frankfurt and Luxembourg, stop here. For information, call Deutsche Touring GmbH in

Frankfurt (tel. 069/79-030). Regional bus service along the Mosel River towns is by RMV Rhein Mosel Verkehrsgesellschaft (tel. 06761/32-38).

By Car   Access by car is via autobahn (A48) on the Koblenz-Trier run, exiting at Wittlich.

ESSENTIALS   Contact **Tourist-Information** in Bernkastel, Gestate 5 (tel. 06531/40-23).

Like Traben-Trarbach (see below), this town is split into twin villages on opposite banks of the Mosel. In a valley of wine towns, Bernkastel stands out as the most colorful, with its old Marktplatz surrounded by half-timbered buildings dating from as early as 1608. In the center of the square stands **St. Michael's Fountain** (17th century), which flows with wine during the annual September wine festival. On a promontory above the town stand the ruins of the 11th-century **Landshut Castle**, worth a visit for the view of the Mosel.

WHERE TO STAY & DINE

MODERATE

DOCTOR WEINSTUBEN, Hebegasse 5, D-5550 Bernkastel-Kues. Tel. 06531/60-81. Fax 06531/62-96. 19 rms (all with bath or shower). TV TEL
$ Rates (including buffet breakfast): 95 DM–105 DM ($62.70–$69.30) single; 150 DM–170 DM ($99–$112.20) double. AE, DC, MC, V. **Closed:** Jan 5–Feb.

This intricately half-timbered building in the town center was the headquarters of the tax collector when it was constructed in 1652. Today it's perhaps the most visually interesting hotel in Bernkastel. Transformed into a tavern back in 1830, it still has many of its original woodcarvings, including an elaborate double balustrade (the motif in vines and fruits) leading to the upper floors. Its cozy guest rooms are furnished in a simple modern style.

The inn serves some of the most savory food in town, with meals beginning at 36 DM ($23.80). Food is offered daily from noon to 2pm and 6 to 10pm. Many guests prefer to sample Mosel wine in the hotel's vine-covered courtyard.

ZUR POST, Gestade 17, D-5550 Bernkastel-Kues. Tel. 06531/20-22. Fax 06531/29-27. 42 rms (all with bath or shower). MINIBAR TV TEL
$ Rates (including buffet breakfast): 95 DM–105 DM ($62.70–$69.30) single; 150 DM–190 DM ($99–$125.40) double. AE, DC, MC, V. **Parking:** Free. **Closed:** Jan.

Constructed in 1827 as a stopover for horseback riders on the local postal routes, this centrally located hotel is today directed by Bernhard Rössling. He maintains the yellow-and-mustard facade in good condition. The well-maintained rooms have both traditional and modern furnishings. A view of the interior will reveal an elegantly crafted stairwell flanked by half-timbered walls and a paneled, beamed dining room where excellent regional cookery is served with 100 varieties of Mosel wine. The restaurant serves meals daily from noon to 2pm and 6 to 9pm. À la carte meals cost 36 DM to 65 DM ($23.80 to $42.90).

INEXPENSIVE

GASTHOF   MOSELBLÜMCHEN,   Schwanenstrasse   10,   D-5550 Bernkastel-Kues. Tel. 06531/23-35. Fax 06531/76-33. 22 rms (all with bath or shower).
$ Rates (including continental breakfast): 65 DM ($42.90) single; 124 DM ($81.80) double. MC, V. **Closed:** Mid-Jan to Mar.

On a narrow cobblestone street for pedestrians only, within walking distance of everything in Bernkastel, this guesthouse is identified by a wrought-iron sign fastened to the corner of the building. Rooms here are clean and charmingly appointed, and some contain TVs. Meals in the restaurant cost 30 DM to 56 DM ($19.80 to $37). It is closed Monday for dinner and all day Tuesday in summer.

RÖMISCHER KAISER, Markt 29, D-5550 Bernkastel-Kues. Tel. 06531/ 30-38. Fax 06531/76-72. 35 rms (all with bath or shower). TV TEL
$ Rates: 85 DM–105 DM ($56.10–$69.30) single; 110 DM–160 DM ($72.60–$105.60) double. Breakfast 18 DM ($11.90) extra. AE, DC, MC, V. **Closed:** Jan–Feb.

The peach-colored facade of this hotel, covering the angle of two downtown streets, has a view of the Mosel from many of the upper windows. The public rooms are decorated almost like a private home, with paintings and Oriental rugs.

Many visitors come here just to dine; the hotel is well known in the region for its gutbürgerlich cookery, using fresh ingredients if at all possible. Like any good restaurant along the Mosel, it features local wines. A separate menu lists all the things anyone could possibly do with prawns, with meals costing 35 DM to 70 DM ($23.10 to $46.20). The restaurant is open daily from 11am to 9:30pm.

4. TRABEN-TRARBACH

37 miles NE of Trier; 64 miles W of Mainz; 11 miles SW of Zell

GETTING THERE **By Train** The Traben-Trarbach Bahnhof lies on the Moselbahn rail line between Trier and Bullay, with frequent service. Phone 0651/21-075 for information.

By Bus Regional bus service along the Mosel River towns is provided by RMV Rhein Mosel Verkehrsgesellschaft (tel. 06761/32-38 for information and schedules).

By Car Access by car is via autobahn A48 (Trier-Koblenz), exiting at Wittlich.

ESSENTIALS For tourist information, contact the **Kurverwaltung und Verkehrsamt** in Traben, Bahnstrasse 22 (tel. 06541/90-11).

Thanks to their central location on the Mosel, halfway between Koblenz and Trier, the twin towns of Traben and Trarbach have become the wine capitals of the Mosel Valley. The gardenlike promenades on both banks of the river are viewpoints for annual international speedboat and waterskiing competitions. The July wine festival attracts visitors from all over Europe to the old wine cellars and taverns of the towns. But behind all the bustle and activity, Traben-Trarbach is proud of its attractions, especially its thermal springs and health resort, **Bad Wildstein,** just south of town.

Above Trarbach, on the east bank of the river, is the 14th-century **Grevenburg Castle,** which, with five other now-in-ruins castles nearby, was the scene of hard-fought battles to gain control of this strategic spot on the Mosel. On the opposite bank, above Traben, are the ruins of **Mont Royal,** a fortress built in the late 17th century by the invading Louis XIV.

WHERE TO STAY & DINE
EXPENSIVE

REMA HOTEL BELLEVUE, Am Moselufer, D-5580 Traben-Trarbach. Tel. 06541/20-65. Fax 06541/25-51. 90 rms. MINIBAR TV TEL **Bus:** Trier-Bullay.
$ Rates (including continental breakfast): 119 DM–145 DM ($78.50–$95.70) single; 190 DM–280 DM ($125.40–$184.80) double. AE, DC, MC, V. **Parking:** Free.

If you plan to stay over, you might try the Rema in Traben, a heavily Germanic structure right on the riverbank. It was created in an ornamental style about 1900 by the architect Moehring, with elaborate timberwork, a domed tower, a highly pitched roof, gables, and dormers. Later, its size was greatly increased with a modern addition. A special feature is the ivy-covered terrace, where you can dine. Inside, stained-glass windows are set in ecclesiastical frames, and overstuffed chairs are drawn up around Victorian fringed "parlor tables," under vaulted ceilings.

MODERATE

BISENIUS, An der Mosel 56, D-5580 Traben-Trarbach. Tel. 06541/68-10. 12 rms (all with shower). **Bus:** Trier-Bullay.
$ **Rates:** 70 DM–95 DM ($46.20–$62.70) single; 130 DM–140 DM ($85.80–$92.40) double. Breakfast 18 DM ($11.90) extra. AE, DC, MC, V. **Parking:** Free.
The Bisenius is a family-run, country villa–style hotel, with balconies, flowers, a sun terrace with a view of the Mosel, and an indoor pool. All units are furnished simply but comfortably. Breakfast is the only meal served.

HOTEL MOSELTOR, Moselstrasse 1, D-5580 Traben-Trarbach. Tel. 06541/65-51. Fax 06541/1-49-22. 11 rms (all with bath or shower). TV TEL **Bus:** Trier-Bullay bus.
$ **Rates** (including continental breakfast): 85 DM–105 DM ($56.10–$69.30) single; 115 DM–165 DM ($75.90–$108.90) double. DC, MC, V. **Parking:** 10 DM ($6.60).

ⓢ You'll find this hotel on the outskirts at Im Otsteil Trarbach. The exterior of this four-story rectangular building, dating from 1838, is a masterpiece of fieldstone masonry from another era. Inside, a charming combination of new construction and antique elements from the original building creates a warm mixture of comfort and convenience.
The Bauer family runs the hotel, and the light cuisine is prepared by chef Ruth Bauer, whose reputation has spread to such a degree that German urbanites come here for a "gastronomic weekend." Bauer's Restaurant is small—only 11 tables—with fixed-price meals costing 42 DM to 110 DM ($27.70 to $72.60). Hours are from noon to 2pm and 6 to 9pm; closed Tuesday. The hotel is open all year, but the restaurant is closed in February.

INEXPENSIVE

ZUM ANKER, Rissbacherstrasse 3, D-5580 Traben-Trarbach. Tel. 06541/15-64. 11 rms, 1 suite. TEL **Bus:** Trier-Bullay.
$ **Rates** (including buffet breakfast): 75 DM–90 DM ($49.50–$59.40) single; 110 DM–130 DM ($72.60–$85.80) double; 150 DM–170 DM ($99–$112.20) suite. No credit cards. **Parking:** 6 DM ($4).
In this riverfront hotel run by Dorothee Wienhues, many of the rooms have balconies facing the Mosel, and if yours doesn't you can still enjoy a cup of coffee or a late-night beer at the café/sun terrace. TVs can be rented for 6 DM ($4) per day. The hotel has a restaurant serving both German and international food daily from noon to 10pm, a snack bar offering fast food, and a wine-and-beer bar. On the terrace facing the Mosel guests can enjoy coffee, lunch, or dinner daily from noon to 10pm.

5. BEILSTEIN

7 miles E of Cochem; 69 miles W of Mainz

GETTING THERE **By Train** The nearest rail station is at Cochem (see below).

By Bus Service, including from Cochem and other points along the Mosel, is available from RMV Rhein Mosel Verkehrsgesellschaft (tel. 06761/32-38 for information and schedules).

By Car Access by car is via autobahn A48 on the Koblenz-Trier run, exiting at Kaiseresch.

ESSENTIALS The nearest tourist office is at Cochem (see below).

On the east bank of the Mosel, this unspoiled medieval wine town has an unusual marketplace hewn right into the rocky hillside. Above the town stands the former cloister church and the ruins of the 12th-century Metternich Castle.

WHERE TO STAY & DINE

INEXPENSIVE

HAUS BURGFRIEDEN, Im Muhlental 63, D-5591 Bielstein. Tel. 02673/ 14-32. Fax 02673/15-77. 72 rms (all with shower). A/C TV
$ **Rates** (including continental breakfast): 50 DM–70 DM ($33–$46.20) single; 100 DM–110 DM ($66–$72.60) double. No credit cards. **Parking:** Free. **Closed:** Dec–Mar.
More a complex of buildings than a single hotel, this downtown establishment has proved popular with locals and visitors alike for more than 25 years. The rooms are simply furnished in a modern style. The chef offers an international menu, specializing in game and fish. Meals begin at 25 DM ($16.50).

HAUS LIPMANN, Marktplatz 3, D-5591 Beilstein. Tel. 02673/15-73. 5 rms (all with shower). TV
$ **Rates** (including continental breakfast): 85 DM ($56.10) single; 100 DM–125 DM ($66–$82.50) double. No credit cards. **Parking:** Free. **Closed:** Mid-Nov to mid-Mar.
S You can sample the wines that made Beilstein famous at its favorite inn, the picturesque Haus Lipmann, in the town center. Time has been kind to this 1795 timbered inn, with rooms located in its main house. For six generations the same family has tended the vast riverside vineyards that have won them acclaim. Try either their Ellenzer Goldbäumchen or their Beilsteiner Schlossberg. The spots for drinking and dining are so tempting that it's difficult making a decision. Most popular in summer, however, is the vine-covered terrace, with a statue of Bacchus, overlooking the Mosel. Of course, there's the antiques-filled tavern or the wood-paneled Rittersaal, with its collection of old firearms and pewter. Candles are lit at night; in the cooler months, fires burn in either the tall walk-in fireplace or the tiny open hearth, with its copper kettle on a crane. Meals cost 28 DM to 52 DM ($18.50 to $34.30). Service is daily from noon to 2pm and 6 to 8pm. The Mosel eel in dill sauce is a classic, but especially delectable is the fresh wild trout. Activities get hectic at grape harvest time.

---

6. COCHEM

57 miles NE of Trier; 32 miles SW of Koblenz

GETTING THERE By Train The Cochem Bahnhof is on the Wasserbillig-Trier-Koblenz rail line, with frequent service between these connecting cities. For information and schedules, phone 02671/19-419.

By Bus Regional bus service along the Mosel is provided by RMV Rhein Mosel Verkehrsgesellschaft (tel. 06571/71-49 for information and schedules).

By Car   Access is via autobahn (A48) on the Koblenz-Trier express highway, exiting either at Ulmen or at Kaisersesch.

ESSENTIALS   For tourist information, contact the **Verkehrsamt,** Enderplatz (tel. 02671/39-71).

In one of the best wine regions of the Mosel Valley, this medieval town is crowded against the left bank of the river by a huge vineyard-covered hill. The town is a typical wine village, with tastings and festivals. But the biggest attraction is **Reichsburg Cochem** (tel. 02671/2-55), a huge castle at the top of the mound behind the town. Originally built in 1027, it was almost completely destroyed by Louis XIV's army in 1689. It has since been restored after the original ground plans, and its medieval ramparts and turrets create a dramatic backdrop for the town. To reach the castle, follow the steep footpath from the center of town; the 15-minute walk is well worth it for the views of the town and the Mosel below. Although you can visit anytime, the interior of the castle is open daily from 9am to 5pm. Guided tours are conducted at regular intervals. Admission is 4 DM ($2.60) for adults and 2 DM ($1.30) for children and students. It is open from mid-March to November.

Cochem, because of its large number of inns, might be your best choice for an overnight stopover between Koblenz and Trier.

WHERE TO STAY

MODERATE

ALTE THORSCHENKE, Brückenstrasse 3, D-5590 Cochem. Tel. 02671/ 70-59. Fax 02671/42-02. 35 rms. MINIBAR
$ Rates (including buffet breakfast): 95 DM–145 DM ($62.70–$95.70) single; 165 DM–225 DM ($108.90–$148.50) double. AE, DC, MC, V. **Parking:** 8 DM ($5.30). **Closed:** Jan 5–Mar 15.

Both a hotel and a wine restaurant, centrally located Alte Thorschenke is one of the oldest and best-known establishments along either side of the Mosel. The romantically conceived building, with its timbers and towers, was originally built in 1332. It became a hotel in 1960, when a modern wing was added. Most of the accommodations are reached via a cantilevered wooden staircase that has creaked for centuries—and probably will for a few more. Of course, there is an elevator in the rear if you want to make the ascent easy on yourself. Twenty rooms contain phones, and TV is available upon request. Nine rooms have four-poster beds.

Not to be ignored are meals in the tavern, accompanied by Mosel wine. In summer, guests often take their lunch at one of the sidewalk tables. Meals range from 50 DM to 78 DM ($33 to $51.50).

Guests of the hotel can visit the 500-year-old castle of Baron von Landenberg in Eller, about 4½ miles from Cochem. There in the old cellars they can enjoy tasting the wines.

LOHSPEICHER, Obergasse 1, D-5590 Cochem. Tel. 02671/39-76. Fax 02671/17-72. 8 rms. A/C MINIBAR TV TEL
$ Rates (including continental breakfast): 75 DM–85 DM ($49.50–$56.10) single; 130 DM–150 DM ($85.80–$99) double. AE, DC, MC. **Parking:** 7.50 DM ($5). **Closed:** Jan–Feb.
A former warehouse for supplies for the local tannery, this generously proportioned 1832 building with hand-hewn beams has been completely renovated into a delightful centrally located hotel, serving excellent meals and offering lodging in well-furnished rooms.

A gourmet meal, at what many consider the best table in town, costs 45 DM to 85 DM ($29.70 to $56.10). Specialties include onion or snail soup, followed by all kinds

of fish and game dishes (try the filet of venison with wild mushrooms in cream sauce).
The restaurant is open from noon to 2pm and 6 to 11pm; closed Tuesday.

MOSELROMANTIK HOTEL-CAFÉ THUL, Brauselaystrasse 27, D-5590
    Cochem-Cond. Tel. 02671/71-34. Fax 02671/53-67. 24 rms (all with bath or
    shower).
$ Rates (including continental breakfast): 68 DM–85 DM ($44.90–$56.10) single;
    130 DM–150 DM ($85.80–$99) double. DC, MC. **Closed:** Dec–Feb.
Comfortably modern, this hotel in the town center offers clean rooms and
gemütlichkeit to guests. Furnishings are in a functional modern style. The dining
room serves good food in a pleasant setting, with meals costing 30 DM to 50 DM
($19.80 to $33).

TRITON, Uferstrasse 10, D-5590 Cochem-Cond. Tel. 02671/2-18. Fax
    02671/5751. 18 rms (all with bath or shower). TV TEL **Directions:** Across the
    river from the town center.
$ Rates: (including continental breakfast): 80 DM–85 DM ($52.80–$56.10) single;
    160 DM–170 DM ($105.60–$112.20) double. AE, DC, MC, V.
One of the finest things about this balconied hotel is the view of the baroque buildings
and the fortified castle that you'll get from your river-view windows. Across the Mosel
from the rest of Cochem, the hotel offers modern rooms. In keeping with the symbol
of the hotel (Neptune's triton), the hotel also has an indoor pool with a sauna, plus a
waterside café/sun terrace built almost on the riverbank.

INEXPENSIVE

AM ROSENHÜGEL, Valwigerstrasse 57, D-5590 Cochem-Cond. Tel.
    02671/13-96. Fax 02671/81-16. 23 rms (all with bath or shower). TV
$ Rates (including buffet breakfast): 60 DM–75 DM ($39.60–$49.50) single; 100
    DM–140 DM ($66–$92.40) double. **Parking:** Free. MC, V. **Closed:** Dec–Jan.
The Goebel family are the hosts at this centrally located hotel, which has balconies
and a sun terrace overlooking the Mosel. Some of the rooms offer spectacular views of
the castle on the hill. Furnishings are in a simple modern style.

BURG HOTEL, Moselpromenade 23, D-5590 Cochem. Tel. 02671/71-
    17. Fax 02671/83-36. 50 rms (all with bath or shower). MINIBAR TV TEL
$ Rates (including buffet breakfast): 75 DM–120 DM ($49.50–$79.20) single; 90
    DM–220 DM ($59.40–$145.20) double. AE, DC, MC, V. **Parking:** Free.
The Müller family has renovated this centrally located inn. The furnishings are
traditional, with a few antiques lending added style, and some rooms have balconies
opening onto views of the Mosel.
    In the restaurant, typical dishes include game fricassée with asparagus and rice,
fresh trout meunière, and rumpsteak with mushrooms. A large selection of the best
Mosel wine is available to accompany your meal. The hotel offers an indoor pool,
sauna, solarium, and TV room.

HAUS ERHOLUNG, Moselpromenade 65, D-5590 Cochem. Tel. 02671/
    75-99. Fax 02671/4362. 10 rms (all with bath or shower).
$ Rates (including continental breakfast): 47 DM–60 DM ($31–$39.60) single; 86
    DM–108 DM ($56.80–$71.30) double. MC. **Parking:** Free. **Closed:** Mid-Nov
    to mid-Mar.
    The restaurant of this pension, on the main street in the town center, is gaily
decorated with hanging pink-and-white lamps and lots of green plants. The
dormers and mansard roof of the house itself indicate that it was probably a
private villa before the addition of the sun terrace. Many of the double rooms are
sunny, with large windows exposing views of the countryside. Your hostess is
Hildegunde Lehmann, who will show you to the sauna and pool and serve you a

wholesome breakfast. Overflow guests are housed in an annex, which opens onto a view of the river and castle.

WHERE TO DINE
MODERATE

HOTEL BRIXIADE, Uferstrasse 13, D-5590 Cochem-Cond. Tel. 02671/30-15.

Cuisine: GERMAN. **Reservations:** Usually not necessary.

$ Prices: Appetizers 10 DM–20 DM ($6.60–$13.20); main courses 20 DM–30 DM ($13.20–$19.80). AE, V.

Open: Lunch daily 11:30am–2:30pm; dinner daily 6–9:30pm.

The Brixiade is a hostelry with an illustrious tradition. Its heyday was the period just preceding World War I, when it was a favorite of Kaiser Wilhelm II and of the poet Joseph von Lauff. The German cuisine is well known as among the best in the area, and you can sit either in the Weinstube or on the garden terrace. If you order Mosel wine here, you'll get the best of the local vintages.

The centrally located hotel also rents 40 comfortably furnished rooms, charging 60 DM to 80 DM ($39.60 to $52.80) daily for singles, 120 DM to 150 DM ($79.20 to $99) for doubles, including a continental breakfast. All rooms have private baths or showers.

PARKHOTEL LANDENBERG, Sehler Anlagen 1, D-5590 Cochem-Sehl. Tel. 02671/71-10.

Cuisine: GERMAN/INTERNATIONAL. **Reservations:** Recommended.

$ Prices: Appetizers 9 DM–16 DM ($5.90–$10.60); main courses 18 DM–32 DM ($11.90–$21.10). AE, DC, MC, V.

Open: Lunch daily noon–2pm; dinner daily 6–9pm. **Closed:** Jan 5–Mar 15.

About a mile from the town's Bahnhof, the Parkhotel Landenberg offers a pleasing panoramic view to the Cochemer-Reichsburg and over the Mosel. The specialties of this region are venison, wild boar, and fish—to be enjoyed with a good bottle of white Mosel wine from the hotel's own cellar.

The 25 rooms in the hotel are comfortably furnished. Singles rent for 95 DM to 145 DM ($62.70 to $95.70) daily, doubles for 155 DM to 250 DM ($102.30 to $165), including a continental breakfast. Facilities include a pool, sauna, and solarium. Parking is 8 DM ($5.30).

WEISSMÜHLE IM ENTERTTAL, D-5590 Cochem. Tel. 02671/89-55.

Cuisine: GERMAN. **Reservations:** Recommended. **Directions:** From the center of Cochem, drive toward autobahn (direction: Koblenz/Trier). The inn is on left of road, 1 mile from Cochem.

$ Prices: Appetizers 8.50 DM–20 DM ($5.60–$13.20); main courses 19 DM–36 DM ($12.50–$23.80); four-course fixed-price menu 70 DM ($46.20). DC, MC, V.

Open: Daily noon–9pm.

Weissmühle is in Enterttal, an idyllic hamlet outside of Cochem. Before or after your meal, you'll enjoy a walk through the streets of this small wine village. Many of the German specialties on the menu are unique to the restaurant and include a series of Wurst dishes, trout, or Spiessbraten grilled to perfection over an open fire.

Also, 36 comfortably furnished rooms are rented. Singles cost 80 DM ($52.80) daily, while doubles go for 150 DM to 190 DM ($99 to $125.40), including a buffet breakfast. Rooms have private baths, phones, and TVs.

EASY EXCURSION
BURG ELTZ

This magnificent castle on the north bank of the Mosel is called **✪ Burg Eltz** (tel. 02672/13-00), above the village of Moselkern and surrounded by woodlands. It lies 12 miles northeast of Cochem and 20 miles southwest of Koblenz. A parking lot,

Antoniuskapelle, can be reached via Münstermaifeld. The lot lies less than a mile from the castle, with buses running between it and the castle every 5 minutes.

This is one of the few medieval castles in the region still intact. The original structure, built from the 12th to the 17th century, has been preserved in all its glory—the romance of the Middle Ages really comes alive here. Completely surrounding a large inner court, the castle houses four separate residences, with original furnishings from the medieval period, including some fine old paintings and tapestries. From April to November 1, the castle is open daily from 9:30am to 5:30pm. Admission is 8 DM ($5.30) for adults and 5.50 DM ($3.60) for children. A wine-tasting cellar and a treasury containing works by goldsmiths and silversmiths, armor, weapons, and other objects of value acquired by the family through the centuries are also open to the public. If you want to fortify yourself before the trek back to town, two small restaurants lie within the castle walls. Access is by autobahn A48 and A61 and Route 49.

CHAPTER 9

THE BLACK FOREST (SCHWARZWALD)

- **WHAT'S SPECIAL ABOUT THE BLACK FOREST (SCHWARZWALD)**
- **1. BADEN-BADEN**
- **2. FREIBURG IM BREISGAU**
- **3. TRIBERG**

When you visit the Black Forest, or *Schwarzwald* in German, a region in southwestern Germany, don't expect to come upon a little elf working on a cuckoo clock in his tiny gingerbread shop. What you will find, however, is nearly as exciting and altogether more enjoyable. The Schwarzwald covers a triangular section of the large state of Baden-Württemberg, roughly 90 miles long and 25 miles wide. The pine- and birch-studded mountains are alive with fairy-tale villages, sophisticated spas, and modern ski resorts, but, sad to say, pollution by acid rain from surrounding industries now threatens one of the most beautiful parts of Germany. The peaks in the southern part of the forest reach as high as 5,000 feet, excellent for skiing in winter and hiking or mountain climbing in summer. The little lakes of Titisee and Schluchsee are popular for boating, swimming—and, of course, winter skating. Fish abound in the streams and lakes, and deer romp through groves of fir.

Besides the cuckoo clock and the many toys manufactured in the Black Forest, this region is noted for another product—Kirschwasser, an unsweetened cherry brandy derived from the fruit of black, twisted cherry trees. This, along with Black Forest bacon and provincial-style rye bread, helps create a memorable meal.

SEEING THE REGION

The ideal way to explore the Schwarzwald is on foot, but time and energy would probably run out before the many scenic attractions did. So motoring is the best alternative. The roads through the forest are excellent, especially the ✪ **Schwarzwald Hochstrasse** (Black Forest High Road or Ridgeway, B500), running almost the entire length of the region, some 100 miles from Baden-Baden to Freudenstadt, then resuming at Triberg and going on to Waldshut on the Rhine, where you can cross the border to Switzerland. This scenic route offers many opportunities to park your car and explore the countryside or to turn off on one of the side roads leading to hospitable villages, ancient castles, and rolling farmlands.

SUGGESTED ITINERARY

Day 1 If you're coming from the north (perhaps Frankfurt), use Baden-Baden as your gateway to the Black Forest, taking a promenade through its parks, relaxing at its baths, and gambling at its casino.

Day 2 Spend a leisurely day driving along the Schwarzwald Hochstrasse from Baden-Baden to Freudenstadt. Continue south to Triberg for the night.

WHAT'S SPECIAL ABOUT THE BLACK FOREST [SCHWARZWALD]

Great Towns/Villages

☐ Baden-Baden, the premier spa of Germany, where Caracalla bathed some 1,800 years ago.

☐ Freiburg im Breisgau, the largest city in the Black Forest, noted for its towering cathedral and Altstadt.

☐ Triberg, deep in the heart of the Black Forest, home of the cuckoo clock.

Ace Attractions

☐ Lichtentaler Allee, in Baden-Baden, a park-promenade along the Oosbach River—planted with exotic shrubs and trees.

☐ Schwarzwald Hochstrasse, Black Forest High Road or Ridgeway, one of Germany's great scenic drives, from Baden-Baden to Freudenstadt and from Triberg to Waldshut.

☐ Wasserfall, outside Triberg, dropping some 530 feet, spilling down in seven stages, the highest waterfall in Germany.

Religious Shrine

☐ Freiburg cathedral, on which construction began in 1200, with a "five-tone wonder bell" from 1258.

Shopping

☐ Haus der 1000 Uhren (House of 1,000 Clocks), in Triberg, cuckoo clocks in all sizes, shapes, and sounds.

Museum

☐ Schwarzwald-Museum, in Triberg, where the olden days of the Black Forest come alive in folklore and handicraft exhibitions.

Music Shrine

☐ Brahmshaus, outside Baden-Baden, where the composer spent his summers, working on the "Lichtentaler Symphony" (No. 2) and other works.

Evening Entertainment

☐ Spielbank, in Baden-Baden, a nighttime extravaganza where, according to some, Dostoyevski wrote *The Gambler* after losing his shirt in the casino.

Days 3–4 Explore Triberg in the morning, visit its House of 1,000 Clocks and see its waterfall, then journey to Freiburg im Breisgau for a two-night stopover. Spend Day 4 exploring Freiburg's cathedral and Altstadt (Old Town).

GETTING THERE

International airports serving the area are in Stuttgart (see Chapter 7) and the Swiss city of Basel. Basel lies only 44 miles from Freiburg, the "capital" of the Black Forest. Trains run north and south through the Rhine Valley, with fast, frequent service to such Black Forest towns as Freiburg and Baden-Baden, where connections are possible throughout Germany. Motorists should take autobahn A5, running the length of the Black Forest. See individual towns for more specific transportation recommendations.

---

1. BADEN-BADEN

69 miles W of Stuttgart; 69 miles NE of Freiburg; 108 miles S of Frankfurt

GETTING THERE By Train Baden-Baden is on major rail lines connecting

Frankfurt and Basel and Stuttgart and Munich, with frequent connections in all directions. Twenty trains arrive daily from Stuttgart (trip time: 1 hour, 15 minutes), 25 trains from Munich (4 hours, 10 minutes), and 45 from Frankfurt (3 hours). For local rail information, call 07221/19-419. If you travel to Baden-Baden by rail, you will arrive at Baden-Oos, north of town. Regrettably, it's an expensive 20-minute taxi ride into the town center.

By Bus   Long-distance bus service is provided to Freudenstadt and Tübingen (line #1070), operated by Deutsche Touring GmbH in Frankfurt (tel. 069/79-030 for information). Regional bus service to Offenburg and Achern Bühl is offered by RVS Regionalbusverkehr GmbH at Offenburg (tel. 0781/70-954).

By Car   Access to Baden-Baden is via autobahn A5 north and south or autobahn A8 east and west. The drive south from Frankfurt takes two hours, from Munich about four hours.

ESSENTIALS   For information, contact the **Haus des Kurgastes,** Augustaplatz 8 (tel. 07221/27-52-00).

In the 19th century, the nobility of Europe discovered Baden-Baden, where the bath-conscious Roman emperor Caracalla had taken the waters more than 1,500 years before. Most of the crowns and titles are dust today, but the legacy left by these Romans and Romanovs had made the resort the most elegant and sophisticated playground in Germany. The clientele may have changed, yet Baden-Baden still evokes an aura of 19th-century privilege, combined with the most up-to-date facilities. By the way, the name Baden-Baden (i.e., Baden in Baden state) was adopted to differentiate the town from another spa, Baden-bei-Wien, near Vienna.

Baden-Baden is the ideal choice for sports and outdoor enthusiasts who would like to settle in for a few days of golf, tennis, or horseback riding. Lovers of horse racing will enjoy the international racing season each August at Iffezheim Track. The surrounding countryside is good for hiking and mountain climbing. During the winter, Baden-Baden is still very active. As the gateway to the Black Forest, it is a convenient center for skiing—after a day on the slopes, you can return to a soothing swim in a thermal pool before a night out at the casino.

Most of the spa's attractions are within walking distance of one another. The heart of Baden-Baden is Leopoldsplatz. From the Hauptbahnhof, Leopoldsplatz may be reached by following the Rheinstrasse, which becomes Langestrasse and then Luisenstrasse as it stretches like a snake all the way to the square. From the square, Sophienstrasse, a major artery of town, runs east to what is considered historic Baden-Baden. In and around the area north of Sophienstrasse are such attractions as the Neues Schloss, the Stifskirche, and several baths, both ancient and modern. From Leopoldsplatz a bridge over the river leads into Goetheplatz, a short walk from the Kurhaus, the Spielbank, and the Trinkhalle. South of the Kurhaus, Lichtentaler Allee is the major promenade boulevard of the spa. Lichtentaler Allee will take you to Lichtental, once a separate town, but now part of Baden-Baden. If you continue south, you can traverse the Schwarzwald Hochstrasse referred to in this chapter's introduction.

WHAT TO SEE & DO

THE LEADING SPAS

Your hotel can give you full information on the facilities available at both the Friedrichsbad and the Caracalla.

FRIEDRICHSBAD, Römerplatz 1. Tel. 07221/27-59-21.
   Mark Twain, writing of his visit to Baden-Baden during a tour of Europe, didn't

think much of the town, although he must have loved the baths: "I fully believe I left my rheumatism in Baden-Baden," he wrote.

It's likely that the waters that did Mark Twain so much good were those of the Friedrichsbad, also known as the Old Baths, built from 1869 to 1877 at the behest of Grand Duke Friedrich von Baden. Following the Roman-Irish method, it takes about two hours to have the complete bath program, which involves a shower; two saunas (from 130°F to 160°F) taken in a white-tile chamber whose vaulted ceiling is decorated with waterbirds; a brush massage soaping; thermal steam baths; and three freshwater baths ranging from warm to 60°F. After a 30-minute period of rest and relaxation, wrapped in a sheet or blanket, you're supposed to feel somewhat rejuvenated. Other types of therapy, including massage, electrotherapy, and hydrotherapy, are also offered.

Admission: 38 DM ($25.10). **Bus:** 1.
Open: Mon–Sat 10am–10pm.

CARACALLA-THERME, Römerplatz 11. Tel. 07221/27-59-40.

The Caracalla-Therme has been made more pleasing visually by the addition of a round colonnaded extension with splashing and cascading pools. You can decide on your own bath system here, and medicinal treatment might include mudbaths, massages, whirlpools, and inhalation therapy. The slightly radioactive water, rich in sodium chloride, comes from artesian wells 6,000 feet under the Florentiner Mountain. Its temperature is around 160°F. Bathers usually begin in cooler pools, working up to the warm water. The baths have a sauna area, with footbaths and sunbaths; sauna temperatures go from 185°F to 200°F. You must wear bathing suits in the pools, but nudity is necessary in the saunas. Also offered are group water gymnastics. The Caracalla has a bar and a cafeteria.

Admission: 18 DM ($11.90) for 2 hours of bathing.
Open: Daily 8am–10pm. **Bus:** 1.

OTHER SIGHTS

The center of Baden-Baden activity is ✪ **Lichtentaler Allee,** the park-promenade along the bank of the Oosbach River (affectionately called Oos—pronounced "ohs"), which runs through the center of town. As you stroll along this promenade, you'll be amazed at the variety not only of exotic shrubs and trees but also of rhododendron, azalea, roses, and zinnia. At the north end of the park, on the banks of the stream, are the buildings of the Kurgarten, including the classical **Kurhaus.**

SPIELBANK, Kaiserallee 1. Tel. 07221/210-60.

✪ Behind its sparkling white columns and facade is the Spielbank, the oldest casino in Germany, where for more than 200 years everyone from Dostoyevski's character Alexei Ivanovich to the Prince of Wales has tested his or her luck at the roulette wheel or the baccarat table. Dostoyevski is supposed to have written *The Gambler* after he lost his shirt, and almost his mind, at the gaming tables here (and in Wiesbaden).

The various casino rooms were designed more than 130 years ago in the style of those in an elegant French château, not unlike Versailles. In all this splendor, you can gamble year round, as have such former patrons as Kaiser Wilhelm I, Bismarck, Marlene Dietrich, and the Aga Khan. Jackets and ties are mandatory for men. To enter the casino during gambling hours, you must possess a valid passport or identification card and be at least 21.

Tours: The historic gaming rooms may be viewed daily 10am–noon on a conducted tour costing 3 DM ($2). If visitors want to gamble later, a full day's ticket is available for 5 DM ($3.30). The minimum take is 5 DM ($3.30), but visitors are not obliged to play. **Bus:** 1.

PUMP ROOM [Trinkhalle], Kaiserallee 3. Tel. 07221/27-52-77.

Most of the older bathing establishments, including the Friedrichsbad and the Caracalla-Therme, are on the opposite side of the Oos, in the heart of the Altstadt. The spa gardens contain the Pump Room (Trinkhalle), where visitors can sip the water. Built in the 19th century, the loggia of the hall is decorated with frescoes depicting Black Forest legends. The springs of Baden-Baden have been recognized for more than 2,000 years, and their composition is almost the same today as when the Romans built their baths here in the 3rd century.

Admission: 4 DM ($2.60).

Open: Daily 10am–5:30pm. **Closed:** Winter. **Bus:** 1.

RÖMANISCHE BADRUINEN, between Friedrichsbad and Caracalla-Therme. Tel. 07221/27-59-36.

The Ruins of the Roman Baths are entered from Römerplatz. The old baths were found in 1847 during the construction of the Friedrichsbad, with the bathhouse for the Roman soldiers. You can see a graphic example of hot-springs baths in ancient times.

Admission: 4 DM ($2.60).

Open: Daily 10am–noon and 1:30–4pm. **Closed:** Nov to Good Friday. **Bus:** 1.

NEUES SCHLOSS AND THE ZÄHRINGER MUSEUM, Schlosstrasse. Tel. 07221/2-55-93.

Above Römerplatz stands the Renaissance castle Neues Schloss, the former residence of the margraves of Baden. The original 1437 building was destroyed by a fire in 1689. The present structure, which is surrounded by a beautiful park, wasn't completed until 1847. The terraces offer an excellent view of the city.

The castle houses the **Zähringer Museum,** containing historical rooms from the 19th century, when the castle was the summer residence of the grand dukes of Baden, as well as documents relating to the Grand Duchy of Baden.

Admission: 4 DM ($2.60) adults, 2 DM ($1.30) children.

Open: Tues–Sun 10am–6pm. **Bus:** 1.

STIFTSKIRCHE/CATHOLIC COLLEGIATE CHURCH, Marktplatz. Tel. 07221/2-49-48.

The Church of St. Peter and Paul, near the Roman baths, was a parish church as far back as 1245. It belonged to a collegiate order from 1452 to 1806. Badly damaged by fire in 1689, the church was rebuilt partly in the baroque style. Features of special interest are the 1467 late Gothic crucifix; the tombs of the margraves of Baden; a late Gothic tabernacle from around 1500; and modern stained-glass windows (1953–56), designed by Willy Oeser.

Admission: Free.

Open: Daily 8am–7pm. **Bus:** 1.

NEARBY ATTRACTIONS

In the Lichtental quarter of Baden-Baden, once a separate town, stands **Brahmshaus,** Maximilianstrasse 85 (tel. 07221/7-11-72). The composer Johannes Brahms came here in 1865 and was to spend all his summer months until 1874 at this residence, working on the "Lichtentaler Symphony" (No. 2), among other works. The museum, containing much Brahms memorabilia, is open Monday, Wednesday, and Friday from 3 to 5pm and Sunday from 10am to 1pm, charging 3 DM ($2) admission. Every two years in May, the Baden-Baden Brahms Days—a music festival with about eight concerts—are held. The next festival will be in 1995. Take bus 1 from the Baden-Baden Hauptbahnhof to Brahmsplatz.

In the same neighborhood, you can visit the **Kloster Lichtental,** Hauptstrasse 40 (tel. 07221/7-23-32). This Cistercian convent has existed without interruption since 1245, when it was founded by Margravine Irmengard of Baden. At the moment, the community consists of 35 nuns. You can visit a 13th-century monastery church and hear a Gregorian choral daily at 5pm. On a conducted tour at 3pm, you're shown the Princes' Chapel and a museum of religious artifacts. Admission is 2 DM ($1.30). In the monastery shop visitors find art objects and can also purchase liqueurs produced by the nuns. Take bus 1 from the Baden-Baden Hauptbahnhof to Klosterplatz.

A notable landmark in Baden-Baden is **Merkur,** a mountain named for a sacrificial stone to the Roman god Mercury, which was discovered here. Until the 17th century, the mountain was known as Grosser Staufen. There are many paths with splendid views, and the Merkur Bergbahn, a mountain railway with a 54° slope, departs daily from 10am to 6pm, charging 6 DM ($4) for a round trip. At the station on top of Merkur are a restaurant, an observation tower, and a nature path. Lawns for sunbathing, with Kneipp facilities, are near the station.

Altes Schloss, Alter Schlossweg 1 (tel. 07221/2-69-48), is an old castle with interesting ruins. From the 11th century to its destruction by fire late in the 16th century, it was known as Hohenbaden Castle, seat of the margraves of Baden. From the tower, there's a panoramic view of Baden-Baden and across the Rhine plain to the Vosges Mountains. Facilities here are a terrace snack shop and parking area. The ruins can be visited for free on Tuesday through Sunday from 10am to 10pm. To reach the castle, leave Baden-Baden by Zahringerstrasse and take the Hohenbaden road north of the spa. You can return on the Gernsbach road. Allow about 1½ hours for this 8-mile jaunt. Bus 15 also runs here.

A summer palace, **Schloss Favorite,** Rastatt-Niederbuhl/Forch (tel. 07222/41-207), 3 miles southeast of Rastatt, was built in the baroque style in the early 18th century for Margravine Sibylla Augusts, the widow of "Türkenlouis" (Margrave Ludwig Wilhelm, so nicknamed because of his Turkish victories). The state rooms contain examples of materials used at the time of its construction—stucco, wood, marble—and such arts-and-crafts techniques as mother-of-pearl inlaying, agate and ivory painting, lacquering, wax modeling, and pearl embroidery. There is also a famous porcelain collection and the original kitchen. Concerts are given here, and there is a café. The scenic park has exotic trees and a Magdelene chapel. Guided tours are given from March to October. Open from 9 to 11am and 2 to 5pm; closed Monday. A separate ticket, costing 4 DM ($2.60) for adults and 2 DM ($1.30) for children, is charged for each of three attractions: (1) ground floor with the original kitchen; (2) state rooms, and (3) porcelain collection. No bus runs here.

A former knight's castle, **Yburg** (tel. 07221/25475), is a 4-mile signposted run south from Baden-Baden, on the Yburg. Little is known about the origin of the castle, but it was mentioned in documents of 1245. Destroyed in the Peasants' War of 1525, it was restored by a margrave of Baden who appreciated its panoramic view of Baden-Baden, the vineyards, the Black Forest, the Rhine plain, and the Vosges Mountains. It can be visited free at any time during the day, and there is a castle restaurant for refreshments. You can climb the 110 steps to the tower, about a 15-minute trek. To reach the castle, take Fremersbergstrasse and Varnhalterstrasse (turn left at the bus stop near the Golf Hotel).

WHERE TO STAY

VERY EXPENSIVE

BRENNER'S PARK HOTEL & SPA, An der Lichtentaler Allee, D-7570 Baden-Baden. Tel. 07221/90-00. Fax 07221/38-772. 100 rms, 29 suites. MINIBAR TV **Bus:** 1.

$ Rates (including continental breakfast): 382 DM–622 DM ($252.10–$410.50) single; 514 DM–1,014 DM ($339.20–$669.20) double; from 1,764 DM ($1164.20) suite. AE, DC, MC, V. **Parking:** 28 DM ($18.50).

The Rolls-Royce of resort hotels in Baden-Baden lies in a large private park facing the River Oos and Lichtentaler Allee. Some of its international habitués wouldn't dare let a year go by without making an appearance here for the cure. It's a glamorous place. Celebrities who have patronized the waters here in the past include Cornelius Vanderbilt and Igor Stravinsky. The rooms offer good taste and comfort; some are air-conditioned. The hotel also rents some of the most luxuriously appointed suites in Germany. The public rooms are fashionably conceived, each providing a rich background for the chic attire of guests.

Dining/Entertainment: A pianist plays every afternoon in the lounge and in the evening at the Oleander-Piano-Bar for dancing. There is gourmet dining in the main restaurant Park or in the Schwarzwald-Stube.

Services: Room service, laundry, dry cleaning.

Facilities: Pool, sauna, solarium, massage-and-fitness studio, Lancaster Beauty Farm. The staff includes an expert team of beauticians and masseurs. Other installations feature modern facilities for diagnosis and therapeutics. Golf, tennis, riding, climbing, and walking on marked paths and promenades can be arranged.

KURHOTEL QUISISANA, Bismarckstrasse 21, D-7570 Baden-Baden. Tel. 07221/34-46. Fax 07221/38-195. 60 rms, 9 suites. MINIBAR TV TEL **Bus:** 1.

$ Rates (including continental breakfast): 185 DM–260 DM ($122.10–$171.60) single; 300 DM–360 DM ($198–$237.60) double; from 450 DM ($297) suite. MC, V. **Parking:** 18 DM ($11.90).

Radiating from the core of a 19th-century villa, the annexes of this hotel contain some of the most up-to-date health facilities anywhere in the Black Forest. You can spend an early morning in group calisthenics, for example, followed by treatments with any one of a dozen skin- and muscle-toning techniques. An evening could be spent savoring the sophisticated cuisine available from the world-class kitchens before retiring to your spacious and well-appointed room. One of the staff will direct you to the center of the spa, eight minutes away by foot.

The guest rooms, furnished with both traditional and modern styling, are beautifully kept and well maintained. The elegant restaurant serves both an international and a regional cuisine, with meals costing from 50 DM to 70 DM ($33 to $46.20); only hotel guests are served. Room service, laundry, and dry cleaning are available.

SCHLOSSHOTEL BÜHLERHÖHE/PLÄTTIG HOTEL, Schwarzwald Hochstrasse 1, D-7580 Bühl 13. Tel. 07226/55-100, or toll free 800/223-6800 in the U.S. Fax 07226/55-777. 90 rms, 20 suites. MINIBAR TV TEL **Bus:** Bühl bus from Baden-Baden.

$ Rates (including continental breakfast): 290 DM–420 DM ($191.40–$277.20) single; 490 DM–620 DM ($323.40–$409.20) double; from 1,050 DM ($693) suite. AE, DC, MC, V. **Parking:** 25 DM ($16.50).

⭐ Long one of the famous landmark hotels of the Black Forest, the Schlosshotel Bühlerhöhe underwent a massive restoration in summer 1988.

Located a few miles from Baden-Baden, the complex embraces not only the Schlosshotel but also a spa clinic and the Plättig Hotel. The three separate buildings have a staff of 300 attending to the needs of clients on a 24-hour basis. The hotel has been fully converted to a world-class standard, the epitome of elegance and comfort, and it's filled with modern amenities yet imbued with the most glamorous styling of yesterday. All rooms are beautifully fitted with superior carpeting and furniture, including original oil paintings, cotton bedding, hairdryers, electronic keys, radios, color TVs, and private safes. Suites are named after famous painters, with originals by the artist so honored.

Dining/Entertainment: The Imperial Restaurant offers a refined Swabian and Alsatian-French cuisine, with a discriminating wine list. The elegantly appointed Schloss Restaurant features both national and regional dishes, with diet and calorie-conscious meals available upon advance order. There is also a piano bar with live music.

Services: Beauty farm offering fitness massages, shiatsu, mud packs, and many other treatments; room service; laundry; dry cleaning.

Facilities: Steam and sauna baths, hot whirlpools, Jacuzzi, underwater massages, Kneipp applications, pool, angling, hunting, horseback riding.

STEIGENBERGER AVANCE BADISCHER HOF, Langestrasse 47, D-7570 Baden-Baden. Tel. 07221/934-0, or toll free 800/223-5652 in the U.S. and Canada. Fax 07221/934-470. 139 rms, 5 suites. MINIBAR TV TEL **Bus:** 1.

$ Rates (including buffet breakfast): 225 DM–265 DM ($148.50–$174.90) single; 340 DM–460 DM ($224.40–$303.60) double; from 530 DM ($349.80) suite. AE, DC, MC, V. **Parking:** 25 DM ($16.50). **Bus:** 1.

With its colonnaded facade, the Badischer Hof is on a busy street in the center of town, but in the back you'll find an elegant garden with a wide balustraded terrace, flower beds, and a lawn around a stone fountain. Once a Capuchin monastery stood on this site, giving way to a spa hotel in 1809. Then the hotel began its career as a social center for famous personalities who spent "the season" there, taking the cure. One of its most distinguished guests, composer Carl Maria von Weber, wrote: "The beautiful dining room with its high ceiling, the tastefully decorated casino, and the fine stone-encased bathing facilities will make this guesthouse more and more popular with the years." And so they have. You'll look in amazement at the four-story-high colonnaded hallway, with its great staircase and encircling balustraded balconies. The public rooms are attractive and old world, and the well-furnished guest rooms are priced according to size and view. Many rooms have private balconies. Those in the monastery building have thermal water piped into their baths.

Dining/Entertainment: Dining is in the Park Restaurant, where an international cuisine is served, with meals costing from 62 DM to 86 DM ($40.90 to $56.80). Vegetarian food is also featured.

Services: Room service, laundry, dry cleaning.

Facilities: Thermal-spring pool, open-air pool.

STEIGENBERGER EUROPÄISCHER HOF, Kaiserallee 2, D-7570 Baden-Baden. Tel. 07221/933-0, or toll free 800/223-5652 in the U.S. or Canada. Fax 07221/2-88-31. 131 rms, 4 suites. MINIBAR TV TEL **Bus:** 1.

$ **Rates** (including buffet breakfast): 235 DM–285 DM ($155.10–$188.10) single; 370 DM–470 DM ($244.20–$310.20) double; from 1,500 DM ($990) suite. AE, DC, MC, V. **Parking:** 25 DM ($16.50).

Opposite the Kurgarten and the casino, the elegant Europäischer Hof is adjacent to the Oos River, which runs at the edge of the Kurpark. Actually, it's a pair of joined hotels that were built during the period when spacious living facilities were considered important and affordable. Its colonnaded central hallway is stunning, and many suites and rooms open onto balconies. The hotel offers well-furnished rooms equipped with radios and color TVs.

Dining/Entertainment: In the restaurant, meals cost from 65 DM to 92 DM ($42.90 to $60.70)—and there is formal old-world service, with a nostalgia for yesteryear. Windows overlooking a park sweep across one entire wall of the restaurant. Open daily from noon to 2pm and 6:45 to 10pm.

Services: Room service, laundry, dry cleaning.

Facilities: Hairdresser, beauty parlor.

EXPENSIVE

BAD-HOTEL ZUM HIRSCH, Hirschstrasse 1, D-7570 Baden-Baden. Tel. 07221/93-90, or toll free 800/223-5652 in the U.S. and Canada. Fax 07221/3-81-48. 58 rms. TEL **Bus:** 1.

$ **Rates** (including buffet breakfast): 125 DM–173 DM ($82.50–$114.20) single; 208 DM–280 DM ($137.30–$184.80) double. AE, DC, MC, V. **Parking:** 16 DM ($10.60).

This beautiful and old-fashioned hotel was operated by the same family from 1689 until it was sold to the Steigenberger chain in 1982. It's a tranquil compound of several buildings where modernization has been constant; the antique furnishings have been retained, making the hotel a living museum of the fine period pieces. The formal dining room is dominated by crystal chandeliers and paneled walls; the Blauer Salon is equally attractive, with blue-velvet provincial armchairs and classic draperies; and there are several sitting and drawing rooms, each tastefully furnished. The interesting old-style guest rooms are individually furnished, as if in a country home; some offer minibars and TVs. All rooms have piped-in thermal water.

The restaurant is reserved for board guests. In summer, guests can drink coffee on the wisteria-shaded terrace. Hotel services include a newsstand, dry cleaning, laundry, a social program, and adaptor plugs.

DER KLEINE PRINZ [The Little Prince], Lichtentalerstrasse 36, D-7570 Baden-Baden. Tel. 07221/34-64. Fax 07221/38-264. 24 rms, 15 suites. MINIBAR TV TEL **Bus:** 1.

$ **Rates** (including buffet breakfast): 150 DM–225 DM ($99–$148.50) single; 250 DM–325 DM ($165–$214.50) double; from 425 DM ($280.50) suite. AE, DC, MC, V. **Parking:** 15 DM ($9.90).

In a century-old baroque building is a small, cozy hotel run by Norberg and Edeltraud Rademacher, who know how to cater to American tastes. Norberg has had 22 years of hotel experience in the United States as director at the Waldorf-Astoria and then at the New York Hilton. He and his wife have totally renovated and upgraded Der Kleine Prinz, offering rooms with baths, cable color TVs (English TV), alarm radios, hairdryers, and, in some cases, air conditioning. Each room has its own special feature—an open fireplace, a tower, a balcony, or a whirlpool bath. The furnishings are antiques or Portuguese pine.

The small ground-floor restaurant is an elegant place for a four-course dinner, costing from 65 DM ($42.90), and you can have drinks at the adjacent lobby bar. Personalized service adds to the attractiveness of this intimate, immaculate little hotel, where room service and laundry facilities are available.

DER QUELLENHOF, Sophienstrasse 27-29, D-7570 Baden-Baden. Tel. 07221/93-80, or toll free 800/528-1234 in the U.S. Fax 07221/28-320. 51 rms, 8 suites. MINIBAR TV TEL **Bus:** 1.

$ **Rates** (including buffet breakfast): 165 DM–195 DM ($108.90–$128.70) single; 270 DM–310 DM ($178.20–$204.60) double; from 450 DM ($297) suite. AE, DC, MC, V. **Parking:** 25 DM ($16.50).

A large modern hotel complex, Der Quellenhof could be your resting point in Baden-Baden. Views of the spa's Wilhelminian architecture are generally spectacular from the balconies of the well-furnished, soundproof rooms, which have all the modern conveniences. Room service, laundry, and dry cleaning are provided.

Its informal restaurant, s'Badstüble, offers many regional and international dishes, including some vegetarian specialties. Meals cost from 35 DM to 55 DM ($23.10 to $36.30).

HAUS REICHERT, Sophienstrasse 4, D-7570 Baden-Baden. Tel. 07221/2-41-91. Fax 07221/2-95-34. 24 rms. TV TEL **Bus:** 1 from the Hauptbahnhof.

$ **Rates** (including continental breakfast): 150 DM ($99) single; 220 DM ($145.20) double. AE, DC, MC, V. **Parking:** 10 DM ($6.60).

Owned by the same family since 1860, Haus Reichert is an inviting place to stay. This five-floor 19th-century hotel has a round tower capped by a funnel-shaped "witch's cap." Inside, the rooms are high-ceilinged and comfortable, although practically none of the original furniture or detailing has survived the many renovations. There is room service. Exercise equipment, a pool, and a sauna are at your disposal, along with a central location not far from the casino.

HOLLAND HOTEL SOPHIENPARK, Sophienstrasse 14, D-7570 Baden-Baden. Tel. 07221/3-56-0. Fax 07221/35-61-21. 75 rms, 5 suites. MINIBAR TV TEL **Bus:** 1.

$ **Rates** (including continental breakfast): 160 DM–205 DM ($105.60–$135.30) single; 230 DM–250 DM ($151.80–$165) double; from 350 DM ($231) suite. AE, DC, MC, V. **Parking:** 15 DM ($9.90).

Kings and princes, along with a well-known composer or two (among them Franz Liszt), have frequented this hotel over some 250 years. Reopened in 1987 after a major renovation, it's now better than ever, with a fine restaurant. Its facade is chiseled sandstone carved into baroque designs of shells and flowers, but its recent modernization has added glass-and-steel porticos. The rooms are stylishly furnished, often in pastels.

At noon, the restaurant offers one of the spa's better buffets, reasonably priced at 33 DM ($21.80). You can dine on regional and international specialties in the evening for 47 DM to 90 DM ($31 to $59.40). Room service, laundry, and dry cleaning are available. English-speaking employees see to your needs with professionalism and skill.

INEXPENSIVE

HOTEL AM MARKT, Marktplatz 18, D-7570 Baden-Baden. Tel. 07221/ 2-27-47. 27 rms (20 with bath or shower). TEL **Bus:** 1 or 3 from Hauptbahnhof to Leopoldsplatz.

$ Rates (including continental breakfast): 45 DM ($29.70) single without bath or shower, 75 DM ($49.50) single with bath or shower; 88 DM ($58.10) double without bath or shower, 120 DM ($79.20) double with bath or shower. AE, DC, MC, V. **Parking:** 6 DM ($4).

Sitting like a pleasant country inn on the old marketplace, Hotel Am Markt is far removed from the grander social life of Baden-Baden. It's in a gem of a location, with the quiet interrupted only by chimes from the church across the square; a tiny terrace café in front has windowboxes of petunias. There is no lounge to speak of, but there is a tavern dining room with wooden dado, deep-set windows, and straight-back country armchairs—in all, a relaxed and informal atmosphere. Innkeeper Herr Bogner offers simply furnished but comfortable rooms. A restaurant is open for house guests from 6 to 9pm daily.

WHERE TO DINE

VERY EXPENSIVE

PARK-RESTAURANT, in Brenner's Park Hotel, Schillerstrasse 6. Tel. 07221/90-00.
Cuisine: INTERNATIONAL. **Reservations:** Required. **Bus:** 1.

$ Prices: Appetizers 18 DM–28 DM ($11.90–$18.50); main courses 45 DM–65 DM ($29.70–$42.90); fixed-price menus 78 DM–105 DM ($51.50–$69.30). AE, DC, MC, V.
Open: Lunch daily noon–2pm; dinner daily 7–9pm.

It is generally conceded that Park-Restaurant serves the best food in Baden-Baden. At the corner of Lichtentaler Allee and Schillerstrasse, this is one of the renowned spa dining rooms of Europe, definitely worth its high price. The cuisine here reaches the peak of the highest world standards, as does the service. The emphasis is on French (Alsatian) dishes, along with regional Badish and Rhine Valley foods. Specialties include terrine of rainbow and salmon trout, followed by roast saddle of venison. For dessert, try an ice-cream soufflé.

STAHLBAD, Augustaplatz 2. Tel. 07221/2-45-69.
Cuisine: CONTINENTAL. **Reservations:** Required. **Bus:** 1.

$ Prices: Appetizers 25 DM–40 DM ($16.50–$26.40); main courses 40 DM–55 DM ($26.40–$36.30); fixed-price menu 98.50 DM ($65). AE, DC, MC, V.
Open: Lunch Tues–Sat 11:30am–2pm; dinner Tues–Sat 7:30–10pm.

Providing dining in the French manner, Stahlbad is a luxury restaurant with a stunning decor. Owner Frau Uschi Monch welcomes you in the dining room. The atmosphere evokes a tavern: Every square inch is covered with a collection of framed prints, copper cooking and serving equipment, antique pewter plates, mugs, and engravings. An open kitchen whets your appetite for the good food being prepared. Some of the continental specialties are peppersteak and venison steak (in hunting season), fresh fish, and lobster thermidor (priced according to weight and lethally expensive). The homemade fettuccine Alfredo with white truffles (in season) is as good as—or better than—any you'll have in Rome.

MODERATE

MÜNCHNER LÖWENBRÄU, Gernsbacher Strasse 9. Tel. 07221/2-23-11.
Cuisine: GERMAN. **Reservations:** Not necessary. **Bus:** 1

$ Prices: Appetizers 10 DM–16 DM ($6.60–$10.60); main courses 16 DM–32 DM ($10.60–$21.10). DC, MC, V.
Open: Daily 11am–11pm.

The spa's most popular summertime beer garden is the Münchner Löwenbräu, in the heart of the Altstadt. The terrace is beneath a copse of clipped and pruned linden trees, and the indoor dining room (open year round) with its curved glass walls is up a flight of stone steps at the rear. Many kinds of German sausage are offered, along with an array of daily changing soup pots, Bavarian specialties, and a wide selection of cheese. Regional devotees order pork knuckles fresh from "the pork knuckle grill." Regulars often ask for the "Löwenbräu platter of bites," which is a hearty plate with everything from black pudding to sliced pork. For dessert, I'd suggest the apple fritters.

ZUM NEST, Rettigstrasse. Tel. 07221/2-30-76.
Cuisine: REGIONAL/CONTINENTAL. **Reservations:** Not necessary. **Bus:** 1.
$ Prices: Appetizers 10 DM–15 DM ($6.60–$9.90); main courses 18 DM–30 DM ($11.90–$19.80). AE, DC, MC, V.
Open: Lunch Fri–Wed 11:30am–2pm; dinner Fri–Wed 5–11pm. **Closed:** Mid-Jan to Feb 8.

Near Leopoldsplatz, Zum Nest consistently serves some of the finest moderately priced food in the Altstadt. In a forestlike wood-paneled room, waitresses in dirndls hurry about with platters filled with food and large mugs of beer. You can enjoy artichokes with hollandaise, sole meunière, and assorted roast meats with Spätzle. The Black Forest ham is always a good choice. Several vegetarian dishes are featured.

NEARBY DINING AT NEUWEIER

It's traditional for people of Baden-Baden to dine at the satellite resort of Neuweier, 6 miles southwest. Here are two suggestions.

EXPENSIVE

SCHLOSS NEUWEIER, Mauberbergstrasse 21. Tel. 07223/5-79-44.
Cuisine: INTERNATIONAL. **Reservations:** Required. **Directions:** 6 miles SW of Baden-Baden via Fremersbergstrasse. **Bus:** 6.
$ Prices: Appetizers 18 DM–24 DM ($11.90–$15.80); main courses 25 DM–50 DM ($16.50–$33); fixed-price menus 68 DM–130 DM ($44.90–$85.80). MC.
Open: Lunch Thurs–Mon noon–3pm; dinner Thurs–Tues 6pm–3am. **Closed:** Several weeks in winter (dates vary).

Schloss Neuweier is a small 12th-century castle entirely surrounded by defensive water fortifications and vineyards belonging to the estate. Its restaurant is not large but offers impeccable service in a decor of tile walls hung with paintings of former inhabitants. The house proudly serves local wines, including an excellent Riesling, and practices international cookery with flair, as reflected by the brisket with horseradish sauce and the baked ray.

ZUM ALDE GOTT, Wienstrasse 10. Tel. 07223/55-13.
Cuisine: BADISCHE. **Reservations:** Required. **Directions:** 6 miles SW of Baden-Baden via Fremersbergstrasse. **Bus:** 6.
$ Prices: Appetizers 18 DM–32 DM ($11.90–$21.10); main courses 38 DM–65 DM ($25.10–$42.90); fixed-price lunches 68 DM–95 DM ($44.90–$62.70); fixed-price dinner 90 DM–150 DM ($59.40–$99). AE, MC, V.
Open: Lunch Sat–Wed noon–3pm; dinner Fri–Wed 6–11pm.

In this very old wine cellar with a terrace restaurant, Wilfried Serr holds forth as one of the most distinguished chefs in the Baden-Baden area. He is ably assisted by his wife, Ilse, who helps guide guests through the refined menu, which is likely to include everything from carpaccio of lamb to terrine of fresh plums. Wild game in season is a fine art here. Try also the Black Forest trout or the sea bass. There are only 12 tables, in soft green and white, and the ambience is bright and cheerful.

NEARBY DINING AT VARNHALT

In the same southwesterly direction as Neuweier, but only 4 miles from central Baden-Baden, Varnhalt is another dining goal.

EXPENSIVE

POSPISIL'S RESTAURANT MERKURIUS, Klosterbergstrasse 2. Tel. 07223/54-74.
    Cuisine: CZECH/FRENCH/BADISCHE. **Reservations:** Required. **Directions:** 4 miles from Baden-Baden via Fremersbergstrasse. **Bus:** 16.
$ **Prices:** Appetizers 12 DM–32 DM ($7.90–$21.10); main courses 37 DM–45 DM ($24.40–$29.70); fixed-price menus 60 DM–125 DM ($39.60–$82.50). AE, DC, MC.
    Open: Lunch Wed–Fri and Sun noon–2pm; dinner Tues–Sun 7–10pm.
A family-run restaurant in a Landhaus-style building, this three-story modern structure has a brown roof and white-stucco walls. Pavel Pospisil imports his produce and meats every day from culinary-conscious Strasbourg, France. The food is an unusual blend of Czech and French specialties wedded harmoniously to Black Forest cuisine. You might opt for an eight-course "surprise menu," selected by the chef, who guarantees you a gastronomic thrill.

MODERATE

GASTHAUS ZUM ADLER, Klosterbergstrasse 15. Tel. 07221/5-72-41.
    Cuisine: GERMAN. **Reservations:** Recommended. **Bus:** 16 from the center of Baden-Baden.
$ **Prices:** Appetizers 12 DM–24 DM ($7.90–$15.80); main courses 20 DM–38 DM ($13.20–$25.10). AE, DC, MC, V.
    Open: Lunch Fri–Wed noon–2:30pm; dinner Fri–Wed 6–9:30pm. **Closed:** Jan 15–30 and Nov 20–30.

Baden-Baden can be intimidatingly chic, so if you're in the mood for an informal, relaxed, and gemütlich experience, you'll appreciate the rusticity of this country inn with reasonably priced German home-cookery. A choice of daily specialties is offered, including fish and game (in season)—carp, roast hare or pheasant, possibly poached salmon or trout in Riesling. The house offers inexpensive wines.

The inn also rents nine moderately priced rooms, a single with shower or bath costing 75 DM ($49.50) daily and a double with shower or private bath renting for 150 DM ($99).

---

2. FREIBURG IM BREISGAU

129 miles SW of Stuttgart; 44 miles N of Basel; 174 miles S of Frankfurt

GETTING THERE **By Train** The nearest major airports are at Basel and Stuttgart, to which Freiburg is connected by frequent trains. It's easy to reach this city via the efficient German Federal Railway, whose fastest trains stop at this junction en route to the Swiss Alps. Daily trains connect Frankfurt to Freiburg in 2 hours, or Hamburg to Freiburg in 8 hours. There are also direct rail connections with Berlin. From Zürich or Basel in Switzerland, easy rail connections to Freiburg can also be made. For rail information for the area, call 0761/19-419.

By Bus Long-distance bus service to such places as Basel is provided by Lines 1066, 1072, and 1077 of the Deutsche Touring GmbH in Frankfurt (tel. 069/79-030).

Call for routes, schedules, and tariffs. Regional bus service to towns around Freiburg is offered by SBG Südbaden Bus GmbH, Central Bus Station, Freiburg (tel. 0761/36-172). This company also offers air service from Freiburg to the EuroAirport Basel-Mulhouse and a Euro-Reglo-Bus between Freiburg and the French cities of Mulhouse and Colmar.

By Car Access by car is via autobahn A5 north and south.

ESSENTIALS Information For tourist information, contact **Freiburg-Information,** Rotteckring 14 (tel. 0761/368-90-90).

Orientation Your arrival is likely to be at the Hauptbahnhof in the northwestern sector. This rail terminus opens onto Bismarckallee. The center of Freiburg is small enough to be explored on foot. If you head east on Eisenbahnstrasse, you will reach the heart of the Altstadt. Colombi Park will be on your left as you walk along. This street will become Rathausgasse, leading into Rathausplatz. From this square a small street with a big name, Franziskanerstrasse, leads to Kaiser-Joseph-Strasse, the main commercial artery of the city. From here, take another small street, Münsterstrasse, to Münsterplatz and the famous cathedral, or Münster.

The largest city in the Black Forest region, Freiburg im Breisgau is often overlooked by visitors because this scenic and interesting city is off the beaten track. Its strategic location at the southern edge of the Black Forest brought the town in 1368 under the rule of the Austrian Habsburgs, which lasted for more than 400 years.

Approached from the Rhine plain on the west, the town is silhouetted against huge mountain peaks towering more than 3,000 feet. Freiburg's situation is responsible for its remarkable climate. In early spring the town is usually bursting into bloom while the mountain peaks are still covered with snow. In the fall the smell of new wine fills the narrow streets while reports of snowfalls on the nearby peaks are already reaching the ears of the townsfolk. The reason for this unusual weather is that Freiburg lies in the path of warm air currents that come up from the Mediterranean through the Burgundy Gap, balanced by the winds from the Black Forest hillsides. The two forces join to make Freiburg a year-round attraction and a sports center. The mountain peaks can be reached by funicular or by car within an hour.

The city is one of great historical significance and is home of a 550-year-old university, which has claimed among its faculty and alumni great scholars; scientists; humanists such as Erasmus; and Martin Waldseemüller, the first geographer to put the name *America* on a map.

WHAT TO SEE & DO

FREIBURG CATHEDRAL, Münsterplatz. Tel. 0761/31-009.

Towering over Münsterplatz, site of a busy weekly market, the cathedral is a grand sight with its unique spire of filigree stonework. The steeple sits on an octagonal belfry, whose historic bells include a five-ton wonder dating from 1258. Although construction was begun in 1200 in Romanesque style, the builders had incorporated the style of every Gothic period—as well as a bit of the Renaissance—by the time it was completed in 1620. The overall look, however, is Gothic, with heavy buttresses above the north and south walls, decorated with statues of biblical characters.

Entering the cathedral through the south door, you'll be in the transept facing an early 16th-century sculpture of the adoration of the Christ child by the magi. Turning left into the nave, you'll see at the far end of the aisle, at the entrance to the tower, a 13th-century statue of the Virgin flanked by two adoring angels, a fine example of French Gothic art. Resting against one of the Renaissance pillars along the aisle is a carved 16th-century pulpit, with stairs winding around the curve of the column. The figures below the stairs are likenesses of the townspeople of the period, including the sculptor.

Of interest throughout the cathedral are stained-glass windows. The oldest are the small round windows in the south transept, which date from the 13th century. Some of these, however, have been removed to the Augustinian Museum and replaced by more recent panels.

The vaulted chancel is a treasure house of art. Most impressive is the painted altarpiece by Hans Baldung Grien, dating from 1516, above the high altar. If you follow the aisle around behind the choir, you can also see the reverse side of the work, depicting the crucifixion. Each of the 12 chapels around the choir has its own important works of art, including the elaborate rococo font in the Stürzel Chapel and a 16th-century altarpiece by Sixt von Staufen in the Locher Chapel.

Admission: 1.50 DM ($1) to climb tower.

Open: Cathedral, daily 10am–6pm; tower, Tues–Sat 10am–5pm, Sun 1–5pm. **Bus:** 10, 11, or 12.

MORE ATTRACTIONS IN THE ALTSTADT

Across Münsterplatz from the cathedral is the **Kaufhaus,** the most colorful building in Freiburg. The Gothic structure, with oriel windows at each end, was originally an ancient emporium to which a balcony was added in 1550. Above the massive supporting arches, the facade is decorated with the statues of four emperors of the Habsburg dynasty, all but one of whom visited Freiburg during their reigns. The red-painted building is still used as the town's official reception hall.

The **Rathaus,** on the attractively planted Rathausplatz just west of Münsterplatz, became a happy marriage of two 16th-century merchants' houses when an arcade was built between them in 1900. The Renaissance houses are in suitable condition, and among the decorations on the oriel windows and facades, the one most commented upon is the relief *The Maiden and the Unicorn.*

AUGUSTINER MUSEUM, Augustinerplatz. Tel. 0761/216-3300.

The Augustiner Museum is housed in the former church and monastery of the Order of St. Augustine and contains the town's finest collection of art, including religious art spanning more than 1,000 years. Among the treasures are some of the original stained-glass windows from the cathedral and the most important part of its medieval gold and silver treasure, brought here for safekeeping. The best works, in the collection of medieval art, include the painting by Mathias Grünewald *The Snow Miracle,* as well as works of Hans Baldung Grien (pupil of Albrecht Dürer). There's also a rich collection of fine late-Gothic wooden sculpture and art nouveau glass objects.

Admission: 4 DM ($2.60) adults, 2 DM ($1.30) children.

Open: Mon–Fri 9:30am–5pm, Sat–Sun 10:30am–5pm. Guided tours conducted Wed and Thurs at 4pm. **Bus:** 10, 11, or 12.

MUSEUM FÜR NEUE KUNST, Marienstrasse 10A. Tel. 0761/216-36-71.

The modern art collection formerly housed in the Augustiner Museum is now at the Museum für Neue Kunst. Painting and sculpture, beginning with examples of German expressionism, Neue Sachlichkeit, and other classic modern works of art, especially by artists of southwest Germany, are displayed here as well as contemporary works.

Admission: Free.

Open: Mon–Fri 9:30am–5pm, Sat–Sun 10:30am–5pm. **Bus:** 10, 11, or 12.

WHERE TO STAY

VERY EXPENSIVE

COLOMBI HOTEL, Rotteckring 16, D-7800 Freiburg. Tel. 0761/2-10-60.

Fax 0761/31-410. 94 rms, 12 suites. MINIBAR TV TEL **Bus:** 10, 11, or 12.

$ Rates: 240 DM–275 DM ($158.40–$181.50) single; 340 DM–500 DM ($224.40–$330) double; from 640 DM ($422.40) suite. Breakfast 18 DM ($11.90) extra. AE, DC, MC, V. **Parking:** 12 DM ($7.90).

⭐ Snow-white walls and angular lines make the Colombi easy to spot in the downtown area. Despite its location, the rooms are quiet and peaceful. Many visitors are likely to be part of one of the business conferences that take place here, but the Colombi caters to independent travelers as well. This is the best hotel in town, and its restaurant (see "Where to Dine," below) is the most outstanding in Freiburg. The accommodations are well furnished and appointed; the suites are especially luxurious. Services include room service, laundry, and dry cleaning.

EXPENSIVE

CENTRAL HOTEL, Wasserstrasse 6, D-7800 Freiburg. Tel. 0761/3-19-70. Fax 0761/319-71-00. 49 rms. MINIBAR TV TEL **Bus:** 10, 11, or 12.

$ Rates (including buffet breakfast): 140 DM–165 DM ($92.40–$108.90) single; 195 DM–250 DM ($128.70–$165) double. AE, DC, MC, V. **Parking:** 12 DM ($7.90).

Near the pedestrian zone and the cathedral is the modern Central Hotel, imaginatively designed with skylights, marble floors, and pleasantly furnished rooms and lobby. A buffet breakfast with a wide choice of dishes is included in the rates. Drinks are offered until midnight in a cozy corner bar.

NOVOTEL FREIBURG, Am Karlsplatz, D-7800 Freiburg. Tel. 0761/38-51-0. Fax 0761/30-767. 115 rms. MINIBAR TV TEL **Bus:** 10, 11, or 12.

$ Rates (including buffet breakfast): 178 DM ($117.50) single; 216 DM ($142.60) double. AE, DC, V. **Parking:** 12 DM ($7.90).

Less than a block from the cathedral, Novotel Freiburg offers comfortable lodgings with modern amenities. Sports facilities include a tennis court, pool, sauna, and nearby squash courts. The hotel's restaurant stays open to midnight, serving meals that begin at 42 DM ($27.70).

PARK HOTEL POST, Eisenbahnstrasse 35, D-7800 Freiburg. Tel. 0761/3-16-83. Fax 0761/31-680. 41 rms. MINIBAR TV TEL **Bus:** 10, 11, or 12.

$ Rates (including continental breakfast): 144 DM–159 DM ($95–$104.90) single; 208 DM–248 DM ($137.30–$163.70) double. MC, V. **Parking:** 14.50 DM ($9.60).

A baroque hotel, with an elaborate zinc cap on its octagonal turret, Park Hotel Post is centrally located within walking distance of the major attractions and the rail station. The interior has been entirely renovated, and each unit is attractively furnished and well kept. Breakfast is the only meal served.

VICTORIA, Eisenbahnstrasse 54, D-7800 Freiburg. Tel. 0761/3-18-81. Fax 0761/33-229. 63 rms. MINIBAR TV TEL **Bus:** 10, 11, or 12.

$ Rates (including buffet breakfast): 140 DM–165 DM ($92.40–$108.90) single; 190 DM–240 DM ($125.40–$158.40) double. AE, DC, MC, V. **Parking:** 14 DM ($9.20).

Ⓢ Less than 400 feet from the Hauptbahnhof, the Victoria is nevertheless peaceful, thanks to its frontage on Colombi Park. The facade is a symmetrical 19th-century rectangle, with big windows and dentil work as well as a wrought-iron balcony above the front door. The interior is lavishly paneled throughout the public rooms. The guest rooms are pleasantly furnished. The hotel also has a cocktail bar and a coffee shop.

ZUM ROTEN BÄREN, Oberlinden 12, D-7800 Freiburg. Tel. 0761/3-69-13. Fax 0761/3-69-16. 25 rms (all with bath or shower). 3 suites. TV TEL **Tram:** 1.

$ Rates (including buffet breakfast): 175 DM–195 DM ($115.50–$128.70) single; 220 DM–250 DM ($145.20–$165) double; 320 DM–380 DM ($211.20–$250.80) suite. AE, DC, MC, V. **Parking:** 12 DM ($7.90).

This is one of the oldest buildings in Freiburg, with parts dating from 1120. A modern wing pleasantly blends in. The interior is delightfully decorated, emphasizing original construction elements along with scattered pieces of antique furniture. The rooms are pleasantly styled and furnished, some with minibars. The restaurant serves traditional food and wine, with a high-standard menu. In summer, you can stop by for a glass of wine or beer on the Weinstube's terrace.

MODERATE

RAPPEN, Münsterplatz 13, D-7800 Freiburg. Tel. 0761/3-13-53. Fax 0761/38-22-52. 19 rms (all with bath or shower). MINIBAR TV TEL **Bus:** 10, 11, or 12.

$ Rates (including buffet breakfast): 130 DM ($85.80) single; 160 DM ($105.60) double. AE, DC, MC, V.

A charming, typical Black Forest inn, the Rappen is marked with a wrought-iron hanging sign, little dormer windows in its steep roof, windowboxes, and shutters. There are three dining rooms, all with beamed ceilings, leaded-glass windows, and coach lanterns. You can dine on the sidewalk terrace or inside, the cuisine being notable for local dishes. Meals cost 28 DM to 62 DM ($18.50 to $40.90). The guest rooms are simply but comfortably furnished; the most desirable accommodations open onto views of the Gothic cathedral.

WHERE TO DINE

EXPENSIVE

EICHHALDE, Stadtstrasse 91. Tel. 0761/5-48-17.
  Cuisine: FRENCH/SEAFOOD. **Reservations:** Required. **Bus:** 14.
$ Prices: Appetizers 14 DM–38 DM ($9.20–$25.10); main courses 39 DM–52 DM ($25.70–$34.30); fixed-price lunch 30 DM–100 DM ($19.80–$66); fixed-price dinner 75 DM–105 DM ($49.50–$69.30). AE, DC, MC, V.
  Open: Lunch Sun–Mon and Wed–Fri noon–2pm; dinner Wed–Mon 6–9:30pm.
The most notable French bistro in town lies in the Herden district. This comfortable, safe haven enjoys a lot of neighborhood patronage (it's a long walk from the center). Fixed-price lunches and dinners are available, along with à la carte meals. The bill of fare is likely to include goose-liver terrine with gelée of port, sea bass in thyme sauce, and salad of turbot with mustard sauce.

HANS-THOMA-STUBE/FALKENSTUBE, in the Colombi Hotel, Rotteck-ring 16. Tel. 0761/2-10-60.
  Cuisine: REGIONAL/FRENCH. **Reservations:** Required. **Bus:** 10, 11, or 12.
$ Prices: Appetizers 18 DM–25 DM ($11.90–$16.50); main courses 44 DM–62 DM ($29–$40.90); fixed-price menus 95 DM–165 DM ($62.70–$108.90). AE, DC, MC, V.
  Open: Lunch daily noon–3pm; dinner daily 6pm–midnight.
The most desirable in Freiburg, this restaurant gives guests special attention. You'll probably find your table discreetly separated from that of your neighbors. The chef prepares a light modern cuisine; dishes might include terrine of turbot, chanterelles over filet of venison, or an array of Atlantic fish dishes sumptuously prepared and impeccably served. Fixed-priced or à la carte meals are available.

WEINSTUBE ZUR TRAUBE, Schusterstrasse 17. Tel. 0761/3-21-90.
  Cuisine: FRENCH/SWABIAN. **Reservations:** Required. **Bus:** 10, 11, or 12
$ Prices: Appetizers 15.50 DM–29 DM ($10.20–$19.10); main courses 32 DM–48 DM ($21.10–$31.70); fixed-price menus 65 DM–85 DM ($42.90–$56.10). AE, MC, V.
  Open: Lunch Tues–Sat noon–2pm; dinner Tues–Sat 6–10pm **Closed:** July 1–15

If your grandmother of German extraction happens to be with you during this trip, she will love this Weinstube that's over 600 years old. The pewter and earthenware dinner services decorating the walls are art objects in their own right, and the ceramic stove is over 300 years old. Cooking here is regional and well prepared, emphasizing game, meat, and fish. Try pike roulade with crab sauce.

MODERATE

GREIFFENEGG-SCHLÖSSLE, Schlossbergring 3. Tel. 0761/3-27-28.

Cuisine: REGIONAL/INTERNATIONAL. **Reservations:** Recommended. **Bus:** 10, 11, or 12.

$ **Prices:** Appetizers 14 DM–24 DM ($9.20–$15.80); main courses 22 DM–35 DM ($14.50–$23.10); fixed-price menu 70 DM ($46.20). AE, DC, MC, V.

Open: Tues–Sun noon–11pm. **Closed:** Feb.

The chef cooks up a storm at this family restaurant. Both fixed-price and simpler à la carte meals are available. In summer, try for a seat on the terrace.

OBERKIRCHS WEINSTUBEN, Münsterplatz 22. Tel. 0761/3-10-11.

Cuisine: GERMAN. **Reservations:** Recommended. **Bus:** 10, 11, or 12.

$ **Prices:** Appetizers 12 DM–18 DM ($7.90–$11.90); main courses 22 DM–32 DM ($14.50–$21.10). MC, V.

Open: Lunch Mon–Sat noon–2pm; dinner Mon–Sat 6:30–9:15pm. **Closed:** Mid-Jan to mid-Feb.

The innkeeper provides excellent regional cooking and comfortable rooms in this traditional Freiburg establishment. In the cellar are dozens of six-foot-high wooden kegs of wine. The setting is pure picture postcard: On a colorful square featuring houses with step-gabled roofs, a wrought-iron sign hangs over the entrance, and tables are set out in front. The main Weinstube is old, with a monumental ceiling-high ceramic stove made with ornate decorative tiles. You get good old-fashioned food here—tasty soups, meat dishes, poultry—and plenty of everything. In season, you might try young pheasant. In the rear is a modern complex, fronting an open patio with a fish pond.

The Weinstube also has 25 excellent rooms, most with private baths or showers. Doubles cost 230 DM ($151.80), and singles rent for 110 DM to 150 DM ($72.60 to $99)—continental breakfast included.

WOLFSHÖHLE, Konviktstrasse 8. Tel. 0761/3-03-03.

Cuisine: ITALIAN. **Reservations:** Recommended.

$ **Prices:** Appetizers 12 DM–18 DM ($7.90–$11.90); main courses 25 DM–38 DM ($16.50–$25.10); fixed-price menus 85 DM ($56.10) and 95 DM ($62.70). AE, DC, MC, V.

Open: Lunch Mon–Sat noon–2pm; dinner Mon–Sat 6–10pm.

Wolfshöhle's warmly paneled ambience might remind you of a gemütlich inn high in the mountains on the border between Italy and the German-speaking world. Cuisine is a sophisticated but fortifying blend of such dishes as avocado with shrimp salad, fettuccine studded with lobster chunks in saffron sauce, ravioli stuffed with thyme and rabbit meat, filet of veal in mushroom-cream sauce, and stuffed oxtail.

EVENING ENTERTAINMENT

Freiburg has a busy cultural life centering around the **Städtischen Bühnen,** Bertoldstrasse 46 (tel. 0761/3-48-74). The Freiburg Symphony plays at the theater for operas, operettas, and musical concerts. In the **Freiburger Stadthallen,** Schwarzwaldstrasse 80 (tel. 0761/7-10-20), both classical and rock concerts are presented, as well as all sorts of shows. Most of these are guest performances. There are many "off-Broadway" theaters, but you must know German to appreciate the presentations.

Weinstuben abound throughout the town, especially around the university, where bars and cafés cater to the students. Cabarets and some jazz clubs also exist.

Ask the tourist office for details of what's on.

3. TRIBERG

86 miles SW of Stuttgart; 38 miles NE of Freiburg

GETTING THERE By Plane The nearest major airport is at Stuttgart, 2½ hours away by train.

By Train Trains arrive daily from Munich (trip time: 4½ hours) and from Frankfurt (trip time: 3 hours). The Triberg Bahnhof is on the Konstanz-Singen-Villingen-Offenburg Schwarzwaldbahn rail line, with frequent connections in all directions. Call 07722/19-419 for schedules and more information.

By Bus Regional bus service in the Black Forest area is provided by SBG Südbaden Bus GmbH at Villingen (tel. 07721/26-075).

By Car Access is via autobahn A5 north and south, exiting at Offenburg and then following the signposted directions along Route 33 south.

ESSENTIALS For tourist information, contact the **Kurverwaltung,** Kurhaus (tel. 07722/8-12-30).

Deep in the heart of the Black Forest, Triberg claims to be the home of the cuckoo clock and also has the highest waterfall in the country.

In the little shops you'll find woodcarvings, music boxes, and other traditional crafts. If you're determined to return from Germany with a cuckoo clock or some other Black Forest timepiece, you may want to visit the ✪ **Haus der 1000 Uhren** (House of 1,000 Clocks) (tel. 07722/10-85), at Triberg-Gemmelsbach, along the B33 between Triberg and Nürnberg, open Monday to Saturday from 9am to 5pm. You'll recognize it immediately because of the giant cuckoo clock and waterwheel in front. A painter of clock faces, Josef Weisser, launched the business in 1824. He was the great-great-grandfather of the present owner. For many generations patrons have been flocking to this shop, with its special clocks and souvenirs. They ship to the United States and take all major credit cards. The store maintains a branch in the town center near the entrance to the waterfall.

WHAT TO SEE & DO

The ✪ **Wasserfall** is exceptional, but be prepared to walk an hour or so to reach it. You park your car in a designated area near the Gutach Bridge and walk along a marked trail daily anytime from 7am to 7pm in summer for a cost of 2 DM ($1.30). The Gutach Falls drop some 530 feet, spilling down in seven stages. At the bottom of the falls is a year-round café/restaurant serving the famed Black Forest cake for which, by then, you will have worked up an appetite.

The **Schwarzwald-Museum** of Triberg, Wallfahrtstrasse (tel. 07722/44-34), brings the olden days of the Black Forest vividly to life with displays of dresses; handcrafts; furnishings; bird music boxes; and, of course, exhibitions of clockmaking. You can also see a mineral exhibit of the area and examples of Black Forest woodworking. Children take delight in a model of the famed Schwarzwaldbahn railway, which really works. From May 1 to September 30, the museum is open daily from 9am to noon; from October 1 to April 30, hours are 10am to noon and 2 to 5pm. Admission is 4 DM ($2.60) for adults and 2 DM ($1.30) for children. The museum is closed from November 15 to December 15.

One of the most beautiful churches in the Black Forest, **Wallfahrtkirche Maria in der Tannen** (Church of Our Lady of the Fir Trees) is within easy reach. Built in the early 18th century, it has superb baroque furnishings, including a remarkable pulpit.

After a visit to the church, you may want to drive to the **Open-Air-Museum**

"Vogtsbauernhof," 7625 Gutach (tel. 07831/230), containing original Black Forest homes dating back as many as four centuries. In the museum you can see artifacts of the old way of life in the Black Forest. In summer, guides may demonstrate weaving on some of the looms and other skills. Visits are possible from April to the end of October, daily from 8:30am to 6pm, for an admission of 5 DM ($3.30) for adults and 2 DM ($1.30) for children. From the A5, from Karlsruhe to Basel, turn off at the Offenburg exit and follow B33 in the direction of Gengenbach, Hausach, and Triberg. At Hausach, turn right in the direction of Gutach.

Most visitors to this part of the world also head 10 miles south from Triberg to reach the **Deutsches Uhrenmuseum** (German Clock Museum), Gerwigstrasse 11 at Fürtwangen (tel. 07723/56-117). It is open April through November daily from 9am to 5pm, charging an admission of 3 DM ($2) for adults and 1 DM (66¢) for children. This museum presents a history of timepieces, including displays of a wide variety of Black Forest clocks, some from the early 18th century. There are many cuckoo clocks. Mechanical music automata and elaborate, complicated timepieces are special features of the collection.

WHERE TO STAY
MODERATE

PARKHOTEL WEHRLE, Marktplatz, D-7740 Triberg. Tel. 07722/8-60-20. Fax 07722/86-02-90. 57 rms, 2 suites. TV TEL

$ Rates: 108 DM–138 DM ($71.30–$91.10) single; 175 DM–200 DM ($115.50–$132) double; from 336 DM ($221.80) suite. Continental breakfast 18 DM ($11.90) per person extra. AE, DC, MC, V. **Parking:** 10 DM ($6.60).

Built in the early 1600s, the Parkhotel Wehrle was acquired around 1730 by the family that has owned it ever since. Its lemon-yellow walls and gabled mansard roof occupy one of the most prominent street corners in town. The main house offers an old-world atmosphere, but forest-loving vacationers often request an accommodation in the chalet in a separate location near the woods. There, a pool and breeze-filled balconies create a modern sylvan retreat. The hotel, both a German Romantik Hotel and a *Relais & Châteaux,* is 1 mile from the Bahnhof. The guest rooms are beautifully furnished and individually decorated, sometimes with antiques. Some accommodations also have minibars. The hotel restaurant is the finest in the area and is recommended separately. Facilities also include an indoor pool, sauna, and fitness room; services include room service and laundry.

RÖMISCHER KAISER, Sommerauerstrasse 35, D-7740 Triberg-Nussbach. Tel. 07722/44-18. Fax 07722/4401. 26 rms. TEL

$ Rates (including continental breakfast): 70 DM–80 DM ($46.20–$52.80) single; 110 DM–145 DM ($72.60–$95.70) double. AE, DC, MC, V. **Parking:** Free. **Closed:** Mid-Nov to mid-Dec.

Just over a mile outside Triberg is a comfortable hotel that has been owned by several generations of the same family since 1840. The exterior is a charmingly preserved Black Forest hotel, with lots of exposed wood, and a restaurant that is recommended separately. Bedrooms are pleasantly furnished.

WHERE TO DINE
VERY EXPENSIVE

PARKHOTEL WEHRELE, Marktplatz. Tel. 07722/8-60-20.
Cuisine: CONTINENTAL. **Reservations:** Required.

$ Prices: Appetizers 14 DM–39 DM ($9.20–$25.70); main courses 30 DM–52 DM ($19.80–$34.30); fixed-price menus 69 DM ($45.50), 89 DM ($58.70), and 128 DM ($84.50). AE, DC, MC, V.

Open: Lunch daily noon–2pm; dinner daily 7–10pm.

Meals here are accompanied by the ticking of a stately grandfather clock, while the clientele relaxes in the comfort of cane-bottomed French-style armchairs. Try such refined dishes as la trûite en croute or saddle of venison in the traditional style with juniperberry-cream sauce and Spätzle. A traditional dessert is apples baked with pine honey and flambéed with Kirschwasser. Some of the game specialties are prepared for two. There is also a selection of veal, fish, and regional specialties. Trout is prepared in about two dozen ways.

MODERATE

RÖMISCHER KAISER, Sommerauerstrasse 35. Tel. 07722/44-18.
Cuisine: CONTINENTAL. **Reservations:** Recommended.
$ Prices: Appetizers 12 DM–18 DM ($7.90–$11.90); main courses 17.50 DM–38 DM ($11.60–$25.10); fixed-price lunch 35 DM ($23.10); fixed-price dinner 32 DM–55 DM ($21.10–$36.30). AE, DC, MC, V.
Open: Lunch Thurs–Tues noon–1:30pm; dinner Thurs–Tues 6–9pm. **Closed:** Mid-Nov to mid-Dec.

Some guests of this hotel, located one mile away on the B33 at Nussbach, consider the views from its restaurant to be the best in the area—on a clear day you can see the mountains of distant Switzerland. However, it is the well-prepared cuisine that has made the restaurant so popular. Fresh fish is available throughout the year. Examples include lake trout served with watercress mousse and wild salmon with lobster-cream sauce and fresh asparagus.

CHAPTER 10

LAKE CONSTANCE (BODENSEE)

- **WHAT'S SPECIAL ABOUT LAKE CONSTANCE (BODENSEE)**
- **1. KONSTANZ (CONSTANCE)**
- **2. MEERSBURG**
- **3. LINDAU**

Even though three nations—Austria, Germany, and Switzerland—share the 162-mile shoreline of this large inland sea, the area around Lake Constance (Bodensee in German) is united in a common cultural and historical heritage. The hillsides sloping to the water's edge are covered with vineyards and orchards and dotted with colorful hamlets and busy tourist centers. The mild climate and plentiful sunshine make Lake Constance a vacation spot for lovers of sun and sand, as well as for sightseers and spahoppers. A well-organized network of cruise ships and ferries links every major center around the lake.

Lake Constance is divided into three lakes, although the name is frequently applied only to the largest of these, the Obersee. The western end of the Obersee separates into two distinct branches: One, the Überlingersee, is a long fjord; the other, the Untersee, is more irregular, jutting in and out of marshland and low-lying woodland. It is connected to the larger lake by a narrow channel—actually, the upper Rhine, whose current flows right through the Bodensee. The blue Felchen, a pikelike fish found only in Lake Constance, furnishes the district with a renowned and tasty specialty.

SUGGESTED ITINERARY

Day 1 Spend the first night in Meersburg, on the north shore, exploring the Altes Schloss and Neues Schloss and taking a tour of the lake.

Day 2 Transfer to the city of Konstanz (Constance), on the south shore, where you can explore the old medieval town and wander through the tropical beauty of Mainau Island.

Day 3 Travel to the lovely island of Lindau for the night. Visit the Haus zum Cavazzen and explore the Old Town and the harbor area.

GETTING THERE

The closest international airport is at Zürich, 47 miles southwest of Konstanz. Munich airport is 141 miles to the north. Intercity trains to Lindau (a possible gateway to lake Constance) arrive frequently from Frankfurt, via Stuttgart and Ulm, and there is also frequent rail service from Munich. Fast and frequent trains also arrive from Basel and Zürich.

Motorists take the B12 from Munich, via Landsberg and Kempton, to reach the lake, while drivers from Frankfurt head south along A81 to Memmingen, transferring to B18.

WHAT'S SPECIAL ABOUT LAKE CONSTANCE (BODENSEE)

Great Towns

☐ Konstanz (Constance), a medieval town, now a lakeside resort, on both banks of the infant Rhine River.

☐ Meersburg, on the north lakeshore, cascading in terraces down the hillside to the water.

☐ Lindau, once a Roman camp, then a free imperial town, and today set on an island at the eastern end of the lake.

Ace Attractions

☐ Mainau Island, a tropical paradise, with palms and orange trees, set into an arm of Lake Constance.

☐ Pleasure cruises along Lake Constance, available at docks at resorts along the 162-mile shoreline.

Historic Castles

☐ Altes Schloss, in Meersburg, with a tower from 628, the oldest German castle still standing.

☐ Neues Schloss, in Meersburg, a baroque castle designed by the leading German architect of the 18th century, Balthasar Neumann.

Religious Shrine

☐ Wallfahrtskirche, outside Meersburg, a pilgrimage basilica dating from the mid-18th century and built in the rococo style.

Museum

☐ Haus zum Cavazzen, in Lindau, the handsomest patrician house on Lake Constance, rebuilt in the baroque style in 1730.

1. KONSTANZ (CONSTANCE)

111 miles S of Stuttgart; 47 miles NE of Zürich

GETTING THERE By Train Konstanz is on the main Konstanz-Singen-Villingen-Offenburg rail line, the Schwarzwaldbahn, with frequent connections to major cities of Germany. For rail information, call 07531/19-419.

By Bus Regional bus service along the lake is offered by SBG Südbaden Bus GmbH at Radolfzell (tel. 07732/25-34).

By Boat Ferry service and lake cruises operate between Konstanz, Mainau Island, Meersburg, Lindau, and Bregenz. The operator is Bodensee Schiffahrtsbetriebe der Deutschen Bundesbahn, Hafenstrasse 6, at Constance (tel. 07531/28-13-98 for schedules and more information).

By Car Access by car is via autobahn A81 from the north.

ESSENTIALS Contact **Tourist-Information,** Bahnhofplatz 13 (tel. 07531/28-43-76).

Crowded against the shores of Lake Constance by the borders of Switzerland, this medieval town had nowhere to grow but northward across the river. The resort city lies on both banks of the infant Rhine as it begins its long journey to the North Sea, a strategic position that made Konstanz the most important city on the lake. Early Celtic dwellings were possibly fortified by the Romans under Claudius in C.E. 41. In the 3rd century, the fort was seized by the Germanic tribes, who later became Christianized and founded a bishop's see around C.E. 580. It was here that Emperor Frederick I Barbarossa made peace with the Lombard states in the 12th century. The city was the site of the Council of Constance, held from 1414 to 1418. The council convened to settle claims of three rivals for the papacy, which it did by electing Pope Martin V. But the act that made it notorious was its seizure of Jan Hus, the religious reformer of Prague, who, despite a promise of safe-conduct, was placed on trial for heresy and later burned at the stake.

In 1531, Konstanz accepted the Reformation and was ceded to Austria after the defeat of the Protestant League, which it had supported. It remained Austrian territory until 1805, when it was returned to Germany. Although Konstanz never regained the political status it had held in the early part of the 16th century, it is today still the economic and cultural center of the district.

Remains of the fortifications of the medieval town, on the left bank of the Rhine, are the Schnetz Tor and a portion of the town wall.

WHAT TO SEE & DO

The best way to see Konstanz is from the water. The ✪ **shoreline** is the most fascinating part, with little inlets that weave in and out around ancient buildings and city gardens. Several pleasure ships offer tours along the city shoreline and across the lake to Meersburg. Ferries to Meersburg leave every 15 minutes during daylight hours; from 10pm to 6am, service is curtailed to one ferry per hour. A round-trip fare from Konstanz to Meersburg costs 15.20 DM ($10). For information and schedules, contact Weisse Bodenseeflotte (tel. 07531/28-13-89) at the harbor in back of the rail station.

During the summer, outdoor concerts are presented in the city gardens. Below the gardens is the **Council Building,** originally constructed as a storehouse in 1388 but used for many meetings during its early years; the most important was the Council of Constance. The hall was restored in 1911 and decorated with murals depicting the history of the town. On the harbor in front of the building is an obelisk erected in memory of Count Ferdinand Zeppelin, a citizen of Konstanz who invented the dirigible airship in the late 19th century.

The towers of the Romanesque **basilica** rise behind the city garden. Begun in 1052 on the foundation of an older cathedral, the church took centuries to complete. The Neo-Gothic spire was added only in 1856. During the Council of Constance, the members of the synod met here. From the top of the tower, a view opens onto the lake and the city.

MAINAU ISLAND Four miles north of Konstanz, in the arm of the Bodensee known as the Überlingersee, is the unusual island of ✪ **Mainau,** a tropical paradise. Here palms and orange trees grow in profusion and fragrant flowers bloom year round, practically in the shadow of the snow-covered Alps. In the center of this botanical oasis is an ancient castle, once a residence of Knights of the Teutonic Order. Both the castle and island are owned by the Swedish Count Lennart Bernadotte, but only the island's gardens and parks can be visited by the public. They are open daily from 7am to 7pm from March to October. Winter hours are 9am to 5pm.

There are four restaurants on the island, but no overnight accommodations. You can reach Mainau either by tour boat from Konstanz or by walking across the small footbridge connecting the island to the mainland north of the city. Admission is 12 DM ($7.90) for adults and 3 DM ($2) for children. The island is open year round, but the flower and garden season lasts only from March to November.

WHERE TO STAY

VERY EXPENSIVE

STEIGENBERGER INSEL HOTEL, Auf der Insel 1, D-7750 Konstanz. Tel. 07531/12-50, or toll free 800/223-5652 in the U.S. and Canada. Fax 07531/26-402. 100 rms, 3 suites. MINIBAR TV TEL **Bus:** 1 or 2.

$ Rates (including continental breakfast): 225 DM–315 DM ($148.50–$207.90) single; 350 DM–500 DM ($231–$330) double; from 580 DM ($382.80) suite. Half-board rates 60 DM ($39.60) per person per day extra. AE, DC, MC, V. **Parking:** 10 DM ($6.60).

Starting life as a Dominican monastery in the 13th century, the Insel is now a first-class hotel. Its situation is prime for the area—on an island, with its own lakeside gardens and dock. The step-gabled building is white, with an inner Romanesque cloister. The well-coordinated guest rooms have patterned fabrics, and the furnishings are fine: Most doubles have a living-room look with sofas, armchairs, and coffee tables.

Dining/Entertainment: The formal restaurant is the Seerestaurant, featuring an international kitchen, with meals costing from 65 DM to 100 DM ($42.90 to $66). It is decorated with Windsor chairs, wood-paneled walls, and planters of flowers, along with church arches and pillars. The less formal Dominikaner Stube specializes in regional German cookery, with meals costing from 50 DM ($33). At twilight, guests gather at the intimate, clublike Zeppelin Bar, whose walls are cluttered with framed letters and documents. (The man who pioneered the airship also turned this abbey into a hotel.)

Services: Room service, laundry, dry cleaning.
Facilities: Lake facilities for swimming.

MODERATE

BUCHNER HOF, Buchnerstrasse 6, D-7750 Konstanz. Tel. 07531/5-10-35. Fax 07531/671-37. 13 rms, 2 suites. TV TEL **Bus:** 1 or 2.
$ Rates (including continental breakfast): 120 DM–160 DM ($79.20–$105.60) single; 160 DM–190 DM ($105.60–$125.40) double; from 230 DM ($151.80) suite. AE, DC, V. **Parking:** 10 DM ($6.60).
A well-proportioned and pristine facade greets guests here. In Petershausen, across the Rhine from Konstanz, you'll find the hotel a short walk from most points of interest. The hotel, incidentally, is named after the composer Hans Buchner, who became the organist of the town cathedral in 1510 and is said to have been one of the first musicians to arrange and catalog the wealth of Gregorian chants he found in the region. Rooms are pleasantly furnished; two include minibars. The hotel has a sauna and solarium.

GOLDENER STERN, Bodanplatz 1, D-7750 Konstanz. Tel. 07531/2-52-28. Fax 07531/21-673. 20 rms (all with bath or shower). TV TEL **Bus:** 1 or 2.
$ Rates (including continental breakfast): 92 DM–120 DM ($60.70–$79.20) single; 150 DM–190 DM ($99–$125.40) double. AE, DC, MC, V. **Parking:** 10 DM ($6.60). **Closed:** Jan.
The Goldener Stern's owner maintains an inviting atmosphere. The green of dozens of healthy plants is reflected in pleasing tones of green in the decor. The rooms are spotlessly maintained. Furnishings are in a modern, streamlined style. Regional meals begin at 42 DM ($27.70).

MAGO HOTEL, Bahnhofplatz 4, D-7750 Konstanz. Tel. 07531/2-70-01. Fax 07531/27-003. 31 rms, 3 suites. MINIBAR TV TEL **Bus:** 1 or 2.
$ Rates (including buffet breakfast): 110 DM–130 DM ($72.60–$85.80) single; 150 DM–190 DM ($99–$125.40) double; from 220 DM ($145.20) suite. MC, V. **Parking:** 10 DM ($6.60).
Within view of the lake, the Mago, serving breakfast only, is just a two-minute walk from the Bahnhof. The entrance is one of those elegantly and rigidly narrow archways with an ornate paneled door set into it. The interior is boldly decorated, with modern chandeliers. Rooms are comfortable and warm.

SEEBLICK, Neuhauser Strasse 14, D-7750 Konstanz. Tel. 07531/81-30. Fax 07531/81-32-22. 85 rms. TV TEL **Bus:** 1.
$ Rates (including continental breakfast): 95 DM–120 DM ($62.70–$79.20) single; 155 DM–210 DM ($102.30–$138.60) double. AE, DC, MC, V. **Parking:** 10 DM ($6.60).
In summer, you'll probably want to spend a lot of time beside the pool of this modern

balconied hotel, whose accommodations are partly contained in a low annex near a landscaped sun terrace. The hotel rents well-furnished rooms. There's also a good restaurant, where meals cost from 45 DM to 66 DM ($29.70 to $43.60). The location is near the casino.

WHERE TO DINE
VERY EXPENSIVE

SEEHOTEL SIBER, Seestrasse 25, D-7750 Konstanz. Tel. 07531/6-30-44.
  Cuisine: CONTINENTAL. **Reservations:** Required. **Bus:** 1.
$ **Prices:** Appetizers 14 DM–42 DM ($9.20–$27.70); main courses 55 DM–74 DM ($36.30–$48.80); fixed-price lunch 58 DM ($38.30); fixed-price dinners 110 DM ($72.60), 140 DM ($92.40), and 160 DM ($105.60). AE, DC, V.
  Open: Lunch daily noon–3pm; dinner daily 6pm–1am.

An outstanding dining choice, the best in Konstanz, is run by Bertold Siber, a celebrated chef in the area. Earlier in his career Herr Siber studied with Paul Bocuse and Roger Verge, the famous French chefs. Today his establishment occupies an art nouveau–style villa near the casino, overlooking the lake. The menu offers a conservative version of cuisine moderne. The offerings change daily, based on the seasonal availability of ingredients. Your meal might begin with lobster terrine with butter and red basil or freshly caught lake trout with an array of seasonings. You might prefer, if featured, roast Barbary goose with Beaujolais sauce or stuffed turbot with lobster (served with freshly picked leaf lettuce). Most guests opt for one of three fixed-price dinners, although à la carte meals are available.

Seehotel Siber is mostly acclaimed as a restaurant, but it is also a *Relais & Châteaux* hotel, renting 12 handsomely furnished double rooms in a building adjacent to the restaurant. Doubles rent for 340 DM to 450 DM ($224.40 to $297).

EXPENSIVE

CASINO RESTAURANT AM SEE, Seestrasse 21. Tel. 07531/6-36-15.
  Cuisine: INTERNATIONAL. **Reservations:** Required. **Bus:** 1.
$ **Prices:** Appetizers 15 DM–28 DM ($9.90–$18.50); main courses 32 DM–55 DM ($21.10–$36.30). AE, DC, MC, V.
  Open: Mon–Sat 5pm–2:30am, Sun 6pm–2am.

If you happen to lose at roulette on one of your casino outings in Konstanz, you can revive your spirits (and drink a few, too) on the lakeside terrace of this casino restaurant. The view is lovely, the cuisine first-rate. The restaurant offers a good choice of dishes, especially fresh fish. Saddle of lamb is a specialty. Everything is backed up by a good wine cellar. Men should wear jackets and ties.

INEXPENSIVE

SCHWEDENSCHENKE, Mainau Island. Tel. 07531/30-31-56.
  Cuisine: REGIONAL/SWEDISH. **Reservations:** Required. **Bus:** 4 from the center of Konstanz.
$ **Prices:** Appetizers 5 DM–20 DM ($3.30–$13.20); main courses 10.50 DM–30 DM ($6.90–$19.80). AE, DC, MC, V.
  Open: Lunch Mon–Sat 11:30am–2:30pm, Tues–Sat 6–9pm, Sun lunch noon–3pm.

Local holiday makers sometimes make a pilgrimage to Mainau Island in Lake Constance for a meal in the country villa housing this old-fashioned restaurant. The chef's specialty is assorted lake fish, including perch, pike perch, and trout. A favorite method of serving this fish is with various sauces, accompanied by fresh spinach and buttered potatoes. You can also try Hungarian goulash, Swedish meatballs in cream sauce, and Tafelspitz (boiled topside of beef with horseradish sauce). Pikeperch filets are served in a spicy sauce of tomatoes, capers, shallots, and mushrooms.

2. MEERSBURG

118 miles S of Stuttgart; 89 miles SE of Freiburg

GETTING THERE   By Plane   Regional flights are possible to Friedrichshafen airport, 12 miles from Meersburg. The nearest international airport is at Zürich, 49 miles away.

By Train   The nearest rail station is in Überlingen, 9 miles away, on the Basel-Singen-Radolfzell-Lindau rail line, with frequent connections in all directions. Telephone 07531/19-419 for more information. The train trip from Frankfurt takes about 4½ hours, from Munich, 3 hours.

By Bus   Buses arrive about every 30 minutes throughout the day from Friedrichshafen, a town with good rail connections to Munich. Regional bus service along Lake Constance is provided by RAB Regionalverkehr Alb-Bodensee GmbH at Friedrichshafen (tel. 07541/22-077 for more information).

By Ferry   Ferry service across Lake Constance, including the transport of cars, is available from Bodensee Schiffahrtsbetriebe (tel. 07541/20-13-89). Links are possible between Friedrichshafen and Romanshorn.

By Car   Access by car is via autobahn A7 from the north or highways 31 and 33. You can drive from Munich in about 3 hours; from Frankfurt in about 4½ hours; and from Stuttgart in 2 hours.

ESSENTIALS   For tourist information, contact the **Kur- und Verkehrsamt,** Kirchstrasse 4 (tel. 07532/8-23-83).

SPECIAL EVENTS   The surrounding vineyards produce excellent wine, and on the second weekend in September wine growers around the lake come over to Meersburg for the Lake Constance Wine Festival.

L ike the towns of the lake district of Italy, this village on the northern shore of Lake Constance cascades in terraces down the hillside until it touches the water. You can drive into town as far as the Neues Schloss, where you can leave your car at the northern edge and explore on foot. The heart of Meersburg is a pedestrian area. In the center, the streets become narrow promenades, and steps wander up and down the hillside.

The town turns south toward the sun. From the dock, both large and small boats set out for all kinds of trips on the water, and water sports are plentiful. As an added attraction, Meersburg has an open-air swimming pool.

One charming little detail of Meersburg is the presence of a town watchman who still makes nightly rounds, keeping alive an ancient tradition.

WHAT TO SEE & DO

Entering the town through the ancient Obertor (Upper Gate), you'll be at the Marktplatz and facing the 16th-century Rathaus, containing a typical German Ratskeller. Leading off from this is Steigstrasse, the most interesting artery, passing between rows of half-timbered houses whose arcades serve as covered walkways above the street.

Nearby at Schlossplatz is the   ✪ **Altes Schloss** (tel. 07532/64-41), with Dagobert's Tower, dating from 628, the oldest German castle still standing intact. The town's most impressive monument is open March to October, daily from 9am to 6pm; and November to February, from 10:30am to 5pm. Admission is 6 DM ($4) for adults and 4 DM ($2.60) for children. Clubs, flails, armor, helmets, and axes—all the relics of a warring age are here, along with 28 fully furnished rooms, decorated with pieces from the various epochs. The bishops of Konstanz lived here until the 18th century, when they moved to the Neues Schloss (see below). At that time, it would have been torn down if the Baron of Lassberg, thrilled with medieval romance, hadn't moved in and preserved it. He invited Annette von Droste-Hülshoff, his sister-in-law (1797–1848). She liked it a lot. As Germany's leading female poet, she was instrumental in having the castle turned into a setting for artists and writers. Her luxuriously furnished former chambers can be visited, as can the murky dungeons and the castle museum with its medieval jousting equipment. Adjoining is the Castle Mill (1620), with a 28-foot wooden waterwheel, the oldest of its kind in Germany.

You go from the medieval to the baroque when you enter **Neues Schloss,** Schlossplatz (tel. 07532/8238-5), which stands facing the Altes Schloss. The leading architect of the 18th century, Balthasar Neumann, was instrumental in some of the later castle's design. Elegant stucco moldings grace the ceilings and walls. Ceiling paintings and frescoes throughout were done by prominent artists and craftsmen of the day. Its hall of mirrors, the Spiegelsaal, is the setting for an international music festival in summer. On the top floor is the **Dornier Museum,** tracing the history of Germany's aircraft and aerospace industries. Admission is 3 DM ($2) for adults and 1.50 DM ($1) for children. The museum is open in Easter to October, daily from 10am to 12:30pm and 1:30 to 5:30pm.

On the promenade below stands the **Great House,** dating from 1505 and housing ticket offices for the railway and steamer lines on Lake Constance. Regular ferry service to Konstanz leaves from the dock on the outskirts of town.

A 15-minute drive from Meersburg is the famous **Wallfahrtskirche** (tel. 07556/60-40), the pilgrimage basilica at Birnau, 3 miles southeast of Überlingen. It dates from the mid-18th century and was built in rococo style, with rose, blue, and beige marble predominating. One statuette here is celebrated. The Germans call it a *Honigschlecker,* or "honey-taster"—it shows a baby sucking a finger as he's yanked out of a nest of bees. It's to the right of the St. Bernard altarpiece. The 15th-century *Mother and Child* above the tabernacle on the main altar is an image of reverence among the devout who flock here.

WHERE TO STAY

EXPENSIVE

TERRASSENHOTEL WEISSHAAR, Stefan-Lochner-Strasse 24, D-7758 Meersburg. Tel. 07532/90-06. Fax 07532/91-91. 26 rms. TV TEL

$ Rates (including continental breakfast): 120 DM ($79.20) single; 210 DM ($138.60) double. MC, V. **Parking:** Free.

Separated from the lake by weeping willows and a slight elevation, the panoramic windows of this hotel with their awnings can be seen from far away. The establishment is proud of its genteel tradition and is acclaimed locally for its garden terrace, where guests flock from the first of March to October. Meals cost from 35 DM to 66 DM ($23.10 to $43.60), and service is daily from noon to 2pm and 4 to 10pm.

MODERATE

GASTHOF ZUM BÄREN, Marktplatz 11, D-7758 Meersburg. Tel. 07532/60-44. 17 rms (all with bath or shower).

$ Rates (including continental breakfast): 70 DM ($46.20) single; 132 DM ($87.10) double. No credit cards. **Parking:** 6.50 DM ($4.30). **Closed:** Mid-Nov to mid-Mar.

A picture-book inn right in the heart of town, this is a five-story corner building with step gables. It has windowboxes overflowing with red geraniums, an ornately decorated corner tower with steeple, plus a tangle of purple wisteria crawling over most of the facade. The innkeepers are the English-speaking Gilowsky-Karrer family—Zum Bären has been owned by their family since 1851. Bären was built in 1605 on the foundations of a building dating from 1250 (the cellar of the original Bären is still there and can be seen). It is furnished with tavern pieces and alpine stools, all resting under beamed ceilings. The guest rooms are most attractive.

The inn has two restaurants serving both regional and international menus, plus vegetarian dishes. Fish from Lake Constance is a specialty. Meals begin at 35 DM ($23.10).

SEEHOTEL ZUR MUNZ, Seestrasse 7, D-7558 Meersburg. Tel. 07532/ 90-90. Fax 07532/77-85. 14 rms (all with shower). TEL

$ Rates (including continental breakfast): 82 DM ($54.10) single; 124 DM–166 DM ($81.80–$109.60) double. MC. **Parking:** 8 DM ($5.30). **Closed:** Nov–Feb.

Only a pedestrian walkway and an iron railing separate the Seehotel zur Munz from the tree-lined lakefront, a fact that brings a lot of business to the lakeside café/restaurant. This balconied hotel has an ambience to make you forget the urban bustle. Bernd and Brigitte Knaus are your hosts.

STRANDHOTEL WILDER MANN, Bismarckplatz 2, D-7758 Meersburg. Tel. 07532/90-11. Fax 07532/90-14. 30 rms, 2 suites. TV TEL

$ Rates (including buffet breakfast): 150 DM–155 DM ($99–$102.30) single; 170 DM–260 DM ($112.20–$171.60) double; from 325 DM ($214.50) suite. No credit cards. **Parking:** 10 DM ($6.60). **Closed:** Dec 15–Jan 31.

Built just beyond a stone embankment that defines the edge of the lake, the facade of this country baroque building is the backdrop for a painted illustration of a traditional folk figure, called *der wilde Mann,* contemplating whether he'll have a stag or a unicorn for supper. The roofline's step-gabled design evokes another era in building construction. The owners rent comfortable and well-maintained rooms. You can enjoy the view on a lakeside terrace and later order a meal in the restaurant for 40 DM ($26.40) and up.

WEINSTUBE LÖWEN, Marktplatz 2, D-7556 Meersburg. Tel. 07532/ 4304-0. Fax 07532/2185. 21 rms. TV TEL

$ Rates (including buffet breakfast): 90 DM–105 DM ($59.40–$69.30) single; 150 DM–180 DM ($99–$118.80) double. AE, DC, MC, V. **Parking:** 7 DM ($4.60).

Weinstube Löwen is an old inn on the market square. Its raspberry-pink facade has green shutters, windowboxes filled with red geraniums, and vines reaching the upper windows under the steep roof. The Fischer family has updated its interior while keeping a homelike ambience. All but a few of the rooms have been modernized in a streamlined functional style. The wood-paneled Weinstube, with a white-ceramic corner stove, serves good food and drink.

HOTEL ZUM SCHIFF, Bismarckplatz 5, D-7758 Meersburg. Tel. 07532/ 60-25. Fax 07532/15-37. 35 rms. TV TEL

$ Rates (including continental breakfast): 80 DM ($52.80) single; 130 DM–180 DM ($85.80–$118.80) double. AE, DC, MC, V. **Parking:** 5 DM ($3.30). **Closed:** Mid-Oct to Mar.

This sprawling hotel, with a red-tile roof and a single square tower, has its sun terrace built directly on the water. The guest rooms are well maintained. At the hotel restaurant, meals go for 30 DM ($19.80) and up. The owners speak English.

WHERE TO DINE
MODERATE

WINZERSTUBE ZUM BECHER, Höllgasse 4. Tel. 07532/90-09.
Cuisine: REGIONAL/GERMAN. **Reservations:** Required.

$ Prices: Appetizers 7.50 DM–25 DM ($5–$16.50); main courses 20 DM–45 DM ($13.20–$29.70); fixed-price lunch 35 DM–48 DM ($23.10–$31.70); fixed-price dinner 68 DM–100 DM ($44.90–$66). AE, DC, V.

Open: Daily 10am–2pm and 5pm–midnight; hot meals served 11:30am–2pm and 6–10pm. **Closed:** Mid-Dec to mid-Jan.

If you've come to Germany with images of a handcrafted Weinstube that radiates a gemütlich warmth, then the Winzerstube zum Becher, near the Altes Schloss, is where you should dine. From a corner, a pea-green tile oven provides heat in winter. The chairs are not that comfortable, but the rest of the beflowered, paneled, and happily cluttered room will guarantee you a pleasant evening. The specialty of the chef is onion-flavored Swabian Rosbraten with Spätzle, along with a host of other specialties, including fresh fish from Lake Constance. A superb set dinner is available—you'll probably spend far more ordering à la carte. When meals are not served, the restaurant offers drinks (mostly wine) and snacks.

3. LINDAU

111 miles SW of Munich; 20 miles S of Ravensburg

GETTING THERE   Connected to the mainland by a road bridge and a causeway for walkers and trains, Lindau is easy to reach. It lies just at the edge of the Austrian frontier and is a transportation link between the western part of Lake Constance and the towns of Austria and Switzerland, which lie directly across the water.

By Train   The Lindau Bahnhof is on the major Basel-Singen-Radolfzell-Lindau and Lindau-Kissleg-Memmingen-Buchloe rail lines, with frequent connections in all directions. Call 08382/19-419 for information and schedules.

By Bus   Regional bus service along Lake Constance is offered by Regionalverkehr Alb-Bodensee GmbH at Friedrichshafen (tel. 07541/22-077).

By Ferry   Ferries link Lindau with Konstanz at the rate of about 5 to 7 per day, depending on season. Before reaching Lindau, boats stop at Meersburg, Mainau, and Friedrichshafen, the entire trip taking three hours. Call the tourist office (see below) for information and schedules.

By Car   Access by car is via autobahn (A7) Ulm/Kempten or A96, as well as Routes 12, 18, 31, and 308.

ESSENTIALS   **Tourist-Information** is at Ludwigstrasse 68 (tel. 08382/26-000).

Growing where a Roman camp, castrum Tiberii, once stood, Lindau dates back to the end of the 9th century. It developed into a central transit trade point between Bavaria and Switzerland. Its medieval status as a free imperial town was lost in 1804, when it became a part of Bavaria.

Its unique setting on an island at the eastern end of Lake Constance made Lindau such a tourist attraction that it outgrew its boundaries and spread to the shores of the mainland. It is today under landmark protection. The garden city, stretching for 5 miles along the shoreline, caters to your every whim—from bathing to baccarat. The island also offers a look into the past of a former free imperial town of the Holy Roman Empire.

At the harbor stand two lighthouses—one, called Mangturm, built in the 1200s, and the other constructed at the tip of a breakwater in 1856. Each tower is some 120 feet tall, and can be climbed by the hearty along narrow spiral staircases. The reward for those who make it to the top is a panoramic vista of the Alps, both Swiss and Austrian. One of the town's most interesting buildings is the Rathaus, dating from the 1400s. The building's frescoes represent scenes from a session of the 1496 diet of the Holy Roman Empire, convened at Lindau. However, it is not just one building but the whole of Lindau that is of interest. You can wander at will through the maze of winding narrow streets and old houses that have stood the test of time.

WHAT TO SEE & DO

Whether you arrive at Lindau by boat or train, a tour of the Ferieninsel (Holiday Island) begins with the **old harbor,** seen from the lakeside promenade. The Mangturm, the old lighthouse, stands on the promenade as a reminder of the heavy fortifications that once surrounded the city. It also marks the point (now filled in) where Lindau was once divided into two islands. The entrance to the harbor is marked by two silhouettes, the 108-foot **New Lighthouse** (19th century) and the **Bavarian Lion,** standing guard as yachts and commercial ships pass by below. From the promenade, you can gaze out past these monuments over the water to the Alps on the opposite side of the lake.

In the center of the town, the **Hauptstrasse** is the main street of the Altstadt. The most easily recognized building is the **Altes Rathaus,** erected in 1422 on the site of a vineyard. The stepped gables are typical of the period, but the building's facade also combines many later styles of architecture. The interior, once used by the Imperial Diet as a council hall, is the town library.

Just north of the Hauptstrasse, with its half-timbered houses, is the town's most familiar landmark, the round **Diebsturm** (Thieves' Tower), featuring its turreted roof. Next to it is the oldest building in Lindau, **St. Peter's Church** (11th century), which houses a war memorial chapel. In the church is a group of frescoes painted by Hans Holbein the Elder.

Returning to the Hauptstrasse, which cuts through the exact center of the island, follow the street eastward to the **Haus zum Cavazzen,** Am Marktplatz (tel. 08382/27-54-05), considered the handsomest patrician's house on Lake Constance. Rebuilt in 1730 in the style of a baroque country mansion, it houses the municipal art collections. Included are exhibits of sculpture and painting from the Gothic, Renaissance, and baroque periods. Some of the rooms are furnished with period pieces showing how wealthy citizens lived in the 18th and 19th centuries. The 18th-century murals on the facade have been restored. Among the rarities shown is a collection of mechanical musical instruments. Demonstrations are given of barrel organs, juke boxes, metal record players, and mechanical pianos, among other instruments. The attraction is visited by guided tour only, conducted in April through October at 3pm and 4:15pm on Tuesday to Sunday. Admission is 5 DM ($3.30); children under 10 enter free.

Passing across Am Marktplatz and by the Collegiate Church and St. Stephen's Church, both baroque, you come to the strange pile of rocks known as **Heathen's Wall,** dating from Roman times. Beyond this is the solitude of the **Stadtgarten** (Town Garden), which, although peaceful during the day, livens up at night when the wheels of the town's casino begin to whirl and spin.

WHERE TO STAY

EXPENSIVE

HOTEL BAYERISCHER HOF, Seepromenade, D-8900 Lindau. Tel. 08382/50-55. Fax 08382/5054. 104 rms. MINIBAR TV TEL

$ Rates (including buffet breakfast): 135 DM–240 DM ($89.10–$158.40) single; 240 DM–490 DM ($158.40–$323.40) double. DC, MC, V. **Parking:** 10 DM–15 DM ($6.60–$9.90). **Closed:** Nov to Easter.

Owned by the Spaeth family, who also own and manage Hotel Reutemann und Seegarten (see below), the Bayerischer Hof is right on the promenade. This hotel is first class in atmosphere and service. The guest rooms are the finest at the resort, each well furnished with traditional styling. Three-quarters of them have a good view; the less desirable units overlook a narrow thoroughfare. Room service, laundry, and dry cleaning are available.

The lounge is luxuriously furnished and decorated, and the hotel also has a cocktail bar. The cuisine offered is among the finest at the resort. Both regional and international dishes are served in the formal dining room, with wide-screened windows opening onto views of the lake.

HELVETIA, Seepromenade, D-8990 Lindau.Tel. 08382/40-02. Fax 08382/40-04. 50 rms. TV TEL

$ Rates (including continental breakfast): 180 DM–240 DM ($118.80–$158.40) single; 250 DM–400 DM ($165–$264) double. Half-board rates 220 DM ($145.20) per person per day. AE, DC, MC, V. **Closed:** Nov–Mar.

In the evening, the rows of lights below the eaves of this symmetrical building with striped sidewalk awnings give an effect like that of a carousel. The management tells me that a dye shop occupied this site in the 12th century, but today the coloring vats have been replaced by barrels of beer and wine, which flow freely to the patrons of this establishment's busy sidewalk café. The interior has big windows, hanging lamps, and an open fireplace. The guest rooms are comfortably and attractively furnished, with a high level of maintenance. Those opening onto the lake are the most desirable (and carry the highest price tags). You can also patronize the hotel's restaurant, where meals begin at 32 DM ($21.10).

LINDAUER HOF Seepromenade, D-8990 Lindau. Tel. 08382/40-64. Fax 08382/24-203. 23 rms, 2 suites. MINIBAR TV TEL

$ Rates (including continental breakfast): 135 DM–165 DM ($89.10–$108.90) single; 185 DM–250 DM ($122.10–$165) double; from 280 DM ($184.80) suite. AE, MC, V. **Parking:** 10 DM ($6.60). **Closed:** Jan 7–Feb.

Right in the center of activity near the harbor, the Lindauer Hof is close to the boat docks and harbor yet only a five-minute walk from the Hauptbahnhof plaza. An eye-catching shuttered and gabled building, it faces a square, with a second-floor water-view terrace. Here you can dine under a flourishing wisteria vine. The lounge has an attractive collection of Empire and Biedermeier furniture. The guest rooms are nicely decorated, each in a unique fashion; try for one with a view of the plaza and lake. Facilities include an indoor pool and sauna.

HOTEL REUTEMANN UND SEEGARTEN, Seepromenade, D-8900 Lindau. Tel. 08382/50-55. Fax 08382/50-54. 64 rms. MINIBAR TV TEL

$ Rates (including continental breakfast): 125 DM–195 DM ($82.50–$128.70) single; 200 DM–325 DM ($132–$214.50) double. DC, MC, V. **Parking:** 10 DM–15 DM ($6.60–$9.90).

Two villas have been joined to make one hotel, standing next to its parent, Bayerischer Hof. Each villa is unique. The Reutemann section has its own waterfront garden, with outdoor furniture amid lemon trees and wisteria vines. It is unselfconsciously and traditionally furnished in fine style. Most rooms are large, and some have tile baths, along with heated towel racks, huge tubs, and endless hot water. The Reutemann has a glassed-in dining room, where good meals are served. The Seegarten has the more attractive facade. It's built like a Bavarian villa, with little flower-filled balconies and trailing vines. It, too, has an informal lakefront garden with flower beds and furniture for sunbathing.

The public rooms are elegant, the guest rooms spacious and handsome, especially the lake-view ones (at higher rates, naturally). A special restaurant for dining and dancing, Zum Lieben Augustin (closed in winter), is a romantic tavern shared with the Bayerischer Hof. Tyrolean chairs and tables are set on two levels, and a small orchestra plays in the background.

MODERATE

HOTEL-GARNI BRUGGER, Bei der Heidenmauer 11, D-8900 Lindau. Tel. 08382/60-86. Fax 08382/41-33. 24 rms (all with shower). MINIBAR TV TEL

$ Rates (including continental breakfast): 75 DM–90 DM ($49.50–$59.40) single; 140 DM–160 DM ($92.40–$105.60) double. Extra bed 55 DM ($36.30). AE, DC, MC, V.

Ⓢ Named after its owners, this breakfast-only hotel is pleasingly proportioned, with a gabled attic and expansive French doors that open onto the balconies in the back. Rooms are up-to-date, furnished in a functional modern style, with lots of light. The latest innovation is a winter garden filled with potted plants. The location is an easy walk from the lake and casino.

INSEL-HOTEL, Maximilianstrasse 42, D-8990 Lindau. Tel. 08382/50-17. Fax 08382/67-56. 28 rms (all with shower). MINIBAR TV TEL

$ Rates (including continental breakfast): 98 DM–120 DM ($64.70–$79.20) single; 168 DM–178 DM ($110.90–$117.50) double. AE, DC, MC, V. **Parking:** 15 DM ($9.90).

Only a quarter mile from the lake, the Insel-Hotel has been completely renovated, with a small reception room, plus an elevator. The upstairs rooms are furnished with modern pieces. The breakfast room opens onto the Maximilianstrasse, a pedestrian zone.

WHERE TO DINE
EXPENSIVE

BISTRO BEAUJOLAIS, Ludwigstrasse 7. Tel. 08382/64-49.
   Cuisine: CONTINENTAL. **Reservations:** Required.
$ **Prices:** Appetizers 18 DM–28 DM ($11.90–$18.50); main courses 40 DM–44 DM ($26.40–$29); fixed-price menus 69 DM ($45.50) and 110 DM ($72.60). DC, V.
   Open: Lunch Wed–Sun 11:30am–2pm; dinner Tues–Sun 6–10:30pm. **Closed:** 3 weeks in Mar.

⭐ Its style is that of a sophisticated but informal bistro, and its walls are the same wine-red as its namesake. Specialties include grilled scampi garnished with fresh melon, zander from Lake Constance, and medallions of seawolf with spinach. You can also order a delectable bouillabaisse, with spicy garlic-flavored rouille.

HOYERBERG SCHLÖSSLE, Hoyerbergstrasse 64, at Lindau-Aeschach. Tel. 08382/2-52-95.
   Cuisine: CONTINENTAL. **Reservations:** Required in restaurant; not necessary in café.
$ **Prices:** Appetizers 14.50 DM–38 DM ($9.60–$25.10); main courses 39 DM–54 DM ($25.70–$35.60); fixed-price menus 94 DM–140 DM ($62–$92.40). AE, DC, MC, V.
   Open: Café Tues–Sat 2–5pm; restaurant Tues–Sat noon–2pm and 6–10:30pm. **Closed:** Jan 15–Feb.

Some of the finest food around Lake Constance is provided at Hoyerberg Schlössle. The location is in a building constructed as a private palace, then turned into an elegant bourgeois residence. Eventually the Schloss was purchased by the city of Lindau. Since 1979, the tenants have been a team of dedicated chefs who have come closer than anyone else to re-creating the ambience of the former Lustschloss. A beautifully decorated inner room with a view of the mountains and lake, or one of two terraces, could be your choice for sampling the continental delicacies produced by head chef Friedbert Lang. These include cream of scampi soup, Bodensee pikeperch stuffed with champagne-flavored herbs, and Allgäuer saddle of venison with small flour dumplings and French beans.

MODERATE

ZUM SÜNFZEN, Maximilianstrasse 1. Tel. 08382/58-65.
   Cuisine: GERMAN/BAVARIAN. **Reservations:** Recommended.
$ **Prices:** Appetizers 9 DM–15 DM ($5.90–$9.90); main dishes 18 DM–35 DM ($11.90–$23.10). AE, DC, MC, V.
   Open: Daily 11:30am–10:30pm. **Closed:** Late Jan to late Feb.

🅢 Owned by the same family that runs the Insel-Hotel, this is an old, all-wood arched house/restaurant, with windows in the antique-glass style. It offers pleasant groups of tables covered with napkins. The food is good and the cost low. Dishes range from roast pork with vegetables to filet of venison. Fresh fish from Lake Constance is a specialty.

CHAPTER 11

THE ROMANTIC ROAD

- **WHAT'S SPECIAL ABOUT THE ROMANTIC ROAD**
1. **ROTHENBURG O.D.T.**
2. **DINKELSBÜHL**
3. **NÖRDLINGEN**
4. **AUGSBURG**
5. **FÜSSEN**
6. **NEUSCHWANSTEIN/ HOHENSCHWANGAU**

No area of Germany is more aptly named than the Romantic Road. Even if the road that runs through central Bavaria isn't romantic itself, the medieval villages and 2,000-year-old towns through which it passes certainly are. The Romantische Strasse stretches for 180 miles between Würzburg in the north and Füssen in the foothills of the Bavarian Alps.

SEEING THE REGION

You may, if you wish, take one of numerous bus tours, accompanied by an English-speaking guide, that traverses the entire route each day, from the middle of March through October. For example, one bus departs Würzburg at 9am, arriving in Füssen at 7:30pm on the same day. Yet another bus leaves Wiesbaden at 7am, picks up passengers in Frankfurt, and is in Munich by 7pm. In the south, buses leave Füssen at 8:15am, arriving in Würzburg at 7:30pm. Buses stop at major sights, but there's little time for extended visits. For detailed routes and information, contact **Deutsche Touring GmbH,** Am Römerhof 17 in Frankfurt (tel. 069/79-03-240).

The best way to see the Romantic Road is by car, stopping whenever the mood suggests and then driving on through miles of vineyards and over streams until you arrive at the alpine passes in the south.

SUGGESTED ITINERARY

Day 1 Spend a day and night wandering the streets of Rothenburg, Europe's finest medieval city.

Day 2 Head south along the Romantic Road, visiting Dinkelsbühl in the morning and having lunch there. In the afternoon continue south to Nördlingen for the night.

Day 3 Leave Nördlingen in the morning and arrive farther south in Augsburg for a day of sightseeing in a city filled with art. Overnight there.

Day 4 Continue south toward the Austrian border, and spend the day exploring Neuschwanstein Castle and Hohenschwangau. Overnight in Füssen.

GETTING THERE

The major international airports for the Romantic Road are Frankfurt, from the north, or Munich from the south. Motorists coming from the north should take the Frankfurt/Nürnberg autobahn toward Würzburg (see Chapter 13). Rail passengers will find Augsburg a major gateway, as that city has frequent service to Frankfurt,

WHAT'S SPECIAL ABOUT THE ROMANTIC ROAD

Great Towns/Villages

☐ Rothenburg ob der Tauber, a former free imperial town that has been preserved as the finest medieval city of Europe.

☐ Dinkelsbühl, still surrounded by medieval walls and towers, a town straight out of a Brothers Grimm fairy tale.

☐ Nördlingen, encircled by fortifications, a well-preserved medieval town.

☐ Augsburg, largest city on the Romantic Road, containing a wealth of art and architecture from the Renaissance.

Ace Attraction

☐ The Romantic Road (Romantische Strasse) itself, stretching for 180 miles through central Bavaria, filled with 2,000-year-old towns and villages.

Religious Shrines

☐ Dom St. Maria of Augsburg, with the oldest stained-glass windows in the world.

☐ Wieskirche (Church of the Meadow), outside Füssen, the most glorious example of German rococo architecture.

Historic Castles

☐ Neuschwanstein Castle, the fairy-tale castle of Ludwig II, which the king never finished because of his mysterious death.

☐ Hohenschwangau Castle, a neo-Gothic castle near Neuschwanstein, where Ludwig II entertained Richard Wagner.

Architectural Highlights

☐ Fuggerei, in Augsburg, eight streets lined with 66 gabled houses, founded in 1519.

Munich, and Stuttgart. Towns along the Romantic Road have rail links, but service is much less frequent.

1. ROTHENBURG OB DER TAUBER

73 miles NE of Stuttgart; 32 miles SE of Würzburg

GETTING THERE   By Plane   The nearest regional airport is Nürnberg; from there, it's a two-hour train ride to Rothenburg.

By Train   You can reach Rothenburg by a daily train arriving from Frankfurt (trip time: 3 hours); from Hamburg (trip time: 5½ hours), or from Berlin (trip time: 7 hours). Rothenburg lies on the Steinach-Rothenburg rail line, with frequent connections to all major German cities, including Nürnberg and Stuttgart. For information, call 09861/19-419.

By Bus   The Romantic Road bus (Deutsche Touring Frankfurt) includes Rothenburg on its itinerary stopovers from March to October. Any travel agent in Germany or abroad can book you a seat. Regular long-distance bus service (lines EH 190 and 190A) services the Romantic Road from such cities as Frankfurt, Würzburg, Augsburg, and Munich, as well as Füssen. For information and reservations, phone 069/79-03-48 in Frankfurt. Regional bus service along the Romantic Road is provided by OVF Omnibusverkehr Franken GmbH at Nürnberg (tel. 0911/24-40-162 for information).

By Car   Access by car is via autobahn A7 on the Würzburg/Ulm run, exiting at Rothenburg.

ESSENTIALS For tourist information, contact **Stadt Verkehrsamt**, Rathaus, D-8803 Rothenburg o.d.T. (tel. 09861/40492). All buses into Rothenburg will deposit you at the rail station; from there, you must make your way through the old medieval city on foot.

Sometimes abbreviated as Rothenburg o.d.T. or just Rothenburg, this city was first mentioned in written records in 804 as Rotinbure, a settlement above ("ob" in German) the Tauber River that grew to be a free imperial city, reaching the apex of its prosperity under Burgermeister Heinrich Toppler, in the 14th century.

Admittedly, if you arrive at Rothenburg's Bahnhof at the northeast corner of town, you may find it hard to believe that this is actually the finest medieval city in Europe. Contemporary life and industry have made an impact, and your first sight as you leave the station will be factories and office buildings. But don't be discouraged—inside those undamaged 13th-century city walls is a completely preserved medieval town, relatively untouched by the centuries that have passed by outside.

WHAT TO SEE & DO

RATHAUS, Marktplatz. Tel. 09861/404-92.

⭐ Rothenburg's town hall consists of an older Gothic section from 1240 and a newer Renaissance structure facing the square. From the 165-foot tower of the Gothic hall you get an overview of the town below. The belfry has quite a history. Fire destroyed the Gothic hall's twin (where the Renaissance hall now stands) in 1501. Prior to the fire, the tower had been used as a sentry's lookout, but from that time on, it became a watchtower for fire. The guards had to ring the bell every quarter hour to show that they were wide awake and on the job.

The new Rathaus, built in 1572 to replace the portion destroyed in the fire, is decorated with intricate friezes, an oriel extending the full height of the building, and a large stone portico opening onto the square. The octagonal tower at the center of the side facing the square contains the grand staircase, leading to the upper hall. On the main floor is the large court room. Here an annual Whitsuntide festival, Der Meistertrunk, is held. In 1631 when the town was conquered by General Tilly, Burgermeister Nusch saved the town from destruction by accepting the general's challenge to drink a tankard of wine in one draught. This sounds like a simple achievement until you see the actual tankard on display at the Reichstadtmuseum—it holds almost 3½ quarts (3¼ liters)!

Admission: Rathaus, free; tower, 2 DM ($1.30) adults, 1 DM (66¢) children.

Open: Rathaus, Mon–Fri 7am–6pm, Sat–Sun 7am–4pm; tower, Apr–Oct daily 9:30am–12:30pm and 1–5pm, winter Sat–Sun noon–3pm.

ST. JAKOBSKIRCHE [Church of St. James], Klostergasse 15. Tel. 09861/7006-220.

⭐ In this vertical Gothic church with three naves, the choir, dating from 1336, is the oldest section. The altar from Friedrich Herlin (1466) is one of the prettiest of the late Gothic period. The fine painted-glass windows in the choir date from the same period. To the left is the tabernacle (1390–1400), which was recognized as a "free place" where condemned criminals could not be touched.

Admission: 2 DM ($1.30) adults, 1 DM (66¢) children.

Open: Apr–Oct, daily 9am–5pm; Nov–Mar, daily 10am–noon and 2–4pm.

REICHSSTADTMUSEUM, Klosterhof 5. Tel. 09861/4-04-58.

The historical collection of Rothenburg is housed in this 13th-century Dominican nunnery. The cloisters are well preserved, and you can visit the convent hall, kitchen, and apothecary and view the ancient frescoes and antiques. The museum collection includes period furniture and art from Rothenburg's more prosperous periods, plus the famous goblet that saved the town. Among the exhibits is the work of Martinus Schwartz, the 1494 *Rothenburg Passion* series, 12 pictures depicting scenes from the suffering of Christ. In the gallery you can also see the works of the English painter

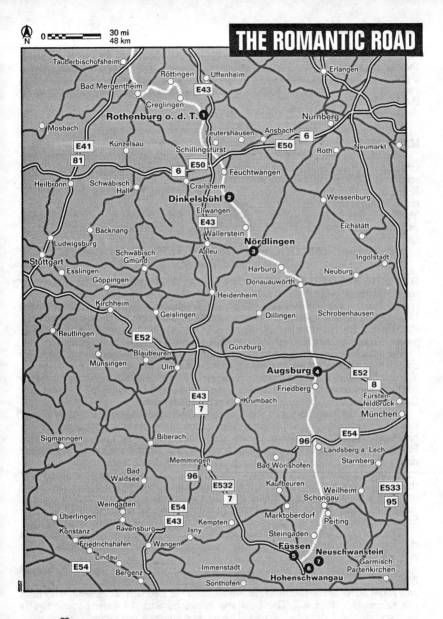

THE ROMANTIC ROAD

N
0 ⊟⊟⊟⊟⊟ 30 mi
48 km

Tauberbischofsheim
Erlangen
Röttingen
Uffenheim
Bad Mergentheim
E43
Creglingen
Rothenburg o. d. T. ❶
Nürnberg
Mosbach
Leutershausen
Ansbach
6
E41
Künzelsau
Schillingsfürst
E50
Roth
Neumarkt
81
Heilbronn
Schwäbisch Hall
6
E50
Feuchtwangen
Crailsheim
Weissenburg
Dinkelsbühl ❷
Ellwangen
E43
Eichstätt
Backnang
Wallerstein
Nördlingen
❸
Ludwigsburg
Schwäbisch Gmünd
Aalen
Stuttgart
Ingolstadt
Esslingen
Harburg
Neuburg
Göppingen
Donauauwörth
Kirchheim
Heidenheim
Geislingen
Dillingen
Schrobenhausen
Reutlingen
E52
Günzburg
Blaubeuren
Münsingen
Ulm
Augsburg ❹
E52
Friedberg
8
E43
Fürstenfeldbruck
7
Krumbach
München
Sigmaringen
Biberach
E54
96
Landsberg a. Lech
Memmingen
Bad Wörishofen
Starnberg
Bad Waldsee
96
E533
Weingarten
E532
Kaufbeuren
Weilheim
95
7
Schongau
E54
Überlingen
Marktoberdorf
Konstanz
E43
Kempten
Peiting
Ravensburg
Isny
Steingaden
Friedrichshafen
Wangen
Füssen
Neuschwanstein
Lindau
❺
❼
Bergenz
E54
Immenstadt
❻
Garmisch-Partenkirchen
Bergenz
Hohenschwangau
Sonthofen

GERMANY

The Romantic Road

❶ Rothenburg ob der Tauber
❷ Dinkelsbühl
❸ Nördlingen
❹ Augsburg
❺ Füssen
❻ Hohenschwangau
❼ Neuschwanstein

Arthur Wasse (1854–1930), whose pictures managed to capture the many moods of the city in a romantic way. The original glazed Elector's Tankard is displayed. There is a Jewish section with gravestones from the Middle Ages and some cult objects. You can also see the new section with archeological objects from prehistoric times up to the Middle Ages.

Admission: 3 DM ($2) adults, 1.50 DM ($1) children.
Open: Apr–Oct, daily 10am–5pm; winter, daily 1–4pm.

KRIMINAL MUSEUM, Burggasse 3. Tel. 09861/53-59.

The only museum of its kind in Europe, the Kriminal Museum is housed in a structure built in 1395 for the Order of the Johanniter, who cared for the sick. It was rebuilt in 1718 in the baroque style, the only edifice of this style still standing in Rothenburg. To give an insight into the life, laws, and punishments of medieval days, on four floors of the building the museum shows the legal history of ten centuries. You'll see chastity belts, women's shame masks, a shame flute for bad musicians, a cage for bakers who baked bread too small or too light, and other mementos of crime and punishment.

Admission: 5 DM ($3.30) adults, 2.50 DM ($1.70) children under 13.
Open: Apr–Oct, daily 9:30am–6pm; Nov–Mar, daily 2–4pm.

A STROLL AROUND THE ARCHITECTURAL HIGHLIGHTS   The only way to see Rothenburg properly is to wander through the town on foot, beginning at the typical hub of any old German village, the **Rathaus,** which is described above. Leaving Marktplatz, walk north on the street that opens off the square between the Rathaus and the tavern. This will lead you to Klingengasse, a narrow old street that passes directly under the Gothic **St. Jakobskirche** (Church of St. James).

For a look at one of the old ramparts, follow Klingengasse northward, from the church to the **Klingentor,** its top portion adorned with four oriels and a ball lantern. You can wander along the covered ramparts of this portion of the wall, and to continue your tour of the town, walk on the wall west and south to the 13th-century Dominican nunnery, housing the **Reichsstadtmuseum.**

From the museum it's just a short walk to **Herrngasse,** once the town's most exclusive street, which leads back to Marktplatz. Many of its half-timbered houses have been converted into shops. On one side of the street is the 13th-century Gothic **Franciscan Church,** with an unusual rood screen separating the east choir from the naves. The church is most notable for its numerous tombs, decorated with sculptures.

At the opposite end of Herrngasse from Marktplatz is the **Burgtor,** the tower that originally led to the Castle of the Hohenstaufen (destroyed in 1425). The tower once had a drawbridge, and although the moat and castle are both gone now, you can still see the holes where the ropes once raised and lowered the bridge and the huge hole, called the peat, through which hot oil or tar could be poured on an enemy.

The gardens where the castle once stood jut out from the rest of the town toward the Tauber River. Across the river from the Burggarten is the **Toppler Castle,** built in 1388 by the famous mayor Toppler.

Take Burggasse for a short distance east and you'll come to the **Kriminal Museum.** From here, it's just a few steps east to Schmiedgasse. Turn down this street and you'll arrive at the **Baumeisterhaus,** home of Leonard Weidmann, who built the Renaissance Rathaus. The facade is decorated with 14 carved stone figures representing the 7 vices and virtues. The interior houses a restaurant.

WHERE TO STAY
VERY EXPENSIVE

EISENHUT (Iron Helmet), Herrengasse 3–5, D-8803 Rothenburg o.d.T. Tel. 09861/70-50. Fax 09861/70-545. 80 rms, 3 suites. MINIBAR TV TEL

$ Rates (including buffet breakfast): 205 DM–225 DM ($135.30–$148.50) single; 285 DM–380 DM ($188.10–$250.80) double; from 580 DM ($382.80) suite. AE, DC, MC, V **Parking:** 15 DM ($9.90)

⭐ The most celebrated inn on the Romantic Road, the Eisenhut is perhaps the finest small hotel in Germany, attracting an international crowd. Four medieval patrician houses, dating from the 12th century, were joined to make this distinctive inn. This virtual museum of antiquity is easy to find, just across the street from the Rathaus.

The main living room has a beamed ceiling, Oriental carpets, ecclesiastical sculpture, and a grandfather clock. The reception lounge continues the theme, with a wooden ceiling, wide staircase, and statuary. The guest rooms are individualized—no two are alike—yours may contain handcarved and monumental pieces or have a 1940s Hollywood touch with a tufted satin headboard.

Most impressive is the three-story galleried dining hall, with ornate classic wood paneling and balconies. There are additional places to dine as well, each richly decorated and furnished, although in sunny weather they're all deserted in favor of the multitiered flagstone terrace on the Tauber. Meals are à la carte, costing 60 Dm to 100 DM ($39.60 to $66). The specialty of the house is filet of lamb with tarragon or pike dumplings in crayfish sauce. Service is daily from noon to 2pm and 6:30 to 9:30pm. There is also a piano bar.

EXPENSIVE

HOTEL BÄREN, Hofbronnengasse 9, D-8803 Rothenburg o.d.T. Tel. 09861/60-31. Fax 09861/48-75. 35 rms. TV TEL
$ Rates (including buffet breakfast): 190 DM–205 DM ($125.40–$135.30) single; 260 DM–330 DM ($171.60–$217.80) double. MC, V. **Parking:** 8 DM ($5.30). **Closed:** Jan 4–Mar 15.

⭐ One of the leading old inns of town, directly south of the Rathaus, dates back to 1577. Though modernized by the Müller family, it still has 15-inch oak beams and ornate wainscoting. Each of the traditional guest rooms is styled differently, with coordinated colors; half of the units also contain minibars.

For quiet moments, the reading-and-writing room has an open fireplace. The centrally located hotel has a spacious, elegant gourmet restaurant, Der Bärenwirt, as well as a cozy Bierstube outfitted with wooden beams and paneling, a tile stove, and an apéritif bar. Meals in the Bärenwirt cost 80 DM to 105 DM ($52.80 to $69.30). You can dine daily from 6 to 10pm.

BURG HOTEL, Klostergasse 1–3, D-8803 Rothenburg o.d.T. Tel. 09861/50-37. Fax 09861/1487. 14 rms, 5 suites. MINIBAR TV TEL
$ Rates (including continental breakfast): 160 DM–190 DM ($105.60–$125.40) single; 190 DM–280 DM ($125.40–$184.80) double; from 320 DM ($211.20) suite. AE, DC, MC, V. **Parking:** 15 DM ($9.90).
Built on top of the old town wall is this large, timbered hotel with a high-pitched roof, flower garden, windowboxes of geraniums, and a picket fence. The dining terrace provides a panoramic view of the Tauber River and the surrounding fields. The interior has been renovated by Gabrielle Berger. All the rooms are unique: One has a four-poster bed of old oak, and others have swagged and draped beds; some are filled with antiques, and some have been done in sleek contemporary style. Breakfast is served in an attractive room done in Louis XVI style, with a view.

GOLDENER HIRSCH, Untere Schmiedgasse 16–25, D-8803 Rothenburg o.d.T. Tel. 09861/70-80. Fax 09861/70-81-00. 80 rms. MINIBAR TEL
$ Rates: 130 DM–200 DM ($85.80–$132) single; 190 DM–315 DM ($125.40–$207.90) double. Breakfast 18 DM ($11.90) extra. AE, DC, MC, V. **Parking:** 15 DM ($9.90). **Closed:** Dec 20–Jan 11.
This first-class hotel is a remake of an inn that dated from 1600. In the heart of town off Wenggasse, it's housed in a rustic building. So popular has this hostelry become that it's annexed another patrician house across the street. The guest rooms are comfortable and homelike, showing a respect for traditional taste. Room service and laundry are available

The Blue Terrace, for dining, offers a panoramic view of the Tauber and the surrounding hills, or you may prefer to take your dinner in the blue-and-white Regency salon. Meals cost from 55 DM to 88 DM ($36.30 to $58.10).

HOTEL MERIAN, Ansbacherstrasse 42, D-8803 Rothenburg o.d.T. Tel. 09861/30-96. Fax 09861/86-787. 32 rms (all with shower). MINIBAR TV TEL
$ Rates (including buffet breakfast): 150 DM–180 DM ($99–$118.80) single; 200 DM–280 DM ($132–$184.80) double. AE, DC, MC, V. **Parking:** Free.

Recently built, the Merian sits beside the old gates of the medieval town, about 400 yards from the Bahnhof. Gisela Schmidt, the proprietor, sees to it that old-fashioned courtesy is offered along with modern comfort and individual service. The rooms are handsomely furnished, each with an alarm radio and a hairdryer. Some rooms also have a terrace. Guests can relax in the conservatory or the bar after a busy sightseeing day.

ROMANTIK HOTEL MARKUSTURM, Rödergasse 1, D-8803 Rothenburg o.d.T. Tel. 09861/20-98. Fax 09861/26-92. 24 rms, 2 suites. TV TEL
$ Rates (including buffet breakfast): 150 DM–200 DM ($99–$132) single; 220 DM–310 DM ($145.20–$204.60) double; from 330 DM ($217.80) suite. AE, DC, MC, V. **Parking:** 12 DM ($7.90). **Closed:** Jan 11–Feb 14.

The Markusturm belongs to the city's history. When it was built in 1264, one of Rothenburg's defensive walls was incorporated into the building. Today that wall has been torn down, except for the section that is part of the hotel, which is still doing a lively business next to St. Mark's Tower. One room has an antique bed that might be strong enough to support the entire hotel. The guest rooms have been modernized but furnished with traditional styling.

HOTEL TILMAN RIEMENSCHNEIDER, Georgengasse 11–13, D-8803 Rothenburg o.d.T. Tel. 09861/20-86. Fax 09861/29-79. 65 rms. TV TEL
$ Rates (including buffet breakfast): 130 DM–210 DM ($85.80–$138.60) single; 180 DM–340 DM ($118.80–$224.40) double. AE, DC, MC, V. **Parking:** 15 DM ($9.90).

Named for the famous sculptor (ca. 1460–1531), the Tilman Riemenschneider has a half-timbered facade rising directly above one of the most visited historic streets of Rothenburg. However, its rear courtyard offers a cool and calm geranium-bedecked oasis from the busy pedestrian traffic in front. One of the most prominent hotels in town, it contains alpine-inspired furniture (often painted in rustic floral motifs), stone floors, lots of mountain-style accessories, and an occasional porcelain stove set into a wall niche. Rooms are well furnished, often stylish. Room service, laundry, and dry cleaning are available, and facilities include a fitness center with a sauna, a turbo-skylab solarium, and two whirlpool baths.

MODERATE

HOTEL GASTHOF GLOCKE, Am Plönlein 1, D-8803 Rothenburg o.d.T. Tel. 09861/30-25. Fax 09861/86-711. 25 rms. TV TEL
$ Rates (including continental breakfast): 93 DM–145 DM ($61.40–$95.70) single; 150 DM–190 DM ($99–$125.40) double. AE, DC, MC, V. **Parking:** 10 DM ($6.60). **Closed:** Dec 24–Jan 6.

The designer of this comfortable hotel took pains to re-create a country-rustic decor. Most meals, drinks, and entertainment take place beneath heavily beamed ceilings, and big windows are framed with frilly curtains. The owners are justifiably proud of their restaurant—with its very complete wine cellar—where meals cost 32 DM to 66 DM ($21.10 to $43.60). They also rent comfortably modern rooms, each with its own TV and radio and often a private balcony. The hotel is south of the town center, off Wenggasse.

HOTEL REICHS-KÜCHENMEISTER, Kirchplatz 8, D-8803 Rothenburg o.d.T. Tel. 09861/20-46. Fax 09861/86-965. 52 rms, 2 suites. TV TEL

$ **Rates** (including buffet breakfast): 95 DM–140 DM ($62.70–$92.40) single; 130 DM–190 DM ($85.80–$125.40) double; from 330 DM ($217.80) suite. AE, DC, MC, V. **Parking:** 10 DM ($6.60).

One of the oldest structures in Rothenburg, near the St. Jacobskirche, is built on different levels. You wander down the corridors to the nicely furnished rooms, all with regionally painted wooden furniture. Some also contain minibars. The hotel has a sauna, whirlpool, steam bath, and solarium. An extra 17 rooms are available in the annex across the street.

In the main restaurant the Franconian regional food is good, the choice wide. I recommend the Reichs-Kuchen "master plate," including a choice of filet of pork, beef, and veal with fresh vegetables. In season, you may prefer a leg of roebuck with mushrooms, potatoes, and cranberries. You might also patronize the Weinstube, whose specialty is "steak from the hot stove."

INEXPENSIVE

BAYERISCHER HOF, Ansbacherstrasse 21, D-8803 Rothenburg o.d.T. Tel. 09861/34-57. Fax 09861/86-56-1. 9 rms (all with shower). TV TEL
$ **Rates** (including continental breakfast): 75 DM–85 DM ($49.50–$56.10) single; 115 DM–135 DM ($75.90–$89.10) double. MC, V. **Parking:** Free. **Closed:** Jan–Feb.

A good hotel, the Bayerischer Hof stands midway between the Bahnhof and the medieval walled city. Petra and Harald Schellhaas welcome guests to their recently renovated, clean, and well-furnished accommodations. The food is very good, with many international and Bavarian specialties.

GASTHOF GOLDENER GREIFEN, Obere Schmiedgasse 5, D-8803 Rothenburg o.d.T. Tel. 09861/22-81. Fax 09861/86-374. 21 rms (12 with bath or shower).
$ **Rates** (including continental breakfast): 42 DM ($27.70) single without bath or shower, 65 DM ($42.90) single with bath or shower; 70 DM ($46.20) double without bath or shower, 108 DM ($71.30) double with bath or shower. AE, MC, V. **Closed:** Aug 22–Sept 2 and Dec 19–Feb 2.

One of the better little inns, Gasthof Goldener Greifen offers not only well-cooked meals at modest prices—from 22 DM ($14.50)—but also comfortable rooms. Just off Marktplatz, in a patrician 1374 house, it stands next door to the prestigious Baumeisterhaus restaurant, recommended below. You can order your morning coffee in the garden amid roses and geraniums. The rooms are simple but offer good comfort, eiderdowns, and hot and cold running water. The dining room is closed on Monday.

WHERE TO DINE
MODERATE

BAUMEISTERHAUS, Obere Schmiedgasse 3. Tel. 09861/34-04.
   Cuisine: FRANCONIAN. **Reservations:** Required for courtyard tables.
$ **Prices:** Appetizers 8 DM–20 DM ($5.30–$13.20); main courses 16 DM–36 DM ($10.60–$23.80); three-course fixed-price lunch 35 DM ($23.10). AE, DC, MC, V.
   Open: Lunch daily 11am–2:30pm; dinner daily 6–9:30pm.

Right off Marktplatz, the Baumeisterhaus is housed in an ancient patrician residence. Built in 1596, it contains what is universally considered the most beautiful courtyard in Rothenburg (which can be visited only by guests). The patio has colorful murals, serenely draped by vines. Try, for an appetizer, the soup of the day. Main dishes are well prepared and attractively served, and desserts are rich and luscious. Even though the cuisine is good, the prices are kept surprisingly moderate.

BLAUE TERRASSE, in the Goldener Hirsch, Untere Schmiedgasse 16. Tel. 09861/70-80.
   Cuisine: FRANCONIAN/INTERNATIONAL. **Reservations:** Recommended

$ Prices: Appetizers 9.50 DM–22 DM ($6.30–$14.50); main courses 35 DM–45 DM ($23.10–$29.70). AE, DC, MC, V.

Open: Lunch daily noon–2pm; dinner daily 6–9pm. **Closed:** Dec–Jan.

The Goldener Hirsch, previously recommended as one of the top hotels, boasts dining facilities that have made it a preferred choice for many nonresidents. The menu changes every season as different produce becomes available.

RATSSTUBE, Marktplatz 6. Tel. 09861/55-11.

Cuisine: FRANCONIAN. **Reservations:** Recommended.

$ Prices: Appetizers 7.50 DM–15 DM ($5–$9.90); main courses 18 DM–32 DM ($11.90–$21.10). MC, V.

Open: Mon–Sat 9am–11pm, Sun noon–6pm. **Closed:** Jan 7–Feb 28.

The Ratsstube enjoys a position right on the market square, one of the most photographed spots in Germany. It's a bustling center of activity throughout the day—a day that begins when practically every Rothenburger stops by for a cup of morning coffee. Inside, a true tavern atmosphere prevails, with hardwood chairs and tables, vaulted ceilings, and pierced copper lanterns. On the à la carte menu are many Franconian wines and dishes, including Sauerbraten and venison, both served with fresh vegetables and potatoes. For dessert, you can order homemade Italian ice cream and a cup of espresso. If you arrive at 9am, the staff will serve you an American breakfast if you wish.

INEXPENSIVE

HOTEL GASTHOF GLOCKE, Am Plönlein 1. Tel. 09861/30-25.

Cuisine: FRANCONIAN. **Reservations:** Recommended.

$ Prices: Appetizers 6.40 DM–16.50 DM ($4.20–$10.90); main courses 15 DM–50 DM ($9.90–$33). AE, DC, MC, V.

Open: Lunch daily 11am–2pm; dinner Mon–Sat 6–9pm. **Closed:** Dec 24–Jan 6.

This traditional hotel and guesthouse (previously recommended) serves regional specialties along with a vast collection of local wine. Meals emphasize seasonal dishes. Service is polite and attentive.

REICHS-KÜCHENMEISTER, Kirchplatz 8. Tel. 09861/20-46.

Cuisine: FRANCONIAN. **Reservations:** Required.

$ Prices: Appetizers 5.50 DM–18 DM ($3.60–$11.90); main courses 14 DM–38 DM ($9.20–$25.10). AE, DC, MC, V.

Open: Lunch daily 11:30am–2pm; dinner daily 6–9:30pm. **Closed:** Tues in Nov–Apr.

Reichs-Küchenmeister might be called an old-fashioned entertainment complex. This hotel near St. Jacobskirche, previously recommended, offers a wide range of gastronomic choices that might include white herring with potatoes, Bavarian liver dumplings with sauerkraut and potatoes, and game stew with noodles and cranberries. You'll find a conservatively decorated Weinstube, a garden terrace, a Konditorei, and traditionally helpful service.

TILMAN RIEMENSCHNEIDER, Georgengasse 11. Tel. 09861/20-86.

Cuisine: FRANCONIAN. **Reservations:** Not necessary.

$ Prices: Appetizers 8 DM–20 DM ($5.30–$13.20); main courses 18 DM–45 DM ($11.90–$29.70); fixed-price menu 22 DM–40 DM ($14.50–$26.40). AE, DC, MC, V.

Open: Lunch daily 11am–2pm; dinner daily 6–9pm.

A traditional old Weinstube is housed in one of the finest hotels in Rothenburg. The chef shows elevated respect for old-fashioned cookery served in generous portions. You might begin with air-dried beef of smoked filet of trout, then follow with poached eel, halibut steak, or loin of pork. Fixed-price and à la carte menus are available.

2. DINKELSBÜHL

58 miles SW of Nürnberg; 71 miles NE of Stuttgart; 65 miles SE of Würzburg

GETTING THERE By Train The nearest Bahnhof is Ansbach, which has several trains arriving daily from such cities as Munich, Nürnberg, and Stuttgart. From Ansbach, Dinkelsbühl can be reached by bus. Train rides from Munich or Frankfurt take about 2½ to 3 hours, depending on the connection. For rail information, telephone 09081/19-419. In summer, it's possible to go from Nördlingen (see below) to Dinkelsbühl on a historic stream rail line, the Bayrische Eisenbahnmuseum. Telephone 09081/98-08 for schedules and information.

By Bus For long-distance bus service along the Romantic Road, refer to "Seeing the Region" at the beginning of this chapter. Regional buses that run along the Romantische Strasse, linking Dinkelsbühl with local towns, are operated by RBA Regionalbus Augsburg GmbH at Donauwörth (tel. 0906/21-727).

By Car To drive to Dinkelsbühl from either Frankfurt or Munich takes about 2½ to 3 hours. Access is via autobahn A7 north and south or Route 25 east.

ESSENTIALS For tourist information, contact **Stadt Verkehrsamt,** Marktplatz (tel. 09851/9-02-40).

SPECIAL EVENTS This dreamy village seems to awaken only once a year for the Kinderzeche (Children's Festival), commemorating the saving of the village by its children in 1632. It is held for 10 days in July. According to the story, the children pleaded with conquering Swedish troops to leave their town without pillaging and destroying it, and got their wish. The pageant includes concerts given by the local boys' band dressed in historic military costumes.

Still surrounded by medieval walls and towers, Dinkelsbühl is straight out of a story by the Brothers Grimm, even down to the gingerbread, which is one of its main products. Behind the ancient walls, originally built in the 10th century, it is a town that retains its quiet, provincial attitude in spite of the great hordes of tourists who come here. The cobblestone streets are lined with fine 16th-century houses, many with carvings and paintings depicting biblical and mythological themes. In the center of town is the late-Gothic **Georgenkirche,** Marktplatz, built between 1448 and 1499, containing a carved Holy Cross Altar from the same period. Many of the pillar sculptures also go back to the 15th century.

WHERE TO STAY & DINE

MODERATE

BLAUER HECHT, Schweinemarkt 1, D-8804 Dinkelsbühl. Tel. 09851/8-11. Fax 09851/814. 44 rms (all with bath or shower). TV TEL
$ Rates (including continental breakfast): 89 DM–119 DM ($58.70–$78.50) single; 130 DM–180 DM ($85.80–$118.80) double. AE, DC, MC, V. **Closed:** Jan 2–31.
This elegant ocher building dating from the 17th century has three hand-built stories of stucco, stone, and tile. The rooms are sunny, large, and comfortable—at least most of them—and come in a variety of color schemes.

DEUTSCHES HAUS, Weinmarkt 3, D-8804 Dinkelsbühl. Tel. 09851/60-58. Fax 09851/79-11. 11 rms. TV TEL
$ Rates (including continental breakfast): 125 DM–155 DM ($82.50–$102.30) single; 160 DM–250 DM ($105.60–$165) double. AE, DC, MC, V. **Parking:** 10 DM ($6.60). **Closed:** Dec 23–Jan 6.

The facade of the Deutschese Haus dates from 1440; it's rich in painted designs and festive woodcarvings. In a niche on the second floor of the arched entrance is a 17th-century madonna. Casually run, Deutsches Haus features a dining room with an elaborately decorated ceiling, inset niches with provincial scenic pictures, and parquet floors. The rooms are unique—you may find yourself in one with a ceramic stove or in another with a Biedermeier desk.

Even if you're a nonresident, you may want to come here to dine in the Altdeutsches Restaurant, one of the finest in Dinkelsbühl. It is intimate and convivial, an attractive rendezvous. À la carte meals cost 36 DM to 70 DM ($23.80 to $46.20). The restaurant serves Franconian and regional specialties daily from 8am to midnight.

EISENKRUG, Dr.-Martin-Luther-Strasse 1, D-8804 Dinkelsbühl. Tel. 09851/60-17. Fax 09851/60-20. 12 rms (all with bath or shower). MINIBAR TV TEL

$ Rates (including continental breakfast): 90 DM ($59.40) single; 125 DM–160 DM ($82.50–$105.60) double. AE, DC, MC, V.

The sienna walls of this centrally located hotel were originally built in 1620. Today the Eisenkrug's forest-green shutters are familiar to practically everyone in town, many of whom celebrate family occasions at its in-house restaurant. There's even a café with al fresco tables in warm weather. The stylish rooms are wallpapered with flowery prints and filled with engaging old furniture. The hotel also offers an additional nine rooms in a guesthouse nearby.

The main restaurant, Zum kleinen Obristen, serves excellent food, as does the historic wine cellar. À la carte meals cost from 62 DM to 105 DM ($40.90 to $69.30). It's also possible to order a fixed-price lunch at 45 DM ($29.70) or a choice of two fixed-price dinners at 60 DM ($39.60) and 108 DM ($71.30). A Franconian cuisine is served in the wine cellar, which is open daily from 5:30pm until the last customer leaves. A gourmet international cuisine is offered in the main restaurant, which serves from noon to 2pm and 6 to 10pm; it's closed on Monday and also Tuesday evening.

GOLDENE ROSE, Marktplatz 4, D-8804 Dinkelsbühl. Tel. 09851/8-31. Fax 09851/61-35. 34 rms (all with bath or shower). MINIBAR TV TEL

$ Rates (including continental breakfast): 75 DM–130 DM ($49.50–$85.80) single; 110 DM–170 DM ($72.60–$112.20) double. AE, DC, MC, V. **Parking:** 5 DM ($3.30).

A landmark in the heart of this village, the intricately timbered Goldene Rose rises three stories, with a steeply pitched roof and windowboxes overflowing with geraniums and petunias. It traces its history back to 1450. The guest rooms are modernized, with comfortable beds.

In the style of a country inn, the dining rooms are more important than the lounges. Adding to the ambience is a wealth of oak, antiques, and portraits of sovereigns (that's Queen Victoria at the bottom of the steps). The à la carte menu offers such tempting items as lobster and crab with dill and rumpsteak Goldene Rose. A good variety of tasty desserts includes fresh raspberries flambé. The cuisine is international with many Franconian and Bavarian specialties. Meals cost 28 DM to 55 DM ($18.50 to $36.30), and service is daily from 11am to midnight.

3. NÖRDLINGEN

81 miles NW of Munich; 59 miles SW of Nürnberg

GETTING THERE   By Plane   The nearest major airport is in Nürnberg, from which either bus or rail connections can be made to Nördlingen.

By Train   Nördlingen lies on the main Nördlingen-Aalen-Stuttgart line, with frequent connections in all directions. Telephone 09081/19-419 for schedules and more information. Nördlingen in summer also operates a historic steam rail line to Dinkelsbühl (see above).

By Bus Long-distance buses operate along the Romantic Road (see "Seeing the Region" at the beginning of this chapter). Regional buses also serve Dinkelsbühl, and they're operated by RBA Regional Bus Stuttgart GmbH at Aalen (tel. 07361/67-140).

By Car Access by car is via autobahn A7 north and south and Route 29 from the east. The drive takes 1½ hours from Munich or 4 hours from Frankfurt.

ESSENTIALS For tourist information, contact the **Verkehrsamt,** Marktplatz 2 (tel. 09081/43-80).

───────────

One of the most irresistible medieval towns along the Romantic Road, Nördlingen is still completely encircled by the well-preserved ✪ **city fortifications** from the 14th and 15th centuries. You can walk around the town on the covered parapet, which passes 11 towers and 5 fortified gates set into the walls.

At the center of the circular-shaped Altstadt within the walls is **Rübenmarkt.** If you stand in this square on market day, you will be swept into a world of the past—the country people have preserved many traditional customs and costumes here, which, along with the ancient houses, create a living medieval city. Around the square stand a number of buildings, including the Gothic Rathaus. A collection of antiquities is displayed in the **Reichsstadt Museum,** Vordere Gerbergasse, which is open from 10am to noon and 1:30 to 4:30pm; it's closed on Monday and from December through February. Admission is 3 DM ($2) for adults and 1.50 DM ($1) for children.

The **Church of St. George,** on the northern side of the square, is the town's most interesting sight and one of its oldest buildings. The Gothic Hallenkirche is from the 15th century. The fan-vaulted interior is decorated with plaques and epitaphs commemorating the town's more illustrious residents of the 16th and 17th centuries. Although the original Gothic altarpiece by Friedrich Herlin (1470) has been placed in the Reichsstadt Museum, a portion of it, depicting the crucifixion, remains in the church. Above the high altar today stands a more elaborate baroque altarpiece. The most prominent feature of the church, however, is the 295-foot French Gothic tower, called the "Daniel." At night, the town watchman calls out from the steeple, his voice ringing through the streets of the town.

WHERE TO STAY

MODERATE

AM RING, Burgermeister-Reiger Strasse 14, D-8860 Nördlingen. Tel. 09081/40-28. Fax 09081/23-170. 39 rms. TV TEL
$ Rates (including continental breakfast): 78 DM–90 DM ($51.50–$59.40) single; 135 DM–170 DM ($89.10–$112.20) double. AE, MC. **Parking:** 10 DM ($6.60). **Closed:** Mid-Dec to Jan 10.
This family-owned hotel with modern amenities should appeal especially to visitors because of its location near the Hauptbahnhof and its dignified guest rooms decorated in streamlined style with lots of light.

KAISER HOTEL SONNE, Marktplatz 3, D-8860 Nördlingen. Tel. 09081/50-67. Fax 09081/23-999. 40 rms (32 with bath). MINIBAR TV TEL
$ Rates (including continental breakfast): 80 DM ($52.80) single without bath, 100 DM ($66) single with bath; 150 DM ($99) double without bath, 195 DM ($128.70) double with bath. AE, DC, MC, V. **Parking:** Free.
In a bull's-eye position, next to the cathedral and the Rathaus, is the Sonne, with a heady atmosphere from having entertained so many illustrious personalities since it opened as an inn in 1405. It has counted emperors, kings, and princes among its guests, including Frederick III, Maximilian I, and Charles V; even Goethe came this way, as did the American astronauts from Apollo 14 and Apollo 17. The interior has been completely modernized, providing tasteful accommodations with comfort.

In a choice of dining rooms, you can order the soup of the day, main courses such as rumpsteak Mirabeau, and fattening German desserts. Meals range from 35 DM to 70 DM ($23.10 to $46.20). It's all quite casual; the waitresses even urge you to finish the food on your plate.

WHERE TO DINE
EXPENSIVE

MEYER'S KELLER, Marienhöhe 8. Tel. 09081/44-93.
   Cuisine: CONTINENTAL. **Reservations:** Required. **Bus:** Local bus to Marktplatz.
$ **Prices:** Appetizers 16 DM–28 DM ($10.60–$18.50); main courses 38 DM–52 DM ($25.10–$34.30); fixed-price lunch 52 DM ($34.30); fixed-price dinner 80 DM–115 DM ($52.80–$75.90). AE, MC.
   Open: Lunch Tues–Sun noon–2pm; dinner Tues–Sun 6–10pm.

The conservatively modern decor here seems a suitable setting for the restrained neue Küche of the talented chef and owner of this place, Joachim Kaiser. The cuisine changes according to the availability of ingredients and the inspiration of the chef; typical selections include roulade of seawolf and salmon with baby spinach and wild rice, John Dory with champagne-flavored tomato sauce, and an impressive array of European wine.

---

4. AUGSBURG

42 miles NW of Munich; 50 miles E of Ulm; 100 miles SE of Stuttgart

GETTING THERE **By Plane** Augsburg's Mühlhausen Airport lies directly on the most important east-west motorway in Bavaria, and it takes three minutes to reach the motorway junction Augsburg-East between Stuttgart and Munich. For flight information, call 0821/70-50-51.

By Train Ninety Euro and Inter-City trains arrive here daily, from all the important German cities. For railway information, call 0821/194-19. Sixty trains per day arrive from Munich (trip time: 30 to 50 minutes); and 35 trains from Frankfurt (3 hours, 5 minutes, to 4½ hours).

By Bus Long-distance bus service (lines EB 190 and 190 A, plus line 189), services the Romantic Road on buses operated by Deutsche Touring GmbH in Frankfurt (tel. 069/79-03-248 for reservations and information). Regional bus service in the area is provided by RBA Regionalbus Augsburg GmbH in Augsburg (tel. 0821/32-64-61).

By Car Access is via autobahn A8 east and west.

ESSENTIALS **Getting Around** The public transportation system in Augsburg consists of three tram and 31 bus lines. This system covers not only the inner city but reaches suburbs as well. Public transportation operates from 5am to midnight daily. Service is provided by Augsburger Verkehrsverband AVV (tel. 821/15-70-07).

Information Contact **Tourist-Information,** Bahnhofstrasse 7 (tel. 0821/50-20-70).

Augsburg is near the center of the Romantic Road and the gateway to the Alps and the south. The 2,000 years that have gone into the creation of this largest city (about 250,000 inhabitants) on the Romantic Road have also made it one of the major sightseeing attractions in southern Germany. Little remains from the early Roman period (it was founded under Tiberius in 15 B.C.E.), but the wealth of art and architecture from the Renaissance is staggering. Over the years Augsburg has been host to many distinguished visitors and has an array of famous native sons. These have included the painters Hans Holbein the Elder and Hans Holbein the Younger, and the playwright Bertolt Brecht. It was to Augsburg that Martin Luther was summoned in 1518 to recant his 95 Theses before a papal emissary. Today, Augsburg is an important industrial center on the Frankfurt-Salzburg Autobahn.

WHAT TO SEE & DO

THE FUGGEREI, at the end of Vorderer Lech. Tel. 0821/3-08-68.

✪ Augsburg has been an important city throughout its history, but during the 15th and 16th centuries it was one of the wealthiest communities in Europe, mainly because of its textile industry and the political and financial power of its two banking families, the Welsers and the Fuggers. The Welsers, who once owned nearly all of Venezuela, have long since faded from the minds of Augsburgers. But the founders of the powerful Fugger family have established themselves forever in the hearts of the townsfolk by an unusual legacy.

The Fuggerei is actually a miniature town, established in 1519 by the Fugger family to house poorer Augsburgers. A master mason fallen on hard times, Franz Mozart, once lived at Mittlere Gasse 14—he was the great-grandfather of Wolfgang Amadeus Mozart. The quarter consists of several streets lined with well-maintained Renaissance houses, as well as a church and administrative offices, all enclosed within walls. As the oldest housing project in the world, it charges tenants rent of only 1.71 DM ($1.10) per year, a rate that has not changed in more than 450 years. Tenants are obligated to pray daily for the souls of their patrons at the restored St. Marcus Church or at home. Residents must be Roman Catholic. The Fugger Foundation still owns the Fuggerei.

A house at Mittlere Gasse 13, next to the one once occupied by Mozart's ancestor, is now the Fuggerei's **museum** (tel. 0821/30-868). The rough 16th- and 17th-century furniture, wood-paneled ceilings and walls, and cast-iron stove, as well as other objects of everyday life, show what it was like to live there in earlier times.

Admission: Museum 1 DM (66¢).

Open: Museum, Mar–Oct daily 9am–6pm. **Tram:** 1.

DOM ST. MARIA, Hoher Weg. Tel. 0821/31-66-353.

The Dom St. Maria of Augsburg has the distinction of containing the oldest stained-glass windows in the world. The Romanesque windows, from the 12th century, are younger than the cathedral itself, which was begun in 944 on the foundation walls of an early Christian baptismal church. The ruins of the original basilica are found in the crypt beneath the west chancel. Partially Gothicized in the 14th century, it stands on the edge of the park, which also fronts the Episcopal Palace, where the basic creed of the Lutheran Reformation was presented at the Diet of Augsburg in 1530. The cathedral remains the episcopal see of the Catholic bishop to this day. The 11th-century bronze doors, leading into the three-aisled nave, are adorned with bas reliefs of a mixture of biblical and mythological characters, including a scene of Adam and Eve. The interior of the cathedral, restored in 1934, contains side altars with altarpieces by Hans Holbein the Elder and Christoph Amberger. The windows in the south transept are the oldest, depicting prophets of the Old Testament in a severe but colorful Romanesque style.

Admission: Free.

Open: Daily 9am–6pm. **Tram:** 1.

ST. ANNE'S, Annastrasse 20. Tel. 0821/30-237.

The third most artistically significant church in Augsburg is St. Anne's, a short walk from the Rathaus. Its most celebrated visitor was Martin Luther in 1518, who, it is said, did not put much faith in his imperial letter of safe conduct and slipped "out the back way" in the middle of the night. Still, his visit must have had a powerful impact, because St. Anne's, then part of a Carmelite monastery, became Protestant some seven years after. It has rich decorations in both the flamboyant Gothic style and the rococo, the latter reflected in its richly adorned frescoes and stuccowork. Dating from 1518, the Fuggerkapelle, or Fugger funeral chapel, is called the first example of the Italian Renaissance style that made its way into Germany from the south. Dürer designed two of the reliefs on the sepulcher. The church owns two works by Lucas Cranach the Elder, including a portrait of Luther. On the second floor, overlooking the cloisters, is a book-lined cell in which Luther found refuge.

Admission: Free.

Open: Daily 9am–6pm. **Tram:** 1.

RATHAUS, Am Rathausplatz 1. Tel. 0821/32-41.

Built by Elias Holl in 1620, the Rathaus was visited by Napoleon in 1805 and 1809. Regrettably, it was also visited by an air raid in 1944, leaving it gutted, a mere shell of a building that had once been known as a palatial eight-story monument to the glory of the Renaissance. The destruction left its celebrated "golden chamber" in shambles. Now, after costly restoration, the Rathaus can be visited by the public. In front of the Rathaus is the Augustus fountain, forged in bronze by the Dutch sculptor Hubert Gerhard in 1594 to commemorate the founding of the town.

Admission: Free.

Open: Daily 10am–6pm. **Tram:** 1.

CHURCH OF ST. ULRICH AND ST. AFRA, Ulrichplatz 19. Tel. 0821/15-60-49.

Extending southward from the Rathaus is the wide Maximilianstrasse, lined with old burghers' houses and studded with fountains by the Renaissance Dutch sculptor Adrien de Vries. Near the southern end of the street is the Hercules Fountain, and behind it, the most attractive church in Augsburg, the Church of St. Ulrich and St. Afra, which was constructed between 1476 and 1500 on the site of a Roman temple. As a tribute to the 1555 Peace of Augsburg, which recognized two denominations, the Catholics and the Lutherans, this church contains both a Catholic and a Protestant church within its walls. The church is 15th-century Gothic, but many of the furnishings, including the three altars representing the birth and resurrection of Christ and the baptism of the Church by the Holy Spirit, are later baroque. The large pulpit looks almost like a pagoda, with decorative angels dressed in Chinese red and gold. The crypt of the church contains the tombs of the Swabian saints, Ulrich and Afra. Ulrich was an Augsburg bishop who died in 973 and Afra a young Roman woman who was martyred because she refused to recant her Christian beliefs. The lance and saddle of St. Ulrich are on display in the sacristy.

Admission: Free.

Open: Daily 9am–6pm. **Tram:** 1.

SCHAEZLERPALAIS, Maximilianstrasse 46. Tel. 0821/324-21-71.

Facing the Hercules Fountain is the Schaezlerpalais, containing the city's art galleries—and what a collection is on display here! Constructed as a 60-room mansion between 1765 and 1770, it was willed to Augsburg after World War II. If only the works of artists who lived in Augsburg during the Renaissance were exhibited, it would be an imposing sight. (Regrettably, however, there is no painting by Titian in all the town, although he was here twice, in 1548 and again in 1551.) Works by local artists are displayed, including Hans Burgkmair, Hans Holbein the Elder, and Hans Holbein the Younger, represented by a fine portrait, who was born in a house nearby. Non-German European masters are represented by Rubens, Veronese, and Tiepolo. The larger number of paintings are by German artists of the Renaissance and baroque periods. One of the most famous of these is Dürer's portrait of Jakob Fugger the Rich, founder of the dynasty that once influenced the elections of the Holy Roman emperors. Besides the art collections, the palace-gallery contains a rococo ballroom, with gilded and mirrored wall panels and a ceiling fresco of the *Four Continents*. Here Marie Antoinette danced the night away on April 28, 1770.

Admission: 3 DM ($2) adults, 1.50 DM ($1) children.

Open: May–Sept, Tues–Sun 10am–5pm; Oct–Apr, Tues–Sun 10am–4pm. **Tram:** 1.

MOZARTHAUS, Frauentorstrasse 30. Tel. 0821/324-21-96.

Augsburg is the native town of the Mozart family. Leopold Mozart was born in Augsburg in 1719. He not only became the father of one of the world's great musical geniuses but also founded the first violin school. The magenta-colored Mozarthaus, north of the Dom, contains a 1785 pianoforte that was built by Johann Andreas Stein, an organ- and piano-maker whose instruments were eagerly sought not only by the young Mozart but also later by Beethoven.

Admission: Free.

Open: Sat–Sun 10am–noon, Mon and Wed–Thurs 10am–noon and 2–5pm, Fri 10am–noon and 2–4pm. **Tram:** 1.

WHERE TO STAY
VERY EXPENSIVE

STEIGENBERGER DREI MOHREN PALASTHOTEL, Maximilianstrasse 40, D-8900 Augsburg. Tel. 0821/5-03-60, or toll free 800/223-5652 in the U.S. or Canada. Fax 0821/15-78-64. 107 rms, 5 suites. MINIBAR TV TEL **Tram:** 1.

$ Rates (including buffet breakfast): 205 DM–270 DM ($135.30–$178.20) single; 292 DM–360 DM ($192.70–$237.60) double; from 525 DM ($346.50) suite. AE, DC, MC, V. **Parking:** 17 DM ($11.20).

Rebuilt in a modern style in 1956, the Steigenberger Drei Mohren Palasthotel was one of the most renowned in Germany before its destruction in a 1944 air raid. It had been a hotel since 1723 and was known to diplomats, composers, and artists; former guests include the Duke of Wellington, Mozart, Goethe, Mascagni, Paganini, and Franklin Roosevelt. The interior treatment of the "Three Moors" incorporates stylish contemporary pieces with traditional furnishings. For example, the drawing room contains a slatted natural-wood ceiling and wall, contrasting with a room-wide mural of Old Augsburg. The guest rooms are restrained and restful, handsomely proportioned, with some reserved for nonsmokers.

Dining/Entertainment: In the formal dining room, an international cuisine is offered. Meals begin at 50 DM ($33). On the breakfast terrace, umbrellas and garden chairs are set in view of flower beds and three free-form fountains.

Services: Room service, laundry, dry cleaning.

Facilities: Staff can arrange golf nearby.

EXPENSIVE

TURM HOTEL, Wittelsbacher Park, D-8900 Augsburg. Tel. 0821/57-70-87. Fax 0821/59-41-16. 185 rms, 11 suites. MINIBAR TV TEL **Tram:** 1.

$ Rates (including continental breakfast): 192 DM–222 DM ($126.70–$146.50) single; 282 DM ($186.10) double; from 320 DM ($211.20) suite. AE, DC, MC, V. **Parking:** Free.

The 35-floor Turm, 10 minutes from the heart of the city, is advertised as the tallest tower hotel in Europe. Students of architecture will see the similarity to Chicago's Marina City in the facade of this rounded and balconied concrete structure thrusting skyward. The hotel, totally renovated and newly furnished in late 1986, offers comfortable sunny rooms with rounded terraces.

The hotel has a sun terrace, and across the street is a fitness center. On the 35th floor, you can dine in one of the two restaurants, La Fontaine and Le Bistro, or have a drink at the piano bar as you look over the housetops of Augsburg.

MODERATE

ALPENHOF, Donauwörther 233, D-8900 Augsburg-Oberhausen. Tel. 0821/4-20-40. Fax 0821/42-04-200. 130 rms (all with bath or shower), 2 suites TV TEL **Directions:** Augsburg-West exit off Autobahn. **Bus:** 52 or 54.

$ Rates (including buffet breakfast): 115 DM–155 DM ($75.90–$102.30) single; 160 DM–200 DM ($105.60–$132) double; from 280 DM ($184.80) suite. AE, DC, MC, V. **Parking:** 10 DM ($6.60).

Set amid a suburbanlike neighborhood near the town center, this stable and solid hotel occupies three interconnected buildings built around 40 years ago. Because of easy access from the Autobahn and ample parking, it appeals to motorists unwilling to negotiate the narrow one-way streets of the Old Town. Quiet and peaceful, the hotel offers modernized rooms and a generous breakfast. There are a bar and conservatively furnished restaurant near the lobby, 24-hour room service, plus a solarium, sauna, and indoor pool.

HOTEL FISCHERTOR, Pfärrie 14-16, D-8900 Augsburg. Tel. 0821/15-60-51. Fax 0821/30-702. 21 rms. MINIBAR TV TEL **Tram:** 1.

$ Rates (including continental breakfast): 98 DM–128 DM ($64.70–$84.50) single; 148 DM–168 DM ($97.70–$110.90) double. Continental breakfast 15 DM ($9.90) extra. AE, DC, MC, V. **Parking:** 9 DM ($5.90).

Near the cathedral, Fischertor is better known for its restaurant than its well-furnished modern rooms, which were added only in 1985 to the already successful restaurant. The contemporary reception area is floored with ruddy-hued stone.

INEXPENSIVE

HOTEL GARNI WEINBERGER, Bismarckstrasse 55, D-8901 Stadtbergen. Tel. 0821/24391-0. 31 rms (26 with bath or shower). TEL **Tram:** 2.

$ Rates (including buffet breakfast): 48 DM ($31.70) single without bath; 95 DM ($62.70) double with bath or shower. No credit cards. **Parking:** Free. **Closed:** Aug 15–30.

One of the least expensive and best budget accommodations in the area lies about 2 miles from the heart of Augsburg, along the Augsburgerstrasse in the western sector. The owner rents light and airy rooms. The place is well patronized by Germans, who know a good bargain, and its café is one of the most popular in the area for snacks.

WHERE TO DINE
VERY EXPENSIVE

HOTEL GREGOR RESTAURANT/CHEVAL BLANC, Landsberger Strasse 62, D-8900 Augsburg 21-Havnstetten. Tel. 0821/8-00-50.
Cuisine: SWABIAN/BAVARIAN/FRENCH. **Reservations:** Recommended. **Bus:** 730, 731, 732, or 733.

$ Prices: Appetizers 20 DM–40 DM ($13.20–$26.40); main courses 45 DM–50 DM ($29.70–$33); four-course fixed-price menu 100 DM ($66); five-course fixed-price menu 130 DM ($85.80). AE, DC, MC, V.
Open: Dinner Tues–Sat 7–10pm.

Five miles south of Augsburg is a rustic country restaurant that retains an antique flavor in spite of new construction. Soups are important, along with such rare treats as wild boar (in season).

It's also possible to stay here in one of the 40 pleasantly furnished guest rooms with private baths, minibars, TVs, and phones. Singles cost 98 DM to 120 DM ($64.70 to $79.20), while doubles go for 145 DM to 180 DM ($95.70 to $118.80)—including continental breakfast.

EXPENSIVE

WELSER KÜCHE, Maximilianstrasse 83. Tel. 0821/3-39-30.
Cuisine: SCHWÄBISH. **Reservations:** Required. **Tram:** 1.

$ Prices: Feasts 59.50 DM ($39.30) and 69.50 DM ($45.90), without drinks. AE, DC, MC.
Open: Dinner seatings daily promptly at 7:30pm.

Come to Welser Küche for a medieval feast eaten at wooden tables. The traditional menu is served nightly by *Knechte* and *Mägde* (knaves and wenches) in 16th-century costumes. A 6- or 8-course menu, called a "Welser Feast," is served, with a dagger and fingers used as utensils. Stone walls, knotty-pine paneling, and stucco arches frame the wooden tables with earthenware pitchers. Many recipes served here were found in a cookbook (found in 1970) that belonged to Philippine Welser, Baroness of Zinnenburg, born in 1527. She was the wife of a Habsburg Archduke Ferdinand II.

It takes about three hours to eat a meal here. Sometimes parties of two or four can be fitted in at the last minute, but reservations should be made as far in advance as possible.

ZUM ALTEN FISCHERTOR [OBLINGER], Pfärrle 14. Tel. 0821/51-86-62.

Cuisine: CONTINENTAL. **Reservations:** Essential. **Tram:** 1.

$ **Prices:** Appetizers 16 DM–32 DM ($10.60–$21.10); main courses 38 DM–55 DM ($25.10–$36.30); fixed-price menus 92 DM ($60.70) and 138 DM ($91.10). AE, DC, MC, V.

Open: Lunch Tues–Sat 11:30am–2pm; dinner Tues–Sat 6–11pm. **Closed:** June 7–21 and Aug 1–15.

In the heart of the historic section, Zum Alten Fischertor is the finest restaurant in Augsburg. Located near the cathedral, it's a charming, intimate 20-seat restaurant offering a changing array of seasonal specialties. The cuisine is presented in unpretentious surroundings; waiters are attentive; and there is a superb collection of wine, more than 200 varieties. A typical meal might include goose-liver terrine with mushrooms and cabbage, sole roulade with crêpes, turbot with chanterelles, or stuffed Bresse pigeon.

MODERATE

DIE ECKE, Elias-Holl-Platz 2. Tel. 0821/51-06-00.

Cuisine: FRENCH/SWABIAN. **Reservations:** Required. **Tram:** 1.

$ **Prices:** Appetizers 14 DM–20 DM ($9.20–$13.20); main courses 22 DM–38 DM ($14.50–$25.10); fixed-price menu 95 DM ($62.70). AE, DC, MC, V.

Open: Lunch daily 11:30am–2pm; dinner daily 6pm–1am.

If you decide to dine here, your name can join a roster of distinguished clients. Since it was founded in the year Columbus sighted the New World, guests have included Hans Holbein the Elder; Wolfgang Amadeus Mozart; and, in more recent times, Rudolf Diesel of engine fame and Bertolt Brecht. (Brecht, it is reported, often showed sharp-tongued irreverence, which tended to irritate diners of more conservative political leanings.) The Weinstube ambience belies the sophisticated cuisine of the chef. Your meal might include such elegant fare as breast of duckling, preceded by a pâté of pheasant or filet of sole in Riesling sauce. Venison dishes are a specialty.

SIEBEN-SCHWABEN-STUBEN, Bürgermeister-Fischer-Strasse 12. Tel. 0821/31-45-63.

Cuisine: SWABIAN. **Reservations:** Recommended. **Tram:** 1.

$ **Prices:** Appetizers 10 DM–16 DM ($6.60–$10.60); main courses 20 DM–36 DM ($13.20–$23.80). AE, DC, MC, V.

Open: Daily 11am–1am.

This unusual place has a high barrel-vaulted ceiling, with half-moon windows. Early in the history of this restaurant the owner conceived the idea of printing the establishment's menu in English and other languages and mailing it regularly to the best clients. Each day a different menu reigns. A hearty Schwabish cuisine is featured, including such dishes as bacon dumplings bedded on cider sauerkraut, a 7 Swabians Pot (tenderloin of pork with Spätzle), and boiled breast of beef with horseradish. For dessert, try the Apfelstrudel with vanilla sauce.

INEXPENSIVE

HOTEL RIEGELE MIT BRÄUSTUBERL, Viktoriastrasse 4. Tel. 0821/3-90-39.

Cuisine: BAVARIAN/SWABIAN. **Reservations:** Not necessary. **Tram:** 1.

$ **Prices:** Appetizers 5.50 DM–18 DM ($3.60–$11.90); main courses 14 DM–38 DM ($9.20–$25.10). AE, DC, MC, V.

Open: Lunch daily 11am–2pm; dinner daily 6–10pm. **Closed:** 2 weeks in Aug (dates vary).

S This restaurant has gutbürgerlich German cookery and a cozy interior that evokes the Black Forest. Luring hungry diners here are traditional specialties, including country-style buffets, coupled with kind and attentive service and reasonable prices. You can try three draft beers with the excellent cuisine. Angus steak and fresh fish are the specialties, along with traditional regional dishes.

---

5. FÜSSEN

57 miles S of Augsburg; 74 miles SW of Munich

GETTING THERE   By Plane   The nearest major airport is at Munich.

By Train   Füssen has a Bahnhof, and trains from Munich or Augsburg arrive frequently throughout the day. For information, call 08362/19-419. A train from Munich takes 2½ hours; from Frankfurt 6 to 7 hours.

By Bus   Long-distance bus service from Augsburg (see above) is provided by line EB 190. Regional service is provided by RVA Regionalverkehr Schwäben Allgau GmbH in Füssen (tel. 08362/37-771). This company runs at least 10 buses a day to the royal castles (see below).

By Car   Access by car is via autobahn A7 from the north and also from Routes 16 and 309.

ESSENTIALS   For tourist information, contact **Kurverwaltung,** Augsburger Torplatz 1 (tel. 08362/70-77).

Depending on which direction you take, Füssen is the beginning or end of the Romantic Road. The town has a number of attractive buildings, including a 15th-century castle once used by the bishops of Augsburg as a summer palace. Füssen's popularity lies in its ideal location as a starting point for excursions into the surrounding countryside. In the foothills of the Bavarian Alps, Füssen is equally enjoyable for winter or summer vacationers. An added attraction is the proximity to the castles of Neuschwanstein and Hohenschwangau.

From Füssen you can take a fascinating excursion to the **○ Wieskirche,** one of the most extravagant and flamboyant rococo buildings in the world, a masterpiece of Dominikus Zimmermann. On the slopes of the Ammergau Alps, lying between Ammer and Lech, the Wieskirche is a noted pilgrimage church, drawing visitors from all over the globe. The location is in an alpine meadow just off the Romantic Road near Steingaden. Inquire at the tourist office for a map and the exact location before setting out. Also, ask if the church will actually be open at the time of your visit. The church, which in German means "in the meadows," was built to honor the memory of Jesus Scourged. With the help of his brother, Johann Baptist, Zimmermann worked on the building from 1746 to 1754. Around the choir the church has "upside down" arches, and its ceiling is richly frescoed. It is amazing that such rich decoration could be crowded into so small a place. The great Zimmermann was so enchanted with his creation that he constructed a small home in the vicinity, and spent the last decade of his life there.

WHERE TO STAY

MODERATE

ALPENBLICK, Uferstrasse 10, D-8958 Füssen-Hopfen am See. Tel.

08362/5-05-70. Fax 08362/50-57-73. 46 rms. TV TEL **Directions:** 3 miles N of Füssen on Augsburger Strasse.

$ Rates: 99 DM–160 DM ($65.30–$105.60) single; 158 DM–220 DM ($104.30–$145.20) double; half board 20 DM ($13.20) per person extra. AE, DC, MC, V. **Parking:** Free.

At Hopfen am See, 3 miles from Füssen, is an attractively designed mountain chalet whose encircling balconies are edged with flowers. From the windows of many of the rooms, guests can see the lake and the Alps. The comfortably furnished units contain TVs and radios, and each has its own balcony. The premises are impeccably maintained in a rustic ambience of wood and hand-painted furniture. On a chilly evening, you might seek out a quiet corner beside the open fireplace in the restaurant. On a panoramic sun terrace, drinks and snacks are served to residents and roadside visitors as well. Meals start at 28 DM ($18.50).

HOTEL CHRISTINE, Weidachstrasse 31, D-8958 Füssen. Tel. 08362/72-29. 15 rms. MINIBAR TV TEL

$ Rates (including continental breakfast): 100 DM–180 DM ($66–$118.80) single; 160 DM–190 DM ($105.60–$125.40) double. No credit cards. **Parking:** Free. **Closed:** Mid-Jan to mid-Feb.

The Christine is one of the best choices, lying five minutes by taxi from the train station in the Weidach district. The long winter months are spent refurbishing the rooms so that they'll be fresh and sparkling to greet spring visitors. Breakfast is served on beautiful regional china as classical music is played in the background. Units are quite spacious, with balconies.

FÜRSTENHOF, Kemptenerstrasse 23, D-8958 Füssen. Tel. 08362/70-06. 15 rms (all with shower). TV TEL

$ Rates (including continental breakfast): 59 DM–75 DM ($38.90–$49.50) single; 116 DM–130 DM ($76.60–$85.80) double. AE, MC. **Parking:** Free. **Closed:** Nov 24–Dec 31.

One of the town's leading hotels offers well-furnished rooms. Here the ceilings are of massive exposed paneling, the full-grained beams set into the modern stucco with taste and craftsmanship. Breakfast is the only meal served.

SEEGASTHOF WEISSENSEE, An der B310, D-8958 Füssen-Weissensee. Tel. 08362/70-95. Fax 08362/23-76. 22 rms (all with bath or shower). MINIBAR TEL **Directions:** 4 miles from central Füssen on B310.

$ Rates (including buffet breakfast): 76 DM–100 DM ($50.20–$66) single; 122 DM–160 DM ($80.50–$105.60) double. No credit cards. **Parking:** Free.

The paneled rooms have sliding glass doors opening onto a balcony overlooking the lake. Each accommodation contains a minibar stocked with beer, wine, and champagne. Breakfast is an appetizing and generous meal of cheese, cold cuts, bread, pastry, eggs, and beverages. The fish that your obliging hosts serve you during dinner might have been caught in the ice-blue waters of the nearby lake, whose far shore you can see from the dining room.

INEXPENSIVE

HOTEL-GASTHOF ZUM HECHTEN, Ritterstrasse 6, D-8958 Füssen. Tel. 08362/79-06. 34 rms (25 with bath or shower), 4 suites.

$ Rates (including continental breakfast): 55 DM ($36.30) single without bath or shower, 65 DM ($42.90) single with bath or shower; 85 DM ($56.10) double without bath or shower, 95 DM ($62.70) double with bath or shower; from 120 DM ($79.20) suite. No credit cards. **Parking:** Free. **Closed:** Nov.

The Pfeiffers have maintained this impeccable guesthouse for generations. Its white-walled facade comes directly to the edge of the centrally located street where it sits. It is one of the oldest guesthouses in town, but it has been unpretentiously and tastefully modernized into a functional format with its own kind of charm. It's laden with a conservative sense of peace and quiet.

STEIG MÜHLE, Alte Steige 3, D-8958 Füssen-Weissensee. Tel. 08362/ 73-73. Fax 08362/31-48. 10 rms (all with bath or shower). **Directions:** From Füssen, take Route 310 toward Kempten, a 5-minute drive.

$ Rates (including buffet breakfast): 35 DM–42 DM ($23.10–$27.70) single; 75 DM–85 DM ($49.50–$56.10) double. No credit cards. **Parking:** 4.50 DM ($3). **Closed:** Nov 23–Dec 24.

S Owners and obliging hosts Josef and Guste Buhmann like things warm and cozy—their guesthouse is almost a cliché of Bavarian charm. It's a pension garni (serving breakfast only), which comes alive with the first breath of spring when the flowerboxes gracing this chaletlike hotel burst into bloom. Rooms open onto a view of the lake or mountains, and many have their own balconies. Six contain TV. They're furnished in a neat, functional style and are kept immaculately clean. The public rooms are often paneled in wood and decorated with local artifacts.

WHERE TO DINE
MODERATE

FISCHERHÜTTE, Uferstrasse 16, Hopfen am See. Tel. 08362/71-03.
  Cuisine: SEAFOOD. **Reservations:** Recommended. **Directions:** 3 miles NW of Füssen in the hamlet of Hopfen am See.

$ Prices: Appetizers 14 DM–19 DM ($9.20–$12.50); main courses 12.50 DM–39.50 DM ($8.30–$26.10). AE, DC, MC, V.
  Open: Lunch daily 11:30am–2pm; dinner daily 6–9:30pm. **Closed:** Mon–Tues from Jan to end of Mar.

At the edge of the lake, within sight of dramatic mountain scenery, lie four gracefully paneled old-fashioned dining rooms, plus a summertime beer garden. Each is laden with antiques and flowers and enjoys a view. A terrace in summer expands the dining area. As its name, Fisherman's Cottage, suggests, the establishment specializes in an array of fish whose origins read a lot like an international atlas of the world: one half of an entire Alaskan salmon (for two); a garlicky version of French bouillabaisse; fresh alpine trout, prepared panfried or with aromatic herbs in the style of Provence; North Atlantic lobster; and grilled halibut. You can precede any of those dishes with a portion of lasagne. A limited array of meat dishes is also offered, as well as succulent desserts.

INEXPENSIVE

ZUM SCHWANEN, Brotmarkt 4. Tel. 08362/61-74.
  Cuisine: SWABIAN/BAVARIAN. **Reservations:** Required.

$ Prices: Appetizers 9 DM–15 DM ($5.90–$9.90); main courses 15 DM–32 DM ($9.90–$21.10). AE.
  Open: Lunch Tues–Sun noon–2pm; dinner Tues–Sat 6–9pm.

A conservatively flavorful blend of Swabian and Bavarian specialties is served to the loyal clients of Zum Schwanen, a small, attractively old-fashioned restaurant. Specialties include homemade sausage, roast pork, lamb, and deer.

---

6. NEUSCHWANSTEIN/ HOHENSCHWANGAU

2 miles E of Füssen; 72 miles SW of Munich

GETTING THERE   By Plane   The nearest major airport is at Munich.

By Train   The nearest rail station is at Füssen (see above).

By Bus   Ten buses a day arrive from Füssen (see above).

By Car   Head east from Füssen along Route B17.

The 19th century saw a great classical revival in Germany, especially in Bavaria, mainly because of the enthusiasm of Bavarian kings for ancient art forms. Beginning with Ludwig I (1786–1868), who was responsible for many Greek-revival buildings in Munich, this royal house ran the gamut of ancient architecture in just three short decades. It culminated in the remarkable flights of fancy of Ludwig II, often called "Mad King Ludwig," who died under mysterious circumstances in 1886. In spite of his rather lonely life and controversial alliances, personal and political, he was a great patron of the arts.

Although the name "Royal Castles" is limited to the castles of Hohenschwangau (built by Ludwig's father, Maximilian II) and Neuschwanstein, the extravagant king was responsible for the creation of three magnificent castles. The remaining two, described in other parts of the book, are Linderhof (near Oberammergau) and Herrenchiemsee (Chiemsee). These pet projects were so close to the king's heart that when his ministers sought to check his extravagance, he became violent.

In 1868, after a visit to the great castle of Wartburg, Ludwig wrote to his good friend, composer Richard Wagner: "I have the intention to rebuild the ancient castle ruins of Hohenschwangau . . . in the true style of the ancient German knight's castle." The following year, construction began on the first of a series of fantastic edifices, a series that stopped only with Ludwig's untimely death in 1886, only five days after he was deposed because of alleged insanity.

Information about the castles and the region in general is available at Kurverwaltung, Rathaus, Münchenerstrasse 2 in Schwangau (tel. 08362/81-98-0).

Note: There are often very long lines at the attractions below in summer, especially August.

NEUSCHWANSTEIN CASTLE, Neuschwansteinstrasse 20. Tel. 08362/81-035.

✪ Neuschwanstein was the fairy-tale castle of Ludwig II. Until the king's death, construction went on for 17 years. After his death, all work stopped, leaving a part of the interior not completed. From 1884 to 1886, Ludwig lived in the rooms on and off for a total of only about six months.

Neuschwanstein was his most ambitious project, set in its isolated location atop a rock ledge high above the Pollat Gorge. The ledge served as the foundation of the castle and because of its unusual configuration, supported portions of the third floor as well as the first. This is obvious in the oddly shaped vestibule on the third floor, at the top of the main staircase of Untersberg marble. This hall, with its colorfully painted Romanesque vaults, is trapezoidal, the walls decorated with scenes from a version of the Siegfried saga.

The doorway off the left side of the vestibule leads to the king's apartments. The study, like most of the rooms, is decorated with wall paintings showing scenes from the Nordic legends (which also inspired Wagner's operas). The theme of the study is the Tannhauser saga, painted by J. Aigner. The only fabric in the room is hand-embroidered silk, used in curtains and chair coverings, all designed with the gold-and-silver Bavarian coat-of-arms.

From the vestibule, you enter the throne room through the doorway at the opposite end. This hall, designed in Byzantine style by J. Hofmann, was never completed. The floor is a mosaic design, depicting the animals of the world. The columns in the main hall are the deep copper red of porphyry. The circular apse where the king's throne was to have stood is reached by a stairway of white Carrara marble. The walls and ceiling are decorated with paintings of Christ in heaven looking down on the 12 Apostles and 6 canonized kings of Europe.

The king's bedroom is the most richly carved in the entire castle. It took 4½ years to complete this room alone, which, aside from the wall painting depicting the legend of Tristan and Isolde, is completely covered in oakwood carvings. The walls are decorated with panels carved to look like Gothic windows. In the center is a large wooden pillar completely encircled with gilded brass sconces. The bed, on its raised platform with its elaborately carved canopy, is the most ornate furnishing in the room. Through the balcony window you can see the 150-foot waterfall in the Pollat Gorge, with the mountains in the distance.

Passing through the winter garden and a grotto with artificial stalactites, you come to the great parlor, whose theme is the Lohengrin saga, expressed in paintings of Heckel and Hauschild. Note the heavy chandelier, holding 48 candles and studded with pieces of colored Bohemian glass.

The fourth floor of the castle is almost entirely given over to the Singer's Hall, the pride of Ludwig II and all of Bavaria. Modeled after the hall at Wartburg, where the legendary song contest of Tannhäuser was supposed to have taken place, this hall is decorated with marble columns and elaborately painted designs interspersed with frescoes depicting the life of Parsifal.

The castle can be visited year round, and in September visitors have the additional treat of hearing Wagnerian concerts in the Singer's Hall. For information and reservations, contact the Verkehrsamt (tourist office) Schwangau, at the Rathaus (tel. 08362/81-98-0). The rooms are open April to October 31, daily from 9am to 5:30pm; in winter, hours are from 10am to 4pm. Admission is 8 DM ($5.30) for adults and 5 DM ($3.30) for children 6 to 15.

To reach Neuschwanstein involves a steep 1-kilometer climb from the car park for Hohenschwangau Castle (see below). This is about a 25-minute walk for the energetic, an eternity for anybody else. To cut down on such a climb, you can take a bus to Marienbrücke, a bridge named for the mother of Ludwig II. The bridge crosses over the Pollat Gorge at a height of 305 feet. From that vantage point you can, like Ludwig, stand and meditate on the glories of the castle and its panoramic surroundings. It costs 3.50 DM ($2.30) for the bus ride up to the bridge, or 2 DM ($1.30) if you'd like to take the bus back down the hill. Marienbrücke is still not at the castle. From the bridge, it is a 10-minute walk to reach Neuschwanstein. This footpath is very steep and not easy for elderly people to negotiate—or for anyone who has trouble walking up or down precipitous hills.

The most traditional way to reach Marienbrücke is by a horse-drawn carriage, costing 7 DM ($4.60) for the ascent, 3.50 DM ($2.30) for the descent. Some readers have objected to the buggy rides, though, complaining that too many people are crowded in. The buggy rides will bring you only to Marienbrücke, so you will still have the steep 10-minute walk to Neuschwanstein.

HOHENSCHWANGAU CASTLE, Alpseestrasse 24. Tel. 08362/81-127.

★ Not as glamorous or spectacular as Neuschwanstein, this neo-Gothic castle nevertheless has a much richer history. The original structure dates back to the Knights of Schwangau of the 12th century. When the knights faded away, the castle began to do so too, helped along by the Napoleonic Wars. When Ludwig II's father, Crown Prince Maximilian (later King Maximilian II), saw the castle in 1832, he purchased it and in four years had it completely restored. Ludwig II spent the first 17 years of his life here and later received Richard Wagner in its chambers, although Wagner never visited Neuschwanstein on the hill above.

The rooms of Hohenschwangau are styled and furnished in a much heavier Gothic mode than those in the castle built by Ludwig. Many are typical of the halls of knights' castles of the Middle Ages in both England and Germany. There is no doubt that the style greatly influenced young Ludwig and encouraged the fanciful boyhood dreams that formed his later tastes and character. Unlike Neuschwanstein, however, this castle has a comfortable look about it, as if it actually were a home at one time, not just a museum. The small chapel, once a reception hall, is still the scene of Sunday mass. The suits of armor and the Gothic arches here set the stage for the rest of the room.

Among the most attractive chambers is the Hall of the Swan Knight, named for the wall paintings depicting the saga of Lohengrin—pre-Wagner and pre–Ludwig II. Note the Gothic grillwork on the ceiling with the open spaces studded with stars. The furniture in the room once reserved for dining is a mixture of period Gothic, overdecorative gifts from admiring subjects, and cherry or maple Biedermeier pieces from the 19th century.

Probably the most authentically Gothic room is the Hall of Heroes. The paintings lining the walls depict the old German saga of Dietrich of Berne. On the long banquet table are centerpieces of gilded bronze decorated with scenes from the Nibelungen saga.

From Ludwig's third-floor bedroom the young king could keep an eye on his castle on the hillside above. As in other rooms, the ceiling of the room was decorated with the typically Gothic stars—with one difference. Here they artificially lit up at night.

Nearby is the music room where Ludwig and Wagner spent long hours entertaining one another at the maple piano. The small chapel in the alcove off the music room was executed by Ludwig. The room also contains an exhibit of emotional letters sent by the king to Wagner, expressing his great admiration for him.

Hohenschwangau is open April to September 30, daily from 9am to 5:30pm; in winter, hours are from 10am to 4pm. Admission is 8 DM ($5.30) for adults and 5 DM ($3.30) for children. Several parking lots nearby enable you to leave your car there while visiting both castles.

WHERE TO STAY & DINE NEARBY

EXPENSIVE

HOTEL LISL AND JÄGERHAUS, Neuschwansteinstrasse 1–3, D-8959 Hohenschwangau. Tel. 08362/8-10-06. Fax 08362/81-107. 53 rms (all with bath or shower). MINIBAR TV TEL **Bus:** Füssen bus.

$ Rates (including buffet breakfast): 110 DM ($72.60) single; 240 DM ($158.40) double. AE, DC, MC, V. **Parking:** Free. **Closed:** Jan to mid-Mar.

This graciously styled villa with an annex across the street was seemingly made to order to provide views as well as comfort. Both houses sit in a narrow valley, surrounded by their own gardens. Here you'll find attractive rooms, some with minibars and TVs. In the main house, two well-styled dining rooms serve meals that average about 35 DM ($23.10). The restaurant features an international as well as a local cuisine.

HOTEL MÜLLER HOHENSCHWANGAU, Alpseestrasse 16, D-8959 Hohenschwangau. Tel. 08362/8-19-90. Fax 08362/81-99-13. 45 rms, 3 suites. TV TEL **Bus:** Füssen bus.

$ Rates (including continental breakfast): 140 DM–200 DM ($92.40–$132) single; 180 DM–240 DM ($118.80–$158.40) double; from 400 DM ($264) suite. AE, DC, MC, V. **Parking:** Free. **Closed:** Nov 20–Dec 31.

The yellow walls, green shutters, and gabled alpine detailing of this hospitable inn are enough incentive for you to stay here. However, its position near the foundation of Neuschwanstein Castle makes it even more alluring. An enlargement and an upgrading in 1984 left the basic Bavarian lines intact yet added extra modern conveniences. On the premises are a well-maintained restaurant lined with burnished pinewood; a more formal evening restaurant with views over a verdantly planted sun terrace; lots of rustic accessories; and comfortable rooms. Nature lovers usually enjoy the opportunity of hiking the short distance to nearby Hohenschwangau Castle.

CHAPTER 12

THE BAVARIAN ALPS

If you walk into a rustic alpine inn along the German-Austrian frontier and ask the innkeeper if he's German, you'll most likely get the indignant response, "Of course not! I'm Bavarian." And he is undoubtedly right, because even though Bavaria is a state of Germany, some older inhabitants can still remember the kingdom of Bavaria, which did not become part of the German Reich until 1918.

The huge province includes not only the Alps but also Franconia, Lake Constance, and the capital city of Munich. However, we will take this opportunity to explore separately the mountains along the Austrian frontier, a world unto themselves. The hospitality of the people of this area is famous. The picture of the plump rosy-cheeked innkeeper who has a constant smile on his or her face is no myth.

Many travelers think of the Alps as a winter vacationland, but you'll find that nearly all the Bavarian resorts and villages boast year-round attractions.

SUGGESTED ITINERARY

Day 1   After leaving Füssen (see Chapter 11), head east for the alpine resort of Garmisch-Partenkirchen, where you can spend the day exploring the Alpspitz region and enjoying views of the towering Zugspitze.

Day 2   Head north to visit the village of Oberammergau in the morning. You can also see other the major attractions in the area, including Schloss Linderhof and Kloster Ettal. Then go southeast for an overnight in the alpine village of Mittenwald.

Day 3   Travel northeast to Chiemsee, where you can visit the Neues Schloss on Herrenchiemsee island. Then head southeast to Berchtesgaden for the night.

Day 4   Stay in Berchtesgaden, filling your busy day visiting the Salzbergwerk Berchtesgaden (salt mines), the Eagle's Nest of Hitler, and Königssee.

GETTING THERE

Munich is the gateway to the region for those arriving by plane. From Munich, Autobahns lead directly to the Bavarian Alps. If you're beginning your tour in Garmisch-Partenkirchen in the west, you should fly into Munich. However, if you'd like to begin your tour in the eastern alps at Berchtesgaden, then Salzburg in Austria is better for plane connections.

InterCity trains have good links to Garmisch and Mittenwald. Berchtesgaden is linked to cities in the north of Germany by Fern-Express trains. Long-distance buses

WHAT'S SPECIAL ABOUT THE BAVARIAN ALPS

Great Towns/Villages

☐ Berchtesgaden, favorite hideaway of Ludwig I, one of the scenic high-lights of the Bavarian Alps.

☐ Garmisch-Partenkirchen, Germany's top alpine resort, famed for skiing and mountain climbing.

☐ Oberammergau, a village of great Bavarian alpine charm, site of a noted passion play.

☐ Mittenwald, straight out of *The Sound of Music*, an alpine village extraordinaire.

Ace Attractions

☐ Königssee, one of the most scenic bodies of water in Europe, lying outside Berchtesgaden.

☐ Obersalzberg, site of Kehlstein, Hitler's "Eagle's Nest," one of the great panoramas of Europe.

☐ Chiemsee, known as the "Bavarian Sea," with two islands, Herrenchiemsee and Frauenchiemsee.

Historic Palaces

☐ Neues Schloss, on Herrenchiemsee, Ludwig II's fantastic attempt to rival the grand palace of Versailles.

☐ Schloss Linderhof, outside Oberammergau, a French rococo palace and architectural fantasy of Ludwig II.

Religious Shrine

☐ Kloster Ettal, founded by Emperor Ludwig the Bavarian in 1330, one of the finest examples of German rococo architecture.

Special Event

☐ Passion play, at Oberammergau, launched in 1634, the world's "longest running show," but staged only once a decade.

don't serve the area well (unless you're on an organized tour) and are an inefficient method of exploring the region. See individual resort sections for bus connections.

1. BERCHTESGADEN

98 miles SE of Munich; 11 miles SE of Bad Reichenhall; 14 miles S of Salzburg

GETTING THERE **By Train** The Berchtesgaden Bahnhof lies on the Munich-Freilassing rail line with frequent connections to Munich. Twelve trains a day arrive from Munich (trip time: 1½ hours). For rail information and schedules, call 08652/19-419. Berchtesgaden also has three mountain rail lines, including Obersalzbergbahn, Jennerbahn, and Hirscheckbahn, going to the mountain plateaus around the resorts. For more information, contact Berchtesgadener Bergbahn AG (tel. 08652/5007) and Obersalzbergbahn AG (tel. 08652/2561).

By Bus Long-distance bus service from Passau as well as from Bad Reichenhall is provided by RBO Regionalbus Ostbayern GmbH in Passau (tel. 0851/73-435). Regional bus service to alpine villages and towns around Berchtesgaden is offered by Verkehrsgesellschaft Regionalverkehr Oberbayern VRO at Berchtesgaden (tel. 08652/5473).

By Car Access by car is via Autobahn A8 from Munich in the north or Route 20 from the south. It takes about 2 hours to drive down from Munich.

ESSENTIALS For tourist information, contact the **Kurdirektion,** Konigsseer Strasse 2 (tel. 08652/50-11).

Ever since Ludwig I of Bavaria chose this resort as a favorite hideaway, the tourist business in Berchtesgaden, situated below the many summits of Watzmann Mountain (8,900 feet at the highest point), has been booming. According to legend, the peaks of the mountain were once a king and his family who were so evil that God punished them by turning them into rocks. The king has evidently not been completely silenced, however, because the Watzmann has been responsible for the deaths of several mountain climbers on the mile-high cliff on its eastern wall.

Many visitors expect to see one of the favorite haunts of Adolf Hitler, since the name Berchtesgaden is often linked with the Führer and the Nazi hierarchy. This is an erroneous impression. Berchtesgaden is an old alpine village with ancient winding streets and a medieval marketplace and castle square. Hitler's playground was actually at Obersalzberg, on a wooded plateau about half a mile up the mountain. Berchtesgaden is very much a quiet Bavarian town.

WHAT TO SEE & DO

The **Stiftskirche** (Abbey Church), dating from 1122, is adjacent to the Königliches Schloss Berchtesgaden. The church is mainly Romanesque, with Gothic additions. One of its ancient twin steeples was destroyed by lightning and rebuilt in 1866. The interior of the church contains many fine works of art, including the high altar with a painting by Zott dating from 1669. In the vestry is a small silver altar donated by Empress Maria Theresa of Austria.

The **Schlossplatz,** partially enclosed by the castle and Stiftskirche, is the most attractive plaza in town. On the opposite side of the square from the church is a 16th-century arcade that leads to the **Marktplatz,** with typically alpine houses and a wooden fountain from 1677 (restored by Ludwig I in 1860). Some of the oldest inns and houses in Berchtesgaden border this square. Extending from the Marktplatz is the **Nonntal,** lined with more old houses, some built into the rocks of the Lockstein Mountain that towers above.

KÖNIGLICHES SCHLOSS BERCHTESGADEN, Schlossplatz 2. Tel. 08652/2085.

Berchtesgaden grew in the Middle Ages around a powerful Augustinian monastery whose monks introduced the art of woodcarving, for which the town is noted to this day. When the town became part of Bavaria in 1809, the abbey was secularized and eventually converted to a palace for the royal family of Wittelsbach. Now it has been converted into a museum, and most of the exhibition is devoted to the royal collection of sacred art, including wood sculptures by the famed artists Veit Stoss and Tilman Riemenschneider. You can also explore a gallery of 19th-century art. There is a collection of Italian Renaissance furniture from the 16th century and three armoires displaying many pistols and guns of the 17th and 18th centuries, plus swords and armor. Precious porcelain and hunting trophies are also shown.

Admission: 7 DM ($4.60) adults, 3 DM ($2) children 6–16.

Open: Easter–Sept, Sun–Fri 10am–1pm and 2–5pm; Oct–Easter, Mon–Fri 10am–1pm and 2–5pm. **Bus:** 9539.

SALZBERGWERK BERCHTESGADEN, Bergwerkstrasse 83. Tel. 08652/60-02-0.

At the eastern edge of town are salt mines once owned by the Augustinian monastery. Operations began here in 1517. The mines contain two types of salt, one suitable only for salt licks for cattle and other animals. The deposits are more than 990 feet thick and still processed today from four galleries or "hills." Visitors on guided tours enter the mine on a small wagonlike train after donning the protective clothing of the miner. After nearly a half-mile ride, they leave the train and explore the

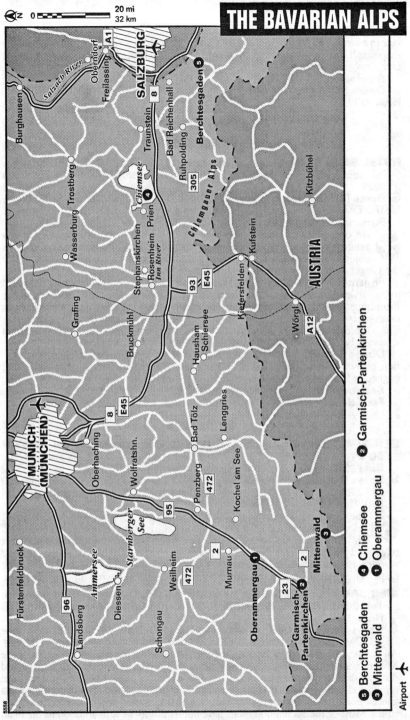

THE BAVARIAN ALPS

20 mi / 32 km

N

Salzach River
Burghausen
Oberndorf
A1
Freilassing
SALZBURG
8
Berchtesgaden
5
Trostberg
Traunstein
Bad Reichenhall
Ruhpolding
Wasserburg
305
Chiemsee
4
Prien
Rosenheim
Stephanskirchen
Chiemgauer Alps
Kitzbühel
Grafing
Inn River
93
E45
Kufstein
Kiefersfelden
AUSTRIA
Bruckmühl
Hausham
Schliersee
Wörgl
A12
Grafing

MUNICH (MÜNCHEN)
8
E45
Oberhaching
Bad Tölz
Lenggries
Wolfratshn.
Penzberg
472
Starnberger See
95
Kochel am See
Mittenwald
3
Fürstenfeldbruck
Ammersee
Weilheim
2
Murnau
2
96
Diessen
472
Oberammergau
1
Landsberg
Schongau
Garmisch-Partenkirchen
23
2

5 Berchtesgaden   4 Chiemsee   2 Garmisch-Partenkirchen
3 Mittenwald   1 Oberammergau

✈ Airport

rest of the mine on foot, sliding down a miner's slide, and enjoying a ride on the salt lake in a ferry. The highlight of the tour is the "chapel," a grotto containing unusually shaped salt formations illuminated to create an eerie effect. The 1½-hour tour can be taken any time of the year, in any weather.

Admission: 14 DM ($9.20) adults, 7 DM ($4.60) children.

Open: May 1–Oct 15, daily 8:30am–5pm; off-season, Mon–Sat 12:30–3:30pm. **Bus:** 9539.

WHERE TO STAY
EXPENSIVE

HOTEL GEIGER, Berchtesgadenstrasse 111, D-8240 Berchtesgaden. Tel. 08652/96-53. Fax 08652/50-58. 45 rms, 2 suites. MINIBAR TV TEL **Bus:** 9539.

$ Rates (including continental breakfast): 110 DM–200 DM ($72.60–$132) single; 160 DM–400 DM ($105.60–$264) double; from 420 DM ($277.20) suite. V. **Parking:** 8 DM ($5.30).

An ornate chalet inn on the upper fringes of Berchtesgaden, the Geiger is a genuine antique. From its terraces, guest rooms, and breakfast rooms, you can enjoy fantastic views of the mountaintops. This remarkable retreat is owned by the Geiger family, who created the hotel more than a century ago.

Biedermeier enthusiasts will revel in the several sitting rooms completely furnished in that style. Any member of the Geiger family will give you the history of any of the furnishings, especially the painting in the paneled drawing room of *Silent Night* (it upset everyone by depicting Mary as awaiting the birth of Jesus on a Bavarian farm). The comfortable rooms are also furnished with antiques. Prices are based on whatever bath facilities you request and whether you have a balcony.

Dining/Entertainment: Dining is a true event here (see separate recommendation below). Guests like to gather in the drawing room for after-dinner coffee and cognac in front of the fireplace.

Services: Massage, laundry, room service.

Facilities: Open-air pool, indoor pool, sauna, solarium, fitness room.

MODERATE

DEMMING, Sunklergässchen 2, D-8240 Berchtesgaden. Tel. 08652/ 50-21. Fax 08652/64-8-78. 34 rms (all with bath or shower), 4 suites. TV TEL **Bus:** 9539.

$ Rates (including buffet breakfast): 78 DM–85 DM ($51.50–$56.10) single; 150 DM ($99) double; from 170 DM ($112.20) suite. AE, DC, MC, V. **Parking:** 6 DM ($4). **Closed:** Nov 20–Dec 31.

The Demming looks like a chalet, but it is truly massive, with four floors of balconied rooms and an annex extending at right angles to the main building. The entire complex is nestled in a depression between two forested hills that offer good views. The reception area contains such artifacts as two wine presses, their wooden screws somewhat weakened by time yet still tinged with the color of the grape. The guest rooms are furnished with alpine pieces. There's an outdoor pool.

VIER JAHRESZEITEN, Maximilianstrasse 20, D-8240 Berchtesgaden. Tel. 08652/50-26. Fax 08652/50-29. 65 rms (all with bath or shower). TEL **Bus:** 9539.

$ Rates (including buffet breakfast): 98 DM–190 DM ($64.70–$125.40) single; 160 DM–250 DM ($105.60–$165) double. AE, DC, MC, V. **Parking:** 6 DM ($4). An old inn with modern extensions, the Vier Jahreszeiten has been in the hands of the Miller family since 1876. It's in the heart of the village and has a colorful and distinguished restaurant (see dining recommendations, below). The inn has been remodeled and improved over the years and now brings a good level of comfort to its guests. Some of the newer units, with tiny sitting rooms and balconies, resemble suites. Most of the accommodations have minibars and TVs. In addition to the main dining room, there's a terrace for summer dining and viewing. The hotel offers an indoor pool, a sauna, and a solarium.

WITTELSBACH, Maximilianstrasse 16, D-8240 Berchtesgaden. Tel. 08652/50-61. Fax 08652/66-304. 29 rms, 3 suites. MINIBAR TV TEL **Bus:** 9539.

$ **Rates** (including buffet breakfast): 80 DM–110 DM ($52.80–$72.60) single; 140 DM–170 DM ($92.40–$112.20) double; from 280 DM ($184.80) suite. AE, DC, MC, V. **Parking:** 6 DM ($4). **Closed:** Mid-Nov to Dec 31.

The Wittelsbach has been stylishly modernized and now offers well-furnished rooms in the heart of Berchtesgaden. It represents a combination of tradition and up-to-date comfort. The rooms are quiet and sunny; most have balconies with fine views of the mountains. Breakfast is the only meal served.

INEXPENSIVE

WATZMANN, Franziskanerplatz 2, D-8240 Berchtesgaden. Tel. 08652/ 20-55. Fax 08652/5174. 38 rms (16 with bath or shower). **Bus:** 9540 or 9541.

$ **Rates** (including continental breakfast): 33 DM–38 DM ($21.80–$25.10) single without bath; 66 DM–72 DM ($43.60–$47.50) double without bath, 76 DM ($50.20) double with shower, 142 DM ($93.70) double with bath. AE, DC, MC, V. **Parking:** Free. **Closed:** Nov until just before Christmas.

Built as part of a brewery 300 years ago, the Watzmann has been altered and expanded many times since. Set opposite the church on the main square, it has one of the largest outdoor terraces in town, a cozy Bavarian-inspired decor, and dozens of turn-of-the-century artifacts derived from local traditions of archery and agriculture. Everyone seems to stop throughout the day or night for a beer, coffee, or lunch. Inside, you'll find huge carved wooden pillars, oak ceilings, wrought-iron chandeliers, and hunting trophies. The simply furnished guest rooms have doors painted with floral murals.

WHERE TO DINE

EXPENSIVE

HOTEL GEIGER, Berchtesgadenstrasse 111. Tel. 08652/96-53.
 Cuisine: BAVARIAN/INTERNATIONAL. **Reservations:** Required. **Bus:** 9539.

$ **Prices:** Appetizers 10 DM–25 DM ($6.60–$16.50); main courses 28 DM–50 DM ($18.50–$33). V.
 Open: Lunch daily noon–2pm; dinner daily 6:30–9pm.

This gabled, extravagantly ornate hotel looks like what every tourist imagines a German hotel to be. Even if you don't stay here, you may want to visit for a meal. Its owner makes guests feel well cared for in a cultivated atmosphere featuring hearty cuisine. Trout and game are specialties. Try the Tafelspitz, delectable boiled beef.

MODERATE

DEMMING-RESTAURANT LE GOURMET, Sunklergässchen 2. Tel. 08652/50-21.
 Cuisine: BAVARIAN/INTERNATIONAL. **Reservations:** Required. **Bus:** 9539.

$ **Prices:** Appetizers 5.50 DM–15 DM ($3.60–$9.90); main courses 12 DM–36 DM ($7.90–$23.80). AE, DC, MC, V.
 Open: Lunch daily 11:30am–2pm; dinner daily 7:30–8:30pm. **Closed:** Nov 1–Dec 19.

The previously recommended Demming hotel contains one of the best restaurants in town. The former wealthy private house looks out over a panoramic view of mountains and forests. Many locals regard dining here as something of an event. Only fresh ingredients are used in the well-prepared dishes, including hearty mountain fare, such as roast beef with chive sauce, plus an array of veal and fish dishes.

HUBERTUSSTUBEN, in the Vier Jahreszeiten, Maximilianstrasse 20. Tel. 08652/50-26.

Cuisine: GERMAN/INTERNATIONAL. **Reservations:** Required.

$ Prices: Appetizers 12 DM–22 DM ($7.90–$14.50); main courses 20 DM–45 DM ($13.20–$29.70). AE, DC, MC, V.

Open: Lunch daily 11:30am–2pm; dinner daily 6–9:30pm.

The Hubertusstuben, directed by the Miller family, has one of the most elaborate menus in Berchtesgaden, and the wine list is also distinguished. A fresh fish soup is presented, and likely dishes are banana steak Bombay and venison steak with vegetables and homemade noodles. For dessert, I'd suggest the apple fritters on walnut ice cream.

EASY EXCURSIONS

✪ **KÖNIGSSEE** This "jewel in the necklace" of Berchtesgaden is one of the most scenic bodies of water in Europe. Its waters appear to be a dark green because of the steep mountains that jut upward from its shores. Low-lying land on the northern edge of the lake contains a car park and a few charming inns and bathing facilities, but the rest of the lake is enclosed by mountains, making it impossible to walk along the shoreline. The only way to explore the waters, unless you're like one of the mountain goats you may see on cliffs above, is by boat. Electric motorboats—no noisy gas-powered launches allowed—carry passengers on tours around the lake throughout the summer and occasionally even in winter. The favorite spot on the Königssee is the tiny flat peninsula on the western bank. It was the site of a basilica as early as the 12th century. Today the Catholic **Chapel of St. Bartholomew** is still used for services (except in winter). The clergy must arrive by boat since there is no other way to approach the peninsula. The adjacent buildings include a fisherman's house and a restaurant where you can sample trout and salmon caught in the crisp, clean waters. At the southern end of the lake you come to the "Salet-Alm," where the tour boat makes a short stop near a thundering waterfall. If you follow the footpath up the hillside, you'll reach the summer pastures used by the cattle of Berchtesgaden Land.

Just over the hill is **Lake Obersee,** part of Königssee until an avalanche separated them eight centuries ago. If you prefer a shorter trip, you can take the boat as far as St. Bartholomew and back. To reach the lake from Berchtesgaden by car, follow the signs south from the town (only 3 miles). It's also a pleasant hour's walk or a short ride by electric train or bus from the center of town.

For information about excursions, call 08652/40-27. An entire tour of Königssee requires about two hours. There are boats in summer every 15 minutes, so getting off one boat and climbing back aboard another is easy if you want to break up your tour. The important stops are at Salet and St. Bartholomew. A round-trip fare for a lake tour is 18 DM ($11.90) for adults and 9 DM ($5.90) for children.

✪ **OBERSALZBERG** The drive from Berchtesgaden to Obersalzberg at 3,300 feet is along one of the most scenic routes in Bavaria. It was here that Hitler settled down in a rented cottage while he completed his book *Mein Kampf*. After he came to power in 1933, he bought Haus Wachenfels and had it remodeled and turned into his Berghof, which became the center for holiday living for such Nazis as Martin Bormann and Hermann Göring.

A major point of interest to visitors is the **Kehlstein,** or Eagle's Nest, which can be reached only by a thrilling bus ride up a 4.5-mile-long mountain road, blasted out of solid rock and considered an outstanding feat of construction and engineering when begun in 1937, under the leadership of Bormann, who intended it as a 50th birthday gift for Hitler. The Eagle's Nest was not, as the name may suggest, a military installation. It was a site for relaxation, a tea house, and was not popular with Hitler, who reportedly visited it only two or three times. To reach the spot, you must enter a tunnel and take a 400-foot elevator ride through a shaft in the Kehlstein Mountain to its summit. The building, with solid granite walls and huge picture windows, houses a mountain restaurant. Called the Kehlsteinhaus, the restaurant is open from the end of May to the end of October (in good weather). Buses from the Hintereck parking lot in Obersalzberg run to the Eagle's Nest about every half hour. At the Eagle's Nest parking lot, you can purchase tickets for the elevator ride to enjoy the breathtaking view from the top. You can also explore the rooms of the original tea house, which include Eva Braun's living room. You can observe the Obersalzberg area below, where Hitler's Berghof once stood, and nearby is the site of the house of Martin Bormann and the SS barracks. To the north you can see as far as Salzburg, Austria, and just below the mountain, to the west, is Berchtesgaden, with its rivers dwindling off into threads in the distance.

For information about trips to Kehlstein, call 08652/54-73. RVO buses (local buses based in Berchtesgaden) run from the Berchtesgaden Post Office to Obersalzberg-Hintereck, and from Hintereck special buses go to the Kehlstein car park. The return journey from Berchtesgaden to Obersalzberg costs 10 DM ($6.60). From Obersalzberg (Hintereck) to the Kehlstein car park is 18 DM ($11.90), and from the car park by elevator to Kehlsteinhaus (the summit) is 4 DM ($2.60). If you're hearty, you can also go from the car park on foot to Kehlsteinhaus in about half an hour. The Kehlstein line operates daily from mid-May to mid-October, during which there are full catering periods at Kehlsteinhaus. The Kehlstein road from Obersalzberg is closed to private vehicles.

The best way to see the area is not on your own but through a company known as **Discover Bavaria Sightseeing Tours,** Königsseerstrasse 15 (tel. 08652/64-971), which is an American-run, Berchtesgaden-based tourist service. It offers guided tours in English of the main highlights of the area, including the Eagle's Nest and Obersalzberg. Tours range from the Bunker Tour to The Sound of Music tour, costing from 12 DM to 30 DM ($7.90 to $19.80), plus entrance fees.

At Obersalzberg, you can walk around the ruins of Hitler's **Berghof.** It was here that the 1938 meeting between Hitler and British Prime Minister Neville Chamberlain resulted in the understanding regarding the Sudetenland known as the Munich Agreement. Chamberlain came away hailing "peace in our time," but the Nazi dictator felt he had merely given the prime minister his "autograph." Hitler continued preparations for World War II. The Berghof was destroyed in 1952 by Bavarian government authorities at the request of the U.S. Army; the Americans did not want a monument to Hitler. The only fully remaining structure from the Nazi compound is a guesthouse behind the General Walker Hotel that is used by U.S. troops stationed in the area. Wear good walking shoes and be prepared to run into some "Verboten!" signs.

The bunkers and air-raid shelter were built by Hitler in 1943. Three thousand laborers completed the work in nine months, connecting all the major buildings of the Obersalzberg area to the underground rooms. Many readers have expressed their disappointment when reaching this site, apparently thinking they would tour Hitler's sumptuously decorated private apartments. A bunker is open for a visit, part of Hitler's air-raid shelter system. Newly opened are prison cells used by Reichsicherheitsdienst (State Security Police) and considered a last refuge for Hitler and other high officials. Entrance to the bunker and prison cells is 5 DM ($3.30), and hours are daily from 9am to 5pm. Guided tours in English are conducted at 4:30pm daily from mid-May to mid-October.

Obersalzberg is becoming an important health resort, with the ruins of Bormann's Gastshof being now the Skytop Lodge, a popular golfing center in summer and a ski site in winter.

WHERE TO STAY

Moderate

HOTEL ZUM TÜRKEN, D-8240 Berchtesgaden-Obersalzberg. Tel. 08652/24-28. Fax 08652/47-10. 17 rms (13 with bath or shower). **Bus:** Obersalzberg bus from Berchtesgaden.

$ Rates (including continental breakfast): 47 DM ($31) single without bath, 80 DM ($52.80) single with shower; 94 DM ($62) double without bath, 160 DM ($105.60) double with bath or shower. AE, DC, MC, V. **Parking:** Free. **Closed:** Tues.

In Obersalzberg, the Hotel zum Türken is legendary. It stands today in the alpine style, with terraces and views for hotel guests only. On its facade is a large painted sign of "The Turk," and the foundation is stone, with the windows framed in shutters. A large handmade sign is written across the hillside, with a rather ominous pronouncement, pointing the way to the "Bunker." The story goes that the original building here was erected by a veteran from the Turkish war. At the turn of the century it was acquired by Karl Schuster, who turned it into a well-known restaurant that drew many celebrities of the day, including Brahms and Crown Prince Wilhelm of Prussia. However, anti-Nazi remarks in the 1930s led to trouble for Herr Schuster, who was arrested. In time, Bormann used the building as a Gestapo headquarters. Air raids and looting in April 1945 led to much destruction of the Türken. Many tourists erroneously think the Türken was Hitler's famed Berghof.

Herr Schuster's daughter, Therese Partner, was able to buy the ruin from the German government for a high price in 1949. She opened a café and then some rooms for overnight visitors. Today, pleasantly furnished units are rented. Rooms don't have minibars, but there is a self-service house bar on the ground floor; likewise, rooms don't have private phones, but there is an international pay phone in the main hallway. The Türken is now run by Frau Ingrid Scharfenberg, granddaughter of Karl Schuster.

---

2. GARMISCH-PARTENKIRCHEN

55 miles SW of Munich; 73 miles SE of Augsburg; 37 miles NW of Innsbruck

GETTING THERE   By Train   The Garmisch-Partenkirchen Bahnhof lies on the major Munich-Weilheim-Garmisch-Mittenwald-Innsbruck rail line with frequent connections in all directions. Twenty trains per day arrive from Munich (trip time: 1 hour, 22 minutes). For rail information and schedules, call 08821/19-419. Mountain rail service to several mountain plateaus and the Zugspitze is offered by Bayerische Zugspitzbahn at Garmisch (tel. 08821/58-058).

By Bus   Both long-distance and regional buses through the Bavarian Alps are provided by RVO Regionalverkehr Oberbayern at Garmisch-Partenkirchen (tel. 08821/51-822).

By Car   Access is via Autobahn A95 from Munich, exiting at Eschenlohe.

ESSENTIALS   For tourist information, contact the **Verkehrsamt,** Richard-Strauss-Platz (tel. 08821/18-06). An unnumbered municipal bus services the town, depositing passengers at Marienplatz or the Bahnhof, from where you can walk to all centrally located hotels. This free bus runs every 15 minutes.

In spite of its urban flair, Garmisch-Partenkirchen, Germany's top alpine resort, has maintained the charm of an ancient village. Even today you occasionally see country folk in traditional costumes, and you may be held up in traffic while the cattle are led from their mountain grazing grounds down through the streets of town.

The symbol of the city's growth and modernity is the **Olympic Ice Stadium,** built for the Winter Olympics of 1936 and capable of holding nearly 12,000 people. On the slopes at the edge of town is the much larger **Ski Stadium,** with two ski jumps and a slalom course. In 1936 more than 100,000 people watched the events in this stadium. Today it is still an integral part of winter life in Garmisch—the World Cup Ski Jump is held here every New Year.

Garmisch-Partenkirchen is a center for winter sports and for summer hiking and mountain climbing. In addition, the town and environs offer some of the most exciting views and colorful buildings in Bavaria. The pilgrimage chapel of **St. Anton,** on a pinewood path at the edge of Partenkirchen, is all pink and silver, inside and out. Its graceful lines are characteristic of the 18th century, when it was built. The adjoining monastery pays tribute to local men who died in the two world wars, a memorial that consists of hundreds of photographs of local men who never returned from the wars. The **Philosopher's Walk** in the park surrounding the chapel is a delightful spot to wander, just to enjoy the views of the mountains around the low-lying town.

WHERE TO STAY

EXPENSIVE

ALPINA HOTEL, Alpspitzstrasse 12, D-8100 Garmisch-Partenkirchen. Tel. 08821/78-30. Fax 08821/71-374. 73 rms, 1 suite. MINIBAR TV TEL **Bus:** Eibsee Bus 1.

$ **Rates** (including buffet breakfast): 130 DM–220 DM ($85.80–$145.20) single; 200 DM–310 DM ($132–$204.60) double; 340 DM ($224.40) suite. AE, DC, MC, V. **Parking:** 10 DM ($6.60).

In this Bavarian hostelry, only three minutes from the Hausberg ski lifts, guests have all sorts of luxury facilities, including a garden with wide lawns and trees and an open patio. Its facade is graced with a wide overhanging roof and Tyrolean-style entranceway and windows. Each of the guest rooms sports a personalized decor: Yours may have a snow-white sofa, chairs, walls, lamps, and carpet, with original paintings as accents; or you may be assigned one with sloped pine ceilings, a Spanish bedspread, and matching armchairs.

Dining/Entertainment: The open tavern dining room has two levels, and there is an extensive brick wine cellar offering a wide and excellent choice. Bavarian and international dishes are served in a beamed rustic dining room and on the sun terrace. Meals begin at 42 DM ($27.70).

Services: Room service, laundry, dry cleaning.

Facilities: Covered pool with recreational terrace, open-air pool, sun terrace.

GRAND HOTEL SONNENBICHL, Burgstrasse 97, D-8100 Garmisch-Partenkirchen. Tel. 08821/70-20. Fax 08821/70-21-31. 90 rms, 3 suites. MINIBAR TV TEL **Directions:** Route 23 toward Oberammergau.

$ **Rates** (including continental breakfast): 160 DM–210 DM ($105.60–$138.60) single; 250 DM–310 DM ($165–$204.60) double; from 450 DM–1,000 DM ($297–$660) suite. AE, DC, MC, V. **Parking:** Free.

The finest hotel in the area is on the hillside overlooking Garmisch-Partenkirchen, **1** mile from the city center and 2 miles from the Bahnhof, with views of the Wetterstein mountain range and the Zugspitze. The rooms have all been renovated and offer a full line of the modern amenities.

Dining/Entertainment: The hotel serves excellent food. You can have light, modern cuisine in the elegant gourmet restaurant, Blauer Salon, or Bavarian specialties in the Zirbelstube. Afternoon coffee and fresh homemade cake are served in the lobby or on the sunny terrace; cocktails are available in the Peacock Bar.

Services: Room service, laundry, dry cleaning.

Facilities: Pool, sauna, solarium, fitness and massage rooms, beauty farm.

KÖNIGSHOF, St.-Martin-Strasse 4, D-8100 Garmisch-Partenkirchen. Tel. 08821/72-70. Fax 08821/72-71-00. 82 rms. TV TEL **Bus:** Eibsee Bus 1.

$ **Rates** (including continental breakfast): 125 DM–180 DM ($82.50–$118.80) single; 185 DM–245 DM ($122.10–$161.70) double. AE, MC, V. **Parking:** 10 DM ($6.60).

This is a holiday resort hotel with a lot of activity inside and out. The exterior is a massive rectangle with large windows and a triple-peaked roofline that evokes a chalet. The spectacular alpine backdrop helps with that impression. You'll find a sauna; pool; massage therapy; a collection of bars, boutiques, and nightclubs; and a bowling alley. The dining room is large and sunny, with oversize windows and a view. Each room is attractively decorated.

OBERMÜHLE, Mühlstrasse 22, D-8100 Garmisch-Partenkirchen. Tel. 08821/70-40. Fax 08821/70-41-112. 97 rms, 5 suites. TV TEL **Directions:** Route 24 (Zugspitzstrasse) toward Griesen.

$ **Rates** (including buffet breakfast): 205 DM–260 DM ($135.30–$171.60) single; 270 DM–350 DM ($178.20–$231) double; from 400 DM ($264) suite. AE, DC, MC, V. **Parking:** Free.

The Wolf family, the owners of this hotel, come from a 300-year-old line of hoteliers. Although the present building was constructed in 1969, they still maintain the traditional hospitality that has characterized their family for so long. Most rooms have balconies with views of the Alps. Nearby are miles of woodland trails crisscrossing through the nearby foothills. Rooms often have style and comfort, some with traditional Bavarian character.

Dining/Entertainment: Bavarian and international dishes are featured in the excellent restaurant. The garden and cozy Weinstube might be places you'll choose to wander through also.

Service: Room service, laundry, babysitting.

Facilities: Indoor pool set below a wooden roof shaped like a modified Gothic arch (at least it's pointed).

POSTHOTEL PARTENKIRCHEN, Ludwigstrasse 49, D-8100 Garmisch-Partenkirchen. Tel. 08821/5-10-67. Fax 08821/78-568. 61 rms. TV TEL **Bus:** Eibsee Bus 1.

$ **Rates** (including continental breakfast): 128 DM–180 DM ($84.50–$118.80) single; 190 DM–290 DM ($125.40–$191.40) double. AE, DC, MC, V. **Parking:** 12 DM ($7.90).

★ After many stages in its development—it was once a posting inn—the Posthotel Partenkirchen has emerged as one of the most prestigious hotels in town, especially with the added asset of its unusually fine restaurant (see my dining suggestions). You feel apart from conventional hotel life here: It's old-world living, and the owners offer personalized service. The hotel's facade is studded with windowboxes of red geraniums, and around the front entrance are decorative murals and designs. The U-shaped rooms are stylish, with antiques and hand-decorated or elaborately carved furnishings. The balconies are sun traps, overlooking a garden and parking for your car, and from them you'll have a view of the Alps.

Dining/Entertainment: Of the two dining rooms, the larger is known for its wooden beamed ceiling, wrought-iron chandeliers, and the huge arches that divide the room, making it more intimate. In the rustic Weinlokal Barbarossa, there are nooks for quiet before- or after-dinner drinks. Musicians provide background music.

Services: Room service, laundry.

Facilities: Golf, tennis, swimming, hiking, mountain climbing, skiing, cycling, hiking, horseback riding, paragliding.

REINDL'S PARTENKIRCHNER HOF, Bahnhofstrasse 15, D-8100 Garmisch-Partenkirchen. Tel. 08821/5-80-25. Fax 08821/73-401. 65 rms, 23 suites. MINIBAR TV TEL **Bus:** Eibsee Bus 1.

$ **Rates:** 130 DM–165 DM ($85.80–$108.90) single; 160 DM–190 DM ($105.60–$125.40) double; suites from 250 DM–400 DM ($165–$264). Breakfast 16 DM ($10.60) extra: AE, DC, MC, V. **Parking:** 12 DM ($7.90). **Closed:** Nov 11–Dec 12.

★ Reindl's was opened in 1911. From the very first it attracted a glittering array of celebrated people. Maintaining high levels of luxury and hospitality, owners Bruni and Karl Reindl have kept this a special Bavarian retreat. The annexes, the Wetterstein and the House Alspitz, have balconies, and the main building has wraparound verandas, giving each room an unobstructed view of the mountains and town. The well-furnished rooms have been redecorated and have all the amenities, including safes.

Dining/Entertainment: The place is also known for Reindl's much-honored restaurant, one of the best in Bavaria, recommended separately.

Services: Room service, laundry.

Facilities: Covered pool, sauna, sun room, beauty farm with slimming gourmet menu, open terrace for snacks, two attractive gardens.

WITTELSBACH, Von-Brug-Strasse 24, D-8100 Garmisch-Partenkirchen. Tel. 08821/5-30-96. Fax 08821/57-312. 60 rms. MINIBAR TV TEL **Bus:** Eibsee Bus 1.

$ Rates (including buffet breakfast): 154 DM–180 DM ($101.60–$118.80) single; 190 DM–250 DM ($125.40–$165) double. Half-board rates 128 DM–185 DM ($84.50–$122.10) per person per day. AE, DC, MC, V. **Parking:** 8 DM ($5.30). **Closed:** Nov 1–Dec 20.

A rocky outcrop of the mountain chains Wetterstein and Zugspitze frames a visitor's view of the front of this fine hotel, with green-and-white verandas and, depending on the season, cascades of flowers or a covering of snow. The Obexer family manages this idyllic spot, maintaining the covered pool in near-Olympic condition, overseeing the dining room's sumptuous buffets, and caring for the needs of clients who vow to return year after year. The hotel is known for its excellent restaurant, serving both Bavarian and continental dishes, with meals costing from 42 DM ($27.70). Room service and laundry facilities are available.

MODERATE

BODDENBERG, Wildenauerstrasse 21, D-8100 Garmisch-Partenkirchen. Tel. 08821/5-10-89. Fax 08821/52-911. 24 rms, 1 suite. TV TEL **Bus:** Kreis Krau.

$ Rates (including continental breakfast): 75 DM–90 DM ($49.50–$59.40) single; 160 DM–180 DM ($105.60–$118.80) double; 220 DM ($145.20) suite. AE, DC, MC, V. **Parking:** Free. **Closed:** Mid-Nov to Dec 31.

The Boddenberg has been run by the same family for 30 years. It can be recognized by its boxy shape, its balconies, and its location near the Olympic Ski Stadium ski jump. If you don't have a car, a bus that stops nearby will take you quickly into town. Many of the sunny rooms sport lots of wooden furniture and wood paneling. Guests have use of a heated open-air pool.

HOTEL HILLEPRANDT, Riffelstrasse 17, D-8100 Garmisch-Partenkirchen. Tel. 08821/28-61. Fax 08821/74-548. 17 rms, 1 suite. TV TEL **Bus:** Eibsee Bus 1.

$ Rates (including buffet breakfast): 82 DM ($54.10) single; 130 DM–148 DM ($85.80–$97.70) double; 160 DM ($105.60) suite. MC, V. **Parking:** Free.

This cozy chalet is close to the Zugspitz Bahnhof and the Olympic Ice Stadium. Its cutout wooden balconies, its attractive garden, and its backdrop of forest-covered mountains give the impression of an old-time alpine building. However, it was completely renovated in 1992 into a streamlined modern comfort. Guests enjoy a fitness room; a sauna; a solarium; a pleasant breakfast room; and the personality of the accommodating owner, Klaus Hilleprandt. Each room opens to a private balcony.

INEXPENSIVE

GÄSTEHAUS TRENKLER, Kreuzstrasse 20, D-8100 Garmisch-Partenkirchen. Tel. 08821/34-39. 10 rms (5 with shower). **Bus:** Eibsee Bus 1.

$ Rates (including continental breakfast): 70 DM–82 DM ($46.20–$54.10) double without shower, 87 DM–90 DM ($57.40–$59.40) double with shower. No credit cards. **Parking:** Free.

⑤ For a number of years Frau Trenkler has made travelers feel well cared for in her guesthouse, which enjoys a quiet central location. She rents five doubles with showers and toilets and five doubles with hot and cold running water. Rooms are simply but comfortably furnished.

GASTHOF FRAUNDORFER, Ludwigstrasse 34, D-8100 Garmisch-Partenkirchen. Tel. 08821/21-76. Fax 08821/71-073. 33 rms (30 with bath or shower). TV TEL **Bus:** Eibsee Bus 1.

$ Rates (including buffet breakfast): 70 DM ($46.20) single without bath or shower, 95 DM ($62.70) single with bath or shower; 120 DM-180 DM ($79.20-$118.80) double with bath or shower. AE, MC, V. **Parking:** Free. **Closed:** Tues.

⑤ The family-owned Gasthof Fraundorfer is directly on the main street of the town, just a five-minute walk from the old church. Its original style has not been updated, and it retains the character of another day. There are three floors under a sloping roof, with a facade brightly decorated with windowboxes of red geraniums and decorative murals depicting a family feast. You'll be in the midst of village-center activities, near interesting shops and restaurants. The guest rooms are pleasant and adequately furnished. Owners Josef and Barbel Fraundorfer are proud of their country-style meals. There is an interesting Bavarian evening with yodeling and dancing nightly, except Tuesday. Dinner reservations are advisable.

In addition, the owners also operate Gastehaus Barbara in back, with 20 more beds, in a typical Bavarian decor, including a Himmelbett ("heaven bed"). A double in their new house costs 140 DM ($92.40).

HAUS LILLY, Zugspitzstrasse 20a, D-8100 Garmisch-Partenkirchen. Tel. 08821/5-26-00. 8 rms (all with bath or shower). **Bus:** Eibsee Bus 1.

$ Rates (including buffet breakfast): 60 DM ($39.60) single; 90 DM ($59.40) double; 140 DM ($92.40) triple or quad. No credit cards. **Parking:** Free.

Many visitors appreciate this spotlessly clean guesthouse that's a 15-minute walk from the Bahnhof. It wins prizes for its copious breakfasts and the personality of its smiling owner, Maria Lechner, whose English is limited but whose hospitality is universal. Each of her cozy rooms includes free access to a kitchen, so that in-house preparation of meals is an option for guests wanting to save money. Breakfast offers a combination of cold cuts; rolls; cheese; eggs; pastries; and coffee, tea, or chocolate.

WHERE TO DINE

MODERATE

ALPENHOF, Am Kurpark 10. Tel. 08821/5-90-55.
   Cuisine: BAVARIAN. **Reservations:** Recommended. **Bus:** Eibsee Bus 1.
$ Prices: Appetizers 6.50 DM-24.50 DM ($4.30-$16.20); main courses 17.50 DM-36.50 DM ($11.60-$24.10); fixed-price lunch 24.50 DM-28.50 DM ($16.20-$18.80). DC, MC, V.
   Open: Lunch daily 11:30am-2pm; dinner daily 5:30-9:30pm. **Closed:** 3 weeks in Nov.

The Alpenhof is widely regarded as the finest restaurant in Garmisch outside the hotel dining rooms. In summer, try for an outside table; in winter, retreat to the cozy interior, which is flooded with sunlight from a greenhouse extension. Renate and Josef Huber offer a variety of Bavarian specialties, as well as trout "any way you want," salmon grilled with mousseline sauce, and ragoût of venison. For dessert, try a soufflé with exotic fruits. An exceptional meal for 28.50 DM ($18.80)—perhaps the best for value at the resort—is presented daily.

OBERMÜHLE, Mühlstrasse 22. Tel. 08821/70-40.
   Cuisine: BAVARIAN/INTERNATIONAL. **Reservations:** Required. **Directions:** Route 24 (Zugspitzstrasse) toward Griesen.
$ Prices: Appetizers 8 DM-30 DM ($5.30-$19.80); main courses 26 DM-60 DM ($17.20-$39.60); four-course fixed-price menu 54 DM ($35.60). AE, DC, MC, V.

Open: Lunch daily noon–2pm; dinner daily 6–10pm.

The decor is not noteworthy here, but an ambience radiates from the golden light of hanging lamps. Part of a previously recommended hotel, this restaurant offers one of the finest lunches at the resort. The menu includes some delectable "fruits of the sea," plus Bavarian meat and poultry dishes.

POSTHOTEL PARTENKIRCHEN, Ludwigstrasse 49, Partenkirchen. Tel. 088221/5-10-67.
   Cuisine: CONTINENTAL. **Reservations:** Required. **Bus:** Eibsee Bus 1.
$ Prices: Appetizers 7.50 DM–24 DM ($5–$15.80); main courses 18 DM–50 DM ($11.90–$33); fixed-price menus 28 DM–75 DM ($18.50–$49.50). AE, DC, MC, V.
   Open: Lunch daily noon–2:15pm; dinner daily 6–9:45pm.

The Posthotel Partenkirchen is renowned for its distinguished continental cuisine—in fact, its reputation is known throughout Bavaria. The interior dining rooms are rustic, with lots of mellow, old-fashioned atmosphere. You could imagine meeting Dürer here. Everything seems comfortably subdued, including the guests. Perhaps the best way to dine here is to order one of the set menus, which change daily, depending on the availability of seasonal produce. The à la carte menu is extensive, featuring such products as game in the autumn. You can order soups such as fresh cauliflower, followed by such main dishes as Schnitzel Cordon Bleu or mixed grill St. James. The Wiener Schnitzel served with a large salad is the best I've had in the resort.

REINDL'S RESTAURANT, in the Partenkirchner Hof, Bahnhofstrasse 15. Tel. 08821/5-80-25.
   Cuisine: CONTINENTAL. **Reservations:** Essential. **Bus:** Eibsee Bus 1.
$ Prices: Appetizers 12 DM–26 DM ($7.90–$17.20); main courses 24 DM–38 DM ($15.80–$25.10); fixed-price lunch 35 DM ($23.10); fixed-price dinner 75 DM–100 DM ($49.50–$66). AE, DC, MC, V.
   Open: Lunch daily 11:30am–2:30pm; dinner daily 6:30pm–midnight. **Closed:** Nov 11–Dec 12.

⭐ One of the best places to eat in Partenkirchen is Reindl's, a first-class restaurant in every sense of the word. The menu is composed according to the season, with cuisine moderne as well as regional Bavarian dishes. The cuisine of France as well as some famous French wines and champagnes, such as Romanée Conti, Château Lafitte Rothschild, and Château Petrus, are represented. Karl Reindl apprenticed at the famous Walterspiel of Munich's Vier Jahreszeiten; he also worked in the kitchens of Claridge's in London, Horcher's in Madrid, and Maxim's in Paris. The restaurant is known for honoring each "food season": For example, if you are here in asparagus season in spring, a special menu will be offered for sampling the dish in all the best-known varieties.

As a good opening to a fine repast, I suggest the scampi salad Walterspiel with fresh peaches, lemon, and tarragon or homemade goose-liver pâté with Riesling jelly. Among main dishes, I recommend coq au Riesling with noodles or veal roasted with Steinpilzen, a special mushroom from the Bavarian mountains. Among the fish dishes, try wild salmon with white and red wine and butter sauce. For dessert, you can select Grand Marnier sabayon with strawberry and vanilla ice cream or something more spectacular—a Salzburger Nockerl for two. Meals cost 38 DM to 70 DM ($25.10 to $46.20), with gourmet feasts (perhaps a lobster dinner) going higher.

INEXPENSIVE

FLÖSSERSTUBEN, Schmiedstrasse 2. Tel. 08821/28-88.
   Cuisine: GREEK/BAVARIAN/INTERNATIONAL. **Reservations:** Recommended. **Bus:** Eibsee Bus 1.
$ Prices: Appetizers 4 DM–12 DM ($2.60–$7.90); main courses 15 DM–30 DM ($9.90–$19.80). AE, MC.
   Open: Lunch daily 11am–2pm; dinner daily 5–10pm (or as late as 1:30am, depending on business).

Ⓢ Regardless of the season, a bit of the Bavarian Alps always seems to flower amid the wood-trimmed nostalgia of this intimate restaurant that lies close to the center of town. On certain evenings, the weathered beams above the dining tables are likely to reverberate with the laughter and good times. You can select a seat at one of the colorful wooden tables or on one of the ox-yoke-inspired stools in front of the spliced saplings that decorate the bar. Moussaka and souvlaki, as well as Sauerbraten and all kinds of Bavarian dishes, are abundantly available.

RESTAURANT-CAFÉ FÖHRENHOF, Frickenstrasse 2. Tel. 08821/66-40.
Cuisine: GERMAN. **Reservations:** Recommended.
$ Prices: Appetizers 4 DM–7 DM ($2.60–$4.60); main courses 15 DM–30 DM ($9.90–$19.80); three-course menu 20 DM–30 DM ($13.20–$19.80). No credit cards.
Open: Lunch daily 11am–3pm; dinner daily 5–9pm. **Closed:** Mar 20–Apr 14; Oct 1–Dec 21.

Ⓢ Built in 1970 and decorated in a pleasing Bavarian style, this establishment is best known for its restaurant. It lies 3 miles north of Garmisch, along the road to Farchant. Copious platters of an appetizing array of homemade specialties include Kellermeister toast, for example, a juicy portion of rumpsteak along with bacon, mushrooms, hollandaise sauce, and salad. If you're in the mood for game (in season), you might enjoy a filet of venison Hubertus with homemade Spätzle, cranberries, and salad. Cheese might follow your main course, then a cream- or chocolate-covered portion of homemade ice cream, followed by a cup of Irish coffee. Children's portions are thoughtfully provided.

The establishment also contains 21 simple but comfortable guest rooms, all with private baths and TVs, a few with views over the mountains. Singles cost 55 DM ($36.30). Double rooms, depending on their size, cost from 90 DM to 150 DM ($59.40 to $99). A buffet breakfast is included in the price.

THE CASINO

You can play French or American roulette, baccarat, or blackjack or have fun with 75 slot machines and poker, blackjack, horseracing, bingo, and roulette machines at **Spielbank Garmisch-Partenkirchen,** Am Kurpark 10 (tel. 08821/5-30-99), open daily from 3pm to 2am. Follow the signs for Spielbank or Parkhaus to walk to the casino, which is in the heart of Garmisch-Partenkirchen. The admission charge is 5 DM ($3.30), and once you're inside, drinks cost from 6 DM ($4) for beer to 15 DM ($9.90) for whisky and soda.

EASY EXCURSIONS

From Garmisch-Partenkirchen, you can see the tallest peak in Germany, the ✪ **Zugspitze,** at the frontier of Austria and Germany. Its summit towers some 9,720 feet above sea level. Ski slopes begin at the **Hotel Schneefernerhaus** at a height of 8,700 feet. For a spectacular view of both the Bavarian and the Tyrolean (Austrian) Alps, go all the way to the peak. The Zugspitze summit can be reached from Garmisch by taking the cogwheel train to the Schneefernerhaus. The train leaves the Zugspitzplatz daily every hour between 7:35am and 3:35pm. Travel time from Garmisch is 65 minutes. The Eibsee cable car (Eibsee-Seilbahn) may be taken from Eibsee, a small lake at the foot of the mountain. It makes the 10-minute run at least every half hour from 8:15am to 5:45pm (in July and August until 6:15pm).

The cable car to the Zugspitze summit (Gipfelseilbahn), a three-minute ride, departs from Sonn Alpin to the summit at least every half hour during the operating hours of the cogwheel train and the Eibsee cable car. The Zugspitze round trip is 51 DM ($33.70) in winter and 60 DM ($39.60) in summer.

The ✪ **Alpspitz** region can also be explored. It's a paradise for hikers and nature lovers in general. From early spring until late fall, its meadows and flowers are a delight, and its rocks evoke a prehistoric world. At altitudes of 4,600 to 6,300 feet, the Alps present themselves in a storybook fantasy. Those who want to explore the northern foot of the Alpspitz can take the Alpspitz round trip by going up with the Alpspitz cable car, over the Hochalm, and back down with the Kreuzeck or Hausberg cable car, allowing time in between for hikes lasting from half an hour to an hour and a half. Snacks are served at the top station of the Alpspitz cable car or at the more rustic Hochalm Chalet.

The Alpspitz cable car to Osterfelderkopf, at a height of 6,300 feet, makes its nine-minute run at least every hour from 8am to 5pm. The round-trip cost is 35 DM ($23.10) for adults and 21 DM ($13.90) for children 4 to 14.

The Hochalm cable car from the Hochalm to Osterfelderkopf makes its four-minute run at least every hour during the operating hours of the Alpspitz cable car. A single ride costs 6 DM ($4) for adults and 4 DM ($2.60) for children.

The Alpspitz round trip with the Osterfelder Cable car, the Hochalm cable car, and the Kreuzcek or Kreuzwankl/Hausberg cable car is 35 DM ($23.10) for adults and 21 DM ($13.90) for children.

These fares and times of departure can fluctuate from season to season. Therefore, for the latest details, check with the tourist office, Kurverwaltung, Richard-Strauss-Platz (tel. 08821/12-06), open Monday to Saturday from 8am to 6pm and Sunday from 10am to noon only.

From Garmisch-Partenkirchen, many other peaks of the Witterstein range are accessible as well, via the 10 funiculars ascending from the borders of the town. From the top of the **Wank** (5,850 feet) to the east, you get the best view of the plateau on which the twin villages of Garmisch and Partenkirchen have grown up. This summit is also a favorite with the patrons of Garmisch's spa facilities because the plentiful sunshine makes it ideal for the *Liegekur* (deck-chair cure).

Another excursion from the town is a hike through the **Partnachklamm Gorge,** lying between the Graseck and Hausberg peaks. After taking the cable car to the first station on the Graseck route, follow the paths along the sides of the slope to the right and trail the river as it cascades over the rocks. The path circles around by crossing the gorge, and returns you to the point where you entered. Many readers have found this one of their most memorable sightseeing adventures in Bavaria. The experience of walking along a rocky ledge just above the rushing river and often behind small waterfalls, while looking up at 1,200 feet of rocky cliffs, always fills me with awe.

3. CHIEMSEE

Prien am Chiemsee: 53 miles SE of Munich, 14 miles E of Rosenheim, 40 miles W of Salzburg

GETTING THERE By Train Prien Bahnhof is on the major Munich-Rosenheim-Freilassing-Salzburg rail line, with frequent connections in all directions. Ten daily trains arrive from Munich (trip time: one hour). For information, call 08051/19-419.

By Bus Regional bus service in the area is offered by RVO Regionalverkehr Oberbayern, Betrieb Rosenheim (tel. 08031/62-006 for schedules and information).

By Car Access by car is via Autobahn (A8) from Munich.

GETTING AROUND From the liveliest resort, Prien, on the west shore, you can reach either Frauenchiemsee or Herrenchiemsee via lake steamers that make regular trips throughout the year. The round-trip fare to Herrenchiemsee is 7 DM ($4.60), or you pay only 13 DM ($8.60) for a round trip to both islands. The steamers, operated by Chiemsee-Schiffahrt Ludwig Fessler, D-8210 Prien am Chiemsee, Postfach 1162 (tel. 08051/60-90), make round trips covering the entire lake. Connections are made from Gstadt, Seebruck, Chieming, Übersee/Feldwies, and Bernau/Felden. Large parking areas are found in Prien-Stock (harbor) and in all the villages around the lake.

Boats leave Prien/Stock about every 20 minutes for Herrenchiemsee (castle of Ludwig II) at the island of Herreninsel from June to September 23 between 9am and 4:30pm. The last return is at 7:25pm.

There is also bus service from the harbor to the DB-station in Prien (Chiemsee-Schiffahrt) and around the lake by RVO. In summer (May to September), guests can enjoy the famous "Chiemseebahn," the last steam-tramway in the world, operating since 1887. It runs from the Prien Bahnhof to the Prien dock every 20 minutes, costing 3.50 DM ($2.30) for a round-trip passage.

ESSENTIALS   For tourist information, contact the **Kur- and Verkehrsamt,** Rathausstrasse 11, in Prien am Chiemsee (tel. 08051/6-90-50).

Known as the "Bavarian Sea," Chiemsee is one of the most beautiful lakes in the Bavarian Alps, in a serene landscape. In the south, the mountains reach almost to the water. Many resorts line the shores of the large lake, but the main attractions of Chiemsee are on its two islands, Frauenchiemsee and Herrenchiemsee.

FRAUENCHIEMSEE   Frauenchiemsee, also called Fraueninsel, is the smaller of the lake's two major islands. Along its sandy shore stands a fishing village whose boats drag the lake for its pike and salmon. At the festival of Corpus Christi, these boats are covered with flowers and streamers, the fishermen outfitted in Bavarian garb, and the young women of the village dressed as brides; as the boats circle the island, they stop at each corner for the singing of the Gospels. The island is also the home of a Benedictine nunnery, founded in 782. The convent is known for a liqueur called Kloster Likör. Sold by nuns in black cowls with white-winged headgarb, it's supposed to be an "agreeable stomach elixir."

HERRENCHIEMSEE   Herrenchiemsee (also called Herreninsel), at Herren-chiemsee 3 (tel. 08051/30-69), is the most popular tourist attraction on the lake because of the fantastic castle,   **۞ Neues Schloss,** begun by Ludwig II in 1878. Never completed because of the king's death in 1886, the castle was to have been a replica of the grand palace of Versailles that Ludwig so admired. A German journalist once wrote this: "The Palace, a monument to uncreative megalomania and as superfluous as the artificial castle ruins of the 19th century, is an imposing postlude of feudal architectural grandeur nonetheless." One of the architects of Herrenchiemsee was Julius Hofmann, whom the king had also employed for the construction of his fantastic alpine castle, Neuschwanstein. When the work was halted in 1886, only the center of the enormous palace had been completed. Surrounded by woodlands of beech and fir, the palace and its formal gardens remain one of the most fascinating of Ludwig's adventures, in spite of their unfinished state.

The palace entrance is lit by a huge skylight over the sumptuously decorated state staircase. Frescoes depicting the four states of existence alternate with Greek and Roman statues set in niches on the staircase and in the gallery above. The vestibule is adorned with a pair of enameled peacocks, the favorite bird of Louis XIV.

The state bedroom is brilliant to the point of gaudiness, as practically every inch of the room has been gilded. On the dais, instead of a throne, stands the richly decorated state bed, its purple-velvet draperies weighing more than 300 pounds. Separating the dais from the rest of the room is a carved wooden balustrade covered with gold leaf. On the ceiling is a huge fresco depicting the descent of Apollo, surrounded by the other gods of Olympus. The sun god's features bear a strong resemblance to those of Louis XIV.

The Great Hall of Mirrors is unquestionably the most splendid hall in the palace and probably the most authentic replica of Versailles. The 17 door panels contain enormous mirrors reflecting the 33 crystal chandeliers and the 44 gilded candelabra. The vaulted ceiling is covered with 25 paintings depicting the life of Louis XIV. At the entrance to what would have been the private apartments of the king (Ludwig spent less than three weeks in the palace) is a smaller hall of mirrors, with mirrored panels set into the marble walls.

The dining room is a popular attraction for visitors because of the table nicknamed "the little table that lays itself." A mechanism in the floor permitted the table to go down to the room below to be cleaned and relaid between each course. Over the table hangs the largest porcelain chandelier in the world, produced by Meissen, the most valuable single item in the whole palace.

The royal bedroom is the only room in the palace to make use of rich solid colors on the walls. Set in gilded panels, royal-blue silk matching the fabric of the draperies and the bed canopy offsets the gilded ceiling and furnishings. Separating the bed from the rest of the room is a gilded balustrade like that in the throne room.

You can visit Herrenchiemsee at any time of the year. In summer, April to September 30, tour hours are daily from 9am to 5pm; off-season hours are from 10am to 4pm. Admission (in addition to the round-trip boat fare) is 6 DM ($4) for adults. Students and children pay 3.50 DM ($2.30).

WHERE TO STAY & DINE

EXPENSIVE

YACHTHOTEL CHIEMSEE, Harrasser Strasse 49, D-8210 Prien am Chiemsee. Tel. 08051/69-60. Fax 08051/51-71. 102 rms, 5 suites. MINIBAR TV TEL

$ Rates (including continental breakfast): 180 DM–350 DM ($118.80–$231) single; 250 DM–350 DM ($165–$231) double; from 550 DM ($363) suite. AE, DC, MC, V. **Parking:** Free.

The best place to stay on the lake is Yachthotel Chiemsee, on the western shore of the "Bavarian Sea." Launched in 1989, the hotel offers attractively furnished rooms, all with king-size beds and balconies or terraces opening onto the water.

Dining/Entertainment: Three restaurants provide the best views along the lake; the main restaurant extends over a lakeside terrace and the marina. Meals range from 48 DM to 82 DM ($31.70 to $54.10).

Services: In winter, the hotel's bus service brings you to the slopes in 10 minutes. Laundry, babysitting, 24-hour room service.

Facilities: Sailing, rowing, tennis, riding, golf (nearby), horse-drawn carriage trips; spa department, beauty care center, sauna, solarium, health and fitness center, outdoor whirlpool, indoor pool.

MODERATE

BAYERISCHER HOF, Bernauerstrasse 3, D-8210 Prien am Chiemsee. Tel. 08051/60-30. Fax 08051/62-917. 47 rms (all with bath or shower). TV TEL

$ Rates (including buffet breakfast): 80 DM ($52.80) single; 140 DM ($92.40) double. V. **Parking:** 8 DM ($5.30). **Closed:** Nov.

S The Estermann family will welcome you to the Bayerischer Hof. The rustic touches in the decor create the illusion that this relatively severe modern hotel is indeed older and more mellow than it is. Of particular note is the painted ceiling in the dining room, where regional meals begin at 28 DM ($18.50). The rest of the hotel is more streamlined—modern, efficient, and quite appealing.

REINHART, Seestrasse 117, D-8210 Prien am Chiemsee. Tel. 08051/69-40. Fax 08051/69-41-00. 24 rms (all with bath or shower). TV TEL

$ Rates: 95 DM–100 DM ($62.70–$66) single; 145 DM–200 DM ($95.70–$132) double. AE, DC, V. **Closed:** Jan to Easter and Oct 20–Dec 10.

This hotel and restaurant borders on the lake, offering three well-appointed floors. You'll find a heated indoor pool; a family-run sauna; and a series of public rooms beautifully decorated with Oriental rugs, warm colors, and chalet chairs. A buffet breakfast comes with a generous portion of yogurt, cheese, and cold cuts. There is access to a nearby golf course.

4. OBERAMMERGAU

59 miles SW of Munich; 12 miles N of Garmisch-Partenkirchen

GETTING THERE By Train The Oberammergau Bahnhof is on the Murnau–Bad Kohlgrum–Oberammergau rail line, with frequent connections in all directions. Through Murnau all major German cities can be reached. Daily trains arrive from Munich in two hours and Frankfurt in seven hours. For rail information and schedules, call 08822/19-419.

By Bus Regional bus service to nearby towns is offered by RVO Regionalverkehr Oberbayern, at Garmisch-partenkirchen (tel. 08821/51-822). Bus 30 goes back and forth between Oberammergau and Garmisch-Partenkirchen.

By Car Many visitors drive here, the trip taking 1½ hours from Munich and 5½ hours from Frankfurt. Take the A95 Munich/Garmisch Partenkirchen Autobahn, exiting at Eschenlohe.

ESSENTIALS For tourist information, contact the **Verkehrsbüro,** Eugen-Pabst-Strasse 9A (tel. 08822/1021).

In this alpine village the world-famous passion play is presented, with performances generally 10 years apart. The next one is scheduled for the year 2000, May through October. Surely the world's longest-running show (in more ways than one), it began in 1634 as the result of a vow taken by the town's citizens after they were spared from the devastating plague of 1633. Lasting about eight hours, the play is divided into episodes, each of which is introduced by an Old Testament tableau connecting predictions of the great prophets to incidents of Christ's suffering.

A visit to Oberammergau is ideal in summer or winter. It stands in a wide valley surrounded by forests and mountains, as well as sunny slopes and green meadows. It has long been known for the skill of its woodcarvers. Here in this village right under the Kofel are farms still intact, as well as first-class hotels, cozy inns, and family boarding houses.

A wide variety of sports is offered. Numerous hiking trails lead through the mountains around Oberammergau to hikers' inns such as the Kolbenalm and the Romanshohe. You can, however, simply go up to the mountaintops on the Laber cable railway or the Kolben chairlift. Not only hikers have a good time in Oberammergau, but also tennis buffs, minigolf players, cyclists, swimmers, hang-gliding enthusiasts, and canoeists. A visit to the recreation center, Wellenberg, is always a special experience. This large alpine swimming complex with its open-air pools, hot water and fountains, sauna, solarium, and restaurant is said to be one of the most beautiful recreation centers in the Alps. The Ammer Valley, of which Oberammergau lies in the center, is a treasure trove for explorers, who use it as a base for visiting such attractions as Linderhof Castle, the Benedictine monastery at Ettal, or Neuschwanstein Castle or Hohenschwangau.

WHAT TO SEE & DO

If you visit Oberammergau in an "off" year, you can still see the **Passionspielhaus,** Passionweise, the modern theater at the edge of town where the passion play is performed. The roofed auditorium holds 4,700 spectators, and the open-air stage is a wonder of engineering, with a curtained center stage flanked by gates opening onto the so-called streets of Jerusalem. The theater and production methods are contemporary, but the spirit of the play is marked by the medieval tradition of involving the entire community in its production. The 124 speaking parts are taken by amateur actors from the surrounding villages. The balance of the community seems to be included in the crowd scenes. The impressive array of scenery, props, and costumes is open to the public daily from 10am to noon and 1:30 to 4:30pm. Admission is 4 DM ($2.60) for adults and 2.50 DM ($1.70) for children.

Aside from the actors, Oberammergau's most respected citizens include another unusual group, the woodcarvers, many of whom have been trained in the woodcarvers' school in the village. In the **Pilate House** on Verlegergasse, you can watch local artists at work, including woodcarvers, painters, sculptors, and potters. You'll see many examples of these art forms throughout the town, on the painted cottages and inns and in the churchyard. Also worth seeing on a walk through the village are the houses with frescoes by Franz Zwink (18th century) that are named after fairy-tale characters, such as the "Hansel and Gretel House" and the "Little Red Riding Hood House."

The **Heimatmuseum,** Dorfstrasse (tel. 08822/32-256), has a notable collection of Christmas crèches, all hand-carved and painted, from the 18th through the 20th century. It is open May 15 to October 15, Tuesday to Saturday from 2 to 6pm. Off-season it is open only on Saturday from 2 to 6pm. Admission is 3 DM ($2) for adults and 1 DM (66¢) for children.

NEARBY ATTRACTIONS

✪ **SCHLOSS LINDERHOF**   Eight miles west of the village, until the late 19th century, stood a modest hunting lodge on a large piece of land owned by the Bavarian royal family. In 1869 "Mad Ludwig" struck again, this time creating a French rococo palace in the Ammergau Mountains. Unlike Ludwig's palace at Chiemsee, the Linderhof was not meant to be a copy of any other structure. And unlike his castle at Neuschwanstein, its concentration of fanciful projects and designs was not limited to the interior of the palace. In fact, the gardens and smaller buildings at Linderhof are, if anything, more elaborate than the two-story main structure.

As you stand on the steps in front of the castle's white stone facade, you'll note that the ground floor is rather plain while the upper story is adorned with relief columns altered with niches occupied by statues of mythological figures. In the center, over the three arched portals, is a large statue of Victory. Towering above the gable with its oval windows is a huge statue of Atlas supporting a world that seems just a bit too much even for him.

The most interesting palace rooms are on the second floor, where ceilings are much higher because of the unusual roof plan. Ascending the winged staircase of Carrara marble, you'll find yourself at the West Gobelin Room (music room), with carved and gilded paneling and richly colored tapestries. This leads directly into the Hall of Mirrors. The mirrors are set in white-and-gold panels, decorated with gilded woodcarvings. The ceiling of this room is festooned with frescoes depicting mythological scenes, including *The Birth of Venus* and *The Judgment of Paris*.

The two side rooms are oval in design, each having a smaller, horseshoe-shaped anteroom. The eastern room is the dining room, mirrored and decorated with marble fireplaces, mythological sculptures, and an elaborately carved and gilded sideboard. The table, like that at Chiemsee, could be raised and lowered through the floor to permit the servants in the room below to reset the various courses without intruding on the shy king's privacy.

The king's bedchamber is the largest room in the palace and is placed in the back, overlooking the Fountain of Neptune and the cascades in the gardens. In the tradition of Louis XIV, who often received visitors in his bedchamber, the king's bed is closed off by a carved and gilded balustrade.

In the popular style of the previous century, Ludwig laid out the gardens in formal parterres with geometrical shapes, baroque sculptures, and elegant fountains. The front of the palace opens onto a large pool with a piece of gilded statuary in its center, from which a jet of water sprays 105 feet into the air.

The steep slopes behind the palace lend themselves well to the arrangement of a long cascade, made up of 32 marble steps and adorned with vases and cherubs. At the base of the cascade is the Fountain of Neptune, surrounded by a bed of flowers. Around these formal terrace and garden designs is the large English garden, merging almost imperceptibly into the thick forests of the Ammergau.

The park also contains several other small but fascinating buildings, including the Moorish Kiosk, where Ludwig often spent hours smoking chibouk and dreaming of himself as an Oriental prince. The magic grotto is unique, built of artificial rock, with stalagmites and stalactites dividing the cavelike room into three chambers. One wall of the grotto is painted with a scene of the Venus Mountain from *Tannhäuser.* The main chamber is occupied by an artificial lake illuminated from below, and in Ludwig's time it had an artificial current produced by 24 dynamo engines. A shell-shaped boat, completely gilded, is tied to a platform called the Lorelei Rock.

The fantasy and grandeur of Linderhof, 8107 Linderhof, Post Ettal (tel. 08822/49-87), is open to the public throughout the year and makes a day trip from Munich, as well as Oberammergau. From April to September 30, hours are 9am to 12:15pm and 12:45 to 5:30pm daily. From October to March 31, the grotto and Moorish Kiosk are closed, but the castle is open from 10am to 12:15pm and 12:45 to 4pm. Admission is 7 DM ($4.60) for adults and 4 DM ($2.60) for children.

Buses run between Oberammergau and Schloss Linderhof seven times per day from 10am; the last bus leaves Linderhof at 5:35pm. A round-trip passage costs 7.20 DM ($4.80).

KLOSTER ETTAL   In a lovely valley sheltered by the steep hills of the Ammergau, ✪ **Kloster Ettal,** Kaiser-Ludwig-Platz at Ettal (tel. 08822/740) was founded by Ludwig the Bavarian in 1330. Monks, knights, and their ladies shared the honor of guarding the statue of the virgin, attributed to Giovanni Pisano. In the 18th century, the golden age of the abbey, there were about 70,000 pilgrims every year. The Minister of Our Lady in Ettal is one of the finest examples of Bavarian rococo architecture in existence. Around the polygonal core of the church is a two-story gallery. An impressive baroque facade was built from a plan based on designs of Enrico Zuccali. Inside, visitors stand under a vast dome, admiring the fresco painted by John Jacob Zeiller in the summers of 1751 and 1752. The abbey lies along the road between Garmisch-Partenkirchen and Oberammergau. Admission free, it is open daily from 9am to 5pm.

Ettal stands 2 miles south of Oberammergau. Buses from Oberammergau leave from the Rathaus and the Bahnhof at the rate of one per hour during the day, with one-way passage costing 4 DM ($2.60).

WHERE TO STAY & DINE
MODERATE

ALOIS LANG, St.-Lukeas-Strasse 15, D-8103 Oberammergau. Tel. 08822/7-60. Fax 08822/4723. 70 rms, 4 suites. TV TEL **Bus:** 30.
$ Rates (including continental breakfast): 90 DM–130 DM ($59.40–$85.80) single; 160 DM–240 DM ($105.60–$158.40) double; from 240 DM ($158.40) suite. AE, DC, MC, V. **Parking:** Free.

Seasoned travelers who have made pilgrimages to the passion play in Oberammergau will recognize the name Alois Lang. It was in 1929 that handsome, long-haired Alois Lang was elected by the village to play the role of Christ in the pageant. Within walking distance of the village center, this inn on the site of Alois's rustic home, run by the Lang family, was built chalet style, with long guest-room extensions. The accommodations are modern, the beds soft; all is kept immaculate.

Meals are elaborate, including sophisticated international specialties in addition to local dishes. You may want to dine in the inner tavern or on the open sun terrace, where you can enjoy a view of the mountains.

Room service, laundering, and babysitting are offered. The inn also boasts a sauna, a fitness center, and the biggest private-hotel park in the area.

HOTEL FRIEDENSHÖHE, König-Ludwig-Strasse 31, D-8103 Oberam-mergau. Tel. 08822/35-98. Fax 08822/4345. 14 rms. TEL **Bus:** 30.

$ Rates (including buffet breakfast): 95 DM ($62.70) single; 160 DM ($105.60) double. AE, DC, MC, V. **Parking:** Free. **Closed:** Oct 25–Dec 20.

The name of the hotel means "peaceful height." Built in 1906, the villa enjoys a beautiful location. It was reconstructed into a pension and café in 1913, and before that it had hosted Thomas Mann, who wrote here. The guest rooms, furnished in tasteful modern style, are well maintained. TVs are available on request.

The Bavarian and international cuisine is known for its taste and the quality of its ingredients. The hotel offers a choice of four dining rooms, including an indoor terrace, with a panoramic view, and an outdoor terrace. Meals begin at 26 DM ($17.20).

HOTEL RESTAURANT BÖLD, König-Ludwig-Strasse 10, D-8103 Ober-ammergau. Tel. 08822/30-21. Fax 08822/71-02. 57 rms. TV TEL **Bus:** 30.
$ Rates (including continental breakfast): 121 DM–131 DM ($79.90–$86.50) single; 176 DM–205 DM ($116.20–$135.30) double. AE, DC, MC, V. **Parking:** Free.

Only a stone's throw from the river, this well-designed chalet hotel offers comfortable public rooms in its central core and well-furnished guest rooms in its contemporary annex. A sauna is offered for guests' relaxation, as are a solarium and whirlpool.

The restaurant features both international and regional cuisine, with meals costing from 35 DM ($23.10). In the bar you'll find a peaceful atmosphere, plus well-prepared cocktails and attentive service. Raimund Hans and family are the hosts.

TURMWIRT, Ettalerstrasse 2, D-8103 Oberammergau. Tel. 08822/30-91. Fax 08822/14-37. 22 rms. MINIBAR TV TEL **Bus:** 30.
$ Rates (including buffet breakfast): 90 DM–110 DM ($59.40–$72.60) single; 140 DM–180 DM ($92.40–$118.80) double. AE, DC, MC, V. **Closed:** Oct 27–Dec 15.

A cozy Bavarian-style hotel, the Turmwirt offers many rooms with private balconies opening onto views of the mountains. A lodging house stood on this spot in 1742, and the present building was constructed in 1889. It has received many alterations and renovations over the past few decades. It's an intricately painted green-shuttered country house, with hints of baroque embellishments on the doors and window frames. The homelike interior is well maintained, with chintz-covered armchairs, wooden banquettes, Oriental rugs, beamed ceilings, and handcrafted cubbyholes with tables and chairs. The owners are three generations of the Glas family. The center of town is an invigorating five-minute walk from the hotel.

WITTELSBACH, Dorfstrasse 21, D-8103 Oberammergau. Tel. 08822/10-11. Fax 08822/66-88. 46 rms. TV TEL **Bus:** 30.
$ Rates (including buffet breakfast): 75 DM–100 DM ($49.50–$66) single; 150 DM–180 DM ($99–$118.80) double. AE, DC, MC, V. **Parking:** Free. **Closed:** Nov 20–Dec and Jan 10–27.

Elisabeth and Julius Streibl own this place, which sprawls over a village street corner. It has light-brown shutters, a red roof with ice catchers on the edges, prominent gables, and yards of balconies with flowers virtually spilling over the edges. The Streibls offer sunny, cozy rooms, all recently renovated. Regardless of season, the dining room has a kind of après-ski ambience where diners relax and linger over drinks.

WOLF RESTAURANT-HOTEL, Dorfstrasse 1, D-8103 Oberammergau. Tel. 08822/30-71. Fax 08822/10-96. 32 rms. TV TEL **Bus:** 30.
$ Rates (including continental breakfast): 65 DM–95 DM ($42.90–$62.70) single; 110 DM–180 DM ($72.60–$118.80) double. AE, DC, MC, V. **Parking:** 10 DM ($6.60). **Closed:** Jan 8–28.

An overgrown Bavarian chalet, the Wolf Restaurant-Hotel is at the heart of village life. Its facade is consistent with others in the area: an encircling balcony, heavy timbering, and windowboxes spilling cascades of red and pink geraniums. Inside it has some of the local flavor, although certain concessions have been made: an elevator, conservative room furnishings, a dining hall with zigzag paneled ceiling, and spoke chairs. Only five singles are available.

The Hafner Stub'n is a rustic place for beer drinking as well as eating light meals. Dining here can be both economical and gracious, with menus ranging from 30 DM to 60 DM ($19.80 to $39.60). There's always a freshly made soup of the day, followed by a generous main course, such as Wiener Schnitzel or roast pork with dumplings and cabbage.

INEXPENSIVE

ALTE POST, Dorfstrasse 19, D-8103 Oberammergau. Tel. 08822/10-91. Fax 08822/10-94. 32 rms (28 with bath or shower). TV TEL **Bus:** 30.

$ Rates (including continental breakfast): 60 DM ($39.60) single without bath, 85 DM ($56.10) single with bath; 120 DM ($79.20) double without bath, 140 DM ($92.40) double with bath. AE, MC, V. **Parking:** 6 DM ($4). **Closed:** Oct 25–Dec 19.

Ⓢ A provincial inn in the center of the village, the Alte Post is built in chalet style—wide overhanging roof, green-shuttered windows painted with decorative trim, a large carved crucifix on the facade, and tables set on a sidewalk under a long awning—it's the social hub of the village. The interior has storybook charm, with a ceiling-high green ceramic stove, alpine chairs, and shelves of pewter plates. The rustic guest rooms have wood-beamed ceilings and wide beds with giant posts; most have views.

The main dining room is equally rustic, with a collection of hunting memorabilia, and there is an intimate drinking bar. The restaurant provides excellent dishes. Meals on the à la carte menu average 25 DM to 45 DM ($16.50 to $29.70).

HOTEL SCHILCHERHOF, Bahnhofstrasse 17, D-8103 Oberammergau. Tel. 08822/47-40. 20 rms (all with shower). **Bus:** 30.

$ Rates (including continental breakfast): 60 DM–75 DM ($39.60–$49.50) single; 100 DM–120 DM ($66–$79.20) double. AE, MC, V. **Parking:** Free. **Closed:** Nov 20–Christmas.

An enlarged chalet with surrounding gardens, the Schilcherof has a modern wing that provides excellent rooms. In summer, the terrace overflows with festive living and lots of beer. Five minutes away lies the passion play theater; also nearby is the Ammer River, which flows through the village. In summer, it's not easy to get a room here unless you reserve well in advance. Although the house is built in the old style, with wooden front balconies and tiers of flowerboxes, it has a fresh look.

---

5. MITTENWALD

66 miles S of Munich; 11 miles SE of Garmisch-Partenkirchen;
23 miles NW of Innsbruck

GETTING THERE   By Train   Mittenwald is reached by almost hourly train service, as it lies on the express rail line between Munich and Innsbruck (Austria). From Munich trip time is from 1½ to 2 hours, depending on the train. It takes about 5 to 6 hours by train from Frankfurt. Telephone 908102/19-419 for information.

By Bus   Regional bus service from Garmisch-Partenkirchen and nearby towns is frequently provided by RVO Regionalverkehr Oberbayern at Garmisch (tel. 08821/51-822 for schedules and information).

By Car   Access by car is via Autobahn A95 from Munich.

ESSENTIALS   For tourist information, contact **Kurverwaltung and Verkehrsamt,** Dammkarstrasse 3 (tel. 08823/3-39-81).

Seeming straight out of *The Sound of Music,* the year-round resort of Mittenwald lies in a pass in the Karwendel Range. Especially noteworthy and photogenic are the painted Bavarian houses with their overhanging eaves. Even the tower of the baroque church is covered with frescoes. On the square stands a monument to Mathias Klotz, who introduced violin making to Mittenwald in 1684. The town is a major international center for this highly specialized craft. The town's museum, with a workshop, has exhibits devoted to violins and other stringed instruments, from their conception through the various stages of their evolution. The **Geigenbau- und Heimatmuseum,** Ballenhausgasse 3 (tel. 8823/25-11), is open Monday to Friday from 10 to 11:45am and 2 to 4:45pm, Saturday and Sunday from 10 to 11:45am, charging an admission of 2 DM ($1.30) for adults and 0.50 DM (30¢) for children.

On daily excursions into the countryside, you are constantly exposed to changes in the scenery of the Wetterstein and Karwendel ranges. Some 80 miles of paths wind up and down the mountains around the village. Besides hiking through the hills on your own, you can take part in mountain-climbing expeditions, trips by horse and carriage, or coach tours from Mittenwald to nearby villages. In the evening you are treated to typical Bavarian entertainment, often consisting of folk dancing and singing, zither playing and yodeling, but you also have your choice of concerts, dance bands, discos, and bars. Mittenwald has good spa facilities, in large gardens landscaped with tree-lined streams and trout pools. Concerts are given during the summer in the music pavilion. The town is a skiing center in winter.

WHERE TO STAY

MODERATE

ALPENROSE, Obermarkt 1, D-8102 Mittenwald. Tel. 08823/50-55. Fax 08823/3720. 44 rms. MINIBAR TV TEL **Bus:** RVO.
$ Rates (including buffet breakfast): 78 DM–95 DM ($51.50–$62.70) single; 150 DM–175 DM ($99–$115.50) double. AE, DC, MC, V. **Parking:** Free.

A particularly inviting place to stay is the Alpenrose, in the center of the village at the foot of a rugged mountain. The facade is covered with decorative designs; windowboxes hold flowering vines. The basic structure of the inn is 14th century, although refinements, additions, and improvements have been made over the years. The present inn is comfortable, with suitable plumbing facilities. The hotel's rooms are divided between the Alpenrose and its annex, the Bichlerhof; they're modernized but often with Bavarian traditional styling.

The tavern room, overlooking the street, has many ingratiating features, including coved ceilings (one decoratively painted), handmade chairs, flagstone floors, and a square tile stove in the center. In the Josefkeller, beer is served in giant steins, and in the evening musicians gather to entertain guests. The dining room provides excellent meals, including Bavarian specialties, costing from 28 DM ($18.50).

BERGHOTEL LATSCHENECK, Kaffeefeld 1, D-8102 Mittenwald. Tel. 08823/14-19. Fax 08823/10-58. 12 rms. TV TEL **Bus:** RVO.
$ Rates (including continental breakfast): 115 DM ($75.90) single; 230 DM–260 DM ($151.80–$171.60) double. No credit cards. **Closed:** Apr 18–May and Nov 25–Dec 31. **Parking:** 6 DM ($4).

Set against a craggy backdrop of rock and forest a short walk above the center of town, this chalet is ringed with green shutters, wraparound balconies, and a flagstone-covered sun terrace. Guests are never far from a vista, since large expanses of the exterior walls are devoted to rows of weatherproof windows that flood the wood-trimmed interior with sunlight. The guest rooms are modern and attractively furnished.

During chilly weather an open fireplace illuminates the knickknack-covered walls of the eating areas, which are open only to guests. The Kranzberg ski lift is nearby, making the place attractive to skiers. A covered pool and a sauna can provide a relaxing prelude to a quiet evening.

GÄSTEHAUS SONNENBICHL, Klausnerweg 32, D-8102 Mittenwald.
Tel. 08823/50-41. Fax 08823/58-14. 20 rms (all with bath or shower). TV TEL
Bus: RVO.

$ **Rates** (including continental breakfast): 75 DM–90 DM ($49.50–$59.40) single; 125 DM–138 DM ($82.50–$91.10) double. No credit cards. **Closed:** Oct 27–Dec 11.

Set into a hillside, this chalet has a view of the village set against a backdrop of the Alps from its balconies. The rooms are freshly decorated in vivid natural colors. The guesthouse is often completely booked, so reserving well in advance is a good idea.

HOTEL POST, Obermarkt 9, D-8102 Mittenwald. Tel. 08823/10-94. Fax 08823/1096. 87 rms, 6 suites. TV TEL **Bus:** RVO.

$ **Rates** (including buffet breakfast): 70 DM–120 DM ($46.20–$79.20) single; 130 DM–206 DM ($85.80–$136) double; from 280 DM ($184.80) suite. No credit cards. **Parking:** 7 DM ($4.60). **Closed:** Nov 22–Dec 17.

The Post is one of the more seasoned, established chalet hotels, dating from 1632. Its delightful breakfast is served on the sun terrace, with a view of the Alps. Although the lobby is basic, the tavern and three restaurants go all-out with mountain-chalet decor—black-and-white beams, a collection of deer antlers, and wood paneling. The guest rooms are furnished in a comfortable standard way. Offered to guests are an indoor pool, massage facilities, and a sauna.

RIEGER HOTEL, Dekan-Karl-Platz 28, D-8102 Mittenwald. Tel. 08823/ 50-71. Fax 08823/56-62. 45 rms. TV TEL **Bus:** RVO.

$ **Rates** (including buffet breakfast): 86 DM–162 DM ($56.80–$106.90) single; 128 DM–218 DM ($84.50–$143.90) double. AE, DC, MC, V. **Parking:** 7 DM ($4.60). **Closed:** Nov 18–Dec.

The Rieger is attractive, whether snow is piled up outside or the windowboxes are cascading with petunias. The living room has a beamed ceiling, wide arches, and a three-sided open fireplace. The indoor pool has a picture-window wall. Add to this a room for sauna and massages (segregated except on Monday, family time, when both sexes join the crowd). Fashionably decorated, the guest rooms are pleasant and comfortable. The dining room, with a view of the Alps, offers meals from 32 DM ($21.10).

INEXPENSIVE

GÄSTEHAUS FRANZISKA, Innsbruckerstrasse 24, D-8102 Mittenwald.
Tel. 08823/50-51. Fax 08823/3893. 16 rms, 4 suites. MINIBAR TEL

$ **Rates** (including buffet breakfast): 55 DM–75 DM ($36.30–$49.50) single; 95 DM–125 DM ($62.70–$82.50) double; 135 DM–165 DM ($89.10–$108.90) suite. AE, V. **Parking:** Free. **Closed:** Early Nov to second week in Dec.

⑤ When Olaf Grothe built this guesthouse, he named it after the most important person in his life—his wife, Franziska. Both have labored to make it the most personalized guesthouse in town by furnishing it tastefully and giving sympathetic attention to the needs of their guests. Each room and suite is furnished with traditional Bavarian styling. All have balconies opening onto mountain views; the suites also have color TVs, safes, and tea or coffee facilities. Snacks are served in the evening; otherwise, breakfast is the only meal served, but there are restaurants nearby.

WHERE TO DINE

MODERATE

RESTAURANT ARNSPITZE, Innsbruckerstrasse 68. Tel. 08823/24-25.
Cuisine: BAVARIAN. **Reservations:** Not necessary. **Bus:** RVO.

$ **Prices:** Appetizers 8 DM–24 DM ($5.30–$15.80); main courses 25 DM–38 DM

($16.50–$25.10); fixed-price lunch 36.50 DM ($24.10); fixed-price dinner 76.50 DM ($50.50). AE.

Open: Lunch Thurs–Mon noon–2pm; dinner daily 6–9pm. **Closed:** Oct 25–Dec 19.

S Housed in a modern chalet hotel on the outskirts of town, the Restaurant Arnspitze is the finest dining room in Mittenwald. The restaurant is decorated in the old style; the cuisine is solid, satisfying, and wholesome. You might order sole with homemade noodles or veal steak in creamy smooth sauce, then finish with the dessert specialty, Guglhupf-parfait Wipfelder. There's an excellent fixed-price lunch.

CHAPTER 13

FRANCONIA & THE GERMAN DANUBE

- **WHAT'S SPECIAL ABOUT FRANCONIA & THE GERMAN DANUBE**
1. **ULM**
2. **BAMBERG**
3. **NÜRNBERG [NUREMBERG]**
4. **WÜRZBURG**
5. **BAYREUTH**

The Renaissance swept across Germany, but it seemed to concentrate its full forces on the part of northern Bavaria that had once been a Frankish kingdom. Franconia today holds some of Germany's greatest medieval and Renaissance treasures. From its feudal cities sprang some of Germany's greatest artists—Albrecht Dürer, Lucas Cranach, Veit Stoss, Adam Krafft, and many others. As a center for cultural events, Franconia draws music lovers from all over to its annual Mozart Festival in Würzburg and Wagner Festival in Bayreuth.

The hillsides of Franconia are dotted with well-preserved medieval castles, monasteries, and churches. The region's architecture owes part of its beauty to the limestone range along the southern edge of the province. And between these hills and the edge of the Bavarian Forest is the upper Danube. It gradually builds force from the many smaller streams flowing out of the Alps and Swabian Jura, and by the time it reaches the Austrian border at Passau, it is large enough to carry commercial ships and barges. Although not as important to the German economy as the Rhine, the Danube was responsible for the growth of several influential towns.

SUGGESTED ITINERARY

Day 1 Begin at Ulm, a former imperial town noted for its Münster (cathedral). Spend a day exploring its old streets.

Day 2 Head north to Würzburg, which has been called a "baroque jewel box," and visit its many attractions.

Day 3 Travel southeast to Nürnberg, which is not the medieval city it was before World War II but is still filled with attractions and sights.

Day 4 Go north to Bamberg in the morning to see its Imperial Cathedral and other attractions. Lunch there, then go east to Bayreuth, of Richard Wagner fame, for the night.

GETTING THERE

Either Frankfurt or Munich can serve as the international gateway to Franconia. From Frankfurt, there are flights into the regional airport at Nürnberg. Fast, efficient intercity trains service the area, including hourly service between Frankfurt and Munich, with stops along the way at Würzburg and Nürnberg.

WHAT'S SPECIAL ABOUT FRANCONIA & THE GERMAN DANUBE

Great Towns/Villages

- ☐ Nürnberg, largest city of Franconia, with many major buildings reconstructed following World War II destruction.
- ☐ Würzburg, one of the loveliest baroque cities in all of Germany, starting point for the Romantic Road.
- ☐ Bamberg, one of the leading medieval cities of Germany, showing traces of 1,000 years of architecture.

Religious Shrines

- ☐ Ulmer Münster, second only to Cologne Cathedral as a huge Gothic structure of Christendom.
- ☐ Cathedral of St. Kilian, in Bamberg, the fourth-largest Romanesque church in Germany.

Artistic Shrine

- ☐ Albrecht Dürer House, in Nürnberg, home of Germany's greatest Renaissance artist.

Museum

- ☐ Germanisches Nationalmuseum, in Nürnberg, an impressive collection of German art and culture, including works by Dürer.

Historic Castle

- ☐ The Residenz, in Bamberg, the last and finest of a long line of German baroque castles from the 17th and 18th centuries.

Special Events

- ☐ Richard Wagner Festival, in Bayreuth, from mid-July until the end of August, drawing opera buffs from around the world.

Bus service among the cities of Franconia is poor, so the train is usually better. Motorists find five Autobahnen cutting through the country, including A3 from Cologne and Frankfurt, A7 from Hamburg, A81 from Stuttgart, A9 from Munich, and A6 from Heilbronn.

---

1. ULM

60 miles SE of Stuttgart; 86 miles W of Munich

GETTING THERE By Train Ulm Hauptbahnhof is on several major and regional rail lines, with frequent connections in all directions to major and minor cities of Germany. More than 40 trains per day arrive from Munich (trip time: 1 hour, 12 minutes), and some 50 trains or more arrive from Stuttgart (45 minutes). Daily trains also arrive from Cologne (4 hours, 6 minutes) and from Frankfurt (4 hours). For rail information and schedules, call 0731/19-419.

By Bus Regional bus service to nearby towns, including to the city of Augsburg, is available from Regional Service Augsburg GmbH, at Neu-Ulm (tel. 0731/73-606).

By Car Access by car is via Autobahn A8 east and west or A7 north and south. It takes about 1½ hours to drive from Munich to Ulm and about 3 hours to drive from Frankfurt to Ulm.

ESSENTIALS Contact **Tourist-Information,** Münsterplatz (tel. 0731/6-41-61).

Some settlement may have existed at Ulm as early as 854, but it officially became a town in 1027 and was soon the leading center of the Duchy of Swabia. It became a free imperial town in 1155, a status that brought it rapidly increasing trade and commerce. It is situated at a strategic spot on the Danube, between the points where the young stream is joined by the Ill River above and the Blau River below, making it a navigable waterway. Ulm's importance as a commercial terminal river port has made it a prosperous city ever since the Middle Ages.

The city's most famous son is Albert Einstein, born here in 1879.

WHAT TO SEE & DO

If you approach the town from the Stuttgart-Munich Autobahn, you'll miss the best view. So sometime during your visit, cross the Danube into Neu Ulm for a look at the gables and turrets of the Altstadt lining the north bank of the river. Here is the **Fishermen's Quarter,** with its little medieval houses and tree-shaded squares. Nearby are the more elaborate Renaissance patrician houses and the Gothic-Renaissance Rathaus.

ULM MÜNSTER, Münsterplatz 1. Tel. 0731/15-11-37.

The spirit of the town is dominated by its major attraction. Before you even reach the city, you'll recognize the skyline by the towering Ulm Münster. Its 530-foot steeple is the tallest in the world, and the Münster is second only to Cologne Cathedral in size. Without the pews, the nave of the church could hold nearly 20,000 people, more than twice the population of Ulm at the time the cathedral was begun in 1377. When Ulm joined the Protestant movement in 1531, work on the building was suspended, not to be continued until 1844 through 1890. Miraculously, the cathedral escaped serious damage during World War II.

The exterior is almost pure German Gothic, even though bricks were often used in the walls along with the more typical stone blocks. The unique feature of Ulm Münster, however, is that the architects placed as much emphasis on horizontal lines as on the vertical. Before entering, stop to admire the main porch, whose three massive arches lead to two Renaissance doors. This section dates from the 14th and 15th centuries and contains a wealth of statues and reliefs.

The five aisles of the cathedral lead directly from the hall below the tower through the nave to the east chancel. The conspicuous absence of a transept heightens the emphasis on the chancel and also increases the length of the nave. Each of the five aisles is enclosed by huge pillars towering into steep arches. The ceiling is swept into net-vaults so high that many of Germany's church steeples could sit comfortably beneath them. The nave is so large that, even with pews, it can accommodate more than 11,000 people at one service.

After going up the central aisle toward the chancel, you'll come to the 15th-century pulpit. Above the canopy is a second pulpit, symbolizing the Holy Spirit. Just to the left is a handsomely decorated tabernacle, containing the elements of the Eucharist. The wood panels, carved with figures, date from 1469 to 1474.

The chancel is entered through baroque iron gates set in the "triumph arch." Above the arch is a fresco depicting the Day of Judgment (1471). The other treasures are diminished by the grand choir stalls carved by Jorg Syrlin the Elder between 1469 and 1474. The 89 seats of dark oak are divided into sections, marked by busts of biblical and other characters. The stalls on the north side of the chancel are adorned with figures of men; those on the south, of women. The panels behind the stalls are decorated with elaborate tracery, containing figures from the Old and New Testaments, as well as several saints.

The most attractive stained-glass windows are in the little Besserer Chapel, on the south side behind the women's choir. The five windows in this room are from the 15th century and depict scenes from the Old and New Testaments. The main south window, from the same period, represents the Day of Judgment in striking colors and figures. Although most of the windows in the side aisles of the nave were destroyed in the war, the tall Gothic windows behind the chancel were preserved.

You can climb the tower as far as the third gallery (768 steps), where you can look out on the town and surrounding countryside over the Danube plain as far as the Alps.

Admission: Tower tickets, 2 DM ($1.30) adults, 1 DM (66¢) children.

Open: Oct–Feb, daily 9am–4:45pm; Mar and Sept, daily 9am–5:45pm; Apr–May, daily 8am–6:45pm; July–Aug, 8am–7:45pm. **Closed:** Sun morning services. **Bus:** 2, 3, or 4.

THE RATHAUS, Marktplatz 1. Tel. 0731/16-10.

The Rathaus was built in 1370 as a warehouse but has served as the town hall since 1419. A Gothic and Renaissance building, it contains ornate murals dating from the mid-16th century. On the south gable are coats-of-arms of cities and countries with which Ulm is linked by commerce. On the east gable is an astronomical clock from 1520. Above the interior staircase is a reproduction of the flying machine constructed by A. L. Berblinger, "the tailor of Ulm." In 1811, he was one of the first people to make a serious attempt to fly.

Admission: Free.

Open: Mon–Fri 8am–4pm. **Bus:** 2, 3, or 4.

ULM MUSEUM, Marktplatz 9. Tel. 0731/161-43-00.

Near the cathedral, the Ulm Museum contains an important collection of arts and crafts produced in Ulm and Upper Swabia from medieval times onward. There are also successive exhibitions of both ancient and modern art, including those of the masters of Ulm. It also has exhibits from the region's prehistory.

Admission: Free.

Open: Tues–Wed and Fri–Sun 10am–5pm, Thurs 10am–8pm. **Bus:** 2, 3, or 4.

WHERE TO STAY
EXPENSIVE

NEU-ULM MÖVENPICK HOTEL, Silcherstrasse 40, D-7910 Neu Ulm.
Tel. 0731/8-01-10. Fax 0731/8-59-67. 132 rms, 5 suites. MINIBAR TV TEL **Bus:** 2, 3, or 4.

$ Rates (including buffet breakfast): 190 DM–230 DM ($125.40–$151.80) single; 230 DM–290 DM ($151.80–$191.40) double; from 360 DM ($237.60) suite. AE, DC, MC, V. **Parking:** 10 DM ($6.60).

This was the first member of the Swiss-owned Mövenpick chain to be built in Germany in 1980. The hotel contains standardized guest rooms, well maintained and attractively decorated. Because of the hotel's location beside the Danube, many rooms feature views of the river. On the premises are a Swiss-inspired restaurant designed in the Mövenpick formula and featuring a salad buffet, along with a café and a pub. Room service and laundry service are available.

MODERATE

HOTEL ENGEL, Löherstrasse 35, D-7900 Ulm-Lehr. Tel. 0731/6-08-84.
Fax 0731/61-03-95. 41 rms. TV TEL **Directions:** 2 miles NW on Route 10, toward Stuttgart.

$ Rates (including buffet breakfast): 128 DM–148 DM ($84.50–$97.70) single; 185 DM–205 DM ($122.10–$135.30) double. AE, DC, MC, V. **Parking:** Free.

Completely overhauled and renovated, this hotel lies outside the center and is a good choice for motorists. The accommodations contain all amenities and rustic furniture of light-grained wood. Much of the establishment's business comes from its informal restaurant, which serves Bavarian specialties. Fixed-price menus, costing 30 DM to 62 DM ($19.80 to $40.90), are served daily from 11am to 11pm. The pub-style bar is open Monday to Saturday from 3pm to about 1am.

GOLDENES RAD, Neuestrasse 65, D-7900 Ulm. Tel. 0731/6-70-48. Fax
0731/61410. 20 rms, (all with bath or shower), 1 suite. MINIBAR TV TEL **Bus:** 2, 3, or 4.

$ Rates (including buffet breakfast): 120 DM–150 DM ($79.20–$99) single; 160

DM–190 DM ($105.60–$125.40) double; from 260 DM ($171.60) suite. AE, V. **Parking:** 8 DM ($5.30).

Because of this hotel's location directly on Münsterplatz, you'll have a view of the cathedral from many of its soundproof windows. The rooms are hospitable, with color-coordinated wallpaper and curtains along with colored-tile baths. The hotel was renovated in 1990.

HOTEL NEUTHOR, Neuer Graben 23, D-7900 Ulm. Tel. 0731/1-51-60.
Fax 0731/15-16-513. 85 rms, 6 suites. MINIBAR TV TEL **Tram:** 1.
$ Rates (including continental breakfast): 150 DM–160 DM ($99–$105.60) single; 180 DM–200 DM ($118.80–$132) double; from 220 DM ($145.20) suite. AE, DC, MC, V. **Parking:** 8 DM ($5.30). **Closed:** Dec 23–Jan 10.
In the town center, this hotel blends harmoniously into the old city yet has a modern interior. The lobby has Oriental rugs, gray-marble floors, and hospitable leather armchairs. The restaurant serves both Franconian and international specialties, with meals ranging from 40 DM to 70 DM ($26.40 to $46.20).

HOTEL UND RASTHAUS SELIGWEILER, D-7900 Ulm-Seligweiler, Autobahn-Ausfahrt Ulm-Ost. Tel. 0731/2-05-40. Fax 0731/205-44-00. 118 rms. MINIBAR TV TEL **Directions:** 5 miles NE on Route 19, toward Heidenheim.
$ Rates (including continental breakfast): 90 DM–115 DM ($59.40–$75.90) single; 125 DM–155 DM ($82.50–$102.30) double. AE, DC, MC, V. **Parking:** 7 DM ($4.60).
From across the meadow, the first thing you'll see is the gold lettering of the word *Hotel* splashed across the top floor of this establishment. The modernized accommodations have soundproof windows and walls. There is also a pool equipped with whirlpool jets, plus three bowling alleys.

ULMER SPATZ, Münsterplatz 27, D-7900 Ulm. Tel. 0731/6-80-81. Fax 0731/602-19-25. 36 rms (all with bath or shower). TV TEL **Bus:** 2, 3, or 4.
$ Rates (including continental breakfast): 108 DM–125 DM ($71.30–$82.50) single; 150 DM–160 DM ($99–$105.60) double. AE.

Set beside the cathedral, Ulmer Spatz is a corner stucco hotel-and-restaurant combination, with most of its simply but comfortably furnished rooms overlooking the cathedral tower. The little Weinstube serves tasty Franconian meals in a mellow setting of wood paneling. Meals cost 38 DM to 65 DM ($25.10 to $42.90) and feature main dishes like roast pork Schwäbish.

WHERE TO DINE

EXPENSIVE

ZUR FORELLE, Fischergasse 25. Tel. 0731/6-39-24.
Cuisine: SWABIAN/CONTINENTAL. **Reservations:** Recommended. **Bus:** 2, 3, 4.
$ Prices: Appetizers 8 DM–22 DM ($5.30–$14.50); main courses 26 DM–42 DM ($17.20–$27.70); fixed-price menus 56 DM ($37) and 98 DM ($64.70). AE, DC, MC, V.
Open: Lunch Mon–Sat 10am–2pm; dinner Mon–Sat 5pm–midnight.
With only 10 tables, owners Renate and Guido Heer have created a sympathetic and cozy environment where Swabian specialties and a continental cuisine moderne share equal billing. They offer homemade parfait of eel, lobster, goose, and stag, or filet of trout (forelle) in puff pastry with mushrooms and slices of smoked ham.

MODERATE

ZUM PFLUGMERZLER, Pfluggasse 6. Tel. 0731/6-80-61.
Cuisine: GERMAN/INTERNATIONAL. **Reservations:** Recommended. **Bus:** 2, 3, or 4.

$ Prices: Appetizers 7.50 DM–20 DM ($5–$13.20); main courses 18 DM–50 DM ($11.90–$33). MC.
   Open: Lunch Mon–Fri noon–2pm; dinner Mon–Fri 5pm–midnight. **Closed:** May 20–June 12.

Intimate, and open later than most restaurants in Ulm, this place might be perfect for an after-concert supper in an old-world setting. The kitchen turns out a variety of Swabian, Bavarian, and international meat and fish dishes.

---

2. BAMBERG

148 miles NW of Munich; 38 miles NW of Nürnberg; 60 miles NE of Würzburg

GETTING THERE   By Train   The Bamberg Bahnhof is on two major rail lines—the Stuttgart-Hof and the Berlin-Munich runs, with frequent connections in both directions. Most visitors arrive by rail from Nürnberg (see below) in just one hour. For rail information and schedules, call 0951/19-419.

By Bus   Regional bus service in the area, with frequent connections to nearby cities such as Nürnberg, is provided by CVF Omnibusverkehr Franken GmbH operating out of Coburg (tel. 09561/75-406).

By Car   Access by car is via Autobahnen A3 from Würzburg or A73 from Nurnberg.

ESSENTIALS   For tourist information, contact the **Stadt Fremdenverkehrs-amt,** Geyersworthstrasse 3 (tel. 0951/2-10-40).

A living piece of history, Bamberg is set in the rolling Franconian hills, where the Regnitz River flows into the Main. It suffered very little damage in World War II. Though not large, it was one of the leading medieval cities of Germany, when it was a powerful ecclesiastical center. The architecture of the town shows evidence of 1,000 years of building, with styles ranging from Romanesque to Gothic, Renaissance to baroque, up to the eclecticism of the 19th century. It has narrow cobblestone streets, ornate mansions and palaces, and impressive churches.

   Bamberg today is actually two towns divided by the river: The ecclesiastical town of the prince-bishopric, of which Bamberg was the capital for 800 years, and the secular town of the world of business and commerce, directed by the burghers. First noted in history as the residence of a count in 902, a century later Bamberg was established as the capital of the Holy Roman Empire by Heinrich II.

   Today Bamberg and beer go together like barley and hops. It's been called "a beer drinker's Eden," outranking Munich in the number of breweries in its city limits. The average Bamberger drinks 50 gallons of beer a year, making the rest of the German people look like teetotalers by comparison. Many brew fanciers journey all the way to Bamberg just to sample Rauchbier, a smoked beer first brewed in 1536.

WHAT TO SEE & DO

Domplatz is dominated by the **Alte Hofhaltung,** the Renaissance imperial and episcopal palace, with a courtyard surrounded by late-Gothic framework buildings. Within the palace are the remains of the original diet (assembly) hall, built in the 11th century. Elaborately decorated and furnished, the palace is noted for its frescoed Kaisersaal and its Chinesisches Kabinet, the latter covered with walls of marquetry. Later, you can explore the rose garden.

   Among the other places of interest is the **Altes Rathaus,** considered the strangest town hall in Germany. Determined not to play favorites between the ecclesiastical and secular sections of the city, the town authorities built this Gothic structure on its own little island in the middle of the Regnitz River—halfway between the two factions—a true middle-of-the-road (or river) political stand. From the island you get the best view of the old fishermen's houses along the river in the section called **"Little Venice."**

NEUE RESIDENZ, Domplatz. Tel. 0951/5-63-51.

Opposite the Alte Hofhaltung is the 17th-century Neue Residenz, the much larger palace of the prince-bishops, showing both Renaissance and baroque influence.

Admission: 3 DM ($2) adults, 2 DM ($1.30) children.

Open: Apr 1–Sept 30, daily 9am–noon and 1:30–5pm; Oct 1–Mar 31, daily 9am–noon and 1:30–4pm. **Bus:** 10.

KAISERDOM (Imperial Cathedral), Domplatz 5, Tel. 0951/502-316.

Begun in 1215 in Romanesque and early-Gothic style and resting on a hillside, the cathedral is a basilica with a double chancel, the eastern one raised on a terrace to compensate for the slope. The massive towers at the four corners of the church dominate Bamberg's skyline. The interior contains some of the most noted religious art in Christendom. Best known is the 13th-century equestrian statue the *Bamberger Reiter*, which represents the idealized Christian king of the Middle Ages. Among the many tombs is that of Emperor Heinrich II, who erected the original cathedral. Tilman Riemenschneider labored more than a decade over this masterpiece and the one devoted to the emperor's wife, Kunigunde (who was suspected of adultery, commemorated in a scene on the tomb). The only papal tomb north of the Alps contains the remains of Pope Clement II, who died in 1047; he is buried in the west chancel. The cathedral may be visited at any time during daylight hours, except during services. The cathedral treasury, a rich collection, may be seen in the Diözesan-museum, Kapitelshaus, Domplatz 5 (tel. 0951/502-325).

Admission: Diözesanmusem, 2 DM ($1.30).

Open: Diözesanmuseum, Tues–Sun 10am–5pm. **Bus:** 10.

E.T.A. HOFFMANN HAUS, Schillerplatz 26. Tel. 0951/87-11-52.

This was the home of the writer, poet, and critic from 1809 to 1813. The little narrow-fronted house is filled with mementos and memorabilia of the storyteller whose strange tales formed the basis of Jacques Offenbach's famous opera *The Tales of Hoffmann.*

Admission: 2 DM ($1.30) adults, 0.50 DM (30¢) children.

Open: Apr–Oct, Tues–Fri 4–5pm, Sat–Sun 10am–noon. **Bus:** 10.

WHERE TO STAY

EXPENSIVE

BAMBERGER HOF BELLEVUE, Schönleinsplatz 4, D-8600 Bamberg. Tel. 0951/9-85-50. Fax 0951/98-55-62. 45 rms, 1 suite. MINIBAR TV TEL **Bus:** 8 or 12.

$ **Rates** (including buffet breakfast): 145 DM–190 DM ($95.70–$125.40) single; 190 DM–280 DM ($125.40–$184.80) double; 850 DM ($561) suite. AE, DC, MC, V. **Parking:** 10 DM ($6.60).

This great old palace of stone, crowned by a tower and facing a little park, was renovated in 1984 with the old style retained. Try to book one of the large guest rooms that has several sitting areas. In the hotel's first-class restaurant, Bamberger Hof, the service is attentive. Set meals start at 50 DM ($33). Room service, laundering, and dry cleaning are offered.

RESIDENZSCHLOSS BAMBERG, Untere Sandstrasse 30–32, D-8600 Bamberg. Tel. 0951/60910. Fax 0951/609-1701. 144 rms, 4 suites. MINIBAR TEL TV **Bus:** 8.

$ **Rates** (including buffet breakfast): 180 DM–230 DM ($118.80–$151.80) single; 230 DM–290 DM ($151.80–$191.40) double; from 480 DM ($316.80) suites. AE, DC, MC, V.

This hotel occupies the ochre-colored baroque walls of what was built in 1787 as a hospital. Constructed by the local archbishop, Ludwig von Erthal, it was the most advanced of its era and functioned as a medical center until 1984. In 1991, much embellished and restored, it reopened as an elegant hotel under management by the Treff group, a respected German chain. Today, the hotel's original chapel continues to function as a venue for local weddings. Other than that, however, the interior decor is a blend of old and new, with all the electronic and service-oriented amenities you'd expect.

Popular with conventioneers who appreciate the meeting rooms, the hotel offers guest rooms either within the original baroque building or slightly less expensive ones within a modern annex connected with the main building via a glass-sided breezeway. The hotel is on a bank of the Regnitz, less than 300 yards from the edge of the old town and across from the new Bamburg Symphony Orchestra building.

The hotel's most glamorous restaurant, the Ludwig von Erthal, is open for dinner only, every night from 6 to 10pm. Main courses, costing from 23 DM to 50 DM ($15.20 to $33), include an array of sophisticated modern dishes based on German antecedents. Buffet breakfasts (included in the room price) and buffet lunches, 35 DM ($23.10) per person, are served amid the garden-inspired decor of The Orangerie. A steambath, a sauna, exercise bikes, and weightlifting equipment are available.

ST. NEPOMUK, Obere Mühlbrucke 5, D-8600 Bamberg. Tel. 0951/2-51-83. Fax 0951/2-66-51. 46 rms (all with shower), 4 suites. MINIBAR TV TEL **Bus:** 18.
$ Rates: 120 DM–140 DM ($79.20–$92.40) single; 190 DM–240 DM ($125.40–$158.40) double; from 360 DM ($237.60) suite. Breakfast 20 DM ($13.20) extra. AE, DC, MC, V. **Parking:** Free.

One of the little gems of Bamberg, its facade dating from 1855, St. Nepomuk was first turned into a guesthouse in 1984. The hotel rooms are well furnished with sleek modern styling; some units overlook the Regnitz. Franconian meals begin at 45 DM ($29.70).

MODERATE

HOTEL ALTENBURGBLICK, 59 Panzerleite, D-8600 Bamberg. Tel. 0951/5-40-23. Fax 0951/56-201. 46 rms. TEL **Bus:** 8, 12, or 18.
$ Rates (including continental breakfast): 70 DM–90 DM ($46.20–$59.40) single; 130 DM–140 DM ($85.80–$92.40) double. MC. **Parking:** 8 DM ($5.30).

Surrounded by majestic deciduous trees, which don't interrupt the fine view from the balconied windows, this modern hotel offers rooms with lots of light. Thirty units contain TVs. Breakfast is the only meal served.

BAROCK HOTEL AM DOM, Vorderer Bach 4, D-8600 Bamberg. Tel. 0951/5-40-31. Fax 0951/5-40-21. 19 rms. MINIBAR TV TEL **Bus:** 8 or 12.
$ Rates (including buffet breakfast): 85 DM–90 DM ($56.10–$59.40) single; 120 DM–140 DM ($79.20–$92.40) double. AE, DC, MC, V. **Closed:** Jan 6–31.

The owners of this symmetrical confection have retained every detail of the original ornamented facade and renovated key areas of the interior. The result is a winning combination of baroque elements in a well-lit modernized building. Each room is attractively furnished. Reservations are important.

Tariffs include a nourishing breakfast (the only meal served) of everything you might expect, plus Wurst and cheese. This meal is served in the most unusual breakfast room in Bamberg—the old cellar—where the management has set up tables with colorful napery under the plastered stone vaulting.

HOTEL BRUDERMÜHLE, Schranne 1, D-8600 Bamberg. Tel. 0951/5-40-91. Fax 0951/51-211. 16 rms (all with shower). TV TEL **Bus:** 8 or 12.
$ Rates (including continental breakfast): 105 DM–110 DM ($69.30–$72.60) single; 140 DM–150 DM ($92.40–$99) double. DC, MC, V.

My favorite ornament on the facade of this white-and-terra-cotta building is a corner statue of a saint being protected by two cherubs. I can't guess the age of the statue, but the building itself dates from 1314, when it was constructed as a mill powered by the

Regnitz River. The hotel couldn't be more centrally located, within a few blocks of the cathedral. The rooms are attractively furnished.

DIE ALTE POST, Heiliggrabstrasse 1, D-8600 Bamberg. Tel. 0951/2-78-48. Fax 0951/27-014. 42 rms (all with shower), 1 suite. TV TEL **Bus:** 8 or 12.

$ Rates (including buffet breakfast): 83 DM–87 DM ($54.80–$57.40) single; 130 DM–140 DM ($85.80–$92.40) double; 240 DM ($158.40) suite. AE, DC, MC, V. **Parking:** 8 DM ($5.30).

One of the most reasonably priced hotels in Bamberg is Die Alte Post, which dates from 1920 and is a five-minute walk from the Bahnhof. The helpful hosts do much to make a guest's stay comfortable in one of the well-maintained units. For the price quoted, you're given a good breakfast with orange juice, fresh cheese, and sausage. There's also a restaurant, Postschänke, serving meals from 15 DM to 30 DM ($9.90 to $19.80). A sauna, fitness room, and solarium are available.

NATIONAL, Luitpoldstrasse 37, D-8600 Bamberg. Tel. 0951/2-41-12. Fax 0951/22-436. 41 rms, 3 suites. MINIBAR TV TEL **Bus:** 5.

$ Rates (including buffet breakfast): 105 DM–125 DM ($69.30–$82.50) single; 155 DM–180 DM ($102.30–$118.80) double; from 215 DM ($141.90) suite. AE, DC, MC, V. **Parking:** 8 DM ($5.30).

Such a grand-looking hotel as the National could be found as easily in Paris as in Bamberg. With its black mansard roof, iron balconies, baroque and classical detailing, and opulent public rooms, you'll quickly understand why. The hotel is small with well-maintained guest rooms.

The National has a bar, furnished in a traditional style, and a formal restaurant, serving a notable cuisine of continental and Franconian specialties, with meals costing 40 DM ($26.40) and up. Room service, laundering, and dry cleaning are provided. There are conference facilities.

ROMANTIK HOTEL-WEINHAUS MESSERSCHMITT, Langestrasse 41, D-8600 Bamberg. Tel. 0951/2-78-66. Fax 0951/26-141. 13 rms, 1 suite. MINIBAR TV TEL **Bus:** 8 or 12.

$ Rates (including buffet breakfast): 75 DM–112 DM ($49.50–$73.90) single; 182 DM ($120.10) double; 215 DM ($141.90) suite. AE, DC, MC, V. **Parking:** 5 DM ($3.30).

The exterior here is a gabled expanse of pale blue and yellow, with baroque patterns carved into the window frames. Inside, dozens of windows, paneling, ceramic ovens, and antiques make a mellow decor. Many of the beds upstairs have meticulously crafted headboards. Otto Pschorn is in charge of this complex and does everything he can, with the assistance of his staff, to be helpful.

INEXPENSIVE

HOTEL GARNI GRAUPNER, Langestrasse 5, D-8600 Bamberg. Tel. 0951/98-04-00. Fax 0951/98-04-040. 30 rms (26 with bath). TEL **Bus:** 4, 5, 8, or 16.

$ Rates (including continental breakfast): 60 DM ($39.60) single without bath, 70 DM ($46.20) single with bath; 120 DM ($79.20) double with bath. AE, MC, V. **Parking:** 6 DM ($4).

Many residents of town know this establishment by its big-windowed café and pastry shop occupying the ground floor. Much renovated, rebuilt, and overhauled over the years, it has a very long tradition (since the 14th century) of accepting overnight guests. You can usually get a room here, perhaps with a view over the old city. The café is open daily from 7am to 7pm.

If the main hotel is full, guests are directed to a **Gästehaus Graupner,** Kapellenstrasse 21A (tel. 0951/2-47-33), about eight blocks away across the canal.

Constructed in the late 1960s, it offers 10 modern rooms for the same price charged in the main hotel. Each room in the annex has a private bath. The same family also owns a rose-garden café, a stone's throw from the cathedral.

WHERE TO DINE

MODERATE

ROMANTIK RESTAURANT-WEINHAUS MESSERSCHMITT, Lange-strasse 41. Tel. 0951/2-78-66.
   Cuisine: FRANCONIAN/INTERNATIONAL. **Reservations:** Not necessary.
   Bus: 8 or 12.
$ **Prices:** Appetizers 10 DM–18 DM ($6.60–$11.90); main courses 22 DM–38 DM ($14.50–$25.10); fixed-price menus 26 DM ($17.20) and 78.50 DM ($51.80). AE, DC, MC, V.
   Open: Daily 9am–11pm.
This pleasant restaurant is over 160 years old, and the sixth generation of the same family runs it. It's known throughout Bamberg for its "Romantik Menu," a complete meal costing 78.50 DM ($51.80). The dishes offered depend on seasonal shopping; in spring you get fresh white asparagus. Freshwater fish are kept in an aquarium. Game is another specialty, and the veal and lamb dishes are prepared with exquisite care.

WÜRZBURGER WEINSTUBE, Zinkenwörth 6. Tel. 0951/2-26-57.
   Cuisine: FRANCONIAN. **Reservations:** Recommended. **Bus:** 8 or 12.
$ **Prices:** Appetizers 5.50 DM–22 DM ($3.60–$14.50); main courses 28 DM–36.50 DM ($18.50–$24.10). AE, DC, MC, V.
   Open: Lunch Thurs–Tues 11:30am–2pm; dinner Thurs–Mon 6–9:30pm.
   Closed: End of Aug to mid-Sept.
On a secluded street near the river, the Würzburger Weinstube is an old, attractive half-timbered inn with a courtyard in front for warm-weather dining. The bottled wines available from the owner, Hans Krebs, will keep you smiling, but don't hesitate to drink the open wine of the house. On the à la carte listing you'll find rainbow trout from nearby streams and tenderloin of pork in cream sauce.

INEXPENSIVE

HISTORISCHER BRAUEREIAUSSCHANK SCHLENKERLA, Dominikan-erstrasse 6. Tel. 0951/5-60-60.
   Cuisine: FRANCONIAN. **Reservations:** Not necessary. **Bus:** 8 or 12.
$ **Prices:** Appetizers 5 DM–6.50 DM ($3.30–$4.30); main courses 17.50 DM–26 DM ($11.60–$17.20). No credit cards.
   Open: Wed–Mon 9:30am–11pm. **Closed:** Jan.
S Clients sit here much as they did in 1678, when the erstwhile brewery was established. The decor is rustic, with long wooden tables and smallish chairs. The price is right, and the gemütlich atmosphere genuine. Wholesome food is served; you can sample such local dishes as Bierbrauervesper (smoked meat and sour milk cheese) or Rauchschinken (smoked ham). Patrons wash down these dishes with a hearty malty brew, Rauchbier, which has a smoky aftertaste.

---

3. NÜRNBERG (NUREMBERG)

105 miles NW of Munich; 140 miles SE of Frankfurt;
127 miles NE of Stuttgart

GETTING THERE   By Plane   Nürnberg Flughafen is 4 miles north of the city center, and it's serviced by such airlines as Lufthansa, which has flights from

Frankfurt, along with several European airlines, such as British Airways and Air France flying in from London and Paris. Flying time from Frankfurt is just 40 minutes. There are also flights to and from Berlin (1 hour, 15 minutes) and to Munich (40 minutes). For airport information and schedules, call 0911/350-62-00.

By Train Nürnberg Hauptbahnhof lies on several major German rail lines, with frequent connections to big cities and many smaller regional towns. Travel time to Frankfurt is 2 hours and 20 minutes; to Berlin, 8 hours; and to Munich, 1 hour and 40 minutes. For rail information and schedules, call 0911/19-419.

By Bus Long-distance bus service from such cities as Munich and Frankfurt is provided by Europabus lines 183 and 189E of the Deutsche Touring GmbH operating out of Frankfurt. For information in Nürnberg, call Reisebüro Olcay at 0911/22-69-92. Regional bus service with frequent connections to neighboring towns is offered by OVF Omnibusverkehr Franken GmbH, Gleissbuhlstrasse 7, in Nürnberg (tel. 0911/244-01-15).

By Boat In 1992 the Main-Danube Canal, linking the Rhine, the Main, and the Danube, opened. For information about river boat connections, call Hafenverwaltung Nürnberg (tel. 0911/64-29-40).

By Car From Munich take Autobahn A9 north; from Frankfurt, head southeast along Autobahn A3. From Berlin, take Autobahn A9 south.

When this, the largest city in Franconia, celebrated its 900th birthday in 1950, the scars of World War II were still fresh. It was once considered the ideal of medieval splendor, but that legacy was lost in the ashes of war. With the exception of Dresden, no other German city suffered such devastation in a single air raid as did Nürnberg. On the night of January 2, 1945, 525 British Lancaster bombers rained fire and destruction on the city that was considered the ideological center of the Third Reich. Many of the most important buildings have been restored or reconstructed.

Visitors in Nürnberg today can see not only the ruins of the ramparts that once surrounded the city but also the Justice Palace, where the War Crimes Tribunal sat in 1946. You can also visit the Zeppelinfeld arena, the huge amphitheater where Hitler staged those dramatic rallies in which a million troops could be reviewed. Hitler's architect, Albert Speer, constructed what has been called a "concrete mecca," though today the grounds have been turned into a park with apartment blocks, a trade fair, and a concert hall. Speer's Congress Hall, larger than the Colosseum in Rome, is today a recording studio and warehouse.

Centuries of art and architecture made Nürnberg a little treasure chest of Germany. Some of the most important churches in Germany are here. Always an important trade center, Nürnberg today is a notable industrial city, still associated with its traditional gingerbread products and handmade toys. The first pocket watches, the Nürnberg eggs, were made here in the 16th century.

ORIENTATION

ARRIVING Your arrival is likely to be on the southern fringe at the Hauptbahnhof, which is also the district for most of the major hotels of the city. Opening onto Bahnhofplatz, the rail center lies on the threshold of the Altstadt. From this square, you can take Königstrasse right into the historical section of Nürnberg.

CITY LAYOUT This historical core can be covered easily on foot—in fact, that is about the only way to explore it. Along the way, you'll pass many pedestrians-only shopping streets. Eventually, you'll reach a pair of bridges spanning the Pegnitz River. Take either of them and continue north until you reach Hauptmarkt, which is the principal plaza of Nürnberg. This is a popular center for tourists, and many cafés are found here. You can continue north from here, going along Winklerstrasse, bypassing the huge Altes Rathaus. You'll also see St. Sebald's Church, opening onto Sebalderplatz (see below). When you reach Albrecht-Dürer-Platz, continue up to no. 39 if you wish to visit the house of this great artist. Or else go up Burgstrasse until you reach the Kaiserburg.

INFORMATION Contact **Tourist Information,** in the Hauptbahnhof (tel. 0911/23-36-32). An additional branch of the agency is in the Rathaus, Am Hauptmarkt (tel. 0911/23-36-35).

GETTING AROUND

Nürnberg and nearby towns, such as Fürth and Erlangen, are linked by a public transport system. Local and regional services, including subways, trams, buses, and trains, are interconnected. For all services, the same ticket can be used. Short-distance single tickets cost 2.20 DM ($1.50); long-distance tickets sell for 2.80 DM ($1.90). If you plan to do much traveling, consider the day ticket, called "runabout ticket," costing 6.10 DM ($4), a worthy investment. For more information, call 0911/27-07-50. To summon a taxi, call 0911/19-410.

WHAT TO SEE & DO

During the 15th and 16th centuries, Nürnberg enjoyed a cultural flowering that made it the center of the German Renaissance, bringing together Italian Renaissance and German Gothic traditions. In the artists' workshops were found such great talents as Albrecht Dürer, Veit Stoss, Peter Vischer, Adam Kraft, and Michael Wolgemut. Koberger set up his printing press here, and Regiomontanus his astronomical observatory. The guilds of the Meistersingers, composed of prosperous artisans, flourished; Wagner made their most famous member, Hans Sachs, the hero of his opera *Die Meistersinger von Nürnberg.*

Nearly all the attractions of the city are within the medieval fortifications, parts of whose walls still remain. Between the main wall (with rampart walks) and the secondary wall once ran the waters of a protective moat. Set at the "corners" of the Altstadt are the massive stone towers of the city gates. Four major gateway towers are intact, and the remains of dozens of others still exist along the ramparts. Crowning the northern periphery of the Altstadt is the Kaiserburg.

The **Helig-Geist-Spital** (Holy Ghost Hospital) was established as early as 1331. The building is supported on arches that span one branch of the Pegnitz River. To reach it, walk up to the Hauptmarkt, crossing the little museum bridge over the Pegnitz River; the Holy Ghost Hospital is to your right.

Possibly the best example of Nürnberg's aesthetic passion is the **Beautiful Fountain** on the Marktplatz. The stone pyramid, 60 feet high, dates from 1396 and is adorned with 30 figures arranged in 4 tiers. Within it is enclosed the symbol of Nürnberg, the journeyman's ring.

ALBRECHT DÜRER HOUSE, Am Tiergartnertor, Albrecht-Dürer-Strasse 39. Tel. 0911/16-22-71.

The town's most popular shrine is the Albrecht Dürer House, just up the cobblestoned Bergstrasse from the Dürer Monument and St. Sebald's Church. It was the home of the greatest German Renaissance artist. Aside from the historical and artistic contents inside, the house is well worth the short walk up the hill. Typical of the half-timbered burghers' houses of the 15th century, the structure is the only completely preserved Gothic house in Nürnberg. The first floors are sandstone, surmounted by two half-timbered stories and a gabled roof with a view of the town below. Dürer bought this house near the medieval city walls in 1509 and painted many of his masterpieces here before his death in 1528. The building houses a museum devoted to the life and works of the multifaceted individual who helped establish Nürnberg as a flourishing cultural center. Many of the rooms are furnished with important historical pieces and contain original etchings and woodcuts, plus copies of Dürer's paintings.

Admission: 3 DM ($2) adults, 1 DM (66¢) children.

Open: Nov–Feb, Tues and Thurs–Fri 1–5pm, Wed 1–9pm, Sat–Sun 10am–5pm; Mar–Oct, Tues and Thurs–Sun 10am–5pm, Wed 10am–9pm. **Bus:** 36 or 46.

ST.-LORENZ-KIRCHE, Lorenzer Platz 10. Tel. 0911/20-92-87.

Across the Pegnitz River is the largest and stateliest church in Nürnberg. Begun in 1270, it took more than 200 years to complete, but the final result is one of Gothic purity, inside and out. The twin towers flank the west portal, with its profusion of sculptures depicting the whole theme of redemption, from Adam and Eve through the last judgment. Upon entering the church, you can appreciate the color and detail in the stained-glass rosette above the portal. The interior is defined by pillars that soar upward to become lost in the vaulting shafts above the nave. Each pillar is adorned with sculptures carrying on the theme introduced at the entrance. The oldest of these works is *Mary with Child,* created about 1285. The continuing theme of the sculptures urges you forward toward the single east choir, the last portion of the church to be completed (1477). *The Angelic Salutation* (1519), carved in linden wood by Veit Stoss, is suspended from the roof of the church just behind the Madonna Chandelier. To the left of the altar is the Gothic Tabernacle, hewn from stone by Adam Kraft (1496), its upthrusting turret repeating the vertical emphasis of the church. Above the high altar is another masterpiece by Stoss, a carved crucifix.

The church is filled with woodcarvings, paintings, and reliefs, seemingly utilizing every artists' workshop that flourished in Nürnberg during the Renaissance. Among these are the painted panels at the beginning of the choir by Michael Wolgemut, Dürer's teacher. In the first chapel on the left off the nave is a sandstone relief of the three saints, Barbara, Catherine, and Agnes (1420). Halfway up the right side is another sandstone relief by Adam Kraft, this one depicting the strangulation of St. Beatrice. The beauty of the church is heightened by the well-preserved stained and painted glass, much of it dating from pre-Dürer Nürnberg.

Admission: Free.

Open: Mon–Sat 9am–5pm, Sun 2–4pm. **U-Bahn 2:** Lorenz-Kirche.

ST.-SEBALDUS-KIRCHE, Sebalderplatz. Tel. 0911/22-45-72.

Consecrated in 1273, this church is a fine example of 13th-century transition from Romanesque to German Gothic. The nave and west choir are late Romanesque, with a narrow chancel containing a simple altar and an ancient bronze baptismal font. The larger east choir, consecrated in 1379, is pure Gothic and contains the most important treasures of the church. Between the two east pillars is a huge 16th-century crucifixion group dominated by a life-size crucifix by Veit Stoss. Just behind the altar is the elaborate shrine of St. Sebald, whose remains are encased in a monument cast in brass by Peter Vischer in 1519. The nave of the church also holds several important works of art, including 14th-century statues of St. Catherine and St. Sebald and the *Madonna with a Halo* (1440). On the outside wall of the east choir is the tomb of the Schreyer-Landauer family, decorated with scenes of the passion and resurrection of Christ.

Admission: Free.

Open: Jan–Mar and Nov, daily 10am–4pm; Apr–May, Sept–Oct, and Dec, daily 9am–6pm; June–Aug, 9am–8pm. **U-Bahn 2:** Lorenz-Kirche.

KAISERBURG, Burgstrasse. Tel. 0911/22-57-26.

The Burg looms above the city from its hilltop at the northern edge of the Altstadt. For more than 500 years, from 1050 to 1571, it was the official residence of the German kings and emperors, including Frederick Barbarossa, the zealous Crusader who entertained such exotic guests as the emperor of Byzantium and the sultan of Tyre within its walls. The castle is divided into three complexes of buildings, indicating its main periods of architecture and history: the Kaiserburg (Imperial Castle), the Burgraves' Castle, and the Municipal Buildings of the Free City.

The oldest portion of the complex is the Pentagonal Tower (1050). It probably dates from the previous palace of the Salian Kings, over which the Burgraves' Castle was constructed. Although the Burgraves' Castle has been in ruins since it was destroyed by fire in 1420, it offers the visitor an interesting look into the layout of a feudal castle. The heavy ramparts with the parapet walks and secret passages were used by the watchmen and guards who protected not only the burgraves but also the emperors, who lived in the inner core of the castle complex.

The Kaiserburg, grouped around the inner court within the ramparts of the Burgraves' Castle, was the residence of the kings and emperors of Germany. Most of the buildings were constructed during the 12th century, centering around the once-magnificent Palas built by Konrad III in 1138. The great Knights' Hall on the ground floor and the Imperial Hall on the floor above look much as they did when King Frederick III rebuilt them in the 15th century, with heavy oak beams and painted ceilings. The rooms are decorated with period Gothic furnishings. Adjoining the Palas is the Imperial Chapel, the most important building in the castle complex. It consists of two chapels, one above the other in cross section but united at the center by an open bay. Thus the emperor could worship with his court in the upper chapel to the same liturgy as the lesser members of his retinue in the lower chapel.

The third set of buildings, built outside the Burgraves' Castle, was erected by the council of Nürnberg in the 14th and 15th centuries when it took over the responsibility of protecting the emperor. This section includes the imperial stables, now housing a youth hostel, the massive bastions of the fortress, the Tiefer Brunnen (Deep Well), and the castle gardens.

Even more impressive than the fortress, however, is the view of the roofs and towers of Nürnberg from its terraces.

Admission (including all parts of the castle): 3 DM ($2) adults, 2 DM ($1.30) children.

Open: Apr–Sept, daily 9am–noon and 12:45–5pm; Oct–Mar, daily 9:30am–noon and 12:45–4pm. **Bus:** 36 or 46.

GERMANISCHES NATIONALMUSEUM [Germanic National Museum], Kartäusergasse 12. Tel. 0911/1-33-10.

✪ The largest museum of German art and culture is just inside the south section of the medieval city walls (near the Hauptbahnhof). Its setting, incorporating the buildings of the former Carthusian monastery into its complex, covers the entire spectrum of German craftsmanship and fine arts from their beginnings to the 20th century. The pre- and early historical section contains finds from the Stone Age to the burial sites of the Merovingians. The extensive painting and sculpture sections include works by two of the city's most important artists, Albrecht Dürer and Veit Stoss. The demonstrations of the boundless variety and richness of German handcrafts play a major role in the museum's orientation toward cultural history. In this area, medieval bronze casting and tapestries, works of goldsmithery, scientific instruments, costumes, arms, armor, and toys are well represented.

During the last few years the folk art section and the section devoted to historical musical instruments have been greatly expanded. The print room and the numismatic collection are among the most comprehensive of the German-speaking world. Many documents from important families are housed in the archive. The active and broad-based scholarly programs of the museum would not be possible without its library of more than 500,000 volumes, including manuscripts, incunabula (early printed books), engraved and illustrated works.

Admission: 5 DM ($3.30) adults, 2 DM ($1.30) children. Free on Sun and public holidays.

Open: Tues–Sun 10am–5pm, Wed 10am–9pm. **U-Bahn 2:** Opernhaus.

TUCHERSCHLÖSSCHEN [Tucher Castle], Hirschelgasse 9. Tel. 0911/231-22-71.

This was the summer residence of Nürnberg's most famous and still existing patrician family, the Tuchers, known for making beer. The structure, built in 1534 by Peter Flotner, contains a small but precious collection of artworks commissioned by the Tuchers since the days of the Renaissance.

Admission: 1.50 DM ($1) adults, 0.60 DM (40¢) children.

Tours: Mon–Thurs at 2, 3, and 4pm; Fri at 9, 10, and 11am; Sun at 10 and 11am. **U-Bahn 2:** Lorenz-Kirche.

SPIELZEUGMUSEUM [Toy Museum], Karlstrasse 13. Tel. 0911/231-32-60.

Nürnberg is a major toy center, and it is only fitting that the city devote a museum to this industry, containing toys made not only in Nürnberg but also around the world. Some date from medieval times. The collections of old dollhouses is vastly amusing, as is a mechanical Ferris wheel. Toys, both hand- and machine made, fill three floors. You'll often see adults (without children) enjoying this museum.

Admission: 5 DM ($3.30) adults, 2.50 DM ($1.70) children.

Open: Tues and Thurs–Sun 10am–5pm, Wed 10am–9pm. **Bus:** 36.

HANDWERKER HOF [Artisans' Courtyard], Königstor.

Entering the Handwerker Hof from Königstrasse is like a walk back into the past where you find yourself in a land of half-timbered houses. Craftspeople can be seen at work making handcrafts that you can purchase as souvenirs. You can also eat many local specialties, such as small pork sausages, Rostbratwurst, which the law says must be served the same day they are made.

Open: Mar 20–Dec 23 Mon–Sat craft shops 10am–6:30pm, restaurants 10:30am–10pm. During Christkindlesmarkt (in Advent), entire establishment daily 10am–6:30pm. **Bus:** 36 or 46.

LOCHGEFÄNGNIS, Rathausplatz. Tel. 0911/231-26-90.

Under the Altes Rathaus is a medieval prison with the original cells and torture chamber, a gruesome attraction.

Admission: 3 DM ($2) adults, 1.50 DM ($1) children.

Open: May 2–Sept 30, Mon–Fri 10am–4pm, Sat–Sun 10am–1pm. **Closed:** Oct–Apr. **Bus:** 36.

VERKEHRSMUSEUM, Lessingstrasse 6. Tel. 0911/219-24-28.

The Verkehrsmuseum, the oldest transport museum in Germany, lies just outside the city wall. Its major exhibit is a reconstruction of the famous train that ran between Nürnberg and Fürth in 1835. Philatelists will be delighted to examine the museum's large postage stamp collection. You can also see stagecoaches and early railroad cars.

Admission: 4 DM ($2.60) adults, 2 DM ($1.30) children.

Open: Daily 9:30am–5pm. **U-Bahn 2:** Opernhaus.

WHERE TO STAY

VERY EXPENSIVE

ATRIUM HOTEL, Münchenerstrasse 25, D-8500 Nürnberg 50. Tel. 0911/4-74-80, or toll free 800/223-5652 in the U.S. or Canada. Fax 0911/47-48-420. 187 rms, 2 suites. MINIBAR TV TEL **Tram:** 9. **Bus:** 36.

$ **Rates** (including buffet breakfast): 229 DM–329 DM ($151.10–$217.10) single; 298 DM–448 DM ($196.70–$295.70) double; from 590 DM ($389.40) suite. Children under 12 stay free in parents' double. AE, DC, MC, V. **Parking:** 15 DM ($9.90). **Closed:** Dec 25–Jan 10.

Whoever designed this hotel was concerned with the distribution of natural light and did everything possible to pierce windows through to the greenery beyond the walls. One of the most modern hotels in Nürnberg, looking like a four-story collection of concrete cubes set up on stilts, it is set in a landscaped park on a manicured lawn five minutes by car from the city center. Rooms are spacious, with all the conveniences you'd expect. The hotel is directly connected to the Meistersingerhalle, used by Nürnbergers for concerts and conventions.

Dining/Entertainment: The hotel also has an attractively formal restaurant, Parkrestaurant Meistersingerhalle, specializing in both continental and Franconian food, with meals costing from 52 DM ($34.30). Rôtisserie Médoc features international grill specialties, plus a Terrace Restaurant, weather permitting, is open from May through September. There is also a dignified bar, Henry's.

Services: Room service, laundry, dry cleaning.
Facilities: Indoor pool, three specially designed rooms for the handicapped.

GRAND HOTEL, Bahnhofstrasse 1, D-8500 Nürnberg 1. Tel. 0911/23-22-0. Fax 0911/232-24-44. 185 rms, 3 suites. A/C MINIBAR TV TEL **U-Bahn 2:** Hauptbahnhof.

$ Rates: 254 DM–305 DM ($167.60–$201.30) single; 318 DM–418 DM ($209.90–$275.90) double; from 800 DM ($528) suite. Buffet breakfast 22 DM ($14.50) extra. AE, DC, MC, V. **Parking:** 15 DM ($9.90).

Across from the Hauptbahnhof, the Grand is a solid six-story blockbuster built "when hotels were really hotels"—that is, before World War I. To ensure quiet in this busy location, all the spacious rooms have soundproof windows.

Dining/Entertainment: The hotel restaurant, Brasserie, offers formal dining, with a cuisine both Franconian and international. Meals cost from 45 DM ($29.70). The best beers and wines by the glass are served in a cozy pub, along with local specialties and light snacks.

Services: Room service, laundry, dry cleaning.
Facilities: Sauna, health club, solarium.

MARITIM, Frauentorgraben 11, D-8500 Nürnberg 70. Tel. 0911/2-36-30. Fax 0911/23-63-823. 316 rms, 9 suites. A/C MINIBAR TV TEL **U-Bahn 2:** Hauptbahnhof.

$ Rates (including buffet breakfast): 293 DM–383 DM ($193.40–$252.80) single; 362 DM–452 DM ($238.90–$298.30) double; from 640 DM ($422.40) suite. AE, DC, MC, V. **Parking:** 14 DM ($9.20).

Built in 1986, the most stylish and sought after hotel in the city is the Maritim, near the Hauptbahnhof and across a busy traffic artery from the southern edge of Nürnberg's medieval fortifications. It offers attractively furnished guest rooms, and the lobby is decorated a bit like a private London club, with checkerboard floors of white and russet marble, leather couches, and mahogany paneling.

Dining/Entertainment: The hotel offers two restaurants—the Nürnberger Stuben, serving both local and international cuisine, and Die Auster, its gourmet dining room. Live piano music is heard nightly in the elegant hotel bar.

Services: Room service, laundry, dry cleaning.
Facilities: Indoor pool, sauna, steam bath, newsstand.

EXPENSIVE

DEUTSCHER HOF, Frauentorgraben 29, D-8500 Nürnberg 70. Tel. 0911/24-94-0. Fax 0911/22-76-34. 50 rms. TV TEL **U-Bahn 2:** Hauptbahnhof.

$ Rates (including breakfast): 150 DM–180 DM ($99–$118.80) single; 200 DM–240 DM ($132–$158.40) double. AE, DC, MC, V.

Two blocks from the Hauptbahnhof, this is one of the most imaginatively decorated modern hotels in Nürnberg, making a bold statement with plaids, full-grained paneling, and sophisticated lighting. The rooms are spacious and bright. The hotel has a rustically decorated wine cellar, Weinstube Bocksbeutelkeller, serving Franconian meals for 32 DM ($21.10) and up.

MODERATE

ALTEA HOTEL CARLTON, Eilgustrasse 13–15, D-8500 Nürnberg 1. Tel. 0911/2-00-30. Fax 0911/200-35-32. 130 rms, 3 suites. MINIBAR TV TEL **U-Bahn 2:** Hauptbahnhof.

$ Rates (including buffet breakfast): 130 DM–215 DM ($85.80–$141.90) single; 150 DM–265 DM ($99–$174.90) double; from 275 DM ($181.50) suite. AE, DC, MC, V. **Parking:** 10 DM ($6.60).

This first-class hotel is considered among the best in Nürnberg. It stands on a quiet street a block from the Hauptbahnhof. Some doubles have a pair of L-shaped sofas with coffee tables so they can serve as combined living-sleeping rooms. Rates are based on the size of the accommodation.

Dining/Entertainment: Though the Carlton has a well-known restaurant, the Zirbelstube, many prefer to have lunch on the stone terrace with its umbrella-shaded tables and flower garden.

Services: Room service, laundry, dry cleaning.
Facilities: Sauna, health club, solarium.
NOTE: The name of this hotel may be changed by 1994.

MODERATE

BURGHOTEL-GROSSES HAUS, Lammsgasse 3, D-8500 Nürnberg 1. Tel. 0911/20-44-14. Fax 0911/22-38-82. 46 rms. MINIBAR TV TEL **Bus:** 36 or 46.
$ Rates (including continental breakfast): 135 DM–170 DM ($89.10–$112.20) single; 170 DM–270 DM ($112.20–$178.20) double. AE, DC, MC, V. **Parking:** 12 DM ($7.90).

This unusual hotel offers the luxury of a heated indoor pool opening onto a tile bar area furnished with plants, antiques, and bar stools; there you can sip your favorite drink and pretend you're in the Caribbean. Even better, your door will practically open into one of the most historic parts of the old city of Nürnberg. Room furnishings are in a functional modern style with carefully chosen colors.

CITY HOTEL, Königstrasse 25-27, D-8500 Nürnberg 1. Tel. 0911/22-56-38. Fax 0911/20-39-99. 21 rms. TV TEL **U-Bahn 2:** Lorenz-Kirche.
$ Rates (including continental breakfast): 100 DM ($66) single; 160 DM ($105.60) double. AE, DC, MC, V. **Parking:** 10 DM ($6.60). **Closed:** 2 weeks after Christmas.

⑤ The City occupies the third, fourth, and fifth floors of an old-fashioned building, just a few steps from Lorenz-Kirche on a wide pedestrian thoroughfare in the historic center. Take a cramped elevator upstairs to the third-floor reception area, where the efficient owner, Frau Elenore Pache, will show you one of her simple but immaculate rooms.

DREI LINDEN, Aussere-Suizbacher-Strasse 1, D-8500 Nürnberg 20. Tel. 0911/53-32-33. Fax 0911/55-40-47. 28 rms. MINIBAR TV TEL **Tram:** 8. **Bus:** 45.
$ Rates (including buffet breakfast): 120 DM–140 DM ($79.20–$92.40) single; 180 DM–220 DM ($118.80–$145.20) double. AE, MC. **Parking:** 8 DM ($5.30).

⑤ The 100th anniversary of this renovated guesthouse was celebrated in 1977 by the third generation of the Zeuner family. You'll find comfort in all the rooms, which come with big soundproof windows. The public rooms are attractively decorated in a modern style.

DREI RABEN, Königstrasse 63, D-8500 Nürnberg 1. Tel. 0911/20-45-083. Fax 0911/23-26-11. 31 rms (all with bath or shower). MINIBAR TV TEL **U-Bahn 2:** Hauptbahnhof.
$ Rates (including buffet breakfast): 120 DM–155 DM ($79.20–$102.30) single; 160 DM–190 DM ($105.60–$125.40) double. AE, DC, MC, V. **Parking:** 13 DM ($8.60).

Owned and operated by Herr and Frau Werner Deibel (who speak English), this modest little establishment stands one block from the station. A three-passenger elevator takes you upstairs to the rooms.

DÜRER-HOTEL, Neutormauer 32, D-8500 Nürnberg 1. Tel. 0911/20-80-91. Fax 0911/22-34-58. 107 rms. MINIBAR TV TEL **Bus:** 36 or 46.

$ Rates (including buffet breakfast): 195 DM ($128.70) single; 200 DM–260 DM ($132–$171.60) double. AE, DC, MC, V. **Parking:** 10 DM ($6.60).

Opened in 1989, the Dürer quickly became one of the best first-class hotels in the city. It stands beside the birthplace of this world-famous artist, from whom it takes its name, right under the castle and near all the major sightseeing attractions. Many of the rooms have quite a bit of character. The Dürer offers the Bistro Bar, a fitness center, and a garage. It serves only breakfast, but you are a short walk from many of the city's leading restaurants. The ambience is one of cozy antique charm, combined with modern amenities. Laundry and dry cleaning are available.

VICTORIA, Königstrasse 80, D-8500 Nürnberg 1. Tel. 0911/20-38-01. Fax 0911/22-74-32. 64 rms. TV TEL **U-Bahn:** Lorenz-Kirche.

$ Rates (including buffet breakfast): 100 DM–110 DM ($66–$72.60) single; 160 DM–230 DM ($105.60–$151.80) double. AE, DC, MC, V. **Parking:** 10 DM ($6.60).

Not far from the Lorenz-Kirche, the entrance to this hotel is identified by restrained carving on the sandstone facade that dates from the 19th century. In 1976, the Victoria was completely renovated and equipped with soundproof windows and doors. The interior is modernized but still has an elegantly curved staircase leading to bright rooms on the second floor.

WEINHAUS STEICHELE, Knorrstrasse 2–8, D-8500 Nürnberg 1. Tel. 0911/20-43-78. Fax 0911/22-19-14. 52 rms. MINIBAR TV TEL **U-Bahn 2:** Weisser Turm.

$ Rates (including continental breakfast): 105 DM–140 DM ($69.30–$92.40) single; 170 DM ($112.20) double. No credit cards. **Parking:** 10 DM ($6.60).

The overflow from the original building spills into a modern annex next door that blends harmoniously with the more antique structure. The central core is a beautifully balanced and handcrafted building of heavy stone blocks with a curved sloping roofline that supports a half-timbered gable.

INEXPENSIVE

DEUTSCHER KAISER, Königstrasse 55, D-8500 Nürnberg 1. Tel. 0911/20-33-41. Fax 0911/24-18-982. 51 rms (34 with bath). TEL **U-Bahn 2:** Hauptbahnhof.

$ Rates (including continental breakfast): 60 DM ($39.60) single without bath, 80 DM–90 DM ($52.80–$59.40) single with bath; 96 DM ($63.40) double without bath, 120 DM–140 DM ($79.20–$92.40) double with bath. AE, DC, MC, V.

Ⓢ Erected in 1889, the Deutscher Kaiser has one of the most attractive old-world exteriors of any of the Nürnberg hostelries. At the top of a vehicle-free pedestrian mall, it is built of gray stone, with steep gables and a highly pitched roof studded with dormers. Three Romanesque-style arches lead into the main lobby. The breakfast room is rather simple yet fresh and clean. The general effect is one of comfort in immaculate surroundings. The Deutscher Kaiser, which has been owned and managed by the same family for more than 80 years, is crowded during December and February, when German tourists reserve ahead. In the basement is Wienerwald restaurant.

WHERE TO DINE

EXPENSIVE

DIE ENTENSTUB'N, Güntersbühlerstrasse 145. Tel. 0911/59-80-413. **Cuisine:** CONTINENTAL. **Reservations:** Required.

$ Prices: Appetizers 14 DM–38 DM ($9.20–$25.10); main courses 38 DM–52 DM ($25.10–$34.30); fixed-price lunch 59 DM ($38.90); fixed-price dinners 84 DM–118 DM ($55.40–$77.90). MC.

Open: Lunch Tues–Fri and Sun noon–2pm; dinner Tues–Sat 6:30–10pm.

Die Entenstub'n is considered by some food critics the best dining spot in Nürnberg. Other restaurants may be better established, but this small and well-decorated place is more in tune with a continental cuisine moderne and sophisticated upscale versions of experimental dishes. It is tastefully appointed with light-grained paneling and depictions of geese, the establishment's namesake. Your main course might be marinated lettuce with strips of braised chicken, carpaccio of beef in truffle-flavored oil, or medallions of seawolf in champagne sauce; among the succulent desserts, you might enjoy the hazelnut torte with fresh fruit. Fixed-price or à la carte meals are served. The restaurant is best reached by taxi since it is hard to find, and there is no tram or bus service.

ESSIGBRÄTLEIN, Am Weinmarkt 7. Tel. 0911/22-51-31.

Cuisine: FRANCONIAN/CONTINENTAL. **Reservations:** Required. **U-Bahn 2:** Karstadt.

$ Prices: Appetizers 16 DM–32 DM ($10.60–$21.10); main courses 40 DM–45 DM ($26.40–$29.70); fixed-price lunch 68 DM ($44.90); fixed-price dinner 89 DM ($58.70) and 108 DM ($71.30). DC, MC, V.

Open: Dinner only, Tues–Sat 7pm–midnight. **Closed:** Jan 1–15; Aug 1–15.

An outstanding gourmet spot, the house dates back to 1550, when it was mentioned for the first time in a chronicle of the city. The oldest original restaurant in Nürnberg, it was a favorite meeting place of wine merchants. At the entrance level is room for only 25 diners. Up one flight is a library and cocktail lounge with a private gastronomic museum. In summer, a small garden restaurant is opened. The kitchen harmoniously blends Franconian fare with continental cuisine moderne offerings. Everything is cooked to order, and only the best and freshest produce from the market is used. A gourmet meal is likely to include many small courses.

GOLDENES POSTHORN, Glöckleingasse 2. Tel. 0911/22-51-53.

Cuisine: FRANCONIAN. **Reservations:** Required. **U-Bahn 2:** Lorenz-Kirche.

$ Prices: Appetizers 20 DM–30 DM ($13.20–$19.80); main courses 24 DM–42 DM ($15.80–$27.70); fixed-price lunch 45 DM ($29.70); fixed-price dinner 58 DM–75 DM ($38.30–$49.50). AE, DC, MC, V.

Open: Lunch Mon–Sat noon–2:30pm; dinner Mon–Sat 6–11:30pm.

Lodged in a building whose history goes back to 1498, the Goldenes Posthorn claims among its mementos a drinking glass used by Albrecht Dürer and a playing card belonging to Hans Sachs from about 1560. However, the present structure was rebuilt in 1960. Once one of Germany's most famous restaurants, it offers modern Franconian cuisine based on regional products. Two special set dinners are offered: a four-course house menu and a five-course Franconian menu for even less. Regular menus feature such dishes as quail stuffed with goose liver and nuts. There are fine wines dating back to 1889.

MODERATE

BÖHMS HERRENKELLER, Theatergasse 19. Tel. 0911/22-44-65.

Cuisine: FRANCONIAN. **Reservations:** Recommended. **U-Bahn 2:** Hauptbahnhof.

$ Prices: Appetizers 6 DM–18 DM ($4–$11.90); main courses 12 DM–30 DM ($7.90–$19.80); three-course fixed-price menu 32 DM ($21.10); four-course fixed-price menu 60 DM ($39.60). DC, MC, V.

Open: Lunch Mon–Sat 11:30am–2pm; dinner Mon–Sat 5:30–10pm. Drinks and cold plates served until midnight. **Closed:** Sun lunch in summer.

Parts of this Weinstube date from 1489, with later additions completed in 1948. You'll get a feeling of history as you sample the well-rounded collection of wine and the gutbürgerlich cookery. The three-course fixed-price menu is an especially good value.

HEILIG-GEIST-SPITAL, Spitalgasse 12. Tel. 0911/22-17-61.

Cuisine: FRANCONIAN. **Reservations:** Not necessary. **Bus:** 536.

$ **Prices:** Appetizers 5.50 DM–12 DM ($3.60–$7.90); main courses 20 DM–50 DM ($13.20–$33); three-course fixed-price menu 42 DM ($27.70). AE, DC, MC, V.

Open: Daily 11am–midnight.

An old tavern entered through an arcade near the river is Nürnberg's largest historical winehouse. Carp is a specialty, priced according to weight. The wine is abundant and excellent, with more than 100 vintages to go with the typical Franconian specialties. Main dishes are hearty and filling. In season, you can order leg of venison with noodles and berries.

NASSAUER KELLER, Karolinenstrasse 2–4. Tel. 0911/22-59-67.

Cuisine: INTERNATIONAL/FRANCONIAN. **Reservations:** Recommended. **U-Bahn 2:** Lorenz-Kirche.

$ **Prices:** Appetizers 6 DM–16.50 DM ($4–$10.90); main courses 17.50 DM–36.50 DM ($11.60–$24.10). AE, DC, MC.

Open: Lunch daily noon–2:30pm; dinner daily 6–10:30pm.

Occupying the cellar of one of the most romantic buildings in Nürnberg, opposite the Lorenz-Kirche, Nassauer Keller specializes in trout and game in season. Main dishes include Wiener Schnitzel and filet of venison with mushrooms and cranberries. You can also sample either filet of pork, roast shoulder of pork, saddle of lamb, or roast duck.

INEXPENSIVE

BRATWURST-HAÜSLE, Rathausplatz 1. Tel. 0911/22-76-95.

Cuisine: FRANCONIAN. **Reservations:** Not necessary. **U-Bahn 2:** Lorenz-Kirche. **Bus:** 86.

$ **Prices:** Appetizers 4.50 DM–6.50 DM ($3–$4.30); main courses 8.50 DM–16 DM ($5.60–$10.60); fixed-price lunch 17.50 DM ($11.60); fixed-price dinner 34 DM ($22.40). No credit cards.

Open: Mon–Sat 10am–10pm.

Because it's opposite the Rathaus, you might make this sausage restaurant a luncheon stopover as you explore historic Nürnberg. In winter, you'll find an open hearth to warm you from the snows, and in summer, this makes a refreshingly cool retreat from the heat. Fixed-price menus include a host of Franconian specialties; most diners, though, prefer a platter of Bratwurst and beer, especially the large student clientele.

HISTORISCHE BRATWURST-GLÖCKLEIN, Im Handwerkerhof. Tel. 0911/22-76-25.

Cuisine: FRANCONIAN. **Reservations:** Recommended. **U-Bahn 2:** Hauptbahnhof.

$ **Prices:** Appetizers 4.50 DM–6 DM ($3–$4); main courses 9.50 DM–16 DM ($6.30–$10.60). No credit cards.

Open: Mon–Sat 10:30am–9pm.

If you want to try Bratwurst in all its variations, this place in the "village" of craftspeople is for you. The kitchen prepares a Bratwurst as a main course, with traditional side dishes, all served on tin plates. Since beer goes perfectly with Wurst, you'll enjoy sampling some of the brews on tap while admiring the craftsmanship of the room, which dates from the Middle Ages. Ham hocks are a specialty. Be careful you don't spend your entire afternoon on the sun terrace—it's that tempting.

WEINHAUS STEICHELE, Knorrstrasse 2. Tel. 0911/20-43-78.

Cuisine: FRANCONIAN/BAVARIAN. **Reservations:** Not necessary. **U-Bahn 2:** Weisser Turm.

$ Prices: Appetizers 6 DM–8.50 DM ($4–$5.60); main courses 16 DM–22 DM ($10.60–$14.50). No credit cards.
Open: Tues–Sat 11am–midnight, Sun 4pm–midnight.

Steichele's walls are covered with polished copper pots, antique display cases lit from within, and hanging chandeliers that are carved into double-tailed sea monsters and other mythical beasts. The specialties are a delight, backed up by a superb wine list. Try roast shoulder of pork with potato balls and sauerkraut or Husarenspiess, with onions, ham, paprika, cucumbers, hot sauce, french fries, and salad.

ZUM WAFFENSCHMIED, Obere Schmiedgasse 22. Tel. 0911/22-58-59.
Cuisine: FRANCONIAN/CONTINENTAL. **Reservations:** Required. **U-Bahn**
2: Lorenz-Kirche.
$ Prices: Appetizers 5.80 DM–21 DM ($3.80–$13.90); main courses 8.50 DM–29 DM ($5.60–$19); fixed-price menu 30 DM–60 DM ($19.80–$39.60). AE, DC, MC, V.
Open: Daily 11am–midnight.

Conveniently located between the Albrecht Dürer House and the Kaiserburg, Zum Waffenschmied is attractively decorated with naturally aged paneling, mustard-colored walls, and bright napery. It serves traditional and continental food to the dozens of regular locals. The chef can cook an entire roast pig as easily as he can concoct Norwegian trout served with a sauce of wild mushrooms and cream, Bresse hen with fresh vegetables, and rack of lamb with rosemary.

4. WÜRZBURG

174 miles NW of Munich; 74 miles SE of Frankfurt;
68 miles NW of Nürnberg

GETTING THERE By Train Würzburg Hauptbahnhof lies on several major and regional rail lines, with frequent connections to all big German cities. Thirty trains per day arrive from Frankfurt (trip time: 1½ hours); 20 trains from Munich (2½ hours), 30 trains from Nürnberg (1 hour, 10 minutes), and several trains from Berlin (5 hours, 50 minutes). For rail information and schedules, call 0931/19-419.

By Bus Long-distance bus service, including connections from Frankfurt, is available on EB 190, a bus operated by Deutsche Touring GmbH in Frankfurt (tel. 069/79-030). Local and regional service, with frequent connections, is provided by WSB Würzburg Strassenbahn GmbH at Würzburg (tel. 0931/80-00-520), and by OVF Ominbusverkehr Franken GmbH, also at Würzburg (tel. 0931/1-69-01).

By Car Access is by Autobahn (A7) from the north and south, or Autobahn (A3) from the east and west.

ESSENTIALS For tourist information, contact **Verkehrsamt,** Pavillon vor dem Hauptbahnhof (tel. 0931/3-74-36).

For Germans, the south begins at Würzburg, one of the loveliest baroque cities in all the country. It has been called a "baroque jewel box." Würzburg is the starting point for the Romantic Road (see Chapter 11) and is also at the junction of the most important motorways in Germany.

Remaining faithful to the Catholic Church throughout the Reformation, this city on the Main has been called "the town of madonnas" because of the more than 100 statues of its patron saint that adorn the housefronts. The best known of these statues is the Patrona Franconiae, a baroque madonna that stands among other Franconian saints along the buttresses of the 15th-century Alte Mainbrücke, Germany's second-oldest stone bridge.

On March 16, 1945, Würzburg was shattered by one bombing raid in 20 minutes. In a miraculous rebuilding program, nearly every major structure has been restored.

WHAT TO SEE & DO

Much of the original splendor of the city was because of the efforts of one man—Balthasar Neumann (1687–1753), the greatest master of the German baroque. His major accomplishment as court architect to the prince-bishop of Würzburg was the Residenz.

THE RESIDENZ (Schloss und Gartenverwaltung Würzburg), Residenzplatz. Tel. 0931/52743.

Begun in 1720 to satisfy Prince-Bishop Johann Philipp Franz von Schonborn's passion for elegance and splendor, the Schloss- und Gartenverwaltung Würzburg is the last and finest of a long line of baroque castles built in Bavaria in the 17th and 18th centuries. The great horseshoe-shaped edifice was completed within 24 years, the joint effort of the best Viennese, French, and German architects working under the leadership of Neumann. Because it was built in such a short time, the castle shows a unity of purpose and design not usually evident in buildings of such size.

Leading upward from the vestibule at the center of the castle is the Treppenhaus (staircase), standing detached in the lower hall and branching into twin stairways at a landing halfway to the second floor. This masterful creation by Neumann is the largest German baroque staircase. The high, rounded ceiling above it is decorated with a huge fresco by Tiepolo. At the center, Apollo is seen ascending to the zenith of the vault. The surrounding themes represent the four corners of the world, the seasons, and signs of the zodiac. The illusion of the painting is so complete that it appears to be overflowing onto the walls of the upper hall.

At the top of the staircase you'll enter the White Hall, where absence of color provides the ideal transition between the elaborate staircase and the connecting Kaisersaal (imperial hall), a culmination of the splendor of the entire castle. Based on Neumann's design, Tiepolo worked on this room in conjunction with the accomplished sculptor and stucco artist Antonio Bossi. The walls of the hall are adorned with three-quarter marble pillars with gilded capitals. In the niches between the columns are original sculptures of Poseidon, Juno, Flora, and Apollo by Bossi. The highlight of the hall, however, is in the graceful combination of the white and gold stucco work, and the brilliantly colored paintings on the upper walls and ceiling. The work is so well done that it is difficult to tell where the paintings leave off and the relief work begins. On the flat part of the ceiling Tiepolo has depicted an allegorical scene of Apollo escorting the bride of Frederick Barbarossa to the emperor. The paintings between the upper, rounded windows glamorize important incidents in the history of Würzburg.

The other important attraction in the Residenz is the court chapel, in the southwest section. Neumann placed the window arches at oblique angles to coordinate the windows with the oval sections, thus creating a muted effect. The rectangular room is divided into five oval sections, three with domed ceilings. Colored marble columns define the sections, their gilded capitals enriching the ceiling frescoes by Byss. Bossi trimmed the vaulting and arches with intricate gilded stucco work. At the side altars, Tiepolo painted two important works: *The Fall of the Angels* on the left and *The Assumption of the Virgin* on the right.

The court gardens, at the south and east sides of the Residenz, are entered through the gate next to the court chapel. The terraces are connected by walks and stairways and end in a large orangerie on the south side. The various gardens are laid out in geometric designs and studded with little statues by Johann Peter Wagner, plus several fountains spouting from sunken parterres.

In the 1945 bombings the whole roof and nearly all the wooden ceilings and the floors of the Residenz were burnt. Only the stone vaults of Neumann in the

Treppenhaus, the White Hall, and the Kaisersaal resisted the fire. Rain could easily have damaged the magnificent Tiepolo ceilings. And it would have had not Lt. John D. Skilton, a U.S. Army officer, intervened. He arranged for lumber to be shipped down the Main, and at Heidingsfeld he set up a sawmill that turned out the planking needed to cover the roofs. The lieutenant also personally financed the whole operation, and anyone who goes to Würzburg today can be grateful for his foresight and generosity.

During the summer, a Mozart festival is held in the upper halls. (For information, phone 0931/37-33-6).

Admission: 4.50 DM ($3) adults, 3 DM ($2) children.

Open: Apr–Sept, Tues–Sun 9am–5pm; Oct–Mar, Tues–Sun 10am–4pm. **Tram:** 1, 5.

THE MARIENBERG FORTRESS, Festung Marienberg. Tel. 0931/4-38-38.

The Marienberg Fortress, over the stone bridge from the Altstadt, was the residence of the prince-bishops from 1253 to 1720, when transition was made to the more elegant Residenz. Although portions of the stronghold have been restored, the combination of age and wartime destruction has taken a serious toll on its thick walls and once-impenetrable ramparts. But what remains is worth a visit. One of the oldest churches in Germany, the 8th-century **Marienkirche,** stands within its walls.

In the former arsenal and Echter bulwark, to the right of the first courtyard, is the **Main Fränkisches Museum,** Festung Marienberg (tel. 0931/4-48-40), housed here since 1946. A treasure house, the museum contains a history of Würzburg in art, from marble epitaphs of the prince-bishops to a carved wood model of the town in 1525. Works include a well-known collection of sculpture by Tilman Riemenschneider, including his *Adam and Eve;* paintings by Tiepolo; sculptures by Peter Wagner; and sandstone figures from the rococo gardens of the prince-bishops' summer palace. A further tribute to one of the few industries of the city, that of winemaking, is paid in the presshouse, the former vaults of the fortress. A look at historic casks and carved cask bases and a large collection of glasses and goblets concludes the exhibitions.

The **Fürstenbau-Museum** (tel. 0931/430-16) is the latest museum situated in the restored princes' wing of the fortress. Here the visitor gets a glimpse of the living quarters and living conditions of the prince-bishops (until 1718). The Section for Urban History offers a stroll through 1,200 eventful years of Würzburg's history. A model of the town shows its appearance in 1525, and another model reveals the destroyed city after the bombing in 1945.

Admission: Museums and castle 3 DM ($2) adults; children under 14 free.

Open: Apr–Oct, Tues–Sun 10am–5pm; Nov–Mar, Tues–Sun 10am–4pm.

MORE ATTRACTIONS

The **Cathedral of St. Kilian** (Dom), Domstrasse (tel. 0931/53691), at the end of Schönbornstrasse, was begun in 1045 and ranks as the fourth-largest Romanesque church in Germany. The east towers date from 1237, and the interior was adorned with high-baroque stuccowork after 1700. The Dom is dedicated to St. Kilian, an Irish missionary to Franconia in the 7th century. Destroyed in the early spring bombings of 1945, the Dom has been rebuilt. The baroque stucco work in the cross aisle and the choir has been preserved. The imposing row of bishops' tombs begins with that of Gottfried von Spitzenberg (circa 1190). Look for the tombstones by Riemenschneider.

Few visitors leave Würzburg without making the drive up to the baroque hilltop church, the bulb-topped **Käppele,** Nikolausberg (tel. 0931/72670), standing majestically on a hill at the southwestern outskirts of the city. Often visited by pilgrims, this church was erected by Neumann in the mid-18th century. It has splendid interior stucco work by J. M. Feichtmayr, along with frescoes by Matthaus Gunther. Visitors come here not only to see the church but also to enjoy the view over Würzburg, the vine-covered hills, and, in the far distance, the Marienberg Fortress.

The most interesting excursion in the area is to **Veitschochheim,** Hafgarten 1 (tel. 0931/9-15-82), about 5 miles away. You can take a Main River excursion (about 30 minutes) to this summer retreat of the prince-bishops of the 17th and 18th centuries. The park with about 200 sculptures is a rococo jewel box. The Parnassus group, carved in the mid-18th century and standing in the center of the lake, depicts Apollo and the Muses. The park is open April to September, daily from 7am to dusk. The palace of the bishops can also be visited Tuesday to Sunday from 9am to noon and 1 to 5pm. The park is free, but to visit the palace it costs 3 DM ($2) for adults and 1.50 DM ($1) for children.

WHERE TO STAY

VERY EXPENSIVE

HOTEL MARITIM, Pleichertorstrasse 5, D-8700 Würzburg. Tel. 0931/ 30-53-0. Fax 0931/18-862. 293 rms, 5 suites. A/C MINIBAR TV TEL **Tram:** 1 or 5.

$ Rates (including buffet breakfast): 219 DM–339 DM ($144.50–$223.70) single; 280 DM–388 DM ($184.80–$256.10) double; from 550 DM ($363) suite. AE, DC, MC, V. **Parking:** 18 DM ($11.90) in 300-car underground garage.

The leading choice in the city is the Maritim, a riverside hotel built with views over the Main in 1984 and linked to the city convention center. Modern and imposingly proportioned, its yellow facade is topped by a baroque-style mansard roof. The guest rooms are well upholstered.

Dining/Entertainment: A comfortable Weinstube and a café are on the premises, but the establishment's gourmet haven is the Palais Restaurant. Shining crystal and carefully crafted paneling, with an amber glow from the lamps, combine to create the most elegant restaurant in town. Lunch is daily from noon to 2:30pm and dinner from 6:30 to 11pm. Both fixed-price and à la carte meals begin at 75 DM ($49.50). The Continental menu changes frequently, but typical dishes include rabbit filet with figs, marinated salmon with coriander, and breast of goose in orange-and-mustard sauce. Perhaps finish with a mango dessert. Reservations are necessary. The hotel also has a large terrace and bar.

Services: Room service, dry cleaning, laundry.

Facilities: Sauna, solarium, indoor pool.

EXPENSIVE

AMBERGER, Ludwigstrasse 17, D-8700 Würzburg. Tel. 0931/5-01-79. Fax 0931/54-136. 71 rms. TV TEL **Tram:** 1 or 5.

$ Rates (including breakfast): 145 DM–160 DM ($95.70–$105.60) single; 210 DM–330 DM ($138.60–$217.80) double. AE, DC, MC, V. **Parking:** 12 DM ($7.90). **Closed:** Dec 24–Jan 6.

Named after the family that owns and runs it, the Amberger is close to the center of town, near the Berlinger Ring. The exterior color scheme is cream and coffee, and the comfortable public rooms have high ceilings and wood moldings. The upper-floor guest rooms have been modernized.

HOTEL REBSTOCK, Neubaustrasse 7, D-8700 Würzburg. Tel. 0931/30-93-0, or toll free in the U.S. 800/528-1234. Fax 0931/30-93-100. 81 rms, 2 suites. MINIBAR TV TEL **Tram:** 1, 3, or 5.

$ Rates (including buffet breakfast): 167 DM–234 DM ($110.20–$154.40) single; 270 DM–339 DM ($178.20–$223.70) double; from 475 DM ($313.50) suite. AE, DC, MC, V. **Parking:** 18 DM ($11.90).

Unique and impressive, the Rebstock is housed in a palace. Through a classical doorway, you enter a wide foyer with carved wooden doors and an old Spanish sea chest. A red carpet leads to the reception area. The interior is tastefully decorated; contemporary furnishings have been coordinated with the old.

The guest rooms are equipped with wall-to-wall draperies and matching sofas.

Hairdryers and baths come with each unit, and 30 rooms are air-conditioned. An architectural feature of the hotel is a winter garden with a fountain, chimney, and bar, replacing an old courtyard.

Dining/Entertainment: The main parquet-floor restaurant has been redecorated, with the hand-painted wooden ceiling indirectly lighted. Gourmet cuisine is served. The Fränkische Weinstube comes with oak beams, stark-white walls, and a gilded baroque painting along with a carved madonna. Here, guests gather for local wine.

Services: Room service, laundry, dry cleaning.
Facilities: Car-rental facilities.

WALFISCH, Am Pleidenturm 5, D-8700 Würzburg. Tel. 0931/5-00-55.
Fax 0931/516-90. 41 rms. MINIBAR TV TEL **Tram:** 1, 3, or 5.
$ Rates (including breakfast): 160 DM–190 DM ($105.60–$125.40) single; 210 DM–280 DM ($138.60–$184.80) double. AE, DC, MC, V. **Parking:** 10 DM ($6.60).

The logo of this appealing hotel is a smiling whale with a laughing cherub on its back. The cherub is holding a bunch of grapes, an appropriate reminder that the Weinstube here serves a good selection of wine and generous portions of traditional Germanic food in its timbered modern dining room. From the windows of the modernized guest rooms you can gaze across the Main as far as Marienberg Castle high on the opposite hill. Most of the units are air-conditioned.

MODERATE

HOTEL ALTER KRANEN, Kärrnergasse 11, D-8700 Würzburg. Tel. 0931/5-00-39. Fax 0931/50-010. 17 rms. TV TEL **Tram:** 1 or 5.
$ Rates: 100 DM–130 DM ($66–$85.80) single; 130 DM–140 DM ($85.80–$92.40) double. Continental breakfast 14 DM ($9.20) extra. AE, DC, MC, V. **Parking:** 10 DM ($6.60).
The Alter Kranen occupies one of a long row of five-story houses on the quay next to the Main. Its yellow facade is highlighted with country-style stencils. Inside you'll find a warm, contemporary environment with thick upholstery and gleaming exposed wood. The hotel has well-maintained rooms, furnished in functional modern style.

FRANZISKANER, Franziskanerplatz 2, D-8700 Würzburg. Tel. 0931/1-50-01. Fax 0931/57-743. 47 rms. TEL **Tram:** 1 or 5.
$ Rates (including continental breakfast): 70 DM–110 DM ($46.20–$72.60) single; 140 DM–190 DM ($92.40–$125.40) double. AE, DC, MC, V. **Closed:** Dec 23–Jan 6.
Sleek and internationally modern, the Franziskaner has an illuminated sign in blue neon identifying the sidewalk parapet leading to the door of your waiting car. However, even if you're on foot, you'll still receive a hearty welcome from the staff. The lobby has attractive black panels surrounded with natural wood, while the breakfast room has fine large windows looking out to the greenery beyond. The guest rooms are well furnished.

GASTHOF GREIFENSTEIN, Hafnergasse 1, D-8700 Würzburg. Tel. 0931/5-16-65. Fax 0931/5-70-57. 42 rms. MINIBAR TV TEL **Tram:** 1, 3, or 5.
$ Rates (including continental breakfast): 98 DM–135 DM ($64.70–$89.10) single; 150 DM–205 DM ($99–$135.30) double. AE, DC, MC, V. **Parking:** 10 DM ($6.60).
Originally built 300 years ago, the Griefenstein was faithfully restored to its original design after partial destruction in 1945 and was enlarged with the construction of a modern wing in back. Easy to spot, with shutters and windowboxes alive with bright geraniums, it's a true tavern, abounding in village atmosphere, just off the Marienkapelle and its food market. The upper-floor rooms have a private entrance

and lots of calm and quiet thanks to their vistas over a pedestrian walkway in back. The economical restaurant offers hearty Teutonic cuisine.

ST. JOSEF, Semmelstrasse 28, D-8700 Würzburg. Tel. 0931/308-68-0. Fax 0931/308-68-60. 35 rms (all with bath or shower). MINIBAR TV TEL **Tram:** 1, 2, 3, or 5.

$ Rates (including buffet breakfast): 87 DM–95 DM ($57.40–$62.70) single; 140 DM–170 DM ($92.40–$112.20) double. **Parking:** 12 DM ($7.90). No credit cards. **Closed:** Aug 2–28 and Dec 22–Jan 7.

⑤ St. Josef has long been recognized as one of the best of the moderate accommodations in the Altstadt. Its owner has been successful in bringing it up-to-date. All rooms are pleasantly furnished and well maintained. Since breakfast is the only meal offered, you'll be directed to the many Weinstuben in the area, or you can pick a dining choice from the listing below. Fresh flowers add a personalized touch to this well-run establishment.

HOTEL UND WEINRESTAURANT SCHLOSS STEINBURG, Auf dem Steinberg, D-8700 Würzburg. Tel. 0931/9-30-61. Fax 0931/9-71-21. 53 rms, 2 suites. MINIBAR TV TEL **Directions:** 2 miles on Route 27, toward Fulda.

$ Rates (including continental breakfast): 120 DM–140 DM ($79.20–$92.40) single; 180 DM–210 DM ($118.80–$138.60) double; from 280 DM ($184.80) suite. AE, DC, MC, V. **Parking:** 10 DM ($6.60).

Amid a cluster of trees, this turreted castle and its outbuildings sprawl high on a hill overlooking Würzburg, about 2 miles away. From the sun terrace, guests appreciate the view of the Main River, the acres of vineyards surrounding the property, and the web of rail lines that carry cargo far into the distance. The foundations of this castle date from the 13th century, but what you see was largely rebuilt around 1900. The comfortable guest rooms have a country nostalgia. The hotel has an indoor pool and a sauna.

SCHÖNLEBER, Theaterstrasse 5, D-8700 Würzburg. Tel. 0931/1-20-68. Fax 0931/16-012. 34 rms (27 with bath or shower). TEL **Tram:** 1, 2, 3, or 5.

$ Rates (including continental breakfast): 65 DM ($42.90) single without bath, 100 DM ($66) single with bath; 110 DM ($72.60) double without bath, 140 DM–170 DM ($92.40–$112.20) double with bath. AE, DC, MC, V. **Parking:** 15 DM ($9.90).

⑤ You'll come across the salmon-colored facade of this family hotel in the central part of historic Würzburg. The ground floor is rented to boutiques that monopolize the two enormous arched windows facing the sidewalk. The upper floors offer smallish but comfortable rooms.

WÜRZBURGER HOF, Barbarossaplatz 2, D-8700 Würzburg. Tel. 0931/5-38-14. Fax 0931/58-324. 36 rms, 10 suites. TV TEL **Tram:** 1 or 2, 3, 5.

$ Rates (including continental breakfast): 95 DM–130 DM ($62.70–$85.80) single; 160 DM–230 DM ($105.60–$151.80) double; from 250 DM ($160) suite. AE, DC, MC, V. **Parking:** 10 DM ($6.60).

You'll recognize the Würzburger Hof by its gabled roofline that curves gracefully inward and its enormous ground-floor rounded windows. The reception area, with an elegant sitting room accented by wall paintings, statues, and fresh flowers, can only be surpassed by the newly renovated high-ceilinged guest rooms. Most rooms are decorated with garlands of fruit and flowers; three are air-conditioned. Your hosts are the Heinen family.

WHERE TO DINE

The town has many Weinstuben, where most of the nightlife occurs. Try a local specialty, Zwiebelkuchen, which is like a quiche Lorraine, and look for a fish specialty, Meefischle. White Franconian wine goes well with local sausage.

MODERATE

RATSKELLER WÜRZBURG, Langgasse 1. Tel. 0931/1-30-21.

Cuisine: FRANCONIAN/FRENCH. **Reservations:** Required. **Tram:** 1, 3, 4, or 5.

$ **Prices:** Appetizers 6.50 DM–19.50 DM ($4.30–$12.90); main courses 20 DM–32 DM ($13.20–$21.10); seven-course fixed-price menu 90 DM ($59.40). AE, DC, MC, V.

Open: Lunch daily 11:30am–2:30pm; dinner daily 5:30–11pm. **Closed:** Mid-Jan to first week in Feb.

The Ratskeller is not only an interesting place to visit but also serves tasty food at reasonable prices. Country cookery is an art here, as reflected by the boiled breast of beef with horseradish sauce and noodles. The English-speaking hosts will help you with menu selections, which feature game in season. They also specialize in local beer and Franconian white wines. The cellar is part of the Rathaus in the center of Würzburg, near the Alte Mainbrücke.

WEINHAUS ZUM STACHEL, Gressengasse 1. Tel. 0931/5-27-70.

Cuisine: FRANCONIAN. **Reservations:** Required. **Tram:** 1, 3, or 5.

$ **Prices:** Appetizers 6.20 DM–13.80 DM ($4.10–$9.10); main courses 19.80 DM–36.80 DM ($13.10–$24.30). MC.

Open: Dinner only, Mon–Sat 4pm–midnight. **Closed:** Aug 15–Sept 10; Jan 1–15.

⑤ While there are dozens of winehouses in Würzburg—many with integrity and character—none is as old as this one, constructed in 1413. The seats and walls have been burnished by the homespun clothing of the hundreds of drinkers and diners who have sated their appetites here for the past 500 years on the conservative cookery. The portions are copious. Try veal Cordon Bleu, peppersteak flavored with cognac, or rumpsteak with onions. Some dishes are so elaborate, such as chateaubriand, that they are prepared only for two. In summer, you can dine in a vine-draped outdoor courtyard.

WEIN-UND-FISCHHAUS SCHIFFBÄUERIN, Katzengasse 7. Tel. 0931/4-24-87.

Cuisine: SEAFOOD. **Reservations:** Recommended. **Tram:** 3 or 4.

$ **Prices:** Appetizers 7.50 DM–16.50 DM ($5–$10.90); main courses 20 DM–40 DM ($13.20–$26.40). No credit cards.

Open: Lunch Tues–Sun 11am–2:30pm; dinner Tues–Sat 5:30–9:30pm. **Closed:** Mid-July to mid-Aug.

One of the best dining spots in the region is this combined winehouse/fish restaurant, across the river in an old half-timbered building on a narrow street, about one minute from the old bridge. The house specializes in pike, carp, char, tench, trout, wels, and eel (blue grilled or frite). Most of these dishes are priced per 100 grams. Soup specialties are fish, snail, lobster, and french onion.

ZUR STADT MAINZ, Semmelstrasse 39, D-8700 Würzburg. Tel. 0931/5-31-55.

Cuisine: FRANCONIAN/INTERNATIONAL. **Reservations:** Recommended. **Tram:** 1 or 5.

$ **Prices:** Appetizers 5.80 DM–24 DM ($3.80–$15.80); main courses 14 DM–41.50 DM ($9.20–$27.40). AE, MC, V.

Open: Tues–Sat 7am–midnight; Sun 7am–3pm. **Closed:** Dec 20–Jan 20.

Since the facade of this 500-year-old guesthouse looks like an elaborately iced wedding cake, the owners probably decided that a sign wasn't necessary: All that identifies this establishment is a discreet "39" and a red-and-white heraldic shield over the street. Since 1430 local residents have come here to savor such delights as the legendary oxtail stew or roasted spareribs.

Zur Stadt Mainz offers some of the best bargain accommodations in Würzburg, with 15 newly renovated rooms with showers and toilets costing 120 DM ($79.20) for a single and 180 DM ($118.80) for a double. The price includes buffet breakfast.

INEXPENSIVE

BACKÖFELE, Ursulinergasse 2. Tel. 0931/5-90-59.
   Cuisine: FRANCONIAN. **Reservations:** Not necessary. **Tram:** 1 or 5.
$ **Prices:** Appetizers 7 DM–19 DM ($4.60–$12.50); main courses 16 DM–35 DM ($10.60–$23.10); seven-course fixed-price menu 98 DM ($64.70). No credit cards.
   Open: Lunch daily 11:30am–2pm; dinner daily 4:30–11:30pm.
There has been a tavern at this address for the past 500 years, and since it's a short walk from both the Residenz and the Rathaus, you'll probably include it for at least one of your meals in Würzburg. Even the locals don't really know whether to call it a beer hall, a wine cellar, or a restaurant. The family owners don't worry about the label: All that matters to them is that traditional food is served, and that it's well prepared, and that it's dished up in copious quantities. Try oxtail in burgundy sauce.

WEINSTUBEN JULIUSSPITAL, Juliuspromenade 19. Tel. 0931/5-40-80.
   Cuisine: FRANCONIAN. **Reservations:** Required. **Tram:** 1, 3, or 5.
$ **Prices:** Appetizers 4.50 DM–7.50 DM ($3–$5); main courses 11.50 DM–17.50 DM ($7.60–$11.60); fixed-price lunch 9.80 DM–18.50 DM ($6.50–$12.20). DC, MC, V.
   Open: Thurs–Tues 10am–midnight. **Closed:** July.
One of the best known of Würzburg's Franconian wine taverns, the Juliusspital is traditionally decorated with paneling and beamed ceiling and is distinguished by a wide range of regional dishes. The restaurant is a top address for wine connoisseurs— you can taste a whole range of characteristic Franconian vintages.

5. BAYREUTH

143 miles N of Munich; 40 miles E of Bamberg; 57 miles NE of Nürnberg

GETTING THERE   By Plane   Lufthansa offers three daily scheduled flights from the Frankfurt Airport to Bayreuth.

By Train   The Bayreuth Hauptbahnhof is on the main Nürnberg-Pregnitz-Bayreuth and the Bayreuth-Weiden rail lines, with good connections. Express trains arrive from Nürnberg every hour. For rail information and schedules, call 0921/19-419.

By Bus   Long-distance bus service to Berlin and Munich is provided by Bayern Express and P. Kühn Berlin GmbH. For information, call Deutsches Reisebüro at Bayreuth (tel. 0921/885-0). Local and regional buses in the area are run by OVF Omnibusverkehr Franken GmbH at Bayreuth (tel. 0921/13-712).

By Car   Access by car is via Autobahn A9 from the north and south.

ESSENTIALS   Contact **Tourist-Information,** Luitpoldplatz 9 (tel. 0921/8-85-88).

SPECIAL EVENTS   The town's claim to fame, of course, is that it is the site of the Richard Wagner Festival. If you arrive in this city during the late summer months, you may think the whole town has turned out to pay homage to the great opera composer, who built his opera house here, lived here, and was buried here following his death in Venice. Indeed, for five weeks each year, everything in Bayreuth centers around the festival.

Warning: During the five weeks of the festival—from mid-July until the end of August—hotelkeepers raise their rates quite a bit. Always firmly establish the rate before booking a room and make reservations far in advance.

Lying in a wide valley on the upper basin of the Roter Main River and located on a major trade route, Bayreuth was early given the protection of a fortified castle by the counts of Andechs-Meranien. The town became the property of the Hohenzollerns in medieval times and grew into one of the leading centers of this part of Germany. In 1810, it became part of Bavaria, and it is the capital of the district of Upper Franconia.

WHAT TO SEE & DO

FESTSPIELHAUS, Schulstrasse. Tel. 0921/2-02-21.

The operas of Wagner are dispensed like a musical eucharist from the Festspielhaus, at the northern edge of town. Pilgrims from all over the world gather here for performances. The theater, designed by the composer himself, is not a beautiful building, but it's an ideal Wagnerian facility, with a huge stage capable of swallowing up Valhalla, and excellent, beautifully balanced acoustics throughout the auditorium. Because of the design, the orchestra never overwhelms the singers. When the festival was opened here in 1876 with the epic *Ring* cycle, it was so well received that the annual tradition has been carried on for most of the 20th century. When the composer died in Venice, his wife, Cosima, daughter of Franz Liszt (who is buried in the cemetery in Bayreuth), took over. Later, Wagner's grandson Wolfgang produced the operas, with exciting staging and the best musicians and singers from all over the world.

Note: Tickets to the festival operas are extremely hard to obtain and usually must be booked as part of a package tour. Tickets cost from 35 DM to 255 DM ($23.10 to $168.30).

Tours: Guided tours (in German only, but with English leaflets available) are conducted only from Apr 1–Oct 31, Tues–Sat at 10, 10:45, and 11:30am and 1:30, 2:15, and 3pm, costing 2 DM ($1.30) adults, 1.50 DM ($1) children. Tours might not be possible during rehearsals and at festival time, and there are no tours in Nov. **Bus:** 2.

MARKGRÄFLICHES OPERNHAUS, Opernstrasse. Tel. 0921/65-313.

This is considered the only authentic as well as the finest baroque theater in Germany. It is still in its original condition. Behind its weathered wooden doors is a world of gilded canopies and columns, ornate sconces, and chandeliers. The house was built under the auspices of the Margravine Wilhelmine, who was known for her taste and her cultivation of the arts. The theater was formally opened in 1748 by her brother, Frederick the Great; up until that time, operas (notably those of Telemann) had been performed in the court theater.

Today the opera house, which seats only 520, is used for Bayreuth's "second" festival—the Franconian Weeks' Festival, usually held late in May. Concerts are also given during the summer.

Tours: Guided tours in German only conducted Tues–Sun for 2 DM ($1.30) adults, 1.50 DM ($1) children.

Open: Apr–Sept, Tues–Sun 9am–noon and 1:20–5pm; Oct–Mar, Tues–Sun 10am–noon and 1:30–3:30pm. **Bus:** 2.

NEUES SCHLOSS [New Palace], Domplatz 8. Tel. 0921/56-351.

The well-preserved Neues Schloss (New Palace), in the center of town, one block from the Markgräfliches Opernhaus, also shows the influence and enlightened taste of the talented and cultured Wilhelmine. Dating from the mid-18th century, when fire nearly destroyed the old palace, it was built in baroque style (with a definite French touch). The apartments of Wilhelmine and her husband, Margrave Friedrich, are decorated in a late rococo style, with period furnishings.

Tours: Guided tours (in German with English leaflets available) cost 2.50 DM ($1.70) adults, 1.50 DM ($1) children. Given Apr 1–Sept 30, daily 9–11:30am and 1:30–4:30pm. Oct–Mar 31, Tues–Sun 10–11:30am and 1:30–3pm. **Bus:** 2.

SCHLOSS ERMITAGE [Hermitage], Route 22, 3 miles northeast of Bayreuth toward Weiden. Tel. 0921/9-25-61.

The margraves of Bayreuth also had a pleasure palace outside the city, the Schloss Ermitage (Hermitage), reached via a road lined with chestnut trees planted in honor of Frederick the Great. This summer palace was built in 1718 as a retreat by Margrave Georg Wilhelm. The structure almost looks as if it had been hewn out of a rock, but the interior again felt the touch of Margravine Wilhelmine. Seek out the Japanese salon and the rococo music room. The castle is set in a park, full of formal as well as English-style gardens. In the gardens, which never close and can be entered at any time, you can see the New Palace of the Hermitage, built around 1750. Its columns are covered with polychrome pebbles in mosaic style, a unique structural element in German architecture. A part of the palace becomes a café in summer, and painting exhibitions are put on here.

Admission: 2 DM ($1.30) adults, 1.50 DM ($1) children.

Open: Apr–Sept, Tues–Sat 9–11:30am and 1–4:30pm; Oct–Mar, Tues–Sat 10–11:30am and 1–2:30pm. **Bus:** 22 runs every 20 minutes during the day.

RICHARD WAGNER MUSEUM [Wahnfried], Richard-Wagner-Strasse 48. Tel. 0921/25-404.

Wagner lived here starting in 1874, and the house remained in his family until as late as 1966. Only the front of the original Wahnfried—which means "supreme peace"—remains intact. Wagner's life comes alive, as music fans view a wide range of memorabilia, including manuscripts, pianos, furnishings, artifacts, even a death mask. If you walk to the end of the garden, fronting the rotunda, you'll see the graves of the composer and his wife, Cosima.

Admission: 3.50 DM ($2.30), 4.50 DM ($3) at festival time.

Open: Daily 9am–5pm. **Bus:** 2.

WHERE TO STAY

EXPENSIVE

BAYERISCHER HOF, Bahnhofstrasse 14, D-8580 Bayreuth. Tel. 0921/ 2-20-81. Fax 0921/22-085. 54 rms, 1 suite. MINIBAR TV TEL **Bus:** 1 or 7.

$ Rates (including continental breakfast): 110 DM–135 DM ($72.60–$89.10) single; 175 DM–250 DM ($115.50–$165) double; 650 DM ($429) suite. DC, MC, V. **Parking:** 9.50 DM ($6.30).

The leading Bayreuth hotel is the Bayerischer Hof, near the Hauptbahnhof, with a small garden. Since 1918, the hotel has been run by three generations of the Seuss family. All in all, the Hof is substantial, combining contemporary and traditional furnishings. Some guest rooms have French pieces; others are Nordic modern in design.

Dining/Entertainment: Guests have a choice of three areas for dining—each of a unique character—although the menu is the same (see the separate recommendation). Entertainment is sometimes provided in the Lounge Bar, open from 6pm to midnight.

Services: Room service, laundry.

Facilities: Indoor pool, sauna, solarium, fitness center.

HOTEL KÖNIGSHOF, Bahnhofstrasse 23, D-8580 Bayreuth. Tel. 0921/ 2-40-94. Fax 0921/12-264. 35 rms. TV TEL **Bus:** 1 or 7.
$ Rates (including buffet breakfast): 105 DM–220 DM ($69.30–$145.20) single; 180 DM–360 DM ($118.80–$237.60) double. AE, DC, MC, V. **Parking:** 12 DM ($7.90).

The stylish opulence of this hotel's gilded, paneled, and rococo interior hints at the kind of grandeur that might have appealed to Frederick the Great. Each of the guest rooms is individually decorated, sometimes with antique furniture and a scattering of fine carpets. Room service and laundry are available.

In the formal dining room, the Königsstuben, crystal chandeliers and gilt trim complement the well-prepared Franconian and continental meals and elaborate desserts. Meals cost from 38 DM to 70 DM ($25.10 to $46.20) depending on seasonal availability of ingredients. Reservations are suggested.

MODERATE

GOLDENER ANKER, Opernstrasse 6, D-8580 Bayreuth. Tel. 0921/6-50- 51. Fax 0921/65-500. 39 rms, 1 suite. TEL **Bus:** 2.
$ Rates (including continental breakfast): 95 DM–140 DM ($62.70–$92.40) single; 150 DM–180 DM ($99–$118.80) double; from 450 DM ($297) suite. MC. **Parking:** 10 DM ($6.60). **Closed:** Dec 20–Jan 10.

This is the unquestioned choice for opera enthusiasts. Next door to the Markgräfliche Opernhaus, it has hosted distinguished composers, singers, operatic stars, and conductors for more than 200 years. Framed photographs on the time-seasoned oak-paneled walls are museum treasures. The guestbook includes signatures of notables like Richard Strauss, Elisabeth Schwarzkopf, Arturo Toscanini, Thomas Mann, Fritz Kreisler, Bruno Walter, William Saroyan, Lauritz Melchior, and Patrice Chéreau. The inn is furnished with fine antiques and Oriental rugs. The guest rooms are individually designed.

HOTEL-GASTHOF SPIEGELMÜHLE, Kulmbacher Strasse 28, D-8580 Bayreuth. Tel. 0921/4-10-91. Fax 0921/47-320. 13 rms (all with bath or shower). TV TEL **Bus:** 1 or 7.
$ Rates (including continental breakfast): 82 DM–97 DM ($54.10–$64) single; 140 DM–150 DM ($92.40–$99) double. DC, MC, V. **Parking:** 8 DM ($5.30).

Its original namesake was built in 1555 as part of a working mill, although the stone walls and tile roof of this country-baroque building were completed about 1796. The high-ceilinged interior, which once was used to grind grain into flour, has been transformed and upgraded into a stylish hotel whose rooms are usually booked far in advance during festival season. There's a bar, plus a breakfast room and a Bierstube/Biergarten, serving traditional, flavorful food.

INEXPENSIVE

BRAUEREI-GASTHOF GOLDENER LÖWE, Kulmbacher Strasse 30, D-8580 Bayreuth. Tel. 0921/4-10-46. Fax 0921/47-777. 12 rms (all with shower). TEL **Bus:** 2.
$ Rates (including continental breakfast): 85 DM–95 DM ($56.10–$62.70) single; 120 DM ($79.20) double. AE, DC, MC, V. **Parking:** 12 DM ($7.90). **Closed:** Dec 24–Jan 10.

With its facade set off by windowboxes loaded with flame-red geraniums, this is an unpretentious, well-managed guesthouse containing pine-trimmed guest rooms and a series of dining rooms devoted to conservative and flavorful German food. The rooms have a Bavarian theme of checker-patterned down comforters and light-grained pinewood trim.

WHERE TO DINE

EXPENSIVE

CUVÉE, Markgrafenallee 15. Tel. 0921/2-34-22.
Cuisine: FRENCH/GERMAN. **Reservations:** Required. **Bus:** 1 or 7.
$ **Prices:** Appetizers 10 DM–22 DM ($6.60–$14.50); main courses 33 DM–43 DM ($21.80–$28.40); fixed-price menus 55 DM ($36.30) and 95 DM ($62.70). MC.
Open: Lunch Tues–Sun 12:30–2pm; dinner Tues–Sun 6pm–1am. **Closed:** Aug 29–Sept 15.

⭐ Owner Wolfgang Hauenstein operates the city's finest restaurant, serving a modern interpretation of regional and nouvelle cuisine. Try, if featured, home-marinated salmon with caviar and quail eggs, avocado mousse with fresh shrimp and salad with curly leaf lettuce, or one of the different dessert parfaits. In addition to a good selection of reds and whites, the wine list has 14 kinds of champagne.

SCHLOSS THIERGARTEN, Oberthiergartener Strasse 36, D-8580 Bayreuth. Tel. 0920/13-14.
Cuisine: CONTINENTAL. **Reservations:** Recommended. **Bus:** 11.
$ **Prices:** Appetizers 15 DM–18 DM ($9.90–$11.90); main courses 35 DM–48 DM ($23.10–$31.70); fixed-price menus 56 DM ($37) and 105 DM ($69.30). AE, DC, MC, V.
Open: Lunch Tues–Sun noon–2:30pm; dinner Tues–Sat 7–10:30pm. **Closed:** Mid-Feb to mid-Mar.

Three and a half miles south of Bayreuth, this building with its hexagonal baroque tower was built as a private hunting lodge. There are two dining rooms, the Kamin (meaning "fireplace") and the Venezianischersalon, whose Venetian chandelier is over 300 years old.

The food derives from the culinary traditions of France, Italy, and Germany and might include lobster risotto with basil, stuffed halibut with caviar sauce and kohlrabi noodles, and terrine of sweetbreads. There is an impressive wine list, and wines are stored in very old cellars with vaulted brick ceilings.

The establishment is also a cozy hotel with eight large rooms boasting all the modern accoutrements. Singles range from 130 DM to 140 DM ($85.80 to $92.40) and doubles from 220 DM to 300 DM ($145.20 to $198)—including breakfast.

MODERATE

HOTEL BAYERISCHER HOF, Bahnhofstrasse 14. Tel. 0921/2-20-81.
Cuisine: FRANCONIAN/INTERNATIONAL. **Reservations:** Recommended. **Bus:** 2 or 9.
$ **Prices:** Appetizers 6 DM–20 DM ($4–$13.20); main courses 22 DM–42 DM ($14.50–$27.70); seven-course fixed-price menu 120 DM ($79.20). DC, MC, V.
Open: Lunch Mon–Fri noon–2pm; dinner Mon–Sat 6–11pm.

Already recommended as a hotel, this establishment is the major place to eat in town, offering a selection of dining spots, with both Franconian and international cooking. The Hans Sachs Stube, an air-conditioned replica of an old inn, has walls covered with pictures of famous singers who have performed in Bayreuth. You can also dine at Spanische Stube or at "ins Max." Each room has a different decor, although the menu—seasonally adjusted—is the same in all three.

INEXPENSIVE

BRAUNBIERHAUS, Kanzleistrasse 15. Tel. 0921/6-96-77.
Cuisine: FRANCONIAN. **Reservations:** Not necessary. **Bus:** 3.

$ Prices: Appetizers 4.50 DM–6 DM ($3–$4); main courses 12 DM–20 DM ($7.90–$13.20). AE.

Open: Lunch Mon–Sat 11:30am–2pm; dinner Mon–Sat 5:30–10:30pm; Sun lunch 11:30am–2pm.

The oldest house in Bayreuth, Braunbierhaus was built in 1430 with foundations that date back to the 13th century. It offers inexpensive and down-to-earth food as well as a special kind of beer. The specialty of the kitchen is a Holzfallersteak, which means "wood cutter's steak," served with hash-brown potatoes and a fresh salad.

CHAPTER 14

BREMEN, LOWER SAXONY & NORTH HESSE

The area between Frankfurt and Hamburg is probably Germany's most neglected tourist area, yet it holds very pleasant surprises. Some of the best-preserved medieval timbered towns stand in the flatlands and rolling hills of Lower Saxony and North Hesse, as well as major spas. Extending from the Netherlands to eastern Germany, this area includes a wide variety in its landscape, from the busy port of Bremen to the isolation of the Lüneburg Heath. It contains one of Germany's best winter resort areas, the **Harz Mountains.** These mountains and the flatlands around the Weser River nearby gave rise to some of the most familiar legends and fairy tales in Western literature.

The Harz Mountains are also extolled for their beauty. As the last stronghold of paganism in Germany, this is still a land of legends and fanciful names. It is said that the last bear was killed in the Harz in 1705, the last lynx in 1817. The wolf has become extinct, but there are wildcats, badgers, deer, and foxes. The beech tree that grows in the Harz range has an unusual size and great beauty, and walnut trees abound. The region is also pocked by limestone caves. Much of the Middle Ages remains in old towns, spared from war damage, with their churches and castles.

SEEING BREMEN, SAXONY & NORTH HESSE

THE FAIRY-TALE ROAD ✪ This is the trail of Jakob and Wilhelm Grimm and the Germany made immortal in their fascinating early 19th-century collection of legends, myths, and fables. Today you can follow the Fairy-Tale Road, a 370-mile journey from Bremen, where the town musicians are memorialized, to Hanau near Frankfurt, where the Brothers Grimm were born. The route goes through some of the prettiest medieval villages in the country, listed on the German Tourist Office's maps of the road and its important sights. At some of the towns marionette shows (in German, but universal in appeal) are given in summer, and museums keep the legends alive, including the one in Ziegenhain in the Schwalm Valley, where costumes that might have been worn by Little Red Riding Hood and her grandmother can be seen.

The characters in the stories by the Brothers Grimm come to life along the road—Rapunzel, Snow White and the Seven Dwarfs, the Goose Girl, Sleeping Beauty, Rumpelstiltskin, and Hansel and Gretel. It was along here that they killed the goose that laid the golden eggs, the two cruel brothers were turned into two black stones, and the Pied Piper played his merry tune that was the lure of rats and children in Hameln. Regardless of plot, the moral was always the same: Good prevails over evil. For more information on the Fairy-Tale Road, contact the **German National Tourist Office,** 122 E. 42nd St., New York, NY 10168-0072 (tel. 212/661-7200).

WHAT'S SPECIAL ABOUT BREMEN, LOWER SAXONY & NORTH HESSE

Great Towns/Villages

☐ Bremen, second only to Hamburg among German ports.

☐ Hannover, ancient seat of the House of Hannover, capital of Lower Saxony.

☐ Celle, a well-preserved ancient town at the edge of a wide expanse of moorland.

☐ Goslar, an ancient Hanseatic town at the foot of the Harz Mountains.

Ace Attractions

☐ The Fairy-Tale Road, a 370-mile journey from Bremen in the footsteps of the story-telling Brothers Grimm.

☐ Lüneburg Heath, covering nearly 300 square miles, filled with beauty spots for the nature lover.

☐ Wilsede National Park, outside Lüneburg, a 100-square-mile sanctuary for plants and wildlife.

For the Kids

☐ Rattenfängerhaus (Ratcatcher's House), in Hameln, where frescoes illustrate the Pied Piper legend.

Religious Shrine

☐ Dom St. Petri, in Bremen, designed in 1043, crowning achievement of the port's Altstadt (Old Town).

Museums

☐ Lower Saxony State Museum, Hannover, one of Germany's most important regional museums.

☐ Bomann Museum, in Celle, another outstanding museum, including a 16th-century farmhouse.

Architectural Highlights

☐ Rathaus, in Lüneburg, a perfect example of blending Gothic and Renaissance styles.

☐ Rathaus, in Goslar, one of the oldest and most impressive town halls in Germany, from the 12th century.

SUGGESTED ITINERARY

Day 1   Start at Bremen, the beginning of the Fairy-Tale Road. After exploring this port city, spend the night there.

Day 2   Head east to Lüneburg and spend the day exploring Lüneburg Heath.

Day 3   Travel south to Celle and visit its palaces and museums, and walk its ancient streets.

Day 4   Go a short distance south to Hannover and enjoy the day seeing the city's attractions.

Day 5   Head southwest to Hameln, of Pied Piper fame, explore the town and lunch there. In the afternoon travel southeast to Goslar for the night.

GETTING THERE

Air passengers use Hannover as the gateway to the region, although Hamburg and Frankfurt are also possibilities. Each airport is within easy commuting distance by rail to all the major attractions along the Fairy-Tale Road. The centers previewed below all have excellent rail connections with the rest of Germany. Hannover and Bremen have the most rail links. Motorists find it easy to reach Hameln and Bremen by Autobahn.

Some cities, including Bremen, are served by long-distance buses. Touring the region by bus would be rather time-consuming, however, and might involve long waits.

---

1. BREMEN

74 miles SW of Hamburg; 76 miles NW of Hannover

GETTING THERE   By Plane   The nearest international airports are at Hannover (see below) and at Hamburg (see Chapter 15).

By Train   Bremen has excellent rail connections with leading German cities. Its Hauptbahnhof lies on major rail lines, including Hamburg-Bremen-Osnabrück-Münster and Hannover-Bremen-Bremerhaven. Thirty trains arrive daily from Hamburg (trip time: 55 minutes to 1 hour); 35 trains from Hannover (1 hour, 5 minutes); 13 trains from Berlin (5 hours), and 50 trains from Frankfurt (4 hours, 15 minutes). For rail information, phone 0421/19-419.

By Bus   Long-distance bus service to Berlin, Magdeburg, Celle, and Cuxhaven is provided by Deutsche Land und See Reisen GmbH at Berlin (tel. toll free 0130/6662). Local bus service to all parts of Bremen and nearby towns is offered by Verkehrsgemeinschaft Bremen/Niedersachsen at Bremen (tel. 0421/559-63-00).

By Car   Access by car is via Autobahn A1 east and west and A27 north and south.

ESSENTIALS   For tourist information, contact the **Verkehrsverein,** Tourist-Information am Bahnhofsplatz (tel. 0421/30-80-00).

When you arrive at "this ancient town by the gray river," you'll be instantly aware that Bremen is closely tied to the sea. The sights and smells of coffee, cacao, tropical fruit, lumber, and tobacco give this port city an international flavor. In the days of transatlantic ocean crossing, most travelers disembarked at Bremerhaven, Bremen's neighbor port 40 miles down the Weser River. Many visitors rush immediately off in all directions from the port, ignoring the treasure right under their noses—Bremen, second only to Hamburg among German ports.

Growing from a little fishing settlement on a sandy slope on the right bank of the river, Germany's oldest coastal city was already a significant port when it was made an episcopal see in 787. In the 11th century, under the progressive influence of Archbishop Adalbert, Bremen became known as the "Rome of the North." During the Middle Ages it was one of the strongest members of the Hanseatic League, and in 1646 it became a free imperial city. It remains one of Europe's most important port cities.

Today, Bremen is not just a city. Together with Bremerhaven, it comprises the smallest of Germany's federal *Lands,* or states. The population of Bremen city is about 550,000.

GETTING AROUND

A single ticket, good for one ride on Bremen's network of trams, costs 2.70 DM ($1.80). Most visitors, however, prefer to invest in a strip of four tram tickets that cost 20 DM ($13.20) for adults and 11 DM ($7.30) for children. If you prefer to travel by taxi, the meter begins at 3.60 DM ($2.40).

Sightseeing tours of Bremen, in both English and German, depart from the Hauptbahnhof. They cost 20 DM ($13.20) for adults and 10 DM ($6.60) for children. From the beginning of May until the end of October, they leave at 10:30am from Monday to Sunday. From November to April, they leave at 10:30am only on Sunday only. Tickets must be obtained at the tourist information kiosk, Verkehrsverein (tel. 0421/30-80-00), opposite the Hauptbahnhof.

You can also ask the tourist office about trips around the harbor, departing from the Martini Church jetty (a three-minute walk from the Marktplatz along

Bottcherstrasse), lasting one and a half hours. From the end of March until the end of October, they leave at 10 and 11:30am and at 1:30, 3:15, and 4:40pm. The cost is 11 DM ($7.30) for adults and 6 DM ($4) for children.

WHAT TO SEE & DO

The most practical way to see Bremen is on foot. If you don't like to explore on your own, guides are available for walking tours as well as for motorcoach tours (see the tourist office for complete details).

THE TOP ATTRACTIONS

The main sights center around the **Marktplatz,** the "parlor" of Bremen life for more than 1,000 years. The 30-foot statue of the city's protector, Roland, a military leader under Charlemagne, erected in 1404, still stands today. The knight bears a shield decorated with an imperial eagle and raises "the sword of justice." Local legend has it that as long as the statue of Roland stands in the Marketplace, Bremen will survive as a free city. During World War II, when this area was hard hit by Allied bombs, extensive measures were taken, with bomb-proof concrete and mountains of sandbags, to protect the statue.

Across the square from the Rathaus stands another example of a happy merger of Gothic and Renaissance architecture, the **Schütting,** a 16th-century guildhall used by the Chamber of Commerce. Somewhat in contrast to these ancient masterpieces is the **Haus der Bürgerschaft,** home of Bremen's Parliament, constructed in 1966. The structure was scaled down to fit in with its surroundings. Even though the architecture is a maze of glass, concrete, and steel, it does not look entirely out of place.

THE RATHAUS, Marktplatz. Tel. 0421/36-10.

The Rathaus has stood here for some 560 years and has seen several periods of transformation. The original Gothic foundations remain basically unchanged, but the upper section reflects the 17th-century Weser Renaissance style in the facade; the tall windows alternate with relief statues of Charlemagne and the electors of the Holy Roman Empire. The upper hall, part of the original structure, contains a beautifully carved oak staircase dating from the early 17th century and a mural (1537) depicting *The Judgment of Solomon* reminds us of the hall's original character as a council chamber and courtroom. In the lower hall are oak pillars and beams supporting the building, and below, the historic wine cellar, the "good Ratskeller of Bremen" (see "Where to Dine" below). At the west end is one of the most recent additions, a sculpture of Bremen's visitors from the land of Grimm—the Bremen Town Musicians. The donkey, dog, cat, and cock are stacked, pyramid style, in a constant pose for the ever-present cameras.

Tours: Inquire at the Tourist-Information at the Bahnhofsplatz (see above). When there is no session of city officials, tours generally begin May through October daily at 10:30am. In off-season, only a Sunday tour at 10:30am is offered. **Tram:** 1, 2, 3, or 5. **Bus:** 30, 31, or 34.

DOM ST. PETRI [St. Peter's Cathedral], Sandstrasse 10–12. Tel. 0421/36-50-40.

Set back from the square, St. Peter's towers majestically over all other buildings in the Altstadt. Originally designed in 1043 as the archbishop's church, it was rebuilt in the 13th, 16th, and 19th centuries. Dating from the early church, however, is the Romanesque east crypt, containing the tomb of Adalbert. Another crypt, from the same period, houses a bronze baptismal font, a fine example of 12th-century workmanship. There is a collection of mummies in the Bleikeller ("Lead Cellar"). These are mummified corpses of workers who fell from the roof during the construction. Their bodies were discovered in 1695.

You can also visit the **Dom Museum,** which is located in the church. It is open all year, charging an entrance fee of 2 DM ($1.30) for adults and 1 DM (66¢) for children. Its hours are the same as those of the cellar and tower in summer, but unlike the other two sights, it remains open in winter as well: Monday to Friday from 1 to 5pm, Saturday from 10am to noon, and Sunday from 2 to 5pm.

Admission: Free to cathedral; 1 DM (66¢) to climb tower.

Open: Cathedral, Mon–Fri 10am–5pm, Sat 10am–noon, Sun 2–5pm; cellar and tower, May–Oct, Mon–Fri 10am–5pm, Sat 10am–noon. **Closed:** Holidays; Nov–Apr. **Bus:** 30, 31, or 34.

MORE ATTRACTIONS

Böttcherstrasse, running from the Marktplatz to the Weser River, is a brick-paved reproduction of a medieval alley, complete with shops, restaurants, museum, and galleries. The brainchild of a wealthy Bremen merchant, Ludwig Roselius, the street was designed to present a picture of Bremen life, past and present. Dedicated in 1926 and rebuilt after World War II, the artery is one of Bremen's biggest attractions. Try to visit around noon, 3pm, or 6pm, when the Meissen bells strung between two gables set up a chorus of chimes for a full 15 minutes. Besides fine handcraft and pottery shops, the street contains buildings of historical significance. **Bus:** 30, 31, or 34.

The **Paula Modersohn-Becker House,** Böttcherstrasse 8 (tel. 0421/32-19-11), is dedicated to Bremen's outstanding contemporary painter and contains many of her best works, including several self-portraits and some still lifes. Next door, the **Roselius House,** at no. 6 (tel. 0421/32-19-11), is a 16th-century merchant's house containing Roselius's collection of medieval objets d'art and furniture. The two houses are open Monday to Thursday from 10am to 4pm, Saturday and Sunday from 11am to 4pm. Admission is 2.50 DM ($1.70) for adults and 1.50 DM ($1) for children. **Bus:** 30, 31, or 34.

The **Schnoor,** the old quarter of Bremen, has undergone restoration by the custodian of ancient monuments. The cottages of this east-end district, once homes of simple fishermen, have been rented to artists and artisans in an effort to revive many old arts and crafts. Sightseers visit not only for the atmosphere but for the unusual restaurants, shops, and art galleries.

The **Rampart Walk** is a green park where the ramparts protecting the Hanseatic city used to stand. The gardens divide the Altstadt from the newer extensions of the city. Extending along the canal (once Bremen's crown-shaped moat), the park is a peaceful promenade just a few short blocks from the Marktplatz. Its major attraction is an ancient windmill, still functioning.

WHERE TO STAY

VERY EXPENSIVE

PARK HOTEL BREMEN, Im Burgerpark, D-2800 Bremen. Tel. 0421/3-40-80, or toll free 800/223-5652 in the U.S. and Canada. Fax 0421/3408-602. 150 rms, 13 suites. MINIBAR TV TEL **Tram:** 5 or 6. **Bus:** 26.

$ Rates (including continental breakfast): 305 DM ($201.30) single; 435 DM ($287.10) double; from 570 DM ($376.20) suite. AE, DC, MC, V. **Parking:** Free outside, 15 DM ($9.90) in garage.

Without question the most outstanding and charming in Bremen, this hostelry is affiliated with the "Leading Hotels of the World" and the Steigenberger reservations network. It occupies an enviable site, a park whose meandering lakes, exotic trees, and zoo are the pride of the city. Despite the hundreds of century-old beeches, oaks, and lindens surrounding it, the hotel is just a short ride from the center of town. Designed in a stately but modernistic Hanseatic style, the Park sits behind a large symmetrical reflecting pool that has a stream of water arcing into the sky. Its terra-cotta dome and evenly proportioned side wings were rebuilt in 1955 to emulate a turn-of-the-century pleasure pavilion.

The hotel offers guest rooms stylishly decorated with soft pastel colors and large windows overlooking the park. Each contains a radio, color TV, and hairdryer.

Dining/Entertainment: An imposing series of dignified public rooms—many designed around oval floor plans—includes a bar and three restaurants, one of which occupies an elegant terrace overlooking the colonies of ducks and songbirds in or around the lake. The hotel's gourmet Park Restaurant is furnished Empire style, serving a continental cuisine. For guests in a hurry, there is the informal bistro, Buten un Binnen.

Services: Limousine service from airport or train station, room service, babysitting, laundry, dry cleaning.

Facilities: Terrace and garden; horseback riding arranged.

EXPENSIVE

HOTEL ZUR POST, Bahnhofsplatz 11, D-2800 Bremen. Tel. 0421/3-05-90, or toll free 800/528-1234 in the U.S. and Canada. Fax 0421/3059-591. 194 rms, 4 suites. MINIBAR TV TEL **Tram:** 1, 5, 6, or 10.

$ **Rates:** 175 DM–280 DM ($115.50–$184.80) single; 207 DM–365 DM ($136.60–$240.90) double; from 385 DM ($254.10) suite. Breakfast 20 DM ($13.20) extra. AE, DC, MC, V. **Parking:** 15 DM ($9.90).

A longtime favorite, the Zur Post offers top-notch facilities and comfort, as well as Bremen's leading restaurant, L'Orchidée. The present structure has had four ancestors, the first built in 1889. The latest renovation has created up-to-date accommodations. In addition to the L'Orchidée, the hotel has two restaurants, including Restaurant-Café Zur Post for fresh fish and Kachelstübchen for regional specialties or steak and salad. Laundry, dry cleaning, and room service are available, and the hotel also has a hairdresser and beauty salon. It's an ideal choice for train passengers, who can refresh themselves in the tropical fitness club.

MODERATE

BREMER HAUS, Löningstrasse 16, D-2800 Bremen. Tel. 0421/3-29-40. Fax 0421/329-44-11. 76 rms. TV TEL **Tram:** 1, 5, 6, or 10.

$ **Rates** (including continental breakfast): 120 DM–140 DM ($79.20–$92.40) single; 150 DM–180 DM ($99–$118.80) double. AE, DC, MC, V. **Parking:** 15 DM ($9.90).

This hotel is one of a long row of buildings a few blocks from the Hauptbahnhof—all painted white to accentuate the low relief of the arched and ornamented windows. The hotel is identified by a double staircase welcoming guests from the sidewalk. Once inside, those guests find modern public and guest rooms and a sun terrace overlooking a flowering garden.

HOTEL MERCURE COLUMBUS, Bahnhofsplatz 5–7, D-2800 Bremen. Tel. 0421/1-41-61. Fax 0421/153-69. 148 rms, 5 suites. MINIBAR TV TEL **Tram:** 1, 5, 6, or 10.

$ **Rates** (including continental breakfast): 140 DM–220 DM ($92.40–$145.20) single; 160 DM–230 DM ($105.60–$151.80) double; from 240 DM ($158.40) suite. AE, DC, MC, V. **Parking:** 12 DM ($7.90).

Behind a glistening white facade across from the ornate brickwork of Bremen's Hauptbahnhof, the Mercure Columbus offers attractive rooms furnished in tasteful tones. A sauna with a relaxing room and a solarium are part of the leisure facilities, and personal services include dry cleaning, laundry, and room service. The Hanseaten Bar is a popular rendezvous.

HOTEL MUNTE AM STADTWALD, Parkallee 299, D-2800 Bremen. Tel. 0421/22-020. Fax 0421/21-98-76. 120 rms. MINIBAR TV TEL **Bus:** 22 or 23.

$ **Rates** (including buffet breakfast): 156 DM ($103) ground-floor single, 210 DM ($138.60) upper-floor single; 180 DM ($118.80) ground-floor double, 260 DM ($171.60) upper-floor double. AE, DC, MC, V. **Parking:** 8 DM ($5.30).

You'll think you're in the country here, because this brick hotel fronts directly on one of Bremen's biggest parks, the Burgerpark. Inside you'll find a wood-ceilinged pool with a sauna and massage table, a sympathetic Weinstube (the Fox), a sunny dining room with a panoramic view of the woods, and guest rooms decorated in woodland colors.

RESIDENCE, Hohenlohestrasse 42, D-2800 Bremen. Tel. 0421/34-10-20. Fax 0421/34-23-22. 40 rms (24 with bath or shower). MINIBAR TV TEL **Tram:** 1, 5, 6, 10.
$ **Rates** (including buffet breakfast): 73 DM ($48.20) single without bath or shower, 115 DM ($75.90) single with bath or shower; 135 DM ($89.10) double without bath or shower, 155 DM ($102.30) double with bath or shower. AE, DC, MC, V. **Parking:** 6 DM ($4).

Advertised as a hotel with a Flemish ambience, the Residence has public rooms that are elegantly high-ceilinged, with polished crisscrossed timbers supporting the chandeliered ceiling of the main salon. You'll find both a sunny breakfast room and a Nordic sauna on the premises. The hotel rents simply furnished rooms. The hotel also has a solarium, plus 24-hour snack and drink service.

WHERE TO DINE

As a seaport, Bremen has developed its own style of cooking, concentrating much of its effort, naturally, on seafood from Scandinavia and the North Sea.

EXPENSIVE

DAS KLEINE LOKAL, Besselstrasse 40. Tel. 0421/71929.
Cuisine: CONTINENTAL. **Reservations:** Required. **Bus:** 1, 5, 6, or 10.
$ **Prices:** Appetizers 6 DM–21 DM ($4–$13.90); main courses 35 DM–47 DM ($23.10–$31); fixed-price menus 55 DM–135 DM ($36.30–$89.10).
Open: Tues–Sun 6–11:30pm. AE, DC, MC, V.

Set in a cozy and comfortably cluttered environment deliberately verging on the kitsch, this intimate restaurant is laden with Teutonic nostalgia. Menu specialties include filet of turbot with chive sauce and spinach, roasted filet of goose with egg noodles, roast filet of beef in peppercorn-cream sauce, and seasonal salads studded with sautéed sweetbreads of veal.

DIE GANS IM SCHNOOR, Schnoor 3–4. Tel. 0421/32-12-18.
Cuisine: HANSEATIC/CONTINENTAL. **Reservations:** Required. **Bus:** 30, 31, or 34.
$ **Prices:** Appetizers 4 DM–35 DM ($2.60–$23.10); main courses 36 DM–45 DM ($23.80–$29.70). Fixed-price menus 80 DM–125 DM ($52.80–$82.50). AE, DC, MC, V.
Open: Dinner only, Mon–Sat 6–11pm (last order).

Located in one of the small-scale medieval houses for which Bremen's town center is known, this is considered one of the culinary stars of the historic district. The interior is laden with historical and/or antique paintings. The restaurant features sophisticated cuisine based partly on local traditions. Specialties include Scottish lamb with rosemary-and-thyme sauce, fisherman's platter with wild rice and three types of fish, and filets of Angus beef with a sauce of whisky, cream, and peppercorns. The dessert menu is particularly imaginative, featuring a pear parfait and an array of sweets made from seasonal berries.

GRASHOFF'S BISTRO & WEINBAR, Contrescarpe 80, Hillmann-Passage. Tel. 0421/1-47-40.
Cuisine: FRENCH. **Reservations:** Required. **Tram:** 1, 5, 6, or 10.
$ **Prices:** Appetizers 14 DM–35 DM ($9.20–$23.10); main courses 38 DM–45 DM ($25.10–$29.70). DC, V.
Open: Mon–Fri 10am–6:30pm, Sat 10am–2pm. Full meals served Mon–Fri noon–6pm, Sat noon–2pm.

Jürgen Schmidt is responsible for the good food prepared in this intimate spot. Many ingredients are imported every day from Paris. His favorite dishes include roast beef Italian style, fresh she-crab soup, gratinée of spinach with mushrooms, filet of turbot in champagne sauce, and goose à l'orange. The host's attention to the wine list is also conscientious, and the walls are covered with shelves containing practically every known variety of liquor and liqueur. You can sit at the bar, sampling "one of everything," or you can have the latest lunch or the earliest dinner in Bremen.

MEIEREI IM BURGERPARK, Im Burgerpark. Tel. 0421/340-86-19.
   Cuisine: CONTINENTAL. **Reservations:** Required. **Tram:** 6.
$ **Prices:** Appetizers 12 DM–26 DM ($7.90–$17.20); main courses 35 DM–49 DM ($23.10–$32.30); fixed-price menus 49 DM ($32.30) and 98 DM ($64.70). AE, DC, MC, V.
   Open: Lunch daily noon–2:30pm; dinner daily 6:30–10pm.

Set in the center of a city park, this lovely restaurant is managed by the previously recommended Park Hotel. Many Bremen residents combine a meal here with a promenade in the park. The restaurant occupies what was originally a local aristocrat's summer house. Sheathed in lacy gingerbread, it is ringed with ornate verandas and contains four dining rooms furnished in Hanseatic style. Typical items include fish consommé with scallops and saffron, fried breast of duck filled with herbs, sautéed squab with forest mushroom risotto, and medallions of monkfish with orange butter and basil sauce. Coffee and pastries are served every afternoon.

L'ORCHIDÉE, in the Hotel zur Post, Bahnhofsplatz 11. Tel. 0421/30-59-888.
   Cuisine: FRENCH/MODERN GERMAN. **Reservations:** Required. **Tram:** 1 or 5, 6, 10.
$ **Prices:** Appetizers 18 DM–32 DM ($11.90–$21.10); main courses 40 DM–55 DM ($26.40–$36.30); five-course fixed-price dinner 93 DM ($61.40); seven-course fixed-price dinner 119 DM ($78.50). AE, DC, MC, V.
   Open: Dinner daily 6:30–10pm. **Closed:** Jan 1–15; July.

⭐ On the sixth floor of this previously recommended hotel, L'Orchidée has an elegantly sophisticated gold, cream, and black decor to go with the candles, silverware, and fine porcelain. Try the terrine of zander and salmon, halibut with two paprika-based sauces, breast of pigeon in red wine, and a dessert specialty of fruitcake parfait with a sauce of red wine and orange. The wine list is extensive.

RATSKELLER, Am Markt. Tel. 0421/32-16-76.
   Cuisine: GERMAN/INTERNATIONAL. **Reservations:** Recommended. **Tram:** 1, 3, 5, 24, or 25.
$ **Prices:** Appetizers 9.50 DM–29 DM ($6.30–$19); main courses 34 DM–49 DM ($22.40–$32.30); fixed-price menus 66 DM ($43.60) and 89 DM ($58.70). AE, DC, MC, V.
   Open: Daily 11am–midnight.

⭐ In the 500-year-old Rathaus is one of Germany's most celebrated dining halls—and certainly one of the best. The wine list is outstanding, probably the longest list of German vintages in the world. Some of the decorative kegs have contained wine for nearly 200 years. It's traditional for friends to gather in the evening over a good bottle of Mosel or Rhine wine. (Beer is not served in the Ratskeller.) A high standard of German and international dishes is offered, along with select regional specialties.

MODERATE

ALTE GILDE, Ansgaritorstrasse 24. Tel. 0421/17-17-12.
   Cuisine: CONTINENTAL. **Reservations:** Recommended. **Tram:** 2 or 3. **Bus:** 6, 25, or 26.
$ **Prices:** Appetizers 8.50 DM–18.50 DM ($5.60–$12.20); main courses 16.50 DM–35 DM ($10.90–$23.10); fixed-price lunch 35 DM–45 DM ($23.10–$29.70). AE, DC, MC, V.
   Open: Mon–Sat 11am–11pm, Sun 11am–3pm.

The Alte Gilde is housed in one of the most ornately decorated houses in Bremen. In spite of the new buildings surrounding it, the 17th-century structure, with its gilt gargoyles and sea serpents, clings tenaciously to the past. The restaurant (entrance on

Hutfilterstrasse) is in the vaulted cellar. The chef prepares many fresh fish dishes, but you might try pork steak à la Kempinski, with poached eggs and béarnaise sauce.

LA VILLA, Goetheplatz 4. Tel. 0421/32-79-63.
   Cuisine: ITALIAN. **Reservations:** Required. **Tram:** 2 or 3.
$ Prices: Appetizers 12 DM–18 DM ($7.90–$11.90); main courses 25 DM–35 DM ($16.50–$23.10). No credit cards.
   Open: Lunch Mon–Sat noon–2:30pm; dinner Mon–Fri 6pm–midnight.

⑤ An attractively contemporary restaurant whose specialty is hearty Italian food, La Villa boasts a flower-dotted garden terrace, ideal for conjuring up images of Italy in springtime. You can order any of the typical dishes, including pasta, veal, and fish. Interesting dishes include ragoût of snails and paper-thin carpaccio with forest-fresh mushrooms.

---

2. HANNOVER

76 miles SE of Bremen; 94 miles S of Hamburg; 179 miles W of Berlin

GETTING THERE   By Plane   Hannover is served by Hannover-Langenhagen International Airport (tel. 0511/73-051), 6 miles north of the city center. Service is served by many international airlines, including Air Canada, Air France, Alitalia, British Airways, KLM, and SAS, with flights to many destinations. Lufthansa also has flights to the leading cities of Germany. Flying time between Hannover and Munich is 1 hour, 10 minutes, and flying time between Frankfurt and Hannover is 50 minutes. For flight information, call 0511/730-52-23. During the day a 20-minute bus shuttle service runs between the airport and the city, depositing passengers at the Hauptbahnhof.

By Train   Hannover lies at the junction of an important network of rail lines linking Scandinavia to Italy and Paris to Moscow. Some 500 trains per day pass through Hannover, with frequent connections not only to major German cities but to leading cities of Europe. Nineteen trains arrive daily from Berlin (trip time: 3 hours, 50 minutes); 40 trains from Frankfurt (2 hours, 21 minutes, or 3 hours, 50 minutes, depending on the train); 40 trains from Hamburg (1 hour, 11 minutes, to 1½ hours). For rail information, call 0511/1281 or 0511/19-419.

By Bus   Long-distance bus service to major German cities is offered by Deutsche Touring Büro Hannover, at the Hauptbahnhof (tel. 0511/329-32-94-19 for information and schedules). Service to Berlin is provided by Bayern Express P. Kühn in Berlin (tel. toll free 0130/7022).

By Car   Access is via Autobahn A1 north or south and from A2 east and west.

ESSENTIALS   Information   Contact **Hannover Information,** located at Ernst-August-Platz 2 (tel. 0511/30-14-22). The local public transport system includes commuter trains of the German Federal Railroad, an extensive underground network, city trams, and bus routes operated by several companies. Very frequent service is provided to all parts of the city and regional towns around Hannover. Information and schedules are available from Regionalverkehr Hannover GmbH in Hannover (tel. 0511/99-00-130).

Orientation   If you arrive by train, you'll debark near the historic core of Hannover. The Hauptbahnhof is right at the heartbeat Ernst-August-Platz, a center of life in the city. From here, you can walk down the pedestrians-only Bahnhofstrasse, one of the most modern and sophisticated shopping malls in Germany, built on two levels. At the end of the street is the Kröpcke, which has been called "the living room" of Hannover. Running in both directions from this square, Georgstrasse leads to the Staatstheater (actually on the Rathenauplatz) along with many popular cafés and restaurants.

Bahnhofstrasse becomes Karmarschstrasse, which leads to a major artery,

Friedrichswall, which heads west to a big square, Friedenrikenplatz. The Altes Rathaus is north of the street, and the more modern Rathaus is south of the street. The new city hall opens onto Maschpark with its lake and museums. The major attraction of Hannover, the Herrenhauser Garten (see below), is in the northwest part of the city.

Every student of English history is aware of the role that the House of Hannover (or Hanover) played in the history of Great Britain. For more than 100 years, until Victoria split the alliance, Britain and Hannover were ruled simultaneously by German monarchs, some of whom preferred to live in their native state (much of the annoyance of the British).

The city of Hannover today has lost much of its political influence, although it is the capital of the province of Lower Saxony. It has instead become one of Germany's hubs of industry, transportation, and commerce. The annual industrial trade fair is a magnet. Held the last 10 days in April, the Hannover Fair has grown to be the largest trade fair in the world. Producers and buyers come from around the globe.

The Green Metropolis is a masterpiece of advanced planning, combining parks and tree-lined streets with bold and imaginative solutions to a large city's traffic problems.

Hannover was selected as the city for World Expo 2000.

WHAT TO SEE & DO

The **Market Church** (Marktkirche), on the Marktplatz, is one of Hannover's oldest structures, built in the mid-14th century. Its Gothic brick basilica houses several religious works, including a 15th-century carved altarpiece and a bronze baptismal font. The **Altes Rathaus,** facing the square, is from 1425. Badly damaged during the war, it has been restored and houses a museum and the civic archives.

HERRENHAUSER GARTEN (Royal Gardens of Herrenhausen), Herrenhauser Strasse 4. Tel. 0511/30-14-22.

★ No matter where you go in Hannover, you will not be far from a park or garden. But if you have time to explore only one of these, it might be the Herrenhauser Garten, the only surviving example of Dutch/Low German early baroque-style gardening. Designers from France, the Netherlands, England, and Italy, as well as Germany, worked together to create this masterpiece of living art. The **Grosse Garten,** from 1666, is the largest, consisting of a rectangle surrounded by a moat. Within the maze of walks and trees are examples of French baroque, rococo, and Low German rose and flower gardens. The Grosse Garten also contains the highest fountain in Europe, shooting jets of water 270 feet into the air, and the world's only existing baroque hedge-theater (1692), where plays by Shakespeare, Molière, and Brecht are still performed today, along with ballets and jazz concerts. The smaller 17th-century **Berggarten,** across the Herrenhauser Strasse from the Grosse Garten, is a botanical garden with houses containing rare orchids and other tropical flowers.

Admission: Adults 2 DM ($1.30); children free.

Open: May–Sept, daily 8am–8pm; off-season, daily 8am–4:30pm. Grosse Garten is illuminated May–Sept, daily after dusk. Ornamental fountains play May–Sept Mon–Fri 11am–12:30pm and 3–5:30pm, Sat–Sun and holidays 11am–1pm and 3–6pm. **U-Bahn:** 4 or 5 to Herrenhauser Garten.

RATHAUS, Am Maschpark. Tel. 0511/168-0.

The "new" Rathaus is a large structure built between 1901 and 1913 on 6,026 beech piles. The building is attractive because of its location in the Maschpark, reflected in a small lake, just a short distance from the extensive artificial Maschsee, frequented by Hannoverians for its beach, boating, and restaurants. It supports the only inclined elevator in Europe other than the one at the Eiffel Tower, which takes visitors up to the 330-foot-high dome. In the dome hall, four different models depict Hannover's history from 1689 to today.

Admission: Elevator ride to dome, 3 DM ($2) adults, 2 DM ($1.30) children.
Open: Rathaus, Mon–Fri 10am–5pm. Elevator runs Mar 20–Oct 31, Mon–Fri hourly 10am–1pm and 1:30–5pm. **U-Bahn:** Markthalle. **Tram:** 10 or 18B.

NIEDERSACHSISCHES LANDESMUSEUM [Lower Saxony State Museum], Am Maschpark 5. Tel. 0511/88-30-51.

One of the most important regional museums in Germany, the Landesmuseum is housed in a neo-Renaissance building near the Maschpark. There is a natural history section, and a prehistoric collection that displays objects that date back 200,000 years, including a rich assortment of bronze vessels, stone utensils, jewelry, coins, and earthenware.

The museum's art gallery contains treasures spanning seven centuries. Outstanding is Meister Bertram von Minden's *Passion Altar* (1390–1400) and other medieval works. You'll see paintings by Rembrandt, Van Dyck, Rubens (his *Madonna*), and the *Four Times of Day* series by Caspar David Friedrich. There are many German and Italian primitives, 17th-century Dutch paintings, and a 19th-century German impressionist collection.

An aquarium was added in 1984, showing a world of exotic fish, amphibians, and reptiles.
Admission: Free.
Open: Tues–Wed and Fri–Sun 10am–5pm, Thurs 10am–7pm. **Tram:** 10 or 18B.

WHERE TO STAY

VERY EXPENSIVE

HOTEL AM LEINESCHLOSS, Am Markte 12, D-3000 Hannover. Tel. 0511/32-71-45. Fax 0511/32-55-02. 81 rms. MINIBAR TV TEL **Tram:** 2 or 8.

$ **Rates** (including continental breakfast): 190 DM–310 DM ($125.40–$204.60) single; 260 DM–380 DM ($171.60–$250.80) double. AE, DC, MC, V. **Parking:** 15 DM ($9.90).

Across from the Rathaus is this surprise discovery: It's the preferred hotel for those who want to be in the heart of the old section, yet it's quiet despite its central location. The generously sized rooms, with their bright colors, are housed in an advanced-design structure. Most units have sitting areas big enough for a leisurely breakfast. The good comfort and individual service may make you want to prolong your stay. The higher tariffs are charged during special exhibitions.

CONGRESS HOTEL AM STADTPARK, Clausewitzstrasse 6, D-3000 Hannover. Tel. 0511/2-80-50. Fax 0511/81-46-52. 252 rms, 4 suites. MINIBAR TV TEL **Tram:** 16.

$ **Rates** (including buffet breakfast): 172 DM–351 DM ($113.50–$231.70) single; 305 DM–455 DM ($201.30–$300.30) double; from 650 DM ($429) suite. AE, DC, MC, V. **Parking:** 15 DM ($9.90).

Near the Hauptbahnhof, this completely modern hotel is made up of three wings arranged at equal distances around a central core that rises high into the Hannoverian skies. Rooms are furnished in a contemporary style.

Dining/Entertainment: The Bristol Grill is one of the best places to eat in Hannover, charging 46 DM to 85 DM ($30.40 to $56.10).

Services: Room service, laundry, dry cleaning.

Facilities: Hairdresser, indoor pool, sauna, massage facilities, bicycle-rental center.

KASTENS HOTEL LUISENHOF, Luisenstrasse 2, D-3000 Hannover. Tel. 0511/30-440. Fax 0511/30-44-807. 160 rms, 5 suites. A/C MINIBAR TV TEL **Tram:** 16 to Stadthalle.

$ **Rates** (including buffet breakfast): 199 DM–375 DM ($131.30–$247.50) single; 248 DM–558 DM ($163.70–$368.30) double; from 900 DM ($594) suite. AE, DC, MC, V. **Parking:** 10 DM ($6.60).

★ Many frequent travelers to Hannover consider this the leading and most traditional hotel in town. Its stately glass-and-stone facade is just minutes from the Hauptbahnhof in the city center. Owned by descendants of Heinrich Kasten, who established it in 1856, the hotel has benefited from a series of modernizations that have enhanced comfort while maintaining conservative good taste. The carefully renovated rooms are stylishly furnished. The English-speaking staff welcomes overseas visitors.

Dining/Entertainment: The lobby-level grill room serves food that is superlative by any standard; a few steps away, a cozy modern pub offers drinks and salads.
Services: Room service, laundry, dry cleaning.
Facilities: Facilities for disabled.

MARITIM HOTEL, Hildesheimerstrasse 34–40, D-3000 Hannover. Tel. 0511/1-65-31. Fax 0511/98-05-105. 291 rms, 6 suites. A/C MINIBAR TV TEL **U-Bahn:** Line 8. **Tram:** 2 or 8.
$ **Rates** (including buffet breakfast): 239 DM–419 DM ($157.70–$276.50) single; 288DM–588 DM ($190.10–$388.10) double; from 690 DM ($455.40) suite. AE, DC, MC, V. **Parking:** 15 DM ($9.90).

One of Hannover's best hotels was built a mile from city center in 1984. An oasis of greenery separates the awnings of the front portico from the street. Many of the well-furnished, up-to-date rooms have narrow private terraces.

Dining/Entertainment: On the premises is a plant-filled restaurant, Le Cordon Rouge, serving a superb cuisine and staffed by a polite, uniformed crew of well-trained personnel. The cuisine is both regional and international, with meals costing from 40 DM to 80 DM ($26.40 to $52.80). The hotel also has a café and a bar.
Service: Laundry, babysitting, room service.
Facilities: Sauna, solarium, indoor pool, health facilities.

SCHWEIZERHOF HANNOVER, Hinüberstrasse 6, D-3000 Hannover. Tel. 0511/3-49-50. Fax 0511/34-95-123. 197 rms, 3 suites. MINIBAR TV TEL **Tram:** 16.
$ **Rates** (including buffet breakfast): 295 DM–480 DM ($194.70–$316.80) single; 395 DM–690 DM ($260.70–$455.40) double; from 950 DM ($627) suite. AE, DC, MC, V. **Parking:** 19.50 DM ($12.90).

★ Built in 1984, this hotel is one of the most imaginatively designed in Hannover. It sits on a quiet street in the central business district, behind a red-brick facade whose angular lines were inspired by medieval Hanseatic models. Any parallels to the past, however, are pleasingly updated by the use of illuminated Plexiglas columns, sweeping expanses of russet-colored marble, and color-coordinated accents of gleaming brass and light-grained wood. It serves an affluent and conservative clientele, often attracting visiting celebrities. Eighty-five of the elegantly furnished rooms are air-conditioned.

Dining/Entertainment: On the lobby level, Schu's Restaurant is one of the most stylish—and one of the best—in the city. It is open daily from noon to 2:30pm and 6pm to midnight. The kitchen prepares such classical and cuisine moderne specialties as lobster salad with green and white asparagus, monkfish medallions with thyme-flavored butter and stuffed zucchini, and calves' kidneys and sweetbreads in red-currant sauce. Fixed-price and à la carte meals range from 78 DM to 120 DM ($51.50 to $79.20). Reservations are important. The hotel also offers the Gourmet's Buffet, with meals beginning at 58 DM ($38.30), and the Zirbelstube, serving a regional cuisine, with meals costing from 35 DM ($23.10).
Services: Room service, laundry, dry cleaning. Airport pickup if arranged in advance.
Facilities: Terrace garden in summer.

EXPENSIVE

HOTEL AM FUNKTURM, Hallerstrasse 34, D-3000 Hannover. Tel. 0511/3-39-80. Fax 0511/339-81-11. 46 rms. TV TEL **Bus:** 20 or 39.

$ Rates (including continental breakfast): 108 DM–250 DM ($71.30–$165) single; 178 DM–310 DM ($117.50–$204.60) double. AE, DC, MC, V. **Parking:** 15 DM ($9.90).

In the city center is one of the best accommodations in Hannover. You should book well in advance. The well-furnished rooms, with private marble-floored baths, have antiques scattered throughout. An Italian restaurant on the premises, Milano, is under separate management.

HOTEL KÖNIGSHOF, Königstrasse 12, D-3000 Hannover. Tel. 0511/31-20-71. Fax 0511/31-20-79. 84 rms. TEL **Bus:** 20 or 39.
$ Rates (including continental breakfast): 188 DM–328 DM ($124.10–$216.50) single; 228 DM–480 DM ($150.50–$316.80) double. Children under 16 half price in parents' room. AE, DC, MC, V. **Parking:** 15 DM ($9.90).

Both the skylights and the modernized crenellations on this hotel's mansard roof make it look like an updated feudal fortress. The hotel was built in 1984 above a glass-and-steel shopping arcade in the town center. Each plushly carpeted room has a couch that converts to a bed. An Italian and Austrian-Heurigen restaurant, under separate management, is on the premises.

MODERATE

LOCCUMER HOF, Kurt-Schumacher-Strasse 16, D-3000 Hannover. Tel. 0511/1-26-40. Fax 0511/13-11-92. 75 rms. MINIBAR TV TEL **Tram:** 16.
$ Rates (including buffet breakfast): 140 DM–205 DM ($92.40–$135.30) single; 160 DM–240 DM ($105.60–$158.40) double. Higher rates during Hannover commercial fairs. AE, DC, MC, V. **Parking:** 10 DM ($6.60).

Ⓢ A short walk from the Hauptbahnhof is one of the best economy finds in the city. The rates are reasonable, considering the general comfort and amenities. The utilitarian rooms are small; the service and frills are minimal. The standard fare in the hotel's dining room is quite good. Meals cost from 42 DM ($27.70).

WHERE TO DINE
VERY EXPENSIVE

GEORGENHOF STERN'S RESTAURANT, Herrenhäuser Kirchweg 20, D-3000 Hannover. Tel. 0511/70-22-44. Fax 0511/70-85-59.
Cuisine: INTERNATIONAL. **Reservations:** Required. **Tram:** 4, 5, or 16.
$ Prices: Appetizers 22 DM–44 DM ($14.50–$29); main courses 48 DM–65 DM ($31.70–$42.90); fixed-price lunch 36 DM ($23.80) and 39.50 DM ($26.10); fixed-price dinner 107.50 DM ($71) and 160 DM ($105.60). AE, DC, MC, V.
Open: Lunch daily noon–3pm; dinner daily 6–11pm.

★ Located in a country inn within a private park near the Herrenhausen Gardens, this restaurant is the finest in Hannover. All selections are well worth the price. A selection of international dishes is featured, including Valencian paella. Seafood and fresh fish, prepared in the continental cuisine-moderne style, will tempt the diner, as will the game dishes. In summer, tables are set on the terrace, overlooking a garden and pond.

The 14-room hotel is the quietest, most secluded retreat in Hannover. Singles range from 150 DM to 240 DM ($99 to $158.40), and doubles cost 220 DM to 300 DM ($145.20 to $198). A continental breakfast is included. The accommodations are clean and pleasant, furnished with a mixture of antiques and some traditional handmade furniture. The Georgenhof is highly recommended for both food and lodging.

EXPENSIVE

ALTE MÜHLE, Hermann-Löns-Park 3, Hannover 71-Kleefled. Tel. 0511/55-94-80.

Cuisine: CONTINENTAL/GERMAN. **Reservations:** Required. **Tram:** 3. **Bus:** 3.

$ **Prices:** Appetizers 15 DM–30 DM ($9.90–$19.80); main courses 32 DM–60 DM ($21.10–$39.60). AE, DC, MC.

Open: Fri–Wed 10am–11pm. **Closed:** Jan 11–28; 3 weeks in July.

This half-timbered building on the outskirts of the city has gained many additions since its construction as a mill back in the 16th century. It sits today in a manicured park, like the clubhouse of an elegant country club. Wild game is a specialty in season, and regional specialties are prepared with flair and served beautifully.

CLICHY, Weissekreuzstrasse 31. Tel. 0511/31-24-47.

Cuisine: CONTINENTAL. **Reservations:** Required. **Tram:** 3 or 7.

$ **Prices:** Appetizers 18 DM–28 DM ($11.90–$18.50); main courses 42 DM–49 DM ($27.70–$32.30); fixed-price meals 55 DM ($36.30) and 125 DM ($82.50). AE.

Open: Lunch Sun–Fri noon–3pm; dinner Mon–Sat 6:30–9:30pm.

If you befriend a native of Hannover, he or she might divulge one of the city's better-kept secrets: the address of this elegantly decorated restaurant a few blocks northeast of the Hauptbahnhof. You'll see an appealing combination of art nouveau and art deco. The menu is a sophisticated cuisine moderne. Meals could include goose-liver pâté in port or fricassée of shellfish in champagne sauce, seawolf in Pernod sabayon, and Barbary goose in cognac.

HINDENBURG KLASSIK, Gneisenaustrasse 55. Tel. 0511/85-85-88.

Cuisine: ITALIAN. **Reservations:** Required. **Tram:** 5, 6, or 16.

$ **Prices:** Appetizers 12 DM–26 DM ($7.90–$17.20); main courses 35 DM–46 DM ($23.10–$30.40); five-course fixed-price menu 75 DM ($49.50). MC.

Open: Lunch Mon–Sat noon–3pm; dinner Mon–Sat 6pm–2am (kitchen closes at 11:30pm). **Closed:** 3 weeks sometime in summer; 2 weeks around Christmas.

The decor of this restaurant runs a fine line between classic and modern, with Oriental rugs and elegant white-upholstered chairs. The walls look like an extension of an art gallery. The owners call the menu modern Italian, meaning impeccably fresh ingredients (fish from all European seas is a specialty) served with unusual variations. Whoever created the dessert menu, I suspect, must have foraged through the tropics to discover the unusual fruits that the chef uses so lavishly. There's a good choice of wine from the best Italian vineyards.

WICHMANN, Hildesheimerstrasse 230, at Hannover 81-Dohren. Tel. 0511/83-16-71.

Cuisine: GERMAN. **Reservations:** Required. **Tram:** 1 or 8.

$ **Prices:** Appetizers 12.50 DM–36 DM ($8.30–$23.80); main courses 35 DM–49 DM ($23.10–$32.30); three-course fixed-price lunch 42 DM ($27.70); four-course fixed-price dinner 100 DM ($66); seven-course fixed-price dinner 130 DM ($85.80). MC, V.

Open: Lunch Tues–Sat noon–3pm; dinner Tues–Sat 6pm–midnight. **Closed:** Holidays.

On the eastern edge of Hannover you'll find this family-owned establishment, a white-walled, shuttered inn with slate walks and carefully tended flowerbeds. It's an oasis of comfort. Guests have a choice of five rooms in which to dine. Cooking is German gutbürgerlich—wholesome, hearty—one of the best samplings of such specialties as fish terrine, rack of lamb, homemade noodles, and an array of wine and cheese from all over Germany.

MODERATE

ALTDEUTSCHE BIERSTUBE, Lärchenstrasse 4. Tel. 0511/34-49-21.

Cuisine: GERMAN. **Reservations:** Required. **U-Bahn:** Lister Platz.

$ **Prices:** Appetizers 7 DM–20 DM ($4.60–$13.20); main courses 27 DM–35 DM ($17.80–$23.10); three-course fixed-price menu 46 DM ($30.40). AE, DC, V.

Open: Lunch Mon–Sat noon–2:30pm; dinner Mon–Sat 6–11pm. **Closed:** Holidays.

With a pleasant decor that has changed very little since its original construction around 1860, this old-fashioned Bierstube has remained stable and solid despite the monumental changes that have transformed the society around it. The unpretentious food is hearty, wholesome, and filling, with the regular fare augmented by seasonal specialties. Three favorites include pork knuckles with sauerkraut, filet of beef, and mixed grills.

MÖVENPICK CAFÉ KRÖPCKE-BARON DE LA MOUETTE, Georgstrasse 35. Tel. 0511/32-43-43.

Cuisine: SWISS. **Reservations:** Recommended. **Tram:** 1, 2, 3, 4, or 5. **Bus:** 21.

$ **Prices:** Appetizers 8 DM–16 DM ($5.30–$10.60); main courses 28 DM–40 DM ($18.50–$26.40). AE, DC, MC, V.

Open: Daily 8am–midnight.

Among the delectable Swiss specialties here, I recently enjoyed Zürcher Geschnetzeltes with Rösti (sliced veal in white-wine creme sauce with Swiss potatoes). Desserts are so elaborate that you'll think you're in Vienna. It's cheaper to dine in the café section.

RATSKELLER, Köbelinger Strasse 60. Tel. 0511/36-36-44.

Cuisine: GERMAN/CONTINENTAL. **Reservations:** Not necessary. **Tram:** 8 or 19.

$ **Prices:** Appetizers 8 DM–18 DM ($5.30–$11.90); main courses 22 DM–50 DM ($14.50–$33). AE, MC, V.

Open: Mon–Sat noon–midnight. **Closed:** July.

The Ratskeller, in the historic Altes Rathaus, as in most German cities, is one of the most popular dining spots for townspeople and visitors alike. Patrons dine in two rooms at tables set under vaulted brick arches. The lunches are among the best bargains in town. From noon to 3pm, a complete luncheon, including soup, main course, and dessert, begins at 34 DM ($22.40).

STEUERNDIEB, Steuerndieb 1. Tel. 0511/69-50-90.

Cuisine: LOCAL GERMAN. **Reservations:** Not necessary. **Tram:** 3 or 7.

$ **Prices:** Appetizers 9 DM–20 DM ($5.90–$13.20); main courses 22 DM–40 DM ($14.50–$26.40); three-course fixed-price menu 38 DM ($25.10); seven-course fixed-price menu 105 DM ($69.30). AE, DC, MC, V.

Open: Mon–Sat 11am–11pm, Sun 11am–6pm.

In 1329, a stone-sided tower was erected about a mile east of central Hannover to guard the lumber produced in Eilenreide forest. (Its name, *Steuerndieb,* translates from the archaic German as "Stop, thieves!") Around 1850, a rustic restaurant was built on the site of that tower, and it has been known ever since for hearty and flavorful food. Many of the specialties are cooked over an open fire, and the restaurant offers a locally inspired menu that, unlike those of many other restaurants, features game year round. Two popular dishes are venison with red cabbage, dumplings, and black-cherry sauce and rabbit with black-pepper sauce and red cabbage.

In 1992, the establishment was enlarged with a modern wing containing eight simple, white-walled guest rooms, each with a private bath, TV, telephone, and view overlooking the forest. Singles cost 90 DM ($59.40), and doubles are 180 DM ($118.80)—with continental breakfasts at 15 DM ($9.90) extra per person.

3. CELLE

28 miles NE of Hannover; 69 miles SE of Bremen; 73 miles S of Hamburg

GETTING THERE By Train Celle Hauptbahnhof is on the Hamburg-Hannover rail line, with frequent connections to major German cities. Forty trains arrive daily from Hannover (trip time: 20 to 30 minutes), and the same number pull in from Hamburg (1 hour, 10 minutes, to 1½ hours, depending on the train). For rail information and schedules, call 05141/19-419.

By Bus   Long-distance bus connections, such as from Hannover, are provided by EB 183, operated by Deutsche Touring GmbH. For information, call 0511/32-94-19 in Hannover. Bus service is also offered to Berlin, Bremerhaven, and Cuxhaven by Deutsche Land und See Reisen GmbH, operating out of Berlin (call toll free 0130/6662).

By Car   Access by car is via Autobahn A7 north and south or else Route 214.

ESSENTIALS   For tourist information, contact the **Verkehrsverein,** Markt 6 (tel. 05141/12-12). Local and regional bus service with frequent connections to all parts of Celle and to nearby towns is offered by RVH Regional Verkehr, Hannover (tel. 0511/99-00-130 for information and schedules).

The well-preserved town of Celle stands at the edge of a silent expanse of moorland, looking like something out of a picture book. Its ancient half-timbered houses were untouched by the war, and the legends carved on their beams seem to live on today. Most of the houses date from the 16th and 17th centuries—the oldest was built in 1526—but they are in such good condition that they could have been built in this century.

One of the landmarks of the town is the **Herzogschloss, Palace of the Dukes of Brunswick and Lüneburg** (tel. 05141/123-73), west of Altstadt, a square Renaissance castle with a tower at each corner. It is surrounded by a moat. The palace's bizarre 16th-century Renaissance chapel was designed by Martin de Vos, with galleries and elaborate ornamentation. The pride of the castle, and of the town, is its baroque theater, the oldest in Germany (1674), still in regular use today. The Ducal Palace is open for guided tours only, at 10 and 11am, noon, and 2, 3, and 4pm; closed Saturday afternoon. Admission is 2 DM ($1.30). **Bus:** 3, 5, or 10.

For a picture of life as lived from the 16th to the 20th century in Celle, visit the **Bomann Museum,** Schlossplatz 7 (tel. 05141/12-372), one of Germany's finest regional museums, with extensive exhibits illustrating the life in the country and in the town. Included is a complete 16th-century farmhouse, as well as rooms from old cottages, period costumes, and Hannoverian uniforms from 1803 to 1866. In the portrait gallery of Brunswick-Lüneburg dukes, you can see pictures of the electors, later kings of England and Hannover. From April to October, it is open daily from 10am to 5pm. From November to March, it is open Monday to Saturday from 10am to 5pm, Sunday and holidays from 10am to 1pm. Admission is 3 DM ($2) for adults and 1.50 DM ($1) for children. **Bus:** 3, 5, or 10.

WHERE TO STAY

EXPENSIVE

FÜRSTENHOF CELLE/RESTAURANT ENDTENFANG, Hannoversche-strasse 55, D-3100 Celle. Tel. 05141/20-10. Fax 05141/201-120. 75 rms, 3 suites. A/C MINIBAR TV TEL **Bus:** 3, 5, or 10.
$ Rates (including continental breakfast): 170 DM–240 DM ($112.20–$158.40) single; 200 DM–400 DM ($132–$264) double; from 480 DM ($316.80) suite. AE, DC, MC. **Parking:** 10 DM ($6.60).

Far superior to any other Celle accommodation, this hotel is quite sophisticated for such a provincial town. Standing at the edge of town, it is a small-scale 17th-century manor house flanked by timbered wings. The brick courtyard in front of the salmon-colored mansion is shaded by a towering chestnut tree. The interior has formal neoclassical paneling and a collection of antiques. A modern annex beyond the rear courtyard contrasts with the main building in its use of refreshing colors in the rooms and apartments. All the doubles have been refurbished.

Dining/Entertainment: Fürstenhof's restaurant, Endtenfang, formal yet warm, is considered one of the best in Lower Saxony. An elegant dining room decorated with painted tapestries, it is known for its "ducal duck," after an old recipe from the court of Celle. The barroom is in the ancient vaults of the mansion. Fine food and wine are the order of the day, with meals costing 82 DM to 115 DM ($54.10 to $75.90). The beer tavern Kutscherstube, built into the old coach house, is more formal, with old wooden tables and farm artifacts; here meals range from 44 DM to 70 DM ($29 to $46.20).

Services: Laundry, room service, babysitting.

Facilities: Tile pool, sauna, massage rooms, beauty parlor, shops.

MODERATE

HOTEL CELLER HOF, Stechbahn 11, D-3100 Celle. Tel. 05141/2-80-61.
Fax 05141/3-46-76. 60 rms. MINIBAR TV TEL **Bus:** 3, 5, or 10.
$ Rates (including continental breakfast): 99 DM–124 DM ($65.30–$81.80) single; 168 DM–176 DM ($110.90–$116.20) double. AE, DC, MC, V. **Parking:** 5 DM ($3.30). **Closed:** Jan.

Celler Hof is on the street where tournaments were once held. Considering the old-world 1890 architecture of the hotel and its neighboring timbered houses, the interior furnishings are incongruously modern, though quite pleasing. The Celler Hof's advertisement of *internationaler Komfort* holds true for all guest rooms.

HOTEL SCHIFFERKRUG, Speicherstrasse 9, D-3100 Celle. Tel. 05141/ 70-15. Fax 05141/6350. 10 rms. TV TEL **Bus:** 3, 5, or 10.
$ Rates (including buffet breakfast): 85 DM–100 DM ($56.10–$66) single; 120 DM–170 DM ($79.20–$112.20) double. MC, V.

The brick-and-timber walls of this comfortable hotel have witnessed more than three centuries of innkeeping tradition. The guest rooms have lace curtains and eiderdowns. There's a bar on the premises, along with a rustic Weinstube and a more formal restaurant with a conservative but tasty German menu.

WHERE TO DINE

MODERATE

HOTEL CELLER TOR, Cellerstrasse 13, D-3100 Celle-Gross Hehlen. Tel. 05141/5-10-11.
Cuisine: GERMAN. **Reservations:** Recommended. **Bus:** 11.
$ Prices: Appetizers 7 DM–20 DM ($4.60–$13.20); main courses 21.50 DM–42.50 DM ($14.20–$28.10); five-course fixed-price dinner 85 DM ($56.10). AE, DC, MC, V.
Open: Mon–Sat 6am–1am, Sun lunch noon–2:30pm.

The Celler Tor, about 2 miles outside town, has a gabled red-tile roof and banks of geraniums. You can get some good shrimp and rice dishes here. Chef Horst Niebuhr also knows how to prepare gutbürgerlich specialties, including wild game in season and ragoût of stag with mushrooms. Celler Tor has 60 of the most desirable guest rooms in the area, costing 139 DM to 195 DM ($91.70 to $128.70) for a single and 188 DM to 296 DM ($124.10 to $195.40) for a double—including continental breakfast. Seven suites are also rented, costing 450 DM ($297). A new section of the hotel contains a saltwater indoor pool, massage facilities, a sauna, a solarium, and a workout room.

HISTORISCHER RATSKELLER, Markt 14. Tel. 05141/2-90-99.
Cuisine: GERMAN. **Reservations:** Recommended. **Bus:** 3, 5, or 10.
$ Prices: Appetizers 8 DM–20 DM ($5.30–$13.20); main courses 26 DM–38 DM ($17.20–$25.10); three-course fixed-price lunch 42 DM ($27.70); five-course fixed-price dinner 70 DM ($46.20). AE, MC, V.
Open: Wed–Mon 10am–midnight. **Closed:** Jan 1–15.

Historischer Ratskeller is a plusher version of the typical Rathaus dining room, with cuisine superior to the usual Ratskeller fare. Attentive waiters are constantly passing by, carrying silver platters heaped with spicy, flavorful German dishes. Complete lunches, including soup and dessert, start at 42 DM ($27.70). At night, the à la carte menu is varied.

STADISCHE UNION CELLE, Thaerplatz 1. Tel. 05141/60-96.
    Cuisine: CONTINENTAL. **Reservations:** Recommended. **Bus:** 3, 5, or 10.
$ Prices: Appetizers 8 DM–22 DM ($5.30–$14.50); main courses 22 DM–60 DM ($14.50–$39.60); five-course fixed-price menu 70 DM ($46.20). AE, DC, MC.
    Open: Tues–Sun noon–11pm.

The view from the terrace of this attractive art nouveau restaurant encompasses the walls of the town castle. The cuisine is imaginatively contrived from fresh ingredients to create frequently changing seasonal specialties. Your meal might include terrine of trout, a three-fish platter of local grilled delicacies swimming in aromatic dill-flavored sauce, and a delectably tempting dessert.

---

4. LÜNEBURG & THE LÜNEBURG HEATH

77 miles NE of Hannover; 82 miles E of Bremen; 34 miles SE of Hamburg

GETTING THERE   **By Train**   Lüneburg Bahnhof lies on two major rail lines, the Hamburg-Hannover line and the Lüneburg-Lübeck-Kiel-Flensburg line, with frequent connections. For rail information and schedules, call 04131/19-419.

By Bus   Long-distance bus service to Berlin is provided by Deutsche Land und See Reisen GmbH at Berlin (tel. toll free 0130/6662 for information). Regional bus service to nearby towns is offered by Verkehrsbetrieb Ost-Hannover GmbH at Lüneburg (tel. 04131/51-003 for information and schedules).

By Car   Access is via Autobahn A7 north and south or Route 4 east from Hamburg.

ESSENTIALS   For tourist information, contact the **Verkehrsverein,** Rathaus, Marktplatz (tel. 04131/3-22-00).

Motorists driving south from Scandinavia through the Baltic port of Lübeck often find themselves on the Old Salt Road leading to the Hanseatic city of Lüneburg. The road was so named because it was the route over which heavy salt deposits of Lüneburg were transported to the Scandinavian countries during the Middle Ages. Most buildings of the Salt City are from its most prosperous period, the 15th and 16th centuries. Although the medieval brick buildings are the most prevalent, seven centuries of architecture are represented in this 1,000-year-old city. The rising gables of the once-patrician houses range from Gothic to Renaissance to baroque.

The **Rathaus,** Am Markt, reached along Auf der Meere, is a perfect example of several trends in architecture and design. You'll enter through a Gothic doorway into a Renaissance hall. The Great Council Room is its most outstanding feature, with sculptures and bas-reliefs by Albert von Soest (1566–84). From the painted beamed ceiling in the Fürstensaal hang chandeliers made of antlers. From May to October, guided tours are conducted at 10am, 11am, noon, 2pm, and 3pm from Tuesday to Friday; 10am, 11am, 2pm, and 3pm on Saturday and Sunday. In winter, there are tours also from Tuesday to Sunday. No tours are conducted on Monday. The cost is 5 DM ($3.30) for adults and 2.50 DM ($1.70) for children. For information, phone 04131/30-92-30. **Bus:** 3.

Because of its heavy salt deposits, Lüneburg remains a spa even today. In the **Kurpark** is a bathing house where visitors take brine mud baths. In the spa gardens there are also indoor swimming pools, sauna baths, and tennis courts.

Lüneburg is the ideal starting point for excursions into the ✪ **Lüneburg Heath** (Lüneburger Heide). The soil of the heath is sandy and is mainly covered with brush and heather, although there are a few oak and beech forests in the northern valleys. The heath covers nearly 300 square miles and includes many beauty spots for the outdoors person.

✪ **Wilsede National Park** is a 100-square-mile sanctuary for plants and wildlife, and for people as well: a peaceful, pastoral scene of shepherds, sheep, and undulating hills. Strict laws enforce the maintaining of the thatched-roof houses and rural atmosphere. The heath is beautiful in late summer and early autumn, when the heather turns shades of deep purple.

WHERE TO STAY
MODERATE

BREMER HOF, Lünestrasse 13, D-2120 Lüneburg. Tel. 04131/3-60-77. Fax 04131/3-83-04. 58 rms (54 with bath or shower). **Bus:** 3.
$ **Rates** (including buffet breakfast): 75 DM ($49.50) single without bath or shower, 160 DM ($105.60) single with bath or shower, 130 DM ($85.80) double without bath or shower, 196 DM ($129.40) double with bath or shower. AE, DC, MC, V. **Parking:** Free.

Ⓢ The logo of this hotel is an illustration of the animal musicians of Bremen, who, with their noise, frightened away the robbers. The facade looks like something out of the 16th century. You'll be only two minutes on foot from Marktplatz, and your room will be modern and sunny. All but four units have phones and TVs. The hotel also has its own restaurant, serving food typical of North Germany and specialties of the Lüneberger Heide region. There are also a bar and a 400-year-old wine cellar. Host Albert Brakel's family has owned this place since 1889.

RESIDENZ-RING HOTEL, Münstermannskamp 8, D-2120 Lüneburg. Tel. 04131/4-50-47. Fax 04131/40-16-37. 35 rms. MINIBAR TV TEL **Bus:** 1 or 6.
$ **Rates** (including buffet breakfast): 105 DM–155 DM ($69.30–$102.30) single; 180 DM–200 DM ($118.80–$132) double. AE, DC, MC, V. **Parking:** 10 DM ($6.60).
The buff-and-brown units of this tasteful hotel are so separated from one another that the place will remind you of an apartment building. Since the establishment is right inside the city's Kurpark, you'll get enough shade to pretend you're in a forest. Inside, you'll find an inviting bar and an up-to-date restaurant, serving both international and regional specialties. The guest rooms are elegant and comfortable.

WELLENKAMP'S HOTEL, Am Sande 9, D-2120 Lüneburg. Tel. 04131/4-30-26. Fax 04131/43-027. 45 rms. TV TEL **Bus:** 3.
$ **Rates** (including continental breakfast): 69 DM–108 DM ($45.50–$71.30) single; 125 DM–175 DM ($82.50–$115.50) double. AE, DC, MC, V.

Ⓢ A building so unusual could only have been designed for public use, and, in fact, this hotel used to be a post office. The reddish brick exterior is in a style that could be described as 19th-century neofortification. One of the public rooms is entirely furnished in vintage Biedermeier. The guest rooms are usually sunny and modern. Today the bins in the cellar that once held coal contain some of the finest wine in the region, attracting locals from far and wide. The restaurant also offers a delectable regional cuisine, with meals beginning at 46 DM ($30.40).

WHERE TO DINE
MODERATE

RATSKELLER, Am Markt 1. Tel. 04131/3-17-57.
Cuisine: GERMAN/CONTINENTAL. **Reservations:** Recommended. **Bus:** 3.
$ **Prices:** Appetizers 8 DM–19 DM ($5.30–$12.50); main courses 15 DM–35 DM ($9.90–$23.10); four-course fixed-price menu 70 DM ($46.20). AE, MC, V.
Open: Thurs–Tues 10am–midnight. **Closed:** Jan 1–15.

A good choice for lunch, dinner, or in between is the Ratskeller. Right on the market square, the dining hall offers a varied menu, including game and regional specialties served according to the season. You can always count on good homestyle cooking in a pleasant setting, backed up by a fine wine list. In addition to North German food, continental dishes are served.

5. HAMELN

28 miles SW of Hannover; 30 miles W of Hildesheim

GETTING THERE By Plane The nearest major airport is Hannover-Langenhagen, 34 miles away, which has good rail tie-ins with Hameln.

By Train Hameln Bahnhof lies on the Hannover-Hameln-Albeken rail line, with frequent connections. Depending on the train, trip time from Hannover ranges from 45 to 55 minutes. For rail information and schedules, call 05151/19-419.

By Bus Local and regional bus service to nearby towns and Hannover is available from RVH Regional Verkehr Hannover (tel. 05151/12-016 for information and schedules).

By Car It takes three hours to reach Hameln from Frankfurt and some six to seven hours to reach Hameln from Munich. From Frankfurt, head northeast along A5; then north on A7, and finally west on Route 1. From Munich take A9 north to Nürnberg, A3 west to Würzburg, then A7 north toward Hannover, and finally Route 1 west to Hameln.

ESSENTIALS For tourist information, contact the **Verkehrsverein,** Deisterallee (tel. 05151/20-26-17).

Halfway from Hannover to Bad Pyrmont or Detmold in Lower Saxony lies Hameln (Hamelin in English), best known for the folktale about the Pied Piper, that famous ratcatcher, immortalized by both Goethe and Robert Browning.

The legend is that in 1284 the town was infested by rats. There appeared a piper who, for a fee, offered to lure the vermin into the Weser River. The ratcatcher kept his bargain; the stingy denizens of Hameln did not, claiming that he was a sorcerer. He reappeared the next Sunday and played a tune that lured all the children, except one lame boy, into a mysterious door in a hill. The children and the Pied Piper were never heard from again. There is some historical basis for the story, inasmuch as there was a departure from Hameln by its children several centuries ago, for a reason no one is sure of today. The story is retold every summer Sunday at noon in a special performance at the **Hochzeitshaus** (Wedding House) on Osterstrasse. In the town shops, you can buy rats made of every conceivable material, even candy.

Hameln traces its history back to the 11th century. Among its most interesting buildings is the **Münster,** dedicated to St. Boniface and built in the Gothic style; overlooking the Weser River, it lies at the end of Backerstrasse. Other attractions include the **Rattenfängerhaus** (Ratcatcher's House), on Osterstrasse, with frescoes illustrating the Pied Piper legend; and the already mentioned Hochzeitshaus, with its trio of attractive gables. The finest houses in the town are built in what is known as the Weser Renaissance style, from the late 16th century. You can admire these nicely sculpted houses as you stroll along pedestrians-only streets.

WHERE TO STAY
EXPENSIVE

DORINT HOTEL HAMELN, 164er Ring 3, D-3250 Hameln. Tel. 05151/ 79-20. Fax 05151/79-21-91. 105 rms. TV TEL **Bus:** 1 or 2.
$ Rates (including continental breakfast): 170 DM–280 DM ($112.20–$184.80)

single; 260 DM–400 DM ($171.60–$264) double. AE, DC, MC, V. **Parking:** 10 DM ($6.60).

The comfortable Dorint Hotel Hameln stands in a park with lots of trees, but is within walking distance of the heart of the Altstadt, at the northern edge of the Burgergarten. It rises like a modern collection of building blocks, its oversize glass walls aimed toward the sunlight. Guests have access to a pool, sauna, solarium, and massage facilities. The hotel has an international restaurant, Brochette, plus a beer pub, Alt Hamelin.

KOMFORT-HOTEL GARNI CHRISTINENHOF, Alte Markstrasse 18, D-3250 Hameln. Tel. 05151/95-080. Fax 05151/43-611. 30 rms. MINIBAR TV TEL **Bus:** 1 or 2.

$ Rates (including buffet breakfast): 110 DM ($72.60) single; 198 DM ($130.70) double. AE, V. **Parking:** Free.

The gabled windows of this half-timbered building that's over 300 years old overlook a cobblestoned street in the middle of the Altstadt. Despite its antique facade, much of its interior is streamlined and modern, with many conveniences. There's a pool beneath the vaulted stone ceiling of the old cellar, plus a sauna, a solarium, and conference rooms. Each well-furnished guest room contains a cable color TV.

ZUR KRONE, Osterstrasse 30, D-3250 Hameln. Tel. 05151/74-11. Fax 05151/74-15. 34 rms, 5 suites. MINIBAR TV TEL **Bus:** 1 or 2.

$ Rates: 150 DM–240 DM ($99–$158.40) single; 180 DM–300 DM ($118.80–$198) double; 300 DM ($198) suite. Buffet breakfast 16 DM ($10.60) extra. AE, DC, MC, V. **Parking:** 10 DM ($6.60).

In the center of this historic town, a 10-minute walk from the Bahnhof, Zur Krone is an old house with antique furniture. The dining rooms are small but numerous. The guest rooms are pleasantly furnished and well cared for.

INEXPENSIVE

HOTEL ZUR BÖRSE, Osterstrasse 41A, D-3250 Hameln. Tel. 05151/70-80. Fax 05151/25-485. 34 rms. TV TEL **Bus:** 1 or 2.

$ Rates (including buffet breakfast): 64 DM–75 DM ($42.20–$49.50) single; 114 DM–130 DM ($75.20–$85.80) double. AE, DC, V. **Parking:** 6 DM ($4).

⑤ Within the walls of the Altstadt, this balconied hotel can be identified by the four peaks of the modern roofline. The interior is refreshingly uncluttered. The guest rooms are spacious and sunny. The hotel has an elevator and a restaurant serving international cuisine.

WHERE TO DINE
MODERATE

KLÜTTURM, Auf dem Klütberg. Tel. 05151/6-16-44.
    Cuisine: GERMAN. **Reservations:** Recommended. **Bus:** 1 or 2.
$ Prices: Appetizers 10 DM–19.50 DM ($6.60–$12.90); main courses 26 DM–45 DM ($17.20–$29.70). AE, MC, V.
    Open: Lunch Wed–Mon noon–2:30pm; dinner Wed–Mon 6–9pm. **Closed:** Jan 15–Feb 10.

Although lovely, the traditional decor here takes second place to the restaurant's panoramic view of the old city. Cooking is traditional, with special care lavished on the dessert wagon, whose confections change every day. In season, the cook will prepare game dishes, and throughout the year you'll find rack of baby lamb with fresh vegetables or entrecôte of beef with escargots.

RATTENFÄNGERHAUS, Osterstrasse 28. Tel. 05151/38-88.
    Cuisine: GERMAN/INTERNATIONAL. **Reservations:** Recommended. **Bus:** 1 or 2.
$ Prices: Appetizers 8 DM–20 DM ($5.30–$13.20); main courses 20 DM–36 DM ($13.20–$23.80). AE, DC, MC, V

Open: Lunch Wed–Mon 11am–2:30pm; dinner Wed–Mon 6–9pm.

Dating from 1603, the Rattenfängerhaus is the Renaissance building referred to earlier as the Ratcatcher's House. The outside is well preserved, and inside are small wood windows, antiques, and pictures. It's practically like eating in a museum. The house specialty is rumpsteak Madagascar with green pepper, potato croquettes, and green beans. Another specialty is Rattenschwanze Balireis with salad and a "mousecatcher" plate, a pork filet.

---

6. GOSLAR

56 miles SE of Hannover; 27 miles S of Braunschweig;
37 miles SE of Hildesheim

GETTING THERE   By Plane   The gateway to Goslar for those using public transport is usually Hannover, site of the nearest major airport. From Hannover, it takes one and a half hours to travel to Goslar by rail.

By Train   Goslar Bahnhof is on the Hannover–Hildesheim–Goslar–Bad Harzburg rail line, with frequent connections. For rail information, call 05321/19-419.

By Bus   Long-distance bus service to Berlin is provided by Bayern Express and P. Kühn (tel. toll free 0130/6662). Regional bus service to all parts of the city and nearby towns is provided by Regionalbus Braunschweig GmbH, Betriebsstelle, Goslar (tel. 05321/2811 for schedules and information).

By Car   Access is via Autobahn A7 north and south, exiting at either Seesen or Rüden.

ESSENTIALS   For tourist information, contact the **Kur- und Fremdenver-kehrsgesellschaft,** Markt 7 (tel. 05321/28-46).

In spite of Goslar's progress and growth, the old portion of the town looks just as it did hundreds of years ago. This ancient Hanseatic and imperial town at the foot of the Harz Mountains owed its early prosperity to the Harz silver mines, which were worked as early as 968. The 600-year-old streets are in use today and the carved, half-timbered houses are still used as homes or offices.

Incidentally, for hikers and other outdoor enthusiasts, Goslar is a suitable starting point for day trips and excursions into the Harz Mountains, where some of Germany's best skiing resorts of the highlands and several spas are found.

For the demonology expert, the Harz region is rich in tales of witchcraft and other folklore. Walpurgis Eve (Witches' Sabbath) is still celebrated in the hills each year on the night of April 30.

Bus tours into the Harz Mountains can be booked at the tourist office (see above). They are organized every Tuesday and Thursday from April to October starting at 2pm.

WHAT TO SEE & DO

To best explore this 1,000-year-old town, park your car, put on a pair of comfortable shoes, and set out on foot through the one-square-kilometer Altstadt. That way you won't miss any of the numerous attractions that await you, beginning with the **Rathaus** on the Marktplatz (tel. 05321/704-241), one of the oldest and most impressive town halls in Germany. Although the hall was begun in the 12th century, the main section was not constructed until 1450. This part of the structure consists of an open portico with Gothic crossvaulting, topped by the burghers' hall. The open arcade on the ground level was used for centuries as a market by the townspeople. The open gallery on the second floor was closed up with stained-glass windows in the 17th century. In the early 1500s the original assembly hall in the Rathaus was turned into a Hall of Homage and was lavishly decorated with a cycle of 55 paintings called

The Incarnation of God in Jesus Christ. The paintings, which cover the walls and ceilings of the room, include not only works depicting the life of Christ but those dealing with other biblical characters as well. Many of the faces are actually the portraits of townspeople of the period. It is open April to October, daily from 10am to 5pm; and November to March, daily from 10am to 4pm. Admission is 3.50 DM ($2.30) for adults and 2 DM ($1.30) for children. Buses A and B run into the city center.

The **Marktplatz,** in front of the Rathaus, was for a long time the town's hub of activity. In the center of the large square is a 13th-century fountain with two bronze basins and the German imperial eagle at the top. Townspeople and visitors alike gather in the square at 6pm each evening to hear the clock concert and to watch the parade, including the zinc miners returning home from the Rammelsberg mines.

The churches of Goslar provide a look into the architectural history of the area. Many of the oldest churches—five had already been built by 1200—have been expanded and altered from their original Romanesque style to their current Gothic appearance. The Romanesque **Marktkirche,** just behind the Rathaus, still has its 700-year-old stained-glass windows and a 16th-century bronze baptismal font. From the Marktplatz, take Rosentorstrasse northward to reach the **Jakobikirche,** which dates from the 11th century. It has been transformed into a Gothic masterpiece, complete with baroque altars. The church contains a *Pietà* by Hans Witten (1520). Farther down the street, the **Neuwerkkirche** has retained its purely Romanesque basilica, and its well-preserved sanctuary contains a richly decorated choir and stucco reliefs. Standing in a garden, it was originally constructed as a Cistercian convent in the late 1100s.

The **Frankenberg Kirche,** on Bergstrasse, is from the 12th century but was completely remodeled in the 1700s. Over the elaborate baroque pulpit and altars hangs the intricately carved "Nun's Choir Gallery," bedecked with gilded saints and symbols.

One of the reminders that Goslar was once a free imperial and Hanseatic city is the **Breites Tor** (Wide Gate), a fortress with 23-foot-thick walls and ramparts stretching to Kaiserplatz, a palatinate of the emperor (tel. 05321/70-43-58). Rebuilt in the 19th century along the lines of its 11th-century original is a Romanesque hall. Within its walls is the 12th-century twin-storied chapel of St. Ulrich, containing the sarcophagus of Emperor Henry III. From May 1 until the end of September, it's open daily from 9:30am to 5pm; in March, April, and October, daily from 10am to 4pm; and from November to February, from 10am to 3pm. Admission is 2.50 DM ($1.70). To reach it, head down Peterstrasse.

For a quick and less exhausting look at the history of Goslar, visit the **Goslarer Museum,** at the corner of Abzuchtstrasse and Königstrasse (tel. 05321/70-43-59), which has displays of the early town, its modes of architecture, and several relics of the past. The museum also contains an exhibition of 1,000 years of mining, including a large geological collection from the Harz Mountains. The Goslarer Museum is open in April to October, Monday through Saturday from 10am to 5pm (Sunday from 10am to 4pm); the rest of the year, it's open Monday through Saturday from 10am to 4pm (Sunday from November to May, from 10am to 1pm). Admission is 2.50 DM ($1.70).

WHERE TO STAY
EXPENSIVE

DER ACHTERMANN, Rosentorstrasse 20, D-3380 Goslar. Tel. 05321/ 2-10-01. Fax 05321/4-27-48. 156 rms. MINIBAR TV TEL **Bus:** A or B.
$ Rates (including buffet breakfast): 119 DM–209 DM ($78.50–$137.90) single; 245 DM–335 DM ($161.70–$221.10) double. AE, DC, MC, V. **Parking:** 10 DM ($6.60).

Der Achtermann was completely gutted and rebuilt. The reputation of this historic structure has spread throughout the Harz region. The rooms are now completely modernized, with all the amenities. In addition to the major dining room, the hotel has an intimate bar and a Bierstube, the latter housed in the circular medieval tower for which the hotel is named.

DORINT-HARZHOTEL KREUZECK, Am Kreuzeck 1–4, D-3380 Goslar 2-Hahnenklee. Tel. 05325/740. Fax 05325/7-48-39. 104 rms, 8 suites. MINIBAR TV TEL

$ **Rates** (including buffet breakfast): 165 DM–205 DM ($108.90–$135.30) single; 225 DM–298 DM ($148.50–$196.70) double; from 320 DM ($211.20) suite. AE, DC, MC, V. **Parking:** Free outdoors; 8 DM ($5.30) in garage.

About 9 miles from Goslar is a well-rated, comfortable hotel set directly on a small lake with beautiful mountain scenery. (To get here by car, take A7, exiting at Seesen. You can also take bus 2434 from Goslar.) The only noise might be the roar of a big stag in the distance. The hotel offers country hospitality and exceptional food, and you may want to drive here for a meal even if you can't stay (see "Where to Dine"). In winter, numerous ski lifts are in the vicinity, as well as an 18.5-mile cross-country ski course. Ice-skating rinks are also nearby. In a horse-drawn sleigh, guests can enjoy an old-fashioned ride. In summer, sports include sailing, windsurfing, hiking, tennis, and bicycle riding.

KAISERWORTH, Markt 3, D-3380 Goslar. Tel. 05321/2-11-11. Fax 05321/21-114. 51 rms. TV TEL **Bus:** A or B.

$ **Rates** (including buffet breakfast): 95 DM–135 DM ($62.70–$89.10) single; 170 DM–260 DM ($112.20–$171.60) double. AE, DC, MC, V. **Parking:** Free. **Closed:** Nov to mid-Dec.

Right in the heart of town, the Kaiserworth is a big old-fashioned hotel. The building dates from 1494 and is considered a sightseeing attraction. Below the eaves are carved baroque statues of the Holy Roman emperors. The hotel's exterior is Gothic, with an arched arcade across the front, topped by a turreted oriel window facing the Marktplatz. The large rooms are designed with an accent on comfort; the corner rooms are big enough to be suites. Room 110 (a corner room) offers the best view of the 6 o'clock concert by the clock on the square.

On the ground floor the hotel has a sedate wood-paneled breakfast room and a vaulted-ceilinged dining room, Die Worth. Step through a 1,000-year-old cistern and you'll be in the cellar restaurant, the Dukatenkeller, with stone pillars and ecclesiastical chairs.

MODERATE

GOLDENE KRONE, Breitestrasse 46, D-3380 Goslar. Tel. 05321/2-27-92. Fax 05321/18-046. 26 rms (12 with shower). TV TEL **Bus:** A or B.

$ **Rates** (including continental breakfast): 50 DM ($33) single without shower, 80 DM ($52.80) single with shower; 90 DM ($59.40) double without shower, 140 DM ($92.40) double with shower. MC, V. **Parking:** 6 DM ($4). **Closed:** Jan 10–31; Nov.

Near the Breites Tor (Wide Gate) is this village inn complete with a friendly innkeeper and his wife, Herr and Frau Fehrenbach, who attend to the rooms and the meals. If you enjoy local color, this is a real find. The rooms are simple but homelike and clean; the food and drink are good and inexpensive.

SCHWARZER ADLER, Rosentorstrasse 25, D-3380 Goslar. Tel. 05321/2-40-01. Fax 05321/24-192. 27 rms (all with bath or shower). TV TEL **Bus:** A or B.

$ **Rates:** 90 DM–115 DM ($59.40–$75.90) single; 140 DM–160 DM ($92.40–$105.60) double. Breakfast 15 DM ($9.90) extra. No credit cards. **Parking:** 8 DM ($5.30).

Wolfgang Schmidt is your gracious host at this modern hotel that benefits from a long tradition of good food, hospitality, and comfort. Rooms are furnished in a simple modern style. The hotel also operates one of the more reasonably priced restaurants in town, with meals starting at 32 DM ($21.10). Specialties of the Harz Mountains and North Germany are served.

WHERE TO DINE
MODERATE

DIE WORTH, in the Kaiserworth, Markt 3. Tel. 05321/2-11-11.
Cuisine: NORTH GERMAN. **Reservations:** Not necessary. **Bus:** A or B.
$ **Prices:** Appetizers 8 DM–15 DM ($5.30–$9.90); main courses 15 DM–35 DM ($9.90–$23.10); fixed-price lunch 35 DM ($23.10). AE, DC, MC, V.
Open: Lunch daily noon–2:30pm; dinner daily 6–9:30pm. **Closed:** Nov to mid-Dec.

The most rustic and also the most attractive dining room in Goslar is Die Worth. Right in the heart of town, the restaurant is a Gothic stone crypt with vaulted ceilings and arches, stained-glass windows, wrought-iron lanterns, and trestle tables. The food is good, and the portions are hearty. In season, roast game is featured with wild mushrooms, mashed apples, and berries; or you can try the Tafelspitz (boiled beef) or the rumpsteak.

DORINT-HARZHOTEL KREUZECK, Am Kreuzeck 1–4, Hahnenklee. Tel. 05325/7-40.
Cuisine: CONTINENTAL. **Reservations:** Required. **Bus:** 2434 from Goslar.
$ **Prices:** Appetizers 8.50 DM–19.50 DM ($5.60–$12.90); main courses 25 DM–45 DM ($16.50–$29.70); fixed-price lunch 25 DM ($16.50); fixed-price dinner 33 DM ($21.80). AE, DC, MC, V.
Open: Lunch daily noon–2:30pm; dinner daily 6–11pm.

In a wooded area south of Goslar, this rustic villa serves a cuisine moderne in its restaurant, Bergkanne. All the products used are the freshest available, with many imported directly from France. Specialties include filet of turbot with fresh mushrooms, juicy steaks poached in butter, and sautéed medallions of Charmoise lamb with fresh vegetables and potatoes dauphinoise. Music and dancing often accompany the meal, which could be capped with a tempting array of fresh sorbets.

GOLDENE KRONE, Breitestrasse 46. Tel. 05321/2-27-92.
Cuisine: INTERNATIONAL/NORTH GERMAN. **Reservations:** Not necessary.
Bus: A or B.
$ **Prices:** Appetizers 9 DM–16 DM ($5.90–$10.60); main courses 20 DM–32 DM ($13.20–$21.10); fixed-price lunch 22 DM–32 DM ($14.50–$21.10); fixed-price dinner 35 DM ($23.10). MC, V.
Open: Thurs–Tues 7am–midnight; hot food served 11am–2pm and 6–9pm.

⑤ Seemingly everyone in town knows about this historic Weinstube on the eastern edge of Goslar. The decor is rustic and cozy, and you'll feel at home with the polite service. In addition to the standard North German dishes, occasional international dishes appear on the changing seasonal menu.

HARZHOTEL BÄREN, Krugwiese 11A. Tel. 05321/78-20.
Cuisine: GERMAN/FRENCH. **Reservations:** Required. **Bus:** A.
$ **Prices:** Appetizers 6.50 DM–30 DM ($4.30–$19.80); main courses 15 DM–60 DM ($9.90–$39.60). DC, MC, V.
Open: Daily noon–11pm.

Music and dancing will often accompany your meal at this modern hotel-restaurant frequented by partying locals. The comfortably rustic Stoppenzieher (corkscrew) could provide a suitable spot for a beer or some schnapps before moving into the main restaurant. Specialties of the house include Harzer river trout and roast piglet.

Hamburg has many faces. A trip through the canals will make you realize why it has been called "Venice of the North." A walk down the neon-lit Reeperbahn at night will revive those old and fading memories of "Sin City Europe." A ride around Alster Lake in center city will reveal the elegance of its finest parks and buildings. A view from the old tower of the baroque Hauptkirche St. Michaelis opens on the steel-and-glass buildings of modern Hamburg. A Sunday-morning visit to the Altona fish market will give you a good look at early shoppers mingling with late-nighters from the Reeperbahn.

Above all, Hamburg has a unique and versatile personality. It's a flexible city—it has had to be to recover from the many disasters during its 1,200-year history. Not the least of these was the almost total destruction of this North Sea port during World War II. But the industrious Hamburgers seized this as an opportunity to rebuild a larger and more beautiful city, with huge parks, impressive buildings, and important cultural institutions.

The Hanseatic port of Hamburg, the second-largest city of Germany, lies on the Elbe River 68 miles from the North Sea and 177 miles northwest of Berlin. It is 74 miles northeast of Bremen and 93 miles north of Hannover. Hamburg has about 1.7 million inhabitants.

1. ORIENTATION

ARRIVING

BY PLANE The **Airport Hamburg-Fuhlsbüttel,** Paul-Baumer-Platz 1–3 (tel. 040/50-750), is 5 miles north of center city. It is served by many scheduled airlines and charter companies, with regular flights to major German airports and many European and intercontinental destinations. Lufthansa (tel. 040/35-955) offers flights to Hamburg from most major German cities, including Berlin, Frankfurt, and Munich. Many national carriers also fly into Hamburg, including Air France from Paris and British Airways from London. There are also direct flights from the United States, offered by both Delta and Lufthansa, and connecting flights available on American Airlines and TWA from Atlanta, Boston, Charlotte, Chicago, Dallas,

WHAT'S SPECIAL ABOUT HAMBURG

Ace Attractions

- ☐ The Reeperbahn, the most famous nightlife district of Europe, everything from fun for the family to tawdry sex shows.
- ☐ Boat tours of the harbor, on both the Inner and Outer Alster, a trip through one of the world's great ports.

Park

- ☐ Carl Hagenbeck's Tierpark, with animal houses and enclosures that are among the most advanced in the world.

Museums

- ☐ Hamburger Kunsthalle, one of the leading art museums of northern Germany, containing a noted masterpiece, the *Graybow Altarpiece*, by Master Bertram.

- ☐ Museum of Hamburg History, which allows visitors of German ancestry to trace their forebears.

Religious Shrines

- ☐ Hauptkirche St. Michaelis, Hamburg's signature landmark, the finest baroque church in North Germany.
- ☐ St. Petri Church, dating from the 12th century, with art from the mid-14th century.
- ☐ St. Jacobi, a 13- to 15th-century hall-church, with masterpieces of world art.

Panoramic Vistas

- ☐ Heinrich-Hertz-Turm, a television tower with an observation platform at 425 feet.

Houston, New York/Newark, Philadelphia, and Washington. For flight information, in Hamburg, phone 040/508-25-57.

The HVV–Hamburger Verkehrsverbund–Air Express bus 110 runs every 10 minutes as a shuttle linking the airport with the city's rapid transit rail network (both U-Bahn and S-Bahn). A bus departs for the airport from the Hamburg Hauptbahnhof every 20 minutes from 5:40am to 9:20pm daily. Airport buses heading for the Hauptbahnhof leave daily from 6:22am to 10:42pm. The one-way fare is 8 DM ($5.30) for adults and 4 DM ($2.60) for children under 12. A taxi from the airport to the city center costs approximately 28 DM ($18.50), with a trip time of 25 minutes.

BY TRAIN There are two major rail stations, centrally located **Hamburg Hauptbahnhof,** Hachmannplatz 10 (tel. 040/3918-346), and **Hamburg-Altona** (tel. 040/3918-2387), lying in the western part of the city. Most passengers arrive at the Hauptbahnhof, although trains from the north of Germany, including Westerland, Kiel, and Schleswig, pull into Altona. The two stations are connected by train and the S-Bahn.

Hamburg has frequent train connections with all major German cities, as well as frequent Continental connections. Eight trains arrive daily from Berlin (trip time: 4 hours); 37 trains from Bremen (54 minutes to 1 hour, 10 minutes); and 45 trains from Hannover (1 hour, 11 minutes, to 1 hour, 55 minutes). For rail information, call 040/19-419.

BY BUS Long-distance bus service is provided by Line EB 183 Europabus from Hannover, Nürnberg, Munich, and Stockholm. Information about bus connections is available from Deutsche Touring GmbH, Büro Hamburg at Hamburg (tel. 040/24-98-18). Autokraft GmbH at Kiel (tel. 0431/71-070) also runs buses between Berlin and Hamburg, as does Gebr. Sperling GmbH from Berlin (tel. toll free 0130/6662).

Regional bus service with frequent connections to nearby towns is provided by Autokraft GmbH (tel. 0431/71-070) and the Hamburger Verkehrsverbund (tel. 040/32-39-11).

BY FERRY Ferry service links Hamburg and Harwich, England. The ferry ship *Hamburg* sails between Harwich and the St. Pauli Landungsbrücken in Hamburg (trip time: 20 hours). For information, call Scandinavian Seaways, Rathausstrasse 12 (tel. 040/389-03-71).

BY CAR Hamburg is reached from all directions in Germany by major expressways: Autobahn A1 from the south and west, A7 from the north and south, A23 from the northwest, and A24 from the east. Road signs and directions to Hamburg are frequently posted.

TOURIST INFORMATION

For visitors to Hamburg, information is offered at several places, covering different types of data, including hotel bookings, port information, and general matters such as tour tickets, planned events, and guide services. Offices are: Tourist Information, Bieberhaus, Hachmannplatz, near the Hauptbahnhof (tel. 040/300-51), open Monday to Friday from 7:30am to 6pm, Saturday from 8am to 3pm; Tourist Information at the airport, Arrival Hall D (tel. 040/300-51-240), open daily from 8am to 11pm; Tourist Information, Hauptbahnhof, Kirchenallee exit (tel. 040/24-87-02-30), open daily from 7am to 11pm; Port Information, St. Pauli Landungsbrücken (tel. 040/300-51-200), open daily from 9am to 6pm; and Hamburg information in the city center, Hanse Viertel shopping mall, entrance Poststrasse (tel. 040/300-51-220), open Monday to Friday and the first Saturday in each month from 9am to 6pm (other Saturdays from 9am to 2pm). Hamburg also maintains a North American representative at 38 W. 32nd St., Suite 1210, New York, NY 10001 (tel. 212/967-3110).

CITY LAYOUT

Hamburg is a showplace of modern architecture; historic structures stand side by side with towering steel-and-glass buildings. The 4.5 square miles of parks and gardens are a vital part of the city. Hamburgers are proud of their 22 square miles of rivers and lakes as well.

The **Alster** is the perfect starting point for a pleasurable exploration of Hamburg. This lake, rimmed by the city's most significant buildings, sparkles with the white sails of small boats and ripples with the movement of motor launches. The lake is divided by the Lombard and John F. Kennedy bridges into the **Binnenalster** (Inner Alster) and the larger **Aussenalster** (Outer Alster). The Binnenalster is flanked on the south and the west by the **Jungfernstieg,** one of Europe's best-known streets and Hamburg's most vital artery and shopping district. For landlubbers, the best view of the Alster is from this "maiden's path."

The **Port of Hamburg** is the world's fifth-largest harbor, stretching for nearly 25 miles along the Elbe River. More than 1,500 ships call each month, connecting it with cities throughout the world. Since 1189, the stretch of water has been one of the busiest centers for trade on the continent, making Hamburg one of Germany's wealthiest cities.

From the Hauptbahnhof, on the eastern fringe of the heart of town in the vicinity of the Binnenalster, two major shopping streets fan out in a southwesterly direction, toward St. Petri Church and the Rathaus. They are **Spitalerstrasse** (reserved for pedestrians) and **Mönckebergstrasse,** paralleling it to the south. These streets contain some of the city's finest stores. Stay on Mönckebergstrasse to reach **Rathausmarkt,** which is dominated by the Rathaus, a Renaissance-style palace.

The center of Hamburg offers opportunities for walking; for example, the eastern shoreline of the Binnenalster opens onto **Ballindamm,** which contains many elegant stores. At the foot of this lake is the Jungfernstieg, already mentioned, but along its western shoreline is yet another main artery, the Neuer Jungfernstieg. At the intersection of the Jungfernstieg and Neuer Jungfernstieg is one of the more fascinating streets of Hamburg, the **Colonnaden,** a colonnade of shops and cafés. In this neighborhood stands the **Hamburgische Staatsoper,** the famous modern opera house.

The city is not so compact, however, that it can be easily covered on foot. Many sections of interest are far apart, and you'll have to depend on public transportation or a taxi to reach them.

NEIGHBORHOODS IN BRIEF

Central Hamburg This is the commercial and shopping district of Hamburg, seat of many of its finest hotels and restaurants. The district centers around Binnenalster and the Rathaus (Town Hall). Boat rides on the Alster lakes form one of the major attractions of the city. Many historic buildings that survived World War II or else were rebuilt stand here, including St. Petri, the oldest surviving structure.

The Harbor Sixty dock basins stretching for some 25 miles of quays, including mooring buoys, constitute one of the world's greatest ports. Maritime vessels from all over Europe, and many parts of the world, carry cargo up the Elbe to dock and unload in this port.

St. Pauli This is the nightlife center of Hamburg, with lots of erotica. The district is split by its famous street, the Reeperbahn, neon lit and dazzling, offering all sorts of nighttime pleasures. Cafés, sex shows, bars, discothèques, and music halls abound.

Altona Formerly a city in its own right, west of Hamburg, this district is now integrated into greater Hamburg. Once settled mainly by Jews and Portuguese, it is the scene of Hamburg's famous Fischmarkt, taking place at dawn every Sunday.

Övelgönne Down the river from Altona, Övelgönne is known for its coterie of sailing freighters. From this river district, you'll have a good vantage point for overseeing the maritime vessels on the Elbe heading for port or else leaving Hamburg for destinations around the globe.

Pösseldorf Northwest of Aussenalster, this is a tree-filled residential district, often with villas dating from the 1800s. Many exemplary buildings of the German Jugendstil style can be seen here. The district is largely occupied by upwardly mobile professional people, including a lot of media stars.

GETTING AROUND

A word to the wise—park your car and use public transportation in this busy and, at times, frantic city.

Practically all public transportation services in the Hamburg area, consisting of U-Bahn (subway), S-Bahn (city rail), A-Bahn (commuter rail), as well as numerous bus routes and harbor ferries, are managed by Hamburg Verkehrsverbund–HVV–Altstadterstrasse. For travel information, available daily from 7am to 8pm, call 040/32-29-11. Tickets are sold at automats and railroad ticket counters.

BY PUBLIC TRANSPORTATION Hamburg's **U-Bahn** is one of the best in Germany, serving the entire downtown area and connecting with the **S-Bahn's** surface trains in the suburbs. This train network is the fastest means of getting around, but the buses offer a good alternative. The advantage of surface travel, of course, is that you get to see more of the city. A one-way fare is 3.40 DM ($2.20) for adults and 1.20 DM (80¢) for children.

You buy your ticket from the driver or from slot machines at stops and stations. If you plan to make a day of it, you can purchase one of the day tickets and travel as often as you like. A day ticket is valid within the city limits from 9am to 6pm Monday through Friday and all day Saturday and Sunday, costing 9.50 DM ($6.30) for one adult and three children (if under 12). A family-group ticket is also available for four adults and three children for 19.50 DM ($12.90). A similar three-day family-group ticket costs 29.50 DM ($19.50).

You can reserve tickets in advance. (Day tickets are valid from the time they are actually issued.) Ask for tourist tickets at Tourist Information in the Hauptbahnhof. For further information on transport services, fares, and special offers, phone 040/32-29-11 from 7am to 8pm.

BY TAXI Taxis are available at all hours by telephoning 040/44-10-11 or 040/68-20-01. For a taxi for the disabled, phone 040/410-54-58. A taxi from the airport to city center costs about 28 DM ($18.50). In town, taxi meters start at 3 DM ($2).

 HAMBURG

American Express The Amex office in Hamburg is at Rathausmarkt 5 (tel. 040/33-11-41). The office is open Monday to Friday from 9am to 5:30pm and Saturday from 9am to noon.

Area Code The telephone area code for Hamburg is **040.**

Babysitters Arrangements can usually be made with your hotel reception desk. Most hotels have sitters on call, often members of the staff earning extra money. If you need a sitter in the evening, make arrangements before noon, and request, if available, an English-speaking sitter.

Bookstores Frensche, Spitalerstrasse 26E (tel. 040/32-75-85), is a good English-language bookstore and also carries a large selection of English-language newspapers and magazines.

Business Hours Most banks are open Monday to Friday from 8:30am to 12:30pm and 1:30 to 3:30pm (many banks stay open until 5:30pm on Thursday). Most businesses and stores are open Monday to Friday from 9am to 6pm and on Saturday from 9am to 2pm (to 4 or 6pm on the first Saturday of the month).

Car Rentals It is not recommended that you rent a car for touring Hamburg, but an automobile might be ideal if you plan to tour the environs. Cars are available at such companies as **Avis,** Drehbahn 15–25 (tel. 040/34-16-51), at **Hertz,** Kirchenallee 33 (tel. 040/280-12-01), and **InterRent Europcar,** Rödingsmarkt 14 (tel. 040/36-22-21).

Consulates The **United States** consulate-general is at Alsterufer 28 (tel. 040/411-71-0); the **United Kingdom** consulate-general is at Harvestehuder Weg 8A (tel. 040/44-60-71); and the **New Zealand** consulate is at Heimhuder Strasse 56 (tel. 040/4425-550).

Climate See "When to Go" in Chapter 2.

Currency See "Information, Entry Requirements & Money" in Chapter 2.

Currency Exchange You can exchange your currency at the **Deutsche Verkehrs-Kredit-Bank** branch at the Hauptbahnhof (tel. 040/30-80-04-75), open daily from 7:30am to 10pm, as well as at its branch at Altona Station (tel. 040/340-37-70), open Monday to Saturday from 7:30am to 1pm and 1:45 to 8pm; Sunday and public holidays from 10am to 1pm and 1:45 to 6pm. **Deutsche Bank** has an airport branch, open daily from 6:30am to 10:30pm.

Dentist A dental clinic, with English-speaking dentists, is available at **St. Georg Hospital,** Lungmühlen Strasse 5 (tel. 040/24-88-01).

Doctor Either the British or American consulate (see above) can recommend English-speaking private doctors in Hamburg. You will also find a staff of English-speaking doctors at **St. Georg Hospital,** Lungmühlen Strasse 5 (tel. 040/24-88-01).

Drugstores   Pharmacies that stock foreign drugs include **Internationale Apotheke,** Ballindamm 39 (tel. 040/33-53-33), open Monday to Friday from 8:30am to 6:30pm and Saturday from 9am to 2pm. **Roth's Alte Englishe Apotheke,** 48 Jungfernstieg (tel. 040/34-39-06), is open Monday to Friday from 8am to 6:30pm and Saturday from 9am to 1pm.

Emergencies   Phone numbers are police, **110;** fire brigade, **112;** physician, **22-80-22;** dentist, **468-32-60;** German Automobile Association (ADAC), **23-99-9.**

Eyeglasses   German optics are among the most precise in the world, and dozens of opticians are available. Your hotel reception desk might recommend one near you or you can go to **Karstat-Billstedt,** Möllner Landstrasse 1 (tel. 040/73-33-81).

Holidays   See "When to Go" in Chapter 2.

Hospitals   A good choice is **St. Georg Hospital,** Lungmühlen Strasse 5 (tel. 040/24-88-01).

Information   See "Tourist Information," above.

Laundry/Dry Cleaning   A number of Laundromats and dry-cleaning establishments are found in Hamburg. Your hotel reception desk will often recommend one nearby. If not, try **Chemische Reinigung,** Friedrich Strasse 30 (tel. 040/31-91-434) for both laundry and dry cleaning.

Library   The **Zentralbibliothek,** Grosse Bleichen 27 (tel. 040/35-606-215), is open Tuesday to Friday from 10am to 6pm and Saturday from 10am to 1pm.

Lost Property   Municipal bus and U-Bahn lost property offices are at Backerbreitergang 73 (tel. 040/35-18-51), open Monday and Thursday from 8am to 3:30pm; Tuesday, Wednesday, and Friday from 8am to noon. Railway and S-Bahn lost property offices are at Stresemannstrasse 114 (tel. 040/39-18-26-86), open Monday to Friday from 7:30am to 3pm.

Luggage Storage/Lockers   These are available at the Hamburg Hauptbahnhof, Hachmannplatz 10 (tel. 040/3918-2387). Lockers cost 3 DM ($2) per day.

Newspapers/Magazines   The *International Herald Tribune* is the most widely distributed English-language newspaper at various kiosks throughout the city, although you can also find copies of *USA Today.* Likewise, the European editions of *Time* and *Newsweek* are widely available.

Photographic Needs   Hamburg abounds with photographic shops in every neighborhood. You can also patronize **Photo Porst,** Dammtorstrasse 12 (tel. 040/34-49-16).

Post Office   The post office at the Hamburg Hauptbahnhof, Hachmannplatz 10 (tel. 040/55-66-125), is convenient. In addition to sending mail and packages, you can make long-distance calls here far cheaper than at your hotel. Telegrams, telexes, and faxes can also be sent from here. It is open 24 hours a day.

Radio   The BBC World Service broadcasts to Hamburg as does the American Forces Network (AFN), which you can hear on 1107AM. For the Voice of America, tune to 1197AM.

Religious Services   Services in all of Hamburg's Protestant churches are generally held Sundays at 10am; St. Michaelis, St. Petri, and St. Jacobi also have services Sunday at 6pm. The English Church of St. Thomas à Becket is at Zeughausmarkt (tel. 040/31-28-05). A Lutheran service in English is held the first Sunday in the month at 6pm at St. Petri, Speersort 10.

Restrooms   Use the word *Toilette* not *Badezimmer.* Sometimes it is labeled WC; sometimes H (*Herren* for men) or F (*Frauen* for women). In the center of Hamburg are several public facilities. You can also patronize the facilities at terminals, restaurants, bars, cafés, department stores, hotels, and pubs.

Safety   Hamburg, like all big cities of the world, has its share of crime. Innocent tourists are often victims. The major crimes are pickpocketing and purse-

and camera-snatching. It is your responsibility to keep your guard up and to be alert. Wear a moneybelt. Store valuables in a hotel safe. Most robberies occur in the big tourist areas, such as the Reeperbahn and the area around the Hauptbahnhof, which can be dangerous at night, but much less so than Frankfurt or Munich.

Shoe Repairs Go to **Mister Minit,** Grosse Berg Strasse 172 (tel. 040/38-02-80).

Taxis See "Getting Around" in this chapter.

Telegrams/Telex/Fax These can be sent from the post office at the Hamburg Hauptbahnhof, Hachmannplatz 10 (tel. 040/55-66-125).

Television There are two national TV channels: ARD (channel 1) and ZDF (channel 2). Sometimes these stations show films in their original language (most often English). The more expensive hotels often have cable TV, with such programs as 24-hour news on CNN.

Transit Info For U-Bahn and S-Bahn rail information, call the Hamburg Hauptbahnhof, Hachmannplatz 10 (tel. 3918-2387).

Water Tap water is safe to drink in Hamburg.

Yellow Pages A knowledge of German is necessary. You can always ask the staff of your hotel to assist you in locating a particular service such as a laundrette or a car-rental company.

2. ACCOMMODATIONS

Hamburg is an expensive city that has an abundance of first-class hotels but a limited number of budget accommodations, especially in center city. During a busy convention period, you may have trouble finding a room on your own. The Hauptbahnhof and Bieberhaus tourist information offices have hotel booking desks. This assistance is also offered at the airport in Arrival Hall A, at Am Lehmsaal Autobahn services (Autobahn A7, northbound side), and Buddikate Autobahn services (Autobahn A1, southbound side, exit Fehmarn, Lübeck).

NEAR THE HAUPTBAHNHOF

VERY EXPENSIVE

ATLANTIC HOTEL KEMPINSKI, An der Alster 72, D-2000 Hamburg 1.
Tel. 040/2-88-80, or toll free in the U.S. 800/426-3135. Fax 040/24-17-29. 256 rms, 13 suites. MINIBAR TV TEL **U-Bahn:** Hauptbahnhof.

$ **Rates:** 349 DM–459 DM ($230.30–$302.90) single; 428 DM–538 DM ($282.50–$355.10) double; from 650 DM ($429) suite. Breakfast 30 DM ($19.80) extra. AE, DC, MC, V. **Parking:** 18 DM ($11.90).

This sumptuous hotel was one of the few buildings in its neighborhood to escape the World War II bombs. It occupies an enviable position near the Aussenalster in a central location filled with trees and imposing villas. Considered the flagship of the Kempinski hotel chain, it boasts a turn-of-the-century maritime theme of Ionic columns with touches of Atlantic blue and glistening white, sumptuous proportions and regal furnishings, a soaring stairwell, and a baronial lobby. The rooms and luxurious suites have housed an array of luminaries from around the world. Some are air-conditioned.

Dining/Entertainment: An elegant bar, the Atrium, opens onto a neoclassical fountain; the pub-style restaurant is Atlantic Mühle. The Atlantic Restaurant, one of the finest dining rooms in North Germany, attracts discriminating gourmets. In a stylishly sophisticated atmosphere, some 55 cooks prepare a modern haute cuisine that is matched by a superb wine list. Meals, averaging 78 DM to 110 DM ($51.50 to $72.60), are served daily from noon to 3pm and 6pm to midnight.

Services: Room service, laundry, dry cleaning, babysitting.

Facilities: Beautifully maintained chlorine-free indoor pool, sauna, solarium.

MARITIM HOTEL REICHSHOF, Kirchenallee 34–36, D-200 Hamburg 1. Tel. 040/24-83-30. Fax 040/248-33-588. 303 rms, 6 suites. MINIBAR TV TEL **U-Bahn:** Hauptbahnhof.

$ Rates (including buffet breakfast): 239 DM–369 DM ($157.70–$243.50) single; 288 DM–448 DM ($190.10–$295.70) double; from 575 DM ($379.50) suite. AE, DC, MC, V. **Parking:** 23 DM ($15.20).

Located next door to the Schauspielhaus, the Reichshof is only a few minutes from the Alster and the Elbe. Still steeped in Hanseatic flair and tradition, it was built in 1910 across from the ornate spire of the Hamburg Hauptbahnhof. At that time, this was the most desirable location for a hotel (accommodations were 3.50 DM [$2.30] a night, regardless of room category). Noteworthy then as the largest hotel in Europe, it boasted a lobby that was a landmark in art deco styling.

In World War II it lost most of its upper floors, but the lobby with its gilded pilasters and marble sheating was left intact. A complete renovation has substantially upgraded the hotel. The guest rooms are now modern, with reproductions of art nouveau furniture and color TVs with in-house movies. The hotel today is a favorite with business travelers; consequently, more than half its rooms are classified as singles.

Dining/Entertainment: Guests enjoy tea in the lounge, and in the evening, they can relax over a drink in the Piano Bar, which offers live music every night (except Sunday), 8pm to 2am. The bar is open daily, 5pm to as late as 5am. The hotel's restaurant, one of the finest in the heart of town, is recommended separately.

Services: Room service, laundry, dry cleaning.

PREM HOTEL, An der Alster 9, D-2000 Hamburg 1. Tel. 040/24-17-26. Fax 040/280-38-51. 52 rms, 3 suites. MINIBAR TV TEL **Bus:** 108.

$ Rates (including continental breakfast): 189 DM–369.70 DM ($124.70–$244) single; 279 DM–454 DM ($184.10–$299.60) double; from 580 DM ($382.80) suite. AE, DC, MC, V. **Parking:** 20 DM ($13.20).

The Prem, an elderly mansion in a beautiful location, has been owned by the Prem family since it was established in 1912. An attractive and sophisticated clientele makes this "white house on the Alster" its home during frequent trips to the city. The glistening white facade overlooks the lake, and the rear faces a quiet garden with umbrella-covered tables. The reception salons show off a personalized collection of French antiques and reproductions. A beautiful Gobelin tapestry hangs in the lobby, and most of the rooms are furnished with white-and-gold Louis XV–style pieces. The garden-facing accommodations are much quieter than the front rooms on the Alster.

Dining/Entertainment: You can enjoy breakfast in the white-and-gold dining room jutting out into the garden. The restaurant also serves well-prepared lunches and dinners, with meals costing from 85 DM ($56.10). Service is formal, and the cuisine is both German and international.

Services: Room service, laundry, dry cleaning.

Facilities: Sauna.

EXPENSIVE

AMBASSADOR, Heidenkampsweg 34, D-2000 Hamburg 1. Tel. 040/23-00-02, or toll free 800/528-1234 in the U.S. and Canada. Fax 040/23-00-09. 124 rms. MINIBAR TV TEL **S-Bahn:** Berliner Tor.

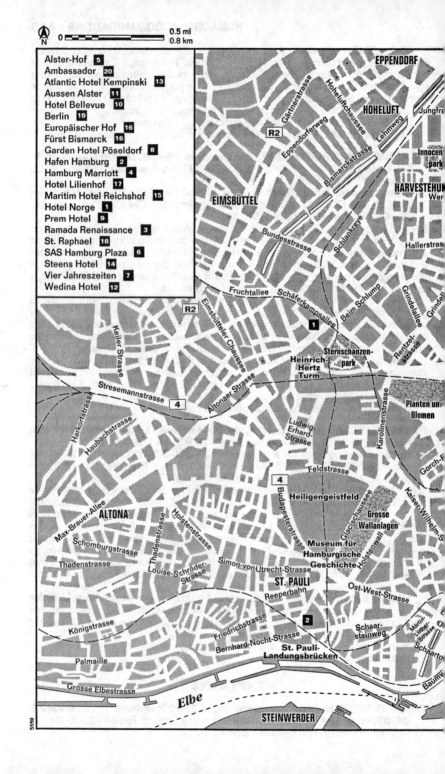

HAMBURG ACCOMMODATIONS

BARMBEK

St. Benedict-strasse

Maria-Louisen-Strasse

Barmbeker Strasse

Osterbekstrasse

Adolph-Schönfelder-Strasse

Weidestrasse

Fernsicht

Bellevue

Sierichstrasse

Hans-Henny-Jahn-Weg

Herderstrasse

Beethovenstrasse

Hamburger Strasse

Oberaltenallee

Hallerstrasse

Mittelweg

Rotherbaumchaussee

Alster-park

Harvesthuder Weg

Herbert-Weichmann-Strasse

UHLENHORST

Winterhuder Weg

5

Lerchenfeld Wartenau

ROTHERBAUM

8

Schöne Aussicht

Mundsburgerdamm

Aussenalster

Schwanenwik

HOHENFELDE

Sechslingspforte

Mühlendamm

75

Mittelweg

7

Alsterufer

Th.-Heuss-Platz

9

10

11

An der Alster

12

Koppelstrasse

Lübecker-strasse

BORGFELDE

Wall-strasse

stavler-Park

Kennedybrücke

Lombardsbrücke

5

13

14

ST. GEORG

Hansaplatz

19

Binnenalster

Balindamm

Hachmannplatz

15

16

4

Jungfernstieg

Possstrasse

17

Steindamm

18

3

Adenauerallee

Kurt-Schumacher-Allee

20

75

Rathaus Stock Exchange

Mönckebergstrasse

Spaldingstrasse

Heidenkampsweg

önckebergstrasse

St. Petri Kirche

Speersort Steinstrasse

Nordkanalstrasse

Hammerbrookstrasse

Domstrasse

Nagelsweg

Holzbr. Matten Sande

Ost-West-Strasse

Dovenfleet

Oberbaumbrücke

Banksstrasse

Amsinckstrasse

Katharinen-strasse

Brooktorkai

$ Rates (including continental breakfast): 165 DM–250 DM ($108.90–$165)
single; 200 DM–240 DM ($132–$158.40) double. AE, DC, MC, V. **Parking:** 20
DM ($13.20).

Seven floors of modern design greet visitors to the Ambassador, a hotel affiliated with
Best Western. The bar, restaurant, pool, and guest rooms are all pleasant places to
spend time. The management blends chain-hotel efficiency with personal service.
Meals cost from 42 DM ($27.70) in the restaurant.

**AUSSEN ALSTER, Schmilinskystrasse 11, D-2000 Hamburg 1. Tel.
040/24-15-57.** Fax 040/280-32-31. 27 rms. MINIBAR TV TEL **U-Bahn:**
Hauptbahnhof.

$ Rates (including continental breakfast): 190 DM–240 DM ($125.40–$158.40)
single; 280 DM–350 DM ($184.80–$231) double. AE, DC, MC, V. **Closed:** Dec
24–27.

Small and exclusive, the Aussen Alster attracts actors, advertising directors,
executives, writers, and artists. Its stylish, ultramodern interior was designed by
one of Germany's most famous architects. This hotel sits on a quiet residential
street, about a five-minute walk from the rail station and a three-minute walk from the
Alster. Its 19th-century facade is painted milk white, capped with an Italianate-
inspired frieze. Managed with panache, the hotel is owned and operated by Hamburg
film producer Klaus Feddermann and his partner, Burkhard Stoelck. The lobby walls
exhibit works of a number of European artists. Rooms are white-walled, angular, and
consciously simple.

Dining/Entertainment: Have a drink in the hotel bar, where on cool nights a
fireplace burns, and then enjoy the international restaurant, Schmilinsky, where Italian
food is a specialty. Meals start at 50 DM ($33).

Services: Laundry, room service.

Facilities: Garden (in back), sauna, solarium.

**HOTEL BELLEVUE, An der Alster 14, D-2000 Hamburg 1. Tel. 040/24-
80-11.** Fax 040/280-33-80. 78 rms. MINIBAR TV TEL **Bus:** 108.

$ Rates (including buffet breakfast): 155 DM–195 DM ($102.30–$128.70) single;
230 DM–250 DM ($151.80–$165) double. AE, DC, MC, V. **Parking:** 12 DM
($7.90).

Many theatrical celebrities make this their Hamburg choice. Just a short ride
from the Hauptbahnhof, facing the Alster, the Bellevue has been considerably
updated. Though some of the larger rooms contain traditional furnishings, the
newer singles are modern, often done in Scandinavian style. Many units contain
cherrywood and rattan pieces; all have trouser presses and hairdryers. The front
windows open onto the lake, but the back rooms are quieter.

The ground-floor Alster Room serves as a breakfast room, and you can enjoy
international cuisine as well as regional specialties in the cozy Pilsner Urquell Stuben.
Live organ music is played after 8pm in the INA bar, where you can enjoy draft
Budweiser and Czech beer.

**BERLIN, Borgfelderstrasse 1–9, D-2000 Hamburg 26. Tel. 040/25-16-
40.** Fax 040/251-64-413. 93 rms. MINIBAR TV TEL **S-Bahn:** Berliner Tor.

$ Rates (including continental breakfast): 162.50 DM–202.50 DM ($107.30–
$133.70) single; 210 DM–250 DM ($138.60–$165) double. Children under 18
stay free in parents' room. AE, DC, MC, V. **Parking:** Free in car park, 22 DM
($14.50) in garage.

At a busy intersection about half a mile from the Hauptbahnhof, the Berlin is a
convenient accommodation, particularly for motorists. Its handsome rooms have
extra-wide beds, radios, hairdryers, and double-glazed windows. Special pleasure is
added by the small basket of fruit in your room on arrival, a newspaper at breakfast,
and a bedtime candy treat. À la carte meals are served in the Brasserie Miro daily from
noon to 3pm and 6 to 10pm. The hotel also has a bar.

EUROPÄISCHER HOF, Kirchenallee 45, D-2000 Hamburg 1. Tel. 040/ 24-82-48. Fax 040/248-24-799. 320 rms. MINIBAR TV TEL **U-Bahn:** Hauptbahnhof.

$ Rates (including continental breakfast): 180 DM–340 DM ($118.80–$224.40) single; 240 DM–420 DM ($158.40–$277.20) double. AE, DC, MC, V. **Parking:** 20 DM ($13.20).

Established in 1925 and still directed by the Berk family, the Europäischer Hof is the largest privately owned hotel in Hamburg. In the city center, the hotel stands across from the Hauptbahnhof. The well-furnished rooms are protected from noise by soundproof windows.

Dining/Entertainment: Two restaurants await visitors, the Chalet and the Jagerstüble, serving both international and regional cuisine. Meals cost from 42 DM ($27.70).

Services: Room service, laundry, dry cleaning.

Facilities: Sauna, solarium, indoor pool, fitness room.

ST. RAPHAEL, Adenauerallee 41, D-2000 Hamburg 1. Tel. 040/24-82-00, or toll free 800/528-1234 in the U.S. and Canada. Fax 040/24-03-33. 130 rms, 3 suites. MINIBAR TV TEL **U-Bahn:** Hauptbahnhof.

$ Rates (including buffet breakfast): 190 DM–230 DM ($125.40–$151.80) single; 230 DM–280 DM ($151.80–$184.80) double; from 350 DM ($231) suite. AE, DC, MC, V. **Parking:** 8 DM ($5.30).

This well-administered hotel on the famous Adenauerallee is constructed of white brick with modern soundproof windows. The interior has the kind of simplicity that soothes and relaxes you after a busy day. The hotel has recently been completely redecorated, with all rooms featuring radios, in-house movies in English, hairdryers, and trouserpresses. A full-service restaurant offers everything from special weekly buffets to late-night snacks. The hotel also has a fitness center with a sauna, a solarium, and a Jacuzzi, plus a sweeping view of Hamburg.

MODERATE

FÜRST BISMARCK, Kirchenallee 49, D-2000 Hamburg 1. Tel. 040/280-10-91. Fax 040/28-01-096. 59 rms. TV TEL **U-Bahn:** Hauptbahnhof.

$ Rates (including continental breakfast): 115 DM–135 DM ($75.90–$89.10) single; 175 DM ($115.50) double. AE, DC, MC, V. **Parking:** 6 DM ($4).

This building looks best when approached through one of Hamburg's frequent mists, when it rises abruptly from a narrow corner lot in all its black, white, and gilded splendor. The interior has been carefully renovated to keep the personalized feeling of being in a special place. The hotel offers modernized, functionally furnished rooms.

STEENS HOTEL, Holzdamm 43, D-2000 Hamburg 1. Tel. 040/244-642. Fax 040/280-3593. 11 rms (all with shower). TV TEL **U-Bahn:** Hauptbahnhof.

$ Rates (including continental breakfast): 100 DM–130 DM ($66–$85.80) single; 170 DM–180 DM ($112.20–$118.80) double. AE, MC, V.

Despite its respectable location a short walk from the Alster and the much more expensive Atlantic Hotel, this century-old house charges reasonable rates. Each simply decorated room contains a private shower, and all but two rooms include a private toilet. Each was renovated in 1989 and is carefully maintained by the live-in owners, the Martin family. The house has functioned as a cost-conscious hotel since the early 1950s. Breakfast is the only meal served.

WEDINA HOTEL, Gurlittstrasse 23, D-2000 Hamburg 1. Tel. 040/24-30-11. Fax 040/280-38-94. 27 rms. TV TEL **Bus:** 108.

$ Rates (including buffet breakfast): 125 DM–155 DM ($82.50–$102.30) single; 170 DM–195 DM ($112.20–$128.70) double; 260 DM ($171.60) triple. AE, DC, MC, V. **Parking:** 15 DM ($9.90). **Closed:** Dec 18–Feb 10.

A family-style hostelry, the Wedina is a minute from the lake and a five-minute walk from the Hauptbahnhof. Most of the rooms open onto a small, informal rear garden. It's a pleasant, quiet retreat (with a pool) that's owned and run by an English-speaking family.

INEXPENSIVE

HOTEL LILIENHOF, Ernst-Merck-Strasse 4, D-2000 Hamburg 1. Tel. 040/241-087. Fax 040/280-1815. 24 rms (8 with shower). TV TEL **U-Bahn:** Hauptbahnhof.

$ Rates (including continental breakfast): 65 DM ($42.90) single without shower, 75 DM–85 DM ($49.50–$56.10) single with shower; 108 DM ($71.30) double without shower, 128 DM ($84.50) double with shower. AE, DC, MC, V.

This unpretentious five-story hotel was built on a sometimes traffic-clogged street in the 1970s. The well-scrubbed rooms are wallpapered and very simple, containing double-insulated windows to keep out some noise. The quieter rooms overlook the rear. None of the rooms contains a toilet, but some offer private showers, and adequate toilet facilities are scattered throughout the hallways.

BINNENALSTER & NEUSTADT

VERY EXPENSIVE

HAMBURG MARRIOTT, ABC Strasse 52, D-2000 Hamburg 36. Tel. 040/35-05-0, or toll free in the U.S. 800/228-9290. Fax 040/3505-1777. 277 rms, 5 studios, 4 suites. A/C MINIBAR TV TEL **U-Bahn:** Gänsemarkt.

$ Rates: 350 DM–380 DM ($231–$250.80) single or double; from 495 DM ($326.70) studio or suite. Continental breakfast 17 DM ($11.20) extra. AE, DC, MC, V. **Parking:** 25 DM ($16.50).

One of the finest hotels in Hamburg opened in 1988. Built on the site of the old Gänsemarkt, where in the Middle Ages geese were sold, the Marriott stands near the Hanse Viertel shopping complex. The surrounding area has become one of the most fashionable in Hamburg, with boutiques, wine bars, shops, and restaurants. Traditional in styling, the hotel offers rooms with private baths floored with marble tile and sinks topped with a slab of polished granite, two phones, and color TVs. The less expensive price is for the standard rooms, and the more expensive tariffs are charged for studios. Lavish suites are also available. One hundred rooms are reserved for nonsmokers.

Dining/Entertainment: Live music begins at 7pm in the lobby-level piano bar. In the newly designed restaurant, American Place, wine and cuisine of California, plus food of New Orleans and Boston, are featured in a casual atmosphere at moderate prices. All popular American holidays and events are celebrated here. The menu ranges from buffet bar salads and sandwiches to full meals, costing from 15 DM to 38 DM ($9.90 to $25.10). Service is daily from noon to 3pm and from 5:30pm to midnight. A special theater menu is also available.

Services: Full concierge services, including babysitting and car rental; 24-hour room service; same-day laundry and dry cleaning (Monday to Friday).

Facilities: Only downtown hotel featuring a pool, sauna, whirlpool, fitness center; also offers Dominique Beauty Farm, ice machines on all floors, fax and computer connections in each room.

RAMADA RENAISSANCE, Grosse Bleichen, D-2000 Hamburg 36. Tel. 040/34-91-80. Fax 040/349-18-431. 211 rms, 3 suites. A/C MINIBAR TV TEL **U-Bahn:** Jungfernstieg.

$ Rates: 295 DM–390 DM ($194.70–$257.40) single; 355 DM–460 DM ($234.30–$303.60) double; from 580 DM ($382.80) suite. Breakfast 27.50 DM ($18.20) extra. AE, DC, MC, V. **Parking:** 25 DM ($16.50).

A 19th-century building with 20th-century comfort, the Ramada Renaissance is a glass-and-hardwood empire of subtle lighting and comfort. From the elegant lobby to the carpeted bar area you'll be fêted by an army of waiters and serenaded by a resident pianist. Accommodations range from well-appointed double-bedded rooms to sumptuously upholstered suites. The hotel was built into the facade of a historic building, and the entire complex was designed with connections to the Hanse Viertel Galerie Passage, Europe's longest shopping arcade (see "Savvy Shopping").

Dining/Entertainment: After drinks in the lounge bar, you can dine at the Noblesse Restaurant.

Services: Room service, laundry, dry cleaning.

Facilities: Whirlpool, sauna.

SAS HAMBURG PLAZA, Marseillerstrasse 2, D-2000 Hamburg 36. Tel. 040/35-02-0. Fax 040/350-23-333. 563 rms, 26 suites. A/C MINIBAR TV TEL **Bus:** 102.

$ Rates: 280 DM–420 DM ($184.80–$277.20) single; 330 DM–490 DM ($217.80–$323.40) double; from 700 DM ($462) suite. Substantial weekend discounts available. Breakfast buffet 27 DM ($17.80) extra. AE, DC, MC, V. **Parking:** 25 DM ($16.50).

There's a hotel in Planten un Blomen Park of real architectural interest: It looks like a collection of narrow black lines banded vertically together. Opened in 1973 and renovated in 1989, this high-rise offers beautifully appointed rooms, many with handsomely paneled walls; all contain individually controlled air conditioning, color TVs, radios, trouser presses, and hairdryers.

Dining/Entertainment: Guests can order South Pacific–inspired dinners at Trader Vic's or sample North German and Scandinavian cuisine in rustic surroundings in the Vierländer Stuben. For coffee, pastries, or drinks, the Galeonen Bar and Lobby Lounge are the choices; later, guests can head for the 26th floor to enjoy a view over Hamburg and the harbor in the nightclub and bar, Top of Town.

Services: 24-hour room service, express laundry, babysitting.

Facilities: Heated pool, sauna, solarium, fitness studio.

VIER JAHRESZEITEN, Neuer Jungfernstieg 9-14, D-2000 Hamburg 36. Tel. 040/3-49-40, or toll free 800/223-6800 in U.S. and Canada. Fax 040/349-46-02. 172 rms, 11 suites. MINIBAR TV TEL **U-Bahn:** Hauptbahnhof.

$ Rates: 365 DM–435 DM ($240.90–$287.10) single; 535 DM–780 DM ($353.10–$514.80) double; from 950 DM ($627) suite. Breakfast 30 DM ($19.80) extra. AE, DC, MC, V. **Parking:** 25 DM ($16.50).

⭐ One of the leading hotels in the world is this warm, mellow establishment, founded in 1897 by Friedrich Haerlin and still a family business. Its position is ideal, right on the Binnenalster. Built in the baronial style, with rich wood paneling, it evokes the grand Edwardian hotels. No two of the rooms are alike. Despite the large size of the hotel, personal service is a hallmark. The prices vary with the view and size of the accommodations.

Dining/Entertainment: The hotel's dining room, Haerlin, bedecked with old tapestries, gold-framed mirrors, and four Dionysian porcelain cherubs, is an attractive setting for excellent international cuisine. There's also the informal Grill Room, where meats are roasted on spits along one wall. The tea room, the two-level Condi (Hamburg's answer to Demel's of Vienna), is a favorite rendezvous point. International bands play in the hotel's own nightclub. There are also a cocktail bar, a wine shop, and a confectioner's shop selling the chef's own pastry.

Services: Room service, laundry, dry cleaning.

Facilities: Horseback riding and golf can be arranged.

EXPENSIVE

ALSTER-HOF, Esplanade 12, D-2000 Hamburg 36. Tel. 040/35-00-76.

Fax 040/350-07-514. 120 rms (97 with bath or shower). MINIBAR TV TEL **U-Bahn:** Gänsemarkt.
$ Rates (including continental breakfast): 135 DM ($89.10) single without bath or shower, 190 DM ($125.40) single with shower; 210 DM–285 DM ($138.60–$188.10) double with bath or shower. AE, DC, MC, V.

The Alster-Hof is a serviceable hotel on a quiet street near the Binnenalster. Its rooms are modernized and functional. Breakfast is the only meal served. One of the better-known hotels of Hamburg, the Alster-Hof is well recommended.

MODERATE

HAFEN HAMBURG, Seewartenstrasse 9, D-2000 Hamburg 1. Tel. 040/ 31-11-30. Fax 040/319-27-36. 252 rms. TV TEL **U-Bahn:** Landungsbrücke.
$ Rates (including continental breakfast): 160 DM–180 DM ($105.60–$118.80) single; 185 DM–210 DM ($122.10–$138.60) double. AE, MC, V. **Parking:** 18 DM ($11.90).

Constructed in the Wilhelmian style, this Hamburg landmark offers splendid views of the river and harbor traffic. The grand staircase is an elaborately twisting wrought-iron fantasy, and the rooms are unusually spacious. If within your budget, book the more expensive harbor-view rooms.

HARVESTEHUDE

VERY EXPENSIVE

GARDEN HOTEL PÖSELDORF, Magdalenenstrasse 60, D-2000 Hamburg 13. Tel. 040/41-40-40. Fax 040/414-04-20. 61 rms. MINIBAR TV TEL **U-Bahn:** Hallerstrasse.
$ Rates (including continental breakfast): 230 DM–300 DM ($151.80–$198) single; 360 DM–420 DM ($237.60–$277.20) double. AE, DC, MC, V. **Parking:** 25 DM ($16.50).

This hotel has had a long history, dating from 1791. Over the years it has entertained many luminaries, including King Christian VIII of Denmark in 1824. The location, however, isn't for everyone. It stands in the Hamburg-Harvestehude district, about a mile from the historic heart of town and some 6 miles from the Hamburg airport. On the western sector of the Outer Alster Lake, it attracts many visitors from the publishing industry. Modern art and well-chosen antiques add to the sophisticated comfort of the rooms.

Dining/Entertainment: The hotel, which serves breakfast only, has a bar adjoining the winter garden.
Services: Room service, laundry, dry cleaning.
Facilities: Terrace garden.

ELMSBÜTTEL

EXPENSIVE

HOTEL NORGE, Schäferkampsallee 49, D-2000 Hamburg 36. Tel. 040/ 44-11-50. Fax 040/441-15-577. 90 rms. MINIBAR TV TEL **U-Bahn:** Christiankirche.
$ Rates (including continental breakfast): 189 DM–229 DM ($124.70–$151.10) single; 243 DM–568 DM ($160.40–$374.90) double. AE, DC, MC, V. **Parking:** 10 DM ($6.60).

The Norge, away from the center in the Elmsbüttel district, offers Norwegian hospitality and a "Gateway to Scandinavia" from the Continent. The hotel is modern

---

⒡FROMMER'S COOL FOR KIDS: HOTELS

Berlin *(see page 446)* Outside the traffic-clogged center, this hotel welcomes parents and houses children under 18 free in their parents' room.

Steens Hotel *(see page 447)* For the family on a budget, this simple but clean and safe hotel is run by a live-in family.

Garden Hotel Pöseldorf *(see page 450)* For the family that can afford it, this traditional hotel in the western sector looks out onto the Outer Alster Lake. Here you'll find cozy comfort in a safe neighborhood.

---

and undistinguished on the outside but warms considerably in its interior. Its Kon-Tiki Grill merits a separate recommendation (see below). The rooms are compact but have many conveniences. Nearly all units are at the lower end of the price scale. Facilities include a pool and sauna, and there's massage service.

HARBURG

MODERATE

SÜDERELBE, Grosser Schippsee 29, D-2000 Hamburg 90. Tel. 040/77-32-14. Fax 040/77-31-04. 21 rms. TV TEL S-Bahn: Harburg.
$ Rates (including continental breakfast): 100 DM–115 DM ($66–$75.90) single; 110 DM–150 DM ($72.60–$99) double. AE, DC, MC, V. **Parking:** 8 DM ($5.30).

Breakfast is the only meal served in this modern hotel in the Harburg district, away from the center of town. Many guests save money by staying here and using public transportation. Each of the quiet, pleasant rooms is filled with contemporary furniture. Some also have minibars.

3. DINING

Hamburg life is tied to the sea, and nothing reflects this more than the cuisine. Lobster from Helgoland, shrimp from Büsum, turbot, plaice, and sole from the North Sea, and fresh oysters in huge quantities make up the Hamburger's diet. Of course, there's also the traditional meat dish, Hamburger steak, called Stuben küchen, and the favorite sailor's dish, Labskaus, made with beer, onions, cured meat, potatoes, herring, and pickle. The eel soup is probably the best known of all Hamburg's typical dishes. Heinrich Heine, who knew the city in his youth, said of Hamburg, "It's manners are from England and its food is from Heaven."

NEAR THE HAUPTBAHNHOF

EXPENSIVE

PETER LEMBCKE, Holzdamm 49. Tel. 040/24-32-90.
Cuisine: NORTHERN GERMAN. **Reservations:** Required. **U-Bahn:** Hauptbahnhof.

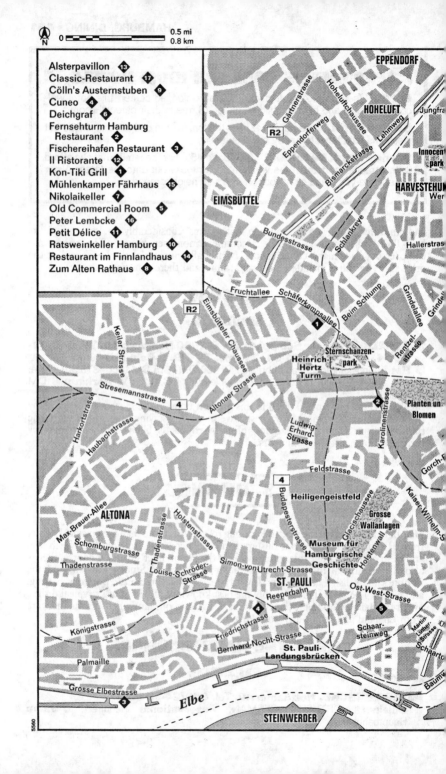

BARMBEK

St. Benedict-strasse

Maria-Louisen-Strasse

Bellevue

Sierichstrasse

Barmbeker-strasse

Osterbekstrasse

Adolph-Schönfelder-Strasse

Hans-Henry-Jahn-Weg

15

Weidestrasse

Fernsic

Herderstrasse

Beethovenstrasse

Hallerstrasse

Alster-park

Bellevue

Herbert-Weichmann-Strasse

Winterhuder Weg

UHLENHORST

5

Hamburger Strasse

Oberaltenallee

Lerchenfeld Wartenau

ROTHERBAUM

Mittelweg

Harvsthuder Weg

Schöne Aussicht

Mundsburgerdamm

Rothenbaumchaussee

Aussenalster

Schwanenwik

HOHENFELDE

Mühlendamm

Th.-Heuss-Platz

Alsterufer

Sechslingspforte

75

Lübecker-strasse

BORGFELDE

stavl-er-Park

14

Kennedybrücke

Lombardsbrücke

An der Alster

Koppelstrasse

Wall-strasse

Binnenalster

16

ST. GEORG

Hansaplatz

Jungfernstieg

Ballindamm

Hachmannplatz

17

Steindamm

12

13

Adenauerallee

11

Mönckebergstrasse

Kurt-Schumacher-Allee

Rathaus Stock Exchange

St. Petri Kirche

10

Speersort Steinstrasse

Spaldingstrasse

Nordkanalstrasse

75

Heidenkampsweg

Mönckebergstrasse

Domstrasse

8

9

Ost-West-Strasse

Holzbr. Marten

7

Katharinen-strasse

Dovenfleet

Oberbaum brücke

Banksstrasse

Bankstrasse

Nagelsweg

Amsinckstrasse

Hammerbrookstrasse

Brooktorkai

$ Prices: Appetizers 12 DM–40 DM ($7.90–$26.40); main courses 22 DM–50 DM ($14.50–$33). AE, DC, MC, V.
Open: Mon–Fri noon–10:45pm, Sat 6–10:45pm.

One of Hamburg's leading restaurants is Peter Lembcke, in an unprepossessing location on the second floor of an Altstadt house. The good-hearted, helter-skelter service adds to the charm, but food is the real attraction here. Lembcke specializes in the cuisine of northern Germany, including the most local dish of all, Labskaus. A house specialty that attracts a loyal following is the eel soup, with dill and fruit swimming in the broth. Possibly more appealing to the foreign palate is the house bouillabaisse. Besides the best Kalbs filet, the restaurant serves excellent steaks. Lembcke's is invariably crowded, and late arrivals without reservations must wait in the foyer, so phone ahead.

BINNENALSTER & NEUSTADT

VERY EXPENSIVE

CÖLLN'S AUSTERNSTUBEN, Brodschrangen 1–5. Tel. 040/32-60-59.
   Cuisine: NORTH GERMAN/CONTINENTAL. **Reservations:** Recommended. **U-Bahn:** Rathausmarkt.
$ Prices: Appetizers 30 DM–40 DM ($19.80–$26.40); main courses 50 DM–80 DM ($33–$52.80). AE, DC, MC, V.
   Open: Mon–Fri 10am–10:30pm (last order), Sat 6–10:30pm (last order).

The original version of this "oyster-eating house" opened in 1761 as a waterfront fish house. After many manifestations, it now occupies much larger quarters, filling about 10 dining rooms, and is considered one of the most stylish and best-liked restaurants in Hamburg. Today, amid carefully maintained paneling, dramatic touches of black, and a strong sense of Teutonic nostalgia, the restaurant serves oysters as well as a sophisticated array of other dishes. These include breast of pheasant in puff pastry with white beans, minestrone studded with lobster meat and served with lobster-stuffed ravioli, schnitzels of salmon in balsamic-vinegar lindenflower sauce, and breast of goose with wild mushrooms and pepper-flavored Bordeaux sauce.

EXPENSIVE

IL RISTORANTE, Grosse Bleichen 16. Tel. 040/34-33-35.
   Cuisine: ITALIAN. **Reservations:** Required. **U-Bahn:** Jungfernstieg.
$ Prices: Appetizers 15 DM–18 DM ($9.90–$11.90); main courses 31 DM–55 DM ($20.50–$36.30); five-course fixed-price menu 95 DM ($62.70). AE, DC, MC.
   Open: Daily noon–midnight.

Perhaps the most fashionable Italian restaurant in Hamburg is located in the heart of town, in a very modern building. Luxurious and rather formal, it's reached by going up a glass-enclosed stairwell. At the top, amid seasonal flowering shrubs, you can enjoy the ambience and the high-quality meals, which use very fresh ingredients. Typical dishes are crayfish in saffron sauce, marinated salmon with green-asparagus mousse, and a cream of carrot and celery soup that is perfect.

PETIT DÉLICE, Grosse Bleichen 21. Tel. 040/34-34-70.
   Cuisine: CONTINENTAL. **Reservations:** Required. **U-Bahn:** Gänsemarkt.
$ Prices: Appetizers 16 DM–34 DM ($10.60–$22.40); main courses 38 DM–48 DM ($25.10–$31.70). No credit cards.
   Open: Lunch Tues–Sat noon–2:30pm; dinner Tues–Sat 6:30–9:30pm.

Petit Délice is part of the rapidly emerging "new Hamburg," a restaurant movement characterized by minimalist decor, *Neue Küche*, and intimate tables. The location of this 10-table bistro is at the rear of In der Galleria, a stylish shopping complex in the city center. The limited menu is based on seasonal shopping and therefore changes frequently. Everything is prepared to order. You might ask for dandelion greens with braised goose liver, which could be followed with a perfectly flavored lamb platter (cooked pink) served with ratatouille and crisply cooked vegetables.

ZUM ALTEN RATHAUS, Börsenbrücke 10. Tel. 040/36-75-70.
   Cuisine: NORTH GERMAN. **Reservations:** Recommended. **U-Bahn:** Rathausmarkt.
$ Prices: Appetizers 12 DM–25 DM ($7.90–$16.50), main courses 28 DM–52 DM ($18.50–$34.30) AE, DC, MC, V.
   Open: Mon–Fri 11:30am–10:30pm (last order).

Situated within the carefully preserved walls of a mid-19th-century building set close to the mouth of the Elbe, in the most historic part of the Altstadt, this restaurant features an appealing array of old-fashioned North German recipes and an enviable collection of antiques. The preferred rendezvous of civic associations, who meet on the upper floors, the restaurant features preparations of herring, goose-liver parfait with black-currant sauce, roast rabbit with aromatic herbs and black-olive sauce, and filet of lamb in rosemary sauce.

MODERATE

DEICHGRAF, Deichstrasse 23. Tel. 040/36-42-08.
   Cuisine: NORTH GERMAN. **Reservations:** Recommended. **U-Bahn:** Rödingsmarkt.
$ Prices: Appetizers 8.50 DM–28 DM ($5.60–$18.50); main courses 23 DM–50 DM ($15.20–$33); three-course fixed-price menu 39.50 DM–50 DM ($26.10–$33); four-course fixed-price menu 70 DM ($46.20); six-course fixed-price menu 90 DM–125 DM ($59.40–$82.50). AE, DC, MC, V.
   Open: Mon–Fri 11am–11pm, Sat 6–11pm. **Closed:** Holidays.

An elegant restaurant, Deichgraf has an unusual collection of antiques, one of which is a 4-foot model of a many-sailed schooner. The restaurant is dedicated to the man who was responsible for the area's dikes and the thousands of men who have maintained them, preventing floods on many occasions. Featured are such northern German specialties as salmon in mustard-flavored dill sauce and fresh seasonal lobster prepared in a number of ways. You can also order several kinds of fondue. Many of the shellfish specialties are sold by weight.

NIKOLAIKELLER, Cremon 36. Tel. 040/36-61-13.
   Cuisine: HAMBURG. **Reservations:** Required. **U-Bahn:** U3 to Rödingsmarkt. **Bus:** 37.
$ Prices: Appetizers 8.50 DM–22.50 DM ($5.60–$14.90); main courses 22 DM–35.80 DM ($14.50–$23.60); five-course Hamburg menu 47.50 DM ($31.40). AE, DC, MC, V.
   Open: Mon–Sat noon–midnight.

S You can see the sprawling maritime facilities of Hamburg from the windows of this place, filled with a no-nonsense crowd of local businesspeople and workers. The Hamburg cuisine includes more than two dozen varieties of herring. You can also order goulash soup Altona style, bacon pancakes topped with cranberries, fresh sole, or salmon. Ample quantities of local beer are provided in oversize mugs.

RATSWEINKELLER HAMBURG, Grosse Johannisstrasse 2. Tel. 040/36-41-53.
   Cuisine: HAMBURG/INTERNATIONAL. **Reservations:** Required. **U-Bahn:** Rathausmarkt.
$ Prices: Appetizers 8 DM–25 DM ($5.30–$16.50); main courses 19 DM–62 DM ($12.50–$40.90); fixed-price menu 42 DM ($27.70). AE, DC, MC, V.
   Open: Mon–Sat 11am–11pm. **Closed:** Holidays.

The city takes pride in the distinguished Ratsweinkeller Hamburg, in business since 1896. The theme is suggested at the entrance, where you'll find a stone statue of Bacchus. The main dining hall has high vaulted ceilings, wood-paneled columns, and large stained-glass windows. One excellent dish is the halibut steak in curry sauce. The fresh sole bonne femme is heavenly and served in large portions; also try the Hamburg crab soup. Listen for the great-grandfather clock to chime the quarter hour, resounding throughout the chambers.

ELMSBÜTTEL

MODERATE

KON-TIKI GRILL, in the Hotel Norge, Schäferkampsallee 49. Tel. 040/441-15-544.

Cuisine: NORWEGIAN. **Reservations:** Required. **U-Bahn:** Christiankirche.

$ Prices: Appetizers 12 DM–22 DM ($7.90–$14.50); main courses 30 DM–50 DM ($19.80–$33); three-course fixed-price dinner 38 DM ($25.10). AE, DC, MC, V.

Open: Lunch daily noon–3pm; dinner daily 6–10:30pm.

Outside the city center in the Elmsbüttel district, this hotel dining room features Norwegian specialties. The buffet is something you'd otherwise have to go to Oslo for. Other specialties include fish, meats, and hot and cold vegetable dishes.

ALTONA

VERY EXPENSIVE

FISCHEREIHAFEN RESTAURANT, Grosse Elbstrasse 143. Tel. 040/38-18-16.

Cuisine: SEAFOOD. **Reservations:** Required. **S-Bahn:** Königinstrasse.

$ Prices: Appetizers 30 DM–60 DM ($19.80–$39.60); main courses 40 DM–70 DM ($26.40–$46.20); six-course fixed-price dinner 95 DM ($62.70). AE, DC, MC, V.

Open: Daily 11:30am–10:30pm.

Established some 35 years ago, the Fischereihafen is considered the best seafood restaurant in Hamburg. Every day the staff buys only the freshest fish and shellfish at the Hamburg auction hall. The menu is changed daily depending on what "fruits of the sea" are available. On the second floor, the place is said to be filled with "fish and VIPs"—the latter including the likes of Chancellor Helmut Kohl and Tina Turner, the former likely to include an appetizer of filet of sole and lobster à la nage or a plate of fresh oysters. The house special is turbot with salmon mousse dotted with truffles. Picture windows open onto a view of the Elbe. The restaurant is a 10-minute taxi ride from the wharf area of Landungsbrücken.

LANDHAUS SCHERRER, Elbchaussee 130. Tel. 040/880-13-25.

Cuisine: CONTINENTAL. **Reservations:** Required. **Bus:** 135.

$ Prices: Appetizers 28 DM–58 DM ($18.50–$38.30); main courses 44 DM–65 DM ($29–$42.90); fixed-price dinner 165 DM ($108.90). AE, DC, MC.

Open: Lunch Mon–Sat noon–2:30pm; dinner Mon–Sat 6:30–10:30pm.

This place was a brewery in its previous incarnation, but the Landhaus is now a citadel of gastronomy on the Elbe River at Altona. It has gained a reputation for correct service and imaginatively prepared cuisine in an amiable setting. Specialties are fresh fish and shellfish, excellent meat, and mushrooms imported from Morocco. An unusual variation might be roast goose with rhubarb in cassis sauce. Dessert might be praline cream or one of 30 types of pastry loading down the sweets trolley. Because of its location in a country house surrounded by trees, it's also popular with locals for wedding receptions.

LE CANARD, Elbchaussee 139. Tel. 040/880-50-57.

Cuisine: CONTINENTAL. **Reservations:** Required. **Bus:** 115.
$ **Prices:** Appetizers 18 DM–75 DM ($11.90–$49.50); main courses 45 DM–115 DM ($29.70–$75.90); fixed-price lunch 68 DM ($44.90); fixed-price dinner 169 DM ($111.50). AE, DC, MC, V.
Open: Lunch Mon–Sat noon–3pm; dinner Mon–Sat 7–11pm.

Northwest of the city center is Le Canard, whose haute cuisine has given it a reputation as one of the best restaurants in Germany. Virtually every major restaurant critic in the country has lauded the unusual cuisine moderne of its imaginative owner-chef, Josef Viehhauser. An unpretentious decor of flowers, framed lithographs, and contemporary accents is made more alluring by the softly discreet lighting. Meals are culinary events. Your elegant repast might include a set of seasonally adjusted dishes, including medallions of lobster garnished with mussels and leaf spinach, suprême of sea bass with herb-flavored sabayon, or Barbary duckling stuffed with goose liver. For dessert you are faced with a wide choice, including melon-flavored cake garnished with strawberry cream and mocha-flavored parfait with mango segments.

BLANKENESE

EXPENSIVE

FLIC FLAC BISTRO, Blankeneser Landstrasse 29. Tel. 040/86-53-45.
Cuisine: FRENCH/GERMAN. **Reservations:** Recommended. **S-Bahn:** Blankenese.
$ **Prices:** Appetizers 14 DM–24 DM ($9.20–$15.80); main courses 30 DM–42 DM ($19.80–$27.70). No credit cards.
Open: Dinner only, Tues–Sun 6pm–midnight.
This attractive bistro awash with unusual lithographs and fresh flowers is the personal statement of its owner, Iris Seybold. Menu items include a full repertoire of French and German cuisine moderne, with an emphasis on fresh vegetables and light sauces.

MODERATE

SAGEBIELS FÄHRHAUS, Blankeneser Hauptstrasse 107. Tel. 040/86-15-14.
Cuisine: GERMAN/ORIENTAL. **Reservations:** Recommended. **Bus:** 46 or 48.
$ **Prices:** Appetizers 10 DM–29 DM ($6.60–$19.10); main courses 23 DM–58 DM ($15.20–$38.30). AE, DC, MC, V.
Open: Daily noon–11pm. **Closed:** Mon in winter.
In a century-old house on a terrace above the Elbe River, 10 miles from the heart of Hamburg, this restaurant has a clear view of ships going up and down the stream. Kaiser Wilhelm once celebrated his birthday here. In the glassed-in dining room, you can enjoy traditional German food, served attractively and capably. One section of the menu is devoted to Oriental cuisine, including tender lamb slices Szechuan with leek and bamboo in orange sauce, sweet-and-sour breast of chicken with fresh pineapple, and young duck. A specialty is three jewels (beef, chicken, and shrimp) in a spicy concoction. Try the garden terrace if the weather is fine.

UHLENHORST

EXPENSIVE

MÜHLENKAMPER FÄHRHAUS, Hans-Henny-Jahnn-Weg 1. Tel. 040/220-73-90.
Cuisine: CONTINENTAL/INTERNATIONAL. **Reservations:** Required. **S-Bahn:** Barmbek.

$ Prices: Appetizers 10.50 DM–28 DM ($6.90–$18.50); main courses 28 DM–75 DM ($18.50–$49.50). AE, DC, MC, V.

Open: Mon–Fri noon–11pm, Sat–Sun 6–10:30pm.

In the Hamburg-Uhlenhorst district, near the Alster Fleet, this family-owned spot has been a Hamburg landmark for some 50 years. A favorite rendezvous of celebrities and the city's most discerning diners, it has a menu that is a virtual encyclopedia of German, French, and international food; the cuisine reflects a light touch, based on North German ingredients. For example, you might enjoy eel in dill jelly; the chef will prepare game specialties or diet dishes per your desire. He excels in such classics as goose liver with truffles. Three hundred varieties of wine are available.

BERGSTEDT

MODERATE

ALTE MÜHLE, Alte Mühle 34, in Bergstedt. Tel. 040/6-04-91-71.
Cuisine: GERMAN. **Reservations:** Recommended. **S-Bahn:** Poppenbüttel.
$ Prices: Appetizers 6.50 DM–20 DM ($4.30–$13.20); main courses 22 DM–36 DM ($14.50–$23.80); four-course fixed-price dinner 55 DM ($36.30). No credit cards.

Open: Wed–Sun 11am–10pm.

In a residential quarter, Alte Mühle sits near a waterfall with an old mill. Homestyle German fare is featured, including pigs' trotters with sauerkraut and potatoes. Many Hamburgers make the journey here just to enjoy the fresh carp with melted butter, horseradish, and potatoes. However, the chef delivers his peak performance when he serves venison with red cabbage. After a satisfying meal, you can walk through the pond-filled woods and watch the horses nearby.

LANGENHORN

EXPENSIVE

ZUM WATTKORN, Tangstedter Landstrasse 230. Tel. 040/520-37-97.
Cuisine: AUSTRIAN. **Reservations:** Required. **U-Bahn:** Langenhorn-Nord.
$ Prices: Appetizers 12 DM–30 DM ($7.90–$19.80); main courses 30 DM–45 DM ($19.80–$29.70); fixed-price menus 59 DM ($38.90) and 79 DM ($52.10). No credit cards.

Open: Lunch Tues–Sun noon–2:30pm; dinner Tues–Sun 6–9pm.

Austrian cuisine is served in generous portions in the popular Biergarten of this

---

 FROMMER'S COOL FOR KIDS: RESTAURANTS

Sagebiels Fährhaus *(see page 457)* Above the Elbe River, children can enjoy watching the ships coming and going as much as they will sampling the German and Oriental food.

Restaurant im Finnlandhaus *(see page 459)* The Finnish specialties are a treat, but they have strong competition from the view of the Binnenalster. Families take an elevator to the top for a panoramic sweep of Hamburg.

Alsterpavillon *(see page 459)* Dining here is like attending a summer festival, as families occupy café tables built right onto the lake, Binnenalster, with boats and yachts clogging the water old-fashioned guesthouse. It's situated outside Hamburg's commercial core in a green oasis of nesting birds and flowering plants. The menu, which changes weekly, makes good use of seasonally available fruits and vegetables.

SPECIALTY DINING
DINING WITH A VIEW
Expensive

RESTAURANT IM FINNLANDHAUS, Esplanade 41. Tel. 040/34-41-32.
   Cuisine: FINNISH/INTERNATIONAL. **Reservations:** Required. **U-Bahn:** Stephansplatz.
$ Prices: Appetizers 10.50 DM–25 DM ($6.90–$16.50); main courses 35 DM–55 DM ($23.10–$36.30); fixed-price lunch 76 DM ($50.20); fixed-price dinner 89 DM ($58.70). AE, DC, MC, V.
   Open: Mon–Fri noon–10pm, Sun 11:30am–3pm.

You'll enjoy panoramic views in the modern glass Finnlandhaus near the Binnenalster. The setting is Finnish, with warm autumnal colors and stylish molded armchairs. Take the elevator to the top, where the restaurant opens onto views of the city and the Alster. From the à la carte menu, a good beginning is warmed smoked salmon. Specialties include Finnish salmon soup, cured salmon, and Finnish moose prepared several ways.

Moderate

ALSTERPAVILLON, Am Jungfernstieg 54. Tel. 040/34-50-52.
   Cuisine: CONTINENTAL. **Reservations:** Recommended. **U-Bahn:** Jungfernstieg.
$ Prices: Appetizers 6.50 DM–22 DM ($4.30–$14.50); main courses 22 DM–50 DM ($14.50–$33). three-course fixed-price menu 35 DM ($23.10). MC, V.
   Open: Daily 11am–8pm.

⭐   At this pavilion built right on the Binnenalster, café tables are placed outside in summer, when the lake takes on a festive air. The Alsterpavillon has been in business for almost two centuries. Heinrich Heine was a regular customer. Sole meunière in chive butter is a superb selection, and other specialties include Strasbourg sauerkraut with pork. A good beginning for any meal is Matjes herring.

FERNSEHTURM HAMBURG RESTAURANT, Lagerstrasse 2–8. Tel. 040/43-80-24.
   Cuisine: CONTINENTAL. **Reservations:** Recommended. **S-Bahn:** Sheruschaure.
$ Prices: Appetizers 10.50 DM–18 DM ($6.90–$11.90); main courses 28 DM–42 DM ($18.50–$27.70); three-course fixed-price dinner 40 DM ($26.40); four-course fixed-price dinner 70 DM ($46.20). AE, DC, MC, V.
   Open: Lunch only, Sat–Sun noon–2:30pm; dinner daily 6–11pm.

The Fernsehturm serves food as good as the view you get while you dine about halfway up Hamburg's 900-foot television tower (in the suburb of Rotherbaum) and the fully air-conditioned room revolves (one complete turn each hour). One of Hamburg's best-known chefs is in charge, and English-speaking waiters are available. The cuisine is continental, and the offerings change with the season. During the afternoon, you can have coffee and cake. Visitors must purchase a 6-DM ($4) ticket to ascend the tower.

HOTEL DINING
Moderate

CLASSIC-RESTAURANT, in the Maritim Hotel Reichshof, Kirchenallee 34-36. Tel. 040/24-83-30.
   Cuisine: INTERNATIONAL/NORTH GERMAN. **Reservations:** Not necessary. **U-Bahn:** Hauptbahnhof.

$ Prices: Appetizers 8 DM–22 DM ($5.30–$14.50); main courses 30 DM–50 DM ($19.80–$33). AE, DC, MC, V.
Open: Lunch daily noon–3pm; dinner daily 6–11:30pm.

For traditionalists who gravitate to lavish belle époque style, this previously recommended hotel near the Hauptbahnhof is a local landmark. The dining room was designed to resemble the one on a favorite transatlantic steamer, *Cap Polonia*. Today, its translucent marble lighting fixtures, carved wooden cherub heads, and art deco glamour make it one of Hamburg's favorite places for before- or after-theater supper. Two of the city's major theaters are a short walk away. Always look for a page on the menu outlining the daily specials. Otherwise, you can select from an extensive à la carte menu, beginning with anything from fresh lobster to Beluga caviar. A local favorite is smoked eel with scrambled eggs. Rich soups are always available, as is a wide selection of fish, including North Sea turbot prepared several ways. You can also enjoy a number of beef dishes or what Germans call *traditionelle Gerichte* (popular dishes), such as veal Züricher style or fried calves' liver with onions, apple slices, and mashed potatoes. Desserts are homemade, ranging from peach Melba to crêpes Reichshof.

LATE-NIGHT DINING
Moderate

OLD COMMERCIAL ROOM, Englische Planke 10. Tel. 040/36-63-19.
  Cuisine: NORTH GERMAN. **Reservations:** Required. **U-Bahn:** St. Pauli.
$ Prices: Appetizers 9.80 DM–18 DM ($6.50–$11.90); main courses 18.50 DM–58 DM ($12.20–$38.30). AE, DC, MC, V.
  Open: Daily 11am–midnight.

Founded in 1643 and located at the foot of St. Michaelis, the sailors' church, the Old Commercial Room is so tied into Hamburg maritime life that many residents consider it the premier sailors' stopover. It is the best place in town to order Labskaus, prepared with devotion by the chef; if you order it, you're given a numbered certificate proclaiming you a genuine Labskaus-eater. You can also order many traditional North German dishes, including fresh fish. Its name, along with that of the street, speaks of the historic mercantile links between Hamburg and England.

LOCAL FAVORITE
Moderate

CUNEO, Davidstrasse 11. Tel. 040/31-25-80.
  Cuisine: ITALIAN. **Reservations:** Required. **U-Bahn:** U-3 to St. Pauli.
$ Prices: Appetizers 6.50 DM–19.50 DM ($4.30–$12.90); main courses 28.50 DM–36.50 DM ($18.80–$24.10). No credit cards.
  Open: Mon–Sat 6:30pm–1:30am. **Closed:** 2 weeks in July (dates vary).

In the St. Pauli neighborhood is this place for good Italian food at reasonable prices. If you're in the area for fun at night and want reliable cookery, head here. Behind an unprepossessing facade, it opens onto crowded rooms that look like an art director's concept of what a Greenwich Village eatery might have been like in the 1930s. Grilled fish is one of the most expensive items on the menu, but you can also order pizza, carpaccio, spaghetti with pesto, gnocchi with Gorgonzola, and Venetian-style liver.

PICNIC FARE & WHERE TO EAT IT

The best place to acquire the makings for an inexpensive picnic lunch is at **Schlemmen im Bahnhof,** Hamburg Hauptbahnhof, Hachmannplatz 10, a collection of stand-up cafés and foods counters in the main rail station. You'll find an array of food items here, including hearty day or delectable sausages and baked potatoes with a variety of toppings (each a meal itself), plus a number of Hamburger seafood specialties. You can also buy beer and wine or soft drinks.

- Nearly 6 million immigrants to America passed through the port of Hamburg between 1850 and 1920.
- Hamburg is called Germany's "millionaires' capital" because so many rich people live there.
- The city is famous for its red-light St. Pauli district, but most locals leave the area to foreign visitors.
- Hamburg is Europe's third-largest port city.
- The first copies of Karl Marx's *Das Kapital* were printed in Hamburg, even though this was forbidden by Bismarck.
- Jungfernstieg, a promenade along the Binnenalster, was named "maidens' walk" because so many young women strolled along it in the 19th century.
- Hamburg's Kunsthalle owns one of Rembrandt's earliest surviving works, *The Presentation in the Temple*, painted when he was only 21.

You can take your picnic to **Planten un Blomen Park,** north of the city center and north of the Botanical Garden (S-Bahn: Dammtor). These gardens were laid out geometrically in 1936. The city of Hamburg uses the gardens to test new species of trees and flowers. An artificially powered cascade flows into the main pool, Grosser Parksee. The park is open daily from 8am to 11:30pm.

4. ATTRACTIONS

Before you tour the city, you can get a good overall view from the tower of the ✪ **Hauptkirche St. Michaelis,** Kravenkamp 4C (Michaeliskirchplatz; tel. 040/376-78-0), Hamburg's favorite landmark. It is considered the finest baroque church in North Germany. The view from the top of the hammered-copper tower is magnificent. The church and tower are open Monday to Saturday from 9am to 5:30pm; Sunday from 11:30am to 5:30pm (in winter, Monday to Saturday from 10am to 4pm; Sunday from 11:30am to 4pm). Take the elevator or climb the 449 steps. U-Bahn: Rödingsmarkt or St. Pauli.

The **Altstadt** actually has little left of the old architecture, but there are a few sights among the canals (fleets) that run through this section from the Alster to the Elbe. The largest of the old buildings is the **Rathaus,** Rathausplatz (tel. 040/36-81-20-62), which is modern compared with many of Germany's town halls. A Renaissance-style structure, it was built in the late 19th century on a foundation of 4,000 oak piles, and has a sumptuous 647-room interior. This seat of the senate and the city council can be visited on guided tours costing 1 DM (66¢). Tours in English are given Monday to Thursday, hourly from 10:15am to 3:15pm; Friday, Saturday, and Sunday from 10:15am to 1:15pm; no tours during official functions. The Rathaus's 160-foot clock tower overlooks the Rathausmarkt and the **Alster Fleet,** the city's largest canal. A visit to the Rathaus can be combined with a stop at the **Hamburg Stock Exchange** on Adolphsplatz (tel. 040/36-74-44), which is back-to-back with the Rathaus. Guided tours are provided Monday to Friday at 11:15am. U-Bahn: Rathausmarkt.

A few blocks away is **St. Petri Kirche,** Mönckebergstrasse (tel. 040/32-44-38), built in the 12th century and renovated in 1842. The lionhead knocker on the main door is the oldest piece of art in Hamburg, dating from 1342. It is open Monday to Friday from 9am to 6pm, Saturday from 9am to 5pm, and Sunday from 9am to noon and 1 to 5pm. U-Bahn: Rathausmarkt.

The nearby 14th-century Gothic church of **St. Jacobi,** Jakobikirchhof 22 (entrance Steinstrasse; tel. 040/32-77-44), damaged in World War II, has been restored. It contains several medieval altars, pictures, and sculptures as well as one of the largest baroque organs in the world (*Arp-Schnitger,* 1693). The church is open Monday through Friday from 10am to 5pm and Saturday from 10am to 1pm.

Hamburg's tallest structure is the 900-foot **Heinrich-Hertz-Turm** (the television tower), Lagerstrasse 2–8 (tel. 040/43-80-24). Visitors can climb to the observation platform, at 425 feet, where there's a restaurant, open daily from 9am to 11pm in summer and from 10am to 10pm in winter (already recommended). To go up in the tower by elevator costs 6 DM ($4). U-Bahn: Sternschanze.

SUGGESTED ITINERARIES

IF YOU HAVE 1 DAY   Take the walking tour of Hamburg (see below), then go for a cruise of the port in the afternoon. Drop into one of the Reeperbahn nightclubs in the evening.

IF YOU HAVE 2 DAYS   Spend Day 1 as outlined above. On Day 2, visit the Hamburger Kunsthalle, then enjoy an afternoon at Carl Hagenbeck's Tierpark. Take lunch at one of the lakeside pavilion restaurants.

IF YOU HAVE 3 DAYS   Spend Days 1 and 2 as outlined above. In the morning, visit Hauptkirche St. Michaelis, a baroque church, and also see the Rathaus (Town Hall), going on a guided tour. Before lunch, see St. Petri Church nearby. In the afternoon, explore the Museum of Hamburg History.

IF YOU HAVE 5 DAYS   Spend Days 1 to 3 as outlined above. On Day 4, visit Willkomm Hoft (Welcome Point), watching the ships from around the world sail into the port of Hamburg. Lunch at Schulauer Fahrhaus in Wedel. Then see the nautical museum in the cellar of the restaurant. In the afternoon, take a pleasure boat ride, with an English commentary, of the Inner and Outer Alster. On Day 5, rent a car or else take the train to visit the old Hanseatic city of Lübeck (see Chapter 16).

MAJOR ATTRACTIONS

MUSEUM OF HAMBURG HISTORY [Museum Für Hamburgische Geschichte], Holstenwall 24. Tel. 040/300-512-50.

Contained in the museum is the Historic Emigration Office, which allows you to trace your roots if your ancestors came through Hamburg. The Hamburg Association for the Protection of Emigrants was founded in 1850 to protect the city's migrant guests from many countries. Ships' agents were required to give authorities complete lists of all passengers, with names, sexes, ages, occupations, and places of origin. The Emigrant Lists, a treasure of America's heritage, survive intact, so if your ancestors include people from Germany, Russia, Poland, or other eastern European countries, you can have their names looked for. This service costs $30 for each year covered in the research, whether the name you want is found or not. The museum also has displays on local history.

Admission: 3 DM ($2) adults, 0.70 DM (50¢) children. Family ticket for parents and children 5 DM ($3.30).

Open: Museum, Tues–Sun 10am–5pm. Emigration office, Tues–Sat 10am–1pm and 2–5pm. **U-Bahn:** St. Pauli.

KUNSTHALLE, Glockengiesser Wall 1. Tel. 040/2486-2612.

This is the leading art museum in northern Germany. One of the most outstanding works is the altarpiece painted for the St. Petri Church in 1379 by Master Bertram, Hamburg's first painter known by name and the leading master of 14th-century Germany. The 24 scenes on the wing-panels are a free adaptation of the medieval text *The Mirror of Human Salvation* and depict the biblical story of mankind from the creation to the flight into Egypt. Particularly interesting is the panel showing the creation of the animals, in which a primitive Christ-like figure is surrounded by creatures from the fish of the sea to the fowl of the air. As a sardonic note, or possibly prophetic, one little fox is already chewing the neck of the lamb next to it. In the center panel of the crucifixion, Master Bertram has depicted prophets, apostles, and saints; in a band above, more prophets appear in medallions. The wise and foolish virgins are lined up above the center shrine.

The museum also contains works by Master Francke, a Dominican monk. The altar of St. Thomas of Canterbury (1424) is the first representation of his murder in the cathedral. There is a remarkable collection of Dutch and local paintings of the 17th century. Van Dyck, Rembrandt, Claude Lorrain, Ruisdael, Tiepolo, Goya, Boucher, and Fragonard are well represented, as is the German school, particularly by Mengs, Graff, and Tischbein. Emphasis is on 19th-century art, beginning with Wilson, Reynolds, and Fuseli. From the Romantic Movement come important works by Caspar David Friedrich and the distinctive visions of Philipp Otto Runge. German impressionists Max Liebermann and Lovis Corinth are exhibited near French painters Manet, Degas, Monet, and Renoir. The 20th century is represented by Munch, Kirchner, Otto Dix, Beckmann, Kandinsky, and Paul Klee. The Kunsthalle also has a collection of contemporary art, ranging from Beuys to Warhol. In addition, seven or eight exhibitions are staged every year, some of international prominence.

Admission: 5 DM ($3.30) adults, 1 DM (66¢) children.
Open: Tues–Sun 10am–6pm. **U-Bahn:** Hauptbahnhof.

CARL HAGENBECK'S TIERPARK, Hagenbeckallee at Stellingen. Tel. 040/540-00-10.

Located in the northwest suburbs, the Tierpark was the first attraction of its kind. This zoo was founded in 1848 and today is home to about 2,100 animals. The unfenced paddocks and the well-tended landscaped park are world-famous. There are sea lion, dolphin, and troparium shows, rides on elephants and camels, a train ride through fairyland, and a spacious children's playground.

Admission: 17 DM ($11.20) adults, 12 DM ($7.90) children.
Open: Daily 8am–6pm. **U-Bahn:** From the Hauptbahnhof in Hamburg almost directly to the entrance (Tierpark), with its bronze elephants, in about 20 minutes.

NEARBY ATTRACTIONS

At **Willkomm-Höft** (Welcome Point), every ship that passes is welcomed in its own language, as well as in German, from sunrise to sunset (8am to 8pm in summer). The ships' national anthems are played as a salute. The point can be reached by car from Hamburg via the Elbchaussee or Ostdorfer Landstrasse to Wedel; the trip takes half an hour. You can also go to Wedel by S-Bahn; a bus will take you to the point, or you can enjoy the 15-minute walk. In the summer, you can take a Hadag riverboat, leaving from St. Pauli Landungsbrüken, an hour's ferry ride.

The station was founded in the late spring of 1952. It is at this point that the sailor first catches sight of the soaring cranes and slipways of the Port of Hamburg. As a vessel comes in, you'll see the Hamburg flag on a 130-foot-high mast lowered in salute. The ship replies by dipping its own flag. More than 50 arriving ships, and as many departing ones, pass Willkomm-Höft within 24 hours.

If you're planning a visit there, you can have lunch at **Schulauer Fährhaus,** Parnasstrasse 29 (tel. 04103/83-094), in Wedel. Attractively situated on the wide lower Elbe, the place is run by the sons of Otto Friedrich Behnke, who founded Willkomm-Höft. The restaurant has a large enclosed veranda, a big open veranda, and a spacious tea garden. Guests are welcomed for breakfast, lunch, tea, or dinner. Fish dishes are a specialty of the kitchen. The wine list is modest but interesting. The restaurant has its own bakery, turning out a tempting array of goodies. Meals cost from 38 DM to 75 DM ($25.10 to $49.50). In April to October, hours are daily 9am to 9pm; in November to March, hours are daily from 10am to 7pm; closed Monday from November to March. No credit cards.

In the cellars of the Schulauer Fährhaus is the **Buddelschiff-Museum,** where more than 150 little vessels are carefully preserved in bottles. The museum is open daily from 10am to 6pm. Admission is 2.50 DM ($1.70) for adults and 1.50 DM ($1) for children.

GARDENS & PARKS

The major park is the **Carl Hagenbeck's Tierpark** (see above), but Hamburg also has many other "green lungs."

FROMMER'S FAVORITE HAMBURG EXPERIENCES

Cruising in a Boat on the Alster In the middle of the city, this pleasure lake, a tributary of the Elbe, is a summer festival, filled with pleasure craft from around the world.

A Night Along the Reeperbahn Notorious (but not quite as bad as its reputation), a nighttime tour of this St. Pauli entertainment district promises something for every taste—and usually lives up to the boast!

The Sunday Fishmarket Between 5 and 10am on Sunday, the Fishmarket at Altona, a tradition since 1703, sells not only fish but also a dusty porcelain coffee pot, a family of ducks, or an 8-foot potted palm. All to the accompaniment of accordion music, with the bars opening at 6am.

A Performance at the Hamburg State Opera One of the leading opera houses of the world, this cultural citadel is likely to enchant with its programs. It's a launching pad for stars who go on to world renown.

Alsterpark lies on the northwest banks of Alster Lake, spread across 175 well-manicured acres. Beautiful shade trees and cultivated gardens greet you at every town. From many places, you'll also have a panoramic view of the Hamburg skyline. Enter on Harvestehuderweg.

The **Hirschpark** is the deer park of Hamburg, whose main entrance is at Mühlenberg. Take the S-Bahn to Blankensee. Landscaped, the park has a game enclosure. You can visit the Hirschparkhaus for an old-fashioned tea with pastries.

Stadtpark, spread across some 450 acres north of the center, has some 20 miles of footpaths and numerous recreational facilities. These include a planetarium, sunbathing areas (Hamburgers often prefer their sun sans attire), and open-air pools. Music concerts are often staged here in summer. Take the U-Bahn to Borgweg in Winterhude.

Finally, **Wallringpark,** entered at Stephansplatz (also the U-Bahn stop), is a beautifully maintained park and garden that is actually a quartet of parks, including the flower garden Planten un Blomen, the Alter Botanischer Garten, and the Kleine and Grosse (big and little) Wallanlagen parks, with many recreational facilities. A miniature railway connects all four parks.

COOL FOR KIDS

Although Hamburg's reputation throughout the world—especially among sailors—is better known for its X-rated entertainment, it is actually a good place for a family vacation.

Carl Hagenbeck's Tierpark is one of Europe's great zoos (see above), and boat tours of the Alster and more lengthy tours of the port of Hamburg also delight kids. Kids also enjoy the many parks of Hamburg (see "Gardens and Parks," above).

WALKING TOUR — HAMBURG

Start: Lombardsbrücke.
Finish: Hauptkirche St. Michaelis.
Estimated Time: 2½ hours, not counting visits to interiors.
Best Time: Daylight hours during clement weather.

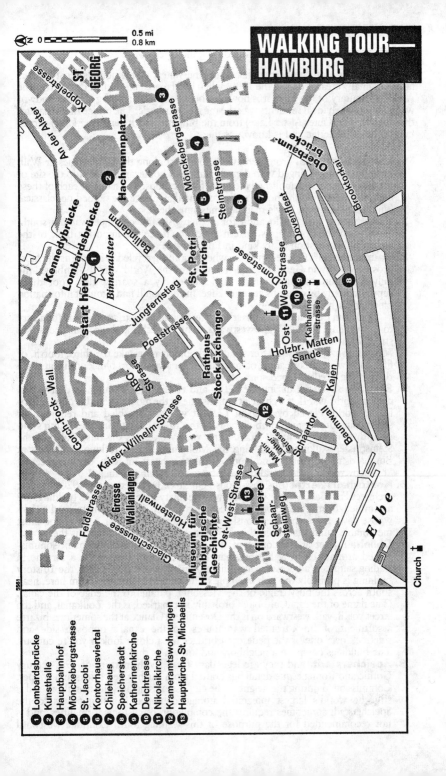

WALKING TOUR—
HAMBURG

0.5 mi
0 0.8 km

ST. GEORG

Koppelstrasse

Hachmannplatz

Kennedybrücke

Lombardsbrücke

An der Alster

start here ★

Binnenalster

Ballindamm

Jungfernstieg

Poststrasse

Gorch-Fock-Wall

ABC Strasse

Rathaus Stock Exchange

Kaiser-Wilhelm-Strasse

Feldstrasse

Grosse

Glacischaussee

Wallanlagen

Holstenwall

Museum für Hamburgische Geschichte

Ost-West-Strasse

Schaar-steinweg

finish here ★

Mönckebergstrasse

Steinstrasse

St. Petri Kirche

Domstrasse

Ost-West-Strasse

Katharinen-strasse

Holzbr. Matten Sande

Kajen

Baumwall

Oberbaum-brücke

Brooktorkai

Dovenfleet

Elbe

Martin-Luther-Strasse

Schaartor Strasse

Church ✚

5561

① Lombardsbrücke
② Kunsthalle
③ Hauptbahnhof
④ Mönckebergstrasse
⑤ St. Jacobi
⑥ Kontorhausviertel
⑦ Chilehaus
⑧ Speicherstadt
⑨ Katherinenkirche
⑩ Deichstrasse
⑪ Nikolaikirche
⑫ Krameramtswohnungen
⑬ Hauptkirche St. Michaelis

Worst Time: After dark, especially during inclement weather.

Begin your tour atop the barrier that spans the waters of Hamburg's most famous lake. Originally created during the 1300s when local merchants built a dam across the Alster (a tributary of the Elbe) it is now the focal point of Hamburg and the body of water about which local residents wax the most enthusiastic. The bridge that separates the Aussenalster (Outer Alster Lake) from the Binnenalster (Inner Alster Lake) carries huge volumes of traffic and is known as the:

1. **Lombardsbrücke.** From here, walk southeast along the Glockengiesser Wall. Inner Hamburg is ringed with densely trafficked boulevards built atop the site of the city's long-ago-demolished medieval fortifications. The name of each of these ends with *wall*. On the boulevard's eastern edge, notice the domed neoclassical building housing the city's main art museum, the:

2. **Kunsthalle.** Note its location for a later visit and continue walking south. Shortly, on the boulevard's eastern edge, you'll see the imposing bulk of the largest railway station of its kind in Europe, the:

3. **Hauptbahnhof.** Opened in 1906, when Hamburg reveled in its role as the most prosperous city in Germany, and rebuilt after the World War II bombings, the railway station contains a main hall capped by a soaring glass roof that's supported only by columns at either edge. Inside, you'll find a tourist information office and a handful of shops.

    Exit from the station and take the underground pedestrian walkway (don't try to brave dense traffic). Walk westward along the calm and pleasant pedestrian street known as the:

4. **Mönckebergstrasse.** After window shopping a bit, take the third, fourth, or fifth narrow alleyway leading off to your left for a very short block until you reach the soaring needle-shaped spire of:

5. **St. Jacobi.** Begun during the 1200s and rebuilt in 1962 after its destruction during World War II, the church contains one of the most famous baroque organs in the world. Played by Bach in 1720, it was disassembled and removed for safekeeping during the bombing raids of the 1940s, along with the church's trio of 15th- and 16th-century altars. After your visit, cross the busy traffic of the Steinstrasse, walking south along the Mohlenhofstrasse, forking gently left at Burchardstrasse. You'll find yourself in the heart of one of the recently "rediscovered" architectural treasure troves of Hamburg, the:

6. **Kontorhausviertel** (Business-House Quarter). Designed in the 1920s by civic architect Fritz Schumacher in the New Objectivity style, many of its buildings are assembled from clinker bricks (irregularly shaped but extremely hard bricks whose flaws are sometimes considered artistically desirable). One of the most memorable buildings within this architecturally acclaimed district is the:

7. **Chilehaus,** set at the corner of the Burchardstrasse and Pumpen. Commissioned around 1920 by businessman Henry Sloman, who made a fortune in trading saltpeter (a necessary ingredient in gunpowder) from Chile, the 10-story building is probably the best example of its kind in Hamburg. From here, head south across the busy traffic of the Messburg, parallel to the edge of the canal. (The name of the canal, although probably not marked, is the Zollkanal, and the street you'll walk westward on is the Dovenfleet.) Glance at the sometimes bizarre assortment of brick-fronted warehouses on the canal's opposite side and sidetrack over one of the pedestrian bridges for a closer look if you're curious. The buildings comprise a neighborhood known as the:

8. **Speicherstadt,** and they are legendary for a lavish mixture of 19th-century Gothic and Romanesque detailings crafted from earth-toned bricks and copper. Commissioned during the height of the city's steamship age, the neighborhood is still the world's largest integrated storage complex. (Gaining access to the Speicherstadt sometimes requires the completion of customs formalities, and is not recommended for the purpose of this walking tour.) Continue westward

(Dovenfleet will have changed its name first to Zippelhaus and then to Bei den Murren) until you reach the green copper spire of the:

9. **Katherinenkirche.** Dedicated during the 1600s to St. Catherine (a princess who was martyred in Alexandria during the 4th century), the baroque church was heavily damaged during World War II and subsequently reconstructed. The environs is probably the oldest residential neighborhood in Hamburg, built during the 1300s and rebuilt after a disastrous fire in 1842.

Continue westward beside the canal along Bei den Murren for about five short blocks, turning right onto Cremon, a narrow street that runs parallel to one of the neighborhood's narrow tributary canals. By now, you'll almost certainly be ready for your much-deserved:

REFUELING STOP The district contains dozens of time-tested cafés and wine bars, many of which spill onto the sidewalk during warm weather, but one of the most consistently reliable eateries is the old-fashioned **Nikolaikeller,** Cremon 28 (tel. 089/36-61-13). Open Monday to Saturday between noon and midnight, it serves 14 preparations of herring (including a popular version with bacon), foaming steins of local beer, coffee, and juicy cuts of steak with onions. Go for the ambience as well as for copious portions and liberal doses of waterfront bravado.

Retrace your steps to the edge of the big canal, turn right, then turn right again onto one of the most historic and well-publicized streets in Hamburg, the:

10. **Deichstrasse.** As you walk north along this street, note the location of no. 42, where the 1842 fire began that eventually left an estimated 20,000 people homeless. No. 27, a warehouse built in 1780, is the oldest of its kind in town. The baroque facade of no. 39 was originally built around 1700. Before you exit from this carefully restored neighborhood, you might wander down some of the intersecting alleyways, particularly any that stretch east toward the neighborhood's tiny Nikolaifleet Canal. At the end of the Diechstrasse, turn right on the Ost-West-Strasse and within about a block notice the soaring spire of the ruined:

11. **Nikolaikirche.** Built during the 19th century in the Neo-Gothic style, it symbolized the mercantile wealth of the German Industrial Age, and boasted a spire that was the second highest in Germany. Today, after bomb attacks during the 1940s, only the tower and crumbling sections of the church's core remain. Never rebuilt, it was declared a monument to those persecuted and killed during the Nazi era. Now walk westward along the wide and busy boulevard identified first as the Ost-West-Strasse, later as the Ludwig-Erhard-Strasse. Within less than a half mile, turn left onto a historic side street, the Krayenkamp, which within a few moments leads you to a collection of famous guild houses known collectively as the:

12. **Krameramtswohnungen** (Shopkeepers Guild Houses). Closely spaced and known for their decorative brickwork, they were built between 1620 and 1626 for the widows of members of the mercantile and shop-owners guild. Though most are privately owned, one (marked "C" at Krayenkamp 10) is open to the public and furnished as it might have been shortly after its construction. (It's open Tuesday to Sunday from 10am to 5pm. Admission free.) At this point, you'll be only a few paces from Hamburg's most famous and most revered landmark, the:

13. **Hauptkirche St. Michaelis.** The premier church of Hamburg, sometimes affectionately known as "Michel," it was built during the 1600s and destroyed three times since then (by lightning in the late 1700s, fire in 1906, and the bombs in the 1940s). Its latest incarnation, complete with the gilt and stucco of the Nordic Baroque manifestation it enjoyed during the 1750s, was finished in 1952. "Michel" is capped with the largest tower clock in Germany (26 feet in diameter), and an observation platform (accessible by elevator or stairs) that affords a sweeping view of Hamburg.

BOAT TOURS

✪ You can tour Hamburg by water, on both the Inner and the Outer Alster, experiencing all the charm of the Alsterpark, the villas, and the sailing boats set against the panorama of towers and church spires. **ATG-Alster-Touristik,** Am Anleger Jungfernstieg (tel. 040/34-11-41), has daily departures every 40 minutes from 10am to 5:15pm, with trips lasting about two hours. The ships leave from the Jungfernstieg quayside. Cassettes with a description of the tour in English, plus a brochure in four languages, are available from the captain. Trips cost 19 DM ($12.50) for adults and 9.50 DM ($6.30) for children. Longer tours are also offered.

ATG-Alster-Touristik, Anleger Jungfernstieg (tel. 040/34-11-41), offers one-hour trips in a comfortable, heated pleasure boat with a commentary in English. The tours leave from Landungsbrücken pier 1. You see modern high-capacity cargo terminals, locks and canals, shipyards and docks, the famous old red-brick warehouse complex (Speicherstadt), and many ships. March through November, the tours leave every 30 minutes from 9am to 6pm. The fare for adults is 14 DM ($9.20), half price for children.

5. SPORTS & RECREATION

BICYCLING The paved walkways that surround the Alster lakes are ideal for bicycling, as are many of the tree-lined boulevards of Hamburg's suburbs. Between May 1 and September 20, the city itself rents bicycles; for information contact the tourist office at the **Bierberhaus,** Hachmannplatz (tel. 040/280-2848), a short walk from the main railway station. Rates begin at 2 DM ($1.30) per hour, or 10 DM ($6.60) per day on Monday to Thursday; rates are doubled on Friday, Saturday, and Sunday. A 100-DM ($66) deposit is required.

BOATING A paddle on the Aussenalster (Outer Alster Lake) can be one of the most relaxing and charming warm-weather activities in Hamburg. **H. Pieper** (tel. 040/24-75-78) and **Alfred Seebeck** (tel. 040/24-76-52) rent rowboats, pedal boats, one-occupant sailing dinghies, and small catamarans, prices beginning at 12 DM ($7.90) per hour. For rentals of larger craft, contact the **Yacht-Schule Bambauer,** Schone Aussicht 20A (tel. 040/220-0030).

JOGGING My personal favorite, either for long promenades or jogging itineraries, is the pedestrian walkway that circumnavigates the Alster lakes. The total perimeter of the larger of the two lakes measures about 4 miles, that of the more congested Binnenalster about 1 mile. Equally suitable for jogging and pedestrian rambles are the string of public parks flanking the northwestern edge of the inner city.

SPECTATOR SPORTS For information about soccer matches and other types of spectator events contact the Hamburger Sportbund (Hamburg Sports Association), Schaferkampsallee 1, 2000 Hamburg 36 (tel. 040/4-12-11).

SWIMMING The rivers and lakes within Hamburg are highly polluted, but there are many pools. Two of the most popular are the **Alster-Schwimmhalle,** Ifflandstrasse 21 (tel. 040/22-30-12), and the **Holthusenbad,** Goernestrasse 21 (tel. 040/47-47-54). The latter has the advantage of artificial waves.

TENNIS AND SQUASH The country that gave the world Steffi Graf and Boris Becker has no lack of tennis facilities. For names and addresses of tennis facilities as well as information about upcoming tournaments, contact the **Tennis-Veranstaltungen,** Hallerstrasse 89 (tel. 040/41-17-82-40). For squash, try the

Squash-Center, Hagenbeckstrasse 124A (tel. 040/54-60-74), where you'll find 17 squash courts, a pool, a sauna, and a solarium.

6. SAVVY SHOPPING

A stroll through the city center is like taking a look at one large international shop window. Hamburg is a city of merchants. In general, stores are open Monday to Friday from 9am to 6:30pm (Saturday from 9am to 2pm; to 4 or 6pm on the first Saturday of the month). Unfortunately, the interesting shops are not concentrated in one location. Two of the oldest and most important shopping streets, **Grosse Bleichen** and **Neuer Wall,** run parallel to the canals, connected transversely by Jungfernstieg and Ufer Strasse on the Binnenalster.

Hamburg is a city of shopping malls, with nine major ones. Even on the grayest, rainiest day in winter, you can shop in Hamburg in relative comfort. The glass-roofed **Hanse Viertel Galerie Passage** is some 220 yards long. Among its stylish and desirable stores, you'll find a sunken Mövenpick Restaurant set within a garden-style interior and illuminated from above by a huge circular skylight. There is also a scattering of cafés, even a stand-up seafood bar where glasses of beer or Sekt are served at tiny tables.

Mönckebergstrasse, a street connecting the main station with the Rathaus, is the city's traditional shopping district, with big department stores such as **Kaufhof,** Mönckebergstrasse 3 (tel. 040/32-14-51), and **Horton,** Mönckebergstrasse 1 (tel. 040/32-81-21). The Mö, as it's called, also has elegant boutiques.

If you walk down Bergstrasse to the second part of the city center, you pass along the **Jungfernstieg,** with tourist boats of the Alster Fleet on the right and a teeming shopping street on the other side. About a block farther along you come to the **Hamburger Hof,** the elegant entrance to one of the most attractive chains of shopping galleries in Europe, with escalators carrying shoppers to upstairs boutiques. At the end of the Jungfernstieg, you can cross Gänsemarkt to **Gänsemarkt Passage,** another shopping gallery, with stores on three levels.

An up-market shopping area of the city is **Eppendorf,** Hamburg's oldest village, first mentioned in written history in 1140. Many prosperous and avant-garde Hamburgers live in the stately 19th-century homes and apartments. The shopping area, from Klosterstern to Eppendorfer Markt, has exclusive boutiques selling fashions from Paris, Milan, and New York, colorful shops with odds and ends for your home, antiques shops, and places where you can not only make purchases but watch goldsmiths, hatmakers, potters, and weavers at work.

The Hamburg fish market, **Fischmarkt,** between Hexenberg and Grosse Elbstrasse, is held every Sunday beginning at 6am. Not just fish but also everything movable is bought and sold at this traditional market, in existence since 1703. Flowers, fruit, vegetables, plants, and pets are for sale. Fresh fish, such as eels, plaice, and cod, direct from the trawlers, is just an incidental item nowadays. The nearby taverns are open to serve Fischmarkt visitors and vendors.

Specific shops worth recommending include the following:

For high-fashion men's clothing, go to **Theo Wormland,** Jungfernstieg 4 (tel. 040/32-62-79). For women's fashions, patronize **Penndorf Das Hamburger Modehaus,** Mönckebergstrasse 10 (tel. 040/32-29-01), a stylish fashion shop. Some of the fashions are from Scotland.

A fine collection of children's clothing can be found at **Die Hamburger Kinderstube,** Jungfernstieg 34 (tel. 040/34-66-46). Traditional high-quality children's wear is tailored to the 1- to 16-year-old market, and "classic fashions" are also sold for young women 18 to 25. The studio's merchandise has its own label (they have their own design studio). The shop is near the U-Bahn Jungfernstieg stop.

One of the city's leading hairdressers is **Marlies Möller.** This *Frisiersalon* is at Tesdorpfstrasse 20 (tel. 040/44-40-01). Perfumes and cosmetics are also sold here.

Besides hair styling and beauty treatments, it also has a large perfume selection. The shop is open Tuesday to Friday from 8:30am to 6pm and Saturday from 8am to 1pm.

One of the leading jewelry stores of Hamburg is **Brahmfeld & Gutruf,** Jungfernstieg 12 (tel. 040/34-61-03). This is one of Germany's oldest jewelers, founded in 1743.

A wide selection of books, including novels, travel maps, and other aids, is found at **Thalia,** Hermannstrasse 18–20 (tel. 040/30-20-701).

For an impressive array of glassware and porcelain, head for **E.B. Lattorff,** Dammtorstrasse 35 (tel. 040/350-90-90), a store that opened its doors in 1882. It has an excellent collection of Meissen china and Hummel figurines, plus china, crystal, and cutlery. There is also a gift department.

Shoes, well made and fashionably styled, are sold to both men and women at **Prange Schuhhaus,** Jungfernstieg 38 (tel. 040/34-31-51).

7. EVENING ENTERTAINMENT

THE PERFORMING ARTS

The state opera, ✪ **Staatsoper,** Dammtorstrasse 28 (tel. 35-17-21), is known throughout the world for its innovative repertoire, and is one of the most important opera houses in Germany. The **Hamburg Ballet,** directed by the American John Neumeier, is also internationally known. The house is one of the most modern in design and in stage facilities in the world. Tickets range from 4 DM to 180 DM ($2.60 to $118.80).

The city's three symphony orchestras and several chamber groups, known for recordings, give frequent concerts throughout the year. At the **Musikhalle,** Karl-Muck-Platz (tel. 040/34-69-20), you can hear performances of the **Hamburg Philharmonic,** the **Hamburg Symphony,** and the **NDR Symphony.** The **Monteverdi-Chor** is famous for interpretations of baroque and Renaissance music. There are also many musical performances in the churches, especially at Easter and Christmas.

To learn of events, buy a copy of *Hamburger Vorschau* for 2.30 DM ($1.50). It's available at various tourist offices, most hotels, and most newsstands. Another helpful magazine that documents all major cultural and entertainment events is *Szene Hamburg,* selling for 4 DM ($2.60) and available at the same places as *Hamburger Vorschau.*

Hamburg is blessed with more than 15 theaters, but for most of these a good knowledge of German is necessary. Plays in English, however, are presented at the **English Theater,** Lerchenfeld 14 (tel. 040/227-70-89); this is the only English-speaking theater in the northern part of Germany. Tickets range from 8 DM to 32 DM ($5.30 to $21.10). Performances are Monday to Saturday at 7:30pm.

If you understand German, then you may want to attend a performance at the **Deutsches Schauspielhaus,** Kirchenallee 39 (tel. 040/24-87-13). It is recognized as one of the outstanding theaters in the German-speaking world, performing both the classics and the avant-garde. Other theaters that perform drama are the **Thaliatheater,** Gerhart-Hauptmann-Platz (tel. 040/328-14-117), and the **Kammerspiele,** Hartungstrasse 9–11 (tel. 040/44-19-690). Kammerspiele stages a wide range of plays, both modern and historical, as well as musical shows, including such productions as *Don Giovanni* and *The Marriage of Figaro.* A new production usually opens every month. Tickets at these theaters range from 10 DM to 51 DM ($6.60 to $33.70).

And for children, for whom language is often not a problem, there is the **Theater für Kinder,** Max-Brauer-Allee 76 (tel. 040/38-25-38). All tickets cost 15 DM ($9.90). Shows are presented at 4:30pm on Thursday and Friday and at 2:30pm and 5pm on Saturday and Sunday.

Hansa Theater, Steindamm 17 (tel. 040/24-14-14), is a North German variety show that claims it's intelligible to all foreigners. The humor is so broad that that's surely true. Each show includes 11 to 14 international attractions, such as acrobatic acts, clowns, dancers, magicians pulling rabbits out of hats, and aerialists balancing on wires above the stage. Each show usually has about 40 performers. There are special tables for smoking and drinking. Two shows are performed Monday to Saturday at 4pm and 8pm, Sunday at 3pm and 7pm. Prices range from 18 DM to 25 DM ($11.90 to $16.50) for the afternoon show, increasing to 25 DM to 29 DM ($16.50 to $19.10) on Saturday and Sunday. For the night show, tickets range from 29 DM to 33 DM ($19.10 to $21.80), going up to 39 DM ($25.70) on Saturday. The season is from September 1 to June 30.

CLUB & MUSIC SCENE

NIGHTCLUB

DIE INSEL, Alsterufer 35. Tel. 040/410-69-55.

The rendezvous of haute Hamburgers, along with the most elegant visitors, is Die Insel. Near the Kennedy-Brücke, opening onto Aussenalster, this is a three-floor town house with a diversity of food, entertainment, and amusement. Around its champagne bar, you'll find members of the German arts and media worlds. It's especially popular as an après-concert rendezvous. The decor is sumptuous; in winter an open fireplace casts a mellow glow. You can dine elegantly here but are likely to spend from 115 DM ($75.90) for a seven-course meal. There is a disco with a round dance floor. Drinks cost from 15 DM ($9.90), and the place is modern, beautiful, up-to-date, and popular with young singles.

Admission: Free.
Open: Daily 8pm–4am.

JAZZ

Hamburg is a leading jazz city.

DENNIS' SWING CLUB, Papenhuderstrasse 25. Tel. 040/229-91-92.

I'm fond of Dennis' Swing Club, in the district north of the center of town called Uhlenhorst. It's a completely informal atmosphere, and it's operated by Dennis Busby, who is not only owner and manager but piano player and bartender as well. Dennis came to Hamburg from Louisiana many years ago. He's been an accompanist to some of the finest stateside jazz talents, and old friends who remember him from those days are always passing through Hamburg. Beer costs 7 DM ($4.60), with whisky beginning at 9.50 DM ($6.30).

Admission: 10 DM–32 DM ($6.60–$21.10), depending on who is appearing.
Open: Daily 8pm–4am, depending on business.

COTTON CLUB, Grossmarkt 50. Tel. 040/34-38-78.

The Cotton Club is legendary. One of the oldest (some 30 years) and the best established of the Hamburg jazz clubs, it has a motto: *Wo Jazz noch Jazz ist* (Where jazz is still jazz). Jazz bands come here from throughout Europe and the United States. Beer costs about 6 DM ($4) per glass, and a small carafe of wine is available for about 6 DM ($4).

Admission: 6 DM–8 DM ($4–$5.30).
Open: Daily 8pm–1am.

ROCK

MARKTHALLE, Klosterwall 9–21, near the Hauptbahnhof. Tel. 040/33-94-91.

One of the best rock venues in Germany often provides a forum for up-and-coming British groups who like to play here. It's a series of boutiques and dining areas set in a marketplace. The performing area is an indoor amphitheater with a stage and a large central section. You can listen to the artists in concert fashion or else view them in theater-in-the-round style. Seats are really backless benches. You're allowed to bring beer or other drinks into the hall as you listen to the music.

Admission: 15 DM–24 DM ($9.90–$15.80).

Open: Hours vary, depending on program.

LOGO, Grindelallee 5. Tel. 040/410-56-58.

Logo, near the university (S-Bahn: Dammtor) is one of the most popular clubs for young college-age visitors to meet their Hamburg contemporaries. It's a small, informal place that often features rock bands, and sometimes well-known singers appear here in concert. Audiences often sit on the floor and enjoy beer, which costs from 5.50 DM ($3.60).

Admission: 10 DM–20 DM ($6.60–$13.20).

Open: Mon–Sat 8am–2am.

FABRIK, Barnerstrasse 36. Tel. 040/39-10-70.

Five minutes from Bahnhof Altona is a cultural center, along the same style as Markthalle. Originally it was an old ammunition depot (circa 1830), until it was burned down. It was rebuilt in the same style. Beer and snacks cost from 6.50 DM to 12 DM ($4.30 to $7.90). Children often come in the afternoon with their parents (hours then are noon to 6pm). After 7:30pm and until midnight (later on Saturday and Sunday), it's a nightclub, offering a mixed program likely to feature rock or even classical music.

Admission: 6 DM–30 DM ($4–$19.80).

THE REEPERBAHN

For the true nightlife of Hamburg, you have to go where the action is, on the Reeperbahn in the St. Pauli quarter. The hottest spots are on a tawdry little side street called Grosse Freiheit, meaning "great freedom." St. Pauli is the sailors' quarter. *Warning:* Be on guard; the area can be dangerous. This section is not for women alone.

The streets are lined with pornography shops, interspersed with clubs with names such as Las Vegas and San Francisco. Be aware that German law requires restaurants and nightclubs to display their price list. Know the cost of your drinks before ordering. Charges for some drinks are ridiculously high. If the management refuses to give you a price list, get up and leave.

In addition to the establishments listed below, other clubs on the same street impose about the same prices, but you should always exercise caution. Stick to beer. Avoid ordering whisky or, especially, "champagne."

Another major tourist attraction is not in a club at all but a street. It's the famous **Herbertstrasse,** which every sailor in town visits when he's in port. For years it's been celebrated as the "street of harlots." These "working girls" sit in windows in this little alleyway, tempting men to come inside. When the curtains are closed, the occupant is "engaged." Exhibitions and "special requests" are catered to in the second and third stories of these little houses. *Warning:* Women walking down this street may be harassed.

COLIBRI, Grosse Freiheit 34. Tel. 040/31-32-33.

The Colibri is not for prudes. Its shows, depicting sexual intercourse between man, woman, beast, or whatever, are among the most erotic you'll see in Germany, but this is the main attraction of Reeperbahn nightlife. You'll pay 40 DM ($26.40) for beer. But don't expect to make one beer last for the whole show. The shows are long, seemingly endless, and 80 attractions are advertised each night.

Admission: 5 DM ($3.30); drink minimum to 40 DM ($26.40).

Open: Daily 8pm–4am.

SAFARI, Grosse Freiheit 24-28. Tel. 040/31-32-33.

The farmer from the environs, in the old seaport without his wife, wants to go on a

"Safari." This is what is known as an "Erotic Cabaret." It offers live sex on the stage, in some actions and forms perhaps unfamiliar to you. Beer costs from 40 DM ($26.40) for the first, 15 DM ($9.90) thereafter.

Admission: 5 DM ($3.30); 40 DM ($26.40) minimum.
Open: Daily 8pm–4am.

MALE STRIPTEASE

CRAZY BOYS, Pulverteich 12. Tel. 040/24-62-85.

It's usually closed in summer, but Crazy Boys is one of the most popular clubs in Hamburg. Every Wednesday night this amusing but risqué cabaret is reserved for women only for the kind of male strip show that has made TV talk shows in America. The rest of the week, the cabaret caters to a predominantly gay male clientele, but not exclusively, as many men take their wives or women friends here as well. Shows begin about 10pm, midnight, and 2am. There's an additional show at 4am on Friday and Saturday. There's also a show at 3:30am but only for women—strip shows, sketches, songs, or whatever are performed. Costumes range from "unusual fantasy" to suits "worn only by Adam."

Admission: 25 DM ($16.50); first drink 18 DM ($11.90).
Open: Mon–Fri 9pm–4am, Sat–Sun 9pm–6am.

DRAG SHOWS

PULVERFASS, Pulverteich 12. Tel. 040/24-97-91.

The best-known drag show, Pulverfass, is usually featured on the "Hamburg by Night" tours. This place is not for the timid. The shows can get downright vulgar, which you'll hear if you know German. Female impersonators from all over Europe appear here, and you can order steaks if you're hungry, costing from 30 DM ($20).

Admission: 20 DM–25 DM ($13.20–$16.50); first drink 18 DM ($11.90).
Shows: Nightly at 8:30 and 11:15pm and 2am.

DISCOTHÈQUES

CHESA, Beim Schlump 15. Tel. 040/45-88-11.

One of the best discothèques is Chesa, which draws an over-25 crowd. It has an English-style decor with a prominent mahogany bar. The main focus of the place is on dancing and conviviality. A glass of beer costs around 12 DM ($7.90). This isn't a place for teenagers.

Admission: Free.
Open: Daily 8pm–4am.

AFTER SHAVE, Spielbudenplatz 7. Tel. 040/319-32-15.

After Shave features not only funk and soul but also jazz and fusion. It's a place for dancing as well as for meeting people, and it draws a crowd in the 20-to-30 age group. The location is near Hamburg's famous Reeperbahn, but that's not why one goes to After Shave. The music is wide-ranging, featuring the latest imports but no hard rock or heavy metal. A bottle of beer costs 7 DM ($4.60). On Tuesday jazz is featured exclusively.

Admission: 8 DM–14 DM ($5.30–$9.20).
Open: Sun and Tues–Thurs 11pm–4am, Fri–Sat 11pm–6am.

DANCE CLUBS

BAYRISCH ZELL, Reeperbahn 110. Tel. 040/31-42-81.

A place to spend a Bavarian night in Hamburg is Bayrisch Zell. It may be on the Reeperbahn, but you could take your great-aunt there, especially if she likes to dance the polka. Clearly an imitation of Munich's famed Hofbrauhaus, Bayrisch Zell attracts couples young and old, and it has plenty of seats for all of them, 1,200 in all. One of the most popular places in the St. Pauli district, it has good cookery, with meals starting at 30 DM ($19.80), with beer from 8 DM ($5.30). If you see someone whom you find attractive, you can ring him or her from your table—that's what those phones are for. Hours are 7pm to 4am daily.

Admission: Free.

Open: Daily 7pm–4am.

CAFÉ KESSE, Reeperbahn 19–21. Tel. 040/31-08-05.

Café Kesse features a "Ball Paradox." That means the women can choose the men as dance partners. The doorman tries to keep out hustlers. Actually, the place is legitimate, even though it wouldn't let Jayne Mansfield in back in the 1950s (she refused to surrender her fur coat at the door). Live bands entertain, and women go there to look for a man. Sandwiches cost around 9 DM ($5.90), with beer going for 7 DM ($4.60).

Admission: Free.

Open: Daily 8pm–4am.

GAY CLUBS

Hamburg, like Berlin, is one of the major gay havens of Europe. Some gay places have a mixed clientele. A little journal, *Dorn Rosa,* distributed at most gay and lesbian bars, contains the latest events, clubs, restaurants, and bars catering to a gay clientele.

SPUNDLOCH, Paulinenstrasse 19. Tel. 040/31-07-98.

The famous Spundloch is sometimes patronized by heterosexual couples, perhaps curiosity seekers. Its elegant bar and disco draw a youngish crowd. Beer costs around 4 DM ($2.60).

Admission: Free.

Open: Sun–Tues and Thurs 9pm–4am, Fri–Sat 9pm–6am.

THE PIT CLUB-SALOON/TOM'S BAR, Pulverteich 17. Tel. 040/24-33-80.

This is a combination leather bar and gay disco near the Hauptbahnhof. A beer will run 5 DM ($3.30).

Admission: Free to 5 DM ($3.30), depending on management's wishes.

Open: Daily 9pm–4am (at least).

THE BAR SCENE

WINE DRINKING

SCHWENDERS, Grossneumarkt 1. Tel. 040/34-54-23.

One of Hamburg's most venerated winehouses is Schwenders. The eponymous Schwenders came from Vienna, bringing style and charm to this old Hanseatic city. The place today often attracts some 400 or more patrons, even though there is room for only 200 to sit down to drink in a belle époque setting filled with nooks and crannies. The music presented might be derived from anything from a Viennese operetta to cabaret, sometimes performed by local, amateur, or temporarily out-of-work musicians. Beer costs from 3 DM ($2), with a bottle of wine beginning at 25 DM ($16.50). Deli cold cuts and excellent cheese will do if you want something to eat with your drinks.

Admission: Free.

Open: Mon–Thurs 4pm–2am, Fri–Sat 4pm–3 or 4am, Sun 5pm–midnight.

ELEGANT BAR

SIMBARI, in the Vier Jahreszeiten, Neuer Jungfernstieg 9–14. Tel. 040/3-49-40.

Perhaps the most elegant bar in Hamburg is the Simbari, in the hotel, Vier Jahreszeiten. It's tiny, intimate, cozy, and select in its clientele. You can sit downstairs or retreat up the steps to a little nook. The overall atmosphere is like that of a conservative gentlemen's club in London. Drinks cost from 15 DM ($9.90). The bar is named for the contemporary pictures and posters of circus performer Nicola Simbari.

Admission: Free.
Open: Daily 11am–3am.

GAMBLING

SPIELBANK HAMBURG, in the Hotel Inter-Continental, Fontenay 10. Tel. 040/44-70-44.

You can play roulette, baccarat, and blackjack at the Spielbank Hamburg. All games are played according to international rules. The minimum stake for roulette is 5 DM ($3.30), and the minimum for blackjack is 10 DM ($6.60).

Admission: 5 DM ($3.30).
Open: Daily 3pm–3am.

CHAPTER 16

SCHLESWIG-HOLSTEIN

1. LÜBECK
- **WHAT'S SPECIAL ABOUT SCHLESWIG-HOLSTEIN**
2. KIEL
3. SCHLESWIG
4. WESTERLAND (SYLT)

You can walk along the dunes and hear the roaring waves breaking fiercely on the rocks. Or you can lie on a tranquil beach while tiny waves lap at your feet. Sounds inconsistent, doesn't it? Not in Schleswig-Holstein. This northernmost province of Germany borders both the turbulent, chilly North Sea and the smooth, gentle Baltic. And between these two bodies of water are rolling groves and meadows, lakes and ponds, and little fishing villages with thatched cottages. Fashionable seaside resorts dot the North and Baltic shorelines and nearby islands. Even in the coldest weather you can swim in heated seawater at the resorts of Westerland and Helgoland. In Kiel you can wander around the harbor and explore Schleswig with its Viking memories.

SUGGESTED ITINERARY

Day 1 From Hamburg, head northeast to Lübeck for a day spent exploring its Altstadt.

Day 2 Travel northwest to Kiel to enjoy a day in this famous port.

Day 3 Move on to the town of Schleswig visiting the interesting museums there, and seeing more of Schleswig-Holstein.

Day 4 Just for fun, journey by rail to the island of Sylt to roam its sand dunes.

GETTING THERE

If you're flying, Hamburg is a good gateway to the region. After that, Lübeck, easily reached from Hamburg by train, becomes the best gateway, with frequent connections. Motorists can easily reach Lübeck from Hamburg via Autobahn A1. Roads are only overcrowded in July and August. Route 105 splits through much of the region. Where the trains end, local buses wait to take you the final lap of the way, linking small towns and villages.

---

1. LÜBECK

57 miles SE of Kiel; 41 miles NE of Hamburg

GETTING THERE By Train Lübeck Hauptbahnhof lies on major rail lines linking Denmark and Hamburg, and also on the Hamburg-Lüneburg-Lübeck-Kiel-Flensburg and the Lübeck-Rostock-Stralsund rail lines, with frequent connections. Forty trains arrive daily from Hamburg (trip time: 40 minutes); and seven trains from Berlin (4 hours, 40 minutes). For rail information, call 0451/8841.

By Bus Long-distance bus service to such cities as Berlin, Kiel, and Flensburg is provided by Autokraft GmbH at Heiligenhafen (tel. 04362/1637), and by Gebr.

WHAT'S SPECIAL ABOUT SCHLESWIG-HOLSTEIN

Great Towns/Villages
☐ Lübeck, a free imperial city for 711 years, hometown of Thomas Mann and Willy Brandt.
☐ Kiel, a port on a perfect natural harbor at the end of a 10-mile-long extension of the Baltic.
☐ Schleswig, former Viking stronghold, one of the oldest towns of northern Germany.

Ace Attractions
☐ Sylt, a long, narrow island, forming the northernmost point of Germany. Westerland is the main town.
☐ Altstadt of Lübeck, the Old Town that was restored or reconstructed after World War II damage.

Architectural Highlight
☐ Rathaus in Lübeck, tracing its origins back to 1230, with Gothic and Romanesque styles.

Religious Shrine
☐ Marienkirche, in Lübeck, one of the most outstanding churches of North Germany and one of the largest Gothic brick churches in the world.

Special Event
☐ Kiel Week in June, a spectacular regatta with a century-old tradition.

Museums
☐ Schleswig-Holstein Museum, in Schleswig, with an exceptional collection of fine and applied arts dating from the Middle Ages.
☐ Viking Museum, outside Schleswig, showing the archeological digs of an ancient Viking town.

Sperling GmbH at Berlin (tel. toll free 0130/6662). Regional bus service, linking the neighboring towns of Lübeck, is offered by Autokraft GmbH at Lübeck (tel. 0451/63839).

By Ferry   Ferry service to and from Denmark is offered by Vogelfluglinie of German Rail (Rodby-Puttgarden). For information and reservations, call 04371/2168 at Puttgarden. Service to and from Sweden is operated by TT Saga Line (Trelleborg-Travemünde; tel. 04502/4021 for bookings), and by Nordo Line (Malmö-Travemünde; tel. 04502/4089 for bookings).

By Car   Access is via Autobahn A1 north and south.

ESSENTIALS   For tourist information, contact the **Touristbüro,** Markt (tel. 0451/1-22-81-06).

It is said that nothing testifies to the wealth of an old European city as much as the size and number of its church spires. If this is so, Lübeck is rich indeed, for no fewer than seven towering steeples punctuate the skyline of this Hanseatic city. It has prospered since it was made a free imperial city in 1226 by Emperor Frederick II. Lübeck held this position for 711 years, until 1937. In addition, it was the capital of the Hanseatic League for centuries, and retains the name Hansestadt Lübeck even though the economic and political importance of the league dissolved in the 17th century.

Once known as the "Queen of the Hanseatic Cities," Lübeck is a city of high-gabled houses, massive gates, and strong towers. The Hanseatic merchants decorated their churches with art treasures and gilded their spires to show off their wealth. Many of these survivors of nearly 900 years of history stand side by side today with postwar housing developments, and the neon lights of the business district shine on the streets and narrow passageways of bygone days.

Lübeck has several famous sons, notably Thomas Mann and Willy Brandt. As a young man, Brandt, who was later the West German chancellor and 1971 Nobel Peace Prize winner, opposed the Nazis so stubbornly that he fled his hometown on a boat to Norway. Mann's novel *Buddenbrooks,* set in his hometown, catapulted the 27-year-old author to international fame in 1902. In 1929, Mann won the Nobel Prize for literature.

The city is the capital of marzipan. According to legend, Lübeckers, riding out a long siege, ran out of flour and started grinding almonds to make bread. So delighted were they with the results, they've been doing it ever since. To sample marzipan on home turf, go to the Niederegger shop across from the Rathaus.

WHAT TO SEE & DO

Lübeck's **✪ Altstadt** is surrounded by the Trave River and its connecting canals, giving it an islandlike appearance. It suffered heavily during World War II, when about one fifth of the city was leveled. Today most damaged buildings have been restored or reconstructed, and Lübeck still offers a wealth of historic attractions. To reach the Altstadt and the attractions outlined below, take bus no. 5, 7, 11, 14, or 16.

Just across the south bridge from the Altstadt, the **Holstentor** (Holsten Gate) is the first monument to greet visitors emerging from the Bahnhof. At one time it was the main town entrance, built in the 15th century as much to awe visitors with the power and prestige of Lübeck as to defend it against intruders. To the outside world the towers look simple and defiant, rather like part of a great palace. But on the city side they contain a wealth of decoration, with windows, arcades, and rich terra-cotta friezes. Within the gate is the municipal museum, **Museum im Holstentor** (tel. 0451/12-241-29), housing a model of Lübeck as it appeared in the mid-17th century. It is open Tuesday to Sunday from 10am to 5pm (to 4pm in winter). Admission is 4 DM ($2.60) adults; children under 14 are free.

The **Salt Lofts,** if viewed from the river side near the Holstentor, are among the most attractive buildings in Lübeck. Dating from as early as the 16th century, they were once used to store salt brought here from Lüneburg before it was sent on to Scandinavia. Each of the six buildings is slightly different, reflecting several trends in Renaissance gabled architecture.

The **Rathaus,** Rathausplatz (tel. 0451/120), traces its origins to 1230. It has been rebuilt several times, but there are remains of the original structure in the vaulting and Romanesque pillars in the cellar and the Gothic south wall. The towering walls have been made with open-air medallions to relieve the pressure on the Gothic-arcaded ground floor and foundations. Tours are conducted Monday to Friday at 11am, noon, and 3pm, costing 3 DM ($2) for adults and 1 DM (66¢) for children.

It is estimated that within an area of 2 square miles around the city hall stand 1,000 medieval houses. Nearby is **Petersgrube,** the finest street in Lübeck, lined with some of the best-restored structures in Europe; one is from as early as 1363.

Museen Behnhaus/Drägerhaus, Königstrasse 9–11 (tel. 0451/122-41-48), was formed from two patrician houses, both entered on Königstrasse, north of Glockengiesser Strasse. They were constructed in a tall, narrow fashion to avoid a heavy tax that was based on frontage. The museum displays mostly German Impressionists and international painting from around 1900, focusing on Edvard Munch of Norway and Gotthardt Kuehl. The museum has an outstanding collection of German Romantic and "Nazarene" painting, especially by Johann Friedrich Overbeck and his school. There is also an exceptional collection of drawings ("cartoons") from Nazarene masters. The Behnhaus part of the museum is housed in the most important neoclassic building in the city. It has a permanent exhibition of contemporary painting, including Schumacher, Schultze, Rainer, Antes, and Kirkeby, along with such 20th-century artists as Kirchner, Beckmann, Lehmbruck, and

Barlach. Both houses are open Tuesday through Sunday, April to September, from 10am to 5pm and Tuesday through Saturday, October to March, from 10am to 4pm. Admission is 3 DM ($2); children under 14 are free.

Buddenbrookhaus, Mengstrasse 4 (tel. 0451/120) near Marienkirche (see below), is the house where the grandparents of Thomas Mann lived. It is a big, solid stone structure with gabled roof and a recessed doorway. Above a leaded-glass fan over the heavy double doors is the date 1758. This is the house Mann described as the home of the family in *Buddenbrooks*. For many years a bank, it was converted into a Mann literary shrine in 1993. The museum highlights not only Thomas Mann, but also his brother, Heinrich Mann, another noted writer. Thomas Mann wrote such classics as *Death in Venice* and *The Magic Mountain*, while Heinrich Mann wrote *Professor Unrat,* the source of the movie *Der Blaue Engel (The Blue Angel)* and other well-received novels. Hours are Tuesday to Sunday from 10am to 5pm, costing an admission of 3 DM ($2); children under 14 are free.

✪ **Marienkirche,** across the Marktplatz from the Rathaus, is the most outstanding church in Lübeck, possibly in northern Germany. Built on the highest point in the Altstadt, it has flying buttresses and towering windows that leave the rest of the city's rooftops at its feet. St. Mary's is undoubtedly a fine example of a Gothic brick church, and one of the largest of its kind in the world. Some of its greatest art treasures were destroyed in 1942, but after the fire was put out, the original painted decoration on the walls and clerestory was discovered. The bells fell in a World War II air raid and embedded themselves in the floor of the church, where they remain to this day. Organ concerts take place during the summer months, carrying on the tradition established by St. Mary's best-known organist, Dietrich Buxtehude (1668–1707).

Haus der Schiffergesellschaft (Seamen's Guild House) is one of the last of the elaborate guild houses of Hanseatic Lübeck, built in 1535 in Renaissance style, with stepped gables and High Gothic blind windows. It's worth seeing just for the medieval furnishings and beamed ceilings in the main hall, now a restaurant (see "Where to Dine" below). A walk through the old streets of Lübeck reveals a continuing use of brick as the local building material (the city insisted on this after fires in the 13th century). The effect is one of unity among all the houses, churches, shops, and guildhalls.

You can take an excursion boat around **Lübeck Harbor,** departing from Trave Landing, right in front of the Hotel Jensen. In season, departures are every half hour, anytime between 10am and 6pm.

WHERE TO STAY
EXPENSIVE

MÖVENPICK HOTEL, Auf der Wallhalbinsel 3, D-2400 Lübeck. Tel. 0451/1-50-40, or toll free in the U.S. 800/333-3333. Fax 0451/15-04-111. 197 rms, 3 suites. MINIBAR TV TEL **Bus:** 1, 3, or 11.
$ **Rates:** 175 DM–195 DM ($115.50–$128.70) single; 195 DM–288 DM ($128.70–$190.10) double; from 338 DM ($233.10) suite. Buffet breakfast 20 DM ($13.20) extra. AE, DC, MC, V. **Parking:** 8 DM ($5.30).

In a garden setting, opening onto a canal, the Mövenpick is right at the entrance to old Lübeck. It's colorful and compact, almost like a motel. The guest rooms are stylishly modern. On the premises is a Café-Konditorei, plus a Bierstube. Tables outside are hedged in by boxes of geraniums. The Mövenpick Restaurant serves tasty specialties, with meals costing 38 DM to 68 DM ($25.10 to $44.90).

MODERATE

HOTEL EXCELSIOR, Hansestrasse 3, D-2400 Lübeck. Tel. 0451/8-80-90. Fax 0451/88-09-99. 64 rms, 2 suites. TEL **Bus:** 1, 3, or 11.
$ **Rates** (including buffet breakfast): 90 DM–160 DM ($59.40–$105.60) single; 140 DM–200 DM ($92.40–$132) double; from 270 DM ($178.20) suite. AE, DC, MC, V. **Parking:** 10 DM ($6.60).

In a symmetrical baroque building with splendid proportions, the Excelsior has an entirely renovated and modernized interior. Some rooms include minibars and TVs. The Excelsior is near Lindenplatz, opposite the central bus station.

JENSEN, An der Obertrave 4–5, D-2400 Lübeck. Tel. 0451/7-16-46. Fax 0451/73-386. 43 rms, 2 suites. MINIBAR TV TEL **Bus:** 5, 7, 11, 14, or 16.

$ Rates (including buffet breakfast): 110 DM–140 DM ($72.60–$92.40) single; 170 DM–200 DM ($112.20–$132) double; from 300 DM ($198) suite. AE, DC, MC, V. **Parking:** 10 DM ($6.60).

One of Lübeck's best moderately priced hotels is the Jensen. Right on a canal, near Holstentor, it offers from its guest-room windows fine views of the Hanseatic brick architecture across the canal. The rooms are modestly furnished in modern style. The buffet breakfast is served in a room with picture windows overlooking the old canal, a delightful way to begin your day. Either lunch or dinner is good in the warmly decorated tavern-style restaurant. Meals cost from 32 DM to 72 DM ($21.10 to $47.50).

KAISERHOF, Kronsforder Allee 11–13, D-2400 Lübeck. Tel. 0451/7-91-011. Fax 0451/79-50-83. 74 rms, 6 suites. MINIBAR TV TEL **Bus:** 2, 7, or 14.

$ Rates (including buffet breakfast): 130 DM–175 DM ($85.80–$115.50) single; 175 DM–220 DM ($115.50–$145.20) double; from 350 DM ($231) suite. AE, DC, MC, V. **Parking:** Free outside, 12 DM ($7.90) in garage.

Two former patrician town houses have been remodeled into the Kaiserhof, standing outside the center on a tree-lined boulevard. The owner has created a fashionable yet homelike environment. Every room is uniquely furnished. An elaborate and authentic Scandinavian sauna opens off the rear garden, and a large pool, a Roman vaporbath, a fitness center, and a solar studio are available.

The hotel does not have a restaurant but offers a limited evening menu, served in the rooms.

WHERE TO DINE

EXPENSIVE

DAS SCHABBELHAUS, Mengstrasse 48–52. Tel. 0451/72-011.
Cuisine: NORTH GERMAN. **Reservations:** Required. **Bus:** 5, 7, 11, 14, or 16.

$ Prices: Appetizers 14 DM–28 DM ($9.20–$18.50); main courses 30 DM–48 DM ($19.80–$31.70); four-course fixed-price menu 74 DM ($48.80); six-course fixed-price menu 92 DM ($60.70). AE, DC, MC, V.

Open: Lunch Mon–Sat noon–3pm; dinner Mon–Sat 6–11pm.

A classic example of Hanseatic architecture on a medieval street, Das Schabbelhaus is installed in two patrician buildings from the 16th and 17th centuries. A wooden staircase and balcony lead to two rooms devoted to memorabilia of Thomas Mann. In the restaurant, ceiling-high studio windows overlook the small gardens; a pair of 15-foot-high armoires hold the restaurant's linen and glassware. The menu includes Lübecker crab soup, fresh items from the sea, and steak.

HISTORISCHER WEINSTUBEN, Heiligen-Geist-Hospital, Koberg 8. Tel. 0451/7-62-34.
Cuisine: INTERNATIONAL. **Reservations:** Recommended. **Bus:** 1 or 3.

$ Prices: Appetizers 12 DM–21 DM ($7.90–$13.90); main courses 32 DM–42 DM ($21.10–$27.70); seven-course fixed-price menu 90 DM ($59.40). AE, DC, MC, V.

Open: Lunch Wed–Mon noon–3pm; dinner Wed–Mon 5pm–1am.

In the basement of one of Lübeck's monuments (Holy Ghost Hospital), you'll find this first-class restaurant and 12th-century wine cellar. Dishes include snails Alsace style and roast curried prawns Bombay style in a sauce of mustard and fresh fruit.

L'ETOILE, Grosse Petersgrube 8. Tel. 0451/7-64-40.
Cuisine: FRENCH/CONTINENTAL. **Reservations:** Recommended. **Bus:** 1

$ Prices: Appetizers 10.50 DM–24 DM ($6.90–$15.80); main courses 34 DM–47 DM ($22.40–$31); three-course fixed-price menu 38 DM ($25.10). No credit cards.
Open: Lunch daily noon–3pm; dinner daily 6–10:30pm.

After years of experience in another restaurant, Michael and Margitta Schunzel decided to open their own establishment inside their art-nouveau home. Regular French food is served in a bistro section and continental cuisine moderne in a restaurant. The menu changes daily but is likely to include rack of lamb with Roquefort sauce or potato soufflé. Italian-style carpaccio, Barbary duckling, and classic French dishes like fresh goose liver are also served.

RATSKELLER, Am Markt 13. Tel. 0451/7-20-44.

Cuisine: NORTH GERMAN. **Reservations:** Required. **Bus:** 5, 7, 11, 14, or 16.
$ Prices: Appetizers 10 DM–24 DM ($6.60–$15.80); main courses 26 DM–55 DM ($17.20–$36.30); four-course fixed-price menu 69 DM ($45.50). AE, DC, MC, V.
Open: Daily 10am–1am.

To reach the dining cellar of the Rathaus, dating from 1235, make your way through the flower vendors on the square outside. You'll enjoy the offerings of the ambitious chef, whose high standards and excellent food are the order of the day. The menu is backed up by a good wine list. As befits a seaport, fish is the house specialty. Wide-ranging delicacies are offered, including some high-priced lobster and caviar. Vegetarian recipes are also on the menu.

MODERATE

HAUS DER SCHIFFERGESELLSCHAFT, Breitestrasse 2. Tel. 0451/7-67-76.

Cuisine: NORTH GERMAN. **Reservations:** Required. **Bus:** 1 or 2.
$ Prices: Appetizers 7.50 DM–19 DM ($5–$12.50); main courses 16 DM–40 DM ($10.60–$26.40). No credit cards.
Open: Tues–Sun 10am–1am.

Opposite the Church of St. Jakobi is this restaurant with memorabilia such as ship models hanging from the ceiling and decorating the walls. Dining in this mellowed Baltic atmosphere is like entering a museum of Hanseatic architecture. The restaurant was once patronized exclusively by sailors and other men of the sea; today good food (and large portions) is served on scrubbed-oak plank tables as you sit in a carved high-backed wooden booth showing coats-of-arms of Baltic merchants. Often you must share a table here. The most expensive items include such elaborate dishes as sole meunière (one pound) with salad. You might want to have a drink in the cocktail bar of the historical Gotteskeller, open Monday to Saturday 6pm to 2am.

LÜBECKER HANSE, Am Kolk 3. Tel. 0451/7-80-54.

Cuisine: FRENCH/GERMAN. **Reservations:** Required. **Bus:** 1, 3, or 11.
$ Prices: Appetizers 8 DM–22 DM ($5.30–$14.50); main courses 22 DM–40 DM ($14.50–$26.40). AE, DC, MC, V.
Open: Lunch Mon–Sat 11:30am–2:30pm; dinner Mon–Sat 6–11:30pm.
Closed: Jan 1–6.

One of the most praised restaurants of Lübeck has an authentically weathered exterior, with dark paneling gracing much of the interior. French food, regional meals, and lots of fresh seafood are offered, and there's also an elaborate salad buffet. Specialties include seafood terrine, bouillabaisse, wild game, and plats du jour.

A LOCAL DESSERT SPECIALTY

J.G. Niederegger, Breitestrasse 89 (tel. 0451/5301-0), sells that "sweetest of all sweetmeats," famous Lübeck marzipan. If you plan to have lunch before coming here, I suggest you skip dessert at the restaurant so you can splurge at this pastry shop, dating from 1806. It's right across from the main entrance to the Rathaus. On the ground floor you can purchase pastries to savor later, or you can go upstairs to a pleasant café where you can order dessert and excellently brewed coffee (the best in Lübeck). Ask for their pastry specialty, a nut torte resting under a huge slab of fresh marzipan. Prices are from 6 DM ($4). Go between 9am and 6:30pm daily. No credit cards. Bus: 5, 7, 11, 14, or 16.

---

2. KIEL

55 miles SE of the Danish border at Flensburg;
60 miles N of Hamburg; 57 miles NW of Lübeck

GETTING THERE **By Plane** The fastest way to reach Kiel is by air. Lufthansa has flights from Frankfurt to Kiel on Sunday to Friday. There are also daily flights from Munich and Hamburg.

By Train The Kiel Hauptbahnhof is on two major rail lines, the Neumünster-Hamburg and the Flensburg-Kiel-Lübeck-Lüneburg lines, with frequent connections. Forty trains arrive from Hamburg daily (trip time: 1 hour, 10 minutes). For rail information and schedules, call 0431/19-419.

By Bus Long-distance bus service to Berlin and Flensburg is provided by Autokraft GmbH at Kiel (tel. 0431/71-070). Local bus service and regional bus service to nearby towns is also offered by Autokraft GmbH. The tourist office (see below) will provide you with schedules.

By Ferry Service between Kiel and Oslo, Norway, is provided by Jahre Line GmbH at Kiel (tel. 0431/97-40-90). Service to and from Kiel and Gothenburg (Göteborg), Sweden, is offered by Stena Line GmbH at Kiel (tel. 0431/90-90).

By Car To reach Kiel from Hamburg, head north along A7; from Lübeck, take Route 76 west.

ESSENTIALS Contact **Tourist Information Kiel,** Sophienblatt 30 (tel. 0431/67910-0).

SPECIAL EVENTS Kiel Week, held each June, is an example of the port's close ties to the sea. This week of special events, held for more than 100 years, includes a spectacular regatta in which hundreds of yachts race on the water of the Kieler Förde. In 1936 and 1972, the Olympic yacht races were held on the waters at Schilksee. Stretches of sandy beach in nearby resorts make the port a Baltic vacation spot as well.

Kiel is the center of the Schleswig-Holstein Music Festival, with performances by musicians such as Yehudi Menuhin, between the end of June and August every year. For more information, contact Tourist Information Kiel (see above).

Even the name of this port and fishing city—it means "haven for ships"—shows the importance of the sea to the growth and prosperity of Kiel. The perfect natural harbor at the end of the 10-mile-long extension of the Baltic Sea made Kiel a center for commerce with other northern European countries. The opening of the Kiel Canal in 1895 connected the Baltic Sea with the North Sea and Western trade.

Although Kiel celebrated its 750th anniversary in 1992, there is little in the way of streets or buildings to make the casual visitor believe that the town ever was anything other than a modern city. Almost all its buildings were destroyed in World War II, and in their place is an admirable example of modern town planning. Kielers are proud of their broad streets, spacious squares, and green parks in the heart of town.

WHAT TO SEE & DO

Most attractions in Kiel center around the harbor, reached by bus no. 8 or 18. For the best overall look at the city and the Roadstead, go to the top of the Rathaus's 350-foot tower. Guided tours are daily at 10:30 and 11:30am from May to mid-October. For a closer view, wander the **Hindenburgufer (Hindenburg Embankment)** stretching for 2 miles along the west side of the fjord, opposite the shipyards. It's also one of the best spots from which to watch the regatta.

If you have the time, take a short steamer trip to one of the nearby Baltic towns, such as Laboe with its sandy beach. Steamers and ferries also connect Kiel with Baltic ports in Norway and Sweden.

The **Schleswig-Holsteinisches Freilichtmuseum** (open-air museum; tel. 0431/6-55-55) is 4 miles outside Kiel. Take the B4 to Neumünster. Farms and rustic country homes, dating from the 16th to the 19th centuries, have been assembled, craftspeople operate shops, and working animals perform tasks. A half-timbered inn serves tasty lunches. The park is open from April 1 to mid-November, Tuesday to Saturday from 9am to 5pm and Sunday from 10am to 6pm. In the off-season it's open only on Sunday from 10am to dusk. Admission is 7 DM ($4.60).

WHERE TO STAY
VERY EXPENSIVE

AVANCE CONTI-HANSA, Schlossgarten 7, D-2300 Kiel. Tel. 0431/5-11-50, or toll free in the U.S. and Canada 800/223-5652. Fax 0431/511-54-44. 164 rms. MINIBAR TV TEL **Bus:** 8 or 18.

$ **Rates** (including continental breakfast): 210 DM–290 DM ($138.60–$191.40) single; 285 DM–340 DM ($188.10–$224.40) double. AE, DC, MC, V. **Parking:** 20 DM ($13.20).

The Avance Conti-Hansa is only a three-minute walk from the pedestrian shopping area. Each room is well equipped, including a trouser press and hairdryer. You can dine at the hotel's well-known restaurant (see below).

MARITIM-BELLEVUE, Bismarckallee 2, D-2300 Kiel. Tel. 0431/3-89-40. Fax 0431/33-84-90. 89 rms, 11 suites. MINIBAR TV TEL **Bus:** 8 or 18.

$ **Rates** (including buffet breakfast): 250 DM–324 DM ($165–$213.80) single; 282 DM–414 DM ($186.10–$273.20) double; from 570 DM ($376.20) suite. AE, DC, MC, V. **Parking:** 20 DM ($13.20).

Rated "superior first class," the Maritim-Bellevue, built in 1972, is a well-appointed convention hotel opening onto the shore promenade of the Baltic. The most expensive doubles are the luxurious corner accommodations. You'll have access to the hotel's pool, sauna, fitness room, solarium, bar, restaurant, and nightclub. Room service, laundry, and dry cleaning are available. The hotel is known locally for its cuisine. Meals cost from 45 DM to 90 DM ($29.70 to $59.40).

EXPENSIVE

HOTEL KIELER YACHT CLUB, Hindenburgufer 70, D-2300 Kiel. Tel. 0431/8-50-55. Fax 0431/85-039. 60 rms. MINIBAR TV TEL **Bus:** 8 or 18.

$ **Rates:** 148 DM–205 DM ($97.70–$135.30) single; 195 DM–235 DM ($128.70–$155.10) double. Continental breakfast 18 DM ($11.90) extra. AE, DC, MC, V. **Parking:** 18 DM ($11.90).

The Kieler Yacht Club is exactly what its name implies—a yacht club with unusually fine guest facilities. It's an old classical building, standing back from the harbor, with an adjoining motel annex of contemporary design. Mastenkeller in the basement is for beer drinking; the restaurant is separately recommended below.

MODERATE

HOTEL ASTOR, Holstenplatz 1, D-2300 Kiel. Tel. 0431/9-30-17. Fax 0431/96-378. 60 rms (all with bath or shower). TV TEL **Bus:** 8 or 18.

$ **Rates** (including buffet breakfast): 110 DM–130 DM ($72.60–$85.80) single; 160 DM–170 DM ($105.60–$112.20) double. AE, DC, MC, V. **Parking:** 8 DM ($5.30).

Ⓢ Within a short walk of the ferryboat station and the Hauptbahnhof, this hotel shares a modern office building with several corporations. The rooms are well appointed. The hotel restaurant, considered one of the best in Kiel, serves an international array of food, with a fixed-price meal beginning at 32 DM ($21.10); it is open Monday to Saturday from 7am to 11pm. The small 10th-floor bar, run by one of Germany's best barmen, is a fashionable place to go.

HOTEL WIKING, Schützenwall 1–3, D-2300 Kiel. Tel. 0431/67-30-51.
Fax 0431/67-30-54. 42 rms (all with bath or shower). MINIBAR TV TEL **Bus:** 8 or 18.

$ Rates (including continental breakfast): 110 DM–140 DM ($72.60–$92.40) single; 160 DM–190 DM ($105.60–$125.40) double. DC, MC, V. **Parking:** 8 DM ($5.30).

Ⓢ The dark facade of this modern hotel is ornamented with heavy-walled balconies, painted a vividly contrasting white. In the center of Kiel, the Wiking offers sunny, well-furnished rooms for prices that are most reasonable by local standards. The restaurant and breakfast rooms have a warm Nordic ambience. The hotel has a sauna and solarium.

WHERE TO DINE

EXPENSIVE

CLAUDIO'S RISTORANTE ALLA SCALA, Königweg 46. Tel. 0431/67-68-67.

Cuisine: ITALIAN. **Reservations:** Required. **Bus:** 8 or 18.

$ Prices: Appetizers 19 DM–24 DM ($12.50–$15.80); main courses 33 DM–48 DM ($21.80–$31.70); fixed-price menus 80 DM ($52.80) and 120 DM ($79.20). AE.

Open: Dinner only, Mon–Sat 7pm–midnight (last order).

In one of the most attractive restaurants in town, chef Claudio Berlese prepares all kinds of light Italian dishes. Specialties are prepared from the day's inventory of lobster, mussels, oysters, game fowl, and fresh vegetables. You might enjoy eggplant stuffed with mozzarella and tomatoes, spaghetti with mussels, or oven-cooked salmon with fresh basil. The choice of wine is tempting.

CONTI-HANSA RESTAURANT, in the Avance Conti-Hansa, Schlossgarten 7. Tel. 0431/5-11-50.

Cuisine: CONTINENTAL. **Reservations:** Recommended. **Bus:** 8 or 18.

$ Prices: Appetizers 17 DM–29 DM ($11.20–$19.10); main courses 23 DM–42 DM ($15.20–$27.70). AE, DC, MC, V.

Open: Mon–Sat noon–11:30pm.

One of Kiel's most elegant restaurants boasts an opulent decor. You might begin with mussel-and-spinach salad, then follow with a main course such as salmon in Riesling sauce or roulade of calves' liver stuffed with wild mushrooms and julienne of vegetables with wild-berry sauce. To the chef, the way food looks is almost as important as the way it tastes.

KIELER YACHT CLUB, Hindenburgufer 70. Tel. 0431/8-50-55.

Cuisine: CONTINENTAL. **Reservations:** Recommended.

$ Prices: Appetizers 17.50 DM–24 DM ($11.60–$15.90); main courses 30 DM–42 DM ($19.80–$27.70); fixed-price menu 75 DM ($49.50). AE, DC, MC, V.

Open: Lunch daily noon–2:30pm; dinner daily 6–10pm.

This dining selection is found in a previously recommended hotel. The bar, a sophisticated hangout, attracts the yachting set. The main attraction, naturally, is seafood. Try the filet of haddock with mustard sauce and potatoes. You can also order saddle of venison with savoy cabbage, another of the chef's specialties.

MODERATE

RESTAURANT IM SCHLOSS, Wall 80. Tel. 0431/9-11-58.

Cuisine: CONTINENTAL. **Reservations:** Required. **Bus:** 1.
$ **Prices:** Appetizers 9 DM–16.50 DM ($5.90–$10.90); main courses 22 DM–32 DM ($14.50–$21.10); three-course fixed-price menu 36 DM ($23.80); seven-course fixed-price menu 98 DM ($64.70). AE, DC, MC, V.
Open: Tues–Sat 9am–midnight; Sun lunch noon–3pm.

The most elegant formal restaurant in Kiel offers superb service, cuisine, and choice of wine. In a stone building overlooking the harbor, the Schloss looks like a museum set in a park. If you reserve, you can get one of the window tables opening onto the water. The cuisine has a creative and lighthearted style, using the freshest of produce. Many fish dishes are from the North German seas. Try, for example, terrine of salmon and zander in cream sauce, followed by filet of lamb breast brushed with white bread crumbs and baked with fresh herbs.

3. SCHLESWIG

30 miles NW of Kiel; 21 miles S of Flensburg

GETTING THERE By Train The Schleswig Bahnhof is on the Flensburg-Neumünster-Hamburg and Westerland-Hamburg rail lines, with frequent connections. Daily trains arrive from Hamburg (trip time: 2 hours, 20 minutes).

By Bus Long-distance bus service to and from Hamburg, Flensburg, and Kiel is provided by Autokraft GmbH at Rendsburg (tel. 04351/24-222).

By Car Access by car is via Autobahn A7 north or south.

ESSENTIALS For tourist information, contact **Städt,** Tourist Information, Plessenstrasse 7 (tel. 04621/81-42-26).

This one-time Viking stronghold on the Schlei (an arm of the Baltic) is Schleswig-Holstein's oldest town, with some 1,200 years of history. It is steeped in the myths and legends that go with such a long history. Even the seagulls have a legend of their own. According to tradition, the birds nesting on Seagull Island in the middle of the Schlei are actually the fellow conspirators of Duke Abel, who in 1250 murdered his own brother, King Eric. The crime was discovered when the king's body, weighted with chains, washed ashore from the Schlei. The duke went mad and eventually died and was impaled and buried in the Tiergarten. But his followers, according to the story, became seagulls, doomed to nest forever on Seagull Island.

WHAT TO SEE & DO

ST. PETER'S CATHEDRAL [Dom St. Petri], Süderdomstrasse 1. Tel. 04621/25-740.
A tour of the attractions usually begins in the Altstadt with a visit to the jewel of Schleswig, St. Peter's Cathedral, a brick Romanesque-Gothic hall-church begun in the 12th century. The towering spire makes the rest of the Altstadt seem like so many dollhouses by comparison. Inside is the outstanding 16th-century *Bordesholm Altarpiece,* a powerful work carved in oak by Hans Brüggemann for the convent at Bordesholm. It was brought to the cathedral in 1666. Its elaborately carved Gothic panels contain nearly 400 figures. The cathedral and cloisters also contain art treasures, including the *Blue Madonna* by J. Ovens and 13th-century frescoes.
Open: May–Sept, Mon–Thurs and Sat 9am–5pm, Fri 9am–3pm, Sun 1–5pm; Apr–Oct, Mon–Thurs and Sat 10am–4pm, Fri 10am–3pm, Sun 1–4pm. **Bus:** 1, 2, 3, 4, or 5.

SCHLOSS GOTTORF, on a small island in the Burgsee, a bay at the west end of the Schlei.
A dam and a bridge connect the island with the town. As you walk around the harbor, the panorama of the Altstadt and the widening bay opens up behind you. The

castle is the largest in Schleswig-Holstein. The foundations date from the original 13th-century ducal palace; the present structure was built mainly in the 16th and 17th centuries and reconditioned since 1948 to house two museums.

The first, the **Provincial Museum of Archeology** (tel. 04621/813-300), has a most remarkable exhibit (in a separate building), the Nydam Boat, a 4th-century ship found in the Nydam marshes in 1863. In the same room are artifacts and weapons found with the ship and corpses preserved in the moor, all adding up to one of the major archeological finds in northern Germany.

The **Schleswig-Holstein State Museum** (tel. 04621/813-222), also housed in the castle, contains an exceptional collection of fine and applied art from medieval times to the 20th century (painting, sculpture, furniture, textiles, weapons). Outstanding are the late Gothic king's hall, the 17th-century ducal living rooms with rich stucco ceilings, and the Renaissance chapel with a private pew for the ducal family decorated with intricate and elaborate carvings and inlays. Two separate buildings east of the castle contain the collections of contemporary art in Schleswig-Holstein, including outstanding works of German expressionism and modern sculpture, plus the ethnological collection with its extensive displays of implements and tools representing the rural life of farmers, artisans, and fishermen.

Admission (including both museums): 5 DM ($3.30) adults, 2 DM ($1.30) children.

Open (museums): Mar–Oct, daily 9am–5pm; Nov–Feb, Tues–Sun 9:30am–4pm. **Bus:** 1, 2, 3, 4, or 5.

WIKINGER MUSEUM, Haithabu. Tel. 04621/81-33-00.

About 1.5 miles from Schleswig is a Viking Museum, opened in 1985, containing the results of archeological excavations of the Viking-age town of Haithabu. Shown are all aspects of daily life, including a Viking longship.

Admission: 4 DM ($2.60).

Open: Apr–Oct, daily 9am–6pm; Nov–Mar, Tues–Fri 9am–5pm, Sat–Sun 10am–6pm. **Transportation:** In summer, you can reach the site by boat, a 20-minute scenic ride. Departures are from Stadthafen, the town quay in Schleswig, south of the cathedral. After you dock it's a 10-minute walk to the museum. In winter, it's a 2-mile walk from the rail station.

WHERE TO STAY

MODERATE

STRANDHALLE, Strandweg 2, D-2380 Schleswig. Tel. 04621/2-20-21.

Fax 04621/2-89-33. 26 rms. TV TEL **Bus:** 1, 2, 3, 4, or 5.

$ Rates (including continental breakfast): 95 DM–140 DM ($62.70–$92.40) single; 150 DM–170 DM ($99–$112.20) double. AE, DC, MC, V. **Parking:** 8 DM ($5.30).

The Strandhalle has been a family-run business since 1905. Actually it's more of a holiday resort—right on the water, with its own rowboats, outdoor pool in a beautiful garden, and indoor pool with steam bath. The owners offer an informal atmosphere in comfortable rooms. You should ask for one opening onto the water, with a view of the yacht harbor. Meals cost 38 DM to 60 DM ($25.10 to $39.60). The wine list contains more than 250 choices.

HOTEL WALDSCHLÖSSCHEN, Kolonnenweg 152, D-2380 Schleswig-Pulverholz. Tel. 04621/38-32-83. Fax 04621/38-31-05. 80 rms. TEL **Directions:** 1 mile SW (no bus).

$ Rates (including continental breakfast): 83 DM–112 DM ($54.80–$73.90) single; 122 DM–160 DM ($80.50–$105.60) double. AE, DC, V. **Parking:** 6 DM ($4).

A mile southwest of town, this elegant country hotel, run by an English-speaking owner, is equipped with every convenience to make your stay interesting and comfortable. You'll notice a rock garden, a gabled house, an elongated annex, and lots of green trees before you enter public rooms that are intimately lit and decorated with tasteful carpeting, warm brick detailing, and wood paneling. The pool is centrally heated year round, and there is a bowling alley, plus a sauna, whirlpool bath, and solarium. The carpeted rooms are completely satisfactory in every way. Forty-five rooms have TVs and 40 contain minibars.

INEXPENSIVE

HOTEL AND RESTAURANT SKANDIA, Lollfuss 89, D-2380 Schleswig.
   Tel. 04621/2-41-90. Fax 04621/299-85. 30 rms. **Bus:** 1 or 2.
$ Rates (including continental breakfast): 60 DM ($39.60) single; 110 DM ($72.60) double. MC, V. **Parking:** Free.
In the center of town is a modern building with pleasing proportions. Inside you'll find a collection of high-ceilinged public rooms, along with small guest rooms decorated with modern wood-grained pieces. The hotel has an excellent kitchen, turning out North German specialties, with meals costing 30 DM ($19.80).

WALDHOTEL AM SCHLOSS GOTTORF, An der Stampfmühle 1, D-2380
   Schleswig. Tel. 04621/2-32-88. Fax 04621/23-289. 9 rms (all with bath or shower). MINIBAR TV TEL **Bus:** 1, 2, 3, 4, or 5.
$ Rates (including continental breakfast): 68 DM–72 DM ($44.90–$47.50) single; 108 DM–120 DM ($71.30–$79.20) double. AE, MC. **Parking:** 6 DM ($4).

⑤ This brick mansion is lodged on a grassy plateau surrounded by a park and pine trees. On the outskirts of Schleswig, en route to the castle, it's a fine bargain as a secluded holiday retreat. There are no lounges to speak of, but the emphasis is placed on the sunny dining room and the comfortable guest rooms (large enough to have breakfast in, unless you prefer your morning coffee on the front terrace).

WHERE TO DINE
MODERATE

OLSCHEWSKI'S, Hafenstrasse 40. Tel. 04621/2-55-77.
   Cuisine: CONTINENTAL. **Reservations:** Required. **Bus:** 1, 2, 3, 4, or 5.
$ Prices: Appetizers 8 DM–19 DM ($5.30–$12.50); main courses 20 DM–40 DM ($13.20–$26.40); fixed-price menus 35 DM ($23.10) and 80 DM ($52.80). AE, MC.
   Open: Lunch Wed–Mon 11:30am–2:30pm; dinner Wed–Sun 5:30–11pm.
In the town center, close to the waterfront, is this cozy well-managed restaurant. You can dine in a glass-sided modern extension or a comfortably unpretentious dining room with views of the Schlei. Your choices may include fresh salad in almost any season, cream of fresh tomato soup, salmon with a tangy cream base or a Riesling sauce, filet of lamb with rosemary, or roast goose.

SCHLOSS KELLER, in the Schloss Gottorf, An der Stampfmühle 1. Tel.
   04621/2-32-88.
   Cuisine: GERMAN. **Reservations:** Not necessary. **Bus:** 1, 2, 3, 4, or 5.
$ Prices: Appetizers 9 DM–22 DM ($5.90–$14.50); main courses 20 DM–32 DM ($13.20–$21.10); three-course fixed-price menu 32 DM ($21.10). AE, MC.
   Open: Lunch daily 11:30am–2:30pm; dinner daily 6–10pm.
A fine choice for dining, Schloss Keller is on the lower level of the castle and hotel (see "What to See & Do" above). There's also a café for light snacks and refreshments. Meals in the pleasant restaurant (which include soup of the day) cost 28 DM to 55 DM ($18.50 to $36.30). The cuisine is typically German, with dishes such as Wiener Schnitzel, rumpsteak, and sole.

---

4. WESTERLAND (SYLT)

13 miles W of the German/Danish border; 120 miles NW of Hamburg

GETTING THERE By Plane   The nearest international airport is at Hamburg (see Chapter 15). But from there you can fly to the regional Westland Airport (tel. 04651/66-96 for information). There is also regularly scheduled air service from Berlin and Bremerhaven.

By Train   The only link between the mainland and the island of Sylt is the railroad causeway running from the mainland town of Niebüll. If you wish to bring your car to the island, you'll have to load it on the train at Niebüll for the slow ride. No advance booking is necessary. You just arrive and take your chances. Passengers are carried free. The Westerland Bahnhof lies on the Westerland-Hamburg and the Westerland-Lübeck rail lines, with frequent connections. Seventeen trains arrive daily from Hamburg (trip time: 2 hours, 40 minutes to 3 hours, 20 minutes, depending on the train). For rail information and schedules, call 04651/24-057.

By Car Ferry   Another way to go is by car-ferry between Hamburg, the Danish island of Romo, which can be reached by highway from Germany, and List, at the northern tip of Sylt. There are at least a dozen crossings in summer, with a much-reduced schedule in winter. Unlike the railway, the car-ferries accept reservations. Call Havneby in Denmark (tel. 0045/75-53-03); or in Germany, the Haus der Reise, Grosse Bergstrasse 154, in Hamburg (tel. 040/38-18-21). In List itself, you can dial 04652/475.

By Bus   Bus service is from Niebüll on the mainland. It's provided by Autokraft GmbH (tel. 04661/87-75 for information).

By Car   Access by car is via Autobahn A7 north or south with a rail car transport between Niebüll and Westerland via the Hindenburg Damm. For information, call 04651/24-057.

ESSENTIALS   For tourist information, contact the **Fremdenverkehrszentrale,** am Bundesbahnhof (tel. 04651/2-40-01).

The long, narrow island of Sylt and its capital, Westerland, from the northernmost point of Germany. Pronounced *"zoolt,"* Sylt lies in the North Sea off the coasts of Denmark and Schleswig-Holstein. In land area, the island is about 36 square miles, its west coast a stretch of beach some 24 miles long. The "Watt" is the name given to the eastern coast, facing the mainland. Pounding winter storms seem to take more and more of the coastline each year, and there are those who think that Sylt will one day disappear into the sea.

People come here to breathe the iodine-rich air and enjoy a climate the Germans call *Reizklima*. Temperatures in midsummer are usually in the low 70s, but rain can come at any minute. This has given rise to the Sylt "mink," or yellow oilskin, which chic visitors wear to protect themselves from the elements. Once it was an island of seafaring folk who earned their living by fishing for herring. Later they turned to whaling. But in the postwar era, Sylt became known as "the St. Tropez of the north," attracting such headliners as Peter Ustinov, Gunther Sachs, Lilli Palmer, and Curt Jurgens. It is now the most exclusive resort in Germany, its hotel prices reflecting its lofty status.

The basic therapy here is sunshine, pure air, and seawater, but in recent years mud baths have also become a method of treatment. The spa has facilities for the treatment of everything from heart disease to skin irritations.

Some of the more remote sections of the dunes have been turned into nudist beaches for purists in the art of sunshine therapy. In addition to bathing, there are facilities in and around Westerland for horseback riding, along with surf, golf, and tennis, as well as more sedentary entertainment such as the theater and concerts.

When the sunlight begins to fade at the end of each day, the Spielbank becomes the center of activity. In the center of town, it is in the same building as the Rathaus. All major games are played here: baccarat, roulette, and blackjack. The Casino bar serves the best drinks in town and is open daily from 5pm.

WHERE TO STAY
VERY EXPENSIVE

HOTEL MIRAMAR, Friedrichstrasse 43, D-2280 Westerland/Sylt. Tel. 04651/85-50. Fax 04651/185-52-22. 94 rms, 8 suites. MINIBAR TV TEL **Bus:** Centrale Omnibus Bahnhof.

$ Rates (including continental breakfast): 145 DM–460 DM ($95.70–$303.60) single; 260 DM–570 DM ($171.60–$376.20) double; from 660 DM ($435.60) suite. AE, DC, MC, V. **Parking:** 12 DM ($7.90).

On a bluff just above the beach, the Miramar is surrounded by an arched veranda. Its public rooms are graced with enormous arched windows with views of the sea. The salon is illuminated from above by an octagonal light, a detail left over from the building's 1903 construction. Regardless of the season, you'll be able to go swimming—in winter in the sunny indoor pool near the sauna and fitness room. The high-ceilinged guest rooms are quite comfortable.

HOTEL ROTH AM STRANDE, Strandstrasse 31, D-2280 Westerland/ Sylt. Tel. 04651/50-91. 55 rms. MINIBAR TV TEL **Bus:** Centrale Omnibus Bahnhof.

$ Rates: 165 DM–208 DM ($108.90–$137.30) single; 316 DM–344 DM ($208.60–$227) double. Breakfast 23 DM ($15.20). MC, V.

Standing at the edge of the sea, this modern hotel would look as much at home in southern Florida as it does in northern Germany. Accommodations are furnished in a functional modern style, each well maintained and comfortably appointed. Many rooms have private balconies overlooking the sea. The hotel has an à la carte restaurant featuring North German specialties, and a Bierstube, as well as a sauna and solarium. Massages can be arranged.

STADT HAMBURG, Strandstrasse 2, D-2280 Westerland/Sylt. Tel. 04651/85-80. Fax 04651/85-82-20. 85 rms, 22 suites. MINIBAR TV TEL **Bus:** Centrale Omnibus Bahnhof.

$ Rates: 168 DM–240 DM ($110.90–$158.40) single; 286 DM–443 DM ($188.80–$292.40) double; from 662 DM ($436.90) suite. Half board 205 DM–420 DM ($135.30–$277.20) per person per day. AE, MC. **Parking:** 12 DM ($7.90).

⭐ The superior hostelry on the island is more like a well-appointed country home than a hotel, its gleaming white entrance reached through a white picket fence with street lanterns. It's built close to the street, next to the casino, and its rear windows overlook a well-kept lawn. The bright and cheerful interior has country-estate furnishings, including wing chairs and floral-covered armchairs. Each room is individually furnished, with homelike touches. You'll want to take your morning meal in the breakfast room, with its blue-and-white ceramic stove. Guests gather on cooler evenings around the open fireplace. The restaurant serves some of the best food at the resort (see below).

EXPENSIVE

HOTEL HANSEAT, Maybachstrasse 1, D-2280 Westerland/Sylt. Tel. 04651/230-23. 21 rms. MINIBAR TV TEL **Bus:** Centrale Omnibus Bahnhof.

$ Rates (including continental breakfast): 120 DM–170 DM ($79.20–$112.20) single; 230 DM–270 DM ($151.80–$178.20) double. AE, MC, V. **Parking:** Free.

Ⓢ The Hanseat is centrally located on a pedestrian walkway. The owner of this family-run establishment offers spacious public rooms and well-maintained guest rooms.

WUNSCHMANN HOTEL, Andreas-Dirks-Strasse 4, D-2280 Westerland/ Sylt. Tel. 04651/50-25. Fax 04651/50-28. 35 rms, 1 suite. TV TEL **Bus:** Centrale Omnibus Bahnhof.

$ Rates: 128 DM–190 DM ($84.50–$125.40) single; 196 DM–336 DM

($129.40–$221.80) double; from 590 DM ($389.40) suite. Breakfast 20 DM ($13.20) extra. AE. **Parking:** 10 DM ($6.60). **Closed:** Mid-Nov to mid-Dec.

⭐ Accommodations are in a complex of modern buildings (with more than two dozen boutiques), but the hotel's inner aura is one of comfortable old-world tranquility. Food is offered in a woodsy and informal dining room. The one-of-a-kind guest rooms are cheerful with strong colors; two offer minibars. The hotel is in the heart of the tourist belt of Westerland, yet only minutes from the sand dunes.

MODERATE

HOTEL CLAUSEN, Friedrichstrasse 20, D-2280 Westerland/Sylt. Tel. 04651/72-25. Fax 04651/28007. 20 rms, 3 suites. TEL

$ Rates (including continental breakfast): 100 DM–140 DM ($66–$92.40) single; 180 DM–240 DM ($118.80–$158.40) double; 250 DM–280 DM ($165–$184.80) suite. AE. **Closed:** Jan.

Set in the heart of Westerland's pedestrian zone, a three-minute walk to the beach, this four-story building was originally built around 1950 and radically modernized in 1992. Today, its congenial English-speaking owners occupy the upper (fourth) floor, devoting the building's lower stories to a series of simple but well-maintained rooms. Breakfast is the only meal served, but many restaurants are nearby.

WHERE TO DINE
VERY EXPENSIVE

JÖRG MÜLLER, Süderstrasse 8. Tel. 04651/2-77-88.
  Cuisine: CONTINENTAL/FRENCH. **Reservations:** Required. **Bus:** Centrale Omnibus Bahnhof.
$ Prices: Appetizers 14 DM–56 DM ($9.20–$37); main courses 48 DM–68 DM ($31.70–$44.90); four-course fixed-price lunch 98 DM ($64.70); four-course fixed-price dinner 136 DM ($89.80); seven-course fixed-price dinner 178 DM ($117.50). AE, DC, MC, V.
  Open: Lunch Wed–Mon 11:30am–2pm; dinner Wed–Mon 6–10pm. **Closed:** Nov 16–21; Dec.

⭐ The most elegant dining on the island is at Jörg Müller, a five-minute walk from the center. The brick building that contains this restaurant is almost a landmark in itself, thanks to its thatched roof, steep gables, and Friesian architecture. Since the culinary star of Sylt, Jörg Müller, took over the premises in 1988, its fame has eclipsed that of every competitor. Menu items change with the seasons and include a blend of continental cuisine moderne with imaginative variations of French recipes, which might include lobster salad with herb-flavored vinaigrette sauce, sliced and braised goose liver with segments of glazed apples, or roast salt-marsh lamb flavored with herbs and served with ratatouille-flavored cream sauce. You can also enjoy local oysters with compote of red shallots and champagne sauce or halibut baked in fennel. For dessert, you might order a compote of fresh fruits with pistachio nuts or feuillete of chocolate served with both light and dark chocolate mousse.

EXPENSIVE

STADT HAMBURG STUBE, Strandstrasse 2. Tel. 04651/85-80.
  Cuisine: GERMAN/FRIESIAN. **Reservations:** Recommended, especially if you're not a hotel guest. **Bus:** Centrale Omnibus Bahnhof.
$ Prices: Appetizers 12 DM–32 DM ($7.90–$21.10); main courses 39 DM–52 DM ($25.70–$34.30); fixed-price lunch 36 DM ($23.80); fixed-price dinner 140 DM ($92.40). AE, MC, V.
  Open: Lunch daily noon–2pm; dinner daily 6–10pm.

⭐ Top-rate cuisine is offered in an attractive setting at Stadt Hamburg Stube. The menu is so wide ranging it makes selection difficult, but among the à la carte listings, the smoothest beginning is the cream of lobster soup. There are many seafood specialties, such as pan-fried fresh North Sea plaice and turbot medallions in saffron sauce with zucchini. Other good dishes are the rack of lamb (raised on the salty grasslands of the island) and a dessert, homemade Rote Grütze—different kinds of berries and cherries topped with vanilla ice cream.

MODERATE

ALTE FRIESENSTUBE, Gaadt 4. Tel. 04651/12-28.
Cuisine: NORTHERN GERMAN/FRIESIAN. **Reservations:** Required. **Bus:** Centrale Omnibus Bahnhof.
$ Prices: Appetizers 8.50 DM–22 DM ($5.60–$14.50); main courses 22 DM–42 DM ($14.50–$27.70). No credit cards.
Open: Dinner only, Tues–Sun 6–10pm. **Closed:** Jan.

The thatched building housing this Stube was constructed in 1648. The menus are written on the wall in a dialect of low German, but someone will gladly assist you in deciphering the offerings, which include regional pork, fish, and beef dishes.

HARDY AUF SYLT, Norderstrasse 65. Tel. 04651/2-27-75.
Cuisine: INTERNATIONAL/NORTHERN GERMAN. **Reservations:** Required.
Bus: Centrale Omnibus Bahnhof.
$ Prices: Appetizers 7.50 DM–16 DM ($5–$10.60); main courses 24 DM–32.50 DM ($15.80–$21.50). AE, DC.
Open: Dinner only, daily 6pm–midnight. **Closed:** Nov 30–Dec 20; Jan 15–Feb 15.

This round, thatched restaurant with a nostalgic interior is run by French gastronomer André Speiser. The decor features furniture dating back to about 1890. Finely worked columns and some imposing old oil portraits adorn the dining area. Beautiful glass lamps and skillfully wrought candlesticks combine to create a relaxed, intimate dinner, with candlelight, soft music, the best of wine, and good food. The menu is adjusted seasonally based on the freshness of produce. There is also a fine selection of French and German wine.

CHAPTER 17

SETTLING INTO BERLIN

I f you had been one of the pilots bringing supplies to the people of West Berlin in the great airlift of 1948 and 1949, you wouldn't recognize the city today. It was Hitler's capital, of course, and because of that dubious distinction it was almost bombed out of existence. Structures of steel and glass now tower over streets where in 1945 only piles of rubble lay. Parks that were once reduced to muddy swampland are again lush forests and gardens. The same optimistic spirit and strength of will that caused the remarkable West Berliners to survive the destruction and the postwar Soviet blockade have created a new Berlin, a metropolis unequaled in Germany now that West Berlin and East Berlin have been united.

Today Berliners wander back and forth in their united city as they did before its division after World War II. A walk between east and west, however, is still a study in contrasts. History may move rapidly, but it cannot transform overnight the city into one Berlin—except politically. On June 20, 1991, the German Parliament voted to move the seat of government from Bonn to Berlin; however, it will take years to make Berlin fully functional as the center of power. The city, nevertheless, is moving quickly to reclaim its stellar position as one of the great capitals of European industry and culture.

Before the war, the section that became East Berlin was the cultural and political heart of Germany; it was here that the best museums, the finest churches, and the most important boulevards lay. When East Berlin became the capital of the Deutsche Demokratische Republik in 1949, it was a metropolis of some one million people. In 1961, the dreaded Berlin Wall stabilized East Berlin by stopping a massive flow of its talent and its work force to the West. The walled-in citizens turned to rebuilding and restoring their city. On November 9, 1989, as future historians will note, East Berlin was the center of a relatively bloodless revolution that rapidly paved the way for reunification and the destruction of the Wall. However, in the 1990s, east Berliners face a devastated economy that will have to be rebuilt before they can become a truly equal partner with their fellow citizens in western Germany.

Berlin stands at the geographical heart of the European continent, lying about halfway between Portugal and Moscow. Embracing an area of about 350 square miles, it is the largest city in Germany, with some 3.5 million inhabitants. It lies 180 miles southeast of Hamburg; 179 miles east of Hannover; and 113 miles northeast of Leipzig.

WHAT'S SPECIAL ABOUT BERLIN

Ace Attractions

☐ The Kurfürstendamm, launched by Bismarck in 1870 to surpass the Champs-Elysées, it is today a bustling neon shopping boulevard celebrating the victory of capitalism.

☐ Brandenburger Tor (Brandenburg Gate), symbolic centerpiece of Imperial Prussia in the 18th century. This landmark straddled the two Berlins of the Cold War years.

☐ Olympic Stadium, designed for 100,000 spectators, this arena was built for Berlin's controversial 1936 Olympic Games, which disappointed Hitler.

☐ Unter den Linden, the architectural showpiece boulevard of Prussian emperors, whose linden trees shaded Goethe, Beethoven, and Schiller.

Museums

☐ Dahlem Museum, assembling within one giant complex the artistic masterpieces (Dürers, Holbeins, Rembrandts, Titians) accumulated by German emperors.

☐ Charlottenburg Palace & Museums, after Potsdam, the greatest 18th-century palace in North Germany.

☐ Museum of the Wall, once a defiant indictment of a brutal Communist regime, now an exhibition of Cold War memories.

☐ Pergamon Museum, containing the fruits of the worldwide archeological digs that mesmerized Germany under the Prussian kaisers.

Park

☐ Zoologischer Garten Berlin, one of Europe's great zoos.

Religious Shrine

☐ Kaiser Wilhelm Memorial Church, with bombed-out ruins deliberately unrepaired, a symbol of the horror of war.

Special Events

☐ International Film Festival, with international cinema artists and aspirants converging on Berlin for two weeks in February.

☐ Jazz-Fest Berlin, everything from mainstream jazz to the most experimental forms, performed in October and November.

1. BERLIN — PAST & PRESENT

Berlin for many centuries has stood at the crossroads of history. It still evokes memories of the not-too-distant past. In the "Golden Twenties," the heyday of intellectual, cabaret, and boulevard life, it saw Marlene Dietrich begin her legendary career in the film *The Blue Angel.* Albert Einstein sketched out his theories of relativity. Lotte Lenya's songs, Kurt Weill's music, the plays of Bertolt Brecht, and the avant-garde films of Fritz Lang were also products of that period.

In the 1930s, Berlin's dubious distinction was to become the capital of Hitler's Third Reich. Hitler's favorite, Leni Riefenstahl, glorified Nazism in film, but the portentous architecture of Albert Speer and Hitler's dreams of architectural glory were never realized. Hitler never liked the city, which had regarded him initially with some skepticism—he did, in fact, consider changing its name from Berlin to Germanica.

Today a metamorphosis is taking place, making the two Berlins into one. Phone systems, transportation, and air arrivals are just some of the thousands of elements that are being blended to make the two cities whole again. Visitors from all over the world are flocking to Berlin to see history in the making, a city in transformation, now in search of another identity.

WHAT IT WAS   The year 1987 marked Berlin's 750th anniversary. These dynamic seven and a half centuries saw Berlin go through many changes. In its earliest recorded history, it was twin cities: the older Cölln and the slightly younger Berlin. Both towns developed from merchant settlements. The first mention of Cölln was in 1237, the first mention of Berlin in 1244. These towns on the River Spree, always closely linked economically, decided to unite as one city in 1307 and surrounded themselves with fortifications. At the crossroads of trade routes of medieval northern Europe, the city flourished.

At the beginning of the 15th century, the Hohenzollerns came to power. To be supreme rulers for five centuries, they made Berlin their seat of power. Hard times were to come. The ravages of the Thirty Years' War (1618–48), along with a series of epidemics, reduced the population to 6,000.

Frederick William (1640–88), the Great Elector, invited the Protestant Huguenots, fleeing religious persecution in France, to Berlin in 1685. Some 6,000 of them arrived, bringing about an economic revitalization of the stagnant Berlin economy. They introduced several industries, including paper mills, glassworks, silk mills, and even tobacco cultivation. In the following years, the city became home to other Protestants from Switzerland and Bohemia. The elector also invited wealthy Jews who had been expelled from Austria to settle in Berlin.

In the meantime, the Hohenzollerns continued to grow in power and possessions, extending their lands to the Russian frontier. Frederick I was crowned "king in Prussia" (as opposed to "of") in 1701. He merged five towns and formed a royal residence, making Berlin the capital in 1709.

Frederick the Great (1712–86), came to the throne in 1740. The king presided over the Silesian Wars, the Seven Years' War, and the partition of Poland. During his reign, Berlin developed as an important commercial city, and became a center of culture and enlightenment; literature and philosophy flourished.

In 1806, Napoleon's troops occupied Berlin, the emperor entering through the Brandenburger Tor, beginning nearly a decade of rule from Paris. This led to the war of liberation from 1813 to 1815. But the peace as promised by the Congress of Vienna in 1815 did not bring the new freedom expected. Following the repression of Frederick William III (1797–1840), the year 1848 brought revolution to the streets. But the rebellion was crushed.

In 1871, Otto von Bismarck (1815–98), the Prussian prime minister, succeeded in uniting Germany for the first time, with a nationalist policy. Berlin became the capital of this new German Empire. Known as the Iron Chancellor, Bismarck instituted an enlightened program of social reform. Berlin continued to grow through all these changes and upheavals. In 1906, its population was reported at 2 million.

World War I arrived in Berlin in 1914, with its dire consequences. Following Germany's defeat and the abdication of the kaiser in November 1918, the first democratic republic was proclaimed in Germany. It was called the Weimar Republic, but in spite of its name, Berlin was still the capital.

By the 1920s Berlin had emerged as the largest industrial power on the Continent, the nerve center of a vast rail network, the home of the German press, and a sophisticated cultural and intellectual center. But the decade was also a time of political turmoil with clashes between the Communists and the Nazis, and the growing power of the Nazi movement.

On January 30, 1933, President von Hindenburg appointed Adolf Hitler chancellor of Germany. The Reichstag (parliament building) was mysteriously burned on February 27, 1933. A reign of terror ensued, culminating in the events of Kristallnacht, November 9, 1938, as Nazi hooligans set fire to synagogues and destroyed the shops of Jewish merchants. Berlin had the infamous distinction of leading Nazi Germany into World War II, a tragic military blunder that would rain Allied destruction on the city and reduce it to rubble.

After the German surrender on May 8, 1945, Berlin, no longer the capital of

Germany, was divided into four zones of occupation: Soviet, U.S., British, and French. The Berlin blockade was launched by the Soviet Union on June 24, 1948, closing roads, rails, and waterways to the west, "trapping" 2.5 million West Berliners without food, supplies, or electricity. The policy was to use mass starvation to bring about a political takeover and occupation. But on June 25, an American transport plane carrying 3 tons of freight landed at Tempelhof Airport in Berlin. The Berlin airlift had begun. Bowing to its success, the Soviet Union lifted the blockade on May 12, 1949. West Berlin further lost status on September 7, 1949, when the Federal Republic of Germany made Bonn its provisional capital. More than ever, West Berlin felt cut off from the rest of Germany. East Berlin was named capital of the German Democratic Republic on October 9, 1949.

On August 13, 1961, the East German government launched the construction of the Berlin Wall to stop the flow of its citizens to the West. At first a barbed-wire barrier, it was turned into a heavily guarded concrete wall. On June 26, 1963, President John F. Kennedy arrived to deliver his now famous "I am a Berliner" line at Schöneberg Rathaus.

In 1972, West Berliners were allowed to visit East Germany, and more than a decade later, in 1986, cultural contacts between East and West Germany were established, just in time for the 1987 celebration of Berlin's 750th anniversary.

Nothing had prepared the world for the sudden events of 1989 and 1990 that led to the dismantling of the Berlin Wall and unification.

WHAT IT IS TODAY   Following partition at the end of World War II, West Berlin forged a new identity. In spite of its decades-long "quadripartite status," it became a vibrant, self-critical city, always receptive to new ideas and change, a major economic and cultural center. It is one of Germany's largest university cities, a leader in development and research. It's a popular destination for tourists and, because of its excellent facilities, is one of Europe's favored sites for trade fairs, congresses, and conventions, attracting 6 million visitors a year.

The panoramic view Berlin visitors see as they arrive by plane is splendid. Few metropolitan areas in the world are blessed with so many lakes, woodlands, and parks, covering about a third of the city's area. Visitors who arrive for the first time are astonished to learn that small farms with fields and meadows still exist.

Berlin is subdivided into boroughs of town-size dimensions, each independently administered from its Rathaus. Each borough has a character of its own, with marketplaces, shopping areas, and service centers. Here and there throughout the city are "villages," with their own warmth and atmosphere. Music, film, and other events of international importance define Berlin as a metropolis. One can dine to the midnight chimes, breakfast outdoors to the beat of a jazz band, or join the strollers along the Kurfürstendamm. Berlin is lively around the clock, with various attractions to suit every taste.

Nothing demonstrates the change in Berlin more than in the Alexanderplatz, the former center of the German Democratic Republic. For a foreigner from the West to reach this massive square was once a formidable undertaking, involving armed border guards, payments of currency fees, and the promise to get out of town (East Berlin) by midnight or else face the consequences.

Now the Friedrichstrasse Bahnhof will take you there from the western part of Berlin. You arrive in this former "People's Paradise" to discover a world of cafés: Umbrellas emblazoned with the logos of Marlboro and Camel cigarettes shade the tables; street vendors sell bananas, once almost impossible to find; a troupe of Bulgarian acrobats may be staging a performance on the square.

IMPRESSIONS

All free men, wherever they live, are citizens of Berlin, and therefore, as a free man, I take pride in the words, "Ich bin ein Berliner"
—JOHN F. KENNEDY, SPEECH IN BERLIN (JUNE 1963)

Right now the city seems to have two of everything: two of the best zoos, two of the best opera companies, two transport systems, two major international airports, two museums of old masters, two museums of Greek and Roman antiquities. Integration will be difficult, and it may take a long time and a lot of hard work and social change before Berlin completes its transition into the indisputable *Hauptstadt* of Germany.

The city's biggest tourist attraction since 1961 is now gone: the Berlin Wall. Where did it go? Virtually everywhere. A piece of it forms a monument in this author's garden in the United States. Edwina Sandys took eight big slabs of it to create a sculpture for Westminster College in Fulton, Missouri. It was here in 1946 that her grandfather, Sir Winston Churchill, used the term "Iron Curtain." The site of the torn-down Berlin Wall is today a bicycle path, part of which is marked with white crosses in honor of those who were killed trying to escape from East Germany. Berliners also push baby strollers along the former "zone of death."

When Heinrich Heine arrived in Berlin in 1819, he exclaimed, "Isn't the present splendid." Were he to arrive today, he might make the same remark.

2. ORIENTATION

ARRIVING

BY PLANE   Prior to the unification of Germany the Eastern Bloc imposed strict rules on which airlines could fly over the eastern sector of Germany and which could legally land its planes at either of the two major Berlin airports. From the roster of allowable airlines, Lufthansa, the flag carrier of West Germany, was omitted.

Since the crumbling of both the Berlin Wall and the restrictions that accompanied it, airlines have scrambled to claim their share of business into Berlin. As might be expected, **Lufthansa** (tel. toll free 800/645-3880) almost immediately reestablished itself as the premier airline.

At press time, Lufthansa did not offer nonstop service to Berlin from North America, preferring instead to route Berlin-bound passengers onto one of the hundred or more flights it offers every day into Berlin from about a dozen cities in western Germany and the rest of Europe. The most popular gateways are Frankfurt and Munich, both of which receive frequent transatlantic flights from Lufthansa's 16 North American cities. Frequent connections are also offered from London, Paris, Athens, Brussels, Cologne, Bremen, Hamburg, Düsseldorf, Stuttgart, and Nürnberg. Lufthansa's flights land in Berlin at Tegel, Tempelhof, or Schönefeld, with Tegel receiving most bigger aircraft.

Lufthansa is not alone in flying to Berlin. **British Airways** (tel. toll free 800/247-9297) offers more flights into the airline capital of Europe (London) than any other airline in the world from the former British Empire. From London's Heathrow Airport, between three and four nonstop flights depart every day for Berlin-Tegel Airport. BA also flies to Berlin from Edinburgh (five times a week) and Birmingham (six times a week).

TWA (tel. toll free 800/892-4141) flies from New York's JFK to Berlin every day in peak season and several times a week at other times. Flights touch down briefly in Brussels en route.

American Airlines (tel. toll free 800/433-7300) inaugurated service to Berlin-Tegel from Chicago's O'Hare in 1992, flying nonstop daily, and offering good connections from other parts of its vast network.

United Airlines (tel. toll free 800/538-2929) flies to Berlin-Tegel nonstop daily from London's Heathrow. To London, United offers frequent service nonstop from San Francisco; New York's JFK; Washington, D.C.'s Dulles; and Newark.

Delta (tel. toll free 800/241-4141) offers nonstop flights every evening from New

York's JFK to Berlin-Tegel. It also offers service from the airline's enormous hub in Atlanta to Berlin, with a brief touchdown in Hamburg.

Getting into the City   Berlin-Tegel Airport (tel. 030/41-011), the newest and most modern airport of Berlin, is 5 miles northwest of center city. Public transportation by bus, taxi, or U-Bahn is convenient to all points in the city. BVG bus 109 runs every 10 minutes from the airport to Bahnhof Zoo in the center. The bus departs from outside the arrival hall, a one-way fare costing 3.20 DM ($2.10). A taxi to center city costs about 29 DM ($19.10) and takes some 20 minutes. No porters are available for luggage handling, but pushcarts are free.

The main terminal has an information counter, offering a free map of the city. There's also a tourist office there, booking arriving passengers into Berlin hotels for a 5-DM ($3.30) fee. It is open daily from 8am to 11pm. Facilities include money-exchange centers, luggage-storage facilities (and locker rentals), a police station, auto-rental kiosks, dining facilities, and a first-aid center. Shops also sell gifts, film, and travel paraphernalia. There's also an airport Novotel with a connecting shuttle between the hotel and the airport.

Berlin-Schönefeld Airport (tel. 030/67-870), once the major airport for East Germany, receives many flights from South America and Asia, as well as Russia, and from cities of Eastern Europe such as Prague. It lies in the eastern part of Berlin, 12 miles southeast of the city center. Airport transfers into the city center are by S-Bahn lines 9 and 10 (trip time: 55 minutes). The S-Bahn station is about a 5-minute walk from the main arrival hall. The S-Bahn will take you to Alexanderplatz where you can transfer to other S-Bahn connections. You can also take bus 59 from the airport to Rudow, where you can transfer to U-Bahn trains for city center locations. Either means of transport costs 3.20 DM ($2.10).

The third airport is **Berlin-Tempelhof** (tel. 030/6909-1), the city's oldest, 4 miles southeast of center city. To handle the overflow from other airports, Tempelhof now receives several flights from German or European cities. Take the U-Bahn (U6) or buses 104, 119, 184, or 341. If you want to go to the city center, bus no. 119 is the most convenient link. All bus fares from Tempelhof into the center cost 3.20 DM ($2.10).

Private bus shuttles among the three airports operate constantly so you can make connecting flights at a different airport.

BY TRAIN   Frankfurt and Hamburg, among other cities, have good rail connections to Berlin. From Frankfurt to Berlin takes about seven hours. Eurailpass and GermanRail passes (see Chapter 2) are valid.

Most arrivals from Western European and western German cities are at the **Bahnhof Zoologischer Garten** (tel. 030/311-02-111), the main train station, called "Bahnhof Zoo," in western Berlin. Lying in the center of the city, close to the Kurfürstendamm, it is well connected for public transportation. Both the U-Bahn and the bus network link this station with the rest of Berlin. Bus no. 109 runs to Berlin-Tegel Airport if you're making connections.

Facilities include a tourist information counter dispensing free maps and tourist brochures. It is open daily from 8am to 11pm. The staff there will also make hotel reservations for 5 DM ($3.30) if you tell them what category of hotel you're seeking. You can also mail letters, exchange currency, and rent lockers. For rail information and schedules, call 030/19-419.

Berlin has two other train stations, the **Berlin Hauptbahnhof** (tel. 030/492-53-47), and **Berlin Lichtenberg** (tel. 030/492-25-31). Many trains from Eastern Europe pull into these two stations, both in eastern Berlin. However, certain trains from the west also service the station, so always make sure you're getting off at the right station, depending on your final destination. S-Bahn 5 connects both of these stations to Bahnhof Zoo.

BY BUS   Regularly scheduled buses operate to and from Berlin from 200 German and continental cities, including Frankfurt, Hamburg, and Munich. Long-distance

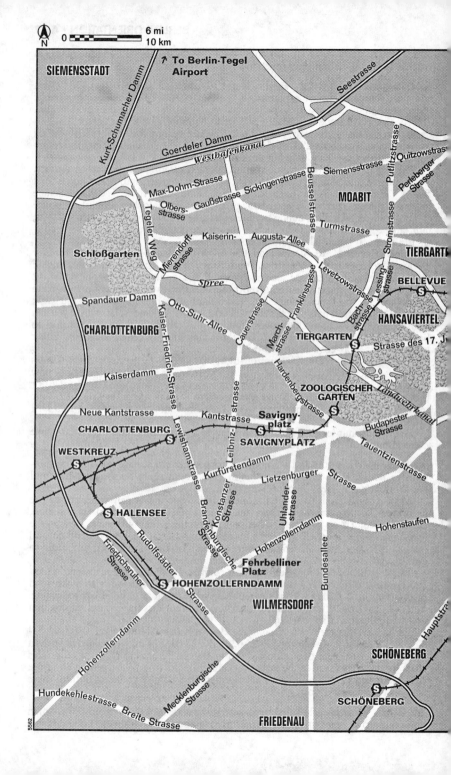

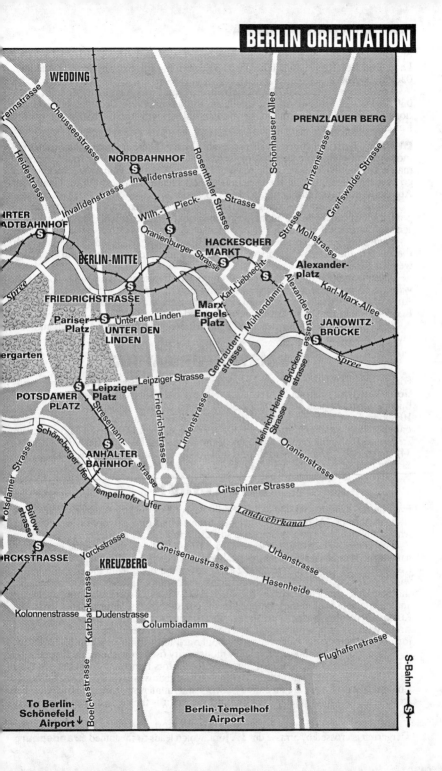

BERLIN ORIENTATION

WEDDING

PRENZLAUER BERG

Chausseestrasse

rennstrasse

Heidestrasse

Schönhauser Allee

Prinzstrasse

Greifswalder Strasse

NORDBAHNHOF

Invalidenstrasse

Invalidenstrasse

Rosenthaler Strasse

Strasse

Mollstrasse

Wilh.- Pieck-

**RTER
ADTBAHNHOF**

Oranienburger Strasse

**HACKESCHER
MARKT**

**Alexander-
platz**

Karl-Liebknecht-

Karl-Marx-Allee

BERLIN-MITTE

Spree

FRIEDRICHSTRASSE

Alexander-Strasse

**JANOWITZ-
BRÜCKE**

**Pariser-
Platz**

Unter den Linden

**Marx-
Engels-
Platz**

Mühlendamm

Brücken-
strasse

Spree

**UNTER DEN
LINDEN**

Gertrauden-
strasse

ergarten

Leipziger Strasse

Lindenstrasse

Leipziger Strasse

Friedrichstrasse

Heinrich-Heine-
Strasse

**POTSDAMER
PLATZ**

**Leipziger
Platz**

Stresemann-

Oranienstrasse

Schöneberger Ufer

Potsdamer Strasse

**ANHALTER
BAHNHOF**

strasse

Tempelhofer Ufer

Gitschiner Strasse

Bülow-
strasse

Landwehrkanal

RCKSTRASSE

Vorckstrasse

Gneisenaustrasse

Urbanstrasse

KREUZBERG

Hasenheide

Kolonnenstrasse

Dudenstrasse

Katzbachstrasse

Columbiadamm

Boelckestrasse

Flughafenstrasse

**To Berlin-
Schönefeld
Airport** ↓

**Berlin-Tempelhof
Airport**

S-Bahn ← Ⓢ ←

bus companies serving Berlin include Autokraft GmbH (tel. 030/33-10-31); Deutsche Land und See Reisen (tel. 030/33-10-31); and Bayern Express & P. Kühn (tel. 030/86-00-960).

Arrivals are at the **ZOB Omnibusbahnhof am Funkturm,** Messedamm 8 (tel. 030/301-80-28 for reservations, schedules, and information). Taxis and bus connections are possible at the station, or you can link up with the U-Bahn at the nearby Kaiserdamm station.

BY CAR   Berlin, of course, is also accessible by car. There are three major routes for motorists traveling from the west of Germany to Berlin. The shorter route (approximately two hours) leads from the town of Helmstedt, east of Hannover. You can also go east from Frankfurt in the direction of Bad Herzfeld toward Berlin. Finally, an Autobahn north of Nürnberg (A9) leads to Berlin.

In case of breakdowns along the Autobahnen, call boxes are placed at strategic points. However, if you are a long way from a box, police cars will often find you and send a tow truck if required.

Eventually, you will reach the Berlin Ring Road or A10 (E55), which encircles both the eastern and western sectors of the city. Chances are, your hotel will be in the western part; if so, follow the signs.

Because many more travelers are going between east and west today (each side wanting to see what was going on on the other), expect heavy traffic delays on Autobahnen, especially on weekends and sunny days when everybody is out touring. Road signs and directions are frequently posted.

Berlin lies 343 miles northeast of Frankfurt, 363 miles north of Munich, and 184 miles southeast of Hamburg.

TOURIST INFORMATION

For tourist information and hotel bookings, head for the **Berlin Tourist Information Center,** Europa-Center (near Memorial Church), entrance on the Budapesterstrasse side (tel. 030/262-60-31), open Monday to Saturday from 8am to 10:30pm, Sunday from 9am to 9pm. Other branches are at the railway station Bahnhof Zoologischer Garten (tel. 030/313-90-63), open Monday to Saturday from 7:30am to 10:30pm; in the main lobby of the Berlin-Tegel Airport (tel. 030/4101-31-34), open daily from 8am to 11pm; and in the Alexanderplatz/TV tower in the eastern part of Berlin (tel. 030/212-45-12), open daily from 8am to 8pm.

CITY LAYOUT

Even before division and unification, Berlin was one of the largest and most complex cities in Europe. Although the city has been united into a more-or-less coherent whole, the marks of past regimes are still discernible in its districts.

The center of activity in the western part of Berlin is the 2½-mile-long street named the **Kurfürstendamm,** but called the Ku'damm by Berliners, who seem to have a habit of irreverently renaming every street and building in the city. Along this wide boulevard you'll find the best hotels, restaurants, theaters, cafés, nightclubs, shops, and department stores. As the showcase of western Berlin, it is the most elegant and fashionable spot in the city, but like the paradox that is western Berlin itself, the Ku'damm combines chic with sleaze. Some visitors walk the entire length of this street, whereas others, not so hale and hearty, give up (as Berliners often do) and head for one of the popular cafés lining the boulevard for a drink or a cup of coffee.

Berlin today is an almost completely modern city risen from the ashes. Regrettably, it is hardly the architectural gem that old-time visitors remember from the pre-Nazi era. It was not rebuilt with the same kind of care that was lavished on such cities as Cologne. Parts of it are architecturally tawdry and uninteresting. Berlin is rich in other attractions, including great museums, but I suspect it is the city's tremendous vitality that attracts so many visitors.

North of the Ku'damm is the huge **Tiergarten,** the city's largest park. The Tiergarten is crossed by Strasse des 17. Juni, which leads to the famed **Brandenburg**

Gate (just north of here is the Reichstag). On the southwestern fringe of the Tiergarten is the **Berlin Zoo,** which we'll visit later. Since Berlin is so spread out (many lakes and pleasure areas are included within its boundaries), you will need to depend on public transportation. From the Ku'damm you can take Hardenbergstrasse, crossing Bismarckstrasse and traversing Otto-Suhr-Allee, which will lead to the Schloss Charlottenburg and museums, one of your major sightseeing goals. The Dahlem Museums are on the southwestern fringe, often reached by going along the Hohenzollerndamm.

The **Brandenburger Tor,** which once separated the two Berlins, is the start of eastern Berlin's most celebrated street, **Unter den Linden,** the cultural heart of Berlin before World War II. It was a street of fashionable hotels, theaters, and cafés. The famous street runs from west to east, cutting a path through the city. It leads to **Museumsinsel,** or Museum Island where the most outstanding museums of eastern Berlin, including the Pergamon Museum, are situated.

As it courses along, Under den Linden crosses another major eastern Berlin artery, **Friedrichstrasse.** If you continue south along the Friedrichstrasse, you will reach the former location of Checkpoint Charlie, a famous site of the Cold War days. No longer a checkpoint, it has a little museum devoted to memories of the dreaded wall.

Under den Linden continues east until it reaches the **Alexanderplatz,** the center of eastern Berlin, with its towering television tower (Fernsehturm).

A short walk away is the newly restored **Nikolai Quarter** (Nikolaiviertel), a neighborhood of bars, restaurants, and shops that evoke life in the prewar days.

NEIGHBORHOODS IN BRIEF

Charlottenburg   Despite its renaming after the bombings of World War II by Berlin wits as Klamottenburg (ragsville), it's probably the wealthiest and most densely commercialized and hotel-rich district of western Berlin. Its centerpiece is Charlottenburg Palace, named for Sophie Charlotte, wife of Prussian ruler Frederick I. The district also contains the world-famous monument to capitalism, the Kurfürstendamm.

Savignyplatz   Located just a few blocks north of the Ku'damm, this tree-lined square and the streets that radiate away from it offer a profusion of bars and restaurants, an engaging aura of permissiveness, and some of the most popular nightclubs and night cafés in Berlin.

Tiergarten   Translated literally as "animal garden," it refers both to the massive swath of urban greenery and to a residential district of the same name. Originally intended as a backdrop to the grand avenues laid out by the German kaisers, it contains the Brandenburg Gate, the German Reichstag (Parliament), the Berlin Zoo, and most of the grandest museums of northern Germany.

Hansaviertel   Sprawling beside the Tiergarten park's northern edge, it contains a series of residential buildings, each designed by a different architect (including Le Corbusier, Walter Gropius, and Alvar Aalto), as the aftermath of an international conference in 1957 of the world's leading designers.

Dahlem   Considered the university district of Berlin, it was originally established as an independent village to the southwest of Berlin's center.

Spandau   Set near the junction of the Spree and Havel rivers, about 6 miles northwest of the city center, Spandau boasts a history of medieval grandeur. Merged with Berlin in 1920, its Altstadt is still intact and, until it was demolished in the early 1990s, so was the legendary Spandau prison.

Kreuzberg   Originally built as tenements during the 19th century to house the workers of a rapidly industrializing Prussia, this has traditionally been the poorest and most overcrowded of Berlin's districts. Today, at least 35% (and perhaps more) of its population is composed of guest workers from Turkey, Yugoslavia, and Greece. Recently, the district has become headquarters for the city's artistic counterculture.

Schöneberg Like Kreuzberg, it was originally an independent suburb of workers' housing. Rebuilt after the war as a solidly middle-class neighborhood, it lies south of the Tiergarten and is rarely visited by foreign tourists.

Grunewald Northwest of the city center, it surprises many newcomers with the sheer sprawl of its 19 square miles of verdant forest and parks. Although 70% of the forest was cut down during the Cold War for fuel, it has been replanted, and serves as it always did as a green lung for the urbanites of Berlin.

Berlin-Mitte Originally conceived as the architectural centerpiece of the Prussian kaisers, it fell under the Eastern zone during the division of Berlin after World War II. As such, its fortunes declined dramatically as the Communist regime infused it with many of their starkly angular monuments. Although many of the district's grand buildings were destroyed, unification has opened its remaining artistic and architectural treasures to the eyes of the world. Its most famous street is Unter den Linden.

Alexanderplatz At the eastern end of Unter den Linden, it once sheltered the kaiser's palace, a monument whose destruction was completed by the East German regime who wanted to rid itself of what might eventually become an ideological monument to the Prussian monarchy. Considered the centerpiece of the former Communist government, it is a large and somewhat sterile square dominated by the tallest building in Berlin, the Sputnik-inspired TV tower.

Museumsinsel (Museum Island) Originally conceived in the 1820s as the showplace for the archeological treasures accumulated during German expeditions abroad, it occupies a complex of neoclassical buildings on an island in the Spree River. Its most famous museum, the Pergamon, contains entire ancient temples that were reconstructed inside, stone by stone.

Nikolaiviertel It was here that Berlin originated during the 1200s and where the neighboring settlements at Cölln and Berlin were formally united in 1432. Located conveniently close to the Alexanderplatz, the Nikolaiviertel is considered the most perfectly restored medieval neighborhood in both Berlins, and a triumph of the restoration skills of the former East German regime.

Köpenick In the southeastern edge of the former eastern zone, this working-class neighborhood traces its history back to the 1000s. Despite the sterility of many of its high-rise apartment blocks, it still bears the provincial and quiet allure of many wooded parks, lakes, and forests.

FINDING AN ADDRESS

As for the numeration of streets, keep in mind that the city sometimes assists you by posting the range of numbers that appear within the context of any particular block, at least within such major arteries as the Kurfürstendamm. These numbers appear on the street signs themselves, helping greatly in finding a particular number within the context of long boulevards. On smaller streets, these numbers are usually not posted on the street signs, requiring searchers to look on the facade of the buildings themselves for guidance. Although some of the city's streets are numbered with the odds on one side and the evens on the other, many (including the Kurfürstendamm) are numbered consecutively up one side of the street and back down the other.

Warning: The names of some eastern Berlin streets and squares with links to the old East German regime have been changed.

MAPS Good maps of Berlin are usually not free, but must be purchased at a bookstore or news kiosks. One of the best of these is the Falk map of Berlin. Despite its full-color detail and comprehensive indexes it sometimes proves awkward to unfold and refold so that a particular neighborhood is exposed to view. If a Falk map is not available anywhere you look, the Europa Press Center (a magazine and newspaper store in the Europa-Center) will usually have a good substitute. Be sure to obtain a recent map showing changes since unification.

3. GETTING AROUND

BY PUBLIC TRANSPORTATION   The Berlin transport system consists of buses, trams (only in eastern Berlin), U-Bahn, and S-Bahn (in eastern Berlin run by the Deutsche Reichsbahn), operating from about 4:30am to 12:30am daily (except for some 44 night buses, 11 night trams, and 2 U-Bahn lines). Public transport throughout Berlin is operated by one authority known as Berliner Verkehrs-Betriebe (BVG), Potsdamer Strasse 188 (tel. 030/216-50-88).

The BVG standard ticket (Einzelfahrschein) costs 3 DM ($2) and is valid for two hours of transportation in all directions, transfers included. Also available at counters and vending machines is the four-ride Multiple Ticket (Sammelkarte) for 10.40 DM ($6.90). On buses only standard tickets can be purchased, and for a ride by tram you have to buy your ticket in advance. Tickets should be kept to the end of the journey; otherwise, a fine of 60 DM ($39.60) has to be paid.

A special service for tourists is the Berlin-Ticket, good for unlimited travel for 24 hours on the U-Bahn, S-Bahn, trams, and buses. It costs 12 DM ($7.90) and can be purchased at the BVG information booth in front of the Bahnhof Zoo as well as at staffed counters of the rapid rail system and at some special vending machines.

All BVG tickets are valid not only in all of Berlin but also within the fare limits of the S-Bahn, in Potsdam's city transport, and in the trams serving Schöneiche, Woltersdorf, and Strausberg.

Two excursion bus lines make some beautiful scenic spots accessible: No. 218 bus line operates from Theodor-Heuss-Platz U-Bahn station near the radio tower via Schildhorn, Grünewald Tower, and Wannsee Beach to Wannsee S-Bahn station, and no. 216 bus line runs from Wannsee S-Bahn station to Pfaueninsel via Moorlake.

BY TAXI   Taxis are available throughout Berlin. The meter starts at 3.60 DM ($2.40), with 1.69 DM ($1.10) added per kilometer traveled. Fares are 1.99 DM ($1.30) per kilometer from midnight to 6am and on Sunday and holidays. For a taxi call 21-02-02, 6902, or 69-10-01.

BY CAR   U.S. rental companies have outlets in Berlin, and arrangements for cars should be made in advance by using toll-free numbers. However, should you need to rent a car in Berlin, you'll find an office of **Hertz** at Berlin-Tegel Airport (tel. 030/410-13-315), and at Budapesterstrasse 39 (tel. 030/261-10-53). **Avis** is also at Berlin-Tegel (tel. 030/410-13-148) and at Budapesterstrasse 43 (tel. 030/261-18-81).

It is not recommended that you use a car for touring Berlin. Free parking places are difficult to come by, and parking is very expensive in public garages. The excellent network of public transportation makes touring by car unnecessary.

Parking   If you're driving into Berlin, chances are that you'll want to safely store your car once you arrive. Many hotels offer parking facilities; otherwise you'll find many parking garages that remain open throughout the day and night. Those located near the Kurfürstendamm and the Europa-Center include the Parkhaus Metropol, Joachimstaler Strasse 14–19; Parkhaus Los-Angeles-Platz, Augsburger Strasse 30; Parkhaus Europa-Center, Nürnberger Strasse 5–7; and the Parkhaus am Zoo, Budapesterstrasse 38. Charges are from 2 DM ($1.30) per hour.

City-Specific Driving Problems   Note that driving in Berlin is a lot like negotiating the streets of any metropolis, except for one sometimes infuriating detail:

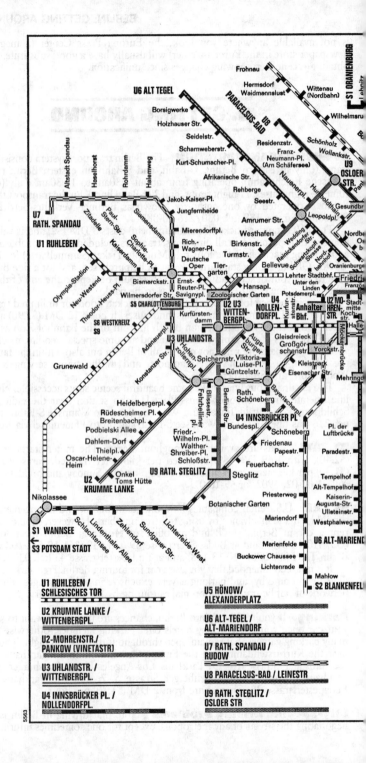

U-BAHN & S-BAHN

S8 BERNAU
Zepernick
Röntgental
S86 BUCH
Karow

S86 BLANKENBURG

Hohen Neuendorf
Bergfelde
Schönfliess
Mühlenbeck-Mönchmühle

Pankow-Heinersdorf

kow

S7 AHRENSFELDE

Raoul-Wallenberg-Str.
Mehrower Allee

U5 HÜNOW

S75 WARTENBURG

U2 PANKOW (VINETASTR.)
Schönhauser Allee
Hohenschönlhausen

Eberswalder Strasse
Senefelderpl.
Ernst-Thälmann-Park
Prenzlauer Allee
Geherenseestr.

Marzahn
Louis-Lewin-Str.
Hellersdorf
Cottbusser Pl.

S5 STRAUSBERG NORD

Poelchaustr.
Springpfuhl

Gottkauer Str.

Rosa-Luxemburg-Pl.
Landsberger Allee
Schillingstr.
Strausbergerpl.
Weberwiese
Rathaus Friedrichshain
Stortkower Str.
Friedrichsfelde Ost.

Kaulsdorf-Nord

Strausberg Stadt
Hegermühle

nauer Str.
Rosenthalerpl.

Weberwiese
Samariterstr.
Magdalenenstr.
Friedrichsfelde
Tierpark
Wuhletal
Biesdorf
Mahlsdorf
Hoppegarten
Neuenhagen
Fredersdorf
Petershagen Nord

Strausberg

erstr.

S7, S75, U5 ALEXANDERPL.
Jannowitzbr.
Frankfurter Allee
Ostkreuz
Lichtenberg

Kaulsdorf
Biesdorf-Süd
Elsterwerdaer Pl.

Klosterstr.
Märkisches Museum
Heinrich-Heine-Moritzpl. Str.
U1 SCHLESISCHES TOR

Rummelsburg
Betriebsbahnhof Rummelsburg

Kottbusser Tor
Görlitzer Bhf.
Warschauer S
Hauptbahnhof

Karlshorst
Wuhlheide

Treptower Park
Plänterwald
Baumschulenweg
Schöneweide

Köpenick
Hirschgarten

Kottbusser Damm

Oberspree

Friedrichshagen

Adlershof
Altglienicke
Grunberg Allee

S86 GRÜNAU
S86 SPINDLERS-FELD

Rahnsdorf
Wilhelmshagen
ERKNER

stern

S9 S10 FLUGHAFEN BERLIN-SCHÖNEFELD
Hermannpl.
Rath. Neukölln
Karl-Marx-Str.
Neukölln

Eichwalde
Zeuthen
Wildau

S6 KÖNIGS WUSTERHAUSEN

U8 LEINESTR

linstr.

Grenz Allee
Blaschko Allee
Parchimer Allee
Britz-Süd
Johannisthaler Ch.
Lipschitz Allee
Wutzky Allee
Zwickauer Damm
RUDOW U7

S5 - CHARLOTTENBURG/ STRAUSBERG NORD

S6 - WESTKREUZ/KÖNIGS WUSTERHAUSEN

S7 - ALEXANDERPLATZ/ AHRENSFELDE

S75 - ALEXANDERPLATZ/ WARTENBURG

S8 - BERNAU/GRÜNAU

S86 - BUCH & BLANKENBURG/ SPINDLERSFELD

S9 - FLUGHAFEN BERLIN-SCHÖNEFELD/WESTKREUZ

S10 - FLUGHAFEN BERLIN-SCHÖNEFELD/BIRKENWERDER

S1 WANNSEE / ORANIENBURG

S2 SCHÖNHOLZ/BLANKENFELDE

S3 POTSDAM STADT/ERKNER

It's almost impossible to turn left on major avenues within former East Berlin. Because of the positioning of metal barriers and tram lines down the middle of major avenues, turning left is usually impossible except at major intersections. There, unfortunately, oversize signs tell you to drive straight on. Many experienced drivers, faced with these conditions, usually opt for a right-hand turn, swing around the block, and then proceed straight across the tram lines wherever a traffic light will allow passage.

BY BICYCLE   Bicycling in Berlin's crushing traffic is not a very appealing prospect. More realistic (and safer) might be the short-term rental of a bicycle to explore the city's outlying parks and forests. Both the U-Bahn and the S-Bahn provide specific compartments for the transport of bicycles, for an extra supplement of 1.70 DM ($1.15). Transport of bicycles, however, is not permitted during rush hour, which is defined as Monday to Friday before 9am and again in the afternoon between 2 and 5:30pm.

On the outskirts you can rent a bike at **Fahrradbüro Berlin,** Hauptstrasse 146 (tel. 030/784-55-62; U-Bahn: Kleistpark). This company charges 12 DM ($7.90) per day, plus a deposit of between 50 DM and 100 DM ($33 and $66), depending on the value of the bicycle. Presentation of a passport or some other form of identification is usually required. Hours are Monday through Wednesday and Friday from 10am to 6pm, Thursday from noon to 7:30pm, and Saturday from 10am to 2pm. In the city and suburbs, try to confine your bicycling to within the cycle zones demarcated with solid red lines that run between the pedestrian sidewalks and the traffic lanes.

BY FOOT   Particularly since the obliteration of the Wall, Berlin offers endlessly interesting pedestrian itineraries, many of which take you through neighborhoods richly imbued with some of the most dramatic history of the 20th century. Remember, however, not to walk on bicycle paths delineated with red lines, lying parallel to the lanes reserved for motor traffic, immediately adjacent ot the sidewalk. If you walk on them, you're likely to be shouted at by cyclists (who know their municipal rights) or even run down. Both the police and everyday citizens do not look favorably on jaywalkers, especially those crossing the busy wide boulevards.

FAST FACTS: BERLIN

American Express   Amex offices are at Uhlandstrasse 173–174 (tel. 030/882-75-75), just off Kurfürstendamm, which services western Berlin, and also at Friedrichstrasse 172 (tel. 030/238-41-02), just off Unter den Linden, which services eastern Berlin. Office hours are Monday through Friday from 9am to 5:30pm and Saturday from 9am to noon. Clients can pick up mail only at the Uhlandstrasse office in the west. Unless you hold an Amex card or traveler's checks, a 2-DM ($1.30) fee will be charged for mail.

Area Code   The telephone area code is **030.**

Babysitters   Many hotels will provide this service for you. Arrangements should be made as far in advance as possible, and you can request an English-speaking sitter. Otherwise, call **Babysitters Service,** Claudiusstrasse 6 (tel. 030/393-59-81).

Bookstores   A good selection of travel guides, maps, and English-language titles are found at **Kiepert,** Hardenbergstrasse 4–5 (tel. 030/311-00-90). Take the U-Bahn to Ernst-Reuter-Platz.

Business Hours   Most **banks** are open Monday to Friday from 9am to either 1 or 3pm. Most other businesses and stores are open from Monday to Friday from 9 or 10am to either 6 or 6:30pm. Saturday hours are from 9am to 2pm. On *langer Samstag,* the first Saturday of the month, shops stay open until 4 or 6pm. Some stores observe late closing on Thursday (usually 8:30pm).

Car Rentals   See "Getting Around" in this chapter.

Climate   See "When to Go" in Chapter 2.

Currency Exchange   There is a facility for exchanging currency at the Bahnhof Zoo, open Monday to Saturday from 8am to 9pm, on Sunday from 10am to 6pm. You can also exchange money at all airports, at major department stores, at any bank, and at American Express offices (see above).

Dentists/Doctors   The Berlin Tourist Office in the Europa-Center (see above) keeps a list of English-speaking dentists and doctors in Berlin. In case of a medical emergency, dial **31-00-31** for information. For a dental emergency, call **11-41.**

Drugstores   If you need a pharmacy (*Apotheke*) at night, go to one on any corner. There you'll find a sign in the window giving the address of the nearest drugstore open at night. This is required by law. Otherwise call 11-41 in western Berlin or 160 in eastern Berlin to find out what's open. Stores calling themselves *Drogeries* are not pharmacies; they dispense sundries and cosmetics, not prescription drugs.

Embassies/Consulates   The **United States** embassy office is at Neustaedtische Kirchstrasse 4–5 (tel. 030/238-51-74). This office handles matters of state between Germany and the United States. For lost passports, visas, or other problems, go to the U.S. consulate, Clayallee 170 (tel. 030/819-74-85). Hours are Monday through Friday from 8:30 to 11:30am. The visa section is open only Monday through Friday from 8:30am to 9:30am. The **United Kingdom** embassy is at Under den Linden 32–34 (tel. 030/220-24-31). The U.K. consulate-general, charged with processing visas and passports, has been relocated to Düsseldorf at Yorkstrasse 19 (tel. 0211/9448-0). For queries about passports, call 0211/9448-236; for visas, call 0211/9448-271. The **Canadian** consulate is at Friedrichstrasse 95 (tel. 030/261-11-61), open Monday through Friday from 8:15am to 12:30pm and 1:30 to 5pm. The **Australian** consulate is in room 253 in the Berlin Hilton, Mohrenstrasse 30 (tel. 030/2382-2041), open Monday through Friday from 9am to noon and 2 to 5pm. Travelers from **New Zealand** should contact the U.K. embassy in Berlin or the New Zealand embassy at Bundeskanzlerplatz in Bonn (tel. 0228/228-07-25).

Emergencies   Call the police at **110;** dial **112** to report a fire or to summon an ambulance.

Eyeglasses   Along the Kurfürstendamm is one of the densest concentrations of optometrists in Berlin, busily crafting everything from eyeglasses to contact lenses. Two good bets would include **Apollo Optik,** Kurfürstendamm 40 (tel. 030/882-5258) and **Goldman City Optik,** Kurfürstendamm 35 (tel. 030/883-8220).

Hairdressers/Barbers   The beauty salon in the **Hotel Bristol,** Kempinski Berlin, Kurfürstendamm 27 (tel. 030/88-43-40), cuts and styles hair for both men and women and has many foreign clients. There are hundreds of other hair salons scattered throughout Berlin; worth mentioning is the **Bloch Haaratelier,** Kurfürstenstrasse 15 (tel. 030/706-4565).

Hospitals   Hotel staffs are usually familiar with the locations of the nearest hospital emergency room, and know how to reach them. If you're dialing personally, call **112** for an ambulance in western Berlin, and **115** for an ambulance in eastern Berlin. For an emergency doctor, dial **31-00-31** in any part of the city, and for the location of an all-night pharmacy, call **11-41.**

Hotlines   For rape crisis advice, contact the **Rape Crisis Center,** Stresemannstrasse 40 (tel. 030/251-28-28). For help with alcohol or alcoholic-related symptoms, contact the Berlin city office against the dangers of addiction (Landesstelle Berlin gegen Suchtgefahren), Gierkezeile 39 (tel. 030/341-85-39). For problems relating to drug use or drug addiction, call the **drug helpline** (tel. 030/24-70-33). For advice and counseling about AIDS and its consequences, contact the **AIDS helpline** (Berliner AIDS-Hilfe, e. V.), Meinekestrasse 12 (tel. 030/883-30-17). For gay bashing or for legal help, call **Schwüles Überfall** at 030/216-33-36).

Information   See "Tourist Information" earlier in this chapter.

Laundry/Dry Cleaning   Deluxe and first-class hotels, even some moderately priced hotels, offer this service, and prices tend to be expensive. A convenient launderette is at **Wasch Center,** Leibnizstrasse 72 (tel. 030/213-88-00), with hours from 6am to 10:30pm daily.

Libraries The **Amerika-Gedenkbibliothek,** Blucherplatz 1, Kreuzberg (tel. 030/6905-0), was founded in 1954 to commemorate the role of the Americans during the Berlin airlift. It's open Monday 4 to 8pm and Tuesday to Saturday from 11am to 3pm (U-Bahn: Hallesches Tor).

Lost Property The general property office is at Tempelhofer Damm 3 (tel. 030/69-91). If you lose property on the public transport system, check with the transit lost-and-found department at Potsdammerstrasse 184 (tel. 030/216-14-13).

Luggage Storage Excess luggage can be stored at the Zoologischer Garten Bahnhof, at the Hauptbahnhof, and at Tegel Airport.

Newspapers/Magazines No major English-language newspapers and magazines are published in Berlin. But copies of British newspapers and copies of the *International Herald Tribune* and *USA Today* are easily available at most newsstands, which also usually carry international editions of *Time* and *Newsweek.*

Photographic Needs Film and other photo equipment are available at **KaDeWe,** Wittenbergplatz (tel. 030/240-171).

Post Office The post office is open 24 hours a day at the Hauptbahnhof (Bahnhof Zoo). If you have mail sent there, have it marked Hauptpostlagernd, Postamt 120, Bahnhof Zoo, D-1000, Berlin 12. Telephone 030/34-09-2330 for information. You can also make long-distance telephone calls here at night.

Radio Radio programs in English can be reached by dialing the following: 87.9AM (or 94 on cable) for the American Forces Network; 90.2FM (87.6 on cable) for the BBC.

Religious Services Berlin is mostly Protestant. Two Protestant congregations that welcome newcomers are the centrally located **Marienkirche,** Kaiser Wilhelm-Strasse (tel. 030/212-44-67), a short walk from the Unter den Linden, and the **Gethsemane Church,** Gethsemanestrasse 9, in the outlying suburb of Prenzlauer Berg (tel. 030/448-42-35). Roman Catholics worship at the diocesan headquarters, **St. Hedwigs Kathedrale,** Bebelplatz (tel. 030/784-3061), off Unter den Linden. The church, whose dome is considered one of the most spectacular anywhere in the north of Germany, holds at least four masses every Sunday. Berlin contains an active Jewish community, whose members welcome visitors. For information about Jewish services, contact the **Judisches Gemeindehaus,** Fasanenstrasse 79-80 (tel. 030/884-20-30).

Restrooms Don't ask for the "bathroom" unless you want to take a bath. A restroom is called a *Toilette,* and public ones are usually labeled WC (water closet). Go into the F for *Frauen* (women) and the H for *Herren* (men). Many public facilities are found throughout Berlin and at all terminals, including the Europa-Center on Tauentzienstrasse. It's customary to tip attendants from 0.30 DM (20¢) to 0.50 DM (30¢).

Safety One unfortunate side effect of unification has been an increase in muggings, bank robberies, bias crimes, and car break-ins. Residents of Berlin have reported feeling unsafe at night, especially in the dimly lit streets of Kreuzberg. (Anyone used to the streets of Los Angeles or New York, however, should find Berlin in many cases safer than their home turf.) Stay alert and be aware of your immediate surroundings, as every city, including Berlin, has its share of criminals. Wear a money belt and don't sling your camera or purse over your shoulder, particularly at night or in crowded places. Keep your valuables in a safety deposit box at your hotel. In case of a robbery or an attack, report the problem immediately to the police. You'll need a police report for any insurance claims, and Berlin police reportedly take a dim (sometimes hostile) view of attempts to avoid including them in immediate reports of street crime.

Shoe Repair Go to the **Wertheim Department Store,** Kurfürstendamm 231 (tel. 030/88-20-610), where you will find a Mister Minit for quick and easy repairs. It is at the eastern end of the Ku'damm (U-Bahn: Kurfürstendamm).

Taxes Governmental value-added tax (VAT) is included in the price of restaurants, hotels, and material goods in Germany. There is no airport departure tax. On many objects, however, temporary visitors to Germany can obtain a refund of the VAT.

Taxis See "Getting Around" in this chapter.

Telegrams/Fax These can be sent from the post office (see "Post Office," above).

Television Many upper-bracket hotels subscribe to cable, including news broadcasts on CNN. Super Channel is a European network telecasting programs in English.

Time Berlin is 6 hours ahead of eastern standard time on the East Coast of the United States or 9 hours ahead of the West Coast. Berlin operates on what is known as Central European Time—except it lags behind 6 minutes, 22 seconds.

Tipping See "Fast Facts: Germany" in Chapter 2.

Water It is said to be safe to drink Berlin water, but locals often ask for bottled mineral water.

Weather For a report on Berlin weather, dial **1164.**

4. ACCOMMODATIONS

Berlin is the scene of frequent international trade fairs, conferences, and festivals, and during these times there are unlikely to be any vacancies in the city. Eastern Berlin has severely limited accommodations, as many of its former hotels have closed, either for massive renovation or for conversion to other purposes, such as offices. It's always wise to make reservations well in advance, especially at the deluxe and first-class hotels.

ON OR NEAR THE KURFÜRSTENDAMM

VERY EXPENSIVE

AM ZOO, Kurfürstendamm 25, D-1000 Berlin 15. Tel. 030/884-37-710. Fax 030/884-37-714. 131 rms, 5 suites. MINIBAR TV TEL **U-Bahn:** Kurfürstendamm.

$ Rates (including buffet breakfast): 170 DM–265 DM ($112.20–$174.90) single; 300 DM–370 DM ($198–$244.20) double; from 445 DM ($293.70) suite. AE, DC, MC, V. **Parking:** 15 DM ($9.90).

The Hotel am Zoo sits snugly on the main street of Berlin. Substantial and well maintained, it was built as a private home in 1900. There are three kinds of well-furnished rooms: Those facing the Ku'damm have triple-glazing on the windows but can still be noisy; rooms facing the inner courtyard are quieter yet get much less light; and those opening onto a parking area are sunny and moderately quiet but with an uninspired view. Incidentally, on his visit to Berlin in the 1930s, author Thomas Wolfe stayed here. Laundry and dry cleaning are available. The hotel also has a bar.

AROSA PARKSCHLOSS, Lietzenburgerstrasse 79–81, D-1000 Berlin 15. Tel. 030/88-00-50. Fax 030/882-45-79. 81 rms, 10 suites. A/C MINIBAR TV TEL **U-Bahn:** Uhlandstrasse.

$ Rates: 225 DM–330 DM ($148.50–$217.80) single; 345 DM–480 DM ($227.70–$316.80) double; from 480 DM ($316.80) suite. Children under 12 stay free in parents' room. Buffet breakfast 18 DM ($11.90) extra. AE, DC, MC, V. **Parking:** 15 DM ($9.90).

The deceivingly austere facade here gives no clue to the charm, style, and flair within. This hotel is strongly recommended for many reasons, especially because it opens

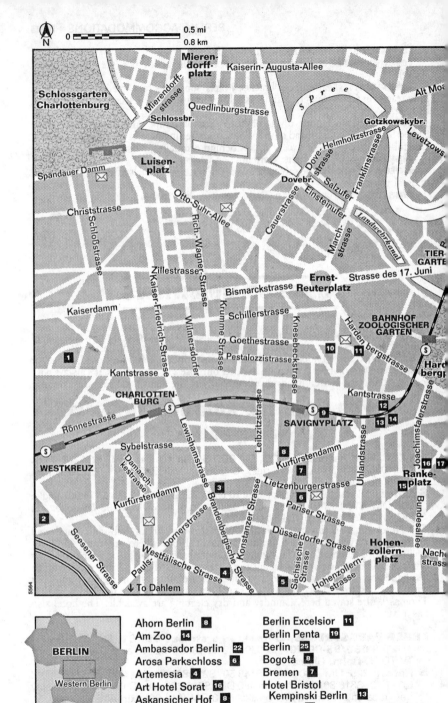

Map labels

N

0.5 mi
0.8 km

Schlossgarten Charlottenburg

Mierendorff-platz

Kaiserin-Augusta-Allee

Mierendorffstrasse

Quedlinburgstrasse

Schlossbr.

S p r e e

Alt Moa

Gotzkowskybr.

Dove-Helmholtzstrasse

strasse

Franklinstrasse

Levetzows

Luisen-platz

Spandauer Damm

Dovebr.

Salzufer

Einsteinufer

Landwehrkanal

Otto-Suhr-Allee

Christstrasse

Schloßstrasse

Zillestrasse

Kaiser-Friedrich-Strasse

Rich.-Wagner-Strasse

Wilmersdorfer

Cauerstrasse

March-strasse

TIER-GARTE

Ernst-Reuterplatz

Strasse des 17. Juni

Bismarckstrasse

Schillerstrasse

BAHNHOF ZOOLOGISCHER GARTEN

Kaiserdamm

Krumme Strasse

Goethestrasse

Knesebeckstrasse

Hardenbergstrasse

Hard berg

Pestalozzistrasse

10

11

1

Kantstrasse

CHARLOTTEN-BURG

Kantstrasse

Rönnestrasse

Lewishamstrasse

Leibnizstrasse

SAVIGNYPLATZ

9

Uhlandstrasse

12

13 **14**

WESTKREUZ

Sybelstrasse

Damaschkestrasse

Kurfürstendamm

8

7

Kurfürstendamm

Joachimstalerstrasse

16 **17**

Ranke-platz

15

Lietzenburgerstrasse

3

6

Pariser Strasse

2

bornerstrasse

Brandenburgische Strasse

Konstanzer Strasse

Düsseldorfer Strasse

Bundesallee

Seesener Strasse

Pauls-

Westfälische Strasse

4

5

Sächsische Strasse

Hohenzollern-strasse

Hohen-zollern-platz

Nache strass

↓ To Dahlem

5564

WESTERN BERLIN ACCOMMODATIONS

Crystal **9**
Domus Berlin **5**
Grand Hotel Esplanade **26**
Hecker's Hotel **10**
Hervis Hotel International **27**
Kronprinz Berlin **2**

Lenz **3**
Mondial **8**
Palace Berlin **20**
President Berlin **24**
Remter **17**
Residenz Berlin **15**

Savoy **12**
Schweizerhof **21**
Seehof Berlin **1**
Steigenberger Berlin **18**
Sylter Hof **23**

onto a rear courtyard and garden with pool and terrace for relaxation, refreshments, and good summer food. The guest rooms are simply styled and functional.

Dining/Entertainment: On the premises are two restaurants, Schneider's Fass and Schneider's Restaurant, as well as Schneider's Bar. The "Fass" has a rough wooden ceiling, heavy beams, alpine chairs, and pine tables and serves an excellent provincial cuisine.

Services: Room service, babysitting, laundry.

Facilities: Open-air pool.

BREMEN, Bleibtreustrasse 25, D-1000 Berlin 15. Tel. 030/881-40-76. Fax 030/882-46-85. 48 rms, 5 suites. MINIBAR TV TEL **Bus:** 109 from Berlin-Tegel Airport to Bahnhof Zoologischer Garten.

$ Rates (including buffet breakfast): 275 DM–320 DM ($181.50–$211.20) single; 340 DM ($224.40) double; from 420 DM ($277.20) suite. Winter discounts available. Children under 12 stay free in parents' room. AE, DC, MC, V.

This first-rate 1960s hotel garni also offers very good service and attracts a long list of habitués, some of whom might like to warble the refrain from "There's a small hotel. . . ." Completely renovated, it is now more inviting than ever. Its well-furnished rooms offer cable TVs, radios, and hairdryers, among other amenities. Some rooms are air-conditioned. You'll be in the center of the Kurfürstendamm, a location that pleases many visitors.

Dining/Entertainment: Breakfast, offered on the fifth floor, is the only meal served, but an inviting lobby bar is open 24 hours.

Services: Room service, laundry, dry cleaning, babysitting, shoeshine machine.

HOTEL BRISTOL KEMPINSKI BERLIN, Kurfürstendamm 27, D-1000 Berlin 15. Tel. 030/88-43-40, or toll free 800/426-3135 in the U.S. Fax 030/883-60-75. 315 rms, 33 suites. A/C MINIBAR TV TEL **U-Bahn:** Kurfürstendamm.

$ Rates: 460 DM–510 DM ($303.60–$336.60) single; 524 DM–664 DM ($345.80–$438.20) double; from 925 DM ($610.50) suite. AE, DC, MC, V. Buffet breakfast 32 DM ($21.10) extra. **Parking:** 22 DM ($14.50).

⭐ It's a legend in Berlin. A century ago Kempinski was the name of one of the most renowned restaurants in Germany. In 1952, it rose out of the debris of World War II to become a landmark hotel, and today it enjoys a position in Berlin similar to that of the Waldorf-Astoria in New York. The lobby sets the relaxed mood, with its fine and comfortable groupings of furniture.

The guest rooms, with their marble bathrooms, match the public rooms in taste. The accommodations are richly carpeted, the furnishings a selection of antique reproductions combined with modern.

Dining/Entertainment: A high-level cuisine is served in both the Restaurant Kempinski, which opens onto a Kurfürstendamm terrace, and the Kempinski Eck. Other discriminating diners prefer the Kempinski Grill, one of the finest in Berlin, for lunch, dinner, or late-night supper. It's open Monday to Saturday from noon to 3pm and 6pm to 2am. The Bristol Bar is low-key, with patent-leather chairs and a pianist playing soft background music.

Services: If you'd like to experience an added touch of class, try the Kempinski Luxury Limousine Service. You can use it for transportation from and to the airport, or for a sightseeing tour, and you'll be riding in an old-fashioned, chauffeur-driven Daimler limousine. Room service, laundry, and dry cleaning are also available.

Facilities: Kempinski Pool, recreation center with indoor pool, sauna, massage facilities, solarium, fitness center, pool bar.

GRAND HOTEL ESPLANADE, Lützowufer 15, D-1000 Berlin 30. Tel. 030/26-10-11. Fax 030/262-91-21. 369 rms, 33 suites. A/C MINIBAR TV TEL **U-Bahn:** Nollendorfplatz or Wittenbergplatz.

$ Rates (including buffet breakfast): 380 DM–470 DM ($250.80–$310.20) single; 450 DM–520 DM ($297–$343.20) double; from 950 DM ($627) suite. AE, DC, MC, V. **Parking:** 20 DM ($13.20).

The most dramatic and sophisticated modern hotel in Berlin is located beside a canal within a 10-minute drive of the commercial center. The disembarkation zone for cars and taxis is enclosed with a cascade of water that flows gracefully down a massive concrete screen. The public rooms incorporate many of the design concepts you'd expect in a museum of modern art, with even a hint of influence from such pop art masters as Andy Warhol. Each of the well-furnished, bright, and cheerful accommodations contains cable TV, video, and sound insulation. Thirty rooms are reserved for nonsmokers.

Dining/Entertainment: There's a beer-restaurant with a neon-encrusted Wurlitzer jukebox (the *Eck-Kneipe*) and a gourmet restaurant devoted to cuisine moderne, the Harlekin. A lavish breakfast buffet is served in the festively decorated Orangerie, and the hotel has its own restaurant ship, the *Esplanade,* with docking space in front of the hotel. See "Evening Entertainment" in Chapter 18 for Harry's New York Bar.

Services: 24-hour room service, laundry, dry cleaning, in-house doctor and nurse, massages, babysitting.

Facilities: Triangular-shaped indoor pool, whirlpool, solarium, sauna, hairdressing salon.

SAVOY, Fasanenstrasse 9–10, D-1000 Berlin 12. Tel. 030/311-03-0, or toll free 800/223-5652 in the U.S. or Canada. Fax 030/311-03-333. 128 rms, 15 suites. MINIBAR TV TEL **U-Bahn:** Kurfürstendamm.

$ Rates: 345 DM–460 DM ($227.70–$303.60) single; 460 DM–530 DM ($303.60–$349.80) double; from 650 DM ($429) suite. Breakfast 25 DM ($16.50) extra. AE, DC, MC, V.

The Savoy is one of the leading hotels of Berlin. Built in 1929, it was the first hotel in the city to have a private bath connected to each room, a revolutionary idea in its day. Over the years, it has attracted some of the most illustrious people of Berlin, as well as a long list of celebrated foreigners, often musicians and artists, including Maria Callas and Herbert von Karajan.

The Savoy has undergone a stylish rehabilitation and offers elegantly furnished rooms that can be rented as either singles or doubles. It is classified as a first-class rather than a deluxe hotel only because of its lack of a pool. The rooms are beautifully furnished in muted colors, and the suites are especially luxurious, each with a hairdryer and trouser press; some are air-conditioned.

Smoothly overseeing the operation is the hotel's outstanding director, Hans Eilers, who has employed a thoughtful, concerned staff. Bodo Wulfert, the reservations director, is a gracious hotelier of much charm. The hotel is one of the founding members of the worldwide Steigenberger Reservations System.

Dining/Entertainment: Breakfast, a copious buffet in the street-level restaurant, can be served on a sixth-floor roof terrace in warm weather. Both the Savoy's restaurant, Belle Epoque (see "Dining," below), and its Times Bar (see "Evening Entertainment" in Chapter 18) are recommended separately.

Services: Laundry, babysitting, room service.

Facilities: Sauna, solarium, fitness club.

STEIGENBERGER BERLIN, Los-Angeles-Platz 1, D-1000 Berlin 30. Tel. 030/2-10-80, or toll free 800/223-5652 in the U.S. or Canada. Fax 030/210-81-17. 397 rms, 11 suites. A/C MINIBAR TV TEL **U-Bahn:** Kurfürstendamm.

$ Rates: 295 DM–450 DM ($194.70–$297) single; 360 DM–530 DM ($237.60–$349.80) double; from 750 DM ($495) suite. Breakfast buffet 26 DM ($17.20) extra. AE, DC, MC, V. **Parking:** 18 DM ($11.90).

No expense seems to have been spared during the 1981 construction of this excellent choice among the expensive modern hostelries of Berlin. The facade boasts a double level of panoramic windows on the ground floor, overlooking the landscaped expanse of the front garden. All the newly decorated rooms have modern conveniences and are handsomely appointed in warm, subdued colors. In the bathroom two sinks and magnifying makeup mirrors are just some of the thoughtful extras. Other amenities include hairdryers, pay videos, soundproof windows, safes, and radios. The more expensive rooms are more spacious.

Dining/Entertainment: The hotel's dining room, the Park Restaurant, one of Berlin's best, offers both classical and modern cuisine. Meals range from 85 DM to 105 DM ($56.10 to $69.30). It is open Tuesday to Sunday from 6pm to midnight. Decorated in an old Berlin style, the less expensive Berliner Stube serves Prussian fare, with meals ranging from 35 DM to 60 DM ($23.10 to $39.60). Excellent pastries are served in the Vienna-styled coffeehouse, Café Charlotte. Drinks are enjoyed in the Hallencafé/Pianobar, which has a stylish art deco decor in tones of cream, rust, turquoise, and black.

Services: Babysitting, 24-hour room service, in-house doctor, laundry, dry cleaning.

Facilities: Pool, sauna, solarium.

EXPENSIVE

AHORN BERLIN, Schlüterstrasse 40, D-1000 Berlin 15. Tel. 030/881-43-44. Fax 030/881-65-00. 27 rms. MINIBAR TV TEL **U-Bahn:** Adenauerplatz.

$ **Rates:** 165 DM–175 DM ($108.90–$115.50) single; 210 DM ($138.60) double. 10 DM ($6.60) per day supplement for kitchenette. Nov–Mar, 20% discounts available. Continental breakfast 15 DM ($9.90) extra. AE, DC, MC, V. **Parking:** Free.

Conveniently located near a corner of the Kurfürstendamm, in a neighborhood liberally sprinkled with Kneipen and restaurants, this is a simple but very clean and cost-conscious hotel. Built in the 1970s, with few frills or architectural embellishments, its rooms have wall-to-wall carpeting. Some of the doubles contain kitchenettes, which are unlocked for a supplemental charge.

ASTORIA, Fasanenstrasse 2, D-1000 Berlin 12. Tel. 030/312-40-67. Fax 030/312-50-27. 33 rms. MINIBAR TV TEL **Bus:** 109 from Berlin-Tegel Airport to Bahnhof Zoologischer Garten.

$ **Rates** (including buffet breakfast): 200 DM ($132) single; 279 DM ($184.10) double. AE, DC, MC, V. **Parking:** 18 DM ($11.90).

The exterior of this rebuilt, modernized hotel, just off the Kurfürstendamm and near Bahnhof Zoo, resembles that of a town house. You can stay here for a moderate amount in a rather expensive section of Berlin. The rooms contain all the necessary comforts and are simply furnished. The miniature breakfast room is restrained with wood paneling and bright walls and chairs. The hotel also has a bar.

KRONPRINZ BERLIN, Kronprinzendamm 1, D-1000 Berlin 31. Tel. 030/89-60-30. Fax 030/89-31-215. 67 rms. MINIBAR TV TEL **U-Bahn:** Adenauerplatz.

$ **Rates** (including buffet breakfast): 185 DM–245 DM ($122.10–$161.70) single; 250 DM–295 DM ($165–$194.70) double. Children 12 and under stay free in parents' room. AE, DC, MC, V.

The facade of this place has remained virtually unchanged since it was constructed in 1894. The owners have renovated the interior into a kind of art deco severity, which doesn't detract from the comfort of the well-appointed rooms, which are each suitable for two, though they can be rented to single travelers. Each accommodation has a balcony, radio, and color TV. If you want a little extra comfort, ask for a Bel-Etage room, one of the newly added and elegantly decorated ones, each more spacious than the others, with larger bathrooms, two private phones, and a private safe. Double-glazed windows cut down on the traffic noise. Many guests congregate in the cozy in-house bar, or in summer they gather with Berliners in the garden under the chestnut trees for draft beer and wine.

RESIDENZ BERLIN, Meinekestrasse 9, D-1000 Berlin 15. Tel. 030/88-

44-30. Fax 030/882-47-26. 80 rms, 4 apartments, 9 suites. MINIBAR TV TEL
U-Bahn: Kurfürstendamm.
$ Rates: 198 DM ($130.70) single with buffet breakfast; 266 DM ($175.60) double
with buffet breakfast; from 310 DM ($204.60) apartment; from 595 DM ($392.70)
suite. Breakfast 20 DM ($13.20) extra for apartment and suite occupants. AE, DC,
MC, V. **Parking:** 12 DM ($7.90).

The neobaroque facade and ornate balconies of the Residenz Berlin were built in
1910 as part of a large and impressive private house. Tastefully upgraded and
completely renovated, it was transformed into a hotel in 1980. There are a
comfortably informal pub-style bar and a well-respected restaurant, Grand-Cru,
whose frescoed ceiling and art nouveau setting contribute to elegant meals. The hotel
lies on one of the residential streets radiating off from the heavily congested inner-city
core that includes the Kaiser Wilhelm Memorial Church and the Europa-Center.

MODERATE

**ARTEMESIA, Brandenburgischestrasse 18, D-1000 Berlin 31. Tel. 030/
87-89-05.** Fax 030/861-86-53. 8 rms (6 with bath or shower). 1 suite. TV TEL
U-Bahn: Konstanzerstrasse.
$ Rates (including continental breakfast): 99 DM ($65.30) single without bath or
shower, 149 DM ($98.30) single with bath or shower; 160 DM ($105.60) double
without bath or shower, 200 DM ($132) double with bath or shower; 220 DM–250
DM ($145.20–$165) suite. Children under 8 stay free in mother's room. Children
6–12 receive 50% discount. AE, MC, V.

Conceived and designed as a hotel for women only, this establishment occupies
the fourth and fifth floors of a residential building near the Kurfürstendamm.
You'll take an elevator from the building's lobby to the hotel, whose interior has
been modernized and set with recessed lighting. In cold weather, a fire sometimes
burns in one of the sitting rooms. You'll usually find a temporary exhibition of art
within the public rooms, which are occasionally rented for women's conferences and
consciousness-raising sessions. On the premises is a rooftop terrace where breakfast is
served on summer mornings, plus a bar.

Each guest room is named after (and dedicated to) the memory of a woman who
influenced the quality of life in Europe, in either science or art. They are outfitted in
shades of white, pink, and turquoise; the suite offers a TV. Children, including boys
up to age 12, can stay here with their mothers.

BOGOTÁ, Schlüterstrasse 45, D-1000 Berlin 15. Tel. 030/881-50-01.
Fax 030/88-35-88. 130 rms (65 with bath; 12 with shower, no toilet). TEL **U-Bahn:**
Adenauerplatz.
$ Rates (including continental breakfast): 70 DM ($46.20) single without bath, 110
DM ($72.60) single with shower (no toilet), 130 DM ($85.80) single with bath; 115
DM ($75.90) double without bath, 165 DM ($108.90) double with shower (no
toilet), 195 DM ($128.70) double with bath. AE, DC, MC, V. **Parking:** 12 DM
($7.90) nearby.

Although you're just off the Kurfürstendamm, when you walk into the Bogotá
you'll think you're in a small town on the northern coast of Spain. When you
hear Spanish spoken, your impression will be confirmed. The lobby is Iberian in
character, with a high-beamed ceiling, an open wooden staircase leading through an
arch to the rooms, a wooden balcony, and a heavy bronze chandelier.

CRYSTAL, Kantstrasse 144, D-1000 Berlin 12. Tel. 030/312-90-47. Fax
030/312-64-65. 33 rms (28 with bath or shower). TEL **S-Bahn:** Savignyplatz.
$ Rates (including continental breakfast): 70 DM–80 DM ($46.20–$52.80) single
without bath or shower, 110 DM–130 DM ($72.60–$85.80) single with bath or
shower; 100 DM ($66) double without bath or shower, 130 DM–150 DM
($85.80–$99) double with bath or shower. AE, MC, V. **Parking:** Free.

Ⓢ A few paces from the manicured garden of the well-located Savignyplatz, a short walk from the Kurfürstendamm, this well-scrubbed, respectable hotel offers cost-conscious accommodation in uncluttered rooms. In contrast to the building's angular modern facade, a traditionally decorated Teutonic Stube, open only to residents, serves an occasional drink but no food; breakfast is the only meal offered here. However, at the doorstep are numerous moderately priced cafés and restaurants.

DOMUS BERLIN, Uhlandstrasse 49, D-1000 Berlin 15. Tel. 030/88-20-41. Fax 030/88-20-410. 73 rms, 3 suites. MINIBAR TEL **Bus:** 249. **U-Bahn:** Spichernstrasse or Hohenzollerndamm.

$ Rates (including buffet breakfast): 145 DM ($95.70) single; 190 DM–215 DM ($125.40–$141.90) double; from 250 DM ($165) suite. AE, DC, MC, V. **Parking:** 8 DM ($5.30). **Closed:** Dec 24–Jan 1.

On a relatively quiet side street off the central Kurfürstendamm, the Domus has generally improved in recent years. It offers rooms that are adequate in size and fairly comfortable. Half of the rooms contain TVs. The hotel is run with notable concern for personalized service. There is a bustling little brasserie-restaurant, where the action overflows onto a sidewalk café.

LENZ, Xantenerstrasse 8, D-1000 Berlin 15. Tel. 030/881-51-58. Fax 030/881-55-17. 29 rms. TV TEL **U-Bahn:** Adenauerplatz.

$ Rates (including continental breakfast): 170 DM ($112.20) single; 180 DM–255 DM ($118.80–$168.30) double. AE, DC, MC, V.

Ⓢ Constructed as a private house just before World War I, the Lenz lies on a residential street a few blocks from the Kurfürstendamm, a short distance from the stopping point for the express bus from Berlin-Tegel Airport. It contains a small but convivial pub-style bar where cold snacks are served, as well as a separate breakfast room. The high-ceilinged rooms have sofas; some also open onto balconies.

INEXPENSIVE

CORTINA, Kantstrasse 140, D-1000 Berlin 12. Tel. 030/313-90-59. 20 rms (6 with bath or shower). TEL **Bus:** 149. **S-Bahn:** Savignyplatz.

$ Rates (including continental breakfast): 60 DM ($39.60) single without bath or shower; 95 DM ($62.70) double without bath or shower, 120 DM ($79.20) double with bath or shower. No credit cards.

The prices at this well-maintained 100-year-old pension just off the Kurfürstendamm won't break the bank. Rates include use of the corridor bath; every room has hot and cold running water. Many doubles have little sitting areas where you can take your morning meal. Two units also contain TVs. It's not a fancy place, yet there's a pleasant feeling of roominess and cleanliness. An English-speaking management helps out too.

NEAR THE MEMORIAL CHURCH & ZOO
VERY EXPENSIVE

AMBASSADOR BERLIN, Bayreutherstrasse 42–43, D-1000 Berlin 30. Tel. 030/21-90-20. Fax 030/219-02-380. 200 rms. MINIBAR TV TEL **U-Bahn:** Wittenbergplatz.

$ Rates (including buffet breakfast): 250 DM–290 DM ($165–$191.40) single; 310 DM–350 DM ($204.60–$231) double. AE, DC, MC, V. **Parking:** 15 DM ($9.90).

The dining rooms and lounges in this upper-class hotel are among the best designed of any Berlin hotel facilities in this price range. The guest rooms, each with soundproof windows, are excellent and well planned. One floor is reserved for nonsmokers.

Dining/Entertainment: The restaurant Schöneberger Krug is comfortable and cozy, serving tasty dishes from both a regional and an international repertoire. The hotel's bar is another attractive rendezvous.

Services: Laundry, valet, babysitting, massage.

Facilities: Heated tropical pool, sun lounge, Finnish sauna, solarium, pool bar.

BERLIN, Lützowplatz 17, D-1000 Berlin 30. Tel. 030/2-60-50, or toll free

800/237-54-69 in the U.S. Fax 030/2605-2715. 490 rms, 6 suites. TV TEL **U-Bahn:** Nollendorfplatz.

$ **Rates:** 330 DM–390 DM ($217.80–$257.40) single; 320 DM–500 DM ($211.20–$330) double; from 725 DM ($478.50) suite. Buffet breakfast 26 DM ($17.20) extra. AE, DC, MC, V. **Parking:** 15 DM ($9.90).

A true international hotel, the Berlin is built in angular modern style, with its own grounds and gardens next to the Tiergarten. Each room is well furnished and rather cozy; many units also have minibars. The best and most expensive rooms are in an air-conditioned modern wing constructed in 1987.

Dining/Entertainment: In addition to its main restaurant, The Grill, the hotel offers Berlin Eck, a typical pub with a local atmosphere serving locally brewed beer and hearty Berliner specialties.

Services: Laundry and dry cleaning, babysitting arranged, room service.

Facilities: In Kurfürstenflügel annex, a beauty shop, fitness room, steam bath, sauna, solarium, souvenir shop, library.

BERLIN EXCELSIOR, Hardenbergstrasse 14, D-1000 Berlin 12. Tel. 030/3199-1. Fax 030/319-92-849. 315 rms, 3 suites. MINIBAR TV TEL **Bus:** 109 from Berlin-Tegel Airport to Bahnhof Zoologischer Garten.

$ **Rates** (including buffet breakfast): 325 DM ($214.50) single; 328 DM–525 DM ($216.50–$346.50) double; from 698 DM ($460.70) suite. Children 2 and under stay free in parents' room. AE, DC, MC, V. **Parking:** 18 DM ($11.90).

The name of the hotel is elaborately set into gray tiles near the entrance of this modern establishment, a few blocks from the Hauptbahnhof. The reception area and the high-ceilinged bar give the feeling of almost unlimited space, with partitions crafted of hardwoods and patterned carpeting muffling the footsteps of the many international guests who stay here every year. Your sleep will be aided by the soundproof windows in the well-furnished and attractively styled rooms. All units have baths tiled in dark colors, plus a collection of electronic devices, including hairdryers, safes, and radios. Some rooms are air-conditioned.

Dining/Entertainment: The Peacock Restaurant serves world-class meals in an aura of intimate simplicity. A second restaurant, the Store House Grill, offers meals from its lava-stone grill and a superb choice of fresh salad in a Mississippi-style atmosphere. Drinks are served at the lobby-level Rum Corner.

Services: Babysitting, room service, in-house physician.

BERLIN PENTA, Nürnbergerstrasse 65, D-1000 Berlin 30. Tel. 030/ 210-07-0, or toll free 800/225-3456 in the U.S. Fax 030/213-20-09. 415 rms, 10 suites. A/C MINIBAR TV TEL **U-Bahn:** Wittenbergplatz or Kurfürstendamm.

$ **Rates:** 318 DM–365 DM ($209.90–$240.90) single; 330 DM–436 DM ($217.80–$287.80) double; from 650 DM ($429) suite. Buffet breakfast 26 DM ($17.20) extra. AE, DC, MC, V. **Parking:** 20 DM ($13.20).

Across from the Europa-Center is this excellent chain-run hotel with soundproofed rooms, each with radio, color TV, and in-house movies. The buffet breakfast is opulent. Special rooms are provided for nonsmokers and the disabled.

Dining/Entertainment: The Globetrotter Restaurant offers elegant dining; the Senator Bistro Bar and the cozy Pinte Bierstube are relaxing places for a drink.

Services: Babysitting, room service, massage.

Facilities: Indoor pool, sauna, solarium, boutique.

PALACE BERLIN, Im Europa-Center, Budapesterstrasse 42, D-1000 Berlin 30. Tel. 030/2502-0, or toll free 800/528-1234 in the U.S. Fax 030/262-65-77. 320 rms, 16 suites. A/C MINIBAR TV TEL **U-Bahn:** Wittenbergplatz.

$ **Rates:** 290 DM–450 DM ($191.40–$297) single; 365 DM–500 DM ($240.90–$330) double; from 650 DM ($429) suite. Children under 12 stay free in parent's room. Buffet breakfast 26 DM ($17.20) extra. AE, DC, MC, V.

In the heart of downtown Berlin next to the Memorial Church, between the Kurfürstendamm and Tauentzienstrasse shopping district, this hotel offers well-furnished rooms, each soundproofed, with hairdryer, trouser press, and radio. In 1989 the Palace added its Casino Wing, and in 1992 it received a massive overhaul. Each unit in the new wing has about 376 square feet and is beautifully appointed. The marble bathrooms offer such amenities as separate bathtubs and showers, cosmetic mirrors, even direct-dial phones and radios.

Dining/Entertainment: Restaurants on the premises offer international, German, and typical Berliner dishes. A buffet breakfast and lunch are served on the second floor with its view of Elephant Gate, entrance to the zoological garden. A small restaurant, First Floor, is the hotel's gourmet dining room, and in the adjacent Europa-Center, you can dine inexpensively at Alt-Nürnberg (see "Dining," below). At the café-restaurant, Tiffany's, you can enjoy homemade pastries, along with various ice creams.

Services: Laundry, room service, babysitting.

Facilities: Next to the Palace is the Thermen am Europa-Center, a large health club with several facilities, including indoor and outdoor pools and sauna. Admission is free to hotel guests.

PRESIDENT BERLIN, An der Urania 16–18, D-1000 Berlin 30. Tel. 030/21-90-30, or toll free 800/528-1234 in the U.S. Fax 030/214-12-00. 186 rms, 7 suites. MINIBAR TV TEL **U-Bahn:** Wittenbergplatz.

$ Rates (including continental breakfast): 255 DM–295 DM ($168.30–$194.70) single; 295 DM–355 DM ($168.30–$234.30) double; from 475 DM ($313.50) suite. Park Consul Club: 295 DM–325 DM ($194.70–$214.50) single; 355 DM–375 DM ($234.30–$247.50) double; 580 DM ($382.80) suite. Children under 14 stay free in parents' room. AE, DC, MC, V. **Parking:** 12 DM ($7.90).

A Best Western hotel, the President Berlin offers four-star comfort at a prestigious central address. Most of the major sights of Berlin are within easy access, and the main shopping centers, the Kurfürstendamm, the Europa-Center, and KaDeWe (the leading department store), are only a few minutes' walk away. Together with its unique atmosphere, this favorite choice offers all the facilities you'd expect of a modern first-class hotel. It rents well-furnished rooms, most of which have air conditioning and are equipped with electronic security locks and hairdryers. In 1993, the hotel added 54 Park Consul Club rooms and a suite in an elegant new section that has its own private lounge.

Dining/Entertainment: Its restaurant, Die Saison, lives up to its name by offering a menu of seasonal specialties, and there is also a hotel bar, the President.

Services: Room service, laundry, babysitting arranged.

Facilities: Fitness center with sauna and steam bath.

SCHWEIZERHOF, Budapesterstrasse 21–31, D-1000 Berlin 30. Tel. 030/2-69-60, or toll free 800/237-5469 in the U.S. Fax 030/269-69-00. 430 rms, 26 suites (all with bath or shower). A/C MINIBAR TV TEL **Bus:** 109 from Tegel Airport to Budapesterstrasse. **U-Bahn:** Bahnhof Zoologischer Garten.

$ Rates: 410 DM–500 DM ($270.60–$330) single; 480 DM–580 DM ($316.80–$382.80) double; from 750 DM ($495) suite. Children under 12 stay free in parents' room. Breakfast 28 DM ($18.50) extra. AE, DC, MC, V. **Parking:** 20 DM ($13.20).

Near the Memorial Church and opposite the zoo, the Schweizerhof offers first-class service, amenities, and comfort with an overall effect of dignified restraint. Increased patronage has led to a new wing of streamlined and substantial rooms. The hotel is one of the largest in Berlin. Rooms are attractively furnished with a number of extras, such as radios, and the fifth floor is exclusively for nonsmokers.

Dining/Entertainment: The Schweizerhof Grill, offering a Helvetian and international cuisine, backed by Swiss wine, is recommendable. You can also dine in the Zunft-Stube and the Schützenstubli, after having a before-dinner drink in the Lobby Bar. For snacks in a cozy atmosphere, there's the Fassbier-Stubli, where good draft beer is served.

Services: Massages, laundry, dry cleaning, room service, nurse on call.

Facilities: Large pool, solarium, sauna, fitness center.

SYLTER HOF, Kurfürstenstrasse 116, D-1000 Berlin 30. Tel. 030/2-12-00. Fax 030/214-28-28. 154 rms, 16 suites. MINIBAR TV TEL **U-Bahn:** Wittenbergplatz.

$ Rates: 250 DM–265 DM ($165–$174.90) single; 360 DM–416 DM ($237.60–$274.60) double; from 560 DM ($369.60) suite. Buffet breakfast 26 DM ($17.20) extra. AE, DC, MC, V. **Parking:** 10 DM ($6.60).

The Sylter Hof, built in 1966, offers rich trappings at good prices. The main lounges are warmly decorated in an old-world style, with chandeliers, Louis XV–style and provincial chairs, and such antiques as an armoire and a grandfather clock. Although small, the guest rooms are warmly appointed, with compact, traditional furnishings. Most of them are singles.

Dining/Entertainment: The bar-lounge serves drinks to guests seated in velvet armchairs nestling on Persian rugs. The dining room is more conservative. Called the Friesenstube, it serves Prussian and continental cuisine.

Services: Shoeshine machines, room service.

Facilities: Beauty salon.

EXPENSIVE

ART HOTEL SORAT, Joachimstalerstrasse 28–29, D-1000 Berlin 15. Tel. 030/88-44-77-55. Fax 030/88-44-77-00. 75 rms. A/C MINIBAR TV TEL **U-Bahn:** Zoologischer Garten.

$ Rates: 225 DM ($148.50) single; 265 DM ($174.90) double. Buffet breakfast 23 DM ($15.20) extra. AE, DC, MC, V.

Built in 1991 on the site of a run-down department store, this is one of the newest and most dramatically minimalist hotels in Berlin. It's been called Berlin's "first boutique hotel." With a decor devoted to high-tech design, bold primary colors, and abundant placements of modern art, it offers cost-conscious lodging to an avant-garde and often youthful clientele. The guest rooms contain white walls and accessories painted in strong tones of blue, yellow, and red. Breakfast is the only meal served, and the hotel contains few facilities. Next door is a chic restaurant/café, the Anteo, serving lunch and dinner.

HECKER'S HOTEL, Grolmanstrasse 35, D-1000 Berlin 12. Tel. 030/88-900. Fax 030/889-0260. 42 rms, 10 suites. MINIBAR TV TEL. **Bus:** 109 from Berlin-Tegel airport to Uhlandstrasse. **U-Bahn:** Uhlandstrasse.

$ Rates: 240 DM–280 DM ($158.40–$184.80) single; 290 DM–330 DM

 FROMMER'S SMART TRAVELER: HOTELS

1. In inexpensive or moderately priced hotels, a room with a shower is cheaper than a room with a private bath. Even cheaper is a room with hot-and-cold running water and a corridor bathroom.
2. Consider a package tour (or book land arrangements with your air ticket). You'll often pay 30% or more less than individual "rack" rates (off-the-street, independent bookings).
3. If Berlin hotels are not full, a little bargaining can bring down the cost of a hotel room. Be polite: Ask if there's a "businessperson's rate," or if schoolteachers get a discount.
4. At less expensive hotels that take credit cards, ask if payment by cash will get you a reduction.
5. If you're going to spend at least a week in Berlin, ask about long-term discounts. Inquire about weekend discounts, which can add up to 50% at hotels patronized by businesspeople.

($191.40–$217.80) double; from 310 DM–350 DM ($204.60–$231) suite. Breakfast buffet 15 DM ($9.90) extra. AE, DC, MC, V. **Parking:** 10 DM ($6.60). Modest but well managed, this pleasant hotel was built in the late 1960s and underwent a substantial renovation in 1990. Known as a "small, private hotel," it enjoys a convenient location near the Ku'damm and the many bars and restaurants around the Savignyplatz. The guest rooms are decorated in tones of rose pink or grayish blue and contain large closets, double-insulated doors, king-size beds, and radios. Six suites contain kitchenettes.

Dining/Entertainment: The hotel's restaurant, Hecker's Deele, is recommended under "Where to Dine." There's also a cozy bar with a rustic Germanic decor.

Services: Room service, laundry.

GREATER CHARLOTTENBURG

This is an area combining private residences, apartment houses, and hotels, about a 5- to 10-minute taxi drive from the Memorial Church and the Kurfürstendamm. On its main artery, Bismarckstrasse, stand the Deutsche Oper and the Schiller-Theater. Actually, Charlottenburg embraces all the hotels we've considered so far. But because the entire district is so large (12 square miles), we've broken it up into the most central accommodations (see above) and those farther afield (see below). It's an area with many sightseeing attractions, including the Funkturm (the radio tower) and Olympic Park.

VERY EXPENSIVE

SEEHOF BERLIN, Lietzensee Ufer 11, D-1000 Berlin 19. Tel. 030/32-00-20. Fax 030/32-002-251. 78 rms, 1 suite. MINIBAR TV TEL **Bus:** 109 from Berlin-Tegel Airport to Bahnhof Zoologischer Garten. **U-Bahn:** Sophie-Charlotteplatz.

$ **Rates:** 195 DM–345 DM ($128.70–$227.70) single; 320 DM–420 DM ($211.20–$277.20) double; 550 DM ($363) suite. Breakfast buffet 24 DM ($15.80) extra. AE, DC, MC, V. **Parking:** 14 DM ($9.20).

An enjoyable but comparatively unknown hotel, in the residential section of Charlottenburg, the Seehof is only 5 minutes from the center by taxi and within walking distance of the Funkturm and surrounding fairgrounds. The hotel borders the lake, Lietzensee, and its beautiful park. The Seehof's blue-and-white checkerboard facade opens onto a tree-shaded street. On the waterside stone terrace in the rear, you can have refreshments, sunbathe, or take your lunch and dinner. You start your day here with a swim in the glassed-in pool, then order breakfast at one of the garden tables. The rooms, most of which overlook the lake and park, have armchairs and cocktail tables for relaxation, plus a desk if you need to do a little work.

Dining/Entertainment: There are two tastefully designed public rooms overlooking the lake, one with its 200-year-old Gobelin, the other with its natural stone wall, planter, and window wall. The main dining room, Restaurant "au Lac," is well designed, and a pianist plays background music. Drinks are available in the rustic tavern bar.

Services: Babysitting, room service, laundry.
Facilities: Sauna, solarium, indoor pool.

EXPENSIVE

AM STUDIO, Kaiserdamm 80-81, D-1000 Berlin 19. Tel. 030/30-20-81. Fax 030/301-95-78. 77 rms. MINIBAR TV TEL **U-Bahn:** Kaiserdamm or Theodor-Heuss-Platz.

$ **Rates** (including continental breakfast): 155 DM–178 DM ($102.30–$117.50) single; 195 DM–255 DM ($128.70–$168.30) double. AE, DC, MC, V. **Parking:** 9 DM ($5.90).

I recommend this hotel, which was built in the 1960s, to those seeking a bright and cheery accommodation. This marble-and-glass structure is near the Olympic Stadium and next to the radio and television center. The guest rooms are pleasantly decorated.

KREUZBERG

EXPENSIVE

HERVIS HOTEL INTERNATIONAL, Stresemannstrasse 97, D-1000 Berlin 61. Tel. 030/261-14-44. Fax 030/261-50-27. 73 rms. MINIBAR TV TEL **U-Bahn:** Möckern Brücke. **S-Bahn:** Anhalter Bahnhof.

$ Rates (including buffet breakfast): 120 DM–220 DM ($79.20–$145.20) single; 205 DM–270 DM ($135.30–$178.20) double. AE, DC, MC, V. **Parking:** Free.

Near the Tiergarten stands a modern hotel just 5 minutes by taxi, or 15 minutes by bus, from the heart of Berlin. The Hervis made its debut in 1968. The rear of this hotel, which overlooks a lawn, looks somewhat like a U-shaped condo in Florida. You'll be able to see the Brandenburg Gate from many of the private rooms. The hotel is within walking distance of the Nationalgalerie and the Philharmonie and stands across the street from the Martin Gropius building (the former arts-and-crafts museum). All rooms are sunny and spacious, decorated with steel-and-wood contemporary furnishings along with patterned wall-to-wall carpeting.

EASTERN BERLIN

VERY EXPENSIVE

BERLIN HILTON, Mohrenstrasse 30, D-1080 Berlin. Tel. 030/23-820, **or** toll-free 800/445-8667 in the U.S. or Canada. Fax 030/2382-4269. 480 rms, 25 suites. A/C MINIBAR TV TEL **U-Bahn:** Friedrichstrasse.

$ Rates: Berlin Hilton: 295 DM–475 DM ($194.70–$313.50) single; 345 DM–525 DM ($227.70–$346.50) double; from 675 DM ($445.50) suite. Buffet breakfast 29 DM ($19.10) extra. Krone Wing: 198 DM–340 DM ($130.70–$224.40) single; 240 DM–370 DM ($158.40–$244.20) double. Special weekend packages available. Buffet breakfast 24 DM ($15.80) extra. AE, DC, MC, V. **Parking:** 25 DM ($16.50).

Originally conceived by the East German government as one of the largest and stylishly modern hotels in eastern Berlin, it celebrated its official opening in 1991, the first hotel to open in either half of the city after the end of the Berlin Wall. Early in 1992, its management was taken over by Hilton International. Today it's the third-largest hotel in Berlin, one of the best located and one of the most popular.

Ⓕ FROMMER'S COOL FOR KIDS: HOTELS

Am Zoo   (see page 509) Families are welcomed in this old-fashioned hotel, where an extra bed for a child can be placed in the parents' room.

Arosa Parkschloss   (see page 509) Ideal for families with small children, this family-operated hotel features everything from infant bathtubs to nursing tables.

Ahorn Berlin   (see page 514) Families like the large rooms that contain small kitchenettes where snacks and light meals can be prepared.

Rising seven floors above a central courtyard, it contains enough accessories, bars, and facilities to keep you fully occupied for at least a week. Visitors register in a two-story lobby where a winter garden blooms prolifically throughout the year on either side of a meandering stream and splashing waterfall.

Set in the most prominent and desirable section of eastern Berlin, the hotel offers comfortably monochromatic rooms, each with a private safe, radio, hairdryer, and video movies; at least half of them overlook the twin churches of one of the city's most dramatic squares, the Gendarmenmarkt.

Located in the same complex as the Berlin Hilton is a less lavish three-star hotel garni (breakfast only), the **Berlin Hilton Krone Wing.** Rooms here are less well accessorized than in its parent hotel, but they are comfortable and less expensive. Krone Wing guests are entitled to use all facilities of the Berlin Hilton.

Dining/Entertainment: The hotel contains eight bars and restaurants, two of which are reviewed in "Where to Dine," below.

Services: 24-hour room service, babysitting, concierge, massage.

Facilities: Health club, saunas, pool with Jacuzzi, rooftop squash court, bowling alleys.

MARITIM GRAND HOTEL, Friedrichstrasse 158–164, D-1080 Berlin. Tel. 030/23-270, or toll free 800/843-3311 in the U.S. Fax 030/23-27-33-62. 327 rms, 22 suites. A/C MINIBAR TV TEL **S-Bahn:** Friedrichstrasse.

$ Rates: 395 DM–515 DM ($260.70–$339.90) single; 480 DM–580 DM ($316.80–$382.80) double; 700 DM–750 DM ($462–$495) junior suite; 800 DM–1,100 DM ($528–$726) senior suite. Buffet breakfast 28 DM ($18.50) extra. AE, DC, MC, V. **Parking:** 25 DM ($16.50).

If the 1930s movie *Grand Hotel,* starring Greta Garbo, were made today, it would have to be set here. Many hotels call themselves grand—this one truly is. The finishing touches were applied in 1987, just in time for the city's 750th anniversary. Of course, following unification, ownership shifted from the East German government to Maritim, a prominent German hotel chain.

Replacing an old and famous landmark, which ended as war rubble, the Grand was constructed by a Japanese company at the reported cost of $120 million. The hotel blends belle époque features with contemporary styling. Its rooms rise, atrium style, above an octagonal lobby whose setting is capped with a lavender-and-pink skylight of intricate stained glass.

The hotel promises "VIP treatment for everyone"—and means it. Rooms come in a wide range of styles, from beautifully appointed standard singles and doubles all the way up to the Schinkel Suite, named to honor the famed early 19th-century architect. Even the bed linens are soft, with down pillows and comforters. Other amenities include chrome fixtures, terry-cloth robes, and fresh flowers.

Dining/Entertainment: No one should visit without exploring the public rooms at the top of a monumental staircase one flight above lobby level. There's the convivial Peacock Bar, whose backdrop is an oversize, oval-shaped window in the form of a peacock. Even more impressive is Club Diana, a faithful copy of the great room of a Teutonic hunting lodge, with dozens of trophies, a blazing fireplace, Oriental carpets, a coffered and paneled ceiling, and an ornate organ for daily concerts in the afternoon. Three of the hotel's four restaurants are so exceptional that they'll be reviewed separately (see "Dining," below).

Services: 24-hour room service, deluxe hairdressing salon.

Facilities: Fitness club, marble pool, saunas, solarium.

METROPOL, Friedrichstrasse 150–153, D-1080 Berlin. Tel. 030/23-875. Fax 030/238-74-209. 341 rms, 40 suites. A/C MINIBAR TV TEL **S-Bahn:** Friedrichstrasse.

$ Rates: 260 DM–385 DM ($171.60–$254.10) single; 310 DM–440 DM ($204.60–$290.40) double; from 550 DM ($363) suite. Buffet breakfast 25 DM ($16.50) extra. AE, DC, MC, V. **Parking:** 10 DM ($6.60).

The Metropol, built in 1977, lies only a short walk from the Friedrichstrasse station, the Brandenburg Gate, and the Reichstag building; it's close to Unter den Linden.

Many businesspeople stay here because of its location opposite the International Trade Center in Friedrichstrasse. All guest rooms are the same size and are furnished with modern wood pieces.

Dining/Entertainment: The hotel has good food in its specialty and grill restaurants, which include Hotelrestaurant Friedrichstadt and the Grillrestaurant (see "Dining," below). Drinks and snacks are served at La Habana.

Services: Hairdresser, in-house physician, limousine service, room service, laundry, dry cleaning.

Facilities: Fitness center with pool, saunas, solarium, massage service, bar.

5. DINING

If it's true that optimism and appetite go hand in hand, Berliners must be among the most optimistic people in Europe. In breads alone, the visitor is likely to be tempted by a dozen varieties. Examples of typical dishes are the Berliner Schlachtplatte (cold plate), pigs' trotters cooked with Sauerkraut and pea purée, or Eisbein (pickled knuckle of pork with Sauerkraut). Venison, wildfowl, and wild boar appear, as do carp and trout, along with an infinite variety of sausages and deli-type cold cuts.

But Berlin does not limit itself to German cuisine—the cuisine of nearly every major nation on the globe is represented here. And don't think that an excellent dinner in Berlin has to be expensive. On the contrary, you can have a memorable dinner in an unheralded wine restaurant or sidewalk café.

ON OR NEAR THE KURFÜRSTENDAMM
VERY EXPENSIVE

BAMBERGER REITER, Regensburgerstrasse 7. Tel. 030/218-42-82.
   Cuisine: CONTINENTAL. **Reservations:** Required. **U-Bahn:** Spichernstrasse.
$ **Prices:** Appetizers 18 DM–60 DM ($11.90–$39.60); main courses 49 DM–56 DM ($32.30–$37); fixed-price lunch 78 DM ($51.50) and 125 DM ($82.50); fixed-price dinner 135 DM ($89.10) and 175 DM ($115.50). AE, DC, V.
   Open: Dinner only, daily 7–10pm. **Closed:** Aug 1–18; Jan 1–15.

Bamberger Reiter is acknowledged by some critics as the city's best restaurant, serving French, German, and Austrian dishes. Don't judge it by its location in an undistinguished 19th-century apartment house. Excellent in its forthright approach to fresh ingredients and meticulous in its preparation and service, the restaurant enjoys a loyal following among Berlin's business elite. The decor evokes old Germany, with lots of exposed wood, mirrors, and fresh flowers. The Raneburger family, Doris and Franz, are your unpretentious hosts.

Don't even attempt to guess what's on the menu the night of your arrival. It might be strips of sautéed pigeon breast with fresh melon, mousse of calves' sweetbreads, or ragoût of shellfish with baby vegetables. The wine list, supervised by Doris herself, is enormous, containing around 20 varieties of champagne alone.

EXPENSIVE

ALT-BERLINER SCHNECKENHAUS, Viktoria-Luise-Platz 12A. Tel. 030/211-20-60.
   Cuisine: CONTINENTAL. **Reservations:** Recommended. **U-Bahn:** Viktoria-Luise-Platz.
$ **Prices:** Appetizers 15 DM–35 DM ($9.90–$23.10); main courses 30 DM–42 DM ($19.80–$27.70). AE.
   Open: Daily 6pm–12:30am (hot food served only until 11:30pm).
This place is recommended for old Prussian-style dining. The interior reveals a high-ceilinged Wilhelmian delight, with German Victorian wooden furniture in all its well-polished splendor. The menu is nostalgic. Snails are a specialty; try, especially,

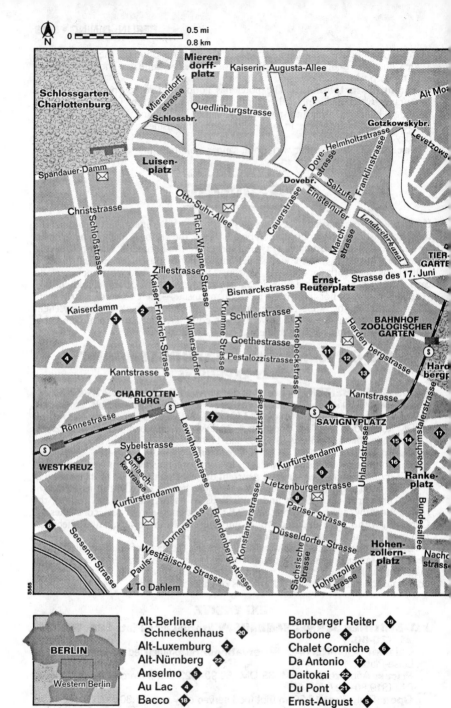

0.5 mi
0
0.8 km
N

Schlossgarten
Charlottenburg

Mierendorff-
platz

Kaiserin- Augusta-Allee

Mierendorffstrasse

Schlossbr.

Quedlinburgstrasse

Spree

Alt Mo

Gotzkowskybr.

Levetzows

Dove- Helmholtzstrasse
strasse

Franklinstrasse

Spandauer-Damm

Luisen-
platz

Dovebr.

Salzufer

Cauerstrasse

Einsteinufer

Christstrasse

Otto-Suhr-Allee

March-
strasse

Landwehrkanal

TIER-
GARTE

Schloßstrasse

Zillestrasse

Rich.-Wagner-Strasse

❶

Strasse des 17. Juni

Ernst-
Reuterplatz

Kaiser-Friedrich-Strasse

Bismarckstrasse

Kaiserdamm

❷

Krumme Strasse

Schillerstrasse

BAHNHOF
ZOOLOGISCHER
GARTEN

❸

Wilmersdorfer

Goethestrasse

Knesebeckstrasse

Harden bergstrasse

S

Haro
bergp

❹

Pestalozzistrasse

❶❶

❶❷

Kantstrasse

❶❸

CHARLOTTEN-
BURG Ⓢ

Rönnestrasse

Leibnizstrasse

Kantstrasse

Ⓢ ❶⓪
SAVIGNYPLATZ

Ⓢ

Lewishamstrasse

❼

Sybelstrasse

❺

Joachimstalerstrasse

WESTKREUZ

Damaschkestrasse

Kurfürstendamm

❶❺ ❶❹

❶❼

Uhlandstrasse

Kurfürstendamm

❾

❶❻

Rankeplatz

Lietzenburgerstrasse

❽

Konstanzerstrasse

Brandenburgstrasse

Pariser Strasse

Bundesallee

❻

bornerstrasse

Düsseldorfer Strasse

Seesener Strasse

Pauls-

Westfälische Strasse

Sächsische Strasse

Hohenzollern-
strasse

Hohen-
zollern-
platz

Nacho
strasse

↓ To Dahlem

5565

BERLIN

Western Berlin

Alt-Berliner
  Schneckenhaus   ⓴
Alt-Luxemburg   ❷
Alt-Nürnberg   ㉒
Anselmo   ❺
Au Lac   ❹
Bacco   ⓲

Bamberger Reiter   ⓳
Borbone   ❸
Chalet Corniche   ❻
Da Antonio   ⓱
Daitokai   ㉒
Du Pont   ㉑
Ernst-August   ❺

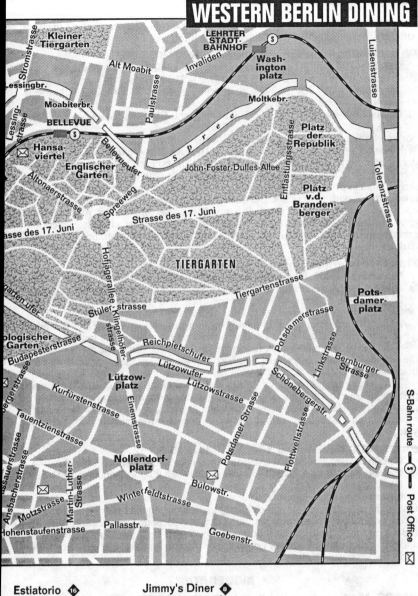

WESTERN BERLIN DINING

Estiatorio **16**
Fioretto **12**
Giraffe **23**
Hard Rock Café **15**
Hardtke's **14**
Hecker's Deele **11**
Hong Kong **9**

Jimmy's Diner **8**
Kopenhagen **23**
Marjellchen **7**
Paris Bar **13**
Ponte Vecchio **1**
San Marino **10**
Schwejk-Prager Gasthaus **21**
Zlata Praha **23**

S-Bahn route ━**S**━ Post Office ⊠

snails Talleyrand-style. Otherwise, you might begin with a galantine of goose breast or Russian cabbage soup. For a main course, I'd recommend onion steak Alsace.

DA ANTONIO, Rankestrasse 26. Tel. 030/218-72-50.
Cuisine: ITALIAN. **Reservations:** Required. **U-Bahn:** Kurfürstendamm.
$ **Prices:** Appetizers 12 DM–25 DM ($7.90–$16.50); main courses 35 DM–42 DM ($23.10–$27.70); four-course fixed-price menu 78 DM ($51.50); seven-course fixed-price menu 110 DM ($72.60). AE, MC, V.
Open: Dinner only, Mon–Sat 6:30pm–midnight. **Closed:** 3 weeks in Oct (dates vary).

For fine Italian food, Da Antonio is one of the most outstanding restaurants in the Wilmersdorf section. Antonio Capiraso and Ciro Ambrosio offer a full repertoire of dishes from both northern and southern Italy. "All you need is to taste the food and then you'll fall in love with it," the owners promise. You can begin with a trio of pastas served as an appetizer, including fettuccine with wild mushrooms in mustard sauce, ravioli stuffed with fresh pesto, and green noodles with pink salmon. For your main course, you might select spicy rack of lamb cooked pink and sliced at your table with great ritual or baby halibut in white mustard sauce. For dessert, chocolate lovers may gravitate to the Schwarzem Dessertteller, a platter that includes parfaits, creams, and dark mousses.

FIORETTO, Carmerstrasse 2. Tel. 030/312-31-15.
Cuisine: ITALIAN. **Reservations:** Recommended. **S-Bahn:** Savignyplatz.
$ **Prices:** Lunch appetizers 15 DM–20 DM ($9.90–$13.20); lunch main courses 30 DM–35 DM ($19.80–$23.10); dinner appetizers 18 DM–25 DM ($11.90–$16.50); dinner main courses 35 DM–42 DM ($23.10–$27.70). AE, V.

This stylish restaurant prides itself on an upscale Italian cuisine. Set behind an ornate facade that might have been removed from an elegant section of Paris, the restaurant is on a quiet residential street off Steinplatz. The apéritif bar near the entrance gives way to a modern dining room outfitted in shades of dusty rose and black lacquer.

The menu changes monthly but includes carpaccio, platters of mixed antipasti, pasta with cêpe mushrooms and shrimp, gnocchi with caviar, several versions of ravioli and rigatoni, agnello (roast lamb) à la Fioretto, chicken breast stuffed with mozzarella and herbs, and turbot filet on a bed of savoy cabbage with balsamic-vinegar sauce.

PARIS BAR, Kantstrasse 152. Tel. 030/313-80-52.
Cuisine: FRENCH. **Reservations:** Recommended. **U-Bahn:** Uhlandstrasse.
$ **Prices:** Appetizers 8.50 DM–36 DM ($5.60–$23.80); main courses 32 DM–50 DM ($21.10–$33). AE.
Open: Daily noon–1am.

One of the most fashionable French bistros in the city enjoys the patronage of film and media personalities. Near the heart of the city, it is decorated in a classic format. The food is invariably fresh and well prepared. You might begin with one of the terrines and then order a grilled steak or grilled fish or oysters if you feel like it. You can finish with classic chocolate mousse.

MODERATE

BACCO, Marburgerstrasse 5. Tel. 030/211-86-87.
Cuisine: ITALIAN. **Reservations:** Recommended. **U-Bahn:** Kurfürstendamm.
$ **Prices:** Appetizers 10.50 DM–20 DM ($6.90–$13.20); main courses 25 DM–45 DM ($16.50–$29.70); fixed-price menu 80 DM–140 DM ($52.80–$92.40). AE, DC, MC, V.
Open: Lunch Mon–Sat noon–3pm; dinner Mon–Sat 6pm–midnight. Dinner only, July–Aug Mon–Sat 6pm–midnight.

Owner and head chef Massimo Mannozzi practices a classical Italian cuisine in this small spot near the Europa-Center. Fish comes from Rungis, the market outside Paris, where he flies three times weekly to buy only the freshest ingredients. A house specialty is the piccata, three little veal steaks with artichokes, mushrooms, tomatoes, and aromatic pepper-flavored wine sauce. Try also black pasta with lobster or any of the Mediterranean fish dishes. The chef also prepares a delectable tagliata with beef and lentils and a succulent loin of lamb. You get good service *con brio* (with flair).

BORBONE, Windscheidstrasse 12. Tel. 030/323-83-05.

Cuisine: ITALIAN. **Reservations:** Required. **Bus:** 10. **U-Bahn:** Wilmersdorf-strasse.

$ Prices: Appetizers 10.50 DM–20 DM ($6.90–$13.20); main courses 28 DM–42 DM ($18.50–$27.70). AE, DC, MC, V.

Open: Mon–Sat noon–midnight.

Small tables are discreetly separated from one another in Borbone, a rather simple and unpretentious place, and the service is efficient. The wine list is extensive, with some legendary expensive bottles, but it also features many reasonable vintages from southern Italy. Notable dishes include filetto al Pepe and fresh filet of beef in cream sauce with green pepper and cognac. Pasta courses are invariably excellent.

ESTIATORIO (also called Fofi), Fasanenstrasse 70. Tel. 030/881-87-85.

Cuisine: GREEK. **Reservations:** Required. **U-Bahn:** Uhlandstrasse.

$ Prices: Appetizers 12 DM–25 DM ($7.90–$16.50); main courses 25 DM–52 DM ($16.50–$34.30). No credit cards.

Open: Dinner daily 7pm–3am.

Estiatorio is decidedly chic. In summer, the doors open and the action spills onto the sidewalk. Otherwise, on a winter's night, you are likely to see some of the more dazzling Berlin personalities around the metal bar, admiring or disapproving of the latest exhibition of contemporary art. John Le Carré used it as a setting for *The Little Drummer Girl*. Estiatorio, the name on the door, means bistro in Greek, but all the habitués call the place Fofi, after its owner. You might begin with a selection of Greek hors d'oeuvres, such as stuffed grape leaves, and then go on to grilled scampi or moussaka. Lamb is also imaginatively prepared. There's more glitz and glitter the later you go.

HARDTKE'S, Meinekestrasse 27A. Tel. 030/881-98-27.

Cuisine: BERLINER. **Reservations:** Required. **U-Bahn:** Kurfürstendamm.

$ Prices: Appetizers 7.50 DM–23 DM ($5–$15.20); main courses 20 DM–30 DM ($13.20–$19.80); three-course fixed-price menu 40 DM ($26.40). No credit cards

Open: Daily noon–1am.

Right off the Kurfürstendamm, Hardtke's is the best all-round moderate restaurant in Berlin for those seeking authentic German cookery. A traditional favorite, it was restored in the old style after being bombed, with dark beams, wood paneling, and wrought-iron chandeliers. It has many cozy booths for leisurely dining. Prices are low; if you want a filling snack, order a Wurstsalat or Matjesfilet (herring). The restaurant is noted for its homemade sausages and its Berliner Eisbein. Try the Sauerbraten.

HECKER'S DEELE, Grolmanstrasse 35, D-1000 Berlin 12. Tel. 030/88-90-0.

Cuisine: WESTPHALIAN. **Reservations:** Recommended. **U-Bahn:** Uhland-strasse.

$ Prices: Appetizers 6.50 DM–23 DM ($4.30–$15.20); main courses 14.50 DM–35.50 DM ($9.60–$33). AE, DC, MC, V.

Open: Daily noon–midnight.

About a block from the Kurfürstendamm, Hecker's zealously guards its time-tested traditional German recipes, such as its way of preparing venison and wild boar (available only during game season), and keeps its prices down. With your main course, you should try a draft beer. Specialties include Sauerbraten with potato, calf's liver, Bratwurst, Knacker (ham sausage), Blutwurst, Leberwurst, and Westphalian ham. Boiled pork knuckles with sauerkraut and mashed peas is a classic favorite. The restaurant is part of a modern hotel previously recommended.

HONG KONG, Kurfürstendamm 210. Tel. 030/881-57-56.

Cuisine: CHINESE. **Reservations:** Not necessary. **U-Bahn:** Kurfürstendamm.

$ Prices: Appetizers 7.50 DM–20 DM ($5–$13.20); main courses 17 DM–40 DM ($11.20–$26.40); three-course fixed-price lunch 18 DM ($11.90); seven-course fixed-price dinner 70 DM ($46.20). AE, DC, MC, V.

Open: Daily noon–midnight.

Hong Kong occupies space on the second floor of a building next to the landmark Paris movie house. Take a small elevator to the restaurant, which is quite stylish, a bit like Raffles in Singapore, with peacock chairs and a version of a Chinese pagoda, with a view of the Ku'damm. The Chinese food here, mostly specialties from the southern provinces, is of fine quality. The menu is large, including such dishes as duckling soup, several shark's-fin specialties, stewed frogs' legs with green pepper, stewed abalone, and special Hong Kong fare such as fried duckling with sweet-and-sour vegetables.

KOPENHAGEN, Kurfürstendamm 203. Tel. 030/881-62-19.

Cuisine: DANISH. **Reservations:** Recommended. **U-Bahn:** Kurfürstendamm.

$ Prices: Appetizers 8.50 DM–22 DM ($5.60–$14.50); main courses 22 DM–38 DM ($14.50–$25.10). AE, MC, V.

Open: Daily noon–midnight.

More than a quarter of a century ago, Copenhagen invaded Berlin (not the other way around). The restaurant operates out of a long, narrow, bistro-style room, with a glass-enclosed entrance overlooking the Ku'damm. Their most famous specialty is smørrebrød (literally, bread and butter), on which they are likely to pile everything from a slice of Danish cheese to steak tartare crowned by a raw egg. These open-face sandwiches, when prepared correctly, are a delight. The selection of smørrebrød is so huge that you may spend half your lunchtime deciding what to order. I favor the marinated herring and roast beef with rémoulade sauce; however, the liver pâté is heartily recommended as well. A special smørrebrød is the aquavit cream cheese. Naturally, you'll want to accompany your meal with a Danish Carlsberg beer. Hot main dishes, Danish-style, are featured as well, including lobster soup. A good main course is game pie with Cumberland sauce and Waldorf salad.

MARJELLCHEN, Mommsenstrasse 9. Tel. 030/883-26-76.

Cuisine: EAST PRUSSIAN. **Reservations:** Required. **U-Bahn:** Adenauerplatz.

$ Prices: Appetizers 8.50 DM–18 DM ($5.60–$11.90); main courses 18.50 DM–35 DM ($12.20–$23.10). DC, MC, V.

Open: Dinner only, daily 5pm–1am. **Closed:** Dec 24–31.

⭐ This is the only restaurant in Berlin specializing in the cuisine of Germany's long-lost province of East Prussia, along with the cuisines of Pomerania and Silesia. Deriving its unusual name from an East Prussian word meaning "young girl," the establishment divides its space among three rooms, the first of which has a Kneipe-style bar dominating it, plus a series of turn-of-the-century photographs of historic buildings in cities that now lie within Poland and the former Soviet Union.

Ramona Azzaro, whose father was Italian and whose East Prussian mother taught her many of the region's most famous recipes, is the creative force here. Amid a Bismarckian ambience of still lifes, vested waiters, and oil lamps, you can enjoy a savory version of red-beet soup with strips of beef, East Prussian potato soup with crabmeat and bacon, falsch Gänsebraten (pork spare ribs stuffed with prunes and bread crumbs "as if the cook had prepared a goose"), marinated elk, and Mecklenburger Kümmelfleisch (lamb with chives and onions).

ZLATA PRAHA, Meinekestrasse 4. Tel. 030/881-97-50.

Cuisine: EASTERN EUROPEAN. **Reservations:** Recommended. **U-Bahn:** Joachimstaler Strasse.

$ Prices: Appetizers 12.50 DM–18 DM ($8.30–$11.90); main courses 22 DM–42 DM ($14.50–$27.70). AE, MC, V.

Open: Daily 5pm–1am.

Zlata Praha serves the best Eastern European cuisine of any restaurant in Berlin. German, French, and Austrian wines are featured. However, the pièce de résistance is the special tap-drawn beer, Pilsner Urquell das Echte. Actually, if your palate isn't Slavic, you may want to steer clear of this brew; otherwise, it makes the perfect drink for toasting your Czech friends at the next table. Most of the food seems inspired by the Prague kitchen. Among the main-dish specialties are Paprika Schnitzel and Sauerbraten. Few can resist the Töpfer Strudel.

INEXPENSIVE

HARD ROCK CAFÉ, Meinekestrasse 21. Tel. 88-46-20.
   Cuisine: AMERICAN. **Reservations:** Not necessary. **U-Bahn:** Kurfürstendamm.
$ Prices: Appetizers 5 DM–15 DM ($3.30–$9.90); main courses 10 DM–30 DM ($6.60–$19.80). MC, V.
   Open: Sun–Thurs noon–midnight, Fri–Sat noon–1am.
This is the local branch of the worldwide chain that successfully mingled rock-and-roll nostalgia with American food. Opened in 1992 on the converted premises of a parking garage, it features part of an early-model Cadillac jutting out from its facade, an always-crowded bar shaped like an oversize guitar, and a restaurant-in-the-round. Popular with visiting rock groups and professional athletes, the place serves two-fisted drinks amid a collection of memorabilia including Uli Roth's 12-string acoustic guitar, Jimi Hendrix's favorite vest, and a microphone used by the Beatles during their early days in Liverpool.
   Menu items feature nachos; salads; Tex-Mex fajitas; steaks; barbecued ribs and chicken; many kinds of burgers; and drinks that include the famous rum, gin, and amaretto mixture known as a Hurricane.

JIMMY'S DINER, Pariser Strasse 41. Tel. 882-31-41.
   Cuisine: AMERICAN/MEXICAN. **Reservations:** Not necessary. **U-Bahn:** Uhlandstrasse.
$ Prices: Appetizers 6.50 DM–12 DM ($4.30–$7.90); main courses 9.50 DM–15 DM ($6.30–$9.90). No credit cards.
   Open: Sun–Thurs 4pm–3am, Fri–Sat 4pm–5am.
This place is all the rage, one of those 1950s-style Stateside diners that often appear in Europe, usually plastered with pictures of James Dean. It's also one of the most popular after-dark spots on the Berlin agenda, because of its late hours. It lies about a 6-minute walk south of the Kurfürstendamm. Here you can satisfy your lust for southern fried chicken or spareribs or go even farther south of the border to enjoy tacos, enchiladas, or chili con carne. Hamburgers are the most popular item. Everything tastes better when washed down with Mexican beer, with country music in the background.

SAN MARINO, Savignyplatz 12. Tel. 313-60-86.
   Cuisine: ITALIAN. **Reservations:** Not necessary. **S-Bahn:** Savignyplatz.
$ Prices: Appetizers 7.50 DM–12 DM ($5–$7.90); main courses 16 DM–35 DM ($10.60–$23.10); pizza from 8 DM ($5.30). AE, MC, V.
   Open: Daily 11am–1am.
This is one of the dozens of trattorie in Berlin. But this is one of the most central, offering reliable cookery over long hours. Many locals drop in just for a pizza. You might begin with antipasto misto or one of the pasta dishes, ranging from lasagne to spaghetti San Marino (with peas, mushrooms, ham, and cream sauce). A wide selection of veal and other meat is offered, including grilled rumpsteak, saltimbocca, and Venetian-style liver. There's a children's menu.

NEAR THE MEMORIAL CHURCH & ZOO

EXPENSIVE

ALT-NÜRNBERG, Berlin Europa-Center. Tel. 261-43-97.
   Cuisine: BAVARIAN. **Reservations:** Recommended weekends. **U-Bahn:** Kurfürstendamm.

$ Prices: Appetizers 12 DM–26 DM ($7.90–$17.20); main courses 28 DM–55 DM ($18.50–$36.30). AE, DC, MC, V.
Open: Daily 11:30am–11pm.

On the ground level, this place handsomely captures the old style of a Bavarian tavern, complete with copper lanterns and wood. The house specialty is a plate of Nürnberger Rostbratwürstl. Each day the chefs prepare a different specialty. You might begin with a typical Berlin pea soup with croûtons or Hungarian goulash. The Wiener Schnitzel is always reliable, as is the herring salad and the pork filet in pepper sauce with broccoli. Inexpensive platters are usually a meal in themselves.

DAITOKAI, Berlin Europa-Center. Tel. 261-80-99.
Cuisine: JAPANESE. **Reservations:** Not necessary. **U-Bahn:** Kurfürsten-damm.
$ Prices: Appetizers 5.50 DM–15 DM ($3.60–$9.90); main courses 42 DM–50 DM ($27.70–$33); fixed-price lunch 40 DM ($26.40); fixed-price dinner 80 DM ($52.80) and 100 DM ($66). AE, DC, MC, V.
Open: Lunch Tues–Sun noon–2:30pm; dinner Tues–Sun 6–10:30pm.
Daitokai, part of a chain, is considered Berlin's leading Japanese restaurant. It lies two floors above street level amid a Japanese-inspired labyrinth of reflecting pools, slate floors that span the water, and low tables. The chefs are artists with their knives, and each dish is artistically arranged. You might begin with a Samurai cocktail, a Sayonara cocktail, or a small pot of saké.

DU PONT, Budapesterstrasse 1. Tel. 261-88-11.
Cuisine: FRENCH. **Reservations:** Required. **Bus:** 9. **U-Bahn:** Bahnhof Zoologischer Garten.
$ Prices: Appetizers 15 DM–18 DM ($9.90–$11.90); main courses 35 DM–45 DM ($23.10–$29.70). AE, DC, MC, V.
Open: Lunch Mon–Fri noon–3pm; dinner Mon–Sat 6pm–midnight.
Du Pont is a restaurant-rôtisserie owned by partners Keuch and Losito. Their modern and stylish restaurant is near the Inter-Continental Hotel, in a modern building designed originally as an architects' firm. It is outfitted in a pleasing collection of neutral colors, but the French cuisine—based on seasonal produce—is the main allure. The daily specials reflect the availability of choice ingredients at the marketplace. Typical listings include filet of veal stuffed with prunes and served with cinnamon sauce, filet of Scottish Black Angus with burgundy sauce, and bacon-wrapped saddle of lamb served with garlic sauce.

MODERATE

GIRAFFE, Klopstockstrasse 2. Tel. 391-47-17.
Cuisine: BERLINER/FRENCH. **Reservations:** Not necessary. **U-Bahn:** Hansaplatz.
$ Prices: Appetizers 5 DM–25 DM ($3.30–$16.50); main courses 20 DM–36 DM ($13.20–$23.80); three-course fixed-price lunch 24 DM–36 DM ($15.80–$23.80). AE, MC.
Open: Tues–Sun noon–9pm.
Set in the Tiergarten, Giraffe derives its name from its location on the ground floor of one of the tallest and narrowest apartment buildings in the city. Situated in a wooded area, it's like a giraffe's neck rising above the plain. Inside is a series of dining rooms. You get hearty cuisine, including five preparations of goose, *Eisbein* (pork knuckle), or pot-au-feu with seafood. In summer, the action spills onto a terrace.

INEXPENSIVE

SCHWEJK-PRAGER GASTHAUS, Ansbacher Strasse 4. Tel. 213-78-92.

Cuisine: CZECH. **Reservations:** Recommended. **U-Bahn:** Wittenbergplatz.
$ Prices: Appetizers 6.50 DM–16.50 DM ($4.30–$10.90); main courses 15
DM–25 DM ($9.90–$16.50). No credit cards.
Open: Dinner only, daily 6pm–1am.

 The taste of Eastern Europe is alive and flourishing at this bistro where
Bohemian specialties are served in generous portions. It's about 2 blocks
from the Memorial Church, in a kind of neighborhood-tavern am-
bience of well-scrubbed tables and regular clients. There's a small bar for drinking.
Much of the food tastes better when washed down with the local Pilsner,
though wine is also available. Typical specialties are crackling broiled pork shanks
(Schweinehaxen) with salad and sauerkraut; good-sized bowls of thick borscht or
liver-noodle soup; and various kinds of "toasts" piled high with meats and vegetables, served with flavorful sauces. Meals here are one of the best bargains
in town. One of a full range of Czechoslovakian liqueurs might round off your
meal.

GREATER CHARLOTTENBURG

EXPENSIVE

ALT-LUXEMBURG, Windscheidstrasse 31. Tel. 323-87-30.
   Cuisine: CONTINENTAL. **Reservations:** Required. **U-Bahn:** Sophie-
Charlotteplatz.
$ Prices: Appetizers 17 DM–35 DM ($11.20–$23.10); main courses 29 DM–45
DM ($19.10–$29.70); fixed-price menus 108 DM ($71.30) and 135 DM ($89.10).
DC, V.
Open: Dinner only, Tues–Sat 7–11pm.

Its dark paneling, evenly spaced mirrors, antique chandeliers, and old-
fashioned chairs create the kind of ambience you might have expected to find in
the early 1900s. Despite the decor, the food here is very tuned in to the neue
Küche–style cuisine. This restaurant is owned and operated by one of Berlin's most
highly respected chefs, Karl Wannemacher. Dishes depend on the season—perhaps
terrine of cauliflower garnished with rondelles of fresh lobster, fresh tomato salad with
quail eggs, breast of goose with honey sauce, and rack of lamb with green beans and
lentils, plus an array of wines.

PONTE VECCHIO, Spielhagenstrasse 3. Tel. 342-19-99.

**Ⓕ FROMMER'S SMART TRAVELER:
RESTAURANTS**

1. Some of the great restaurants of Berlin offer fixed-price luncheons at such
   reasonable prices that the kitchen actually loses money.
2. Select set luncheons or dinners when offered—many represent at least a
   30% saving over à la carte menus.
3. Look for the daily specials on any à la carte menu. They're invariably fresh,
   and often carry a lower price tag than regular à la carte listings.
4. Drink the house wine served in a carafe—it's only a fraction of the price of
   bottled wine.
5. Berliner's colony of Turkish, Asian, Indian, and Greek restaurants often offer
   good dining value.
6. Check to see if the main course comes with vegetables. If it does (as is often
   the case), you don't have to order too many side dishes.

Cuisine: TUSCAN. **Reservations:** Required. **U-Bahn:** Bismarckstrasse.

$ **Prices:** Appetizers 12 DM–25 DM ($7.90–$16.50); main courses 32 DM–45 DM ($21.10–$29.70). DC.

Open: Dinner only, Wed–Mon 6:30–11pm. **Closed:** July 1–Aug 4.

Filled with Italian charm and Tuscan flavors, Ponte Vecchio hosts an appreciative crowd of Berliners, some of whom consider it their preferred place to eat. Typical dishes include carpaccio with fresh mozzarella and ripe tomatoes, many variations of veal dishes, assorted shellfish with basil and olive oil, spinach salad with warm bacon, and even a spicy hot version of penne all'arrabiatta.

MODERATE

ERNST-AUGUST, Sybelstrasse 16. Tel. 324-55-76.

Cuisine: FRENCH/INTERNATIONAL. **Reservations:** Required. **U-Bahn:** Adenauerplatz.

$ **Prices:** Appetizers 8 DM–14.50 DM ($5.30–$9.60); main courses 21 DM–32 DM ($13.90–$21.10). No credit cards.

Open: Wed–Sun 6:30pm–1am (kitchen stops serving hot food at midnight). **Closed:** July 15–Aug 15.

Serving a discerning clientele, this place is pleasantly overdecorated with dozens of antique pieces of bric-a-brac. Offerings might include seven variations of pork filet or two variations of filet of hare. Typical dishes are pork filet with garlic, tomatoes, and cheese or rumpsteak flavored with herbs in a green-pepper sauce. The chef's specialty is filet steak, served in many variations—especially a succulent version, the Ernst-August, with herb butter.

GRUNEWALD

EXPENSIVE

CHALET CORNICHE, Königsallee 5B. Tel. 892-85-97.

Cuisine: CONTINENTAL. **Reservations:** Required. **Bus:** 19.

$ **Prices:** Appetizers 12 DM–26 DM ($7.90–$17.20); main courses 38 DM–48 DM ($25.10–$31.70); six-course fixed-price menu 110 DM ($72.60). AE, DC, MC, V.

Open: Mon–Sat 6pm–1am, Sun noon–1am.

The self-styled "chi-chi" atmosphere here is helped by the open fireplace and a view through the panoramic window overlooking the Hallensee. The most prominent feature is a giant beech tree around which the restaurant is built. The chef prepares a conservative cuisine moderne, using very fresh but often very expensive ingredients. Menu specialties depend on the shopping and the season. You might begin with herb-flavored potato soup with strips of salmon or fresh oysters, then follow with breast of Barbary goose in soy sauce, sweetbreads in tarragon butter with mustard sauce, or saddle of lamb provencal. The carte shows 100 varieties of wine.

HEMINGWAY'S, Hagenstrasse 18. Tel. 825-45-71.

Cuisine: INTERNATIONAL/CONTINENTAL. **Reservations:** Required. **Bus:** 19.

$ **Prices:** Appetizers 20 DM–24 DM ($13.20–$15.90); main courses 36 DM–42 DM ($23.80–$27.70); three-course fixed-price lunch 55 DM ($36.30); four-course fixed-price dinner 85 DM ($56.10); six-course fixed-price dinner 115 DM ($75.90). AE, DC, MC, V.

Open: Lunch daily noon–3pm; dinner daily 7pm–midnight, although guests often linger until 2am.

Berlin seems an unlikely setting for a restaurant honoring Papa, but this one works. It even catches the author's informality by spelling his name with a small *h*. In fact, the man himself might feel at home here, as it is vaguely neocolonial, somewhat like an elegant old-style Cuban hacienda, with lots of latticework and white wicker. A meeting place for gourmets, it is 5 minutes by taxi from the center. A classic cuisine moderne menu is presented. There's a limited selection of high-quality meat dishes, as the chefs seem to feel more at home with seafood. You might select turbot and salmon with two kinds of caviar or orange-flavored carpaccio of salmon with hollandaise sauce. Everything is fresh here. In season fresh asparagus is prominently featured, and in summer, fresh berries make up the most tempting desserts. Perhaps they'll appear in a raspberry parfait or as fresh strawberries with Grand Marnier sauce. The wine list is well chosen and exclusive.

SCHÖNEBERG

MODERATE

RATSKELLER SCHÖNEBERG, Schöneberg Rathaus, John-F.-Kennedy-Platz. Tel. 783-21-27.
  Cuisine: CONTINENTAL. **Reservations:** Not necessary. **U-Bahn:** Schöneberg.
$ Prices: Appetizers 8 DM–22 DM ($5.30–$14.50); main courses 12.50 DM–50 DM ($8.30–$33). AE, DC, MC, V.
  Open: Mon–Fri 11am–10pm, Sun 11am–3pm. **Closed:** Dec 25–Jan 1.
This Ratskeller is on the square that became famous in 1963, when President Kennedy made his now legendary *"Ich bin ein Berliner"* speech. Many Americans, when visiting the square and the Freedom Bell inside, like to stop here. The wines are good and can be ordered with one of the luncheons. Main dishes are fairly ambitious, including such offerings as steak Diane and veal Schnitzel Cordon Bleu, with fresh salad and french fries. The day's soup is invariably tasty.

WAIDMANNSLUST

VERY EXPENSIVE

ROCKENDORF'S RESTAURANT, Düsterhauptstrasse 1. Tel. 402-30-99.
  Cuisine: CONTINENTAL. **Reservations:** Required. **S-Bahn:** Waidmannslust.
$ Prices: Fixed-price lunch 98 DM–170 DM ($64.70–$112.20); fixed-price dinner 170 DM–220 DM ($112.20–$145.20). AE, DC, MC, V.
  Open: Lunch Tues–Sat noon–2pm; dinner Tues–Sat 7–9:30pm. **Closed:** Dec 22–Jan 7; June 28–July 21.
Rockendorf's occupies the primary position in a 19th-century art nouveau villa near the Englischer Garten in north Berlin, a 20-minute taxi ride from the center. Chef Siegfried Rockendorf, whose name graces this elegant restaurant, often sticks to the classical French cuisine, which he prepares beautifully. However, he frequently extends his creativity to continental cuisine moderne, concocting some strikingly original dishes. Perhaps you'll try his fresh jellied aspic with cucumber sauce, filet of turbot in Ricard sauce, or goosemeat pâté in sauterne with cranberries. The innovative thinking of Herr Rockendorf also reaches the borders of China, with his bouillon of wild quail, served with breast of quail over fresh quail eggs. The furnishings of this restaurant are restrained. Fixed-price menus are featured, including two choices at lunch and two at dinner.

SPANDAU

MODERATE

ZITADELLEN-SCHANKE, Strasse am Juliusturm. Tel. 334-21-06.
  Cuisine: GERMAN. **Reservations:** Recommended. **U-Bahn:** Zitadelle.
$ Prices: Appetizers 9.50 DM–18 DM ($6.30–$11.90); main courses 20 DM–40 DM ($13.20–$26.40); fixed-price menu 65 DM–85 DM ($42.90–$56.10). AE, DC, MC, V.
  Open: Tues–Sun 11:30am–11pm.

You'll find a traditional Germanic decor embellishing this historic restaurant behind the ancient stone walls of Spandau Citadel. The soft candlelight and open fireplace provide a cozy and relaxing ambience. The chefs cook time-honored specialties yet also experiment with neue Küche. Some of their better concoctions include wild boar pâté with St. Lucie cherry sauce; Rippenbraten mit Krusten (roast ribs with white cabbage salad); ground filet with steamed dumplings; and Wallenstein grill platter for two, consisting of stuffed quails, beef filet, and loin of pork. An average three-course meal will cost 50 DM ($33). The weekly special, called Spiesbratenessen, is served as a fixed-price meal every Sunday beginning at 6pm; the cost is 65 DM ($42.90). On Friday, Saturday, and Sunday evenings, you can enjoy a medieval banquet with ballad singing by an open fire.

EASTERN BERLIN

EXPENSIVE

BORCHARDT, Französische Strasse 47. Tel. 030/229-3144.
  Cuisine: FRENCH/INTERNATIONAL. **Reservations:** Recommended. **U-Bahn:** Friedrichstrasse.
$ Prices: Lunch appetizers 10 DM–18 DM ($6.60–$11.90); lunch main courses 25 DM–30 DM ($16.50–$19.80); dinner appetizers 20 DM–27 DM ($13.20–$17.80); dinner main courses 31 DM–45 DM ($20.50–$29.70). AE.
  Open: Lunch daily 12:30–3:15pm; dinner daily 6:30pm–midnight.

⭐ This is the most stylish and talked about restaurant in eastern Berlin. Set at the edge of one of the city's most famous squares, the Gendarmenmarkt, it was built in 1853 as the home of F. W. Borchardt, a caterer to Prussian monarchs. The establishment eked out a modest income as a fish restaurant until 1955, and then it was a somewhat somber disco in the 1970s. It was revitalized and redefined in 1992.

Amid the marble, gilt, and cream-colored stucco of the dining room, you're likely to see luminaries from the worlds of German finance, industry, and cinema, as well as such notables as movie star Sir Anthony Hopkins and designer Karl Lagerfeld.

Menu items change according to the season and availability of ingredients but have included fish goulasch with green asparagus, stuffed lamb shoulder Toulouse style with green beans and potatoes gratin, salmon filet in horseradish crust with beetroot sauce, and a succulent array of freshly prepared desserts.

LA COUPOLE, in the Berlin Hilton, Mohrenstrasse 30. Tel. 030/23-820.
  Cuisine: CONTINENTAL. **Reservations:** Recommended. **U-Bahn:** Friedrichstrasse.
$ Prices: Appetizers 16 DM–22 DM ($10.60–$14.50); main dishes 45 DM–52 DM ($29.70–$34.30); fixed-price menu (six to eight courses) 105 DM–120 DM ($69.30–$79.20). AE, DC, MC, V.
  Open: Dinner only, daily 6–11pm (last order).

⭐ Considered one of the finest restaurants in all Berlin, this stylish enclave enjoys a superb reputation for culinary innovation as well as sweeping views over the famous twin churches of the Gendarmenmarkt. Partially sheathed in California pinewood, with murals crafted from Japanese chalk sketches, the restaurant has a highly theatrical open kitchen and a whimsical ceiling fresco, compared by some critics to the work of Marc Chagall. The menu changes with the season and the inspiration of the chef but might include turbot in champagne sauce with asparagus, carpaccio of pigeon with celery and wild greens, and poached flounder in Riesling sauce.

LE GRAND RESTAURANT SILHOUETTE, in the Maritim Grand Hotel, Friedrichstrasse 158. Tel. 030/2-09-20.
  Cuisine: INTERNATIONAL. **Reservations:** Required. **S-Bahn:** Friedrichstrasse.

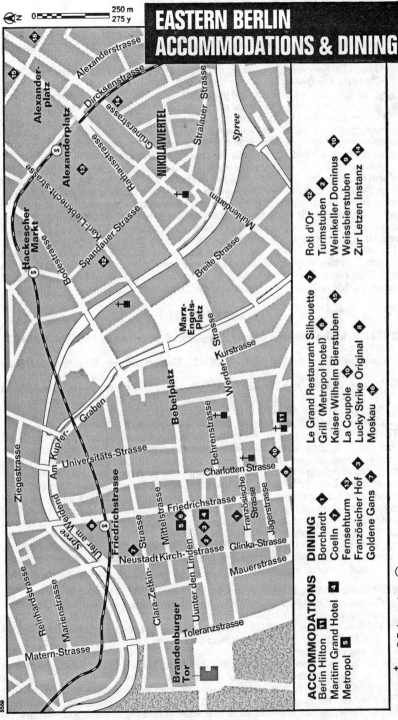

EASTERN BERLIN
ACCOMMODATIONS & DINING

0 — 250 m / 275 y

ACCOMMODATIONS
Berlin Hilton 11
Maritim Grand Hotel 4
Metropol 5

DINING
Borchardt 1
Coelln 7
Fernsehturm 13
Französicher Hof 3
Goldene Gans 7
Le Grand Restaurant Silhouette 7
Grill (Metropol hotel) 6
Kaiser Wilhelm Bierstuben 10
La Coupole 15
Lucky Strike Original 8
Moskau 16
Roti d'Or 12
Turmstuben 2
Weinkeller Dominus 10
Weissbierstuben 9
Zur Letzen Instanz 14

Church ✝
S-Bahn route Ⓢ

NIKOLAIVIERTEL

$ Prices: Appetizers 14 DM–28 DM ($9.20–$18.50); main courses 30 DM–90 DM ($19.80–$59.40); five-course fixed-price menu 130 DM ($85.80); seven-course fixed-price menu 160 DM ($105.60). AE, DC, MC, V.

Open: Dinner only, Mon–Sat 6pm–midnight (restaurant remains open until 3am).
Closed: July 6–Aug 2.

⭐ By any critic's standards, this posh restaurant, offering both classic cuisine and cuisine moderne, is the finest in eastern Berlin. It definitely is the place to go if you can afford it. To reach it, take an elevator in the lobby of this previously recommended hotel to the seventh floor. There you'll encounter a Jugendstil maroon-and-white decor with sculpted plaster ceilings, bronze statues, and sinuously paneled window moldings to mask the room's modern construction.

An attentive staff will propose such selections as a tempting offering of hors d'oeuvres, including freshly smoked fish straight from the ovens, thinly sliced salmon from the Baltic, and the special terrine (made with pike perch, trout, and smoked eel, softened with chive mousse). For your soup selection, the choice might be a pheasant pot-au-feu or double duck broth. Main dishes include stewed venison in juniper-cream sauce, médaillons of veal with lobster slices and oysters, and sliced knuckle of veal au gratin. Desserts are sumptuous, including an ice soufflé with tropical fruits. The wine list, including an international array of some 300 labels, also offers some eastern Germany vintages, made from grapes grown in little vineyards along the Saale and Elbe rivers. After 10pm, there is dance music emanating from a piano and occasionally from a small group of stringed instruments as well.

MODERATE

COELLN, in the Maritim Grand Hotel, Friedrichstrasse 158. Tel. 030/23-27-32-48.

Cuisine: BERLINER/INTERNATIONAL. **Reservations:** Required. **S-Bahn:** Friedrichstrasse.

$ Prices: Appetizers 8 DM–20 DM ($5.30–$13.20); main courses 18 DM–40 DM ($11.90–$26.40); three-course fixed-price menu 36 DM ($23.80); seven-course fixed-price dinner 120 DM ($79.20). AE, DC, MC, V.

Open: Lunch daily noon–4pm; dinner daily 6pm–midnight.

The Coelln is named after the neighborhood in which it sits. (Around 1150, Cölln and Berlin were neighbor towns.) This is the gracious main dining room of this previously recommended deluxe hotel. To reach it, ascend to the second floor. Beneath neobaroque ceilings of sculpted plaster, white is the dominant color, supplemented by pastel tones. Both Berlin specialties and international dishes are offered, enhanced by wines from Germany and abroad. Menus are subject to seasonal changes but could include hors d'oeuvres, sautéed calves' brains, and Beluga caviar. You might start with seafood soup or game soup with wild mushrooms, followed by a main dish such as halibut in orange mousse, haunch of wild boar braised in burgundy, or médaillons of veal filet in calvados. One part of the menu is reserved strictly for old Berlin cuisine, including famous Löffelerbsen (yellow split-pea soup) and salt knuckle of pork with sauerkraut. Desserts are lavish.

ERMELER HAUS, Märkisches Ufer 10. Tel. 030/279-40-28.

Cuisine: GERMAN/CONTINENTAL. **Reservations:** Required. **U-Bahn:** Märkisches Museum.

$ Prices: Appetizers 7 DM–28 DM ($4.60–$18.50); main courses 28 DM–45 DM ($18.50–$29.70); seven-course fixed-price menu 120 DM ($79.20). AE.

Open: Daily 11am–midnight.

Guests dine in rococo splendor in this converted 16th-century town house. It's as close as you can come in the capital to dining in an old-world manner. The waiters wear tails. Once the private home of a tobacco merchant, it stands beside a canal on Fischerinsel. There's an elegant café, plus a terrace. The economical section is the beer hall in the cellar. But well-dressed Berliners prefer dancing in the wine restaurant, on

Friday and Saturday from 7pm to midnight, with its cherubic ceilings and gilt moldings. You might try, for example, rack of venison with pepper sauce, scallops in butter sauce, or stuffed beef filet with oysters.

FRANZÖSISCHER HOF, Jägerstrasse 56. Tel. 030/229-39-69.

Cuisine: FRENCH/GERMAN. **Reservations:** Recommended. **U-Bahn:** Hausvogteiplatz.

$ Prices: Appetizers 16 DM–24 DM ($10.60–$15.80); main courses 25 DM–38 DM ($16.50–$25.10). AE, DC, MC, V.

Open: Daily 11am–midnight. **Closed:** Dec 24.

Französischer Hof opened its art-nouveau doors in 1989. It fills two floors connected by a graceful belle époque staircase, evoking a turn-of-the-century Parisian bistro. Dishes might include cold fish canapés, saddle of lamb, and flambéed filet Stroganoff with almond-studded dumplings.

GOLDENE GANS, in the Maritim Grand Hotel, Friedrichstrasse 158. Tel. 030/23-27-35-46.

Cuisine: GERMAN. **Reservations:** Recommended. **S-Bahn:** Friedrichstrasse.

$ Prices: Appetizers 10.50 DM–20 DM ($6.90–$13.20); main courses 18 DM–38 DM ($11.90–$25.10); three-course fixed-price menu 50 DM ($33). AE, DC, MC, V.

Open: Daily noon–midnight.

⑤ The "Golden Goose" of this previously recommended deluxe hostelry is a deliberate contrast to the beaux-arts glamour containing it. This rustic and gemütlich Stube lies one flight above the lobby level of the Grand. It has a wooden ceiling, colorfully embroidered napery, and an open-to-view kitchen. Cuisine is based on Thuringian recipes vividly evocative of old Germany. Although cholesterol counters shun it, the special appetizer of the kitchen (even though it doesn't appear on the menu) is goose fat with mixed pickles and freshly baked rolls. The restaurant's namesake goose appears in three preparations that are very Thuringian and very much a delicacy. A host of other regional dishes are also offered.

LUCKY STRIKE ORIGINAL, Georgen Strasse 2–5, beneath S-Bahn arches 177–180. Tel. 030/694-4848.

Cuisine: NEW ORLEANS CAJUN. **Reservations:** Recommended. **S-Bahn:** Friedrichstrasse.

$ Prices: Appetizers 9 DM–15 DM ($5.90–$9.90); main courses 20 DM–32 DM ($13.20–$21.10). AE, DC, MC, V.

Open: Breakfast and lunch daily 10am–5pm; dinner daily 6pm–midnight; Fri–Sat late-night suppers midnight–2am.

Only the crumbling of the Berlin Wall and the unification of Germany could have made this restaurant possible. It lies across the river from the Pergamon Museum, near the corner of Friedrichstrasse, within a quartet of interconnected bunkers whose vaulted ceilings gave shelter to Nazi officers and their wives during Allied bombing raids. In 1993, a New Orleans–based investor, Michael Black, teamed up with two German-born music-industry entrepreneurs to create this unusual restaurant.

You'll enter an almost surrealistically claustrophobic doorway set into a concrete facade where the bullet scars of World War II are still visible. Above your head, across an overhead bridge, rumble the trains from S-Bahn, adding a shudder to the whole experience. Declared a historic monument, the premises retains the nine-foot-thick reinforced concrete walls in some places, although windows have been inserted into others for a postmodern effect. The mood is 1940s beebop mingled with Cajun spice. Part of the restaurant's allure derives from the old-fashioned oak-and-mahogany bar that the owners imported from Allentown, Pennsylvania. From it are dispensed deceptively potent drinks (including Hurricanes and Bayou Slides).

In keeping with the establishment's New Orleans inspiration, the place serves late breakfasts throughout the day. The rest of the day, you'll find handpacked hamburgers, Acadian-style seafood gumbo, shrimp Créole, southern fried chicken, and Big Daddy's barbecued ribs. Live bayou-inspired music is sometimes performed in one of the inner rooms on a schedule discerned only by phoning in advance. There may be a music cover charge of 20 DM [$13.20] per person.)

MOSKAU, Karl-Marx-Allee 34. Tel. 030/279-28-69.
   Cuisine: RUSSIAN. **Reservations:** Required. **U-Bahn:** Schillingstrasse.
$ **Prices:** Appetizers 8 DM–18 DM ($5.30–$11.90); main courses 20 DM–30 DM ($13.20–$19.80); five-course fixed-price menu 85 DM ($56.10). AE, DC, MC, V.
   Open: Dinner only, Sun–Thurs 6–11pm, Fri–Sat 6pm–2am.
You'll find this restaurant/café devoted to Russian cuisine about a 10-minute walk from the Alexanderplatz. Specialties include chicken Tabaka and Bauernteller (a Russian farmer's dish). Other dishes include borscht, chicken Kiev, and beef Stroganoff. Of course, you can order Russian vodka, even Russian champagne (listed as SU-Sekt). A coffee bar, Mokkabar, is on the premises. A Tanzcafé is open from 3pm to midnight on Friday and Saturday. Shows are presented, and admission is 15 DM ($9.90).

WEINKELLER DOMINUS, in the Berlin Hilton, Mohrenstrasse 30. Tel. 030/23-820.
   Cuisine: PRUSSIAN. **Reservations:** Recommended. **U-Bahn:** Friedrich-strasse.
$ **Prices:** Appetizers 10 DM–16 DM ($6.60–$10.60); main courses 23 DM–29 DM ($15.20–$19.10). Wine 6.50 DM–8 DM ($4.30–$5.30) per glass, or 44 DM–50 DM ($29–$33) per bottle. AE, DC, MC, V.
   Open: Dinner only, daily 6–11pm (last order).
Its stone vaulting and thick masonry are modified copies of a 13th-century wine cellar that stood here before the 1944 bombings. Today, re-created in painstaking Gothic detail, they are contained within the cellar of the previously recommended hotel. Here you'll find the type of hearty and flavorful fare that goes best with cold weather and wine. Specialties include an array of smoked meat, cheese, and pork, veal, and beef dishes that have tempted the palates of Berliners for centuries. Most unusual about the place, however, is the selection of wine produced in former East Germany. Relatively unknown, they include such vintages as Meissen and Saale-Unstrut, both increasingly sought after in western Germany.

ZUR LETZEN INSTANZ, Waisenstrasse 14–16. Tel. 030/242-55-28.
   Cuisine: GERMAN. **Reservations:** Not necessary. **S-Bahn:** Kloster Strasse.
$ **Prices:** Appetizers 6 DM–20 DM ($4–$13.20); main courses 18 DM–22 DM ($11.90–$14.50); fixed-price lunch 18 DM ($11.90); five-course fixed-price dinner 50 DM ($33). No credit cards.
   Open: Mon 4pm–midnight, Tues–Sat 11am–midnight, Sun 11am–4pm.
Reputedly Berlin's oldest restaurant, dating from 1525, Zur Letzen Instanz in its day was frequented by everybody from Napoleon to Beethoven. Prisoners used to stop off here for one last beer before going to jail.
   It is contained within two floors of a baroque building whose facade is ornamented with a row of stone bas-reliefs of medieval faces. The location, just outside the crumbling brick wall that once ringed medieval Berlin, is not far from the historic core of the Nikolaikirche. Double doors open on a series of small woodsy rooms, one with a bar and ceramic *Kachelofen* (stove). At the back a circular staircase leads to another series of rooms, where every evening at 6, only food and wine (no beer) are served. On both floors you can select from a limited and old-fashioned menu of Berlin staples, including Eisbein (haunch of boiled pork garnished with sauerkraut); you might begin with Gulaschsuppe.

INEXPENSIVE

KAISER WILHELM BIERSTUBEN, Karl-Liebknecht-Strasse 11. Tel. 030/282-42-68.
   Cuisine: BERLINER. **Reservations:** Not necessary. **S-Bahn:** Alexanderplatz.

$ Prices: Appetizers 3 DM–8 DM ($2–$5.30); main courses 8 DM–20 DM ($5.30–$13.20). AE, MC, V.
Open: Daily 11am–10:30pm.

Before the collapse of the Berlin Wall, this cavernous old-fashioned beer hall was one of the most popular lunchtime venues in the eastern sector. Today, its location overlooking the Alexanderplatz and its reasonable prices guarantee a rollicking business throughout the lunch and dinner hours. Forget about cuisine moderne here. What you get is typical home-style Berliner cookery, with such dishes as knuckle of pork with pickled cabbage, thick pea soup, potato pancakes, various types of smoked Wurst, and Sauerbraten with dumplings.

KREUZBERG

MODERATE

EXIL, Paul-Lincke-Ufer 44A. Tel. 030/612-70-37.
   Cuisine: AUSTRIAN. **Reservations:** Required. **U-Bahn:** Kottbusser Tor.
$ Prices: Appetizers 8.50 DM–16.50 DM ($5.60–$10.90); main courses 20.50 DM–40.50 DM ($13.50–$26.70). No credit cards.
   Open: Tues–Sun 7pm–3am (kitchen closes at 1am).

Exil is appropriately named. It's in the Kreuzberg sector. This sector for at least two decades or more has been the haven of guest workers, such as Turks and Yugoslavs, but now is acquiring a different reputation among certain fashionable people, including artists and writers, who want to avoid tourist haunts. A lot of people connected with the theater come here, and in summer they can sit outside and enjoy a table placed along the canal bank. Of course, the weather has to cooperate; otherwise, guests retreat inside to order traditional Austrian cuisine, including Tafelspitz, boiled beef with horseradish sauce. The portions are extremely generous.

MUNDART, Muskauerstrasse 33–34. Tel. 030/61-22-061.
   Cuisine: CONTINENTAL. **Reservations:** Recommended. **U-Bahn:** Kottbusser Tor.
$ Prices: Appetizers 12 DM–30 DM ($7.90–$19.80); main courses 26 DM–32 DM ($17.20–$21.10). No credit cards.
   Open: Dinner only, Wed–Sun 6:30–11pm.

The Mundart is a bit of a discovery—a straightforward restaurant. Decidedly informal, the place has a simple but tasteful decor and food that's prepared fresh daily. All the dishes I've sampled have been well made, well sauced, and well flavored. These include terrine of venison with mustard sauce and, for a main dish, rumpsteak or Tafelspitz.

SPECIALTY DINING

HOTEL DINING

Moderate

BELLE ÉPOQUE, in the Savoy, Fasanenstrasse 9–10. Tel. 030/311-03-0.
   Cuisine: FRENCH. **Reservations:** Recommended. **U-Bahn:** Kurfürstendamm.
$ Prices: Appetizers 10.50 DM–23 DM ($6.90–$15.20); main courses 28 DM–40 DM ($18.50–$26.40). AE, DC, MC, V.
   Open: Lunch daily noon–3pm; dinner daily 6–11:30pm.

On the ground floor of this previously recommended first-class hotel is one of the finest hotel dining rooms in Berlin. The Belle Époque lives up to its name with a turn-of-the-century ambience of champagne, white colors, and crystal chandeliers—all in a Berlin landmark that survived World War II bombs. Everything is prepared to order, and only the finest and freshest ingredients are used. Watch for the weekly specials, as they tend to follow seasonal changes in the market. For example, when spring asparagus comes in, it appears on the menu in many variations. Or from September to December, you are likely to be treated to game specialties, including pheasant or deer. One week will be devoted to Hungarian cuisine, another to the table of Norway.

The chefs are also aware of calorie-conscious patrons, so many dishes reflect a lighthearted approach. Typical menu selections include king prawns provençal style, with mushroom rice and chicory salad; tender pot-roasted chicken with mushrooms; and médaillons of venison with chanterelles. One salad recently enjoyed was made with forest mushrooms, avocado, and grapefruit sections. Several dishes are served flambé style, including luscious crêpes Suzette with walnut ice cream.

GRILLRESTAURANT, in the Hotel Metropol, Friedrichstrasse 150–153. Tel. 030/203-07-272.
   Cuisine: INTERNATIONAL. **Reservations:** Recommended. **S-Bahn:** Friedrich-strasse.
$ **Prices:** Appetizers 8 DM–15 DM ($5.30–$9.90); main courses 26 DM–32 DM ($17.20–$21.10). AE, DC, MC, V.
   Open: Dinner only, daily 5pm–midnight.
This cosmopolitan spot attracts everybody from Japanese industrialists to the Western expense-account circuit. The savory cuisine depends on fresh ingredients. The setting is on the lobby level of this previously recommended hotel, an elegant decor with dark modern paneling and polished stone. Specialties from the charcoal grill include venison steak with cranberries, served with chanterelles, and filet steak filled with beef marrow and coated with béarnaise sauce. You might also enjoy larded filet of rabbit in sherry-flavored cream sauce. Two persons can order braised knuckle of veal in cream sauce. Some dishes are smoked on the premises, including wild boar ham. Desserts feature chocolate mousse and a salad of fresh fruits.

DINING WITH A VIEW

Expensive

AU LAC, in the Seehof Berlin, Lietzensee Ufer 11. Tel. 030/32-00-20.
   Cuisine: CONTINENTAL. **Reservations:** Required summer; recommended other times. **U-Bahn:** Sophie-Charlotteplatz.
$ **Prices:** Appetizers 14 DM–26 DM ($9.20–$17.20); main courses 36 DM–45 DM ($23.80–$29.70); fixed-price lunch 45 DM ($29.70); fixed-price dinner 75 DM ($49.50). AE, DC, MC, V.
   Open: Lunch daily noon–3pm; dinner daily 6–11:30pm.
Under a lavishly frescoed ceiling, with a medieval theme, diners enjoy one of the best views in western Berlin. The terrace overlooks the lake, complete with willow trees and swans. Additional satellite dining rooms are available for more intimate dinners. The setting is airy and bright, with dusty-rose and beige furnishings, in a sort of Italian provincial style. The menu changes based on seasonal ingredients, but you can count on such dishes as the famous Berliner Kartoffelsuppe (potato soup) or Tafelspitz (boiled beef) in the style revered by the last emperor of Austria. Main dishes might include entrecôte in red-wine sauce or a perfectly done rack of lamb. Desserts tend to be luscious, like the Grand Marnier parfait with orange sauce.

LATE-NIGHT DINING

Moderate

HEINZ HOLL, Damaschkestrasse 26. Tel. 030/323-14-04.

Cuisine: GERMAN. **Reservations:** Required. **U-Bahn:** Adenauerplatz.
$ **Prices:** Appetizers 10.50 DM–25 DM ($6.90–$16.50); main courses 21.50 DM–35 DM ($14.20–$23.10). AE, MC.
Open: Mon–Sat 7pm–1am. **Closed:** Holidays; July 13–Aug 7.

West of the center, Heinz Holl has gained a reputation as a select dining spot and somewhat of a social center. Your host is Heinz Holl, who has a devoted local following among theater and media personalities. Savor the recipes that much of Berlin seems to want, including a stuffed cabbage roll so large it could feed a family of four. Other main courses include venison Gulasch, Tafelspitz, and veal Stroganoff. You might begin with potato soup with wild mushrooms. All the action takes place in a charmingly cluttered Berlin bistro ambience. The place, which has both a front and a back room (you're exiled to Siberia there), is decorated with kitsch from all over the world, including a 1984 Florida license plate.

RESTE FIDELE, Bleibtreustrasse 41. Tel. 030/881-16-05.
Cuisine: CONTINENTAL. **Reservations:** Recommended. **S-Bahn:** Savigny-platz.
$ **Prices:** Appetizers 6 DM–15 DM ($4–$9.90); main courses 20 DM–29 DM ($13.20–$19.10). AE, DC, MC, V.
Open: Daily 11am–2am.

The establishment's French name is a translation of the name of the street on which it is located. Most of its allure and energy are produced by a Croat, Ivan Vranjes, who runs it. He offers a successful and charming re-creation of a French bistro in red-walled rooms whose timbered ceilings evoke a country inn. You can enjoy smoked eel, filet of wild goose with cranberries, mixed fish platters, and some of the best rumpsteak (prepared in about six ways) in Berlin.

DINING WITH A VIEW

Expensive

FUNKTURM, Messedamm. Tel. 030/303-829-96.
Cuisine: CONTINENTAL. **Reservations:** Required. **Bus:** 104, 105, 110, or 149. **U-Bahn:** Kaiserdamm.
$ **Prices:** Appetizers 12.50 DM–29 DM ($8.30–$19.10); main courses 32 DM–45 DM ($21.10–$29.70). AE, DC, MC, V.
Open: Lunch daily noon–3pm; dinner daily 6–10pm.

Dining in towers enjoys a vogue in Germany. Berlin is not without its high-rise cuisine, and the Funkturm scores by serving a good continental cuisine, but the local Berlin dishes are most notable. Try, for example, braised leg of beef with mixed vegetables and potatoes. A more international offering is the sole meunière. Lobster soup, cream of potato soup, or duck consommé makes a good beginning.

Moderate

FERNSEHTURM, Alexanderplatz. Tel. 030/24-040.
Cuisine: GERMAN. **Reservations:** Not accepted. **S-Bahn:** Alexanderplatz.
$ **Prices:** Appetizers 8 DM–16 DM ($5.30–$10.60); main courses 22 DM–40 DM ($14.50–$26.40). MC, V.
Open: Tele-Café on top of the tower, daily 8am–11pm. Main restaurant, daily 10am–midnight. Café, Sun–Thurs 10am–10pm, Fri–Sat 10am–1am. Self-service restaurant on ground level, daily 6am–midnight.

Since Fernsehturm is housed in the television tower, you can visit its Tele-Café just for the view and coffee. For more serious dining, there is the main restaurant, featuring such specialties as herring filets in apple-cream sauce, pork cutlets with ham and cheese, and a fish platter. Adjoining it is Tagescafé, where you can order coffee, cake, and ice cream. On the ground level is a self-service restaurant where you can order pea soup with Bockwurst, a typical dish of pigs' trotters with sauerkraut and potato salad. Young Berliners come here for evening dancing to contemporary music.

VEGETARIAN
Inexpensive

LA MASKERA, Gustaf Müller Strasse 1. Tel. 030/784-12-27.
   Cuisine: VEGETARIAN. **Reservations:** Not necessary. **U-Bahn:** Kleistpark.
$ **Prices:** Appetizers 8 DM–12 DM ($5.30–$7.90); main courses 10 DM–25 DM ($6.60–$16.50). V.
   Open: Dinner only, daily 5pm–midnight.

Established in 1972, La Maskera has been a consistently popular vegetarian restaurant. Set on the street level of an old-fashioned building, it contains two dining rooms, one reserved for nonsmokers. Depending on the evening, music may range from recorded versions of Edith Piaf to modern jazz. Only dinner is served, usually accompanied by beer or wine. You can select from an array of antipasti, followed by an al dente version of Mediterranean verduro misto with cream sauce; whole-grain pizzas (said to be the only ones of their kind in Berlin); and several preparations of tofu, including one with Gorgonzola sauce.

LOCAL FAVORITES
Moderate

BLOCKHAUS NIKOLSKOE, Nikolskoer Weg (route B-39), Wannsee. Tel. 030/805-29-14.
   Cuisine: GERMAN/RUSSIAN. **Reservations:** Recommended. **Directions:** S-Bahn to Wannsee suburb, then bus A6 to Nikolskoer-Weg stop, then walk to restaurant through a forest.
$ **Prices:** Appetizers 8 DM–22 DM ($5.30–$14.50); main courses 18 DM–38.50 DM ($11.90–$25.40); fixed-price menu 35 DM–85.50 DM ($23.10–$56.40). AE, DC, MC, V.
   Open: May–Oct, Fri–Wed 10am–10pm; Nov–Apr, Fri–Wed 10am–8pm.

⑤ This restaurant, at Am Wannsee und an der Havel, is a holdover from the Berlin of yesterday. The ancestors of present-day Berliners came here on a summer weekend to drink schnapps and beer on the terraces overlooking the Havel River. The elaborate trim on the log cabin that gives this place its name dates from 1819. It's patterned in the Russian style after the original was rebuilt following a fire. Historians tell me the house was a present from King Friedrich Wilhelm III to his daughter, Charlotte, on the occasion of her wedding to the man who was later to become Czar Nicholas I. Nicholas, after accepting the gift from his father-in-law, commissioned the construction of a Russian church, Peter-Pauls-Kirche, on a nearby hill. You can choose to sit either on the sun terrace or inside the wooden-walled dining room, with a ceramic stove at one end. Many come here just to order drinks or to have salads, sandwiches, and Würste on the terrace.

Inexpensive

GROSSBEERENKELLER, Grossbeerenstrasse 90, Kreuzberg. Tel. 030/251-30-64.
   Cuisine: GERMAN. **Reservations:** Recommended. **U-Bahn:** Möckern Brücke.
$ **Prices:** Appetizers 7.50 DM–15 DM ($5–$9.90); main courses 15 DM–32 DM ($9.90–$21.10); three-course fixed-price menu 40 DM ($26.40). No credit cards.
   Open: Mon–Fri 4pm–2am, Sat 6pm–2am. **Closed:** July 5–27.

This underground Keller in a historic century-old restaurant escaped the World War II bombings. You'll see people here who have probably been mentioned in the Berlin newspapers in recent months, many of them prominent in politics and the arts. Dozens of beer steins hang from the rafters, their images dimly reflected in the polished paneling of the walls. Specialties are bacon or herring salad with scrambled eggs; a tempting selection of steaming hot soups (homemade every day); steaks and Schnitzels; and enough combinations of Knockwurst, hot or cold, to make any Prussian happy. You'll find it most crowded for late-night suppers.

SUNDAY BRUNCH
Expensive

ALTER MARKT, in the Hotel Schweizerhof, Budapesterstrasse 21–31. Tel. 030/269-60.
 Cuisine: BUFFET BRUNCH. **Reservations:** Required. **U-Bahn:** Bahnhof Zoologischer Garten.
$ Prices: Fixed-price brunch 50 DM ($33) adults, 25 DM ($16.50) children under 12. AE, DC, MC, V.
 Open: Sunday noon–3pm. **Closed:** July–Aug.
Perhaps the finest place for an old-fashioned Sunday brunch, Berliner-style, the Alter Markt looks like a large market. In fair weather, guests enjoy the terrace. The Sunday brunch is a large buffet with almost every dish associated with breakfast, ranging from freshly baked French croissants to dark and grainy Berliner breads, from smoked ham to scrambled eggs, from Swiss-style Muesli to fruit yogurts. Often a jazz band entertains, and one section is a kiddies' corner with toys.

PICNIC FARE & WHERE TO EAT IT

The best place to secure the makings for a delectable picnic is at the leading department store of Berlin, **KaDeWe** (Kaufhaus des Westens), Wittenbergplatz (tel. 21-210), which is noted for its sprawling sixth-floor food emporium. Here you'll be tempted with an array of items ranging from the freshest of breads and fruits to grilled chicken, sausage, salad, and Leberkäs. You can also buy a bottle of wine or soft drinks and juices. The store is open Monday through Friday from 9am to 6:30pm and Saturday from 9am to 2pm.

The best place for that picnic is the **Tiergarten** of Berlin, a park and "green lung" stretching northwest of Bahnhof Zoo.

 ## FROMMER'S COOL FOR KIDS: RESTAURANTS

Jimmy's Diner *(see page 529)* When your kid demands Stateside burgers and hungers for tacos and enchiladas, take him or her to this 1950s American-style diner.

Fernsehturm *(see page 541)* Kids delight in going to the top of this television tower. Later, on the ground level you can enjoy inexpensive self-service food, with very good ice cream for dessert.

Blockhaus Nikolskoe *(see page 542)* Ever since King Friedrich Wilhelm III gave this place to his daughter, Charlotte, Berliners have been taking their kids here to dine while overlooking the Havel River.

CHAPTER 18

WHAT TO SEE & DO IN BERLIN

In the midst of the daily whirl of working, shopping, dining, and entertainment, Berliners along the Kurfürstendamm in the western part of the city often glance at a sobering reminder of less happy days. At the end of the street stands the **Kaiser Wilhelm Memorial Church,** Breitscheidplatz (tel. 24-50-23), severely damaged in World War II. Only the shell of the old Neo-Romanesque bell tower (1895) remains. You can wander through the ruins Tuesday through Saturday from 10am to 4:30pm. In striking contrast to the ruins, a new church has been constructed west of the old tower, seating 1,200 people in its octagonal hall, and lit solely by the thousands of colored-glass windows set into the honeycomb framework. Dedicated in 1961, the church has an overall look best described by the nickname given it by Berliners, "lipstick and powder box." Ten-minute services are held in the church daily at 5:30 and 6pm for those going home from work. A Saturday concert is staged at 6pm. U-Bahn: Kurfürstendamm. An English-language worship service is held daily at 9am from June through August.

This remarkable combination of old and new is what Berlin is all about. Although there is more new than old in this city, which suffered perhaps more than any other European metropolis (except Warsaw) during World War II, Berlin offers a multitude of sights for the visitor.

SUGGESTED ITINERARIES

If You Have 1 Day   Rise early and visit the Brandenburg Gate, symbol of Berlin, and walk down Unter den Linden, having coffee and pastry at the Operncafé. Then head for Dahlem to visit the Gemäldegalerie, seeing some of the world's greatest masterpieces. Afterward, go to Charlottenburg Palace and its museums to see the celebrated bust of Queen Nefertiti in the Egyptian Museum. In the evening walk along the Kurfürstendamm, visit the Kaiser Wilhelm Memorial Church, and dine in a local restaurant.

If You Have 2 Days   Spend Day 1 as outlined above. On Day 2, return to eastern Berlin and visit the Pergamon Museum on Museum Island, seeing the Pergamon Altar. Explore the National Gallery and the Bode Museum, and then head for Alexanderplatz. Take the elevator up for a view from its television tower, before exploring Nikolai Quarter on foot.

If You Have 3 Days Spend Days 1 and 2 as outlined above. On Day 3, go to Potsdam (see Chapter 19).

If You Have 5 Days Spend Days 1 through 3 as outlined above. On Day 4, return to the museums of Dahlem, this time to visit the Sculpture Gallery and the Ethnographical Museum in the morning. In the afternoon return to Charlottenburg Palace and explore the Historical Apartments and in the evening visit the modern Europa-Center for drinks and dinner. On Day 5, "mop up" some of the sights you might have missed. Take both of our walking tours of Berlin (see below) and call at the Cold War's Checkpoint Charlie, with its Museum Haus am Checkpoint Charlie. If time remains, visit the Berlin Zoo and attend a cabaret in the evening.

1. THE TOP ATTRACTIONS

MUSEUMS

The old Berlin of prewar days was proud of its fine art museums. But war doesn't respect persons or objects, and the art collections of Berlin suffered during and after World War II. Although many paintings were stored in inoperative salt mines during the war, many larger works, including eight paintings by Rubens and three by Van Dyck, were destroyed by fire. Part of the surviving art stayed in the East, including a wealth of ancient art, treasures that remind us of the leading position held by German archeologists in the 19th and 20th centuries in the study of ancient civilizations. Of the paintings relegated to the West, which passed from nation to nation in the late 1940s like so many decks of cards, most have now been returned to Berlin and are permanently ensconced in the Dahlem Picture Gallery.

THE DAHLEM MUSEUMS, Arnimallee 23–27. Tel. 030/83-01-1.
The **Gemäldegalerie (Picture Gallery)** is one of Germany's finest galleries. Of the nearly 1,500 paintings in its possession, more than 600 are on display.
The ground floor has several rooms devoted to early German masters, with panels from altarpieces dating from the 13th, 14th, and 15th centuries. Note the panel of *The Virgin Enthroned with Child* (1350), surrounded by angels that resemble the demons so popular in the later works of Hieronymus Bosch. Eight paintings make up the Dürer collection in the adjacent rooms, including several portraits.
Two contemporaries of Dürer, Albrecht Altdorfer and Lucas Cranach the Elder, are represented by paintings of *The Rest on the Flight into Egypt*. Note the contrasts between the two works, the former in the Renaissance style, with a town as the background setting and tiny angels playing in an elegant fountain in the foreground. Cranach, on the other hand, chose a quiet pastoral setting and confined the colors and action to the characters themselves.
Another ground-floor gallery is given over entirely to Italian painting. Here are five Raphael madonnas, works by Titian (*The Girl with a Bowl of Fruit*), Fra Filippo Lippi, Botticelli, and Correggio (*Leda with the Swan*). Also there are early Netherlands paintings from the 15th and 16th centuries (van Eyck, van der Weyden, van der Goes, Bosch, and Brueghel).
The floor above is devoted mainly to Flemish and Dutch masters of the 17th century, with no fewer than 15 works by Rembrandt alone. Among the most famous of the great painter's works in the Dahlem is the warmly human *Head of Christ*. One painting, famous for years as a priceless Rembrandt, *The Man with the Golden Helmet,* was proved by radioactive testing in 1986 to be by some other painter of Rembrandt's era who imitated the master's style. This remarkable painting is now accepted as an independent original. Several portraits and biblical scenes make up the

❓ DID YOU KNOW . . . ?

- In 1920, at the peak of German inflation, the U.S. dollar traded in Berlin at 4.20 billion marks.
- In 1945, 98 million cubic yards of Berlin wartime rubble made up one-seventh of all the debris in Germany. In all, the Allies dropped 45,000 tons of bombs on Berlin.
- Berliners have 5 dogs per 100 inhabitants.
- Berlin is the city with the most Turkish inhabitants outside Turkey.
- Berliners call Otto Lilienthal, an engineer and factory owner, "the first flying human being" because his flying machines lifted 100 yards above the ground.
- In Berlin, every 10th inhabitant is a foreigner.
- From 1966 to his suicide in 1987, Rudolf Hess was the only prisoner at Spandau Prison, whose upkeep cost 1 million DM yearly.

balance of this excellent collection. Although several works by Rubens were burned during the war, you can still see 19 on display here, including the charming *Child with a Bird* and one of his landscapes, showing milkmaids tending cattle.

The rest of the building is occupied by several other exhibitions, including the **Sculpture Gallery,** with 1,200 works, including a bas-relief in Carrara marble by Donatello of a serene *Madonna and Child* (1422). The **Prints and Drawings Collection** contains several pen-and-ink drawings by Dürer, including his signed (1511) sketch of *The Holy Family at Rest.* There are 150 drawings by Rembrandt.

Museum für Völkerkunde (Ethnographical Museum) houses arts and artifacts from Africa, the Far East, the South Seas, and South America. Many of the figures and ritualistic masks are grotesquely beautiful, presenting a striking contrast in art, especially after a visit to the gallery of paintings. In addition to all the above museums, the Dahlem houses the **Museums of Far Eastern Art, Islamic Art,** and **Indian Art.**

The museum has a good restaurant where you can have hot meals, including meat, potatoes, and salads, daily from 11:30am to 2:30pm as well as cold dishes for the rest of the day during museum hours.

Admission: 4 DM ($2.60) adults, 2 DM ($1.30) children.

Open: All collections, Tues–Fri 9am–5pm, Sat–Sun 10am–5pm. **Bus:** 101, 110, or 180. **U-Bahn:** Dahlem-Dorf.

SCHLOSS CHARLOTTENBURG (CHARLOTTENBURG PALACE) & MUSEUMS

Charlottenburg lies in the quarter of Berlin of the same name, just west of the Tiergarten. In addition to viewing the exhaustive collections in the palace buildings, you can enjoy a relaxing ramble through Schlossgarten Charlottenburg, where, just a few years ago, lay a field of mud and swampland created by the ravages of war. The gardens have been restored and landscaped much as they were in the days of Friedrich Wilhelm II. In the formal gardens are two rows of cypresses leading to a lake complete with swans and other waterfowl. To the west of the cypress grove, between the English Gardens and the Prehistory Museum, stands the **Mausoleum,** practically unharmed during the war. Beneath its small temple are the tombs of King Friedrich Wilhelm II and Queen Luise, sculptured by Rauch, as well as several other interesting funerary monuments of the Prussian royal family.

SCHLOSS CHARLOTTENBURG, Luisenplatz. Tel. 030/32-09-11.

⭐ Perhaps Napoleon exaggerated a bit in comparing Schloss Charlottenburg to the great Versailles when he invaded Berlin in 1806, but in its heyday Charlottenburg was the most elegant residence for the Prussian rulers outside the castle in Potsdam. Begun in 1695 as a summer palace for the Electress Sophie Charlotte, patron of philosophy and the arts and wife of King Frederick I (Elector Frederick III), the little residence got out of hand until it grew

DAHLEM MUSEUMS

TOP FLOOR
(not shown)
Prints and Drawings
Collection
Museum für Völkerkunde
(East Asia)

UPPER FLOOR
3 Museum für Völkerkunde
  (South Seas)
4 Skulpturengalerie
5 Gemäldegalerie
6 Museum für Völkerkunde
  (Africa)
7 Museum für Islamische Kunst
8 Museum für Ostasiatische
  Kunst
9 Museum für Völkerkunde
  (South Asia)
10 Special exhibitions

GROUND FLOOR
1 Museum für Indische Kunst
2 Museum für Völkerkunde
  (America)
3 Museum für Völkerkunde
  (South Seas)
4 Skulpturengalerie
5 Gemäldegalerie

LOWER FLOOR
A Lecture Room
B Young People's Museum
C Cafeteria
D Museum for the Blind

UPPER FLOOR
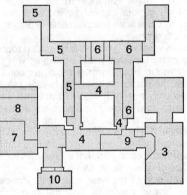

GROUND FLOOR
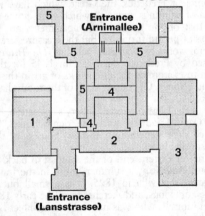

Entrance
(Arnimallee)

Entrance
(Lansstrasse)

LOWER FLOOR

into the massive structure you see today, branching out in long, narrow wings from the main building. When you visit the palace, you should plan on spending the day, since it contains not only the royal apartments but several museums as well.

When you pass the heavy iron gates and enter the courtyard, you'll immediately encounter a baroque equestrian Statue of the Great Elector himself, by Andreas Schlüter. The main entrance to the palace is directly behind, marked by the 157-foot-high cupola capped by a gilded statue of Fortune. Inside, you'll find a columned rotunda with stucco reliefs depicting the virtues of the Prussian princes in mythological terms.

From this vestibule, you can take guided tours of the Historical Apartments. If you wish to prepare for what you'll be seeing, you can buy the English translation of the guide's lecture in book form at the ticket counter.

Parts of the palace were badly damaged during the war, but most of it has now been completely restored. Many furnishings were saved, especially the works of art, and are again on display. The main wing contains the apartments of Frederick I and his "philosopher queen." Of special interest in this section is the **Reception Chamber,** in the left projection of the wing. This large room is decorated with frieze panels, vaulted ceilings, and mirror-paneled niches. The tapestries on the walls (1730) depict men featured in Plutarch's *Lives*. Included are scenes of Pericles in battle and the sacrifice of Theseus on Delos.

At the far end of the west wing is the **Porcelain Chamber,** which is decorated solely by various pieces of Oriental porcelain, hung on the walls, standing on pedestals, some even partly inserted into the walls or suspended by metal rings. The unusual effect is heightened by the profusion of mirrors.

The **New Wing** (Knobelsdorff Flügel), built from 1740 to 1746, contains the apartments of Frederick the Great, which have in essence been converted into a museum of paintings, many of which were either collected or commissioned by the king. Most of the ground-floor apartments are galleries of portraits mixed with examples of period furniture, but the treasures are on the upper floor. Here you can see several works by Watteau, including *The Trade Sign of the Art Dealer Gersaint,* purchased by Frederick the Great in 1745 for the concert hall of the palace. In addition to examining the fine works of art in this wing, note the decoration on the walls and ceilings. Of course, many of the rooms have been virtually reproduced since the war.

Part of the New National Gallery's collection, the early 19th-century paintings of Caspar David Friedrich, Karl Friedrich Schinkel, Karl Blechen, Karl Spitzweg, and others of their generations, is now housed in the Galerie der Romantik in the Knobelsdorff Flügel.

At the far eastern end of the schloss, in back of the Knobelsdorff-Flügel, is the **Schinkel Pavilion,** a summer house in the Italian style. Karl Friedrich Schinkel constructed this villa in 1825. It is a small but noteworthy museum, containing paintings, drawings, and sketches from the early 1800s—some of the sketches are by Schinkel himself, who was not only an architect but also an artist.

At the far end of Schlossgarten Charlottenburg is the **Belvedere,** close to the River Spree. This former royal teahouse presents an exhibition of exquisite Berlin porcelain, much of it from the 1700s.

Tours: Guided tours of the Historical Rooms (in German), Tues–Sun 10am–5pm, leaving every hour. Combined ticket for all buildings and historical rooms, 8 DM ($5.30) adults, 4 DM ($2.60) children under 14. English translation of guide's lecture on sale at the ticket counter. **U-Bahn:** Sophie-Charlotte-Platz or Richard-Wagner-Platz. **Bus:** 109, 121, 145, or 204.

ÄGYPTISCHES MUSEUM, Schlossstrasse 70. Tel. 030/320-91-261.

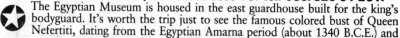

The Egyptian Museum is housed in the east guardhouse built for the king's bodyguard. It's worth the trip just to see the famous colored bust of Queen Nefertiti, dating from the Egyptian Amarna period (about 1340 B.C.E.) and

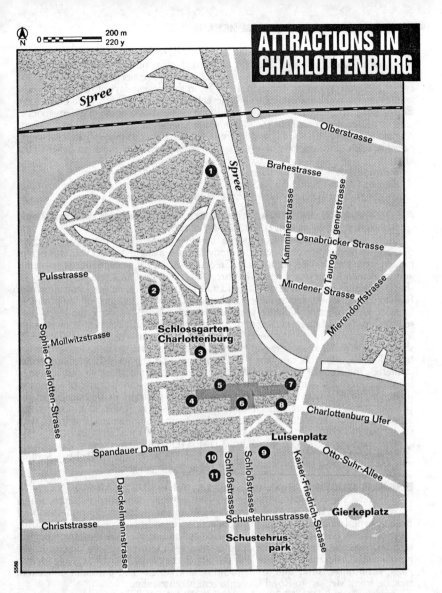

ATTRACTIONS IN CHARLOTTENBURG

Spree

Olberstrasse

Brahestrasse

Kamminerstrasse

Osnabrücker Strasse

Taurog-generstrasse

Pulsstrasse

Mindener Strasse

Mierendorffstrasse

Sophie-Charlotten-Strasse

Mollwitzstrasse

Schlossgarten Charlottenburg

Spree

Schinkel Pavilion

Charlottenburg Ufer

Luisenplatz

Spandauer Damm

Otto-Suhr-Allee

Kaiser-Friedrich-Strasse

Schloßstrasse

Danckelmannstrasse

Christstrasse

Schustehrusstrasse

Gierkeplatz

Schustehrus-park

BERLIN

Charlottenburg

Ägyptisches Museum ❾	Museum für Vor- und Frühgeschichte ❹
Antikensammlung ❿	Schinkel Pavilion ❼
Belvedere ❶	Schloss Charlottenburg ❺
Bröhan Museum ⓫	Schlossgarten Charlottenburg ❸
New Wing (Knobelsdorff-Flügel) ❽	Statue of the Great Elector ❻
Mausoleum ❷	

discovered in 1912. The bust, stunning in every way, is all by itself in a dark first-floor room, illuminated by a spotlight. It is believed that the bust never left the studio in which it was created but served as a model for other portraits of the queen. The left eye of Nefertiti was never drawn in. In 1945, in the closing days of the war the bust was mysteriously taken from East Berlin, eventually to turn up here. In addition, look for the head of Queen Tiy and the world-famous head of a priest in green stone.

The museum also contains the monumental Kalabasha Gateway built by Emperor Augustus around 30 B.C.E., a gift from Egypt. Other displays feature jewelry, papyrus, tools, and weapons, as well as objects relating to the Egyptian belief in the afterlife.

Admission: 4 DM ($2.60) adults, 2 DM ($1.30) children.

Open: Mon–Thurs 9am–5pm, Sat–Sun 10am–5pm. **U-Bahn:** Sophie-Charlotte-Platz or Richard-Wagner-Platz. **Bus:** 9, 54, 62, or 74.

ANTIKENSAMMLUNG [Museum of Greek and Roman Antiquities], Schlossstrasse 1. Tel. 030/320-91-215.

In the west guardhouse, just opposite the Egyptian Museum, this great collection of world-famous works of antique decorative art was inaugurated in 1960. It is rich in pottery from ancient Greece and Italy; Greek, Etruscan, and Roman bronze statuettes and implements; ivory carvings, glassware, objects in precious stone, and jewelry of the Mediterranean region, as well as gold and silver treasures; mummy portraits from Roman Egypt, wood and stone sarcophagi, and a small number of sculptures in marble. The collection includes some of the finest Greek vases of the black- and red-figured style dating from the 6th to the 4th century B.C.E. The best-known vase is a large Athenian wine jar (amphora) found in Vulci, Etruria, dating from 490 B.C.E. It shows a satyr with lyre and the god Hermes. As the artist's name is not known, he has been dubbed, after this vase, the "Berlin painter." Of the several excellent bronze statuettes, the Zeus of Dodone (470 B.C.E.) shows the god about to cast a bolt of lightning. From the sculpture department you can see a rare portrait of Cleopatra (from Alexandria) that is one of the three known portraits of this queen. In the Brandenburg-Prussian art collection, acquired in 1698 in Rome, is an exceptional bronze statue of the goddess Luna descending from the firmament. It is inlaid with silver, and in 1871 the Prussians dubbed it "the pearl of the collection."

Admission: 4 DM ($2.60) adults, 2 DM ($1.30) children.

Open: Mon–Thurs 9am–5pm, Sat–Sun 10am–5pm. **U-Bahn:** Sophie-Charlotte-Platz or Richard-Wagner-Platz. **Bus:** 9, 54, 62, or 74.

BRÖHAN MUSEUM, Schlosstrasse 1A. Tel. 030/321-40-29.

Adjoining the Antikensammlung, this is a privately controlled museum, which makes it unique in the Charlottenburg family of museums. It honors a professor, Karl Bröhan, who launched this Jugendstil collection. Jugendstil (named for the magazine *Jugend*) is the German version of art nouveau, and at the time Professor Bröhan started collecting, this art was viewed as having little merit. Many objects in the museum date from the end of the 19th century to the eve of World War II and include glass, furnishings, silver and gold, painting, and vases. The porcelain collection, ranging from Meissen to Royal Copenhagen, is outstanding.

Admission: 5 DM ($3.30) adults, 2.50 DM ($1.70) children.

Open: Tues–Sun 10am–6pm. **U-Bahn:** Sophie-Charlotte-Platz or Richard-Wagner-Platz.

MUSEUM FÜR VOR- UND FRÜHGESCHICHTE, Langhansbau. Tel. 030/320-91-233.

This museum of pre- and protohistory, in the western extension of the palace facing Klausener Platz, contains five rooms devoted to art and artifacts discovered mainly in Europe and the Near East. The rooms have exhibits grouped into the ages of man, from 1 million B.C.E. up to the first millennium C.E.

Admission: 4 DM ($2.60) adults, 2 DM ($1.30) children.

Open: Mon–Thurs 9am–5pm, Sat–Sun 10am–5pm. **U-Bahn:** Sophie-Charlotte-Platz or Richard-Wagner-Platz. **Bus:** 9, 54, 62, or 74.

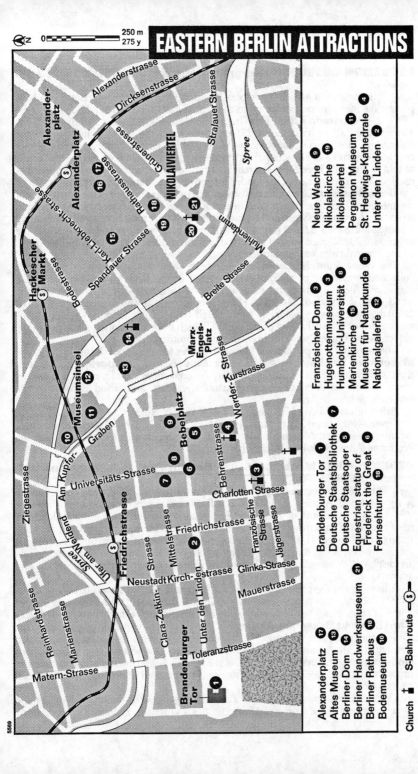

EASTERN BERLIN ATTRACTIONS

0 — 250 m / 275 y

N

Alexanderplatz
Alexanderstrasse
Dircksenstrasse
Stralauer Strasse
Grünerstrasse
Spree
NIKOLAIVIERTEL
Karl-Liebknecht-strasse
Rathausstrasse
Bodestrasse
Spandauer Strasse
Hackescher Markt
Muhlendamm
Breite Strasse
Marx-Engels-Platz
Werder- Strasse
Kurstrasse
Museumsinsel
Am Kupfer-
Graben
Bebelplatz
Behrenstrasse
Ziegestrasse
Universitäts-Strasse
Charlotten Strasse
Am Weiden
Spree am Weiden
Ufer am
Friedrichstrasse
Strasse
Mittelstrasse
Friedrichstrasse
Französische Strasse
Jägerstrasse
Neustadt Kirch-strasse
Glinka-Strasse
Mauerstrasse
Reinhardstrasse
Marienstrasse
Clara-Zetkin-
Unter den Linden
Toleranzstrasse
Matern-Strasse
Brandenburger Tor

Alexanderplatz 17
Altes Museum 13
Berliner Dom 14
Berliner Handwerksmuseum 21
Berliner Rathaus 18
Bodemuseum 10

Brandenburger Tor 1
Deutsche Staatsbibliothek 7
Deutsche Staatsoper 5
Equestrian statue of Frederick the Great 6
Fernsehturm 18

Französicher Dom 3
Hugenottenmuseum 3
Humboldt-Universität 8
Marienkirche 15
Museum für Naturkunde 8
Nationalgalerie 12

Neue Wache 9
Nikolaikirche 19
Nikolaiviertel
Pergamon Museum 11
St. Hedwigs-Kathedrale 4
Unter den Linden 2

✝ ■ **Church**   ⑤ **S-Bahn route**

5569

MUSEUMSINSEL MUSEUMS

PERGAMON MUSEUM, Kupfergraben, Museumsinsel. Tel. 030/203-55-444.

⭐ The Pergamon Museum complex houses several departments. But if you have time for only one exhibit, go to the central hall of the U-shaped building to see the **Pergamon Altar.** This Greek altar (180–160 B.C.E.) is so large that it has a huge room all to itself. Some 27 steps lead from the museum floor up to the colonnade. Most fascinating is the frieze around the base, tediously pieced together over a 20-year period. Depicting the struggle of the Olympian gods against the Titans as told in Hesiod's *Theogony,* the relief is strikingly alive, with its figures projected as much as 6 feet from the background. This, however, is only part of the attraction of the **Department of Greek and Roman Antiquities,** housed in the north wing of the museum. Here you'll also find a Roman market gate discovered in Miletus and sculptures from many Greek and Roman cities, including a statue of a goddess holding a pomegranate (575 B.C.E.) found in southern Attica, where it had lain beneath the ground for 2,000 years. So well preserved was the goddess that you can still see flecks of the original paint on her garments.

The **Near East Museum,** in the south wing, contains one of the largest collections anywhere of antiquities discovered in the lands of ancient Babylonia, Persia, and Assyria. Among the exhibits is the Processional Way of Babylon with the Ishtar Gate, dating from 580 B.C.E.; these monuments, as well as the throne room of Nebuchadnezzar, were decorated with glazed bricks. Cuneiform clay tablets document much of the civilization of the period, which created ceramics, glass, and metal objects while Europe was still overrun with primitive tribes.

The museum's upper level is devoted to the **Museum of Islamic Art,** the **Museum of Far Eastern Art,** and the **Museum of Ethnography.** Although these suffered great losses during the war, the collections contain many noteworthy items. Of special interest are the miniatures, carpets, and wood carvings in the Museum of Islamic Art.

Admission: 4 DM ($2.60) adults, 2 DM ($1.30) children.

Open: Usual hours, daily 9am–5pm. Mon–Tues only parts of museum are open, including Near East Museum and three halls of ancient architecture, including the Pergamon Altar. **S-Bahn:** Hackescher Markt.

BODEMUSEUM, Monbijoubrücke, Bodestrasse 1–3, Museumsinsel. Tel. 030/20355-0.

⭐ The Bodemuseum contains one of the most significant Egyptian collections in the world. At the end of World War II, West Berliners broke up a set when they secured the bust of Nefertiti. The head of her husband, King Akhenaton, remained in the eastern sector, where it is today. Exhibits vary in size from the huge sphinx of Hatshepur (1490 B.C.E.) to fragments of reliefs from Egyptian temples. Of special interest is the Burial Cult Room, where coffins, mummies, and grave objects are displayed along with lifesize X-ray photographs of the mummies of humans and animals.

Adjoining the Egyptian Museum is the **Papyrus Collection,** containing about 25,000 documents of papyrus, ostraca, parchment, limestone, wax, and wood in eight different languages. On the opposite side of the staircase is the **Museum of Early Christian and Byzantine Art,** with a rich display of early Christian sarcophagi, Coptic and Byzantine sculpture, icons, and even gravestones dating from the 3rd through the 18th century. Also on the lower level is a section of the **Sculpture Collection,** with several pieces from the churches and monasteries, including a sandstone pulpit support by Anton Pilgram (1490) carved in the shape of a medieval craftsman.

Upstairs you'll find a part of the **Art Gallery,** devoted mainly to German and Dutch painting of the 15th and 16th centuries and Italian, Flemish, Dutch, English, and French masters of the 14th through the 18th century.

Admission: 4 DM ($2.60) adults, 2 DM ($1.30) children.
Open: Wed–Sun 9am–5pm. **S-Bahn:** Hackescher Markt.

NATIONALGALERIE (National Gallery), Bodestrasse, Museumsinsel. Tel. 030/20-35-50.

The Nationalgalerie mainly contains 19th- and 20th-century painting and sculpture. The Nazi campaign against degenerate art depleted this collection during World War II, but you can still see quite a few works by Cézanne, Rodin, Degas, Liebermann, Tischbein, and Corinth. Many of the German works of the 19th century show scenes of court life at Wilhelm I's "Königsberg." The best of these are by Adolph von Menzel (1815–1905), who also is represented in the numerous sketches and drawings included in the museum. You can also see several paintings by one of Germany's greatest portrait artists, Max Liebermann (1847–1935). On the top floor is a large collection of watercolors, many satirical.

Admission: 4 DM ($2.60) adults, 2 DM ($1.30) children.
Open: Wed–Sun 10am–6pm. **S-Bahn:** Karl-Liebknecht-Platz or Friedrichstrasse.

TIERGARTEN MUSEUMS

NEUE NATIONALGALERIE (New National Gallery), Potsdamerstrasse 50. Tel. 030/2666.

In its modern glass-and-steel home designed by Ludwig Miès van der Rohe (1886–1969), just south of the Tiergarten, the Neue Nationalgalerie, a continually growing collection of contemporary art, European as well as American, is a sort of sequel to the art at Dahlem. Here are works of 19th- and 20th-century artists, with a concentration on such French impressionists as Manet, Renoir, Monet, and Pissarro. The collection of German artwork starts with Adolph von Menzel's paintings from about 1850.

The 20th-century collection includes works by Max Beckmann, Edvard Munch, and E. L. Kirchner—*Brandenburger Tor* (1929) is among the most popular—as well as a few paintings by Francis Bacon, Dufy, Picasso, Max Ernst, and Paul Klee, as well as American artists, such as Barnett Newman.

The hours of food service in the **café** on the ground floor are similar to the opening hours. Hot meals are served only between 11:30am to 3pm.

Admission: Permanent collection, 4 DM ($2.60) adults, 2 DM ($1.30) children; temporary exhibitions, 4 DM–8 DM ($2.60–$5.30).
Open: Tues–Fri 9am–5pm, Sat–Sun 10am–5pm. **Closed:** Jan 1; May 1; Dec 24–25 and 31; Tues after Easter and Whitsunday. **Bus:** 34, 129, 148, or 248. **U-Bahn:** Kurfürstenstrasse.

KUNSTGEWERBEMUSEUM, Matthäikirchplatz. Tel. 030/266-29-02.

Opposite the Philharmonie is the Kunstgewerbemuseum, a museum of applied art and crafts. Room after room is devoted to domestic and ecclesiastical art from the Middle Ages through the 20th century. Its most outstanding exhibition is the Guelph Treasure, a collection of medieval church treasures in gold and silver. In the basement are rooms devoted to contemporary design from the Bauhaus to Charles Eames and Memphis. Collections of Venetian glass, Italian majolica, and German Renaissance goldsmiths' work, as well as 18th-century porcelain figurines, are outstanding. The treasures include such art nouveau works as a translucent opal-and-enamel box by Eugène Feuillâtre. The cafeteria is open from 10am to 4:30pm.

Admission: 4 DM ($2.60) adults, 2 DM ($1.30) children.
Open: Tues–Fri 9am–5pm, Sat–Sun 10am–5pm. **U-Bahn:** Kurfürstenstrasse. **S-Bahn:** Potsdamer Platz. **Bus:** 129, 142, 148, 248, or 348.

MUSIKINSTRUMENTEN MUSEUM (Museum of Musical Instruments), Tiergartenstrasse 1. Tel. 030/25-48-10.

In 1888, a well-meaning group of musicologists established a museum devoted to the preservation of antique musical instruments. During World War II, both the museum building and many of its exhibits were fire-bombed. The postwar German economic boom, however, replenished this organization's inventory and procured a new premises in the Tiergarten. Today, the museum contains valuable musical instruments from the Renaissance and the baroque era—including a collection of charmingly decorated harpsichords; clavichords; spinets; trombones; harps; zithers; guitars; and the almost-forgotten glass harmonica, for which Mozart and some of his contemporaries wrote compositions. Although set behind glass, some of the instruments lie adjacent to recording machines that reproduce some of their curiously tinny sounds.

Admission: Free.
Open: Tues–Fri 9am–5pm, Sat–Sun 10am–5pm. **Closed:** Jan 1, Tues after Easter and after Whitsunday, May 1, Dec 24–25 and 31. **U-Bahn:** Kurfürstenstrasse, then bus 148 or 248. **Bus:** 129 from the Ku'damm.

2. MORE ATTRACTIONS

OTHER MUSEUMS

BRÜCKE-MUSEUM, Bussardsteig 9. Tel. 030/831-20-29.

A considerable proportion of the work of Karl Schmidt-Rottluff is displayed in this one-story museum at the edge of the Grünewald, along with the works of a group of expressionist artists known as *Die Brücke* (The Bridge), who gathered in Dresden in 1905. One of my favorite German artists, Ernst Ludwig Kirchner (1880–1938), was the leader of Die Brücke. His pictures were sharply patterned and colored, the figures distorted. The Nazi government burned many of his paintings, and before the outbreak of World War II he committed suicide.

Admission: 4 DM ($2.60) adults, 2 DM ($1.30) children.
Open: Wed–Mon 11am–5pm. **Bus:** 129. **U-Bahn:** Dahlem-Dorf.

BERLIN MUSEUM, Lindenstrasse 14. Tel. 030/2586-28-39.

The Berlin Museum is housed in what was once the Court of Justice, built in late baroque style in 1735. These former law courts have been converted into a museum of the city of Berlin, with exhibits depicting the life of its citizenry from the 17th to the 20th century.

Admission: 4 DM ($2.60) adults, 2 DM ($1.30) children.
Open: Tues–Sun 10am–10pm. **U-Bahn:** Hallesches Tor, then bus 141, or a 10-minute walk.

KÄTHE-KOLLWITZ-MUSEUM, Fasanenstrasse 24. Tel. 030/882-52-10.

Probably more than any other museum in Germany, this one reflects the individual sorrow of the artist whose work it contains. Some visitors call it a personalized revolt against the agonies of war, as well as a welcome change from the unrelenting commercialism of the nearby Ku'damm. Established in 1986, it was inspired by Berlin-born Käthe Kollwitz—ardent socialist, feminist, and pacifist—whose stormy social commentary led to the eventual banning of her works by the Nazis.

The first woman elected to the Prussian Academy of the Arts, she resigned her position there in 1933 to protest Hitler's rise to power. Her husband, Karl Kollwitz, was a physician who chose to practice on a working-class street in what later became part of Berlin's eastern zone, Weissenburgerstrasse (now called Kollwitzstrasse). In 1943, Allied bombing drove Käthe to the countryside near Dresden, where she died in 1945, a guest of the former royal family of Saxony in their castle at Moritzburg.

Many Kollwitz works show the agonies of wartime separation of mother and child, probably the result of her losing a son in Flanders during World War I and a grandson

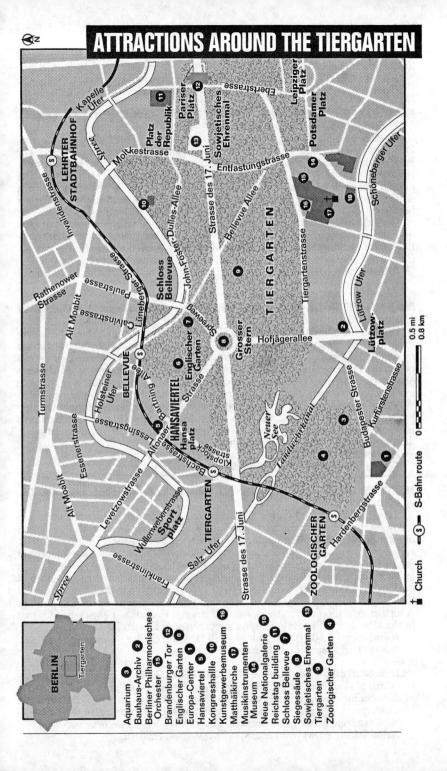

ATTRACTIONS AROUND THE TIERGARTEN

BERLIN

Tiergarten

Aquarium ③
Bauhaus-Archiv ②
Berliner Philharmonisches
Orchester ⑮
Brandenburger Tor ⑫
Englischer Garten ⑥
Europa-Center ①
Hansaviertel ⑤
Kongresshalle ⑩
Kunstgewerbemuseum ⑯
Matthäikirche ⑰
Musikinstrumenten
Museum ⑭
Neue Nationalgalerie ⑱
Reichstag building ⑪
Schloss Bellevue ⑦
Siegessäule ⑧
Sowjetisches Ehrenmal ⑨
Tiergarten ⑬
Zoologischer Garten ④

✝ ■ Church

S ⓢ S-Bahn route

0   0.5 mi
0   0.8 km

during World War II. The lower floors of the museum are devoted to woodcuts and lithographs, the upper floors to particularly poignant sculptures.

Admission: 6 DM ($4) adults, 3 DM ($2) children and students.
Open: Wed–Mon 11am–6pm. **U-Bahn:** Uhlandstrasse.

MUSEUM FÜR VERKEHR UND TECHNIK [Transport Museum], Trebbinerstrasse 9. Tel. 030/25-48-40.

Holding an equal fascination for adults and children is the Transport Museum. One commentator once wrote, "If it flies, rolls, or floats, you'll find it here." The museum displays models of trains and trams, as well as spacecraft and even a copy of Columbus's *Santa Maria,* which sailed to the New World. An early aeronautical pioneer, Berlin-born Otto Lilienthal, who died in 1896, is also honored. His achievements in "flying models" were said to have been studied by the Wright brothers.

Since this museum was bulging with displays, a second wing has opened. It took over the freightyard of the old-time Anhalter Bahnhof, where the fictional Sally Bowles arrived in Isherwood's Berlin stories, which were the basis for the musical *Cabaret.* If you want to go there, ask at the main museum for directions.

Admission: 4 DM ($2.60) adults, 2 DM ($1.30) children.
Open: Tues–Fri 9am–6pm, Sat–Sun 10am–6pm. **Bus:** A129.

MARTIN-GROPIUS-BAU GALLERY, Stresemannstrasse 110. Tel. 030/25-48-60.

In 1981, the Martin-Gropius-Bau Gallery opened in a location about a 12-minute stroll from the Tiergarten. *The New York Times* called it one of the "most dramatic museums in the world." It contains the **Museum Berlinische Galerie,** with works of art, architecture, and photography of the 19th and 20th centuries; the **Jewish Museum;** and the **Werkbund Archiv.** On the ground floor are changing exhibitions of different character. The building lies near the site of the former Berlin Wall, and the eastern part of the museum opens onto the leveled former Gestapo headquarters, which were adjoining. It makes for a fascinating stroll to look at this building, whose exterior terra-cotta friezes were not restored. If they were damaged, destroyed, or left intact, that is how they remain today.

Admission: 6 DM ($4) adults, 3 DM ($2) children.
Open: Tues–Sun 10am–8pm. **S-Bahn:** Anhalter Bahnhof.

MUSEUM HAUS AM CHECKPOINT CHARLIE, Friedrichstrasse 44. Tel. 030/251-10-31.

This small building houses exhibits depicting the tragic events leading up to and following the erection of the former Berlin Wall. You can see some of the instruments of escape used by East Germans, including chair lifts, false passports, hot-air balloons, and even a minisub. Photos document the building of the wall, the establishment of escape tunnels, and the postwar history of both parts of Berlin from 1945 until today, including the airlift. One of the most moving exhibits is the display on the staircase of drawings by schoolchildren who, in 1961 to 1962, were asked to depict both halves of Germany in one picture. You can also see works by well-known international painters. A further exhibition depicts the nonviolent struggle for human rights, especially that of the 1989 and 1991 revolutions in the countries of Eastern Europe.

Admission: 7.50 DM ($5) adults, 4.50 DM ($3) children.
Open: Daily 9am–10pm. **U-Bahn:** Kochstrasse.

ALTES MUSEUM, Lustgarten. Tel. 030/203-55-0.

North of Karl-Liebknecht-Platz in the Lustgarten section of the square, this is one of the most impressive buildings of the architect, Karl Friedrich Schinkel. Considered his masterpiece, it is graced by 18 Ionic columns and offers changing exhibitions— perhaps exquisite drawings by Botticelli along with postwar German art.

Admission: 1 DM (66¢) adults, 0.50 DM (30¢) children.

Open: Wed–Sun 10am–5pm. **S-Bahn:** Karl-Liebknecht-Platz.

MUSEUM FÜR NATURKUNDE [Museum of Natural History], Invalidenstrasse 43. Tel. 030/289-72-540.

The Natural History Museum is attached to Humboldt-Universität. Among the exhibits illustrating evolutionary phases is the original skeleton of the gigantic reptile *Brachiosaurus brancai,* which terrified the world some 150 million years ago. The 60 million-plus natural science objects contained here make this one of the largest museums of its kind in the world. Displays trace the evolution of organic life as well as inorganic matter. Mineralogical, zoological, and paleontological departments make up the vast collections. An arboretum is attached to the museum.

Admission: 4 DM ($2.60) adults, 2 DM ($1.30) children.
Open: Tues–Sun 9:30am–5pm. **U-Bahn:** Unter den Linden.

HUGENOTTENMUSEUM [Huguenot Museum], Gendarmenmarkt. Tel. 030/229-17-60.

In the tower of the Französischer Dom are displayed documents, maps, historic pictures, and objects relating to the spread and status of the Huguenots who were forced to flee Louis XIV's France and found new homes in Berlin and Brandenburg. This relatively small museum contains archives and a Huguenot library.

Admission: 4 DM ($2.60) adults, 2 DM ($1.30) children.
Open: Tues–Wed and Sat 10am–5pm, Thurs 10am–6pm, Sun 11:30am–5pm.
Closed: Mon and Fri, but church and tower can be visited 10am–5pm.

OTTO-NAGEL-HAUS, Am Märkischen Ufer 16–18. Tel. 030/279-14-02.

At the Otto Nagel House, about 1,100 yards from Museum Island, the Nationalgalerie exhibits works of German artists between World War I and World War II. Among them are works by such famous artists as Ernst Barlach; Otto Dix; Karl Hofer; Käthe Kollwitz; Ludwig Meidner; and, of course, Otto Nagel (1894–1967), for whom the museum is named. Nagel depicted the plight of blue-collar workers in Berlin in the 1920s and 1930s.

Admission: 4 DM ($2.60) adults, 2 DM ($1.30) children.
Open: Sun–Thurs 9am–5pm. **S-Bahn:** Märkisches Museum.

MÄRKISCHES MUSEUM, Am Köllnischen Park 5. Tel. 030/270-05-14.

The full cultural history of Berlin is displayed in one of the most prominent buildings on the banks of the Spree. The museum is operated by the municipal council. The 42 rooms contain collections of artifacts from excavations, plus such art treasures as Slav silver items and finds from the Bronze Age. The history of Berlin's theaters and literature, the arts in Berlin and in the March of Brandenburg, and sections dedicated to the life and work of Berlin artists, may be seen here. Most visitors like the array of mechanical musical instruments.

Admission: 2 DM ($1.30) adults, 1 DM (66¢) children.
Open: Wed–Fri 10am–6pm, Sat–Sun 10am–5pm. **U-Bahn:** Markisches Museum.

WESTERN BERLIN ATTRACTIONS

OLYMPIA-STADION, Olympischer Platz 3. Tel. 030/304-06-76.

Built in 1936 by Werner March for the 11th Olympic Games, the Olympia-Stadion, seating 100,000 people, was the first in Europe to supply all the facilities necessary for modern sports. Hitler expected to see the "master race" run off with all the awards in the 1936 Olympics, and you can imagine his disappointment when an African American, Jesse Owens, took four gold medals for the U.S. team.

The stadium area covers a total of 330 acres, including a swimming stadium, a hockey arena, tennis courts, and riders' exhibition grounds. But the main attraction is the arena, so large that if the seats were laid end to end, they would stretch for more than 25 miles. The playing field in its center lies 47 feet below ground level. You can take the elevator to the top of the 260-foot platform where the Olympic bell hangs. From this point you have a panoramic view of Berlin to the east. Since the Olympic Stadium lies northwest of the Funkturm (see below), you can reach it in a few minutes by a brisk walk.

Admission: 2 DM ($1.30).
Open: Daily 8am–5pm. **U-Bahn:** Olympia-Stadion.

FUNKTURM [Radio Tower], Messedamm. Tel. 030/303-829-96.

Nearly every sizable town in Germany seems to have a television tower, but this steel-frame construction predates them all—in fact, it predates television. Erected from 1924 to 1926, it sits on a base of porcelain pedestals. Popularly called the "Tall Dwarf," the tower has been converted to a television transmitter, but if you visit here it will likely be either for the restaurant (at 170 feet) or for the view of Berlin and its environs (as far as Potsdam) from the observation platform at 457 feet. The elevator reaches the top in half a minute.

Admission: Viewing platform, 5 DM ($3.30); 3 DM ($2) for elevator to restaurant.
Open: Elevator, daily 10am–11pm. **U-Bahn:** Kaiserdamm. **S-Bahn:** Westkreuz.

ADDITIONAL EASTERN BERLIN ATTRACTIONS

REBUILT NIKOLAI QUARTER

Nikolaiviertel, a historic site in the eastern part of the city, was restored in time for the city's 750th anniversary in 1987. Here, on the banks of the Spree River, is where Berlin was born. Many of the old buildings in the area were completely rebuilt after having been destroyed in World War II. The restoration has recaptured some of the old flavor of the city.

The area is named for the **Nikolaikirche** (Church of St. Nicholas) Nikolai-kirchplatz, off Spandauerstrasse (tel. 030/24-31-31-46). The church, built in the 14th century and, as such the oldest in Berlin, was constructed on the remains of a Romanesque church from the 13th century. In its reconstruction, 800-year-old skeletons were found. No longer a church, the restored building is now used to display the results of archeological digs following the bombing of Berlin. Since 1982 the church has had two towers again, as it did at the turn of the 20th century. The new south tower is topped by a golden weathervane with the Berlin bear and the date 1981 to commemorate the start of the rebuilding of the Nikolai Quarter. Charging 2 DM ($1.35) for admission, it is open Monday from 10am to 5pm, Thursday from 10am to 6pm, Friday from 10am to 4pm, Saturday from 10am to 6pm, and Sunday from 10am to 5pm. U-Bahn: Klosterstrasse.

The **Gerichtslaube,** seat of early jurisdiction, and the 18th-century **Ephraim Palace** were also rebuilt. New structures were built in the old style to house apartments, boutiques, shops, cafés, and restaurants, all reflecting old Berlin.

The historic center was unused for decades. Around the Nikolaikirche a number of former burgher houses were reconstructed using photographs. Once again old Berlin has such quaint street names as Eiergasse (Egg Alley), Propstrasse (Provost Street), Rosstrasse (Horse Street), Molkenmarkt (Milk Market), and Mühlendamm.

On Church Square, the house in which Gotthold Ephraim Lessing lived from 1752 to 1755 was restored. On Mühlendamm, the famous Ephraim Palace was rebuilt using original parts of the facade and interior. The rounded baroque facade was once popularly known as "Berlin's most beautiful corner." On Mühlendamm, there is also the **Berliner Handwerksmuseum** showing the development of Berlin crafts between the 13th and the 19th centuries.

In Eiergasse stands Zum Paddenwirt, a restaurant, while the Zur Rippe is on Molkenmarkt, originally the center of the medieval town. Propstrasse proudly shows restored burgher houses from the 17th through the 19th century. The Zum Nussbaum restaurant used to be in one of the oldest gable houses on Fischerinsel

(Fisherman's Isle). It became famous through its habitués, who included Heinrich Zille and Otto Nagel.

Next to the Spree, a bronze sculpture of St. George slaying the dragon was recently erected. It was made in 1853 by August Kiss, a pupil of Christian Daniel Rauch, for the Castle of Berlin. In Poststrasse, the Kurfürst House and the Grell, the Schubert and Knoblauch houses have all been reconstructed. Of special interest is the Kaak, a bird with a grinning human face and donkey's ears that symbolizes the insults and ridicule thrown at those once pilloried here.

OTHER ATTRACTIONS

The strolling street of eastern Berlin is the world-famous **Unter den Linden** (see Walking Tour 2, below), beginning at the Brandenburg Gate. One of its most famous landmarks, other than Humbolt Universität, is the **equestrian statue of Frederick the Great,** the "enlightened despot" of Prussia. In 1945, this statue was shipped to Potsdam, but it was returned in 1980.

The **Berliner Rathaus,** or Town Hall, on Rathausstrasse (S-Bahn: Alexanderplatz), was once a Neo-Renaissance structure built between 1861 and 1869. Reconstructed after war damage, it now has a clock tower above its main portal. In its cellar is a restaurant serving old Berlin specialties.

The **Deutsche Staatsbibliothek** (National Library) stands at Unter den Linden 8 (S-Bahn: Friedrichstrasse). Built in the neo-baroque style, it was constructed between 1903 and 1914. On the eve of World War II, the National Library had some 3.8 million volumes. After war destruction, the collection has now grown to more than 5 million. There are a dozen reading rooms. Hours are Monday through Friday from 9am to 9pm and Saturday from 9am to 5pm.

One of the most important churches of Berlin is **St. Hedwigs-Kathedrale,** Bebelplatz (U-Bahn: Hausvogteiplatz), a baroque cathedral that architect Jean-Laurent Legeay modeled on the Pantheon in Rome. Work on this building began in 1747. The church was consecrated in 1773 and was named for the wife of Duke Henry of Silesia. Destroyed by fire in World War II, it was reconstructed between 1952 and 1963. The original structure of the dome has been preserved, although the interior is modern.

Another landmark of Berlin is the **Berliner Dom,** Karl-Liebknecht-Platz (also the S-Bahn stop), which was designed by Julius Raschdorff in the style of the Italian High Renaissance. Construction lasted from 1894 to 1905. The Dom was built on the site of a cathedral frequented by Frederick the Great in 1750. World War II brought massive destruction, and restoration efforts have been slow. The cathedral is open to visitors Monday through Wednesday and Friday from noon to 4pm and Saturday from 10am to 1pm.

In 1969, East Berliners constructed a massive **Fernsehturm** (TV tower) on Alexanderplatz (tel. 030/242-33-33), the second-highest structure in Europe (1,100 feet), second only to the tower in Moscow. It's worthwhile to take the 60-second elevator ride to the observation platform, 610 feet above the city. From this isolated vantage point you can clearly distinguish most landmarks. On the floor above, you can enjoy a piece of cake and cup of coffee as the Tele-Café slowly revolves, making one complete turn every hour. The elevator to the top costs 5 DM ($3.30) for adults and 2.50 DM ($1.70) for children. The tower is open daily from 9am to 11:30pm (U-Bahn or S-Bahn: Alexanderplatz).

At the foot of the Fernsehturm stands one of Berlin's oldest churches, the brick Gothic **Marienkirche** (St. Mary's), opening onto Kaiser-Wilhelm-Strasse (tel. 030/212-44-67). Constructed in the 15th century, it is especially notable for the wall painting depicting *The Dance of Death* (1475), discovered beneath a layer of whitewash in the entrance hall of the church in 1860. Also worth seeing is the marble baroque pulpit carved by Andreas Schlüter (1703).

On the opposite side of the Fernsehturm stands **Alexanderplatz,** center of activity in the east of the city. Several modern buildings line the square, including an HO Department Store and the Congress Hall. Information and tickets pertaining to events in Berlin are available at the Berolina House on the square, open Monday to Friday from 9am to 7pm (Saturday to 4pm).

ZOO & GARDENS

TIERGARTEN, from the Bahnhof Zoo to the Brandenburger Tor.

 Originally laid out as a private park for the Electors of Prussia, this is the largest green space in central Berlin, covering just under 1 square mile, with more than 14 miles of meandering walkways. Late in the 19th century, partially to placate growing civic unrest, it was opened to the public, with a layout that was formalized by one of the leading landscape architects of the era, Peter Josef Lenné.

The park was devastated during World War II, and the few trees that remained were chopped down as fuel as Berlin shuddered through the winter of 1945 to 1946. By 1947, it had been converted into a series of weed patches and carefully guarded vegetable gardens, a sad remnant of its former glory. Beginning in 1955, trees were replanted, with alleyways, canals, ponds, and flower beds rearranged more or less in their original patterns through the cooperative efforts of many landscape architects, among them Heinrich Dathe. Today, the Tierpark is one of the most-visited places in Berlin on warm afternoons, popular with joggers and (sometimes naked) sunbathers.

The park's largest monuments include the Berlin Zoo, described below, and the **Golden Goddess of Victory** *(Die Siegessäule),* which perches atop a soaring red-granite pedestal from a position in the center of the wide boulevard (Strasse des 17. Juni) that neatly bisects the Tiergarten into roughly equivalent sections. Originally erected by the Kaisers in front of the Reichstag, in 1938 it was moved into its present location as a suitable backdrop for Hitler's military parades.

The most important church in the Tiergarten is **Matthäikirche** or the Church of St. Matthew, opening onto the Matthäikirchplatz. It is the only remaining building from the 1800s, as its neighbors were destroyed in the war. Designed by August Stüler in 1846, it is built of a mottled red-and-white brick. Closed to the public today, it was once the major church for the high society of Berlin.

The final famous monument within the Tiergarten is the relatively small but elegantly baroque **Schloss Bellevue** (Bellevue Palace), which was built in 1785 on the banks of the Spree as a summer house for the younger brother of Frederick the Great, Prince Augustus Ferdinand. Hitler used it before the war as his official guest

---

FROMMER'S FAVORITE BERLIN EXPERIENCES

Promenades along Unter den Linden and the Kurfürstendamm Visitors don't know Berlin until they've strolled the Ku'damm, called the showcase of Western capitalism (glossy, store-lined), or Unter den Linden, Prussian centerpiece of the Berlin-Mitte district.

Kneipen Crawling These pubs or taverns are tantamount to London's famed tradition of "pub crawling." Whether you want breakfast or a beer at 4am, Kneipen exist in every neighborhood waiting to claim you.

A Night of Culture Berlin is home to the Berliner Philharmonisches Orchester, one of the world's leading orchestras. The baton of the late Herbert von Karajan is no longer raised, but the Philharmonie is still the stage for some of the world's finest music.

Strolling the Nikolai Quarter A symbol of Berlin's desire to bounce back after war damage, this charming 16th-century neighborhood has been rebuilt—ideal for leisurely strolls of its narrow streets, lit by gas lanterns, with its period taverns and churches.

house, entertaining within its walls Soviet Foreign Minister Molotov, after whom the famous incendiary device was named.

From 1959 (when it was restored after wartime ruin) until unification, it served as the official Berlin residence of the West German president. The palace and its grounds are best defined as a semiprivate park at the northern edge of the much larger expanse of the Tiergarten, with 50 acres of landscaping and on its western edge an English-inspired garden called the **Englischer Garten.**

Except for unusual situations involving national security, the western edge (the English gardens) are usually open to the public every day from 8am until dusk. At press time, plans were being formed to move the German president's official residence from Schloss Bellevue to the former German Crown Prince's Palace on Unter den Linden in a few years. The **Victory Column,** Grosser Stern (tel. 030/391-29-61), has a 157-foot-high observation platform that is reached after a climb up a spiral 290-step staircase. It is open from April to mid-November; visiting hours are Monday from 1 to 5:30pm and Tuesday through Sunday from 9am to 5:30pm. Take bus 100 to Grosser Stern.

ZOOLOGISCHER GARTEN BERLIN [Berlin Zoo], Hardenbergplatz 8. Tel. 030/25-40-10.

In Berlin, with its surprisingly large proportion of green parkland in comparison to many big cities of Europe, you can see the oldest and finest zoo in Germany, founded in 1844. A short walk north from the main street of town, the Ku'damm, it occupies almost the entire southwest corner of the Tiergarten.

Until World War II, the zoo boasted thousands of animals of every imaginable species and description, many familiar to Berliners by nicknames. The tragedy of the war struck here as well as in the human sections of Berlin, and by the end of 1945, only 91 animals had survived. For the past 45 years, however, the city has been rebuilding its large and unique collection, until today there are more than 13,000 animals, some housed here to prevent their becoming extinct. The zoo has the most modern birdhouse in Europe, with more than 550 species. Furthermore, great and small cats from all over the world can be seen in the Carnivore House. The zoo's most valuable inhabitant is a giant panda. In the Nocturnal House the visitors can watch the way of life of nocturnal animals. The monkey center is a popular spot, and you can see breeding groups of apes (no fewer than 8 gorillas, 12 orangutans, and 7 chimpanzees). There are also large open ranges where wild animals roam in simulated natural habitats.

In the center of the zoo is a large restaurant.

The **aquarium** is as impressive as the adjacent zoo. Its collection of more than 9,000 fish, reptiles, amphibians, and other animals holds a fascination for every visitor. The second floor is devoted entirely to creatures that live exclusively underwater, with one section for saltwater fish and one for those that live in lakes and streams. Benches are set up along the viewing promenade so you can sit and watch your favorite turtle or octopus for as long as you wish. But even more intriguing is the terrarium, with a crocodile collection, Komodo monitors, and tuataras. You can even walk into the terrarium on a bridge over the reptile pit—but don't lose your balance. Around the outside are several glass cases containing a large collection of snakes, lizards, and turtles, and a large terrarium at the corner with giant tortoises. On the third floor, you can watch the world of insects and amphibians.

Admission: Zoo, 9 DM ($5.90) adults, 4.50 DM ($3) children. Aquarium, 8 DM ($5.30) adults, 4 DM ($2.60) children. Combined ticket for zoo and aquarium, 13.50 DM ($8.90) adults, 6.50 DM ($4.30) children.

Open: Daily 9am–6pm. **U-Bahn:** Bahnhof Zoo.

BOTANISCHER GARTEN [Botanical Garden], Königin-Luise-Strasse 6–8, Dahlem. Tel. 030/830-06-0.

In the Dahlem quarter of western Berlin, near the Dahlem Museum, the huge Botanischer Garten contains vast collections of European and exotic plants in the open and in 15 greenhouses. Among the most popular are the big palm house, one of the largest in the world, with its palms, bamboos, and tropical flowers, and the

Victoria house, where *Victoria amazonica* and *Victoria cruziana* are in bloom in late summer. In the open, the section representing the vegetation of the temperate regions of the northern hemisphere is most noteworthy. There are also a large arboretum and several special collections, such as a garden for the blind and waterplants.

A unique approach to botany is represented in the **Botanical Museum** near the entrance to the gardens. Here you can see dioramas and exhibit cases portraying the history and significant facts of plant life around the world.

Admission: Garden 3 DM ($2); children under 14 free.

Open: Garden, daily 9am–8pm (closes at dusk in winter); museum, Tues–Sun 10am–5pm. **S-Bahn:** Botanischer Garten.

COOL FOR KIDS

If you arrive in Berlin with your family, don't worry about small children getting bored. There's plenty for them to do.

The most exciting place to take them is the **Berlin Zoo** (see above). There, the most famous celebrity, among a cast of 10,000 or so, is Bao-Bao, the celebrated panda. His compound is always surrounded by crowds of children. The zoo has a cliff compound for the monkeys, an aquarium, a crocodile house, an underground nocturnal animal center, and even a children's zoo where the animals welcome a cuddle. It also offers playgrounds.

In addition, the tourist office can direct families to certain children's farms where the kiddies can do more than just see the animals: They can actually join in the fun, lending a helping hand and learning farm experience firsthand.

Fun for the whole family is virtually guaranteed at Berlin's many fairs and festivals, including the Spring Festival, the Park Festival at Britz, the Steglitz Borough Festival, the German-American Festival, the Oktoberfest, and the Christmas fairs.

Grips-Theater, Altonaerstrasse 22 (tel. 030/391-40-04), has gained a reputation in Europe for its bright, breezy productions for children. Matinees, costing 10 DM ($6.60) for all ages, are Tuesday through Friday at 10am and Saturday and Sunday at 3pm. Evening performances, when tickets cost 22 DM ($14.50) per person, are Tuesday through Sunday at 7:30pm. Take bus no. 106 or 123.

SPANDAU CITADEL

One of the most popular day-trips from the heart of the city is to Spandau district in northwest Berlin. Head up Am Juliusturm and you'll eventually reach this suburb, which was incorporated into Berlin in 1920. It is one of the oldest parts of Altmark, receiving its city charter back in 1232. The Hohenzollern electors of Brandenburg turned it into a summer residence, and in time it became the chief military center of Prussia, housing the imperial war treasury.

The **Spandauer Zitadelle,** or Spandau Citadel Am Juliusturm (tel. 030/339-12-97), stands at the confluence of the Spree and Havel. The Julius Tower (Juliusturm) and the Palast are the oldest buildings still standing, the only remaining parts of the castle, which was built in the 13th and 14th centuries. In the main building, accessible by footbridge, is a local history museum. The citadel is open Tuesday to Friday from 9am to 5pm and Saturday and Sunday from 10am to 5pm. Entrance price is 1.50 DM ($1) for adults and 1 DM (66¢) for children. The U-Bahn stop is Zitadelle.

The citadel has had a checkered past, and it's been besieged by everybody from the French to the Prussians. It has also been a state prison. However, it was not here that the remaining leader of the Nazi hierarchy, Rudolf Hess, was housed but at Spandau Prison in Wilhelmstrasse, in the middle of Spandau. Following the death of Hess in 1987, the prison was demolished. Hess, born in 1894, was appointed deputy Führer in 1933, but parachuted into Scotland, where he was arrested and interned until the end of the war. He was sentenced to life imprisonment at Nürnberg in 1946, and thus began his lonely vigil at Spandau. He was guarded—at great expense to all countries—by the Americans, Russians, French, and British. Attempts by the son of the former war criminal to get him released were unsuccessful.

3. SPECIAL-INTEREST SIGHTSEEING

FOR THE ARCHITECTURE LOVER

In World War II, one out of every three Berliners lost his or her home. After the rubble was cleared it took the united effort of many of the world's greatest architects to create contemporary Berlin. The **Hansaviertel,** or Hansa Quarter (U-Bahn to Hansaplatz), was a direct result of the great Interbau (international builders' exhibition) of 1957, when architectural designers from 22 nations constructed homes and apartments in this district, along with shops, schools, churches, a cinema, library, and a museum. The excitement here is in the variety: Each of the nearly 50 architects, including Gropius, Niemeyer, and Duttman, was able to express himself in his own way. Even Le Corbusier submitted a design for an apartment house, but the structure would have been too gigantic for the quarter. You can see it today where it was built in the less congested western section, near the Olympic Statium. The **Corbusier House,** called Strahlende Stadt (radiant city), is Berlin's largest housing complex, and one of the biggest in Europe. Its 530 apartments (more than 1,000 rooms) can house up to 1,400 people. Typical of the architect's style, this tremendous building rests on stilts.

Despite the urgency at creating new housing, the architects of the rebuilt Berlin were also encouraged to design centers for the performing arts. One of the most controversial of these projects was the **Congress Hall** (Kongresshalle), on John-Foster-Dulles-Allee. Set within the Tiergarten, just west of the Brandenburg Gate and the Soviet War Memorial, it was conceived as the American contribution to the 1957 International Building Exhibition. Constructed of reinforced concrete with a 60-foot-high vaulted ceiling that reminded some viewers of an oversize flying saucer, it was immediately christened "The Pregnant Oyster" by irreverent Berliners. Tragically, its ceiling collapsed on a hot summer night in 1980, and although it has been rebuilt, the structure is today used mainly for conventions.

Berlin's tallest building sits in the heart of the city's activity. The 22-story **Europa-Center,** between Tauentzienstrasse and Budapesterstrasse (U-Bahn: Kurfürstendamm), just across the plaza from the Kaiser Wilhelm Memorial Church, is the largest self-contained shopping center and entertainment complex in Europe. This town-within-a-town opened in 1965 and has been fascinating Berliners and outsiders alike ever since. Besides its three levels of shops, restaurants, nightclubs, bars, and movie houses, it contains dozens of offices; a car park; and an observation roof, Aussichtsplatform, from which you can view the city. Hours are daily from 9am to midnight (until 10pm in winter). Admission is 3 DM ($2) to the observation roof.

BAUHAUS ARCHIV MUSEUM FUR GESTALTUNG (Bauhaus Museum), Klingelhoferstrasse 14. Tel. 030/25-40-020.

Even if you're not a student of architecture or design, you should be fascinated by the Bauhaus Museum; it will bring you closer to the ideas and concepts of modern design and architecture and where they originated. The Bauhaus was founded by Walter Gropius in 1919 at Weimar. (He was later to become a longtime resident of the United States.) This school was largely responsible for establishing a curriculum for the teaching of industrial design throughout the Western world. The Bauhaus artists were kicked out of Weimar in 1925, moving to Dessau and then to Berlin, where the institute dissolved itself in 1933.

Admission: 4 DM ($2.60).
Open: Wed–Mon 10am–5pm. **U-Bahn:** Nollendorfplatz. **Bus:** 100, 106, 129, or 341.

FRIEDRICHSWERDERSCHE KIRCHE—SCHINKELMUSEUM, Werderstrasse. Tel. 030/208-13-23.

Installed in the deconsecrated Friedrichswerdersche Kirche, one of the most famous churches of Berlin before the war, the Schinkelmuseum is right off Karl-Liebknecht-Platz, at the corner of Niederlagstrasse. The twin Gothic portals of the old church shelter a bronze of St. George slaying the dragon. Inside, the museum is devoted to the memory of Karl Friedrich Schinkel, the architect of the early 19th century. He was responsible for designing many of the great palaces and monuments of Berlin that survived, along with his legend, until 1944 and 1945. In this museum his memory and records of his great accomplishments live on.

Admission: 2 DM ($1.30) adults, 1 DM (66¢) children.
Open: Wed–Sun 10am–6pm. **U-Bahn:** Hausvogteiplatz.

NEUE WACHE (New Guardhouse), Unter den Linden 4. No phone.
Planned as a memorial to German war dead, Neue Wache was constructed by the great architect K. F. Schinkel in 1816. A large brick-constructed pile, it is graced with a Doric portico in front, looking like a Greek temple. In 1931, the inside was transformed to honor the dead of World War I; in 1960, the East German government converted it into a monument honoring the victims of fascism and militarism. In its Hall of Honor, contained within a crystal cube, the eternal flame burns.

Bus: 57.

FOR VISITING AMERICANS

SCHÖNEBERG RATHAUS, John-F.-Kennedy-Platz. Tel. 030/7831.
Of special interest to Americans, this political center of West Berlin administration and parliamentary life since 1948 was the scene of John F. Kennedy's memorable "Ich bin ein Berliner" speech on June 26, 1963. Berliners have renamed the square around the building the John-F.-Kennedy-Platz. Built in 1911, the facade of the hall is not as outstanding as the interior. Here you'll find many paintings, especially portraits of political leaders of the past, and an exhibition of the history of the Schöneberg quarter of Berlin. Note the eight tinted-glass panels in the vestibule with scenes of various sections of Berlin, each with its own coat-of-arms.

From the 237-foot-high tower of the hall, a replica of the Liberty Bell is rung every day at noon. A gift from the American people in 1950, the Freedom Bell, as it is called, symbolized U.S. support for the West Berliners during the days of the Cold War. The document chamber contains a testimonial bearing the signatures of 17 million Americans who gave their moral support in the struggle.

Admission: Free.
Open: Wed and Sun 10am–4pm. **U-Bahn:** Schöneberg.

FOR THE LITERARY ENTHUSIAST

BRECHT-WEIGEL-MUSEUM, Chausseestrasse 125. Tel. 030/282-99-16.
Theater buffs may also want to seek out the house occupied by Bertolt Brecht (1898–1956), the German poet and playwright who lived in the United States during World War II but returned to live in East Berlin until his death. It was in East Berlin that he created his own "epic theater" company, the acclaimed Berliner Ensemble, with which he often expressed leftist and antimilitarist themes. Berlin-Mitte retains the Bertolt-Brecht-Haus as the Bertolt Brecht Center, in an old tenement house not far from the Berlin-Friedrichstrasse station. This was where Brecht and his wife, the noted actress Helene Weigel, lived from 1953 until their deaths. The museum houses the artists' living and working rooms and the Brecht and Weigel Archives containing 350,000 manuscripts, typescripts, collections of his printed works, press cuttings, playbills, and sound documents.

Admission: 2 DM ($1.30) adults, 1 DM (66¢) children.
Open: Tues–Wed and Fri 10am–noon, Thurs 10am–noon and 5–7pm, Sat 9:30am–noon and 12:30–2pm. **U-Bahn:** Zinnowitzer Strasse.

WORLD WAR II SIGHTS

SOWJETISCHES EHRENMAL (Soviet War Memorial), in Treptower Park, along the Spree, with an entrance on Puschkinallee at the park.

The Soviet War Memorial is the final resting place of more than 5,000 Soviet soldiers. Entering the park, you pass between two huge red-granite pylons in the form of stylized flags, each towering over a bronze sculpture of a kneeling Soviet soldier. The cemetery consists of 5 large communal graves flanked by 16 raised stone sarcophagi on which bas-reliefs portray the events of World War II. At the end of the Grove of Honor stands the Memorial Statue, atop the Mausoleum, which contains the Book of Honor, listing the victims of the war who are buried here. Much of this memorial was constructed from marble from Hitler's demolished chancellery.

S-Bahn: Tiergarten.

SITE OF THE REICHS CHANCELLERY, Vosstrasse and Toleranzstrasse.

Many readers have asked the way to Hitler's bunker, where, on April 30, 1945, the Third Reich came to an end with the suicide of the German dictator. Although the chancellery once stood within walking distance of Checkpoint Charlie of Cold War fame, it does not exist today. The Russians bombed the area totally, and bulldozed what was left; the Communists did not want to create a memorial of any kind to Hitler. The site today is an open space. Only a mound of rubble marks the spot where the Nazi nerve center once stood. At one time the marble-and-glass building was vast, with Fascist state art adorning its great halls. The bunker was built 50 feet below ground, following the bombing of Hitler's military headquarters. The site of the building is at the northwest corner of Vosstrasse and Toleranzstrasse. The mound marking the Führerbunker is located inside the so-called death strip where many East Germans lost their lives in the postwar era trying to escape to the West. You can get an idea of the grandeur of the building by walking around the Thälmannplatz U-Bahn station or at the Soviet War Memorial in Treptower Park. The walls of the station are lined with red marble taken from the chancellery.

U-Bahn: Thälmannplatz, the last stop.

TOPOGRAPHY OF TERROR, Niederkirchenstrasse.

Once the Gestapo Headquarters was the most feared place in Europe. Many who entered it for interrogation never came out alive. Allied bombing reduced it to rubble. However, the government has partly excavated some of its cellars to reveal rooms used for torture, which was said to be especially brutal and sadistic. There's also an exhibition called "Topography of Terror."

Admission: Free.

Open: Tues–Sun 10am–6pm. **Bus:** 129.

ON JEWISH HISTORY

JÜDISCHER FRIEDHOF [Jewish Cemetery], Herbert-Baumstrasse, Weissensee.

In one of the suburbs of eastern Berlin, the famous Jewish cemetery, Jüdischer Friedhof, in Weissensee, was opened in 1880. It contains some 110,000 graves of the former Jewish residents of Berlin. Because you may have a hard time finding it on your own, it's recommended that you take a taxi there. Many distinguished artists, musicians, and scientists, as well as religious leaders, are buried here. Some of the tombs are of Jewish soldiers who fought on the German side in World War I. Back then, of course, many Jews were filled with a strong sense of German nationalism and showed great bravery at the front fighting against the Allies. A memorial honors Jewish victims murdered during the Nazi era. Many graves are of Jews who chose to face suicide in 1942 rather than a long, lingering death in one of the concentration camps. Many visitors from the West visit the cemetery, seeking the graves of long-departed ancestors.

Open: May–Sept, daily 8am–6pm; Oct–Apr, daily 8am–4 or 5pm.

NEUE SYNAGOGE, Oranienburgerstrasse 28.

Kept as a reminder of the Nazi's death grip are the ruins of a synagogue at Oranienburgerstrasse 28, which was firebombed during Kristallnacht, November 9 and 10, 1938. On that "night of broken glass," Jewish places of worship throughout the country were devastated by firebombs, and this one has been left standing as a memorial, untouched since the Nazi era.

Directions: Follow Friedrichstrasse (S-Bahn stop) to Oranienburgerstrasse, then turn right for 5 blocks. The ruins lie on the left side of the street as you appraoch. It's a long walk, across the river and past the Bahnhof.

HAUS DER WANNSEE-KONFERENZ. Grosser Wannsee 56. Tel. 030/805-00-10.

In a leafy Berlin suburb on January 20, 1942, a villa became the site of one of the most notorious conferences in history: Nazi bureaucrats and SS officials met here to map plans to commit genocide upon European Jewry. The villa was built after World War I by a German industrialist, then acquired by the SS in 1940 for use as a hotel for their highest-ranking officers.

In 1992, the villa was opened as a memorial to the Holocaust, a photographic exhibition of men, women, and children who were sent to their deaths. This exhibit is not for the squeamish, with its horrible images, including disfigured victims of Nazi medical experiments. One document—signed in 1944 by Dr. Josef Mengele—certifies to the shipment of a 12-year-old Gypsy boy's head to a laboratory. Mengele, of course, was the infamous "medical director" of Auschwitz.

The minutes of the conference were kept by Adolf Eichmann, the sallow-faced SS functionary who later mapped out the transport logistics for sending millions of Jews to their deaths. The exhibit was financed by the Berlin Senate. Nearly all the pictures on display were official Nazi photographs. As they put it at the trials at Nürnberg, "No government in history ever did a better job of photographing and documenting its crimes against humanity."

Admission: Free.

Open: Tues–Fri 10am–6pm, Sat–Sun 2–6pm. **S-Bahn:** Wannsee or Nikolassee.

WALKING TOUR 1 — KURFÜRSTENDAMM

Start: Nollendorfplatz.
Finish: Savignyplatz.
Estimated Time: 2 hours, not counting shopping or visits to interiors.
Best Time: Daylight hours during clement weather.
Worst Time: After dark or Sunday, when shops are usually closed.

This tour takes you through the heart of Berlin's most commercialized district, the Kurfürstendamm. The street was built upon forests and farmland by Prince Otto von Bismarck, Prussian-born unifier of 19th-century Germany. He envisioned its broad flanks as a site for aristocratic villas and designated that its verdant central barrier be reserved for the horseback riding of "the upper classes." He encouraged the construction of the now-ruined Kaiser Wilhelm Memorial Church. Begin your tour at the:

1. **Nollendorfplatz,** a busy junction of U-Bahn lines 1 and 4. Exit from the square's southern edge, walk south along the Maaßenstrasse, then turn right (west) in a block onto the Nollendorfstrasse. At no. 17 is the:
2. **Former residence of writer Christopher Isherwood,** whose short stories about Berlin during the 1920s and 30s evoked the decadence of a world eventually to be swept away by the Nazis.

    Follow the Nollendorfstrasse to its end, then turn right on the Eisenacher Strasse. Within 2 blocks, turn left and walk west along the Kleiststrasse. Near the corner of the An der Uraniastrasse, you'll see the first of several pieces of modern sculpture created for Berlin's 750th birthday celebration in 1987. On the northeastern corner of the intersection lies the:
3. **Postmuseum,** whose exhibits commemorate some of the little-known tri-

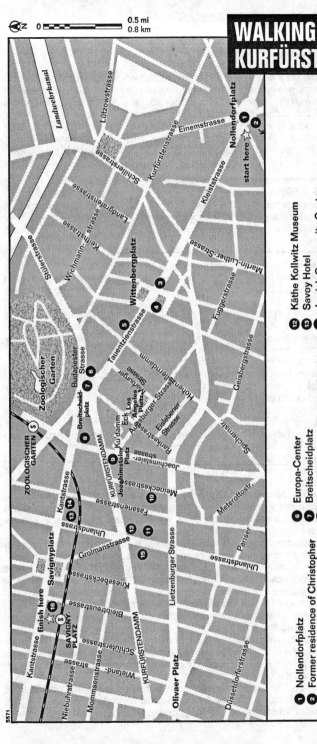

WALKING TOUR—KURFÜRSTENDAMM

1 Nollendorfplatz
2 Former residence of Christopher Isherwood
3 Postmuseum
4 Wittenbergplatz
5 Tauentzienstrasse
6 Europa-Center
7 Breitscheidplatz
8 Kaiser Wilhelm Memorial Church
9 Kurfürstendamm
10 Meinekestrasse
11 Villa Grisebach
12 Käthe Kollwitz Museum
13 Savoy Hotel
14 Jewish Community Center
15 Mengenlehr Uhr (Set-Theory Clock)
16 Savignyplatz

S — S-Bahn route

umphs of human communications, including a series of early telephones, telex, and telegraph machines. After your visit, retrace your steps to the Kleitstrasse and continue walking west until you reach the:

4. **Wittenbergplatz,** where you'll find a flea market whose individual stallowners maintain weekly open hours that are as random and unpredictable as Berlin itself. Now, descend into the bowels of Berlin's bedrock for a look at Wittenbergplatz's Jugendstil U-Bahn station. Considered one of Germany's best examples of civic art nouveau design, it was built in 1913 and renovated in the mid-1980s. After resurfacing, head for Wittenbergplatz's southwestern edge, where rises one of Berlin's most prestigious shopping emporiums, the Kaufhaus des Westens, known affectionately as the KaDeWe (pronounced Kah-DAY-vay).

REFUELING STOP An express elevator will carry you to the top floor of the **KaDeWe,** Tauentzienstrasse 21–24 (tel. 030/21-21-0), to an elegant snack bar, the Feinschmeckerétage. There, shoppers stop for an afternoon quaff of champagne, a tiny but succulent quiche, a salmon salad, or a platter of ultrafresh oysters.

From the KaDeWe, descend to the busy:

5. **Tauentzienstrasse.** Known before the war for its inventories of shoes from throughout the world, its merchandise today is more varied. In the street's center rises yet another sculpture dedicated to the city's 750th anniversary, this one entitled *Berlin,* by German artists Bridget and Martin Denninghoff. Assembled from twisted tubes of chrome-nickel alloy, its tortured planes in dynamic juxtaposition symbolize the contrasting faces of a city once divided but newly united. Looming now on your right in angular Cold War kitsch rises the architecturally controversial bulk of the:

6. **Europa-Center.** Built during an era when West Berlin struggled to assert itself (and to survive), it symbolizes better than any other building in Berlin the gutsy and often brash commercialism of West Berlin during the Cold War. The interior bristles with restaurants, movie theaters, shops, and fast-food emporiums. (The elevator to the top will carry visitors to an observation platform where the view encompasses the urban sprawl of Berlin and the fertile plains of long-ago Prussia.) After your visit, descend onto the pavement of the:

7. **Breitscheidplatz,** a large plaza usually packed with visitors. Rising in ruined splendor ahead of you is the building that symbolizes the indefatigable spirit of Berlin itself, the:

8. **Kaiser Wilhelm Memorial Church.** Once the largest and proudest of Bismarck's monuments, it stands today in unrepaired Neo-Gothic grandeur, a reminder to future generations of the price war can exact from a society. Now walk southwest onto the most famous boulevard of Berlin, the:

9. **✪ Kurfürstendamm.** A road of sorts has existed here since the 16th century. It was later used as a riding path for hunting parties headed toward the rich game preserves of the Grunewald forest. The boulevard enjoyed its heyday during the 1920s, when American writer Thomas Wolfe described it as the "largest coffeehouse in Europe." After the destruction and firebombings of 1943 and 1944 (when three-quarters of the avenue's aristocratic villas were demolished), the boulevard was rebuilt in a universally modern and angular style. Take the second left and walk south along the:

10. **Meinekestrasse,** which contains some of the very few remaining belle époque town houses. At the end of the block, turn right onto the Leitzenburger Strasse, then turn right (north) onto the relatively pristine Fasanenstrasse, where soon, at no. 25, will loom the ornate bulk of the:

11. **Villa Grisebach.** An elegant, once-private home, its Jugendstil premises are today used for a changing array of art exhibitions. Next door, at no. 24, is the:

12. **Käthe Kollwitz Museum.** The museum contains the woodcuts, etchings,

drawings, and sculpture produced by one of the most visible feminists and socialists of the Weimar era, in a town house whose opulence contradicts the socialist ideals of the late artist (1867–1945). After your visit, continue to walk north along the Fasanenstrasse, cross over the busy traffic of the Kurfürstendamm. At no. 9, you'll see one of the most historically interesting hotels of Berlin, the:

13. **Savoy.** Today widely recognized as one of the most charming and elegant in Berlin, its premises served during World War II as the site of the Japanese embassy to the Third Reich. Some vicious hand-to-hand fighting took place here as the Japanese opposed the takeover of their embassy by the incoming waves of Russian soldiers.

REFUELING STOP **Times Bar,** on the ground floor of the Savoy, Fasanenstrasse 9–10 (tel. 030/311-03-0), serves stiff drinks, platters of such snacks as marinated herring with capers, and views of some of the most stylish people in Berlin. As its name implies, there's also a selection of English-language newspapers hanging in racks, which might remind you of a comfortable club in London.

Nearby, at no. 79–80 Fasanenstrasse, you'll see the:

14. **Jewish Community Center** (Jüdischer Gemeindehaus). Once the site of the richest and most impressive synagogue in Berlin, it remains as a memorial to the some 6,000 members of Berlin's Jewish community today. A primary Nazi target during the looting and destruction of *Kristallnacht* (November 9, 1938), it was burned to the ground. After the war, the site of the original building was transformed into a community center and memorial to the former 20,000 members of Berlin's prewar Jewish community. Now, return to the Ku'damm, cross the lanes of the surging traffic, and turn to the right. Within a few blocks, near the corner of Uhlandstrasse, you'll spot the high-tech:

15. **Mengenlehr Uhr** (or Set-Theory Clock). Designed by Dieter Binninger and inspired by the layout of a Chinese abacus, the circa 1975 clock is probably the most distinctive timepiece in Europe. (To tell the time, think in "Base 5," learn to count sequential rows of flashing rectangles, and do some fast arithmetic. If you don't succeed, do as the Berliners do and try to appreciate it as a work of electronic sculpture.) Know at this point that the Ku'damm continues for at least another mile. (If you decide to continue to explore the Ku'damm, note that at the avenue's western terminus, within the Rathenauplatz, lies one artist's subjective appraisal of modern life. There, Wolf Vostell's montage of two Cadillacs partially buried in concrete reigns supreme as one of the most tongue-in-cheek sculptures in Berlin.

For the moment, however, sidetrack from the Ku'damm at Uhlandstrasse, taking its left-hand fork northwest onto Grolmanstrasse for about a block until you reach:

16. **Savignyplatz,** a grassy square known for its rows of cafés and beer halls, nightclubs, and turn-of-the-century apartment buildings. In the 1920s, this neighborhood was famous as one of the most avant-garde in Berlin, making it a prime target of Nazi Brownshirt attacks.

WALKING TOUR 2 — THE SITE OF THE FORMER WALL TO UNTER DEN LINDEN

Start: Moritzplatz.
Finish: Nikolaikirche.
Estimated Time: 4 hours.

Best Time: Daylight hours during clement weather.
Worst Time: After dark, when bad lighting and the possibility of ongoing construction makes access hazardous.

In August 1961, the ideological rift between East and West Berlin adopted a tangible form with the tragic but hasty construction of the Berlin Wall. For more than 28 years, the wall symbolized the division of a nation otherwise united by language, history, and experience.

In 1989, the wall started to fall, like Jericho's. By 1990, its demolition—undertaken at night—was in full swing, much to the delight of souvenir hunters around the world. Collectors purchased pieces of the wall for as much as $100,000 and hauled them off as relics of a dying era.

Today, only isolated remnants of the wall remain in place, usually with green spaces around them destined to enhance their status as historic relics of the Cold War. Know before you embark on this tour that the former "No Man's Land" between the eastern and western zones is now among the most hotly contested real estate in Europe. Even during the lifetime of this edition, parts of this walking tour may become outdated because of the district's ongoing transformation.

Your tour begins in Kreuzberg district, within former West Berlin, at the:

1. **Moritzplatz.** This was known before the wartime bombings as the publishing center of the German-speaking world, but its importance dried up almost overnight after the suppression of newspapers under the Communist regime. From here, walk for a few paces west along the Oranienstrasse. Within less than a block, veer right (north) onto:

2. **Stallschreiber Strasse.** Within one block, the street will pass through what was known for almost 30 years as the "Death Zone," which claimed the life of all but a lucky handful of persons trying to escape from the eastern zone. Turn left at the Alte Jakobstrasse, a residential street once divided midway along its length by the formidable Berlin Wall. Although most traces of the wall are now gone, an acute observer can notice distinct differences between the styles of architecture, the state of building maintenance, and the methods of pavement construction on the two sides of the street. Turn right onto Kommandanten, then left onto Lindenstrasse. At the corner of Lindenstrasse and Oranienstrasse, you'll see the headquarters of:

3. **Axel Springer Verlag** (Axel Springer Publishers). Constructed during the height of the Cold War, it was deliberately placed adjacent to the Berlin Wall by the company's pugnacious director, who considered its skyscraping bulk a symbol of defiance against the Communist regime whose territory lay only a few feet away. The building today houses the executive offices for three of Germany's biggest-selling newspapers, *Berliner Morgenpost, Bild,* and *Die Welt.* Since unification, the company has enlarged its premises by building a new wing jutting into what was formerly the much-feared "No Man's Land."

Now, retrace your steps north for a block along the Lindenstrasse, turning left (west) along the Zimmerstrasse. Within 3 blocks, at the:

4. **Corner of Zimmerstrasse and Charlottenstrasse,** you'll see the site where one of the most widely publicized dramas of the Cold War occurred. A cross marks the spot where, in 1962, 18-year-old Peter Fechter was shot as he attempted to climb over the Berlin Wall within the sightlines of a horrified crowd of West Berliners, photojournalists, and U.S. soldiers. From here, walk another block west to the corner of the Zimmerstrasse and the Friedrichstrasse, where you'll see the:

5. **Site of Checkpoint Charlie.** For decades, this spot was probably the tensest border crossing in the world. Checkpoint Charlie was created in 1961 when U.S. tanks moved up the Friedrichstrasse to assert Allied claims onto the western sector of the defeated capital of the Third Reich. A prefabricated metal-sided hut was lowered by crane into the middle of the street, provoking three of the tensest

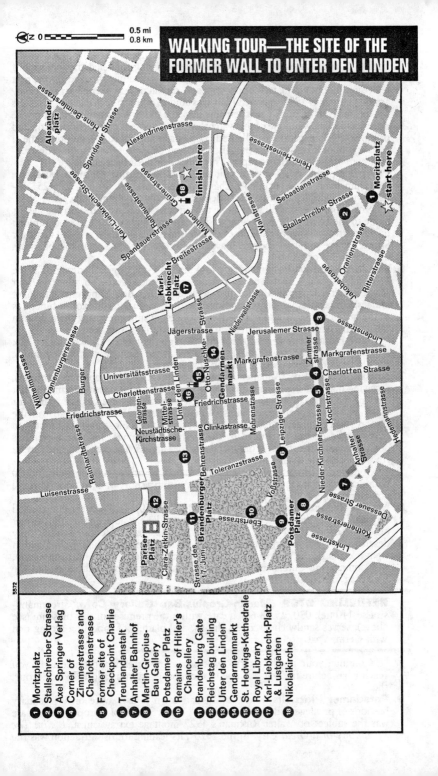

WALKING TOUR—THE SITE OF THE FORMER WALL TO UNTER DEN LINDEN

0.5 mi
0.8 km

Alexanderplatz

Hans-Beimlerstrasse

Alexandrinenstrasse

Spandauer Strasse

Heinr-Heinestrasse

Moritzplatz
start here

Sebastianstrasse

Stallschreiber Strasse

finish here

Karl-Liebknecht-Strasse

Grünerstrasse

Rathausstrasse

Wallstrasse

Oranienstrasse

Jakobstrasse

Ritterstrasse

Spandauerstrasse

Mühlend

Breitestrasse

Karl-Liebknecht Platz

Lindenstrasse

Oranienburgerstrasse

Burger

Niederwallstrasse

Jerusalemer Strasse

Jägerstrasse

Zimmer strasse

Markgrafenstrasse

Markgrafenstrasse

Charlotten Strasse

Wilhelmstrasse

Universitätsstrasse

Otto-Nuschke-strasse

Gendarmen-markt

Kochstrasse

Friedrichstrasse

Charlottenstrasse

Georgen-strasse

Mittel-strasse

Unter den Linden

Friedrichstrasse

Mohrenstrasse

Nieder-Kirchner-Strasse

Anhalter Strasse

Hedemannstrasse

Reinhardstrasse

Neustädtische-Kirchstrasse

Glinkastrasse

Leipziger Strasse

Voßstrasse

Dessauer Strasse

Luisenstrasse

Behrenstrasse

Toleranzstrasse

Ebertstrasse

Potsdamer Platz

Kothenerstrasse

Linkstrasse

Pariser Platz

Clara-Zetkin-Strasse

Brandenburger Platz

Strasse des 17. Juni

Ebertstrasse

5572

1. Moritzplatz
2. Stallschreiber Strasse
3. Axel Springer Verlag
4. Corner of Zimmerstrasse and Charlottenstrasse
5. Former site of Checkpoint Charlie
6. Treuhandanstalt
7. Anhalter Bahnhof
8. Martin-Gropius-Bau Gallery
9. Potsdamer Platz
10. Remains of Hitler's Chancellery
11. Brandenburg Gate
12. Reichstag building
13. Unter den Linden
14. Gendarmenmarkt
15. St. Hedwigs-Kathedrale
16. Royal Library
17. Karl-Liebknecht-Platz & Lustgarten
18. Nikolaikirche

weeks of the Cold War as U.S. and Soviet troops stared at each other over the barrels of their tanks. For years, this border crossing funneled the majority of non-German visitors through its forbidding series of double-locked doors, past television monitors, luggage inspectors, and the humorless skepticism of heavily armed guards. In 1992, the metal hut was sold to a group of American investors for its souvenir value. All that remains in place today is a small segment of the once-forbidding wall, one of the watchtowers, and potent comparisons of the fall of the Soviet Empire to the collapsed grandeur of ancient Rome. At press time, a consortium of investors were preparing the foundation for the eventual construction here of a massive skyscraper, The American Business Center.

At this point, don't miss a visit to the **Checkpoint Charlie Museum** (Museum Haus am Checkpoint Charlie), Friedrichstrasse 44 (tel. 030/251-10-31), whose exhibits are more fully described in "More Attractions," above.

Now, continue to walk west along the Zimmerstrasse, which soon changes its name to the Nieder-Kirchner-Strasse. Take an optional detour for about a block to the north, walking to the corner of the Strasse des Friedens and the Liepziger Strasse, where you'll see the gray masonry of one of the most adaptable buildings in German history, the:

6. Treuhandanstalt. Its bureaucratic-looking bulk was originally designed as the Hermann Göring–directed headquarters for the Third Reich's air ministry. After 1945, it served as the Communist regime's Haus des Ministerien (Cabinet Offices). Today, despite ongoing renovation of its cavernous interior, it functions as the headquarters of a government agency responsible for easing the transition of eastern German industries from the public to the private sector.

Now, retrace your steps to the south, then go right and walk west for a block along the Anhalter Strasse. You'll soon arrive at the ruins of what served during the 1920s as the third-largest railroad station in Europe, the:

7. Anhalter Bahnhof (Anhalter Railway Station). Long an important terminus, receiving many of the crowned heads of Europe on official visits during the last days of the Prussian monarchs, this railroad station was used as the setting for many of Hitler's propaganda films. When the Berlin Wall cut off most of the station's access routes, West Berlin officials demolished those parts of the station that weren't already devastated by the wartime bombings. Today, the premises contains one of the station's original decorative arches, a soccer field, and several rows of badly weathered masonry.

Continue your walk west along the Anhalter Strasse, turning right (north) within a block onto the Stresemannstrasse. Within a short walk, at no. 110, you'll come upon the:

8. Martin-Gropius-Bau Gallery (tel. 030/25-48-60). Deliberately constructed on the site of the former Berlin Wall, immediately adjacent to the former headquarters of the Nazi Gestapo, this unusual art collection is more fully described in "More Attractions," above. A mirror-image building, set within what used to be the eastern zone and which at press time was under renovation, will contain the bureaucratic spillover from governmental offices within the Reichstag, described below.

REFUELING STOP **Martin-Gropius-Bau Gallery Café,** Stresemann-strasse 110 (tel. 030/25-48-60), a café within the premises of this museum (see above), serves sandwiches, coffee, drinks, and platters of food in a setting rich with German art.

Continue your northwesterly walk along the Stresemannstrasse until you reach what before the war was one of the most glamorous addresses in Europe, the:

9. Potsdamer Platz. Its hotels, cafés, and town houses were once legendary bastions of privilege and chic. Called the "Times Square of Europe," the square was the subject of Walter Ruttman's 1927 montage extravaganza, *Berlin: The Symphony of a Great City.* In the 1920s, its leading tourist attraction was the cupola-topped complex of restaurants, Kempinski's Haus Vaterland. Its street lamps boasted the first electric illumination in Europe, and more than 550 trams used to pass through it every hour. In 1920, with the advent of the motorcar, it was the setting for Germany's first traffic light; during the height of the Third Reich, it bordered the most important power centers of the German Empire, including the now-demolished Chancellery. During the Cold War, any hopes of rebuilding the bombed-out neighborhood were squashed by its division among three occupation zones. Today, Potsdamer Platz is one of the most depressing sites in Berlin, functioning as the site of circus performances and as a giant parking lot. Despite the hopes of civic planners to return the square to prewar glory, at least half of the landscape around it was snapped up in 1990 at deflated prices by Daimler-Benz, and its architectural future remains uncertain.

The neighborhood you're traversing was filled during World War II with the densest concentration of Nazi administrative buildings in Germany, known collectively as the *Regierungsviertel*. As you walk north along Ebertstrasse, look at the barren mound to your right. Difficult to discern, it's noticeable only as a deliberately understated bump in the hard-packed earth. It is the subject of hotly contested civic debates as well as an endless source of political embarrassment, and its role within the New Germany remains uncertain, especially as the value of the land it occupies continues to rise. This innocuous mound is the deliberately unpublicized:

10. **Remains of Hitler's Chancellery.** From the premises encircling it, the most powerful military machine in European history was directed. Reluctant to have the site of Hitler's suicide canonized by defeated Germans after World War II, Soviet soldiers demolished the once-massive building brick by brick following their occupation of the eastern zone, and here they established the broadest point of their impassible "No Man's Land." According to local legend, none of the Soviet-trained guard dogs patrolling the site during the Cold War would ever go near it unless forced, and even today, despite the efforts of several gardeners, no vegetation ever seems to grow there.

At this point, facing north, you'll be within the sightlines of the world-famous:

11. **Brandenburg Gate** (Brandenburger Tor), inspired by the Propylea of Athen's Parthenon and originally constructed in 1789 as a focal point for the grand avenues surrounding it. Its neoclassical grandeur marked for many years the boundary line between East and West Berlin. The gate also represents an early act of cooperation between the sectors of the once-divided city. When the Quadriga (a chariot drawn by four horses) atop the gate was destroyed during the war and the gate badly damaged, the West Berlin senate arranged for a new Quadriga to be hammered in copper and presented to the administration of East Berlin to place atop the newly repaired colonnade.

From the base of the Brandenburg Gate, walk north a short distance toward the Spree River to the large square called Platz der Republik. At the eastern edge of the square rises a rebuilt structure, gutted by a suspicious 1933 fire at the time of Hitler's rise to power, the:

12. **Reichstag** building. Designed in neo-Renaissance style, it was designated as the official seat of the German government after unification. Unfortunately, the growing pains of the new administration has required more room than the building contains. At press time, there remained considerable uncertainty over which government functions would remain in Bonn and which would be moved to Berlin. Despite the rapidly changing functions of this building, it continues to retain a powerful hold on the imagination of any student of the Nazi era.

Now, retrace your steps south to the base of the Brandenburg Gate and notice the broad, eastward-stretching panorama of one of the most famous thoroughfares in Europe:

13. **Unter den Linden.** The palaces and cafés that once lined this boulevard were legendary throughout Europe for a clientele that included virtually every famous artist and politician in the history of the German-speaking world. Various

monarchs planted symmetrical rows of trees, including Friedrich Wilhelm, the Great Elector, who decreed that anyone cutting down one of his lindens should have his hand amputated. Hitler, seemingly in defiance of monarchical tradition, cut all of them down to widen the boulevard for military parades. The East German communists replanted them after World War II and restored many of the neoclassical palaces and Humboldt University buildings lining its edges today.

Despite these efforts, the prewar gaiety and glamour of Unter den Linden has never returned. Despite its formal beauty and the glimmerings of street life along certain stretches, much of the east-to-west expanse remains monumental, monotonous, and lifeless.

REFUELING STOP   Operncafé, Unter den Linden 5 (tel. 030/200-02-56), was the most famous coffeehouse of prewar Berlin, occupying a section of a palace constructed in 1733 but destroyed during Allied bombing raids. Now restored, it has plenty of old-world charm and dispenses all sorts of drinks, light meals, snacks, and ice cream. Upstairs, you can order complete lunches and dinners.

Turn right at the fourth street on your right, the Charlottenstrasse, which within a few blocks runs into one of the most monumental squares in the former eastern sector, the:

14. Gendarmenmarkt. Despite its antique appearance, this graceful baroque square was reduced to rubble during World War II. Rebuilt in its original format by the Communists (who called it Platz der Akademie), it received its original form under Frederick the Great in the 1780s, when he ordered the rebuilding of two earlier (and more modest) churches along the lines of Santa Maria dei Miracoli and Santa Maria in Montesanto in the Piazza del Popolo in Rome. Both churches were built as symmetrical ornaments to flank the edges of the early 19th-century Schauspielhaus (theater) that arises between them.

Exit from the square's northeast corner, walking east for a few steps along Französische Strasse. Turn left at the Hedwigskirchgasse, and, when it funnels into the Bebelsplatz, admire the enormous dome of:

15. St. Hedwigs-Kathedrale, which now functions as a Roman Catholic cathedral. Begun in 1747 by Frederick the Great, probably as a gesture to appease his troublesome subjects in Catholic Silesia, it was the only Catholic church in Berlin, and it remained so until the mid-1880s. Plagued with structural problems early in its construction, with a copper-sheated dome designed after the Pantheon in Rome, it's a much simpler building than the one Frederick originally hoped for. Opposite the church on the Bebelplatz, completed in 1780, is the:

16. Royal Library (Königliche Bibliothek), part of Humboldt University. Modeled on the Royal Palace (Die Hofburg) in Vienna, the curved wings of the structure prompted irreverent Berliners to christen it the "Kommode" (chest of drawers).

Continue your walk east along Unter den Linden, which will become narrower and then end at:

17. Karl-Liebknecht-Platz and the **Lustgarden.** Before unification, the two together were known as Marx-Engels-Platz, considered the showcase of the East German state. Once the much-heralded site of the Kaiser's Palace, which was damaged during World War II and then completely demolished by the communists as a symbol of capitalistic decadence, the square is now a monument to the yearning for modernity of the old East German regime. Sadly, many of the graceless and angular buildings erected by the Communists were declared unfit for use after unification because of the massive asbestos content.

Exit from the Karl-Liebknecht-Platz and the Lustgarden by walking northeast on Karl-Liebnecht-Strasse. After several blocks, turn right onto Spandauer Strasse. Within two blocks, you'll reach one of the prides of the former East German program of historic restoration, a neighborhood that is quickly blossoming into a haven of coffeehouses, art galleries, and nightspots—the Nikolaiviertel. A warren of laboriously restored medieval and baroque buildings, the neighborhood's centerpiece is the:

18. Nikolaikirche. Berlin's oldest parish church has two spires that have become an emblem of the united city. Built of brick on foundations dating from the 13th century, the church boasts a refreshingly simple interior where, in 1307, Berlin and its neighbor, Cölln, decided to unite.

ORGANIZED TOURS

Because of its size Berlin can be difficult to navigate on your own. Therefore you may need the security of an organized tour. The best ones are operated by **Severin & Kühn,** Berliner Stadtrundfahrt, Kurfürstendamm 216 (second floor; tel. 030/883-10-15). Across from the Bristol Hotel Kempinski Berlin, this agency offers a host of tours.

Their 2-hour Berlin City Tour leaves at 11am, 1:30pm, and 4pm daily, costing 30 DM ($19.80); it takes in the most important attractions of Berlin, including Europa-Center, Unter den Linden, and the Brandenburg Gate.

The 3-hour Big Berlin Tour departs at 10am daily, costing 41 DM ($27.10); it visits Kreuzberg Forest, with a stopover at the Egyptian Museum.

In the environs, the most interesting tour is the 7½-hour Potsdam–Sans Souci, with a guided visit to the summer residence of Frederick the Great and a visit to the Cecilienhof, where the Potsdam Conference of 1945 was conducted. Departures are Tuesday through Sunday at 9:30am, costing 95 DM ($62.70).

BOAT EXCURSIONS   You might not think of a boat as a means of traveling in Berlin, but many operate here, and a boat ride can become quite an outing when you tire of museums and the cafés along the Kurfürstendamm. The lakes of Wannsee (known as "Kleiner" and "Grösser," depending on their size) are the major targets in summer. Sand has been imported from some of the North Sea beaches, and on a hot day the **Wannsee Strandbad** is packed. The lake fills with sailboats.

Berliners, who boast that their city has more bridges than Venice, deliver 30 percent of their freight by boat. The Spree and Havel rivers—ranging from narrow channels to large lakes—snake through the city. A network of locks and canals form a lacelike gridwork. During the Cold War, many waterways were blocked, but now they are open again, filled with floating Berliners or foreign visitors. You can take tours that are short rides for close-up views of the inner city or daylong adventures along the Spree and Havel, the latter often turning into beer-drinking fests.

Berliners can also escape the concrete of the downtown area for boat rides through forests and hills. The best-known boat operator is **Stern und Kreis-schiffahrt,** Sachlbernstrasse 60 (tel. 030/803-87-50 or 810-00-40). Among its many boats, it has a lake steamer shaped like a whale, called *Moby Dick.* This or another of the firm's craft departs from a point near the terminus of U-Bahn line no. 6 at Tegel. Walk through the suburb of Tegel to the Greenwich Promenade 10 minutes from the U-Bahn station. Boats operate between March and late September. A 4½-hour trip leaves from Tegel at 10:30am and 12:40pm, costing 13 DM ($8.60) for adults and half price for children. A longer tour encompasses the Tegelsee, the Hohenzollernkanal, the Ploetzensee locks, the Charlottenburger Lake, the Spree River, Havel Lake, Spandau, and Wannsee, the latter the site of the notorious Wannsee Conference of January 20, 1942, where Hitler and SS officials completed details for the "final solution" to exterminate European Jewry. For information, call the numbers listed above. Reservations are usually necessary.

In eastern Berlin, there are boat excursions on the Spree. For a scenic boat ride through the waterways of the city, check with **Weisse Flotte,** whose white-painted vessels dock at Treptower Park (tel. 030/271-22-37). They operate daily between late April and early October, usually leaving about eight times a day. The cost of a trip is 13 DM ($8.60) for adults, half price for children. After a round trip through the lakes at Luisenhain, I'd suggest you get off in Köpenick, near the Mecklenburger Dorf, which is a reconstruction of a typical 19th-century village in the north of Germany. In the open-air restaurant you can obtain light meals. All Berlin specialties are accompanied by the brew, of course.

4. SPORTS & RECREATION

JOGGING   Head for the vast and verdant leafiness of the **Grunewald,** criss-crossed with pedestrian and cyclists' paths. Set on the city's western edge, it's appropriate for very long endurance tests and a respite from the city's congestion. Closer to the center is the **Tiergarten,** which offers the advantage of intense doses of history because of its many monuments and memorials. Also appropriate are the grounds of **Charlottenburg Castle,** whose perimeter measures about 2 miles.

RIDING   If it intrigues you, do as the Kaisers did and embark on an equestrian jaunt by renting a horse from the **Reitschule Onkel Toms Hütte,** Onkel-Tom-Strasse 172 (tel. 030/813-2081).

SPECTATOR SPORTS   For Berliners, soccer is the most popular sport. For information about which teams are playing in town on any given day, ask the receptionist at your hotel, refer to the daily newspaper or to the weekly magazine *Berlin Programm,* or contact the AMK Berlin, Messedamm 22, D-1000 Berlin 19 (tel. 030/30-38-0).

SWIMMING   Berlin has dozens of pools. One of the best equipped, (once the pride of the East German Communist regime) is the **Sports and Recreation Center,** Landsbergee Allee 77 (tel. 030/83-320). Here you'll find a swimming pool, a diving pool, a wave pool, an assortment of waterfalls, a jet pool, sauna and solarium facilities, a weight room, and about a half-dozen restaurants and snack bars. (Also on the premises is a bowling alley.)

A worthy competitor (just east of Tempelhof Airport) is the **BLUB Badeparadis Lido,** Buschkrugallee 64 (tel. 030/606-6060), with indoor and outdoor pools, six saunas, a steam room, solariums, and a water slide that is supposed to be the highest and longest in Europe.

For one of the closest approximations of the spa ritual in the heart of Berlin, head for the **Europa-Center,** where a company named Thermen, Nürnbergerstrasse 7 (tel. 030/261-6032), offers an array of heated pools, saunas, massage facilities, and solariums. For outdoor swimming during the hot months, there are beaches at the **Wannsee,** one of Europe's largest lake beaches. (Take the S-Bahn to the Nikolaisee and follow the hordes of bathers heading toward the water's edge.)

TENNIS AND SQUASH   Try **Tennis & Squash City,** Brandenburgischestrasse 31, in the district of Wilmersdorf (tel. 030/87-90-97), where you'll find almost a dozen squash courts and seven tennis courts. Closer to the center is the Tennisplätze am Ku'damm, Cicerostrasse 55A (tel. 030/89-66-30).

5. SAVVY SHOPPING

Store prices in Berlin are considered more reasonable than those often charged in German cities like Hamburg, Düsseldorf, Cologne, and Munich. The reason, perhaps, is that Berlin lacks the substantial moneyed class found in these other prosperous cities.

The central shopping destinations are Kurfürstendamm, Tauentzienstrasse, Am Zoo, and Kantstrasse. You might also want to walk up streets that intersect with Tauentzienstrasse: Marburger, Ranke, and Nürnberger.

Bric-a-brac collectors need not leave western Berlin empty-handed—head for Kantstrasse. Frankly, many items are junk, but perhaps you'll find something appealing. **Ku'damm-Karree,** Kurfürstendamm 206–208 (tel. 030/883-10-71), contains 35 shops in its shopping arcade at the corner of Knesebeckstrasse. You can buy old books, prints, jewelry, clothing, whatever, and patronize two theaters, or 26 bars and restaurants here. Take the U-Bahn to Uhlandstrasse.

ANTIQUES

ASTORIA, Bleibtreustrasse 50. Tel. 030/312-83-04.

Some of the 20th century's most memorable decorative accessories were produced in the 1920s and 1930s, just before Europe was blasted apart by World War II. One store that does its best to pay this period homage is Astoria, whose buyers frequently scour the antiques markets of France, England, and Germany. Inside, you'll find dressers, mirrors, lamps, tables, and jewelry, as well as a handful of recent reproductions.

HARMEL'S, Damaschkestrasse 24. Tel. 030/324-22-92.

Most of the inventory was gathered in England and France, a commentary on the relative scarcity—because of wartime bombing—of genuine German antiques. The carefully chosen stock stresses furniture, jewelry, and accessories from the Victorian and Edwardian eras.

ART GALLERIES

GALERIE BRUSBERG, Kurfürstendamm 213. Tel. 030/882-76-82.

This reigns as one of the most visible and influential art galleries in Germany. Established in the 1960s by Dieter Brusberg, it counts itself lucky to occupy the second floor of one of the only never-bombed buildings along the Kurfürstendamm. (Built around 1900, it housed the residences of army officers and physicians.) For years, the gallery has handled the work of Max Ernst, Salvador Dalí, Joan Miró, Picasso, and René Magritte. Since unification, it has placed special emphasis on painters of the old Eastern bloc, most notably Bernhard Heisig, Wolfgang Mattheuer, and Werner Tübke. Paintings begin at around 6,000 DM ($3,960). No one will bother you if you drop in just for a look.

GALERIE PELS-LEUSDEN AND VILLA GRIESBACH AUKTIONEN, Fasanenstrasse 25. Tel. 030/882-68-11.

The gallery building is considered a historic monument in its own right. Built in the 1880s by architect Hans Grisebach as his private home, it devotes two floors to 19th- and 20th-century mostly German art. (A scattering of French and American paintings from the same era are also displayed.) Prices begin at 250 DM ($165) for the least expensive lithograph but can go much higher. In November and June, the building functions as headquarters and display area for two of Berlin's most visible art auctions. Nearby is the Käthe Kollwitz Museum.

LADENGALLERIE, Kurfürstendamm 64. Tel. 030/881-42-14.

Small and personalized, this one-room art gallery specializes in month-long shows featuring individual German artists. Exhibitions have a museumlike air and are often worth a visit on your way along the Kurfürstendamm.

ZILLE HOF, Fasanenstrasse 14. Tel. 030/313-43-33.

Dusty and claustrophobic, this somewhat peculiar shop is precariously located amid some of Berlin's most expensive real estate, near the exclusive Savoy Hotel. Set next to the overhang of the S-Bahn tracks, it contains a curious mixture of value and junk that for some visitors evokes memories of Berlin prior to World War II.

CHINA & PORCELAIN

HELMUT TIMBERG, Kurfürstendamm 214. Tel. 030/881-91-58.

✪ Helmut Timberg offers the finest array of exquisite Meissen dinner plates in Berlin. He also displays and sells Dresden ware, including sculpture and chandeliers. This is one of the most famous porcelain outlets in Europe.

ROYAL PORCELAIN FACTORY, Wegelystrasse 1. Tel. 030/39-00-90.

✪ Known as KPM, the Royal Porcelain Factory has been in existence since 1763. The Hohenzollern dynasty turned it into Prussia's answer to Meissen in Saxony. Patterns are handmade and hand-painted and based for the most part on designs from the 18th and 19th centuries. Prices are royal too. Products from this factory carry a distinctive official signature, an imperial orb and the letters KPM. Guided tours let you look at the beautiful work of the employees, and you can buy exquisite pieces of porcelain here. If you don't have time to visit the main headquarters, you can look at a good selection of its offerings at **KPM,** Kurfürstendamm 26A (tel. 030/881-18-02).

DEPARTMENT STORES

KAUFHAUS DES WESTENS, Wittenbergplatz. Tel. 030/21-21-0.

✪ Known popularly as KaDeWe (kah-DAY-vay), this is a luxury department store about 2 blocks from the Kurfürstendamm. The huge store, whose name means "department store of the west," was established some 75 years ago. Of all the extravagant items on display, it is known mainly for its food department on the sixth floor, which is open Monday to Friday from 9am to 6:30pm and on Saturday from 9am to 2pm. This has been called the greatest food emporium in the world. The finest in German sausages are displayed, some 1,000 varieties. But not only that—delicacies from all the world are shipped in. Sit-down counters are available for sipping Sekt or ordering tasty dishes and desserts. After proper fortification, you can explore the six floors of merchandise. KaDeWe is more than a department store—one shopper called it a "collection of first-class specialty shops."

WERTHEIM, Kurfürstendamm 231. Tel. 030/88-20-61.

In the heart of the city near the Kaiser Wilhelm Memorial Church and the Europa-Center, this is a good all-around store to stock up on travel aids and general basics. It is also the distributor of a number of perfumes, clothing for all the family, jewelry, electrical devices, household goods, photography supplies, and souvenirs. It also has one of the largest restaurants in Berlin with a grand view over half the city. The department store also has a shoe-repair section.

DESIGN

ROSENTHAL, Kurfürstendamm 226. Tel. 030/881-70-51.

If you're seeking modern design, head here for contemporary Rosenthal designs, which are made in two villages in Bavaria. Some Berliners come here to shop for wedding gifts. In addition to Rosenthal porcelain, you'll find Boda glassware along with elegantly modern tableware.

FASHION

E. BRAUN & CO., Kurfürstendamm 43. Tel. 030/881-34-62.

This is one of the most exclusive clothing stores in Berlin, ideal for women and men. It distributes such prestigious designer names as Chanel and Valentino, along with Christian Dior and Leonard. It also offers Chester Barrie, Kiton, and Hermès designs for men and carries part of the Salvatore Ferragamo line, along with deluxe accessories.

MODENHAUS HORN, Kurfürstendamm 213. Tel. 030/881-40-55.
Berlin is one of the world's most fashion-conscious cities, and here you can look at a sample of what is *au courant* for chic women.

SONIA RYKIEL, Kurfürstendamm 186–187. Tel. 030/882-17-74.
This is the only shop in Germany devoted exclusively to this successful French fashion mogul. Ms. Rykiel, in addition to designing some of the most sophisticated hotel interiors in Paris, also designed the interior of this shop, which opened in 1990—a showcase of the stylish and fashionable wear. Even a Sonia Rykiel T-shirt is expensive, however.

JEWELRY

GALERIE LALIQUE, Bleibtreustrasse 47. Tel. 030/881-97-62.
Considered one of the more unusual jewelry stores in Berlin, this emporium stocks the original designs of about 50 German-based designers. Most pieces sold here are modern interpretations using more precious colored stones (sapphires, rubies, and emeralds, as well as diamonds) than you might have expected. Despite the similarity of the store's name with that of the French glass designer, it does not sell crystal or glassware.

LEATHER

ETIENNE AIGNER, Kurfürstendamm 197. Tel. 030/883-72-33.
Leather goods, especially shoes, are sold at the top-rated Etienne Aigner, along with stylish clothes for both men and women.

MARKETS

If you're a flea market buff, you'll also find a large flea market going strong every Saturday and Sunday on **Strasse des 17. Juni** (tel. 030/322-81-99), west of the Tiergarten S-Bahn station.

ANTIK & FLOHMARKT, Friedrichstrasse S-Bahn station, Berlin-Mitte. Tel. 030/215-02-129.
You might want to check out the action at one of the latest flea markets in Berlin, occupying part of the S-Bahn station in old East Berlin. Some 100 vendors try to tempt buyers with porcelain, odds and ends, bits of junk, brassware, and assorted bric-a-brac, even mementos of World War II. It is open Wednesday through Monday from 11am to 5pm.

TURKISH BAZAAR, bank of the Maybachufer, Kreuzberg. Tel. 030/6809-29-26.
This place has been converted by guest workers into a Turkish Bazaar. Take the U-Bahn to Kottbusser Tor. You'll think you're in Istanbul, as you wander about checking over the jewelry, glassware, onyx, and copper items. You can take time out to enjoy Turkish coffee with baklava, perhaps ordering some kebabs if you want to have lunch.

PEWTER

BERLINER ZINNFIGUREN KABINETT, Knesebeckstrasse 88. Tel. 030/31-08-02.

The entire Prussian army—that is, in miniature—is for sale at Berliner Zinnfiguren Kabinett. The army comes in pewter. All figures are hand-molded, hand-painted, and hand-carved, an art form famous in Germany for many, many years. The least expensive soldier always is sold unpainted, but you can pay considerably for a fully rounded, hand-painted figure. These figures depict warriors from the ancient Greek empire up to fashion models in contemporary costume of the 1980s. Students of the two world wars will appreciate the 20th-century German soldiers. The business has been owned by three generations of the Scholtz family.

SHOPPING CENTER

EUROPA-CENTER, Tauentzienstrasse.
The average shopper with average requirements will head first for the Europa-Center in the heart of the western city. Take the U-Bahn to Kurfürstendamm. Here, in addition to the Berlin casino and a number of restaurants and cafés, you'll find a dazzling array of 100 shops, Berlin's largest indoor shopping center, topped by the Mercedes-Benz star. The merchandise is wide ranging, running up and down the price-scale ladder.

6. EVENING ENTERTAINMENT

In Berlin, nightlife runs around the clock, and much of it starts after 11pm. Of course, for those who like to go to bed at that time, there is still much to see and do before 11pm, including attending floor shows, cabarets, live music houses, a gambling casino, operas, chamber music or orchestral concerts, and theater.

To find out what's happening, pick up a copy of *Berlin Programm*, which offers a detailed guide to current events, be it concerts or shows. The cost is 2.80 DM ($1.90). Biweekly magazines include *Tip* at 3.70 DM ($2.40) and *Zitty* at 3.30 DM ($2.20), each packed with listings of local events.

THE PERFORMING ARTS

OPERA & CLASSICAL MUSIC

BERLINER PHILHARMONISCHES ORCHESTER (Berlin Philharmonic), Matthäikirchstrasse 1. Tel. 030/25-48-80.
The Berlin Philharmonic is one of the world's premier orchestras. For many years under the direction of the renowned Herbert von Karajan, it now has Claudio Abbado as music director. You can purchase tickets for performances at the office in the main lobby of the orchestra hall Monday to Friday from 3:30 to 6pm and Saturday and Sunday from 11am to 2pm. It is not possible to place orders by phone. If you're staying in a first-class or deluxe hotel, you can usually get the concierge to obtain seats for you. Of the 2,218 seats, none is more than 100 feet from the rostrum. The location is in the Tiergarten sector; the hall can be reached from the center of the Ku'damm by taking bus no. 129.
Tickets: 14 DM–103 DM ($9.20–$68).

DEUTSCHE OPER BERLIN, Bismarckstrasse 35. Tel. 030/34-381 for information, or 341-02-49 for ticket sales.
In Charlottenburg is one of the world's great opera houses, built on the site of the prewar opera house that enjoyed world fame. The present structure is a notable example of modern theater architecture that seats 1,885. The house attracts opera lovers from all over the world. The company is willing to tackle a

Puccini favorite, a Janácek rarity, or a modern work, and they have a complete Wagner repertoire. There is a ballet company that performs once a week. Concerts, including Lieder evenings, are also presented on the opera stage. U-Bahn: Deutsche Oper.
Tickets: 12 DM–130 DM ($7.90–$85.80).

DEUTSCHE STAATSOPER [German State Opera], Unter den Linden 7. Tel. 030/208-22-14.

If you can get a ticket to a performance at the Deutsche Staatsoper, by all means go. It often presents some of the finest opera in the world, along with a regular repertoire of ballet and concerts. The box office generally sells tickets from noon to 6pm on Monday to Saturday and from 4 to 6pm on Sunday. However, if you visit near the end of summer, the opera will be closed. U-Bahn: Französische Strasse.
Tickets: 6 DM–45 DM ($4–$29.70).

KOMISCHE OPER [Comic Opera], Behrensstrasse 55–57. Tel. 030/229-25-55.

A visit to another Berlin performing venue in the east might be in order. The Komische Oper lies between the S-Bahnhof Friedrichstrasse and the U-Bahnhof Stadtmitte. The opera is known for its avant-garde productions. Orchestral concerts and light operas are also performed here. The box office is open Monday to Friday 2 to 6pm, Saturday 10am to 6pm, and Sunday 1 hour before the performance. U-Bahn: Französische Strasse.
Tickets: 5 DM–60 DM ($3.30–$39.60).

THEATER DES WESTENS, Kantstrasse 12. Tel. 030/31-90-30.

The lighter muse of the musical is at home at the Theater des Westens, built in 1896 and located between the Berlin Zoo and Kurfürstendamm. The box office is open Tuesday through Saturday from 10am to 6pm and Sunday from 3 to 6pm. U-Bahn: Kurfürstendamm.
Tickets: 15 DM–86 DM ($9.90–$56.80).

THEATER

The city's most distinguished theater is the Staatliche Schauspielbühnen Berlin. There are three theaters under this umbrella. The largest is the **Schiller-Theater,** Bismarckstrasse 110 (tel. 030/312-65-05). Classic plays, as well as modern drama, are presented; often plays are commissioned. You are likely to see anything, perhaps Shakespeare's *Macbeth.* A smaller stage at this theater is the **Werkstatt** (Workshop) for new or experimental pieces. The third theater is the **Schlosspark-Theater,** Schloss Strasse 48 (tel. 030/793-15-15). Tickets range from 10 DM to 52 DM ($6.60 to $34.30) in the Schiller-Theater and from 8 DM to 51 DM ($5.30 to $33.70) in the Schlosspark-Theater. Tickets for the Werkstatt are 20 DM ($13.20) for all seats. The three theaters produce about 25 to 30 shows per season. They are closed from late July until late August. U-Bahn: Ernst-Reuter-Platz for the Schiller-Theater and Werkstatt. S-Bahn: Steglitz for the Schlosspark-Theater.

SCHAUBÜHNE AM LEHNINER PLATZ, Kurfürstendamm 153. Tel. 030/89-00-23.

Schaubühne am Lehniner Platz is considered by some to be one of the most important German-language theaters in the country. The location is at the east end of the Kurfürstendamm, near Lehniner Platz. Three plays can be presented at the same time because of its three different stages. The box office is open Monday to Saturday from 11am to 6:30pm and Sunday and holidays from 3 to 6:30pm. Most performances are Tuesday to Sunday at 8:30pm. Closed: July. Bus: 119 or 129.
Tickets: 15 DM–50 DM ($9.90–$33).

BERLINER ENSEMBLE, Am Bertolt-Brecht-Platz 1. Tel. 030/288-81-55.

One of the most famous theaters is the Berliner Ensemble, which the late playwright, Bertolt Brecht, co-creator of *The Threepenny Opera,* founded in 1948. Brecht's wife, the great actress Helene Weigel, played a role in the founding and was its long-time director. Works by Brecht and other guest playwrights are presented here, and most seats are reasonably priced. The box office is open Monday through Saturday from 11am to 6:30pm and Sunday from 3 to 6:30pm. Most performances are presented at 7pm on Tuesday to Sunday. S-Bahn: Friedrichstrasse.

Tickets: 12 DM–40 DM ($7.90–$26.40).

CLUB & MUSIC SCENE

CABARET

Most popular among visitors to Berlin is the kind of nightspot depicted in the musical *Cabaret,* with floor-show patter and acts full of satire aimed at both the political and the social scene.

LA VIE EN ROSE, Europa-Center, Tauentzienstrasse. Tel. 030/323-60-06.

The major cabaret and revue theater of Berlin is found in the cellar of the Europa-Center. The show is a musical revue, including singing, dancing, and beautiful costumes. Spoken words are as often in English as in German, because the cabaret attracts a largely international crowd. The doors always open 30 minutes before the evening's first show.

Admission: 25 DM ($16.50); 35 DM ($23.10) minimum.

Open: Tues–Fri and Sun, show at 10pm; Sat, shows at 8pm, 10pm, and midnight. **Bus:** 119 or 129.

DANCE CLUBS

BIG EDEN, Kurfürstendamm 202. Tel. 030/882-61-20.

Big Eden bills itself as a dance paradise for 2,000 people. The latest electronic gimmicks, all zany, decorate this unique place, the creation of the fertile mind of Rolf Eden, since 1968 Berlin's most successful disco operator. The strobe system alone may send you into a trance. Here, you'll find a mélange of Berlin youth, in every conceivable form of dress (or lack of it), dancing to recorded music. As befits the means of most of the clientele, prices are kept low. Drinks start at 4 DM ($2.60).

Admission: Sun–Thurs free; Fri–Sat 7 DM ($4.60).

Open: Sun–Thurs 8pm–4am, Fri–Sat 8pm–7am. **U-Bahn:** Uhlandstrasse.

CAFÉ KEESE, Bismarckstrasse 108. Tel. 030/312-91-11.

What the Germans call a "ball paradox" is offered at Café Keese—a fancy way of saying that the women have a chance to ask the men to dance, instead of the other way around. People go here who actually like to dance the traditional way. The orchestra plays music quite slowly at times, and the place is often jammed, especially on Saturday night. If you're a lone male and fear the women will mob you if you make an appearance on the floor, you can remain perched at the bar. Incidentally, the management reserves the right to kick out any male patron who turns down a female's request to dance! The Keese sees itself as something of a matrimonial bureau—always announcing new statistics about the number of people who have met and fallen in love on its premises and later got married. Men and women are requested to wear formal attire. Inside, you can order a beer at 7 DM ($4.60)—the cheapest way to spend an evening here, incidentally—or most whiskies at 12 DM ($7.90) a shot.

Admission: Sun–Thurs free, although there's a minimum drink charge of 7 DM ($4.60); Fri–Sat 14 DM ($9.20).

Open: Mon–Thurs 8pm–3am, Fri–Sat 8pm–4am, Sun 4pm–1am. **U-Bahn:** Ernst-Reuter-Platz.

CHIP, Berlin Hilton, Mohrenstrasse 30. Tel. 030/23820.

Located in the basement of Berlin's third-largest hotel, Chip is one of the city's most unusual and appealingly glossy discos. Its high-tech battery of accessories includes an array of laserlike lights and a fog machine that adds a surrealistic mist to the crowded dance floor. Recent video clips play simultaneously to an international crowd of nightclubbing patrons. Beer costs 5 DM ($3.30).

Admission: 20 DM ($13.20).

Open: Daily 9pm–dawn.

DSCHUNGEL [Jungle], Nürnbergerstrasse 53. Tel. 030/218-66-98.

One of the most fashionable rendezvous points in town attracts everybody from film personalities to German tennis star Boris Becker. Berlin's beau monde gathers downstairs before heading upstairs to the disco or up a spiral staircase to a favored balcony spot for drinks. The price of a beer is 5 DM ($3.30). Although this place opens at 11pm, no one with any social pizzazz shows up before 1am.

Admission: 10 DM ($6.60) Fri–Sat; free other nights.

Open: Wed–Mon 11pm–4am. **U-Bahn:** Ku'damm or Wittenbergplatz.

EIERSCHALE, Rankestrasse 1. Tel. 030/882-53-05.

Eierschale means "eggshell" in German. There is live music of one kind or another here nightly beginning at 9:30pm. Possibilities include country and western; rock and roll; and, on Friday and Saturday only, jazz. Beer costs from 4.50 DM ($3), and when music is presented there is an admission charge. It is a Berlin tradition to visit the Eierschale for its fixed-price Sunday brunch, served from 8am to 2pm and costing 13.50 DM ($8.90).

Admission: 4 DM ($2.60), which is applied to your first drink, when there's live music.

Open: Sun–Thurs 8am–2am, Fri–Sat 8am–4am. **U-Bahn:** Kurfürstendamm.

METROPOL, Nollendorfplatz 5, Schöneberg. Tel. 030/216-41-22.

One of the leading nightclubs in town happily blends straights and gays in what used to be a cinema. On Friday and Saturday nights, it is a standard disco. On those nights, a beer costs from 6 DM ($4). On every other night of the week concerts are presented at 8pm, lasting 90 minutes, with a total venue, including after-concert time lingering at the bar, of around 3 hours. The place is usually empty by 11pm. Most clients are in the 18-to-40 age group.

Admission: Disco nights, 10 DM ($6.60); concerts, 15 DM–35 DM ($9.90–$23.10).

Open: Sun–Thurs 8–11pm, Fri–Sat 10pm–8am. **U-Bahn:** Nollendorfplatz.

QUASIMODO, Kantstrasse 12A. Tel. 030/312-80-86.

Beer and wine—as well as live music—flow nightly in this pub-cum-soundstage. Popular with rockers from 20 to 30, it offers beer from 5 DM ($3.30). The music is rock, jazz, funk, whatever.

Admission: 10 DM–30 DM ($6.60–$19.80).

Open: Daily 9pm–1 or 3am. **U-Bahn:** Bahnhof Zoo. **Closed:** Aug.

DRAG SHOWS

Ever since the 1920s, when George Grosz was doing his savage caricatures and Greta Garbo, then unknown, was slipping around the town undetected, drag acts have been a staple of Berlin nightlife. Today's scene still goes on, the only problem being that it lacks a Christopher Isherwood to record it.

CHEZ NOUS, Marburgerstrasse 14. Tel. 030/213-18-10.

The show at Chez Nous has gone on to world fame, attracting an essentially straight clientele. The setting has been called mock Louis XIV. This club books some of the best transvestite acts in Europe, everything from a sultry, boa-draped striptease star from Rio de Janeiro to a drag queen who looks like a gun moll from the 1940s. Shows are nightly at 8:30 and 11pm. Sometimes, but only rarely, a late show at 1am will be offered on a Saturday night (but call about that). The first drink costs 30 DM ($19.80), which is the minimum.

Admission: 15 DM ($9.90).

Shows: Daily 8:30 and 11pm. **U-Bahn:** Wittenbergplatz.

GAY & LESBIAN BERLIN

On the gay circuit, Berlin has a trio of bars (Tom's, the Pool Disco, and the Knast Bar), sometimes jokingly referred to as "the Bermuda Triangle." Young men often bar-hop from one to the other. Motzstrasse is the center of many other gay and lesbian bars.

BEGINE CAFE-UND-KULTURZENTRUM FÜR FRAUEN, Potsdamer-strasse 139. Tel. 030/215-14-14.

For women, Café-und-Kulturzentrum für Frauen, established in 1986, is one of Berlin's most visible headquarters for feminists and the most obvious launching pad for women seeking to meet other women. Within its inner sanctum is a changing array of art exhibitions, poetry readings, German-language discussions, lectures, and social events. You can phone in advance to learn the program. The premises are occasionally transformed into a disco. At the bar, women can order a glass of wine for 4.50 DM ($3) or a cappuccino for 3.50 DM ($2.30).

Admission: Free.

Open: Daily 6pm–1am. **Bus:** 19 or 48.

KNAST BAR, Fuggerstrasse 34. Tel. 030/218-10-26.

The Knast is the leading leather bar of Berlin. No entrance fee is charged, and beer costs from 5.50 DM ($3.60).

Open: Daily 11pm–dawn. **U-Bahn:** Wittenbergplatz.

LIPSTICK, Richard-Wagner-Platz 5. Tel. 030/342-81-26.

This lesbian dance hall is hot, at least as of this writing. It perhaps attracts more lesbians than any other venue in town. On Tuesday, Thursday, or Sunday, men (mainly gay) are allowed in as well. The first Friday of the month draws a largely mixed crowd. Beer costs from 5.50 DM ($3.60).

Admission: 5 DM ($3.30).

Open: Daily 10pm–5am. **U-Bahn:** Deutsche Oper.

POOL DISCO, Motzstrasse 90. Tel. 030/218-75-29.

Usually very animated and crowded, this is the most popular gay disco in the western sector, attracting mostly young men in their 20s. Beer costs from 5.50 DM ($3.60).

Admission: 5 DM ($3.30) Fri–Sat; otherwise free.

Open: Wed and Fri–Sun 11pm–5am. **U-Bahn:** Wittenbergplatz.

TOM'S BAR, Motzstrasse 19. Tel. 030/213-45-70.

Tom's becomes crowded after 11pm, with young gay men flocking to the hottest dance club in the city. A beer costs from 5 DM ($3.30).

Admission: Free, except 5 DM ($3.30) on Fri–Sat.

Open: Daily 10pm–6am. **U-Bahn:** Wittenbergplatz.

WU WU, Kleistrasse 4. Tel. 030/213-63-92.

Wu Wu is a place for younger gay men—or, in the words of one client, "blue-jean babies." Of course, older men are always welcome. Beer costs 5 DM ($3.30).

Admission: Free, except 3 DM ($2) cover on Fri–Sat.

Open: Daily 10pm–7am. Shows presented Sun at 11:30pm. **U-Bahn:** Wittenbergplatz.

BAR & CAFE SCENE

CAFÉ LIFE

At its zenith, the mid-19th century, Berlin was famous for its cafés. Max Krell, an editor, once wrote: "Cafés were our homeland. They were the stock exchange of ideas, site of intellectual transactions, futures' market of poetic and artistic glory and defeat." Many of the most famous ones, such as the grand coffeehouses of Unter den Linden in East Berlin, or those celebrated in the post–World War I era among artists and writers—the Café des Westens and the Romanisches Café—didn't survive the Allied air raids of World War II. Some did survive in tattered remains; others fled to such points as Frankfurt; and many relocated from East Berlin to West Berlin following World War II. Coffeehouses, however, are still going strong in Berlin. They've changed with the times, but every true Berliner has his or her favorite. It is said that a person can tell who you are by the café you frequent. So, in your search for self-identity, I'll offer the following selections.

CAFÉ ADLON, Kurfürstendamm 69. Tel. 030/883-76-82.

At the turn of the century, the imposing neoclassical decor, overstuffed sofas, and formal waiters made this one of the most prestigious cafés in its neighborhood. Today, only a bit tattered around the edges, with a clientele considerably less formal than in days gone by, it still offers charming summertime vistas from its sidewalk tables and a view of Berlin kitsch from its interior. You'll find a huge selection of cakes, priced from 4.50 DM ($3). Coffee costs 6 DM ($4).

Open: Daily 10am–midnight. **U-Bahn:** Kurfürstendamm.

CAFÉ/BISTRO LEYSIEFFER, Kurfürstendamm 218. Tel. 030/882-78-20.

A relative newcomer when compared to the venerable ages of its better-established competitors, this family-operated gathering place was established in the early 1980s within what had been the Chinese embassy. Some of the ornate moldings and lighting fixtures are still in place from earlier times plus a pair of gilded lions guarding the entrance next door. The street level contains a pastry-and-candy shop, but most clients climb the flight of stairs to a marble-and-wood-sheathed café with a balcony overlooking the busy Ku'damm. A breakfast served here is one of the most elegant in town: Parma ham, smoked salmon, a freshly baked baguette, French butter, and—to round it off—champagne. During the rest of the day, the Leysieffer offers different hot and cold platters, including veal cutlets and beef in horseradish sauce, with meals costing from 20 DM ($13.20). You could also visit just for coffee and dessert (the apple strudel or the fruit-studded tiramisu would be a good choice), which together would cost about 10 DM ($6.60).

Open: Mon-Sat 9am–8pm, Sun 10am–7pm. **U-Bahn:** Uhlandstrasse.

CAFÉ KRANZLER, Kurfürstendamm 18–19. Tel. 030/882-69-11.

✪ Originally established in 1825, Café Kranzler is on the eastern side of town, near Unter den Linden. About a hundred years later, it packed up its porcelain, busy waiters, and—with its arts-oriented clientele in tow—moved to the (then) less imposing district around Kurfürstendamm, where it quickly becomes fashionable. Like almost everything else along the street, it rose from the ashes of World War II ready to thrive in what had become the new center of western Berlin. Today you'll find an unashamedly modern establishment, with striped canopies, sidewalk tables and chairs, and two floors of densely packed tables. Owned by Swiss inventors, the café/restaurant has a selection of such Swiss specialties as shredded veal Zürich style, which you can eat with such Swiss wines as Fendant, one of the array of ever-changing daily specials, a pastry from the buffet, and a choice from the wide selection of ice creams. Meals cost 25 DM to 50 DM ($16.50–$33). Beer costs 6.80 DM ($4.50); liquor starts at 4 DM ($2.60).

Open: Daily 8am–midnight. **U-Bahn:** Kurfürstendamm.

CAFÉ MOHRING, Kurfürstendamm 215. Tel. 030/881-20-75.

Set behind a belle époque awning and a bevy of outdoor tables, this café is the survivor of a tradition begun in 1898 that welcomed political and literary opinions of all persuasions. From the terrace you'll have a view of the deliberately unrepaired tower of the Kaiser Wilhelm Memorial Church. The fresh flowers and the many older women who linger over pastries contribute to the strong impression of a bygone era. Cakes cost from 4.25 DM ($2.80); breakfast starts at 9 DM ($5.90). Meals range from 10 DM to 30 DM ($6.60 to $19.80).

Open: Daily 7am–midnight. **U-Bahn:** Uhlandstrasse.

OFFENBACH STUBEN, Stubbenkammerstrasse 8. Tel. 030/448-41-96.

Offenbach Stuben has a theatrical flair, honoring the creator of the grand opera *The Tales of Hoffmann.* In fact, this is an independently run eatery, reportedly subsidized by two of the leading theaters of the capital, the Berlin Comic Opera and the Metropol Theater. It presents an array of international dishes and Berliner specialties at around 35 DM ($23.10) for dinner. Coffee costs 3.50 DM ($2.30). The cuisine includes such dishes as veal steak with ham and mushrooms. Reservations are needed.

Open: Daily 7pm–2am. **S-Bahn:** Prenzlauer.

OPERNCAFÉ, Unter den Linden 5. Tel. 030/200-02-56.

⭐ The leading café of eastern Berlin is a good choice if you're visiting the Staatsoper next door. The building is a remodeled version of a former structure built for royalty in 1733. The atmosphere is traditional, but the interior is of today. You have a choice of places at which to eat, drink, or dine. In the cellar is a bar, on the street floor is a café, and upstairs are two restaurants. The café has a small dance floor with a bandstand. An orchestra plays in the evening until 9:30. Lots of green plants and framed theater prints add extra glamour. Tuesday to Saturday from 10am, you can order light snacks, Berliner cakes, tea, and coffee. Dinner often costs from 30 DM ($19.80). The second-floor Weinrestaurant offers more formal dining where specialties include curried pork and porterhouse steak for two. Meals cost from 60 DM ($39.60) here. On a lower level is the Nachtbar. In the café, coffee costs from 3.50 DM ($2.30). At least 70 varieties of drinks are offered.

Open: Nachtbar, daily 9:30pm–4:30am; café, daily 8:30am–midnight; restaurants, daily 11am–midnight. **U-Bahn:** Französische Strasse.

CLASSIC WINE CELLAR

HISTORISCHER WEINKELLER, Alt-Pichelsdorf 32. Tel. 030/361-80-56.

Squat and unpretentious, this inn lies on a cobbled street about a mile west of the Olympia-Stadion. Established in 1753, it has survived wars and all sorts of disasters and might be the site of one of your more interesting evenings in Berlin. In winter, the staff lights a sugarcone and performs the medieval ceremony of "burning the punch" three times a week: Wednesday, Friday, and Saturday between 10 and 11pm. The punch, a kind of hot spiced wine, costs 10 DM ($6.60) per glass; as the flame burns, you're supposed to make a wish. On other nights, you can order beer or any of more than 100 German wines at prices that begin at 6.50 DM ($4.30) per glass. You can also order full meals, priced at 25 DM to 40 DM ($16.50 to $26.40). (If you plan to dine, you should reserve in advance.) The setting is a highly atmospheric vaulted cellar, although during summer, the place expands into a rustically nostalgic beer garden.

Open: Daily noon–2pm. **U-Bahn:** Olympia-Stadion.

BEER GARDENS

LORETTA IM GARTEN, Lietzenburgerstrasse 89. Tel. 030/882-33-54.

This beer garden is surprisingly rustic for such a midcity location. It offers both waiter service and self-service. It has wooden banquettes and paneling, with a handful of outdoor toys to amuse your children as you drink; there's even a Ferris wheel. It also offers live musical acts, including country and western, folk, and rock and roll. Beer costs from 6 DM ($4). You can also enjoy hearty Berliner and German regional dishes, with meals beginning at 16 DM ($10.60).

Open: Daily 10am–1am. **Closed:** Mid-Oct to Mar 31. **U-Bahn:** Uhlandstrasse.

WIRTSHAUS ZUM LÖWEN, Hardenbergstrasse 29. Tel. 030/26-21-02-0.

One of the most gemütlich places in Berlin is Wirtshaus zum Löwen, a pub in the city center directly opposite the Kaiser Wilhelm Memorial Church. It is attractively decorated, and even in winter you get the feeling of sitting out under the chestnut trees although you're snug and warm inside. In summer you can soak up the atmosphere in the beer garden. Every night, a band plays for dancing and singing, with the guests joining in, creating a happy feeling like that found at the Oktoberfest in Munich. The kitchen offers good plain German food, including Bavarian specialties; hot meals start at 10 DM ($6.60). Also served is Munchener Löwenbräu, typical German beer, costing 6.50 DM ($4.30) for half a liter. The best time to come here to enjoy the atmosphere is from 7pm to midnight.

Open: Sun–Thurs 10am–midnight, Fri–Sat until 2am. **U-Bahn:** Zoologischer Garten.

ZENNER, Alt-Treptow 14–17. Tel. 030/272-72-11.

Berlin's largest and oldest beer garden is Zenner, which opened in 1727 in the eastern sector. This pleasure pavilion beside the River Spree in Alt-Treptow, a former fishing village, is housed in a tavern in a neoclassical building. Meals cost from 30 DM ($19.80), and there are many places for drinking, ranging from an upstairs café to a beer garden under linden trees. Beer starts at 4 DM ($2.60). There's dancing on Friday and Saturday, live music on Sunday, and disco action on Monday. You can also rent boats to go for a spree on the Spree.

Open: Tues–Thurs and Sun 11am–8pm, Mon and Fri–Sat 11am–1am. **S-Bahn:** Planterwald.

ELEGANT BARS

HARRY'S NEW YORK BAR, in the Grand Hotel Esplanade, Lützowufer 15. Tel. 030/26-10-11.

Harry's is an aggressively stylized bar with minimalist decor. Entirely sheathed in slabs of polished dark-gray granite and studded with red-leather armchairs, pop art, and photographs of all the American presidents, it is modeled after that famous watering hole, Harry's Bar in Paris. Its drinks menu is a monument to the oral traditions of the IBF (International Bar Flies) Society and includes such favorites as "Mizner's Dream" (created in 1962 for the Boca Raton Hotel Club in Florida) and the 1964 classic, "The Petrifier" (ingredients unlisted), for two. Frequent visitors consider the "Dirty Harry," "Bill's Knockout Punch," and the "Flying Elephant" far more prosaic. In all, the menu lists almost 200 drinks—a small library by anyone's standards—as well as a limited selection of food items.

Suitable dress includes everything from leather jackets and microskirts with tights to business suits. Beer costs from 7 DM ($4.60), with more elaborate concoctions going for 14 DM ($9.20) and up.

Open: Daily noon–2 to 7am, depending on business. **U-Bahn:** Nollendorfplatz.

TIMES BAR, in the Savoy Hotel, Fasanenstrasse 9–10. Tel. 030/311-03-0.

One of the special bars of Berlin is the cozy and intimate Times Bar, almost like a wood-paneled library in someone's private home. Dedicated to *The Times* (London), whose latest edition is often displayed in the window, this bar is a comfortable rendezvous point. Guests sit in leather upholstered chairs, enjoying the English-language newspapers and the style and quiet charm of the place. In addition to drinks, light meals can also be had for about 25 DM ($16.50). Perhaps you'd like some lobster soup or a bowl of velvety ice cream. Drinks cost from 13 DM ($8.60).

Open: Daily 6pm–1am or "later," depending on needs of patrons. **U-Bahn:** Bahnhof Zoo.

FINDING A KNEIPE

It has long been the custom of a typical Berliner to find a favorite Kneipe in which to relax after work or to meet sympathetic friends (or be introduced to new ones). A Kneipe is the equivalent of a Londoner's local pub. Usually (but not always) these are cozy rendezvous places. There are hundreds of Kneipen in Berlin. I can only get you started by recommending a handful.

AX-BAR, Leibnizstrasse 34. Tel. 030/313-85-94.

Off Kantstrasse is a hangout for movie people and Berlin literati. The bar is well decorated, but there's no sign on the door. They like to keep it discreet here. You can order Kleinigkeiten or tasty snacks with your beer or wine. Viennese-style meals cost 25 DM to 40 DM ($16.50 to $26.40). Of course, many come here just to drink, paying from 5 DM ($3.30) for beer or from 10 DM ($6.60) for a mixed drink. The most popular time to eat here is around 9pm, when it's best to reserve in advance.

Open: Tues–Sun 7pm–3am. **U-Bahn:** Savignyplatz.

GASTSTÄTTE HOECK (Wilhelm Hoeck), Wilmersdorferstrasse 149. Tel. 030/341-31-10.

You'll find this place on a street lined with department stores and shops that are almost deserted after 6pm. Set behind a brightly illuminated facade jammed with slogans for local beers, it is distinctly divided into two very different sections. You (and half of the rest of the neighborhood) can have a drink in the very rowdy, sometimes raucous bar area, where—among other dramas—a clown may be playing the harmonica. The separate dining room serves traditional food. You can choose from more than a dozen kinds of beer (if in doubt, just ask for my favorite, Pilsner Urquell) and wine by the glass. Meals start at 30 DM ($19.80), and hot food is served Monday through Saturday from 11am to 11pm. Beer costs from 4.50 DM ($3).

Open: Daily 8am–midnight. **U-Bahn:** Bismarckstrasse.

LUTTER UND WEGNER 1811, Schlüterstrasse 55. Tel. 030/881-34-40.

Established just after World War II, the restaurant was named after a gastronomic and social landmark, Lutter und Wegner, which in Wilhelmian days attracted Berlin's leading actors. With the original namesake, dating from1811, isolated in bombed-out obscurity in East Berlin, its owners set up this very successful grandchild in West Berlin in 1945. No one will mind if you remain in the outermost of the two rooms, at the stand-up bar, with a drink. If you want to dine, however, phone in advance, be on time, and be prepared to wait. Specialties include a soup of smoked trout and salmon with cranberry-cream sauce. Meals range from 35 DM to 42 DM ($23.10 to $27.70). Beer costs 5.50 DM ($3.60); liquor starts at 10 DM ($6.60).

Open: Restaurant, daily 6:30pm–midnight; bar, daily 6:30pm–3am. **S-Bahn:** Savignyplatz.

ZWIEBELFISCH, Savignyplatz 7–8. Tel. 030/31-73-63.

Zwiebelfisch has long been a favorite hangout of artists, writers, and newspaper people. It also attracts U.S. jazz artists after they finish their gigs of the evening in other Berlin clubs. Gossip is easily exchanged, and companions and friends easily met. There is a limited menu in case you want more than libations. Find a seat at one of the spacious wooden tables, where you can order drinks from 6 DM to 10 DM ($4 to $6.60); snacks and small platters of food cost from 7.50 DM to 15 DM ($5 to $9.90).

Open: Daily noon–6am. **S-Bahn:** Savignyplatz.

GAMBLING

SPIELBANK, at the Europa-Center (entrance on Budapesterstrasse). Tel. 030/25-00-89-0.

One of the biggest attractions for visitors is the Spielbank. Inside you'll find a number of roulette tables, in addition to tables for baccarat, blackjack, and other games. The bar is the longest in Berlin, and it's a watering spot between rounds at the tables. There's also a restaurant serving expensive international cuisine. Male guests should wear jackets and ties (no jeans or tennis shoes are allowed). It is important to bring along your passport.

Admission: 5 DM ($3.30); minimum bets 5 DM ($3.30). **U-Bahn:** Kurfurstendamm.

Open: Daily 3pm–3am.

CHAPTER 19
EASTERN GERMANY

A visit to the former country of East Germany today is to see history in the making. It is a land of dynamic change . . . and problems. But, even so, a visit here in the 1990s will provide stories you can tell your grandchildren. While there's still time, you can even buy souvenir chunks of the former Berlin Wall. Before the wall was erected in 1961, some four million East Germans escaped to the West.

The section the Soviet Union carved out of Germany after World War II was roughly the size of Ohio, its population less than a third of the Federal Republic's. Yet in the postwar era, East Germany rose to become an important industrial power. But all of what had been widely publicized as "the economic miracle" came apart in 1989, when East Germany stood as the "poor relation" to its economically powerful neighbor. Shortages of resources had taken their toll, and the economic machinery of the country was revealed to have steadily eroded. Party leaders, notably hard-liner Erich Honecker, were arrested, even as he prophesied, "The wall will last for at least another half century to protect our republic from thieves." Although he and other Communist party bosses preached self-sacrifice to their people, they were exposed as living "high off the hog," enjoying great luxury while literally stealing millions from the treasury.

In fall 1989, some two-thirds of the country's 16.7 million inhabitants crossed the once-feared border to visit West Germany. For many, it was the first time they'd ever set foot in West Berlin, even though they might have lived within a quarter of a mile of the border for 40 years. For an older generation, it was "coming home" again, with memories of a West Berlin that didn't exist any more.

Many stayed to live permanently in the western section. Others stocked up on consumer goods and planned to return next weekend. Still others, such as one eastern Berlin restaurant owner, fled to the western section only to return when the Honecker government collapsed under the furtive chants of "We are the people."

As it moves into the mid-1990s, the big question facing what is now eastern Germany is how to reinvent itself both economically and politically. Following unification, the question remained, "How will eastern Germany retain its separate identity?"

Many eastern Germans prefer the term "reassociation" instead of unification. Others fear that even though they may ultimately benefit economically from a more capitalistic system, there will be a period of difficult economic adjustment. Eastern Germans also fear that problems may be imported from the western section—notably crime and drugs—problems from which they have been relatively free since World War II. Integrating the two countries is proving difficult. Eastern Germany has a decaying infrastructure, chronic shortages, and an outmoded technology. But its citizens are an intelligent, educated, hardworking people—even a great people—and

WHAT'S SPECIAL ABOUT EASTERN GERMANY

Great Towns

☐ Potsdam, a baroque town on the Havel River, often called the Versailles of Germany.

☐ Leipzig, hometown of Richard Wagner, which Goethe pronounced *klein Paris*, or Paris in miniature.

☐ Dresden, once called "Florence on the Elbe," now partially restored after its fire bombing in 1945.

☐ Weimar, symbol of German culture, a 1,000-year-old town set at the edge of the Thuringian Forest.

Palaces

☐ Sans Souci, in Potsdam, with its terraces and gardens, summer residence of Frederick the Great.

☐ Cecilienhof, also at Potsdam, site of the 1945 Potsdam Conference with Truman and Stalin.

Religious Shrine

☐ Thomaskirche, in Leipzig, whose choirmaster was Johann Sebastian Bach, who lived in the city until his death in 1750.

Literary Shrine

☐ Schillerhaus, a small farmhouse outside Leipzig, former residence of Friedrich von Schiller, greatest name in German literature after Goethe.

Museums

☐ Zwinger, palace complex at Dresden, a quadrangle of pavilions and galleries with masterpieces of world art.

☐ Goethe National Museum, in Weimar, where the poet lived from 1782 to 1832.

Historical Site

☐ Buchenwald, outside Weimar, Nazi concentration camp and death chamber where mass murders occurred from 1937 to 1945.

they can rebuild a new society, just as they rebuilt after World War II when much of the country lay in ruins.

As everybody knows, Germany was split into four zones at the end of the war. East Germany consisted mainly of three former states—Saxony, Thuringia, and Mecklenburg—and parts of Prussia. The boundaries of East Germany were formed by the Baltic Sea in the north and Poland in the east. Parts of German territory were surrendered to Poland in the aftermath of World War II.

A NEW FRONTIER IN TRAVEL

Eastern Germany has beautiful scenery and monuments, and, perhaps more important, in some of the more remote parts of the country, you will think you've wandered into a time warp, seeing rural Germany as it must have existed in 1928. All that will change one day, but for the moment it allows you to wander far off the beaten path of standardized European itineraries.

Eastern Germany is a land of mountainous scenery (one part, in fact, is called "Saxon Switzerland"), heavy forests, and gently rolling plains. Rural traditions, now largely abandoned in most parts of western Germany, still linger in some parts of the east. There are no traffic jams on the roads as you make your way through the Harz Mountains, the Thuringian Forest, or along the Elbe River. Gasoline stations are few and far between, and many of the back roads are in poor condition. Again, that situation will change with time.

You'll visit cities that rose out of ashes, including Dresden. Many East German cities were collections of bomb-blackened ruins and shell-pocked buildings in 1945. A remnant of once-powerful Prussia, and later a faded piece of real estate left over from the gaudy dream of the Hitlerian Reich, East Germany appeared to face a bleak future. Now, florid baroque palaces are being restored, and hotels of modern comfort are being built to join those that already exist.

Eastern Germany, once a dreaded, feared nation in the West—often connected in our minds with spy novels—is extending a welcome to visitors today as never before.

It's always good to arrive somewhere with a hotel reservation, because rooms are still limited, and many are filled with Germans from the west driving over to see what the eastern part of their country looks like after all these years.

SUGGESTED ITINERARY

Day 1   While still based in Berlin, you can spend a day exploring Potsdam and its Sans Souci palace and gardens.

Days 2–3   Head south to Leipzig, exploring many of its attractions in the afternoon. In the morning on Day 3, visit Lutherstadt Wittenberg, center of the German Reformation, then return to Leipzig in the afternoon to see the sights you didn't see on Day 2.

Days 4–5   Go to Dresden and spend the day exploring its palace complex of museums and galleries at the Zwinger. Try to attend a performance of the opera in the evening. While still based in Dresden, take an excursion through the Spreewald (forest of the River Spree) and visit the porcelain factory at Meissen.

Days 6–7   Go west to Weimar and spend a day exploring its literary and artistic shrines. On Day 7, while still based in Weimar, see the former concentration camp of Buchenwald in the morning. In the afternoon make an excursion to Erfurt, where Luther was a monk for about 5 years.

GETTING THERE

Potsdam, of course, is a virtual suburb of Berlin, but getting around the rest of eastern Germany is easier than it's ever been. Some 1,000 miles of Autobahnen and about 7,000 miles of secondary highways cut across the eastern part. Train schedules are a bit chaotic, as the German Federal Railways rapidly incorporates the former East German system into its vast network.

Reservations are mandatory when traveling by rail through eastern Germany, as demand for seats is great. Consult a travel agent. Since 1991, long-distance bus service links Berlin with Dresden and Leipzig. Service is still not frequent, however, as buses exist mainly to supplement the rail network.

---

1. POTSDAM

15 miles SW of Berlin; 87 miles NE of Leipzig; 92 miles NE of Magdeburg

GETTING THERE   By Train   Potsdam Hauptbahnhof is on the major Reichsbahn rail lines, with frequent connections. There are 29 daily rail connections to the rail stations of Berlin, taking 23 minutes to the Bahnhof Zoo in Berlin and 54 minutes to the Berliner Hauptbahnhof. There are also 14 trains daily to and from Hannover (trip time: 3 to 3½ hours, depending on the train), and 15 daily trains to Nürnberg (6 to 6½ hours). For rail information in Potsdam, call 0331/220-94. Potsdam can also be reached by the S-Bahn lines S3, S4, and S5 of the Berlin rapid-transit system, connecting at Wannsee station, with lines R1, R3, and R4. Travel time on these lines from Berlin to Potsdam is 30 minutes. For more information, call BVG Berlin (tel. 0331/216-50-88).

By Bus Regional bus service with frequent connections between Berlin and Potsdam is available at Wannsee station (bus no. 133) in Berlin. Service is provided by Verkehrsverband Potsdam. For travel information and schedules, call Europäisches Reiseburo at Potsdam (tel. 0331/220-94). Long-distance bus service to such cities as Magdeburg, Celle, Bremen, and Cuxhaven and to the Harz Mountains is offered by Deutsche Land und See Reisen GmbH at Berlin (tel. 0331/33-10-31).

By Car Access is via Autobahn E30 east and west or E53 north and south. Allow about 30 minutes to drive here from Berlin.

ESSENTIALS For tourist information, contact **Potsdam-Information,** Friedrich-Ebert-Strasse 5 (tel. 0331/211-00).

Of all the tours possible from Berlin, the three-star attraction is the baroque town of Potsdam on the Havel River, often called Germany's Versailles.

From the beginning of the 18th century, it was the residence and garrison town of the Prussian kings. Soviet propagandists once called it a "former cradle of Prussian militarism and reactionary forces." World attention focused on Potsdam from July 17 to August 2, 1945, when the Potsdam Conference shaped postwar Europe.

Potsdam, although mainly visited for its historic sights, lakes, and parks, is a major industrial center. On the main rail line to Magdeburg, the city is known for its beautiful chain of lakes formed by the Havel. Surrounded by a wooded range of hills, the town was beautifully planned architecturally, with large parks and many green areas. The center of town is Sans Souci Park, with palaces and gardens, which lies to the west of the historic core. In the northern part of the town is the New Garden, lying on the Heiliger See, a mile northwest of Sans Souci. This garden contains Cecilienhof Palace (see below). The third large garden district of the city lies north of the town district of Bebelsberg, the "German Hollywood," where Marlene Dietrich rose to fame in the 1920s. In the late 1930s, Josef Goebbels ordered the filming of anti-Semitic Nazi propaganda films. After World War II, the studios here cranked out Communist propaganda films attacking "Western imperialism."

WHAT TO SEE & DO

At Potsdam, a British air raid on April 14, 1945, destroyed much of the center of the old city, but the major attraction, Sans Souci Park and its palace buildings, survived.

SANS SOUCI PARK, Zur historischen Mühle. Tel. 0331/220-51.

With its palaces and gardens, Sans Souci (or Sanssouci) Park was the work of many architects and sculptors. The park covers an area of about a square mile. Once at Potsdam, you might consider an organized tour of the park and various places. Take tram no. 94 or 96 or bus no. 612, 614, 631, 632, 692, or 695 to reach the sights below.

Frederick II (called "the Great") chose Potsdam rather than Berlin as his permanent residence. The style of the buildings he ordered erected is called Potsdam rococo, an achievement primarily of Georg Wenzeslaus von Knobelsdorff.

Knobelsdorff built **Sans Souci** (or **Sanssouci**) **Palace,** with its terraces and gardens, as a summer residence for Frederick II. The palace was inaugurated in 1747 and called Sans Souci, meaning "free from worry." It is a long one-story building crowned by a dome and flanked by two round pavilions. Of all the rooms, the music salon is the supreme example of the rococo style. The elliptically shaped Marble Hall is the largest in the palace. As a guest of the king, Voltaire visited in 1750. A small bust of Voltaire commemorates that sojourn. Sans Souci is open daily in April to September from 9am to 5pm; in November to January daily from 9am to 3pm; and in

February, March, and October daily from 9am to 4pm; closed on the first and third Monday of every month. Admission is 6 DM ($4) for adults and 3 DM ($2) for children to both Sans Souci Palace and Bildergalerie (below).

The **Bildergalerie** (Picture Gallery), Östlicher Lustgarden (tel. 0331/226-55), was built between 1755 and 1763. Its facade is similar to that of Sans Souci Palace. The interior is considered one of the most flamboyant in Germany. A collection of some 125 paintings is displayed, including works from both the Italian Renaissance and the baroque period. Dutch and Flemish masters are also exhibited. Such artists as Rubens, Terbrugghen, Van Dyck, Vasari, and Guido Reni, as well as Caravaggio, are represented. Concerts at the Potsdam Park Festival take place here. The Bildergalerie is open the same hours as Sans Souci.

West of Sans Souci is the **Orangerie,** built between 1851 and 1864. It was based on designs of Italian Renaissance palaces. Its purpose was to shelter southerly plants during the cold months. In the central core, with its twin towers, is the Raphael Hall, with 47 copies of that master's paintings. In addition, you can visit five lavishly decorated salons. Admission is 6 DM ($4) for adults and 3 DM ($2) for children.

The largest building in the park is the **Neues Palais,** Sans Souci Park (tel. 0331/220-51), built between 1763 and 1769, at the end of the Seven Years' War. Frederick II called it a *fanfaronade.* Crowning the center is a dome. The Three Graces bear the crown on the lantern. The rooms were used as a residence for members of the royal family. Filled with paintings and antiques, they were decorated in the rococo style. The most notable chamber is the Hall of Shells, with its fossils and semiprecious stones. At the palace theater, also in the rococo style, concerts take place every year from April to November. Keeping the same hours as Sans Souci, the Neues Palais charges 6 DM ($4) for adults and 3 DM ($2) for children. It is closed the second and fourth Monday of every month.

SCHLOSS CHARLOTTENHOF, south of Okonomieweg. Tel. 0331/97-27-74.

Schloss Charlottenhof was built between 1826 and 1829 to the designs of Karl Friedrich Schinkel, the greatest master of neoclassical architecture in Germany. He erected the palace in the style of a villa and designed most of the furniture inside.

Neighboring the palace, the **Roman Baths** are on the north of the artificial lake known as "machine pond," or Maschinenteich. This group of buildings was constructed between 1829 and 1835, based in part on designs by Schinkel. The baths were strictly for the romantic love of antiquity, having no practical purpose.

Admission: 3 DM ($2) adults, 2 DM ($1.30) children.

Open: Apr–Sept, daily 9am–5pm; Nov–Jan, daily 9am–3pm; Feb–Mar, and Oct, daily 9am–4pm. **Closed:** 4th Thurs of every month. **Tram:** 1 or 4.

NEUER GARTEN, on Heiliger See. Tel. 0331/231-41.

On the Heiliger See, or "holy lake," in the northern part of Potsdam lies the Neuer Garten, about a mile northwest of Sans Souci. The nephew and successor to Frederick the Great, Frederick William II, ordered the gardens laid out.

Admission: Free.

Open: Same hours as Sans Souci. **Bus:** 695.

CECILIENHOF PALACE, Neuer Garten. Tel. 0331/225-79.

North of the 200-acre park, Cecilienhof Palace was completed in the style of an English country house and is recommended as a hotel and a luncheon stopover (see "Where to Stay" and "Where to Dine," below). It was ordered built by Kaiser Wilhelm II between 1913 and 1917. The 176-room mansion became the new residence of Crown Prince Wilhelm of Hohenzollern. It was occupied as a royal residence until March 1945, when the crown prince and his family fled to the West, taking many of their possessions with them.

Cecilienhof was the headquarters of the 1945 Potsdam Conference. For the conference, 36 rooms had to be quickly reconditioned. Truman represented the United States, and Stalin, of course, represented the Soviet Union. Churchill at first represented Great Britain, but at the time of the actual signing on August 2, 1945,

Clement R. Attlee had replaced him. It is possible to visit the studies of the various delegations and to see the large round table, made in Moscow, where the actual agreement was signed.

Admission: 3 DM ($2) adults, 1.50 DM ($1) children.

Open: May–Oct, Tues–Sun 9am–5:15pm; Nov–Apr, Tues–Sun 9am–4:45pm.

Bus: 695.

WHERE TO STAY
EXPENSIVE

HOTEL MERCURE, Lange Brücke, 0-1561 Potsdam. Tel. 0331/46-31.
Fax 0331/23-496. 208 rms, 4 suites. MINIBAR TV TEL **Tram:** 91, 92, 93, or 94.

$ **Rates** (including continental breakfast): 190 DM–240 DM ($125.40–$158.40) single; 235 DM–290 DM ($155.10–$191.40) double; from 375 DM ($247.50) suite. AE, DC, MC, V. **Parking:** 15 DM ($9.90).

One of the best of the high-rise hotels lies at the entrance to the city on the route nearest Berlin, rising over the Havel River, on the site of the old winter Cecilienhof Palace. (Under Communist rule, it was known as Hotel Potsdam.)

It features a number of amenities, including a sauna, massage service, and a shop where you can purchase souvenirs. Dancing and entertainment are provided by the nightclub, Bellevue. Its major restaurants are the Havellandgrill and the Fortuna, with meals costing from 32 DM to 70 DM ($21.10 to $46.20). It also has a café, a tearoom, and a garden restaurant that is popular in summer.

HOTEL SCHLOSS CECILIENHOF, Neuer Garten, 0-1561 Potsdam. Tel. 0331/231-41. Fax 0331/22-498. 40 rms. (all with bath or shower), 3 suites. MINIBAR TV TEL **Bus:** 695.

$ **Rates** (including continental breakfast): 150 DM–270 DM ($99–$178.20) single; 260 DM–340 DM ($171.60–$224.40) double; from 525 DM ($346.50) suite. AE, DC, MC, V. **Parking:** Free.

The Hotel Cecilienhof was recommended earlier as a sightseeing attraction. However, many visitors who pass through here don't realize that it's possible for guests to stay in this lovely tranquil setting. The palace was built from 1913 to 1917 in the style of an English country manor house, and it was the residence of Crown Prince Wilhelm. The government converted a residential wing into one of the most charming hotels in the country. Residents can take their meals in the palace dining room, enjoying a first-class cuisine of both international and regional specialties.

WHERE TO DINE
EXPENSIVE

HOTEL SCHLOSS CECILIENHOF, Neuer Garten. Tel. 0331/231-41.
Cuisine: GERMAN/INTERNATIONAL. **Reservations:** Required. **Bus:** 695.

$ **Prices:** Appetizers 15 DM–22 DM ($9.90–$14.50); main courses 24 DM–42 DM ($15.80–$27.70); fixed-price menus 35 DM ($23.10) and 130 DM ($85.80). AE, DC, MC, V.

Open: Daily 11:30am–11pm.

Previously recommended as a hotel and also endorsed as a sightseeing attraction (see "What to See & Do," above), the Hotel Schloss Cecilienhof also makes the most desirable luncheon stopover in a city not distinguished for its cuisine. In this once royal residence, site of the conference that drew Harry Truman and Joseph Stalin, you can dine on a menu that borrows freely from both the East and the West, even including some Ukrainian specialties. Try the peppersteak or beef roulade. The restaurant is about half an hour's walk from Sans Souci.

MODERATE

MINSK, Am Brauhausberg, Max-Planck-Strasse 10. Tel. 0331/236-36.

Cuisine: GERMAN. **Reservations:** Recommended. **Tram:** 91, 95, or 96 to Schwimmhalle am Brauhausberg.

$ **Prices:** Appetizers 8 DM–16 DM ($5.30–$10.60); main courses 15 DM–32 DM ($9.90–$21.10). MC, V.

Open: Daily 11am–6pm and 7pm–midnight.

⑤ Minsk takes its name from Potsdam's so-called "sister city" in Russia. Often overrun by bus tours, it is nevertheless a winning candidate for well-prepared, albeit rather plain, German cuisine. Try the roast goose or one of the pork specialties. The ideal place to enjoy your meal is on the al fresco terrace if the weather is right. In the evening dance music is played.

VILLA KELLERMAN, Mangerstrasse 34–36. Tel. 0331/215-72.

Cuisine: ITALIAN/INTERNATIONAL. **Reservations:** Recommended. **Bus:** 695.

$ **Prices:** Appetizers 7 DM–19 DM ($4.60–$12.50); main courses 16 DM–41 DM ($10.60–$27.10); fixed-price lunches 27 DM–35 DM ($17.80–$23.10); fixed-price dinners 60 DM–85 DM ($39.60–$56.10). AE.

Open: Tues–Sun noon–midnight.

In 1878, one of the courtiers in the service of the Prussian monarchs built this elegant villa on the shore of Heileger See. During the 1920s, it was used by the respected German author Bernhardt Kellerman as the place where he wrote some of his best work. After a Cold War stint as a base for Russian officers, it now functions as one of the most innovative and talked-about restaurants in Potsdam. The classically Italian cuisine attracts a diverse clientele well-placed within the new Germany's worlds of finance and the arts.

Your meal might include marinated carpaccio of seawolf; a mixed platter of antipasti; spaghetti with scampi, herbs, and garlic; ravioli stuffed with cheese, spinach, and herbs; John Dory in butter-and-caper sauce; and an aray of veal and beef dishes. The wine list represents mostly Italian vintages.

INEXPENSIVE

RESTAURANT BÖRSE & BEERBAR MARKTLAUSE, Brandenburger Strasse 35–36. Tel. 0331/225-05.

Cuisine: GERMAN. **Reservations:** Recommended. **Tram:** 91, 95, or 96.

$ **Prices:** Appetizers 5.50 DM–12 DM ($3.60–$7.90); main courses 12 DM–24 DM ($7.90–$15.80). AE, MC, V.

Open: Sun–Mon 11am–11pm, Tues–Sat 11am–midnight.

In the heart of the Altstadt (Old Town), close to the central bus station, this is an intimate family-type restaurant where English is spoken. In the 18th century it was a wine distillery. You might begin with a small salad Börse or onion soup with cheese croûtons. The chef also does a clear oxtail soup. Main dishes include herring housewife style, chicken fricassée with asparagus, and a Sauerbraten Rhinerlander style. You can also order entrecôte in red wine or a rumpsteak.

---

2. LEIPZIG

102 miles SW of Berlin; 68 miles NW of Dresden; 78 miles NE of Erfurt

GETTING THERE By Plane Leipzig-Schkeuditz International Airport (tel. 0341/391-36-16), lies 7 miles northwest of the city center. Lufthansa links Leipzig with major German cities, such as Munich and Berlin, and also some continental destinations. For complete information, call Lufthansa at Reichstrasse 18 (tel. 0341/273-31-32) in Leipzig. An airport bus runs between the airport and the Leipzig Hauptbahnhof in the center every 30 minutes daily from 6:30am to 9:40pm (trip time:

40 minutes). Taxis are also available, meeting all arriving planes, but it will cost from 35 DM ($23.10) to reach the center of the city in about 25 to 30 minutes, depending on traffic.

By Train   The Leipzig Hauptbahnhof, Platz der Republik (tel. 0341/72-40), is on the major Deutsche Reichsbahn rail line, with frequent connections to German cities. Seventeen trains arrive daily from Berlin (trip time: 2 hours, 10 minutes to 2 hours, 50 minutes, depending on the train). Twenty-three trains arrive from Dresden (1 hour, 35 minutes, to 2 hours), and 15 trains arrive from Frankfurt in the west (5 hours). For rail information and schedules, call 0341/72-40.

By Bus   Long-distance bus service to such cities as Berlin is provided by Leipziger Verkhehrsbetriebe. Buses depart from the east side of the main rail station. For bus information and schedules, call 0341/29-17-77. Regional bus service to nearby towns around Leipzig is also provided by Leipzer Verkehrsbetriebe (tel. 0341/393-70 for information and schedules).

By Car   Access is via the Halle-Dresden Autobahn east and west or the E51 Autobahn north and south.

ESSENTIALS Information   Head first for the **Leipzig-Information,** Sachsenplatz 1 (tel. 0341/795-90). It is open Monday to Friday from 9am to 12:30pm and 1:30 to 4pm, Saturday from 10am to noon. There you will be given a map pinpointing the major sights. This place becomes a beehive of activity at the time of the annual trade fairs. The inner city of Leipzig is served by a public transit system of trams, light railways, and buses, with frequent service to all parts of the city. The service is operated by Leipziger Verkehrsbetriebe (tel. 0341/39-370 for more information and schedules).

Orientation   Leipzig is a large city, but its historic core is compact enough to be covered on foot (in fact, that's about the only way to explore it). The **Hauptbahnhof** lies directly north of the center, opening onto the **Platz der Republik.** Some of the streets, such as **Richard-Wagner-Strasse,** directly south of the square, are named after artists or composers. Directly south of this square is a greenbelt with a body of water, called **Schwanenteich.** The opera house is at the southern sector of this park, its other side opening onto **Augustus-Platz,** headquarters of the University of Leipzig. Katharinenstrasse runs west of the heartbeat square, **Sachsenplatz.** In its southern corner is the restored **Rathaus,** opening onto **Marktplatz.** A short stroll west of here will lead to Thomaskirche, the 1,000-year-old Gothic church where Bach is buried. This major attraction will be covered under "What to See & Do," below.

SPECIAL EVENTS   Chances are, your visit to Leipzig will be during one of the **annual trade fairs,** held around March and again in September. These great fairs date from the Middle Ages, first under the auspices of the margraves of Meissen and later under the electors of Saxony. Revived by the Communists after World War II, today they draw business representatives from more than 50 countries. A lot of people who come to them are concerned with the publishing industry, as Leipzig is the principal center of eastern German publishing and has been an important publishing center since the 16th century. The city is also a literary center; many German authors live in and around Leipzig.

Leipzig is called the "metropolis of fairs," but it also enjoys renown as a center of music. Richard Wagner was born here in 1813, and Johann Sebastian Bach (you'll surely see a statue of him) is closely associated with Leipzig. Leipzig stands above the junction of three tiny rivers, the Elster, the Parthe, and the Pleisse.

Because of its strategic value as a rail center, both the RAF and the U.S. Air Force bombed Leipzig heavily in 1943, 1944, and 1945, but it has been rebuilt, more or less well. Leipzig is once again a major rail terminus. From its Hauptbahnhof, with 26 platforms the largest in Europe, lines radiate to all the chief German cities, and from there to the rest of Europe.

Outdistanced only by Berlin, Leipzig is the economic and cultural center of eastern Germany. It still has some narrow streets and houses from the 16th and 17th centuries. The heart of Leipzig is encircled by a "ring" road, as in Vienna.

WHAT TO SEE & DO

MAJOR ATTRACTIONS

MUSIKINSTRUMENTEN-MUSEUM [Museum of Musical Instruments], University of Leipzig, Täubschenweg 2. Tel. 0341/29-46-58.
This museum collects, cares for, and exhibits treasures of musical culture, chiefly Italian, German, and French instruments of the 16th to the 19th century. Perhaps you'll be able to attend one of the concerts that are sometimes played with historical instruments.
Admission: 3 DM ($2).
Open: Tues–Thurs 2–5pm, Fri and Sun 10am–1pm, Sat 10am–3pm. **Tram:** 4, 6, 8, 10, 11, or 13.

THOMASKIRCHE [St. Thomas Church], Thomas-Gasse. Tel. 0341/28-22-74.
A towering figure in the history of music, master of the contrapuntal style, Johann Sebastian Bach (1685–1750) lived in Leipzig from 1723 until his death. Unlike Wagner, he wasn't born in the city. However, he spent the most creative years of his life there. He was a choirmaster at Thomaskirche (St. Thomas Church) on Thomas-Gasse, which has been handsomely restored after World War II damage. It has a high-pitched roof built in 1496. The church, just off Marktplatz, grew up on the site of a 13th-century monastery. The city's Thomaner Choir presents concerts every Sunday morning and Friday evening—when it's in residence. The choir is popular all over the country, and often it is on tour, keeping alive the memory of Bach. Bach was buried just in front of the altar. Both Mozart and Mendelssohn performed here, and Richard Wagner was christened here in 1813.
Admission: Free.
Open: Daily 9am–6pm. **Tram:** 4, 6, 8, 10, 11, or 13.

ALTES RATHAUS, Marktplatz 1. Tel. 0341/709-21.
The Altes Rathaus, from the 16th century, stands on the Renaissance Marktplatz, from the 12th century. Again, Allied bombs rained down on it, but it has been restored. Inside, you'll find the Stadtgeschichtliches Museum, chronicling the city's history, both cultural and political.
Admission: 3 DM ($2) adults, 1.50 DM ($1) children.
Open: Tues–Fri 10am–6pm, Sat–Sun 10am–4pm. **Tram:** 4, 6, 8, 10, 11, or 13.

SCHILLERHAUS, Menckstrasse 42. Tel. 0341/58-31-87.
In this small farmhouse in Gohlis, a suburb of Leipzig, Johann Christoph Friedrich von Schiller, a friend of Goethe's and, after him, the greatest name in German literature, wrote his "Ode to Joy" in 1785. The poem was incorporated in the great final movement of Beethoven's Ninth Symphony.
Admission: 2 DM ($1.30) adults, 1 DM (66¢) children.
Open: Tues–Wed and Fri–Sat 11am–5pm. **Tram:** 20 or 24.

BACHMUSEUM, Thomaskirchhof 16. Tel. 0341/78-66.
The Bachmuseum contains the largest collection of Bach archives in Germany.

Many mementos of the composer are found within. The museum is in the shadow of Thomaskirche.

Admission: 2 DM ($1.30) adults, 1 DM (66¢) children.

Open: Apr–Sept, daily 10am–6pm; Oct–Mar, daily 9am–5pm. **Tram:** 20, 21, or 24.

ZOOLOGISCHER GARTEN LEIPZIG, Pfaffendorfer-Strasse 29. Tel. 0341/29-10-01.

Here animals—many wild ones, of course—are bred in order to help conserve endangered species. The zoo was founded in 1878 and is internationally known for the breeding of big carnivores. There is also the biggest aquarium in Eastern Germany. You can dine at the restaurant on the grounds.

Admission: 5 DM ($3.30) adults, 2 DM ($1.30) children.

Open: Year round, daily 8am–7pm. **Tram:** 20 or 24.

MUSEUM DER BILDENDEN KUNSTE, Georgi-Dimitroff-Platz 1. Tel. 0341/31-31-02.

The city's museum of modern art concentrates mainly on the 20th century, although many works are from the 19th century. Of its some 2,500 paintings and sculptures, included are works by such artists as Dürer, Rubens, Rembrandt, Rodin, and van Eyck. The building was constructed in 1888 as the home of the Supreme Court of the Reich and changed into a museum in 1952. One section displays exhibits relating the story of Georgi Dimitroff, once head of the Communist party in Bulgaria. Hitler accused Dimitroff and other Communist leaders of responsibility for the Reichstag fire. They were tried in this building, in what Hitler thought would be a great blow against the Communists and a victory for the Nazis. Dimitroff was interrogated by Hermann Göring. The plan backfired, however, when the Leipzig jury acquitted the defendants. In the carefully preserved courtroom, tapes of the Reichstag trial are played.

Admission: 5 DM ($3.30) adults, 2.50 DM ($1.70) children.

Open: Tues, Thurs, and Sun 9am–5pm; Wed 1–7:30pm. **Tram:** 3, 5, 8, 12, or 13.

MORE ATTRACTIONS

Goethe, who was a student at Leipzig, called the city "klein Paris," or Paris in miniature. This city has long been closely linked to the names of eminent personages. A Bach memorial was opened in the reconstructed Bose House on the occasion of the 300th anniversary of the birth of the composer. The historic restaurant Auerbachs Keller was the setting for one of the scenes of Goethe's *Faust,* and there are many productions of Wagner's *Ring* at the Leipzig Opera House. The German Library, the **Deutsche Bücherei,** is the central archive of German literature, which can be visited only with special permission. It is reputed to possess every item of German literature ever published. It also has a copy of *Iskra,* the Bolshevik newspaper that Lenin came here to print secretly in 1900.

Founded in 1409, the **University of Leipzig,** Universitätsstrasse, has contributed greatly to the cultural growth of the city. At the time of Hitler's ill-fated Third Reich, it was the largest university in Germany. It was rechristened Karl Marx University by the East Germans, but the name Universität Leipzig was restored in 1990.

Contrary to popular belief, the Thomaskirche isn't the oldest in Leipzig. That distinction belongs to **Nikolaikirche,** Nikolaistrasse, erected in 1165. Many works by Bach, including the *St. John Passion,* were first performed at this church.

A gateway leads to **Nasch Market,** the city's best-known square; and a short walk nearby takes you to **Königshaus,** which for many centuries was the headquarters of the Saxon monarchs who ruled Leipzig.

The **Neues Rathaus** on Burgplatz was erected on the site of the old Pleissenburg, the citadel where Martin Luther in 1519 held a momentous disputation.

The **Neues Gewandhaus** (tel. 0341/713-20) faces the Neues Opernhaus across Augustus-Platz. The famous **Gewandhaus Orchestra,** founded in 1781, saw some of its greatest days under the baton of Felix Mendelssohn, who died in Leipzig in 1847. Its other famous conductors have included Wilhelm Furtwängler, Bruno Walter, and, more recently, Kurt Masur. Concerts, ballets, and other premier events are staged in this modern structure, which opened in 1981. Recitals are presented on a mammoth organ. Tram: 4, 5, 12, 13, or 15.

The **Neues Opernhaus** is at Augustus-Platz (tel. 0341/29-10-36). However, you should go to the tourist office for concert information and hard-to-get tickets.

Going out Strasse des 18. Oktober will take you to a memorial honoring the famed 1813 battle. Along the way, see a pre–World War I Russian Orthodox church, built in the Byzantine style as a monument to the 22,000 soldiers killed at Leipzig; and also the fairgrounds, which come alive during the annual trade fairs. At the far end, the memorial, the **Völkerschlachtdenkmal,** Süd-Friedhof (tel. 0341/861-19-62), was dedicated in 1913 to the combined Prussian, Austrian, and Russian armies who defeated the Grande Armée of Napoléon. It rises some 300 feet in the air. Climb to the top for a view of Leipzig.

At the memorial is a museum, open daily from 9am to 4pm, charging no admission, devoted to the history of Leipzig, including a diorama of the famous 1813 battle fought here. Some historians call this "The Battle of Leipzig," and others more pretentiously refer to it as "The Battle of Nations." At any rate, it's known in all European history books as the battle that led to the defeat of Napoléon and the destruction of his Grande Armée. Tram no. 15 from the Hauptbahnhof runs here.

WHERE TO STAY

VERY EXPENSIVE

INTER-CONTINENTAL LEIPZIG, Gerberstrasse 15, 0-7010 Leipzig. Tel. 0341/7990, or toll free 800/327-0200 in the U.S. or Canada. Fax 0341/799-1229. 445 rms, 18 suites. MINIBAR TV TEL **S-Bahn:** Hauptbahnhof.

$ **Rates:** 350 DM–440 DM ($231–$290.40) single or double; from 550 DM ($363) suite. Continental breakfast 19 DM ($12.50) extra. AE, DC, MC, V. **Parking:** 20 DM ($13.20).

A silver-and-concrete high-rise, the former Merkur, taken over by the Inter-Continental group in 1993, was built in 1981. Much improved, it receives guests from all over the world, maintaining fine international standards. It lies in the heart of Liepzig, five minutes from the Altes Rathaus, and is the city's tallest building. It has a spacious and elegant lobby, with comfortably furnished rooms.

Dining/Entertainment: For breakfast or à la carte dining in the evening, your choice is Restaurant Brühl, containing a piano bar and wine cellar. A lunch buffet with a Saxon cuisine is served in the Wintergarten, and low-priced Saxon dishes are offered in a beer house called the Pub. The hotel also has a casino.

Services: 24-hour room service, same-day laundry, massage.

Facilities: Health club with indoor pool, solarium, sauna, fitness machines, two bowling lanes, business center, beauty salon.

MARITIM ASTORIA, Platz der Republik, 0-7010 Leipzig. Tel. 0341/722-20. Fax 0341/722-47-47. 323 rms, 5 suites. TV TEL **S-Bahn:** Hauptbahnhof.

$ **Rates** (including continental breakfast): 249 DM–339 DM ($164.30–$223.70) single; 336 DM–456 DM ($221.80–$301) double; from 500 DM ($330) suite. AE, DC, MC, V. **Parking:** 20 DM ($13.20).

Across from one of the most famous railroad stations in Europe, the four-star Maritim Astoria—known for decades as the Hotel Astoria—was taken over by the Maritim chain in 1992. Since 1915, the date of its opening, it has been a meeting place for leading figures in not only politics and business but also the arts and sports. The hotel offers good hospitality, combining personal comfort in the guest rooms, with fine cuisine and select wines. Try for a room on one of the upper floors, as many guests find them more desirable.

Dining/Entertainment: Not only German regional dishes but also international cuisine are served in the hotel's restaurant, the Galerie, decorated in the

Chippendale style, and in the City Restaurant, with its cycle of paintings by the Leipzig artist Professor Werner Tubke. The Astoria Bar is for night owls.

Services: Hairdresser, massage.

Facilities: Sauna, solarium, fitness room, car-rental office.

EXPENSIVE

STADT LEIPZIG, Richard-Wagner-Strasse 1–5, 0-7010 Leipzig. Tel. 0341/2-14-50. Fax 0341/214-56-00. 348 rms (all with bath or shower). MINIBAR TV TEL **Tram:** 10 or 21. **S-Bahn:** Hauptbahnhof.

$ Rates (including continental breakfast): 160 DM–240 DM ($105.60–$158.40) single; 265 DM–330 DM ($174.90–$217.80) double. AE, DC, MC, V. **Parking:** Free.

The Stadt Leipzig stands on a street honoring the famous "hometown boy." A postwar modern hotel from the 1960s, it lies across from the Hauptbahnhof, built back from attractively landscaped grounds in downtown Leipzig, with rows of trees setting off the blue-and-white facade. This hotel shelters well-maintained but often very small units. The Stadt Leipzig also has two restaurants, a café, and a nightclub. The higher prices are charged only during trade fairs.

WHERE TO DINE

MODERATE

APELS GARTEN, Kolonnadenstrasse 2. Tel. 0341/28-50-93.

Cuisine: GERMAN. **Reservations:** Recommended. **Tram:** 4, 6, 8, 10, 11, or 13.

$ Prices: Appetizers 6 DM–14 DM ($4–$9.20); main courses 20 DM–28 DM ($13.20–$18.50). AE, DC, MC, V.

Open: Mon–Sat 11:30am–11:30pm, Sun 11am–3pm.

Its name commemorates a 400-year-old garden (the Apels Garten) whose boundaries were almost eliminated during the Cold War. Rising from the site of that garden, you'll find a modern mid-1980s building whose street level contains a conservatively decorated restaurant known for its homestyle and traditional German food. Specialties include potato soup studded with slices of sausage, roast goose with potatoes and vegetables, grilled Wurst with potatoes and red cabbage, Sauerbraten with onions and red cabbage, pan-fried fish filets with kohlrabi, roulades of pork with sautéed onions, marinated rack of lamb with white beans, and roast quail or seasonal versions of venison.

AUERBACHS KELLER, Mädlerpassage, Grimmaischestrasse 2–4. Tel. 0341/211-60-34.

Cuisine: GERMAN. **Reservations:** Recommended. **S-Bahn:** Hauptbahnhof.

$ Prices: Appetizers 6.50 DM–10.50 DM ($4.30–$6.90); main courses 22 DM–28 DM ($14.50–$18.50); three-course fixed-price lunch 36 DM ($23.80); five-course fixed-price menu 82 DM ($54.10). AE, DC, MC, V.

Open: Daily 10am–midnight.

Many visitors to Leipzig eat at their hotels. However, I suggest that you escape for at least one night to dine at the most famous restaurant in the city, Auerbachs Keller. This is the restaurant and tavern where Goethe, in *Faust,* staged his debate between Faust and Mephistopheles. It's still there, amazingly, after all that bombing. It lies off the market square, close to the Altes Rathaus. The cellar dates from 1530 and has a series of murals from the 16th century, representing the legend on which the play *Faust* was based. The food is good. The chefs prepare mainly regional dishes of Saxony, often employing Faustian names that sound more ominous than they are: Mephisto-Fleisch, or Mephistopheles' meat, and Teufelstoast. You can order from a fine selection of wine and beer.

STADTPFEIFFER, Augustusplatz 8. Tel. 0341/713-23-89.

Cuisine: CONTINENTAL. **Reservations:** Required. **Tram:** 8, 10, 11, 13, or 20.

$ Prices: Appetizers 6.50 DM–18 DM ($4.30–$11.90); main courses 28 DM–32 DM ($18.50–$21.10); four-course fixed-price lunch 48 DM ($31.70); eight-course fixed-price dinner 90 DM ($59.40). AE, V.

Open: Lunch Mon–Sat 11am–3pm; dinner Mon–Sat 6pm–midnight.

Stadtpfeiffer occupies space in the concert hall. This restaurant opened in 1982, and for the theme of its decor chose the musical troupes who traveled all over Germany in the 1400s. The name *Pfeiffe* is that of an old woodwind instrument. Such a theatricalized setting attracts many media-related figures who appreciate the good food and service. The chef uses high-quality ingredients in such dishes as stuffed loin of pork with mushroom-cream sauce or thinly sliced filet of veal.

WEINRESTAURANT "FALSTAFF," Georgiring 9. Tel. 0341/28-64-03.

Cuisine: CONTINENTAL. **Reservations:** Recommended. **S-Bahn:** Hauptbahnhof.

$ Prices: Appetizers 6.50 DM–22 DM ($4.30–$14.50); main courses 22 DM–36 DM ($14.50–$23.80); fixed-price lunch 32 DM ($21.10); fixed-price dinner 65 DM ($42.90). AE, MC, V.

Open: Lunch daily 11:30am–3pm; dinner daily 6pm–12:30am.

One of the most elegant restaurants near the Hauptbahnhof and more commodious than you'd expect, this place sits within a short distance of the opera house. If you'd like a predinner drink, the uniformed maître d' will usher you across Persian carpets to the art nouveau–style, dark-paneled bar in the rear. Afterward, you'll be shown a table in the modern high-ceilinged dining room. You can select a fine continental and eastern German repast that might begin with smoked eel on toast and go on to Thuringian beef with onions or pork steak stuffed with ham and cheese. The Viennese hen is also reliable.

INEXPENSIVE

THÜRINGER HOF, Burgstrasse 19-23. Tel. 0341/20-98-84.

Cuisine: GERMAN/EASTERN EUROPEAN. **Reservations:** Not necessary. **Tram:** 5, 11, 13, or 29.

$ Prices: Appetizers 6.50 DM–8 DM ($4.30–$5.30); main courses 14 DM–20 DM ($9.20–$13.20). AE, MC, V.

Open: Daily 11am–10pm.

Long a popular beer cellar in the Altstadt, Thüringer Hof draws young people (especially on weekends) who fill its tables in a fairly elegant setting with carved baroque accents. Waiters in white aprons hurry about, carrying mugs of beer and large platters of food. You get classic German fare here, along with a sampling of dishes from Eastern Europe. Your selection of soups, for example, might come from Ukraine or from Hungary. There's even a peppery dash of Mexico in the pork steak platter. One of the most popular dishes is broiled chicken with apple-flavored red cabbage and potatoes.

EASY EXCURSIONS

LUTHERSTADT WITTENBERG

This is the city forever associated with Martin Luther, attracting pilgrims from all over the world. It was the center of the German Reformation. Wittenberg had not one, but two famous sons, and both men are honored with statues in front of the Rathaus. Its other celebrated son was the humanist, Philipp Melanchthon (1497–1560). The Protestant reformer and scholar was a friend of Luther's and later of Calvin's.

Wittenberg lies 42 miles northeast of Leipzig and 62 miles southwest of Berlin. Access by car is via Autobahn E5 north and south or else Highway 187 east or Highway 2 north and south. The Wittenberg Bahnhof is on the major Deutsche Reichsbahn rail line (Halle-Berlin), with frequent connections. It's an hour by train from Leipzig. For travel information, call Europäisches Reisebüro at Wittenberg (tel. 03491/27-59). Stop in at **Wittenberg-Information,** Collegienstrasse 8 (tel. 03491/22-39), and ask for a map pinpointing the attractions of the city.

Both Luther and Melanchthon are buried in the **Schlosskirche,** Schlossplatz (tel. 03491/25-85), which dates from the 15th century (but was rebuilt in the 19th century). It was on the Schlosskirche doors that Luther nailed his Ninety-five Theses in 1517. The 1858 bronze doors bear the Latin text of the theses. Hours are Tuesday through Sunday from 10am to noon and 2 to 5pm. Entrance is 1 DM (66¢).

Part of an Augustinian monastery in which Luther lived has been turned into the **Lutherhalle Wittenberg** at Collegienstrasse 54 (tel. 03491/26-71), and the parish church in which Luther preached is from the 14th century. An oak tree marks the spot outside the Elster gate where Luther publicly burned the papal bull of excommunication in 1520. It is open Tuesday through Sunday from 9am to 5pm. Admission is 4 DM ($2.60).

You can also visit the **Stadtkirche,** Kirchplatz (tel. 03491/32-01), with an altar by Lucas Cranach the Elder, who was once the Bürgermeister of Wittenberg. It is open Monday through Saturday from 10am to noon and 2 to 5pm and Sunday from 11am to noon and 2 to 5pm. Entrance is 1 DM (66¢).

Where to Stay & Dine: Moderate

GOLDENER ADLER, Markt 7, 0-4600 Wittenberg. Tel. 03491/20-53. Fax 0451/20-54. 40 rms. **Bus:** Bahnhof bus.

$ Rates (including continental breakfast): 98 DM–148 DM ($64.70–$97.70) single; 110 DM–160 DM ($72.60–$105.60) double. AE, V. **Parking:** Free.

This good little hotel offers newly renovated guest rooms, some with TVs and phones. You can also visit the hotel dining room, which serves meals for 25 DM to 48 DM ($16.50 to $31.70).

EISLEBEN (LUTHERSTADT)

The leader of the German Reformation, Martin Luther, was born and died in this old Prussian town, which lies on a southeastern spur of the Harz Mountains, about 25 miles west of Halle. Access by car is via Autobahn B6 or State Highway B80. The Eisleben Bahnhof has frequent connections to Halle. For travel information, call 03475/29-57.

The town is divided into an Old Town and a New Town: **Altstadt and Neustadt.**

The house at the end of Lutherstrasse, in which Luther was born in 1483, was damaged by fire in 1689 but rebuilt in its present Gothic Franconian town-house style and used for a long time as a free school for homeless children. You can see the room in which he was born, as well as exhibits tracing his life story. You can view a wood carving, the **Luther Swan,** inspired by the prophetic statement of the early Bohemian reformer, John Hus, about the swan (taken later to be Luther) who was to follow him.

At the end of his life the ailing Luther returned to his birthplace, and here he died in 1546, in a house near the Market Square, where a memorial statue to him stands. A museum here contains his deathbed, death mask, and coffin shroud, and you can see the room where he died.

In Eisleben you can also see the font where Luther was baptized in the late-Gothic **Peter-Paul-Kirche.** For tourist information, go to Fremdenverkehrsverein, Hallesche Strasse 6 (tel. 03475/21-24).

NAUMBURG

If you have unlimited time for eastern Germany, you might seek out the medieval town of Naumburg, in the Halle district, lying between Leipzig and Weimar. A former district of Saxony, it lies 29 miles southwest of Halle. In the 10th century, it was a stronghold of the margraves of Meissen.

Lying on the Saale River, the town of 32,000 people is reached by car via Autobahn E49 or State Highway 180. The Naumburg Bahnhof is on rail lines from Leipzig, Erfurt, and Berlin, with frequent connections. For local rail information, call 03445/24-13 in Naumburg.

Built in the Romanesque Transition style, the **Cathedral of St. Peter and St. Paul** dates from the early 13th century and is known for its huge crypt and towers. Look inside for the hand-carved folk figures. In the Rathaus, opening on Wilhelm-Pieck-Platz, is a good **Ratskeller,** serving beer, hearty food, and a local wine that is quite dry.

3. DRESDEN

123 miles S of Berlin; 69 miles SE of Leipzig

GETTING THERE By Plane   The local airport, Dresden-Klotsche (tel. 0351/58-31-41), lies 6 miles north of center city. The airport is served by Lufthansa, Air France, KLM, and other international carriers, with regularly scheduled flights to 11 German cities, including Berlin, Munich, and Frankfurt, as well as to other major European cities. For flight information, call 0351/495-60-13. A shuttle bus (no. 99) runs from the airport to the city center (trip time: 20 minutes).

By Train   Dresden has two main rail stations, the Hauptbahnhof, Wiener Platz, and the Dresden-Neustadt, Schlesischer Park. Trams no. 3 and 11 connect the two terminals. The city is served by the Deutsche Reichsbahn rail line, with frequent connections to major and regional cities, including Berlin and Leipzig. Fifteen trains arrive daily from Berlin (trip time: 2 hours, 20 minutes), and 12 trains pull in from Frankfurt in the west (trip time: 7 to 8 hours, depending on the train). For rail information and schedules, call Europäisches Reiseburo GmbH (tel. 0351/486-52-64 in Dresden).

By Car   Access is via Autobahn E40 from the west; Autobahn E5 from the north (Rostock, Berlin) or from the south.

Dresden was once called "Florence on the Elbe." Throughout Europe, prewar Dresden was celebrated for its architecture and art treasures. Then came the night of February 13, 1945. The Allies, presumably in an attempt to crush the morale of the German people, rained down phosphorus and high-explosive bombs on Dresden, a city with no military targets. If you're interested in the subject, you might want to read the Kurt Vonnegut novel *Slaughterhouse Five.* It is estimated that some 35,000 Dresdeners were sucked into the devastating fire storm that engulfed the historic city. However, because refugees had crowded into the city at the time, no one knows for sure exactly what the body count was. Some sources have claimed as many as 135,000, or even 300,000. However, the 35,000 body count is the figure generally given. By morning the Dresden of legend was but a memory. The bombing of this great city of art is considered one of the major tragedies of World War II, and there are those, especially the old Communist regime, who have compared its destruction to that of Hiroshima.

For many long and dreary years after the war, Dresden, the third-largest city in eastern Germany, no longer resembled the city on the Elbe painted by Canaletto. Most of it still doesn't, but much of the familiar silhouette has been belatedly restored. Bouncing back from disaster, Dresden is nevertheless a major sightseeing target, especially its "centerpiece," the museum-packed Zwinger (see "What to See & Do," below).

Regrettably, the city has recently become a center for neo-Nazi skinheads, who often single out foreigners, especially African, Polish, and Vietnamese, as targets of attack. All foreigners should take caution, however, and be especially careful walking the streets at night. The area north of the Elbe has seen the most violence.

ORIENTATION

INFORMATION   Before tackling Dresden, which is a virtual "museumland," you should head first to the **Information Center,** Pragerstrasse (tel. 0351/495-50-25). Hours from April to October are Monday through Saturday from 9am to 8pm and Sunday and public holidays from 9am to noon. From November through March, hours are Monday through Saturday from 9am to 6pm and Sunday and public holidays from 9am to noon. Here you can purchase a map you'll definitely need.

The **Central Post Office** is at St. Petersburger Strasse 26 (tel. 0351/495-41-65), entered at Pragerstrasse. It is open Monday through Friday from 8am to 6pm, Saturday 9am to noon, and Sunday 10am to 11am.

CITY LAYOUT   Today, a pedestrian mall, **Pragerstrasse,** once the fashionable Champs-Élysées of Dresden, cuts through the city "that rose from the ashes." The street is lined with modern, heavy, gray commercial buildings—a valley, not a peak, in socialist architecture. However, its severity is relieved by fountains and benches. On those benches you'll find many foreign tourists. Prague Street runs from the Altmarkt to the Hauptbahnhof. The Altmarkt itself is the historic hub of the city, with its Palace of Culture, or **Kulturpalast,** built in 1969.

Dresden consists of both an **Altstadt** and a **Neustadt.** Actually, since the war both terms have been a misnomer. Since it has been rebuilt, the Altstadt is newer than the Neustadt. The old and new towns are connected by four road bridges and one railway bridge, of which the Augustus is the best known.

Work continues on the **Royal Palace** (Schloss). Already the Georgentor, the main gate, has returned to its original appearance and the fine Renaissance facade has been restored. Some have projected 2006 as the completion date of this palace, which would be Dresden's 800th anniversary.

The most pleasant place for a stroll is the city's main park, **Blüherpark,** lying directly south of Altstadt.

GETTING AROUND

One of the major means of transport in Dresden is the tram, a modern, reliable, low-energy system for getting around. The public transportation network also consists of city-suburb trains and 28 bus lines, with frequent service to all parts of the city. For information, call Dresdner Verkehrsbetriebe AG in Dresden (tel. 0351/520-01). Also, you can take trips on the big paddlesteamers that ply the River Elbe from central moorings below the Brühl Terrace. You can take trips from April to October on one of the ships belonging to the **Weisse Flotte** (White Fleet) (tel. 0351/502-26-11).

Even if you don't make a river trip, it's exciting to watch as the paddlesteamers lower their funnels to pass under a bridge. One of Dresden's most celebrated bridges is called Blaues Wunder (Blue Wonder), a tribute to the bridge-building genius applied here at the turn of the century. The funicular railway, the first of its kind in the world, built from 1898 to 1900, takes passengers to the viewing site at Loschwitzhöhe.

WHAT TO SEE & DO

The restoration of old buildings in the "monumental zones" has been tremendous. Ruins from the war can still be seen, most notably in the baroque **Frauenkirche** (Church of Our Lady), at Neumarkt, built between 1726 and 1743 and once known throughout Europe for its cupola. The blackened hulk remains, supposedly a deliberate decision on the part of the government to remind the passerby of "the horrors of modern warfare." It stands today, a ghostly reminder of what happened to this *Kunststadt,* or city of art.

Some of Dresden's famous churches have been restored, however. The **Hofkirche,** also at Neumarkt, built in the rococo style with a slender clock tower, rises some 300 feet. It was elevated to the status of cathedral by the Vatican following its restoration. The **Kreuzkirche** (Church of the Cross) stands at the Altmarkt. This church is the home of the Kreuzchor, the famous boys' choir of Dresden.

Of Dresden's many parks and gardens, the most visited is the **Grosser Garten,** which lies to the southeast of the Altstadt. The park was mapped out in 1676 and today contains a zoo and a botanical garden. In the center is a Lustschloss (pleasure palace) built in 1670.

As the court of the 17th-century princes of Saxony, Dresden enjoyed renown throughout Europe. Its Palace of Electors and Kings is still in ruins from World War II, but so fascinating are these ruins that they form one of the major attractions of the city. However, the **Zwinger** (palace complex) at Postplatz is a series of beautiful baroque buildings that have been restored and turned into a collection of museums, some 20 in all.

The Zwinger is a large quadrangle of pavilions and galleries. It was here that Augustus the Strong, the elector of Saxony (he was also the king of Poland), staged tournaments that dazzled the townsfolk. He also kept dozens of concubines here, as he was reportedly something of a sexual athlete. His physique was called Herculean, his temperament Rabelaisian, but he had a great love of the arts. It was this monarch who started the collection of paintings that in time was supplemented by his son.

The Zwinger was initially conceived by M. D. Pöppelmann as the forecourt of the castle. In its center are formal gardens, fountains, and promenades, forming a deep curving bay enclosed by pavilions. The Renaissance-style building is from 1846, and the exterior is decorated with sculptures of such celebrated figures as Goethe, Dante, and Michelangelo. To reach the Zwinger and its museums, take tram no. 1, 2, 4, 7, 8, 11, 12, 14, or 17 to Postplatz.

The most important museum is the ✪ **Gemäldegalerie Alte Meister,** Sophienstrasse (tel. 0351/484-01-20), open Tuesday to Sunday from 9am to 5pm, charging an admission of 5 DM ($3.30) for adults and 2.50 DM ($1.70) for children. The gallery, considered one of the best on the Continent, has as its showpiece Raphael's *Sistine Madonna.* You find also Giorgione's *Sleeping Venus; The Martyrdom of St. Sebastian* by Antonello da Messina; Titian's *Tribute Money;* and many famous works by Veronese, Tintoretto, Correggio, and Annibale Carracci. You'll also see paintings by Jan van Eyck, Rubens, Rembrandt, Vermeer, Dürer, Cranach, Holbein, and many other important painters.

Staatliche Kunstsammlungen Historisches Museum, Zwinger (tel. 0351/48-40-126), displays an ornamental collection of weaponry that is truly stunning, if a bit frightening. It is open Tuesday through Sunday from 9am to 5pm, charging adults 3 DM ($2) and children 2 DM ($1.30).

In the **Porcelain Museum** (Porzellansammlung) (tel. 0351/484-01-27), a vast array of one of the best-known crafts of Dresden is exhibited. The collection of porcelain, which was begun by Augustus II, is considered the second biggest on earth. Meissen porcelain tends to dominate the exhibit, but the collection is wide-ranging, even taking in work from China and Japan. The museum is open Friday through Wednesday from 10am to 6pm. Admission is 3 DM ($2).

The glass-domed **Albertinum** (tel. 0351/495-30-56), originally from 1559, is another museum complex, this one on Brühl Terrace, housing the state art collection. It's open Friday through Wednesday from 9am to 5pm, charging an admission of 7 DM ($4.60) for adults and 3.50 DM ($2.30) for children. Its most famous attraction is the Green Vault, or Grünes Gewölbe, a dazzling exhibition of jewelry and other treasures from the 16th to the 18th century. The museum complex also contains the **Galerie Neue Meister** (tel. 0351/495-30-56), with paintings by an array of artists from Gauguin to Corot. Admission is 5 DM ($3.30) for adults and 2.50 DM ($1.70) for children. Hours are Tuesday through Sunday 9am to 5pm. Tram: 1, 3, 5, 7, or 8.

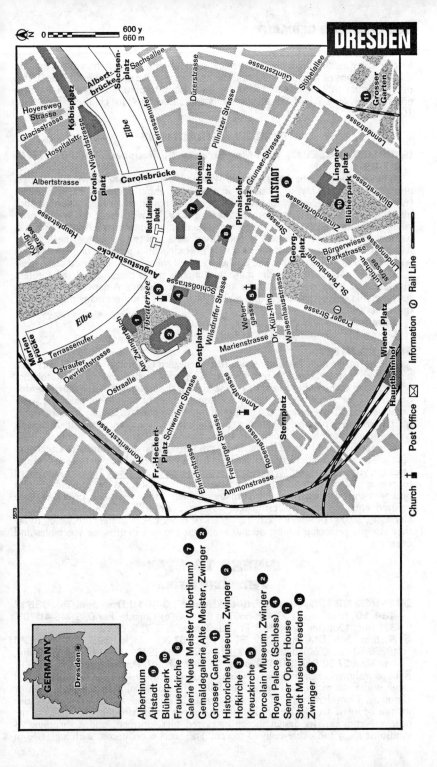

DRESDEN

Church ✝ Post Office ⊠ Information ⓘ Rail Line ▬▬▬

GERMANY
Dresden●

Albertinum ⑦
Altstadt ⑨
Blüherpark ⑩
Frauenkirche ⑥
Galerie Neue Meister (Albertinum) ⑦
Gemäldegalerie Alte Meister, Zwinger ②
Grosser Garten ⑪
Historiches Museum, Zwinger ②
Hofkirche ③
Kreuzkirche ⑤
Porcelain Museum, Zwinger ②
Royal Palace (Schloss) ④
Semper Opera House ①
Stadt Museum Dresden ⑧
Zwinger ②

Stadtmuseum Dresden, Wilsdruffer Strasse 2 (tel. 0351/495-23-02), contains a rich display on Dresden's history. Perhaps no exhibit more fascinates visitors than do the photographs of Dresden following the bombings at the end of World War II. It is open Monday to Thursday and Saturday from 10am to 6pm, Sunday from 10am to 6pm. Admission is 2 DM ($1.30) for adults and 1 DM (66¢) for children. Tram: 9 or 10.

NEARBY ATTRACTIONS

INDIANER MUSEUM, Karl-May-Strasse 5, Radebeul. Tel. 0351/76-27-23.

A fascination with the American Old West and especially with Native Americans is present in all Germany, and notably in Radebeul, about 5 miles west of Dresden (Autobahn Dresden-Neustadt), where the popular German writer Karl May lived until his death in 1912. May wrote about prairies and Native Americans and frontier villains even though he never visited the United States until after his last book was written. However, he collected Native American artifacts and started the Indianer Museum in a log cabin built near his villa in Radebeul, a project completed by his widow in 1928 and opened to the public. Much of the material displayed came from later acquisitions, and today the museum contains peace pipes, tomahawks, totem poles, crafts, moccasins, and many other items of Native American lore. May's restored villa nearby was opened to the public in 1985. It houses many mementos of the writer's life.

Admission: 5 DM ($3.30) adults, 3 DM ($2) children.
Open: Daily 9am–5pm. **Tram:** 4 or 5.

SORB COUNTRY.

One of the most fascinating side trips in eastern Germany is to the history-rich Sorb country. If you're returning from Dresden to Berlin along the Autobahn, get off at the Lübbenau exit. This section of the country is called **Spreewald,** or forest of the Spree, and it's nearly 100 square miles of woodland, pastures, and a canal network. Drive toward the port (Hafen), where you can usually hire someone, often a woman in national costume, to pilot you in a canoe along these canals. Several waterside cafés are found along the canals, serving food and drink.

The area is still inhabited by the Sorbs, who speak a language similar to Czech and Polish. The Sorbs are descendants of Slavic tribes who settled here in the 6th century. Over the years, they have faced tremendous persecution, but they always fought hard to preserve their culture. They were particularly persecuted by the Nazis, who outlawed their language and killed many of them. However, since 1949 they have enjoyed equal rights. It is estimated that there are still 100,000 Sorbs living in Germany, 30,000 of whom inhabit cottages or other places in the Spreewald. Today they enjoy a protected landscape and are often engaged in growing vegetables and fruit.

WHERE TO STAY
VERY EXPENSIVE

DRESDEN HILTON, An der Frauenkirche 5, 0-8010 Dresden. Tel. 0351/484-10, or toll free 800/445-8667 in the U.S. or Canada. Fax 0351/48-41-700. 321 rms, 12 suites. MINIBAR TV TEL **Tram:** 3, 5, 7, 8, or 12.

$ Rates: 345 DM–405 DM ($227.70–$267.30) single; 395 DM–455 DM ($260.70–$300.30) double; 650 DM–780 DM ($429–$514.80) suite. Buffet breakfast 27.50 DM ($18.20) extra. AE, DC, MC, V. **Parking:** 15 DM ($9.90).

Built as a showcase of the eastern German tourist infrastructure in 1990, this hotel came under the managerial control of Hilton International after the unification of Germany. Considered one of the best hotels in the eastern area, its conservative mansard-roofed facade blends harmoniously with the baroque buildings on the nearby Neumarkt. Its design incorporates red tiles, dormers, and a sheathing of sandstone slabs and ochre-colored stucco. The hotel is connected with a glassed-in passageway to a 19th-century library, the Sekundogenitur, which contains two restaurants and an array of banqueting and conference rooms.

Dining/Entertainment: The hotel contains 11 restaurants and cafés, 2 of which are recommended below. Other eateries include a bistro, a Bierclub, a Viennese coffeehouse, and a wine cellar.

Services: 24-hour room service, laundry, babysitting, concierge to arrange city tours.

Facilities: Fitness club with pool, sauna, solarium.

MARITIM BELLEVUE, Grosse Meissner Strasse 15, 0-8060 Dresden. Tel. 0351/5-66-20. Fax 0351/5-59-97. 328 rms, 16 suites. MINIBAR TV TEL **Tram:** 4 or 5.

$ Rates (including continental breakfast): 339 DM–449 DM ($223.70–$296.30) single; 448 DM–538 DM ($295.70–$355.10) double; from 750 DM ($495) suite. AE, DC, MC, V. **Parking:** 20 DM ($13.20).

The Maritim Bellevue, which opened in spring 1985, stands on the most attractive part of the bank of the Elbe, and a look out the hotel's windows and from its terraces to the opposite bank makes you feel as if this must be the spot from which Canaletto painted his magnificent scenes. The hotel building incorporates Dresden's only double court, which was formerly the Royal Chancellery. The court survived the 1945 bombing and is now a protected monument that has carefully integrated into the hotel, giving a feel of special elegance and style. Whether you stay in the old part of the building or in the new section, you'll find the rooms well appointed, with carpeting, and comfortable armchairs. Half are air-conditioned.

Dining/Entertainment: Five eating places offer a variety of cuisine, together with consistently good service. Restaurants include the Palais, the Buri-Buri (recommended separately), the Canaletto (recommended separately), the Elbterrasse with its summer terrace, and the Wackerbarths Wine Cellar. Guests can enjoy drinks in the foyer bar.

Services: Room service, babysitting, laundry.

Facilities: Fitness club with indoor pool, solarium, "bronzarium," saunas, bowling alleys, a massage room; shopping arcade with boutiques, shops.

EXPENSIVE

MERCURE NEWA, St. Petersburger Strasse 34, 0-8010 Dresden. Tel. 0351/4-81-40. Fax 0351/495-51-37. 310 rms, 8 suites. TV TEL **Tram:** 3, 5, 7, 8, or 9.

$ Rates (including continental breakfast): 240 DM–290 DM ($158.40–$191.40) single; 290 DM–340 DM ($191.40–$224.40) double; from 400 DM ($264) suite. AE, DC, MC, V. **Parking:** 15 DM ($9.90).

Surrounded by a flat expanse of green lawn, opposite Dresden's Hauptbahnhof, with another high-rise set immediately behind it, this buff-and-beige rectangle is supported by an even-larger one-story rectangle containing a popular glass-walled restaurant. There is also the Spezialitäten-restaurant, as well as a Café Baltik, along with two salons, the Repin and Puschkin. You can dine here for as little as 32 DM ($21.10) per meal. The rooms are standard but comfortable; some units contain minibars. In all, the hotel is big, bustling, and fairly anonymous, often filled with tour groups. You'll find a sauna and solarium too. If you're assigned a room on one of the upper floors, you'll have a spectacular city view.

MODERATE

KÖNIGSTEIN, Pragerstrasse 101, 0-8012 Dresden. Tel. 0351/485-63-42. Fax 0351/495-40-54. 306 rms, 9 suites. TV TEL **Tram:** 3, 5, 7, 8, 10, 11, or 15.

$ Rates (including continental breakfast): 155 DM–175 DM ($102.30–$115.50) single; 185 DM–205 DM ($122.10–$135.30) double; 250 DM ($165) suite. AE, DC, MC, V. **Parking:** 15 DM ($9.90).

The Königstein stands across from the Mercure Newa (see above), also at the Hauptbahnhof. It was built near a pedestrian walkway planted with masses of flowers, which change seasonally. It's a big building, with an anonymous facade pierced by uninterrupted horizontal lines of glass. The rooms in fair weather are sunny and decorated in a predictably utilitarian modern style. Some units contain minibars. Other facilities include a restaurant, a roof garden, and a sauna. The restaurant is restricted to residents for most of the day.

MARTHA HOSPIZ, Nieritzstrasse 11, 0-8060 Dresden-Neustadt. Tel. 0351/5-24-25. Fax 0351/5-32-18. 36 rms. TV TEL **Tram:** 3, 5, 7, 8, 10, 11, or 15.

$ Rates (including continental breakfast): 130 DM ($85.80) single; 190 DM–230 DM ($125.40–$151.80) double. MC, V. **Parking:** Free.

Planned and conceived before unification, this simple but comfortable hotel opened in 1991 in a quiet location five minute's walk from the commercial heart of modern Dresden. Rising four stories, it contains few amenities other than its breakfast room and offers conservatively modern guest rooms decorated in either blue or brown.

WHERE TO DINE
EXPENSIVE

BURI-BURI, in the Maritim Bellevue, Grosse Meissner Strasse 15. Tel. 0351/56-620.
  Cuisine: POLYNESIAN. **Reservations:** Recommended. **Tram:** 4 or 5.
$ Prices: Appetizers 10.50 DM–21 DM ($6.90–$13.90); main courses 22 DM–45 DM ($14.50–$29.70); four-course fixed-price menu 65 DM ($42.90). AE, DC, MC, V.
  Open: Dinner only, daily 6pm–1am.

Buri-Buri brings the exotic flavors of the South Seas to conservative Dresden. You'll think you're at Trader Vic's as you peruse the menu of lush tropical food and drink. Meals include a selection of Polynesian hors d'oeuvres. You might follow with filet Waikiki or one of the spicy meat curries. My favorite is "carpetbag steak."

CANALETTO, in the Maritim Bellevue, Grosse Meissner Strasse 15. Tel. 0351/56-620.
  Cuisine: CONTINENTAL. **Reservations:** Recommended. **Tram:** 4 or 5.
$ Prices: Appetizers 10.50 DM–26 DM ($6.90–$17.20); main courses 28 DM–48 DM ($18.50–$31.70); fixed-price dinner 75 DM–120 DM ($49.50–$79.20). AE, DC, MC, V.
  Open: Dinner only, daily 6pm–1am.

✪ Perhaps the finest (and most expensive) restaurant in Dresden, Canaletto uses only the best meats and produce. Its chefs and service are world-class, and diners enjoy the candlelit setting in the vaulted room of this previously recommended hotel. You might begin with smoked North Sea oysters or game soup with Pernod-flavored venison quenelles and almond crêpes. For a main course, you try gin-pickled venison cutlet garnished with chanterelles and pâté, peppersteak, or veal in cream sauce with morels in the style of Zurich.

ROSSINI, in the Dresden Hilton, An der Frauenkirche 5. Tel. 0351/484-10. Tram: 3, 5, 7, 8, or 12.
  Cuisine: ITALIAN. **Reservations:** Not necessary.
$ Prices: Appetizers 9 DM–21 DM ($5.90–$13.90); main courses 22 DM–35 DM ($14.50–$23.10). AE, DC, MC, V.
  Open: Lunch daily 12:30–3pm; dinner daily 7pm–midnight.

Considered the finest and most upscale restaurant within the previously recommended hotel, the Rossini offers Italian cuisine within a stylish decor of black-lacquer furniture and white walls and napery. Located one floor above the hotel's lobby, it presents a welcome relief from too constant a diet of the Teutonic specialties that are the standard fare in many other local restaurants. The menu features a changing array of dishes based on the cuisines of north and south Italy; these might include chicken-liver pâté in marsala wine, a buffet of Sicilian antipasti, carpaccio of swordfish marinated in marsala vinaigrette, Sicilian-style fish soup, or grilled lamb with anchovy sauce. Dessert might be a cassata made with ricotta cheese and candied fruit or a granita (sorbet) of oranges and lemons floating on white wine.

MODERATE

GRUNER BAUM, in the Dresden Hilton, An der Frauenkirche 5. Tel. 0351/484-10.
  Cuisine: GERMAN/INTERNATIONAL. **Reservations:** Not necessary. **Tram:** 3, 5, 7, 8, or 12.
$ Prices: Appetizers 8 DM ($5.30); main courses 25 DM–35 DM ($16.50–$23.10); fixed-price "business lunch" 33 DM ($21.80); Thurs–Fri fish buffet supper 46 DM ($30.40). AE, DC, MC, V.
  Open: Daily 6:30am–1am; business lunch Mon–Fri noon–3pm.

Set amid burgeoning plants and trees of what's probably the most dramatic hotel lobby in Dresden, this restaurant remains open throughout the day for coffee, snacks, and meals. One of the most popular events is the fish buffet, served every Thursday and Friday from 6 to 11pm, when the bounty of the north Atlantic is spread in an imaginative all-you-can-eat display. At other times, a flavorful and imaginative à la carte menu of German dishes is available, including soup with mushrooms and wild herbs, kohlrabi soup studded with tiny balls of freshly made cheese, salmon-potato soup with strips of goose breast, and grilled John Dory baked in an herb coating in herb sauce. Desserts include several kinds of berried yogurts, pastries, and a marzipan parfait with amaretto.

MEISSNER WEINKELLER, Hauptstrasse 1B. Tel. 0351/558-14.
  Cuisine: CONTINENTAL. **Reservations:** Recommended. **Tram:** 4 or 5.
$ Prices: Appetizers 6 DM–10.50 DM ($4–$6.90); main courses 18 DM–32 DM ($11.90–$21.10); "Saxon menu of the day" 52 DM ($34.30). AE, DC, MC, V.
  Open: Dinner only, Sun–Fri 6pm–midnight, Sat 6pm–1am.

Perhaps the most popular dining place in Dresden is across from the "golden man" statue near the Maritim Bellevue. In summer, it has outdoor tables. An arched stone door leads down to the cellar, and upstairs the place has a modern café decor with a large central bar. It has a devoted following among the young people of town. The chef's specialty is a mixed grill including chicken, pork médaillons, and beef médaillons. You can also order beef fondue and flambé steak.

OPERNRESTAURANT, Theaterplatz 2. Tel. 0351/484-2511.
  Cuisine: GERMAN/INTERNATIONAL. **Reservations:** Recommended. **Tram:** 1, 2, 4, 7, 8, 11, 12, 14, or 17.
$ Prices: Appetizers 9 DM–13 DM ($5.90–$8.60); main courses 20 DM–32 DM ($13.20–$21.10). Fixed-price menus 30 DM–95 DM ($19.80–$62.70) AE, DC, MC, V.
  Open: Daily noon–midnight.

One floor above street level in a modern building that shares the same square as Dresden's historic opera house, this is considered a stylish and sophisticated venue for lunch, afternoon coffee or snacks, dinner, or late-night supper. The decor might remind you of that in a private London or Berlin club, with upholstered banquettes, potted trees, modern accessories, and original artwork. Recorded classical music, sometimes derived from performances at the nearby opera, might play softly as you dine.

Menu specialties include tartare of raw marinated salmon served with asparagus tips and toast, a paprika-laden version of pork goulasch, roulades of beef stuffed with onions and herbs, and freshly prepared pastries.

INEXPENSIVE

LUISENHOF, Bergbahnstrasse 8. Tel. 0351/368-42.

Cuisine: SAXON/CONTINENTAL. **Reservations:** Recommended. **Directions:** Follow signs from center to funicular station.

$ Prices: Appetizers 5.50 DM–18 DM ($3.60–$11.90); main courses 18 DM–32 DM ($11.90–$21.10); fixed-price lunch 30 DM ($19.80). AE, DC, MC, V.

Open: Tues–Sun 11:30am–midnight.

For my final meal in Dresden, I go to Luisenhof, where, however good the food is, it takes second place to the magnificent view. Take the funicular railway up to the restaurant site, which has been called "the balcony of Dresden," high above the city. You can see the reemerging baroque skyline of the historic, carefully restored buildings and bridges. Try to avoid going here on weekends, when it is sure to be thronged with people—some of the many tourists who visit Dresden every day. Try the Sauerbraten specialty or salmon on spinach leaves.

RATSKELLER, in the cellar of the Rathaus, Dr.-Külz-Ring 19. Tel. 0351/488-29-50.

Cuisine: SAXON/CONTINENTAL. **Reservations:** Recommended. **Bus:** 75.

$ Prices: Appetizers 6 DM–10.50 DM ($4–$6.90); main courses 15 DM–28 DM ($9.90–$18.50). AE, MC, V.

Open: Sun–Fri 11am–midnight, Sat 11am–1am.

Here it's easy to strike up a conversation if there's no language problem, as tables are shared. You can get Sauerbraten and Wiener Schnitzel, along with plain roast beef and Hungarian goulash. Potatoes—boiled, fried, roasted, mashed, whatever—are always served. Desserts are simple, usually a fruit compote or ice cream.

UNGARISCHE GASTSTÄTTE SZEGED, Wilhofstrasse 6, 2nd floor. Tel. 0351/495-13-71.

Cuisine: HUNGARIAN. **Reservations:** Not necessary. **Tram:** 2, 12, or 14.

$ Prices: Appetizers 6.50 DM–10 DM ($4.30–$6.60); main courses 15 DM–30 DM ($9.90–$19.80). AE, DC, MC, V.

Open: Daily noon–11pm.

This is the place to go for food cooked from old Hungarian recipes, as well as latter-day additions inspired by the cuisine of Budapest. If you're hungry for a little paprika, this is the restaurant for you. À la carte meals include roast pork stuffed with goose liver in paprika-cream sauce, Budapest-style rumpsteak covered with liver ragoût, and Hungarian-style roast chicken. There's a coffee bar downstairs in the street-side café.

EVENING ENTERTAINMENT

Between the Elbe and the Zwinger, Dresden's **✪ Semper Opera House,** Theaterplatz 2 (tel. 0351/48-42-328), was designed by Gottfried Semper, the architect who mapped out the famous picture gallery of Dresden. The opera house, at which both Wagner and Weber conducted, was completed in 1878 in a Renaissance style. What you see today, standing on the western side of Theaterplatz, is the work of restorers who have brought the two-tiered facade and interior of the Italian Renaissance-style building back to life. Careful attention was paid to the replacement of the paintings and decorations used by Semper when the place was built, and the fine acoustics for which the opera house was known have been restored. The stage was altered somewhat to allow for use of modern technology, and fewer seats were designed to allow for more comfort (the old auditorium held 1,700 persons; the new, 1,323). The Semper Opera House was reopened in 1985. Good seats can be purchased for 60 DM to 80 DM ($39.60 to $52.80). The opera company takes a vacation from mid-July to September. Concerts are also performed in summer in the courtyards of the Zwinger. Tram: 1, 2, 4, 7, 8, 11, 12, 14, or 17.

The **Dresden Philharmonic** appears at the Kulturpalast, in the Altmarkt (tel. 0351/486-60).

Your hotel or the tourist office will have a complete listing of these cultural events.

4. MEISSEN

14 miles NW of Dresden; 108 miles S of Berlin; 53 miles E of Leipzig

GETTING THERE **By Train** The Meissen Bahnhof is on the Deutsche Reichsbahn rail line, with frequent connections to Dresden and other major and regional cities. For rail information, call Europäisches Reisebüro in Meissen (tel. 03521/33-53).

By Bus Regional buses connecting Dresden with Meissen are operated by Verkehrsgesellshaft Meissen (consult the tourist office—see below—for a schedule of connections), or ask at the tourist information center at Dresden (see above).

By Car Access is via Autobahn E40 from Dresden or E49 from Leipzig.

By Boat If you're in Dresden in summer, the best way to go to Meissen is by boat. The Weisse Flotte (tel. 0351/502-26-11) leaves two times a day from Dresden's Brühl Terrace, the fortified embankment on the other side of the Hofkirche. You get to enjoy the scenery along the Elbe.

ESSENTIALS For tourist information, contact **Fremdenverkehrsamt Meissen,** An der Frauenkirche 3 (tel. 03521/45-44-70).

Few Western visitors stay overnight in Meissen, as accommodations are severely limited. The "city of porcelain" is most often visited on a day trip from Dresden. Since 1710, Meissen has been known around the world as the center of the manufacture of Dresden china. The early makers of this so-called "white gold" were virtually held prisoner within Meissen. The princes who ruled the city didn't want the secret of the porcelain to escape. Of course it did, and rivals imitated it. The city is still known for its factories making porcelain, glass, and pottery.

Meissen lies on both banks of the Elbe. The Altstadt was built on the left bank. It is a very old town, dating from 929.

WHAT TO SEE & DO

Towering over the town is the Gothic-style **Dom,** Domplatz 7 (tel. 03521/24-90), built between 1260 and 1450 and one of the smallest cathedrals in Germany. Up to 1400, the bishops of the diocese of Meissen had their seat next to the cathedral, and Saxon rulers were buried here, the first interred in 1428. Inside the cathedral are works of art, including a painting by Lucas Cranach the Elder, along with rare Meissen porcelain. The cathedral has been Protestant since the 16th century. It is open daily from 9am to 4:30pm, charging 2.50 DM ($1.70) for adults and 1.20 DM (80¢) for children.

Sharing the castle quarter with the cathedral is **Albrechtsburg Castle,** Domplatz (tel. 03521/29-20), where the first Meissen porcelain was made. The castle construction began in 1471 and went on intermittently until 1525, with restoration in the late 19th century. From 1710 to 1864 it was the site of the Meissen Porcelain Manufactory. It is open Tuesday through Sunday from 10am to 6pm; closed in January. Admission is 4 DM ($2.60).

Guided tours go through the **Staatliche Porzellan-Manufaktur,** Talstrasse 9 (tel. 03521/45-85-41), Tuesday and Sunday from 8:30am to 4pm. You can see how the centuries-old manufacture of Meissen china is still carried on, many times using the same designs. It was established back in 1710, not long after Johann Friedrich Böttger first succeeded in producing fine red stoneware in 1707 and then, in 1708, European white hard-paste porcelain.

Böttger, an apprentice pharmacist, had taken up alchemy, conducted various experiments, and claimed to be able to make gold. Augustus the Strong, Elector of Saxony and King of Poland, had him put behind bars when he heard of this and ordered Böttger to prove his claim—which the latter labored at for many years, eventually producing "white gold," or porcelain.

On the premises you can visit the **Porcelain Museum,** the oldest in Europe, plus the workshop, for 10 DM ($6.60) for adults and 8 DM ($5.30) for children.

The terraces of the nearby vineyards in the Elbe Valley produce fine wines, for which Meissen has been known for 1,000 years, including the hard-to-obtain Meissner Domherr.

WHERE TO DINE
MODERATE

VINCENZ RICHTER, An der Frauenkirche 12. Tel. 03521/32-85.
   Cuisine: SAXON. **Reservations:** Recommended.
$ **Prices:** Appetizers 13.50 DM–18 DM ($8.90–$11.90); main courses 20 DM–28 DM ($13.20–$18.50); fixed-price menu 30 DM ($19.80). AE, DC, MC, V.
   Open: Tues–Sat 3–11pm.

An exciting choice, if you don't mind the steep walk down and back, is Vincenz Richter. Just off the Market Square, this vine-covered restaurant is privately owned. It stands on a terrace in a building dating from 1523 (the present wine tavern was established in 1706). However, here you can sample the famous wines of Meissen and get simple, hearty Saxon food.

INEXPENSIVE

DOMKELLER, Domplatz 9. Tel. 03521/45-20-34.
   Cuisine: SAXON. **Reservations:** Not necessary.
$ **Prices:** Appetizers 5 DM–13 DM ($3.30–$8.60); main courses 8 DM–22 DM ($5.30–$14.50). DC, V.
   Open: Sun and Tues–Thurs 11am–8pm, Fri–Sat 11am–10:30pm.

Closely associated with the city's cathedral, deep within a masonry-sided cellar, this has been a historic rendezvous since 1755. Many of the important historical figures of Germany, both secular and ecclesiastical, have passed through its portals and perhaps enjoyed a platter of its hearty fare. Today, the tradition continues, with such filling and flavorful dishes as Eisbein, Sauerbraten, and roast goose—all served in a tavernlike setting.

---

5. WEIMAR

162 miles SW of Berlin; 14 miles E of Erfurt

GETTING THERE   By Train   The Weimar Bahnhof is on the major Deutsche Reichsbahn rail lines, linking Erfurt and Leipzig and also Weimar with Dresden. There are frequent daily connections in both directions. For rail information and schedules, call Europäisches Reisebüro in Weimar at 03643/26-82.

By Bus   Regional buses to all parts of the city and the surrounding area are offered by Verkehrsgesellschaft Weimar (tel. 03643/28-07 for schedules and information).

By Car   Access is via Autobahn E40 east and west.

ESSENTIALS   You may want to head first for Weimar's tourist agency, the **Weimar Informationscentrum,** Marktstrasse 4 (tel. 03643/21-37), which is open Monday from 10am to 6pm, Tuesday to Friday from 9am to 6pm, and Saturday from 9am to 1pm. You can purchase a map, which will be most helpful in orientation.

Before World War II, Weimar was a symbol of German culture. Lucas Cranach the Elder worked here in the 16th century, and from 1708 to 1717 Bach was court organist. Under the Dowager Duchess Anna Amalia and her son, Charles Augustus II, it reached its peak as a cultural center. In 1775 Goethe came to reside at their court, and he attracted such men as Herder and Schiller. Later in the 19th century Franz Liszt was musical director, and under his auspices, Wagner's *Lohengrin* had its first performance.

It was at Weimar that the German national assembly met in February 1919, in the aftermath of World War I, and drafted a constitution that created the Weimar Republic, a democratic republic that was, regrettably, to dissolve into a dictatorship 14 years later.

After Dresden and Berlin, Weimar is the chief destination in eastern Germany for the lover of German culture. The 1,000-year-old town lies on the edge of the Thuringian Forest. A 19th-century writer called it "one of the most walkable towns of Europe"—and so it is. Its existence goes back to the 9th century.

Unlike many eastern German cities, Weimar still retains much of its old flavor, with narrow winding streets left over from the Middle Ages and high-pitched gables and roofs. There is no town in the east that has so many important monuments of German classical history that were spared from the bombings of World War II.

WHAT TO SEE & DO

GOETHE NATIONAL MUSEUM, Am Frauenplan 1. Tel. 03643/620-41.

The principal attraction of the town is the Goethe National Museum, where the poet lived from 1782 to 1832. It's an example of a German nobleman's baroque house, built in 1709. There are 14 exhibition rooms, some pretty much as Goethe and his wife, Christiane Vulpius, left them. There is much original art in the house, and the library contains more than 5,000 volumes. The writer's mineral collection is here also. At Weimar, Goethe held the post of minister of state, and although his reputation rests today on his writing, the rooms in which he lived reveal his diverse interest in science as well (he was an early advocate of the belief in the common origin of all animal life, for example). He died in Weimar on March 22, 1832.

Admission: 5 DM ($3.30) adults, 3 DM ($2) children.
Open: Tues–Sun 9am–5pm. **Bus:** 1, 4, 6, 8, or 71.

GOETHES GARTENHAUS, Im Park an der Ilm. Tel. 03643/24-72.

In a park on the Ilm River is a plain wood cottage with a high-pitched roof—this is where the poet retreated for most of his summers to contemplate nature and anatomy. Goethe selected this house as his first residence when he came to Weimar. Even after he moved to other quarters, he still came here seeking peace and tranquility, describing the park around him as "infinitely beautiful."

Admission: 3 DM ($2) adults, 2 DM ($1.30) children.
Open: Daily 9am–noon and 1–5pm. **Bus:** 1, 4, 6, 8, or 71.

SCHILLERHAUS, Schillerstrasse 12. Tel. 03643/620-41 for information provided by the Goethe National Museum.

The Schillerhaus contains the rooms in which this great poet and philosopher lived. After his friend Goethe, Schiller is the greatest name in German literature. Schiller lived here with his family from 1802 to 1805. A museum displays mementos of his life and work. It also has a collection of costumes from productions of dramas by Schiller. The attic rooms have been refurnished as they were believed to have been in Schiller's day. He wrote his last works here, including *Wilhelm Tell*.

The Schillerhaus is opposite the Gänsemännchen, a copy of the Nürnberg Gänsemännchen from 1530.

Admission: 5 DM ($3.30) adults, 3 DM ($2) children.
Open: Mon and Wed–Sun 9am–5pm. **Bus:** 1, 4, 6, 8, or 71.

LISZT HOUSE, Marienstrasse 17. Tel. 03643/643-86.

The house of yet another famous artist, Franz Liszt (1811–86), can also be visited, as it has been turned into a museum. The Liszt House is where the Hungarian composer and pianist spent the last period of his life. It is said that he "strove to express the deepest romantic emotion in his playing and compositions." His daughter,

Cosima, was to become the wife of Richard Wagner. A two-story building, the Liszt House was once the home for the royal gardeners of Weimar. You'll find several mementos, both personal and musical, from the composer's life, including communications between Liszt and his son-in-law. You can also see a piano at which he played and taught his pupils.

Admission: 3 DM ($2) adults, 2 DM ($1.30) children.

Open: Tues–Sun 9am–1pm and 2–5pm. **Bus:** 4, 6, 8, or 71.

KUNSTSAMMLUNGEN ZU WEIMAR, Burgplatz 4. Tel. 03643/618-31.

Erected under the guidance of Goethe in 1789, this structure was completed in 1803 (the previous castle had burned down in 1774; only a tower survived). In one of the wings is a series of galleries dedicated not only to Schiller and Goethe but to two other famous names associated with Weimar: Johann Gottfried Herder (1744–1803), the German critic and philosopher who was a pioneer of the Sturm und Drang movement, and Christoph Martin Wieland (1733–1813), the poet and critic who wrote the satirical romance *The Republic of Fools.* The ground floor displays works by Lucas Cranach the Elder. On some of the upper floors you can see art of the famous Bauhaus movement, led by Walter Gropius, which once flourished in Weimar until it was expelled. The school of design, Das Staatliche Bauhaus Weimar, was principally responsible for revolutionizing the teaching of sculpture, painting, industrial arts, and architecture throughout the Western world. Followers around the globe may have been impressed, but not the good people of Weimar. They "tolerated" the school until 1925, bombarding it in the press, until it finally moved to Dessau, where it was to survive until the Nazis closed it in 1933, claiming it was a center of "Communist intellectualism."

Admission: 4 DM ($2.60) adults, 2 DM ($1.30) children.

Open: June–Aug, Tues–Sun 10am–6pm; Sept–May, Tues–Sun 9am–5pm. **Bus:** 5.

WITTUMSPALAIS, Am Palais 3. Tel. 03643/76-71-44.

Follow Rittergasse until the end, when you come upon the Wittumspalais, once the residence of Dowager Duchess Anna Amalia. The old ducal dowerhouse is devoted to mementos of the German classical Enlightenment. Under the Dowager Duchess Anna Amalia and her son, Charles Augustus, Weimar reached its peak as a cultural center.

Admission: 3 DM ($2) adults, 2 DM ($1.30) children.

Open: Tues–Sun 9am–noon and 1–5pm. **Bus:** 4, 6, or 8.

STADTKIRCHE ST. PETER AND PAUL, Herderplatz 8. Tel. 03643/23-28.

In a more ecclesiastical vein, you can follow Vorwerksgasse to the Gothic church, the Stadtkirche St. Peter and Paul, with an altarpiece by Lucas Cranach the Elder.

Admission: 1 DM (66¢).

Open: Daily 10am–noon and 2–4pm. **Bus:** 4 or 6.

RÖMISCHES HAUS, Im Park an der Ilm. Tel. 03643/76-71-47.

In the Goethepark you can see the neoclassical summer residence of Carl August, the Römisches Haus, located near Belvedere Allee on the other side of the Ilm River. The duke wanted to please Goethe, whose fondness for Roman architecture was well known.

Admission: 2 DM ($1.30) adults, 1 DM (66¢) children.

Open: Sun–Mon and Wed 9am–noon and 1–5pm. **Bus:** 8 or 11.

NIETZSCHE HOUSE, Humboldtstrasse 36. Tel. 03643/76-71-49.

Here Friedrich Nietzsche (1844–1900) spent the last 3 years of his life. The Nietzsche archives are stored here. They were arranged by his sister, Elisabeth Förster-Nietzsche (1846–1935).

Admission: 2 DM ($1.30).

Open: Tues–Sun 1–5pm. **Bus:** 6.

CHÂTEAU OF BELVEDERE [Schloss Belvedere], 2 miles south of Weimar. Tel. 03643/64-039.

The baroque Château of Belvedere has an open-air theater where stage productions were presented in Goethe's day. This was a favorite retreat of Anna Amalia and the "enlightened" Weimar set, including Carl August. It was a hunting seat and pleasure schloss in the 18th century. An orangerie was built, along with the open-air theater and an English-style park. A collection of historical coaches is here. In the château are displays of dainty rococo art.

Admission: 3.50 DM ($2.30) adults, 2 DM ($1.30) children.
Open: Mar–Oct, Tues–Sun 10am–6pm. **Bus:** 12.

TIEFURT PALACE [Schloss Tiefurt], on the outskirts of Weimar in the village of Tiefurt. Tel. 03643/30-38.
This was formerly the site of another summer retreat for Duchess Anna Amalia. Guests today can wander through its pavilions and gardens.

Admission: 3 DM ($2) adults, 2 DM ($1.30) children.
Open: Tues–Sun 9am–1pm and 2–5pm. **Directions:** Go east along Tiefurter Allee. **Bus:** 3 from Gotheplatz; Tiefurt is the last stop.

MORE ATTRACTIONS

On the Marktplatz, you can view the **Lucas Cranach the Elder House,** which is decorated with carved bouquets and Neptunian adventures. The painter spent his final years here.

In the **cemetery,** south of the town center, Am Posseckschen Garten, you see the controversial **Denkmal der März Gefallenen,** a monument to the revolutionaries whose slaughter in 1919 hastened the exit of Gropius from Weimar, along with his Bauhaus followers. But most Germans visit the cemetery today to pause in tribute at the grand ducal family vault, where Goethe and Schiller, friends in life, also lie side by side in death. The **Goethe-Schiller Mausoleum,** once the family vault of the Weimar dynasty, is on a terrace above the steps. It was built from 1825 to 1826 according to plans drawn up by Coudray, who consulted Goethe on the design and construction. Schiller was entombed here in 1827 and Goethe in 1832, both in oak coffins. Visiting hours are daily 9am to 1pm and 2 to 5pm. Admission is free. A chapel in Russian church style is on the south side of the mausoleum. It was built in 1859 for Maria Pavlovna, daughter-in-law of Duke Carl August.

BUCHENWALD The worst for last. The Buchenwald bus (no. 6) from Weimar's Hauptbahnhof goes to **Nationale Mahn- und Gedenkstätte Buchenwald,** Ettersberg (tel. 03643/67-481), Hitler's concentration camp and death chamber where Jews, Slavs, political prisoners, including the Communist leader Ernst Thalmann, and other condemned people were confined and brutally murdered from 1937 until 1945, when the final prisoners, starving and diseased and awaiting extermination, were released by the U.S. Army. On the Ettersberg, 4 miles northwest of Weimar, Buchenwald was the last sight that some 56,000 unfortunate souls saw before their extermination. Officially, it was called a work camp, so Buchenwald did not count the millions dead that Auschwitz did. However, atrocities practiced at this camp have made the name of Buchenwald synonymous with human perversity. For example, Ilse Koch, who has entered history as the notorious "bitch of Buchenwald," was said to have ordered lampshades made from human skin. It is reminiscent of a similar camp, Dachau, outside Munich.

Buchenwald virtually eliminated the Jewish population of eastern Germany—that is, those who had not already fled. It is estimated that a quarter of a million people were sent here during the camp's reign of terror. A memorial with a cluster of "larger-than-life" people, victims of fascism, was created by Professor Fritz Cremer to honor the victims of 32 nations who lost their lives at Buchenwald.

The atrocities continued under the Soviet occupation forces when they ran the camp from 1945 to 1951. It is believed they sent thousands of prisoners here to die, those suspected of being Nazis, although many historians believe that many were innocent. The Soviets also fatally tortured victims here, as mass graves nearby testify. All this was "hushed up" until the winter of 1989, when the Soviet atrocities along with Nazi atrocities became part of the onerous Buchenwald legend. Before that time, the Soviets had attempted to exploit the museum as a showcase illustrating "the suffering of Soviet soldiers and the German Communists." But the museum has been changed to illustrate history more accurately.

Hours are Tuesday to Sunday from 9am to 4:30pm. Admission is free.

WHERE TO STAY
VERY EXPENSIVE

FLAMBERG HOTEL ELEPHANT, Am Markt 19, 0-5300 Weimar. Tel. 03643/614-71. Fax 03643/653-10. 102 rms, 3 suites. MINIBAR TV TEL **Bus:** 11 or 71.

$ Rates (including continental breakfast): 195 DM–290 DM ($128.70–$191.40) single; 300 DM–360 DM ($198–$237.60) double; from 410 DM ($270.60) suite. AE, DC, MC, V. **Parking:** Free. **Closed:** Jan–Feb.

The most famous accommodation in Weimar is the Elephant. The elegant facade of this circa 1696 building is set off with stone corner mullions; a beautifully weathered terra-cotta roof; a series of elongated bay windows stretching from the second to the third floors; and, best of all, a frontage onto the old marketplace containing a dried-up fountain dedicated to Neptune. Many celebrities have visited this hotel, including Tolstoy and Bach, but its most notorious guest was Adolf Hitler. The Elephant became known, however, through the Thomas Mann novel *Lotte in Weimar* (published in English as *The Beloved Returns*). It has comfortably furnished rooms.

WEIMAR HILTON, Belvedere Allee 25, 0-5300 Weimar. Tel. 03643/72-20, or toll free 800/445-8667 in the U.S. or Canada. Fax 03643/722-7412. 288 rms, 6 suites. A/C MINIBAR TV TEL **Bus:** 1.

$ Rates: 295 DM ($194.70) single; 355 DM ($234.30) double; 560 DM ($369.60) suite. Buffet breakfast 25 DM ($16.50) extra. AE, DC, MC, V. **Parking:** 15 DM ($9.90).

Ironically, the excellence of its construction and the lavishness of its materials were a deliberate choice of the former East German government, which designed and supervised the building of this hotel a few months before unification. In 1992, the administration was taken over by Hilton International, which today considers it one of the finest properties in the former eastern zone. It rises six stories above Goethe Park, a swath of greenery known for the opulence of its still-intact residences and embassies during the long-ago days of the Weimar Republic. Its lobby is considered one of the most dramatic anywhere, with sunflooded skylights, glass walls, and a soothing sense of calm and quiet. The guest rooms contain furniture crafted from light-grained wood, pastel colors, and many amenities.

Dining/Entertainment: The Kolonnaden Bar services the Bistro Thalia and the Restaurant Esplanade/Trattoria Esplanade, both of which are separately recommended.

Services: 24-hour room service, concierge staff capable of arranging local sightseeing tours, babysitters, massage.

Facilities: Impressive indoor pool, two saunas, hairdressing salon, fitness center.

EXPENSIVE

HOTEL RUSSISCHER HOF, Goetheplatz 2, 0-5300 Weimar. Tel. 03643/77-40. Fax 03643/62-337. 84 rms, 1 suite. TV TEL **Bus:** 11 or 71.

$ Rates (including buffet breakfast): 140 DM–155 DM ($92.40–$102.30) single; 210 DM–280 DM ($138.60–$184.80) double; from 425 DM ($280.50) suite. AE, DC, MC, V. **Parking:** 10 DM ($6.60).

Built in 1805 by Russian aristocrats as a suitable residence for their visits to the court of Weimar, the Russischer Hof sports a dark-green-and-white facade opening onto one of the most important squares in the center of town. Inside, graceful, pastel-colored rooms, elegant and intimate, form the public rooms. The guest rooms are in a modern annex behind the hotel; 18 offer minibars. Of course, the decoration isn't equal to the opulence of the original core, yet each accommodation is suitably furnished and comfortable.

WHERE TO DINE
EXPENSIVE

RESTAURANT ESPLANADE/TRATTORIA ESPLANADE, in the Weimar Hilton, Belvederer Allee 25. Tel. 03643/72-20.

Cuisine: GERMAN/INTERNATIONAL/ITALIAN. **Reservations:** Not necessary. **Bus:** 1.

$ Prices: Appetizers 10 DM–20 DM ($6.60–$13.20); main courses 35 DM–42 DM ($23.10–$27.70). AE, DC, MC, V.

Open: Lunch daily noon–3pm; dinner daily 6–11pm.

Adjacent to the lobby of the previously recommended hotel, this attractive restaurant is flooded with sunlight from its large windows, and neatly decorated with conservatively modern accessories. Most of its floor space is devoted to a repertoire of German and international dishes, including an array of superfresh salads, filet steak in pepper sauce, Sauerbraten with dumplings and red cabbage, and filet of sole in a sauce of white wine and butter. One section of the restaurant, the Trattoria Esplanade, contains a series of tables devoted exclusively to Italian cuisine.

MODERATE

BISTRO THALIA, in the Weimar Hilton, Belvederer Allee 25. Tel. 03643/72-20.

Cuisine: THURINGIAN. **Reservations:** Not necessary. **Bus:** 1.

$ Prices: Appetizers 7 DM–15 DM ($4.60–$9.90), main courses 25 DM–35 DM ($16.50–$23.10). AE, DC, MC, V.

Open: Dinner only, daily 6–11pm.

Some diners consider Thalia the most interesting restaurant in this previously recommended hotel. Its decor is entirely devoted to the 19th-century theatrical traditions that made Weimar the envy of the Teutonic world. Antique lithographs of almost-forgotten productions and a scattering of antique costumes lend nostalgia for the glories of German civilization as you dine. Menu items include Sauerbraten with dumplings and braised red cabbage, many grilled meats and Wursts, pork Schnitzels in gravy with fried onions, and an impressive selection of wine and beer.

FLAMBERG HOTEL ELEPHANT, Am Markt 19. Tel. 03643/614-71.

Cuisine: GERMAN. **Reservations:** Recommended. **Bus:** 11 or 71.

$ Prices: Appetizers 7.50 DM–20 DM ($5–$13.20); main courses 22 DM–30 DM ($14.50–$19.80); three-course fixed-price lunch 40 DM ($26.40); five-course fixed-price dinner 80 DM ($52.80). AE, DC, MC, V.

Open: Both restaurants, Mon–Sat 11:30am–midnight, Sun 11:30am–3pm.

Closed: Jan–Feb.

In the hotel are two restaurants, The Anna Amalia, on the main floor, is the more formal. In a modern, skylit, airy, and spacious room with good service, international meals feature such dishes as filet Stroganoff, three pork médaillons, and beefsteak Cubano with pineapple.

The less formal **Elephantkeller,** reached by a flight of stone steps from a separate entrance, is an elegant light-colored room whose vaults rest on square travertine columns. A specialty is Zwiebelmarkt salads, made of onions from the famous onion market that is still held each October, a tradition dating from 1653.

WEISSER SCHWAN, Frauentorstrasse 23. Tel. 03643/617-15.

Cuisine: THURINGIAN/INTERNATIONAL. **Reservations:** Recommended. **Bus:** 7 or 71.

$ Prices: Appetizers 7.50 DM–15 DM ($5–$9.90); main courses 26 DM–40 DM

($17.20–$26.40); three-course fixed-price lunch 36.50 DM ($24.10); four-course fixed-price lunch 50 DM ($33); seven-course fixed-price dinner 95 DM ($62.70). AE, DC, MC, V.

Open: Sun and Tues–Thurs noon–11pm, Fri–Sat noon–midnight.

One of Weimar's leading restaurants specializes in a regional kitchen, using fresh produce and the best of the local beef, game, and poultry dishes. In the center of Weimar, it is convenient for dining, especially if you're visiting the Goethe House right near by. The atmosphere is mellow, and the building, containing various rooms, dates from the early 16th century. The library is still preserved. Along with the Thuringian specialties, known especially for fish and grilled meats, international dishes are featured.

INEXPENSIVE

RATSKELLER, Stadthaus im Markt. Tel. 03643/641-42.
 Cuisine: THURINGIAN. **Reservations:** Required. **Bus:** 7 or 71.
$ **Prices:** Appetizers 5.50 DM–10.50 DM ($3.60–$6.90); main courses 15 DM–30 DM ($9.90–$19.80). MC.
 Open: Mon–Sat 11:30am–midnight, Sun 11:30am–3:30pm.
You'll descend a flight of stairs into a pair of dining rooms in the Ratskeller. The first is vaulted and white, the second more modern and paneled, with a prominent bar. Everything is clean, correct, and proper. You might begin with goose liver on toast, following with Schnitzel, gulasch with mixed salad, or pork cutlets prepared four different ways.

EASY EXCURSIONS

ERFURT

After a 15-mile train ride beginning at the Weimar Hauptbahnhof, you'll reach 1,200-year-old Erfurt, 81 miles southwest of Leipzig. Erfurt, with a population of 216,000, is the capital of Thuringia. It has frequent connections to Weimar. For rail information, phone Europäisches Reiseburo in Erfurt at 0361/570-00. Access by car is via Autobahn E40 east and west and State Highway 4. After arriving, head for the Erfurt information bureau at Bahnhofstrasse 37 (tel. 0361/2-62-67), where you can find out what's happening locally and what might be open during your visit.

On the Gera River, the city, part of the Land of Thuringia, lies right on the Autobahn from Berlin to Frankfurt am Main.

The Augustinian monastery, where the reformer Luther was a monk for some 5 years, is now used as an orphanage. Gardens originally cultivated by monks just grew and grew, and Erfurt today is world-famous as a horticultural center, known for its wide variety of flowers and vegetables. An international horticultural exhibition is held annually in Cyriaksburg Park.

One of the curiosities of the town is the **Krämer brücke** (Shopkeepers' Bridge), from the 14th century, with houses on both sides, nearly three dozen in all. Spanning the Gera, the bridge is now filled with bookstalls, cafés, and antiques shops, and you'll certainly want to spend some time here browsing.

Well-preserved patrician mansions built in both the Gothic and the Renaissance style are the historic town's dominant features. Many of its narrow streets are lined with half-timbered houses. These houses, for the most part, stood before World War II. Miraculously, Erfurt was one of the few towns of its size in Eastern Germany that wasn't virtually leveled in the bombing raids. The American army liberated it in the spring of 1945 before turning it over to the Russians.

The ecclesiastical center of town is the **Domberg**, where two Catholic churches stand side by side, their 15th-century walls almost closing in on each other at one point. The **cathedral**, Domplatz, begun in the 12th century, was later rebuilt in the 13th century in the Gothic style. It contains many ecclesiastical treasures and some 15th-century stained glass. The Dom is open May through October on Monday through Friday from 9 to 11:30am and 12:30 to 5pm, Saturday from 9 to 11:30am and

12:30 to 4:30pm, and Sunday from 2 to 4pm. From November through April, it is open Monday through Saturday from 10am to 11:30am and 12:30 to 4pm and Sunday from 2 to 4pm. Its neighbor, keeping the same hours, is the **Church of St. Severus.**

The most beautiful churches of Erfurt, "rich in towers," are the Romanesque **Peterskirche,** dating from the 12th and 14th centuries; the **Predigerkirche,** a 13th-century house of worship of the Order of Mendicant Friars; and three churches from the early Middle Ages—**Agidienkirche, Michaeliskirche,** and **Allerheiligengeistkirche.** The tourist office (see above) will give you a map pinpointing all the locations. Most of them can be reached on foot.

Of special interest is the **Steinerne Chronik** (Chronicle of Stone) in Michaelisstrasse, a combination of architectural styles from different eras.

Where to Stay & Dine: Expensive

ERFURTER HOF, Am Bahnhofsvorplatz 0-5010 Erfurt. Tel. 0361/53-10. Fax 0361/646-10-21. 173 rms, 5 suites. TV TEL

$ Rates: 200 DM–250 DM ($132–$165) single; 250 DM–380 DM ($165–$250.80) double; from 500 DM ($330) suite. Buffet breakfast 25 DM ($16.50) extra. AE, DC, MC, V. **Parking:** 15 DM ($9.90).

This was at one time a very grand hotel, and over the years it has hosted many famous guests, among them the then chancellor of West Germany, Willy Brandt, who came here in 1970 seeking reconciliation with the DDR. The most expensive hotel in town, near the Bahnhof, it has many tall windows; small wrought-iron balconies embellish a facade done in sculptured limestone. Inside are six restaurants, a nightclub, and a flower shop. The hotel's guest rooms are comfortable although plainly furnished; 86 contain minibars.

The Kellerrestaurant offers meals beginning at 28 DM ($18.50), and the main dining room, Erfordia, features regional and continental cuisine at prices ranging from 35 DM to 72 DM ($23.10 to $47.50).

HOTEL KOSMOS, Juri-Gagarin-Ring 126, 0-5010 Erfurt. Tel. 0361/55-10. Fax 0361/55-12-10. 321 rms (all with shower). MINIBAR TV TEL

$ Rates (including continental breakfast): 175 DM–230 DM ($115.50–$151.80) single; 205 DM–315 DM ($135.30–$207.90) double. AE, DC, MC, V. **Parking:** Free.

Constructed in 1981 halfway between the station and the town center, the Kosmos is one of the Erfurt's better hotels. Its rooms are modern and sunny, though decorated in a rather sterile format. The Galaxis restaurant offers meals from 34 DM ($22.40).

EISENACH

This historic town lies on the northwestern slopes of the Thuringian Forest at the confluence of the Nesse and Horsel rivers, 30 miles west of Erfurt. The Eisenach Bahnhof receives frequent daily trains from Erfurt (see above). For rail information and schedules, call Europäisches Reiseburo (tel. 03691/51-61). Access by car is via Autobahn E40 east and west. At the **Eisenach-Information,** Bahnhofstrasse 3 (tel. 03691/48-95), pick up a map that will locate the monuments for you.

Eisenach is best known as the site of **Wartburg Schloss,** which stands on a hill 600 feet above the town. Hitler called Wartburg Castle "the most German of German castles" and engaged in a battle with local authorities to take down their cross and replace it with a swastika. This ancient castle from 1400 belonged to the landgraves of Thuringia. It has now been turned into a regional museum. Once it was the home of the medieval Minnesanger poets, who were immortalized by Wagner in *Tannhäuser.* Students of Martin Luther will know that it was at this castle that, upon his return from the Diet of Worms in 1521, he hid out until he could complete his translation of the Bible. He is also said to have "fought the Devil with ink" at Wartburg. Hours are 8:30am to 4pm daily. Admission is 5 DM ($3.30) for adults and 3 DM ($2) for children.

For 2.50 DM ($1.70), you can take a miniature train, the **Wartburg Express,** which will deliver you to the castle. Or you can walk down the Wartburger Allee from the Bahnhof and follow the signs to the castle.

Eisenach is also associated with Johann Sebastian Bach, who was born here in 1685. The **Bachhaus,** Am Frauenplan 21 (tel. 03691/37-14), contains many mementos of the Bach family, along with a collection of musical instruments. It is now a museum, open April through September on Monday from noon to 5:45pm and Tuesday through Sunday from 9am to 5:45pm. From October through March, hours are Monday from 1 to 4:45pm and Tuesday through Sunday from 9am to 4:45pm. Admission is 5 DM ($3.30) for adults and 2 DM ($1.30) for children. Bus: 3.

The house where Fritz Reuter lived from 1868 to 1874, known as the **Reuterhaus,** is also a museum, commemorating this German novelist who made *Plattdeutsch* a literary language. Although arrested for high treason in 1833 and condemned to death by the Prussian government, he was later set free in a general amnesty. He died in Eisenach on July 12, 1874. The museum also has a Wagner collection. Hours and admission charges are the same as for Bachhaus.

You can also visit the **Lutherhaus** of the Cotta family, Lutherplatz 8 (tel. 49-83), where the famous reformer stayed as a schoolboy. Hours are 9am to 1pm and 2 to 5pm Monday to Saturday, 2 to 5pm on Sunday. Admission is 3 DM ($2) for adults and 1.50 DM ($1) for children. Bus: 1 or 5.

Where to Stay & Dine: Expensive

DER KAISERHOF, Wartburger Allee 2, 0-5900 Eisenach. Tel. 03691/32-74. Fax 03691/3653. 85 rms, 4 suites. MINIBAR TV TEL **Bus:** 3.

$ Rates (including continental breakfast): 125 DM–165 DM ($82.50–$108.90) single; 165 DM–285 DM ($108.90–$188.10) double; from 350 DM ($231) suite. AE, DC, MC, V. **Parking:** 10 DM ($6.60).

Der Kaiserhof is one of the best places to stay in town. This historic hotel was recently renovated following unification and has taken on a new life. Rooms are simply furnished, and the hotel has a restaurant, plus a gift shop. Dining is in the Turmschanke, where regional meals cost from 30 DM ($19.80), or in the Zwinger, where light or hearty fare costs 20 DM ($13.20) for a meal.

WARTBURG HOTEL, Auf der Wartburg, 0-5900 Eisenach. Tel. 03691/51-11. Fax 03691/5111. 32 rms. MINIBAR TV TEL **Transportation:** Taxi from station (no bus).

$ Rates (including continental breakfast): 210 DM ($138.60) single; 280 DM ($184.80) double. AE, MC. **Parking:** 5 DM ($3.30).

Two miles from the center of town is this historic castle, where Martin Luther was once a guest. Other famous visitors have included Richard Wagner and Johann Sebastian Bach. Many rooms open onto views of the countryside. The hotel has been restored, and its guest rooms are comfortably but plainly furnished. The hotel also has a regional restaurant where meals range from 20 DM to 50 DM ($13.20 to $33).

A. GLOSSARY

Altstadt old part of a city or town
Apotheke pharmacy
Bad spa (also bath)
Bahn railroad, train
    Bahnhof railroad station
    Bergbahn funicular
    Hauptbahnhof main railroad station
    Seilbahn cable car
    Stadtbahn (S-Bahn) commuter railroad
    Strassenbahn streetcar, tram
    Untergrundbahn (U-Bahn) subway, underground system in a city
Baroque ornate, decorated style of art and architecture in the 18th century, characterized by use of elaborate ornamentation and gilding
Bauhaus style of functional design for architecture and objects, originating in early 20th century in Germany
Berg mountain
Biedermeier solid, bourgeois style of furniture design and interior decoration in the mid-19th century
Der Blaue Reiter group of nonfigurative painters, founded in Munich in 1911 by Franz Marc and Wassily Kandinsky
Die Brücke group of avant-garde expressionist painters originating in Dresden around 1905
Brunnen spring or well
Burg fortified castle
Dom cathedral
Domplatz cathedral square
Drogerie shop selling cosmetics, sundries
"Evergreen" alpine traditional music
Gastarbeiter foreign worker
Gasthof inn
Gemütlichkeit (gemütlich) comfort, coziness, friendliness
Gutbürgerlich German home cooking
Hotel garni hotel that serves no meals or serves breakfast only
Kaufhaus department store
Kneipe bar for drinking, may serve snacks
Konditorei café for coffee and pastries
Kunst art
Marktplatz market square
Messegelände exhibition center, fairgrounds
Neue Küche cuisine moderne
Neustadt new part of city or town
Rathaus town or city hall
    Altes Rathaus old town hall
    Neues Rathaus new town hall (currently used as such)
Ratskeller restaurant in Rathaus cellar serving traditional German food
Schauspielhaus theater for plays
Schloss palace, castle

Spielbank casino
Stadt town, city
Tor gateway
Turm tower
Verkehrsamt tourist office
Weinstube wine bar or tavern serving meals
Wilhelmian decorative style of the late 19th century

B. MENU TERMS

SOUPS [Suppen]

Erbsensuppe pea soup
Gemüsesuppe vegetable soup
Hühnerbruhe chicken broth
Kartoffelsuppe potato soup

Gulaschsuppe goulash soup
Linsensuppe lentil soup
Nudelsuppe noodle soup
Ochsenschwanzsuppe oxtail soup

MEATS [Wurst, Fleisch & Geflügel]

Aufschnitt cold cuts
Brathuhn roast chicken
Bratwurst grilled sausage
Deutsches Beefsteak hamburger
  steak
Eisbein pigs' knuckles
Ente duck
Gans goose
Hammel mutton
Kalb veal
Kaltes Geflügel cold poultry
Kassler Rippchen pork chops

Lamm lamb
Leber liver
Nieren kidneys
Ragout stew
Rinderbraten roast beef
Rindfleisch beef
Sauerbraten sauerbraten
Schinken ham
Schweinebraten roast pork
Truthahn turkey
Wiener Schnitzel veal cutlet
Wurst sausage

FISH [Fisch]

Aal eel
Forelle trout
Hecht pike
Karpfen carp
Krebs crawfish

Lachs salmon
Makrele mackerel
Rheinsalm Rhine salmon
Schellfisch haddock
Seezunge sole

EGGS [Eier]

Eier in der Schale boiled eggs
Rühreier scrambled eggs
Spiegeleier fried eggs

Mit Speck with bacon
Verlorene Eier poached eggs

SANDWICHES [Belegte Brote]

Käsebrot cheese sandwich
Schinkenbrot ham sandwich

Schwarzbrot mit
  Butter pumpernickel w/butter
Wurstbrot sausage sandwich

SALADS [Salat]

Gemischter Salat mixed salad
Gurkensalat cucumber salad

Kopfsalat lettuce salad
Rohkostplatte raw vegetable platter

VEGETABLES [Gemüse]

Artischocken artichokes
Blumenkohl cauliflower
Bohnen beans
Bratkartoffeln fried potatoes
Erbsen peas
Grüne Bohnen string beans
Gurken cucumbers
Karotten carrots
Kartoffelbrei mashed potatoes
Kartoffelsalat potato salad
Knödel dumplings
Kohl cabbage

Reis rice
Rote Rüben beets
Rotkraut red cabbage
Salat lettuce
Salzkartoffeln boiled potatoes
Sauerkraut sauerkraut
Spargel asparagus
Spinat spinach
Steinpilze boletus mushrooms
Tomaten tomatoes
Vorspeisen hors d'oeuvres
Weisse Ruben turnips

DESSERTS [Nachtisch]

Blatterteiggebäck puff pastry
Bratapfel baked apple
Käse cheese
Kloss dumpling
Kompott stewed fruit
Obstkuchen fruit tart

Obstsalat fruit salad
Pfannkuchen sugared pancakes
Pflaumenkompott stewed plums
Teegebäck tea cakes
Torten pastries

FRUITS [Obst]

Ananas pineapple
Apfel apple
Apfelsine orange
Banane banana
Birne pear

Erdbeeren strawberries
Kirschen cherries
Pfirsich peach
Weintrauben grapes
Zitrone lemon

BEVERAGES [Getränke]

Bier beer
Ein Dunkles a dark beer
Ein Helles a light beer
Milch milk
Rotwein red wine

Schokolade chocolate
Eine Tasse Kaffee a cup of coffee
Eine Tasse Tee a cup of tea
Tomatensaft tomato juice
Wasser water

CONDIMENTS & TABLE ITEMS

Brot bread
Brötchen rolls
Butter butter
Eis ice
Essig vinegar
Gabel fork
Glas glass
Löffel spoon

Messer knife
Platte plate
Pfeffer pepper
Sahne cream
Salz salt
Senf mustard
Tasse cup
Zucker sugar

COOKING TERMS

Gebacken baked
Gebraten fried
Gefüllt stuffed
Gekocht boiled

Geröstet broiled
Gut durchgebraten well done
Nicht durchgebraten rare
Paniert breaded

C. WEIGHTS & MEASURES

LENGTH

1 millimeter (mm)	=	0.04 inches (*or* less than ¹⁄₁₆ in.)
1 centimeter (cm)	=	0.39 inches (*or* under ½ in.)
1 meter (m)	=	39 inches (*or* about 1.1 yards)
1 kilometer (km)	=	0.62 miles (*or* about ⅔ of a mile)

To convert kilometers to miles, multiply the number of kilometers by 0.62. Also use to convert speeds from kilometers per hour (kmph) to miles per hour (mph).
To convert miles to kilometers, multiply the number of miles by 1.61. Also use to convert speeds from mph to kmph.

CAPACITY

1 liter (l)	=	33.92 ounces	=	2.1 pints	=	1.06 quarts
	=	0.26 U.S. gallons				
1 Imperial gallon	=	1.2 U.S. gallons				

To convert liters to U.S. gallons, multiply the number of liters by 0.26.
To convert U.S. gallons to liters, multiply the number of gallons by 3.79.
To convert Imperial gallons to U.S. gallons, multiply Imperial gallons by 1.2.
To convert U.S. gallons to Imperial gallons, multiply U.S. gallons by 0.83.

WEIGHT

1 gram (g)	=	0.04 ounces (*or* about a paperclip's weight)
1 kilogram (kg)	=	35.2 ounces
	=	2.2 pounds
1 metric ton	=	2,205 pounds = 1.1 short ton

To convert kilograms to pounds, multiply the number of kilograms by 2.2.
To convert pounds to kilograms, multiply the number of pounds by 0.45.

TEMPERATURE

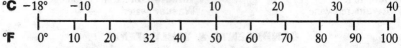

°C	−18°	−10	0	10	20	30	40
°F	0° 10	20	32 40	50 60	70	80 90	100

To convert degrees Celsius to degrees Fahrenheit, multiply °C by 9, divide by 5, then add 32 (example: 20°C × 9/5 + 32 = 68°F).
To convert degrees Fahrenheit to degrees Celsius, subtract 32 from °F, then multiply by 5, then divide by 9 (example: 85°F − 32 × 5/9 = 29.4°C).

INDEX

GENERAL INFORMATION

DESTINATIONS

Key to abbreviations *B* = Budget; *E* = Expensive; *I* = Inexpensive; *M* = Moderate; *VE* = Very
expensive; * = Author's favorite; $ = Super Value Choice

Please Send Me the Books Checked Below:

FROMMER'S COMPREHENSIVE GUIDES
(Guides listing facilities from budget to deluxe,
with emphasis on the medium-priced)

	Retail Price	Code		Retail Price	Code
☐ Acapulco/Ixtapa/Taxco 1993–94	$15.00	C120	☐ Jamaica/Barbados 1993–94	$15.00	C105
☐ Alaska 1994–95	$17.00	C130	☐ Japan 1992–93	$19.00	C020
☐ Arizona 1993–94	$18.00	C101	☐ Morocco 1992–93	$18.00	C021
☐ Australia 1992–93	$18.00	C002	☐ Nepal 1994–95	$18.00	C126
☐ Austria 1993–94	$19.00	C119	☐ New England 1993	$17.00	C114
☐ Belgium/Holland/ Luxembourg 1993–94	$18.00	C106	☐ New Mexico 1993–94	$15.00	C117
☐ Bahamas 1994–95	$17.00	C121	☐ New York State 1994–95	$19.00	C132
☐ Bermuda 1994–95	$15.00	C122	☐ Northwest 1991–92	$17.00	C026
☐ Brazil 1993–94	$20.00	C111	☐ Portugal 1992–93	$16.00	C027
☐ California 1993	$18.00	C112	☐ Puerto Rico 1993–94	$15.00	C103
☐ Canada 1992–93	$18.00	C009	☐ Puerto Vallarta/Manzanillo/ Guadalajara 1992–93	$14.00	C028
☐ Caribbean 1994	$18.00	C123	☐ Scandinavia 1993–94	$19.00	C118
☐ Carolinas/Georgia 1994–95	$17.00	C128	☐ Scotland 1992–93	$16.00	C040
☐ Colorado 1993–94	$16.00	C100	☐ Skiing Europe 1989–90	$15.00	C030
☐ Cruises 1993–94	$19.00	C107	☐ South Pacific 1992–93	$20.00	C031
☐ DE/MD/PA & NJ Shore 1992–93	$19.00	C012	☐ Spain 1993–94	$19.00	C115
☐ Egypt 1990–91	$17.00	C013	☐ Switzerland/Liechtenstein 1992–93	$19.00	C032
☐ England 1994	$18.00	C129	☐ Thailand 1992–93	$20.00	C033
☐ Florida 1994	$18.00	C124	☐ U.S.A. 1993–94	$19.00	C116
☐ France 1994–95	$20.00	C131	☐ Virgin Islands 1994–95	$13.00	C127
☐ Germany 1994	$19.00	C125	☐ Virginia 1992–93	$14.00	C037
☐ Italy 1994	$19.00	C130	☐ Yucatán 1993–94	$18.00	C110

FROMMER'S $-A-DAY GUIDES
(Guides to low-cost tourist accommodations and facilities)

	Retail Price	Code		Retail Price	Code
☐ Australia on $45 1993–94	$18.00	D102	☐ Mexico on $45 1994	$19.00	D116
☐ Costa Rica/Guatemala/ Belize on $35 1993–94	$17.00	D108	☐ New York on $70 1992–93	$16.00	D016
☐ Eastern Europe on $30 1993–94	$18.00	D110	☐ New Zealand on $45 1993–94	$18.00	D103
☐ England on $60 1994	$18.00	D112	☐ Scotland/Wales on $50 1992–93	$18.00	D019
☐ Europe on $50 1994	$19.00	D115	☐ South America on $40 1993–94	$19.00	D109
☐ Greece on $45 1993–94	$19.00	D100			
☐ Hawaii on $75 1994	$19.00	D113	☐ Turkey on $40 1992–93	$22.00	D023
☐ India on $40 1992–93	$20.00	D010	☐ Washington, D.C. on $40 1992–93	$17.00	D024
☐ Ireland on $40 1992–93	$17.00	D011			
☐ Israel on $45 1993–94	$18.00	D101			

FROMMER'S CITY $-A-DAY GUIDES
(Pocket-size guides with an emphasis on low-cost tourist accommodations and facilities)

	Retail Price	Code		Retail Price	Code
☐ Berlin on $40 1994–95	$12.00	D111	☐ Madrid on $50 1992–93	$13.00	D014
☐ Copenhagen on $50 1992–93	$12.00	D003	☐ Paris on $45 1994–95	$12.00	D117
☐ London on $45 1994–95	$12.00	D114	☐ Stockholm on $50 1992–93	$13.00	D022

FROMMER'S WALKING TOURS
(With routes and detailed maps, these companion guides point out
the places and pleasures that make a city unique)

	Retail Price	Code		Retail Price	Code
☐ Berlin	$12.00	W100	☐ Paris	$12.00	W103
☐ London	$12.00	W101	☐ San Francisco	$12.00	W104
☐ New York	$12.00	W102	☐ Washington, D.C.	$12.00	W105

FROMMER'S TOURING GUIDES
(Color-illustrated guides that include walking tours, cultural and historic
sites, and practical information)

	Retail Price	Code		Retail Price	Code
☐ Amsterdam	$11.00	T001	☐ New York	$11.00	T008
☐ Barcelona	$14.00	T015	☐ Rome	$11.00	T010
☐ Brazil	$11.00	T003	☐ Scotland	$10.00	T011
☐ Florence	$ 9.00	T005	☐ Sicily	$15.00	T017
☐ Hong Kong/Singapore/			☐ Tokyo	$15.00	T016
Macau	$11.00	T006	☐ Turkey	$11.00	T013
☐ Kenya	$14.00	T018	☐ Venice	$ 9.00	T014
☐ London	$13.00	T007			

FROMMER'S FAMILY GUIDES

	Retail Price	Code		Retail Price	Code
☐ California with Kids	$18.00	F100	☐ San Francisco with Kids	$17.00	F004
☐ Los Angeles with Kids	$17.00	F002	☐ Washington, D.C. with Kids	$17.00	F005
☐ New York City with Kids	$18.00	F003			

FROMMER'S CITY GUIDES
(Pocket-size guides to sightseeing and tourist accommodations and
facilities in all price ranges)

	Retail Price	Code		Retail Price	Code
☐ Amsterdam 1993–94	$13.00	S110	☐ Montreál/Québec		
☐ Athens 1993–94	$13.00	S114	City 1993–94	$13.00	S125
☐ Atlanta 1993–94	$13.00	S112	☐ New Orleans 1993–94	$13.00	S103
☐ Atlantic City/Cape			☐ New York 1993	$13.00	S120
May 1993–94	$13.00	S130	☐ Orlando 1994	$13.00	S135
☐ Bangkok 1992–93	$13.00	S005	☐ Paris 1993–94	$13.00	S109
☐ Barcelona/Majorca/			☐ Philadelphia 1993–94	$13.00	S113
Minorca/Ibiza 1993–94	$13.00	S115	☐ Rio 1991–92	$ 9.00	S029
☐ Berlin 1993–94	$13.00	S116	☐ Rome 1993–94	$13.00	S111
☐ Boston 1993–94	$13.00	S117	☐ Salt Lake City 1991–92	$ 9.00	S031
☐ Cancún/Cozumel 1991–			☐ San Diego 1993–94	$13.00	S107
92	$ 9.00	S010	☐ San Francisco 1994	$13.00	S133
☐ Chicago 1993–94	$13.00	S122	☐ Santa Fe/Taos/		
☐ Denver/Boulder/Colorado			Albuquerque 1993–94	$13.00	S108
Springs 1993–94	$13.00	S131	☐ Seattle/Portland 1992–93	$12.00	S035
☐ Dublin 1993–94	$13.00	S128	☐ St. Louis/Kansas		
☐ Hawaii 1992	$12.00	S014	City 1993–94	$13.00	S127
☐ Hong Kong 1992–93	$12.00	S015	☐ Sydney 1993–94	$13.00	S129
☐ Honolulu/Oahu 1994	$13.00	S134	☐ Tampa/St.		
☐ Las Vegas 1993–94	$13.00	S121	Petersburg 1993–94	$13.00	S105
☐ London 1994	$13.00	S132	☐ Tokyo 1992–93	$13.00	S039
☐ Los Angeles 1993–94	$13.00	S123	☐ Toronto 1993–94	$13.00	S126
☐ Madrid/Costa del			☐ Vancouver/Victoria 1990–		
Sol 1993–94	$13.00	S124	91	$ 8.00	S041
☐ Miami 1993–94	$13.00	S118	☐ Washington, D.C. 1993	$13.00	S102
☐ Minneapolis/St.					
Paul 1993–94	$13.00	S119			

Other Titles Available at Membership Prices

SPECIAL EDITIONS

	Retail Price	Code		Retail Price	Code
☐ Bed & Breakfast North America	$15.00	P002	☐ Marilyn Wood's Wonderful Weekends (within a 250-mile radius of NYC)	$12.00	P017
☐ Bed & Breakfast Southwest	$16.00	P100	☐ National Park Guide 1993	$15.00	P101
☐ Caribbean Hideaways	$16.00	P103	☐ Where to Stay U.S.A.	$15.00	P102

GAULT MILLAU'S "BEST OF" GUIDES
(The only guides that distinguish the truly superlative from the merely overrated)

	Retail Price	Code		Retail Price	Code
☐ Chicago	$16.00	G002	☐ New England	$16.00	G010
☐ Florida	$17.00	G003	☐ New Orleans	$17.00	G011
☐ France	$17.00	G004	☐ New York	$17.00	G012
☐ Germany	$18.00	G018	☐ Paris	$17.00	G013
☐ Hawaii	$17.00	G006	☐ San Francisco	$17.00	G014
☐ Hong Kong	$17.00	G007	☐ Thailand	$18.00	G019
☐ London	$17.00	G009	☐ Toronto	$17.00	G020
☐ Los Angeles	$17.00	G005	☐ Washington, D.C.	$17.00	G017

THE REAL GUIDES
(Opinionated, politically aware guides for youthful budget-minded travelers)

	Retail Price	Code		Retail Price	Code
☐ Able to Travel	$20.00	R112	☐ Kenya	$12.95	R015
☐ Amsterdam	$13.00	R100	☐ Mexico	$11.95	R128
☐ Barcelona	$13.00	R101	☐ Morocco	$14.00	R129
☐ Belgium/Holland/ Luxembourg	$16.00	R031	☐ Nepal	$14.00	R018
☐ Berlin	$13.00	R123	☐ New York	$13.00	R019
☐ Brazil	$13.95	R003	☐ Paris	$13.00	R130
☐ California & the West Coast	$17.00	R121	☐ Peru	$12.95	R021
☐ Canada	$15.00	R103	☐ Poland	$13.95	R131
☐ Czechoslovakia	$15.00	R124	☐ Portugal	$16.00	R126
☐ Egypt	$19.00	R105	☐ Prague	$15.00	R113
☐ Europe	$18.00	R122	☐ San Francisco & the Bay Area	$11.95	R024
☐ Florida	$14.00	R006	☐ Scandinavia	$14.95	R025
☐ France	$18.00	R106	☐ Spain	$16.00	R026
☐ Germany	$18.00	R107	☐ Thailand	$17.00	R119
☐ Greece	$18.00	R108	☐ Tunisia	$17.00	R115
☐ Guatemala/Belize	$14.00	R127	☐ Turkey	$13.95	R027
☐ Hong Kong/Macau	$11.95	R011	☐ U.S.A.	$18.00	R117
☐ Hungary	$14.95	R118	☐ Venice	$11.95	R028
☐ Ireland	$17.00	R120	☐ Women Travel	$12.95	R029
☐ Italy	$18.00	R125	☐ Yugoslavia	$12.95	R030

We can wire money to every major city in Europe almost as fast as you can say, "Zut alors! J'ai perdu mes valises."

How fast? We can send money in 10 minutes or less, to 13,500 locations in over 68 countries. That's faster than any other international money transfer service. And when you're *sans* luggage, every minute counts.

For more information call 49-69-21050 in Frankfurt or visit your nearest American Express® Travel Service Office. In the United States call 1-800-MONEYGRAM.

MoneyGram
INTERNATIONAL MONEY TRANSFERS.